Touring Europe

Central and South East (Europe), Benelux and Scandinavia

Also available:

C000283950

© The Caravan Club Limited 2020
Published by The Caravan and Motorhome Club Limited
East Grinstead House, East Grinstead
West Sussex RH19 1UA

General Enquiries: 01342 326944
Travel Service Reservations: 01342 316101
Red Pennant Overseas Holiday Insurance: 01342 336633
Website: camc.com

Editor: Kate Walters
Publishing service provided by Fyooz Ltd
Printed by Stephens & George Ltd
Merthyr Tydfil
ISBN 978-1-9993236-3-9

Maps and distance charts generated from Collins Bartholomew Digital Database
Maps ©Collins Bartholomew Ltd 2020, reproduced by permission of HarperCollins Publishers.

Cover from **£60***

Red Pennant Overseas Holiday, Breakdown and Emergency Insurance

- Roadside assistance & Recovery including repatriation.

- Travel Insurance including cancellation and medical emergencies.

- Cover is available for multiple trips in a year, or for single trips up to 365 days**

- Friendly emergency services team
  Based at our Head Office, our multi-lingual team are ready to help when you need us.

For full details of cover offered, including limitations and exclusions that apply, a sample of the policy wording is available upon request.

Call 01342 336 633 or visit camc.com/redpennant

Welcome...

...to another year of touring across Europe!

Wherever and however you travel, people who camp (whether in a caravan, motorhome, campervan or tent) share a sense of adventure and freedom that you don't get from other types of holidays.

However as we enter 2020 we are still in a period of uncertainty regarding the UK's position in the European Union and what will happen when we leave. While it is unlikely that Brexit will stop us from touring the EU, you might need to plan further ahead and do more research before you travel.

At the time of this book going to press much of what will change once the UK leaves the EU is unknown, and therefore it is very difficult to advise on issues such as border controls, customs, visa requirements and pet passports. Therefore you're strongly advised to check this information before you travel, especially if the UK has already left or will leave the EU while you're travelling. Check camc.com/overseas for our most up-to-date advice.

So as you start another year of touring adventures, I would like to thank you for continuing to buy and contribute to these guides. If you can, please spare five minutes to fill in one of the site report forms at the back of this book or visit camc.com/europereport to let us know what you think about the sites you've stayed on this year. Happy touring!

Kate Walters

Kate Walters, Editor

Contents

How to use this guide

The Handbook..6
Country Introductions.........................6
Campsite Entries..................................6
Campsite Fees......................................6
Sites Maps & Satellite Navigation......6
Site Report Forms................................7
Acknowledgements..............................8
Explanation of a Campsite Entry.........9
Guide to symbols................................10
Site description abbreviations...........11

Planning your trip

Documents...14
Camping Key Europe...........................14
Driving Licence...................................14
Passport..15
Pet Travel Scheme (PETS)...................16
Travelling with Children......................16
Vehicle documents.............................17
Visas..17
Insurance..18
Car, Motorhome and Caravan Insurance.................18
Holiday Travel Insurance....................19
Holiday Insurance for Pets..................20
Home Insurance..................................20
Customs..21
Caravans and Vehicles.......................21
Currency..21
Customs Allowances..........................21
Medicines..22
Prohibited and restricted goods........23
Personal Possessions.........................23
Plants & Foods................................... 23
Money..24
Local Currency....................................24
Foreign Currency Bank Accounts.......24
Prepaid travel cards...........................25
Credit & Debit Cards...........................25
Emergency Cash.................................25
Crossing the channel..........................26
Booking Your Ferry.............................26
On the Ferry..26
Channel Tunnel...................................27
Pets..27
Gas...27
Club Sites near Ports..........................28
Ferry Routes and Operators...............29

Motoring advice

Motoring Advice..................................30
Preparing for Your Journey.................30
Driving in Europe.................................31
Fuel..31
Low Emission Zones............................32
Motorhomes Towing Cars...................32
Priority & Roundabouts.......................32
Public Transport..................................33
Pedestrian Crossings..........................33
Traffic Lights..33
Motoring Equipment...........................34
Essential Equipment...........................34
Child restraint systems.......................34
Fire Extinguisher.................................34
Lights...34
Nationality Plate (GB/IRL)...................35
Reflective Jackets................................35
Route Planning....................................35
Seat Belts..36
Spares..36
Towbar...37
Tyres..37
Winter Driving.....................................37
Warning Triangles...............................38
Essential Equipment Table.................38
Route Planning Maps................... 40-45
Mountain Passes & Tunnels...............46
Mountain roads...................................46
Mountain Pass Information.................47
Table and Map Information.................47
Major Mountain Passes Table – Alpine..................48
Major Rail Tunnels Table – Alpine......57
Major Road Tunnels Table – Alpine....58
Mountain Passes & Tunnels Maps............60

During your stay

Keeping in Touch.................................64
Telephones..64
Accessing the Internet........................65
Radio & Television...............................66
Medical Matters..................................67
European Health Insurance Card (EHIC)...............67
Travel Insurance.................................68
First Aid...68
Accidents & Emergencies...................68
Sun Protection....................................69
Tick-Bourne Encephalitis and Lyme Disease..........69
Water & Food.......................................69
Returning Home..................................69

Electricity & Gas 70
Electricity – General Advice 70
Electrical Connections – CEE17 70
Hooking up to the Mains.............................71
Reversed Polarity 72
Shaver Sockets 72
Gas – General Advice................................72
Safety & Security..74
Beaches, Lakes & Rivers 74
Campsite Safety..74
On The Road..76
Personal Security.......................................77
Money Security 78
Winter sports 79
British Consular Services Abroad............................79

Campsites

Booking a Campsite 80
Caravan Storage 81
Facilities & Site Description 81
Finding a Campsite 82
Overnight Stops 82
Municipal Campsites...................................82
Naturist Campsites 82
Opening Dates 83
Pets on Campsites.....................................83
Prices..84
Registering on Arrival 84
General Advice 85

Site listings

Austria
Country Introduction 86
Site Entries..93
Distance Chart / Sites Location Map 108
Belgium
Country Introduction 110
Site Entries..117
Distance Chart / Sites Location Map 125
Croatia
Country Introduction 127
Site Entries..133
Distance Chart / Sites Location Map 140
Czech Republic
Country Introduction 142
Site Entries..149
Distance Chart / Sites Location Map 154
Denmark
Country Introduction 156
Site Entries..164
Distance Chart / Sites Location Map 174

Finland
Country Introduction 176
Site Entries.. 183
Distance Chart / Sites Location Map 187
Germany
Country Introduction 189
Site Entries.. 198
Distance Chart / Sites Location Maps 248
Greece
Country Introduction 254
Site Entries.. 261
Distance Chart / Sites Location Map 266
Hungary
Country Introduction 268
Site Entries.. 275
Distance Chart / Sites Location Map 278
Italy
Country Introduction 280
Site Entries.. 289
Distance Chart / Sites Location Map 318
Luxembourg
Country Introduction 323
Site Entries.. 328
Sites Location Map 332
Netherlands
Country Introduction 333
Site Entries.. 340
Distance Chart / Sites Location Map 356
Norway
Country Introduction 358
Site Entries.. 369
Distance Chart / Sites Location Maps 384
Poland
Country Introduction 387
Site Entries.. 394
Distance Chart / Sites Location Map 398
Slovakia
Country Introduction 400
Site Entries.. 407
Distance Chart / Sites Location Map 409
Slovenia
Country Introduction 411
Site Entries.. 417
Distance Chart / Sites Location Map 421
Sweden
Country Introduction 423
Site Entries.. 432
Distance Chart / Sites Location Maps 444
Switzerland
Country Introduction 447
Site Entries.. 455
Distance Chart / Sites Location Map 467

Site Report Forms 470
Subject Index... 478

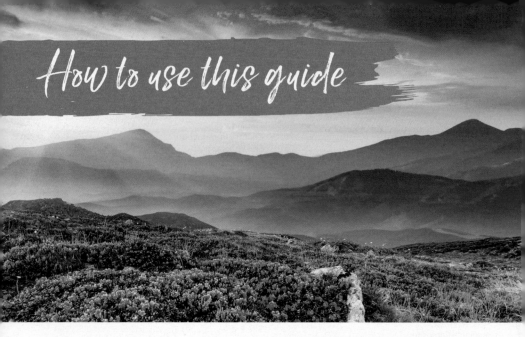

How to use this guide

The Handbook

This includes general information about touring in Europe, such as legal requirements, advice and regulations.

Country Introductions

Following on from the Handbook chapters you will find the Country Introductions containing information, regulations and advice specific to each country. You should read the Country Introduction in conjunction with the Handbook chapters before you set off on your holiday.

Campsite Entries

After the country introduction you will find the campsite entries listed alphabetically under their nearest town or village. Where there are several campsites shown in and around the same town they will be listed in clockwise order from the north.

To find a campsite all you need to do is look for the town or village of where you would like to stay, or use the maps at the back of the book to find a town where sites are listed.

For an explanation of the site entries and a guide to symbols please see the following pages. You'll also find a guide to site entries on the fold out on the rear cover.

Campsite Fees

Campsite entries show high season fees per night for an outfit plus two adults. Prices given may not include electricity or showers, unless indicated. Outside of the main holiday season many sites offer discounts on the prices shown and some sites may also offer a reduction for longer stays.

Campsite fees may vary to the prices stated in the site entries, especially if the site has not been reported on for a few years. You are advised to always check fees when booking, or at least before pitching, as those shown in site entries should be used as a guide only.

Site Maps

Each town and village listed alphabetically in the site entry pages has a map grid reference number, e.g. 3B4. The map grid reference number is shown on each site entry.

The maps can be found at the end of each country section. The reference number will show you where each town or village is located, and the site entry will tell you how far the site is from that town. Place names are shown on the maps in two colours:

Red where we list a site which is open all year (or for at least eleven months of the year)

Black where we only list seasonal sites which close in winter.

These maps are intended for general campsite location purposes only; a detailed road map or atlas is essential for route planning and touring.

The scale of the map means that it isn't possible to show every town or village where a campsite is listed, so some sites in small villages may be listed under a nearby larger town instead.

Satellite Navigation

Most campsite entries now show a GPS (sat nav) reference. There are several different formats of writing co-ordinates, and in this guide we use decimal degrees, for example 48.85661 (latitude north) and 2.35222 (longitude east).

Minus readings, shown as -1.23456, indicate that the longitude is west of the Greenwich meridian. This will only apply to sites in the west of France, most of Spain and all of Portugal as the majority of Europe are east of the Greenwich meridian.

Manufacturers of sat navs all use different formats of co-ordinates so you may need to convert the co-ordinates before using them with your device. There are plenty of online conversion tools which enable you to do this quickly and easily - just type 'co-ordinate converter' into your search engine.

Please be aware if you are using a sat nav device some routes may take you on roads that are narrow and/or are not suitable for caravans or large outfits.

The GPS co-ordinates given in this guide are provided by members and checked wherever possible, however we cannot guarantee their accuracy due to the rural nature of most sites. The Caravan and Motorhome Club cannot accept responsibility for any inaccuracies, errors or omissions or for their effects.

Site Report Forms

With the exception of campsites in The Club's Overseas Site Booking Service (SBS) network, The Caravan and Motorhome Club does not inspect sites listed in this guide. Virtually all of the sites listed in Touring Europe are from site reports submitted by users of these guides.

Sites which are not reported on for five years are deleted from the guide, so even if you visit a site and find nothing has changed we'd still appreciate an update to make sure that the site isn't archived.

You will find site report forms towards the back of the book, or you can submit them at camc.com/europereport - use the abbreviated site report form if you are reporting no changes, or only minor changes, to a site entry. The full report form should be used for new sites or if sites have changed a lot.

Please submit reports as soon as possible. Information received by mid August will be used wherever possible in the next edition of Touring Europe. Reports received after that date are still very welcome and will appear in the following edition. The editor is unable to respond individually to site reports submitted due to the large quantity that we receive.

Tips for Completing Site Reports

- If possible fill in a site report form while at the campsite. Once back at home it can be difficult to remember details of individual sites, especially if you visited several during your trip.

- When giving directions to a site, remember to include the direction of travel, e.g. 'from north on D137, turn left onto D794 signposted Combourg' or 'on N83 from Poligny turn right at petrol station in village'. Wherever possible give road numbers, junction numbers and/or kilometre post numbers, where you exit from motorways or main roads. It is also helpful to mention useful landmarks such as bridges, roundabouts, traffic lights or prominent buildings.

We very much appreciate the time and trouble you take submitting reports on campsites that you have visited; without your valuable contributions it would be impossible to update this guide.

Acknowledgements

Thanks go to the AIT/FIA Information Centre (OTA), the Alliance Internationale de Tourisme (AIT), the Fédération International de Camping et de Caravanning (FICC) and to the national clubs and tourist offices of those countries who have assisted with this publication.

Every effort is made to ensure that information provided in this publication is accurate. The Caravan and Motorhome Club Ltd has not checked these details by inspection or other investigation and cannot accept responsibility for the accuracy of these reports as provided by members and non-members, or for errors, omissions or their effects. In addition The Caravan and Motorhome Club Ltd cannot be held accountable for the quality, safety or operation of the sites concerned, or for the fact that conditions, facilities, management or prices may have changed since the last recorded visit. Any recommendations, additional comments or opinions have been contributed by people staying on the site and are not those of The Caravan and Motorhome Club.

The inclusion of advertisements or other inserted material does not imply any form of approval or recognition, nor can The Caravan and Motorhome Club Ltd undertake any responsibility for checking the accuracy of advertising material.

Explanation of a Campsite Entry

Site map grid reference

Distance and direction of the site from the centre of the listing town in kilometres (or metres), together with the aspect of the site (urban, rural or coastal).

GPS co-ordinates – latitude and longitude in decimal degrees. Minus figures indicate that the site is west of the Greenwich meridian

The town under which the campsite is listed, as shown on the relevant Sites Location Map at the end of each country's site entry pages

Campsite name

Campsite address.

Site information shown by symbols, a guide to which can be found on the next page or inside the rear cover. Where further information is available (e.g. a price for dogs or if a toilet block is heated) is shown after the symbol.

Site contact details, including telephone number, email address and website address where available.

OSSIACH *D3 (1km SW Rural)* *46.66388, 13.97500*
Terrassen Camping Ossiacher See, Ostriach 67, 9570
Ossiach **(04243) 436; martinz@camping.at;**
www.terrassen.camping.at

🛖 €3 👫(htd) WD 🚿 🔥 ♿ 🍴 🖩 💻 🦋 🛶 🍸 ① 🐕 🛒 🚲 ✐

Leave A10/E55/E66 at exit for Ossiachersee, turn L onto B94 twd Feldkirchen & shortly R to Ossiach Süd. Site on lake shore just S of Ossiach vill.
Lge, mkd, pt shd, terr, EHU (4-10A) €3; gas; bbq; sw; red long stay; twin axles; TV; ccard acc; clsd 1200-1500 LS; games area; horseriding; games rm; windsurfing; bike hire; fishing; tennis; watersports; CKE. *"Ideal Carinthian lakes, Hochosterwitz castle & excursions into Italy; parking adj; cash machine; beautiful scenery; many activities; excel san facs; pitches sm and diff for big o'fits; dogs confined to pitches next to entrance; but site in lovely location."*
€41.00, 1 May-30 Sep, G05.   **2019**

Directions to the site are shown in bold text.

Comments and opinions of tourers who have visited the site shown in italic text

Additional site information, including pitch information and electric information. For details of the abbreviations used please see the following pages.

The year in which the site was last reported on by a visitor. Sites are archived if we don't receive a report for 5 years so please consider sending in a report if you visit a site with an older date shown.

Guide price for 2 adults, an outfit and a pitch in high season.

Booking reference for a site the Club's Overseas Travel Service work with, i.e. bookable via the Club.

Opening dates for the site, may give specific dates or the general months of opening. If no dates are present the site will be open all year, as shown by the 🔢 in the symbols section.

Guide to symbols

Symbol	Explanation
12	The site is open all year. Some sites may decide to close if they are not busy so call ahead out of season.
	Dogs are allowed on site, usually at an extra cost (shown if known). Please see the description or member comments for any restrictions.
	Toilets available. If followed by (cont) they will be continental style toilets.
WD	Chemical toilet disposal.
	Showers available.
	Family bathroom or baby and toddler room on site. Facilities may vary.
	Toilet and/or shower facilities available for disabled guests on site. Facilities may vary.
	Laundry facilities available. Facilities and costs may vary.
	Electric hook ups are available. See the description for details of the amperage, costs and any further information.
MSP	Motorhome service point. Low level waste discharge point for motor caravans; fresh water tap and rinse facilities should also be available
	Quiet site - set in a peaceful location although at busy times you may still experience noise from other site users.

Symbol	Explanation
	Wi-Fi available, usually at an extra cost.
	Bar on site or nearby if followed by nr.
	Restaurant on site or nearby if followed by nr.
	Snack bar, cafe or takeaway on site.
	Shop on site or nearby if followed by nr.
	Playground or play area on site. Age restrictions may apply.
	Entertainment on site - this may either be evening entertainment or organised daytime activities or excursions.
	Pool on site. Where known the listing will specify if heated (htd), covered (covrd).
	Paddling pool for younger children on site
	Beach nearby, followed by the distance and information about the type of beach where known.

Site Description Abbreviations

Each site entry assumes the following unless stated otherwise:

Level ground, open grass pitches, drinking water on site, clean wc unless otherwise stated (own sanitation required if wc not listed), site is suitable for any length of stay within the dates shown.

aspect
   urban – within a city or town, or on its outskirts
   rural – within or on edge of a village or in open countryside
   coastal – within one kilometre of the coast

size of site
   sm – max 50 pitches
   med – 51 to 150 pitches
   lge – 151 to 500 pitches
   v lge – 501+ pitches

pitches
   hdg pitch – hedged pitches
   mkd pitch – marked or numbered pitches
   hdstg – some hard standing or gravel

levels
   sl – sloping site
   pt sl – sloping in parts
   terr – terraced site

shade
   shd – plenty of shade
   pt shd – part shaded
   unshd – no shade

Site Facilities

adv bkg -
   acc - advance booking accepted
   rec – advance booking recommended
   req - advance booking required

beach - symbol followed by:
   1km – distance to beach
   sand beach – sandy beach
   shgl beach – shingle beach

bus/metro/tram
   Public transport within 5km

chem disp
   Dedicated chemical toilet disposal facilities;
   chem disp (wc) – no dedicated point; disposal via wc only

CKE
   Camping Key Europe accepted

CL-type
   Very small, privately-owned, informal and usually basic, farm or country site similar to those in the Caravan and Motorhome Club's network of Certificated Locations

el pnts - symbol followed by:
   Mains electric hook-ups available for a fee;
   inc – cost included in site fee quoted
   10A – amperage provided
   conn fee – one-off charge for connection to metered electricity supply
   rev pol – reversed polarity may be present (see Electricity and Gas section

Eng spkn
   English spoken by campsite reception staff

gas
   Supplies of bottled gas available on site or nearby

Mairie
   Town hall (France); will usually make municipal campsite reservations

NH
   Suitable as a night halt

open 1 Apr-15 Oct
   Where no specific dates are given, opening dates are assumed to be inclusive, ie Apr-Oct – beginning April to end October
   (NB: opening dates may vary from those shown; check before travelling, particularly when travelling out of the main holiday season)

phone
   Public payphone on or adjacent to site

pool - symbol followed by:
   Indoor – indoor pool
   htd – heated pool
   covrd – indoor pool or one with retractable cover

red CCI/CCS
   Reduction in fees on production of a Camping Card International or Camping Card Scandinavia

BBQ
barbecues allowed (may be restricted to a separate, designated area)

serviced pitch
Electric hook-ups and mains water inlet and grey water waste outlet to pitch;
all – to all pitches
50% – percentage of pitches

shwrs - symbol followed by:
inc – cost included in site fee quoted

ssn
Season;
high ssn – peak holiday season
low ssn – out of peak season

50% statics
Percentage of static caravans/mobile homes/chalets/fixed tents/cabins or long term seasonal pitches on site, including those run by tour operators

sw
Swimming nearby;
1km – nearest swimming
lake – in lake
rv – in river

TV
TV rm – separate TV room (often also a games room)
TV (pitch) – cable or satellite connections to pitches

Other Abbreviations

AIT	Alliance Internationale de Tourisme
a'bahn	Autobahn
a'pista	Autopista
a'route	Autoroute
a'strada	Autostrada
adj	Adjacent, nearby
alt	Alternative
app	Approach, on approaching
arr	Arrival, arriving
avail	Available
Ave	Avenue
bdge	Bridge
bef	Before
bet	Between
Blvd	Boulevard
C	Century, eg 16thC
c'van	Caravan
CC	Caravan and Motorhome Club
ccard acc	Credit and/or debit cards accepted (check with site for specific details)
cent	Centre or central
clsd	Closed
conn	Connection
cont	Continue or continental (wc)
conv	Convenient
covrd	Covered
dep	Departure
diff	Difficult, with difficulty
dir	Direction
dist	Distance
dual c'way	Dual carriageway
E	East
ent	Entrance/entry to
espec	Especially
ess	Essential
excel	Excellent
facs	Facilities
FIA	Fédération Internationale de l'Automobile
FICC	Fédération Internationale de Camping & de Caravaning
FFCC	Fédération Française de Camping et de Caravaning
FKK/FNF	Naturist federation, ie naturist site
foll	Follow

fr	From
g'ge	Garage
gd	Good
grnd(s)	Ground(s)
hr(s)	Hour(s)
immac	Immaculate
immed	Immediate(ly)
inc	Included/inclusive
indus est	Industrial estate
INF	Naturist federation, ie naturist site
int'l	International
irreg	Irregular
junc	Junction
km	Kilometre
L	Left
LH	Left-hand
LS	Low season
ltd	Limited
mkd	Marked
mkt	Market
mob	Mobile (phone)
m'van	Motor caravan
m'way	Motorway
N	North
narr	Narrow
nr, nrby	Near, nearby
opp	Opposite
o'fits	Outfits
o'look(ing)	Overlook(ing)
o'night	Overnight
o'skts	Outskirts
PO	Post office
poss	Possible, possibly
pt	Part
R	Right
rd	Road or street
rec	Recommend/ed
recep	Reception
red	Reduced, reduction (for)
reg	Regular
req	Required
RH	Right-hand
rlwy	Railway line
rm	Room
rndabt	Roundabout
rte	Route
RV	Recreational vehicle, ie large motor caravan
rv/rvside	River/riverside

S	South
san facs	Sanitary facilities ie wc, showers, etc
snr citizens	Senior citizens
sep	Separate
sh	Short
sp	Sign post, signposted
sq	Square
ssn	Season
stn	Station
strt	Straight, straight ahead
sw	Swimming
thro	Through
TO	Tourist Office
tour ops	Tour operators
traff lts	Traffic lights
twd	Toward(s)
unrel	Unreliable
vg	Very good
vill	Village
W	West
w/end	Weekend
x-ing	Crossing
x-rds	Cross roads

Documents

Camping Key Europe

Camping Key Europe (CKE) is a useful touring companion. Not only does it serve as ID at campsites, meaning that you don't have to leave your passport at reception, it also entitles you to discounts at over 2200 sites.

CKE also offers third-party liability insurance for families including up to three children, which provides cover for loss or damage that occurs while on site. For more information on the scheme and all its benefits visit www.campingkey.com.

You can purchase the CKE from the Club by calling 01342 336633, or it is provided free for Red Pennant Overseas Holiday Insurance customers taking out 'Motoring' cover.

If you are using a CKE or CCI card as ID at a site, make sure that you collect your card when checking out. Also check that you have been given your own card instead of someone else's.

Driving Licence

A full (not provisional), valid driving licence should be carried at all times when driving abroad. You must produce it when asked to do so by the police and other authorities, or you may be liable for an immediate fine and confiscation of your vehicle(s).

If your driving licence is due to expire while you are away it can be renewed up to three months before expiry - contact the DVLA if you need to renew more than three months ahead.

Rules regarding driving with a provisional licences vary across Europe, so you may not be entitled to drive in some EU countries unless you have a full licence.

All EU countries recognise the photocard driving licence introduced in the UK in 1990, subject to the minimum age requirements (normally 18 years for a vehicle with a maximum weight of 3,500 kg carrying no more than 8 people).

Old-style green paper licences or Northern Irish licences issued before 1991 should be updated before travelling as they may not be recognised by local authorities.

Passport

In many EU countries everyone is required to carry photographic ID at all times. Enter next-of-kin details in the back of your passport and keep a separate photocopy. It's also a good idea to leave a photocopy of it with a relative or friend at home.

You can also scan or take a photo of your passport to keep saved on your smart phone or in a cloud storage service so you are able to access it while you're away.

The following information applies to British passport holders only. For information on passports issued by other countries you should contact the local embassy.

Applying for a Passport

Each person travelling out of the UK (including babies) must hold a valid passport - it is no longer possible to include children on a parent's passport. A standard British passport is valid for ten years, or 5 years for under 16s.

All newly issued UK passports are now biometric, also known as e-passports, which contain a microchip with information which can be used to authenticate the holder's identity.

Full information and application forms are available from main post offices or from the Identity & Passport Service's website, www.gov.uk where you can complete an online application. Allow at least six weeks for first-time passport applications, for which you may need to attend an interview at your nearest Identity and Passport Service (IPS) regional office. Allow three weeks for a renewal application or replacement of a lost, stolen or damaged passport.

Passport Validity

Most countries in the EU only require your passport to be valid for the duration of your stay. However, in case your return home is delayed it is a good idea make sure you have six month's validity remaining. Any time left on a passport (up to a maximum of nine months) will be added to the validity of your new passport on renewal.

Schengen Agreement

The Schengen Agreement allows people and vehicles to pass freely without border checks from country to country within the Schengen area (26 countries). Where there are no longer any border checks you should still not attempt to cross land borders without a full, valid passport. It is likely that random identity checks will be made for the foreseeable future in areas surrounding borders. The United Kingdom and Republic of Ireland do not fully participate in the Schengen Agreement.

Due to the current migrant crisis in Europe some countries have temporarily restored their borders. A current list of countries affected is available on the EU website: **ec.europa.eu/home-affairs/what-we-do/policies/borders-and-visas/schengen/reintroduction-border-control_en**.

Pets resident anywhere in the British Isles (excluding the Republic of Ireland) are able to travel freely within the British Isles and are not subject to PETS rules.

For details of how to obtain a Pet Passport visit www.defra.gov.uk or call 0370 241 1710.

Returning to the UK

On your return to the UK with your pet you will need to visit a vet between 24 and 120 hours prior to your return journey in order for your pet to be treated for tapeworm. The vet will need to sign your pet passport - ensure that they put the correct date against their signature or you may not fall within the correct time range for travel. Ask your campsite to recommend a local vet, or research vets near to the port you will be returning from before you travel.

Regulations for Pets

Some campsites do not accept dogs at all and some have restrictions on the number and breed of dogs allowed. Visit camc.com/overseasadvice for more information and country specific advice.

In popular tourist areas local regulations may ban dogs from beaches in the summer months.

Pet Travel Scheme (PETS)

The Pet Travel Scheme (PETS) allows owners of dogs, cats and ferrets from qualifying European countries, to bring their pets into the UK (up to a limit of five per person) without quarantine. The animal must have an EU pet passport, be microchipped and be vaccinated against rabies. Dogs must also have been treated for tapeworm. It also allows pets to travel from the UK to other EU qualifying countries.

There are country specific regulations regarding certain breeds of dogs. You can't import breeds classed as dangerous dogs to many countries, and other breeds will require additional documentation. For more information or to find out which breeds are banned or restricted visit camc.com/pets or call us on 01342 336766.

Travelling with Children

Some countries require evidence of parental responsibility for people travelling alone with children, especially those who have a different surname to them (including lone parents and grandparent). The authorities may want to see a birth certificate, a letter of consent from the child's parent (or other parent if you are travelling alone with your own child) and some evidence as to your responsibility for the child.

For further information on exactly what will be required at immigration contact the Embassy or Consulate of the countries you intend to visit.

Vehicle documents

Caravan Proof of Ownership (CRIS)

In Britain and Ireland, unlike most other European countries, caravans are not formally registered in the same way as cars. This may not be fully understood by police and other authorities on the Continent. You are strongly advised, therefore, to carry a copy of your Caravan Registration Identification Scheme (CRIS) document.

MOT Certificate

Carry your vehicle's MOT certificate (if applicable) as you may need to show it to the authorities if your vehicle is involved in an accident, or in the event of random vehicle checks. If your MOT certificate is due to expire while you are away you should have the vehicle tested before you leave home.

Tax

While driving abroad you still need to have current UK vehicle tax. If your vehicle's tax is due to expire while you are abroad you may apply to re-license the vehicle at a post office, by post, or in person at a DVLA local office, up to two months in advance.

Since October 2014 the DVLA have no longer issued paper tax discs - EU Authorities are aware of this change.

Vehicle Registration Certificate (V5C)

You must always carry your Vehicle Registration Certificate (V5C) and MOT Certificate (if applicable) when taking your vehicle abroad. If yours has been lost, stolen or destroyed you should apply to a DVLA local office on form V62. Call DVLA Customer Enquiries on 0300 790 6802 for more information.

Hired or Borrowed Vehicles

If using a borrowed vehicle you must obtain a letter of authority to use the vehicle from the registered owner. You should also carry the Vehicle Registration Certificate (V5C).

In the case of hired or leased vehicles, including company cars, when the user does not normally possess the V5C, ask the company which owns the vehicle to supply a Vehicle On Hire Certificate, form VE103, which is the only legal substitute for a V5C. The BVRLA, the trade body for the vehicle rental and leasing sector, provide advice on hired or leased vehicles - see www.bvrla.co.uk or call them on 01494 434747 for more information.

If you are caught driving a hired vehicle abroad without this certificate you may be fined and/or the vehicle impounded.

Visas

British citizens holding a full UK passport do not require a visa for entry into any EU countries, although you may require a permit for stays of more than three months. Contact the relevant country's UK embassy before you travel for information.

British subjects, British overseas citizens, British dependent territories citizens and citizens of other countries may need visas that are not required by British citizens. Again check with the authorities of the country you are due to visit at their UK embassy or consulate. Citizens of other countries should apply to their own embassy, consulate or High Commission.

Insurance

Car, Motorhome and Caravan Insurance

It is important to make sure your outfit is covered whilst you are travelling abroad. Your car or motorhome insurance should cover you for driving in the EU, but check what you are covered for before you travel. If you are travelling outside the EU or associated countries you'll need to inform your insurer and may have to pay an additional premium.

Make sure your caravan insurance includes travel outside of the UK, speak to your provider to check this. You may need to notify them of your dates of travel and may be charged an extra premium dependent on your level of cover.

The Caravan and Motorhome Club's Car, Caravan Cover and Motorhome Insurance schemes extend to provide policy cover for travel within the EU free of charge, provided the total period of foreign travel in any one year does not exceed 270 days for Car and Motorhome Insurance and 182 for Caravan Insurance. It may be possible to extend this period, although a charge may apply.

Should you be delayed beyond these limits notify your broker or insurer immediately in order to maintain your cover until you can return to the UK.

If your outfit is damaged during ferry travel (including while loading or unloading) it must be reported to the carrier at the time of the incident. Most insurance policies will cover short sea crossings (up to 65 hours) but check with your insurer before travelling.

Visit camc.com/insurance or call 01342 336610 for full details of our Caravan Cover or for Car or Motorhome Insurance call 0345 504 0334.

European Accident Statement

Your car or motorhome insurer may provide you with a European Accident Statement form (EAS), or you may be given one if you are involved in an accident abroad. The EAS is a standard form, available in different languages, which gives all parties involved in an accident the opportunity to agree on the facts. Signing the form doesn't mean that you are accepting liability, just that you agree with what has been stated on the form. Only sign an EAS if you are completely sure that you understand what has been written and always make sure that you take a copy of the completed EAS.

Vehicles Left Behind Abroad

If you are involved in an accident or breakdown abroad which prevents you taking your vehicle home, you must ensure that your normal insurance will cover your vehicle if left overseas while you return home. Also check if you're covered for the cost of recovering it to your home address.

In this event you should remove all items of baggage and personal belongings from your vehicles before leaving them unattended. If this isn't possible you should check with your insurer if extended cover can be provided. In all circumstances, you must remove any valuables and items liable for customs duty, including wine, beer, spirits and cigarettes.

Legal Costs Abroad

If an accident abroad leads to you being taken to court you may find yourself liable for legal costs – even if you are not found to be at fault. Most UK vehicle insurance policies include cover for legal costs or have the option to add cover for a small additional cost – check if you are covered before you travel.

Holiday Travel Insurance

A standard motor insurance policy won't cover you for all eventualities, for example vehicle breakdown, medical expenses or accommodation so it's important to also take out adequate travel insurance. Make sure that the travel insurance you take out is suitable for a caravan or motorhome holiday.

Remember to check exemptions and exclusions, especially those relating to pre-existing medical conditions or the use of alcohol. Be sure to declare any pre-existing medical conditions to your insurer.

The Club's Red Pennant Overseas Holiday Insurance is designed specifically for touring holidays and can cover both motoring and personal use. Depending on the level of cover chosen the policy will cover you for vehicle recovery and repair, holiday continuation, medical expenses and accommodation.

Visit camc.com/redpennant for full details or call us on 01342 336633.

Holiday Insurance for Pets

Taking your pet with you? Make sure they're covered too. Some holiday insurance policies, including The Club's Red Pennant, can be extended to cover pet expenses relating to an incident normally covered under the policy – such as pet repatriation in the event that your vehicle is written off.

However in order to provide cover for pet injury or illness you will need a separate pet insurance policy which covers your pet while out of the UK. For details of The Club's Pet Insurance scheme visit camc.com/petins or call 0345 504 0336.

Home Insurance

Your home insurer may require advance notification if you are leaving your home unoccupied for 30 days or more. There may be specific requirements, such as turning off mains services (except electricity), draining water down and having somebody check your home periodically. Read your policy documents or speak to your provider.

The Club's Home Insurance policy provides full cover for up to 90 days when you are away from home (for instance when touring) and requires only common sense precautions for longer periods of unoccupancy. See camc.com/homeins or call 0345 504 0335 for details.

Personal Belongings

The majority of travellers are able to cover their valuables such as jewellery, watches, cameras, laptops, and bikes under a home insurance policy. This includes the Club's Home Insurance scheme.

Specialist gadget insurance is now commonly available and can provide valuable benefits if you are taking smart phones, tablets, laptops or other gadgets on holiday with you. The Club offers a Gadget Insurance policy - visit camc.com/gadget or call 01342 779413 to find out more.

Customs

Caravans and Vehicles

You can temporarily import a caravan, trailer tent or vehicle from one EU country to another without any Customs formalities. Vehicles and caravans may be temporarily imported into non-EU countries generally for a maximum of six months in any twelve month period, provided they are not hired, sold or otherwise disposed of in that country.

If you intend to stay longer than six months, dispose of a vehicle in another country or leave your vehicle there in storage you should seek advice well before your departure from the UK.

Borrowed Vehicles

If you are borrowing a vehicle from a friend or relative, or loaning yours to someone, you should be aware of the following:

- The total time the vehicle spends abroad must not exceed the limit for temporary importation (generally six months).
- The owner of the caravan must provide the other person with a letter of authority.
- The owner cannot accept a hire fee or reward.

- The number plate on the caravan must match the number plate on the tow car.
- Both drivers' insurers must be informed if a caravan is being towed and any additional premium must be paid.

Currency

You must declare cash of €10,000 (or equivalent in other currencies) or more when travelling between the UK and a non-EU country. The term 'cash' includes cheques, travellers' cheques, bankers' drafts, notes and coins. You don't need to declare cash when travelling within the EU.

For further information contact HMRC Excise & Customs Helpline on 0300 200 3700.

Customs Allowances

Travelling within the European Union

If you are travelling to the UK from within the EU you can bring an unlimited amount of most goods without being liable for any duty or tax, but certain rules apply. The goods must be for your own personal use, which can include use as a gift (if the person you are gifting the goods to reimburses you this is not classed as a gift), and you must have paid duty and tax in the country where you purchased the goods. If a customs official suspects that any goods are not for your own personal use they can question you, make further checks and ultimately seize both the goods and the vehicle used to transport them. Although no limits are in place, customs officials are less likely to question you regarding your goods if they are under the following limits:

- 800 cigarettes
- 400 cigarillos
- 200 cigars
- 1kg tobacco
- 10 litres of spirits

- 20 litres of fortified wine (e.g. port or sherry)
- 90 litres of wine
- 110 litres of beer

The same rules and recommended limits apply for travel between other EU countries.

Travelling Outside the EU

There are set limits to the amount of goods you bring back into the UK from countries outside of the EU. All goods must be for your own personal use. Each person aged 17 and over is entitled to the following allowance:

- 200 cigarettes, or 100 cigarillos, or 50 cigars, or 250g tobacco
- 1 litre of spirits or strong liqueurs over 22% volume, or 2 litres of fortified wine, sparkling wine or any other alcoholic drink that's less than 22% volume
- 4 litres of still wine
- 16 litres of beer
- £390 worth of all other goods including perfume, gifts and souvenirs without having to pay tax and/or duty
- For further information contact HMRC National Advice Service on 0300 200 3700.

Medicines

There is no limit to the amount of medicines you can take abroad if they are obtained without prescription (i.e. over the counter medicines). Medicines prescribed by your doctor may contain controlled drugs (e.g. morphine), for which you will need a licence if you're leaving the UK for 3 months or more. Visit www.gov.uk/travelling-controlled-drugs or call 020 7035 0771 for a list of controlled drugs and to apply for a licence.

You don't need a licence if you carry less than 3 months' supply or your medication doesn't contain controlled drugs, but you should carry a letter from your doctor stating your name, a list of your prescribed drugs and dosages for each drug. You may have to show this letter when going through customs.

Personal Possessions

Visitors to countries within the EU are free to carry reasonable quantities of any personal possessions such as jewellery, cameras, and electrical equipment required for the duration of their stay. It is sensible to carry sales receipts for new items in case you need to prove that tax has already been paid.

Prohibited and Restricted Goods

Regardless of where you are travelling from the importation of some goods into the UK is restricted or banned, mainly to protect health and the environment. These include:

- Endangered animals or plants including live animals, birds and plants, ivory, skins, coral, hides, shells and goods made from them such as jewellery, shoes, bags and belts.
- Controlled, unlicensed or dangerous drugs.
- Counterfeit or pirated goods such as watches, CDs and clothes; goods bearing a false indication of their place of manufacture or in breach of UK copyright.

- Offensive weapons such as firearms, flick knives, knuckledusters, push daggers, self-defence sprays and stun guns.
- Pornographic material depicting extreme violence or featuring children

This list is not exhaustive; if in doubt contact HMRC on 0300 200 3700 (+44 2920 501 261 from outside the UK) or go through the red Customs channel and ask a Customs officer when returning to the UK.

Plants and Food

Travellers from within the EU may bring into the UK any fruit, vegetable or plant products without restriction as long as they are grown in the EU, are free from pests or disease and are for your own consumption. For food products Andorra, the Channel Islands, the Isle of Man, San Marino and Switzerland are treated as part of the EU. From most countries outside the EU you are not allowed to bring into the UK any meat or dairy products. Other animal products may be severely restricted or banned and it is important that you declare any such products on entering the UK. For up to date information contact the Department for Environment, Food and Rural Affairs (Defra) on 0345 33 55 77 or +44 20 7238 6951 from outside the UK. You can also visit www.defra.gov.uk to find out more.

Money

Being able to safely access your money while you're away is a necessity for you to enjoy your break. It isn't a good idea to rely on one method of payment, so always have a backup plan. A mixture of a small amount of cash plus one or two electronic means of payment are a good idea.

Traveller's cheques have become less popular in recent years as fewer banks and hotels are willing or able to cash them. There are alternative options which offer the same level of security but are easier to use, such as prepaid credit cards.

Local Currency

It is a good idea to take enough foreign currency for your journey and immediate needs on arrival, don't forget you may need change for tolls or parking on your journey. Currency exchange facilities will be available at ports and on ferries but rates offered may not be as good as you would find elsewhere.

The Post Office, banks, exchange offices and travel agents offer foreign exchange. All should stock Euros but during peak holiday times or if you need a large amount it may be sensible to pre-order your currency. You should also pre-order less common currencies. Shop around and compare commission and exchange rates, together with minimum charges.

Banks and money exchanges in central and eastern Europe won't usually accept Scottish and Northern Irish bank notes and may be reluctant to change any sterling which has been written on or is creased or worn.

Foreign Currency Bank Accounts

Frequent travellers or those who spend long periods abroad may find a Euro bank account useful. Most such accounts impose no currency conversion charges for debit or credit card use and allow fee-free cash withdrawals at ATMs. Some banks may also allow you to spread your account across different currencies, depending on your circumstances. Speak to your bank about the services they offer.

Prepaid Travel Cards

Prepaid travel money cards are issued by various providers including the Post Office, Travelex, Lloyds Bank and American Express.

They are increasingly popular as the PIN protected travel money card offers the security of Traveller's Cheques, with the convenience of paying by card. You load the card with the amount you need before leaving home, and then use cash machines to make withdrawals or use the card to pay for goods and services as you would a credit or debit card. You can top the card up over the telephone or online while you are abroad. However there can be issues with using them with some automated payment systems, such as pay-at-pump petrol stations and toll booths, so you should always have an alternative payment method available.

These cards can be cheaper to use than credit or debit cards for both cash withdrawals and purchases as there are usually no loading or transaction fees to pay. In addition, because they are separate from your bank account, if the card is lost or stolen you bank account will still be secure.

Credit and Debit Cards

Credit and debit cards offer a convenient way of spending abroad. For the use of cards abroad most banks impose a foreign currency conversion charge of up to 3% per transaction. If you use your card to withdraw cash there will be a further commission charge of up to 3% and you will be charged interest (possibly at a higher rate than normal) as soon as you withdraw the money.

There are credit cards available which are specifically designed for spending overseas and will give you the best available rates. However they often have high interest rates so are only economical if you're able to pay them off in full each month.

If you have several cards, take at least two in case you encounter problems. Credit and debit 'Chip and PIN' cards issued by UK banks may not be universally accepted abroad so check that your card will be accepted if using it in restaurants or other situations where you pay after you have received goods or services

Contact your credit or debit card issuer before you leave home to let them know that you will be travelling abroad. In the battle against card fraud, card issuers frequently query transactions which they regard as unusual or suspicious, causing your card to be declined or temporarily stopped. You should always carry your card issuer's helpline number with you so that you can contact them if this happens. You will also need this number should you need to report the loss or theft of your card.

Dynamic Currency Conversion

When you pay with a credit or debit card, retailers may offer you the choice of currency for payment, e.g. a euro amount will be converted into sterling and then charged to your card account. This is known as a 'Dynamic Currency Conversion' but the exchange rate used is likely to be worse than the rate offered by your card issuer, so will work out more expensive than paying in the local currency.

Emergency Cash

If an emergency or theft means that you need cash in a hurry, then friends or relatives at home can send you emergency cash via money transfer services. The Post Office, MoneyGram and Western Union all offer services which, allows the transfer of money to over 233,000 money transfer agents around the world. Transfers take approximately ten minutes and charges are levied on a sliding scale.

Crossing the Channel

Booking Your Ferry

If travelling at peak times, such as Easter or school holidays, make reservations as early as possible. Each ferry will have limited room for caravans and large vehicles so spaces can fill up quickly, especially on cheaper crossings. If you need any special assistance request this at the time of booking.

When booking any ferry crossing, make sure you give the correct measurements for your outfit including bikes, roof boxes or anything which may add to the length or height of your vehicle - if you underestimate your vehicle's size you may be turned away or charged an additional fee.

The Caravan and Motorhome Club is an agent for most major ferry companies operating services. Call The Club's Travel Service on 01342 316 101 or see camc.com/ferries to book.

The table at the end of this section shows ferry routes from the UK to the Continent and Ireland. Some ferry routes may not be operational all year, and during peak periods there may be a limit to the number of caravans or motorhomes accepted. For the most up-to-date information visit camc.com/ferries or call the Club's Travel Services team.

On the Ferry

Arrive at the port with plenty of time before your boarding time. Motorhomes and car/caravan outfits will usually either be the first or last vehicles boarded onto the ferry. Almost all ferries are now 'drive on – drive off' so you won't be required to do any complicated manoeuvres. You may be required to show ferry staff that your gas is switched off before boarding the ferry.

Be careful using the ferry access ramps, as they are often very steep which can mean there is a risk of grounding the tow bar or caravan hitch. Drive slowly and, if your ground clearance is low, consider whether removing your jockey wheel and any stabilising devices would help.

Vehicles are often parked close together on ferries, meaning that if you have towing extension mirrors they could get knocked or damaged by people trying to get past your vehicle. If you leave them attached during the ferry crossing then make sure you check their position on returning to your vehicle.

Channel Tunnel

The Channel Tunnel operator, Eurotunnel, accepts cars, caravans and motorhomes (except those running on LPG) on their service between Folkestone and Calais. You can just turn up and see if there is availability on the day, however prices increase as it gets closer to the departure time so if you know your plans in advance it is best to book as early as possible.

On the Journey

You will be asked to open your roof vents prior to travel and you will also need to apply the caravan brake once you have parked your vehicle on the train. You will not be able to use your caravan until arrival.

Pets

It is possible to transport your pet on a number of ferry routes to the Continent and Ireland, as well as on Eurotunnel services from Folkestone to Calais. Advance booking is essential as restrictions apply to the number of animals allowed on any one crossing. Make sure you understand the carrier's terms and conditions for transporting pets. Brittany Ferries ask for all dogs to be muzzled when out of the vehicle but this varies for other operators so please check at the time of booking.

Once on board pets are normally required to remain in their owner's vehicle or in kennels on the car deck and you won't be able to access your vehicle to check on your pet while the ferry is at sea. On longer crossings you should make arrangements at the on-board information desk for permission to visit your pet in order to check its well-being. You should always make sure that ferry staff know your vehicle has a pet on board.

Information and advice on the welfare of animals before and during a journey is available on the website of the Department for Environment, Food and Rural Affairs (Defra), www.defra.gov.uk.

Gas

UK based ferry companies usually allow up to three gas cylinders per caravan, including the cylinder currently in use, however some may restrict this to a maximum of two cylinders. Some operators may ask you to hand over your gas cylinders to a member of the crew so that they can be safely stored during the crossing. Check that you know the rules of your ferry operator before you travel.

Cylinder valves should be fully closed and covered with a cap, if provided, and should remain closed during the crossing. Cylinders should be fixed securely in or on the caravan in the position specified by the manufacturer.

Gas cylinders must be declared at check-in and the crew may ask to inspect each cylinder for leakage before travel.

The carriage of spare petrol cans, whether full or empty, is not permitted on ferries or through the Channel Tunnel.

LPG Vehicles

Vehicles fully or partially powered by LPG can't be carried through the Channel Tunnel. Gas for domestic use (e.g. heating, lighting or cooking) can be carried, but the maximum limit is 47kg for a single bottle or 50kg in multiple bottles. Tanks must be switched off before boarding and must be less than 80% full; you will be asked to demonstrate this before you travel.

Most ferry companies will accept LPG-powered vehicles but you must let them know at the time of booking. During the crossing the tank must be no more than 75% full and it must be turned off. In the case of vehicles converted to use LPG, some ferry companies also require a certificate showing that the conversion has been carried out by a professional - before you book speak to the ferry company to see what their requirements are.

Club Sites Near Ports

If you've got a long drive to the ferry port, or want to catch an early ferry then an overnight stop near to the port gives you a relaxing start to your holiday. The following table lists Club sites which are close to ports.

Club Members can book online at camc.com or call 01342 327490. Non-members can book by calling the sites directly on the telephone numbers below when the sites are open.

Please note that Commons Wood, Fairlight Wood, Hunter's Moon and Old Hartley are open to Club members only. Non-members are welcome at all other sites listed below.

Port	Nearest Club Site	Tel No.
Cairnryan	New England Bay	01776 860275
Dover, Folkestone, Channel Tunnel	Bearsted	01622 730018
	Black Horse Farm*	01303 892665
	Daleacres	01303 267679
	Fairlight Wood	01424 812333
Fishguard, Pembroke	Freshwater East	01646 672341
Harwich	Cambridge Cherry Hinton*	01223 244088
	Commons Wood*	01707 260786
Holyhead	Penrhos	01248 852617
Hull	York Beechwood Grange*	01904 424637
	York Rowntree Park*	01904 658997
Newcastle upon Tyne	Old Hartley	0191 237 0256
Newhaven	Brighton*	01273 626546
Plymouth	Plymouth Sound	01752 862325
Poole	Hunter's Moon*	01929 556605
Portsmouth	Rookesbury Park	01329 834085
Rosslare	River Valley	00353 (0)404 41647
Weymouth	Crossways	01305 852032

Site open all year

Ferry Routes and Operators

Route	Operator	Approximate Crossing Time	Maximum Frequency
Belgium			
Hull – Zeebrugge	P & O Ferries	12-14 hrs	1 daily
France			
Dover – Calais	P & O Ferries	1½ hrs	22 daily
Dover – Calais	DFDS Seaways	1½ hrs	10 daily
Dover – Dunkerque	DFDS Seaways	2 hrs	12 daily
Folkestone – Calais	Eurotunnel	35 mins	3 per hour
Newhaven – Dieppe	DFDS Seaways	4 hrs	2 daily
Plymouth – Roscoff	Brittany Ferries	6 hrs	2 daily
Poole – St Malo (via Channel Islands)*	Condor Ferries	5 hrs	1 daily (May to Sep)
Portsmouth – Caen	Brittany Ferries	6 / 7 hrs	3 daily (maximum)
Portsmouth – Cherbourg	Brittany Ferries	3 hrs	2 daily (maximum)
Portsmouth – Le Havre	Brittany Ferries	3¼ / 8 hrs	1 daily (minimum)
Portsmouth – St Malo	Brittany Ferries	9 hrs	1 daily
Ireland – Northern			
Cairnryan – Larne	P & O Irish Sea	1 / 2 hrs	7 daily
Liverpool (Birkenhead) – Belfast	Stena Line	8 hrs	2 daily
Cairnryan – Belfast	Stena Line	2 / 3 hrs	7 daily
Ireland – Republic			
Cork – Roscoff*	Brittany Ferries	14 hrs	1 per week
Dublin – Cherbourg	Irish Ferries	19 hrs	1 per week
Fishguard – Rosslare	Stena Line	3½ hrs	2 daily
Holyhead – Dublin	Irish Ferries	2-4 hrs	Max 4 daily
Holyhead – Dublin	Stena Line	2-4 hrs	Max 4 daily
Liverpool – Dublin	P & O Irish Sea	8 hrs	2 daily
Pembroke – Rosslare	Irish Ferries	4 hrs	2 daily
Rosslare – Cherbourg*	Irish Ferries	19½ hrs	3 per week
Rosslare – Cherbourg	Stena Line	19 hrs	3 per week
Rosslare – Roscoff*	Irish Ferries	19½ hrs	4 per week
Netherlands			
Harwich – Hook of Holland	Stena Line	7 hrs	2 daily
Hull – Rotterdam	P & O Ferries	11-12 hrs	1 daily
Newcastle – Ijmuiden (Amsterdam)	DFDS Seaways	15½ hrs	1 daily
Spain			
Portsmouth – Bilbao	Brittany Ferries	24 / 32 hrs	1 - 3 per week
Portsmouth or Plymouth – Santander	Brittany Ferries	20 / 32 hrs	4 per week

*Not bookable through The Club's Travel Service.
Note: Services and routes correct at time of publication but subject to change.

Motoring advice

Preparing for Your Journey

The first priority in preparing your outfit for your journey should be to make sure it has a full service. Make sure that you have a fully equipped spares kit, and a spare wheel and tyre for your caravan – it is easier to get hold of them from your local dealer than to have to spend time searching for spares where you don't know the local area.

Club members should carry their UK Sites Directory & Handbook with them, as it contains a section of technical advice which may be useful when travelling.

The Club also has a free advice service covering a wide range of technical topics – download free information leaflets at camc.com/advice or contact the team by calling 01342 336611 or emailing technical@camc.com.

For advice on issues specific to countries other than the UK, Club members can contact the Travel Service Information Officer, email: travelserviceinfo@camc.com or call 01342 336766.

Weight Limits

From both a legal and a safety point of view, it is essential not to exceed vehicle weight limits. It is advisable to carry documentation confirming your vehicle's maximum permitted laden weight - if your Vehicle Registration Certificate (V5C) does not state this, you will need to produce alternative certification, e.g. from a weighbridge.

If you are pulled over by the police and don't have certification you will be taken to a weighbridge. If your vehicle(s) are then found to be overweight you will be liable to a fine and may have to discard items to lower the weight before you can continue on your journey.

Some Final Checks

Before you start any journey make sure you complete the following checks:

- All car and caravan or motorhome lights are working and sets of spare bulbs are packed
- The coupling is correctly seated on the towball and the breakaway cable is attached
- Windows, vents, hatches and doors are shut
- On-board water systems are drained
- Mirrors are adjusted for maximum visibility
- Corner steadies are fully wound up and the brace is handy for your arrival on site

- Any fires or flames are extinguished and the gas cylinder tap is turned off. Fire extinguishers are fully charged and close at hand.
- The over-run brake is working correctly.
- The jockey wheel is raised and secured, the handbrake is released.

Driving in Europe

Driving abroad for the first time can be a daunting prospect, especially when towing a caravan. Here are a few tips to make the transition easier:

- Remember that Sat Navs may take you on unsuitable roads, so have a map or atlas to hand to help you find an alternative route.
- It can be tempting to try and get to your destination as quickly as possible but we recommend travelling a maximum of 250 miles a day when towing.
- Share the driving if possible, and on long journeys plan an overnight stop.
- Remember that if you need to overtake or pull out around an obstruction you will not be able to see clearly from the driver's seat. If possible, always have a responsible adult in the passenger seat who can advise you when it is clear to pull out. If that is not possible then stay well back to get a better view and pull out slowly.
- If traffic builds up behind you, pull over safely and let it pass.
- Driving on the right should become second nature after a while, but pay particular attention when turning left, after leaving a rest area, petrol station or site or after a one-way system.
- Stop at least every two hours to stretch your legs and take a break.

Fuel

Grades of petrol sold on the Continent are comparable to those sold in the UK; 95 octane is frequently known as 'Essence' and 98 octane as 'Super'. Diesel may be called 'Gasoil' and is widely available across Europe. E10 petrol (containing 10% Ethanol) can be found in certain countries in Europe. Most modern cars are E10 compatible, but those which aren't could be damaged by filling up with E10. Check your vehicle handbook or visit www.acea.be and search for 'E10' to find the publication 'Vehicle compatibility with new fuel standards'.

Members of The Caravan and Motorhome Club can check current average fuel prices by country at camc.com/overseasadvice.

Away from major roads and towns it is a good idea not to let your fuel tank run too low as you may have difficulty finding a petrol station, especially at night or on Sundays. Petrol stations offering a 24-hour service may involve an automated process, in some cases only accepting credit cards issued in the country you are in.

Automotive Liquefied Petroleum Gas (LPG)

The increasing popularity of dual-fuelled vehicles means that the availability of LPG – also known as 'autogas' or GPL – has become an important issue for more drivers.

There are different tank-filling openings in use in different countries. Currently there is no common European filling system, and you might find a variety of systems. Most Continental motorway services will have adaptors but these should be used with care – see www.autogas.ltd.uk for more information.

Low Emission Zones

Many cities in countries around Europe have introduced 'Low Emission Zones' (LEZ's) in order to regulate vehicle pollution levels. Some schemes require you to buy a windscreen sticker, pay a fee or register your vehicle before entering the zone. You may also need to provide proof that your vehicle's emissions meet the required standard. Before you travel visit www.lowemissionzones.eu for maps and details of LEZ's across Europe. Also see the Country Introductions later in this guide for country specific information.

Motorhomes Towing Cars

If you are towing a car behind a motorhome, our advice would be to use a trailer with all four wheels of the car off the ground. Although most countries don't have specific laws banning A-frames, there may be laws in place which prohibit motor vehicle towing another motor vehicle.

Priority and Roundabouts

When driving on the Continent it can be difficult to work out which vehicles have priority in different situations. Watch out for road signs which indicate priority and read the Country Introductions later in this guide for country specific information.

Take care at intersections – you should never rely on being given right of way, even if you have priority; especially in small towns and villages where local traffic may take right of way. Always give way to public service and military vehicles and to buses and trams.

In some countries in Europe priority at roundabouts is given to vehicles entering the roundabout (i.e. on the right) unless the road signs say otherwise.

Public Transport

In general in built-up areas be prepared to stop to allow a bus to pull out from a bus stop when the driver is signalling his intention to do so.

Take particular care when school buses have stopped and passengers are getting on and off.

Overtaking trams in motion is normally only allowed on the right, unless on a one way street where you can overtake on the left if there is not enough space on the right. Do not overtake a tram near a tram stop. These may be in the centre of the road. When a tram or bus stops to allow passengers on and off, you should stop to allow them to cross to the pavement. Give way to trams which are turning across your carriageway. Don't park or stop across tram lines; trams cannot steer round obstructions!

Pedestrian Crossings

Stopping to allow pedestrians to cross at zebra crossings is not always common practice on the Continent as it is in the UK. Pedestrians expect to wait until the road is clear before crossing, while motorists behind may be taken by surprise by your stopping. The result may be a rear-end shunt or vehicles overtaking you at the crossing and putting pedestrians at risk.

Traffic Lights

Traffic lights may not be as easily visible as they are in the UK, for instance they may be smaller or suspended across the road with a smaller set on a post at the roadside. You may find that lights change directly from red to green, bypassing amber completely. Flashing amber lights generally indicate that you may proceed with caution if it is safe to do so but you must give way to pedestrians and other vehicles.

A green filter light should be treated with caution as you may still have to give way to pedestrians who have a green light to cross the road. If a light turns red as approached, continental drivers will often speed up to get through the light instead of stopping. Be aware that if you brake sharply because a traffic light has turned red as you approached, the driver behind might not be expecting it.

Motoring Equipment

Essential Equipment

The equipment that you legally have to carry differs by country. For a full list see the Essential Equipment table at the end of this chapter. Please note equipment requirements and regulations can change frequently. To keep up to date with the latest equipment information visit camc.com/overseasadvice.

Child Restraint Systems

Children under 10 years of age are not permitted to travel in front seats of vehicles, unless there are no rear seats in the vehicle, the rear seats are already occupied with other children, or there are no seat belts in the rear. In these situations a child must not be placed in the front seats in a rear-facing child seat, unless any airbag is deactivated. Children up to 10 must travel in an approved child seat or restraint system, adapted to their size. A baby up to 13kg in weight must be carried in a rear facing baby seat. A child between 9kg and 18kg in weight must be seated in a child seat. A child from 15kg in weight up to the age of 10 can use a booster seat with a seat belt.

Children must not travel in the front of a vehicle if there are rear seats available. If they travel in the front the airbag must be deactivated and again they must use an EU approved restraint system for their size.

Fire Extinguisher

As a safety precaution, an approved fire extinguisher should be carried in all vehicles. This is a legal requirement in several countries in Europe.

Lights

When driving in on the right headlights should be adjusted if they are likely to dazzle other road users. You can do this by applying beam deflectors, or some newer vehicles have a built-in adjustment system. Some high-density discharge (HID), xenon or halogen lights, may need to be taken to a dealer to make the necessary adjustment.

Remember also to adjust headlights according to the load being carried and to compensate for the weight of the caravan on the back of your car. Even if you do not intend to drive at night, it is important to ensure that your headlights are correctly adjusted as you may need to use them in heavy rain, fog or in tunnels. If using tape or a pre-cut adhesive mask remember to remove it on your return home.

All vehicle lights must be in working condition. If your lights are not in working order you may be liable for a fine of up to €450 and confiscation of your vehicle is a possibility in some European countries.

Headlight-Flashing

On the Continent headlight-flashing is used as a warning of approach or as an overtaking signal at night, and not, as is commonly the case in the UK, an indication that you are giving way. Be more cautious with both flashing your headlights and when another driver flashes you. If a driver flashes his headlights they are generally indicating that he has priority and you should give way, contrary to standard practice in the UK.

Hazard Warning Lights

Hazard warning lights should not be used in place of a warning triangle, but should be used in addition to it.

Nationality Plate

A nationality plate must be fixed to the rear of both your car or motorhome and caravan. Checks are made and a fine may be imposed for failure to display a nationality plate correctly. If your number plates have the Euro-Symbol on them there is no requirement to display an additional GB sticker within the EU and Switzerland. If your number plate doesn't have the EU symbol or you are planning to travel outside of the EU you will need a GB sticker.

GB is the only national identification code allowed for cars registered in the UK.

Reflective Jackets / Waistcoats

If you break down outside of a built-up area it is normally a legal requirement that anyone leaving the vehicle must be wearing a reflective jacket or waistcoat. Make sure that your jacket is accessible from inside the car as you will need to put it on before exiting the vehicle. Carry one for each passenger as well as the driver.

Route Planning

It is always a good idea to carry a road atlas or map of the countries you plan to visit, even if you have Satellite Navigation. You can find information on UK roads from Keep Moving – www.keepmoving.co.uk or call 09003 401100. Websites offering a European route mapping service include www.google.co.uk/maps, www.mappy.com or www.viamichelin.com.

Satellite Navigation/GPS

European postcodes don't cover just one street or part of a street in the same way as UK postcodes, they can cover a very large area. GPS co-ordinates and full addresses are given for site entries in this guide wherever possible, so that you can programme your device as accurately as possible.

It is important to remember that sat nav devices don't usually allow for towing or driving a large motorhome and may try to send you down unsuitable roads. Always use your common sense, and if a road looks unsuitable find an alternative route.

Use your sat nav in conjunction with the directions given in the site entries, which have been provided by members who have actually visited. Please note that directions given in site entries have not been checked by the Caravan and Motorhome Club.

In nearly all European countries it is illegal to use car navigation systems which actively search for mobile speed cameras or interfere with police equipment (laser or radar detection).

Car navigation systems which give a warning of fixed speed camera locations are legal in most countries with the exception of France, Germany, and Switzerland where this function must be de-activated.

Seat Belts

The wearing of seat belts is compulsory throughout Europe. On-the-spot fines will be incurred for failure to wear them and, in the event of an accident failure to wear a seat belt may reduce any claim for injury. See the country introductions for specific regulations on both seat belts and car seats.

Spares

Caravan Spares

It will generally be much harder to get hold of spare parts for caravans on the continent, especially for UK manufactured caravans.

It is therefore advisable to carry any commonly required spares (such as light bulbs) with you.

Take contact details of your UK dealer or manufacturer with you, as they may be able to assist in getting spares delivered to you in an emergency.

Car Spares

Some car manufacturers produce spares kits; contact your dealer for details. The choice of spares will depend on the vehicle and how long you are away, but the following is a list of basic items which should cover the most common causes of breakdown:

- Radiator top hose
- Fan belt
- Fuses and bulbs
- Windscreen wiper blade
- Length of 12V electrical cable
- Tools, torch and WD40 or equivalent water repellent/ dispersant spray

Spare Wheel

Your local caravan dealer should be able to supply an appropriate spare wheel. If you have any difficulty in obtaining one, the Club's Technical Department can provide Club members with a list of suppliers on request.

Tyre legislation across Europe is more or less consistent and, while the Club has no specific knowledge of laws on the Continent regarding the use of space-saver spare wheels, there should be no problems in using such a wheel provided its use is in accordance with the manufacturer's instructions. Space-saver spare wheels are designed for short journeys to get to a place where it can be repaired and there will usually be restrictions on the distance and speed at which the vehicle should be driven.

Towbar

The vast majority of cars registered after 1 August 1998 are legally required to have a European Type approved towbar (complying with European Directive 94/20) carrying a plate giving its approval number and various technical details, including the maximum noseweight. Your car dealer or specialist towbar fitter will be able to give further advice.

All new motorhomes will need some form of type approval before they can be registered in the UK and as such can only be fitted with a type approved towbar. Older vehicles can continue to be fitted with non-approved towing brackets.

Tyres

Tyre condition has a major effect on the safe handling of your outfit. Caravan tyres must be suitable for the highest speed at which you can legally tow, even if you choose to drive slower.

Most countries require a minimum tread depth of 1.6mm but motoring organisations recommend at least 3mm. If you are planning a long journey, consider if they will still be above the legal minimum by the end of your journey.

Tyre Pressure

Tyre pressure should be checked and adjusted when the tyres are cold; checking warm tyres will result in a higher pressure reading. The correct pressures will be found in your car handbook, but unless it states otherwise to add an extra 4 - 6 pounds per square inch to the rear tyres of a car when towing to improve handling. Make sure you know what pressure your caravan tyres should be. Some require a pressure much higher than that normally used for cars. Check your caravan handbook for details.

Tyre Sizes

It is worth noting that some sizes of radial tyre to fit the 13" wheels commonly used on older UK caravans are virtually impossible to find in stock at retailers abroad, e.g. 175R13C.

After a Puncture

A lot of cars now have a liquid sealant puncture repair kit instead of a spare wheel. These should not be considered a permanent repair, and in some cases have been known to make repair of the tyre impossible. If you need to use a liquid sealant you should get the tyre repaired or replaced as soon as possible.

Following a caravan tyre puncture, especially on a single-axle caravan, it is advisable to have the non-punctured tyre removed from its wheel and checked inside and out for signs of damage resulting from overloading during the deflation of the punctured tyre.

Winter Driving

Snow chains must be fitted to vehicles using snow-covered roads in compliance with the relevant road signs. Fines may be imposed for non-compliance. Vehicles fitted with chains must not exceed 50 km/h (31mph).

They are not difficult to fit but it's a good idea to carry sturdy gloves to protect your hands when handling the chains in freezing conditions. Polar Automotive Ltd sells and hires out snow chains, contact them on 01892 519933, www.snowchains.com, or email: polar@snowchains.com.

In Andorra winter tyres are recommended. Snow chains must be used when road conditions necessitate their use and/or when road signs indicate.

Warning Triangles

In almost all European countries it is compulsory to carry a warning triangle which, in the event of vehicle breakdown or accident, must be placed (providing it is safe to do so) on the carriageway at least 30 metres from the vehicle. In some instances it is not compulsory to use the triangle but only when this action would endanger the driver.

A warning triangle should be placed on the road approximately 30 metres (100 metres on motorways) behind the broken down vehicle on the same side of the road. Always assemble the triangle before leaving your vehicle and walk with it so that the red, reflective surface is facing oncoming traffic. If a breakdown occurs round a blind corner, place the triangle in advance of the corner. Hazard warning lights may be used in conjunction with the triangle but they do not replace it.

Essential Equipment Table

The table below shows the essential equipment required for each country. Please note that this information was correct at the time of going to print but is subject to change.

For up to date information on equipment requirements for countries in Europe visit camc.com/overseasadvice.

Country	Warning Triangle	Spare Bulbs	First Aid Kit	Reflective Jacket	Additional Equipment to be Carried/Used
Andorra	Yes (2)	Yes	Rec	Yes	Dipped headlights in poor daytime visibility. Winter tyres recommended; snow chains when road conditions or signs dictate.
Austria	Yes	Rec	Yes	Yes	Winter tyres from 1 Nov to 15 April.*
Belgium	Yes	Rec	Rec	Yes	Dipped headlights in poor daytime visibility.
Croatia	Yes (2 for vehicle with trailer)	Yes	Yes	Yes	Dipped headlights at all times from last Sunday in Oct - last Sunday in Mar. Spare bulbs compulsory if lights are xenon, neon or LED. Snow chains compulsory in winter in certain regions.*
Czech Rep	Yes	Yes	Yes	Yes	Dipped headlights at all times. Replacement fuses. Winter tyres or snow chains from 1 Nov - 31st March.*
Denmark	Yes	Rec	Rec	Rec	Dipped headlights at all times. On motorways use hazard warning lights when queues or danger ahead.
Finland	Yes	Rec	Rec	Yes	Dipped headlights at all times. Winter tyres Dec - Feb.*
France	Yes	Rec	Rec	Yes	Dipped headlights recommended at all times. Legal requirement to carry a breathalyser, but no penalty for non-compliance.

Country	Warning Triangle	Spare Bulbs	First Aid Kit	Reflective Jacket	Additional Equipment to be Carried/Used
Germany	Rec	Rec	Rec	Rec	Dipped headlights recommended at all times. Winter tyres to be used in winter weather conditions.*
Greece	Yes	Rec	Yes	Rec	Fire extinguisher compulsory. Dipped headlights in towns at night and in poor daytime visibility.
Hungary	Yes	Rec	Yes	Yes	Dipped headlights at all times outside built-up areas and in built-up areas at night. Snow chains compulsory on some roads in winter conditions.*
Italy	Yes	Rec	Rec	Yes	Dipped headlights at all times outside built-up areas and in poor visibility. Snow chains from 15 Oct - 15 April.*
Luxembourg	Yes	Rec	Rec	Yes	Dipped headlights at night and daytime in bad weather.
Netherlands	Yes	Rec	Rec	Rec	Dipped headlights at night and in bad weather and recommended during the day.
Norway	Yes	Rec	Rec	Rec	Dipped headlights at all times. Winter tyres compulsory when snow or ice on the roads.*
Poland	Yes	Rec	Rec	Rec	Dipped headlights at all times. Fire extinguisher compulsory.
Portugal	Yes	Rec	Rec	Rec	Dipped headlights in poor daytime visibility, in tunnels and in lanes where traffic flow is reversible.
Slovakia	Yes	Rec	Yes	Yes	Dipped headlights at all times. Winter tyres compulsory when compact snow or ice on the road.*
Slovenia	Yes (2 for vehicle with trailer)	Yes	Rec	Yes	Dipped headlights at all times. Hazard warning lights when reversing. Use winter tyres or carry snow chains 15 Nov - 15 Mar.
Spain	Yes (2 Rec)	Rec	Rec	Yes	Dipped headlights at night, in tunnels and on 'special' roads (roadworks).
Sweden	Yes	Rec	Rec	Rec	Dipped headlights at all times. Winter tyres 1 Dec to 31 March.
Switzerland (inc Liechtenstein)	Yes	Rec	Rec	Rec	Dipped headlights recommended at all times, compulsory in tunnels. Snow chains where indicated by signs.

NOTES:
1) All countries: seat belts (if fitted) must be worn by all passengers.
2) Rec: not compulsory for foreign-registered vehicles, but strongly recommended
3) Headlamp converters, spare bulbs, fire extinguisher, first aid kit and reflective waistcoat are strongly recommended for all countries.
4) In some countries drivers who wear prescription glasses must carry a spare pair.
5) Please check information for any country before you travel. This information is to be used as a guide only and it is your responsibility to make sure you have the correct equipment.

* For more information and regulations on winter driving please see the Country Introduction.

FRANCE
Basel
Zürich
Innsbruck
AUSTRIA
Szombathely
Veszprém
BERN
Graz
Luzern
Nagykar
SWITZERLAND
Klagenfurt
Maribor
Pé
LIECHTENSTEIN
Lausanne
Bolzano
SLOVENIA
Genève
Trento
LJUBLJANA
ZAGREB
Milano
Verona
Trieste
Slavons
Karlovac
Bro
Torino
Venezia
Rijeka
FRANCE
Pula
CROATIA
Banj
Genova
Bologna
BOSN
HERZE
Zeni
Nice
Zadar
MONACO
San Marino
Firenze
Ancona
Split
Livorno
Dubro
Bastia
Perugia
ITALY
Ajaccio
Corse
(Corsica)
(France)
L'Aquila
Pescara
A d r i a t i c S
Campobasso
ROMA
Olbia
Sassari
Napoli
Ba
Potenza
Sardegne
(Sardinia)
(Italy)
N
W   E
S
Cagliari
T y r r h e n i a n
S e a
Nicastro
Cat
	Motorways
	Major roads
	Main roads
	Ferry routes
⊕	Major airports

Messina
Reggio di Cala
Palermo
Sicilia
(Sicily)
Catania
M e d i t e r
Bizerte
Menzel
Bourguiba
Skikda
Annaba
L'Ariana
Ben Arous
Siracusa
Tunis
Guelma

Mountain roads

Mountain Passes

Mountain passes can create difficult driving conditions, especially when towing or driving a large vehicle. You should only use them if you have a good power to weight ratio and in good driving conditions. If in any doubt as to your outfit's suitability or the weather then stick to motorway routes across mountain ranges if possible.

The tables on the following pages show which passes are not suitable for caravans, and those where caravans are not permitted. Motorhomes aren't usually included in these restrictions, but relatively low powered or very large vehicles should find an alternative route. Road signs at the foot of a pass may restrict access or offer advice, especially for heavy vehicles. Warning notices are usually posted at the foot of a pass if it is closed, or if chains or winter tyres must be used.

Caravanners are particularly sensitive to gradients and traffic/road conditions on passes. The maximum gradient is usually on the inside of bends but exercise caution if it is necessary to pull out. Always engage a lower gear before taking a hairpin bend and give priority to vehicles ascending. On mountain roads it is not the gradient which puts strain on your car but the duration of the climb and the loss of power at high altitudes: approximately 10% at 915 metres (3,000 feet) and even more as you get higher. To minimise the risk of the engine overheating, take high passes in the cool part of the day, don't climb any faster than necessary and keep the engine pulling steadily. To prevent a radiator boiling, pull off the road safely, turn the heater and blower full on and switch off air conditioning. Keep an eye on water and oil levels. Never put cold water into a boiling radiator or it may crack. Check that the radiator is not obstructed by debris sucked up during the journey.

A long descent may result in overheating brakes; select the correct gear for the gradient and avoid excessive use of brakes. Even if you are using engine braking to control speed, caravan brakes may activate due to the overrun mechanism, which may cause them to overheat.

Travelling at altitude can cause a pressure build up in tanks and water pipes. You can prevent this by slightly opening the blade valve of your portable toilet and opening a tap a fraction.

Mountain Pass Information

The dates of opening and closing given in the following tables are approximate. Before attempting late afternoon or early morning journeys across borders, check their opening times as some borders close at night.

Gradients listed are the maximum which may be encountered on the pass and may be steeper at the inside of curves, particularly on older roads.

Gravel surfaces (such as dirt and stone chips) vary considerably; they can be dusty when dry and slippery when wet. Where known to exist, this type of surface has been noted.

In fine weather winter tyres or snow chains will only be required on very high passes, or for short periods in early or late summer. In winter conditions you will probably need to use them at altitudes exceeding 600 metres (approximately 2,000 feet).

Tunnels

Long tunnels are a much more commonly seen feature in Europe than in the UK, especially in mountainous regions. Tolls are usually charged for the use of major tunnels.

Dipped headlights are usually required by law even in well-lit tunnels, so switch them on before you enter. Snow chains, if used, must be removed before entering a tunnel in lay-bys provided for this purpose.

'No overtaking' signs must be strictly observed. Never cross central single or double lines. If overtaking is permitted in twin-tube tunnels, bear in mind that it is very easy to underestimate distances and speed once inside. In order to minimise the effects of exhaust fumes close all car windows and set the ventilator to circulate air, or operate the air conditioning system coupled with the recycled air option.

If you break down, try to reach the next lay-by and call for help from an emergency phone. If you cannot reach a lay-by, place your warning triangle at least 100 metres behind your vehicle. Modern tunnels have video surveillance systems to ensure prompt assistance in an emergency. Some tunnels can extend for miles and a high number of breakdowns are due to running out of fuel so make sure you have enough before entering the tunnel.

Tables and Maps

Much of the information contained in the following tables was originally supplied by The Automobile Association and other motoring and tourist organisations. The Caravan and Motorhome Club haven't checked this information and cannot accept responsibility for the accuracy or for errors or omissions to these tables.

The mountain passes, rail and road tunnels listed in the tables are shown on the following maps. Numbers and letters against each pass or tunnel in the tables correspond with the numbers and letters on the maps.

Converting Gradients

20% = 1 in 5	11% = 1 in 9
16% = 1 in 6	10% = 1 in 8
14% = 1 in 7	8% = 1 in 12
12% = 1 in 8	6% = 1 in 16

Abbreviations

MHV	Maximum height of vehicle
MLV	Maximum length of vehicle
MWV	Maximum width of vehicle
MWR	Minimum width of road
OC	Occasionally closed between dates
UC	Usually closed between dates
UO	Usually open between dates, although a fall of snow may obstruct the road for 24-48 hours.

Major Alpine Mountain Passes

Before using any of these passes, please read the advice at the beginning of this chapter.

	Pass Height In Metres (Feet)	From To	Max gradient	Conditions and Comments
1	**Achenpass** (Austria – Germany) 941 (3087)	Achenwald Glashütte	4%	UO. Well-engineered road, B181/307. Gradient not too severe.
2	**Albula** (Switzerland) 2312 (7585)	Tiefencastel La Punt	10%	UC Nov-early Jun. MWR 3.5m (11'6") MWV 2.25m (7'6") Inferior alternative to the Julier; fine scenery. Not recommended for caravans. Alternative rail tunnel.
3	**Allos** (France) 2250 (7382)	Colmars Barcelonette	10%	UC early Nov-early Jun. MWR 4m (13'1") Very winding, narrow, mostly unguarded pass on D908 but not difficult otherwise; passing bays on southern slope; poor surface, MWV 1.8m (5'11"). Not recommended for caravans.
4	**Aprica** (Italy) 1176 (3858)	Tresenda Edolo	9%	UO. MWR 4m (13'1"). Fine scenery: good surface; well-graded on road S39. Narrow in places; watch for protruding rock. Not recommended for caravanners to attempt this pass E or W. Poor road conditions, repairs reduce width drastically.
5	**Aravis** (France) 1498 (4915)	La Clusaz Flumet	9%	OC Dec-Mar. MWR 4m (13'1"). Fine scenery; D909, fairly easy road. Poor surface in parts on Chamonix side. Some single-line traffic.
6	**Arlberg** (Austria) 1802 (5912)	Bludenz Landeck	13%	OC Dec-Apr. MWR 6m (19'8"). Good modern road B197/E60 with several pull-in places. Steeper fr W easing towards summit; heavy traffic. Caravans prohibited. Parallel road tunnel (tolls) available on E60 (poss long queues).
7	**Ballon d'Alsace** (France) 1178 (3865)	Giromagny St Maurice-sur-Moselle	11%	OC Dec-Mar. MWR 4m (13'1") Fairly straightforward ascent/descent; narrow in places; numerous bends. On road D465.
8	**Bayard** (France) 1248 (4094)	Chauffayer Gap	14%	UO. MWR 6m (19'8") Part of the Route Napoléon N85. Fairly easy, steepest on the S side with several hairpin bends. Negotiable by caravans from N-to-S via D1075 (N75) and Col-de-la-Croix Haute, avoiding Gap.
9	**Bernina** (Switzerland) 2330 (7644)	Pontresina Poschiavo	12.50%	OC Dec-Mar. MWR 5m (16'5") MWV 2.25m (7'6") Fine scenery. Good with care on open narrow sections towards summit on S-side; on road no. 29.
10	**Bracco** (Italy) 613 (2011)	Riva Trigoso Borghetto di Vara	14%	UO. MWR 5m (16'5") A two-lane road (P1) more severe than height suggests due to hairpins and volume of traffic; passing difficult. Rec cross early to avoid traffic. Alternative toll m'way A12 available.

Before using any of these passes, please read the advice at the beginning of this chapter.

	Pass Height in Metres (Feet)	From To	Max gradient	Conditions and Comments
11	**Brenner (Europabrücke)** (Austria – Italy) 1374 (4508)	Innsbruck *Vipiteno/Sterzing*	14%	UO. MWR 6m (19'8") On road no. 182/12. Parallel toll m'way A13/A22/E45 (6%) suitable for caravans. Heavy traffic may delay at Customs. Pass road closed to vehicles towing trailers.
12	**Brouis** (France) 1279 (4196)	Nice *Col-de-Tende*	12.50%	UO. MWR 6m (19'8") Good surface but many hairpins on D6204 (N204)/S20. Steep gradients on approaches. Height of tunnel at Col-de-Tende at the Italian border is 3.8m (12'4) Not recommended for caravans.
13	**Brünig** (Switzerland) 1007 (3340)	Brienzwiler Station *Giswil*	8.50%	UO. MWR 6m (19'8") MWV 2.5m (8'2") An easy but winding road (no. 4); heavy traffic at weekends; frequent lay-bys. On-going road improvement (2009) may cause delays – check before travel.
14	**Bussang** (France) 721 (2365)	Thann *St Maurice-sur-Moselle*	7%	UO. MWR 4m (13'1") A very easy road (N66) over the Vosges; beautiful scenery.
15	**Cabre** (France) 1180 (3871)	Luc-en-Diois *Aspres-sur-Buëch*	9%	UO. MWR 5.5m (18') An easy pleasant road (D93/D993), winding at Col-de-Cabre.
16	**Campolongo** (Italy) 1875 (6152)	Corvara-in-Badia *Arabba*	12.50%	OC Dec-Mar. MWR 5m (16'5") A winding but easy ascent on rd P244; long level stretch on summit followed by easy descent. Good surface, fine scenery.
17	**Cayolle** (France) 2326 (7631)	Barcelonnette *Guillaumes*	10%	UC early Nov-early Jun. MWR 4m (13'1") Narrow, winding road (D902) with hairpin bends; poor surface, broken edges with steep drops. Long stretches of single-track road with passing places. Caravans prohibited.
18	**Costalunga (Karer)** (Italy) 1745 (5725)	Bolzano *Pozza-di-Fassa*	16%	OC Dec-Apr. MWR 5m (16'5") A good well-engineered road (S241) but mostly winding with many blind hairpins. Caravans prohibited.
19	**Croix** (Switzerland) 1778 (5833)	Villars-sur-Ollon *Les Diablerets*	13%	UC Nov-May. MWR 3.5m (11'6") A narrow, winding route but extremely picturesque. Not recommended for caravans.
20	**Croix Haute** (France) 1179 (3868)	Monestier-de-Clermont *Aspres-sur-Buëch*	7%	UO on N75. MWR 5.5m (18') Well-engineered road (D1075/N75); several hairpin bends on N side.
21	**Falzárego** (Italy) 2117 (6945)	Cortina-d'Ampezzo *Andraz*	8.50%	OC Dec-Apr. MWR 5m (16'5") Well-engineered bitumen surface on road R48; many blind hairpin bends on both sides; used by tour coaches.

Before using any of these passes, please read the advice at the beginning of this chapter.

Pass Height In Metres (Feet)	From To	Max gradient	Conditions and Comments
㉒ Faucille (France) 1323 (4341)	Gex Morez	10%	UO. MWR 5m (16'5") Fairly wide, winding road (N5) across the Jura mountains; negotiable by caravans but probably better to follow route via La Cure-St Cergue-Nyon.
㉓ Fern (Austria) 1209 (3967)	Nassereith Lermoos	8%	UO. MWR 6m (19'8") Obstructed intermittently during winter. An easy pass on road 179 but slippery when wet; heavy traffic at summer weekends. Connects with Holzleiten Sattel Pass at S end for travel to/from Innsbruck– see below.
㉔ Flexen (Austria) 1784 (5853)	Lech Rauzalpe (nr Arlberg Pass)	10%	UO. MWR 5.5m (18') The magnificent 'Flexenstrasse', a well-engineered mountain road (no. 198) with tunnels and galleries. The road from Lech to Warth, N of the pass, is usually closed Nov–Apr due to danger of avalanche. Not recommended for caravans.
㉕ Flüela (Switzerland) 2383 (7818)	Davos-Dorf Susch	12.50%	OC Nov–May. MWR 5m (16'5") MWV 2.3m (7'6") Easy ascent from Davos on road no. 28; some acute hairpin bends on the E side; bitumen surface.
㉖ Forclaz (Switzerland – France) 1527 (5010)	Martigny Argentière	8.50%	UO Forclaz; OC Montets Dec-early Apr. MWR 5m (16'5") MWV 2.5m (8'2") Good road over the pass and to the French border; long, hard climb out of Martigny; narrow and rough over Col-des-Montets on D1506 (NS06).
㉗ Foscagno (Italy) 2291 (7516)	Bormio Livigno	12.50%	OC Nov–May. MWR 3.3m (10'10") Narrow and winding road (S301) through lonely mountains, generally poor surface. Long winding ascent with many blind bends; not always well-guarded. Descent includes winding rise and fall over the Passo-d'Eira 2,200m (7,218'). Not recommended for caravans.
㉘ Fugazze (Italy) 1159 (3802)	Rovereto Valli-del-Pasubio	14%	UO. MWR 3.5m (11'6") Very winding road (S46) with some narrow sections, particularly on N side. The many blind bends and several hairpin bends call for extra care. Not recommended for caravans.
㉙ Furka (Switzerland) 2431 (7976)	Gletsch Realp	11%	UC Oct-Jun. MWR 4m (13'1") MWV 2.25m (7'6") Well-graded road (no. 19) with narrow sections (single track in place on E side) and several hairpin bends on both ascent and descent. Fine views of the Rhône Glacier. Beware of coaches and traffic build-up. Not recommended for caravans. Alternative rail tunnel available.
㉚ Galibier (France) 2645 (8678)	La Grave St Michel-de-Maurienne	12.50%	UC Oct-Jun. MWR 3m (9'10") Mainly wide, well-surfaced road (D902) but unprotected and narrow over summit. From Col-du-Lautaret it rises over the Col-du-Telegraphe then 11 more hairpin bends. Ten hairpin bends on descent then 5km (3.1 miles) narrow and rough; easier in N to S direction. Limited parking at summit. Not recommended for caravans. (Single-track tunnel under the Galibier summit, controlled by traffic lights; caravans are not permitted).
㉛ Gardena (Grödner-Joch) (Italy) 2121 (6959)	Val Gardena Corvara-in-Badia	12.50%	OC Dec-Jun. MWR 5m (16'5") A well-engineered road (S243), very winding on descent. Fine views. Caravans prohibited.

Before using any of these passes, please read the advice at the beginning of this chapter.

	Pass Height in Metres (Feet)	From To	Max gradient	Conditions and Comments
32	**Gavia** (Italy) 2621 (8599)	Bormio *Ponte-di-Legno*	20%	UC Oct-Jul. MWR 3m (9'10") MWV 1.8m (5'11") Steep, narrow, difficult road (P300) with frequent passing bays; many hairpin bends and gravel surface; not for the faint-hearted; extra care necessary. Not recommended for caravans. Long winding ascent on Bormio side.
33	**Gerlos** (Austria) 1628 (5341)	Zell-am-Ziller *Wald im Pinzgau*	9%	UO. MWR 4m (13'1") Hairpin ascent out of Zell to modern toll road (B165); the old, steep, narrow and winding route with passing bays and 14% gradient is not rec but is negotiable with care. Views of Krimml waterfalls. Caravans prohibited.
34	**Gorges-du-Verdon** (France) 1032 (3386)	Castellane *Moustiers-Ste Marie*	9%	UO. MWR probably 5m (16'5") On road D952 over Col-d'Ayen and Col-d'Olivier. Moderate gradients but slow, narrow and winding. Poss heavy traffic.
35	**Grand St Bernard** (Switzerland – Italy) 2469 (8100)	Martigny *Aosta*	11%	UC Oct-Jun. MWR 4m (13'1") MWV 2.5m (8' 2") Modern road to entrance of road tunnel on road no. 21/E27 (UO), then narrow but bitumen surface over summit to border; also good in Italy. Suitable for caravans using tunnel. Pass road feasible but not recommended. See *Road Tunnels* in this section.
36	**Grimsel** (Switzerland) 2164 (7100)	Innertkirchen *Gletsch*	10%	UC mid Oct-late Jun. MWR 5m (16'5") MWV 2.25m (7'6") A fairly easy, modern road (no. 6) with heavy traffic at weekends. A long winding ascent, finally hairpin bends; then a terraced descent with six hairpins (some tight) into the Rhône valley. Good surface; fine scenery.
37	**Grossglockner** (Austria) 2503 (8212)	Bruck-an-der-Grossglocknerstrasse *Heiligenblut*	12.50%	UC late Oct-early May. MWR 5.5m (18') Well-engineered road (no. 107) but many hairpins; heavy traffic; moderate but very long ascent/descent. Negotiable preferably S to N by caravans. Avoid side road to highest point at Edelweissespitze if towing, as road is very steep and narrow. Magnificent scenery. Tolls charged. Road closed from 2200-0500 hrs (summer). Alternative Felbertauern road tunnel between Lienz and Mittersil (toll).
38	**Hahntennjoch** (Austria) 1894 (6250)	Imst *Elmen*	15%	UC Nov-May. A minor pass. Caravans prohibited.
39	**Hochtannberg** (Austria) 1679 (5509)	Schröcken *Warth (nr Lech)*	14%	OC Jan-Mar. MWR 4m (13'1") A reconstructed modern road (no. 200). W to E long ascent with many hairpins. Easier E to W. Not recommended for caravans.
40	**Holzleiten Sattel** (Austria) 1126 (3694)	Nassereith *Obsteig*	12.50%	(12.5%), UO. MWR 5m (16'5") Road surface good on W side; poor on E. Light traffic; gradients no problem. Not recommended for caravans.
41	**Iseran** (France) 2770 (9088)	Bourg-St Maurice *Lanslebourg*	11%	UC mid Oct-late Jun. MWR 4m (13'1") Second highest pass in the Alps on road D902. Well-graded with reasonable bends, average surface. Several unlit tunnels on N approach. Not recommended for caravans.

Pass Height In Metres (Feet)	From To	Max gradient	Conditions and Comments
42 Izoard (France) 2360 (7743)	Guillestre *Briançon*	12.50%	UC late Oct-mid Jun. MWR 5m (16'5") Fine scenery. Winding, sometimes narrow road (D902) with many hairpin bends; care required at several unlit tunnels near Guillestre. Not recommended for caravans.
43 Jaun (Switzerland) 1509 (4951)	Bulle *Reidenbach*	14%	UO. MWR 4m (13'1") MWV 2.25m (7'6") A modern but generally narrow road (no. 11); some poor sections on ascent and several hairpin bends on descent.
44 Julier (Switzerland) 2284 (7493)	Tiefencastel *Silvaplana*	13%	UO. MWR 4m (13'1") MWV 2.5m (8'2") Well-engineered road (no. 3) approached from Chur via Sils. Fine scenery. Negotiable by caravans, preferably from N to S, but a long haul and many tight hairpins. Alternative rail tunnel from Thusis to Samedan. See *Rail Tunnels* in this section.
45 Katschberg (Austria) 1641 (5384)	Spittal-an-der-Drau *St Michael*	20%	UO. MWR 6m (19'8") Good wide road (no. 99) with no hairpins but steep gradients particularly from S. Suitable only light caravans. Parallel Tauern/Katschberg toll motorway A10/E55 and road tunnels.
46 Klausen (Switzerland) 1948 (6391)	Altdorf *Linthal*	10%	UC late Oct-early Jun. MWR 5m (16'5") MWV 2.30m (7'6") Narrow and winding in places, but generally easy in spite of a number of sharp bends. Caravans prohibited between Unterschächen and Linthal (no. 17).
47 Larche (della Maddalena) (France – Italy) 1994 (6542)	La Condamine-Châtelard *Vinadio*	8.50%	OC Dec-Mar. MWR 3.5m (11'6") An easy, well-graded road (D900); long, steady ascent on French side, many hairpins on Italian side (S21). Fine scenery; ample parking at summit.
48 Lautaret (France) 2058 (6752)	Le Bourg-d'Oisans *Briançon*	12.50%	OC Dec-Mar. MWR 4m (13'1") Modern, evenly graded but winding road (D1091), and unguarded in places; very fine scenery; suitable for caravans but with care through narrow tunnels.
49 Leques (France) 1146 (3760)	Barrême *Castellane*	8%	UO. MWR 4m (13'1") On Route Napoléon (D4085). Light traffic; excellent surface; narrow in places on N ascent. S ascent has many hairpins.
50 Loibl (Ljubelj) (Austria – Slovenia) 1067 (3500)	Unterloibl *Kranj*	20%	UO. MWR 6m (19'8") Steep rise and fall over Little Loibl pass (E652) to 1.6km (1 mile) tunnel under summit. Caravans prohibited. The old road over the summit is closed to through-traffic.
51 Lukmanier (Lucomagno) (Switzerland) 1916 (6286)	Olivone *Disentis*	9%	UC early Nov-late May. MWR 5m (16'5") MWV 2.25m (7'6") Rebuilt, modern road.
52 Maloja (Switzerland) 1815 (5955)	Silvaplana *Chiavenna*	9%	UO. MWR 4m (13'1") MWV 2.5m (8'2") Escarpment facing south; fairly easy, but many hairpin bends on descent; negotiable by caravans but possibly difficult on ascent. On road no. 3/S37.

Before using any of these passes, please read the advice at the beginning of this chapter.

Pass Height In Metres (Feet)	From To	Max gradient	Conditions and Comments
53 **Mauria** (Italy) 1298 (4258)	Lozzo di Cadore / Ampezzo	7%	UO. MWR 5m (16'5") A well-designed road (S52) with easy, winding ascent and descent.
54 **Mendola** (Italy) 1363 (4472)	Appiano/Eppan / Sarnonico	12.50%	UO. MWR 5m (16'5") A fairly straightforward but winding road (S42), well-guarded, many hairpins. Take care overhanging cliffs if towing. The E side going down to Bolzano is not wide enough for caravans, especially difficult on busy days, not recommended for caravans.
55 **Mont Cenis** (France – Italy) 2083 (6834)	Lanslebourg / Susa	12.50%	UC Nov–May. MWR 5m (16'5") Approach by industrial valley. An easy highway (D1006/S25) with mostly good surface; spectacular scenery; long descent into Italy with few stopping places. Alternative Fréjus road tunnel available.
56 **Monte Croce-di-Comélico (Kreuzberg)** (Italy) 1636 (5368)	San Candido / Santo-Stefano-di-Cadore	8.50%	UO. MWR 5m (16'5") A winding road (S52) with moderate gradients, beautiful scenery.
57 **Montgenèvre** (France – Italy) 1850 (6070)	Briançon / Cesana-Torinese	9%	UO. MWR 5m (16'5") Easy, modern road (N94/S24), some tight hairpin bends, good road surface on French side; road widened & tunnels improved on Italian side, in need of some repair but still easy. Much used by lorries; may need to give way to large vehicles on hairpins.
58 **Monte Giovo (Jaufen)** (Italy) 2094 (6870)	Merano / Vipiteno/Sterzing	12.50%	UC Nov–May. MWR 4m (13'1") Many well-engineered hairpin bends on S44; good scenery. Caravans prohibited.
Montetts (See Forclaz)			
59 **Morgins** (France – Switzerland) 1369 (4491)	Abondance / Monthey	14%	UO. MWR 4m (13'1") A lesser used route (D22) through pleasant, forested countryside crossing French/Swiss border. Not recommended for caravans.
60 **Mosses** (Switzerland) 1445 (4740)	Aigle / Château-d'Oex	8.50%	UO. MWR 4m (13'1") MWV 2.25m (7'6") A modern road (no. 11). Aigle side steeper and narrow in places.
61 **Nassfeld (Pramollo)** (Austria – Italy) 1530 (5020)	Tröpolach / Pontebba	20%	OC Late Nov–Mar. MWR 4m (13'1") The winding descent on road no. 90 into Italy has been improved but not rec for caravans.
62 **Nufenen (Novena) (Switzerland)** 2478 (8130)	Ulrichen / Airolo	10%	UC Mid Oct–mid Jun. MWR 4m (13'1") MWV 2.25m (7'6") The approach roads are narrow, with tight bends, but the road over the pass is good; negotiable with care. Long drag from Ulrichen.
63 **Oberalp** (Switzerland) 2044 (6706)	Andermatt / Disentis	10%	UC Nov–late May. MWR 5m (16'5") MWV 2.3m (7'6") Much improved and widened road (no.19) but narrow in places on E side; many tight hairpin bends, but long level stretch on summit. Alternative rail tunnel during the winter. Not recommended for caravans.

	Pass Height In Metres (Feet)	From To	Max gradient	Conditions and Comments
64	**Ofen (Fuorn)** (Switzerland) 2149 (7051)	Zernez Santa Maria-im- Münstertal	12.50%	UO. MWR 4m (13'1") MWV 2.25m (7'6") Good road (no. 28) through Swiss National Park.
65	**Petit St Bernard** (France – Italy) 2188 (7178)	Bourg-St Maurice Pré-St Didier	8.50%	UC mid Oct-Jun. MWR 5m (16'5") Outstanding scenery, but poor surface and unguarded broken edges near summit. Easiest from France (D1090); sharp hairpins on climb from Italy (S26). Caravans prohibited.
66	**Pillon** (Switzerland) 1546 (5072)	Le Sépey Gsteig	9%	OC Jan-Feb. MWR 4m (13'1") MWV 2.25m (7'6") A comparatively easy modern road.
67	**Plöcken (Monte Croce-Carnico)** (Austria – Italy) 1362 (4468)	Kötschach Paluzza	14%	OC Dec-Apr. MWR 5m (16'5") A modern road (no. 110) with long, reconstructed sections; OC to caravans due to heavy traffic on summer weekends; delay likely at the border. Long, slow, twisty pull from S, easier from N.
68	**Pordoi** (Italy) 2239 (7346)	Arabba Canazei	10%	OC Dec-Apr. MWR 5m (16'5") An excellent modern road (S48) with numerous blind hairpin bends; fine scenery; used by tour coaches. Long drag when combined with Falzarego pass.
69	**Pötschen** (Austria) 982 (3222)	Bad Ischl Bad Aussee	9%	UO. MWR 7m (23') A modern road (no. 145). Good scenery.
70	**Radstädter-Tauern** (Austria) 1738 (5702)	Radstadt Mauterndorf	16%	OC Jan-Mar. MWR 5m (16'5") N ascent steep (road no. 99) but not difficult otherwise; but negotiable by light caravans using parallel toll m'way (A10) through tunnel.
71	**Résia (Reschen)** (Italy – Austria) 1504 (4934)	Spondigna Pfunds	10%	UO. MWR 6m (19'8") A good, straightforward alternative to the Brenner Pass. Fine views but no stopping places. On road S40/180.
72	**Restefond (La Bonette)** (France) 2802 (9193)	Barcelonnette St Etienne-de-Tinée	16%	UC Oct-Jun. MWR 3m (9'10") The highest pass in the Alps. Rebuilt, resurfaced road (D64) with rest area at summit – top loop narrow and unguarded. Winding with hairpin bends. Not recommended for caravans.
73	**Rolle** (Italy) 1970 (6463)	Predazzo Mezzano	9%	OC Dec-Mar. MWR 5m (16'5") A well-engineered road (S50) with many hairpin bends on both sides; very beautiful scenery; good surface.
	Rombo (See Timmelsjoch)			
74	**St Gotthard (San Gottardo)** (Switzerland) 2108 (6916)	Göschenen Airolo	10%	UC mid Oct-early Jun. MWR 6m (19'8") MHV 3.6m (11'9") MWV 2.5m (8'2") Modern, fairly easy two- to three-lane road (A2/E35). Heavy traffic. Alternative road tunnel.

Before using any of these passes, please read the advice at the beginning of this chapter.

	Pass Height in Metres (Feet)	From To	Max gradient	Conditions and Comments
75	San Bernardino (Switzerland) 2066 (6778)	Mesocco Hinterrhein	10%	UC Oct-late Jun. MWR 4m (13'1") MWV 2.25m (7'6") Easy modern road (A13/E43) on N and S approaches to tunnel, narrow and winding over summit via tunnel suitable for caravans.
76	Schlucht (France) 1139 (3737)	Gérardmer Munster	7%	UO. MWR 5m (16'5") An extremely picturesque route (D417) crossing the Vosges mountains, with easy, wide bends on the descent. Good surface.
77	Seeberg (Jezersko) (Austria – Slovenia) 1218 (3996)	Eisenkappel Kranj	12.50%	UO. MWR 5m (16'5") An alternative to the steeper Loibl and Wurzen passes on B82/210; moderate climb with winding, hairpin ascent and descent. Not recommended for caravans.
78	Sella (Italy) 2240 (7349)	Selva Canazei	11%	OC Dec-Jan. MWR 5m (16'5") A well-engineered, winding road; exceptional views of Dolomites. Caravans prohibited.
79	Sestriere (Italy) 2033 (6670)	Cesana-Torinese Pinarolo	10%	UO MWR 6m (19'8") Mostly bitumen surface on road R23. Fairly easy; fine scenery.
80	Silvretta (Bielerhöhe) (Austria) 2032 (6666)	Partenen Galtur	11%	UC late Oct-early Jun. MWR 5m (16'5") Mostly reconstructed road (188); 32 easy hairpin bends on W ascent; E side more straightforward. Tolls charged. Caravans prohibited.
81	Simplon (Switzerland – Italy) 2005 (6578)	Brig Domodóssola	11%	OC Nov-Apr. MWR 7m (23") MWV 2.5m (8'2") An easy, reconstructed, modern road (E62/S33), 21km (13 miles) long, continuous ascent to summit; good views, many stopping places. Surface better on Swiss side. Alternative rail tunnel fr Kandersteg in operation from Easter to September.
82	Splügen (Switzerland – Italy) 2113 (6932)	Splügen Chiavenna	13%	UC Nov-Jun. MWR 3.5m (11'6") MHV 2.8m (9'2") MWV 2.3m (7'6") Mostly narrow, winding road (S36), with extremely tight hairpin bends, not well guarded; care also required at many tunnels/galleries. Not recommended for caravans.
83	Stelvio (Italy) 2757 (9045)	Bormio Spondigna	12.50%	UC Oct-late Jun. MWR 4m (13'1") MLV 10m (32') Third highest pass in Alps on S38; 40-50 acute hairpin bends either side, all well-engineered; good surface, traffic often heavy. Hairpin bends too acute for long vehicles. Not recommended for caravans.
84	Susten (Switzerland) 2224 (7297)	Innertkirchen Wassen	9%	UC Nov-Jun. MWR 6m (19'8") MWV 2.5m (8'2") Scenic, well-guarded road (no. 11); easy gradients and turns; heavy weekend traffic. East side easier than west. Negotiable by caravans (rec small/medium sized only) with care, not for the faint-hearted. Large summit parking area.
85	Tenda (Tende) Italy – France 1321 (4334)	Borgo-San Dalmazzo Tende	9%	UO. MWR 6m (19'8") Well-guarded, modern road (S20/ND6204) with several hairpin bends; road tunnel (height 3.8m) at summit narrow with poor road surface. Less steep on Italian side. Caravans prohibited during winter.

	Pass Height In Metres (Feet)	From To	Max gradient	Conditions and Comments
86	**Thurn** (Austria) 1274 (4180)	Kitzbühel _Mittersill_	8.50%	UO. MWR 5m (16'5") MWV 2.5m (8' 2") A good road (no. 161) with narrow stretches; N approach rebuilt. Several good parking areas.
87	**Timmelsjoch (Rombo)** (Austria – Italy) 2509 (8232)	Obergurgl _Moso_	14%	UC mid Oct–Jun. MWR 3.5m (11'6") Border closed at night 8pm to 7am. On the pass (road no 186/S44b) caravans are prohibited. (toll charged), as some tunnels on Italian side too narrow for larger vehicles. Easiest N to S.
88	**Tonale** (Italy) 1883 (6178)	Edolo _Dimaro_	10%	UO. MWR 5m (16'5") A relatively easy road (S42); steepest on W; long drag. Fine views.
89	**Tre Croci** (Italy) 1809 (5935)	Cortina-d'Ampezzo _Auronzo-di-Cadore_	11%	OC Dec–Mar. MWR 6m (19'8") An easy pass on road R48; fine scenery.
90	**Turracher Höhe** (Austria) 1763 (5784)	Predlitz _Ebene-Reichenau_	23%	UO. MWR 4m (13'1") Formerly one of the steepest mountain roads (no. 95) in Austria; now improved. Steep, fairly straightforward ascent followed by a very steep descent; good surface and mainly two-lane; fine scenery. Not recommended for caravans.
91	**Umbrail** (Switzerland – Italy) 2501 (8205)	Santa Maria-im-Münstertal _Bormio_	9%	UC Nov–early Jun. MWR 4.3m (14'1") MWV 2.3m (7'6") Highest Swiss pass (road S38); mostly tarmac with some gravel surface. Narrow with 34 hairpin bends. Not recommended for caravans.
92	**Vars** (France) 2109 (6919)	St Paul-sur-Ubaye _Guillestre_	9%	OC Dec–Mar. MWR 5m (16'5") Easy winding ascent and descent on D902 with 14 hairpin bends; good surface.
93	**Wurzen (Koren)** (Austria – Slovenia) 1073 (3520)	Riegersdorf _Kranjska Gora_	20%	UO. MWR 4m (13'1") Steep two-lane road (no. 109), otherwise not particularly difficult; better on Austrian side; heavy traffic summer weekends; delays likely at the border. Caravans prohibited.
94	**Zirler Berg** (Austria) 1009 (3310)	Seefeld _Zirl_	16.50%	UO. MWR 7m (23"). South facing escarpment, good, modern road (no. 171). Heavy tourist traffic and long steep descent with one hairpin bend into Inn Valley. Steepest section from hairpin bend down to Zirl. Caravans not permitted northbound and not recommended southbound.

Technical information by courtesy of the Automobile Association. Additional update and amendments supplied by caravanners and tourers who have themselves used the passes and tunnels. The Caravan and Motorhome Club has not checked the information contained in these tables and cannot accept responsibility for their accuracy, or for any errors, omissions, or their effects.

Major Alpine Rail Tunnels

Before using any of these tunnels, please read the advice at the beginning of this chapter.

	Tunnel	Route	Journey Time	General Information and Comments	Contact
A	**Albula** (Switzerland) 5.9 km (3.5 miles)	**Chur – St Moritz** Thusis to Samedan	80 mins	MHV 2.85m + MWV 1.40m or MHV 2.50m + MWV 2.20 This tunnel no longer operates a car transport service, but there are regular passenger transport services.	Thusis (081) 2884716 Samedan (081) 2885511 www.rhb.ch
B	**Furka** (Switzerland) 15.4 km (9.5 miles)	**Andermatt – Brig** Realp to Oberwald	15 mins	Hourly all year from 6am to 9pm weekdays; half-hourly weekends. MHV 3.5m Saturdays in February and March are exceptionally busy.	(027) 9277777 www.mgbahn.ch
C	**Oberalp** (Switzerland) 28 km (17.3 miles)	**Andermatt – Disentis** Andermatt to Sedrun	60 mins	MHV 2.50m 2-6 trains daily when the Oberalp Pass is closed for winter.. Advance booking is compulsory.	(027) 9277777 www.mgbahn.ch
D	**Lötschberg** (Switzerland) 14 km (8.7 miles)	**Bern – Brig** Kandersteg to Goppenstein	15 mins	MHV 2.90m Frequent all year half-hourly service. Journey time 15 minutes. Advance booking unnecessary; extension to Hohtenn operates when Goppenstein-Gampel road is closed.	Kandersteg (0)900 553333 www.bls.ch/autoverlad
E	**Simplon** (Switzerland – Italy)	**Brig – Domodossola** Brig to Iselle	20 mins	10 trains daily, all year.	(0)900 300300 http://mct.sbb.ch//mct/autoverlad
	Lötschberg/ Simplon Switzerland – Italy	**Bern – Domodossola** Kandersteg to Iselle	75 mins	Limited service Easter to mid-October up to 3 days a week (up to 10 times a day) and at Christmas for vehicles max height 2.50m, motor caravans up to 5,000 kg. Advance booking compulsory.	(0)900 553333 www.bls.ch
F	**Tauerbahn** (Austria)	**Bad Gastein – Spittal an der Drau** Böckstein to Mallnitz	11 mins	East of and parallel to Grossglockner pass. Half-hourly service all year.	(05) 1717 http://autoschleuse.oebb.at
G	**Vereina** (Switzerland) 19.6 km (11.7 miles)	**Klosters – Susch** Selfranga to Sagliains	18 mins	MLV 12m Half-hourly daytime service all year. Journey time 18 minutes. Restricted capacity for vehicles over 3.30m high during winter w/ ends and public holidays. Steep approach to Klosters.	(081) 2883737 www.rhb.ch

NOTES: Information believed to be correct at time of publication. Detailed timetables are available from the appropriate tourist offices. Always check for current information before you travel.

Major Alpine Road Tunnels

Before using any of these tunnels, please read the advice at the beginning of this chapter.

	Tunnel	Route and Height above Sea Level	General Information and Comments
H	Arlberg (Austria) 14 km (8.75 miles)	Langen to St Anton 1220m (4000')	On B197 parallel and to S of Arlberg Pass which is closed to caravans/trailers. Motorway vignette required; tolls charged. www.arlberg.com
I	Bosruck (Austria) 5.5 km (3.4 miles)	Spital am Pyhrn to Selzthal 742m (2434')	To E of Phyrn pass; with Gleinalm Tunnel (see below) forms part of A9 a'bahn between Linz & Graz. Max speed 80 km/h (50 mph). Use dipped headlights, no overtaking. Occasional emergency lay-bys with telephones. Motorway vignette required; tolls charged.
J	Felbertauern (Austria) 5.3 km (3.25 miles)	Mittersill to Matrei 1525m (5000')	MWR 7m (23'), tunnel height 4.5m (14'9"). On B109 W of and parallel to Grossglockner pass; downwards gradient of 9% S to N with sharp bend before N exit. Wheel chains may be needed on approach Nov-Apr. Tolls charged.
K	Frejus (France – Italy) 12.8 km (8 miles)	Modane to Bardonecchia 1220m (4000')	MWR 9m (29'6"), tunnel height 4.3m (14'). Min/max speed 60/70 km/h (37/44 mph). Return tickets valid until midnight on 7th day after day of issue. Season tickets are available. Approach via A43 and D1006; heavy use by freight vehicles. Good surface on approach roads. Tolls charged. www.sftrf.fr
L	Gleinalm (Austria) 8.3 km (5 miles)	St Michael to Fiesach (nr Graz) 817m (2680')	Part of A9 Pyhrn a'bahn. Motorway vignette required; tolls charged.
M	Grand St Bernard (Switzerland – Italy) 5.8 km (3.6 miles)	Bourg-St Pierre to St Rhémy (Italy) 1925m (7570')	MHV 4m (13'1"), MWV 2.55m (8'2.5"), MLV 18m (60'). Min/max speed 40/80 km/h (24/50 mph). On E27. Passport check, Customs & toll offices at entrance; breakdown bays at each end with telephones; return tickets valid one month. Although approaches are covered, wheel chains may be needed in winter. Season tickets are available. Motorway vignette required; tolls charged. For 24-hour information tel: (027) 7884400 (Switzerland) or 0165 780902 (Italy), www.letunnel.com
N	Karawanken (Austria – Slovenia) 8 km (5 miles)	Rosenbach to Jesenice 610m (2000')	On A11. Motorway vignette required; tolls charged.
O	Mont Blanc (France – Italy) 11.6 km (7.2 miles)	Chamonix to Courmayeur 1381m (4530')	MHV 4.7m (15'5"), MWV 6m (19'6") On N205 France, S26 (Italy). Max speed in tunnel 70 km/h (44 mph) – lower limits when exiting; min speed 50 km/h. Leave 150m between vehicles; ensure enough fuel for 30km. Return tickets valid until midnight on 7th day after issue. Season tickets are available. Tolls charged. www.tunnelmb.net

Before using any of these tunnels, please read the advice at the beginning of this chapter.

	Tunnel	Route and Height above Sea Level	General Information and Comments
P	**Munt La Schera** (Switzerland – Italy) 3.5 km (2 miles)	**Zernez to Livigno** 1706m (5597')	MHV 3.6m (11'9"), MWV 2.5m (8'2"). Open 24 hours; single lane traffic controlled by traffic lights; roads from Livogno S to the Bernina Pass and Bormio closed Dec-Apr. On N28 (Switzerland). Tolls charged. Tel: (081) 8561888, www.livigno.eu
Q	**St Gotthard** (Switzerland) 16.3 km (10 miles)	**Göschenen to Airolo** 1159m (3800')	Tunnel height 4.5m (14'9"), single carriageway 7.5m (25') wide. Max speed 80 km/h (50 mph). No tolls, but tunnel is part of Swiss motorway network (A2). Motorway vignette required. Tunnel closed 8pm to 5am Monday to Friday for periods during June and September. Heavy traffic and delays high season. www.gotthard-strassentunnel.ch
-	**Ste Marie-aux-Mines** 6.8 km (4.25 miles)	**St Dié to Ste-Marie-aux-Mines** 772m (2533')	Re-opened October 2008; the longest road tunnel situated entirely in France. Also known as Maurice Lemaire Tunnel, through the Vosges in north-east France from Lusse on N159 to N59. Tolls charged. Alternate route via Col-de-Ste Marie on D459.
R	**San Bernardino** (Switzerland) 6.6 km (4 miles)	**Hinterrhein to San Bernadino** 1644m (5396')	Tunnel height 4.8m (15'9"), width 7m (23'). On A13 motorway. No stopping or overtaking; keep 100m between vehicles; breakdown bays with telephones. Max speed 80 km/h (50 mph). Motorway vignette required.
S	**Tauern and Katschberg** (Austria) 6.4 km (4 miles) & 5.4km (3.5 miles)	**Salzburg to Villach** 1340m (4396') & 1110m (3642')	The two major tunnels on the A10, height 4.5m (14'9"), width 7.5m (25'). Motorway vignette required; tolls charged.

NOTES: *Dipped headlights should be used (unless stated otherwise) when travelling through road tunnels, even when the road appears well lit. In some countries police make spot checks and impose on-the-spot fines. During the winter wheel chains may be required on the approaches to some tunnels. These must not be used in tunnels and lay-bys are available for the removal and refitting of wheel chains. Much of the information contained in the table was originally supplied by The Automobile Association and other motoring and tourist organisations. Updates and amendments are supplied by caravanners and tourers who have themselves used the passes and tunnels.*

The Caravan and Motorhome Club has not checked the information contained in these tables and cannot accept responsibility for their accuracy, or for any errors, omissions, or for their effects.

Keeping in Touch

Telephones

You might need to use a telephone at some point while you're away, whether to keep in touch with family and friends or call ahead to sites. Even if you don't plan to use one, it's best to make sure you have access to a phone in an emergency.

International Direct Dial Calls

Each country has a unique dialing code you must use if phoning from outside that country. You can find the international dialing code for any country by visiting www.thephonebook.bt.com. First dial the code then the local number. If the area code starts with a zero this should be omitted.

The international access code to dial the UK from anywhere in the world is 0044.

Ringing Tones

Ringing tones vary from country to country, so may sound very different to UK tones. Some ringing tones sound similar to error or engaged tones that you would hear on a UK line.

Using Mobile Phones

Mobile phones have an international calling option called 'roaming' which will automatically search for a local network when you switch your phone on. The EU abolished roaming charges in 2017, but you should contact your service provider to check if there are any charges for your tariff.

Storing telephone numbers in your phone's contact list in international format (i.e. use the prefix of +44 and omit the initial '0') will mean that your contacts will automatically work abroad as well as in the UK.

Global SIM Cards

If you're planning on travelling to more than one country consider buying a global SIM card. This will mean your mobile phone can operate on foreign mobile networks, which will be more cost effective than your service provider's roaming charges. For details of SIM cards available, speak to your service provider or visit www.0044.co.uk or www.globalsimcard.co.uk.

You may find it simpler to buy a SIM card or cheap 'pay-as-you-go' phone abroad if you plan to make a lot for local calls, e.g. to book campsites or restaurants. This may mean that you still have higher call charges for international calls (such as calling the UK).

Before buying a different SIM card, check with you provider whether your phone is locked against use on other networks.

Hands-Free

Legislation in Europe forbids the use of mobile or car phones while driving except when using hands-free equipment. In some European countries it is now also illegal to drive while wearing headphones or a headset - including hands-free kits.

If you are involved in an accident whilst driving and using a hand-held mobile phone, your insurance company may refuse to honour the claim.

Accessing the internet

If you have a phone plan that includes mobile data then you should be able to use this as normal within the European Union. Check with you network provider, and please note that this is likely to change if the UK leaves the EU.

Internet Access

Wi-Fi is available on lots of campsites in Europe, the cost may be an additional charge or included in your pitch fee. Most larger towns may have internet cafés or libraries where you can access the internet, however lots of fast food restaurants and coffee chains now offer free Wi-Fi for customers so you can get access for the price of a coffee or bite to eat.

Many people now use their smartphones for internet access. Another option is a dongle – a device which connects to your laptop to give internet access using a mobile phone network. While these methods are economical in the UK, overseas you will be charged data roaming charges which can run into hundreds or thousands of pounds depending on how much data you use. If you plan on using your smartphone or a dongle abroad speak to your service provider before you leave the UK to make sure you understand the costs or add an overseas data roaming package to your phone contract.

Making Calls from your Laptop

If you download Skype to your laptop you can make free calls to other Skype users anywhere in the world using a Wi-Fi connection. Rates for calls to non-Skype users (landline or mobile phone) are also very competitively-priced. You will need a computer with a microphone and speakers, and a webcam is handy too. It is also possible to download Skype to an internet-enabled mobile phone to take advantage of the same low-cost calls – see www.skype.com.

Club Together

If you want to chat to other members either at home or while you're away, you can do so on The Club's online community Club Together. You can ask questions and gather opinions on the forums at camc.com/together.

Radio and Television

The BBC World Service broadcasts radio programmes 24 hours a day worldwide and you can listen on a number of platforms: online, via satellite or cable, DRM digital radio, internet radio or mobile phone. You can find detailed information and programme schedules at www.bbc.co.uk/worldservice.

Whereas analogue television signals were switched off in the UK during 2012, no date has yet been fixed for the switch off of analogue radio signals.

Digital Terrestrial Television

As in the UK, television transmissions in most of Europe have been converted to digital. The UK's high definition transmission technology may be more advanced than any currently implemented or planned in Europe. This means that digital televisions intended for use in the UK might not be able to receive HD terrestrial signals in some countries.

Satellite Television

For English-language TV programmes the only realistic option is satellite, and satellite dishes are a common sight on campsites all over Europe. A satellite dish mounted on the caravan roof or clamped to a pole fixed to the drawbar, or one mounted on a foldable free-standing tripod, will provide good reception and minimal interference. Remember however that obstructions to the south east (such as

tall trees or even mountains) or heavy rain, can interrupt the signals. A specialist dealer will be able to advise you on the best way of mounting your dish. You will also need a satellite receiver and ideally a satellite-finding meter.

The main entertainment channels such as BBC1, ITV1 and Channel 4 can be difficult to pick up in mainland Europe as they are now being transmitted by new narrow-beam satellites. A 60cm dish should pick up these channels in most of France, Belgium and the Netherlands but as you travel further afield, you'll need a progressively larger dish. See www.satelliteforcaravans.co.uk (created and operated by a Club member) for the latest changes and developments, and for information on how to set up your equipment.

Medical Matters

Before You Travel

You can find country specific medical advice, including any vaccinations you may need, from www.nhs.uk/healthcareabroad, or speak to your GP surgery. For general enquiries about medical care abroad contact NHS England on 0300 311 22 33 or email england.contactus@nhs.uk.

If you have any pre-existing medical conditions you should check with your GP that you are fit to travel. Ask your doctor for a written summary of any medical problems and a list of medications , which is especially important for those who use controlled drugs or hypodermic syringes.

Always make sure that you have enough medication for the duration of your holiday and some extra in case your return is delayed. Take details of the generic name of any drugs you use, as brand names may be different abroad, your blood group and details of any allergies (translations may be useful for restaurants).

An emergency dental kit is available from High Street chemists which will allow you temporarily to restore a crown, bridge or filling or to dress a broken tooth until you can get to a dentist.

A good website to check before you travel is www.nathnac.org/travel which gives general health and safety advice, as well as highlighting potential health risks by country.

European Health Insurance Card

Before leaving home apply for a European Health Insurance Card (EHIC). British residents temporarily visiting another EU country are entitled to receive state-provided emergency treatment during their stay on the same terms as residents of those countries, but you must have a valid EHIC to claim these services.

To apply for your EHIC visit www.ehic.org.uk, call 0300 330 1350 or pick up an application form from a post office. An EHIC is required by each family member, with children under 16 included in a parent or guardian's application. The EHIC is free of charge, is valid for up to five years and can be renewed up to six months before its expiry date. Before you travel remember to check that your EHIC is still valid.

An EHIC is not a substitute for travel insurance and it is strongly recommended that you arrange full travel insurance before leaving home regardless of the cover provided by your EHIC. Some insurance companies require you to have an EHIC and some will waive the policy excess if an EHIC has been used.

If your EHIC is stolen or lost while you are abroad contact 0044 191 2127500 for help. If you experience difficulties in getting your EHIC accepted, telephone the Department for Work & Pensions for assistance on the overseas healthcare team line 0044 (0)191 218 1999 between 8am to 5pm Monday to Friday. Residents of the Republic of Ireland, the Isle of Man and Channel Islands, should check with their own health authorities about reciprocal arrangements with other countries.

Travel Insurance

Despite having an EHIC you may incur high medical costs if you fall ill or have an accident. The cost of bringing a person back to the UK in the event of illness or death is never covered by the EHIC.

Separate additional travel insurance adequate for your destination is essential, such as the Club's Red Pennant Overseas Holiday Insurance – see camc.com/redpennant.

First Aid

A first aid kit containing at least the basic requirements is an essential item, and in some countries it is compulsory to carry one in your vehicle (see the Essential Equipment Table in the chapter Motoring – Equipment). Kits should contain items such as sterile pads, assorted dressings, bandages and plasters, antiseptic wipes or cream, cotton wool, scissors, eye bath and tweezers. Also make sure you carry something for upset stomachs, painkillers and an antihistamine in case of hay fever or mild allergic reactions.

If you're travelling to remote areas then you may find it useful to carry a good first aid manual. The British Red Cross publishes a comprehensive First Aid Manual in conjunction with St John Ambulance and St Andrew's Ambulance Association.

Accidents and Emergencies

If you are involved in or witness a road accident the police may want to question you about it. If possible take photographs or make sketches of the scene, and write a few notes about what happened as it may be more difficult to remember the details at a later date.

For sports activities such as skiing and mountaineering, travel insurance must include provision for covering the cost of mountain and helicopter rescue. Visitors to the Savoie and Haute-Savoie areas should be aware that an accident or illness may result in a transfer to Switzerland for hospital treatment. There is a reciprocal healthcare agreement for British citizens visiting Switzerland but you will be required to pay the full costs of treatment and afterwards apply for a refund.

Sun Protection

Never under-estimate how ill exposure to the sun can make you. If you are not used to the heat it is very easy to fall victim to heat exhaustion or heat stroke. Avoid sitting in the sun between 11am and 3pm and cover your head if sitting or walking in the sun. Use a high sun protection factor (SPF) and re-apply frequently. Make sure you drink plenty of fluids.

Tick-Borne Encephalitis (TBE) and Lyme Disease

Hikers and outdoor sports enthusiasts planning trips to forested, rural areas should be aware of tick-borne encephalitis, which is transmitted by the bite of an infected tick. If you think you may be at risk, seek medical advice on prevention and immunisation before you leave the UK.

There is no vaccine against Lyme disease, an equally serious tick-borne infection, which, if left untreated, can attack the nervous system and joints. You can minimise the risk by using an insect repellent containing DEET, wearing long sleeves and long trousers, and checking for ticks after outdoor activity.

Avoid unpasteurised dairy products in risk areas. See www.tickalert.org or telephone 01943 468010 for more information.

Water and food

Water from mains supplies throughout Europe is generally safe, but may be treated with chemicals which make it taste different to tap water in the UK. If in any doubt, always drink bottled water or boil it before drinking.

Food poisoning is potential anywhere, and a complete change of diet may upset your stomach as well. In hot conditions avoid any food that hasn't been refrigerated or hot food that has been left to cool. Be sensible about the food that you eat – don't eat unpasteurised or undercooked food and if you aren't sure about the freshness of meat or seafood then it is best avoided.

Returning Home

If you become ill on your return home tell your doctor that you have been abroad and which countries you have visited. Even if you have received medical treatment in another country, always consult your doctor if you have been bitten or scratched by an animal while on holiday. If you were given any medicines in another country, it may be illegal to bring them back into the UK. If in doubt, declare them at Customs when you return.

Electricity and Gas

Electricity

General Advice

The voltage for mains electricity is 230V across the EU, but varying degrees of 'acceptable tolerance' mean you may find variations in the actual voltage. Most appliances sold in the UK are 220-240V so should work correctly. However, some high-powered equipment, such as microwave ovens, may not function well – check your instruction manual for any specific instructions. Appliances marked with 'CE' have been designed to meet the requirements of relevant European directives.

The table below gives an approximate idea of which appliances can be used based on the amperage which is being supplied (although not all appliances should be used at the same time). You can work it out more accurately by making a note of the wattage of each appliance in your caravan. The wattages given are based on appliances designed for use in caravans and motorhomes. Household kettles, for example, have at least a 2000W element. Each caravan circuit will also have a maximum amp rating which should not be exceeded.

Electrical Connections – EN60309-2 (CEE17)

EN60309-2 (formerly known as CEE17) is the European Standard for all newly fitted connectors. Most sites should now have these connectors, however there is no requirement to replace connectors which were installed before this was standardised so you may still find some sites where your UK 3 pin connector doesn't fit. For this reason it is a good idea

Amps	Wattage (Approx)	Fridge	Battery Charger	Air Conditioning	LCD TV	Water Heater	Kettle (750W)	Heater (1kW)
2	400	✓	✓					
4	900	✓	✓		✓	✓		
6	1300	✓	✓	*	✓	✓	✓	
8	1800	✓	✓	✓**	✓	✓	✓	✓**
10	2300	✓	✓	✓**	✓	✓	✓	✓**
16	3600	✓	✓	✓	✓	✓	✓	✓**

*	Usage possible, depending on wattage of appliance in question
**	Not to be used at the same time as other high-wattage equipment

to carry a 2-pin adapter. If you are already on site and find your connector doesn't fit, ask campsite staff to borrow or hire an adaptor. You may still encounter a poor electrical supply on site even with an EN60309-2 connection.

If the campsite does not have a modern EN60309-2 (CEE17) supply, ask to see the electrical protection for the socket outlet. If there is a device marked with IDn = 30mA, then the risk is minimised.

Hooking Up to the Mains

Connection should always be made in the following order:

- Check your outfit isolating switch is at 'off'.
- Uncoil the connecting cable from the drum. A coiled cable with current flowing through it may overheat. Take your cable and insert the connector (female end) into your outfit inlet.
- Insert the plug (male end) into the site outlet socket.
- Switch outfit isolating switch to 'on'.
- Use a polarity tester in one of the 13A sockets in the outfit to check all connections are correctly wired. Never leave it in the socket. Some caravans have these devices built in as standard.

It is recommended that the supply is not used if the polarity is incorrect (see Reversed Polarity).

Warnings:

If you are in any doubt of the safety of the system, if you don't receive electricity once connected or if the supply stops then contact the site staff.

If the fault is found to be with your outfit then call a qualified electrician rather than trying to fix the problem yourself.

To ensure your safety you should never use an electrical system which you can't confirm to be safe. Use a mains tester such as the one shown on the right to test the electrical supply.

Always check that a proper earth connection exists before using the electrics. Please note that these testers may not pick up all earth faults so if there is any doubt as to the integrity of the earth system do not use the electrical supply.

Disconnection

- Switch your outfit isolating switch to 'off'.
- At the site supply socket withdraw the plug.
- Disconnect the cable from your outfit.

Motorhomes – if leaving your pitch during the day, don't leave your mains cable plugged into the site supply, as this creates a hazard if the exposed live connections in the plug are touched or if the cable is not seen during grass-cutting.

Reversed Polarity

Even if the site connector meets European Standard EN60309-2 (CEE17), British caravanners are still likely to encounter the problem known as reversed polarity. This is where the site supply 'live' line connects to the outfit's 'neutral' and vice versa. You should always check the polarity immediately on connection, using a polarity tester available from caravan accessory shops. If polarity is reversed the caravan mains electricity should not be used. Try using another nearby socket instead. Frequent travellers to the Continent can make up an adaptor themselves, or ask an electrician to make one for you, with the live

and neutral wires reversed. Using a reversed polarity socket will probably not affect how an electrical appliance works, however your protection is greatly reduced. For example, a lamp socket may still be live as you touch it while replacing a blown bulb, even if the light switch is turned off.

Shaver Sockets

Most campsites provide shaver sockets with a voltage of 220V or 110V. Using an incorrect voltage may cause the shaver to become hot or break. The 2-pin adaptor available in the UK may not fit Continental sockets so it is advisable to buy 2-pin adaptors on the Continent. Many modern shavers will work on a range of voltages which make them suitable for travelling abroad. Check you instruction manual to see if this is the case.

Gas

General Advice

Gas usage can be difficult to predict as so many factors, such as temperature and how often you eat out, can affect the amount you need. As a rough guide allow 0.45kg of gas a day for normal summer usage.

With the exception of Campingaz, LPG cylinders normally available in the UK cannot be exchanged abroad. If possible, take enough gas with you and bring back the empty

Site hooking up adaptor

Adaptateur de prise au site (secteur)
Campingplatz-anschluss (netz)

Extension lead to outfit

Câble de rallonge à la caravane
Verlâengerungskabel zum wohnwagen

Site outlet
Prise du site
Campingplatz-Steckdose

Mains adaptor
Adaptateur Secteur
Netzanschlußstacker

16A 230V AC

cylinders. Always check how many you can take with you as ferry and tunnel operators may restrict the number of cylinders you are permitted to carry for safety reasons.

The full range of Campingaz cylinders is widely available from large supermarkets and hypermarkets, although at the end of the holiday season stocks may be low. Other popular brands of gas are Primagaz, Butagaz, Totalgaz and Le Cube. A loan deposit is required and if you are buying a cylinder for the first time you may also need to buy the appropriate regulator or adaptor hose.

If you are touring in cold weather conditions use propane gas instead of butane. Many other brands of gas are available in different countries and, as long as you have the correct regulator, adaptor and hose and the cylinders fit in your gas locker these local brands can also be used.

Gas cylinders are now standardised with a pressure of 30mbar for both butane and propane within the EU. On UK-specification caravans and motorhomes (2004 models and later) a 30mbar regulator suited to both propane and butane use is fitted to the bulkhead of the gas locker. This is connected to the cylinder with a connecting hose (and

sometimes an adaptor) to suit different brands or types of gas. Older outfits and some foreign-built ones may use a cylinder-mounted regulator, which may need to be changed to suit different brands or types of gas.

Warnings:

- Refilling gas cylinders intended to be exchanged is against the law in most countries, however you may still find that some sites and dealers will offer to refill cylinders for you. Never take them up on this service as it can be dangerous; the cylinders haven't been designed for user-refilling and it is possible to overfill them with catastrophic consequences.

- Regular servicing of gas appliances is important as a faulty appliance can emit carbon monoxide, which could prove fatal. Check your vehicle or appliance handbook for service recommendations.

- Never use a hob or oven as a space heater.

The Caravan and Motorhome Club publishes a range of technical leaflets for its members including detailed advice on the use of electricity and gas – you can request copies or see camc.com/advice-and-training.

Safety and security

EU countries have good legislation in place to protect your safety wherever possible. However accidents and crime will still occur and taking sensible precautions can help to minimise your risk of being involved.

Beaches, Lakes and Rivers

Check for any warning signs or flags before you swim and ensure that you know what they mean. Check the depth of water before diving and avoid diving or jumping into murky water as submerged objects may not be visible. Familiarise yourself with the location of safety apparatus and/or lifeguards.

Use only the designated areas for swimming, watersports and boating and always use life jackets where appropriate. Watch out for tides, undertows, currents and wind strength and direction before swimming in the sea. This applies in particular when using inflatables, windsurfing equipment, body boards, kayaks or sailing boats. Sudden changes of wave and weather conditions combined with fast tides and currents are particularly dangerous.

Campsite Safety

Once you've settled in, take a walk around the site to familiarise yourself with its layout and locate the nearest safety equipment. Ensure that children know their way around and where your pitch is.

Natural disasters are rare, but always think about what could happen. A combination of heavy rain and a riverside pitch could lead to flash flooding, for example, so make yourself aware of site evacuation procedures.

Be aware of sources of electricity and cabling on and around your pitch – electrical safety might not be up to the same standards as in the UK.

Poison for rodent control is sometimes used on sites or surrounding farmland. Warning notices are not always posted and you are strongly advised to check if staying on a rural site with dogs or children.

Incidents of theft on campsites are rare but when leaving your caravan unattended make sure you lock all doors and shut windows. Conceal valuables from sight and lock up any bicycles.

Children

Watch out for children as you drive around the site and don't exceed walking pace.

Children's play areas are generally unsupervised, so check which are suitable for your children's ages and abilities. Read and respect the displayed rules. Remember it is your responsibility to supervise your children at all times.

Be aware of any campsite rules concerning ball games or use of play equipment, such as roller blades and skateboards. When your children attend organised activities, arrange when and where to meet afterwards. You should never leave children alone inside a caravan.

Fire

Fire prevention is important on sites, as fire can spread quickly between outfits. Certain areas of southern Europe experience severe water shortages in summer months leading to an increased fire risk. This may result in some local authorities imposing restrictions at short notice on the use of barbecues and open flames.

Fires can be a regular occurrence in forested areas, especially along the Mediterranean coast during summer months. They are generally extinguished quickly and efficiently but short term evacuations are sometimes necessary. If visiting forested areas familiarise yourself with local emergency procedures in the event of fire. Never use paraffin or gas heaters inside your caravan. Gas heaters should only be fitted when air is taken from outside

the caravan. Don't change your gas cylinder inside the caravan. If you smell gas turn off the cylinder immediately, extinguish all naked flames and seek professional help.

Make sure you know where the fire points and telephones are on site and know the site fire drill. Make sure everyone in your party knows how to call the emergency services.

Where site rules permit the use of barbecues, take the following precautions to prevent fire:

- Never locate a barbecue near trees or hedges.
- Have a bucket of water to hand in case of sparks.
- Only use recommended fire-lighting materials.
- Don't leave a barbecue unattended when lit and dispose of hot ash safely.
- Never take a barbecue into an enclosed area or awning – even when cooling they continue to release carbon monoxide which can lead to fatal poisoning.

Swimming Pools

Familiarize yourself with the pool area before you venture in for a swim - check the pool layout and identify shallow and deep ends and the location of safety equipment. Check the gradient of the pool bottom as pools which shelve off sharply can catch weak or non-swimmers unawares.

Never dive or jump into a pool without knowing the depth – if there is a no diving rule it usually means the pool isn't deep enough for safe diving.

For pools with a supervisor or lifeguard, note any times or dates when the pool is not supervised. Read safety notices and rules posted around the pool.

On the Road

Don't leave valuables on view in cars or caravans, even if they are locked. Make sure items on roof racks or cycle carriers are locked securely.

Near to ports British owned cars have been targeted by thieves, both while parked and on the move, e.g. by flagging drivers down or indicating that a vehicle has a flat tyre. If you stop in such circumstances be wary of anyone offering help, ensure that car keys are not left in the ignition and that vehicle doors are locked while you investigate.

Always keep car doors locked and windows closed when driving in populated areas. Beware of a 'snatch' through open car windows at traffic lights, filling stations or in traffic jams. When driving through towns and cities keep your doors locked. Keep handbags, valuables and documents out of sight at all times.

If flagged down by another motorist for whatever reason, take care that your own car is locked and windows closed while you check outside, even if someone is left inside.

Be particularly careful on long, empty stretches of motorway and when you stop for fuel. Even if the people flagging you down appear to be officials (e.g. wearing yellow reflective jackets or dark, 'uniform-type' clothing) lock your vehicle doors. They may appear to be friendly and helpful, but could be opportunistic thieves. Have a mobile phone to hand and, if necessary, be seen to use it.

Road accidents are a increased risk in some countries where traffic laws may be inadequately enforced, roads may be poorly maintained, road signs and lighting inadequate, and driving standards poor. It's a good idea to keep a fully-charged mobile phone with you in your car with the number of your breakdown organisation saved into it. On your return to the UK there are increasing issues with migrants attempting to stowaway in vehicles, especially if you're travelling through Calais.

The UK government have issued the following instructions to prevent people entering the UK illegally:

- Where possible all vehicle doors and storage compartments should be fitted with locks.

- All locks must be engaged when the vehicle is stationary or unattended.
- Immediately before boarding your ferry or train check that the locks on your vehicle haven't been compromised.
- If you have any reason to suspect someone may have accessed your outfit speak to border control staff or call the police. Do not board the ferry or train or you may be liable for a fine of up to £2000.

Overnight Stops

Overnight stops should always be at campsites and not at motorway service areas, ferry terminal car parks, petrol station forecourts or isolated 'aires de services' on motorways where robberies are occasionally reported. If you decide to use these areas for a rest then take appropriate precautions, for example, shutting all windows, securing locks and making a thorough external check of your vehicle(s) before departing. Safeguard your property, e.g. handbags, while out of the caravan and beware of approaches by strangers.

For a safer place to take a break, there is a wide network of 'Aires de Services' in cities, towns and villages across Europe, many specifically for motorhomes with good security and overnight facilities. They are often less isolated and therefore safer than the motorway aires. It is rare that you will be the only vehicle staying on such areas, but take sensible precautions and trust your instincts.

Personal Security

Petty crime happens all over the world, including in the UK; however as a tourist you are more vulnerable to it. This shouldn't stop you from exploring new horizons, but there are a few sensible precautions you can take to minimise the risk.

- Leave valuables and jewellery at home. If you do take them, fit a small safe in your caravan or lock them in the boot of your car. Don't leave money or valuables in a car glovebox or on view. Don't leave bags in full view when sitting outside at cafés or restaurants, or leave valuables unattended on the beach.
- When walking be security-conscious. Avoid unlit streets at night, walk away from the kerb edge and carry handbags or shoulder bags on the side away from the kerb. The less of a tourist you appear, the less of a target you are.

- Keep a note of your holiday insurance details and emergency telephone numbers in more than one place, in case the bag or vehicle containing them is stolen.

- Beware of pickpockets in crowded areas, at tourist attractions and in cities. Be especially aware when using public transport in cities.

- Be cautious of bogus plain-clothes policemen who may ask to see your foreign currency or credit cards and passport. If approached, decline to show your money or to hand over your passport but ask for credentials and offer instead to go to the nearest police station.

- Laws and punishment vary from country to country so make yourself aware of anything which may affect you before you travel. Be especially careful on laws involving alcohol consumption (such as drinking in public areas), and never buy or use illegal drugs abroad.

- Respect customs regulations - smuggling is a serious offence and can carry heavy penalties. Do not carry parcels or luggage through customs for other people and never cross borders with people you do not know in your vehicle, such as hitchhikers.

The Foreign & Commonwealth Office produces a range of material to advise and inform British citizens travelling abroad about issues affecting their safety - www.gov.uk/foreign-travel-advice has country specific guides.

Money Security

We would rarely walk around at home carrying large amounts of cash, but as you may not have the usual access to bank accounts and credit cards you are more likely to do so on holiday. You are also less likely to have the same degree of security when online banking as you would in your own home. Take the following precautions to keep your money safe:

- Carry only the minimum amount of cash and don't rely on one person to carry everything. Never carry a wallet in your back pocket. Concealed money belts are the most secure way to carry cash and passports.

- Keep a separate note of bank account and credit/debit card numbers. Carry your credit card issuer/bank's 24-hour UK contact number with you.

- Be careful when using cash machines (ATMs) – try to use a machine in an area with high footfall and don't allow yourself to be distracted. Put your cash away before moving away from the cash machine.

- Always guard your PIN number, both at cash machines and when using your card to pay in shops and restaurants. Never let your card out of your sight while paying.

- If using internet banking do not leave the PC or mobile device unattended and make sure you log out fully at the end of the session.

Winter Sports

If you are planning a skiing or snowboarding holiday you should research the safety advice for your destination before you travel. A good starting point may be the relevant embassy for the country you're visiting. All safety instructions should be followed meticulously given the dangers of avalanches in some areas.

The Ski Club of Great Britain offer a lot of advice for anyone taking to the mountains, visit their website www.skiclub.co.uk to pick up some useful safety tips and advice on which resorts are suitable for different skill levels.

British Consular Services Abroad

British Embassy and Consular staff offer practical advice, assistance and support to British travellers abroad. They can, for example, issue replacement passports, help Britons who have been the victims of crime, contact relatives and friends in the event of an accident, illness or death, provide information about transferring funds and provide details of local lawyers, doctors and interpreters. But there are limits to their powers and a British Consul cannot, for example, give legal advice, intervene in court proceedings, put up bail, pay for legal or medical bills, or for funerals or the repatriation of bodies, or undertake work more properly done by banks, motoring organisations and travel insurers.

If you are charged with a serious offence, insist on the British Consul being informed. You will be contacted as soon as possible by a Consular Officer who can advise on local procedures, provide access to lawyers and insist that you are treated as well as nationals of the country which is holding you. However, they cannot get you released as a matter of course.

British and Irish embassy contact details can be found in the Country Introduction chapters.

Campsites

The quantity and variety of sites across Europe means you're sure to find one that suits your needs – from full facilities and entertainment to quiet rural retreats. If you haven't previously toured outside of the UK you may notice some differences, such as pitches being smaller or closer together. In hot climates hard ground may make putting up awnings difficult.

In the high season all campsite facilities are usually open, however bear in mind that toilet and shower facilities may be busy. Out of season some facilities such as shops and swimming pools may be closed and office opening hours may be reduced. If the site has very low occupancy the sanitary facilities may be reduced to a few unisex toilet and shower cubicles.

Booking a Campsite

To save the hassle of arriving to find a site full it is best to book in advance, especially in high season. If you don't book ahead arrive no later than 4pm (earlier at popular resorts) to secure a pitch, after this time sites fill up quickly. You also need to allow time to find another campsite if your first choice is fully booked.

You can often book directly via a campsite's website using a credit or debit card to pay a deposit if required. Please be aware that some sites regard the deposit as a booking or admin fee and will not deduct the amount from your final bill.

Overseas Travel Service

The Club's Overseas Travel Service offers members an site booking service on over 250 campsites in Europe. Full details of these sites plus information on ferry special offers and Red Pennant Overseas Holiday Insurance can be found in the Club's Venture Abroad brochure – call 01342 327410 to request a copy or visit camc.com/overseas.

Overseas Site Booking Service sites show heir booking code (e.g. G04) at the end of their listing. We can't make reservations for any other campsites in this guide.

Overseas Site Night Vouchers

The Club offers Overseas Site Night Vouchers which can be used at over 300 Club inspected sites in Europe. The vouchers cost £21.95 each (2019 cost) and you'll need one voucher per night to stay on a site in low season and two per night in high season. You'll also be eligible for the Club's special packaged ferry rates when you're buying vouchers. For more information and the view the voucher terms and conditions visit www.camc.com/overseasoffers or call 01342 327 410.

Caravan Storage

Storing your caravan on a site in Europe can be a great way to avoid a long tow and to save on ferry and fuel costs. Before you leave your caravan in storage always check whether your insurance covers this, as many policies don't.

If you aren't covered then look for a specialist policy - Towergate Insurance (tel: 01242 538431 or www.towergateinsurance.co.uk) or Look Insurance (tel: 0333 777 3035 or www.lookinsuranceservices.co.uk) both offer insurance policies for caravans stored abroad.

Facilities and Site Description

All of the site facilities shown in the site listings of this guide have been taken from member reports, as have the comments at the end of each site entry. Please remember that opinions and expectations can differ significantly from one person to the next.

The year of report is shown at the end of each site listing – sites which haven't been reported on for a few years may have had significant changes to their prices, facilities, and opening dates. It is always best to check any specific details you need to know before travelling by contacting the site or looking at their website.

Sanitary Facilities

Facilities normally include toilet and shower blocks with shower cubicles, wash basins and razor sockets. In site listings the abbreviation 'wc' indicates that the site has the kind of toilets we are used to in the UK (pedestal style). Some sites have footplate style toilets and, where this is known, you will see the abbreviation 'cont', i.e. continental. European sites do not always provide sink plugs, toilet paper or soap so take them with you.

Waste Disposal

Site entries show (when known) where a campsite has a chemical disposal and/or a motorhome service point, which is assumed to include a waste (grey) water dump station and toilet cassette-emptying point. You may find fewer waste water disposal facilities as on the continent more people use the site sanitary blocks rather than their own facilities.

Chemical disposal points may be fixed at a high level requiring you to lift cassettes in order to empty them. Disposal may simply be down a toilet. Wastemaster-style emptying points are not very common in Europe. Formaldehyde chemical cleaning products are banned in many countries. In Germany the 'Blue Angel' (Blaue Engel) Standard, and in the Netherlands the 'Milieukeur' Standard, indicates that the product has particularly good environmental credentials.

Finding a Campsite

Directions are given for all campsites listed in this guide and most listings also include GPS co-ordinates. Full street addresses are also given where available. The directions have been supplied by member reports and haven't been checked in detail by The Club.

For information about using satellite navigation to find a site see the Motoring Equipment section.

Overnight Stops

Many towns and villages across Europe provide dedicated overnight or short stay areas specifically for motorhomes, usually with security, electricity, water and waste facilities. These are known as 'Aires de Services', 'Stellplatz' or 'Aree di Sosta' and are usually well signposted with a motorhome icon. Facilities and charges for these overnight stopping areas will vary significantly.

Many campsites in popular tourist areas will also have separate overnight areas of hardstanding with facilities often just outside the main campsite area. There are guidebooks available which list just these overnight stops, Vicarious Books publish an English guide to Aires including directions and GPS

co-ordinates. Please contact 0131 208 3333 or visit their website www.vicarious-shop.com.

For security reasons you shouldn't spend the night on petrol station service areas, ferry terminal car parks or isolated 'Aires de Repos' or 'Aires de Services' along motorways.

Municipal Campsites

Municipal sites are found in towns and villages all over Europe, in particular in France. Once very basic, many have been improved in recent years and now offer a wider range of facilities. They can usually be booked in advance through the local town hall or tourism office. When approaching a town you may find that municipal sites are not always named and signposts may simply state 'Camping' or show a tent or caravan symbol. Most municipal sites are clean, well-run and very reasonably priced but security may be basic.

These sites may be used by seasonal workers, market traders and travellers in low season and as a result there may be restrictions or very high charges for some types of outfits (such as twin axles) in order to discourage this. If you may be affected check for any restrictions when you book.

Naturist Campsites

Some naturist sites are included in this guide and are shown with the word 'naturist' after their site name. Those marked 'part naturist' have separate areas for naturists. Visitors to naturist sites aged 16 and over usually require an INF card or Naturist Licence - covered by membership of British Naturism (tel 01604 620361, visit www.british-naturism.org.uk or email headoffice@british-naturism.org.uk) or you can apply for a licence on arrival at any recognised naturist site (a passport-size photograph is required).

Opening Dates and Times

Opening dates should always be taken with a pinch of salt - including those given in this guide. Sites may close without notice due to refurbishment work, a lack of visitors or bad weather. Outside the high season it is always best to contact campsites in advance, even if the site advertises itself as open all year. Most sites will close their gates or barriers overnight – if you are planning to arrive late or are delayed on your journey you should call ahead to make sure you will be able to gain access to the site. There may be a late arrivals area outside of the barriers where you can pitch overnight. Motorhomers should also consider barrier closing times if leaving site in your vehicle for the evening.

Check out time is usually between 10am and 12 noon – speak to the site staff if you need to leave very early to make sure you can check out on departure. Sites may also close for an extended lunch break, so if you're planning to arrive or check out around lunchtime check that the office will be open.

Pets on Campsites

Dogs are welcome on many sites, although you may have to prove that all of their vaccinations are up to date before they are allowed onto the site. Certain breeds of dogs are banned in some countries and other breeds will need to be muzzled and kept on a lead at all times. A list of breeds with restrictions by country can be found at camc.com/pets.

Sites usually charge for dogs and may limit the number allowed per pitch. On arrival make yourself aware of site rules regarding dogs, such as keeping them on a lead, muzzling them or not leaving them unattended in your outfit.

In popular tourist areas local regulations may ban dogs from beaches during the summer. Some dogs may find it difficult to cope with changes in climate. Also watch out for diseases transmitted by ticks, caterpillars, mosquitoes or sandflies - dogs from the UK will have no natural resistance. Consult your vet about preventative treatment before you travel.

Visitors to southern Spain and Portugal, parts of central France and northern Italy should be aware of the danger of Pine Processionary

Caterpillars from mid-winter to late spring. Dogs should be kept away from pine trees if possible or fitted with a muzzle that prevents the nose and mouth from touching the ground. This will also protect against poisoned bait sometimes used by farmers and hunters.

In the event that your pet is taken ill abroad a campsite should have information about local vets.

Most European countries require dogs to wear a collar identifying their owners at all times. If your dog goes missing, report the matter to the local police and the local branch of that country's animal welfare organisation.

See the Documents section of this book for more information about the Pet Travel Scheme.

Prices and Payment

Prices per night (for an outfit and two adults) are shown in the site entries. If you stay on site after midday you may be charged for an extra day. Many campsites have a minimum amount for credit card transactions, meaning they can't be used to pay for overnight or short stays. Check which payment methods are accepted when you check in.

Sites with automatic barriers may ask for a deposit for a swipe card or fob to operate it.

Extra charges may apply for the use of facilities such as swimming pools, showers or laundry rooms. You may also be charged extra for dogs, Wi-Fi, tents and extra cars.

A tourist tax, eco tax and/or rubbish tax may be imposed by local authorities in some European countries. VAT may also be added to your campsite fees.

Registering on Arrival

Local authority requirements mean you will usually have to produce an identity document on arrival, which will be held by the site until you check out. If you don't want to leave your passport with reception most sites accept a document such as the Camping Key Europe (CKE) or Camping Card International (CCI).

CKE are available for Club members to purchase by calling 01342 336633 or are free to members if you take out the 'motoring' level of cover from the Club's Red Pennant Overseas Holiday Insurance.

General Advice

If you've visiting a new site ask to take a look around the site and facilities before booking in. Riverside pitches can be very scenic but keep an eye on the water level; in periods of heavy rain this may rise rapidly.

Speed limits on campsites are usually restricted to 10 km/h (6 mph). You may be asked to park your car in a separate area away from your caravan, particularly in the high season.

The use of the term 'statics' in the campsite reports in this guide may to any long-term accommodation on site, such as seasonal pitches, chalets, cottages, fixed tents and cabins, as well as static caravans.

Complaints

If you want to make a complaint about a site issue, take it up with site staff or owners at the time in order to give them the opportunity to rectify the problem during your stay.

The Caravan and Motorhome Club has no control or influence over day to day campsite operations or administration of the sites listed in this guide. Therefore we aren't able to intervene in any dispute you should have with a campsite, unless the booking has been made through our Advanced Booking Service - see listings that have a booking code at the end of the entry (e.g. G04).

Campsite Groups

Across Europe there are many campsite groups or chains with sites in various locations.

You will generally find that group sites will be consistent in their format and the quality and variety of facilities they offer. If you liked one site you can be fairly confident that you will like other sites within the same group.

If you're looking for a full facility site, with swimming pools, play areas, bars and restaurants on site you're likely to find these on sites which are part of a group. You might even find organised excursions and activities such as archery on site.

📍 Hallstatt

Highlights

From bustling, cosmopolitan cities, packed with culture, to stunning natural landscapes that will take your breath away, Austria is a rich and varied country that caters to every taste.

The Alps offer endless appeal for those looking to enjoy an active, outdoor holiday while the picturesque towns and villages that punctuate the landscape are ideal for relaxing and soaking up the local culture.

Austria is an important centre for European culture; in particular music. As the birthplace of many notable composers – Mozart, Strauss and Haydn to name just a few – Austria is a magnet for classical music fans.

When it comes to food, one of Austria's most famous dishes is strudel, and there are many different varieties of flavours and types available. The oldest strudel recipes can be found in a handwritten cookbook from 1696 at the Vienna City Library.

Major towns and cities

- Vienna – enjoy a slice of sachertorte in this historic capital.
- Linz – a city of arts and music on the banks of the Danube.
- Graz – the old town is filled with sights and is on the UNESCO World Heritage List.
- Salzburg – this fairytale city was the birthplace of Mozart.

Attractions

- Schönbrunn Palace – a Baroque palace in the heart of Vienna.
- Hallstatt – this Alpine village has a fascinating history as well as picturesque views.
- Grossglockner Alpine Road – the highest road in Austria with unparalleled mountain views.
- Innsbruck – a renowned winter sports centre packed with historical sights.

Find out more

www.austria.info
E: info@austria.info Tel: 0043 (0)1 58 86 60

Country Information

Population (approx): 8.7 million

Capital: Vienna

Area: 83,870 sq km

Bordered by: Czech Republic, Germany, Hungary, Italy, Liechtenstein, Slovakia, Slovenia, Switzerland

Terrain: Mountainous in south and west; flat or gently sloping in extreme north and east

Climate: Temperate; cold winters with frequent rain in the lowlands and snow in the mountains; moderate summers, sometimes very hot

Highest Point: Grossglockner 3,798m

Language: German

Local Time: GMT or BST + 1, i.e. 1 hour ahead of the UK all year

Currency: Euros divided into 100 cents; £1 = €1.16, €1 = £0.87 (October 2019)

Telephoning: From the UK dial 0043 for Austria and omit the initial zero of the area code of the number you are calling.

Emergency numbers: Police 133; Fire brigade 122; Ambulance 144, or dial 112 for any service (operators speak English).

Public Holidays 2020: Jan 1, 6; Apr 13; May 1, 21; Jun 1, 11; Aug 15; Oct 26 (National Day); Nov 1, 15 (Vienna only); Dec 8, 25, 26.

School summer holidays last the whole of July, August and early September

Entry Formalities

Due to the current migrant crisis in Europe some countries have temporarily restored their borders. A current list of countries affected is available on the EU website: **ec.europa. eu/home-affairs/what-we-do/policies/ borders-and-visas/schengen/reintroduction- border-control_en**. At the time of going to print Austria has restored their borders with Hungary and Slovenia.

British and Irish passport holders may stay in Austria for up to three months without a visa. Visitors arriving at a campsite or hotel must complete a registration form.

Medical Services

Minor matters can be dealt with by staff at pharmacies (apotheke). Pharmacies operate a rota system for out of hours access; when closed a notice is often displayed giving the addresses of the nearest open pharmacies.

Free treatment is available from doctors and hospital outpatient departments as long as the doctor is contracted to the local health insurance office (Gebietskrankenkasse). To be covered for hospital treatment you will need a doctor's referral. In-patient treatment will incur a daily non-refundable charge for the first 28 days.

Only a limited amount of dental treatment is covered under the state healthcare system. You will need to present your European Health Insurance Card (EHIC) to receive treatment.

Opening Hours

Banks: Mon-Fri 8am-12.30pm & 1.30pm-3pm (5.30pm Thu), main branches don't close for lunch; closed Sat/Sun. (Hours may vary).

Museums: Mon-Fri 10am-6pm (summer), 9am-4pm (winter); Sat, Sun & public holidays 9am-6pm.

Post Offices: Mon-Fri 8am-12pm & 2pm-6pm; city post offices don't close for lunch; in some towns open Sat 9am-12pm.

Shops: Mon-Fri 8am-6pm; some open until 7.30pm Thu; some close 12pm-2pm for lunch; Sat 8am-5pm; some open Sun and public holidays.

Safety and Security

Most visits to Austria are trouble-free, but visitors should take sensible precautions to avoid becoming a victim of crime at crowded tourist sites and around major railway stations and city centre parks after dark. Pickpockets and muggers operate in and around the city centre of Vienna.

Drivers, especially on the autobahns in Lower Austria, should be wary of bogus plain clothes police officers. In all traffic-related matters police officers will be in uniform and unmarked vehicles will have a flashing sign in the rear window which reads 'Stopp –Polizei – Folgen'. If in any doubt contact the police on the emergency number 133 or 112 and ask for confirmation. The winter sports season lasts from December to March, or the end of May in higher regions. If you plan to ski contact the Austrian National 8.5

British Embassy

JAURESGASSE 12
1030 VIENNA
Tel: +43 (1) 716130
www.ukinaustria.fco.gov.uk/en/

Irish Embassy

ROTENTURMSTRAßE
16-18, 1010 VIENNA
Tel: +43 (0)1 715 4246
www.embassyofireland.at

Documents

Driving Licence

If you hold a UK driving licence which does not bear your photograph you should carry your passport as further proof of identity, or obtain a photocard licence.

Money

Cash dispensers (Bankomaten) have instructions in English. Major credit cards are widely accepted in large cities although a number of small hotels, shops and restaurants may refuse. Visa and Mastercard are more readily accepted than American Express and Diner's Club.

Passport

You are advised to carry your passport or photocard licence at all times.

Vehicle(s)

You should carry your vehicle registration certificate (V5C), insurance details and MOT certificate.

Driving

Alcohol

The maximum permitted level of alcohol in the bloodstream is 0.049%, i.e. lower than that permitted in the UK. Penalties for exceeding this limit are severe. A lower limit of virtually zero (0.01%) applies to drivers who have held a full driving licence for less than two years.

Breakdown Service

The motoring organisation, ÖAMTC, operates a breakdown service 24 hours a day on all roads.

The emergency number is 120 throughout the country from a land line or mobile phone. Motorists pay a set fee, which is higher at night; towing charges also apply. Payment by credit card is accepted.

Members of AIT and FIA affiliated clubs, such as the Caravan and Motorhome Club, qualify for reduced charges on presentation of a valid Club membership card.

Child Restraint System

Children under 14 years of age and less than 1.5 metres in height must use a suitable child restraint system for their height and weight when travelling in the front and rear of a vehicle. Children under 14 years aren't allowed to travel in two seater sports cars.

Children under 14 years of age but over 1.35 metres are allowed to use a 3-point seat belt without a special child seat, as long as the seat belt does not cut across the child's throat or neck.

Fuel

Most petrol stations are open from 8am to 8pm. Motorway service stations and some petrol stations in larger cities stay open 24 hours. Fuel is normally cheaper at self-service filling stations.

LPG (flüssiggas) is available at a limited number of outlets – a list should be available on www.oeamtc.at.

Lights

Dipped headlights must be used in poor visibility or bad weather. Headlight flashing is used as a warning of approach, not as an indication that a driver is giving way.

Motorways

Orange emergency telephones on motorways are 2 km to 3 km apart. A flashing orange light at the top of telephone posts indicates danger ahead.

Whenever congestion occurs on motorways and dual carriageways drivers are required to create an emergency corridor. Drivers in the left-hand lane must move as far over to the left as possible, and drivers in the central and right-hand lanes must move as far over to the right as possible to provide access for emergency vehicles.

Motorway Tolls (Vehicles under 3,500 kg)

Drivers of vehicles under 3,500 kg using motorways and expressways (A and S roads) must purchase a motorway vignette (sticker). One vignette covers your caravan as well. Vignettes may be purchased at all major border crossings into Austria and from OeAMTC offices, larger petrol stations and post offices in Austria. A two-month vignette is available for a car (with or without a trailer) or a motorhome at a cost of €26.20. Also available are a 10 day vignette at €9 and a one year vignette at €87.30 (2015 tariffs).

Failure to display a vignette incurs a fine of at least €120, plus the cost of the vignette. Credit cards or foreign currency may be used in payment. If you have visited Austria before, make sure you remove your old sticker.

There are special toll sections in Austria which are excluded from the vignette and where the toll needs to be paid at respective toll points. These include A10 Tauern tunnel, A13 Brenner motorway and S16 Alberg tunnel.

Motorway Tolls (Vehicles over 3,500 kg)

Tolls for vehicles over 3,500 kg are calculated according to the number of axles and EURO emissions category and are collected electronically by means of a small box (called the GO-Box) fixed to your vehicle's windscreen.

They are available for a one-off handling fee of €5 from around 220 points of sale – mainly petrol stations – along the primary road network in Austria and neighbouring countries, and at all major border crossing points.

You can pre-load a set amount onto your Go box or pay after you have travelled. Tolls are calculated according to the number of axles on a vehicle; those with two axles are charged between €0.156 and €0.211 per kilometre + 20% VAT, according to the vehicle's emissions rating. Visit www.go-maut.at to register for the scheme. Telephone 0043 19551266 or email info@go-maut.at for help before you travel. Operators speak English.

This distance-related toll system does not apply to a car/caravan combination even if its total laden weight is over 3,500 kg, unless the laden weight of the towing vehicle itself exceeds that weight.

Parking

Regulations on the parking of motorhomes and caravans vary according to region, but restrictions apply in areas protected for their natural beauty or landscape and beside lakes. If in doubt, ask the local municipality. You cannot leave a caravan without its towing vehicle in a public place.

A zigzag line marked on the road indicates that parking is prohibited. Blue lines indicate a blue zone (Kurzparkzone) where parking is restricted to a period for up to two hours and you need to purchase a voucher (Parkschein) from a local shop, bank or petrol station.

Most cities have 'Pay and Display' machines, parking meters or parking discs, and in main tourist areas the instructions are in English. Illegally-parked cars may be impounded or clamped. Large areas of Vienna are pedestrianised and parking places are limited. However, there are several underground car parks in Vienna District 1.

Priority

Outside built-up areas, road signs on main roads indicate where traffic has priority or if there are no signs priority is given to traffic from the right.

Buses have priority when leaving a bus stop. Do not overtake school buses with flashing yellow lights which have stopped to let children on and off. Trams have priority even if coming from the left.

In heavy traffic, drivers must not enter an intersection unless their exit is clear, even if they have priority or if the lights are green.

Prohibited Equipment

Dashboard cameras are not allowed in Austria.

Roads

Austria has a well developed and engineered network of roads classified as: federal motorways (A roads), expressways (S' roads), provincial (B roads) and local (L roads). There are over 2180km of motorways and expressways.

Road Signs and Markings

Most signs conform to international usage. The following are exceptions:

Diversions

Street lights not on all night

Tram turns at yellow or red

You may be stopped and fined in Austria for using roads that prohibit trailers and caravans. This is indicated by the below sign:

If there is an additional sign which shows a weight limit, then this indicates the maximum gross vehicle weight of the trailer. You can also find these signs with a length limit.

Some other signs that are also in use which you may find useful Include:

Austrian	English Translation
Abblendlicht	Dipped headlights
Alle richtungen	All directions
Bauarbeiten	Roadworks

Austrian	English Translation
Durchfahrt verboten	No through traffic
Einbahn	One-way street
Fussgänger	Pedestrians
Beschrankung für halten oder parken	Stopping or parking restricted
Lawinen gefahr	Avalanche danger
Links einbiegen	Turn left
Raststätte	Service area
Raststätte Rechts einbiegen	Turn right
Strasse gesperrt	Road closed
Überholen verboten	No passing
Umleitung	Detour

Speed Limits

	Open Road (km/h)	Motorway (km/h)
Car Solo	100	130
Car towing caravan/trailer	80	100
Motorhome under 3500kg	100	130
Motorhome 3500-7500kg	70	80

Exceptions

If the total combined weight of a car and caravan outfit or a motorhome exceeds 3,500 kg the speed limit on motorways is reduced to 80 km/h (50 mph) and on other roads outside built-up areas to 70 km/h (43 mph).

On motorways where the speed limit for solo vehicles is 130 km/h (81 mph) overhead message signs may restrict speed to 100 km/h (62 mph). Between 10pm and 5am solo cars are restricted to 110 km/h (68 mph) on the A10 (Tauern), A12 (Inntal), A13 (Brenner) and A14 (Rheintal). There is a general speed limit of 60 km/h (37 mph) on most roads in the Tyrol, unless indicated otherwise. There is a speed limit of 50km/h in build up areas unless otherwise indicated by road signs. A built-up area starts from the road sign indicating that place name as you enter a town or village.

Some sections of the A12 and A13 are limited to 100km/h, day and night.

The minimum speed on motorways, as indicated by a rectangular blue sign depicting a white car, is 60 km/h (37 mph). A number of towns have a general speed limit of 30 km/h (18 mph), except where a higher speed limit is indicated.

Traffic Lights

At traffic lights a flashing green light indicates the approach of the end of the green phase. An orange light combined with the red light indicates that the green phase is imminent.

Traffic Jams

In recent years traffic has increased on the A1 from Vienna to the German border (the West Autobahn). There are usually queues at the border posts with Czech Republic, Slovakia and Hungary. As a result, traffic has also increased on the ring road around Vienna and on the A4 (Ost Autobahn).

Other bottlenecks occur on the A10 (Salzburg to Villach) before the Tauern and Katschberg tunnels, the A12 (Kufstein to Landeck) before the Perjen tunnel and before Landeck, and the A13 (Innsbruck to Brenner) between Steinach and the Italian border. Busy sections on other roads are the S35/S6 between Kirchdorf or Bruck an der Mur and the A9, the B320/E651 in the Schladming and Gröbming areas, and the B179 Fern Pass.

Violation of Traffic Regulations

Police can impose and collect on-the-spot fines of up to €90 from drivers who violate traffic regulations. For higher fines you will be required to pay a deposit and the remainder within two weeks. An official receipt should be issued. A points system operates which applies to drivers of Austrian and foreign-registered vehicles.

Winter Driving

From 1 November to 15 April vehicles, including those registered abroad, must be fitted with winter tyres marked M&S (mud & snow) on all wheels when there is snow or ice on the road. Snow chains are allowed on roads fully covered by snow or ice, as long as road surfaces will not be damaged by the chains. The maximum recommended speed for vehicles with snow chains is generally 50 km/h.

Between 15 November to 15 March vehicles weighing over 3500kg are required to have winter tyres on at least one of the driving axles, regardless of the road conditions. They must also carry snow chains, and use them where road signs indicate that they are compulsory.

It is the driver's legal responsibility to carry the required winter equipment; therefore, it is essential to check that it is included in any hire car.

Essential Equipment

First aid kit

All vehicles must carry a first aid kit kept in a strong, dirt-proof box.

Reflective Jackets/ Waistcoats

If your vehicle breaks down or you are in an accident you must wear a reflective jacket or waistcoat when getting out of your vehicle (compliant with EU Standard EN471). This includes when setting up a warning triangle. It is also recommended that a passenger who leaves the vehicle, for example, to assist with a repair, should also wear one. Keep the jackets within easy reach inside your vehicle, not in the boot.

Warning Triangle

An EU approved warning triangle must be used if the vehicle breaks down, has a puncture or is involved in an accident.

Touring

Austria is divided into nine federal regions, namely Burgenland, Carinthia (Kärnten), Lower Austria (Niederösterreich), Salzburg, Styria (Steiermark), Tyrol (Tirol), Upper Austria (Oberösterreich), Vienna (Wien) and Voralberg.

A 10-15% service charge is included in restaurant bills, but it is customary to add a further 5% tip if satisfied with the service.

The Vienna Card offers unlimited free public transport and discounts at museums, restaurants, theatres and shops. The Card is valid for three days and is available from hotels, tourist information and public transport offices; see www.wienkarte.at.

A Salzburg Card and an Innsbruck Card are also available – see www.austria.info/uk or contact the Austrian National Tourist Office for more information.

Camping and Caravanning

There are approximately 500 campsites in Austria, around 150 of which are open all year, mostly in or near to ski resorts.

Casual/wild camping is not encouraged and is prohibited in Vienna, in the Tyrol and in forests and nature reserves. Permission to park a caravan should be obtained in advance from the owners of private land, or from the local town hall or police station in the case of common land or state property.

Cycling

There is an extensive network of cycle routes, following dedicated cycle and footpaths, such as the 360 km cycle lane that follows the Danube. Many cities encourage cyclists with designated cycle lanes. A Citybike hire scheme operates in Vienna from more than 60 rental offices situated close to underground/metro stations. See www.citybikewien.at for more information or email kontakt@citybikewien.at. There are eight signposted mountain bike routes between 10 and 42 kilometres long in the Vienna woods.

Cycle helmets are compulsory for children under 12 years, or 15 years in Lower Austria (Niederösterreich).

Bikes may be carried on the roof or rear of a car. When carried at the rear, the width must not extend beyond the width of the vehicle, and the rear lights and number plate must be visible.

Electricity and Gas

Current on campsites varies from 4 - 16 amps. Plugs have two round pins and most campsites have CEE connections. Electricity points tend to be in locked boxes, so you will need to check polarity on arrival before the box is locked. Arrangements also need to be made for the box to be unlocked if making an early departure.

Some sites in Austria make a one-off charge for connection to the electricity supply, which is then metered at a rate per kilowatt hour (kwh) The full range of Campingaz cylinders is widely available.

Public Transport & Local Travel

All major cities have efficient, integrated public transport systems including underground and light rail systems, trams and buses. Two to five people travelling as a group by train can buy an Einfach-Raus-Ticket (ERT), which is good for a day's unlimited travel on all Austrian regional trains – see www.oebb.at (English option) for more information or ask at any station.

In Vienna there are travel concessions on public transport for senior citizens (show your passport as proof of age). Buy a ticket from a tobacconist or from a ticket machine in an underground station. Otherwise single tickets are available from vending machines in the vehicles themselves – have plenty of coins ready. Tickets are also available for periods of 24 and 72 hours. Children under six travel free and children under 15 travel free on Sundays, public holidays and during school holidays.

Car ferry services operate throughout the year on the River Danube, and hydrofoil and hovercraft services transport passengers from Vienna to Bratislava (Slovakia) and to Budapest (Hungary).

ABERSEE *B3* (3km N Rural) *47.74040, 13.40665*
Seecamping Primus, Schwand 39, 5342 Abersee
06227 3228; seecamping.primus@aon.at
🏕️ �📶 🏔️ 🔥 🗑️ 🚿 ⚭ 🐕 ⛱️ 🦮 nr 🏧 🏊

**B158 fr St Gilgen to Strobl. After 3 km turn L.
Camp is last but one.** Med, mkd, pt shd, EHU (10A);
sw; twin axles; bus 1km; Eng spkn; games area;
CCI. *"Very helpful owner; beautiful area nr shipping
on lake; ideal for boating; excel; mountain views."*
€25.70, 25 Apr-30 Sep. **2016**

ABERSEE *B3* (3km SE Rural) *47.71336, 13.45138*
Camping Schönblick, Gschwendt 33, 5342
Abersee (06137) 7042; laimer.schoenblick@
aon.at; www.camping-schoenblick.at
🐕 €2.90 🏕️ ⚭ 📶 🏔️ 🗑️ ⚭ 🦋 ⓦ nr 🏊

Fr B158 at km 36 dir Schiffstation & site in 1km on L.
Med, mkd, hdstg, pt shd, pt sl, terr, EHU (10A) inc; gas;
sw nr; 40% statics; ccard acc; CKE. *"Beautiful, friendly,
family-run site nr lakeside opp St Wolfgang town; ferry
stn; excel san facs but stretched at busy times; walks &
cycle path fr site; vg site."* **€26.90, 1 May-15 Oct.**
2019

ABERSEE *B3* (1.5km NW Rural) *47.73656, 13.43250*
Camping Wolfgangblick, Seestrasse 115, 5342
Abersee (06227) 3475; camping@wolfgangblick.at;
www.wolfgangblick.at
🐕 €3.70 🏕️ ⚭ ⓦ 🏔️ 🗑️ ⚭ 🦋 🍽️ ⓦ 🔥 🏊 🏧

**Fr B158 fr St Gilgen, on ent Abersee turn L at km
34 twds lake. Site in 1km foll sp to site.** Med, mkd,
hdstg, pt shd, EHU (12A) metered; 50% statics; Eng
spkn; ccard acc. *"Pleasant site; gd, friendly family run
site by lake; helpful owners; beautiful scenery; excel
for walking & cycling; lake adj; on bus rte to Salzburg
and local vills; poss cr, adv bkg advised."*
€32.50, 1 May-30 Sep. **2019**

ABERSEE *B3* (2.5km NW Rural) *47.73910, 13.40065*
Camping Birkenstrand Wolfgangsee, Schwand 4,
5342 Abersee (06227) 3029; camp@birkenstrand.at;
www.birkenstrand.at
🐕 €3.40 🏕️ ⚭ ⓦ 🏔️ 🗑️ ⚭ 🦋 🚿 🍽️ nr ⓦ nr 🔥 🏊 nr 🏧 🖊️

**Fr B158 fr St Gilgen, on ent Abersee turn L at km 32
twds lake. Site on both sides of rd in 1km.** 4*, Med,
mkd, unshd, pt sl, EHU (10A) metered; bbq; sw nr;
TV; 20% statics; Eng spkn; adv bkg acc; boat hire; golf
15km; bike hire. *"Excel area for walking, cycling; lovely
situation; immac site; ACSI card acc; new facs (2015)."*
€25.00, 27 Mar-31 Oct. **2016**

ABERSEE *B3* (3km NW Rural) *47.73945, 13.40245*
Romantik Camping Wolfgangsee Lindenstrand,
Schwand 19, 5342 St Gilgen (06227) 32050;
camping@lindenstrand.at; www.lindenstrand.at
🐕 €3.70 🏕️ (htd) ⓦ 🗑️ ⚭ 🦋 ⓦ nr 🏊 🏧

**Fr St Gilgen take B158 dir Bad Ischl. In 4km at km
32 foll sp Schwand, site on L on lakeside.** Lge, mkd,
hdstg, pt shd, serviced pitches; EHU (10A) metered;
10% statics; phone; bus; Eng spkn; adv bkg acc;
ccard acc; watersports; CKE. *"Lovely site; rec adv
bkg for lakeside pitches; elec conn by staff; lake adj,
no probs in water; poss req long leads; bus & boat to
local towns & Salzburg; continental plugs high ssn."*
€23.60, 1 Apr-31 Oct. **2019**

ASCHACH AN DER DONAU *B3* (16km N Rural)
48.42026, 13.98400 **Camping Kaiserhof,** Kaiserau 1,
4082 Aschach-an-der-Donau (07273) 62210;
kaiserhof@aschach.at; www.pension-kaiserhof.at
🏕️ (htd) ⓦ 🏔️ 🗑️ ⚭ 🦋 🍽️ 🔥 🖊️ 🏊

**Fr town cent foll site sp. Site adj rv & Gasthof
Kaiserhof.** Sm, pt shd, EHU; red long stay;
80% statics; Eng spkn; ccard acc; CKE. *"Beautiful
location on Danube."* **€19.00, 15 Apr-30 Sep.** **2016**

ATTERSEE *B3* (16km S Rural) *47.80100, 13.48266*
Inselcamping, Unterburgau 37, 4866 Unterach-am-
Attersee (07665) 8311; camping@inselcamp.at;
www.inselcamp.at
🐕 €2 🏕️ ⓦ 🗑️ ⚭ 🦋 🔥 🏊 🏊 shgl

**Leave A1 at junc 243 St Georgen/Attersee, foll
B151 to Unterach fr Attersee vill. Site sp on app
to Unterach.** Med, pt shd, EHU (6-16A); gas; sw;
25% statics; Eng spkn; adv bkg acc; CKE. *"Excel site
next to lake with sw; helpful owner; 5 min walk to
attractive town; conv Salzburg & Salzkammergut; lots
to see locally; clsd 1200-1400; gd boat trips; extra for
lakeside pitches - some with boat mooring; vg san facs;
adv bkg for over 6 days."* **€24.00, 1 May-15 Sep.**
2018

BAD AUSSEE *C3* (11km E Rural) *47.63783, 13.90365*
Campingplatz Gössl, Gössl 201, 8993 Grundlsee
(03622) 81810; office@campinggoessl.com;
www.campinggoessl.com
🐕 €1 🏕️ ⚭ 🏔️ 🗑️ ⚭ 🦋 🍽️ nr ⓦ nr 🔥 nr 🏊

**Fr B145 foll sp to Grundlsee, then along lake to
Gössl at far end. Ent adj gasthof off mini-rndbt, site
on L.** Med, EHU (10A) metered + conn fee; sw nr; bus;
adv bkg acc; fishing. *"Excel walking cent; scenery v
beautiful; boating (no motor boats); local gasthofs vg;
daily bus & ferry services; v clean facs."*
€17.00, 1 May-31 Oct. **2019**

BAD GLEICHENBERG *C4* (3km E Rural) *46.87470, 15.93360* **Camping Feriendorf in Thermenland,** Haus Nr 240, 8344 Bairisch-Kölldorf **(03159) 3941;** camping.bk@aon.at; www.bairisch-koelldorf.at
12 🐕 €0.70 👪(htd) 🚿 ♨ ⚡ 🅿 ∥ MSP 🦋 🍴 ⑪ 🛒 🏛 🏊(covrd)

Exit A2 at Gleisdorf Süd onto B68 dir Feldbach. Take B66 dir Bad Gleichenberg & at 2nd rndabt turn L, site sp. 4*, Med, unshd, EHU (16A) metered; gas; bbq; sw; 10% statics; adv bkg acc; bike hire; golf 3km; tennis 600m; games area. **€20.00**   **2016**

BLUDENZ *C1* (2km N Rural) *47.16990, 9.80788* **Terrassencamping Sonnenberg,** Hinteroferstrasse 12, 6714 Nüziders **(05552) 64035;** sonnencamp@aon.at; www.camping-sonnenberg.com
🐕 €3-4.50 👪(htd) 🚿 🅿 ∥ 🦋 🍴 ⑪ 🛒nr 🏛 ♿

Exit A14/E60 junc 57 onto B190 N, foll sp Nüziders & foll site sp thro Nüziders vill. Med, hdstg, mkd, pt shd, terr, EHU (5-13A) metered over 4kw; red long stay; TV; phone; Eng spkn; adv bkg acc; sep car park. *"Friendly, v helpful owners; superb facs; beautiful scenery - extra for Panorama pitches at top of site; excel mountain views; excel walking; lifts to mountains; ltd opening hrs for recep - use phone at bldg on L at main ent; no arr after 2200 hrs but sep o'night area; rec bk in adv in high ssn; gd for m'vans; highly rec; excel site; gd value."* **€32.60, 27 Apr-6 Oct.**   **2019**

BLUDENZ *C1* (3km S Rural) *47.14651, 9.81630* **Auhof Camping,** Aulandweg 5, 6706 Bürs **(05552) 67044;** auhof.buers@aon.at; www.buers.at
12 👪(htd) 🚿 🅿 ∥ ⑪ 🛒nr 🛒

Exit A14/E60 junc 59 dir Bludenz/Bürs, then Brand. Site sp in 300m at Zimba Park shopping cent on edge of sm indus est. Med, unshd, EHU (4A); gas. *"Friendly, tidy, clean site on wkg farm; conv Arlberg Tunnel, m'way, Liechtenstein & mountain resorts; muddy in wet; conv NH for m'way; lovely owners."* **€23.00**   **2016**

BRUCK AN DER GROSSGLOCKNERSTRASSE *C2* (0.9km SW Urban) *47.28386, 12.81736* **Sportcamp Woferlgut,** Krössenbach 40, 5671 Bruck-an-der-Grossglocknerstrasse **(06545) 73030;** info@sportcamp.at; www.sportcamp.at
12 🐕 €5.50 👪 🅿 WD 🚿 ♨ ⚡ 🅿 ∥ MSP 🍴 ⑪ 🛒 🏛 ♿ 🏊(htd)

Exit A10 junc 47 dir Bischofshofen, B311 dir Zell-am-See. Take 2nd exit to Bruck, site sp fr by-pass, & foll sps thro town to site. 4*, Lge, pt shd, serviced pitches; EHU (10-16A) €2.20 conn fee & €0.80 per kw; sw nr; red long stay; TV; 80% statics; phone; bus to Zell-am-Zee & glacier; Eng spkn; adv bkg acc; ccard acc; tennis; games rm; sauna. *"Extended facs area with R numbered pitches preferable; excel site for sh or long stay; gym & fitness cent; ski cent; farm produce; big pitches; excel mntn walking, local horseriding; helpful recep; tour ops tents & statics; excel for young/teenage families; vg san facs; indoor play area; warm welcome; sm supmkt nrby & plenty of rests & cafes; excel."* **€37.80, G06.**   **2018**

See advertisement

BRUCK AN DER MUR *C4* (4km W Urban) *47.40311, 15.22755* **Camping Raddörf'l,** Bruckerstrasse 110, 8600 Oberaich **(03862) 51418;** info@gasthofpichler.at; www.gasthofpichler.at
🐕 €2 👪 🚿 🅿 ∥ 🍴 🛒 🛒nr 🏛

Fr S6 take Oberaich exit 4km W of Bruck. Foll site sp (in opp dir to vill of Oberaich), go under rlwy bdge, turn L at T-junc. Site is 300m on L at Gasthof Pichler, ent thro car park. Sm, pt shd, EHU (10A) inc; CKE. *"Gd NH; site (10 o'fits max) in orchard at rear of Gasthof; gd rest; cramped."* **€21.00, 1 May-1 Oct.**   **2015**

DELLACH IM DRAUTAL *D2* (1km S Rural) *46.73085, 13.07846* **Camping Waldbad,** 9772 Dellach-im-Drautal (Kärnten) **(04714) 234-18 or (04714) 288;** info@camping-waldbad.at; www.camping-waldbad.at

🐕 €2.50 ♦♦ ⓌⒹ ♨ ♻ & ▤ ⁄ ⭐ 🦋 Ⓨ Ⓣ ⑭ ♿ ☎ ⚠ ⚲

Clearly sp on B100 & in vill of Dellach on S side or Rv Drau. Med, hdg, mkd, pt shd, EHU (6A) inc; gas; 5% statics; adv bkg acc; ccard acc; games rm; games area. *"Peaceful, wooded site; htd pool complex, paddling pool adj; waterslide adj; vg leisure facs adj."* **€31.00, 1 May-30 Sep.** **2019**

DOBRIACH *D3* (2km S Rural) *46.77020, 13.64788* **Komfort Campingpark Burgstaller,** Seefeldstrasse 16, A-9873 Döbriach (Kärnten) **04246 7774; info@ burgstaller.co.at; www.burgstaller.co.at**

🗓 🐕 €4.10 ♦♦ ⓌⒹ ♨ ♻ & ▤ ⁄ ⭐ 🦋 Ⓨ Ⓣ nr ⑭ nr ☎ ⚠ ⚲
🏊 (htd)

Fr on A10/E55/E66 take exit Millstätter See. Turn L at traff lts on B98 dir Radenthein. Thro Millstatt & Dellach, turn R into Döbriach, sp Camping See site on L by lake after Döbriach. V lge, hdg, mkd, pt shd, EHU (6-10A) inc; gas; sw; TV; 10% statics; Eng spkn; adv bkg acc; solarium; golf 8km; bike hire; games area; horseriding; boating; sauna; CKE. *"Organised walks & trips to Italy; excel rest; private san facs avail; cinema; some pitches tight; fantastic facs."* **€28.90** **2019**

DOBRIACH *D3* (2km SW Urban) *46.76811, 13.64809* **Camping Brunner am See,** Glanzerstrasse 108, 9873 Döbriach **(04246) 7189 or 7386; office@camping-brunner.at; www.camping-brunner.at**

🗓 🐕 €5 ♦♦ ⓌⒹ ♨ & ▤ ⁄ ⭐ Ⓣ ⑭ ♿ ☎ ⚠

Fr Salzburg on A10 a'bahn take Seeboden-Millstatt exit bef Spittal. Foll rd 98 N of Millstattersee to camping sp. Med, pt shd, EHU (6A) inc; adv bkg acc; ccard acc; tennis; watersports; CKE. *"Great site with excel, clean san facs; pool 300m; gd size pitches; lakeside location; supmkt nrby & rests in vicinity; superb scenery."* **€34.40** **2019**

EBEN IM PONGAU *C3* (1.5km S Rural) *47.39932, 13.39566* **See-Camping Eben,** Familie Schneider, Badeseestraße 54, 5531 Eben I Pg **06458 8231 or 0664 450 2000; info@seecamping-eben.at; www.seecamping-eben.at**

🗓 🐕 €3 ♦♦ (htd) ♨ ♻ ▤ ⁄ ⭐ 🦋 Ⓨ Ⓣ

Head E on A10, take exit 60 - Eben. Turn L onto B99. R onto Badeseestr. Campsite 800m on the L. Med, pt shd, EHU (16A) inc; train 800m; adv bkg acc; games area. *"Helpful owners; saunas; steam rm; lake adj; direct access fr mountains; clean & well organise; gd site."* **€30.00** **2019**

EHRWALD *C1* (3km SW Rural) *47.38249, 10.90222* **Camping Biberhof,** Schmitte 8, 6633 Biberwier (Tirol) **(05673) 2950; info@biberhof.at; www.biberhof.at**

🗓 🐕 €1.90 ♦♦ ⓌⒹ ♨ ♻ ▤ ⁄ ⭐ 🦋 Ⓨ Ⓣ ⚲ ⚠

Fr Reutte, leave B179 sp Lermoos. In Leermoos cent turn R sp Biberwier. At t-junc in Biberwier turn L sp Ehrwald. Site on R in 300mtrs. Med, mkd, hdstg, pt shd, EHU (10A); bbq; twin axles; 80% statics; bus adj; Eng spkn; adv bkg acc; games area. *"Site under power cables; sometimes noisy; trampoline, volleyball, wall climbing, table tennis, walking/cycle rtes adj; mountain views; 3 scenic vill; pool at Lermoos 2km; outstanding san facs; drying rm; beautiful setting; generous pitches; clean san facs; free gd wifi; ideal NH."* **€29.50** **2018**

EHRWALD *C1* (3km W Rural) *47.40250, 10.88893* **Happy Camp Hofherr,** Garmischerstrasse 21, 6631 Lermoos **(05673) 2980; info@camping-lermoos.com; www.camping-lermoos.com**

🗓 🐕 ♦♦ (htd) ⓌⒹ ♨ ▤ ⁄ ⭐ 🦋 Ⓨ ⑭ ☎ nr ⚠

On ent Lermoos on B187 fr Ehrwald site located on R. Med, pt shd, pt sl, EHU (16A) metered; gas; TV (pitch); 40% statics; phone; adv bkg acc; ccard acc; site clsd 1 Nov-mid Dec; tennis. *"Ideal for walks/cycling; v picturesque; adj park; ask for guest card for discount on ski lifts etc; ski lift 300m; excel san facs; htd pool 200m; superb rest (clsd Mon & Tue eve); family run site."* **€29.70** **2019**

EISENSTADT *B4* (16km SE Rural) *47.80132, 16.69185* **Storchencamp Rust,** Ruster Bucht, 7071 Rust-am-Neusiedlersee (Burgenland) **(02685) 595; office@gmeiner.co.at; www.gmeiner.co.at**

🐕 €4 ♦♦ ⓌⒹ ♨ ▤ ⁄ ⭐ ⚲ ☎

Fr Eisenstadt take rd to Rust & Mörbisch. In Rust foll sps to site & Zee; lakeside rd to ent. Lge, pt shd, EHU (16A) €3; sw nr; 60% statics; boating. *"Nr Hungarian border; attractive vill with nesting storks."* **€30.00, 1 Apr-31 Oct.** **2019**

ENGELHARTSZELL *B3* (1km NW Rural) *48.51238, 13.72428* **Camp Municipal an der Donau,** Nibelungenstrasse 113, 4090 Engelhartszell **(0664) 8708787; tourismus@engelhartszell.ooe.gv.at; www.camping-audonau.at**

♦♦ ⓌⒹ ♨ & ▤ ⁄ ⭐ Ⓣ ⚲ ⚠

Fr Passau (Germany) exit SE on B130 along Rv Danube. Site on L in approx 28km just bef Engelhartszell adj municipal pool complex. Sm, unshd, EHU (6A) metered; 50% statics; bus nr. *"Excel, clean, friendly site on rvside; pool adj; Danube cycleway passes site."* **€22.60, 15 Apr-15 Oct.** **2016**

AUSTRIA

FURSTENFELD *C4* (2km NW Rural) *47.05631, 16.06255* **Camping Fürstenfeld,** Campingweg 1, 8280 Fürstenfeld **(03382) 54940; camping.fuerstenfeld@chello.at; www.camping-fuerstenfeld.at**

🏕 €2 👥 WD ♨ 🖴 ⊙ ⚡ ✗ ♿ 🍴 🍽 Ⓖ nr ⚒ 🛒 nr ✗ 🚴 ⛴

Exit A2/E59 sp Fürstenfeld onto B65. Site well sp fr town cent. 4*, Med, pt shd, pt sl, EHU (10A) €2.30 (poss long lead req); 25% statics; phone; golf 5km; waterslide; rv fishing; CKE. *"Pleasant rvside site; ltd facs but clean; conv Hungarian border."* **€21.00, 15 Apr-15 Oct.** **2016**

GMUND (KARNTEN) *C3* (6km NW Rural) *46.94950, 13.50940* **Terrassencamping Maltatal,** Malta 6, 9854 Malta **(04733) 234; info@maltacamp.at**

🏕 €4 👥 (htd) WD ♨ ♿ 🖴 ⊙ ✗ MP 🍴 🍽 Ⓖ ♨ 🛒 ⚒ /Δ
🚴 (htd) 🎿

Exit A10/E14 onto B99 to Gmünd. Foll sp Malta & after 6km site sp, on R next to filling stn. 5*, Lge, mkd, pt shd, terr, serviced pitches; EHU (10A) inc; bbq; 5% statics; phone; adv bkg acc; tennis; games area; canoeing; sauna; games rm; trout fishing; CKE. *"Gmund & Spittal gd shopping towns; Millstättersee 15km, Grossglocknerstrasse 1hr's drive; magnificant area with rvs, waterfalls, forests & mountains; guided walks; vg rest; children's mini farm; excel site."* **€30.00, 1 Apr-31 Oct.** **2019**

GNESAU *D3* (1km W Rural) *46.77966, 13.95062* **Camping Hobitsch,** Sonnleiten 24, 9563 Gnesau (Kärnten) **(0676) 6032848; office@camping-hobitsch.at; www.camping-hobitsch.at**

🏕 €1.50 👥 WD ♨ 🖴 ✗ 🍴 🍽 Ⓖ nr ♨ 🛒 nr /Δ 🚴

Site sp on B95. Sm, pt shd, EHU €3.50; Eng spkn; tennis; games area. *"Beautiful setting in meadow; excel san facs; adj to cycle path."* **€16.60, 1 May-30 Sep.** **2016**

GRAN *C1* (1km N Rural) *47.51000, 10.55611* **Comfort-Camp Grän,** Engetalstrasse 13, 6673 Grän (Tirol) **(05675) 6570; info@comfortcamp.at; www.comfortcamp.at**

🏕 €4 👥 (htd) WD ♨ ♿ ⊙ ✗ 🍴 🍽 🍴 Ⓖ ♨ 🛒 nr /Δ
🚴 (covrd, htd)

Leave A7 (Germany) at Oy exit, foll 310 via Wertach, Oberjoch to Gran. Rtes fr Sonthofen or Reutte only suitable for MH's. 4*, Med, mkd, unshd, pt sl, terr, EHU (16A) 0.75 per kWh; gas; bbq; TV; 20% statics; phone; bus; Eng spkn; adv bkg acc; games rm; solarium; CKE. *"Ski-rm facs avail; private bthrms avail extra cost; vg facs; luxurious facs, sauna, massage; beautiful area; cable car nrby; walking/cycle rtes fr site; ACSI site."* **€36.00, 10 May-1 Nov & 15 Dec-16 Apr.** **2018**

GRAN *C1* (6km W Rural) *47.50825, 10.49468* **Panoramacamp Alpenwelt,** Kienzerle 3, 6675 Tannheim **(05675) 43070; alpenwelt@tirol.com; www.tannheimertal-camping.com**

🏕 €3.50 👥 (htd) WD ♨ ♿ ♿ 🖴 ✗ 🍴 🍽 🍴 Ⓖ 🛒 /Δ 🚴

Fr N leave A7 junc 137 Oy-Mittelberg onto B310 to Oberjoch, then B199 to Tannheim. Fr S on B198 dir Reutte, turn onto B199 at Weissenbach to Tannheim. 5*, Med, mkd, hdstg, unshd, terr, serviced pitches; EHU (16A) metered; sw nr; TV (pitch); 30% statics; Eng spkn; adv bkg acc; sauna; CKE. *"Excel site & san facs; ski lift 2km; ski bus; gd walking/cycling area; lovely views; pool 4km; wifi at cafe."* **€36.00, 20 Dec-19 Apr & 1 May-30 Oct.** **2017**

GRAZ *C4* (7km SW Urban) *47.02447, 15.39719* **Stadt-Camping Central,** Martinhofstrasse 3, 8054 Graz-Strassgang **(0316) 697824 or 0676 3785102 (mob); office@reisemobilstellplatz-graz.at; www.reisemobilstellplatz-graz.at**

🏕 👥 WD ♨ ♿ 🖴 ✗ MP 🍴 🍽 🍴 Ⓖ nr 🛒 nr /Δ

Fr A9/E57 exit Graz-Webling, then dir Strassgang onto B70, site sp on R after Billa supmkt & filling stn. Med, mkd, hdstg, pt shd, EHU (6A) inc; gas; bbq; 20% statics; bus to city; tennis. *"Pleasant, conv site; reg bus service fr the nrby main rd (no traff noise); dogs free; pool, paddling pool adj; free ent superb lido (pt naturist); site manager v helpful; mainly MH."* **€30.00, 1 Apr-31 Oct.** **2017**

GREIFENBURG *D2* (2km E Rural) *46.74744, 13.19448* **Fliergercamp am See,** Seeweg 333, 9761 Greifenburg (Kärnten) **(04712) 8666; info@fliegercamp.at; www.fliegercamp.at**

12 🏕 👥 (htd) ♨ ♿ ♿ 🖴 ✗ MP 🍴 🍽 Ⓖ nr ♨ 🛒 nr

Leave A10 & J139 onto 100 dir Lienz. Site on L after 15km, mkd & visible fr rd. Med, hdg, mkd, pt shd, EHU (16A) inc; gas; sw nr; twin axles; 20% statics; Eng spkn; ccard acc; games area; CCI. *"Gd cycling; vg site; pool adj; well run."* **€24.00** **2015**

GREIN *B3* (0.7km SW Urban) *48.22476, 14.85428* **Campingplatz Grein,** Donaulände 1, 4360 Grein **07268 21230; office@camping-grein.at; www.camping-grein.at**

🏕 €2.50 👥 WD ♨ 🖴 ✗ 🍴 🍽 Ⓖ nr ♨ 🛒 nr /Δ

Sp fr A1 & B3 on banks of Danube. Med, pt shd, EHU (6-10A) €3; gas; red long stay; 10% statics; canoeing; fishing; CKE. *"Friendly, helpful owner lives on site; recep in café/bar; vg, modern san facs; htd covrd pool 200m; open air pool 500m; lovely scenery; quaint vill; gd walking; excursions; conv Danube cycle rte & Mauthausen Concentration Camp."* **€33.00, 1 Mar-31 Oct.** **2019**

HALL IN TIROL *C2* (6km E Rural) *47.28711, 11.57223*
Schlosscamping Aschach, Hochschwarzweg 2,
6111 Volders **(05224) 52333; info@schlosscamping.
com; www.schlosscamping.com**

🐕 €2.50 ♦♦ ⌷ ᴡᴅ ♨ 🗑 ∥ ᴹˢᴾ ⵠ 🍽 ① 🖩 🏊 ⌂ 🛝(htd)

**Fr A12 leave at either Hall Mitte & foll sp to Volders,
or leave at Wattens & travel W to Volders (easiest
rte). Site well sp on B171. Narr ent bet lge trees.**
Lge, mkd, pt shd, pt sl, EHU (16A) €2.70 (long cable
req some pitches, adaptor lead avail); gas; bbq; red
long stay; TV; phone; bus 250m; Eng spkn; adv bkg
acc; ccard acc; horseriding; tennis; CKE. *"Well-run,
efficient, clean site with vg, modern facs & helpful
management; few water & waste points; grassy pitches;
beautiful setting & views; gd walking/touring; arr early
to ensure pitch; excel."* **€29.00, 1 May-20 Sep.**
                                                      2017

HALL IN TIROL *C2* (1km NW Urban) *47.28423,
11.49658* **Schwimmbad-Camping,** Scheidensteinstrasse
26, 6060 Hall-in-Tirol **(05223) 5855550; h.niedrist@
hall.at; www.hall.ag**

🐕 ♦♦ ᴡᴅ ♨ & 🗑 ∥ ᴹˢᴾ ⵠ ① 🖩 ⌂

**Exit A12/E45/E60 at junc 68 at Hall-in-Tirol. Cross
rv strt into town & foll camp sp fr 2nd turn L; site
on B171. Diff ent.** 3*, Med, pt shd, EHU (6A) €2.50;
red long stay; 15% statics; bus; Eng spkn; adv bkg
acc; tennis adj; CKE. *"Well-cared for site; friendly
welcome; vg, modern facs, poss stretched high ssn;
local excursions, walking; pt of sports complex; Hall
pretty, interesting medieval town; mini golf adj;
frequent music festivals; less cr than Innsbruck sites; no
twin axles; htd pool adj; walk to town; conv for m'vans;
NB m'vans only 1 Oct-30 Apr for €7.50 per night."*
€28.00, 1 May-30 Sep.   **2015**

"That's changed – Should I let the Club know?"

If you find something on site that's different
from the site entry, fill in a report and let us
know. See camc.com/europereport.

HALLEIN *B2* (5km NW Rural) *47.70441, 13.06868*
Camping Auwirt, Salzburgerstrasse 42, 5400 Hallein
(06245) 80417; info@auwirt.net; www.auwirt.com

🐕 €2 ♦♦ ᴡᴅ ♨ & 🗑 ∥ ⵠ 🍽 ① 🖩 ⌂ 🛁

**Exit A10/E55 junc 8 onto B150 sp Salzburg Süd, then
B159 twd Hallein. Site on L in 4km.** Med, pt shd, EHU
(10A) €3; bus to Salzburg at site ent; Eng spkn; adv
bkg acc; CKE. *"Mountain views; cycle path to Salzburg
nr; gd san facs & rest; conv salt mines at Hallein &
scenic drive to Eagles' Nest; conv for Berchtesgaden;
friendly helpful family owners; flat site; excel."*
€36.00, 26 Mar-8 Oct, 9 Apr-5 Oct & 1 Dec-31 Dec.
                                                      2017

HALLSTATT *C3* (1km S Rural) *47.55296, 13.64786*
Camping Klausner-Höll, Lahnstrasse 201, 4830
Hallstatt **(06134) 6134 or 8322; camping@
hallstatt.net; camping.hallstatt.net**

🐕 €3 ♦♦ ᴡᴅ ♨ 🗑 ∥ 🍽 ① nr 🖩 🏊 ⌂

**On exit tunnel 500m thro vill, site on R nr lge filling
stn.** Med, pt shd, EHU (16A) €1 per person; sw; red
long stay; Eng spkn; ccard acc; boat trips; CKE. *"Excel,
level site; gd, clean san facs; chem disp diff to use; conv
Salzkammergut region, Hallstatt salt mines, ice caves;
pretty town 10 mins walk; family run site; relaxed &
friendly; walks; idyllic quiet setting with mountains
all around; cycle path around lake; pool adj; supmkt
300m."* **€40.00, 15 Apr-15 Oct.**   **2019**

"I like to fill in the reports as I travel from site to site"

You'll find report forms at the back of this
guide, or you can fill them in online at
camc.com/europereport.

HIRSCHEGG *C3* (0.5km N Rural) *47.02300, 14.95325*
Campingplatz Hirschegg, Haus No. 53, 8584
Hirschegg **info@camping-hirschegg.at;
www.camping-hirschegg.at**

12 🐕 €1 ♦♦ ᴡᴅ ♨ 🗑 ∥ 🐾 ⵠ 🍽 nr ① nr 🖩 nr ⌂ 🛝

**Exit A2 junc 224 Modriach N. At T-junc foll sp to
Hirschegg & in cent of vill turn R at petrol stn. Site
in 300m on L by fire stn.** Med, mkd, hdg, pt shd, EHU
(10A) €2; sw nr; 30% statics; adv bkg acc. *"Excel,
family-run site."* **€18.00**   **2016**

IMST *C1* (1.5km S Rural) *47.22861, 10.74305*
Caravanpark Imst-West, Langgasse 62, 6460 Imst
**(05412) 66293; info@imst-west.com;
www.imst-west.com**

12 🐕 €1.80-€2 ♦♦ ᴡᴅ ♨ 🗑 ∥ ᴹˢᴾ 🐾 🍽 ① nr 🖩 nr ⌂

**Fr A12/E60 exit Imst-Pitztal onto B171 N dir Imst. In
1km at rndabt turn L and sweep R round Billa store.
Immed turn L & L again to site (sp).** Med, mkd, pt shd,
pt sl, EHU (6-10A) €3; gas; Eng spkn. *"Gd cent for Tirol,
trips to Germany & en rte for Innsbruck; lovely views;
pool 1.5km; immac new san facs (2015); ski lift 2km;
free ski bus; gd."* **€28.00**   **2017**

INNSBRUCK *C1* (9.5km SW Rural) *47.23724, 11.33865* **Camping Natterersee,** Natterer See 1, 6161 Natters **(0512) 546732; info@natterersee.com; www.natterersee.com**

12 ⊼ €4.50 (htd) 🚻 ⊠ ♨ ♿ 🚿 ╱ MSP ⚲ 🍴 ⊞ 🛒 🛎 ⚠ ⚓

App Innsbruck fr E or W on A12 take A13/E45 sp Brenner. Leave at 1st junc sp Innsbruck Süd, Natters. Foll sp Natters - acute R turns & severe gradients (care across unguarded level x-ing), turn sharp R in vill & foll sp to site. Take care on negotiating ent. Narr rds & app. Fr S on A13 Brennerautobahn exit junc 3 & foll dir Mutters & Natters. 5*, Med, pt shd, sl, EHU (10A)€3.75; gas; bbq; sw; TV; bus to Innsbruck; Eng spkn; adv bkg acc; ccard acc; bike hire; waterslide; games rm; tennis; clsd 1 Nov-mid Dec; games area; CKE. *"Well-kept site adj local beauty spot; lakeside pitches gd views (extra charge); gd, scenic cent for walking & driving excursions; gd for children; friendly, helpful staff; excel modern san facs; some sm pitches & narr site rds diff lge o'fits; fantastic setting; sep car park high ssn; no dogs Jul/Aug; guided hiking; special shwr for dogs; excel."* **€42.00, G01.** **2018**

"We must tell the Club about that great site we found"

Get your site reports in by mid-August and we'll do our best to get your updates into the next edition.

INNSBRUCK *C1* (7km W Rural) *47.26339, 11.32629* **Camping Kranebittehof,** Kranebitter Allee 216, 6020 Innsbruck-Kranebitten **(0512) 281958; info@kranebitterhof.at; www.kranebitterhof.at**

12 ⊼ 🚻 (htd) WD 🚾 ♿ 🚿 ╱ MSP ⚲ ⊞ 🛒

Fr W fork L after Zirl bef main rd rv bdge, sp Innsbruck & foll B171 for 5km. Fr S on A13 fr border foll dir Bregenz on A12 exit Kranebitten & foll sp to site. Sharp ent on R. Med, mkd, hdstg, pt shd, pt sl, terr, EHU (6-10A) inc; red long stay; 20% statics; bus; Eng spkn; ccard acc; CKE. *"Excel, refurbished site in lovely situation; vg, modern san facs; some m'way & airport noise; hiking; friendly, helpful staff; ski lift 5km; site easy to find fr m'way, excel rest on site."* **€25.00** **2016**

INNSBRUCK *C1* (7.5km W Urban) *47.25307, 11.32661* **Campingplatz Pizzeria Stigger,** Bahnhofstraße 10, 6176 Völs **(0512) 303533; campingvoels@aon.at; www.camping-stigger.at**

12 🚻 WD 🚾 ⊠ 🍴 ⊞ 🛒 nr

Exit A12/E60 at Völs exit & foll site sp. 1*, Sm, pt shd, EHU inc; bus adj; Eng spkn; ccard acc; CKE. *"Gd; pool 200m; conv Innsbruck; few lge pitches and quite expensive."* **€28.00** **2018**

JENBACH *C2* (6.5km NW Rural) *47.42156, 11.74043* **Camping Karwendel,** 6212 Maurach **(05243) 6116; info@karwendel-camping.at; www.karwendel-camping.at**

12 ⊼ €3 🚻 (htd) WD 🚾 ⊠ 🧺 ╱ ⚲ 🍴 ⊞ 🛒 nr ⚠

Exit A12/E45/E50 junc 39 onto B181. Foll sp Pertisau & Maurach. In 8km (climbing fr a'route turn L at Maurach. Foll rd thro vill, turn L at T-junc, then strt across rndabt twd lake. Site sp past recycling cent. Med, unshd, EHU (10A) metered; sw nr; TV; 80% statics; golf 4km; site clsd Nov. *"In open country, glorious views of lake & mountains; diff access lge o'fits; site neglected & rundown."* **€36.00** **2019**

KALS AM GROßGLOCKNER *C2* (3km N Rural) *47.01912, 12.63680* **National Park Camping,** Berg 22, A9981 Kals am Großglockner **(043) 4852 67389; info@nationalpark-camping-kals.at; www.nationalpark-camping-kals.at**

🚻 (htd) WD 🚾 ⊠ ╱ MSP

Fr 108 (Leinz - Millersill) take L26 to Kals am Großglockner. Site thro vill in abt 2km well sp. Care needed at 3 way rd junc at end of vill, take ctr rd. 4*, Med, mkd, unshd, terr, EHU 10A; CKE. *"Excel, brand new purpose built site in Hohe Tauren Nat Park at 1460m; superb san facs."* **€30.00, 1 Apr-31 Oct.** **2015**

KITZBUHEL *C2* (3km NW Rural) *47.45906, 12.3619* **Campingplatz Schwarzsee,** Reitherstrasse 24, 6370 Kitzbühel **(05356) 62806; office@bruggerhof-camping.at; www.bruggerhof-camping.at**

12 ⊼ €5.50 🚻 (htd) WD 🚾 ⊠ ♿ 🚿 ╱ MSP 🍴 ⊞ nr 🛒 ⚠

Site sp fr Kitzbühel dir Kirchberg-Schwarzsee. Lge, pt shd, pt sl, EHU (16A) metered; gas; sw nr; TV (pitch); 80% statics; phone; bus; Eng spkn; adv bkg acc; ccard acc; sauna; CKE. *"Gd walks, cable cars & chair lifts; vg, well-maintained site; poss mosquito & vermin prob; some pitches in statics area; friendly owner; well equipped with lots of activities; excel saunas (site naturist in sauna area only); gd for families."* **€50.00** **2019**

KLAGENFURT *D3* (5km W Rural) *46.61826, 14.25641* **Camping Wörthersee,** Metnitzstrand 5, 9020 Klagenfurt am wörthersee (Kärnten) **(0463) 287810; info@campingfreund.at; www.camping-woerthersee.at**

⊼ €4.90 🚻 WD 🚾 ♿ ╱ 🦋 ⊞ ⚠ ⚓ 🏊 sand adj

Fr A2/E66 take spur to Klagenfurt-West, exit at Klagenfurt-Wörthersee. Turn R at traff lts & immed L at rd fork (traff lts), then foll sp to site. Lge, shd, EHU (10A) inc; 10% statics; bus; ccard acc; sauna; bike hire. *"V clean facs; local tax €3.50 per visit."* **€39.40, 1 May-30 Sep.** **2019**

KLOSTERNEUBURG *B4* (0.7km N Rural) *48.31097, 16.32810* **Donaupark Camping Klosterneuburg,** In der Au, 3402 Klosterneuburg **(02243) 25877; campklosterneuburg@oeamtc.at; www.camping klosterneuburg.at**

🏕 ♦♦(htd) ⓦ ⚓ ♿ ☐ ⁄ ⓂⓈⓅ ☂ ⍾ ⑪nr ♨ ▣ /Ⅲ\

Fr A22/E59 exit junc 7 onto B14, site sp in cent of town behind rlwy stn. After passing Klosterneuburg Abbey on L turn 1st R (sharp turn under rlwy). Site immed ahead. 4*, Med, mkd, pt shd, EHU (6-12A) €3; gas; bbq; cooking facs; TV; 5% statics; phone; bus, train to Vienna; ccard acc; bike hire; boat hire; tennis; CKE. *"Well-organised, popular site; leisure cent adj; vg san facs; helpful staff; sm pitches; htd pools adj; conv Danube cycle path & Vienna; church & monastery worth visit."* **€36.00, 13 Mar-5 Nov.** **2017**

KOSSEN *B2* (3km SE Rural) *47.65388, 12.41544* **Eurocamping Wilder Kaiser,** Kranebittau 18, 6345 Kössen **(05375) 6444; info@eurocamp-koessen.com; www.eurocamp-koessen.com** '

12 🏕 ☐ €4-6 ♦♦(htd) ⓦ ⚓ ♨ ☐ ⁄ ⓂⓈⓅ ⍾ ☂ ⑪ ♨ ▣ /Ⅲ\ ♪

Leave A12 at Oberaudorf/Niederndorf junc, head E on 172 thro Niederndorf & Walchsee to Kössen. Strt across at rndabt, in 1km turn R sp Hinterburg Lift. At next junc turn R & site located after 400m. 5*, Lge, mkd, pt shd, serviced pitches; EHU (6A) metered + conn fee; gas; TV (pitch); 50% statics; Eng spkn; adv bkg acc; ccard acc; games area; sauna; tennis; golf 2km; solarium; CKE. *"Lovely site; excel play area & organised activities; htd pool adj; rafting, hang-gliding & canoeing 1km; excel."* **€39.90** **2019**

KOTSCHACH *D2* (1km SW Rural) *46.66946, 12.99153* **Alpencamp,** Kötschach 284, 9640 Kötschach-Mauthen **(04715) 429; info@alpencamp.at; www.alpencamp.at**

12 🏕 ☐ €2 ♦♦(htd) ⓦ ⚓ ♿ ☐ ⁄ ⓂⓈⓅ ☂ ⍾ ⑪nr ♨ ▣ /Ⅲ\ ♨ (covrd, htd)

At junc of rds B110 & B111 in Kötschach turn W onto B111, foll camp sps to site in 800m on L. 4*, Med, mkd, pt shd, EHU (16A) inc; TV; phone; Eng spkn; ccard acc; games rm; bike hire; tennis; waterslide; site clsd 1 Nov-14 Dec; bike hire; tennis 400m; sauna; games area. *"Useful for Plöcken Pass; cycle tracks on rv bank nrby; vg san facs; friendly, helpful owner; vg site."* **€19.00** **2016**

LANDECK *C1* (0.5km W Urban) *47.14263, 10.56147* **Camping Riffler,** Bruggfeldstrasse 2, 6500 Landeck **(05442) 64898; info@camping-riffler.at; www.camping-riffler.at**

12 🏕 ♦♦♦ ⓦ ⚓ ☐ ⁄ ⑪nr ▣nr /Ⅲ\

Exit E60/A12 at Landeck-West, site in 1.5km, 500m fr cent on L. Sm, pt shd, EHU (10A) €2.70 (poss rev pol); gas; ccard acc; bike hire; site clsd May; CKE. *"Well-kept, clean, friendly site; sm pitches; dogs free; narr rds; recep open 1800-2000 LS - site yourself & pay later; pool 500m; excel NH."* **€25.00** **2016**

LIENZ *C2* (6km SE Rural) *46.80730, 12.80350* **Camping Seewiese,** Tristachersee 2, 9900 Tristach **(04852) 69767; seewiese@hotmail.com; www.campingtirol.com**

🏕 ☐ €3 ♦♦♦ ⓦ ⚓ ☐ ⁄ ⓂⓈⓅ ☂ ⍾ ⍽ ⑪ ♨ /Ⅲ\

On B100 to Lienz dir Tristach, turn sharp L after rlwy underpass & rv bdge to by-pass Trisach. Turn R after 4km opp golf course. Steep (11%) climb to site. Sp. 4*, Med, hdstg, pt shd, sl, EHU (6-16A) €2.70; gas; sw nr; TV; phone; bus high ssn to Tristach; Eng spkn; bike hire; tennis; CKE. *"Fairly secluded, relaxing site; htd pool 5km; mountain views; gd walks; gd san facs; helpful owner."* **€36.00, 15 May-14 Sep.** **2015**

LIENZ *C2* (2km S Rural) *46.81388, 12.76388* **Dolomiten-Camping Amlacherhof,** Lake rd 20, 9908 Amlach Lienz **(04852) 62317 or 69917 62317-1 (mob); info@amlacherhof.at; www.amlacherhof.at**

🏕 ☐ €2.90 ♦♦♦(htd) ⓦ ⚓ ♨ ♿ ☐ ⁄ ⓂⓈⓅ ☂ ⍾ ⍽ ⑪nr ♨ /Ⅲ\ ♨ (htd)

S fr Lienz on B100, foll sp in 1.5km to Amlach. In vill, foll site sp. 4*, Med, hdg, mkd, pt shd, EHU (16A) metered inc; bbq; TV; 5% statics; bus adj; Eng spkn; adv bkg acc; site clsd 1 Nov-15 Dec; games rm; golf 7km; tennis; bike hire. *"Excel touring cent; many mkd walks & cycle rtes; cable cars, ski lifts 3km; attractive, historic town; excel, scenic site; local taxes €5."* **€32.40, 1 Mar-31 Oct.** **2019**

LIEZEN *C3* (11km SW Rural) *47.52061, 14.13080* **Camping Putterersee,** Hohenberg 2A, 8943 Aigen **(03682) 22859; camping.putterersee@aon.at; www.camping-putterersee.at**

🏕 ☐ €2.20 ♦♦♦(htd) ⓦ ⚓ ♿ ☐ ⁄ ☂ ⍾ ⍽ ⑪ ♨ ▣nr /Ⅲ\ ⌖

S on A10 fr Salzburg, exit 63 for E651/B320 twds Hohenberg. Foll sp. Med, pt shd, pt sl, EHU (13A); gas; bbq; sw; twin axles; Eng spkn; adv bkg acc; bike hire; boat hire; fishing; games rm; CKE. *"Excel san facs; gd views, walking & cycling; v helpful staff; vg."* **€21.00, 15 Apr-31 Oct.** **2015**

LINZ *B3* (14km SE Rural) *48.23527, 14.37888* **Camping-Linz am Pichlingersee,** Wienerstrasse 937, 4030 Linz **(0732) 305314; office@camping-linz.at; www.camping-linz.at**

🏕 ☐ €1.90 ♦♦♦(htd) ⓦ ⚓ ♿ ☐ ⁄ ⓂⓈⓅ ⍾ ⑪ ♨ ▣

Exit A1/E60 junc 160; take Enns dir; go L on 1st rndabt; do not go under rndabt thro underpass; site is sp on R. Med, mkd, pt shd, EHU (6A) inc; gas; cooking facs; sw nr; red long stay; 40% statics; bus; Eng spkn; adv bkg acc; tennis. *"Excel modern san facs, well-run, family-run site; friendly staff; site clsd 1300-1500; gd walks around lake; monastery at St Florian worth visit; conv NH; gd."* **€26.50, 15 Mar-15 Oct.** **2017**

LOFER *C2* (2km SE Rural) *47.57500, 12.70804*
Camping Park Grubhof, St Martin 39, 5092 St Martin-bei-Lofer (06588) 82370; home@grubhof.com; www.grubhof.com

Clear sps to camp at ent on rd B311 Lofer to Zell-am-See. Site on L after garden cent. Lge, pt shd, serviced pitches; EHU (10A) €2; phone; bus to Salzburg; adv bkg acc; CKE. "*Beautiful scenery; roomy, peaceful site; excel san facs; adult only & dog free areas; fitness cent; sh walk to vill; highly rec; mountain views; some meadowside and rvside pitches; delightful rest/bar; excel.*"
€36.00, 1 Jan-23 Mar, 11 Apr-2 Nov, 6 Dec-31 Dec, G04. 2018

See advertisement

LUNZ AM SEE *B4* (0.9km E Urban) *47.86194, 15.03638* **Ötscherland Camping**, Zellerhofstrasse 23, 3293 Lunz-am-See (07486) 8413; info@oetscherland camping.at; www.oetscherlandcamping.at

Fr S on B25 turn R into Lunz-am-See. In 300m turn L, cross rv & take 1st L, site on L on edge of vill. Sm, hdstg, pt shd, EHU (16A) inc; sw nr; 80% statics; Eng spkn. "*Excel walking; immac facs; winter skiing; vg site on Rv Ybbs & Eisenstrasse.*" **€19.50** 2016

MARBACH AN DER DONAU *B4* (1km W Rural) *48.21309, 15.13828* **Campingplatz Marbacher**, Granz 51, 3671 Marbach-an-der-Donau (07413) 20733; info@marbach-freizeit.at; www.marbach-freizeit.at

Fr W exit A1 junc 100 at Ybbs onto B25. Cross Rv Danube & turn R onto B3. Site in 7km. Fr E exit A1 junc 90 at Pöchlarn, cross rv & turn L onto B3 to Marbach, site sp. Med, mkd, pt shd, EHU (16A) €1.9; bbq; sw; 5% statics; Eng spkn; adv bkg acc; ccard acc; bike hire; boat hire; tennis 800m; watersports; CKE. "*Beautiful, well-managed site; sm, narr pitches; excel facs & staff; gd rst & bar; gd cycling & watersports; v clean facs; gd NH fr m'way or longer stay for touring.*"
€25.40, 1 Apr-31 Oct. 2019

MARIAZELL *B4* (4km NW Rural) *47.79009, 15.28221* **Campingplatz am Erlaufsee**, Erlaufseestrasse 3, 8630 St Sebastien-bei-Mariazell (03882) 4937 or (066460) 644400 (mob); gemeinde@st-sebastian.at; www.st-sebastian.at

On B20 1km N of Mariazell turn W sp Erlaufsee. Site in 3km on app to lake, turn L thro car park ent to site. Med, pt shd, pt sl, EHU (12A) metered; bus high ssn. "*Cable car in Mariazell; beach nrby; pilgrimage cent; all hot water by token fr owner.*"
€16.30, 1 May-15 Sep. 2016

MATREI IN OSTTIROL *C2* (0.5km S Rural) *46.99583, 12.53906* **Camping Edengarten**, Edenweg 15a, 9971 Matrei-in-Osttirol (04875) 5111; info@ campingedengarten.at; www.campingedengarten.at

App fr Lienz on B108 turn L bef long ascent (bypassing Matrei) sp Matrei-in-Osttirol & Camping. App fr N thro Felbertauern tunnel, by-pass town, turn R at end of long descent, sps as above. Med, pt shd, EHU (10A); gas; 10% statics; bus. "*Gd mountain scenery; helpful owner; beautiful views; pool 300m; pretty town; some rd noise during daytime.*"
€32.00, 1 Apr-31 Oct. 2019

MATREI IN OSTTIROL *C2* (23km W Rural) *47.01912, 12.63695* **Camping Kals Am Großglockner**, Burg 22, 9981 Kals am Großglockner 04852 67389; info@ nationalpark-camping-kals.at; www.nationalpark-camping-kals.at

Fr 108 Matrei in Osttirol to Lienz, exit at Huben onto L26 to Kals. 3km after vill foll sp to Dorfertal. National Park campsite on L. Med, unshd, EHU metered; twin axles; Eng spkn; ccard acc; CCI. "*Excel site; ski bus; excel walking & climbing.*"
€31.50, 17 May-13 Oct. 2019

MAYRHOFEN *C2* (1km N Rural) *47.17617, 11.86969*
Camping Mayrhofen, Laubichl 125, 6290 Mayrhofen
(05285) 6258051; camping@alpenparadies.com;
www.alpenparadies.com

🐕 €4.50 ♦♦ wc 🚿 ♿ 🚮 ⊘ mp ♈ 🄌 ⓘ 🍴 🝰nr ⚠ ⛵

Site at N end of vill off B169. Lge, hdstg, mkd, pt shd,
EHU (10A) metered; gas; 50% statics; adv bkg
acc; bike hire; sauna; CKE. *"Modern san facs; diff
for lge o'fits, narr rds; some factory noise; gd rest."*
€31.20, 1 Jan-31 Oct & 15 Dec-31 Dec. **2019**

MELK *B4* (3km N Urban) *48.24298, 15.34040*
Donau Camping Emmersdorf, Bundesstrasse 133,
3644 Emmersdorf-an-der-Donau **(02752) 71707;**
office@emmersdorf.at; www.emmersdorf.at

🐕 ♦♦ wc 🚿 ♿ 🚮 ⊘ ⓘ 🝰nr 🝰nr

Fr A1 take Melk exit. Turn R, foll sp Donaubrücke,
cross rv bdge. Turn R, site 200m on L, well sp.
Sm, hdg, mkd, pt shd, EHU (6A) inc; bbq; phone; ccard
acc; games rm; bike hire; tennis; fishing; CKE. *"Liable to
close if rv in flood; clean facs; noise fr rd & disco w/end;
attractive vill; vg."* **€20.50, 1 May-30 Sep.** **2019**

MELK *B4* (6km NE Rural) *48.25395, 15.37115*
Campingplatz Stumpfer, 3392 Schönbühel **(02752)**
8510; office@stumpfer.com; www.stumpfer.com

🐕 ♦♦ wc 🚿 ⊘ ⓘ 🚮 🝰nr

Exit A1 junc 80. Foll sp for Melk on B1 as far as junc
with B33. Turn onto B33 (S bank of Danube) for 2km
to Schönbühel. Site on L adj gasthof, sp. Sm, pt shd,
EHU (10-16A) €2.40 or metered; gas; red long stay;
Eng spkn; adv bkg acc; ccard acc; CKE. *"On beautiful
stretch of Danube; arr early for rvside pitch; abbeys in
Melk & Krems worth visit; lower end site unrel in wet;
helpful staff; vg facs but poss stretched high ssn; cycle
path adj."* **€28.50, 1 Apr-31 Oct.** **2017**

MELK *B4* (3.6km NW Rural) *48.23347, 15.32888*
Camping Fährhaus Melk, Kolomaniau 3, 3390 Melk
(02752) 53291; info@faehrhaus-melk.at;
www.faehrhaus-melk.at

♦♦ 🚮 ⊘ ♈ ⓘnr 🚮 🝰nr ⚠

Skirt Melk on B1, immed after abbey at traff lts,
turn N on bdge over rv (sp). Site in 700m.
Sm, pt shd, EHU (6A) inc; bbq; fishing. *"Basic site
but adequate; abbey adj & boating on Danube; NB all
sites on banks of Danube liable to close if rv in flood."*
€12.50, 1 Apr-31 Oct. **2016**

MICHELDORF IN OBERÖSTERREICH *B3* (4km S
Rural) *47.851081, 14.146745* **Schön Camping,** Schön
60, 4563 Micheldorf **(07582) 60917; reservierung@
schoen-menschen.at; schoen-menschen.at**

🐕 ♦♦ 🚮 ♿ ⊘ ⊘ mp 🦋 ⓘ 🚮 ⚠ (indoor)

Fr m'way J28 take rd 138 N dir Micheldorf, foll
Schon camping sp (not Schon-Menschen sp) to
avoid 3.1m rlwy bdge. Narr country rd. Drive thro
complex to camping area at top. Hdstg, pt shd, pt
sl, EHU inc; cooking facs; sw nr; phone; bus on rd
138; Eng spkn; adv bkg acc. *"Literally self service,
pay in honesty box by facs bldg; part of disabled
complex; free minigolf, access to indoor pool;
walks witin site and local area; cafe (ltd hrs); vg."*
€25.50, 1 May-30 Sep. **2019**

MILLSTATT *D3* (4km SE Rural) *46.78863, 13.61418*
Camping Neubauer, Dellach 3, 9872 Millstatt-am-See
(04766) 2532; info@camping-neubauer.at;
www.camping-neubauer.at

🐕 €2.50 ♦♦ (htd) wc 🚮 ♿ ⊘ ⊘ 🦋 ♈ 🍴 ⓘnr 🚮 🝰nr ⚠ 🚣

Exit A10/E55 dir Seeboden & Millstatt. Take lakeside
rd B98 fr Millstatt to Dellach, R turn & foll sp
camping sp. Med, mkd, hdstg, pt shd, terr, EHU (6A)
inc; gas; bbq; sw; 10% statics; ccard acc; tennis; golf
6km; bike hire; watersports. *"Gd touring base; easy
access to Italy; superb scenery with lakes & mountains;
gd walks; excel facs; boat trips nr; gd rest; steep narr
rd's to pitches, tractor avail to help; pt shd on lake
pitches."* **€31.70, 1 May-15 Oct.** **2019**

MITTERSILL *C2* (1km E Rural) *47.27761, 12.49267*
Camping Schmidl, Museumstrasse 6, 5730 Mittersill
(06562) 6158

🐕 ♦♦ wc 🚮 ⊘ 🦋 🝰nr

Fr Zell-am-See or Kitzbühel, exit to Mittersill,
fr town sq foll camping sp past hospital.
Sm, pt shd, EHU (15A) inc. *"Friendly & welcoming;
useful stop bef Felbertauern tunnel; conv Krimml
waterfall & Grossglockner; large CL type with pitches
for 10 o'fits; gd for NH."* **€12.00, 1 May-30 Sep.** **2015**

MONDSEE *B3* (5km SE Rural) *47.82956, 13.36554*
Austria Camp, Achort 60, 5310 St Lorenz **(06232)**
2927; office@austriacamp.at; austriacamp.at

🐕 €2.90 ♦♦ wc 🚮 ♿ ⊘ ⊘ mp 🦋 🍴 ⓘ 🚮 ⚠ 🚣

Exit A1/E55/E60 junc 265 onto B154. In 4km at
St Lorenz at km 21.4 turn L onto unclassified
rd to site in 600m at lakeside. Fr SW via Bad
Ischl, at St Gilgen take Mondsee rd; 500m after
Plomberg turn R at St Lorenz; Austria Camp sps
clear. Med, shd, EHU (6A) €2.90; sw; 45% statics;
adv bkg acc; boat launch; sauna; fishing; bike hire;
golf nr; tennis; CKE. *"Gd, clean san facs; gd rest;
friendly, family-run site; no arrivals bet 1200 & 1500."*
€30.00, 1 Apr-30 Sep. **2015**

MURAU *C3* (3km W Rural) *47.10791, 14.13883*
Camping Olachgut, Kaindorf 90, 8861 St Georgen-ob-Murau (03532) 2162 or 3233; office@olachgut.at; www.olachgut.at

12 🐕 €3 👫 wc 🚿 ♿ 🚽 ∥ MSP 🦋 ♟ 🍴 ⊕ 🍴 🏊 nr 🏧 🚲

Site sp on rd B97 bet Murau & St Georgen. Med, pt shd, EHU (16A) inc; gas; sw; 40% statics; adv bkg acc; sauna; horseriding; bike hire; games area. *"Rural site nr rlwy; ski lift 2.5km."* **€30.00**   **2019**

> ## "Satellite navigation makes touring much easier"
>
> Remember most sat navs don't know if you're towing or in a larger vehicle – always use yours alongside maps and site directions.

MURECK *D4* (0.7km S Rural) *46.70491, 15.77240*
Campingplatz Mureck, Austrasse 10, 8480 Mureck (03472) 210512; m.rauch@mureck.steiermark.at; www.mureck.gv.at/tourismus-freizeit/campingplatz

🐕 €3.50 👫 wc 🚿 ♿ 🚽 ∥ 🦋 🍴 ⊕ 🍴 🏊 nr 🏧

Fr Graz on A9, turn E at junc 226 onto B69 sp Mureck. NB: Low archway in Mureck. Med, mkd, hdstg, shd, EHU (10A) inc; bbq; red long stay; 30% statics; phone; adv bkg acc; ccard acc; bike hire; fishing; tennis; games area; CKE. *"Off beaten track in pleasant country town; htd pool complex inc waterslide adj; pt of leisure complex; gd, modern san facs."* **€23.00, 1 May-3 Nov.**   **2016**

NASSEREITH *C1* (2.5km SE Rural) *47.30975, 10.85466* **Camping Rossbach,** Rossbach 325, 6465 Nassereith (05265) 5154; rainer.ruepp@gmx.at; www.campingrossbach.com

12 🐕 €1.50 (htd) 👫 wc 🚿 ♿ 🚽 ∥ MSP 🦋 🍴 ⊕ 🍴 🏊 🏧 🛷 (htd) 🔥

On ent vill of Nassereith turn E & foll dir Rossbach/Dormitz, site in 1.5km. Foll sm green sps. Narr app. 4*, Med, mkd, pt shd, EHU (6A); bbq; TV; 5% statics; phone; adv bkg acc; fishing; games rm; CKE. *"Mountain views; friendly welcome; ACSI prices; ski lift 500m; ski bus; pitch in various sep areas; vg san facs."* **€23.50**   **2017**

NAUDERS *C1* (4km S Rural) *46.85139, 10.50472*
Alpencamping, Bundestrasse 279, 6543 Nauders (05473) 87217; info@camping-nauders.at; www.camping-nauders.at

🐕 €2 👫 (htd) wc 🚿 ♿ 🚽 ∥ 🍴 ⊕ 🍴 🏊

On W side of B180 just bef Italian border. Sm, hdstg, unshd, EHU €1.90; gas; phone; ccard acc; CKE. *"Conv NH for Reschen pass; gd touring base; excel cycling, walking; excel san facs."* **€25.00, 1 Jan-16 Apr, 30 Apr-15 Oct, 20 Dec-31 Dec.**
                  2016

NEUSTIFT IM STUBAITAL *C1* (0.5km NE Rural) *47.10977, 11.30770* **Camping Stubai,** Stubaitalstrasse 94, 6167 Neustift-im-Stubaital (05226) 2537; info@campingstubai.at; www.campingstubai.at

12 🐕 €2.60 👫 (htd) wc 🚿 ♿ 🚽 ∥ MSP 🍴 ⊕ 🍴 nr 🏊 nr 🏧

S fr Innsbruck on B182 or A13, take B183 dir Fulpmes & Neustift. Site sp, in vill opp church & adj Billa supmkt. If app via A13 & Europabrucke, toll payable on exit junc 10 into Stubaital Valley. 4*, Med, mkd, pt shd, pt sl, terr, EHU (6A) €2.90; 50% statics; Eng spkn; adv bkg acc; games rm; sauna; CKE. *"Friendly, family-run site; pitches nr rv poss flood; recep open 0900-1100 & 1700-1900 - barrier down but can use farm ent & find space; htd pool 500m; excel mountain walking & skiing; lovely location."* **€34.00**   **2017**

NEUSTIFT IM STUBAITAL *C1* (6km SW Rural) *47.06777, 11.25388* **Camping Edelweiss,** Volderau 29, 6167 Neustift-im-Stubaital (05226) 3484; info@camping-edelweiss.at; camping-edelweiss.at

12 🐕 €3 👫 (htd) wc 🚿 🚽 ∥ MSP 🦋 ⊕ 🍴

Fr B182 or A13 exit junc 10 take B183 to Neustift, site on R at Volderau vill. Med, hdstg, unshd, EHU (4A) €3; gas; 30% statics; phone; bus. *"Excel peaceful site in scenic valley; vg, modern san facs; haphazard mix of statics & tourers; winter skiing."* **€18.00**   **2019**

OBERNBERG AM INN *B3* (1km SW Rural) *48.31506, 13.32313* **Panorama Camping,** Saltzburgerstrasse 28, 4982 Obernberg-am-Inn (07758) 30024 or 173 2306 571 (mob); obernberg-panoramacamping@aon.at; http://obernberg-panoramacamping.jimdo.com

12 👫 wc 🚿 🚽 ∥ 🦋 🍴 ⊕ nr 🏊 nr

Exit A8/E56 junc 65 to Obernberg. Then take dir Braunau, site well sp. Sm, hdg, pt shd, pt sl, serviced pitches; EHU (10A) metered or €2 (poss rev pol); Eng spkn; adv bkg acc; tennis 800m. *"Friendly, excel sm site; site yourself if office clsd; nr to border; spectacular views; san facs clean; gd walking, birdwatching; o'night m'vans area; network of cycle paths around vills on other side of rv; pool 800m; pleasant walk to town past rv viewpoint."* **€29.00**   **2015**

OETZ *C1* (10km S Rural) *47.13533, 10.9316* **Ötztal Arena Camp Krismer,** Mühlweg 32, 6441 Umhausen (05255) 5390; www.oetztalcamping.com; www.oetztal-camping.at

12 🐕 €2.60 👫 wc 🚿 🚽 ∥ 🦋 ♟ 🍴 ⊕ 🏊 nr 🏧

Fr A12 exit junc 123 S onto B186 sp Ötztal. S of Ötztal turn L into Umhausen vill & foll site sp. 4*, Med, mkd, pt shd, pt sl, EHU (16A) metered (poss rev pol); gas; bbq; sw; phone; Eng spkn; adv bkg req. *"Well-run site; immac facs; lots of local info given on arr; friendly owners; poss diff pitching on some sh pitches; pool 200m; excel cent for Stuibenfal waterfall (illuminated Wed night high ssn) & Ötztaler Valley; pool & lake sw 200m; wonderful scenery; gd walking fr site; narr app rd; very cr in high ssn."* **€29.00**   **2018**

OSSIACH *D3* (1km SW Rural) *46.66388, 13.97500*
Terrassen Camping Ossiacher See, Ostriach 67, 9570
Ossiach **(04243) 436; martinz@camping.at;**
www.terrassen.camping.at

🏕 €3 ♟(htd) ⬚ 📶 ♨ ⚲ ⬚ 🚿 ⧫ 🦋 ⌖ ▽ ⊕ 🚽 🛒 ⚱ ✒

**Leave A10/E55/E66 at exit for Ossiachersee, turn
L onto B94 twd Feldkirchen & shortly R to Ossiach
Süd. Site on lake shore just S of Ossiach vill.**
Lge, mkd, pt shd, terr, EHU (4-10A) €3; gas; bbq; sw;
red long stay; twin axles; TV; ccard acc; clsd 1200-
1500 LS; games area; horseriding; games rm;
windsurfing; bike hire; fishing; tennis; watersports;
CKE. *"Ideal Carinthian lakes, Hochosterwitz castle
& excursions into Italy; parking adj; cash machine;
beautiful scenery; many activities; excel san facs;
pitches sm and diff for big o'fits; dogs confined to
pitches next to entrance; but site in lovely location."*
€41.00, 1 May-30 Sep, G05. **2019**

POYSDORF *A4* (1km W Urban) *48.66454, 16.61168*
Veltlinerland Camping, Laaerstrasse 106, 2170
Poysdorf **(02552) 20371; veltlinerlandcamping.
poysdorf@gmx.at; www.poysdorf.at**

🏕 🐕 ⬚ 🚿 ⧫ 🦋 ⊕ 🛒 ⚱

**Fr rd 7/E461 at traff lts in Poysdorf turn W onto
rd 219 dir Laa an der Thaya. Site sp on R in approx
1km on edge of park.** Sm, mkd, hdstg, unshd, terr,
EHU (6A) €2.20; sw nr; 50% statics; Eng spkn; tennis.
*"Gd, under-used site 1hr N of Vienna; htd wc & shwrs at
park adj (key issued); no other site in area; conv Czech
border."* **€13.00, 1 May-31 Oct.** **2016**

PRUTZ *C1* (0.6km NE Rural) *47.07955, 10.6588*
Aktiv-Camping Prutz, Pontlatzstrasse 22, 6522 Prutz
(05472) 2648; info@aktiv-camping.at;
www.aktiv-camping.at

12 🏕 €3 ♟(htd) ⬚ 📶 ♨ ⚲ ⬚ 🚿 ⌖ ▽ ⊕ 🚽 ⚱

**Fr Landeck to Prutz on rd B180 turn R at Shell stn
over rv bdge, site sp.** 4*, Med, hdg, mkd, pt shd, EHU
(16A) inc; gas; sw nr; red long stay; TV; 20% statics;
Eng spkn; adv bkg acc; ccard acc; bike hire; site clsd
Nov; CKE. *"Excel, clean facs; gd views; o'night m'vans
area; pool complex in vill; office clsd 1000-1630 - find
pitch & pay later; walks & cycle rtes; conv NH en rte
Italy & for tax-free shopping in Samnaun, Switzerland;
gd site; cards given for free bus travel."* **€32.00** **2015**

PURBACH AM NEUSIEDLERSEE *B4* (1km SE Rural)
47.90958, 16.70580 **Storchencamp Purbach,**
Türkenhain, 7083 Purbach-am-Neusiedlersee
(Burgenland) **(02683) 5170; office@gmeiner.co.at;**
www.gmeiner.co.at

🏕 🐕 €2.90 ♟(htd) ⬚ 📶 ♨ ⬚ 🚿 ⧫ 🦋 ▽ ⊕ 🛒 ⚱

**Exit A4/E6 junc 43 onto B50 at Neuseidl-am-See to
Purbach. Site sp in town nr pool complex.** Sm, pt
shd, EHU (6A) €2.30; bbq; 80% statics; bus/train 1km;
Eng spkn; games area. *"Open field for tourers; excel
sw complex adj free with local visitor card; free public
transport & red ent to museums etc; modern facs; conv
NH."* **€17.50, 1 Apr-31 Oct.** **2016**

RATTENBERG *C2* (4.5km N Rural) *47.45670, 11.88084*
Seen-Camping Stadlerhof, Seebühel 15, 6233
Kramsach-am-Reintalersee **(05337) 63371; camping.
stadlerhof@chello.at; www.camping-stadlerhof.at**

12 🏕 €4.90 ♟(htd) ⬚ 📶 ♨ ⚲ ⬚ 🚿 ⧫ 🦋 ⌖ ▽ ⊕ 🚽 🛒 nr ⚱
🚤(htd) 🎣

**Exit A12/E45/E60 junc 32 Rattenberg dir Kramsach.
At rndabt turn R, then immed L & foll sp 'Zu den
Seen' & site sp. Site on L at Lake Krumsee.** 5*, Lge,
mkd, hdstg, pt shd, pt sl, EHU (10A) inc; gas; bbq;
sw nr; TV (pitch); 50% statics; phone; adv bkg acc;
games rm; bike hire; fishing; tennis; sauna. *"Beautiful,
well laid-out site in lovely setting; excel san facs."*
€35.80 **2019**

RATTENBERG *C2* (4km NE Rural) *47.46198, 11.90708*
Camping Seehof, Moosen 42, 6233 Kramsach-am-
Reintalersee **(05337) 63541; info@camping-seehof.
com; www.camping-seehof.com**

12 🏕 €5 ♟(htd) ⬚ 📶 ♨ ⚲ ⬚ 🚿 ⧫ 🦋 ⌖ ▽ ⊕ 🚽 🛒 ⚱ 🚤

**Exit A12/E45/E60 junc 32 sp Kramsach, foll sp
'Zu den Seen' for 5km. Site immed bef Camping
Seeblick-Toni Brantlhof.** 5*, Med, mkd, pt shd,
EHU (6-13A) €3; bbq; sw; red long stay; TV (pitch);
30% statics; phone; Eng spkn; adv bkg acc; ccard acc;
bike hire; games rm; solarium; horseriding nr; CKE. *"Friendly
staff; gd views fr some pitches; gd, modern san facs; gd
rest; Excel site, local walks, excel museum next door;
local taxes €2."* **€33.00** **2019**

REUTTE *C1* (1km S Rural) *47.47763, 10.72258*
Camping Reutte, Ehrenbergstrasse 53, 6600 Reutte
**(05672) 62809 or (06641) 858279 (mob); camping-
reutte@aon.at; www.camping-reutte.com**

12 🏕 €2 ♟(htd) ⬚ 📶 ♨ ⬚ 🚿 ⧫ 🦋 ⊕ 🛒

**Foll B179 (Fern pass rd), exit at Reutte Süd. Site sp
in 1.5km on L.** Med, mkd, hdstg, pt shd, EHU (16A)
€2.40; TV (pitch); phone; Eng spkn; adv bkg acc; CKE.
*"Conv for Fern Pass; barriers clsd 2100; clean, popular
site; excel; ski lift 500m; pool adj; free guest cards for
facs & transport."* **€29.70** **2016**

RIED IM OBERINNTAL *C1* (0.6km E Rural) *47.05480,
10.65630* **Camping Dreiländereck,** Gartenland 37,
6531 Ried Im Oberinntal **05472 6025; info@tirol
camping.at; www.tirolcamping.at**

12 🏕 €4 ♟(htd) ⬚ 📶 ♨ ⚲ ⬚ 🚿 ⧫ 🦋 ⌖ ▽ ⊕ 🚽 🛒 nr

**Fr Landeck take 180 twd Reschenpass. Exit at Ried
& foll sp.** Sm, unshd, EHU (15A) metered; sw nr;
twin axles; TV; bus adj; Eng spkn; adv bkg acc; CCI.
*"Wellness cent; conv to vill shops; bike hire; helpful
owners; gd clean san facs; adventure sports fac nrby;
gd site."* **€40.60** **2019**

AUSTRIA

ST ANTON AM ARLBERG *C1* (2km E Rural) *47.14505, 10.33890* **Camping Arlberg,** Strohsack 235c, 6574 Pettneu-am-Arlberg (Tirol) **(05448) 222660; info@ camping-arlberg.at; www.camping-arlberg.at**

🏕 🕴📶 ▥ ⚒ ᵴ 🅿 🚐 (covrd, htd) 🎿

Fr W on S16/E60, thro Arlberg tunnel, then take Pettneu exit after St Anton to N; site sp in 200m. 4*, Lge, hdg, mkd, pt shd, EHU (16A) metered; twin axles; 10% statics; phone; bus; Eng spkn; adv bkg acc; sauna; fishing. *"Mountain views; htd private bathrms & sat TV each pitch; o'night m'vans area; beauty treatments avail; excel site;ski & boot rm; ski bus; ski lift 1km; wellness ctr adj with pool; site fees inc free bus, cable car & sw pool for 1 day."* **€30.00, 1 Jan-30 Apr, 1 Jun-31 Sep & 1 Dec-31 Dec.** **2017**

ST JOHANN IM PONGAU *C2* (1km S Urban) *47.34141, 13.19793* **Camping Kastenhof,** Kastenhofweg 6, 5600 St Johann-im-Pongau (06412) 5490; info@kastenhof.at; www.kastenhof.at

12 🏕 🕴(htd) ▥ ⚒ 🚐 ⲙ 🅿 ❄ ⓘ nr ⛴ 🅰

Take A10 S fr Salzburg onto B311 for Alpendorf. Go over rv & turn L into Liechtensteinklamm twd St Johann, site on L, sp. 1*, Med, unshd, EHU (15A) metered + €2 conn fee; TV (pitch); 10% statics; bus; adv bkg acc; sauna; CKE. *"Conv Tauern tunnel, Grossglockner Hochalpenstrasse, Zell-am-See; gd clean site."* **€28.00** **2018**

ST JOHANN IN TIROL *C2* (12km SE Rural) *47.46845, 12.55440* **Tirol Camp,** Lindau 20, 6391 Fieberbrunn (Tirol) **(05354) 56666; office@tirol-camp.at; www.tirol-camp.at**

🏕 €8 🕴(htd) ▥ ⚒ 🚐 ⲙ 🅿 ❄ ⓘ ⲁ ⛴ 🅰 🎿 (covrd, htd)

Fr St Johann thro vill of Fieberbrunn, site sp at end of vill. Turn R up to Streuböden chair lift, site 200m on L. 4*, Lge, pt shd, terr, EHU (6A) metered; sw; TV; 30% statics; phone; train; adv bkg acc; ccard acc; games area; tennis; waterslide; sauna. *"Superb site & facs; gd base for skiing, gd walking; wellness cent; trips to Innsbruck & Salzburg; noise fr adj farm."* **€38.00, 1 Jan-12 Apr, 11 May-1 Nov & 9 Dec-31 Dec.** **2015**

ST MICHAEL IM LUNGAU *C3* (0.2km S Rural) *47.09685, 13.63706* **Camping St Michael,** Waaghausgasse 277, 5582 St Michael-im-Lungau (06477) 8276; camping-st.michael@sgb.at; www.camping-sanktmichael.at

12 🏕 🕴📶 ▥ ⚒ ⲙ 🅿 ⓘ nr ⛴ nr 🅰

Exit junc 104 fr A10/E55, site sp at turn into vill, then on L after 200m bef hill. Sm, pt shd, EHU (16A) €3.50 (poss rev pol); gas; adv bkg acc; ccard acc; CKE. *"Delightful site adj vill; excel san facs (shared with adj sports club); ski lift 1km; pool adj; poss full if arr after 6pm, but o'flow area avail."* **€20.00** **2016**

ST PETER AM KAMMERSBERG *C3* (3km ESE Rural) *47.17905, 14.21671* **Camping Bella Austria,** Peterdorf 100, 8842 St Peter-am-Kammersberg **(03536) 73902; info@camping-bellaustria.com; www.camping-bellaustria.com**

🏕 €2 🕴(htd) ▥ ⚒ ᵴ 🚐 ⲙ 🅿 ❄ ❄ ❄ ⓘ ⲁ ⛴ 🅰 🎿 (htd)

Fr B96 turn N onto L501 into Katschtal Valley dir Oberdorf, Althofen & St Peter-am-Kammersberg. Site sp. 4*, Lge, hdstg, pt shd, EHU (16A) inc; sw; TV; 70% statics; Eng spkn; adv bkg acc; sauna; games area; bike hire. *"Superb walking area; excel."* **€26.00, 12 Apr-28 Sep.** **2019**

ST PRIMUS *D3* (0.8km N Rural) *46.58569, 14.56598* **Strandcamping Turnersee Breznik,** Unternarrach 21, 9123 St Primus **(04239) 2350; info@breznik.at; www.breznik.at**

🏕 €2.40 🕴(htd) ▥ ⚒ ᵴ 🚐 ⲙ 🅿 ❄ ❄ ❄ ⓘ 🅰

Exit A2 at junc 298 Grafenstein onto B70. After 4km turn R & go thro Tainach, St Kanzian twd St Primus. Site is on W side of Turnersee. 5*, Lge, mkd, pt shd, serviced pitches; EHU (6A) inc; bbq; sw; TV; 30% statics; adv bkg acc; fishing; golf 2km; tennis 500m; games area; bike hire; games rm; CKE. *"Lovely situation; cinema rm; excel site."* **€20.40, 16 Apr-2 Oct.** **2016**

ST VEIT AN DER GLAN *D3* (6km NE Rural) *46.80245, 14.41260* **Camping Wieser,** Bernaich 8, 9313 St Georgen-am-Längsee (Kärnten) **(04212) 3535; info@ campingwieser.com; www.campingwieser.com**

🕴📶 ▥ ⚒ 🚐 ⲙ 🅿 ❄ Y ⓘ ⛴ nr 🅰

Fr St Veit take B317 NE dir Freisach. After 4km turn R to Bernaich, St Georgen. Site sp on L after 500m. Med, mkd, pt shd, terr, EHU (10A) inc; sw nr; TV; phone; CKE. *"Farm site; pool 5km; friendly owner."* **€27.00, 1 May-10 Oct.** **2016**

ST WOLFGANG IM SALZKAMMERGUT *B3* (1km W Rural) *47.74277, 13.43361* **Seeterrassen Camping Reid,** Ried 18, 5360 St Wolfgang/Salzkammergut **(06138) 3201; camping-ried@aon.at; www.seeterrassencamping-ried.at**

🏕 €4 🕴(htd) ▥ ⚒ 🚐 ⲙ 🅿 Y ⓘ ⲁ ⛴ 🅰

Fr Salzburg take B158 thro St Gilgen dir Bad Ischl. Exit at sp Strobl & foll sp St Wolfgang. Go thro tunnel to avoid town cent, foll rd along lake to site. Sm, pt shd, pt sl, terr, EHU (16A) metered; gas; sw nr; TV; 10% statics; phone; Eng spkn; watersports adj; tennis nr; fishing adj; CKE. *"Mountain rlwy stn nr; lake views; gd touring base; easy walk into town; friendly site; v clean san facs."* **€30.20, 16 Apr-31 Oct.** **2019**

SALZBURG *B2* (3km N Rural) *47.82843, 13.05221*
Panorama Camping Stadtblick, Rauchenbichler
strasse 21, 5020 Salzburg **(0662) 450652; info@
panorama-camping.at; www.panorama-camping.at**

🐕 €2 ♟(htd) ⬛ ♨ ▣ ∥ ᴹᴾ ⑨ 🍽 ⓗ 🧺

Fr A1/E55/E60 exit 288 Salzburg Nord/Zentrum & at
end of slip rd turn R & sharp R at traff lts, site sp.
If coming fr S, foll ring rd to W then N.
Med, mkd, hdstg, pt shd, terr, EHU (4A) inc (long lead
req some pitches); gas; red long stay; phone; bus to
town nrby (tickets fr recep); Eng spkn; adv bkg acc;
CKE. *"Conv a'bahn; views of Salzburg; cycle track by rv
to town; Salzburg card avail fr recep; sm pitches - rec
phone ahead if lge o'fit; v helpful family owners; vg
rest; excel, modern san facs; cash only; rec arr early;
also open some dates in Dec & Jan; excel; 'Sound of
Music' Tour; v conv for Salzburg; gd views; beautiful
city; helpful owner."*
€37.00, 1 Jan-8 Jan, 20 Mar-5 Nov, 6 Dec-17 Dec.
                                                    2017

> ## "There aren't many sites open at this time of year"
>
> If you're travelling outside peak season
> remember to call ahead to check site opening
> dates – even if the entry says 'open all year'.

SALZBURG *B2* (5km SE Urban) *47.78058, 13.08985*
Camping Schloss Aigen, Weberbartlweg 20, 5026
Salzburg-Aigen **(0662) 622079; camping.aigen@
elsnet.at; www.campingaigen.com**

🐕 €1 ♟ ⬛ ♨ ∥ 🦮 🍽 ⓗ ♨ 🧺

Fr S leave A10/E55 at junc 8 Salzburg-Süd & take
B150 twds Salzburg on Alpenstrasse. Turn R at
rndabt dir Glasenbach, then L into Aignerstrasse.
1km S of Aigen stn turn R into Glasenstrasse & foll
sps to site. Lge, pt shd, pt sl, EHU (6-16A) €2.50; gas;
red long stay; bus to town 700m; adv bkg acc; CKE.
*"Friendly, family-run site; washing machine avail; sl
pitches v slippery & boggy when wet; excel rest; conv
for city, gd walks."* **€26.50, 1 May-30 Sep.**   **2019**

SCHARNSTEIN *B3* (2.5km NE Rural) *47.91580,
13.97372* **Almcamp Schatzlmühle,** Viechtwang 1A,
4644 Scharnstein **07615 20269; office@almcamp.at;
www.almcamp.at**

🐕 €2 ♟ ⬛ ♨ ⛄ 🦮 ∥ ᴹᴾ 🦮 ⑨ 🍽 ⓗ 🧺 ⚠

Fr A1 take exit 207 Vorchtdorf to Pettenbach on
the L536. Head twd Scharnstein on 120. Turn R 2km
bef vill (dir Viechtwang). Foll sp. Alt take A9, exit
5, dir Scharnstein. Sm, mkd, hdstg, hdg, pt shd, EHU
(16A); bbq; twin axles; TV; 10% statics; phone; Eng
spkn; adv bkg acc; games area; games rm; CCI. *"Child
friendly; family run site; site by rv, scenic location;
gd cycling & walking rtes; htd, excel site & san facs."*
€28.00, 12 Mar-31 Oct.   **2019**

SEEFELD IN TIROL *C1* (1.6km NW Rural) *47.33661,
11.17756* **Alpin Camp,** Leutascherstrasse 810, 6100
Seefeld **(05212) 4848; info@camp-alpin.at;
www.camp-alpin.at**

12 🐕 €3 ♟ ⬛ ♨ 🦮 ∥ ᴹᴾ 🦮 ⑨ ⓗ nr 🧺 ⚠

Fr N on B177/E533 turn W into Seefeld. Thro main
rd, turn R sp Leutasch, site on L in 2km. Apps fr SE &
SW via v steep hills/hairpins, prohibited to trailers.
3*, Med, hdstg, pt shd, pt sl, terr, EHU (16A) €2.80 or
metered; gas; 10% statics; bus to town; Eng spkn; adv
bkg acc; golf 1.5km; site clsd Nov; bike hire. *"Excel site;
htd, covrd pool 1.5km; sauna & steambath inc; excel
facs; friendly owners; vg walking; delightful setting; ski
tows at gate; lovely vill; free bus to town/funicular."*
€42.00   **2018**

SILLIAN *D2* (4km E Rural) *46.74583, 12.46315*
Camping Lienzer Dolomiten, Tassenbach 191,
9918 Strassen-bei-Sillian **(04842) 5228; camping-
dolomiten@gmx.at; www.camping-tirol.at**

12 🐕 €2 ♟ ⬛ ♨ ▣ ∥ ᴹᴾ ⑨ 🍽 ⓗ nr 🧺 nr

B100 fr Sillian dir Lienz, turn R after filling stn, over
level x-ing, then immed R; site sp. 3*, Med, mkd,
hdstg, unshd, pt sl, EHU (6A) €2; sw; red long stay;
25% statics. *"Informal, peaceful site; clean facs; ski lift
3km; helpful staff; mountain views."* **€28.50**   **2016**

SOLDEN *C1* (1km S Rural) *46.95786, 11.01193*
Camping Sölden, Wohlfahrtstrasse 22, 6450 Sölden
**(05254) 26270; info@camping-soelden.com;
www.camping-soelden.com**

🐕 €3 ♟ ⬛ ♨ 🦮 ▣ ∥ ᴹᴾ 🦮 ⑨ ⓗ nr 🧺 nr ⚠

Turn L off main rd at cable car terminal. Turn R at rv
& foll narr track on rv bank for about 200m, turn R
into site. Med, mkd, pt shd, pt sl, terr, serviced pitches;
EHU (10A) metered; gas; Eng spkn; adv bkg acc; ccard
acc; site clsd mid-Apr to mid-Jun approx; gym; sauna;
og-washing facs. *"Excel for touring or climbing in upper
Ötz Valley; pitches tight for lge o'fits; superb site; excel
san facs."* **€33.00, 1 Jan-12 Apr & 27 Jun-31 Dec.**
                                                    2015

SPITTAL AN DER DRAU *D3* (5.6km NE Urban)
46.81510, 13.52001 **Strandcamping Winkler,**
Seepromenade 33, 9871 Seeboden **04 76 28 19 27;
http://www.campsite.at/strandcamping-winkler**

🐕 €4 ♟ ⬛ ♨ ▣ ∥ ᴹᴾ ⚠

Leave A10 Villach-Salzburg at junc 139 twd
Seeboden. Cont along main st across 2 rndabts &
turn R down narr rd sp Strandcamping Winkler.
Sm, mkd, pt shd, pt sl, EHU (16A); sw nr; twin axles;
Eng spkn; adv bkg acc; CCI. *"Cycling & walking rtes
rnd beautiful Millstätter; gd site."*
€36.50, 1 May-1 Oct.   **2019**

AUSTRIA

SULZ IM WIENERWALD *B4* (1km N Rural) *48.10510, 16.13348* **Camping Wienerwald,** Leopoldigasse 2, 2392 Sulz-im-Wienerwald (0)664 4609796; ww-camp@aon.at; www.camping-wienerwald.at

€1.20 ⬆⬇ ⬛ ⬛ ⬛ ✚ ⬛ ✚ ⬛ ⬛ nr ⬛ nr

Leave A21/E60 at junc 26 dir Sittendorf, Foll sp to site at Sulz (7km fr m'way). Sm, mkd, pt shd, pt sl, EHU (6A) €1.90 (poss long lead req); 10% statics. *"Conv Vienna - 25km; gd walks."*
€17.00, 15 Apr-15 Oct. 2016

TELFS *C1* (9km SW Rural) *47.27510, 10.98661* **Camping Eichenwald,** Schiess-Standweg 10, 6422 Stams (05263) 6159; info@camping-eichenwald.at or info@tirol-camping.at; www.tirol-camping.at

12 ⬛ €2.50 ⬆⬇(htd) ⬛ ⬛ ⬛ ✚ ⬛ ✚ ⬛ ⬛ ✚ ⬛ ⬛ ⬛ nr /⬛
⬛ (htd)

Exit A12 at exit Stams-Mötz, foll B171 sp Stams. Turn R into vill, site behind monastery nr dry ski jump; steep app. 4*, Med, pt shd, terr, EHU (6A) €2.70; gas; TV; Eng spkn; adv bkg acc; games rm; bike hire; tennis 500m; games area; CKE. *"Beautiful views; friendly owner; private bthrms some pitches; statics (sep area); vg site; gd rest; san facs v clean."*
€31.00 2018

VELDEN AM WORTHERSEE *D3* (8km E Rural) *46.61890, 14.10565* **Camping Weisses Rössl,** Auenstrasse 47, Schiefling-am-See, 9220 Velden-Auen (04274) 2898; office@weisse-roessl-camping.at; www.weisses-roessl-camping.at

⬛ €3 ⬆⬇(htd) ⬛ ⬛ ⬛ ⬛ ✚ ⬛ ⬛ ⬛ /⬛ ⬛

Fr A2 exit 335 dir Velden. At rndabt bef town fol sp twd Maria Wörth for 9km on S side of Wörthersee. Site on R up hill. Lge, hdstg, pt shd, pt sl, terr, EHU (16A) inc; gas; bbq; sw nr; TV; phone; Eng spkn; CKE. *"Gd."* **€24.50, 1 May-30 Sep.** 2016

VILLACH *D3* (7km NE Rural) *46.65641, 13.89196* **Camping Bad Ossiacher See,** Seeuferstrasse 109, 9520 Annenheim (04248) 2757; office@camping-ossiachersee.at; www.camping-ossiachersee.at

⬆⬇(htd) ⬛ ⬛ ⬛ ⬛ ⬛ ✚ ⬛ ✚ ⬛ ⬛ ⬛ ⬛ /⬛

Fr A10/E55/E66 exit sp Villach/Ossiacher See onto B94. Turn R for St Andrä sp Süd Ossiacher See. Site on L in 300m. Lge, pt shd, EHU (10-16A) inc; bbq; sw nr; twin axles; 5% statics; phone; Eng spkn; adv bkg acc; ccard acc; tennis; games area; sailing; waterskiing. *"Well-kept site; barrier clsd 1200-1400; handy NH even when wet; Annenheim cable car; lge level grass pitches; excel."* **€35.60, 7 Apr-26 Oct.** 2017

WAIDHOFEN AN DER THAYA *A4* (1km SE Rural) *48.81113, 15.28839* **Campingplatz Thayapark,** Badgasse, 3830 Waidhofen-an-der Thaya (02842) 50356 or 0664 5904433 (mob); stadtamt@ waidhofen-thaya.gv.at; www.waidhofen-thaya.at/ Campingplatz_Thayapark

⬆⬇ ⬛ ⬛ ⬛ ⬛ ✚ ⬛ ✚ ⬛ ⬛ ⬛ nr ⬛ nr ⬛ nr /⬛

Site sp fr town cent. Med, pt shd, EHU (10A) €2.30; TV (pitch); 5% statics; CKE. *"Quiet site nr attractive town; pool 300m; recep open 0800-1000 & 1600-1800."* **€14.80, 1 May-30 Sep.** 2016

WERFEN *C2* (4km S Rural) *47.44501, 13.21165* **Camping Vierthaler,** Reitsam 8, 5452 Pfarrwerfen (06468) 57570; vierthaler@camping-vierthaler.at; www.camping-vierthaler.at

⬛ ⬆⬇ ⬛ ⬛ ⬛ ✚ ⬛ ✚ ⬛ ⬛ ⬛ /⬛

Fr A10 exit 43 or 44 sp Werfen/Pfarrwerfen. Turn S onto B159 twd Bischofshofen. After 2km site on L bet rd & rv. 1*, Sm, pt shd, EHU (10-16A) €2; gas; 10% statics; adv bkg rec; ccard acc; rafting; fishing. *"Scenic site; friendly owners; htd pool 2km; Werfen castle & ice caves worth a visit; cycle path; walking; ltd san facs, sometimes stretched."* **€22.00, 15 Apr-30 Sep.** 2018

"That's changed – Should I let the Club know?"

If you find something on site that's different from the site entry, fill in a report and let us know. See camc.com/europereport.

WIEN *B4* (9km E Urban) *48.20861, 16.44722* **Aktiv-Camping Neue Donau,** Am Kleehäufel, 1220 Wien-Ost (01) 2024010; neuedonau@campingwien.at; www.campingwien.at

⬛ €4.50 ⬆⬇(htd) ⬛ ⬛ ⬛ ✚ ⬛ ✚ ⬛ ⬛ ⬛ /⬛

Take A21-A23, exit sp Olhafen/Lobau. After x-ing Rv Danube turn R, sp Neue-Donau Sud. In 150m turn L at traff lts after Shell g'ge; site on R. Fr E on A4 turn R onto A23 & take 1st slip rd sp N-Donau after x-ing rv Danube. Lge, unshd, serviced pitches; EHU (16A) €4 (poss rev pol); bus/metro to city 1km; Eng spkn; adv bkg acc; ccard acc; tennis; games area; CKE. *"Conv Vienna; lovely site; excel facs but poss stretched high ssn; poss v cr due bus tours on site; cycle track to city cent (map fr recep); 3 classes of pitch (extra charge for serviced); recep clsd 1200-1430; standard san facs."* **€32.00, 15 Apr-30 Sep.** 2019

WIEN *B4* (13km W Urban) *48.21396, 16.2505*
Camping Wien-West, Hüttelbergstrasse 80, 1140
Wien **(01)** 9142314; west@campingwien.at;
www.campingwien.at

🛏 €4.50 ♦♦ WD ♨ 🖫 ⩗ MP ⧉ ♨ ⧖ 🄰

Fr Linz, after Auhof enter 3 lane 1-way rd. On app
to traff lts get into L hand (fast) lane & turn L at
traff lts. At next lts (Linzerstrasse) go strt over into
Hüttelburgstrasse & site is uphill. Fr Vienna, foll sp
A1 Linz on W a'bahn & site sp to R 100m bef double
rlwy bdge. After this turn L on rd with tramlines &
foll to v narr section, R at traff lts. Lge, mkd, hdstg,
pt shd, EHU (16A) €4; 10% statics; bus; Eng spkn; adv
bkg acc; ccard acc; CKE. *"Rec arr early; gd bus service
to U-Bahn & city cent - tickets fr recep + Vienna Card;
clean facs, but poss stretched high ssn & ltd LS; poss
travellers; site poss unkempt LS; sm pitches; sep car
park; site clsd Feb; well run; well position for Vienna."*
€36.00, 1 Jan-31 Jan & 16 Feb-31 Dec.   2017

WORGL *C2* (13km SE Rural) *47.43068, 12.14990*
Camping Reiterhof, Kelchsauerstrasse 48, 6361
Hopfgarten **(05335)** 3512; info@campingreiterhof.at;
www.campingreiterhof.at

12 🐕 €2.20 ♦♦ (htd) WD ♨ ♨ ♿ 🖫 ⩗ MP 🦋 ⧖ nr ⊕ nr
⧖ nr 🄰

Fr Wörgl S on B170, thro Hopfgarten, site sp on R
dir Kelchsau. 4*, Med, mkd, pt shd, EHU (10A) €2.80;
45% statics; Eng spkn; adv bkg acc; CKE. *"V friendly, v
welcoming, helpful staff; immac san facs; ski lift 2km;
excel for families or couples; lge recreation park adj;
htd pool 200m; excel walking & cycling area; free ski
bus; excel."* **€18.00   2016**

**"I like to fill in the reports as I
travel from site to site"**

You'll find report forms at the back of this
guide, or you can fill them in online at
camc.com/europereport.

ZELL AM SEE *C2* (7km N Rural) *47.37740, 12.79583*
Campingplatz Bad Neunbrunnen, Neunbrunnen 56,
5751 Maishofen **(06542)** 68548 or **(0664)** 3512282
(mob); camping@neunbrunnen.at; www.camping-
neunbrunnen.at

12 🐕 ♦♦ WD ♨ 🖫 ⩗ MP 🦋 ⧖ 🍽 ⊕ ♨ ⧖ 🄰

Foll B311 N fr Zell-am-See dir Saalfelden; 500m
after Maishofen turn L bef tunnel & foll site sp.
Med, mkd, hdstg, unshd, EHU (10A) €2.20; sw; ccard
acc; fishing; games rm. *"Vg, scenic site; cycle & walking
tracks fr site; winter sports area; vg rest."* **€19.50
                                                    2015**

ZELL AM SEE *C2* (6km SE Rural) *47.30133, 12.8150*
Panorama Camp Zell am See, Seeuferstrasse 196,
5700 Zell am See **(06542)** 56228; info@panorama
camp.at; www.panoramacamp.at

12 🛏 €3.80 ♦♦ WD ♨ 🖫 ♨ ⩗ MP 🦋 ⧖ ⧖ 🄰

S fr Zell on B311 sp Salzburg (using tunnel). At 3rd
rndabt turn L dir Thumersbach, site on L in 1.5km,
sp. Med, hdg, pt shd, serviced pitches; EHU (16A)
metered + conn fee; red long stay; TV; 30% statics;
bus; Eng spkn; adv bkg acc; CKE. *"Conv Salzburg &
Krimml falls; clsd 1200-1330; cycle & footpaths round
lake adj; helpful owners; excel facs; peaceful site; nicely
laid out site with adequate pitches; owners take you
to pitch and make elec conn; shop nr; rest nr; pizzas &
rolls fr recep; lovely view of mountains; easy access."*
€33.50   2019

**"We must tell the Club about
that great site we found"**

Get your site reports in by mid-August and we'll
do our best to get your updates into the next
edition.

ZWETTL *A4* (12km E Rural) *48.58956, 15.31805*
Campingplatz Lichtenfels, Friedersbach 69, 3533
Friedersbach **(02826)** 7492 or 0664 5746866 **(mob)**;
forstverwaltung@thurnforst.at; www.thurnforst.at

🛏 ♦♦ WD ♨ 🦋 🍽

Fr E on B38 fr Zwettl on app Rastenfeld look for rv
bdge & ruins of castle. Site sp on L. Med, pt shd, bbq;
sw nr; 40% statics; games area. *"Pretty lake setting;
open air concerts in ruins of castle high ssn; friendly
owner; v clean facs."* **€15.50, 1 May-10 Oct.   2016**

France and Andorra

Central and South East Europe, Benelux and Scandinavia

Spain and Portugal

Landeck to Wien (Vienna) = 550km

© Collins Bartholomew Ltd 2020

Belgium

Ghent

Highlights

Although a country of two halves, with French-speaking Wallonia making up the southern part of the country, and Dutch-speaking Flanders the north, Belgium is very much united when it comes to delicious cuisine, fascinating historic attractions and breathtaking architecture.

With several UNESCO world heritage sites, a diverse landscape and a range of museums and art galleries, you will be spoilt for choice when deciding how best to spend your time in this delightful country.

Most people associate Belgium with chocolate, mussels and beer, but there are other products which share an equal amount of tradition. Lace making has been practiced in Belgium for centuries, Bruges still renowned for the intricate designs and delicacy of its product.

Belgium has also played an important role in the development of comics, and can boast Georges Remi (Hergé), the creator of Tintin, and Pierre Culliford (Peyo) the man behind the smurfs amongst its talented celebrities.

Major towns and cities

- Brussels - this historic city is Belgium's capital.
- Ghent - a city filled with beautiful buildings and important museums.
- Antwerp - Belgium's largest city is filled with stunning landmarks.
- Liège - famous for its folk festivals and for hosting a large annual Christmas Market.

Attractions

- Grand-Place, Brussels - this opulent central square is a UNESCO World Heritage site.
- Gravensteen Castle, Ghent - a magnificent 12th century castle that houses a museum.
- Historic Centre, Bruges - the medieval architecture of the city centre is a must-see.
- Ypres - an ancient town filled with historic monuments, including the Menin Gate.

Find out more

www.visitbelgium.com
E: tourist@visit.brussels T: 0032 (2) 513 89 40

Country Information

Population (approx): 11.5 million
Capital: Brussels (population approx 1 million)
Area: 30,528 sq km

Bordered by: France, Germany, Luxembourg, Netherlands

Terrain: Flat coastal plains in north-west; central rolling hills; rugged Ardennes hills and forest in south-east.

Climate: Mild winters with snow likely in the Ardennes. Cool summers, rain any time of the year; coast can be windy

Coastline: 66km

Highest Point: Signal de Botrange 694m

Languages: Flemish, French, German

Local Time: GMT or BST + 1, i.e. 1 hour ahead of the UK all year

Currency: Euros divided into 100 cents; £1 = €1.16, €1 = £0.87 (October 2019)

Emergency numbers: Police 112, Fire Brigade 112, Ambulance 112.

Public Holidays 2020: Jan 1; Apr 13; May 1, 21; June 1; Jul 21 (National Day); Aug 15; Nov 1, 11 (Armistice Day); Dec 25.

School summer holidays extend over July and August.

Entry Formalities

British and Irish passport holders may visit Belgium for up to three months without a visa. Passports must be valid for at least 3 months after your departure.

Medical Services

The standard of health care is high. Emergency medical and hospital treatment is available at a reduced cost on production of a European Health Insurance Card (EHIC). Check whether a doctor you wish to see is registered with the national health service (conventionné/ geconventioneerd) or offers private healthcare. You will have to pay for services provided but 75% of the cost of treatment and approved medicines will be refunded if you apply to a local Sickness Fund Office with your EHIC.

At night and at weekends at least one local pharmacy will remain open and its address will be displayed in the window of all local pharmacies.

Opening Hours

Banks: Open hours vary from one bank to another, however usual open hours are Mon-Fri 9am-12pm & 2pm-4pm; Sat 9am-12pm (some banks).

Museums: Tue-Sun 10am-5pm; most museums close Monday.

Shops: Mon-Sat 10am-6pm or 8pm (supermarkets); some close 12pm-2pm; most shops closed Sunday.

Safety and Security

Belgium is relatively safe for visitors but you should take the usual sensible precautions to avoid becoming a victim of muggers, bag-snatchers and pickpockets, especially at major railway stations and on the public transport in Antwerp and Brussels.

There have been recent reports of thefts from luggage racks on high-speed trains. Keep your possessions close to you, especially when the train is in a station and could be grabbed.

Belgium shares with the rest of Europe an underlying threat from terrorism. Attacks could be indiscriminate and against civilian and tourist targets. The area around Brussels hosts a number of international institutions (EU, NATO) which are sensitive locations where you should be vigilant.

British Embassy
AVENUE D'AUDERGHEM 10
1040 BRUXELLES
Tel: (02) 2876211
www.ukinbelgium.fco.gov.uk/en/
public.brussels@fco.gov.uk

Irish Embassy
RUE FROISSART - FROISSARTSTRAAT 50
1040 BRUXELLES
Tel: (02) 2823400
www.embassyofireland.be
brusselsembassy@dfa.ie
There is also an Honorary Consulate in Antwerp.

Documents

Money

Major credit cards are widely accepted by shops, hotels, restaurants and petrol stations.

Carry your credit card issuer or bank's 24-hour UK contact numbers in case of loss or theft of your cards. If you have difficulty reporting the theft of your card(s) to your UK bank or credit card company, ask the Belgian group 'Card Stop' to send a fax to your UK company to block your card. Card Stop's telephone number is (070) 344344.

Passport

Belgian law requires everyone to carry some form of identification, for example passport or photocard driving licence, at all times.

Vehicle(s)

You should carry your vehicle registration certificate (V5C), insurance details and MOT certificate (if applicable).

Driving

Accidents

The police must be called after an accident if an unoccupied stationary vehicle is damaged or if people are injured. If it isn't necessary to call the police to the scene of the accident you must still report it at the local police station within 24 hours.

Alcohol

The maximum permitted level of alcohol is 50 milligrams in 100 millilitres of blood, i.e. lower than in the UK (80 milligrams). Penalties for exceeding this limit are severe including suspension of driving licence and a possible jail sentence.

Breakdown Service

The Touring Club Royal de Belgique (TCB) operates a breakdown service 24 hours a day throughout the country, tel (070) 344777.

On motorways, use the roadside telephones called 'telestrade' which are controlled by the police and are situated approximately every 2km. Ask for 'Touring Secours' or, when in the north of the country, 'Touring Wegenhulp'. It will be necessary to pay a fee which is variable depending on the time of day.

Child Restraint System

Children under 1.35m must be seated in a child seat or child restraint when travelling in the front or rear seat of a vehicle. If a child seat/restraint is not available, i.e. when two child restraint systems are being used on rear seats and there isn't enough space for a third to be placed, a child must travel in the back of the vehicle using an adult seat belt. If the child is three years or under they must not travel in a vehicle without being seated in a child seat/restraint.

The child restraint must correspond to the child's weight and be of an approved type. A rear facing child restraint must not be used on a front seat with a front air bag unless it is deactivated.

Fuel

Petrol stations on motorways and main roads are open 24 hours and credit cards are generally accepted. Others may close from 8pm to 8am and often all day Sunday.

LPG, also known as GPL, is widely available at many service stations.

Motorways

Belgium has a network of approximately 1,750km of motorways. Although Belgian motorways are toll free for most vehicles, there is a toll for vehicles over 3,500kg.

Service areas usually have a petrol station, restaurant, shop, showers and toilets. Rest areas have picnic facilities. For detailed information see www.autosnelwegen.net.

Some motorways are so heavily used by lorries that the inside lane may become heavily rutted and/or potholed. These parallel ruts are potentially dangerous for caravans travelling at high speed. It is understood that parts of the A2/E314 and A3/E40 are particularly prone to this problem.

Parking

Blue zones indicating limited parking are used to denote where vehicles must display a parking disc on Monday to Saturday, from 9am to 6pm. Discs are available from police stations, petrol stations and some shops. Outside blue zones a parking disc must also be used where the parking sign has a panel showing the disc symbol. Parking areas are also regulated by parking meters and if these exist inside a blue zone parking discs must not be used, except if the parking meter or ticket machine is out of action. Illegally parked vehicles may be towed away or clamped.

Do not park in a street where there is a triangular sign 'Axe Rouge/Ax Rode'.

Pollution

From 1 November to 31 March during levels of high pollution, known as pollution peaks, restrictions are imposed on driving in Brussels. There are different levels of restriction, from reduced speed limits to a total ban on driving, depending on the severity of the pollution. When in place restrictions are announced on local media and an electronic signs around the city. Visit www.brussels.be and search for 'pollution peak' for more information.

Priority

You should take great care to obey the 'priority to the right' rule which is designed to slow traffic in built-up areas. Drivers must give priority to vehicles joining from the right, even if those vehicles have stopped at a road junction or stopped for pedestrians or cyclists, and even if you are on what appears to be a main road. Exemptions to this rule apply on motorways, roundabouts and roads signposted with an orange diamond on a white background.

Trams have priority over other traffic. If a tram or bus stops in the middle of the road to allow passengers on or off, you must stop.

From 2014 a 'Zip Merging' rule has been in place in Belgium. Where a lane is ending or closed, drivers in that lane must continue to where that lane starts to close up before merging into the open lane. Drivers in the lane which remains open must give way in turn to the drivers merging into their lane.

Roads

Roads are generally in good condition and well lit, however, some stretches of motorways have poor surfacing and signs to advise drivers to slow down. Traffic is fast and the accident rate is high, especially at weekends, mainly due to speeding.

Road Signs and Markings

Roads signs and markings conform to international standards. A sign has been introduced prohibiting the use of cruise control. This sign will normally only be encountered on motorways where there is a risk of multiple crashes due to congestion or road works. Where this particular sign shows a weight limit, the prohibition applies to drivers of vehicles with a higher maximum permitted weight.

Destination road signs can be confusing because a town may be signposted either by its French or its Flemish name, according to the predominant language in that particular area.

The most important of these towns are:

Flemish	French
Aalst	Alost
Aken (Aachen)	Aix-la-Chapelle (Germany)
Antwerpen	Anvers
Bergen	Mons
Brugge	Bruges
Brussel	Bruxelles
Doornik	Tournai
Gent	Gand
Geraardsbergen	Grammont
Ieper	Ypres
Kortrijk	Courtrai
Leuven	Louvain
Luik	Liège
Mechelen	Maline
Namen	Namur
Rijsel	Lille (France)
Roeselare	Roulers
Tienen	Tirlemont
Veurne	Furnes

Generally signposts leading to and on motorways show foreign destination place names in the language of the country concerned. e.g. German. Exceptions do occur, particularly on the E40 and E314 where city names may be given in Flemish or French.

Roads with the prefix N are regional roads; those with numbers 1 to 9 radiate from Brussels. Motorways have the prefix A and have blue and white signs. When route planning through Belgium follow the green European road numbers with the prefix E which may be the only road numbers displayed.

Road signs you may see include the following:

You may pass right or left

Cyclists have priority over turning traffic

Cyclists have priority at junction

Use of Cruise Control prohibited

Speed Limits

	Open Road (km/h)	Motorway (km/h)
Car Solo	90*	120
Car towing caravan/trailer	90*	120
Motorhome under 3500kg	90*	120
Motorhome 3500-7500kg	90*	90

*70 in Flanders

Whilst the general speed limit in built-up areas is 50 km/h (31mph), lower limits of 30 km/h (18 mph) or 20 km/h (12mph) may be imposed and indicated by signs in residential areas, town centres and near schools. Brussels city centre is a 30 km/h (18mph) speed limit zone. The start and finish points of these zones are not always clearly marked. Vehicles over 3,500 kg in weight are restricted to 90 km/h (56mph) outside built-up areas and on motorways.

Traffic Jams

During good weather roads to the coast, the Ardennes and around Brussels and Antwerp are very busy during the weekends.

Other busy routes are the E40 (Brussels to Ostend), the E25 (Liège to Bastogne and Arlon), the E411 (Brussels to Namur and Luxembourg), and the N4 from Bastogne to Arlon around the border town of Martelange caused by motorists queuing for cheap petrol in Luxembourg. Avoid traffic on the E40 by taking the R4 and N49, and on the E411 by taking the N4 Bastogne to Marche-en-Famenne and Namur. These routes are heavily used and consequently the road surface can be poor.

Traffic Lights

A green light (arrow) showing at the same time as a red or amber light means that you can turn in that direction providing you give way to other traffic and pedestrians. An amber light, possibly flashing, in the form of an arrow inclined at an angle of 45 degrees to the left or to the right, shows that the number of traffic lanes will be reduced.

Tunnels

Three road tunnels go under the River Scheldt at Antwerp. In the Liefkenhoeks tunnel on road R2 to the north of the city a toll of €17.60-19.00 (2018) for vehicles over 2.75m in height. Vehicles under 2.75m are charged €4.95-6.00. If you're towing your caravan will be included within this height categorisation. The Kennedy Tunnel on road R1 to the south of the city is toll-free but is heavily congested in both directions for much of the day. The smallest tunnel, the Waasland Tunnel is part of the N59a and is also toll-free.

Violation of Traffic Regulations

The police may impose on-the-spot fines on visitors who infringe traffic regulations such as speeding and parking offences. If you can't pay on the spot your vehicle(s) may be impounded or your driving licence withdrawn. Fines can be paid in cash or with a debit or credit card - make sure you get an official receipt.

In an effort to improve road safety the authorities have increased the number of speed traps throughout the country in the form of cameras and unmarked police vehicles.

Vehicles of 3,500 kg or over are not allowed to use the left lane on roads with more than three lanes except when approaching a fork in a motorway when vehicles have to move to the left or right lane

Essential Equipment

First aid kit

It is not compulsory for foreign registered vehicles to carry a first aid kit, but it is still recommended.

Warning Triangle

An EU approved warning triangle must be used if the vehicle breaks down, has a puncture or is involved in an accident.

Reflective Jacket/ Waistcoat

If you have broken down or are in an accident where stopping or parking is prohibited, you must wear a reflective jacket or waistcoat when getting out of your vehicle, or face a €58.00 fine. Anyone leaving the vehicle should also wear one. Keep the jacket(s) to hand in your vehicle, not in the boot.

Touring

Flemish is spoken in the north of Belgium, whilst French is spoken in the south. Brussels is bi-lingual. English is widely spoken.

Prices in restaurants are quoted 'all inclusive' and no additional tipping is necessary. Smoking is severely restricted in public places including restaurants and cafés.

Carrier bags are generally not provided in supermarkets, so take your own.

When visiting Brussels visitors may buy a Brussels Card, valid for 24, 48 or 72 hours, which offers free access to virtually every major museum in the city and unlimited use of public transport, together with discounts at a number of other attractions. The pass is available from the tourist information office in the Hotel de Ville and from many hotels, museums and public transport stations, or visit www.brusselscard.be to buy online.

Camping and Caravanning

There are more than 900 campsites in Belgium, most of which are near the coast or in the Ardennes. Coastal sites tend to consist largely of mobile homes/statics and can be very crowded at the height of the holiday season. A local tourist tax is usually included in the rates charged.

Twin-axle caravans are not permitted on municipal sites in and around Antwerp. Caravans and vehicles longer than 6 metres are prohibited from Liège city centre.

Casual/wild camping is prohibited in Flanders. Elsewhere permission must first be sought from the landowner or police. Camping is not permitted alongside public highways for more than a 24-hour period, nor is it permitted in lay-bys, in state forests or along the seashore, or within a 100 metre radius of a main water point, or on a site classified for the conservation of monuments.

Cycling

Belgium is well equipped for cyclists, with an extensive network of signposted cycling routes. Cycle lanes are marked on the carriageway by means of a broken double white line or by circular signs depicting a white bicycle on a blue or black background.

Bikes may be carried at the rear of a vehicle as long as its width doesn't extend beyond the width of the vehicle or more than one metre from the rear, and providing the rear lights and number plate remain visible.

Electricity and Gas

The current on most campsites varies from 4 - 16 amps although on some it is as low as 2 amps. Plugs have two round pins. CEE connections are not yet available at all sites.

Use a mains tester to test a connection before hooking up as problems are more common in Belgium than other EU countries. Issues may include reversed polarity, no earth and/or incorrectly alternating current.

The full range of Campingaz cylinders are available.

Public Transport

Anyone under the age of 25 is entitled to free or reduced prices on public transport in Brussels. During periods of severe air pollution public transport in that region is free to all.

Brussels and Antwerp have metro systems and extensive networks of trams and buses. Tram and bus stops are identified by a red and white sign and all stops are request stops; hold out your arm to stop a bus or tram. Tickets, including 10-journey and one-day travel cards, are available from vending machines at metro stations and some bus stops, newsagents, supermarkets and tourist information centres.

The MOBIB Smartcard, similar to an Oyster card, can be purchased and topped up at metro station kiosks, supermarkets and newsagents, and is valid for all STIB public transport in Brussels (including trams, buses and metros).

Belgium has a good train network and most main routes pass through Antwerp, Brussels or Namur. Trains are modern, comfortable and punctual and fares are reasonable. Buy tickets before boarding the train or you may be charged a supplement.

Brussels

AISCHE EN REFAIL *B3* (0.4km E Rural) *50.59977, 4.84335* **Camping du Manoir de Là-Bas,** Route de Gembloux 180, 5310 Aische-en-Refail **(081) 655353; europa-camping.sa@skynet.be; www.camping-manoirdelabas.be**

🐕 €3 ♦♦ WD ♨ ♂ ⚹ 🗐 ⁄ MSP 🐾 ♈ ① 🖈 ⚐ nr ⚠ ✦ ⚓ (htd) ⛲

Fr E411/A4 exit junc 12 & foll sps to Aische-en-Refail. Site on o'skts of vill. 2*, Lge, pt shd, pt sl, EHU (6A) inc; gas; bbq; 50% statics; phone; Eng spkn; adv bkg acc; fishing; tennis; games rm; CKE. *"Friendly staff; site little run down; ltd hot water; poor san facs, dated & long way fr pitches; some sats are narr; recep far side of chateau; gd rest & bar (clsd in Sep); site needs updating (2014); poor; NH only; sm pitches; rec NH only."* **€25.00, 1 Apr-31 Oct.**   **2017**

ANTWERPEN *A3* (6km NW Urban) *51.23347, 4.39261* **Camping De Molen,** Thonelaan - Jachthavenweg 6, St Annastrand, 2050 Antwerpen **(03) 2198179; info@camping-de-molen.be; www.camping-de-molen.be**

12 ♦♦ WD ♨ ⚹ ⁄ ♈ ① nr ⚐ nr

Clockwise on ring rd, take 1st exit after Kennedy tunnel, exit 6. R at traff lts, 3rd L where cannot go strt on (rv on R), site on R in 1km on bank of Rv Schelde. Or on ent Antwerp foll sp Linkeroever, go strt on at 3 traff lts, then turn L & foll camping sp. Fr A14/E17 exit junc 7 & foll sp for Linkeroever Park & Ride until site sp appear, then foll sp. 2*, Med, pt shd, EHU (10A) inc (poss rev pol) - €30 deposit for adaptor/cable; bus nrby; Eng spkn; adv bkg rec. *"Popular site; max 14 nt stay; pedestrian/cycle tunnel to city cent 1km; metro 1km; gd for rollerblading, cycling; friendly, helpful staff; mosquitoes poss a problem; san facs satisfactory; 30 min walk or bus to city cent; site tired."* **€28.00**   **2016**

ARLON *D3* (2km N Urban) *49.70215, 5.80678* **Camping Officiel Arlon,** 373 Rue de Bastogne, Bonnert, 6700 Arlon **(063) 226582; campingofficiel@skynet.be; www.campingofficielarlon.be**

12 🐕 €2 ♦♦ WD ♨ ♂ ⚹ 🗐 ⁄ ♈ ♈ 🖈 ⚐ nr ⚠ ⚓

Fr E411 exit junc 31 onto N82 Arlon for 4km, turn twd Bastogne on N4. Site sp on R. 2*, Med, pt shd, pt sl, EHU (6-10A) €2.40 (check earth); gas; bbq; red long stay; TV; Eng spkn; adv bkg acc; CKE. *"Charming, clean, well laid out, pretty site; levelling blocks/ramps req - supplied by site; c'vans tight-packed when site busy; 5km approx to Luxembourg for cheap petrol; Arlon interesting town; vg NH & longer stay; thoroughly rec for stop over; cash only; 3 hdstgs for m'van; new pool; san facs updated, v clean; busy but organised; gd vet 0.5m."* **€24.50**   **2018**

ARLON *D3* (7.6km N Rural) *49.74833, 5.78697* **Camping Sud,** 75 Voie de la Liberté, 6717 Attert **(063) 223715; info@campingsudattert.com; www.campingsudattert.com**

🐕 €2 ♦♦ (htd) WD ♨ 🗐 ⁄ 🐾 ♈ ① ♂ ⚐ ⚠ ⚓

Off N4 Arlon rd on E side of dual c'way. Sp to site fr N4 (500m). U-turn into site ent. 4*, Med, hdg, mkd, hdstg, pt shd, EHU (5-10A) €2.50 (check earth); bbq; red long stay; phone; bus; Eng spkn; adv bkg acc; CKE. *"Vg, well-organised site; special NH pitches; fishing & walking; peaceful site; v friendly staff; highly rec."* **€25.00, 1 Apr-15 Oct.**   **2019**

BASTOGNE *C3* (1.6km WNW Urban) *50.00340, 5.69525* **Camping de Renval,** 148 Route de Marche, 6600 Bastogne **(061) 212985; www.campingderenval.be**

🐕 €2 ♦♦ (htd) WD ♨ ♂ 🗐 ⁄ 🐾 ♈ ♂ ⚐ nr ⚠ ⚓

Fr N leave A26 exit 54, foll Bastogne sp. Fr Marche-en-Famenne dir, exit N4 at N84 for Bastogne; site on L in 150m opp petrol stn. Fr E foll Marche, in 1km site on R opp petrol stn. 3*, Med, hdstg, pt shd, pt sl, terr, EHU (10A) inc (poss rev pol); bbq; 95% statics; ccard acc; site clsd Jan; games area; tennis. *"Take care speed bumps; helpful staff; clean san facs but long walk fr tourers' pitches; gd security; facs ltd LS; gd NH."* **€23.00, 1 Feb-31 Dec.**   **2019**

BRUGGE *A2* (5km E Urban) *51.20722, 3.26305* **Camping Memling,** Veltemweg 109, 8310 Sint Kruis **(050) 355845; info@camping-memling.be or info@brugescamping.be; www.camping-memling.be or www.brugescamping.be**

12 🐕 €2 ♦♦ (htd) WD ♨ 🗐 ⁄ ♈ ♈ ♈ ① nr ⚐ nr

Exit A10 junc 8 Brugge. In 2km turn R onto N397 dir St Michiels & cont 2km to rlwy stn on R. Turn R under rlwy tunnel & at 1st rndbt take dir Maldegem onto ring rd & in a few kms take N9 sp Maldegem & St Kruis. After 3km at traff lts adj MacDonalds, turn R & immed L sp Camping to site on R in 400m past sw pool. Fr Gent exit E40 sp Oostkamp & foll Brugge sp for 7km to N9 as above. 2*, Med, mkd, hdstg, pt shd, EHU (6A) inc (poss rev pol); red long stay; 13% statics; bus 200m; Eng spkn; adv bkg req; ccard acc; bike hire; CKE. *"Busy site; red LS as no shwrs/rest/bar; friendly, helpful owners; recep open 0800-2200 (all day to 2200 high ssn); arr early high ssn to ensure pitch; LS site yourself & report to recep; conv Zeebrugge ferry (30mins) & allowed to stay to 1500; conv bus svrs every 20 mins to Bruges; htd pool adj; adv bkgs taken but no pitch reserved; m'van pitches sm, rec pay extra for standard pitch; clean new san facs (2016); cycle rte or 35 min walk to Bruges; nice site; rec."* **€32.00**   **2018**

Campsite Ter Duinen — De Haan – Belgian Coast

De Haan situated at the Belgian coast is famous for its Belle Epoque buildings and the English cottage-styled houses. The historical city of Bruges, Ostend and the scenic city of Damme are only 15 minutes distance. It is only a 600 m. walk to the sea, the adjacent leisure park offers you subtropical pool complex and a covered play arena. Opportunities for riding and hiring bikes are close by.

www.campingterduinen.be | Wenduinsesteenweg 143 B-8421 De Haan | Tel +32 (0)50 413593

BELGIUM

BRUGGE *A2* (4km S Urban) *51.19634, 3.22573*
Motorcaravan Park, Off ring rd R30, Buiten Katelijnevest, Brugge

Exit A10 at junc 7 twd Brugge. After going under rlwy bdge, turn R on ring rd immed after marina to dedicated mv parking adj coach parking, nr marina. Med, hdstg, pt shd, EHU (10A) inc. *"M'vans only; in great location - gd view of canal; sh walk to town cent thro park; rec arr early high ssn; washrm nr; if full, take ticket & park in coach park opp; NH only; vg for city ctr; narr spaces; traff noise; bef leaving pay at machine & leave thro coach pk; gd."* **€25.00** 2018

> ## "There aren't many sites open at this time of year"
>
> If you're travelling outside peak season remember to call ahead to check site opening dates – even if the entry says 'open all year'.

BRUGGE *A2* (13km SW Urban) *51.18448, 3.10445*
Recreatiepark Klein Strand, Varsenareweg 29, 8490 Jabbeke **(050)** 811440; info@kleinstrand.be; www.kleinstrand.be

Fr W leave A10/E40 at Jabbeke exit, junc 6; turn R at rndabt & in 100m turn R into narr rd. Foll site to statics car pk on L & park - walk to check-in at recep bef proceeding to tourer site in 400m. Fr E leave A10/E40 at junc 6 (Jabbeke) turn L at 1st rndabt. Drive over m'way twd vill. Turn L at next rndabt & foll site sp into site car pk as above. Out of ssn carry on along rd to recep by lake. 4*, V lge, hdg, mkd, pt shd, EHU (10A) inc; gas; bbq; sw nr; TV; 75% statics; bus to Brugge; Eng spkn; ccard acc; bike hire; fishing; tennis; watersports; games rm; CKE. *"Busy site; vg touring base; lge pitches; no o'fits over 12m; wide range of entmnt & excursions; direct access to lake adj; bus every 20 mins."* **€39.00, H15.** 2017

BRUXELLES *B2* (13km N Rural) *50.93548, 4.38226*
Camping Grimbergen, Veldkantstraat 64, 1850 Grimbergen **(0479)** 760378 **or (02)** 2709597; camping-grimbergen@webs.com; camping-grimbergen.webs.com

Fr Ostend on E40/A10 at ringrd turn E & foll sp Leuven/Luik (Liège)/Aachen. Exit junc 7 N sp Antwerpen/Grimbergen N202. At bus stn traff lts turn R twd Vilvoorde N211. Turn L at 2nd traff lts (ignore no L turn - lorries only). Site sp 500m on R. Ent via pool car pk. 3*, Med, hdg, pt shd, pt sl, EHU (10A) €4; phone; bus to city (hourly) 200m; Eng spkn; adv bkg acc; bike hire; CKE. *"Well-run, popular site - rec arr early; gd, clean, modern san facs; helpful staff; sh walk to town; train to Brussels fr next vill; red facs LS; gates clsd 1130-1400 and 2000 onwards; gd rest by bus stop; conv Brussels; excel san facs; rec; pool adj; gd NH."* **€22.00, 1 Apr-25 Oct.** 2019

BRUXELLES *B2* (13km E Urban) *50.85720, 4.48506*
RCCC de Belgique, Warandeberg 52, 1970 Wezembeek **(02)** 7821009; info@campingbrussels.be; www.rcccb.com

Leave ringrd RO at junc 2 sp Kraainem turning E. In 140m 1st intersection on dual c'way (by pedestrian x-ing) turn L into Wezembeek. Foll orange camping sp taking rd to the R around church. Foll rd to crest of hill. Site on L bet houses. Narr ent, easy to miss. 2*, Med, mkd, hdstg, pt shd, pt sl, terr, EHU (6A) inc (poss rev pol & no earth); 65% statics; Eng spkn; adv bkg acc; ccard acc; CKE. *"Poss diff for lge o'fits due narr site ent, v tight corners, metro nr; gates clsd 1200-1400 & 2200-0800; raised kerbs; updated san facs (2015); gd for metro into Brussels fr Kraainem; welcoming wardens; no Eng spkn; unkept."* **€22.50, 1 Apr-30 Sep.** 2018

DE HAAN *A1* (2.6km ENE Coastal) *51.28330, 3.05610* **Camping Ter Duinen,** Wenduinesteenweg 143, Vlissegem, 8421 De Haan **(050) 413593;** lawrence.sansens@scarlet.be; www.campingter-duinen.be

🛏 €5.75 ♦♦(htd) ⓦ 🛁 ♨ ♿ 🖥 ∥ MP 🦋 �🍴 ♨ 🛒 Ⓜ

⛺ shgl 500m

Exit A10/E40 junc 6 Jabbeke onto N377 dir De Haan. Go thro town dir Wenduine, site on R in 4km. 3*, Med, mkd, pt shd, EHU (6A) inc; bbq; sw nr; 85% statics; phone; tram nrby; Eng spkn; adv bkg req; horseriding 1km; fishing 200m; golf 4km; CKE. *"Neat, clean, well-managed site; friendly staff; poss long walk to excel san facs inc novelty wcs!; water complex 1km; htd pool 200m; conv ferries, Bruges; bike hire 200m; excel; hot dish water req tokens, mkt in nrby towns."* **€40.00, 15 Mar-15 Oct.** **2019**

See advertisement opposite

DE PANNE *A1* (3km S Rural) *51.08288, 2.59094* **Camping Ter Hoeve,** Duinhoekstraat 101, 8660 Adinkerke **(058) 412376; info@campingterhoeve.be;** www.camping-terhoeve.be

12 ♦♦ ⓦ 🛁 ♨ ∥ MP 🛒 Ⓜ ⛺ 2km

Leave Calais-Ostend m'way at junc 1 (ignore junc 1a) dir De Panne. Foll rd past theme park (Plopsaland), L at filling stn, site 1km on L. 2*, Lge, hdg, pt shd, EHU (4A) €3.50 (poss no earth); 60% statics; tram 1km. *"Nice pitches; lge grassed area for tourers & hdstg area for late arr/early dep; barrier clsd 2200-0800 - go to visitors' car park on R bef booking in; v busy site high ssn, phone to check opening times LS; conv Dunkerque ferries & Plopsaland park; some daytime noise fr nrby theme park; tram tickets avail at filling stn; coin operated dishwash water; san facs dated & clsd LS; Oct-Mar by appointment only; under new management (2018)."* **€16.50** **2018**

DINANT *C3* (2km N Urban) *50.27722, 4.89694* **Camping Communal Devant-Bouvignes,** 1 Quai de Camping, 5500 Dinant **(082) 224002;** camping.communal@dinant.be; www.dinant.be

12 🛏 ♦♦(htd) ⓦ 🛁 ♨ ∥ 🛒 nr Ⓜ

Exit E11 junc 20 onto N936; drive to cent of Dinant (steep descent) to T-junc; turn R onto N92; cont along rv for 1.5km; site on L after bend. Med, pt shd, EHU (16A) €3; sw; 50% statics; bus at ent; adv bkg acc. *"Excel situation on rv bank; dogs free; scruffy san facs; 25 min walk to interesting town."* **€25.00** **2017**

DOCHAMPS *C3* (0.7km ESE Rural) *50.23080, 5.63180* **Panorama Campsite Petite Suisse,** Al Bounire 27, 6960 Dochamps **(084) 444030; info@petitesuisse.be;** www.petitesuisse.be

12 🛏 €5 ♦♦(htd) ⓦ 🛁 ♨ ♿ 🖥 ∥ MP 🦋 ⟟ 🍴 � ♨ 🛒 Ⓜ 🦮 (htd) 🎣

Fr E25, take N89 (La Roche) at Samrée turn R onto N841 headed twrds Dochamp. Turn R into rd sp Al Bounire and foll sp to site. 4*, Lge, hdstg, mkd, pt shd, pt sl, terr, EHU (10A) inc; gas; bbq; TV; 50% statics; phone; adv bkg acc; ccard acc; games area; waterslide; games rm; tennis; CKE. *"Outstanding facs; beautiful spot; busy, popular, excel site."* **€35.50** **2017**

EEKLO *A2* (7km E Rural) *51.18093, 3.64180* **Camping Malpertuus,** Tragelstraat 12, 9971 Lembeke **(09) 3776178;** campingmalpertuus@telenet.be; www.vkt.be

12 🛏 ♦♦(htd) ⓦ 🛁 ♿ 🖥 ∥ MP 🦋 🍴 Ⓜ nr 🛒 nr

Exit A10/E40 junc 11 onto N44 dir Aalter & Maldegem. Foll sp Eekloo onto N49 & then foll sp Lembeke, site sp. Med, pt shd, EHU (4A) €3; gas; 85% statics; phone; bus 300m; Eng spkn; adv bkg acc; CKE. *"Gd site in lovely area; friendly staff; entmnt/ events at w/end; gd size pitches; gd site; unisex facs."* **€20.00** **2018**

EUPEN *B4* (3km SW Rural) *50.61457, 6.01686* **Camping Hertogenwald,** Oestraat 78, 4700 Eupen **(087) 743222; info@camping-hertogenwald.be;** www.camping-hertogenwald.be

12 🛏 €1.60 ♦♦(htd) ⓦ 🛁 ♿ 🖥 ∥ 🦋 🍴 � ♨ 🛒 nr Ⓜ

Fr German border customs on E40 a'bahn for Liège, take 2nd exit for Eupen. In Eupen L at 3rd traff lts & 1st R in 100m. Drive thro Eupen cent, foll sp to Spa. Camping sp immed at bottom of hill, sharp hairpin R turn onto N629, site on L in 2km. 3*, Med, unshd, EHU (6A) inc (long lead req & poss no earth); 90% statics; phone; Eng spkn; games area. *"Sm tourer area; clean site adj rv & forest; htd covrd pool 3km; muddy after rain; gd walking & cycling beside rv; conv Aachen."* **€18.00** **2016**

GHENT *A2* (14km SW Rural) *51.00508, 3.57228* **Camping Groeneveld,** Groenevelddreef 14, Bachte-Maria-Leerne, 9800 Deinze **(09) 3801014; info@ campinggroeneveld.be; www.campinggroeneveld.be**

🛏 €2 ♦♦(htd) ⓦ 🛁 ♨ ∥ MP 🦋 ⟟ 🍴 ⓐ ♨ 🛒 nr Ⓜ 🎣

E or W E40/E10 on Brussels to Ostend m'way exit junc 13 at sp Gent W/Drongen. Take N466 sp Dienze. Approx 1km beyond junc with N437, turn L just after 2nd 70 km/h sp down narr side rd - house on corner has advert hoarding. Site on L opp flour mill. Sm sp at turning. Med, hdg, pt shd, EHU (10A) inc (poss no earth); red long stay; TV; 40% statics; phone; Eng spkn; adv bkg acc; fishing; CKE. *"Gd welcome; additional san facs at lower end of site; office open 1900-2000 LS but staff in van adj san facs, or site yourself; barrier (€25 deposit for card) clsd until 0800; do not arr bef 1400; 1km fr Ooidonk 16th Castle; OK NH; gd site; bus to vill; some pitches tight; cash only."* **€24.00, 1 Apr-4 Oct.** **2018**

GHENT *A2* (4km W Urban) *51.04638, 3.68083*
Camping Blaarmeersen, Zuiderlaan 12, 9000 Gent
(09) 2668160; camping.blaarmeersen@gent.be;
www.blaarmeersen.be

🐕 €1.25 ♦♦(htd) ⬚ ⬛🖩☕ ⚟ 🍽 🏇👤🏊⛰

Exit A10/E40 Brussels-Ostend m'way at junc 13 sp
Gent W & Drongen. At T-junc turn onto N466 twd
Gent. In 4km cross canal then turn R to site, sp (3
rings) Sport & Recreatiecentrum Blaarmeersen.
Fr Gent cent foll N34 twd Tielt for 1km past city
boundary & turn L to site; adj lake & De Ossemeersen
nature reserve. NB Due to rd layout, rec foll camping
sp on app to site rather than sat nav. 4*, Lge, mkd,
hdg, pt shd, serviced pitches; EHU (10A) metered +
conn fee €1.25 (poss rev pol); sw nr; 5% statics; phone;
bus to Gent; Eng spkn; ccard acc; tennis; watersports.
*"Clean, well-organised, busy site; beautiful lake with
path around; helpful staff; rest gd value; full sports facs
adj; passport req; gd cycle track fr site; cycle into cent
avoiding main rd; gd location for walks & activities; no
dep bef 0815 hrs; poss travellers LS; pitches muddy
when wet; pool adj; some m'van pitches sm & v shd;
excel."* **€31.00, 1 Mar-3 Nov.** 2015

GODARVILLE *B2* (12km E Rural) *50.50501, 4.39928*
Camping Trieu du Bois, Rue Picolome, 63 6238 Luttre
(Pont-a-Celles) (Hainaut) Belgique **(071) 845937 or
(0477) 200343; trieudubois@hotmail.com;**
www.trieudubois.be

12 🐕 ♦♦ ⬚ ⬛ ⚟ 🦋

Fr J21 Luttre, foll sp twrds Luttre. After 1km at
T-junc turn L. Site on R after 1km. Sm, hdg, pt shd,
EHU (6A) €2; bbq; twin axles; 20% statics; Eng spkn;
adv bkg acc. *"Conv for Waterloo & Brussels; adj canal
path dir fr site; fair."* **€15.00** 2017

GODARVILLE *B2* (2km S Rural) *50.48794, 4.29318*
Camping Domaine Claire-Fontaine, 11 Ave
Clémenceau, 7160 Godarville **(064) 443675; sites.**
voiesdeau@hainaut.be

🐕 ♦♦ ⬚ ⬛🖩 ⚟ 🍽 🏊⛰

Exit A15/E42 junc 18 onto N59 to Godarville, site sp.
3*, Lge, unshd, EHU (6A) inc; bbq; sw; 85% statics;
phone; ccard acc; games area; CKE. *"Facs better than
1st impression but avoid san facs nr touring area &
avoid area outside barrier; helpful warden; NH only."*
€22.00, 1 Mar-31 Oct. 2016

HAN SUR LESSE *C3* (0.3km N Urban) *50.12727,
5.18773* **Camping Aire Gîte d'Etape,** Rue du Gîte
d'Etape 10, 5580 Han-sur-Lesse **(084) 377441; gite.**
han@gitesdetape.be; www.gitesdetape.be/han

12 ♦♦ ⚟ 🖩 👤🏊 ✂

Exit A4/E411 junc 23 sp Ave-et-Auffe & Rochefort.
Go over 2 rv bdges then immed L & 1st R. Site on L.
Sm, hdstg, unshd, EHU 10A; games area. *"M'van
only; excel; attendant calls; v conv for show caves."*
€11.00 2018

HAN SUR LESSE *C3* (5km SW Rural) *50.11178,
5.13308* **Camping Le Roptai,** Rue Roptai 34, 5580
Ave-et-Auffe **(084) 388319; info@leroptai.be;**
www.leroptai.be

12 🐕 €1.50 ♦♦ ⬚ ⬛ ⚟ 🦋 🍽 👤🏊⛰ 🛶(htd)

Fr A4 exit 23 & take N94 dir Dinant. At bottom of
hill turn R onto N86. Turn L in vill of Ave, foll sp,
200m to L. 3*, Med, mkd, hdstg, pt shd, pt sl, terr, EHU
(6A) €1.80; gas; TV; 80% statics; Eng spkn; adv bkg
acc; site clsd Jan; CKE. *"Some pitches awkwardly sl;
generally run down & poor facs; ltd facs LS; NH only."*
€23.50 2019

HAN SUR LESSE *C3* (0.2km NW Urban) *50.12632,
5.18478* **Camping Le Pirot,** Rue Joseph Lamotte 3,
5580 Han-sur-Lesse **(084) 377280; han.tourisme@
skynet.be; www.valdelesse.be**

🐕 ♦♦ ⬚ ⚟ 🦋 🍽 nr 👤 🏊 nr

Exit A4/E411 junc 23 sp Ave-et-Auffe & Rochefort.
Go over 1st bdge then L immed bef 2nd bdge in Han
cent; sh, steep incline. 1*, Sm, unshd, EHU (10A) inc
(poss rev pol); bus adj; adv bkg acc; ccard acc; CKE.
*"Excel position on raised bank of rv; adj attractions
& rests; interesting town; helpful staff; basic, dated
san facs; conv NH or sh stay in attractive town."*
€20.00, 1 Apr-15 Nov. 2015

"That's changed – Should I let the Club know?"

If you find something on site that's different
from the site entry, fill in a report and let us
know. See camc.com/europereport.

HASSELT *B3* (12km NE Rural) *50.99775, 5.42537*
Camping Holsteenbron, Hengelhoefseweg 9, 3520
Zonhoven **011 817140; camping.holsteenbron@
telenet.be; www.holsteenbron.be**

🐕 €1 ♦♦(htd) ⬚ ⬛🖩 ⚟ 🦋 🍽 ⛰

Leave A2 junc 29 twd Hasselt; turn L at 1st traff
lts in 1km, foll sp thro houses & woods for 3km.
Site is NE of Zonhoven. Med, hdstg, hdg, mkd,
pt shd, EHU (6A) inc; TV; 30% statics; phone;
Eng spkn; games area; CKE. *"Pleasant, happy site
in woodland; gd touring base; friendly owners."*
€22.00, 1 Apr-13 Nov. 2016

HOTTON *C3* (0.9km NW Urban) *50.27085, 5.43833*
Camping Eau Zone, rue des Fonzays 10, 6990 Hotton
(084) 477715; campingeauzone@hotmail.be;
www.campingeauzone.be

🛉 ♦️⬛ ⬛ ♿ 🖊 ⛺ 🍽️ ♨️

E411 exit 18 to Marche then N86 to Hotton, over bdge in Hotton, turn L twds Melreux, foll rv and sp. Sm, pt shd, EHU (10A); bbq; twin axles; 20% statics; phone; Eng spkn; adv bkg rec; CKE. *"Site conv for Hotton caves; public transport 1km; easy walk to town; gd NH."* **€20.00, 1 Mar-30 Nov.** 2015

HOUTHALEN *B3* (4km E Rural) *51.03222, 5.41613*
Camping De Binnenvaart (formerly Kelchterhoef), Binnenvaartstraat, 3530 Houthalen-Helchteren
(011) 526720; debinnenvaart@limburgcampings.be;
www.limburgcampings.be

12 ♦️(htd) ⬛ ⛲ ⬛ 🖊 🐾 ⛺ ♨️ ⚡ 🚿 🌊

Exit A2/E314 junc 30 N. In 2km at x-rds turn L, in 2km at rndabt turn R into Binnenvaartstraat, then foll site sp. 2*, Lge, mkd, pt shd, EHU (16A) inc; sw nr; TV; 40% statics; Eng spkn; adv bkg acc. *"Press button at ent for access; friendly welcome; lge serviced pitches; excel NH or longer."* **€26.00** 2017

KOKSIJDE *A1* (2km W Rural) *51.10287, 2.63066*
Camping Noordduinen, Noordduinen 12, 8670 Koksijde aan Zee (058) 512546 or 0477 276469 (mob);
roos@campingbenelux.be; www.camping noordduinen.be

12 🐾 €2.50 ♦️⬛ ⛲ ⬛ 🖊 🐾 ⚡ 🔥nr ⛱ sand 3km

Exit A18/E40 junc 1A onto N8. Foll sp Koksijde to rndabt, strt over into Leopold III Laan, site on L. Do not use SatNav. Sm, hdg, hdstg, pt shd, EHU €2.50; 80% statics; bus 500m; Eng spkn; adv bkg acc; CKE. *"Gd site; adj cycle rte to Veurne - attractive, historic town; san facs now closer to pitches."* **€30.00** 2017

MARCHE EN FAMENNE *C3* (6.5km NW Rural) *50.24911, 5.27978* **Camping Le Relais,** 16 Rue de Serinchamps, 5377 Hogne (0475) 423049; info@ campinglerelais.com; www.campinglerelais.com

12 🐾 ♦️(htd) ⬛ ⛲ ♨️ ⬛ 🖊 ⚡ ♨️ ⛺

Sp fr N4 bet Marche-en-Famenne & Namur. Fr Namur ent immed R under new bdge. 3*, Med, unshd, pt sl, EHU (10A) €2.50; TV; 30% statics; adv bkg acc; CKE. *"V pleasant; lake adj; gd, clean facs but dated (2015); conv for N4."* **€20.50** 2015

NAMUR *C3* (9km SW Rural) *50.44164, 4.80182*
Camping Les Trieux, 99 Rue Les Tris, 5020 Malonne
(081) 445583 or 473 810742 (mob); camping.les.
trieux@skynet.be; www.campinglestrieux.be

♦️(htd) ⬛ ⛲ ⬛ 🖊 🗺️ 🐾 ⛺

Fr Namur take N90 sp Charleroi, after 8km take L fork sp Malonne (camp sp at junc). After 400m turn L at camp sp & site at top of 1 in 7 (13%) hill, approx 200m. To miss steep hill, fr Namur take Dinant (N92) S. In 2km R at camping sp. Take care at hairpin in 200m. Foll site sps. Located up steep, but surfaced rd. Med, mkd, pt shd, terr, EHU (10A) €2; TV; 50% statics; phone; Eng spkn; CKE. *"Friendly owners; pretty site, but steep - take care ent pitch; pitches diff for lge o'fits; basic san facs but clean; NH only."* **€21.00, 1 Apr-31 Oct.** 2015

NEUFCHATEAU *D3* (2.5km SW Rural) *49.83305, 5.41721* **Camping Spineuse,** Rue de Florenville, 6840 Neufchâteau 061 27 73 20; info@camping-spineuse. be; www.camping-spineuse.be

12 🐾 €1.25 ♦️(htd) ⬛ ⛲ ⬛ 🖊 🗺️ 🐾 ⛺ 🍽️ ♨️ ⚡ ♨️ 🔥nr ♨️ ⛱

Fr A4/E411 exit junc 26 or junc 27 fr E25 to Neufchâteau. Take N85 dir Florenville, site is 3rd on L. Ent easy to miss. 3*, Med, pt shd, EHU (16A) €3; TV; 30% statics; phone; Eng spkn; ccard acc. *"Pleasant, pretty site; poss diff lge o'fits if site full; vg san facs; some flooding after heavy rain."* **€28.50** 2018

NIEUWPOORT *A1* (1.5km NE Rural) *51.13324, 2.76031* **Parking De Zwerver,** Brugsesteenweg 16, 8620 Nieuwpoort (0474) 669526; de_zwerver@ telenet.be

12 ♦️⬛ ⛲ ♿ ⬛ 🗺️ ♨️

Nr Kompass Camping - see dirs under Kompass Camping. Site behind De Zwerver nursery. Sm, mkd, hdstg, unshd, bbq. *"M'vans only; coin & note operated facs; modern & efficient; walking/cycling dist to town cent & port."* **€0.50** 2016

NIEUWPOORT *A1* (3km E Rural) *51.12960, 2.77220* **Kompascamping Nieuwpoort,** Brugsesteenweg 49, 8620 Nieuwpoort (058) 236037; nieuwpoort@ kompascamping.be; www.kompascamping.be

🐾 €3.20 ♦️(htd) ⬛ ⛲ ♨️ ⬛ 🖊 🐾 ⛺ 🍽️ ⚡ ♨️ ♨️ 🌊
⛱ (covrd, htd) 🏊

Exit E40/A18 at junc 3 sp Nieuwpoort; in 500m turn R at full traff lts; after 1km turn R at traff lts; turn R at rndabt & immed turn L over 2 sm canal bdgs. Turn R to Brugsesteenweg, site on L approx 1km. Fr Ostende on N34 (coast rd) turn L at rndabt after canal bdge as above. 4*, V lge, hdg, mkd, hdstg, pt shd, EHU (10A) inc; gas; red long stay; 50% statics; adv bkg acc; tennis; bike hire; waterslide; golf 10km; CKE. *"Well-equipped site; helpful staff; boat-launching facs; sep area for sh stay tourers; sports/games area adj; very busy w/ends; excel cycle rtes; conv Dunkerque ferry; excel facs; superb san facs; lge site."* **€44.00, 23 Mar-5 Nov, H19.** 2018

NIEUWPOORT *A1* (16km S Rural) *51.02401, 2.84370* **De Ijzerhoeve,** Kapellestraat 4, B-8600 Diksmuide **(51)** 439439 or **(472)** 961220; info@ deijzerhoeve.be; www.deijzerhoeve.be

♞ €1 ♦️♦️ 🚿 ♿ ♿ 💧 💦 🐕 ₪ nr

Fr Ypres take N369 to Diksmuide. Turn L onto N35, L again strt after bdge then R onto Kapellestraat. Site in 1km on R. Sm, unshd, EHU (6A); red long stay; TV; 50% statics; phone; bus; Eng spkn; adv bkg acc. *"Site conv & cheap; renovation in progress(2017); gd."* **€14.00, 1 Apr-31 Oct.** 2017

OOSTENDE *A1* (6km NE Rural) *51.24366, 2.98002* **Camping T Minnepark,** Zandstraat 105, 8450 Bredene-Dorp **(059)** 322458; info@minnepark.be; www.minnepark.be

12 ♞ €1 ♦️♦️ 🚿 🏊 💦 🐕 🐕 💧 ₪ 🏪 🌊 sand 2km

Fr Ostend take N34 sp Blankenberge. After tunnel under rlwy turn R sp Brugge. Cross canal & turn L at traff lts in 300m. In 2km after water tower, turn L at X-rds. at Mini rndabt turn R pass Aldi. Site on L in 1km after Zanpolder (sm yellow sp on L). V lge, unshd, EHU (16A) €1 (poss rev pol); TV (pitch); 75% statics; Eng spkn; adv bkg rec. *"Lge pitches; friendly, helpful staff; warm welcome; excel, well-run, well maintained family run site; excel san facs; conv ferries, Bruges & coast; lge pitches; conv for exploring Brugge, Ghent, Ypres & coast."* **€30.00** 2019

OTEPPE *B3* (0.5km N Rural) *50.58239, 5.12455* **Camping L'Hirondelle Château,** Rue de la Burdinale 76A, 4210 Oteppe **(085)** 711131; info@lhirondelle.be; www.lhirondelle.be

♞ €2.50 ♦️♦️ 🏊 🍴 💦 🐕 🐕 ₪ 🍴 🌊 💧 🏪 🌊

App fr E A15/E42 at exit 8; turn W on N643 for 1.5km; turn at sp on R for Oteppe. In vill 3km pass church to x-rds & R by police stn: site 150m on L. Fr W exit A15 at exit 10 onto N80, turn R onto N652 at Burdinne for Oteppe - easier rte. V lge, shd, pt sl, EHU (6A) inc; gas; bbq; 75% statics; ccard acc; games area; waterslide; tennis; CKE. *"Site in grnds of chateau; excel facs for children; touring pitches at top of site poss diff (steep); gd area for walking, fishing; conv NH; v quiet LS."* **€29.00, 1 Apr-31 Oct.** 2019

PHILIPPEVILLE *C2* (11km NW Rural) *50.23920, 4.45927* **Camping Le Chesle,** 1 rue d'Yves, 5650 Vogenee **(071)** 612632; info.camping.chesle@gmail. com; www.chesle.be

♞ ♦️♦️ 🚿 ♿ 💧 💦 🐕 🍴 💧 🏪

N5 Charleroi-Philippeville, exit Yves Gomezee. After rlwy, turn R to Vogenee and foll sp. Med, unshd, pt sl, EHU (16A); bbq; TV; 50% statics; bus 1km; Eng spkn; adv bkg acc; CKE. *"Pleasant walking rtes fr site, ask for map; cycling poss, but v hilly; vg; v friendly, helpful owners."* **€24.60, 1 Feb-15 Dec.** 2018

ROCHEFORT *C3* (0.5km E Rural) *50.15947, 5.22609* **Camping Communal Les Roches,** 26 Rue du Hableau, 5580 Rochefort **(084)** 211900 or **(479)** 261759 **(mob)**; campingrochefort@lesroches.be; www.lesroches.be

♞ ♦️♦️(htd) 🚿 🏊 ♿ 💧 💦 MSP 🐕 🍴 ₪ nr ⊕ nr 💧 nr 🏪 🌊

Fr Rochefort cent on N86 & turn L at rndabt, then 1st R. Site well sp. 4*, Lge, hdg, mkd, hdstg, unshd, pt sl, serviced pitches; EHU (16A) metered; bbq; TV; 50% statics; phone; bus 250m; Eng spkn; ccard acc; games rm; tennis; games area. *"Vg, well-managed, pleasant, refurbished site; pool high ssn adj; gd walking; sh walk to charming town; gd, modern clean san facs; v popular site; rest at w-ends only."* **€27.00, 1 Apr-11 Nov.** 2018

SINT MARGRIETE *A2* (2.6km NW Rural) *51.2860, 3.5164* **Camping De Soetelaer,** Sint Margrietepolder 2, 9981 Sint Margriete **(09)** 3798151; camping. desoetelaer@telenet.be; www.desoetelaer.be

♦️♦️ 🚿 🏊 💦 🐕 🐕 ₪ nr

Fr E on N49/E34 to Maldegem or fr W on N9 or N49 turn N onto N251 to Aardenburg (N'lands), then turn R twd St Kruis (N'lands) - site situated 1.5km strt on fr St Margriete (back in Belgium). Med, mkd, pt shd, serviced pitches; EHU (6A) inc; Eng spkn; adv bkg acc; CKE. *"Vg, clean site; excel, modern san facs; peace & quiet, privacy & space; highly rec for relaxation; o'fits pitched v close end to end."* **€24.00, Easter-15 Oct.** 2019

SOUMAGNE *B3* (3.5km S Rural) *50.61099, 5.73840* **Domaine Provincial de Wégimont,** Chaussée de Wégimont 76, 4630 Soumagne **(04)** 2372400; wegimont@prov-liege.be; www.prov-liege.be/ wegimont

12 ♞ ♦️♦️(htd) 🚿 🏊 ♿ 💦 🍴 ⊕ 💧 🏪 🌊

Exit A3 at junc 37 onto N3 W twd Fléron & Liège. In 500m at traff lts turn L sp Soumagne. In Soumagne at traff lts form R dir Wégimont, site on top of hill on R directly after bus stop. Med, hdg, pt shd, pt sl, EHU (16A) inc poss rev pol; bbq; 70% statics; bus; site clsd Jan; tennis; games area; CKE. *"Welcoming site in chateau grnds (public access); pool adj high ssn; clean facs; conv sh stay/NH nr m'way."* **€13.50** 2016

SPA *C4* (1.6km SE Rural) *50.48559, 5.88385* **Camping Parc des Sources,** Rue de la Sauvenière 141, 4900 Spa **(087)** 772311; info@parcdessources.be; www.parcdessources.be

♞ €1.50 ♦️♦️(htd) 🚿 🏊 ♿ 💧 💦 MSP 🐕 🍴 💧 ₪ nr 🏪 🌊

Bet Spa & Francorchamps on N62, sp on R. Med, mkd, pt shd, pt sl, EHU (10A) €2.75; gas; 60% statics; phone. *"Excel facs, modern lndry, beautiful location, nr forest; friendly & helpful staff."* **€25.00, 25 Mar-31 Oct.** 2016

STEKENE *A2* (4km SW Rural) *51.18366, 4.00730*
Camping Vlasaard, Heirweg 143, 9190 Stekene
(03) 7798164; info@camping-vlasaard.be;
www.camping-vlasaard.be

ⵗ(htd) 🆆 ⵠ ⅋ ♿ ⵗ ⌁ Ⓣ ⓗ 🝙 ⵂ nr ⛰ ⛵

Fr N49 Antwerp-Knokke rd, exit sp Stekene. In
Stekene, take dir Moerbeke, site on L in 4km.
V lge, mkd, unshd, serviced pitches; EHU (16A);
75% statics; Eng spkn; ccard acc; games area.
€18.00, 7 Jan-20 Dec. 2016

"I like to fill in the reports as I travel from site to site"

You'll find report forms at the back of this
guide, or you can fill them in online at
camc.com/europereport.

TOURINNES LA GOSSE *B3* (0.5km SW Rural)
50.77952, 4.73657 **Camping au Val Tourinnes,** Rue
du Grand Brou 16A, 1320 Tourinnes-la-Grosse
(010) 866642; campingopassage@gmail.com;
www.opassage.be

🄵🅸 ⵗ €4 ⵗ(htd) 🆆 ⵠ ⅋ ♿ 🦋 ⅌ ♿ nr ⛰

Fr N on E40/A3 m'way exit junc 23 onto N25 S dir
Hamme-Mille. In Hamme-Mille turn L at traff lts,
site on R in 2km. Or fr S on E411/A4 exit junc 8 onto
N25 to Hamme-Mille & turn R at traff lts, then as
above. Don't use site name on Sat Nav. 2*, Sm, hdg,
pt shd, EHU (2A) €4, (10A) €8; twin axles; Eng spkn;
adv bkg acc; ccard acc; lake fishing. *"New owners
(2019), will be gd when finished; at present only a few
EHU pitches; some pitches diff to access due to grass
kerbs; vg, modern san facs; access tight for lge o'fits;
airshow 1st w/end July; peaceful, quirky site; fair."*
€20.00 2019

TOURNAI *B2* (2km SE Urban) *50.59967, 3.41349*
Camp Municipal de l'Orient, Jean-Baptiste Moens 8,
7500 Tournai **(069) 222635; campingorient@tournai.be**

🄵🅸 ⵗ(htd) 🆆 ⵠ ⅋ 🝙 nr

Exit E42 junc 32 R onto N7 twd Tournai. L at 1st
traff lts, foll sp Aquapark, L at rndabt, site immed
on L (no sp). 4*, Med, hdg, hdstg, pt shd, serviced
pitches; EHU (10A) inc (poss rev pol/no earth) or
metered; gas; Eng spkn; adv bkg req; CKE. *"Well-kept
site in interesting area & old town; facs stretched high
ssn, but excel site; take care raised kerbs to pitches;
max length of c'van 6.5m due narr site rds & high hdgs;
helpful wardens; lake adj; E side of site quietest; htd;
indoor pool adj; EHU had no earth on a nbr of pitches;
rest, bar & playgrnd at leisure complex adj (50% disc
to campers); handy for Lille and Dunkerque ferries."*
€16.00 2018

TURNHOUT *A3* (9.6km SW Rural) *51.28253, 4.83750*
Recreatie de Lilse Bergen, Strandweg 6, 2275
Lille-Gierle **(014) 557901; info@lilsebergen.be;**
www.lilsebergen.be

🄵🅸 ⵗ €5 ⵗ(htd) 🆆 ⵠ 🝙 ⅋ 🝙 ⅌ Ⓣ ⓗ 🝙 ⛰ ⵙ ⛵

Exit A21/E34 junc 22 N dir Beerse; at rndabt foll sp
Lilse Bergen. Site in 1.5km. 3*, Lge, mkd, shd, EHU
(10A) inc; bbq; sw; 60% statics; phone; Eng spkn; adv
bkg acc; ccard acc; bike hire; tennis; games area; sep
car park; watersports; CKE. *"Site sep pt of lge leisure
complex; pitches amongst pine trees; modern san facs,
poss streteched high ssn; excel for children/teenagers."*
€26.50 2016

VIRTON *D3* (3km NE Rural) *49.57915, 5.54892*
Camping Colline de Rabais, 1 Rue Clos des Horlès,
6760 Virton **(063) 571195; info@collinederabais.be;**
www.collinederabais.be

🄵🅸 ⵗ €3.25 ⵗ(htd) 🆆 ⵠ 🝙 ♿ ⅋ ♿ 🦋 ⅌ Ⓣ ⓗ 🝙 ⛰ ⛵

Take junc 29 fr A4/E411 onto N87, 2km fr Virton
turn into wood at site sp. At end of rd bef lge
building turn R, then 3rd turn R at phone box.
4*, Lge, pt shd, pt sl, terr, EHU (16A) €3.20; sw nr; TV
(pitch); 20% statics; phone; Eng spkn; adv bkg acc;
ccard acc; bike hire; tennis 1km; fishing 1km; CKE.
"Pleasant site; gd facs." **€14.00** 2016

WAASMUNSTER *A2* (2.4km N Rural) *51.12690,
4.08455* **Camping Gerstekot,** Vinkenlaan 30, 9250
Waasmunster **(0323) 7723424; campinggerstekot.
be@gmail.com; www.gerstekot.be**

🄵🅸 ⵗ(htd) 🆆 ⵠ 🝙 ♿ ⅋ ♿ 🦋 ⅌ Ⓣ 🝙 ⵂ ⛰

Exit A14/E17 at junc 13 Waasmunster onto N446 S;
take 1st L in 100m into Patrijzenlaan & L again into
Vinkenlaan, foll camp sp. Med, mkd, pt shd, EHU (16A)
inc; bbq; TV; 95% statics; phone; adv bkg acc; ccard acc;
games area; games rm; CKE. *"Busy at w/end; water use
metered; key req for shwrs; gd."* **€18.00** 2016

WESTENDE *A1* (0.4km SW Coastal) *51.15728,
2.76561* **Camping Westende,** Westendelaan 341,
8434 Westende **(058) 233254; info@camping
westende.be; www.campingwestende.be**

ⵗ €2 ⵗ(htd) 🆆 ⵠ ♿ ⅋ ♿ 🦋 ⅌ ♿ ⓗ 🝙 ⵂ nr ⛰ ⵙ(htd)

ⵜ sand 1km

Fr Middelkerke foll N318; just after Westende vill
church take dir Nieupoort, site on L in 150m.
Lge, mkd, unshd, EHU (10A) inc; gas; 90% statics;
phone; bus; Eng spkn; CKE. *"Sm but tidy touring area;
friendly owners; beach nrby; tram 1km; excel cycling;
gd."* **€34.00, 1 Apr-14 Nov.** 2016

BELGIUM

YPRES/IEPER *B1* (3km E Urban) *50.8467, 2.8994*
Camping Jeugdstadion, Bolwerkstraat 1, 8900
Leper, Ypres **(057) 217282; info@jeugdstadion.be;**
www.jeugdstadion.be

🐕 €1 ⭑⭑⭑(htd) [WD] ⛺ ⳥ [MSP] ⳣ 🗑 nr ⛺

Fr S ent town cent on N336, after rlwy x-ing turn
R at rndabt onto ring rd & L at 2nd rndabt, foll
camping sp. Site in 300m on L, sp fr ring rd. If app
town cent fr N on N8 fr Veurne take ring rd N37; at
rndabt turn L, site in 300m on L, well sp. Fr N38 in
Ypres turn off at rndabt sp Industrie/Jeugdstadion,
take 2nd L, site at end. NB site open all year for
m'vans. 2*, Med, hdstg, hdg, mkd, pt shd, pt sl, EHU
(10A) inc (poss rev pol); Eng spkn; adv bkg rec; ccard
acc; bike hire. *"Automatic registration/check out
avail when office clsd; peaceful, well-refurbished site;
conv WW1 battle fields & museums; 10 min walk to
Menin Gate for daily Last Post Ceremony; helpful
staff; gd, modern san facs; sports park adj; soft grass
pitches - ask for one with 'rubber tracks' to avoid
sinking; hdstg m'van (OAY with own san facs only)
pitches in sep area like an Aire; site poss v full local
public hols; pool adj; site not fully enclsd; excel, clean,
tidy, well run site; rec; noise fr adj processing plant."*
€15.00, 1 Mar-12 Nov. 2019

"We must tell the Club about that great site we found"

Get your site reports in by mid-August and we'll
do our best to get your updates into the next
edition.

YPRES/IEPER *B1* (10km SW Rural) *50.78643, 2.82035*
Camping Ypra, Pingelaarstraat 2, 8956 Kemmel-
Heuvelland **(057) 444631; camping.ypra@skynet.be;**
www.camping-ypra.be

🐕 €1.90 ⭑⭑⭑(htd) [WD] ⛺ 🗑 ⳣ 🦋 🍽 ⑭ nr 🗑 ⛺

On N38 Poperinge ring rd turn S at rndabt onto
N304. Foll sp Kemmel. Site on R in 12km on N edge
of Kemmel. 3*, Med, mkd, hdstg, pt shd, pt sl, EHU
(16A) inc (poss rev pol); 90% statics; Eng spkn; adv
bkg acc; CKE. *"Clean, well-maintained site; gd, modern
san facs, but ltd; helpful, friendly staff; access to some
pitches poss diff; interesting rest in vill; conv for WW1
battlefields; pitches varied sizes; poss noise fr club hse
& bar; gd."* **€22.00, 1 Mar-30 Nov.** 2019

ZELE *A2* (6.5km SW Rural) *51.05273, 3.97996*
Camping Groenpark, Gentsesteenweg 337, 9240
Zele **(09) 3679071; Groenpark@scarlet.be;**
www.campinggroenpark.be

🐕 ⭑⭑⭑(htd) [WD] ⛺ ⳣ [MSP] 🦋 🍽 nr ⑭ ⳥ 🗑 nr ⛺

Fr A14 Ghent/Antwerp, J12 S onto N47. In 10km
turn Ronto N445 to Overmeer. Site on L (flags) in
10km. 3*, Sm, mkd, pt shd, EHU (10A) inc; bbq; sw
nr; TV; 10% statics; tram; Eng spkn; adv bkg acc; CKE.
*"Nr Park & Ride to Ghent; wooded area for tourers;
gd; pleasant site; nice walk around lake; sm site in tall
pines 50mtrs fr Donkmeer Lake; v pretty; not well
maintained; fair."* **€25.00, 31 Mar-1 Oct.** 2018

Map legend:
- France and Andorra
- Central and South East Europe, Benelux and Scandinavia
- Spain and Portugal

Eupen to Turnhout = 122km

Distance chart (distances in km). Each city is listed against the cities preceding it, reading left to right:

City	Distances
Zeebrugge	—
Ypres	68
Turnhout	176, 167
Tournai	174, 58, 113
Philippeville	185, 127, 195, 86
Oudenaarde	119, 37, 91, 65, 25
Oostende	138, 193, 170, 56, 25, 86
Namur	179, 62, 120, 175, 177, 72, 140
Mons	137, 67, 193, 62, 72, 48, 160, 151
Mechelen	90, 81, 137, 96, 116, 54, 146, 146, 137
Malmedy	163, 168, 102, 268, 226, 242, 166, 304, 272, 263
Luxembourg City	116, 234, 225, 155, 329, 310, 270, 304, 328, 331
Liège	180, 56, 107, 129, 62, 214, 172, 175, 105, 232, 212
Leuven	80, 215, 24, 87, 62, 144, 119, 177, 29, 161, 143
Kortrijk	129, 203, 299, 242, 115, 76, 144, 62, 35, 146, 147, 29, 74
Huy	174, 69, 36, 150, 68, 96, 100, 34, 198, 165, 91, 148, 205, 197
Hasselt	74, 189, 51, 43, 199, 110, 80, 164, 97, 202, 156, 211, 55, 217, 156
Gent	145, 141, 48, 88, 155, 272, 210, 82, 121, 120, 70, 29, 71, 106, 78, 201
Eupen	191, 67, 239, 117, 42, 130, 26, 144, 164, 99, 249, 207, 155, 211, 122, 269, 70
Dinant	127, 147, 125, 62, 159, 92, 125, 101, 109, 85, 28, 205, 164, 30, 131, 177, 189, 205
Clervaux (Luxembourg)	113, 82, 231, 180, 120, 60, 56, 132, 199, 190, 120, 36, 294, 255, 142, 344, 293, 263
Charleroi	159, 55, 129, 110, 56, 79, 84, 64, 89, 46, 63, 115, 166, 71, 26, 93, 161, 151, 170
Bruxelles (Brussels)	60, 181, 280, 190, 234, 97, 55, 188, 315, 253, 123, 136, 27, 69, 136, 123, 166, 158, 89, 264
Brugge	154, 32, 207, 97, 183, 131, 83, 67, 226, 185, 166, 25, 89, 264, 121, 71, 182, 203, 155, 263, 263
Bastogne	177, 113, 118, 187, 70, 133, 117, 58, 82, 149, 242, 84, 207, 196, 127, 302, 149, 141, 244, 277, 302, 128
Ath	216, 39, 288, 189, 166, 63, 67, 120, 136, 61, 245, 172, 123, 274, 188, 132, 262, 28, 123, 302, 277, 155, 90
Arlon	233, 112, 135, 154, 207, 230, 180, 129, 123, 102, 274, 207, 196, 127, 122, 302, 81, 155, 244, 127, 132, 90, 128
Antwerpen	81, 262, 196, 107, 26, 73, 130, 253, 207, 27, 166, 157, 46, 102, 171, 288, 226, 30, 155, 71, 128, 77, 40, 121
Aalter	83, 196, 26, 73, 130, 253, 207, 27, 166, 157, 46, 102, 171, 288, 226, 30, 155, 71, 128, 77, 40, 121
Aalst	48, 53, 217, 50, 178, 76, 29, 82, 210, 121, 163, 33, 114, 109, 70, 59, 127, 244, 182, 51, 89, 90, 93, 108, 67, 99, 100, 90

Hvar

Highlights

Croatia's Adriatic coast is a land of sun, beauty and history. Soaked in culture going back thousands of years, there are so many different sights to see, from the 16th century walls of Dubrovnik to the Roman amphitheatre in Pula.

With countless galleries, museums and churches to discover, as well as an exquisite natural landscape to explore, there truly is something for everyone.

Licitars are brightly decorated biscuits made of sweet honey dough. Often given as a gift at celebrations such as Christmas or weddings, they are an integral part of Croatian identity dating from the 16th century.

Croatia is well known for its carnivals, festivals and celebrations, which take place throughout the year. Some of the most important are the Spring Procession of Queens from Gorjani, the Bell Ringer's Pageant from the Kastav Area and the Festivity of St. Blaise, Dubrovnik's patron saint.

Major towns and cities

- Zagreb – the capital of Croatia has a rich history that dates from Roman times.
- Rijeka – Croatia's principal port city overlooking the Adriatic.
- Split – the centre of the city is built around an ancient Roman palace.
- Osijek – a gastronomic centre, and the best place to try a traditional dish.

Attractions

- Dubrovnik – a wonderfully-preserved medieval walled city with plenty to see.
- Plitvice Lakes - a stunning series of lakes and waterfalls set in an enchanting woodland.
- Pula Arena – this ancient Roman amphitheatre is one of the best preserved in the world.
- Diocletian's Palace – an ancient monument that makes up the heart of Split.

Find out more

www.croatia.hr
E: info@htz.hr T: 0038 5 14 55 64 55

Country Information

Population (approx): 4.2 million

Capital: Zagreb

Area: 56,540 sq km, divided into 20 counties

Bordered by: Bosnia-Herzegovina, Hungary, Serbia, Montenegro and Slovenia

Terrain: Flat plains along border with Hungary; low mountains and highlands near Adriatic coast and islands

Climate: Mediterranean climate along the coast with hot, dry summers and mild, wet winters; continental climate inland with hot summers and cold winters

Coastline: 5,835km (inc 4,058km islands)

Highest Point: Dinara 1,830m

Language: Croatian

Local Time: GMT or BST + 1, i.e. 1 hour ahead of the UK all year

Currency: Kuna (HRK) divided into 100 lipa; £1 = HRK 8.59, HRK 10 = £1.16 (October 2019)

Emergency Numbers: Police 192; Fire brigade 193; Ambulance 194. Or dial 112 and specify the service you need.

Public Holidays in 2020: Jan 1, 6; Apr 13; May 1; Jun 11, 22, 25 (National Day); Aug 5 (Thanksgiving Day), 15; Oct 8 (Independence Day); Nov 1; Dec 25, 26.

Some Christian Orthodox and Muslim festivals are also celebrated locally. School summer holidays take place from the last week in June to the end of August.

Entry Formalities

British and Irish passport holders may visit Croatia for up to three months without a visa.

Unless staying at official tourist accommodation (hotel or campsite) all visitors are obliged to register at the nearest police station or tourist agency within 24 hours of arrival. Campsites should carry out this function for their guests but make sure you check with them. If you fail to register you may receive a fine or you may have to leave Croatia.

British citizens intending to stay for an extended period should seek advice from the Croatian Embassy.

Medical Services

For minor ailments, first of all consult staff in a pharmacy (ljekarna).

Emergency hospital and medical treatment is available at a reduced cost on production of a valid EHIC. You will be expected to pay a proportion of the cost (normally 20%). Only basic health care facilities are available in outlying areas and islands

Opening Hours

Banks: Mon-Fri 7am-7pm; Sat 7am-1pm.

Museums: Tue-Sun 10am-5pm; most close Mon and some close Sun afternoons.

Post Offices: Mon-Fri 7am-7pm (2pm in small villages). In major towns or tourist places, post offices on duty are open until 9pm.

Shops: Mon-Fri 8am-8pm; Sat & Sun 8am-2pm.

Safety and Security

The level of street crime is low, but you should be aware of pickpockets in major cities, coastal areas (e.g. pavement cafés) and take sensible precautions when carrying money, credit cards and passports.

Beware of people trying to make you pull over when driving, either by requesting help or indicating that something is wrong with your vehicle. If possible wait until you are in a populated area before pulling over to check.

If you are planning to travel outside the normal tourist resorts you should be aware that there are areas affected by the war, which ended in 1995, where unexploded mines remain. These include Eastern Slavonia, Brodsko-Posavska County, Karlovac County, areas around Zadar County and in more remote areas of the Plitvice Lakes National Park. See the Croatian Mine Action Centre's website at www.hcr.hr/en/protuminUvod.asp for more specific information about mine-affected areas.

Croatia shares with the rest of Europe an underlying threat from terrorism. Attacks could be indiscriminate and against civilian targets, including places frequented by tourists.

British Embassy

UL IVANA LUČIĆA 4
HR-10000 ZAGREB
Tel: (01) 6009100
www.british.embassyzagreb@fco.gov.uk

Irish Honorary Consulate

MIRAMARSKA 23 (EUROCENTER)
10000 ZAGREB
Tel: (01) 6310025
irish.consulate.zg@inet.hr

TRUMBICEVA OBALA 3
21000 SPLIT
Tel: (021) 343715
9csain@cpad.hr

Customs Regulations

Customs Posts

Main border crossings are open 24 hours a day.

Foodstuffs

Up to 10kg of meat and meat products and 10kg of dairy products may be imported from EU countries. If you are entering from outside the EU, you can bring 2kg of meat products as long as they are in sealed packages.

Documents

Driving Licence

Full, valid British driving licence are recognised but if you have an old-style green licence then it is advisable to change it for a photocard licence in order to avoid any local difficulties.

Green Card

While an International Motor Insurance Certificate (Green Card) is not necessary, you should ensure that your vehicle insurance includes cover for Croatia.

If you are driving to or through Bosnia and Herzegovina (for example, along the 20 km strip of coastline at Neum on the Dalmatian coastal highway to Dubrovnik) you should ensure that you have obtained Green Card cover for Bosnia and Herzegovina. For Club members insured under the Club's Motor Insurance schemes full policy cover is available for this 20km strip, however you must ask at the time of taking out or renewing your insurance policy for one that specifically covers Bosnia. If you have difficulties obtaining this cover before departure Club members can contact the Club's Travel Service Information Officer for advice, email travelserviceinfo@camc.com. Alternatively, temporary third-party insurance can be purchased at the country's main border posts, or in Split and other large cities. It is not generally obtainable at the Neum border crossing itself.

As an alternative, you can take the ferry from Ploče to Trpanj on the Pelješac peninsula and avoid the stretch of road in Bosnia and Herzegovina altogether. There are frequent ferries during summer months, but be aware that motorhome drivers are sometimes requested to reverse onto them.

Money

Visitors may exchange money in bureaux de change, banks, post offices, hotels and some travel agencies but you are likely to get the best rates in banks. Exchange slips should be kept in order to convert unspent kuna on leaving the country. Many prices are quoted in both kuna and euros, both are widely accepted.

Most shops and restaurants accept credit cards. There are cash machines in all but the smallest resorts.

The police are warning visitors about a recent increase in the number of forged Croatian banknotes in circulation, especially 200 and 500 kuna notes. Take care when purchasing kuna and use only reliable outlets, such as banks and cash points.

Passport

You must be able to show some form of identification if required by the authorities and, therefore, should carry your passport or photocard driving licence at all times.

Vehicle(s)

Carry your vehicle registration certificate (V5C), insurance details and MOT certificate (if applicable).

Driving

Accidents

Any visible damage to a vehicle entering Croatia must be certified by the authorities at the border and a Certificate of Damage issued, which must be produced when leaving the country. In the event of a minor accident resulting in material damage only, call the police and they will assist with the exchange of information between drivers and will issue a Certificate of Damage to the foreign driver. You should not try to leave the country with a damaged vehicle without this Certificate as you may be accused of a 'hit and run' offence.

Confiscation of passport and a court appearance within 24 hours are standard procedures for motoring accidents where a person is injured.

The Croatian Insurance Bureau in Zagreb can assist with Customs and other formalities following road accidents, tel: (01) 4696600, email: huo@huo.hr or see www.huo.hr.

Alcohol

The general legal limit of alcohol is 50 milligrams in 100 millilitres of blood, i.e. less than the level in the UK (80 milligrams). For drivers of vehicles over 3,500 kg and for drivers under 24 years of age the alcohol limit is zero. The general legal limit also applies to cyclists.

It is prohibited to drive after having taken any medicine whose side-effects may affect the ability to drive a motor vehicle.

Breakdown Service

The Hrvatski Auto-Klub (HAK) operates a breakdown service throughout the country, telephone 987 (or 01987 from a mobile phone) for assistance. On motorways use the roadside emergency phones which are placed at 2km intervals. Towing and breakdown services are available 24 hours a day in and around most major cities and along the coast in summer (6am to midnight in Zagreb).

Child Restraint Systems

Children under the age of 12 are not allowed to travel in the front seats of vehicles, with the exception of children under 2 years of age who can travel in the front if they are placed in a child restraint system adapted to their size. It must be rear-facing and the airbag must be de-activated.

Children up to 5 years old must be placed in a seat adapted to their size on the back seat. Children between the ages of 5 and 12 must travel on the back seat using a 3 point seat belt with a booster seat if necessary for their height.

Fuel

Petrol stations are generally open from 7am to 7 or 8pm, later in summer. Some of those on major stretches of road stay open 24 hours a day. Payment by credit card is widely accepted. LPG (Autogas) is fairly widely available.

Lights

Dipped headlights are compulsory at all times, regardless of weather conditions, from the end of October to the end of March and in reduced visibility at other times of the year. It is compulsory to carry spare bulbs, however this rule does not apply if your vehicle is fitted with xenon, neon, LED or similar lights.

Motorways

There is just over 1250km of motorways, with the major stretches being shown in the table below. Tolls (cestarina) are levied according to vehicle category. Electronic display panels above motorways indicate speed limits, road conditions and lane closures. Information on motorways can be found on www.hac.hr.

Motorway Tolls

Class 1   Vehicle with 2 axles, height up to 1.3m measured from front axle) excluding vans

Class 2   Vehicle with 2 or more axles, height up to 1.3m (measured from front axle), including car + caravan or trailer, motorhomes and vans.

Class 3   Vehicle with 2 or 3 axles, height over 1.3m (measured from front axle), including van with trailer

Class 4   Vehicle with 4 or more axles, height over .3m (measured from front axle)

Tolls can be paid in cash or by credit card. Details of toll prices can be found in English at www.hac.hr.

Parking

Lines at the roadside indicate parking restrictions. Traffic wardens patrol roads and impose fines for illegal parking. Vehicles, including those registered outside Croatia, may be immobilised by wheel clamps.

Roads

In general road conditions are good in and around the larger towns. The Adriatic Highway or Jadranksa Magistrala (part of European route E65) runs the whole length of the Adriatic coast and is in good condition, despite being mostly single-carriageway. Minor road surfaces may be uneven and, because of the heat-resisting material used to surface them, may be very slippery when wet. Minor roads are usually unlit at night.

Motorists should take care when overtaking and be aware that other drivers may overtake unexpectedly in slow-moving traffic. The standard of driving is generally fair.

Road Signs and Markings

Road signs and markings conform to international standards. Motorway signs have a green background; national road signs have a blue background.

Speed Limits

	Open Road (km/h)	Motorway (km/h)
Car Solo	90-110	130
Car towing caravan/trailer	80	90
Motorhome under 3500kg	90-110	130
Motorhome 3500-7500kg	80	90

In addition to complying with other speed limits, drivers under the age of 25 must not exceed 80 km/h (50 mph) on the open road, 100 km/h (62 mph) on expressways and 120 km/h (74 mph) on motorways.

Traffic Jams

During the summer, tailbacks may occur at the border posts with Slovenia at Buje on the E751 (road 21), at Bregana on the E70 (A3) and at Donji Macelj on the E59 (A1). During July and August there may be heavy congestion, for example at Rupa/Klenovica and at other tourist centres, and on the E65 north-south Adriatic Highway. This is particularly true on Friday evenings, Saturday mornings, Sunday evenings and holidays.

Queues form at ferry crossings to the main islands.Road and traffic conditions can be viewed on the HAK website (in English), www. hak.hr or tel: (01) 4640800 (English spoken) or (072) 777777 while in Croatia for round-the-clock recorded information.

Violation of Traffic Regulations

The police may impose on-the-spot fines for parking and driving offences. If you are unable to pay the police may confiscate your passport. Motoring law enforcement, especially for speeding offences, is strictly observed.

Winter Driving

It is compulsory to carry snow chains in your vehicle and they must be used if required by the weather conditions (5cm of snow or black ice). The compulsory winter equipment in Croatia consists of a shovel in your vehicle and a set of snow chains on the driving axel.

Essential Equipment

First aid kit

All vehicles, including those registered abroad, must carry a first aid kit.

Reflective Jacket/ Waistcoat

It is obligatory to carry a reflective jacket inside your car (not in the boot) and you must wear it if you need to leave your vehicle to attend to a breakdown, e.g. changing a tyre. It is also common sense for any passenger leaving the vehicle to also wear one.

Warning Triangle(s)

All motor vehicles must carry a warning triangle. If you are towing a caravan or trailer you must have two warning triangles.

Touring

There are a number of national parks and nature reserves throughout the country, including the World Heritage site at the Plitvice lakes, the Paklenica mountain massif, and the Kornati archipelago with 140 uninhabited islands, islets and reefs. Dubrovnik, itself a World Heritage site, is one of the world's best-preserved medieval cities, having been extensively restored since recent hostilities.

While Croatia has a long coastline, there are few sandy beaches; instead there are pebbles, shingle and rocks with man-made bathing platforms.

The Croatian National Tourist Board operates 'Croatian Angels', a multi-lingual tourist information and advice service available from the end of March to mid-October, tel: 062 999 999 or 00385 62 999 999 from outside Croatia.

Croatia originated the concept of commercial naturist resorts in Europe and today attracts an estimated 1 million naturist tourists annually. There are approximately 20 official naturist resorts and beaches and numerous other unofficial or naturist-optional 'free' beaches. Smoking is prohibited in restaurants, bars and public places. A service charge is general included in the bill. English is widely spoken.

Camping and Caravanning

There are more than 150 campsites in Croatia including several well-established naturist sites, mainly along the coast. Sites are licensed according to how many people they can accommodate, rather than by the number of vehicles or tents, and are classed according to a grading system of 1 to 4 stars. There are some very large sites catering for up to 10,000 people at any one time but there are also many small sites, mainly in Dalmatia, situated in gardens, orchards and farms.

Many sites open from April to October; few open all year. They are generally well-equipped.

A tourist tax is levied of between HRK 4 and HRK 7 per person per day according to region and time of year.

Casual/wild camping is illegal and is particularly monitored at beaches, harbours and rural car parks. Most campsites have overnight areas for late arrivals and there are a number of rest areas established along main roads for overnight stays or brief stopovers.

Electricity and Gas

Current on campsites ranges from 10 to 16 amps. Plugs have 2 round pins. There may not be CEE connections and a long cable might be required.

Campingaz cylinders are not available, so take a good supply of gas with you.

Public Transport

Rail travel is slow and cab be unreliable. By contrast the bus network offers the cheapest and most extensive means of public transport. Buy bus tickets when you board or from kiosks, which you must validate once on board. Trams operate in Zagreb and you can buy tickets from kiosks.

Coastal towns and cities have regular scheduled passenger and car ferry services. Most ferries are drive-on/drive-off – see www.jadrolinija.hr for schedules and maps.

Car ferries operate from Ancona, Bari, Pescara and Venice in Italy to Dubrovnik, Korèula, Mali Lošinj, Poreè, Pula, Rijecka, Rovinj, Sibenik, Split, Starigrad, Vis and Zadar. Full details from:

VIAMARE LTD
SUITE 108, 582 HONEYPOT LANE
STANMORE
MIDDX HA7 1JS
Tel: 020 8206 3420

Email: ferries@viamare.com
www.viamare.com

BIOGRAD NA MORU *B3* (12km NW Coastal) *44.00532, 15.36748* **Autokamp Filko,** Aleksandar Colic 23207 Sveti Petar Na Moru **02 33 91 177;** info@autokamp-filko.hr; www.autokamp-filko.hr

🔢 🐕 🏕 ⬜ ⬛ ☂ 💧 Y ℗ ⚡ shgl

On D8 bet Zadar & Biograd Na Moru at Sv Petar NM. 1st camp on the R by sea. Sm, pt shd, 30% statics; Eng spkn. *"Some pitches by water on hdstg with views across to islands; dir access fr rd; ideal LS; gd."* **HRK 170** 2019

DUBROVNIK *C4* (10km S Coastal) *42.62444, 18.19301* **Autocamp Matkovica,** Srebreno 8, 20207 Dubrovnik **(020) 485867;** u.o.matkovica@hotmail.com

🔢 🐕 ♿ ⬜ 🏕 ⬛ 💧 Y nr ℗ nr ☂ shgl adj

Fr Dubrovnik S on coast rd. At Kupari foll sp to site behind Camping Porto. 1*, Sm, mkd, shd, EHU (6A) inc; phone; bus 200m; Eng spkn. *"Well-kept site; friendly, helpful owners; cash only; san facs old but clean; water bus to Dubrovnik 1km."* **HRK 135** 2019

DUBROVNIK *C4* (7km S Coastal) *42.62471, 18.20801* **Autocamp Kate,** Tupina 1, 20207 Mlini **(020) 487006;** info@campingkate.com; www.campingkate.com

🐕 HRK4 ♿ ⬜ 🏕 ⬛ 💧 Y nr ℗ ☂ shgl 200m

Fr Dubrovnik on rd 8 foll sp Cavtat or Čilipi or airport into vill of Mlini. Fr S past Cavtat into Mlini. Site well sp fr main rd. Sm, hdstg, pt shd, pt sl, terr, EHU (10-16A) inc; bbq; red long stay; phone; bus to Dubrovnik 150m; Eng spkn; adv bkg acc; CKE. *"Family-run site in lovely setting; v helpful, hard-working, welcoming owners; vg clean facs; boats fr vill to Dubrovnik; long, steep climb (steps) down to beach."* **HRK 173, 4 Apr-27 Oct.** 2017

FAZANA *A3* (1km S Coastal) *44.91717, 13.81105* **Camping Bi-Village,** Dragonja 115, 52212 Fažana **(052) 300300;** info@bivillage.com; www.bivillage.com

🐕 HRK37 ♿ (htd) ⬜ 🏕 ♿ 💧 MSP ☂ Y ℗ ⚡ ☂ ⚓ 🏊 ☂ shgl adj

N fr Pula on rd 21/A9/E751 at Vodnjan turn W sp Fažana. Foll sp for site. 4*, V lge, mkd, pt shd, EHU (10A) inc; gas; bbq; 30% statics; phone; bus; Eng spkn; adv bkg acc; ccard acc; bike hire; waterslide; golf 2km; tennis 1km; boat hire; games area; watersports; CKE. *"Excel, modern, clean san facs; private bthrms avail; site surrounded by pine trees; some beachside pitches; conv Brijuni Island National Park; excel leisure facs for families; vg cycle paths; no emptying point for Wastemaster; vg; prices vary per ssn."* **HRK 342, 20 Apr-14 Oct.** 2017

KARLOVAC *B2* (12km SW Rural) *45.41962, 15.48338* **Autocamp Slapić,** Mrežničke Brig, 47250 Duga Resa **(098) 860601;** autocamp@inet.hr; www.campslapic.hr

🐕 HRK20 ♿ ⬜ 🏕 ♿ 💧 Y nr ℗ nr ☂ nr 🚐

Exit A1/E65 junc 3 for Karlovac; strt over traff lts immed after toll booth sp Split & Rijecka.Take D23 to Duga Resa; turn L by church in Duga Resa; cont over bdge & turn R; foll rd keeping rv on your R; cont thro vill of Mrnžnički Brig in 3km; site sp in another 1km. NB new bdge at Belavici. Site well sp fr Duga Resa. 4*, Sm, mkd, pt shd, EHU (16A) HRK30; bbq; sw nr; phone; train to Zagreb 500m; Eng spkn; adv bkg acc; ccard acc; canoeing; fishing; games area; tennis; bike hire. *"Friendly, pleasant, family-owned site in gd location on rv; lovely area; gd bar/rest; gd clean facs; lge pitches; long hoses req LS; easy drive into Zagreb; excel; new, superb sans block (2014); poss noise fr daytrippers; rds to site narr."* **HRK 220, 1 Apr-31 Oct.** 2019

KORENICA *B3* (1.5km NW Urban) *44.76527, 15.68833* **Camping Borje,** Vranovaca bb, 53230 Korenica **(053) 751790;** info@np-plitvicka-jezera.hr; np-plitvicka-jezera.hr/camp-borje

🐕 HRK20 ♿ (htd) ⬜ 🏕 ♿ 💧 ⬛ MSP ☂ Y ℗ ☂ nr 🚐

Exit A1/A6 at Karlovac & take rd 1/E71 S dir Split. Site on R approx 15km after Plitvička Jezera National Park, well sp. 3*, Med, mkd, pt shd, sl, EHU (10A) inc; bbq; sw nr; twin axles; Eng spkn; adv bkg acc; ccard acc; CKE. *"Vg, clean, well-kept, spacious, sl site - levelling poss tricky; gd, modern, immac facs; helpful staff; well run by Plitvicka National Park; excel for visiting the Lakes & waterfalls; free bus runs to park at 1030 and returns at 1730; excel; mountain views."* **HRK 250, 1 Apr-15 Oct.** 2019

LABIN *A2* (3km SW Rural) *45.08179, 14.10167* **Mini Camping Romantik,** HR-52220 Labin, Kapelica 47b **(911) 396423;** mario.braticic@pu.t-com.hr

🐕 ♿ ⬜ 🏕 ♿ 💧 🦋 ☂ 🚐 🏊

Fr Labin on A21/E751, take 5103 twds Koramomacno for 2km. Site sp on this rd. Turn L into sm lane. Foll sp. 3*, Sm, hdstg, mkd, unshd, EHU (10A); bbq; cooking facs; 10% statics; Eng spkn; adv bkg rec; games area. *"Sm family site; 4 mkd and 4 unmkd pitches; v friendly, helpful, lovely family run site; 2km walk to old Labin."* **HRK 164, 24 Apr-15 Oct.** 2016

CROATIA

MOLUNAT *D4* (0.5km N Coastal) *42.45298, 18.4276*
Autokamp Monika, Molunat 28, 20219 Molunat
(020) 794557; info@camp-monika.hr

12 ⌂ HRK8 ♦♦♦ wc ⊟ ↗ MP 🦋 ♀ ♈ ⊕ ⛽ ♨ sand adj

Site well sp in Molunat off Adriatic Highway E65.
Sm, pt shd, terr, EHU (6A) HRK20; bbq; bus; Eng spkn.
*"Gd site close to Montenegro border & in quiet cove;
sea view fr all pitches; owner's wine & olive oil for sale;
beautiful views, v quiet LS; v friendly & helpful owner;
highly rec."* **HRK 135** **2019**

OMIS *C4* (1.5km W Coastal) *43.44040, 16.67960*
Autocamp Galeb, Vukovarska bb, 21310 Omiš **(021)
864430; camping@galeb.hr; www.camp.galeb.hr**

12 ⌂ HRK33 ♦♦♦ wc ⚓ ♨ ⚐ ⊟ ↗ MP ♀ ♈ ⊕ ⛽ 🔥 nr ⚠ ♨
♨ sand

Site sp on rd 2/E65 fr Split to Dubrovnik.
3*, Lge, mkd, pt shd, serviced pitches; EHU (16A) inc;
gas; bbq (elec, gas); red long stay; 50% statics; bus;
ccard acc; bike hire; games area; tennis; white water
rafting; watersports; CKE. *"Excel, well-maintained site
in gd position; private bthrms avail; extra for waterside
pitch; clean san facs; suitable young children; easy walk
or water taxi to town; v friendly staff; excel new rest,
with set breakfast."* **HRK 281, X02.** **2018**

OREBIC *C4* (2.6km ENE Coastal) *42.982485,
17.205609* **Camping Lavanda,** Dubravica bb, HR
20250 Orebič **(385) 20454484; info@lavanda-
camping.com; www.lavanda-camping.com**

⌂ ♦♦♦ wc ⚓ ♨ ⚐ ↗ MP 🦋 ♀ ♈ ⊕ ⛽ ⚠ 🔥 ♨

On main rd 1km bef Orebic app fr Trpanj.
4*, Med, hdstg, mkd, pt shd, terr, EHU (16A); bbq; TV;
5% statics; phone; bus adj; Eng spkn; adv bkg acc;
sauna; CKE. *"Brand new site (2018); excel san facs;
dog shwr; ATM; beach for dogs; ferry to island avail;
great views fr almost every pitch; supmkt 500m; petrol
200m; excel."* **HRK 177, 15 Apr-31 Oct.** **2018**

POREC *A2* (10km N Coastal) *45.29728, 13.59425*
Camping Lanterna, Lanterna 1, 52465 Tar **(052) 404
500; lanterna@valamar.com; www.camping-
adriatic.com/camp-lanterna**

⌂ HRK 55 ♦♦♦ wc ⚓ ♨ ⚐ ⊟ ↗ MP ♀ ♈ ⊕ ⛽ ⚠ ♨ ♨ ⛵ ⛴
♨ shgl adj

**Site sp 5km S of Novigrad (Istria) & N of Poreč on
Umag-Vrsar coast rd.** 4*, V lge, hdstg, mkd, hdg,
pt shd, pt sl, terr, EHU (10A); gas; bbq; 10% statics;
phone; adv bkg req; ccard acc; bike hire; watersports;
games area; boat launch; tennis; CKE. *"V busy,
well-run site; excel san facs & leisure facs; 2 hydromassage pools; noise fr ships loading across bay; bkg
fee; although many san facs they may be a long walk;
variety of shops; gd sightseeing; extra for seaside/hdg
pitch; vg."* **HRK 355, 12 Apr-10 Oct, X10.** **2019**

POREC *A2* (8km NW Coastal) *45.25680, 13.58350*
Naturist-Center Ulika (Naturist), 52440 Poreč (Istra)
**(052) 436325; reservations@plavalaguna.hr;
www.lagunaporec.com**

⌂ HRK48 ♦♦♦ ⚓ ♨ ⚐ ⊟ ↗ 🦋 ♀ ♈ ⊕ ⛽ ♨ ⚠ 🔥 ♨ shgl

Site sp on rd fr Poreč to Tar & Novigrad. 4*, V lge,
shd, pt sl, EHU (6A) HRK23; red long stay; 9% statics;
adv bkg acc; ccard acc; watersports; tennis. *"Excel
site; picturesque shore; vg facs; poss far fr some
pitches; lge site, bike useful for getting around."*
HRK 287, 8 Apr-1 Oct. **2017**

PRIMOSTEN *B4* (2km N Coastal) *43.60646, 15.92085*
Auto Kamp Adriatic, Huljerat BB, 22202 Primošten
**(022) 571223; camp-adriatiq@adriatiq.com;
www.autocamp-adriatiq.com**

⌂ HRK32 ♦♦♦ wc ⚓ ♨ ⚐ ⊟ ↗ MP 🦋 ♀ ♈ ⊕ ⛽ 🔥 ♨ ⚠ ♨ shgl adj

Off Adriatic Highway, rd 8/E65, sp. 3*, V lge, hdstg,
unshd, pt sl, terr, EHU (16A) inc; gas; Eng spkn;
watersports; games area; tennis; boat hire; CKE. *"Gd
sea views; excel san facs; diving cent; some pitches
poss diff to get onto; beautiful views fr beach."*
HRK 190, 7 Apr-31 Oct. **2016**

PULA *A3* (10km S Coastal) *44.82393, 13.85069*
Camping Indije, Indije 96, 52203, Banjole, Pula **052
573066; info@arenaturist.hr; arenacamps.com**

⌂ €4 ♦♦♦ wc ⚓ ♨ ⚐ ⊟ ↗ MP ♀ ♈ ⊕ ⛽ ⚠ 🔥 ♨

**Fr Pula ring rd, drive twd Premantura. At Banjole,
exit rndbt 1st R and foll site sp.** 2*, Lge, mkd, pt shd,
pt sl, terr, EHU (10A); bbq; red long stay; twin axles;
TV; 20% statics; phone; Eng spkn; adv bkg acc; games
area; bike hire; CKE. *"Watersports/diving; mkd walks &
cycle tracks; vg site."* **HRK 222, 21 Apr-25 Sep.** **2016**

PULA *A3* (7km S Coastal) *44.82290, 13.85080*
Camping Peškera, Indije 73 52100 Banjole/Pula (Istra)
**052 573209; info@camp-peskera.com; www.camp-
peskera.com**

⌂ HRK22 ♦♦♦ wc ⚓ ♨ ↗ MP 🦋 ♀ ♈ ⊕ nr ⛽ ♨ shgl adj

**Fr N take A9 to Pula. Cont on m'way twd
Premantura. Exit at Banjole, cont twd Indije.
Campsite is 100m after Indije.** 3*, Sm, pt shd, pt sl,
EHU; bus 0.5km; Eng spkn; adv bkg acc; ccard acc; CCI.
*"Beautiful situation; helpful & friendly owners; gd clean
san facs; vg."* **HRK 276, 1 Apr-31 Oct.** **2019**

PULA *A3* (8km S Rural) *44.82472, 13.85885*
Camping Diana, Castagnes b b, 52100 Banjole
**(385) 99 293 1963 or (385) 99 738 0313; kristijan.
modrusan@gmail.com; www.camp-diana.com**

♦♦♦ wc ↗ 🦋 ♀ ♈ ⊕ ♨ nr ⚠ ⛴ ♨

**Fr Pula ring rd foll sp Premantura & Camping Indije.
Site 1km bef Cmp Indije.** 3*, Sm, pt shd, pt sl, EHU
(16A) inc; adv bkg acc; tennis; games area. *"Pleasant
site in garden setting; gd range of facs; immac san facs;
welcoming family owners; narr ent poss diff for lge
o'fits."* **HRK 254, 15 May-22 Sep.** **2016**

CROATIA

PULA *A3* (9km S Coastal) *44.82012, 13.90252*
Autocamp Pomer, Pomer bb, 52100 Pula **052 573746;**
acpomer@arenaturist.hr; www.arenacamps.com

🏕 HRK23 ♦♦ ⓦ ♨ ⅃ 🚽 ∥ 🦋 ⓣ ① 🍴 🐟 ⚠ ✎ 🌲 shgl adj

**Fr N on A9 to Pula, take exit to Pula. At bottom
of hill turn L after filling stn & foll dir Medulin/
Premantura. In Premantura turn L by Consum
supmkt & foll sp to Pomer & site.** Med, mkd, shd, terr,
EHU (16A) HRK21 (long lead poss req); bbq;
10% statics; phone; Eng spkn; adv bkg acc;
watersports; fishing; games area; CKE. *"Clean san facs
poss stretched high ssn; friendly owner; quiet, relaxing
site."* **HRK 127, 21 Apr-15 Oct.** **2016**

> ## "There aren't many sites open at this time of year"
>
> If you're travelling outside peak season
> remember to call ahead to check site opening
> dates – even if the entry says 'open all year'.

RAKOVICA *B3* (7km SW Rural) *44.95020, 15.64160*
Camp Korana, Plitvička Jezera, 47246 Drežnik
Grad **(053) 751888;** autokamp.korana@np-
plitvicka-jezera.hr; www.np-plitvicka-jezera.hr

🏕 HRK23 ♦♦ ⓦ ♨ 🚽 ∥ 🔲 ⓣ ⅃ ① 🍴 🐟

**On A1/E59 2km S of Grabovac, site on L. Site is 5km
N of main ent to Plitvička Nat Park, sp.** Lge, hdstg,
pt shd, pt sl, EHU (16A) inc (poss long lead req); own
san req; bbq; 10% statics; Eng spkn; ccard acc; CKE.
*"Lovely site, v busy; poss long way fr facs; gd new san
facs but inadequate for size of site; efficient, friendly
site staff; poss muddy in wet; bus to National Park
(6km) high ssn; gd rest."* **HRK 232, 1 Apr-31 Oct.**
2018

RIZVANUSA *B3* (10km W Rural) *44.49580, 15.29165*
Eco Camp Rizvan City, Rizvanuša 1, 53000 Gospić
053 57 33 33; info@adria-velebitica.hr; www.camp-
rizvancity.com

🏕 ♦♦ ⓦ ♨ ⅃ ♿ 🔲 ∥ 🔲 🦋 ⓣ ⚠

**Fr A1 take exit 12 (Gospic). Head 10km E twd
Karlobag on highway 25. Turn L off main rd into Vill
Rizvanusa. Camp 500m.** Sm, pt shd, EHU (16A); bbq;
twin axles; Eng spkn; adv bkg acc; games area. *"Walks,
high rope course; quad & jeep safari; archery; paintball;
zip line; wall climbing; giant swing; bike trails; vg."*
HRK 150, 1 Mar-1 Nov. **2019**

ROVINJ *A2* (5km N Coastal) *45.10444, 13.62527*
Camping Valdaliso, Monsena b.b, 52210 Rovinj
(052) 805505; ac-valdaliso@maistra.hr;
www.campingrovinjvrsar.com

♦♦ (htd) ⓦ ♨ ♨ ♿ 🔲 ∥ 🔲 🦋 ⓣ ⅃ ① 🍴 🐟 ⚠ ✎ 🌲 shgl adj

**N fr Rovinj dir Valalta for 2km, turn W to coast,
site sp.** 3*, Lge, hdg, hdstg, mkd, pt shd, pt sl, EHU
(10A) inc; gas; bbq; TV (pitch); 10% statics; phone;
bus; Eng spkn; adv bkg acc; ccard acc; waterslide; bike
hire; games area; tennis; games rm; CKE. *"Pretty site
in olive trees; use of all amenities in hotel adj; excel
modern san facs; poss waterlogged after heavy rain;
excel; water taxi; facs stretched if site full; pitches
uneven; closing in Sep 2015 for redevelopment."*
HRK 288, 12 Apr-26 Sep. **2015**

ROVINJ *A2* (7km N Coastal) *45.12287, 13.62970*
Campsite Valalta Naturist (Naturist), Cesta Za
Valaltu-Lim 7, 52210 Rovinj (Istra) **052 804800;**
valalta@valalta.hr; www.valalta.hr

♦♦ ⓦ ♨ ♨ ♿ 🔲 ∥ 🔲 🦋 ⓣ ⅃ ① 🍴 🐟 ⚠ ✎ 🏊 🚿 🌲

7km NW fr Rovinj. Foll signs to Valalta.
5*, V lge, hdg, mkd, hdstg, pt shd, EHU (16A); bbq;
twin axles; TV; phone; Eng spkn; adv bkg acc; games
area; games rm; waterslide; bike hire. *"Excel site."*
HRK 450, 1 May-1 Oct. **2019**

ROVINJ *A2* (0.7km NW Coastal) *45.09472, 13.64527*
Autocamp Porton Biondi, Aleja Porton Biondi 1,
52210 Rovinj **(052) 813557;** portonbiondi@web.de;
www.portonbiondirovinj.com

🏕 HRK24 ♦♦ ♨ ♿ ∥ 🦋 ① 🍴 🐟 nr ✎ 🌲 shgl nrby

Site sp on ent Rovinj. 3*, Lge, shd, pt sl, terr, EHU inc;
red long stay; adv bkg acc; ccard acc; watersports;
CKE. *"Gd site within walking dist Rovinj old town;
beautiful views; new san facs; sm pitches not
suitable lge o'fits & care needed when ent site;
excel rest; 2nd & subsequent nights at red rate."*
HRK 207, 15 Mar-31 Oct. **2018**

ROVINJ *A2* (5km NW Coastal) *45.10909, 13.61974*
Camping Amarin, Monsena bb, 52210 Rovinj
(052) 802000; ac-amarin@maistra.hr; www.camping
rovinjvrsar.com

🏕 HRK47 ♦♦ ⓦ ♨ ♿ ∥ 🔲 🦋 ⓣ ⅃ ① 🍴 🐟 ⚠ ✎
🏊 (htd) 🚿 🌲 shgl adj

Fr town N in dir Valalta, turn L & foll site sp.
3*, V lge, mkd, pt shd, pt sl, EHU (10A) inc; TV;
30% statics; phone; Eng spkn; adv bkg acc; ccard acc;
sports facs; tennis; bike hire; waterslide; CKE. *"Excel
site; clean, well-maintained san facs & pool; gd entmnt;
views of town & islands; lovely situation in pine & olive
trees; water taxi to town; some pitches obstructed by
trees & uneven; wifi hotspots but free."*
HRK 302, 20 Apr-30 Sep. **2018**

SELCE *A2* (1.3km SE Coastal) *45.15361, 14.72488*
Autocamp Selce, Jasenová 19, 51266 Selce **(051)**
764038; autokampselce@jadran-crikvenica.hr;
www.jadran-crikvenica.hr

HRK17 shgl adj

Thro Selce town cent, site is 500m SE of town, sp.
2*, Lge, hdstg, pt shd, pt sl, terr, EHU (10A) HRK27;
red long stay; TV; phone; ccard acc; CKE. *"Wooded
site; seaside location; helpful staff; long stay; blocks &
wedges ess; san facs run down & neglected; long lead
rec; door security."* **HRK 247, 1 Apr-15 Oct.   2019**

SENJ *A3* (6km NW Coastal) *45.04403, 14.87817*
Autocamp Sibinj, Sibinj 9, 51252 Klenovica **(051)**
796916; milieijko.tomijanovic@ri.hinet.hr

shgl adj

Fr Novi Vinodolski, take rd S. In approx 12km
site sp. 2*, Med, pt shd, sl, terr, EHU (10A). *"Well-
run site; clean facs but in need of modernising;
magnificent views; poss open all yr; noisy rd; NH only."*
HRK 152, 1 May-31 Oct.   2016

SIBENIK *B3* (10km NE Rural) *43.80063, 15.94210*
Camp Krka, Skocici 21, 22221 Lozovac **(022)** 778495;
goran.skocic@si.t-com.hr; www.camp-krka.hr

nr

Exit A1 at junc 22 Šibenik, turn E at T-junc, thro
tunnel & site in approx 4km. Fr main coast rd at
Sibenik turn N onto rte 33 twd Drniš. After 15km
turn L dir Skradin, site sp on L. 3*, Med, hdstg, pt shd,
EHU (16A) HRK23 (poss rev pol, check earth);
10% statics; Eng spkn; CKE. *"Pleasant, basic site in
orchard; friendly owner; B&B; gd modern san facs; conv
Krka National Park & Krka gorge; gd; clean new shwr/
wc facs (2014); rest, cheap basic food."*
HRK 151, 1 Apr-30 Oct.   2019

SIBENIK *B3* (4km S Coastal) *43.69925, 15.87942*
Camping Solaris, Hotelsko Naselje Solaris, 22000
Šibenik **(022)** 364000; info@solaris.hr;
www.solaris.hr

(htd) nr

Sp fr E65 Zadar-Split rd, adj hotel complex.
4*, V lge, hdg, mkd, pt shd, serviced pitches; EHU
(6A) inc; bbq; red long stay; TV; bus; ccard acc; bike
hire; waterslide; tennis; sauna; watersports; CKE.
*"Well-situated in olive & pine trees; mv service pnt
nr; some pitches adj marina; excel, modern san facs."*
HRK 225, 15 Apr-31 Oct.   2019

See advertisement

SPLIT *B4* (8km E Coastal) *43.50451, 16.52598*
Camping Stobreč-Split, Sv Lovre 6, 21311 Stobreč
(021) 325426; camping.split@gmail.com;
www.campingsplit.com

12 HRK45 sand

Fr N foll E65 & m'way thro Split to sp Stobreč. Site
sp R off E65 at traff lts in Stobreč. 4*, Lge, hdstg,
mkd, shd, pt sl, EHU (16A) inc (long lead poss req); bus
to Split; Eng spkn; games area. *"Superb, well-run site
in lovely setting with views; helpful, welcoming staff;
gd facs; own sandy beach; public footpath thro site; rec
arr early to secure pitch; gd value for money; highly rec;
Diocletian's Palace worth a visit; excel; wellness ctr -
pool, sauna, gym."* **HRK 278   2017**

TUHELJSKE TOPLICE *B2* (0km S Urban) *46.06583,
15.78513* **Camping Terme Tuhelj,** Ljudevita Gaja 4,
49215 Tuhelj **(049)** 203000; info@terme-tuhelj.hr;
www.terme-tuhelj.hr

HKR25 (htd)

N fr Zagreb on A2 for approx 24km, exit junc 5
Zabok & foll rds 24/301/205 to sp Tuheljske Toplice.
Check in at Hotel Toplice. Sm, pt shd, EHU (6A)
HRK25; TV; phone; bus; Eng spkn; adv bkg acc; games
area; games rm; waterslide. *"Gd, conv Zagreb & gd
alt to Zagreb site; thermal spa adj."*
HRK 210, 1 Apr-31 Oct.   2016

UMAG *A2* (6km S Coastal) *45.39271, 13.54193*
Autocamp Finida, Križine br 55A, 52470 Umag **(052)**
756296; camp.finida@instraturist.hr; www.istra
camping.com

🏕 HRK25 ♥♥ [wc] ⛺ ♨ 🔵 ☁ ✎ [MSP] 🦋 ♈ 🍴 ⑪ 🍴 ♨ 🚲 ⚠ ⤴ shgl adj

Site clearly sp. 4*, Lge, mkd, pt shd, pt sl, EHU
(10A) inc; red long stay; TV; 50% statics; phone;
bus; Eng spkn; adv bkg acc; ccard acc; bike hire;
CKE. "*Gd base for touring Istria; gd, clean, modern
facs; lovely site amongst oak trees; friendly staff.*"
HRK 125, 23 Apr-30 Sep. 2016

ZADAR *B3* (3.5km N Coastal) *44.13408, 15.21115*
Falkensteiner Camping Zadar (formerly Autocamp
Borik), Majstora Radovana 7, 23000 Zadar **(023)**
206 555 602; reservations.campingzadar@
falkensteiner.com; www.falkensteiner.com

♥♥ [wc] ⛺ 🔵 ✎ [MSP] 🍴 ⑪ 🍴 ♨ ⚠ ⤴ shgl

Exit A2 at Zadar 1/West, cont for approx.19 km.
In Zadar, turn R at 2nd x-rds with traff lts and
take the bypass (dir Nin, Vir). Cont across 2 x-rds
(dir Puntamika). In 70m turn R to Falkensteiner
Resort Borik. 3*, V lge, shd, EHU (10A) inc; own san
req; phone; bus 450m; Eng spkn; ccard acc; tennis;
watersports; CKE. "*Pt of resort complex of 6 hotels;
facs poor & some cold water only; poor security; gd
sw beach; gd rests nrby; site run down; NH only.*"
HRK 229, 1 May-30 Sep. 2016

"That's changed – Should I let the Club know?"

If you find something on site that's different
from the site entry, fill in a report and let us
know. See camc.com/europereport.

ZAGREB *B2* (12km SW Urban) *45.77389, 15.87778*
Camping Motel Plitvice, Lučko, 10090 Zagreb **(01)**
6530444; motel@motel-plitvice.hr; www.motel-
plitvice.hr

♥♥ (htd) [wc] ⛺ 🔵 ✎ 🍴 ⑪ 🍴 ♨

Site at motel attached to Plitvice services on A3/
E70. Access only fr m'way travelling fr N, otherwise
long m'way detour fr S. Lge, pt shd, EHU (16A)
inc; TV; phone; bus to town fr site; ccard acc; tennis;
CKE. "*Ask at motel recep (excel Eng) for best way
back fr city &/or details minibus to city; Zagreb well
worth a visit; site shabby but facs clean & adequate
- stretched when site full & in need of update.*"
HRK 168, 1 May-30 Sep. 2016

ZAGREB *B2* (16km W Rural) *45.80217, 15.82696*
Camp Zagreb, Jezerska 6, 10437 Rakitje
(01) 3324567; info@campzagreb.com; www.camp
zagreb.com

[12] 🐕 ♥♥ ⛺ ♨ 🔵 ☁ ✎ [MSP] 🦋 ♈ 🍴 ⑪ 🍴 ⚠

Exit A3 J2 sp Bestovje. Turn R and cont for approx
3km. At rndabt before x-ing over m'way turn R. Cont
for 1km. Site on L. 4*, Med, hdg, mkd, pt shd, EHU
(16A); bbq; sw; twin axles; 5% statics; train 1km; Eng
spkn; adv bkg acc; games rm; bike hire; CKE. "*Excel
site; lake adj; sauna & massage; kayak & bike hire; horse
trail; public trans 1.5km; free shuttle to rlw stn into city
ctr.*" **HRK 256** 2018

ZAOSTROG *C4* (0.5km SE Coastal) *43.13925,
17.28047* **Camp Viter,** Obala A.K. Miosica 1, 21334
Zaostrog (Dalmatija) **098 704018; info@camp-viter.**
com; www.camp-viter.com

🏕 HRK25 ♥♥ [wc] ⛺ ✎ [MSP] 🦋 ♈ 🍴 nr ⑪ nr 🍴 nr ⤴

Foll Camp Viter signs 600m on R after Zaostrog sp.
Sm, hdstg, pt shd, EHU (16A) HRK25; bbq; twin axles;
Eng spkn; adv bkg acc; CCI. "*Very helpful, friendly
owners; vg.*" **HRK 237, 1 Apr-31 Oct.** 2019

ZATON *B3* (1.5km N Coastal) *44.23434, 15.16605*
Camping Zaton Holiday Resort, Široka ulica bb,
23232 Zaton **023 280215; camping@zaton.hr;**
www.zaton.hr

🏕 HRK65 ♥♥ (htd) [wc] ⛺ 🔵 ☁ ✎ [MSP] 🦋 ♈ 🍴 ⑪ 🍴 ♨ ⚠ ✏ 🚿 🛥 ⤴ sand adj

Site 16km NW of Zadar on Nin rd. Pt of Zaton
holiday vill. Wel sp. 3*, V lge, pt shd, EHU (10A) inc;
gas; 15% statics; phone; adv bkg acc; ccard acc; games
area; boat hire; watersports; tennis; CKE. "*Excel,
well-run, busy site; own beach; excel, modern san facs;
cent of site is 'vill' with gd value shops & rests; gd for
all ages; nr ancient sm town of Nin, in walking dist;
conv National Parks; v expensive outside ACSI discount
period but has first class facs and nrby town well worth
a visit; Croatia's best campsite; superbly laid out &
equipped.*" **HRK 480, 1 May-30 Sep.** 2019

BRAC ISLAND

BOL *C4* (0.5km W Urban/Coastal) *43.26373, 16.64799*
Kamp Kito (formerly Konobo Kito), Braćke Ceste bb,
21420 Bol **(021) 635551 or 635091; info@camping-**
brac.com; www.camping-brac.com

[12] 🐕 ♥♥ [wc] ⛺ ✎ 🦋 ⑪ ⤴ 500m

Take ferry fr Makarska to Brač & take rd 113/115 to
Bol (37km). On o'skrts do not turn L into town but
cont twd Zlatni Rat. Pass Studenac sup'mkt on R,
site on L. Sm, pt shd, EHU (16A) HRK20; gas; bbq; TV;
10% statics; Eng spkn; adv bkg acc. "*Excel for beaches
& boating; gd local food in rest; vg, friendly, family-run
site; clean, well-equipped; well worth effort to get
there.*" **HRK 141** 2016

CRES ISLAND

MARTINSCICA *A3* (1km NW Coastal) *44.82108, 14.34298* **Camping Slatina,** 51556 Martinščica **(051) 574127; info@camp-slatina.com; www.camp-slatina.com**

🛗 HRK23 ⛺ ⓦ ♨ ⚓ ♿ 🖭 ∥ MSP 🦋 ⍾ 🍴 ⑪ 🛒 🏪 ⚒ 🛁 shgl adj

Fr Cres S on main rd sp Mali Lošinj for 17km. Turn R sp Martinščica, site in 8km at end of rd. 4*, V lge, hdg, hdstg, shd, terr, EHU (10A) inc (long lead req); 20% statics; phone; Eng spkn; adv bkg acc; ccard acc; boat launch. *"Site on steep slope; newest san facs superb; beautiful island; dog & car washing facs; vg supmkt; ATM on site."* **HRK 234, 19 Mar-10 Oct.**

2016

KRK ISLAND

BASKA *A3* (1.4km SW Coastal) *44.965613, 14.747772* **Baška Beach Camping Resort,** Put Zablaca 40, 51523 Baska 552 465010; camping@valamar.com; www.camping-adriatic.com

🛗 🐕 ⛺ ♨ ♿ 🖭 ∥ MSP 🦋 ⍾ ⑪ 🛒 🏪 ⚒ 🛶 (htd) 🛁

Drive over bdge to islnd of KRK (no chge on Sun) and take main rd 103 to Krk, then on to the southern tip of islnd and Baska. Site sp on ent town. 4*, Lge, mkd, pt shd, EHU (16A) inc; bbq; twin axles; TV; 20% statics; phone; bus adj; Eng spkn; adv bkg acc; sauna; sports area; bike hire; CKE. *"Excellent, new san facs (2018); kids club; rest adj; perfect experience creator; free use of pool & gym at Baska Wellness Ctr; excel site."* **HRK 396, 19 Apr-6 Oct.** **2018**

KRK *A3* (4km SE Coastal) *45.01638, 14.62833* **Autocamp Pila,** Šetalište Ivana Brusića 2, 51521 Punat **(051) 854020; pila@hoteli-punat.hr; www.hoteli-punat.hr**

🛗 HRK32 ⛺ ⓦ ♨ ⚓ ♿ 🖭 ∥ MSP 🦋 ⍾ ⑪ 🛒 🛒nr 🏪 ⚒ 🛁 adj

Take coast rd, rte 2 twd Split. At Kraljevica, turn R onto rd 103 over Krk toll bdge. Foll sp for Krk, Punat. Site sp at T-junc after Punat Marina & vill. 3*, Lge, pt shd, serviced pitches; EHU (10-16A) inc; cooking facs; TV; 80% statics; ccard acc; fishing; watersports; CKE. *"Well-run, big site; clean facs; gd for families with sm children; boat hire; boat trips; sm picturesque vill; lots to do; poss cr."* **HRK 347, 12 Apr-18 Oct.** **2019**

NJIVICE *A2* (0.4km N Coastal) *45.16971, 14.54701* **Kamp Njivice,** 51512 Njivice **(051) 846168; reservation@kampnjivice.hr; www.kampnjivice.com**

🛗 HRK24.50 ⛺ ⓦ ♨ ⚓ ♿ 🖭 ∥ MSP 🦋 ⍾ 🍴 ⑪ 🛒 ⚒ shgl adj

8km S of Krk Bdge on rd 102 turn R to Njivice. Site not well sp but foll sp to hotel area N of town cent. 2*, V lge, shd, EHU (6-10A) HRK28; 60% statics; phone; bus; Eng spkn; ccard acc; CKE. *"Less cr than other Krk sites; gd facs."* **HRK 173, 1 May-30 Sep.**

2016

LOSINJ ISLAND

MALI LOSINJ *A3* (4km NW Coastal) *44.55555, 14.44166* **Camping Village Poljana,** Privlaka 19, 51550 Mali Lošinj **(051) 231726 or (0365) 520682; www.campingpoljana.com**

🛗 HRK61 ⛺ ⓦ ♨ ⚓ ♿ 🖭 ∥ MSP 🦋 ⍾ 🍴 ⑪ 🛒 🏪 ⚒ shgl

On main island rd 1km bef vill of Lošinj, sp. Two ferries a day fr Rijeka take car & c'van on 2hr trip to island. 3*, V lge, shd, pt sl, terr, EHU (6-16A) inc; gas; 50% statics; phone; adv bkg acc; ccard acc; bike hire; tennis; games area; boat hire; watersports; CKE. *"Site in pine forest; private washrms avail; sw with dolphins nrby; sep naturist beach."* **HRK 312, 24 Mar-31 Oct.**

2016

RAB ISLAND

LOPAR *A3* (3km E Coastal) *44.82345, 14.73735* **Hotel Village San Marino,** 51281 Lopar **(051) 775133; ac-sanmarino@imperial.hr; www.rab-camping.com**

🛗 HRK29 ⛺ ⓦ ♨ ⚓ ♿ 🖭 ∥ MSP 🍴 ⑪ 🛒 🏪 ⚒ 🛁 sand adj

Fr Rab town N to Lopar, sp ferry. At x-rds turn R sp San Marino, site sp. 3*, V lge, mkd, hdstg, shd, terr, EHU (16A) inc; TV; 10% statics; phone; bus; Eng spkn; adv bkg acc; ccard acc; games area; tennis; watersports; CKE. *"Superb, family site on delightful island; pitches on sandy soil in pine woods."* **HRK 187, 1 Apr-30 Sep.**

2016

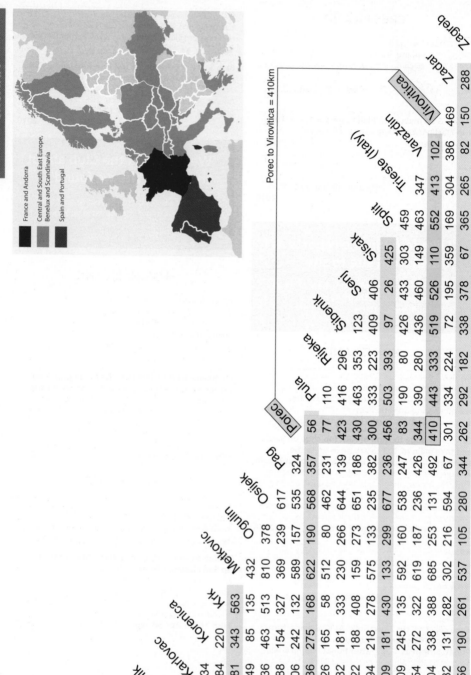

Legend:
- France and Andorra
- Central and South East Europe, Benelux and Scandinavia
- Spain and Portugal

Porec to Virovitica = 410km

	Dubrovnik	Karlovac	Korenica	Krk	Metković	Ogulin	Osijek	Pag	Porec	Pula	Rijeka	Šibenik	Senj	Sisak	Split	Trieste (Italy)	Varaždin	Virovitica	Zadar
Karlovac	526																		
Korenica	439	134																	
Krk	659	184	220																
Metković	96	481	343	563															
Ogulin	524	49	85	135	432														
Osijek	902	336	463	513	810	378													
Pag	465	288	154	327	369	239	617												
Porec	678	206	242	132	589	157	535	324											
Pula	711	236	275	168	622	190	568	357	56										
Rijeka	601	126	165	58	512	80	462	231	77	110									
Šibenik	305	282	181	333	230	266	644	139	423	416	296								
Senj	251	322	188	408	159	273	651	186	430	463	353	123							
Sisak	667	94	218	278	575	133	235	382	300	333	223	409	406						
Split	225	309	181	430	133	299	677	236	456	503	393	97	26	425					
Trieste (Italy)	684	209	245	135	592	160	538	247	83	190	80	426	433	303	459				
Varaždin	670	154	272	322	619	187	236	426	344	390	280	436	460	149	463	347			
Virovitica	777	204	338	388	685	253	131	492	410	443	333	519	526	110	552	413	102		
Zadar	377	232	131	282	302	216	594	67	301	334	224	72	195	359	169	304	386	469	
Zagreb	572	56	190	261	537	105	280	344	262	292	182	338	378	67	365	265	82	150	288

Legend (Roads):
- Motorways
- Major roads
- Main roads

Legend (Sites):
- All year site(s)
- Seasonal site(s)
- No sites listed
- 200m +
- 0–200m

AUSTRIA

SLOVAKIA

HUNGARY

SLOVENIA

SERBIA

BOSNIA-HERZEGOVINA

MONTENEGRO

ITALY

ADRIATIC SEA

WIEN
BRATISLAVA
BUDAPEST
Graz
Maribor
Nagykanizsa
LJUBLJANA
Tuheljske Toplice
VARAŽDIN
Pécs
Novo Mesto
ZAGREB
VIROVITICA
Sombor
Trieste
KARLOVAC
SISAK
OSIJEK
Umag
Opatija
POREČ
Vrsar
Rovinj
OGULIN
Labin
Njivice
Fažana
Rabac
KRK
SENJ
PULA
Cres
Beska
Rakovica
Martinščica
Lopar
KORENICA
Bihać
Mali Lošinj
Banja Luka
PAG
Rizvanusa
Stangrad
Paklenica
Zaton
ZADAR
Novigrad
(Dalmatia)
Biograd na Moru
SARAJEVO
ŠIBENIK
Primošten
Trogir
SPLIT
Omiš
BRAČ
Bol
Mostar
Hvar
HVAR
Zaostrog
Orebić
METKOVIĆ
KORČULA
DUBROVNIK
PODGORICA
Molunat

CRES
KRK
RAB
LOŠINJ
PAG
MURTER

A2
A4
A3
A1/A6
A6
A3
A5
A3
A1
A7
A8
A9

0   50   100   150 kms
0   50   100 mls

© Collins Bartholomew Ltd.2020

Czech Republic

Prague

Highlights

Lying in the heart of Europe, the Czech Republic is renowned for its ornate castles, fantastically preserved medieval buildings, and numerous other cultural sights.

Considered to be one of the most beautiful cities in the world, the capital, Prague, is a wonderful mix of traditional and modern with treasures old and new waiting to be discovered around every corner.

Traditions are important in the Czech Republic, one of which takes places on the 30th of April – Walpurgis Night. Known as pálení čarodějnic (the burning of the witches), this is a night of bonfires and celebrations throughout the country.

The Czech Republic is the home of Bohemian glass or crystal, which is international renowned for its beauty, quality and craftsmanship. They are immensely popular as gifts and souvenirs and are one of the best known Czech exports.

Major towns and cities

- Prague – home to an impressive castle and old town.
- Brno – filled with gorgeous architecture and historic sights.
- Plzeň – famous worldwide for Pilsner beer, created here in 1842.
- Olomouc – a quaint city of cobbled streets and historic buildings.

Attractions

- Wenceslas Square, Prague – bursting with monuments, restaurants and shops.
- Český Krumlov – the old town is a UNESCO site and the castle houses a theatre.
- Kutná Hora – Founded in the 12th century, this city houses many spectacular churches.
- Hrad Karlšstejn – this imposing gothic castle is one of the most famous in the country.

Find out more

www.czechtourism.com
E: czechtourism@czechtourism.cz
T:0042 (0)22 1580 111

Country Information

Population (approx): 10.6 million

Capital: Prague

Area: 78,864 sq km

Bordered by: Austria, Germany, Poland, Slovakia

Terrain: Diverse landscape with rolling hills and plains in the west (Bohemia) surrounded by low mountains; higher hills and heavily forested mountains in the east (Moravia)

Climate: Temperate continental with warm, showery summers and cold, cloudy, snowy winters

Highest Point: Snezka 1,602m

Language: Czech

Local Time: GMT or BST + 1, i.e. 1 hour ahead of the UK all year

Currency: Czech crown (CZK) £1 = CZK 29.65, CZK 100 = £3.37 (October 2019)

Emergency numbers: Police 158; Fire brigade 150; Ambulance 155 (operators speak English) or 112.

Public Holidays in 2020: Jan 1; Apr 10, 23; May 1, 8 (National Liberation Day); Jul 5, 6; Sep 28 (St Wenceslas), Oct 28 (Independence Day); Nov 17; Dec 24, 25, 26.

School summer holidays are from the beginning of July to the end of August.

Entry Formalities

British and Irish passport holders may visit the Czech Republic for up to three months without a visa. If intending to stay longer, visitors must register with the police.

Due to the current migrant crisis in Europe some countries have temporarily restored their borders. A current list of countries affected is available on the EU website: **ec.europa.eu/ home-affairs/what-we-do/policies/borders- and-visas/schengen/reintroduction-border- control_en**. At the time of going to print the Czech Republic hasn't restored its borders, but neighbouring Austria and Germany have.

Medical Services

For minor ailments first consult staff at a pharmacy (lékárna) who can give advice and are sometimes able to sell drugs normally only available on prescription in the UK. Language may be a problem outside Prague; if you need particular drugs or a repeat prescription, take an empty bottle or remaining pills with you. For more serious matters requiring a visit to a doctor go to a medical centre (poliklinika) or hospital (nemocnice).

British nationals may obtain emergency medical and hospital treatment and prescriptions on presentation of a European Health Insurance Card (EHIC). You may have to make a contribution towards costs. Make sure that the doctor or dentist you see is contracted to the public health insurance service, the CMU (most are), otherwise you will have to pay in full for private treatment and for any prescription medicines and the Czech insurance service will not reimburse you. See www.cmu.cz, email info@cmu.cz for advice on healthcare in the Czech Republic.

In parts of the country where few foreign visitors venture, medical staff may not be aware of the rights conferred on you by an EHIC. If you have difficulties contact the British Embassy in Prague.

Outbreaks of hepatitis A occur sporadically, particularly in the Prague and Central Bohemia areas, and immunisation is advised for long-stay visitors to rural areas and those who plan to travel outside tourist areas. Take particular care with food and water hygiene.

Opening Hours

Banks: Mon-Fri 9am-5pm. Some foreign exchange bureaux in Prague are open 24 hours.

Museums: Tue-Sun 10am-6pm; closed Monday

Post Offices: Mon-Fri 8am-6pm, some open on Saturday morning; main post office in Prague (Jindrisska Street 14) is open 2am-12am

Shops: Mon-Fri 9am-6pm, small shops usually close at lunchtime; Sat 9am-1pm; some food shops open on Sundays

Safety and Security

There is a high incidence of petty theft, particularly in major tourist areas in Prague, and pickpocketing is common at popular tourist attractions. Care should be taken around the main railway station and on public transport particularly routes to and from Prague Castle where pickpockets may operate.

Beware of fake plain-clothes police officers asking to see your foreign currency and passport. If approached, don't get out your passport. You can call 158 or 112 to check if they are genuine officers, or offer to go to the nearest police station or find a uniformed officer. No police officer has the right to check your money or its authenticity.

If your passport, wallet or other items are lost or stolen you should report the incident immediately to the nearest police station and obtain a police report. A police station that is used to dealing with foreign travellers is at Jungmannovo Námìstí 9, Praha 1, 24 hour telephone number 974 851 750; nearest metro: Müstek. Any theft of property must be reported in person to the police within 24 hours in order to obtain a crime number.

The Czech Republic shares with the rest of Europe an underlying threat from terrorism. Attacks could be indiscriminate and against civilian targets, including tourist attractions.

British Embassy

THUNOVSKÁ 14
118 00 PRAGUE 1
Tel: 257402111
www.ukinczechrepublic.fco.gov.uk
Email: ukinczechrepublic@fco.gov.uk

Irish Embassy

VELVYSLANECTVÍ IRSKA
TRŽIŠTĚ 13, 118 00 PRAHA 1
Tel: 257011280
www.embassyofireland.cz
Email: pragueembassy@dfa.ie

Documents

Driving Licence

The Czech Republic authorities require foreign drivers to carry a photocard driving licence. If you still have an old-style driving license you should update it to a photocard before you travel, or obtain an International Driving Permit to accompany your old-style licence. The minimum driving age is 18.

Money

The best place to exchange foreign currency is at banks, where commission rates are generally lower. In Prague some foreign exchange bureaux are open 24 hours. Scottish and Northern Irish bank notes will not be changed. Never exchange money with vendors on the street as notes are often counterfeit.

Credit cards are often accepted in tourist areas. Cash points are widely available but take care using them from a personal security point of view. Many retail outlets accept Euros.

Passport

You must have a valid passport to enter Czech Republic. It is recommended that your passport is valid after your planned departure date in case of an unforeseen emergency, which may prevent you from leaving. British nationals with passports in poor condition have been refused entry so you should ensure that your passport is in an acceptable state.

If you hold a British passport where your nationality is shown as anything other than British Citizen contact the Czech Embassy in London to determine whether you require a visa for entry.

Vehicle(s)

Carry your vehicle registration certificate (V5C), insurance details and MOT certificate (if applicable). If you are not the owner of the vehicle you are advised to carry a letter of authority from the owner permitting you to drive it.

Driving

Accidents

If an accident causes injury or damage in excess of CZK 100,000 it must be reported to the police immediately. You should wait at the scene of the accident until the police arrive and then obtain a police report. If your vehicle is only slightly damaged it is still a good idea to report the accident to the police as they will issue a certificate which will facilitate the exportation of the vehicle.

Alcohol

It is prohibited to drink alcohol before or whilst driving. No degree of alcohol is permitted in the blood and driving under the influence of alcohol is considered a criminal offence. This rule also applies to cyclists and horse riders. Frequent random breath-testing takes places and drivers are likely to be breathalysed after an accident, even a minor one.

Breakdown Service

The motoring organisation ÚAMK provides roadside assistance and towing services 24 hours a day, telephone 1230 or 261104123. Emergency operators speak English. Breakdown assistance is provided for all motorists at a basic cost of approximately CZK 400 for 30 minutes + CZK 24 per kilometre travelled, payable in cash (2015). Extra charges apply at night, at weekends and for towing.

The vehicles used for road assistance are yellow Skodas, bearing the ÚAMK and/or ARC Transistance logos or the words 'Silniční Služba', together with the telephone number of the emergency centre. ÚMAK also uses the services of contracted companies who provide assistance and towing. These vehicles are also marked with the ÚAMK logo and the telephone number of the emergency centre.

Child Restraint System

Children under 1.5m in height must use a suitable child restraint conforming to ECE standard 44/03 or 44/04. If in the front seat, the restraint must be rear facing with any airbag deactivated. If there are no seatbelts fitted children over the age of 3 may travel in the rear of the vehicle without a child restraint.

Fuel

Some petrol stations on main roads, international routes and in main towns are open 24 hours a day. Most accept credit cards.

Diesel pumps are marked 'Nafta'. LPG is called 'Autoplyn' or 'Plyn' and is widely available at many filling stations. A list of these is available from the ÚAMK and a map is available from filling stations, or see www.lpg.cz and click on 'Čerpací stanice'.

Motorways

There are approximately 1240 km of motorways and express roads. New sections of motorways are being built and on some motorways junctions are being renumbered to correspond with kilometre markers.

There is a good network of service areas with petrol stations, restaurants and shops, together with rest areas with picnic facilities. Emergency telephones connected to the motorway police are placed at 2 km intervals.

Emergency corridors are compulsory on motorways and dual carriageways. Drivers must create a corridor at least 3m wide for emergency vehicles whenever congestion occurs. Drivers in the left-hand lane must move as far to the left as possible, and drivers in the central and right-hand lanes move to the right.

Motorway Tolls (vehicles under 3,500kg)

To use motorways and express roads you must purchase a vignette (sticker) which must be displayed on the right hand side of your windscreen. This is available from post offices, ÚAMK branch offices, petrol stations and border posts. Old Vignettes must be removed.

Charges in 2019 are CZK 1,500 for an annual vignette, CZK 440 for one month and CZK 310 for 10 days. For more information please visit www.motorway.cz/stickers.

Motorway Tolls (vehicles over 3,500kg)

Vehicles over 3,500kg will need to purchase an electronic tag to calculate tolls. You can find a full list of distribution points and a toll calculator (tolls vary by time and day of the week) at www.mytocz.com/en.

Parking

Vehicles may only be parked on the right of the road. In a one-way road, parking is also allowed on the left.

Continuous or broken yellow lines indicate parking prohibitions or restrictions. Illegally-parked vehicles may be clamped or towed away.

Prague city centre is divided into parking zones: orange and green zones are limited to two and six hours respectively between 8am and 6pm, and blue zones are for residents only.

Priority

At uncontrolled intersections which are not marked by a priority road sign, priority must be given to vehicles coming from the right. Where there are priority signs, these may easily be missed and care is therefore needed at junctions which, according to recent visitors, may have no road markings.

Trams turning right have priority over traffic moving alongside them on the right. Drivers must slow down and, if necessary, stop to allow buses and trams to merge with normal traffic at the end of a bus lane. On pedestrian crossings pedestrians have right of way, except if the vehicle approaching is a tram.

Roads

Czech drivers are sometimes described as reckless (particularly when overtaking). Speeding is common and the law on the wearing of seat belts is sometimes ignored.

In general roads are in a good condition and well-signposted. Roads are being upgraded and many have new numbers. It is essential, therefore, to have an up-to-date road map or atlas.

Road Signs and Markings

Road signs and markings conform to international standards. Continuous white lines indicate no overtaking, but are often ignored.

The following road signs may be encountered:

Czech	English Translation
Bez poplatků	Free of charge
Chod'te vlevo	Pedestrians must walk on the left
Dálkový provoz	By-pass
Nebezpečí smyku	Danger of skidding
Nemocnice	Hospital
Objízdka	Diversion
Pozor děti	Attention children
Průjezd zakázán	Closed to all vehicles
Rozsvit' světla	Lights needed
Úsek častých nehod	Accident blackspot
Zákaz zastavení	Stopping prohibited

Speed Limits

	Open Road (km/h)	Motorway (km/h)
Car Solo	90	130
Car towing caravan/trailer	80	80
Motorhome under 3500kg	90	130
Motorhome 3500-7500kg	80	80

Motorhomes over 3,500 kg and cars towing a caravan or trailer are restricted to 80 km/h (50 mph) on motorways and main roads and lower limits in urban areas. Speed limits are strictly enforced and drivers exceeding them may be fined on the spot. Police with radar guns are much in evidence.

The use of radar detectors is prohibited and GPS systems which indicate the position of fixed speed cameras must have that function deactivated.

Traffic Lights

A traffic light signal with a green arrow shows that drivers may turn in that direction. If a yellow walking figure accompanies the signal, pedestrians may cross the road and drivers must give them right of way. A green light lit at the same time as a red or yellow light means that drivers may turn in the direction indicated by the arrow, giving way to other traffic and pedestrians.

An illuminated speed signal indicates the speed at which to travel in order to arrive at the next set of traffic lights when they are green.

Traffic Jams

The volume of traffic has increased considerably in recent years, particularly in and around Prague, including its ring road. Traffic jams may also occur on the E50/D1 (Prague-Mirošovice), the E48/R6 (Prague-Kladno), the E50/D5 (Plzeň-Rozvadov) and on the E50/D1 (Prague-Brno).

Traffic may be heavy at border crossings from Germany, Austria and Slovakia, particularly at weekends, resulting in extended waiting times. Petrol is cheaper than in Germany and you may well find queues at petrol stations near the border. Traffic information can be obtained from the ÚAMK Information Centre: tel 261104333, or www.uamk.cz.

Vehicles over 3,500 kg

Vehicles over 3,500 kg are subject to an electronic toll (mýto) and vehicle owners must register with the toll-collection service to obtain an on-board device called a Premid which must be fixed on your windscreen inside the vehicle and for which a deposit is required.

Tolls vary according to, emissions category, weight and distance driven. You must be able to show your vehicle documentation when obtaining the device but if your vehicle registration certificate (V5C) does not give an emissions category, then your vehicle will be classified in category Euro 2 for the purposes of this system. For more information please visit www.premid.cz before you travel.

Violation of Traffic Regulations

The police are authorised to impose and collect on-the-spot fines up to CZK 5,000 and to withdraw a driving licence in the case of a serious offence. An official receipt should be obtained. Efforts are under way to improve enforcement of traffic regulations and a points system has been introduced, together with stricter penalties.

Winter Driving

Winter tyres are compulsory from 1 November to 31 March on all wheels of vehicles up to 3.5 tonnes when there is compacted snow or ice on the road. They are also compulsory whenever the temperature is lower than 4°C and there is a possibility of snow or ice on the road. On roads where there are winter tyres signs (see below) , the regulations apply even if the road surface is free of snow and ice, regardless of the weather.

Sign for winter tyres (if shown with a line through indicates the end of restriction)

Vehicles over 3,500 kg must be fitted with winter tyres on the driving wheels or carry snow chains. A full list of roads where this rule applies can be found on www.uamk.cz.

Essential Equipment

First aid kit

You are required to carry a basic first aid kit in your vehicle.

Lights

Dipped headlights are compulsory at all times, regardless of weather conditions. Bulbs are more likely to fail with constant use and it is recommended that you carry a complete set of spares.

Drivers are required to signal when leaving a roundabout and when overtaking cyclists.

Reflective Jacket/ Waistcoat

If your vehicle has broken down, or in the event of an emergency, you must wear a reflective jacket or waistcoat on all roads, carriageways and motorways when getting out of your vehicle. Passengers who leave the vehicle, for example to assist with a repair, should also wear one. Jackets should, therefore, be kept inside your vehicle, and not in the boot. These must be of an EU standard EN471.

Warning Triangles

You must carry a warning triangle, which must be placed at least 100m behind the vehicle on motorways and highways and 50m behind on other roads. Drivers may use Hazard Warning lights in conjunction with the warning triangle.

Touring

It is not necessary to tip in restaurants but if you have received very good service add 10% to the bill or round it up.

Smoking is not permitted in public places (including public transport) and restaurant owners must provide an area for non-smokers.

A Prague Card offers entrance to over 50 tourist attractions and discounts on excursions and activities. It is available from tourist offices, main metro stations, some travel agents and hotels or order online from www.praguecard.com.

German is the most widely spoken foreign language and a basic understanding is particularly helpful in southern Bohemia. However, many young people speak English.

Camping and Caravanning

Campsites are divided into four categories from 1 to 4 stars. Normally campsites are open from May to mid September, although some campsites stay open all year. They usually close at night between 10pm and 6am.

Campsites are generally good value and in recent years many have upgraded their facilities. Privacy in the showers may be a problem due to a shortage of, or lack of, shower curtains and only a communal dressing area.

Some sites have communal kitchen facilities which enable visitors to make great savings on their own gas supply.

Motorhomes are recommended to carry a very long hose with a variety of tap connectors. Refill the onboard tank whenever possible as few sites have easily accessible mains water.

Casual/wild camping is not permitted and fines are imposed for violation of this law, especially in national parks. It is prohibited to sleep in a caravan or motorhome outside a campsite.

Cycling

There are around 2,500km of cycle tracks, known as Greenways, in tourist areas. A long-distance cycle track links Vienna and Prague and there are many tracks linking the Czech Republic to Austria and Poland. Helmets are compulsory for cyclists under the age of 18.

Electricity and Gas

Current on campsites varies between 6 and 16 amps. Plugs have two round pins. A few campsites have CEE connections but not many. Reversed polarity may be encountered.

You may find that Campingaz 907 cylinders are available from large DIY warehouses.

Public Transport

Prague city centre is very congested, so park outside and use buses, trams or the metro which are efficient and cheap. There are guarded Park and Ride facilities at a number of metro stations around Prague.

Public transport tickets must be purchased before travelling and are available from newspaper stands ('Trafika'), tobacconists, convenience stores and from vending machines at stations. Special tourist tickets are available for one or three days. Tickets must be validated before the start of your journey at the yellow machines at metro stations or on board trams and buses, including before boarding the funicular tram at Petřín. Failure to do so may result in an on-the-spot fine.

Take extra care when in the vicinity of tram tracks and make sure you look both ways. Trams cannot stop quickly nor can they avoid you if you are on the track.

As a pedestrian you may be fined if you attempt to cross the road or cross tram tracks within 50 metres of a designated crossing point or traffic lights. You may also be fined if you cross at a pedestrian crossing if the green pedestrian light is not illuminated.

For reasons of safety and economy use major taxi companies wherever possible. If you telephone to order a taxi these companies are usually able to tell you in advance the type, number and colour of the car allocated to you. If you do pick up a taxi in the street always check the per kilometre price before getting in. The price list must be clearly displayed and the driver must provide a receipt if requested.

BEROUN *B2* (10km NE Rural) *50.0115, 14.1505*
Camping Valek, Chrustenice 155, 267 12
Chrustenice **tel 311 672 147; info@campvalek.cz;**
www.campvalek.cz

🐕 CZK80 ♦♦ 🅆 🛆 🖪 ⚊ 🐾 ➤ ⟂ 🍴 ⓓ 🛒 🏊 /⋀ 🚿

SW fr Prague on E50; take exit 10 twd Loděnice
then N to Chrustenice. Foll sp. Lge, pt shd, EHU
(10A) CZK100; bbq; red long stay; TV; 10% statics;
phone; Eng spkn; adv bkg acc; tennis; CKE. *"Vg
location; money change on site; entmnt (w/end); excel
rest; metro to Prague at Zličín (secure car park adj)."*
CZK 430, 1 May-30 Sep.   2016

BESINY *C1* (0.5km SW Rural) *49.29533, 13.32086*
Eurocamp Běšiny, Běšiny 150, 339 01 Běšiny
**tel 376 375 011; eurocamp@besiny.cz; www.euro
camp.besiny.cz**

12 🐕 ♦♦(htd) 🅆 🛆 🖪 ⚊ 🐾 ➤ 🍴 ⓓ 🛒nr 🏊 ⛵

Fr E53/rd 27 take rd 171 twd Sušice. Site just
outside vill on L. Med, unshd, EHU (6A) inc; bbq;
cooking facs; 50% statics; adv bkg acc; ccard acc;
games area; tennis; CKE. *"Pleasant setting; nrby vill
drab."* **CZK 303**   2016

BRECLAV *D3* (6km NW Rural) *48.78549, 16.82663*
Autocamp Apollo, Charvátská Nová Ves, 691 44
Břeclav **tel 519 340 414; info@atcapollo.cz;**
www.atcapollo.cz

🐕 CZK30 ♦♦ 🅆 🛆 ⚊ ⓓnr 🛒nr

Fr Breclav take Lednice rd. Site is 3km S of Lednice
vill. Lge, pt shd, pt sl, EHU CZK30; sw nr; bus; CKE.
*"Fair sh stay; site in beautiful area; excel cycling &
walking; Lednice Castle worth a visit; poss school
parties."* **CZK 280, 1 May-30 Sep.**   2016

"There aren't many sites open at this time of year"

If you're travelling outside peak season
remember to call ahead to check site opening
dates – even if the entry says 'open all year'.

BRNO *C3* (21km W Rural) *49.21182, 16.40745*
Camping Oáza, Náměstí Viléma Mrštíka 10, 66481
Ostrovačice **tel 606 457 448; info@kempoaza.cz;**
www.kempoaza.cz

♦♦ 🅆 🛆 🖪 ⚊ 🐾 ⓓnr 🛒 /⋀ 🚿

Leave E65/E50 Prague-Brno at junc 178 for
Ostrovačice. At T-junc in vill turn L, site on R 100m.
Sm, pt shd, pt sl, EHU (10A) inc; CKE. *"Excel CL-type
site, v clean facs; friendly, helpful lady owner; narr
uneven ent poss diff lge o'fits; poss unrel opening
dates; super."* **CZK 365, 1 Apr-31 Oct.**   2019

BUDISOV NAD BUDISOVKOU *B4* (0.8km SE Urban)
49.79089, 17.63668 **Autokemp Budišov,** Nábřeží č.
688, 747 87, Budišov nad Budišovkou **tel 736 767 588;**
autokemp@budisov.cz; www.autokemp.budisov.cz

🐕 CZK30 ♦♦ 🛆 🐾 ➤ 🍴 ⓓ 🛒nr /⋀ 🚿

Ent town fr E on rd 443; at T junc turn L sp; foll rd
which will take you under rlwy; site on R in 100m.
Sm, unshd, sl, EHU (6A) CZK80; bbq; 50% statics; CKE.
*"Space for 20 vans only, with 4 elec pnts; mini golf
onsite & bike hire avail; valid vaccination card req for
dogs."* **CZK 240, 1 May-30 Sep.**   2016

CESKE BUDEJOVICE *C2* (22km N Rural) *49.13701,
14.47413* **Camping Kostelec,** Kostelec 8, 373
41 Hluboká nad Vltavou **tel 731 272 098; info@
campingkostelec.nl; www.campingkostelec.nl**

🐕 ♦♦ 🅆 🛆 🖪 ⚊ 🐾 ➤ 🍴 ⓓ 🛒 /⋀ 🏊 🍴

Fr České Budějovice N twd Hluboká nad Vltavou,
then foll unnumbered rd thro forest to Poněšice
& Kostelec for approx 14km. Med, pt shd, pt sl,
terr, EHU (10A) inc; gas; bbq (elec, gas); bus adj;
Eng spkn; adv bkg acc; games rm; fishing; CKE.
*"Remote, peaceful site; gd walking; dogs free;
conv Prague, České Budějovice & Český Krumlov."*
CZK 570, 30 Apr-15 Sep.   2016

CESKY KRUMLOV *C2* (11km NE Rural) *48.83954,
14.37525* **Camping Paradijs,** Rajov 26, 38101
Cesky Krumlov **tel 776 898 022; jakesova.jana@
centrum.cz; www.camping-paradijs.eu**

♦♦ 🛆 🛆 ➤ 🍴 🍴

NE of Cesky Krumlov on rte 39 heading twrds Cesky
Budejovice. Site sp at bottom of hill.
Sm, mkd, pt shd, Eng spkn; adv bkg req; games rm.
*"A sm picturesque rural site beside rv; narr app rd, not
suitable for lge o'fits; clean but ltd san facs; rafting &
canoeing avail."* **CZK 483, 1 Apr-15 Oct.**   2017

DOMAZLICE *C1* (11km SE Rural) *49.40314, 13.05763*
Autocamping Hájovna, Na Kobyle 209, 345 06
Kdyně **tel 379 731 233; automotoklub@kdyne.cz;**
www.camphajovna.cz

🐕 CZK45 ♦♦ 🛆 🖪 ⚊ 🐾 ➤ 🍴 ⓓnr 🛒 /⋀ 🚿

In Kdyně going twd Klatovy on rd 22, turn L at end
of town sq; then 1st R twd cobbled rd (for 300m);
site on L in 2km. 3*, Med, hdstg, pt shd, pt sl, EHU
(10A) CZK70 (poss rev pol); TV; 10% statics; phone;
CKE. *"Hořovský Týn & Domažlice interesting towns; gd
walking; friendly owner; ltd level pitches."*
CZK 240, 1 May-30 Sep.   2016

FRENSTAT *C4* (750km NW Urban) *49.551722, 18.204618* **Autokemp Frenstat Pod Radhostem,** Dolni 1807, 74401 Frenstat pod Radhostem **tel 556 836 624 or 607 265 107; autokemp@ mufrenstat.cz; www.autokemp-frenstat.cz**

[12] 🐕 CZK35 ♯♯ [wc] ⛱ ♨ ♿ 🖪 ⅄/ 🍴 Ⅳ ⓘ 🅿 🦋 🛒(htd) 🌊

Fr S on 58 turn R at Aquapark, site on L in 250m. Med, hdstg, mkd, hdg, pt shd, EHU (10A) CZK100; cooking facs; red long stay; 25% statics; 25m; Eng spkn; adv bkg acc; games area; bike hire. *"Vg site aimed at families/young people; all rds mkd for cycling; school parties visit LS; easy walk to town; gd hill walks & mountain biking area; excel outdoor museum in Roznov."* **CZK 395** **2018**

FRYDEK MISTEK *B4* (5km SW Rural) *49.66459, 18.31161* **Autokemp Olešná,** Nad Přehradou, 738 02 Frýdek-Místek **tel 558 434 806; olesna@tsfm.cz; www.autokempolesna.cz**

🐕 CZK25 ♯♯ [wc] ⛱ ⅄/ 🦋 🍴 ⓘ 🛒

Nr Tesco on S side of E462/rte 48 on lakeside. 1*, Sm, unshd, sl, EHU (10A); cooking facs; Eng spkn; fishing. *"Unisex san facs; individual shwr cabins."* **CZK 230, 1 May-30 Sep.** **2016**

FRYMBURK *D2* (1km S Rural) *48.65556, 14.17008* **Camping Frymburk,** Frymburk 20/55, 382 79 Frymburk **tel 380 735 284 or 733 745 435; info@ campingfrymburk.cz; www.campingfrymburk.cz**

🐕 CZK60 ♯♯ [wc] ⛱ 🖪 ⅄/ 🦋 🍴 ⓘ 🅿 🛒 ⚓ 🔥

Fr Černa on lake, take rd 163 dir Loucovice to site. Fr Český Krumlov take Rožmberk nad Vltavou rd, turn R at Větřni on rd 162 sp Světlik. At Frymburk turn L to Lipno then site 500m on R on lake shore. 4*, Med, pt shd, sl, terr, EHU (6A) inc; sw; TV; 10% statics; adv bkg acc; bike hire; fishing; boat hire; boating. *"Beautiful lakeside site; modern, clean san facs; some pitches poss tight for lge o'fits; gd rest nrby; v friendly, helpful Dutch owners; private san facs some pitches; gd walking; adv bkg rec bef 1st Apr."* **CZK 764, 29 Apr-25 Sep.** **2016**

JIHLAVA *C3* (8km S Rural) *49.44732, 15.59911* **Autocamping Pávov,** Pávov 90, 586 01 Jihlava **tel 776 293 393; camp@pavov.com; www.pavov.com**

🐕 ♯♯ ⛱ 🖪 ⅄/ ⓘ 🛒 ⚠

Fr D1/E50/E65 exit junc 112 sp Jihlava. Foll sp Pávov & site for 2km. Fr N/S on rte 38, nr a'bahn pick up sp for Pávov. Recep in adj pension/rest. 2*, Med, mkd, unshd, EHU (6A); sw nr; 30% statics; fishing; tennis. *"Grand Hotel in Jihlava gd; m'way noise; friendly rest."* **CZK 135, 1 May-30 Sep.** **2016**

KARLOVY VARY *B1* (5.5km NNE Rural) *50.26450, 12.90013* **Autokamp Sasanka,** Sadov 7, 360 01 Sadov **tel 353 590 130 or 603 202 051 (mob); campsadov@seznam.cz**

🐕 CZK50 ♯♯ [wc] ⛱ ♨ ⅄/ [MBP] Ⅳ 🍴 🅿 🛒 ⚠

Fr Karlovy Vary on rd 13/E442 NE twds Chomutov, exit to Sadov, site sp. 3*, Med, pt shd, pt sl, EHU (16A) CZK60 (poss rev pol); red long stay; CKE. *"Lovely, well-run site; friendly, helpful staff; modern, clean san facs; picturesque vill of Loket a must; excel bus service fr vill to Karlovy Vary; take care height restriction on app to Tesco fr m'way; rec; excel."* **CZK 458, 1 Apr-31 Oct.** **2018**

KLATOVY *C1* (19km S Rural) *49.28177, 13.24003* **Camping U dvou Orecha,** Splz 13 Strážov na Sumava 34024 **tel (0420) 376 382 421; info@ camping-tsjechie.nl; www.camping-tsjechie.nl**

♯♯ ⛱ 🖪 ⅄/ 🦋 🍴 🍴 🛒

Fr Klatovy twrds Nýrsko on 191, after Janovice turn L twrds Strážov, after 5.5km in Strážov turn R sp Desenice. Site sp on L after 2.4km. Sm, pt shd, terr, EHU 10A; Eng spkn; adv bkg acc; CKE. *"Delightful, vg CL type site; warm welcome fr friendly, helpful Dutch owners."* **CZK 545, 1 May-1 Oct.** **2018**

KUTNA HORA *B2* (3km NE Urban) *49.96416, 15.30250* **Autocamp Transit,** Malín 35, 284 05 Kutná Hora **tel 327 523 785; egidylada@seznam.cz; www.transit.zde.cz**

🐕 ♯♯ ⛱ ⅄/ 🍴 ⓘ 🛒

Fr N on rd 38 fr Kolín, turn R immed after flyover onto rd No 2 then turn L twrds town, In 1km turn L immed bef rlwy bdge. Sm, pt shd, EHU (16A); cooking facs; TV; phone; bus 800m; Eng spkn; CKE. *"Poss noise fr nrby rlwy; sw high ssn; family run; Int UNESCO World Heritage Town; clean, well-kept, with garden area."* **CZK 390, 1 Apr-30 Sep.** **2017**

LIPNO NAD VLTAVOU *D2* (3km W Rural) *48.63891, 14.20880* **Autocamp Lipno Modřín,** 382 78 Lipno nad Vltavou **tel 380 736 272; camp@lipnoservis.cz; www.campinglipno.cz**

🐕 CZK70 ♯♯ [wc] ⛱ ♿ ⅄/ 🦋 🍴 🍴 🅿 🛒 ⚠

Site sp on rd 163 on lakeside. 1*, Lge, mkd, unshd, EHU (6A) inc; sw; 10% statics; adv bkg acc; games area; bike hire; tennis; boat hire. *"Pleasant, popular site; htd pool complex 500m."* **CZK 660, 1 Apr-30 Sep.** **2016**

LITOMERICE *A2* (2km SE Urban) *50.53185, 14.13899*
Autocamping Slavoj, Střelecký Ostrov, 412 01
Litoměřice **tel 416 734 481 or 777 687 667 (mob);**
kemp.litomerice@post.cz; www.autokemp
litomerice.com

🐾 CZK30 ⁞⁞ 🚾 ♨ ⚊ ╱ ⊕ 🅿︎ 🔥 ⚓

Fr N on rd 15 N of rv make for bdge over Rv Elbe
(Labe) sp Terezín; R down hill immed bef bdge
(cobbled rd), L under rlwy bdge, L again, site 300m
on R bef tennis courts at sports cent beside rv.
Fr S on rd 15 turn L immed after x-ing rv bdge to
cobbled rd. 3*, Sm, pt shd, EHU (8-16A) CZK75;
10% statics; Eng spkn; tennis; CKE. *"Friendly, family-
run site; gd, modern san facs; vg rest; 10 mins walk
town cent; Terezín ghetto & preserved concentration
camp; v friendly."* **CZK 430, 1 May-30 Sep.**   2019

LITOMYSL *B3* (1.5km E Urban) *49.86776, 16.32440*
ATC Primátor Camping, Strakovská, 570 01 Litomyšl
tel 461 612 238 or 732 148 723 (mob); primator@
camplitomysl.cz; www.camplitomysl.cz

🐾 CZK45 ⁞⁞ 🚾 ♨ ⚊ ╱ ⊕ nr ⚓ nr ⚓

Fr S on E442/35 turn R at sp on edge of town, site
on L in 500m. 3*, Sm, hdstg, pt shd, sl, EHU (6A)
CZK60; TV; 80% statics; Eng spkn; CKE. *"Worth visit
to Litomyšl - steep walk; easy (paid) parking in town
sq; pool 300m; sports facs 300m; vg san facs; v sl site;
friendly owner."* **CZK 210, 1 May-30 Sep.**   2016

MOHELNICE *B3* (1.5km NW Urban) *49.78308,
16.90808* **Autocamping Morava,** ul Petra Bezruče 13,
789 85 Mohelnice **tel 583 430 129;** info@atc-morava.
cz; www.atc-morava.cz

⁞⁞ ⚊ ╱ ❦ ⚓ ⊕ nr 🅿︎ ⚓ ⚓ 🔥

Fr E keep on D35/E442 to town boundary, turn
R down rd 35. Site sp 300m on R. 3*, Lge, pt shd,
EHU (10A) inc; TV; 20% statics; Eng spkn; bike hire;
tennis; CKE. *"Pleasant, well-run site; v quiet LS;
hourly trains to Olomouc; excel modern san fac."*
CZK 188, 15 May-15 Oct.   2016

NACHOD *B3* (8km SW Rural) *50.39866, 16.06302*
Autocamping Rozkoš, Masaryka 836, 552 03 Česká
Skalice **tel 491 451 112 or 491 451 108;**
atc@atcrozkos.com; www.atcrozkos.com

12 🐾 CZK30 ⁞⁞ ⚊ ♨ ⚐ ╱ ⊕ 🅿︎ ⚓ ⚓ ✎ ⚓

On rd 33/E67 fr Náchod dir Hradec Králové, site sp
2km bef Česká Skalice on lakeside. V lge, EHU (16A)
CZK70; sw nr; 10% statics; ccard acc; bike hire;
windsurfing school; watersports; sauna. *"Lovely
countryside."* **CZK 290**   2016

NOVE STRASECI *B2* (6km NW Rural) *50.17221,
13.83951* **Camping Bucek,** Trtice 170, 271 01 Nové
Strašecí **tel 313 564 212;** info@campingbucek.cz;
www.campingbucek.cz

🐾 CZK60 ⁞⁞ 🚾 ⚊ ♨ ╱ 🆖 ❦ 🏕 ⚓ ⊕ 🅿︎ ⚓ nr ⚓ ⚓ (htd)

Site sp fr E48/rd 6, 2km S of Řevničov on lakeside &
approx 40km fr Prague. 4*, Med, mkd, pt shd, pt sl,
EHU (6A) inc; bbq; sw nr; TV; Eng spkn; boating adj.
"Helpful owner; modern san facs; gd walks in woods."
CZK 630, 1 May-3 Sep.   2016

ORLIK NAD VLTAVOU *C2* (5km S Rural) *49.52458,
14.15563* **Camping Velký Vír,** Kožlí 23, 398 07
Oriik nad Vltavou **tel 382 275 192;** obec.kozli@
seznam.cz; www.velkyvir.cz

🐾 CZK30 ⁞⁞ 🚾 ⚊ ╱ ❦ ⊕ 🅿︎ ⚓ ⚓

Fr Milevsko head W on rte 19; turn N to Orlík vill;
foll camp sp 7km N to Velký Vír. Med, unshd, pt sl,
EHU (6A) CZK70; sw nr; 10% statics; adv bkg acc;
tennis; CKE. *"V quiet site by rv; few EHU & may not
work."* **CZK 210, 1 May-30 Sep.**   2016

PODEBRADY *B2* (2km SE Rural) *50.13549, 15.13794*
Autocamping Golf, U Nové Vodárny 428, 290 01
Poděbrady **tel 325 612 833;** ATCAutokemp@gmail.
com; www.kemp-golf.cz

🐾 CZK20 ⁞⁞ 🚾 ⚊ ╱ ❦ ⚓ 🅿︎

Fr D11/E67 (Prague/Poděbrady) take Poděbrady
exit N onto rd 32 for 3km; at junc with rte 11/E67
turn W sp Poděbrady (care needed, priority not
obvious); site sp on L on E edge of town; site opp
town name sp 400m down lane; app fr E if poss.
3*, Med, pt shd, EHU (long cable req) CZK80; own san
rec; CKE. *"Conv for touring area; gd supmkt with
parking in town; basic site."*
CZK 260, 1 May-31 Sep.   2016

PRAHA *B2* (6km N Urban) *50.11694, 14.42361*
Camping Sokol Trója, Trojská 171a, 171 00 Praha 7
tel 233 542 908 or 283 850 486; tj.sokol.troja@quick.cz
or info@camp-sokol-troja.cz; www.camp-sokol-
troja.cz

12 🐾 CZK50 ⁞⁞ ⚊ ♨ ╱ 🅿︎ ⚓ ⚓

Fr Pilsen (E50/D5) head into cent to rte D8/E55 sp
Treplice. Foll N to Trója sp. Immed after rv x-ing
take exit under rte 8 & foll camp sp & site on L 100m
past Autocamp Trojská. Fr Dresden on E55/D8 foll
sp to Centrum to Trója exit on R, foll camping sp.
NB: There are 5 sites adj to each other with similar
names. Best app fr Treplice. 2*, Med, hdstg, pt
shd, EHU (10A) CZK100; ccard acc; CKE. *"Easy tram
transport to city; Trója Palace & zoo 1km; v helpful,
friendly owner; bar & rest gd value; noise fr bar; facs
basic & run down (2017); hostel; 10 min walk to shops."*
CZK 520   2018

PRAHA *B2* (20km S Rural) *49.93277, 14.37294*
Camp Matyáš, U Elektrárny, 252 46 Vrané nad
Vltavou **tel 257 761 228 or 777 016073 (mob);**
campmatyas@centrum.cz; www.camp-matyas.com

🏕 ♦♦ 🅦 ⛺ 🅰 ⊘ ♨ ♈ ⵣ ① ♿ 🅿 ⛰ 🅰

Fr Plzen take E50/D5 NE twd Prague.Take E48/E50
heading approx SE twd R4. Exit onto R4 sp
Strakonice. Exit R4 twd Zbraslav. Enter vill, turn L
in Sq. Foll rd to cross major bdge over Rv Vltava.
After bdge turn immed R. Foll this rd keeping rv
on your R. Camp is on R in 6km. 3*, Med, pt shd,
EHU (10A) CZK120; cooking facs; sw nr; bus, train
to city; Eng spkn; adv bkg acc; fishing adj; CKE. *"In
lovely location; friendly owners; train & tram service to
Prague (1 hr); boat trips on Rv Vltava; superb family
site."* **CZK 550, 1 Apr-30 Sep.** **2016**

PRAHA *B2* (10km SW Urban) *50.05583, 14.41361*
Caravan Camping Praha, Císařská Louka 162, Smíchov,
150 00 Praha 5 **tel 257 317 555; info@caravan**
camping.cz; www.caravancamping.cz

12 ♦♦ 🅦 ⛺ 🅰 ⊘ 🦋 ① ♿ 🅿

Foll dir as for Prague Yacht Club C'van Park. This
site just bef on R, look for lge yellow tower.
Sm, unshd, EHU CZK95; Eng spkn; CKE. *"V helpful
gd staff; busy sh stay site on island; conv for Prague
cent metro - St Wenceslas Sq 15/20mins; no privacy in
shwrs; san fanc modernised & v clean (2015); v busy."*
CZK 600 **2015**

PRAHA *B2* (10km SW Urban) *50.06233, 14.41331*
Praha Yacht Club Caravan Park, Cisarská Louka 599,
Smíchov, 150 00 Praha 5 **tel 257 318 387 or 060**
2343701 (mob); caravanpark.cl@gmail.com;
www.volny.cz/convoy

12 🐕 CZK57 ♦♦ 🅦 ⛺ 🅰 ⊘ 🦋 🅿 nr

Fr E50 access only poss fr S by travelling N on W
side of rv. After complex junc (care needed), turn
sharp R bef Shell petrol stn to Cisařská Island, foll
rd to end. Nr C'van Camping CSK. Diff app fr N due
no L turns on Strakonická. Sm, pt shd, EHU (16A)
CZK95; adv bkg acc; ccard acc; tennis 100m. *"Boats
for hire; launch trips on rv; water taxi fr Prague, book
at site recep; helpful staff; friendly, secure site; san facs
clean & adequate; unmkd pithces; excel location; views
of city; milk etc avail fr Agip petrol stn on Strakonická;
busy site, rec arr early; 5 min to ferry & metro to
Prague."* **CZK 484** **2017**

PRAHA *B2* (14km SW Rural) *50.04388, 14.28416*
Camp Drusus, Třebonice 4, 155 00 Praha 5 **tel 235**
514 391; drusus@drusus.com; www.drusus.com

🐕 CZK30 ♦♦ 🅦 ⛺ 🅰 ⊘ 🅼🅿 ♈ ⵣ 🅰

Fr Plzeň take E50/D5 to exit 1/23 Třebonice, then
E50 dir Brno. Fr Brno exit E50/D5 at junc 19 sp
Řeporyje, site in 2km, sp. 1*, Med, pt shd, sl, EHU
(10A) CZK110; gas; cooking facs; red long stay; TV;
10% statics; bus; Eng spkn; adv bkg acc; ccard acc;
games area; CKE. *"Reg bus service to Prague nrby,
tickets fr site; owner v helpful; vg."*
CZK 617, 1 Apr-15 Oct. **2018**

PRAHA *B2* (12km NW Rural) *50.09890, 14.33569*
Camping Džbán, Nad Lávkou 5, Vokovice, 160 00
Praha 6 **tel 725 956 457 or 777 327 595; info@**
campdzban.eu; www.campdzban.eu

🐕 CZK60 ♦♦ 🅦 ⛺ 🅰 ⊘ ♈ ⵣ ① ♿ 🅿 ⛷

Exit 28 off ring rd onto rd 7 Chomutov-Prague; site
approx 4km after airport twd Prague; at traff lts on
brow of hill just bef Esso stn on L turn L; take 2nd L
& strt on for 600m; site adj go-kart racing.
3*, Lge, unshd, pt sl, EHU (10A) CZK90; tram 200m;
Eng spkn; ccard acc; tennis; games area; CKE. *"Tram
direct to Prague (Republic Sq) 25 mins, tickets at
bureau; gd security; long way bet shwrs & wcs; san facs
old but clean; communal male shwrs; narr pitches; new
Metro."* **CZK 681, 1 May-30 Sep.** **2016**

ROZNOV POD RADHOSTEM *C4* (2km NE Rural)
49.46654, 18.16376 **Camping Rožnov,** Radhošťská
940, 756 61 Rožnov pod Radhoštěm **tel 731 504 073;**
camproznov@seznam.cz; www.camproznov.cz

♦♦ (htd) 🅦 ⛺ 🅰 ⊘ 🦋 ① nr 🅿 🅰 ⛷ (htd)

On rd 35/E442; on E o'skts of Rožnov on N of rd
200m past ent to Camping Sport, take L fork opp
Benzina petrol stn (site sp obscured by lamp post).
4*, Med, pt shd, EHU (16A) CZK60; 60% statics;
phone; Eng spkn; ccard acc; tennis; CKE. *"Welcoming;
gd cooking & washing facs; pitches v close together;
basic, worn san facs; annexe; nr open-air museum
(clsd Mon); gd walking cent; cycle to town thro park."*
CZK 469, 1 May-31 Oct. **2018**

STERNBERK *B3* (2km N Rural) *49.74800, 17.30641*
Autocamping Šternbek, Dolní Žleb, 785 01
Šternberk **tel 585 011 300; info@campsternberk.cz;**
www.campsternberk.cz

🐕 CZK30 ♦♦ 🅦 ⛺ 🅰 ⊘ 🦋 ♈ ① nr 🅿 🅰

Fr Olomouc take rte 46 to Šternberk. At Šternberk
go thro town cent & foll sp Dalov, site just bef vill
of Dolní Žleb. Or circumnavigate to W on rds 444
& 445, site sp. Med, pt shd, EHU (10A) CZK75 (poss
rev pol); cooking facs; TV; 30% statics; phone; adv bkg
acc; CKE. *"Gd, clean facs even when full; helpful staff."*
CZK 215, 15 May-15 Sep. **2016**

STRIBRO *B1* (16km NE Rural) *49.79073, 13.16869*
Transkemp Hracholusky, 330 23 Hracholusky
tel 420 337 914 113 or 420 728 470 650; info@
hracholusky.com; www.hracholusky.com

♦♦ 🅦 ⛺ 🅰 ⊘ ① 🅿 nr 🅰 shgl adj

Fr Ulice bet Stribro & Plzen on rte 5/E50 turn N,
sp Plesnice, & foll vill sp to site in 4km at E end of
lake. Med, unshd, pt sl, EHU inc (adaptor for hire); sw;
25% statics; Eng spkn; adv bkg acc; waterskiing;
boating. *"Lake steamer trips; gd sh stay/NH; gd
location on lakeside; fair site; facs basic."*
CZK 270, 1 May-31 Dec. **2019**

STRMILOV C2 (2km SE Rural) 49.14956, 15.20890
Autokemp Komorník, 378 53 Strmilov **tel 384 392 468;**
recepce@autokempkomornik.cz; www.autokemp
komornik.cz

🐕 CZK40 ♨ ⬛ ♿ ⚲ 🚲 ☂ ⊕ 🅿 🌡 ⚠ 🏕 sand adj

Sp fr rd 23 at Strmilov. Lge, pt shd, pt sl, EHU (10A)
CZK75 (long lead rec); bbq; 20% statics; CKE. "V
pleasant setting by lake; lake adj; clean, modern san
facs; gd rest & bar; conv Telč & Slavonice historic
towns." CZK 215, 1 Jun-15 Sep.   **2016**

TABOR C2 (6km E Rural) 49.40985, 14.73157
Autocamping & Hotel Knížecí Rybník, Měsice 399,
39156 Tábor **tel 381 252 546;** knizecak@seznam.cz;
www.knizecirybnik.cz

12 🐕 CZK50 ♨ ⬛ ⚲ ⊕ 🅿 🌡

On N side of rd 19 fr Tábor to Jihlava, in woods
by lake adj hotel. 3*, Lge, mkd, hdg, pt shd, EHU
(6-10A) CZK60; sw nr; 10% statics; ccard acc; fishing;
tennis; CKE. "Pleasant, lakeside site; modern san facs."
CZK 200   **2016**

"I like to fill in the reports as I travel from site to site"

You'll find report forms at the back of this
guide, or you can fill them in online at
camc.com/europereport.

TELC C2 (10km NW Rural) 49.22785, 15.38442 **Camp
Velkopařezitý,** Řásná 10, 58856 Mrákotín **tel 567 379
449;** campvelkoparezity@tiscali.cz; www.camp
velkoparezity.cz

12 🐕 CZK30 ♨ ⬛ ♿ ⚲ ⊕ 🌡 ☂ 1km

Exit Telč on Jihlava rd; turn L in 300m (sp) & foll sp
to site beyond Rásná. Well sp fr Telč. Steep site ent.
Sm, pt shd, pt sl, EHU CZK100; 10% statics. "Friendly
atmosphere; poor san facs; gd walking & cycling; Telč
wonderful World Heritage site." CZK 270   **2016**

TREBON C2 (1km S Rural) 48.99263, 14.76753
Autocamp Třeboňsky Ráj, Domanin 285, 37901
Třeboň **tel 384 722 586;** info@autocamp-trebon.cz;
www.autocamp-trebon.cz

🐕 CZK60 ♨ ⬛ ♿ ⚲ 🚲 ⚲ 🎣 Y ⊕ 🅿 🌡 ⚠ ⚲

Exit town by rd 155 sp Borovany heading SW.
Site on L just past lake. Note: site Not accessible
fr other end of this rd. 3*, Med, pt shd, pt sl, EHU (6A)
CZK70 (long cable req & poss rev pol); bbq; cooking
facs; sw; twin axles; TV; 5% statics; phone; bus 2km;
Eng spkn; adv bkg acc; bike hire; games area; games
rm; boat hire; CKE. "Attractive unspoilt town; helpful
owner; facs stretched when site full; insect repellant
rec; gd cycle paths; gd rest on site; indiv shwrs but
no curtains, changing area opp shwr; gd cycle paths."
CZK 340, 27 Apr-30 Sep.   **2018**

TURNOV A2 (6km SSE Rural) 50.5580, 15.1867
Autocamping Sedmihorky, Sedmihorky 72, 51101
Turnov **tel 481 389 162;** camp@campsedmihorky.cz;
www.campsedmihorky.cz

12 🐕 CZK50 ♨ ⬛ ♿ ⚲ ⚲ Y ⊕ 🅿 🌡 ⚠

Fr rte 35/E442 fr Turnov. Turn SW over rlwy x-ing at
camping sp S of Sedmihorky. 300m along ave take
1st R. 3*, Lge, pt shd, pt sl, EHU (16A) CZK60; sw;
phone; Eng spkn; ccard acc; bike hire; CKE. "V beautiful
site in National Park, sometimes called Bohemian
Paradise; v busy site high ssn; dep bef 1000 otherwise
charge for extra day; excel site." CZK 370   **2018**

VRCHLABI A3 (1km S Rural) 50.61036, 15.60263
Holiday Park Liščí Farma, Dolní Branná 350,
54362 Vrchlabí **tel 499 421 473;** info@liscifarma.cz;
www.liscifarma.cz

12 🐕 CZK20 ♨ (htd) ⬛ ♿ ⚲ 🅿 🚲 Y ⊕ 🌡 nr ⚠
⚲ ⚲

S fr Vrchlabí on rd 295, site sp. 4*, Lge, mkd, pt shd,
EHU (6A) CZK125; cooking facs; TV; adv bkg acc;
ccard acc; games area; bike hire; golf 5km; canoeing;
horseriding 2km; tennis; sauna. "Private bthrms avail."
CZK 220   **2016**

ZAMBERK B3 (1km E Urban) 50.08638, 16.47527
Autocamping Jan Kulhanek, U koupaliště, 564 01
Žamberk **tel 465 614 755;** kemp@orlicko.cz;
www.autocamping.cz

🐕 CZK50 ♨ ⚲ ⚲ 🚲 Y nr ⊕ nr 🌡 nr

Fr Zamberk cent on rd 11, foll sp. Sm, pt shd, EHU
(16A) CZK70; cooking facs; TV; 50% statics; phone;
bus adj, train 1km; Eng spkn; CKE. "Site is pt of sports
cent & aqua park with many diff facs inc mini golf,
volleyball & bowling; playgrnd, pool, games area,
games rm at sports cent; site leaflet avail at recep
showing town plans with supmkt & info office; gd site."
CZK 241, 1 Apr-31 Oct.   **2016**

ZNOJMO C3 (8km N Rural) 48.92018, 16.02588
Camping Country, 67152 Hluboké Mašůvky **tel 515
255 249;** camping-country@cbox.cz; www.camp-
country.com

🐕 CZK50 ♨ ⬛ ♿ ⚲ 🚲 ⚲ ⊕ 🌡 nr ⚠ ⚲

N fr Znojmo on E59/38 4km; turn E on 408
to Přímětice; then N on 361 4km to Hluboké
Mašůvky. Sharp turn into site fr S. 4*, Med, pt shd,
sl, EHU (16A) CZK80 (long lead poss req); sw nr; TV;
20% statics; Eng spkn; tennis; bike hire; horseriding;
CKE. "Gd, clean, well-manicured site; v helpful owner
& family; not easy to find level pitch; excel meals."
CZK 400, 1 May-30 Oct.   **2016**

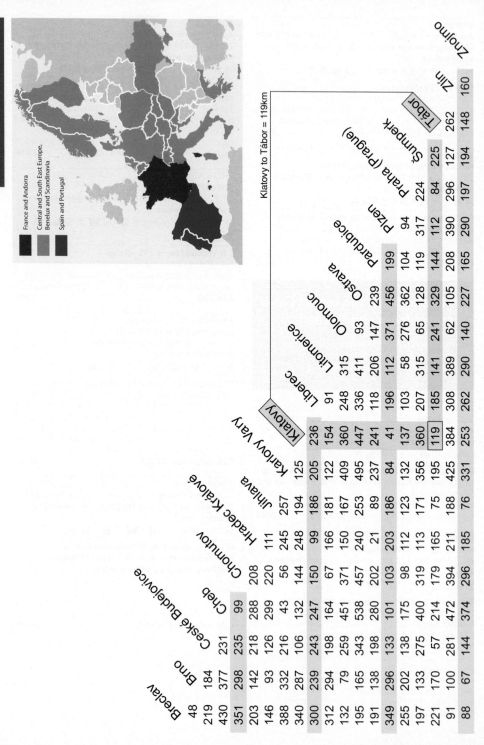

Map legend:
- France and Andorra
- Central and South East Europe, Benelux and Scandinavia
- Spain and Portugal

Klatovy to Tábor = 119km

City	Břeclav	Brno	České Budějovice	Cheb	Chomutov	Hradec Králové	Jihlava	Karlovy Vary	Klatovy	Liberec	Litoměřice	Olomouc	Ostrava	Pardubice	Plzeň	Praha (Prague)	Šumperk	Tábor	Zlín
Brno	48																		
České Budějovice	219	184																	
Cheb	430	377	231																
Chomutov	351	298	235	99															
Hradec Králové	203	142	218	288	208														
Jihlava	146	93	126	299	220	111													
Karlovy Vary	388	332	216	43	56	245	257												
Klatovy	340	287	106	132	144	248	194	125											
Liberec	300	239	243	247	150	99	186	205	236										
Litoměřice	312	294	198	164	67	166	181	122	154	91									
Olomouc	132	79	259	451	371	150	167	409	360	248	315								
Ostrava	195	165	343	538	457	240	253	495	447	336	411	93							
Pardubice	191	138	198	280	202	21	89	237	241	118	206	147	239						
Plzeň	349	296	133	101	103	203	186	84	41	196	112	371	456	199					
Praha (Prague)	255	202	138	175	98	112	123	137	137	103	58	276	362	104	94				
Šumperk	197	133	275	400	319	113	171	356	360	207	315	65	128	119	317	224			
Tábor	221	170	57	214	179	165	75	195	119	185	141	241	329	144	112	84	225		
Zlín	91	100	281	472	394	188	211	425	384	308	389	62	105	208	390	296	127	262	
Znojmo	88	67	144	374	296	185	76	331	253	262	290	140	227	165	290	197	194	148	160

© Collins Bartholomew Ltd 2020

Motorways
Major roads
Main roads

All year site(s)
Seasonal site(s)
No sites listed

200m +
0–200m

150 kms
90 mls

155

Aarhus

Highlights

Regularly found high on the list of the happiest nations on earth, Denmark is a friendly country that welcomes everyone. You can enjoy a charming, fairytale atmosphere working together with modern cities at the forefront of design and sustainability,

The landscape, too, is enchanting, and the beautiful sandy beaches, lakes, river and plains are a delight to explore, and ideal for cyclists.

The smørrebrød, a traditional open sandwich made with rye bread, salad and meat or fish, is perhaps one of Denmark's most famous dishes. Equally renowned is the Danish pastry - known locally as Vienna bread or wienerbrød. You'll find these at bakeries throughout the country.

A traditional Scandinavian drink, Akvavit is believed to have originated in Denmark in the 16th century. The spirit takes its distinct flavour from herbs and spices and is often sipped slowly from a small shot glass.

Major towns and cities

- Copenhagen – Denmark's bustling capital city is a perfect mix of old and new.
- Aarhus – this compact city is well known for its musical heritage.
- Odense – one of the country's oldest cities, and home of Hans Christian Anderson.
- Aalborg – a vibrant city with an atmospheric waterfront.

Attractions

- Tivoli Gardens, Copenhagen – one of the oldest amusement parks in the world.
- Kronborg Castle, Helsingør – This renaissance castle is a UNESCO site.
- Frederiksborg Castle, Hillerød – a palatial residence that now houses a museum.
- Skagen Beaches – 60km of white, sandy beaches and stunning, rugged coastline.

Find out more

www.visitdenmark.com
E: contact@visitdenmark.com T: 0045 (0) 32 88 99 00

Country Information

Population (approx): 5.6 million

Capital: Copenhagen

Area: 43,094 sq km (excl Faroe Islands and Greenland)

Bordered by: Germany

Terrain: Mostly fertile lowland, undulating hills, woodland, lakes and moors

Climate: Generally mild, changeable climate without extremes of heat or cold; cold winters but usually not severe; warm, sunny summers; the best time to visit is between May and September

Coastline: 7,400km

Highest Point: Ejer Bavnehøj 173m

Languages: Danish

Local Time: GMT or BST + 1, ie 1 hour ahead of the UK all year

Currency: Krone (DKK) divided into 100 øre; £1 = DKK 8.64, DKK 10 = £1.16 (October 2019)

Emergency numbers: Police 112 (114 for non-urgent calls); Fire brigade 112; Ambulance 112 (operators speak English).

Public Holidays 2020: Jan 1; Apr 9,10, 12, 13; May 8, 21, 31; Jun 1; Dec 25, 26.

School summer holidays extend from end June to mid August.

Entry Formalities

Visas are not required by British or Irish passport holders for a stay of up to three months. Visitors planning to stay longer should contact the Danish Embassy in London before they travel - find contact details at www.denmark.org.uk.

Due to the current migrant crisis in Europe some countries have temporarily restored their borders. A current list of countries affected is available on the EU website: **ec.europa.eu/home-affairs/what-we-do/policies/borders-and-visas/schengen/reintroduction-border-control_en**. At the time of going to print Denmark has restored their border with Germany and may extend this to all borders.

Medical Services

The standard of healthcare is high. Citizens of the UK are entitled to the same emergency medical services as the Danish, including free hospital treatment, on production of a European Health Insurance Card (EHIC). Tourist offices and health offices (kommunes social og sundhedforvaltning) have lists of doctors and dentists who are registered with the public health service. For a consultation with a doctor you may have to pay the full fee but you will be refunded if you apply to a local health office if they are registered with the Danish Public Health Service. Partial refunds may be made for dental costs and approved medicines. Prescriptions are dispensed at pharmacies (apotek).

Opening Hours

Banks: Mon-Fri 10am-4pm (Thu to 6pm). In the Provinces opening hours vary from town to town.

Museums: Tue-Sun 9am/10am-5pm; most close Mon.

Post Offices: Mon-Fri 9am/10am-5pm/6pm, Sat 9am/10am-12pm/2pm or closed all day.

Shops: Mon-Fri 9am-5.30pm (Fri to 7pm); Sat 9am-1pm/2pm; supermarkets open Mon-Fri 9am-7pm & Sat 9am-4pm/5pm; open on first Sunday of the month 10am-5pm. Most shops close on public holidays but you may find some bakers, sandwich shops, confectioners and kiosks open.

Regulations for Pets

Between April and September all dogs must be kept on a lead. This applies not only on campsites but throughout the country in general.

Safety and Security

Denmark has relatively low levels of crime and most visits to the country are trouble-free. The majority of public places are well lit and secure, most people are helpful and often speak good English. Visitors should, however, be aware of pickpocketing or bag-snatching in Copenhagen, particularly around the central station and in the Christiania and Nørrebro areas, as well as in other large cities and tourist attractions. Car break-ins have increased in recent years; never leave valuables in your car.

Denmark shares with the rest of Europe a general threat from terrorism. Attacks could be indiscriminate and against civilian targets in public places, including tourist sites.

British Embassy

KASTELSVEJ 36-40
DK-2100 Copenhagen Ø
Tel: 35 44 52 00
www.ukindenmark.fco.gov.uk/en

There are also Honorary Consulates in Aabenraa, Åarhus, Fredericia and Herning

Irish Embassy

ØSTBANEGADE 21
DK-2100 Copenhagen Ø
Tel: 35 47 32 00
www.embassyofireland.dk

Documents

Money

Some shops and restaurants, particularly in the larger cities, display prices in both krone and euros and many will accept payment in euros.

Major credit cards are widely, but not always, accepted. Credit cards are not normally accepted in supermarkets. Cash machines are widespread. A 5% surcharge is usually applied to credit card transactions. Some banks and/or cash machines may not accept debit cards issued by non-Danish banks.

It is advisable to carry your passport or photocard driving licence if paying with a credit card as you may well be asked for photographic proof of identity. Carry your credit card issuers'/banks' 24-hour UK contact numbers in case of loss or theft of your cards.

Passport

Your passport must be valid for the proposed duration of your stay, however in case of any unforeseen delays it is strongly recommended to have a period of extra validity on your passport.

Vehicle(s)

Carry your vehicle documentation, including vehicle registration certificate (V5C), certificate of insurance and MOT certificate (if applicable).

You may be asked to produce your V5C if driving a motorhome over the Great Belt Bridge between Funen and Zealand in order to verify the weight of your vehicle. For more information see the 'Motorways' section of this introduction.

The minimum age you can drive, with a valid driver's licence, is 17.

Driving

Alcohol

The level of alcohol cannot exceed 50 milligrams (0.05%) in 100 millilitres of blood which is lower than in the UK. Drivers caught over this limit will be fined and their driving licence withdrawn. Police carry out random breath tests.

Breakdown Service

24 hours assistance is available from SOS Dansk Autohjaelp (Danish Automobile Assistance) call Tel: 70 10 80 90.

The hourly charge between Monday and Friday is DKK 638 + VAT and an administration charge; higher charges apply at night and at weekends and public holidays. On-the-spot repairs and towing must be paid for in cash.

On motorways use the emergency telephones, situated every 2 km, to call the breakdown service. The telephone number to dial in case of an accident is 112.

Child Restraint System

Children under three years of age must be seated in an approved child restraint system adapted to their size. Children over three years old and under 1.35 metres in height must be seated in an approved child restraint suitable for both their height and weight. If the vehicle is fitted with an active airbag children must not be placed in the front seat in a rear-facing child seat.

Fuel

Some petrol stations in larger towns stay open 24 hours a day and they often have self-service pumps which accept DKK 50, 100 and occasionally DKK 200 notes. Few display instructions in English and it is advisable to fill up during normal opening hours when staff are on hand. Unleaded petrol pumps are marked 'Blyfri Benzine'. Major credit cards are normally accepted.

LPG (Autogas or Bilgas) is available from a handful of BP, OK, Q8, Uno-X, YX, Shell and Statoil service stations – the Danish Tourist Board publishes a list of outlets on its website www.visitdenmark.com.

Lights and Indicators

Dipped headlights are compulsory at all times, regardless of weather conditions. Bulbs are more likely to fail with constant use and you are recommended to carry spares.

On motorways drivers must use their hazard warning lights to warn other motorists of sudden queues ahead or other dangers such as accidents.

By law indicators must be used when overtaking or changing lanes on a motorway and when pulling out from a parked position at the kerb.

Low Emission Zones

Low Emission zones are in operation in many large cities. The rules affect all diesel powered vehicles over 3,500kg, which must meet European Emission Standard 4 (EURO 4). All vehicles over 3,500kg must display an Environmental Zone sticker (Eco-label) You can order the Eco-label online from www.applusbilsyn.dk for DKK 93 or visit a car inspection station in Denmark where the Eco-label will cost DKK 165.
Vehicles which do not meet European Emission Standard 4 are not allowed into the Low Emission Zone. A fine of DKK 20,000 (Approximately £1900 in 2015) is payable for non-compliance.

Motorways

There are approximately 1,000 km of motorways, mainly two-lane and relatively uncongested. No tolls are levied except on bridges. Lay-bys with picnic areas and occasionally motorhome service points are situated at 25 km intervals. These often also have toilet facilities. Service areas and petrol stations are situated at 50 km intervals and are generally open from 7am to 10pm.

Parking

Parking prohibitions and limitations are indicated by signs. Hours during which parking is not allowed are displayed in black for weekdays, with brackets for Saturdays and in red for Sundays and public holidays. Parking meters and discs are used and discs are available free of charge from post offices, banks, petrol stations and tourist offices. The centre of Copenhagen is divided into red, green and blue zones and variable hourly charges apply round the clock Monday to Friday (Saturday to 5pm; Sunday and public holidays free). 'Pay and display' tickets may be bought from machines with cash or a credit card. Cars must be parked on the right-hand side of the road (except in one-way streets). An illegally parked vehicle may be removed by the police.

Priority

At intersections where there are 'give way' or 'stop' signs and/or a transverse line consisting of triangles (shark's teeth) with one point facing towards the driver, drivers must give way to traffic at an intersection. If approaching an intersection of two roads without any signs you must give way to vehicles coming from the right. Give way to cyclists and to buses signalling to pull out. On the Danish islands take care as many people travel by foot, bicycle or on horseback.

Roads

Roads are generally in good condition, well-signposted and largely uncongested and driving standards are fairly high.

Caravanners should beware of strong crosswinds on exposed stretches of road. Distances are short; it is less than 500 km (310 miles) from Copenhagen on the eastern edge of Zealand, to Skagen at the tip of Jutland, and the coast is never more than an hour away.

Road Signs and Markings

Signs directing you onto or along international E-roads are green with white lettering. E-roads, having been integrated into the Danish network, usually have no other national number.

Signs above the carriageway on motorways have white lettering on a blue background. Signs guiding you onto other roads are white with red text and a hexagonal sign with red numbering indicates the number of a motorway exit.

Primary (main roads) connecting large towns and ferry connections have signs with black numbers on a yellow background. Secondary (local) roads connecting small towns and primary routes are indicated by signs with black numbers on a white background. Signs of any colour with a dotted frame refer you to a road further ahead. Road signs themselves may be placed low down and, as a result, may be easy to miss. 'Sharks teeth' markings at junctions indicate stop and give way to traffic on the road you are entering.

General roads signs conform to international standards. You may see the following:

Place of interest

Recommended speed limits

Dual Carriage-way ends

The following are some other common signs:

Danish	English Translation
Ensrettet kørsel	One-way street
Fare	Danger
Farligt sving	Dangerous bend
Fodgægerovergang	Pedestrian crossing
Gennemkørsel forbudt	No through road
Hold til hojre	Keep to the right
Hold til venstre	Keep to the left
Omkørsel	Diversion
Parkering forbudt	No parking
Vejen er spærret	Road closed

Speed Limits

	Open Road (km/h)	Motorway (km/h)
Car Solo	80-90	110-130
Car towing caravan/trailer	70	80
Motorhome under 3500kg	80-90	110-130
Motorhome 3500-7500kg	70	70

Vehicles over 3,500 kg are restricted to 70 km/h (44 mph) on the open road and on motorways. It is prohibited to use radar detectors.

Traffic Jams

British drivers will enjoy the relatively low density of traffic. At most, traffic builds up during the evening rush hours around the major cities of Copenhagen, Århus, Aalborg and Odense. During the holiday season traffic jams may be encountered at the Flensburg border crossing into Germany, on the roads to coastal areas, on approach roads to ferry crossings and on routes along the west coast of Jutland.

Toll Bridges

The areas of Falster and Zealand are linked by two road bridges, 1.6 km and 1.7 km in length respectively.

The areas of Funen and Zealand are linked by an 18 km suspension road bridge and rail tunnel known as the Great Belt Link (Storebæltsbroen), connecting the towns of Nyborg and Korsør. The toll road is part of the E20 between Odense and Ringsted and tolls for single journeys on the bridge are shown in Table 1 below (2015 prices subject to change).

Table 1 – Great Belt Bridge

Vehicle(s)	Price
Solo Car up to 6 metres	DKK 240
Car + trailer/caravan	DKK 365
Motorhome (under 3,500 kg) under 6 metres	DKK 240

Vehicle(s)	Price
Motorhome (under 3,500kg) over 6 metres	DKK 365
Motorhome (over 3,500 kg) up to 10 metres	DKK 610
Motorhome (over 3,500 kg) over 10 metres	DKK 965

You may be asked to produce your Vehicle Registration Certificate (V5C) to verify the weight of your vehicle. Day return and weekend return tickets are also available. For more information see www.storebaelt.dk/english.

The 16 km Øresund Bridge links Copenhagen in Denmark with Malmö in Sweden and means that it is possible to drive all the way from mainland Europe to Sweden by motorway. The crossing is via a 7.8 km bridge to the artificial island of Peberholm, and a 4 km tunnel. Tolls for single journeys (payable in cash, including euros, or by credit card) are levied on the Swedish side, and are shown in Table 2 below (2015 prices subject to change).

Table 2 – Øresund Bridge

Vehicle(s)	Price
Solo Car or motorhome up to 6 metres	€50
Car + caravan/trailer or motorhome over 6 metres	€ 100

Speed limits apply, and during periods of high wind the bridge is closed to caravans. Bicycles are not allowed. Information on the Øresund Bridge can be found on www.oeresundsbron.com.

On both the Øresund and Storebælts bridges vehicle length is measured electronically and even a slight overhang over six metres, e.g. towbars, projecting loads and loose items, will result in payment of the higher tariff.

Violation of Traffic Regulations

The police are authorised to impose and collect on-the-spot fines for traffic offences. Driving offences committed in Denmark are reported to the UK authorities.

Essential Equipment

Reflective Jacket

It is recommended, though not compulsory, to carry a reflectorised jacket on board the vehicle in the event the driver has to step out of the car in an emergency.

Warning Triangle

An EU approved red warning triangle must be used if the vehicle breaks down, punctures or is involved in an accident.

Touring

The peak holiday season and school holidays are slightly earlier than in the UK and by mid-August some attractions close or operate reduced opening hours.

Service charges are automatically added to restaurant bills although you may round up the bill if service has been good, but it is not expected. Tips for taxi drivers are included in the fare. Smoking is not allowed in enclosed public places, including restaurants and bars. The 3,500 km Marguerite Route, marked by brown signs depicting a flower (see below), takes motorists to the best sights and scenic areas in Denmark.

A route map and guide (in English) are available from bookshops, tourist offices and Statoil service stations all over Denmark. Stretches of the route are not suitable for cars towing caravans as some of the roads are narrow and twisting.

The capital and major port, Copenhagen, is situated on the island of Zealand. Grundtvig Cathedral, Amalienborg Palace and the Viking Museum are well worth a visit, as are the famous Tivoli Gardens open from mid April to the third week in September and again for a few days in October and from mid November to the end of December (excluding Christmas). The statue of the Little Mermaid, the character created by Hans Christian Andersen, can be found at the end of the promenade called Langelinie. Copenhagen is easy to explore and from there visitors may travel to the north of

Zealand along the 'Danish Riviera' to Hamlet's castle at Kronborg, or west to Roskilde with its Viking Ship Museum and 12th century cathedral.

A Copenhagen Card (CPH Card) offers unlimited use of public transport throughout Greater Copenhagen and North Zealand, free entry to over 60 museums and attractions and discounts at restaurants and other attractions. Cards are valid for 24 or 72 hours and may be purchased from selected tourist offices, travel agents, hotels and railway stations or online from www.visitcopenhagen.com. Two children up to the age of nine are included free of charge on an adult card. The Copenhagen Card is also available to buy via a mobile app.

National Parks in the country include Thy National Park near Thisted along Jutland's north-west coast, Mols Bjerge National Park in eastern Jutland and Wadden Sea National Park in the south-west of the country.

English is widely spoken.

Camping and Caravanning

Denmark has approximately 500 approved, well-equipped, annually inspected campsites. A green banner flies at each campsite entrance, making it easy to spot. Campsites are graded from 1 to 5 stars, many having excellent facilities including baby-changing areas, private family bathrooms, self-catering cooking facilities and shops. Prices are regulated and there is very little variation.

All except the most basic 1-star sites have water and waste facilities for motorhomes and at least some electric hook-ups. You may find it useful to take your own flat universal sink plug. During the high season it is advisable to book in advance as many Danish holidaymakers take pitches for the whole season for use at weekends and holidays resulting in minimal space for tourers.

A Camping Key Europe (CKE) or Camping Card International (CCI) is required on all campsites.

Approximately 190 campsites have a 'Quick Stop' amenity which provides safe, secure overnight facilities on or adjoining campsites, including the use of sanitary facilities. Quick Stop rates are about two thirds of the regular camping rate but you must arrive after 8pm and leave by 10am next morning. A list of Quick Stop sites may be obtained from local tourist offices or downloaded from DK-Camp www.dk-camp.dk.

Wild camping is prohibited on common or State land, in stopping bays and parking sites, in the dunes, or on the beaches, unless there is an organised camp site. Farmers or landowners may allow you to pitch on their land, but you must always seek permission from them is advance.

Cycling

Although not as flat as the Netherlands, Denmark is very cyclist-friendly and many major and minor roads, including those in all major towns, have separate cycle lanes or tracks. They have their own traffic lights and signals. Cyclists often have the right of way and, when driving, you should check cycle lanes before turning left or right.

In Åarhus and Copenhagen city centre bicycles are free to use between mid-April and November - you will need to pay a refundable deposit. Simply look for one of the many bicycle racks around the central area; see www.visitcopenhagen.com for more information.

There are many separate cycle routes, including eleven national routes, which may be long distance, local or circular, mainly on quiet roads and tracks. Local tourist offices can provide information. When planning a route, take the (often strong) prevailing westerly winds into account.

Bicycles may be carried on the roof of a car as well as at the rear. When carried at the rear, the lights and number plate must remain visible.

Electricity and Gas

Current on campsites varies between 6 and 16 amps, a 10 amp supply being the most common. Plugs have 2 round pins. Some sites have CEE17 electric hook-ups or are in the process of converting. If a CEE17 connection is not available site staff will usually provide an adaptor. Visitors report that reversed polarity is common.

Campingaz 904 and 907 butane cylinders are readily available from campsites, or some Statoil service stations and at camping or hardware shops. If travelling on to Norway, Statoil agencies there will exchange Danish propane cylinders.

Public Transport

Public transport is excellent and you can buy a variety of bus, train and metro tickets at station kiosks and at some supermarkets. Children under the age of 12 travel free on buses and metro trains in the Greater Copenhagen area when accompanied by an adult. Tickets must be purchased for dogs and bicycles.

Numerous car ferry connections operate daily between different parts of the country. The ferry is a common mode of transport in Denmark and there may be long queues, especially at weekends in summer. The most important routes connect the bigger islands of Zealand and Funen with Jutland using high-speed vessels on day and night services. Vehicle length and height restrictions apply on routes between Odden (Zealand) and Århus and Æbeltoft (Jutland) and not all sailings transport caravans – check in advance. The Danish Tourist Board can provide general information on car ferry services or contact Scandlines for information on inter-island services including timetables and prices - www.scandlines.dk, email scandlines@scandlines.com or telephone 0045 (0) 33 15 15 15.

International ferry services are particularly busy during July and August and it is advisable to book in advance. Popular routes include Frederikshavn to Gothenburg (Sweden), Helsingør to Helsingborg (Sweden), Copenhagen to Oslo (Norway), and Rødby to Puttgarden in Germany (this route involves a road bridge which is occasionally closed to high-sided vehicles because of high winds). The ferry route from Copenhagen to Hamburg is a good alternative to the busy E45 motorway linking Denmark and Germany.

Copenhagen

Sites in Denmark

AABENRAA *B3* (2.7km S Coastal) *55.02490, 9.41461*
Fjordlyst Aabenraa City Camping, Sønderskovvej 100,
6200 Aabenraa **tel 45 74 62 26 99; mail@fjordlyst.dk;
www.fjordlyst.dk**

🐾 DKK10 🏕 📶 🔥 ♿ 🛒 🚐 MSP 🦋 ⛺ 🍽 🎮 🐕 500m

**Fr S take E45 & exit at junc 72 to Aabenraa. Foll Rd 42
then turn L onto Rd 24. Site sp on R.** 3*, Med, mkd, pt
shd, sl, terr, EHU (16A) DKK35; bbq; twin axles; TV;
10% statics; bus adj; Eng spkn; adv bkg acc; games
area; CCI. *"Scenic location with views over the bay;
excel facs; friendly, helpful staff; some steep slopes on
site rds; vg."* **DKK 225, 19 Mar-23 Sep.** **2016**

AALBORG *B1* (3km W Urban) *57.05500, 9.88500*
Strandparken Camping, Skydebanevej 20, 9000
Aalborg **tel 98 12 76 29; info@strandparken.dk;
www.strandparken.dk**

🐾 DKK10 🏕 📶 🔥 ♿ 🚐 MSP ⛺ 🍽 nr 🎮

**Turn L at start of m'way to Svenstrup & Aalborg W,
foll A180 (Hobrovej rd) twd town cent. Turn L bef
Limfjorden bdge onto Borgergade for 2km, site on
R. Fr N turn R after bdge onto Borgergade.** 3*, Med,
shd, EHU (10A) DKK30 (poss rev pol); cooking facs;
TV; 10% statics; phone; bus nr; Eng spkn; adv bkg
acc; ccard acc; CKE. *"Gd cent for town & N Jutland;
gd security; facs block excel; pool adj; card for elec."*
DKK 248, 24 Marr-11 Sep. **2016**

AALESTRUP *B2* (1km E Rural) *56.69166, 9.49991*
Aalestrup Camping, Aalestrup Campingplads,
Parkvænget 2, 9620 Aalestrup **tel 22 79 92 64;
pouledb@ofir.dk; www.rosenparken.dk**

🏕 📶 🔥 🚐 MSP 🦋 🍽 nr 🎮

**Fr E45 turn W onto rd 561 to Aalestrup; 500m after
junc with rd 13 turn L into Borgergade, cross rlwy
line. Site sp.** 1*, Med, pt shd, EHU DKK30. *"Free ent
beautiful rose garden; gd touring base; friendly staff."*
DKK 125, 1 Mar-1 Nov. **2016**

AARHUS *C2* (8km N Rural) *56.22660, 10.16260*
Åarhus Camping, Randersvej 400, Lisbjerg, 8200
Åarhus Nord **tel 86 23 11 33; info@aarhuscamping.dk;
www.aarhuscamping.dk**

12 🐾 DKK10 🏕 📶 🔥 ♿ 🚐 MSP ⛺ 🍽 🎮 (htd)

**Exit E45 junc 46 Århus N, then to Ikea rndabt. Then
foll sp Lisbjerg & head for smoking factory chimney.
Site 400m N of Lisbjerg.** 3*, Med, pt shd, pt sl, EHU
(16A) metered; gas; bbq; cooking facs; TV; 10% statics;
phone; adv bkg acc; golf 10km; games area; CKE.
*"Conv Århus; gd, tidy site; modern san facs; conv for
bus into Aarhus, helpful owner; elec cards for shwrs."*
DKK 203 **2015**

AARHUS *C2* (8km S Coastal) *56.11030, 10.23209*
Blommehaven Camping, Ørneredevej 35, 8270
Højbjerg **tel 86 27 02 07; info@blommenhaven.dk;
www.blommenhaven.dk**

🐾 DKK10 🏕 📶 🔥 ♿ 🚐 MSP 🦋 🍽 🎮 sand adj

**Fr S on E45 at junc 50 take rd 501 twd Århus. In
10km this becomes 01 ring rd. Take 2nd R Dalgas
Ave, at T-junc turn L & immed R into Strandvejen.
Site 3km on L in Marselisborg Forest.**
3*, Lge, mkd, hdg, pt shd, terr, EHU DKK35; bbq;
cooking facs; TV; 4% statics; phone; bus; Eng spkn;
adv bkg acc; Quickstop o'night facs. *"Some pitches
sm & bare earth; helpful staff; clean facs; easy reach
woods, cliffs & beach; conv for open-air museum."*
DKK 251, 18 Mar-23 Oct. **2016**

AARS *B2* (2km N Rural) *56.81530, 9.50695* **Aars
Camping,** Tolstrup Byvej 17, 9600 Aars **tel 98 62 36 03;
aarscampingplads@gmail.com; www.aarscamping.dk**

🏕 (htd) 📶 🔥 ♿ 🚐 MSP 🦋 ⛺ 🍽 🎮

**Fr E45 exit junc 33 W to Aars on rd 535. Turn N onto
rd 29 (Aggersundvej), site sp.** 3*, Med, pt shd, pt sl,
EHU (16A) DKK30; gas; bbq; cooking facs; TV;
10% statics; Eng spkn; adv bkg acc; ccard acc;
horseriding; tennis; CKE. *"Vg."*
DKK 150, 1 Apr-1 Nov. **2016**

ALBAEK *C1* (9.6km N Coastal) *57.64433, 10.46179*
Bunken Camping, Ålbækvej 288, Bunken Klitplantage,
9982 Ålbæk **tel 98 48 71 80; info@bunkenstrand
camping.dk; www.bunkenstrandcamping.dk**

🐾 DKK15 🏕 📶 🔥 ♿ 🚐 MSP 🍽 🎮 🐕 sand 150m

Site in fir plantation E of A10. 3*, V lge, hdg, pt shd,
EHU DKK39 (poss rev pol); gas; cooking facs; TV;
phone; adv bkg acc; boating; fishing. *"Beautiful site in
trees; spacious pitches."* **DKK 215, 3 Apr-18 Oct.**
2016

ASSENS *B3* (12km N Coastal) *55.33400, 9.89002*
Sandager Naes Camping, Strandgårdsvej 12, DK 5610
Assens **tel 45 64 79 11 56; info@sandagernaes.dk;
www.sandagernaes.dk**

🐾 🏕 📶 🔥 ♿ 🚐 MSP ⛺ 🍽 🎮 (htd) 🐕 0.5km

**Fr E20, take exit 57 dir Assens. R at Sandager &
foll sp.** Med, hdg, mkd, pt shd, pt sl, EHU (13A); bbq;
cooking facs; TV; 50% statics; phone; Eng spkn; adv
bkg acc; games area; games rm; waterslide; CCI. *"Excel
site."* **DKK 330, 23 Mar-15 Sep.** **2019**

ASSENS *B3* (1.6km W Urban/Coastal) *55.26569, 9.88390* **Camping Assens Strand,** Næsvej 15, 5610 Assens **tel** (45) 63 60 63 62; assens@campone.dk; www.campone.dk/assens

🏕DKK25 ♦♦♦ 🚿 ▲ ♨ ὕ ▣ ⌿ ▥ ▨ ⚏ ⚠ 🏊 sand adj

Site on beach at neck of land W of town adj marina. 3*, Med, pt shd, EHU (10A) DKK30; gas; TV; 20% statics; phone; adv bkg acc; watersports; fishing. *"Pleasant site on beach."*
DKK 215, Easter-13 Sep. 2016

BILLUND *B3* (12km SE Rural) *55.68877, 9.26864* **Randbøldal Camping,** Dalen 9, 7183 Randbøl **tel** 75 88 35 75; info@randboldalcamping.dk; www.randboldalcamping.dk

12 🏕DKK20 ♦♦♦ (htd) ▣ ▲ ♨ ὕ ▣ ⌿ ▥ 🦋 ὑ 🍺 ⚠

Fr Vejle take Billund rd. After approx 18km take L turn to Randbol & Bindebolle. Foll sp, site located approx 5km on L. 3*, Med, shd, pt sl, EHU (10A) DKK35; cooking facs; sw; TV; 15% statics; phone; Eng spkn; adv bkg acc; ccard acc; fishing nr; waterslide nr. *"Wooded site nr rv & trout hatchery; facs stretched high ssn; conv Legoland & Lion Park."* **DKK 234** 2016

BOGENSE *C3* (2km SW Urban/Coastal) *55.56144, 10.08530* **Bogense Strand Camping,** Vestre Engvej 11, 5400 Bogense **tel** 64 81 35 08; info@bogensecamp.dk; www.bogensecamp.dk

🏕DKK20 ♦♦♦ ▣ ▲ ♨ ὕ ▣ ⌿ ▥ 🦋 ὑ 🍺 ⚠ 🏊 ⚏ 🏊 shgl adj

Fr E20 at junc 57 & take 317 NE to Bogense. At 1st traff lts turn L for harbour, site sp at side of harbour. Lge, pt shd, EHU (12A) DKK35; cooking facs; TV; 10% statics; phone; adv bkg acc; CKE. *"Well-run site; excel facs; interesting sm town 5 mins walk."*
DKK 325, 3 Apr-18 Oct. 2016

BORRE *D3* (6km SE Rural) *54.97971, 12.52198* **Camping Møns Klint,** Klintevej 544, 4791 Magleby **tel** 55 81 20 25; camping@klintholm.dk; www.campingmoensklint.dk

🏕 ♦♦♦ ▣ ▲ ὕ ⌿ ▥ 🦋 ⚏ ὑ 🍺 ⚠ 🏊 ⚏ shgl 3km

Site nr end of metalled section of rd 287 fr Stege to E of Magleby, site sp. 3*, Lge, pt shd, pt sl, EHU (10A) DKK40; gas; cooking facs; TV; 20% statics; phone; Eng spkn; adv bkg acc; ccard acc; boating; games area; bike hire; tennis; fishing; CKE. *"150m chalk cliffs adj - geological interest; much flora, fauna, fossils; gd walks; friendly staff; excel facs."*
DKK 292, 1 Apr-31 Oct. 2016

BRAEDSTRUP *B2* (6.3km SSE Rural) *55.93552, 9.65314* **Gudenå Camping Brædstrup,** Bolundvej 4, 8740 Brædstrup **tel** 75763070; info@gudenaa camping.dk; www.gudenaacamping.dk

🏕DKK10 ♦♦♦ (htd) ▣ ▲ ♨ ὕ ▣ ⌿ ▥ 🦋 ⚏ 🍴 ὑ ⚠ 🏊

Fr Silkeborg take rd 52 twds Horsens; site sp R off rd 52 approx 4km fr Braedstrup. 3*, Sm, mkd, unshd, EHU (10A) metered; bbq; TV; 25% statics; adv bkg rec; games rm; CKE. *"Sm, attractive site beside Rv Gudenå; v well run fam site; fishing fr site; excel san facs."*
DKK 223, 29 Apr-27 Sep. 2015

COPENHAGEN *D3* (13km S Urban) *55.582578, 12.628996* **Copenhagen Camping,** Bachersmindevej 11, DK-2791 Dragør **tel** 32 94 20 07; info@ copenhagencamping.dk; copenhagencamping.dk

12 🏕 ♦♦♦ (htd) ▣ ▲ ♨ ▥ ⚏ 🏊

Exit E20 at junc 18. Lge, hdstg, hdg, unshd, 60% statics; Eng spkn; adv bkg acc; ccard acc; CKE. *"Gd; some airport noise; barrier clsd 2300-0700; of for short stay to visit Copenhagen."* **DKK 220** 2019

ENGESVANG *B2* (3km N Rural) *56.18736, 9.35627* **Bøllingsø Camping,** Kragelundvej 5, 7442 Engesvang **tel** 86 86 51 44; post@bollingso-camping.dk; www.bollingso-camping.dk

🏕DKK10 ♦♦♦ (htd) ▣ ▲ ♨ ὕ ▣ ⌿ ▥ 🦋 ⚏ nr ὑ 🍺 ⚠ 🏊 ⚏

Fr A13 dir Viborg, turn E to N of Engesvang & foll minor rd so Kragelund. Site on L 1km after museum. 3*, Med, mkd, pt shd, pt sl, EHU (16A) DKK30; cooking facs; TV; 2% statics; phone; adv bkg acc; lake fishing 250m; games area; CKE. *"Conv NH for A13; well-kept family site; clean, dated facs; nr Danish lake district."*
DKK 170, 1 Apr-1 Oct. 2016

ESBJERG *A3* (13km NW Rural/Coastal) *55.54359, 8.33921* **Sjelborg Camping,** Sjelborg Standvej 11, Hjerting, 6710 Esbjerg Vest **tel** 75 11 54 32; info@ sjelborg.dk; www.sjelborg.dk

♦♦♦ ▣ ▲ ♨ ὕ ▣ ⌿ ▥ 🦋 ὑ 🍺 ⚠ 🏊 shgl nr

Fr Esbjerg take coast rd N twds Hjerting & Sjelborg. At T-junc, Sjelborg Vej, turn L & in 100m turn R onto Sjelborg Kirkevej (camping sp); in 600m turn L into Sjelborg Strandvej (sp); site on R in 600m. 3*, Lge, mkd, hdg, pt shd, EHU (10A)€4.50; phone; bus to town; adv bkg acc; fishing; golf 5km. *"Excel, well maintained site in a quiet country setting; superb facs & activities all ages; lake adj; spacious on edge of conservation area; mkd walks & bird sanctuary; v welcoming & friendly."* **DKK 190, 11 Apr-20 Sep.** 2015

FAABORG *C3* (8.5km W Coastal) *55.10568, 10.10776* **Bøjden Strandcamping,** Bøjden Landevej 12, 5600 Bøjden **tel** 63 60 63 60; info@bojden.dk; www.bojden.dk

🏕DKK15 ♦♦♦ (htd) ▣ ▲ ♨ ὕ ▣ ⌿ ▥ ⚏ ⚏ nr 🍺 ⚠ ✎ 🏊 (htd) 🏊 ⚏ sand adj

Rd 8 W fr Fåborg dir Bøjden/Fynshav, site sp nr ferry. 5*, Lge, mkd, hdg, pt shd, pt sl, terr, serviced pitches; EHU (16A) DKK31; cooking facs; TV; 80% statics; Eng spkn; adv bkg acc; ccard acc; games rm; golf 12km; bike hire; sep car park; boat hire. *"Excel family site with activity cent; blue flag beach; sea views fr pitches; interesting area; excel facs."*
DKK 395, 9 Apr-22 Oct. 2017

DENMARK

FREDERIKSHAVN *C1* (2km N Coastal) *57.46415,
10.52778* **Nordstrand Camping A/S (Formerly
TopCamp),** Apholmenvej 40, 9900 Frederikshavn
**tel 98 42 93 50; info@nordstrand-camping.dk;
www.nordstrand-camping.dk**

🐕 DKK12 👫 WD ⚍ ♨ ⚲ 🖃 🏊 🛒 (covrd) 🌲 1km

Fr E45/Rd40 foll rd N twd Skagen to outside town
boundary (over rlwy bdge), turn R at rndabt into
Apholmenvej; site sp. 4*, Lge, mkd, unshd, EHU
(10A); gas; red long stay; TV; 10% statics; phone; Eng
spkn; adv bkg acc; ccard acc; excursions; CKE. *"Vg
NH for ferries; recep open 24hrs peak ssn; well-run,
clean site; some pitches sm; cycle track to town."*
DKK 305, 14 Mar-24 Sep. **2017**

GRASTEN *B3* (2km SW Coastal) *54.9007, 9.57121*
Lærkelunden Camping, Nederbyvej 17-25, Rinkenæs,
6300 Gråsten **tel 74 65 02 50; info@laerkelunden.dk;
www.laerkelunden.dk**

🐕 👫 WD ⚍ ♨ ⚲ & 🖃 MP 🐾 🛒 (covrd, htd) 🌲 sand adj

Fr Kruså E on rd 8 twds Gråsten & Sønderborg; on
E o'skts of Rinkenæs turn R Nederbyvej (car dealer
on corner) & foll sp to site in 400m. 4*, Lge, hdstg,
unshd, pt sl, serviced pitches; EHU (10A) DKK30; gas;
bbq; cooking facs; TV; 10% statics; phone; Eng spkn;
ccard acc; boat launch; sauna; solarium; CKE. *"Gd
sailing/surfing; views over Flensburg fjord; coastal
footpath; gd cent for S Jutland & N Germany; excel;
lovely, well run site."* **DKK 317, 21 Mar-22 Oct.**
2017

GRENAA *C2* (4km S Coastal) *56.38957, 10.91213*
Grenaa Strand Camping, Fuglsangsvej 58, 8500 Grenå
**tel 86 32 17 18; info@722.dk; www.grenaastrand
camping.dk**

🐕 DKK30 👫 WD ⚍ ♨ ⚲ 🖃 MP 🛒 /⛰ 🌲 sand 250m

Fr Grenå harbour foll coast rd due S foll sp. 3*, V lge,
unshd, EHU (10A) DKK35; gas; TV; 10% statics; phone;
adv bkg acc; solarium. *"Conv for ferries to Sweden;
busy site."* **DKK 264, 1 Apr-16 Sep.** **2016**

HADERSLEV *B3* (13.6km S Coastal) *55.15313, 9.49424*
Vikaer Strand Camping, Dundelum 29, Djernaes,
6100 Haderslev **tel 74 57 54 64; info@vikaercamp.dk;
www.vikaercamp.dk**

🐕 DKK 12 👫 WD ⚍ & 🖃 MP 🐾 🛒 ⛰

S on Katsund twd Lille Klingbjerg, turn R onto Lille
Klingbjerg, L onto Højgade, R onto Møllepladsen,
L to stay on Møllepladsen then take rte 170 to
Diernæs Strandvej for 10.9km, then take 1st R onto
Ny Erlevvej for 450m, turn L onto Omkørselsvejen/
Rte 170, cont to foll Rte 170 for 8.1km, go thro 1
rndbt, turn L onto Diernæsvej Strandvej for 2.3km
foll Diernæs Strandvej to Dundelum, L onto Diernæs
Strandvej, R to stay on same rd, R onto Dundelum, L
to stay on Dundelum and site on R. Lge, mkd, unshd,
pt sl, EHU (10-16A); Eng spkn; CCI. *"Super site, many
outlets for children; lovely beach; immac san facs."*
DKK 240, Easter-31 Oct. **2019**

HANSTHOLM *B1* (4km E Coastal) *57.10913, 8.66731*
Hanstholm Camping, Hamborgvej 95, 7730
Hanstholm **tel 97 96 51 98; info@hanstholm-
camping.de; www.hanstholm-camping.dk**

12 🐕 DKK10 👫 (htd) WD ⚍ ♨ ⚲ 🖃 /⛰ MP 🐾 ⚍ 🛒 /⛰ 🌲 (htd)
🛁 🌲 sand 1km

Ent town fr S on rte 26. At rndabt turn R onto coast
rd sp Vigsø. Site on L in about 4km. 3*, Lge, hdg,
mkd, pt shd, pt sl, EHU (10A) DKK40; gas; bbq; TV;
30% statics; phone; Eng spkn; adv bkg acc; ccard acc;
horseriding; sauna; fishing; CKE. *"Fine view of North
Sea coast; nr wildlife area; gd cycling/walking on
coast path; excel, busy, well-maintained site; generous
pitches; gd rest; excel childrens facs."* **DKK 230**
2016

HEJLSMINDE *B3* (9km N Coastal) *55.41109, 9.59228*
Gronninghoved Strand Camping, Mosvigvej 21,
6093 Sjolund **tel 75 57 40 45; info@gronninghoved.dk;
www.gronninghoved.dk**

🐕 👫 WD ⚍ ♨ ⚲ & 🖃 /⛰ MP 🐾 🛒 /⛰ 🌲 (htd) 🛁 🌲 shgl 0.2km

Fr E45 at exit 65 take 25 twds Kolding. At lights
turn R onto 170. After 3.4km turn L sp Sjolund.
On entry Sjolund take 1st L sp Gronninghoved.
Take 2nd R in Gronninghoved, then 1st L, foll sp
to site. 4*, Lge, mkd, hdg, pt shd, pt sl, EHU (10A)
DKK37; cooking facs; twin axles; TV; 75% statics;
Eng spkn; adv bkg acc; games area; games rm; CKE.
"Excel site; tennis, mini golf, billards & waterslide."
DKK 270, 18 Mar-15 Sep. **2016**

HELSINGOR *D2* (3km NE Urban/Coastal) *56.04393,
12.60433* **Helsingør Camping Grønnehave,**
Strandalleen 2, 3000 Helsingør **tel 49 28 49 50 or
25 31 12 12; campingpladsen@helsingor.dk;
www.helsingorcamping.dk**

12 👫 WD ⚍ & 🖃 /⛰ 🛒 /⛰ ⛰

Site in NE o'skts of town, twd Hornbæk. Site nr
beach o'looking channel to Sweden on E side of
rd. Foll sps on app or in town (beware: sp are sm
& low down). 2*, Med, pt shd, EHU (10A) DKK30;
cooking facs; 25% statics; phone. *"10 min walk to
Hamlet's castle; 20 min walk to town & stn; gd train
service to Copenhagen; max stay 14 days 15 Jun-15
Aug; Baltic ships w/end mid-Aug; v busy/cr high ssn."*
DKK 217 **2019**

HELSINGOR *D2* (13km SSW Coastal) *55.93949,
12.51643* **Niva Camping,** Sølyst Allé 14, 2290 Nivå
**tel 49 14 52 26; nivaacamping@post8.tele.dk;
www.nivaacamping.dk**

🐕 👫 (htd) WD ⚍ ♨ ⚲ 🖃 /⛰ MP 🏊 ⊕ nr 🛒 /⛰ 🌲 800m

Take coast rd bet Copenhagen & Helsingør. Fr N foll
sp to Nivå, & site 500m fr main rd, sp. Fr S site 2km
after vill. 2*, Lge, mkd, hdstg, pt shd, pt sl, EHU (16A);
bbq; cooking facs; twin axles; TV; 10% statics; Eng
spkn; adv bkg acc; ccard acc; fishing adj; games rm;
CKE. *"Conv Helsingborg ferry, Copenhagen, Kronborg
Castle (Hamlet); excel san facs; vg location; quiet; best
site in Zealand; excel help; upper level pitches quietest
& coolest if hot."* **DKK 240, 31 Mar-30 Sep.** **2019**

For a guide to symbols see the fold out on the rear cover

HELSINGOR *D2* (10km NW Urban) *56.08104, 12.51348* **Skibstrup Camping,** Stormlugen 20, 3140 Ålsgårde **tel 49 70 99 71; info@skibstrup-camping.dk; www.skibstrup-camping.dk**

🐕 ♦♦♦ WD 📷 ♁ ♿ 🖳 ⊿ MSP 🦋 📶 nr 🔺 ⚓ 🚣 ♨ ⚓ 500m

Fr Helsingør take N coast rd to Ålsgårde; then foll site sp. 3*, Lge, shd, EHU (10A) DKK35; cooking facs; TV; 10% statics; phone; adv bkg acc; ccard acc. *"Pleasant site amongst trees; conv for ferry & Copenhagen."* **DKK 150, 1 Apr-31 Oct.** 2015

HILLEROD *D2* (1km SW Urban) *55.9246, 12.2941* **Hillerød Camping,** Blytækkervej 18, 3400 Hillerød **tel 48 26 48 54; info@hillerodcamping.dk; www.hillerodcamping.dk**

🐕 DKK10 ♦♦♦ WD 📷 ♁ ♿ 🖳 ⊿ MSP 🦋 ⑪ nr 📶 🔺 nr 📶

Fr Roskilde or Copenhagen on A16 twd Hillerød, take 1st L at traff lts sp Hillerød & Frederiksborg Slot Rv233. Site in town cent, not well sp. Med, pt shd, pt sl, EHU (10A) DKK40 (long lead poss req); gas; cooking facs; TV; phone; bus, train nr; Eng spkn; adv bkg acc; ccard acc; bike hire; CCI. *"Frederiksborg castle in town cent; gd base for N Seeland; 30 min by train to Copenhagen; v helpful, charming owner; common/dining rm; pleasant, well-run site; excel, new san facs 2010; no mkd pitch, but owner positions o'fits carefully; many personal touches - eg courtyard with herbs, fruit trees, candles & torches; best site."* **DKK 240, 12 Apr-19 Oct.** 2019

HIRTSHALS *C1* (5km SW Coastal) *57.55507, 9.93254* **Tornby Strand Camping,** Strandvejen 13, 9850 Tornby **tel 98 97 78 77; mail@tornbystrand.dk; www.tornbystrand.dk**

12 🐕 DKK5 ♦♦♦ WD 📷 ♁ ♿ 🖳 ⊿ MSP 🦋 🛒 📶 nr 📶 🔺 sand 1km

Take rd 55 fr Hjørring twd Hirtshals. In 12km turn L sp Tornby Strand & Camping, site on L in 200m. 3*, Lge, pt shd, EHU (16A) DKK30; gas; TV; 75% statics; phone; Eng spkn; adv bkg acc; CKE. *"Useful for ferries to Kristiansand, Arendal, Faroe & Iceland; helpful owner."* **DKK 254** 2016

HIRTSHALS *C1* (1.5km W Urban) *57.58650, 9.94583* **Hirtshals Camping,** Kystvejen 6, 9850 Hirtshals **tel 98 94 25 35; info@hirtshals-camping.dk; www.dk-camp.dk/hirtshals**

🐕 DKK10 ♦♦♦ WD 📷 ♁ ♿ ⊿ MSP 🦋 ⑪ nr 📶 🔺 200m

Located 16km N of Hjørring. Turn L off rd 14 3km SW of Hirtshals & site on L. Fr ferry foll sp town cent, then site sp. 3*, Med, unshd, terr, EHU (10A) DKK30; sw nr; TV; phone; bike hire; fishing 200m. *"Open site on cliff top; san facs dated; friendly staff; conv ferries; on coastal cycle path; late arr area; busy but efficient; conv for NH."* **DKK 225, 25 Mar-31 Oct.** 2016

HJORRING *C1* (14km W Urban) *57.47375, 9.80100* **Lønstrup Camping,** Møllebakkevej 20, Lonstrup, 9800 Hjørring **tel 45 21 44 56 37; loenstrupcamping@ mail.dk; www.campingloenstrup.dk**

🐕 10DKK ♦♦♦ (htd) WD 📷 ♁ ♿ 🖳 ⊿ MSP 🦋 📶 🔺 500m

Fr E39 take Exit 3 dir Hjørring for Rte 35 twd Rte 55. Turn R onto Lonstrupvej. Foll sp to site. Med, mkd, pt shd, EHU (10A) 35DKK; bbq; cooking facs; twin axles; 30% statics; bus 200m; Eng spkn; adv bkg acc; CCI. *"Vg site; friendly, helpful family owned; lge units may be tight access; close to sm vill & coast."* **DKK 245, 28 Mar-29 Sep.** 2019

HOLBAEK *D3* (4km E Coastal) *55.71799, 11.76020* **FDM Holbæk Fjord Camping,** Sofiesminde Allé 1, 4300 Holbæk **tel 59 43 50 64; c-holbaek@fdm.dk**

12 🐕 DKK15 ♦♦♦ (htd) WD 📷 ♁ ♿ 🖳 ⊿ MSP 🦋 📶 ⑪ 🛒 📶 🔺 📶 🔺 (htd) ♨

Fr Rv21 exit junc 20 (fr N) or junc 18 (fr S) & foll sp to harbour. Turn R (E) at harbour - Munkholmvej. Approx 1.5km along Munkholmvej, after traff lts, turn L into Sofiesminde Allé dir marina. Site on R, close to marina. 3*, Lge, hdg, mkd, pt shd, EHU (10A) inc; gas; bbq; cooking facs; TV; 80% statics; phone; adv bkg acc; ccard acc; sauna; golf nr; games area; bike hire; games rm; fishing nr; watersports nr. *"Well-run site in attractive position; helpful staff; pitches poss tight lge o'fits; whirlpool; spa; clean san facs; no o'fits over 10m high ssn; gd walks & cycle tracks."* **DKK 328, H17.** 2015

HORSENS *B2* (6km W Rural/Coastal) *55.85928, 9.91747* **Husodde Strand Camping,** Husoddevej 85, 8700 Horsens **tel 75 65 70 60; camping@husodde.dk; www.husodde-camping.dk**

12 🐕 DKK10 ♦♦♦ WD 📷 ♁ ♿ 🖳 ⊿ MSP 🦋 ⑪ nr 📶 🔺 📶 🔺 sand adj

Site sp to R of Horsens-Odder rd (451), foll rd to fjord, site sp. 3*, Med, mkd, pt shd, pt sl, EHU (10A) DKK35; bbq; cooking facs; TV; 10% statics; phone; Eng spkn; fishing adj; CKE. *"Lovely location; lge pitches; well-maintained, well-managed site; friendly welcome; pool 3km; cycle tracks."* **DKK 238** 2015

HVIDE SANDE *A2* (7.6km S Coastal) *55.94975, 8.15030* **Nordsø Camping & Badeland,** Tingodden 3, Årgab, 6960 Hvide Sande **tel 75 52 14 82; info@ dancamps.dk; www.dancamps.dk**

🐕 DKK20 ♦♦♦ (htd) WD 📷 ♁ ♿ 🖳 ⊿ MSP 🦋 🍽 ⑪ 🛒 📶 🔺 📶 🔺 ⊿ (covrd, htd) ♨ 🔺 sand 200m

Fr E20 take exit 73 onto rd 11 to Varde. Then take rd 181 twd Nymindegab & Hvide Sande. 3*, Lge, hdstg, unshd, serviced pitches; EHU (10A) DKK30; TV; 10% statics; phone; adv bkg acc; fishing; waterslide; tennis; sauna. *"Well-maintained facs; extra charge seaview pitches; private san facs avail; vg."* **DKK 199, 15 Apr-31 Oct.** 2016

DENMARK

JELLING *B3* (13km NW Rural) *55.83138, 9.29944*
Topcamp Riis & Feriecenter, Østerhovedvej 43,
Riis 7323 Give **tel 75 73 14 33; info@riisferiepark.dk;
www.riisferiepark.dk**

🛉 DKK20 ♨ ⬚ ♨ ⚷ ⬚ ✓ ⬚ ✗ ✗ ♈ ♈ 🛒 🏔 ✗
⚓ (htd) 🏖

Fr S exit E45 at junc 61, turn L & foll rd 28 for approx
8km. Turn R onto rd 441 for 15km, then turn R into
Østerhovedvej for 2km & turn L into site. Or fr N
on E45 exit junc 57, turn R & foll rd for 25km; turn
L & foll 442 for 500m; turn R into Østerhovedvej &
cont for 1.5km; turn R into site. 4*, Med, hdstg, mkd,
hdg, pt shd, serviced pitches; EHU (13A) inc; gas; bbq;
TV; 60% statics; phone; adv bkg acc; ccard acc; sauna;
fishing 3.5km; golf 4km; bike hire; games rm; jacuzzi;
waterslide; CKE. *"Attractive, well laid-out, well-run site
in beautiful countryside; jacuzzi; fitness cent; vg san
facs; no o'fits over 15m high ssn; conv for Legoland,
Safari Park, Center Mobilium museum in Billund, lakes
& E coast; excel; recep 0800-2200; friendly & relaxed;
spacious pitches."* **DKK 430, 19 Mar-25 Sep, H11.**
                                                    2019

"We must tell the Club about that great site we found"

Get your site reports in by mid-August and we'll
do our best to get your updates into the next
edition.

KARISE *D3* (5km S Rural) *55.27086, 12.22281*
Lægårdens Camping, Vemmetoftevej 2A, Store
Spjellerup, 4653 Karise **tel 56 71 00 67; info@
laegaardenscamping.dk; www.laegaardenscamping.dk**
12 🛉 DKK10 ♨ (htd) ⬚ ⬚ ⬚ ✓ ⬚ ⬚ nr 🏔 ✗ 3km

Turn S off rd 209 in Karise, site sp. 2*, Med, mkd, hdg,
pt shd, EHU DKK30; TV; 60% statics; Eng spkn; adv
bkg acc; CKE. **DKK 150**   **2016**

KOBENHAVN *D3* (10km N Coastal) *55.74536, 12.58331*
Camping Charlottenlund Fort, Strandvejen 144B,
2290 Charlottenlund **tel 39 62 36 88; camping@
gentofte.dk; www.campingcopenhagen.dk**
♨ ⬚ ⬚ ⬚ ✓ ⬚ ♈ ✗ nr ⬚ nr ✗ sand

**Take København-Helsingør coast rd O2/152, site on
seaside 2km N of Tuborg factory.** Sm, mkd, hdstg,
shd, EHU (10A) metered; cooking facs; bus; Eng spkn;
adv bkg rec; ccard acc; CKE. *"Experimentarium Science
Park at Tuborg brewery; in grnds of old moated fort;
conv Copenhagen & Sweden; gd facs but inadequate
high ssn; quiet but noisy during mid-summer festivities;
friendly staff."* **DKK 260, 30 Apr-6 Sep.**   **2019**

KOBENHAVN *D3* (9km W Urban) *55.67055, 12.43353*
DCU Absalon Camping, Korsdalsvej 132, 2610
Rødovre **tel 36 41 06 00; copenhagen@dcu.dk;
www.camping-absalon.dk**
12 🛉 DKK23 ♨ (htd) ⬚ ⬚ ⬚ ⬚ ✓ ⬚ ♈ ⬚ nr ⬚ 🏔 🏖

Fr E55/E20/E47 exit junc 24 dir København, site on L
in 1km, sp. Or fr København foll A156 W for 9km. Sp
Rødovre then Brøndbyøster, shortly after this site
sp to R at traff lts; ent on L after 100m down side
rd, sp. 2*, V lge, hdg, mkd, unshd, pt sl, EHU (10-16A)
DKK30 or metered + conn fee; gas; bbq; cooking facs;
twin axles; TV; 10% statics; bus/train nr; Eng spkn;
adv bkg acc; ccard acc; games area; golf 10km; games
rm; CKE. *"Well located nr Brøndbyøster rlwy stn & bus
Copenhagen (rail tickets fr recep); some pitches unrel in
wet & dusty when dry; vg, modern san facs; office clsd
1200-1400 LS; htd pool 300m; sep area for c'vans &
m'vans; helpful staff; cycle rte to city; excel site; v well
run; fitness rm; outdoor chess; attrac & boat trips can
be booked; muddy when wet."* **DKK 260**   **2018**

KOLDING *B3* (16km E Coastal) *55.46777, 9.67972*
Gammel Ålbo Camping, Gammel Aalbovej 30, 6092
Sønder Stenderup **tel 75 57 11 16; camping@
gl-aalbo.dk; www.gl-aalbo.dk**
12 🛉 ♨ (htd) ⬚ ⬚ ⬚ ✓ ⬚ ♈ 🛒 ✗ shgl adj

Foll rd SE fr Kolding to Agtrup then on to Sønder
Bjert & Sønder Stenderup. Foll site sp thro vill twd
coast, site at end of rd. 3*, Med, hdg, hdstg, pt shd,
terr, EHU (16A) DKK38.50; 10% statics; Eng spkn;
fishing; boat hire; CKE. *"Well-kept, relaxing
site o'looking Lillebælt; skin-diving; v cr in high ssn."*
DKK 224   **2015**

KOLDING *B3* (5km S Urban) *55.46290, 9.47290*
Kolding City Camp, Vonsildvej 19, 6000 Kolding
**tel 75 52 13 88; info@koldingcitycamp.dk;
www.koldingcitycamp.dk**
12 🛉 DKK20 ♨ (htd) ⬚ ⬚ ⬚ ⬚ ✓ ⬚ ♈ ⬚ nr ✗ 🏔

E45 (Flensbury-Frederikshavn) take exit 65 at
Kolding Syd twrds Kolding; at 1st traff lts turn R site
800m on L. 3*, Lge, pt shd, pt sl, EHU (10A) DKK40;
gas; bbq; cooking facs; TV; phone; bus to town; Eng
spkn; adv bkg acc; ccard acc; fishing 5km; tennis; CKE.
*"Friendly & v quiet; conv NH Legoland; htd covrd pool
3km; vg san facs; gd site; level pitches; private san facs
avail; full kitchen facs."* **DKK 301**   **2019**

KORSOR *C3* (10km SE Rural) *55.28991, 11.2649*
Boeslunde Camping, Rennebjergvej 110, 4242
Boeslunde **tel 58 14 02 08; info@campinggaarden.dk;
www.campinggaarden.dk**
🛉 DKK10 ♨ ⬚ ⬚ ⬚ ⬚ ✓ ⬚ ✗ ♈ 🛒 🏔 🏖 ✗ 1.5km

Take rd 265 S out of Korsør & in 8km, bef
Boeslunde at camping sp, turn R. Site on L in
2km. 3*, Med, pt shd, pt sl, EHU DKK30 (long lead
poss req); gas; TV (pitch); phone; adv bkg acc; CKE.
"Gd size, grassy pitches; well kept; gate barrier."
DKK 235, 1 Apr-1 Oct.   **2018**

MIDDELFART *B3* (11km NE Coastal) *55.51948, 9.85025* **Vejlby Fed Camping,** Rigelvej 1, 5500 Vejlby Fed **tel** 64 40 24 20; mail@vejlbyfed.dk; www.vejlbyfed.dk

🐕 DKK20 ⁜ ⓌⒹ ♨ ♿ 🅿 ☇ MP ⁇ 🍴 🎣 🕹 🏔 ⚓(htd) 🖳

𝒯 sand adj

Exit E20 junc 57 or 58. Site sp in Vejlby Fed, NE fr Middelfart dir Bogense, on coast. 4*, Lge, mkd, pt shd, EHU (10A) DKK39; cooking facs; 30% statics; phone; Eng spkn; adv bkg acc; sauna; fishing; tennis; boating; CKE. **DKK 430, 15 Mar-14 Sep.**   2019

MIDDELFART *B3* (5km NW Rural) *55.51694, 9.68225* **Gals Klint Camping,** Galsklintvej 11, 5500 Middelfart **tel** 64 41 20 59; mail@galsklint.dk; www.galsklint.dk

🐕 ⁜(htd) ⓌⒹ ♨ ♿ 🅿 ☇ MP 🦋 ①r 🔋 🏔 𝒯shgl adj

Fr W on E20 take rd 161. At 2 traff lts turn L & cross Little Belt Bdge. In 300m turn R into Galsklintvej & foll sp. 3*, Lge, hdg, mkd, pt shd, EHU (16A) DKK28; bbq; cooking facs; 10% statics; Eng spkn; adv bkg acc; ccard acc; boat hire; fishing; CKE. *"Site surrounded by forest; gd cycling/walking; vg; well run mod facs shoreside next woodland."*
DKK 208, 18 Mar-3 Oct.   2016

NYBORG *C3* (4km N Coastal) *55.35853, 10.78660* **Gronnehave Strand,** Regstrupvej 83, 5800 Nyborg **tel** 65 36 15 50; info@gronnehave.dk; www.gronnehave.dk

🐕 ⁜(htd) ⓌⒹ ♨ ♿ 🅿 ☇ MP 🦋 ⁇ 🔋nr 🏔 𝒯adj

10 mins N on Skaboeshusevej - sp. Fr E20 junc 46 turn N and foll sp. 3*, Med, mkd, unshd, terr, EHU (10A) DKK36; TV; Eng spkn; games area. *"Friendly owner; gd views; bdge to Zeeland; vg."*
DKK 261, 29 Mar-23 Sep.   2019

NYBORG *C3* (3km SE Coastal) *55.30457, 10.82453* **Nyborg Strandcamping,** Hjejlevej 99, 5800 Nyborg **tel** 65 31 02 56; mail@strandcamping.dk; www.strandcamping.dk

🐕 ⁜ ⓌⒹ ♨ ♿ 🅿 ☇ MP ⁇ ①nr 🔋 🏔 𝒯sand adj

Exit E20 at junc 44. Turn N, site sp in 1km. 3*, Lge, mkd, pt shd, EHU (10A) metered; gas; TV; 50% statics; phone; Eng spkn; adv bkg acc; fishing; golf 1km; CKE. *"Conv m'way, rlwy & ferry; excel views of bdge; gd facs; gd site; well difined pitches next to beach."*
DKK 256, 13 Apr-21 Sep.   2019

NYBORG *C3* (13km S Rural) *55.23693, 10.8080* **Tårup Stand Camping,** Lersey Allé 25, Tårup Strand, 5871 Frørup **tel** 65 37 11 99; mail@taarupstrandcamping.dk; www.taarupstrandcamping.dk

🐕 ⁜(htd) ⓌⒹ ♨ ♿ 🅿 ☇ MP 🦋 ⁇ 🏔 𝒯shgl

S fr Nyborg take 163 twds Svendborg; after 6.5km turn L sp Tårup. In 2.7km turn L sp Tårup Strand. Site 1.5km on R. 3*, Med, mkd, EHU (6-10A) DKK26; TV; 70% statics; phone; adv bkg acc; ccard acc; games rm; CKE. *"Quiet family site; excel views of bdge; fishing; excel site."* **DKK 222, 4 Apr-21 Sep.**   2019

ODENSE *C3* (5km S Rural) *55.36966, 10.39316* **DCU Camping Odense,** Odensevej 102, 5260 Odense **tel** 66 11 47 02; odense@dcu.dk; www.camping-odense.dk

12 🐕 DKK23 ⁜(htd) ⓌⒹ ♨ ♿ 🅿 ☇ MP 🦋 ⁇ ①nr 🔋 🏔 ⚓ 🖳

Exit E20 junc 51 foll sp 'centrum' (Stenlosevej). After rndabt site on L just after 3rd set traff lts. Ent to R of petrol stn. 3*, Lge, mkd, hdg, pt shd, EHU (16A) DKK30; gas; bbq; cooking facs; twin axles; TV; 10% statics; phone; bus; Eng spkn; adv bkg acc; ccard acc; games area; games rm; CKE. *"Hans Christian Andersen's hse; many attractions; excel, friendly, family-run site; busy high ssn & facs stretched; easy bus access to town cent; lovely, easy cycle rte into town cent; excel san fac; pitches tight for larger units; quick stop area for MH; sep c'van & MH areas; pitches muddy when wet; excel."* **DKK 380**   2018

"I need an on-site restaurant"

We do our best to make sure site information is correct, but it is always best to check any must-have facilities are still available or will be open during your visit.

ODENSE *C3* (11km W Rural) *55.3894, 10.2475* **Campingpladsen Blommenslyst,** Middelfartvej 494, 5491 Blommenslyst **tel** 65 96 76 41; info@blommelyst-camping.dk; www.blommenslyst-camping.dk

🐕 DKK10 ⁜(htd) ⓌⒹ ♨ ♿ 🅿 ☇ MP 🦋 🔋 🏔

Exit E20 onto 161 (junc 53); sp 'Odense/Blommenslyst', site on R after 2km; lge pink Camping sp on side of house. 2*, Sm, shd, pt sl, EHU (4A) DKK30; 10% statics; bus; Eng spkn; adv bkg req; CKE. *"Picturesque setting round sm lake; gd, clean, rustic facs; welcoming owners; frequent bus to town outside site; excel; lovely site."*
DKK 168, 5 Jan-20 Dec.   2019

RANDERS *B2* (8km SW Rural) *56.44984, 9.95287* **Randers City Camp,** Hedevej 9, Fladbro, 8920 Randers **tel** 45 29 47 36 55; info@randerscitycamp.dk; www.randerscitycamp.dk

12 🐕 DKK10 ⁜(htd) ⓌⒹ ♨ ♿ 🅿 ☇ MP 🦋 ⁇ 🔋 🏔 ⚓(covrd, htd)

Take exit 40 fr E45 & turn twd Randers. Approx 100m fr m'way turn R at traff lts dir Langå. Site clearly sp in 3km & also sp fr rd 16. 3*, Lge, mkd, pt shd, terr, EHU (10A) DKK35; bbq; cooking facs; twin axles; TV; 50% statics; phone; bus 0.5km; Eng spkn; adv bkg acc; ccard acc; games rm; golf adj; fishing; CKE. *"On heather hills with view of Nørreå valley; rec arr early for pitch with view; golf course; Randers tropical zoo; ideal for walkers, cyclist & runners; fishing; gd."* **DKK 239**   2017

RIBE *B3* (2km SE Rural) *55.31725, 8.75952* **Parking Storkesøen,** Haulundvej 164, 6760 Ribe **tel 75 41 04 11;** info@storkesoen.dk; www.storkesoen.dk

🔟 ♯♦ⓌⓄ ♨ ⚡ ⊒

Fr S on rte 11, turn R at 1st rndabt onto rte 24 & R at next rndabt. Site 100m on R, sp fishing. Fr S on rte 24, at 1st rndabt after rlwy turn L, site 200m on R. M'vans only - check in at fishing shop on R. Sm, hdstg, unshd, EHU (5A/16A) inc; own san req; lake fishing. *"Picturesque, quiet site o'looking fishing lakes; walking dist Denmark's oldest city; m'vans & c'vans acc, ideal NH; fishing shop; vg facs."* **DKK 140   2016**

RIBE *B3* (2.4km NNW Rural) *55.34115, 8.76506* **Ribe Camping,** Farupvej 2, 6760 Ribe **tel 75 41 07 77;** info@ribecamping.dk; www.ribecamping.dk

🔟 🐕 DKK15 ♯♦(htd) ⓌⓄ ♨ ⚡ ⊒ ♨ 🦋 ⚓ ♔ ♨ ⚡ /Ⅲ
🛶 (htd)

Fr S foll A11 by-pass W of Ribe to traff lts N of town; turn W off A11 at traff lts; site 500m on R. Fr N (Esbjerg ferry) to Ribe, turn R at traff lts sp Farup. Site on R, sp. 3*, Lge, pt shd, serviced pitches; EHU (10A) DKK35; gas; cooking facs; TV; 10% statics; phone; adv bkg acc; ccard acc; games rm; Quickstop o'night facs; CKE. *"Ribe oldest town in Denmark; much historical interest; helpful, friendly staff; well-run; excel, modern san facs; conv Esbjerg ferry."*
DKK 271   2016

RINGKOBING *A2* (5km E Rural) *56.08856, 8.31659* **Ringkøbing Camping,** Herningvej 105, 6950 Ringkøbing **tel 97 32 04 20;** info@ringkobingcamping.dk; www.ringkøbingcamping.dk

🐕 DKK10 ♯♦ ⓌⓄ ♨ ⚓ ♔ ♨ /Ⅲ 🦋 ♨ ♨ /Ⅲ 🌳 sand 3km

Take rd 15 fr Ringkøbing dir Herning, site on L. 3*, Med, hdg, mkd, pt shd, EHU (10A) DKK29; gas; TV; phone; adv bkg acc; Quickstop o'night facs. *"Beautiful site in mixed forest; friendly welcome; excel facs; gd walks; 3km to fjord; 14km to sea."*
DKK 226, 1 Apr-30 Sep.   2016

ROSKILDE *D3* (4km N Rural) *55.67411, 12.07955* **Roskilde Camping,** Baunehøjvej 7-9, 4000 Veddelev **tel 46 75 79 96;** mail@roskildecamping.dk; www.roskildecamping.dk

♯♦(htd) ⓌⓄ ♨ ⚓ ♔ ♨ /Ⅲ 🦋 ♨ ① ♨ /Ⅲ 🌳 shgl

Leave rd 21/23 at junc 11 & turn N on rd 6 sp Hillerød. Turn R onto rd 02 (E ring rd); then rejoin 6; (watch for camping sp). At traff lts with camping sp turn L twds city & foll site sp. 3*, Lge, mkd, pt shd, pt sl, EHU (10A) DKK30; own san req; gas; TV; Eng spkn; adv bkg acc; ccard acc; games rm; watersports; CKE. *"Beautiful views over fjord; nr Viking Ship Museum (a must) - easy parking; beautiful Cathedral; excel rest & shop open 0800-2000; bus service to stn, frequent trains to Copenhagen; ltd flat pitches; lovely site; immac, new state of the art san facs block with card for ent (2014); v welcoming & helpful staff."*
DKK 225, 31 Mar-23 Sep.   2019

RY *B2* (4km NW Rural) *56.10388, 9.74555* **Birkede Camping,** Lyngvej 14, 8680 Ry **tel 86 89 13 55;** info@birkhede.dk; www.birkhede.dk

🐕 ♯♦ ⓌⓄ ♨ ⚓ ♔ ♨ /Ⅲ MSP ♨ ♔ ① ♨ /Ⅲ 🛶(htd)

Fr S on rd 52 exit onto rd 445 to Ry, then foll sp N on rd dir Laven. Turn R in 1km to site on lakeside. Clearly sp in cent of Ry. 3*, Lge, mkd, pt shd, pt sl, EHU (10A) metered + conn fee; gas; cooking facs; TV; phone; Eng spkn; adv bkg acc; bike hire; golf 10km; fishing; boat hire; games rm; CKE. *"Gd site."*
DKK 260, 11 Apr-21 Sep.   2019

"Satellite navigation makes touring much easier"

Remember most sat navs don't know if you're towing or in a larger vehicle – always use yours alongside maps and site directions.

RY *B2* (7km NW Rural) *56.12421, 9.71055* **Terrassen Camping,** Himmelbjergvej 9a, 8600 Laven **tel 86 84 13 01;** info@terrassen.dk; www.terrassen.dk

🐕 DKK15 ♯♦ ⓌⓄ ♨ ⚓ ♔ ♨ /Ⅲ MSP 🦋 ♔ ① nr ♨ nr /Ⅲ 🐾
🛶 (htd)

In Silkeborg take Århus rd 15 to Linå. In Linå turn R for Laven. In Laven turn R parallel to lake; site up hill on R in 300m. Sharp turn R into ent. 4*, Lge, pt shd, terr, EHU (10A) DKK32; gas; sw; TV; 15% statics; phone; adv bkg acc; ccard acc; games area; sauna; fishing. *"Excel views of lake & woods; pet zoo; British owner; Jutland's lake district."*
DKK 268, 11 Apr-14 Sep.   2019

SAEBY *C1* (3km N Coastal) *57.35498, 10.51026* **Hedebo Strandcamping,** Frederikshavnsvej 108, 9300 Sæby **tel 98 46 14 49;** info@hedebocamping.dk; www.hedebocamping.dk

🐕 ♯♦(htd) ⓌⓄ ♨ ⚓ ♔ ♨ /Ⅲ MSP 🦋 ♔ ♀ ① ♨ ♨ /Ⅲ 🛶(htd)
🌳 adj

Sp on rd 180. 3*, Lge, mkd, hdg, unshd, EHU (10A) DKK40; bbq; cooking facs; 60% statics; phone; bus adj; Eng spkn; adv bkg acc; CKE.
DKK 250, 31 Mar-7 Sep.   2016

SAEBY *C1* (3.7km N Coastal) *57.36000, 10.50861* **Svalereden Camping And Hytteby,** Frederikshavnsvej 112b, 9900 Frederikshavn **tel 98 46 19 37;** info@ svaleredencamping.dk; svaleredencamping.dk

🔟 🐕 ♯♦(htd) ♨ ⚓ ♔ ♨ /Ⅲ 🦋 ♔ ♨ /Ⅲ 🌳

Take coastal rte 180, exit 13 and 12. Site bet Frederikshavn & Saeby. 3*, Med, EHU (16A); bbq; twin axles; TV; bus; Eng spkn; adv bkg acc; ccard acc; games area; CKE. *"Conv for Frederikshavn-Gothenburg ferry; outstanding san facs; excel."*
DKK 280   2017

SAKSKOBING *C3* (0.8km W Urban) *54.79840, 11.64070* **Sakskøbing Camping,** Saxes Allé 15, 4990 Sakskøbing **tel 45 54 70 45 66 or 45 54 70 47 57; sax@sport.dk; www.saxcamping.dk**

N fr Rødby exit E47 at Sakskøbing junc 46, turn L twd town: at x-rds turn R. In 300m turn R into Saxes Allé, site sp. 3*, Med, hdg, mkd, pt shd, EHU (6A) DKK30; gas; cooking facs; phone; adv bkg acc; fishing. *"Conv for Rødby-Puttgarden ferry; pool 100m; gd touring base; excel site in pretty area; v welcoming & friendly."* **DKK 194, 15 Mar-28 Sep.** **2019**

SILKEBORG *B2* (12km W Rural) *56.14869, 9.39697* **DCU Hesselhus Camping,** Moselundsvej 28, Funder, 8600 Silkeborg **tel 86 86 50 66; hesselhus@dcu.dk; www.camping-hesselhus.dk**

Take rd 15 W fr Silkeborg twd Herning; after 6km bear R, sp Funder Kirkeby, foll camping sps for several km to site. 3*, Lge, mkd, pt shd, EHU DKK35; gas; TV; 40% statics; phone; adv bkg acc; CKE. *"Great family site; beautiful natural surroundings; 1 hr fr Legoland; busy at w'ends."* **DKK 144** **2016**

SINDAL *C1* (2km W Rural) *57.46785, 10.17851* **Sindal Camping,** Hjørringvej 125, 9870 Sindal **tel 98 93 65 30; info@sindal-camping.dk; www.sindal-camping.dk**

On rte 35 due W of Frederikshavn on S side of rd. 3*, Lge, mkd, hdg, pt shd, EHU (16A) metered; gas; bbq; twin axles; red long stay; TV; 50% statics; phone; Eng spkn; adv bkg acc; games area; bike hire; golf 3km; CKE. *"Train & bus v conv; lovely beaches 30 mins; excel modern san facs; helpful owners; hg rec; excel."* **DKK 220** **2017**

"There aren't many sites open at this time of year"

If you're travelling outside peak season remember to call ahead to check site opening dates – even if the entry says 'open all year'.

SKAELSKOR *C3* (1km NW Rural) *55.25648, 11.28461* **Skælskør Nør Camping,** Kildehusvej 1, 4230 Skælskør **tel 58 19 43 84; kildehuset@cafeer.dk; www.campnor.dk**

Exit E20 junc 42 sp Korsør. Take rd 265 S sp Skælskør, site on L just bef town, nr Kildehuset Rest. 4*, Med, mkd, unshd, EHU (10A) DKK35; cooking facs; TV; 80% statics; phone; Eng spkn; adv bkg acc; ccard acc; CKE. *"Lovely location by lake in nature reserve; woodland walks; excel facs; helpful owners."* **DKK 221** **2018**

SVENDBORG *C3* (7km SE Coastal) *55.0537, 10.6304* **Svendborg Sund Camping (formerly Vindebyøre),** Vindebyørevej 52, Tåsinge, 5700 Svendborg **tel 21 72 09 13 or 62 22 54 25; maria@svendborgsund-camping.dk; www.svendborgsund-camping.dk**

Cross bdge fr Svendborg (dir Spodsbjerg) to island of Tåsinge on rd 9; at traff lts over bdge turn L, then immed 1st L to Vindeby, thro vill, L at sp to site. 3*, Med, pt shd, pt sl, EHU DKK30; bbq; cooking facs; TV; 10% statics; phone; adv bkg acc; ccard acc; boat hire; bike hire; CKE. *"V helpful owners; swipe card for facs; excel touring base & conv ferries to islands; beautiful views; o'night area; immac, excel site; narr sandy beach."* **DKK 225, 18 Mar-27 Sep.** **2015**

TARM *A2* (1.5km S Rural) *55.89309, 8.51278* **Tarm Camping,** Vardevej 79, 6880 Tarm **tel 30 12 66 35; tarm.camping@pc.dk; www.tarm-camping.dk**

Fr rd 11 S of Tarm take exit twds Tarm; immed turn R, site on L in 500m, sp. 3*, Med, mkd, pt shd, EHU (10A) DKK30; gas; cooking facs; 10% statics; phone; Eng spkn; adv bkg acc; CKE. *"Friendly & helpful staff; vg."* **DKK 168, 27 Mar-4 Oct.** **2015**

THISTED *B2* (1km SE Coastal) *56.95226, 8.71286* **Thisted Camping,** Iversensvej 3, 7700 Thisted **tel 97 92 16 35; mail@thisted-camping.dk; www.thisted-camping.dk**

On side of fjord on o'skts of Thisted, sp fr rd 11. 3*, Med, unshd, pt sl, EHU (16A) DKK30; gas; bbq; cooking facs; TV; Eng spkn; adv bkg acc; fishing; games rm; CKE. *"Attractive views fr some pitches; nice, friendly, helpful, well run site; grnd soft aft heavy rain; easy walk to town; gd facs."* **DKK 240** **2016**

THORSMINDE *A2* (0.5km N Coastal) *56.37626, 8.12251* **Thorsminde Camping,** Klitrosevej 4, 6990 Thorsminde **tel 20 45 19 76; mail@thorsminde camping.dk; www.thorsmindecamping.dk**

On rd 16/28 to Ulfborg, turn W twd coast & Husby Klitplantage. Turn N onto rd 181 to Thorsminde, 1st turn R past shops, site sp. 3*, Lge, unshd, EHU (10A) DKK30; cooking facs; TV; 10% statics; phone; adv bkg acc; sauna. *"Pleasant site; helpful staff; excel sea fishing."* **DKK 200, 8 Apr-23 Oct.** **2016**

DENMARK

TONDER *B3* (5km W Rural) *54.93746, 8.80008*
Møgeltønder Camping, Sønderstrengvej 2, Møgeltonder,
6270 Tønder **tel 74 73 84 60; info@mogeltonder
camping.dk; www.mogeltondercamping.dk**

[12] ♜ DKK10 ♦↟(htd) [WD] ♨ ⚲ ♿ 🖾 ✎ [MSP] 🦋 ♈ ♨ ♨ 🏊(htd)

**N fr Tønder thro Møgeltønder (avoid cobbled main
rd by taking 2nd turning sp Møgeltønder) site sp
on L in 200m outside vill.** 3*, Lge, mkd, pt shd, EHU
(10A) DKK25; bbq; cooking facs; TV; 25% statics;
phone; Eng spkn; adv bkg acc; CKE. *"Gd cycle paths;
beautiful & romantic little vill adj; Ribe worth visit
(43km); friendly owner."* **DKK 234** **2019**

VEJERS STRAND *A3* (12km S Coastal) *55.54403,
8.13386* **Hvidbjerg Strand Feriepark,** Hvidbjerg
Strandvej 27, 6857 Blåvand **tel 75 27 90 40; info@
hvidbjerg.dk; www.hvidbjerg.dk**

♜ DKK30 ♦↟ [WD] ♨ ⚲ ♿ 🖾 ✎ [MSP] 🦋 ♈ ♨ ♨ 🦿
♨ (covrd, htd) ♈ sand

**Exit rd 11 at Varde on minor rd, sp Blåvand, turn L
at sp to Hvidbjerg Strand 2km; site 1km on L.**
5*, V lge, hdg, pt shd, serviced pitches; EHU (6A) inc;
gas; cooking facs; TV; 10% statics; phone; adv bkg acc;
ccard acc; tennis; games area. *"Superb facs; excel
family site; young groups not acc."*
DKK 453, 7 Apr-22 Oct. **2019**

VEJLE *B3* (2km ENE Urban) *55.7151, 9.5611* **Vejle
City Camping,** Helligkildevej 5, 7100 Vejle **tel 75 82
33 35; info@vejlecitycamping.dk; www.vejlecity
camping.dk**

♜ DKK5 ♦↟ [WD] ♨ ⚲ ♿ 🖾 ✎ [MSP] 🦋 ♨ ♨ ♨ ♈ sand 2km

**Exit E45 m'way at Vejle N. Turn L twd town. In 250m
turn L at camping sp & 'stadion' sp.** 3*, Med, pt shd,
pt sl, EHU (6-10A) DKK30; cooking facs; red long stay;
TV; phone; Eng spkn; adv bkg acc; ccard acc. *"Site adj
woods & deer enclosure; quickstop o'night facs; walk
to town; conv Legoland (26km); lovely well kept site;
helpful friendly staff."* **DKK 255, 19 Mar-25 Sep.**
2016

VIBORG *B2* (15km N Rural/Coastal) *56.53452,
9.33117* **Hjarbæk Fjord Camping,** Hulager 2, Hjarbæk,
8831 Løgstrup **tel 86 64 23 09; info@hjarbaek.dk;
www.hjarbaek.dk**

[12] ♜ DKK10 ♦↟(htd) [WD] ♨ ⚲ ♿ 🖾 ✎ 🦋 ♈ 🍽 Ⓟ ♨ ♨ 🏊
♈ sand adj

**Take A26 (Viborg to Skive) to Løgstrup, turn R (N)
to Hjarbæk, keep R thro vill, site sp.** 3*, Lge, mkd, pt
shd, terr, EHU metered; gas; bbq; cooking facs; TV;
3% statics; phone; Eng spkn; adv bkg acc; ccard acc;
lake fishing; CKE. *"Friendly & well-run; gd views; close
to attractive vill & harbour."* **DKK 299** **2019**

VINDERUP *B2* (6.7km ESE Rural) *56.45901, 8.86918*
Sevel Camping, Halallé 6, Sevel, 7830 Vinderup
**tel 97 44 85 50; mail@sevelcamping.dk; www.sevel
camping.dk**

[12] ♜ DKK6 ♦↟(htd) [WD] ♨ ⚲ ♿ 🖾 ✎ [MSP] 🦋 Ⓟ nr ♨ ♨ nr ♨

**Fr Struer on rd 513. In Vinderup L nr church then
R past Vinderup Camping. Site sp on R on edge
of vill.** 2*, Sm, hdg, pt shd, pt sl, EHU (16A) DKK30;
cooking facs; 10% statics; Eng spkn; adv bkg acc; ccard
acc; CKE. *"Family-run site; pleasant, helpful owners;
picturesque, historic area."* **DKK 182** **2016**

VORDINGBORG *D3* (3.6km W Urban/Coastal)
55.00688, 11.87509 **Ore Strand Camping,** Orevej
145, 4760 Vordingborg **tel 55 77 8822; mail@
orestrandcamping.dk; www.orestrandcamping.dk**

[12] ♦↟ [WD] ♨ ⚲ ♿ ✎ [MSP] 🦋 ♨ ♈ shgl adj

**Fr E55/47 exit junc 41 onto rd 59 to Vordingborg
7km. Turn R at site sp into Ore, site on L.** 3*, Med, pt shd,
EHU (6A) DKK30; cooking facs; phone; Eng spkn; adv
bkg acc; ccard acc. *"Gd touring cent; fine views if nr
water; interesting old town."* **DKK 140** **2015**

"That's changed – Should I let the Club know?"

If you find something on site that's different
from the site entry, fill in a report and let us
know. See camc.com/europereport.

AERO ISLAND

MARSTAL *C3* (2km S Urban/Coastal) *54.84666,
10.51823* **Marstal Camping,** Eghovedvej 1, 5960
Marstal **tel 63 52 63 69; mail@marstalcamping.dk;
www.marstalcamping.dk**

[12] ♜ DKK15 ♦↟ [WD] ♨ ⚲ ♿ 🖾 ✎ [MSP] 🍽 nr Ⓟ nr ♨ ♨

**Fr Ærøskobing ferry to E end of Ærø Island, thro
town of Marstal & turn R at harbour twd sailing
club; site adj to club.** 3*, Med, mkd, pt shd, EHU (16A)
DKK48; bbq; TV; 10% statics; phone; adv bkg acc;
ccard acc; CKE. **DKK 160** **2016**

BORNHOLM ISLAND

GUDHJEM *A1* (2km S Coastal) *55.19566, 14.98602*
Sannes Familiecamping, Melstedvej 39, 3760 Melsted
**tel 56 48 52 11; sannes@familiecamping.dk;
www.familiecamping.dk**

🏕 ♨ ⓦ ♨ ⚲ 🖳 ⫽ 🅼 💐 ♈ ⓗ nr ⛴ 🎠 ⚓ (htd) 🛥
⛱ sand adj

SW fr Gudhjem on rd 158, in 2km site on L. Pass
other sites. NB: Bornholm Is can be reached by ferry
fr Sassnitz in Germany or Ystad in Sweden. 4*, Med,
mkd, hdstg, pt shd, terr, EHU (6A) DKK30; gas; TV;
10% statics; phone; Eng spkn; adv bkg acc; ccard acc;
bike hire; fishing; sauna; fitness rm; CKE. *"Friendly &
helpful staff; gd cycle paths in area; bus service fr site."*
DKK 270, 1 Apr-18 Sep. **2016**

NEXO *A1* (5.5km S Urban/Coastal) *55.02895,
15.11130* **FDM Camping Balka Strand,** Klynevej 6,
Snogebæk, 3730 Nexø **tel 56 48 80 74; c-balka@fdm.dk;
www.balka.fdmcamping.dk**

🏕 DKK15 ♨ (htd) ⓦ ♨ ⚲ 🖳 ⫽ 🅼 💐 ♈ ⓗ nr ⛴ 🎠
⛱ sand 200m

Fr ferry at Rønne on rd 38 to Nexø, foll sp to site N
of Snogebæk. 3*, Lge, mkd, pt shd, EHU (6A) DKK49;
bbq; cooking facs; TV; 10% statics; adv bkg acc; ccard
acc; windsurfing 1km; fishing 500m; games area;
bike hire; golf 5km. *"Superb beach; vg touring base
Bornholm Is."* **DKK 217, 25 Apr-13 Sep.** **2016**

"I like to fill in the reports as I travel from site to site"

You'll find report forms at the back of this
guide, or you can fill them in online at
camc.com/europereport.

RONNE *A1* (1km S Coastal) *55.08978, 14.70565*
Galløkken Camping, Strandvejen 4, 3700 Rønne **tel
56 95 23 20; info@gallokken.dk; www.gallokken.dk**

🏕 ♨ (htd) ⓦ ♨ ⚲ 🖳 ⫽ 🅼 💐 ♈ ⓗ nr ⛴ 🎠 ⛱ sand 200m

Fr Rønne cent foll dir airport, site well sp. 3*, Med,
mkd, hdg, pt shd, EHU (13A) DKK31; bbq; cooking
facs; TV; 10% statics; adv bkg acc; bike hire; games rm;
tennis 1km. *"Lovely location; private san facs avail; gd,
modern san facs."* **DKK 200, 1 May-31 Aug.** **2016**

LANGELAND ISLAND

LOHALS *C3* (0.4km W Urban) *55.13383, 10.90578*
Lohals Camping, Birkevej 11, 5953 Lohals **tel 62 55 14
60; mail@lohalscamping.dk; www.lohalscamping.dk**

12 🏕 ♨ ♨ ⚲ 🖳 ⫽ 🅼 💐 ♈ ⓗ nr ⛴ 🎠 ⚓ (htd) 🛥
⛱ sand 1km

On island of Langeland. Cross to Rudkøbing, fr
island of Tåsinge, then 28km to N of island (only 1
main rd); site in middle of vill nr ferry to Sjælland
Island. 3*, Med, shd, EHU (10A) DKK35; TV;
10% statics; phone; adv bkg acc; tennis; bike hire;
fishing; boat hire; games area. *"Conv ferry (Lohals-
Korsor) 500m."* **DKK 210** **2016**

ROMO ISLAND

HAVNEBY *A3* (2km N Coastal) *55.09883, 8.54395*
Kommandørgårdens Camping, Havnebyvej 201, 6792
Rømø **tel 74 75 51 22; info@kommandoergaarden.
dk; www.kommandoergaarden.dk**

12 🏕 DKK20 ♨ (htd) ⓦ ♨ ⚲ 🖳 ⫽ 🅼 💐 ⓗ ⚓ ⛴ 🎠
⚓ (htd) 🛥 ⛱ sand 1km

Turn S after exit causeway fr mainland onto rd
175 sp Havneby. Site on L in 8km. 3*, V lge, mkd, pt
shd, EHU (10A) DKK35; gas; TV; 30% statics; phone;
adv bkg acc; tennis. *"Family-owned site; wellness &
beauty cent on site; ferry to German island of Sylt."*
DKK 240 **2016**

Finland

Northern Lights

Highlights

Finland is a country filled with vast forests, crystal clear lakes and a diverse range of flora and fauna. With the Northern Lights visible from Lapland, the outstanding natural world is one of Finland's finest assets, with a vast, pristine wilderness that captures the imagination.

The cities of Finland are not to be missed, with vibrant atmospheres, museums, galleries, delicious restaurants and gorgeous architecture in spades.

Saunas are an important part of life in Finland, and have been for hundreds of years. They are used as a place to relax with friends and family and are generally sociable spaces.

Design and fashion have always been popular in Finland, with one of its most famous companies, Marimekko, a huge contributor to fashion in the 20th century.

Visit Svalbard to witness the unique spectacle of the Midnight Sun. This natural phenomenon occurs each year around the summer solstice.

Major towns and cities

- Helsinki – this capital city is a hub of shopping and architecture.
- Tempere – Finland's cultural home with theatrical, musical and literary traditions.
- Turku – Finland's oldest city and a former European City of Culture.
- Oulu – a quirky city where many technology companies, including Nokia, are based.

Attractions

- Olavinlinna Castle, Savolinna – a medieval stone fortress that houses several exhibitions.
- Lapland– This region is famous for the midnight sun and the Northern Lights.
- Repovesi National Park – a stunning natural area with plenty of walking and hiking trails.
- Temppeliaukio Kirkko, Helsinki – This church is built directly into solid rock.

Find out more

www.visitfinland.com
E: helsinki.tourist.info@hel.fi T: 0035 (0) 82 95 05 80 00

Country Information

Population (approx): 5.5 million

Capital: Helsinki

Area: 338,145 sq km

Bordered by: Norway, Sweden, Russia

Terrain: Flat, rolling, heavily forested plains interspersed with low hills and over 60,000 lakes; one third lies within the Arctic Circle

Climate: Short, warm summers; long, very cold, dry winters; the best time to visit is between May and September

Coastline: 1,250km (excluding islands)

Highest Point: Haltiatunturi 1,328m

Languages: Finnish, Swedish

Local Time: GMT or BST + 2, ie 2 hours ahead of the UK all year

Currency: Euros divided into 100 cents; £1 = €1.16, €1 = £0.87 (October 2019)

Emergency numbers: Police 112; Fire brigade 112; Ambulance 112 (operators speak English)

Public Holidays 2020: Jan 1, 6; Apr 10, 12, 13; May 1, 21, 31; Jun 20; Oct 31; Dec 6, 25, 26.

School summer holidays from early June to mid-August.

Border Posts

The main border posts with Sweden are at Tornio, Ylitornio and Kaaresuvanto. Those with Norway are at Kilpisjärvi, Kivilompolo, Karigasniemi, Utsjoki Ohcejohka and Nuorgam. Border posts are open day and night. The Finnish-Russian border can only be crossed by road at certain official points – contact the Finnish Tourist Board for details.

Border guards patrol the area close to the Russian border and it is important, therefore, to carry identification at all times when visiting the region.

Entry Formalities

Holders of British and Irish passports are permitted to stay up to three months in any six month period in Finland before a visa is required. Campsites and hotels register foreign guests with the police within 24 hours of arrival.

Medical Services

The local health system is good and Finland generally has a high level of healthcare. British citizens are entitled to obtain emergency health care at municipal health centres on presentation of a European Health Insurance Card (EHIC). Treatment will either be given free or for a standard fee. Dental care is provided mainly by private practitioners.

There is a non-refundable charge for hospital treatment, whether for inpatient or outpatient visits. Refunds for the cost of private medical treatment may be obtained from Sickness Insurance Department, KELA, (www.kela.fi) up to six months from the date of treatment.

Prescribed drugs can be obtained from pharmacies (apteekki), some of which have late opening hours. Some medicines that are available in stores and supermarkets in other countries, such as aspirin and various ointments, are only available in pharmacies in Finland.

Mosquitoes are abundant and very active during damp summers, particularly in the north of Finland. The use of mosquito repellant and a topical cream to prevent bites becoming infected is highly recommended.

Opening Hours

Banks: Mon-Fri 9.15am-4.15pm.

Museums: Check locally as times vary.

Post Offices: Mon-Fri 9am-5pm. During winter some post offices may stay open until 6pm.

Shops: Mon-Fri 7am/8am/9am-9pm; Sat 7am/8am/9am/10am-6pm; Sun noon-6pm (some supermarkets until 11pm). On the eve of a public holiday some shops close early.

Safety and Security

The crime rate is relatively low in Finland although the tourist season attracts pickpockets in crowded areas. You should take the usual commonsense precautions to safeguard your person and property.

There is a low threat from international terrorism but you should be aware of the global risks of indiscriminate terrorist attacks which could be against civilian targets in public places, including tourist sites.

British Embassy

ITÄINEN PUISTOTIE 17, 00140 HELSINKI
Tel: (09) 22865100 Fax: (09) 22865262
www.ukinfinland.fco.gov.uk
info.helsinki@fco.gov.uk

There are also Honorary Consulates in Åland Islands, Jyväskylä, Kotka, Kuopio, Oulu, Rovaniemi, Tampere, Turku and Vaasa.

Irish Embassy

EROTTAJANKATU 7A, FIN-00130 HELSINKI
Tel: (09) 6824240
www.embassyofireland.fi

Documents

Driving Licence/Vehicle(s)

When driving you should carry your driving licence, vehicle registration certificate (V5C), insurance certificate plus MOT certificate (if applicable).

Money

Currency may be exchanged at banks and at bureaux de change.

Major credit cards are widely accepted and cash machines are widespread.

Carry your credit card issuers'/banks' 24-hour UK contact numbers in case of loss or theft of your cards.

Passport

You should carry your passport at all times.

Driving

Accidents

Accidents must be reported to the police and if a foreign motorist is involved the Finnish Motor Insurers Bureau (Liikennevakuutuskeskus) should also be informed. Their address is Bulevardi 28, FIN-00120 Helsinki, tel (09) 40 450 4700/4750, www.lvk.fi./en. At the site of an accident other road users must be warned by the use of a warning triangle.

Alcohol

The maximum permitted level of alcohol is 50 milligrams in 100 millilitres of blood, i.e. lower than that permitted in the UK (80 milligrams). It is advisable to adopt the 'no drink and drive' rule at all times as anyone exceeding this limit will be arrested immediately and could face a prison sentence. Breath tests and blood tests may be carried out at random.

Breakdown Service

The Automobile & Touring Club of Finland, Autoliitto, has approximately 300 roadside patrols manned by volunteers and these can be called out at weekends and on public holidays. At other times, or if the Autoliitto patrol cannot be reached, contracted partners will provide assistance. For 24-hour assistance telephone (0)200 8080. Charges are made for assistance and towing, plus a call-out fee.

Emergency telephone boxes are installed around Helsinki, Kouvola, Jamsa, and Rovaniemi, and on the roads Kouvola-Lappeenranta-Imatra-Simpele and Rovaniemi-Jaatila. Drivers are connected to the national breakdown service.

Child Restraint System

Children under the height of 1.35m must be seated in a suitable child restraint.

If there is not a child restraint/seat available children of 3 years or older must travel in the rear seat using a seat belt or other safety device attached to the seat. Unless in a taxi a child under the age of 3 must not travel in a vehicle without a child restraint. It is the responsibility of the driver to ensure all children under the age of 15 years old are correctly and safely restrained.

Fuel

Petrol stations are usually open from 7am to 9pm on weekdays and for shorter hours at weekends, although a few stay open 24 hours. Their frequency reduces towards the north, so it is advisable not to let your tank run low. Credit cards are accepted at most manned petrol stations. There are many unmanned stations, which have automatic petrol pumps perated with bank notes or credit cards. It is understood that automatic payment machines at petrol pumps do not accept cards issued outside Finland.

LPG is not available.

Motorways

There are 700km of motorway (moottoritie) in Finland linking Helsinki, Tampere and Turku. No tolls are levied. There are no emergency phones located on motorways. In the case of breakdown on a motorway drivers of all vehicles must use a warning triangle.

Parking

A vehicle that has been illegally or dangerously parked may be removed by the police and the owner fined. Parking fines may be enforced on the spot, the minimum charge being €10. Parking meters operate for between 15 minutes and four hours; the free use of unexpired time is allowed. In some built-up areas you will need a parking disc obtainable from petrol stations or car accessory shops.

8 - 17
Restriction applies 8-17 hrs (Mon-Fri)

(8-13)
Restriction applies 8-13 hrs (Sat)

8 - 14
Restriction applies 8-14 hrs (Sun)

In some towns streets are cleaned on a regular basis and road signs indicate which day the cleaning takes place and, therefore, when the street should be kept clear of parked vehicles. Vehicles which cause an obstruction will be removed and drivers fined.

If you have a low emission car you may be entitled to 50% off parking fees in Helsinki. To qualify for this reduction the parking fees must be made by mobile phone and you will need to have obtained a green sticker with the letter 'P' from the Helsinki town authorities, which then needs to be attached to the windscreen. For further information visit www.easypark.fi or www.nextpark.com.

Priority

At intersections, vehicles coming from the right have priority, except when otherwise indicated. The approach to a main road from a minor road is indicated by a sign with a red triangle on a yellow background. When this sign is supplemented by a red octagon with STOP in the centre, vehicles must stop before entering the intersection. Trams and emergency vehicles, even coming from the left, always have priority. Vehicles entering a roundabout must give way to traffic already on the roundabout, i.e. on the left.

Roads

In general there is a good main road system, traffic is light and it is possible to cover long distances quickly, but there are still some gravelled roads in the countryside which have speed restrictions to avoid windscreens being broken by loose stones. During the spring thaw and during the wet season in September, gravelled roads may be in a poor condition. Roadworks take place during the summer months and sections under repair can extend for many miles.

There are large numbers of elk in Finland and they often wander across roads, especially at dawn and dusk. The same applies to reindeer in Lapland. Warning signs showing approximate lengths of danger zones are posted in these areas. If you collide with an elk, deer or reindeer you must notify the police.

The Finnish Transport Agency operates an information service on weather and road conditions, recommended driving routes and roadworks, tel 0295 020 600 or visit www.liikennevirasto.fi.

Road Signs and Markings

Road markings are generally white. Road signs conform to international conventions. Signs for motorway and end of motorway are on a green background while those for main roads are on a blue background. The following signs may also be found:

Finnish	English Translation
Aja hitaasti	Drive slowly
Aluerajoitus	Local speed limit
Kelirikko	Frost damage
Kokeile jarruja	Test your brakes
Kunnossapitotyö	Roadworks (repairs)
Lossi färja	Ferry

Finnish	English Translation
Päällystetyötä	Roadworks (resurfacing)
Tulli	Customs
Tie rakenteilla	Roadworks (road under construction)
Varo irtokiviä	Beware of loose stones

Speed Limits

	Open Road (km/h)	Motorway (km/h)
Car Solo	80-100	120
Car towing caravan/trailer	80	80
Motorhome under 3500kg	100	100
Motorhome 3500-7500kg	80	80

On all roads outside built-up areas, other than motorways, differing speed limits between 70 and 100 km/h (44 and 62 mph) apply – except where vehicles are subject to a lower limit – according to the road quality and traffic. Where there is no sign, the basic speed limit is usually 80 km/h (50 mph) on main roads and 70 km/h (44 mph) on secondary roads, whether solo or towing. The road sign which indicates this basic limit bears the word 'Perusnopeus' in Finnish, and 'Grundhastighet' in Swedish.

Reduced speed limits apply from October to March and these are generally 20 km/h (13 mph) lower than the standard limits.

The maximum speed limit for motorhomes up to 3,500kg is 100 km/h (62 mph).

Recommended maximum speed limits are indicated on some roads by square or rectangular signs bearing white figures on a blue background. The maximum speed limit in residential areas is 20 km/h (13 mph).

Slow moving vehicles must let others pass wherever possible, if necessary by moving onto the roadside verge. Maintain a sufficient distance behind a slow moving vehicle to allow an overtaking vehicle to pull in front.

Radar detectors are prohibited.

Violation of Traffic Regulations

The police can impose, but not collect, fines when road users violate traffic regulations. Fines should be paid at banks.

Winter Driving

Winter tyres are compulsory from 1 December to 28 February. Snow chains may be used temporarily when conditions necessitate.

The main arctic road leads from Kemi on the Gulf of Bothnia through Rovaniemi to the Norwegian border. During the winter, all high volume, main roads are kept open including routes to Norway and Sweden. In total between 6,000 and 7,000km of roads are mainly kept free of ice and snow by the use of salt. Other roads will consist of compacted snow. Drivers should expect winter conditions as early as October.

Essential Equipment

Lights

Dipped headlights are compulsory at all times, regardless of weather conditions. Bulbs are more likely to fail with constant use and you are recommended to carry spares.

Reflective Jacket/ Waistcoat

Pedestrians must wear reflective devices during the hours of darkness (any type of reflector is acceptable). If you get out of your vehicle you are required to wear one and the standard reflective jacket is probably the best option for driver and passengers.

Warning Triangles

All vehicles must carry a warning triangle and use it when broken down.

Touring

Both Finnish and Swedish are official languages. As a result, many towns and streets have two names, e.g. Helsinki is also known as Helsingfors, and Turku as Åbo. Finnish street names usually end 'katu', while Swedish street names usually end 'gatan' or 'vägen'. Swedish place names are more commonly used in the south and west of the country.

Smoking is not permitted in public buildings, restaurants or bars, except in designated smoking zones, nor on public transport.

The Helsinki Card offers free entry to several major museums and other attractions, and unlimited travel for 24, 48 or 72 hours on public transport, plus discounts for sightseeing, restaurants, shopping, concert tickets, sports, etc. For more information see www.helsinkicard.fi.

The sale of wine and spirits is restricted to Alko shops which are open Monday to Friday until 6pm or 8pm, Saturday until 4pm or 6pm, and closed on Sunday and public holidays. Medium strength beer is also sold in supermarkets and other stores.

A service charge is generally included in most restaurant bills and tips are not expected, but if the service has been good it is customary to round up the bill.

Most lakes are situated in the south east of the country and they form a web of waterways linked by rivers and canals, making this a paradise for those who enjoy fishing, canoeing and hiking. In Lapland the vegetation is sparse, consisting mostly of dwarf birch. Reindeer roam freely so motorists must take special care and observe the warning signs. Rovaniemi is the biggest town in Lapland, just south of the Arctic Circle. It has a special post office and 'Santa Claus Land'.

A number of 'Uniquely Finnish' touring routes have been established including the King's Road along the south coast which takes you through many places of interest including Porvoo, a small town with well-preserved, old, wooden houses, Turku, the former capital, and the famous Imatra waterfall near the southern shore of Lake Saimaa. Swedish influence is evident in this area in local customs, place names and language. These 'Uniquely Finnish' touring routes are marked with brown sign posts; contact the Finnish Tourist Board for more information.

Southern and central Finland are usually snow covered from early December to mid or late April, although in recent years the south coast has had little or no snow. Northern Finland has snow falls from October to May and temperatures can be extremely low. Thanks to the Gulf Stream and low humidity, Finland's winter climate does not feel as cold as temperature readings might indicate but if you plan a visit during the winter you should be prepared for harsh weather conditions.

In the summer many Finnish newspapers have summaries of main news items and weather forecasts in English and radio stations have regular news bulletins in English. English is taught in all schools and is widely spoken.

Camping and Caravanning

There are around 150 campsites in Finland. Campsites are graded from 1 to 5 stars according to facilities available. Most have cabins for hire in addition to tent and caravan pitches, and most have saunas.

At some sites visitors who do not already have one must purchase a Camping Key Europe, which replaced the Camping Card Scandinavia (CCS) in 2012. The Camping Key is valid across Europe and you may purchase it for €16 on arrival at your first campsite or from local tourist offices - for more information visit www.camping.fi.

During the peak camping season from June to mid August it is advisable to make advance reservations. Prices at many campsites may double (or treble) over the midsummer holiday long weekend in June and advance booking is essential for this period. Approximately 70 campsites stay open all year.

Casual or wild camping may be allowed for a short period - one or 2 days. For longer periods, permission must be obtained from the landowner. Camping may be prohibited on public beaches and in public recreation areas where campers are often directed to special areas, many of which have facilities provided free of charge.

Cycling

Finland is good for cyclists as it is relatively flat. Most towns have a good network of cycle lanes which are indicated by traffic signs. In built up areas pavements are sometimes divided into two sections, one for cyclists and one for pedestrians. It is compulsory to wear a safety helmet.

Electricity and Gas

Current on campsites is usually between 10 and 16 amps. Plugs are round with two pins. Some sites have CEE connections.

Butane gas is not generally available and campsites and service stations do not have facilities for replacing empty foreign gas cylinders. You will need to travel with sufficient supplies to cover your needs while in Finland or purchase propane cylinders locally, plus an adaptor. The Club does not recommend the refilling of cylinders.

The Midnight Sun and Northern Lights

Areas within the Arctic Circle have 24 hours of daylight in the height of summer and no sun in winter for up to two months. There are almost 20 hours of daylight in Helsinki in the summer.

The Northern Lights (Aurora Borealis) may be seen in the arctic sky on clear dark nights, the highest incidence occurring in February/March and September/October in the Kilpisjärvi region of Lapland when the lights are seen on three nights out of four.

The Order of Bluenosed Caravanners

Visitors to the Arctic Circle from anywhere in the world may apply for membership of the Order of Bluenosed Caravanners which will be recognised by the issue of a certificate by the International Caravanning Association (ICA).

For more information contact bluenosed@ icacaravanning.org and attach a photograph of yourselves and your outfit under any Arctic Circle signpost, together with the date and country of crossing and the names of those who made the crossing.

This service is free to members of the ICA (annual membership £20); the fee for non-members is £5. Coloured plastic decals for your outfit, indicating membership of the Order, are also available at a cost of £4. Cheques should be payable to the ICA. For more information visit www.icacaravanning.org.

Public Transport & Local Travel

The public transport infrastructure is of a very high standard and very punctual. You can buy a variety of bus, train, tram and metro tickets at public transport stations, HKL service points, newspaper kiosks and shops all over the country. Single tickets, which are valid for 60 minutes, can be purchased from ticket machines, bus and tram drivers or train conductors. Tourist tickets valid for one, three or five days can also be purchased from kiosks, ticket machines and bus and tram drivers and are valid on all forms of public transport including the Suomenlinna ferry.

Within the Helsinki city area you may hire city bicycles in the summer for a token fee (refundable) from one of 26 Citybike stands.

Vehicle ferries operate all year on routes to Estonia, Germany and Russia and it is now possible to enjoy a visa free ferry trip to St Petersburg for up to 72 hours from Helsinki; see www.visitfinland.com for a link to more information or contact the Finnish Tourist Board.

Internal ferry services (in Finnish 'lossi') transport motor vehicles day and night. Those situated on the principal roads, taking the place of a bridge, are state-run and free of charge. There are regular services on Lake Paijanne, Lake Inari and Lake Pielinen, and during the summer vessels operate daily tours as well as longer cruises through Finland's lake region. Popular routes are between Hameenlinna and Tampere, Tampere and Virrat, as well as the Saimaa Lake routes. Full details are available from the Finnish Tourist Board.

HAMINA *C4 (7km SE Coastal) 60.52644, 27.25191*
Hamina Camping, Vilniementie 375, 49400 Hamina
**(40) 1513446; camping.hamina@gmail.com;
hamina-camping.fi**

†¶†(htd) **⚓ ✓ MSP ❦ ❞ ⊺ ♿ ☂**sand

**Fr Hamina take rte 7/E18 dir Vaalimaa E. In 3km
turn R rd 3513 sp Virolahti, site sp.** 3*, Med, hdstg,
pt shd, EHU (16A); twin axles; 20% statics; CKE. *"Site
in pine forest; secluded pitches; attractive coastline;
conv for visiting Russia & Kings Rte; sm museum at
Virolahti worth visit; facs poss stretched when site full;
interesting town; site under refurb (2016); helpful staff;
gd."* **€26.50, 1 May-18 Sep.**   **2017**

HANKO/HANGO *B4 (4km NE Coastal) 59.85271,
23.01716* **Camping Silversand,** Hopeahietikko, 10960
Hanko Pohjoinen **(019) 248 5500; cornia@cornia.fi;
www.www.cornia.fi**

†¶† wd **⚓ ♿ ✓ MSP ❞** Ⓝr **â ☂ ⚏**

Site sp fr rd 25. 3*, Lge, shd, EHU (16A) inc; cooking
facs; TV; 10% statics; Eng spkn; ccard acc; sauna;
boat hire; fishing; games rm; bike hire; CKE.
"Beautiful location on edge of sea in pine forest."
€30.60, 25 Apr-30 Sep.   **2016**

HELSINKI/HELSINGFORS *C4 (14km ENE Urban/
Coastal) 60.20668, 25.12116* **Rastila Municipal
Camping,** Karavaanikatu 4, Vuosaari, 00980 Helsinki
**(09) 31078517; rastilacamping@hel.fi; www.hel.fi/
rastila**

12 †¶† wd **⚓ ♿ ☐ ✓ MSP ❦ ❞ ⓘ â ☲**nr **☂ ⚏**sand 1.2km

**E fr Helsinki on rte 170, over Vuosaari bdge; or get
to ring rd 1, turn E dir Vuosaari, site sp. Also sp fr
Silja & other ferry terminals & fr rte 170 to Porvoo.
Also sp on rte 167. Fr N on E75 exit at Ring I then
immed L fork. Foll 101, 170 then sp.** 3*, V lge, hdstg,
pt shd, EHU (16A) €4.50; cooking facs; red long stay;
TV; 10% statics; Eng spkn; ccard acc; games rm;
sauna; CKE. *"Conv Helsinki & district; pleasant site; gd
san facs; helpful staff; poss ssn workers but site clean &
tidy; metro nr; weekly rates avail; best place we stayed
at."* **€37.00**   **2016**

INARI *B1 (0.5km SE Rural) 68.90233, 27.0370* **Holiday
Village/Lomakylä Inari,** Inarintie 26, 99780 Inari **(016)
671108; info@lomakyla-inari.fi; www.saariselka.fi/
lomakylainari**

12 🐕 †¶† wd **⚓ ♿ ☐ ✓ MSP ❞ ⓘ**nr **â ☲**nr **⚏ ☂**sand adj

**Fr S on rte 4/E75, site on R app Inari, clearly sp. Fr N
on E75 500m past town cent, site on L, sp.**
3*, Sm, hdstg, unshd, EHU (16A) inc (long lead poss
req) no earth; bbq; sw nr; twin axles; 40% statics; bus
500m; Eng spkn; ccard acc; canoe hire; sauna; CKE.
*"Gd for walking; midnight sun cruises on Lake Inari;
excel Lapp museum; motorboat hire; poss boggy in
wet; poss low voltage if site full; some lge pitches
suitable RVs & lge o'fits; clean site; boat/canoe hire; fab
Sami ctr in vill."* **€25.00**   **2017**

IVALO *B1 (2km S Rural) 68.64369, 27.52714* **Holiday
Village Näverniemi,** 99800 Ivalo **(016) 677601;
naverniemen@lomakyla.inet.fi; www.narkka.com**

†¶† wd **⚓ ☐ ✓ ❦ ⓘ â ☲ ⚏ ⚏**

Sp on W side of rte 4/E75. Lge, unshd, EHU (10A)
€2.50; sw nr; TV; adv bkg acc; ccard acc; sauna; CKE.
*"Gd cent for birdwatchers; rvside site; reindeer herds
nr site; insufficient el hook-ups; helpful, friendly owner;
phone ahead early ssn to check open - poss flooding
during spring thaw."* **€26.00, 1 Jun-30 Sep.**   **2016**

IVALO *B1 (4km S Rural) 68.62475, 27.54296* **Ivalo
River Camping,** Kerttuojantie 1, 99800 Ivalo **(400)
395046; info@ivalorivercamping.com; www.ivalo
rivercamping.com**

🐕 †¶† **⚓ ✓ ❞ â ☲**

**At side of Rte4/E75, on R when travelling N. Sp on
Rte 4/E75. Pt of petrol stn & café.** Sm, hdstg, pt shd,
pt sl, EHU; cooking facs; 50% statics; Eng spkn; adv
bkg acc; CKE. *"Gd cent for birdwatching; conv NH; only
site open in mid May; gd."* **€20.00, May-Sep.**   **2016**

JUUKA *C3 (35km SE Rural) 63.04004, 29.70994* **Koli
Freetime Oy,** Kopravaarantie 27, Juuka **010 322 3040;
koli@kolifreetime.fi; www.kolifreetime.fi**

🐕 †¶†(htd) wd **⚓ ♿ ☐ ✓ MSP ❦ ❞ ⊺ â ⚏ ☂**sand adj

**Site is well sp on rte 6 heading N of Juuka. Turn off
onto gravel rd as indicated for 2km.** Sm, pt shd, sl,
EHU (16A) inc; bbq; sw nr; twin axles; TV; 10% statics;
Eng spkn; adv bkg acc; ccard acc; games rm; CKE.
*"Sauna inc; sm site on edge of lake with sw; in forest;
nature walks; 10km fr Koli & nearest supmkt; vg."*
€28.00   **2016**

JYVASKYLA *C3 (4km N Urban) 62.25536, 25.6983*
Laajis Camping, Laajavuorentie 15, 40740 Jyväskylä
207 436 436; laajis@laajis.fi; www.laajis.fi

12 🐕 †¶†(htd) wd **⚓ ♿ ✓ MSP ❦ ❞ ⓘ â ☲**nr **⚏**

**Well sp fr N on E75 & E63 fr S, site sp adj youth
hostel.** Med, mkd, hdstg, unshd, EHU (16A) inc;
cooking facs; red long stay; TV (pitch); Eng spkn;
sauna; CKE. *"Facs stretched if site full; htd pool 3km;
ski lift/jumps adj; c'vans only."* **€29.00**   **2016**

KAMMENNIEMI *B4 (7km NW Rural) 61.65423,
23.77748* **Camping Taulaniemi,** Taulaniementie
357, 34240 Kämmenniemi **(03) 3785753;
taulaniemi@yritys.soon.fi; www.taulaniemi.fi**

†¶†(htd) wd **⚓ ☐ ✓ ❦ ⓘ ⚏**

**Fr Tampere take rte 9/E63 dir Jyvaskyla. In 10km
take rte 338 thro Kämmenniemi. Foll sp Taulaniemi
on unmade rd to lakeside site.** 3*, Sm, unshd, pt sl,
terr, EHU (16A) €3; cooking facs; TV; adv bkg acc;
boat hire; sauna; CKE. *"Beautiful site."*
€30.50, 1 Jun-31 Sep.   **2017**

FINLAND

KARIGASNIEMI *B1* (0.9km NW Rural) *69.39975,*
25.84278 **Camping Tenorinne,** Ylätenontie 55,
99950 Karigasniemi **040 832 8487; camping@
tenorinne.com; www.tenorinne.com**
👪 (htd) 🚐 🔄 ⚫ ∕ 🦯 ⊕ nr 🏪 nr 🏧

N of town cent on rd 970 Karigasniemi to Utsjoki.
Sm, pt shd, EHU (16A) €4; TV; 10% statics; ccard acc;
sauna; CKE. **€26.00, 5 Jun-20 Sep.** 2016

KILPISJARVI *A1* (4.6km SSE Rural) *69.01413,*
20.88235 **Kilpisjärvi Holiday Village,** Käsivarrentie
14188, 99490 Kilpisjärvi **(0400) 396684;**
www.tundrea.com
12 👪 (htd) 🚐 🔄 👶 ⚫ ∕ 🦯 Y ⊕ ∕ 🏪 nr

On main rd 21 almost opp g'ge, in middle of vill, sp.
Lge, hdstg, unshd, EHU (10A) inc; bbq; cooking facs;
bus adj; Eng spkn. *"Gd NH to/fr N Norwegian fjords;
access to Saana Fells for gd walking/trekking; winter
sports cent."* **€20.00** 2016

KOKKOLA *B3* (2.5km N Coastal) *63.85500, 23.11305*
Kokkola Camping, Vanhansatamanlahti, 67100
Kokkola **(06) 8314006; info@kokkola-camping.fi;**
www.kokkola-camping.fi
👪 🚐 🔄 👶 ∕ 🦯 🏪 🏧 sand adj

Exit A8 at Kokkola onto rte 749. Site on R, sp fr town.
Med, pt shd, EHU inc; cooking facs; games area; sauna;
CKE. *"Lovely site, no adv bkg; call ahead in winter for
pitching instructions."* **€30.00, 1 Jun-31 Aug.** 2016

KUHMO *C3* (3km SE Rural) *64.11898, 29.57771*
Kalevala Caravan Parking, Vainamoinen 2, 88900
Kuhmo **(086) 557111; kalevalan.kuntoutuskoti@
kalevalankk.fi; www.hyvinvointisampo.fi**
12 👪 🔄 ∕

Fr Kajaani on 76 turn R in ctr of town to 912
Kalevala (brown sp). After 1.6km turn L onto 912.
Site on R. Obtain key fr Hyvinvoiti Sampo (old
peoples home) on R as you enter. Site at bottom of
hill. Hdstg, EHU (10A). *"Clean modern san facs; waste
water & chem disp in town (ask recep)."* **€10.00** 2016

KUOPIO *C3* (9km SW Rural) *62.86432, 27.64165*
Rauhalahti Holiday Centre, Kiviniementie, 70700
Kuopio **(017) 473000; sales@visitrauhalahti.fi;**
www.visitrauhalahti.fi
12 👪 (htd) 🚐 🔄 👶 ∕ 🦯 Y ⊕ 🏪 🏧

Well sp fr rte 5 (E63). Site 1.5km fr E63 dir Levänen,
on Lake Kallavesi. 4*, Lge, hdstg, pt shd, pt sl, EHU
(16A) inc; gas; cooking facs; sw; TV; adv bkg rec; ccard
acc; sauna; boat trips; watersports; CKE. *"Hdstg for
cars, grass for van & awning; ltd services Sept-May."*
€35.00 2016

KUUSAMO *C2* (5km N Rural) *66.00143, 29.16713*
Camping Rantatropiikki, Kylpyläntie, 93600
Kuusamo/Petäjälampi **(08) 8596000; myyntipalvelu.
tropiikki@holidayclub.fi**
12 🐎 👪 (htd) 🚐 🔄 ∕ 🦯 🏪 ⊕ sand

Three sites in same sm area on rd 5/E63, sp. Med, pt
shd, EHU (10A) inc; sw; ccard acc; sauna; tennis; bike
hire; CKE. *"Conv falls area; pool in hotel adj; LS site
recep at hotel 500m past site ent."* 2016

LAHTI *C4* (5km N Rural) *61.01599, 25.64855*
Camping Mukkula, Ritaniemenkatu 10, 15240 Lahti
(03) 7535380; tiedustelut@mukkulacamping.fi;
www.mukkulacamping.fi
12 👪 (htd) 🚐 🔄 👶 ∕ 🦯 🏪 Y nr ⊕ nr 🏪 nr 🏧

Fr S on rte 4/E75 foll camping sps fr town cent.
3*, Med, pt shd, EHU (10A) inc; cooking facs; sw;
TV; ccard acc; tennis; bike hire; fishing; sauna; CKE.
"Beautiful lakeside views." 2016

LAHTI *C4* (8km NW Rural) *61.01872, 25.56387*
Camping Messila, Rantatie 5, 15980 Hollola **3876290;**
messila@campingmessila.fi; www.campingmessila.fi
12 👪 (htd) 🚐 ∕ 🦯 Y ⊕ ∕ 🏧 sand

Off A12 onto Messilantie (N), foll rd to lakeshore.
Lge, hdg, mkd, hdstg, pt shd, EHU (16A) €5; bbq; sw
nr; twin axles; Eng spkn; CKE. *"Gd sized pitches; barrier;
v welcoming; well kept; next to marina; golf nr; conv
for Lahti; vg."* **€26.00** 2017

LIEKSA *D3* (3km SW Rural) *63.30666, 30.00532*
Timitranniemi Camping, Timitra, 81720 Lieksa **(04)
51237166; loma@timitra.com; www.timitra.com**
👪 🚐 🔄 ∕ ⊕ nr 🏪 🏧

Rte 73, well sp fr town on Lake Pielinen. 3*, Med, pt
shd, pt sl, EHU (16A) €4; cooking facs; sw; TV; ccard
acc; bike hire; sauna; boat hire; fishing; CKE. *"Pt of
recreational complex; Pielinen outdoor museum worth
visit."* **€28.00, 20 May-10 Sep.** 2016

MERIKARVIA *B4* (3km SW Coastal) *61.84777,*
21.47138 **Mericamping,** Palosaarentie 67, 29900
Merikarvia **(04) 00 719589; info@mericamping.fi;**
www.mericamping.fi
👪 🚐 ∕ 🦯 🏪 ⊕ ∕ 🏧 adj

Fr E8 foll sp to Merikarvia, site sp 2km W beyond
main housing area. Med, mkd, unshd, EHU €5; Eng
spkn; ccard acc; CKE. *"Vg site on water's edge; some
cottages; friendly, helpful staff."*
€22.00, 1 Jun-31 Aug. 2016

MUONIO *B1* (3km S Rural) *67.93333, 23.6575*
Harrinivan Lomakeskus, Harrinivantie 35, 99300
Muonio **400 155 110; sales@harriniva.fi;**
www.harriniva.fi

∦(htd) ⱳ ♨ ⚡ 🐾 🏕 ⵣ ⓣ 🅿nr ⟋⟍

On E8 5km S of Muonio, well sp on R going S.
Sm, hdstg, pt shd, pt sl, EHU (16A) €4; bbq; twin axles;
Eng spkn; adv bkg acc; ccard acc; rv; CCI. *"Canoe hire
for white water rafting; huskies; san facs stretch in high
ssn; fair."* **€32.00, 1 Jun-30 Sep.** 2019

NOKIA *B4* (5km S Rural) *61.44798, 23.49247*
Camping Viinikanniemi, Viinikanniemenkatu, 37120
Nokia **(400) 420772; info@viinikanniemi.com;**
www.viinikanniemi.com

12 🐕 ∦(htd) ⱳ ♨ ⛲ ⚡ 🐾 MSP 🦋 🏕 ⓣ🅿 ⟋⟍ ✎

SW fr Tampere on rd 12, site well sp. 4*, Med, mkd,
hdstg, pt shd, pt sl, EHU (16A) €5.90-10; gas; bbq;
sw nr; 10% statics; Eng spkn; adv bkg acc; ccard acc;
fishing; games area; bike hire; boat hire; CKE. *"Excel
site; conv Tampere."* **€21.00** 2016

NURMES *C3* (4km SE Rural) *63.53274, 29.19889*
Hyvärilä Camping, Lomatie 12, 75500 Nurmes **(013)**
6872500; hyvarila@nurmes.fi; www.hyvarila.com

🐕 ∦∦(htd) ⱳ ♨ ⚡ 🐾 MSP 🦋 ⓣ🅿nr ⟋⟍

**On rte 73 to Lieksa, turn R 4km fr rte 6/73 junc.
Well sp on Lake Pielinen. Check in at hotel.** 3*, Lge,
unshd, EHU (16A) €5; sw; red long stay; 10% statics;
ccard acc; sauna; games area; tennis; CKE. *"Gd
base for N Karelia; pt of recreational complex."*
€24.00, 1 Jun-15 Sep. 2016

OULU/ULEABORG *B2* (6km NW Coastal) *65.0317,
25.4159* **Camping Nallikari,** Leiritie 10, Hietasaari,
90500 Oulu/Uleåborg **(08) 55861350; nallikari.
camping@ouka.fi; www.nallikari.fi**

12 🐕 ∦∦(htd) ⱳ ♨ ⛲ ⚡ 🐾 MSP 🦋 🏕 ⓣnr ⵣ🅿 ⟋⟍ ✎

**Off Kemi rd. Sp fr town & rte 4/E75 fr Kemi.
(Do not take Oulu by-pass app fr S).** Lge, pt shd, EHU
(16A) €4.50; bbq; cooking facs; sw nr; TV; 20% statics;
ccard acc; sauna; games area; bike hire; CKE. *"Gd
cycling; spa adj; pool adj; excel modern services block."*
€23.00 2016

PELLO *B2* (1km NW Rural) *66.78413, 23.94540*
Camping Pello, Nivanpääntie 58, 95700 Pello
050 3606611; pello.camping@gmail.com;
www.travelpello.fi/palvelu/camping-pello

∦∦(htd) ⱳ ♨ ⚡ 🐾 MSP 🦋 ⓣnr 🅿nr ⟋⟍

Foll site sp fr town cent. Med, hdstg, pt shd, EHU
(16A) inc; 30% statics; Eng spkn; ccard acc; boat hire;
rv fishing adj; sauna. *"Rvside pitches avail - insects!"*
€21.00, 1 Jun-20 Sep. 2016

PERANKA *C2* (2km E Rural) *65.39583, 29.07094*
Camping Piispansaunat, Selkoskyläntie 19, 89770 P
eranka **(040) 5916784 or (0400) 387615; piispan
saunat@elisanet.fi; piispansaunat@elisanet.fi**

🐾 ∦∦ ⱳ ♨ 🐾 🦋 ⵣ 🅿nr ⟋⟍

**Take rte 5/63 N or S; at Peranka turn E on rd 9190
for 2km; site on R in trees.** Sm, hdstg, shd, pt sl, EHU
(10A) €4; bbq; cooking facs; sw nr; Eng spkn; fishing;
sauna; CKE. **€25.00, 1 Jun-31 Aug.** 2016

PORVOO/BORGA *C4* (2km S Rural) *60.3798,
25.66673* **Camping Kokonniemi,** Uddaksentie 17,
06100 Porvoo **(452) 550074; myynti@suncamping.fi**

∦∦ ⱳ ♨ ⚡ 🐾 ⓣnr ⵣ🅿nr ⟋⟍

**Fr E on rte 7/E18 m'way ignore 1st exit Porvoo,
site sp fr 2nd exit.** 3*, Med, hdstg, sl, EHU (16A)
€5; Eng spkn; ccard acc; sauna; CKE. *"Access to old
town & rv walk; conv Helsinki & ferry; nice welcome;
v clean; ideal NH or longer; Porvoo interesting."*
€33.00, 1 Jun-26 Aug. 2017

PUNKAHARJU *D4* (9km NW Rural) *61.80032,
29.29088* **Punkaharjun Camping,** Tuunaansaarentie
4, 58540 Punkaharju **29 007 4050; info@punkaharju
resort.fi; www.punkaharjuresort.fi**

12 ∦∦ ⱳ ♨ ⚡ 🐾 🏕 ⓣ ⵣ🅿 ⟋⟍

27km SE of Savonlinna on rte 14 to Imatra, sp on R.
4*, Med, pt shd, EHU (16A) €7; sw; TV; ccard acc;
waterslide; fishing; tennis; games area; sauna; CKE.
*"Theme park nrby (closes 15/8); Kerimäki, world's
largest wooden church; Retretti Art Cent adj."*
€24.00 2016

RAUMA *B4* (3km NW Coastal) *61.13501, 21.47085*
Poroholma Camping, Poroholmanti 8, 26100 Rauma
(02)533 5522; info@poroholma.fi;
www.poroholma.fi

12 🐕 ∦∦ ⱳ ♨ ⚡ 🐾 ⵣ ⓣ 🅿 ⟋⟍ ⯑sand

**Enter town fr coast rd (8) or Huittinen (42). Foll
campsite sp around N pt of town to site on coast.
Site well sp.** 3*, Lge, shd, pt sl, EHU (16A) €5; ccard
acc; sauna; CKE. *"Attractive, peaceful location on
sm peninsula in yacht marina & jetty for ferry (foot
passengers only) to outlying islands; pool 250m; excel
beach; warm welcome fr helpful staff; clean facs."*
€25.00 2016

ROVANIEMI *B2* (7km E Rural) *66.51706, 25.84678*
Camping Napapiirin Saarituvat, Kuusamontie 96,
96900 Saarenkylä **(016) 3560045; reception@
saarituvat.fi; www.saarituvat.fi**

🐾 ⵣ ∦∦(htd) ⱳ ♨ ⚡ 🐾 🦋 🏕 ⓣ 🅿nr ⟋⟍

**Fr town cent take rd 81, site on R at side of rd on
lakeside. NB ignore 1st campsite sp after 2km.** Sm,
pt shd, terr, EHU (16A) €5.50; bbq; Eng spkn; adv
bkg acc; sauna; CKE. *"Excel; friendly staff; vg base for
Santa Park & Vill."* **€32.50, 20 May-9 Sep.** 2019

FINLAND

ROVANIEMI *B2 (1km SE Urban) 66.49743, 25.74340*
Ounaskoski Camping, Jäämerentie 1, 96200
Rovaniemi **(016) 345304; ounaskoski-camping@
windowslive.com**

🛉 ⅋⅋(htd) ⊡ ⚎ ⚲ ⅋ ⊟ ⅋ ⅁ 🦋 ⁂ ⊕nr ⅋ ⅀ ⚠ ⅋sand

**Exit rte 4 onto rte 78 & cross rv. Over bdge turn S on
rvside along Jäämerentie. Site on R in approx 500m
immed bef old rd & rail bdge, sp.** 3*, Med, mkd, hdstg,
unshd, EHU (16A) inc; bbq; cooking facs; sw; twin
axles; TV; 10% statics; bus 500m; Eng spkn; adv bkg
acc; ccard acc; sauna; bike hire; CKE. *"Helpful staff;
excel site beside rv in parkland; gd facs; suitable RVs
& twin axles; 9km fr Arctic Circle; 6km to Santa Park,
'official' home of Santa; Artikum Museum worth visit;
easy walk to town cent; gd flea mkts; excel san facs."*
€38.50, 21 May-24 Sep. **2017**

SAVONLINNA *C4 (7km W Rural) 61.86216, 28.80513*
Camping Vuohimäki, Vuohimäentie 60, 57600
Savonlinna **(015) 537353 or (045) 2550073;
savonlinna@suncamping.fi; www.suncamping.fi**

🛉 ⅋⅋ ⊡ ⚎ ⚲ ⅋ ⊟ ⅋ 🦋 ⁂ ⅂ ⊕ ⅋ ⅀nr ⚠

**On rte 14, 4km W of Savonlinna turn L immed after
bdge twd Pihlajaniemi; site sp for approx 4km on R.**
4*, Med, EHU (16A) €5; sw; 10% statics; bus; Eng spkn;
adv bkg acc; ccard acc; watersports; sauna; bike hire;
CKE. *"Gd area for touring; lake trips; views over lake; gd
san facs."* **€31.00, 10 Jun-22 Aug.** **2016**

TORNIO *B2 (3km SE Rural) 65.83211, 24.19953*
Camping Tornio, Matkailijantie, 95420 Tornio **(016)
445945; camping.tornio@co.inet.fi; www.camping
tornio.com**

⅋⅋ ⚎ ⚲ ⅋ ⊟ ⅋ 🦋 ⅋ ⅀nr ⚠

**App Tornio on E4 coast rd fr Kemi sp on L of dual c/
way; turn L at traff lts then immed R. Site well sp.**
3*, Lge, pt shd, EHU (16A) €4; cooking facs; TV; ccard
acc; sauna; tennis; bike hire; CKE. *"Poss boggy in wet."*
€28.00, 5 May-30 Sep. **2016**

TURKU/ABO *B4 (12km SW Rural) 60.42531, 22.10258*
Ruissalo Camping (Part Naturist), Saaronniemi,
20100 Turku **(02) 2625100; ruissalocamping@
turku.fi**

12 ⅋⅋(htd) ⊡ ⚎ ⚲ ⅋ ⊟ ⅋ 🅼 🦋 ⁂ ⊕nr ⅋ ⅀ ⚠ ⅋sand adj

**Well sp fr m'way & fr Turku docks; recep immed
after sharp bend in a layby.** 3*, Med, hdstg, pt shd,
EHU (16A) inc; TV; 10% statics; bus; Eng spkn; ccard
acc; watersports; sauna; games area; CKE. *"Conv for
ferry; modern, clean san facs; sep area for naturists; ltd
EHU some parts."* **€32.00** **2016**

VAASA/VASA *B3 (3km NW Coastal) 63.1008, 21.57618*
Top Camping Vaasa, Niemeläntie 1, 65170 Vaasa
**(0)20 7961 255; vaasa@topcamping.fi; www.top
camping.fi/vaasa**

🛉 ⅋⅋(htd) ⊡ ⚎ ⚲ ⅋ ⊟ ⅋ 🅼 ⅂ ⅀ ⚠

Fr town cent foll sp to harbour (Satama), site sp.
3*, Lge, pt shd, EHU (10A) €7; red long stay; TV;
10% statics; ccard acc; sauna; bike hire; CKE.
€29.50, 25 May-10 Aug. **2016**

VIRRAT *B4 (6km SE Rural) 62.20883, 23.83501*
Camping Lakarin Leirintä, Lakarintie 405, 34800
Virrat **(03) 4758639; lakari@virtainmatkailu.fi;
www.virtainmatkailu.fi**

⅋⅋(htd) ⊡ ⚎ ⅋ 🦋 ⅋ ⚠

**Fr Virrat on rte 66 twd Ruovesi. Fr Virrat pass info/
park & take 2nd L, then 1st L. Site 1.7km on R
(poor surface), sp.** Med, pt shd, pt sl, EHU (16A)
€3.40; sw nr; 50% statics; Eng spkn; sauna; boating;
fishing; CKE. *"Beautiful lakeside pitches."*
€20.00, 1 May-30 Sep. **2016**

VUOSTIMO *C2 (2km SW Rural) 66.95783, 27.50350*
Camping Kuukiurun, Sodankyläntie, 98360
Vuostimo **(0) 400 199 184; office@kuukiuru.fi;
www.kuukiuru.fi**

12 🛉 ⅋⅋ ⊡ ⚎ ⅋ 🦋 ⅋

**N fr Kemijarvi on rd 5, site on R of rd leaving
Vuostimo adj rv.** Sm, mkd, unshd, pt sl, EHU inc;
TV; 80% statics; fishing; sauna; boat hire. *"Beautiful,
peaceful site; x-country skiing; friendly owners."* **2016**

ALAND ISLANDS

SUND *A4 (12km SE Coastal) 60.21252, 20.23508*
Puttes Camping, Bryggvägen 40, Bomarsund, 22530
Sund **(018) 44040; puttes.camping@aland.net;
www.visitaland.com/puttescamping**

🛉 ⅋⅋ ⊡ ⚎ ⚲ ⅋ ⊟ ⅋ 🅼 🦋 ⅂ ⊕ ⅋ ⅀ ⅋shgl adj

**N fr Mariehamn on rd 2 for 40+ km, site at
Bomarsund fortress ruins.** 3*, Med, pt shd, pt sl, EHU
(10A) inc; bbq; cooking facs; 5% statics; phone; bus
adj; Eng spkn; adv bkg acc; games area; bike hire; CKE.
"Basic, but clean & welcoming; vg."
€12.00, 15 May-11 Sep. **2016**

VARDO *A4 (4km N Coastal) 60.27073, 20.38819*
Sandösunds Camping, Sandösundsvägen, 22550
Vårdö **(018) 47750; info@sandocamping.aland.fi;
www.sandocamping.aland.fi**

🛉 ⅋⅋(htd) ⊡ ⚎ ⚲ ⅋ ⊟ ⅋ 🅼 🦋 ⁂
⅂ ⊕ ⅋ ⅀ ⚠ ⅋sand adj

Site sp fr ferry at Hummelvik & fr rd 2.
3*, Med, pt shd, pt sl, EHU (10A) €4 (long lead poss
req); bbq; cooking facs; 5% statics; phone; Eng spkn;
adv bkg acc; bike hire; kayak hire; games area; CKE.
"Well-run site in beautiful location; excel facs."
€14.00, 15 Apr-31 Oct. **2016**

Map legend:
- France and Andorra
- Central and South East Europe, Benelux and Scandinavia
- Spain and Portugal

Kuusamo to Turku = 848 km

Distance table (km). Row city to column city:

	Forssa	Hanko	Helsinki	Hämeenlinna	Ivalo	Joensuu	Jyväskylä	Kajaani	Kemijärvi	Kokkola	Kouvola	Kuopio	Kurikka	Kuusamo	Kyyjärvi	Lahti	Lappeenranta	Mikkeli	Muonio	Nurmes	Oulu	Pori	Rovaniemi	Savonlinna	Sodankylä	Tampere	Tornio	Turku	Vaasa
Hanko	150																												
Helsinki	114	129																											
Hämeenlinna	56	195	100																										
Ivalo	1091	1238	1122	1041																									
Joensuu	464	546	439	410	839																								
Jyväskylä	238	380	271	187	848	244																							
Kajaani	555	664	556	500	623	229	313																						
Kemijärvi	889	1031	920	835	268	600	646	384																					
Kokkola	417	544	493	391	709	428	241	244	505																				
Kouvola	192	271	143	134	1037	310	192	436	821	432																			
Kuopio	383	493	382	332	800	135	145	170	557	314	264																		
Kurikka	263	390	345	245	882	449	230	385	679	174	356	335																	
Kuusamo	792	910	803	740	406	460	552	245	140	420	750	415	585																
Kyyjärvi	318	474	389	278	802	332	118	293	599	120	245	686	420	503															
Lahti	127	219	107	73	1017	336	170	450	813	409	61	282	704	339	137														
Lappeenranta	275	354	220	221	1062	236	220	437	820	459	82	266	682	296	215	147													
Mikkeli	258	341	231	204	957	208	114	330	718	356	99	162	579	127	233	105	129												
Muonio	975	1121	1004	918	325	782	732	568	275	590	922	670	420	686	945	901	840	945											
Nurmes	514	624	512	459	720	130	272	110	479	393	420	764	339	901	414	363	290	764	660										
Oulu	580	723	612	529	510	392	340	180	308	197	286	212	212	496	290	508	551	363	390	278									
Pori	127	257	242	180	1019	507	273	555	817	531	405	292	725	212	290	236	387	669	900	535	510								
Rovaniemi	807	941	831	747	287	550	561	339	85	302	750	510	192	725	513	774	774	730	230	429	471	730							
Savonlinna	362	449	333	310	958	142	207	332	717	440	162	325	578	577	155	232	155	593	839	272	447	471	671						
Sodankylä	929	1070	960	876	160	691	680	466	108	548	879	640	248	702	904	858	904	722	166	560	352	862	131	798					
Tampere	88	140	165	148	1144	549	304	615	943	434	274	448	501	364	217	217	578	501	1027	577	632	138	710	355	841				
Tornio	317	453	418	316	827	494	282	304	626	120	430	379	283	217	363	363	349	79	711	461	317	668	123	576	252	621			
Turku	344	429	320	288	875	118	125	250	634	355	190	75	353	848	242	217	87	756	206	362	390	714	855	444	986	153	764		
Vaasa																							444	540	668	245	448	428	
Varkaus																							586	88	714	276	494	346	396

Germany

Berlin

Highlights

Home to beautiful landscapes, architectural delights and diverse cities, Germany has a rich culture and history for you to discover. Berlin is undoubtedly one of the culture and arts capitals of the world, while the picturesque timbered villages and castles have inspired countless works of literature, film and art.

Often thought of as the home of beer and bratwurst, Germany has much more to offer on a gastronomic level, with Riesling wine, Black Forest Gateaux and Stollen just some of the treats that are waiting to be discovered and enjoyed.

Germany is the home of the modern car, and its automobile industry is one of the most innovative in the world. BMW, Audi, Porsche and Mercedes all have museums to visit.

Oktoberfest, the largest beer festival in the world, is held annually in Munich and attracts people from around the globe. This 17-day festival only serves traditional beers that are brewed within Munich city limits.

Major towns and cities

- Berlin – this capital is an exciting city of culture and science.
- Hamburg – enjoy stunning and varied architecture in this gorgeous city.
- Munich – a magnificent city of culture and technology.
- Cologne – this city is brimming with bars, restaurants and pubs.

Attractions

- Neuschwanstein, Füssen – this fairytale castle inspired Sleeping Beauty's palace.
- Holstentor, Lübeck – a UNESCO relic of the medieval city fortifications.
- Cologne Cathedral – This gothic cathedral is Germany's most visited landmark.
- Lindau – an enchanting island town boasting beautiful architecture and wonderful gardens.

Find out more

www.germany.travel
E: hallo@visitberlin.de T: 0049 (0) 69 97 46 40

Country Information

Population (approx): 81million

Capital: Berlin (population approx 3.4 million)

Area: 357,050 sq km

Bordered by: Austria, Belgium, Czech Republic, Denmark, France, Luxembourg, Netherlands, Poland, Switzerland

Terrain: Lowlands in north; uplands/industrialised belt in the centre; highlands, forests and Bavarian alps in the south

Climate: Temperate throughout the year; warm summers and cold winters; rain throughout the year

Coastline: 2,389km

Highest Point: Zugspitze 2,962m

Language: German

Local Time: GMT or BST + 1, i.e. 1 hour ahead of the UK all year

Currency: Euros divided into 100 cents; £1 = €1.16, €1 = £0.87 (October 2019)

Emergency numbers: Police 112; Fire brigade 112; Ambulance 112. Operators speak English

Public Holidays 2020: Jan 1, 6; Apr 10, 12, 13; May 1, 21; June 1, 11; Aug 15; Oct 3, 31; Nov 1, 18; Dec 25, 26.

Public holidays vary according to region. The dates shown here may not be celebrated throughout the country. School summer holidays also vary by region but are roughly July to mid/end Aug or Aug to mid Sept.

Entry Formalities

Due to the current migrant crisis in Europe some countries have temporarily restored their borders. A current list of countries affected is available on the EU website: **ec.europa. eu/home-affairs/what-we-do/policies/ borders-and-visas/schengen/reintroduction- border-control_en**. At the time of going to print Germany has restored their borders with Austria.

British and Irish passport holders may stay in Germany for up to three months without a visa. While there are no Customs controls at Germany's borders into other EU countries, when you enter or leave the Czech Republic and Poland you may still have to show your passport.

Regulations for Pets

Certain breeds of dogs, such as pit bull terriers and American Staffordshire terriers, are prohibited from entering Germany unless you have a Certificate of Personality Test, which must be given by a vet on entering Germany. Other breeds such as Dobermann, Mastiff and Rottweiler may need to be kept on a lead and muzzled in public, including in your car. You are advised to contact the German embassy in London before making travel arrangements for your dog and check the latest available information from your vet or from the PETS Helpline on 0370 241 1710.

Medical Services

Local state health insurance fund offices offer assistance round-the-clock and telephone numbers can be found in the local telephone directory. EU citizens are entitled to free or subsidised emergency care from doctors contracted to the state health care system on presentation of a European Health Insurance Card (EHIC). Private treatment by doctors or dentists is not refundable under the German health service. You will be liable for a percentage of prescribed medication charges at pharmacies and this is also non-refundable. Pharmacies offer an all-night and Sunday service and the address of the nearest out-of-hours branch will be displayed on the door of every pharmacy.

There is a fixed daily charge for a stay in hospital (treatment is free for anyone under 18 years of age) which is not refundable. If you are required to pay an additional patient contribution for treatment then reduced charges apply to holders of an EHIC. For refunds of these additional charges you should apply with original receipts to a local state health insurance fund office.

Opening Hours

Banks: Mon-Fri 8.30am-12.30pm & 1.30pm-3.30pm (to 5pm or 6pm on Thurs).

Museums: Check locally as times vary.

Post Offices: Mon-Fri 7/8am-6/8pm; Sat 8am-12pm.

Shops: Mon-Fri 8/9am-6pm/8pm. Sat 8/9am-12/4pm; bakers may be open Sun mornings.

Safety and Security

Most visits to Germany are trouble free but visitors should take the usual commonsense precautions against mugging, pickpocketing and bag snatching, particularly in areas around railway stations, airports in large cities and at Christmas markets. Do not leave valuables unattended.

Germany shares with the rest of Europe a general threat from terrorism. Attacks could be indiscriminate and against civilian targets in public places, including tourist sites. You should maintain a high level of vigilance at all times.

British Embassy

WILHELMSTRASSE 70, D-10117 BERLIN
Tel: (030) 204570,
www.ukingermany.fco.gov.uk/en/

British Consulates-General

OststraBe 86, 40210
DÜSSELDORF
Tel: (0211) 94480
MÖHLSTRASSE 5, 81675 MÜNCHEN
Tel: (089) 211090

Irish Embassy

JÄGERSTRASSE 51, 10117 BERLIN
Tel: (030) 220720
www.embassyofireland.de

There are also Irish Honorary Consulates in Frankfurt, Hamburg, Köln (Cologne) and München (Munich).

Documents

Passport

It is a legal requirement to carry your passport at all times. German police have the right to ask to see identification and for British citizens the only acceptable form of ID is a valid passport.

Money

The major debit and credit cards, including American Express, are widely accepted by shops, hotels, restaurants and petrol stations. However, you may find that credit cards are not as widely accepted in smaller establishments as they are in the UK, including many shops and campsites, due to the high charges imposed on retailers, and debit cards are preferred. Cash machines are widespread and have instructions in English.

British visitors have been arrested for possession of counterfeit currency and the authorities advise against changing money anywhere other than at banks or legitimate bureaux de change.

Carry your credit card issuers'/banks' 24-hour UK contact numbers in case of loss or theft of your cards.

Vehicle(s)

Carry your valid driving licence, insurance and vehicle documents with you in your vehicle at all times. It is particularly important to carry your vehicle registration document V5C, as you will need it if entering a low emission zone (see later in this chapter for more information).

If you are driving a hired or borrowed vehicle, you must be in possession of a letter of authorisation from the owner or a hire agreement.

Driving

Roads in Germany are of an excellent standard but speed limits are higher than in the UK and the accident rate is greater. Drivers undertaking long journeys in or through Germany should plan their journeys carefully and take frequent breaks.

Accidents

In the event of a road accident the police must always be called even if there are no injuries.

Alcohol

The maximum permitted level of alcohol is 50 milligrams per 100 millilitres of blood, i.e. lower than that in the UK (80 milligrams). For novice drivers who have held a driving licence for less than two years, and for drivers under the age of 21, no alcohol is permitted in the bloodstream. Penalties for driving under the influence of alcohol or drugs are severe.

Breakdown Service

The motoring organisation Allgemeiner Deutscher Automobil-Club (ADAC) operates road patrols on motorways and in the event of a breakdown, assistance can be obtained by calling from emergency phones placed every 2 km. Members of clubs affiliated to the AIT or FIA, such as The Caravan and Motorhome Club, must ask specifically for roadside assistance to be provided by ADAC as they should be able to receive assistance free of charge. You must pay for replacement parts and towing. ADAC breakdown vehicles are yellow and marked 'ADAC Strassenwacht'.

If ADAC Strassenwacht vehicles are not available, firms under contract to ADAC provide towing and roadside assistance, against payment. Vehicles used by firms under contract to ADAC are marked 'Strassendienst im Auftrag des ADAC'.

On other roads the ADAC breakdown service can be reached 24 hours a day by telephoning 01802-22 22 22 (local call rates) or 22 22 22 from a mobile phone.

Child Restraint Systems

Children under three years of age must be placed in an approved child restraint and cannot be transported in a vehicle otherwise. Children of three years and over must travel in the rear of vehicles. Children under 12 years old and 1.5 metres in height must be seated in an approved child restraint. If a child restraint won't fit into the vehicle because other children are using a child restraint, then children of three years and over must use a seat belt or other safety device attached to the seat.

Fuel

Most petrol stations are open from 8am to 8pm. In large cities many are open 24 hours. In the east there are fewer petrol stations than in the south and west. Some have automatic pumps operated using credit cards.

LPG (autogas or flussiggas) is widely available. You can view a list of approximately 800 outlets throughout the country, including those near motorways, from the website www. autogastanken.de (follow the links under 'Tanken' and 'Tankstellan-Karte). On some stretches of motorway petrol stations may be

few and far between, e.g. the A45, A42 and A3 to the Dutch border, and it is advisable not to let your fuel tank run low.

Lights

Dipped headlights are recommended at all times and must always be used in tunnels, as well as when visibility is poor and during periods of bad weather. Bulbs are more likely to fail with constant use and you are recommended to carry spares.

Low Emission Zones

A large number of German cities and towns now require motorists to purchase a 'Pollution Badge' (Umwelt Plakette) in the form of a windscreen sticker in order to enter city centre 'Umwelt' or green zones. The areas where restrictions apply are indicated by signs showing coloured vignettes, the colour of the vignette issued (red, yellow or green) depending on your vehicle's engine type and its Euro emission rating.

You must present your vehicle registration document, V5C, at an 'Umwelt Plakette' sales outlet, which can be found at vehicle repair centres, car dealers, MOT (Tüv) stations and vehicle licensing offices and it is understood that badges are also available from ATU motoring supplies shops. The cost varies between €5 and €10 + VAT and postage.

Failure to display a badge could result in a fine of €40. Enforcement is managed by the police, local authorities and traffic wardens. Older vehicles without a catalytic converter or a particulate filter (generally emission-rated Euro 1) will not be issued with a badge and will not be permitted to enter the centres of those cities and towns participating in the scheme.

Visit www.lowemissionzones.eu or www. umwelt-plakette.de (you may also be able to purchase your badge here before you travel to Germany).

Motorways

With around 12,845 toll free kilometres, Germany's motorways (autobahns) constitute one of the world's most advanced and efficient systems. For a complete list of autobahns, including the location of all junctions and roadworks in progress, see www.autobahn-online.de.

Some motorways are so heavily used by lorries that the inside lane has become heavily rutted. These parallel ruts are potentially dangerous for caravans travelling at high speed and vigilance is necessary. It is understood that the A44 and A7 are particularly prone to this problem. Caution also needs to be exercised when driving on the concrete surfaces of major roads.

On motorways emergency telephones are placed at 2 km intervals; some have one button to request breakdown assistance and another to summon an ambulance. Other telephones connect the caller to a rescue control centre. A vehicle that has broken down on a motorway must be towed away to the nearest exit.

There are hundreds of motorway service areas offering, at the very least, a petrol station and a restaurant or cafeteria. Tourist information boards are posted in all the modern motorway service areas. Recent visitors have reported an increase in service facilities just off Autobahn exit ramps, in particular with 'Autohof' (truck stops). The facilities at Autohofs are reported to be comparable to service areas, but usually with considerably lower prices.

Parking

Zigzag lines on the carriageway indicate a stopping (waiting) and parking prohibition, e.g. at bus stops, narrow roads and places with poor visibility, but double or single yellow lines are not used. Instead look out for 'no stopping', 'parking prohibited' or 'no parking' signs.

Except for one-way streets, parking is only permitted on the right-hand side. Do not park in the opposite direction to traffic flow. Parking meters and parking disc schemes are in operation and discs may be bought in local shops or service stations.

Priority

At crossroads and junctions, where no priority is indicated, traffic coming from the right has priority. Trams do not have absolute priority over other vehicles but priority must be given to passengers getting on or off stationary trams. Trams in two-way streets must be overtaken on the right. Drivers must give way to a bus whose driver has indicated his intention to pull away from the kerb. Do not overtake a stationary school bus which has stopped to let passengers on or off. This may be indicated by a red flashing light on the bus.

Traffic already on a roundabout has right of way, except when signs show otherwise. Drivers must use their indicators when leaving a roundabout, not when entering.

Always stop to allow pedestrians to cross at marked pedestrian crossings. In residential areas where traffic-calming zones exist, pedestrians are allowed to use the whole street, so drive with great care.

Road Signs and Markings

Most German road signs and markings conform to the international pattern. Other road signs that may be encountered are:

Keep distance shown

Street lights not on all night

Lower speed limit applies in the wet

Recommended route on motorways

One way street

Tram or bus stop

German	English Translation
Einsatzfahrzeuge Fre	Emergency vehicles only
Fahrbahnwechsel	Change traffic lane
Freie Fahrt	Road clear
Frostchaden	Frost damage
Gefährlich	Danger
Glatteisgefahr	Ice on the road
Notruf	Emergency roadside telephone
Radweg Kreuzt	Cycle-track crossing
Rollsplitt	Loose grit
Stau	Traffic jam
Strassenschaden	Road damage
Umleitung	Diversion
Vorsicht	Caution

Road signs on motorways are blue and white, whereas on B roads (Bundesstrasse) they are orange and black. If you are planning a route through Germany using E road numbers, be aware that E roads may be poorly signposted and you may have to navigate using national A or B road numbers.

Speed Limits

	Open Road (kmph)	Motorway (kmph)
Solo Car	100	130
Car towing caravan/trailer	80*	80
Motorhome under 3500kg	100	130
Motorhome 3500-7500kg	80	100

* 100 km/h (62 mph) if your car and caravan passes a TUV test in Germany (test costs €70 and takes 2 hours to complete)

There is a speed limit of 50 km/h (31 mph) in built-up areas for all types of motor vehicles, unless otherwise indicated by road signs. A built-up area starts from the town name sign at the beginning of a town or village.

The number of sections of autobahn with de-restricted zones, i.e. no upper speed limit, is diminishing and the volume of traffic makes high speed motoring virtually impossible. Regulations on many stretches of two-lane motorway restrict lorries, together with cars towing caravans, from overtaking.

Speed cameras are frequently in use but they may be deliberately hidden behind crash barriers or in mobile units. A GPS navigation system which indicates the location of fixed speed cameras must have the function deactivated. The use of radar detectors is prohibited.

A car towing a caravan or trailer is prohibited to 80km/h (50 mph) on motorways and other main roads. You may occasionally see car/caravan combinations displaying a sign indicating that their maximum permitted speed is 100 km/h (62 mph). This is only permitted for vehicles that have passed a TUV test in Germany, who will then need to apply for a sticker at a Zulassungsstelle. The application process can be complicated as some Zulassungsstelles will insist they see a registration certificate for your caravan. Obtaining a 100km/h sticker without a registration certificate is best done in Aachen as they are the only Zulassungsstelle familiar with this process. If you are having difficulty at a different Zulassungsstelle ask them to call the Zulassungsstelle in Aachen to confirm that a registration document is not required.

In bad weather when visibility is below 50 metres, the maximum speed limit is 50 km/h (31 mph) on all roads.

Towing

Drivers of cars towing caravans and other slow-moving vehicles must leave enough space in front of them for an overtaking vehicle to get into that space, or they must pull over from time to time to let other vehicles pass.

If you are towing a car behind a motorhome, our advice would be to use a trailer with all four wheels of the car off the ground. Although Germany doesn't have a specific law banning A-frames, they do have a law which prohibits a motor vehicle towing another motor vehicle. Outside built-up areas the speed limit for such vehicle combinations is 80 km/h (50 mph) or 60 km/h (37 mph) for vehicles over 3,500 kg.

Traffic Jams

Roads leading to popular destinations in Denmark, the Alps and Adriatic Coast become very congested during the busy holiday period of July and August and on public holidays. In those periods traffic jams of up to 60 km are not unheard of.

Congestion is likely on the A3 and A5 north-south routes. Traffic jams are also likely to occur on the A7 Kassel-Denmark, the A8 Stuttgart-Munich-Salzburg and on the A2 and A9 to Berlin. Other cities where congestion may occur are Würzburg, Nürnberg (Nuremberg), Munich and Hamburg. Alternative routes, known as U routes, have been devised; those leading to the south or west have even numbers and those leading to the north or east have odd numbers. These U routes often detour over secondary roads to the following motorway junction and the acquisition of a good road map or atlas is recommended.

ADAC employs 'Stauberater' (traffic jam advisors) who are recognisable by their bright yellow motorbikes. They assist motorists stuck in traffic and will advise on alternative routes.

Upgrading of motorways to Berlin from the west and improvements to many roads in the old east German suburbs may result in diversions and delays, and worsened traffic congestion.

Violation of Traffic Regulations

Police are empowered to impose and collect small on-the-spot fines for contravention of traffic regulations. Fines vary according to the gravity of the offence and have in recent years been increased dramatically for motorists caught speeding in a built-up area (over 50 km/h – 31 mph). A deposit may be required against higher fines and failure to pay may cause the vehicle to be confiscated.

It is an offence to use abusive language, or make rude gestures in Germany, including to other drivers while driving. It is also an offence to stop on the hard shoulder of a motorway except in the case of mechanical failure - please note that running out of fuel is not classed as a mechanical failure so you may be liable for a fine of up to €20 if you do run out of fuel and stop on the hard shoulder.

It is illegal for pedestrians to cross a road when the red pedestrian light is displayed, even if there is no traffic approaching the crossing. Offenders could be fined and will find themselves liable to all costs in the event of an accident.

Winter Driving

All vehicles, including those registered outside Germany, must be fitted with winter tyres (or all season tyres) during winter conditions, bearing the mark 'M+S' (Mud + Snow) or the snowflake symbol. Failure to use them can result in a fine and penalty points. There must also be anti-freeze in the windscreen cleaning fluid.

The use of snow chains is permitted and for vehicles fitted with them there is a maximum speed limit of 50 km/h (31 mph).
In mountainous areas the requirement for chains is indicated by signs. The use of spiked tyres is not authorised.

Essential Equipment

First Aid Kit

Drivers of German registered vehicles must carry a first aid kit but this is not a legal requirement for foreign visitors.

Lights

Dipped headlights are recommended at all times and must always be used in tunnels, as well as when visibility is poor and during periods of bad weather. Bulbs are more likely to fail with constant use and you are recommended to carry spares.

Touring

German food is generally of high quality and offers great regional range and diversity. In the country there is at least one inn – 'gasthof' or 'gasthaus' – in virtually every village. A service charge is usually included in restaurant bills but it is usual to leave some small change or round up the bill by 5-10% if satisfied with the service.

Smoking is generally banned on public transport and in restaurants and bars, but regulations vary from state to state.

The German National Tourist Board (GNTB) produces guides to walking and cycle paths throughout the country, as well an extensive range of other brochures and guides. The individual tourist offices for the 16 federal states can also supply a wealth of information about events, attractions and tourist opportunities within their local regions. Obtain contact details from the GNTO.

Christmas markets are an essential part of the run-up to the festive season and they range in size from a few booths in small towns and villages, to hundreds of stalls and booths in large cities. The markets generally run from mid November to 22 or 23 December.

There are 32 UNESCO World Heritage sites in Germany, including the cities of Lübeck, Potsdam and Weimar, the cathedrals of Aachen, Cologne and Speyer, together with numerous other venues of great architectural and archaeological interest.

The Berlin Welcome Card is valid for 2, 3 or 5 days and includes free bus and train travel (including free travel for three accompanying children up to the age of 14), as well as discounted or free entrance to museums, and discounts on tours, boat trips, restaurants and theatres. It can be extended to include Potsdam and the Museuminsel and is available from tourist information centres, hotels and public transport centres or from www.visitberlin. de. A 3 day museum card – SchauLUST-MuseenBERLIN – is also available, valid in more than 60 national museums in and around the city.

Other cities, groups of cities or regions also offer Welcome Cards, including Bonn, Cologne, Dresden, Düsseldorf, Frankfurt, Hamburg, Heidelberg and Munich. These give discounts on public transport, museums, shopping, dining and attractions. Enquire at a local tourist office or at the German National Tourist Office in London.

Camping and Caravanning

There are approximately 3,500 campsites in Germany, which are generally open from April to October. Many (mostly in winter sports areas) stay open in winter and have all the necessary facilities for winter sports enthusiasts. Sites may have a very high proportion of statics, usually in a separate area. In the high summer season visitors should either start looking for a pitch early in the afternoon or book in advance.

Campsites are usually well equipped with modern sanitary facilities, shops and leisure amenities, etc. Some sites impose a charge for handling rubbish, commonly €1 to €2 a day. Separate containers for recycling glass, plastic, etc, are now the norm.

A daily tourist tax may also be payable of up to €2 or €3 per person per night.

Naturism is popular, particularly in eastern Germany, and sites which accept naturists will generally display a sign 'FKK'.

Many sites close for a two hour period between noon and 3pm (known as Mittagsruhe) and you may find barriers down so that vehicles cannot be moved on or off the site during this period. Some sites provide a waiting area but where a site entrance is off a busy road parking or turning may be difficult.

For a list of small sites (up to 150 pitches) see www.kleincamp.de.

Casual/wild camping is discouraged and is not allowed in forests and nature reserves. In the case of private property permission to pitch a tent or park a caravan should be obtained in advance from the owners, or on common land or state property, from the local town hall or police station.

Cycling

There is an extensive network of over 70,000 km of cycle routes across all regions. Children under eight years are not allowed to cycle on the road. Under 10 year olds may ride on the pavement but must give way to pedestrians and dismount to cross the road. Bicycles must have front and rear lights and a bell.

Cyclists can be fined €25 for using a mobile phone while cycling and €10 for using earphones.

Electricity and Gas

Current on campsites varies between 2 and 16 amps, 6 to 10 amps being the most common. Plugs have two round pins. Most campsites have CEE connections.

Many sites make a one-off charge – usually €1 or €2 however long your stay – for connection to the electricity supply, which is then metered at a rate per kilowatt hour (kwh) of approximately €0.50-€0.70, with or without an additional daily charge. This connection charge can make one night stays expensive. During the summer you may find only a flat, daily charge for electricity of €2-€5, the supply being metered during the rest of the year.

Campingaz is available and the blue cylinders in general used throughout Europe may be exchanged for German cylinders which are green-grey. At some campsites in winter sports areas a direct connection with the gas mains ring is available and the supply is metered.

Public Transport

Most major German cities have underground (U-bahn), urban railway (S-bahn), bus and tram systems whose convenience and punctuality are renowned. Pay your fare prior to boarding public transport using the automated ticketing machines. Your ticket must then be date stamped separately using the machines on board the vehicle or at the entry gates at major stops. Daily tickets permit the use of trains, buses and trams.

A number of car ferries operate across the Weser and Elbe rivers which allow easy touring north of Bremen and Hamburg. Routes across the Weser include Blexen to Bremerhavn, Brake to Sandstedt and Berne to Farge. The Weser Tunnel (B437) connects the villages of Rodenkirchen and Dedesdorf, offering an easy connection between the cities of Bremerhaven and Nordenham. Across the Elbe there is a car ferry route between Wischhafen and Glückstadt. An international ferry route operates all year across Lake Constance (Bodensee) between Konstanz and Meersburg. There is also a route between Friedrichshafen and Romanshorn in Switzerland.

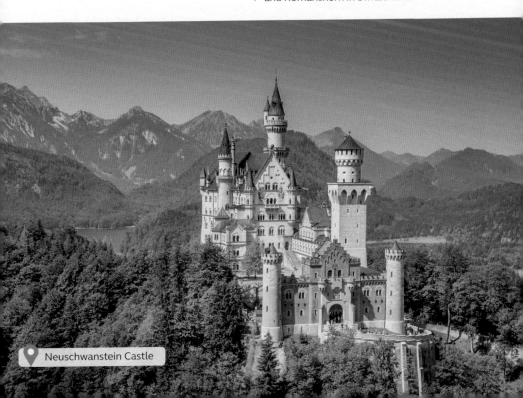

Neuschwanstein Castle

AACHEN *1A4* (18km SE Rural) *50.69944, 6.22194*
Camping Vichtbachtal, Vichtbachstrasse 10, 52159
Roetgen-Mulartshütte **(02408) 5131;** camping@
vichtbachtal.de; www.vichtbachtal.de

12 ♀♀ ⓦ ⌂ ⬛ ♨ ☂ ⓗ ᵤᵣ ⬛ ⚲

On E40/A44 exit junc 3 Aachen/Brand onto B258
dir Kornelimünster. In 5km at R-hand bend turn L
sp Mulartshütte. Thro Venwegen. Site ent on L 50m
bef T-junc app Mulartshütte, site sp. 3*, Med, shd, pt
sl, EHU (16A) €1.50 or metered (rev pol); 80% statics;
site clsd Nov; CKE. "*Sm area for tourers; v friendly
Eng spkn owners; gd site for visiting Aachen; gd walks
adj; gd bus service to Aachen; v pretty wooded area.*"
€21.50   2016

AACHEN *1A4* (3.5km SE Urban) *50.76140, 6.10285*
Aachen Platz für Camping, Branderhoferweg 11,
52066 Aachen-Burtscheid **(0241) 6088057;** mail@
aachen-camping.de; www.aachen-camping.de

12 ♀ ♀♀(htd) ⓦ ⌂ ⚙ ♨ ☂

Exit A44 junc 2 onto L233 Monschauerstrasse dir
Aachen. In 3.8km at outer ring rd Adenauer Allee
L260 turn R, then in 800m L at 2nd traff lts onto
Branderhoferweg twd Beverau. Site on R at bottom
of hill. 2*, Sm, mkd, hdstg, pt shd, EHU (16A) inc; bus
500m; Eng spkn. "*Nice, clean, well-run municipal site;
gd, modern san facs; max stay 5 nights; excel o'night
stop; rec arr bef 1600 high ssn; ideal Xmas mkts; gd
conv site; close to city cent; open access site; fair.*"
€15.00   2015

"There aren't many sites open at this time of year"

If you're travelling outside peak season
remember to call ahead to check site opening
dates – even if the entry says 'open all year'.

ALPIRSBACH *3C3* (2km N Rural) *48.35576, 8.41224*
Camping Alpirsbach, Grezenbühler Weg 18-20,
72275 Alpirsbach **(07444) 6313;** info@camping-
alpirsbach.de; www.camping-alpirsbach.de

12 ♀ €1 ♀♀ ⓦ ⌂ ⚙ ♨ ☂ ☂ ☂ ⓗ ⬛ ⚲

On B294 leave Alpirsbach twds Freudenstadt.
1st site sp on L. 4*, Med, pt shd, serviced pitches;
EHU (16A) metered; gas; red long stay; 10% statics;
Eng spkn; tennis; golf 5km; CKE. "*Excel site; helpful,
informative & friendly owner; vg welcome, free bottle
of local beer per person; immac san facs; gd rest; gd
walking; o'night area for m'vans €10; guest card for
free transport on some local transport; some rvside
pitches (v shd).*" **€30.00**   2019

ALSFELD *1D4* (11km W Rural) *50.73638, 9.15222*
Camping Heimertshausen, Ehringshäuserstrasse,
36320 Kirtorf-Heimertshausen **(06635) 206;** info@
campingplatz-heimertshausen.de; campingplatz-
heimertshausen.de

♀ €1 ♀♀ ⌂ ⬛ ♨ ☂ ⓗ ⬛ ⚲ ⚲

Exit A5 junc 3 Alsfeld West onto B49 dir Frankfurt.
Turn R in vill of Romrod to Heimertshausen & L to
site. Site also sp fr B62. Med, shd, EHU (10-16A) €2
or metered; 65% statics; Eng spkn; adv bkg acc; CKE.
"*Beautiful, wooded area; lovely 'hunting lodge' type
cosy rest; bar/food open Jul/Aug; clsd 1300-1500
& 2200-0800; htd pool adj; o'night m'vans area; site
run down (2015); facs dated but clean & adequate.*"
€27.50, 1 Apr-30 Sep.   2015

ALTENBERG *4G1* (1km W Rural) *50.76666, 13.74666*
Camping Kleiner Galgenteich (Naturist), Galgenteich
3, 01773 Altenberg **(035056) 31995;** mail@camping-
erzgebirge.de; www.camping-erzgebirge.de

12 ♀ €1 ♀♀ ⓦ ⌂ ⬛ ♨ ☂ ☂ ⓨ ⓗ ⬛ ⚲

Leave A4 at Dresden-Nord onto B170 sp Zinnwald
then Altenberg. On SW side of B170; clearly sp.
Lge, pt shd, pt sl, EHU (10A) metered + conn fee; sw
nr; 50% statics; sailing adj. "*Sep area for naturists; ski
lift 500m; site clsd in Nov.*" **€21.00**   2016

ALTENBURG *2F4* (12km NNE Rural) *51.045799,
12.500404* See Camping Altenburgh-Pahna, 04617
Pahna **(03434) 351914;** camping-pahna@t-online.de;
www.camping-pahna.de

12 ♀ €2.50 ♀♀(htd) ⓦ ⌂ ⚙ ♨ ☂ ☂ ⓨ ☰ ⓗ ⬛ ⚲ ⚲

A4 exit 60 (Ronneburg) then B7 to Altenburg. B93
direction Leipzig, right B7 direction Frohburg, foll sp
at Eschefeld. 4*, V lge, pt shd, serviced pitches; EHU
€2; bbq; cooking facs; sw; red long stay; 25% statics;
Eng spkn; adv bkg acc; lake adj; games area; CKE. "*Vg;
nature walks; conv Dresden, Leipzig & Colditz; quiet LS
but busy on w/ends and hg ssn.*" **€24.00**   2019

ALTENKIRCHEN *2F1* (9km W Coastal) *54.62905,
13.22281* **Caravancamp Ostseeblick,** Seestr. 39a,
18556 Dranske **(03839) 18196;** www.caravancamp-
ostseeblick.de

♀ ♀♀ ⓦ ⌂ ⚙ ♨ ☂ ⓨ

Clearly sp fr main rd bet Kuhle & Dranske.
Sm, hdstg, hdg, mkd, pt shd, EHU €2.50; twin axles;
20% statics; Eng spkn; adv bkg rec. "*Excel; sea adj.*"
€23.00, 1 Apr-31 Oct.   2017

ALTENSTEIG *3C3* (3km W Rural) *48.58456, 8.57866*
Schwarzwald Camping Altensteig, Im Oberen Tal 3-5,
72213 Altensteig **(07453) 8415; info@schwarzwald
camping.de; www.schwarzwaldcamping.de**

12 ⌂ €2 ⋔ wc ⚍ ⛌ ⌀ ✿ Ⓨ ⓘ

Take Obere Talstrasse (L362) due W fr town ctr. Aft
2km site on L. Easy access. Sm, pt shd, EHU; bbq;
twin axles; 75% statics; Eng spkn; games area. *"Gd;
table tennis, beach volleyball, boating, walking fr site;
Black Forest; cross country skiing."* **€23.00   2017**

AUGSBURG *4E3* (7km N Rural) *48.41168, 10.92371*
Camping Bella Augusta, Mühlhauserstrasse 54B,
86169 Augsburg-Ost **(0821) 707575; info@
caravaningpark.de; www.caravaningpark.de**

12 ⌂ €2.55 ⋔ wc ⚍ ⌀ MP Ⓨ nr ⛟ ⟋

Exit A8/E52 junc 73 dir Neuburg to N, site sp.
2*, Lge, pt shd, EHU (10A) inc; sw nr; 80% statics;
ccard acc; boating. *"V busy NH; excel rest; camping
equipment shop on site; vg san facs but site looking
a little run down; noise fr a'bahn; cycle track to town
(map fr recep); vg; nice lake."* **€31.00   2019**

AUGSBURG *4E3* (8km N Rural) *48.43194, 10.92388*
Camping Ludwigshof am See, Augsburgerstrasse 36,
86444 Mühlhausen-Affing **(08207) 961724; info@
campingludwigshof.de; www.campingludwigshof.de**

⌂ €2 ⋔ wc ⚍ ⌀ MP ✿ Ⓨ ⓘ ⚘ ⛟ nr ⟋

Exit A8/E52 junc 73at Augsburg Ost/Pöttmes exit;
foll sp Pöttmes; site sp on L on lakeside.
3*, Lge, unshd, EHU (16A) €3.50 (long cable req); bbq;
sw; twin axles; red long stay; 70% statics; bus; Eng
spkn; ccard acc; tennis; CKE. *"Pleasant site; unmkd
field for tourers, close to san facs; both 6A panel & 16A
panels for EHU -16A only accepts German type of plug;
beautiful clean, modern facs; nr A8 m'way; conv NH on
way to E Italy; clsd 1300-1500; gd for long stay, special
rates can be negotiated; poss need long cable as EHU
in corner of field."* **€31.50, 1 Apr-31 Oct.   2018**

AUGSBURG *4E3* (9km NE Rural) *48.4375, 10.92916*
Lech Camping, Seeweg 6, 86444 Affing-Mühlhausen
**(08207) 2200; info@lech-camping.de; www.lech-
camping.de**

⌂ €3 ⋔ (htd) wc ⚍ ⛌ ⌀ MP ⚘ Ⓨ ⓘ ⛟ nr

Exit A8/E52 at junc 73 Augsburg-Ost; take rd N sp
Pöttmes; site 3km on R. 5*, Sm, hdstg, mkd, pt shd,
EHU (16A); bbq; sw nr; bus to Augsburg, train Munich;
Eng spkn; adv bkg rec; ccard acc; boating. *"Lovely,
well-ordered site; friendly, helpful owners; excel san
facs; gd play area; deposit for san facs key; camping
accessory shop on site; cycle rte to Augsburg; excel
NH for A8; excel site espec lakeside pitch; statics (sep
area); c'vans close together; constant rd noise; recep
shut 12-2pm."* **€36.50, 15 Apr-15 Sep, G19.   2018**

BAD ABBACH *4F3* (6km W Rural) *48.93686, 12.01992*
Campingplatz Freizeitinsel, Inselstraße 1a, D93077
Bad Abbach **(09405) 9570401 or (0176) 96631729;
info@campingplatz-freizeitinsel.de; www.camping
platz-freizeitinsel.de**

⋔ wc ⚍ ⛌ ⌀ ⚍ MP ✿ Ⓨ ⓘ ⟋

A93 Regensburg, exit Pentling B16 dir twrds
Kelheim. Cont on B16 past Bad Abbach and take
next exit R to Poikam/Inselbad. Over rv and foll
rd round to R past Poikam sp. At junc turn R sp
Inselbad. Site on R. Med, mkd, EHU; bbq; cooking
facs; sw nr; twin axles; 20% statics; Eng spkn; adv
bkg acc; bike hire; CKE. *"New (2014) family run
developing site; vg, modern, clean facs; some deluxe
serviced pitches avail with supp; gd area for touring,
cycling & walking; nrby lake, sw & thermal baths; gd
rest in vill 1km; train to Regensburg 1km; excel site."*
€28.00, 25 Mar-31 Oct & 27 Nov-18 Dec.   2017

BAD BIRNBACH *4G3* (800km N Rural) *48.450201,
13.094024* **Camping Theresienhof,** Breindoblweg 6,
84364 Bad Birnbach **(08563) 963244; www.camping-
theresienhof.de**

12 ⌂ ⋔ (htd) wc ⚍ ⛌ ⌀ MP ✿

Off B388 W fr A3 fr Schaarding. Hdstg, mkd, pt shd,
terr, EHU (16A); bbq (charcoal, elec, gas); cooking
facs; twin axles; adv bkg rec; bike hire. *"Ideal stopover."*
NP 26.9   2019

BAD BRAMSTEDT *1D2* (1km N Rural) *53.9283, 9.8901*
Kur-Camping Roland, Kielerstrasse 52, 24576 Bad
Bramstedt **(04192) 6723**

⌂ €2 ⋔ wc ⚍ ⛌ ⌀ ⓘ nr ⚘ ⛟

Exit A7 junc 17 dir Bad Bremstedt; site sp, ent
immed at Nissan g'ge at top of hill at start of dual
c'way. Fr N exit A7 junc 16 dir Bad Bremstedt;
site on L in 4km. 3*, Sm, shd, EHU (6-16A) €2 &
metered; Eng spkn; CKE. *"Excel CL-type site; friendly
owner; EHU not rec if site v full; gd sh stay/NH."*
€24.00, 1 Apr-31 Oct.   2017

BAD DOBERAN *2F1* (10km N Coastal) *54.15250,
11.89972* **Ferien-Camp Borgerende (Part Naturist),**
Deichstrasse 16, 18211 Börgerende **(038203) 81126;
info@ostseeferiencamp.de; www.ostseeferien
camp.de**

⌂ €4 ⋔ wc ⚍ ⛌ ⌀ MP ✿ Ⓨ ⓘ ⚘ ⛟ ⟋ ⚏ 🌴 shgl adj

In Bad Doberan, turn L off B105 sp Warnemunde.
In 4km in Rethwisch, turn L sp Börgerende. In 3km
turn R at site sp. 5*, V lge, hdg, unshd, EHU (10-16A)
€3; cooking facs; 10% statics; phone; bus 500m;
Eng spkn; games area; bike hire; sauna; CKE. *"Excel
beaches; o'night m'vans area; cycle paths; sep naturist
beach; excel site."* **€35.00, 21 Mar-30 Oct.   2016**

BAD DURKHEIM *3C2* (3km NE Rural) *49.47361, 8.19166* **Knaus Campingplatz Bad Dürkheim,** In den Almen 3, 67098 Bad Dürkheim **(06322) 61356; badduerkheim@knauscamp.de; www.knauscamp.de**

12 ♿ (htd) wc ♨ ♿ ♻ ⊟ ⊘ MSP ⊕ ♨ ⚠ ☂ sand adj

Fr S on A61/E31 exit junc 60 onto A650/B37 twds Bad Dürkheim. At 2nd traff lts turn R, site sp nr local airfield. Fr N on A6 exit junc 19 onto B271 to Bad Dürkheim. At traff lts after Ungstein turn L dir Lugwigshafen, at next traff lts turn L, then 1st R. Site at end of rd. Ent strictly controlled. Site well sp fr all dir on town o'skts. 4*, V lge, mkd, pt shd, EHU (16A) €2.50; gas; bbq; sw nr; red long stay; TV; 45% statics; phone; bus; Eng spkn; tennis; bike hire; sauna; solarium; golf 8km; games area; CKE. "Well-equipped, busy site in vineyards; sm, well-worn pitches; some modern san facs - all clean; m'van o'night facs; no access 1300-1500; gd pool in Bad Dürkheim; wine-fest & wurst-fest Sep excel; conv NH Bavaria & Austria." **€36.50** 2015

"That's changed – Should I let the Club know?"

If you find something on site that's different from the site entry, fill in a report and let us know. See camc.com/europereport.

BAD DURKHEIM *3C2* (3km S Rural) *49.43741, 8.17036* **Campingplatz im Burgtal,** Waldstrasse 105, 67157 Wachenheim **(06322) 9580-801; touristinfo@ vg-wachenheim.de; www.wachenheim.de**

♿ €1 ♿ wc ♨ ♿ ⊟ ⊘ MSP ⊕ ♨ ⚠

Fr Bad Dürkheim, take B271 S dir Neustadt for approx 2km. After passing Villa Rustica rest area, turn L for Wachenheim, then R. Go strt at traff lts, up hill thro vill (narr). Site on L. Med, hdg, mkd, hdstg, pt shd, serviced pitches; EHU (16A) inc; 50% statics; tennis; golf 12km; CKE. "Forest walks in Pfalz National Park; in heart of wine-tasting country; v busy during wine festival - adv bkg rec; helpful owners; gd facs; site bit shabby (2017); upper area unshd." **€27.50, 1 Mar-30 Nov.** 2019

BAD EMS *3B2* (7km E Rural) *50.32773, 7.75483* **Camping Lahn-Beach,** Hallgarten 16, 56132 Dausenau **(02603) 13964; info@canutours.de; www.camping platz-dausenau.de**

♿ ♿ wc ♨ ♿ ⊟ ⊘ MSP ⊕ ♨ ⚠

Foll rv E fr Bad Ems twd Nassau on B260/417. At ent to vill of Dausenau turn R over bdge, site visible on S bank of Lahn Rv. Med, pt shd, EHU (6-16A) metered + conn fee; 40% statics; adv bkg acc; bike hire; boat launch; sep car park. "Pleasant situation; interesting rv traff & sightseeing around Lahn Valley; liable to flood at v high water; gd san facs." **€23.50, 1 Apr-31 Oct.** 2015

BAD FALLINGBOSTEL *1D2* (3km NE Rural) *52.87686, 9.73147* **Camping Bohmeschlucht,** Vierde 22, D 29683 Fallingbostel-Vierde **(05162) 5604; campingplatz-hoehmeschlucht@t-online.de; www.boehmeschlucht.de**

12 ♿ ♿ wc ♨ ♿ ⊟ ⊘ MSP ♈ ♉ ⊕ ♨ nr ⚠

A7 junc 47 Bad Fallingbostel. Foll sp Dorfmark/ Soltau. On leaving Fallingbostel, go strt at rndabt and cont for approx 1 km. Site sp on R. 4*, Med, mkd, pt shd, EHU (16A) - €2; bbq; sw; 60% statics; Eng spkn; adv bkg acc; games rm. "Excel walking, cycling & boat/ canoe tours fr site; vg rest; library; helpful staff; excel for exploring Luneburger Heide, Hamburg or Walsrode Bird Park; excel site." **€21.00** 2019

BAD FUSSING *4G3* (3km S Urban) *48.33236, 13.31577* **Fuchs Kur Camping,** Falkenstraße 14, 94072 Bad Fussing **(0853) 7356; info@kurcamping-fuchs.de; www.kurcamping-fuchs.de**

12 ♿ €2 ♿ wc ♨ ♿ ⊟ ⊘ ♈ ⊕ ⚠

Fr A3 Nurnberg-Passau, take exit 118 dir Egglfing. Foll sp. 4*, Med, mkd, hdstg, EHU inc; 10% statics; Eng spkn; adv bkg acc; ccard acc; CKE. "Gd NH; gd value; vg." **€23.00** 2015

BAD FUSSING *4G3* (3km S Rural) *48.33255, 13.31440* **Kur-Camping Max,** Falkenstrasse 12, 94072 Egglfing-Bad Füssing **(08537) 96170; info@campingmax.de; www.campingmax.de**

12 ♿ €2 ♿ (htd) wc ♨ ♿ ⊟ ⊘ MSP ♈ ♉ ♉ ⊕ nr ♨ ♨ ⚠ ✎

Across frontier & bdge fr Obernberg in Austria. Site sp in Egglfing. On B12 Schärding to Simbach turn L immed bef vill of Tutting sp Obernberg. Site on R after 7km, sp. 5*, Med, pt shd, EHU (16A) metered + conn fee; cooking facs; sw; TV; 20% statics; fishing; golf 2km; tennis 2km; bike hire; CKE. "Gd rest for snacks & meals on site; well managed site; excel clean facs; wellness cent; thermal facs in Bad Füssing; pool 3km; private san facs avail; new indoor thermal bath & outdoor sw pool (2014)." **€22.60** 2019

BAD GANDERSHEIM *1D3* (2km E Rural) *51.86694, 10.04972* **Kur-Campingpark,** 37581 Bad Gandersheim **(05382) 1595; info@camping-bad-gandersheim. de; www.camping-bad-gandersheim.de**

12 ♿ €1 ♿ wc ♨ ♿ ⊟ ⊘ MSP ♈ ⊕ ♨ ⚠

Exit A7/E45 at junc 67 onto B64 dir Holzminden & Bad Gandersheim. Site on R shortly after Seboldshausen. 4*, Lge, pt shd, EHU (10A) metered + conn fee; 40% statics; bike hire. "Excel; pool 1.5km; always plenty of space; sep o'night area." **€25.00** 2019

BAD KOSEN *2E4* (1.5km S Rural) *51.12285, 11.71743* **Camping an der Rudelsburg,** 06628 Bad Kösen **(034463) 28705; campkoesen@aol.com; www.campingbadkoesen.de**

♿ €2 ♿ wc ♨ ♿ ⊟ ⊘ ♈ ♉ ⊕ nr ♨ ♨ nr ⚠

Site sp fr town. 4*, Med, pt shd, EHU (16A) metered + conn fee; gas; 10% statics; CKE. "O'night m'vans area." **€24.40, 23 Mar-1 Nov.** 2016

BAD KREUZNACH *3C2* (8km N Rural) *49.88383, 7.85712* **Campingplatz Lindelgrund,** Im Lindelgrund 1, 55452 Guldental **(06707) 633; info@lindelgrund.de; www.lindelgrund.de**

🐕 €1.50 ♦♦♦ �🚰 ⌂ ⚡ ♨ ⊕ ⚓ ⋀

Fr A61 exit junc 47 for Windesheim. In cent immed after level x-ing, turn L & pass thro Guldental. Site sp on R in 500m. Sm, hdstg, pt shd, terr, EHU (10-16A) €2 or metered; red long stay; 60% statics; tennis; golf 12km. *"Lovely, peaceful site; friendly, helpful staff; wine sold on site; narr gauge rlwy & museum adj; gd NH; htd covrd pool 2km; san facs nr touring pitches; conv base for Rhine & Mosel Valleys."* **€22.00, 1 Mar-15 Dec.** **2016**

BAD NEUENAHR AHRWEILER *3B1* (8km W Rural) *50.53400, 7.04800* **Camping Dernau,** Ahrweg 2, 53507 Dernau **(02643) 8517; www.camping-dernau.de**

🐕 €1 ♦♦♦ (htd) ⚡ ⌂ ⚓ ♨ MSP ⚓nr ⋀

Exit A61 junc 30 for Ahrweiler. Fr Ahrweiler on B267 W to Dernau, cross rv bef Dernau & turn L into Ahrweg, site sp. 3*, Sm, hdstg, shd, EHU (16A) €2; bus, train. *"In beautiful Ahr valley - gd wine area; train to Ahrweiler Markt rec; immac, modern san facs; v nice."* **€17.00, 1 Apr-31 Oct.** **2019**

BAD RIPPOLDSAU *3C3* (7km S Rural) *48.38396, 8.30168* **Schwarzwaldcamping Alisehof,** Rippold sauerstrasse 8, 77776 Bad Rippoldsau-Schapbach **(07839) 203; camping@alisehof.de; www.alisehof.de**

12 🐕 €2 ♦♦♦ (htd) ⚡ ⌂ ♨ ⚓ ⊟ ♨ ⚓ 🦋 ♈ ⊕ ⚓ ⚓ ⋀ ✎

Exit A5/E35 junc 55 Offenburg onto B33 dir Gengenbach & Hausach to Wolfach. At end of Wolfach vill turn N dir Bad Rippoldsau. Site on R over wooden bdge after vill of Schapbach. 2 steep passes fr other dir. 5*, Med, mkd, pt shd, pt sl, serviced pitches; EHU (16A) metered + conn fee; gas; red long stay; 20% statics; phone; Eng spkn; adv bkg acc; CKE. *"Highly rec; clean, friendly site; site clsd 1230-1430; many gd walks in area; not a NH."* **€28.20** **2019**

BAD SEGEBERG *1D2* (5km NE Rural) *53.96131, 10.33685* **Klüthseecamp Seeblick,** Stripdorfer Weg, Klüthseehof 2, 23795 Klein Rönnau **(04551) 82368; info@kluethseecamp.de; www.kluethseecamp.de**

🐕 €2 ♦♦♦ ⚡ ⌂ ♨ ⚓ ⊟ ♨ ♈ 🦋 ♈ ⊕ ⚓ ⚓ ⋀ ⚓ (htd)

Exit A21 junc 13 at Bad Sedgeberg Süd onto B432; turn L sp Bad Sedgeberg; cont on B432 dir Scharbeutz & Puttgarden thro Klein Rönnau, look out for sp, site on R. 5*, V lge, pt shd, serviced pitches; EHU (16A) inc; gas; bbq; sw nr; twin axles; TV; 75% statics; bus adj, train to Hamburg, Lübeck; Eng spkn; adv bkg acc; ccard acc; fishing; golf 6km; games rm; horseriding; tennis; bike hire; CKE. *"Spacious, well-kept nr lakeside site; relaxing atmophere; lge pitches; sauna; steam rm; helpful staff; gd facs & pool; site clsd Feb; wide range of activities; spa; gd cycling, walking; conv Hamburg, Lübeck; excel; peaceful 50 min lakeside walk to town; excel."* **€25.00, 1 Jan-31 Jan & 1 Mar-31 Dec, G12.** **2018**

BAD TOLZ *4E4* (7km S Rural) *47.70721, 11.55023* **Alpen-Camping Arzbach,** Alpenbadstrasse 20, 83646 Arzbach **(08042) 8408; info@alpen-campingplatz.de; www.alpen-campingplatz.de**

12 🐕 ♦♦♦ ⚡ ⌂ ♨ ⚓ ♨ 🦋 ♈ ♈ ⊕ ⚓nr ⋀ ⚓ (covrd)

S fr Bad Tölz on B13. Exit Lenggries, turn R to cross rv & R on Wackersburgerstrasse twds Arzbach; in 5km on ent Arzbach turn L. Site ent past sw pool. 3*, Med, hdstg, pt shd, EHU (10-16A) €2; gas; bbq; sw nr; twin axles; 50% statics; bus 300m; Eng spkn; adv bkg acc; tennis 100m; CKE. *"Gd walking, touring Bavarian lakes, excel facs & rest; care needed with lge c'vans due trees & hedges; vg site with superb rest; easy eccess to Munich; excel."* **€24.00** **2018**

BAD URACH *3D3* (11km E Rural) *48.48598, 9.50761* **Camping Lauberg,** Hinter Lau 3, 72587 Römerstein-Böhringen **(07382) 1509; info@lauberg.de; www.lauberg.de**

12 🐕 €1.50 ♦♦♦ (htd) ⚡ ♨ ⚓ ♨ 🦋 ♈ ♈ ⊕ ⚓ ⋀

Fr Bad Urach, take rd twd Grabenstetten & foll sp to Böhringen, then sp to site. NB Rd to Grabenstetten avoids long, steep climb on B28. 3*, Med, mkd, unshd, terr, serviced pitches; EHU (16A) metered + conn fee; bbq; red long stay; 80% statics; adv bkg acc. *"Ideal walking area, castles, caves, Bad Urach baths; winter sports; htd pool 9km; ski lift 5km."* **€16.50** **2015**

BAD WILDBAD IM SCHWARZWALD *3C3* (9km E Rural) *48.73745, 8.57623* **Camping Kleinenzhof,** Kleinenzhof 1, 75323 Bad Wildbad **(07081) 3435; info@kleinenzhof.de; www.kleinenzhof.de**

12 🐕 €2.90 ♦♦♦ ⚡ ⌂ ♨ ⚓ ⊟ ♨ MSP 🦋 ⊕ ⚓ ⚓ ⋀ ✎ ⚓ (covrd, htd)

Fr Calmbach foll B294 5km S. Site sp on R, in rv valley. Fr Bad Wildbad site is on L. 5*, Lge, pt shd, pt sl, serviced pitches; EHU (16A) metered + conn fee; gas; red long stay; 80% statics; adv bkg acc; sauna; bike hire. *"Nature trails fr site; o'night m'vans area; clsd 1300-1500; mountain views; distillery on site; modern san facs; ski lift 8km; sm pitches."* **€27.80** **2018**

BAD WILDBAD IM SCHWARZWALD *3C3* (7km S Rural) *48.69777, 8.52027* **Camping Kälbermühle,** Kälbermühlenweg 57, 75323 Bad Wildbad **(07085) 7322 or 7353; information@kaelbermuehle.de**

12 🐕 €0.80 ♦♦♦ ⚡ ♨ ⚓ ♨ 🦋 ⋀

Take Enzklösterle rd S fr Bad Wildbad, site sp on rv bank. 2*, Med, pt shd, EHU (16A) metered + conn fee; 60% statics; bus; adv bkg acc. *"Friendly owners; beautifully kept, peaceful site; superb rest; mkd forest walks; gd; no cc/debit cards."* **€23.00** **2015**

GERMANY

BAMBERG *4E2* (5km S Rural) *49.86138, 10.91583*
Camping Insel, Am Campingplatz 1, 96049 Bamberg-
Bug **(0951) 56320; buero@campinginsel.de;**
www.campinginsel.de

[12] 🐕 €1.10 ♨(htd) [wc] ⚓ ♨ ⅙ 🗑 ⚡ [MP] 🦋 ⅀ 🛒 /🛆

Exit A70/E48 junc 16 or A73 exit Bamberg-Süd onto
B22 dir Würzburg. Site on L of rd along Rv Regnitz.
Bug sm vill suburb of Bamburg to S of rv. Fr S on
A3 exit junc 79 dir Bamben. In 12km turn L dir
Pettstadt; turn R at rndabt, site in 2km. 4*, Lge, pt
shd, EHU (16A) metered (long lead poss req); gas; red
long stay; TV; 20% statics; bus to Bamburg; Eng spkn;
clsd 1300-1500 & 2300-0700; CKE. *"Lovely historic
town, Unesco; cash only; rvside site; excel cycle facs
to town; bus to town €1.50; excel, modern san facs;
family run site; gd rest; beautiful walk thro park by
rvside; UNESCO World Heritage town; new lgr san facs
for 2015."* **€29.50** **2015**

BENSERSIEL *1B2* (0km W Coastal) *53.67531, 7.57001*
Familien & Kurcampingplatz Bensersiel, 26427
Esens-Bensersiel **(04971) 917121; info@bensersiel.de;**
www.bensersiel.de

♨ [wc] ⚓ ⅙ 🗑 ⚡ [MP] ⅀ 🛒 /🛆 ⚿ 🏊(htd) 🎾 adj

Fr B210 turn N at Ogenbargen; thro Esens to
Bensersiel. Site adj to harbour in cent of vill -
clearly sp. V lge, unshd, EHU (16A) €2.50; gas; TV;
70% statics; adv bkg acc; tennis; bike hire; games area.
*"Cycling country; spa cent nrby; gd boat trips; gd san
facs; open site adj sea; gd access vill, rests & island
ferries; elec metered after 3 days - if staying longer,
check meter on arr."* **€17.00, Easter-15 Oct.** **2017**

BERCHTESGADEN *4G4* (5km NE Rural) *47.64742,
13.03993* **Camping Allweglehen,** Allweggasse 4,
83471 Berchtesgaden-Untersalzberg **(08652) 2396;**
camping@allweglehen.de; www.allweglehen.de

[12] 🐕 €2.95 ♨(htd) [wc] ⚓ ♨ ⅙ 🗑 ⚡ 🦋 ⅌ ⅀ ⊕ 🛒 /🛆
⚿ 🚠(htd)

On R of rd B305 Berchtesgaden dir Salzburg, immed
after ent Unterau; sp. App v steep in places with
hairpin bend; gd power/weight ratio needed. 4*, Lge,
hdstg, pt shd, pt sl, terr, serviced pitches; EHU (16A)
metered + conn fee; 20% statics; phone; bus 500m;
adv bkg rec; ccard acc; CKE. *"Gd touring/walking
cent; wonderful views some pitches; cycles; beautiful
scenery; Hitler's Eagles' Nest worth visit (rd opens mid-
May) - bus fr Obersalzburg; ski lift; site rds poss o'grown
& uneven; steep app some pitches - risk of grounding
for long o'fits; friendly, family-run site; excel rest."*
€45.50 **2019**

BERGEN *1D3* (9km E Rural) *52.80443, 10.10376*
Camping am Örtzetal, Dicksbarg 46, 29320 Oldendorf
(05052) 3072; www.campingplatz-oldendorf.de

[12] 🐕 €1.50 ♨ [wc] ⚓ 🗑 ⚡ 🦋 ⅀ ⊕ nr 🛒 🛒 nr /🛆

Fr S, exit A7/E45 junc 52 dir Celle, in 5km turn L sp
Winsen, Belsen & Bergen. Fr N exit A7/E45 at junc
45 onto B3 to Bergen. Foll rd to Bergen. In Bergen
foll sp Hermannsburg. In about 7km at T-junc turn
R, then 1st L sp Eschede & Oldendorf. In Oldendorf
turn L at 2nd x-rds. Site on R in 1km. Lge, pt shd,
EHU (6A) metered + conn fee; 40% statics; phone;
bike hire; CKE. *"Ideal for walking & cycling on Lüneburg
Heath; conv Belsen memorial; welcoming, friendly
owner; htd pool 4km; peaceful site; barrier clsd 1300-
1500."* **€17.00** **2016**

BERLIN *2G3* (23km SW Rural) *52.4650, 13.16638* **DCC**
Campingplatz Gatow, Kladower Damm 207-213,
14089 Berlin-Gatow **(030) 3654340; gatow@**
dccberlin.de; www.dccberlin.de

[12] 🐕 €2 ♨(htd) [wc] ⚓ ♨ ⅙ 🗑 ⚡ [MP] ⅀ 🛒 nr /🛆 🛶 sand 1km

Fr A10 to W of Berlin turn E on rd 5 sp Spandau/
Centrum. Go twd city cent & after 14km turn R onto
Gatowerstrasse (Esso g'ge) sp Kladow/Gatow. Site
6.5km on L almost opp Kaserne (barracks).
3*, Med, pt shd, EHU (10-16A) metered + conn fee;
gas; 60% statics; bus at gate; Eng spkn; CKE. *"Excel
site; bus tickets fr friendly recep; frequent bus to Berlin
cent at gate; highly rec; excel, clean san facs; bicycles
can be taken on nrby Kladow ferry to Wannsee S Bahn;
gates close bet 1300 & 1500 and at 2200; rec."* **€26.50**
2016

> ## "I like to fill in the reports as I travel from site to site"
>
> You'll find report forms at the back of this
> guide, or you can fill them in online at
> camc.com/europereport.

BERLIN *2G3* (26km SW Rural) *52.55111, 13.24900*
City Campingplatz Hettler & Lange, Bäkehang 9a,
14532 Kleinmachnow-Dreilinden **(033203) 79684;**
kleinmachnow@city-camping-berlin.de; www.city-
camping-berlin.de

[12] 🐕 €2 ♨(htd) [wc] ⚓ ♨ 🗑 ⚡ [MP] 🦋 ⊕ 🛒 /🛆

Fr S exit A115/E51 junc 5 sp Kleinmachnow, turn
L at T-junc & cont to rndabt. Turn L & foll site sp in
800m. 3*, Lge, pt shd, pt sl, EHU (6A) €2.50; gas; sw
nr; phone; bus nr; Eng spkn; adv bkg acc; boat hire;
CKE. *"Excel location on canal side; immac, modern san
facs; twin axles by arrangement; gd walking in woods;
gd public transport conv Berlin 45 mins - parking at
Wannsee S-bahn (family ticket avail for bus & train); v
busy sandy site under trees; 20 min walk to bus stop;
vg."* **€24.00** **2018**

BERLIN *2G3* (13km NW Urban) *52.54861, 13.25694* **City-Camping Hettler & Lange,** Gartenfelderstrasse 1, 13599 Berlin-Spandau (030) 33503633; spandau@ city-camping-berlin.de; www.hettler-lange.de

12 🐕 €2 ♦♦ wo ♨ 🖵 ∥ ⊤ ① ☎nr

Fr N on A111/A115/E26 exit junc 10 sp Tegel Airport & head W on Saatwinkler Damm. Fr S on A100 exit junc 11 onto Saatwinkler Damm. Cont 3.2km to traff lts, turn R, then R again immed bef 2nd bdge. Site on island in rv. Med, shd, pt sl, EHU (16A) €2; Eng spkn; ccard acc; CKE. *"Conv Berlin; 15 min walk to bus stn; gd location beside a canal but aircraft noise; gd san facs; NH/sh stay only; poss to cycle along canal to Potsdam."* **€22.50**　　　　　　　　　　**2019**

"We must tell the Club about that great site we found"

Get your site reports in by mid-August and we'll do our best to get your updates into the next edition.

BERNKASTEL KUES *3B2* (2km SW Rural) *49.90883, 7.05600* **Knaus Campingpark (formerly Kueser Werth Camping),** Am Hafen 2, 54470 Bernkastel-Kues (06531) 8200; www.knauscamp.de

🐕 ♦♦(htd) wo ♨ ⅄ 🖵 ∥ MSP ⊤nr ① ☎ /瓜

A'bahn A1/48 (E44) exit Salmtal; join rd sp Bernkastel. Bef rv bdge turn L sp Lieser, thro Lieser cont by rv to ent on R for boat harbour, foll camping sp to marina. Diff access via narr single-track rd. 3*, Lge, mkd, pt shd, EHU (16A); bbq; 10% statics; bus 1km; Eng spkn; adv bkg acc; CKE. *"Excel cent for touring Mosel Valley; covrd pool 2km; Bernkastel delightful sm town with gd parking, sailing, boat excursions, wine cent; cycle lanes; site low on rv bank - poss flooding in bad weather; efficient staff; gd site; not rec for NH/sh stay high ssn as pitches & position poor; san facs old but gd condition; newly taken over by Knaus."* **€22.00, 1 Apr-31 Oct.**　　**2017**

BERNKASTEL KUES *3B2* (3km NW Rural) *49.93736, 7.04853* **Camping Schenk,** Hauptstrasse 165, 54470 Bernkastel-Wehlen (06531) 8176; info@camping-schenk.de; www.camping-schenk.com

🐕 ♦♦(htd) wo ♨ ⅄ 🖵 ∥ MSP 🐾 ⊤ ① ☎nr ♨ ☎nr /瓜 ⚓

On Trier/Koblenz rd B53, exit Kues heading N on L bank of rv & site on R in 4km at Wehlen, sp. Steep exit. Med, mkd, hdstg, pt shd, pt sl, terr, serviced pitches; EHU (16A) metered + conn fee; gas; 40% statics; phone; bus; Eng spkn; adv bkg acc; CKE. *"In apple orchard on Rv Mosel; price according to pitch size; friendly helpful owners; debit cards acc; pool deep - not suitable non-swimmers; poorly ventilated san facs; rv walks & cycle path to town."* **€21.00, 19 Mar-31 Oct.**　　**2016**

BERNKASTEL KUES *3B2* (4km NW Rural) *49.94122, 7.04653* **Weingut Studert-Prum,** Uferallee 22, 54470 Bernkastel Kues (06531) 2487; info@studert-pruem. de; www.studert-pruem.com

🐕 wo MSP ∥ ⊤nr ① ☎nr

Fr Bernkastel-Kues, co N on W Bank of Rv Mosel, site on R in 4km at ent to Wehlen. Adj to Camp Schenk. Sm, hdstg, mkd, unshd; terr, own san rec; adv bkg acc. *"M'homes only; no san facs; terr site with lovely views of Rv Mosel; covrd pool 2km; vineyards; sh walk to pretty vill; walk/cycle path by rv; boat trips; wineries; excel."* **€10.00, 1 Apr-31 Oct.**　　**2016**

BIELEFELD *1C3* (8km SW Rural) *52.00624, 8.45681* **Campingpark Meyer Zu Bentrup,** Vogelweide 9, 33649 Bielefeld (0521) 4592233; bielefeld@ meyer-zu-bentrup.de; www.camping-bielefeld.de

🐕 €2 ♦♦ wo ♨ ⅄ 🖵 ∥ MSP 🐾 ⊡ ⊤ /瓜

Fr N or S on A2 - At interchange 21 take A33 Osnabruck. Cont till m'way ends, cont onto A61 dir Bielefeld. After 2km take A68 exit, dir Osnabruck/ Halle West. Site on L after 3km. 3*, Lge, unshd, pt sl, EHU (10-16A) €1.50; cooking facs; 70% statics; games area; games rm; CKE. *"Vg; immac but dated san facs (2015); conv for Bielefeld; well maintained; warm welcome; excel shop at adj fruit farm."* **€25.00, 1 Mar-30 Nov.**　　**2018**

BINGEN *3C2* (3km E Urban) *49.97029, 7.93916* **Camping Hindenburgbrucke,** Bornstrasse 22, 55411 Kempton-Bingen (06721) 17160; bauer-schorsch.de; www.bauer-schorsch.de

♦♦ wo ♨ ⅄ ∥ ⊤ ① ♨ /瓜

Foll rd on Rhine twd Mainz, site on L bef traff lts. Turn into tarmac rd, bear R, L under rlwy bdge, strt to site ent by Rhine. Lge, hdg, unshd, EHU (watch rev pol); bbq; twin axles; 40% statics; bus/train adj. *"Open site on W bank of Rhein; staff conn elec pnts; lovely position for sh stay; mosquitoes abound; close to Rüdesheim-Bingen ferry, vineyards, castles, cruising."* **€19.00, 1 May-31 Oct.**　　**2019**

BONN *1B4* (13km SE Rural) *50.65388, 7.20111* **Camping Genienau,** Im Frankenkeller 49, 53179 Bonn-Mehlem (0228) 344949; genienau@freenet.de

12 🐕 €2 ♦♦ wo ♨ ⅄ 🖵 ∥ ① ☎nr ☎nr

Fr B9 dir Mehlem, site sp on Rv Rhine, S of Mehlem. Med, pt shd, EHU (6A) €3 or metered; 60% statics; bus; Eng spkn; CKE. *"Excel site on rv bank; liable to flood when rv v high; nr ferry to cross Rhine; late arr no problem; san facs up steps but disabled facs at grnd level; lots to see & do."* **€20.00**　　**2016**

GERMANY

BOPPARD *3B2* (6km NE Rural) *50.24888, 7.62638* **Camping Sonneneck,** 56154 Boppard **(06742) 2121; kontakt@camping-sonneneck.de; www.camping park-sonneneck.de**

🏕 €2.40 ♦♦ ⓌⒹ ♨ � 🏊 ⊟ ✉ ⓂⓅ Ⓣ ⓗ 🅰 🏊 ⚂ ♨ shgl nr

On Koblenz-Mainz rd B9, on W bank of Rhine, in vill of Spay. 4*, Lge, mkd, pt shd, serviced pitches; EHU (4A) €2.50; gas; 10% statics; phone; Eng spkn; fishing; sauna; CKE. *"V pleasant staff; night watchman; clean san facs, poss long way fr pitches; ltd waste water points; extra for rvside pitch; crazy golf; 18-hole golf 2km; site poss liable to flood; gd cycle path along Rhine; gd NH."* **€25.00, 1 Apr-31 Oct.**   **2015**

BRANDENBURG AN DER HAVEL *2F3* (9km E Rural) *52.39833, 12.43665* **Camping und Ferienpark am Plauer See,** Plauer Landstrasse 200, 14774 Brandenburg **33 81 80 45 44; info@camping-plauersee.de; www.camping-plauersee.de**

12 🏕 ♦♦ ⓌⒹ ♨ ☆ ⊟ ✉ ⓂⓅ 🦮 Ⓣ ⓗ 🅰 ♨

Fr A2 take 102 to Brandenburg. L onto 1, cont 4km. Just after sp for Plauerhof is a campsite sp. Turn L & foll rd for 1.5km to site on the side of lake. Med, mkd, pt shd, pt sl, EHU (10A) €1.90; bbq; 75% statics; Eng spkn; adv bkg acc; games area; bike hire; CCI. *"Next to sm lake; boat, cycles & BBQ hire; nr historic town of Brandenburg; vg site, mainly statics but tourers and MH given gd pitches next to lake; gd rest and bar; rec Potsdam."* **€33.00**   **2019**

BRAUNEBERG *3B2* (0.9km W Rural) *49.90564, 6.97603* **Wohnmobilstellplatz Brauneberger Juffer,** Moselweinstraße 101, 54472 Brauneberg **6534 933 333; mfrollison@yahoo.co.uk or info@brauneberg.de; www.brauneberg.de**

12 🏕 ⓌⒹ ✉ ⓂⓅ 🦮

Fr NE of A1 take exit 127-Klausen onto L47 twds Mulheim. Cont onto L158, then turn L onto B53. Supermkt 20m fr site ent which is down side rd twds rv. Sm, mkd, hdg, hdstg, pt shd, EHU (16A); bbq; sw nr; bus 100m; Eng spkn. *"Aire-type site; no adv bkg; Gd cycle paths along rv; vg site."* **€10.00**   **2019**

BRAUNLAGE *2E4* (12km SE Rural) *51.65697, 10.66786* **Campingplatz am Bärenbache,** Bärenbachweg 10, 38700 Hohegeiss **(05583) 1306; campingplatz-hohegeiss@t-online.de; www.campingplatz-hohegeiss.de**

12 🏕 €1.50 ♦♦ (htd) ⓌⒹ ♨ ☆ � ⊟ ✉ ⓂⓅ 🦮 🍴 Ⓣ ⓗ 🅰 🏊 nr ♨ 🏊 (htd) 🎿

Fr Braunlage S on B4 thro Hohegeiss; site sp on L downhill (15%) on edge of town. 4*, Med, hdg, mkd, pt shd, terr, EHU (10A); bbq; cooking facs; 10% statics; Eng spkn; adv bkg acc; bike hire. *"Gd walking; friendly; walking dist to vill; vg."* **€22.50**   **2019**

BREISACH AM RHEIN *3B4* (7km E Rural) *48.03104, 7.65781* **Kaiserstuhl Camping,** Nachwaid 5, 79241 Ihringen **(07668) 950065; info@kaiserstuhlcamping.de; www.kaiserstuhlcamping.de**

🏕 €2.50 ♦♦ ⓌⒹ ♨ ☆ � ⊟ ✉ ⓂⓅ 🦮 Ⓣ ⓗ nr 🅰 🏊 nr 🅰

Fr S exit A5/E35 junc 64a, foll sp twds Breisach, then camping sp to Ihringen. At Ihringen site sp dir Merdingen. Fr N exit junc 60 & foll sp. Med, unshd, EHU (16A) metered + conn fee; red long stay; 10% statics; tennis adj; golf 8km; CKE. *"Can get cr in high ssn; htd pool adj."* **€32.00, 15 Mar-31 Oct.**   **2019**

BREMEN *1C2* (16km SW Rural) *53.01055, 8.68972* **Marchencamping (formerly Camp Wienberg),** Zum Steller See 83, 28816 Stuhr-Gross Mackenstedt **(04206) 9191; info@maerchen-camping.com; maerchen-camping.com**

12 🏕 €2 ♦♦ (htd) ⓌⒹ ♨ ☆ ⊟ ✉ ⓂⓅ Ⓣ ⓗ 🅰 🏊 🅰 ♨ 🏊

Exit A1/E37 junc 58a onto B322 sp Stuhr/Delmenhorst. Foll Camping Steller See sp. Sp also call site Marchen Camping. Lge, mkd, hdstg, pt shd, pt sl, EHU (16A) metered or €3; TV; 50% statics; Eng spkn; adv bkg acc; ccard acc; bike hire; CKE. *"Helpful staff; basic facs; gd."* **€20.50**   **2018**

BREMEN *1C2* (17km SW Rural) *53.00694, 8.69277* **Campingplatz Steller See,** Zum Stellersee 15, 28817 Stuhr-Gross Mackenstedt **(04206) 6490; steller.see@t-online.de; www.steller-see.de**

♦♦ (htd) ⓌⒹ ♨ ☆ � ⊟ ✉ ⓂⓅ 🍴 Ⓣ ⓗ 🅰 🏊 nr 🅰 ♨

Exit A1/E37 junc 58a onto B322 sp Stuhr/Delmenhorst. Foll site sp. 3*, Lge, unshd, EHU (10-16A) inc; gas; bbq; sw nr; red long stay; 80% statics; phone; adv bkg acc; ccard acc; games area; CKE. *"Site officially clsd but owner may accommodate you; well-appointed, clean, lakeside site; immac san facs; friendly owners; conv NH fr m'way & for trams to Bremen; gd space, easy to position; vg."* **€35.00, 1 Apr-3 Oct.**   **2018**

BREMEN *1C2* (5km NW Rural) *53.11483, 8.83263* **Camping Hanse (formerly Camping am Stadtwaldsee),** Hochschulring 1, 28359 Bremen **(0421)30746825**

12 🏕 €4 ♦♦ (htd) ⓌⒹ ♨ ☆ � ⊟ ✉ ⓂⓅ 🍴 Ⓣ ⓗ 🅰 🏊 🅰

Fr A27 take exit 19 for Universitat, foll sp for Universitat and camping. Site on L in 1km after leaving University area. 3*, Lge, hdstg, mkd, pt shd, EHU (16A) metered; gas; bbq; cooking facs; sw nr; red long stay; 10% statics; phone; bus 100m; Eng spkn; adv bkg acc; ccard acc; CKE. *"Excel, spacious lakeside site; superb san facs; cycle path to beautiful city; gd bus service; v gd rest adj; spacious pitches but unkept & poorly maintained."* **€35.50**   **2017**

BRIESELANG *2F3* (5km W Rural) *52.57138, 12.96583*
Campingplatz Zeestow im Havelland, 11 Briese langerstrasse, 14665 Brieselang **(033234) 88634;** info@campingplatz-zeestow.de; www.camping platz-zeestow.de

12 ⛺ €2 � ᵂᴰ ♨ ♿ 🔧 / ⊕ 🛒

Exit A10/E55 junc 27; turn W dir Wustermark; site on L after canal bdge in 500m. 3*, Lge, unshd, pt sl, EHU (16A) metered; gas; 75% statics; bus; CKE. "Gd NH nr a'bahn; facs dated but clean; 13km fr Berlin & 25km fr Potsdam; fair." **€14.00**   2016

BRUGGEN *1A4* (2km SE Rural) *51.23416, 6.19815*
Camping-Forst Laarer See, Brüggenerstrasse 27, 41372 Niederkrüchten **(02163) 8461 or 0172 7630591 (mob);** info@campingforst-laarersee.com; www.campingforst-laarersee.com

12 ⛺ €1 ♦♦ (htd) ᵂᴰ ♨ ♿ 🔧 / ᴹˢᴾ 🦋 Ⴑ ⊕ nr 🛒 nr /1\

Fr A52 junc 3 or A61 junc 3 - take B221 to Brüggen, turn R at 1st traff lts into site. Lge, pt shd, pt sl, EHU (16A) inc; bbq; 80% statics; Eng spkn; adv bkg acc; games area; CKE. "Unspoilt area nr pretty town; many leisure amenities nr site - gd for children; vg site; ltd touring pitches; pleasant site with lake; walking/bike paths." **€21.00**   2016

BUHL *3C3* (7km NW Rural) *48.72719, 8.08074*
Ferienpark & Campingplatz Adam, Campingstrasse 1, 77815 Bühl-Oberbruch **(07223) 23194;** info@camping platz-adam.de; www.campingplatz-adam.de

12 ⛺ €2.50 ♦♦ ᵂᴰ ♨ ♿ 🔧 / ᴹˢᴾ 🦋 Ⴑ ⊕ 🛒 /1\ ✐

Exit A5 at Bühl take sp Lichtenau & foll sp thro Oberbruch, then L twd Moos to site in 500m. If app on rd 3 take rd sp W to Rheinmünster N of Bühl. Site sp to S at W end of Oberbruch. 4*, Lge, mkd, hdstg, pt shd, serviced pitches; EHU (10A) €3; sw; red long stay; 60% statics; Eng spkn; adv bkg acc; ccard acc; sailing; tennis; fishing; boating; CKE. "Excel, clean san facs; conv for Strasbourg, Baden-Baden & Black Forest visits; o'night area tarmac car park; extra for lakeside pitches; if recep clsd use area outside gate; vg; excel camp with own lake; gd rest; friendly staff; handy for m'way but still quiet; o'night tarmac area excel for NH but worth a longer stay; highly rec; 45 mins to Europe Pk." **€28.00**   2017

BURGEN *3B2* (0.6km N Rural) *50.21457, 7.38976*
Camping Burgen, 56332 Burgen **(02605) 2396;** info@ camping-burgen.de; www.camping-burgen.de

⛺ €2 ♦♦ 🔧 / ᴹˢᴾ ⊕ nr 🛒 /1\ ✐ 🚣

Leave A61 at J39; foll B411 twds Dieblich to reach S bank of Mosel; turn L and foll B49 for approx 12km; site on L bet rd and rv bef vill. Sat nav uses rte thro vill, not suitable. 4*, Med, mkd, unshd, EHU (10A) metered + conn fee (poss rev pol); gas; 30% statics; Eng spkn; boat launch; CKE. "Scenic area; ideal for touring Mosel, Rhine & Koblenz areas; gd shop; poss liable to flood; lovely, clean site; gd san facs; rec."
€23.00, 11 Apr-19 Oct.   2019

CALW *3C3* (12km SW Rural) *48.67766, 8.68990*
Camping Erbenwald, 75387 Neubulach-Liebelsberg **(07053) 7382;** info@camping-erbenwald.de; www.camping-erbenwald.de

12 ⛺ €2 ♦♦ ᵂᴰ ♨ ♿ 🔧 / ᴹˢᴾ 🦋 ♈ Ⴑ ⊕ 🛒 /1\
🏊 (htd) ⛷

On B463 S fr Calw, take R slip rd sp Neubulach to go over main rd. Foll Neubulach sp until camping sp at R junc. Site well sp. 4*, Lge, mkd, hdg, pt shd, EHU (10A) metered; 60% statics; phone; Eng spkn; adv bkg acc; games area. "Gd size pitches; child-friendly site; no vehicles in or out fr 1300-1500; excel; cash only."
€22.00   2019

CANOW *2F2* (2km E Rural) *53.19636, 12.93116*
Camping Pälitzsee, Am Canower See 165, 17255 Canow **(039828) 20220;** info@mecklenburg-tourist.de; www.mecklenburg-tourist.de

12 ⛺ €2 ♦♦ ᵂᴰ ♨ ♿ / 🦋 Ⴑ ⊕ nr 🛒 /1\

Fr N on B198 turn S dir Rheinsberg to Canow vill, site sp. Lge, pt shd, EHU (16A) metered or €3; sw; 50% statics; adv bkg acc; boating. "Canow charming vill; vg touring base for lakes." **€20.00**   2016

CHEMNITZ *2F4* (10km SW Rural) *50.76583, 13.01444*
Waldcampingplatz Erzgebirgsblick, An der Dittersdorfer Höhe 1, 09439 Amtsberg **(0371) 7750833;** info@waldcamping-erzgebirge.de; www.waldcamping-erzgebirge.de

12 ⛺ ♦♦ (htd) ᵂᴰ ♨ ♿ 🔧 / ᴹˢᴾ 🛒 /1\

Fr A4 take A72 S & exit junc 15. Foll sp 'Centrum' & join 'Südring' ring rd. Turn onto B174 & foll sp Marienberg twd junc with B180. Site sp 500m fr junc. Med, mkd, pt shd, EHU (16A) metered; gas; red long stay; TV; bus 800m; Eng spkn; games area; site clsd 6-27 Nov; CKE. "Gd san facs; relaxing site; gd walking; dogs free; vg standard of site." **€17.00** 2016

CHIEMING *4F4* (2km NW Rural) *47.902103, 12.519891*
Camping Seehäusl, Beim Seehäusl 1, 83339 Chieming **(8664) 303;** www.camping-seehaeusl.de

⛺ ♦♦ (htd) ᵂᴰ ♨ ♿ 🔧 / ᴹˢᴾ 🦋 ♈ Ⴑ ⊕ /1\ ♨ lake, shgl

J109 N off A8 twrds Chieming. Foll sp. Diff access for v lge o'fits (narr lane) 4*, Med, hdstg, mkd, pt shd, EHU (16A); bbq (elec, gas); sw nr; twin axles; Eng spkn; adv bkg rec; ccard acc; fishing; watersports. "Gd san facs." **€32.50, 1 Apr-1 Oct.**   2019

COBURG *4E2* (15km SW Rural) *50.19433, 10.83809*
Campingplatz Sonnland, Bahnhofstrasse 154, 96145 Sesslach **(09569) 220;** info@camping-sonnland.de; www.camping-sonnland.de

12 ⛺ €1.50 ♦♦ (htd) ᵂᴰ ♨ 🔧 / ᴹˢᴾ ⊕ nr 🛒 nr /1\

Exit A73 junc 10 Ebersdorf onto B303 W. Then at Niederfüllbach turn S onto B4, then turn W dir Sesslach. Site sp N of Sesslach dir Hattersdorf; turn R at sp opp filling stn, site in 150m. Med, mkd, hdstg, pt shd, terr, serviced pitches; EHU (16A) metered; bbq; sw; 70% statics; adv bkg acc; CKE. "Sesslach unspoilt, medieval, walled town; site well laid-out." **€21.50**   2016

COCHEM 3B2 (1.5km N Rural) 50.15731, 7.17360
Campingplatz am Freizeitzentrum, Moritzburger strasse 1, 56812 Cochem (02671) 4409; info@ campingplatz-cochem.de; www.campingplatz-cochem.de

🐕 €3 �♦ ⬛ ⬛ ✏ MP ① nr ⬛ ⬛nr ⚓

On rd B49 fr Koblenz, on ent town go under 1st rv bdge then turn R over same bdge. Foll site sp. 3*, Lge, mkd, pt shd, pt sl, EHU (10-16A) €2.50 + conn fee (some rev pol); gas; 10% statics; bike hire; CKE. "Gd, clean site adj Rv Mosel; pitches tight & poss diff access fr site rds; gd for children; easy walk along rv to town; train to Koblenz, Trier, Mainz." €23.00, 1 Apr-31 Oct. **2016**

COCHEM 3B2 (6km SE Rural) 50.10999, 7.23542
Campingplatz Happy-Holiday, Moselweinstrasse, 56821 Ellenz-Poltersdorf (02673) 1272; www.camping-happy-holiday.de

🐕 €1.50 ♦(htd) ⬛ ⬛ ✏ ❓ ⵙ ① ⬛ ⬛

Fr Cochem, take B49 S to Ellenz; site sp on bank of Rv Mosel. Med, shd, pt sl, EHU (6A) metered; gas; 70% statics; Eng spkn; fishing; watersports. "Pleasant situation; gd value rest; pool 300m; clean facs; conv touring base." €19.50, 1 Apr-31 Oct. **2019**

COCHEM 3B2 (7km SE Rural) 50.13253, 7.23029
Campingplatz Bruttig, Am Moselufer, 56814 Bruttig-Fankel (02671) 915429; www.campingplatz-bruttig.de

♦(htd) ⬛ ⬛ ✏ ❓ ⵙ ⬛ ⚓

Leave Cochem on B49 twd Trier. In 8km turn L over bdge to Bruttig-Fankel. Thro vill, site on R on banks Rv Mosel. Sm, mkd, pt shd, EHU (16A) metered; sw nr; 50% statics; phone; Eng spkn. "Pleasant site in pretty vill; gd walking, cycling; Mosel boat trips fr Bruttig." €16.00, Easter-31 Oct. **2016**

COCHEM 3B2 (15km S Rural) 50.09162, 7.16319
Campingplatz zum Feuerberg, 56814 Ediger-Eller (02675) 701; info@zum-feuerberg.de; www.zum-feuerberg.de

🐕 €2 ♦ ⬛ ⬛ ✏ MP ❤ ❓ ⵙ ⬛ ⬛nr ⚓ ≋

On A49 fr Cochem to Bernkastel Kues, just bef vill of Ediger on L - 17km by rd. Lge, mkd, hdg, EHU (16A) metered + conn fee; gas; 40% statics; phone; bus, train to Cochem; Eng spkn; adv bkg acc; bike hire; CKE. "Well-kept site in lovely area; charming vill; boat mooring; helpful staff; facs at 1st floor level, via key (deposit); gd selection of rests & pubs; rv bus high ssn; gd touring base; gd; pitches next to rv cost more." €23.00, 18 Mar-31 Oct. **2016**

COLBITZ 2E3 (3km NE Rural) 52.33158, 11.63123
Campingplatz Heide-Camp, Angerschestrasse, 39326 Colbitz (039207) 80291; info@heide-camp-colbitz.de; www.heide-camp-colbitz.de

12 🐕 €2.80 ♦ ⬛ ⬛ ⬛ ✏ MP ❤ ① nr ⬛ ⬛nr ⚓

Exit A2/E30 junc 70 onto B189 N dir Stendal. In Colbitz foll sp Angern. Site in 2km. 4*, Lge, mkd, pt shd, EHU (6-16A) metered + conn fee; gas; 20% statics; Eng spkn; adv bkg acc; ccard acc; games area; CKE. "Site on woodland, lge pitches." €19.00 **2019**

"I need an on-site restaurant"

We do our best to make sure site information is correct, but it is always best to check any must-have facilities are still available or will be open during your visit.

COLDITZ 2F4 (4km E Rural) 51.13083, 12.83305
Campingplatz am Waldbad, Im Tiergarten 5, 04680 Colditz (034381) 43122; info@campingplatz-colditz.de; www.campingplatz-colditz.de

🐕 €1 ♦ ⬛ ⬛ ✏ ① ⬛nr

Fr Leipzig A14 to Grimma, foll B107 to Colditz. Cross rv, foll B176 sp Dobeln. Turn L immed bef town exit sp. After 1km turn R at camping sp. Foll track thro woods for 500m, site on R immed after sw pool. 4*, Med, pt shd, pt sl, EHU (10A) inc; 30% statics; phone; Eng spkn; sauna; CKE. "V nice peaceful site; gd clean facs; gd value; tight turn into site fr narr rd; helpful, friendly manager & staff; 30 mins walk to Colditz Castle; leisure cent adj; sm rest 200m; new chem point." €19.00, 1 Apr-30 Sep. **2015**

CREGLINGEN 3D2 (3.5km S Rural) 49.43945, 10.04210 **Campingpark Romantische Strasse,** Münster 67, 97993 Creglingen-Münster (07933) 20289; camping.hausotter@web.de; www.camping-romantische-strasse.de

🐕 €1 ♦(htd) ⬛ ⬛ ⬛ ✏ MP ❤ ❓ ⵙ ① ⬛ ⬛nr ⚓ ≋(covrd, htd) 🏊

Fr E43 exit A7/junc 105 at Uffenheim. At edge of Uffenheim turn R in dir of Bad Mergentheim; in approx 17km at T-junc turn L for Creglingen, thro vill & then R sp Münster with camping sp - approx 8km further. Site on R after Münster. (Avoid rte bet Rothenburg & Creglingen as includes some v narr vills & coaches). 4*, Med, pt shd, serviced pitches; EHU (6A) €2.20; bbq; 20% statics; phone; sauna; bike hire; lake fishing; CKE. "Site ent needs care; helpful owner; lovely welcome; excel rest & facs; Romantische Strasse with interesting medieval churches locally; gd cent for historic towns; clsd 1300-1500; gd value; facs stretched high ssn; poss long walk fr facs." €24.00, 15 Mar-15 Nov. **2017**

DAUN *3B2* (19km SE Rural) *50.13111, 6.93331*
Feriendorf Pulvermaar, Auf der Maarhöhe,
Vulkanstrasse, 54558 Gillenfeld **(06573) 287; info@
feriendorf-pulvermaar.de; www.feriendorf-
pulvermaar.de**

🔢 🏕 €1 👫 ⬛ ⛺ 🅿 🚿 ⋈ 🍴 🎾 ⌂ ⚓

**Fr A1/A48/E44 exit junc 121 onto B421 dir Zell/
Mosel. After approx 5km turn R to Pulvermaar,
site sp nr lakeside.** 3*, Med, pt shd, sl, EHU (16A)
metered + conn fee; bbq; 60% statics; Eng spkn; adv
bkg acc; fishing adj; games area; CKE. *"Conv Mosel
valley & Weinstrasse; attractive site; helpful owner."*
€21.00 2016

DINKELSBÜHL *3D3* (2km NNE Rural) *49.08194,
10.33416* **DCC Campingpark Romantische Strasse,**
Kobeltsmühle6, 91550 Dinkelsbühl **(09851) 7817;
campdinkelsbuehl@aol.com; www.campingplatz-
dinkelsbuehl.de**

🔢 🏕 €1 👫 ⬛ ⛺ ♿ ⛽ 🅿 🚿 🍴 ⋈ 🎾 ⌂ ⚓

**On Rothenburg-Dinkelsbühl rd 25. Turn sharp L at
camp sp immed bef rlwy x-ing (at Jet petrol stn) at
N end of town. Site on R in 1km on lakeside. Or exit
A7/E43 junc 112; turn R at T-junc. Site well sp.**
4*, Lge, mkd, pt shd, terr, EHU (10-16A) metered; gas;
sw; 40% statics; phone; adv bkg acc; ccard acc; site
clsd 1300-1500 & 2200-0800; boating; dog wash; CKE.
*"Pitches poss long way fr san facs; gd, modern san facs;
NH area with easy access; close to beautiful medieval
town (25min walk); m'van o'night area with EHU; quiet,
peaceful, well-equipped & well-managed site; excel
rest; gd cycle paths in area; gd; recep open 9-1230 &
1500-1700."* **€23.00** 2019

"Satellite navigation makes touring much easier"

Remember most sat navs don't know if you're
towing or in a larger vehicle – always use yours
alongside maps and site directions.

DONAUESCHINGEN *3C4* (7km SE Rural) *47.93754,
8.53422* **Riedsee-Camping,** Am Riedsee 11, 78166
Donaueschingen **(0771) 5511; info@riedsee-camping.
de; www.riedsee-camping.de**

🔢 🏕 €3.50 👫 ⬛ ⛺ ♿ 🅿 🚿 🍴 ⌂ ⋈ ⚓ 🚲

Fr Donaueschingen on B31 to Pfohren vill, site sp.
Lge, mkd, pt shd, EHU (16A) metered, €0.50 (check
for rev pol); sw; 90% statics; Eng spkn; ccard acc; bike
hire; golf 9km; boating; tennis; CKE. *"Vg facs; clean,
well-run site; sm pitches; site busy at w/end; office clsd
Mon (poss LS only); gd value rest; conv Danube cycle
way."* **€24.00** 2016

DONAUWORTH *4E3* (5km SE Rural) *48.67660,
10.84100* **Donau-Lech Camping,** Campingweg 1,
86698 Eggelstetten **(09090) 4046; info@donau-
lech-camping.de; www.donau-lech-camping.de**

🔢 🏕 €2.20 👫 (htd) ⬛ ⛺ 🅿 🚿 ⋈ 🍴 ⛲ 🎾 ⌂ nr ⚓ nr ⌂

**Fr B2 take Eggelstetten exit & foll sp to vill. Site
immed bef vill on R, foll 'Int'l Camping' sp.** 4*, Med,
hdg, mkd, hdstg, pt shd, EHU (16A) inc (some rev pol);
gas; sw; 80% statics; phone; Eng spkn; adv bkg acc;
archery; golf nr; boat hire; site clsd Nov; fishing nr;
horseriding nr; CKE. *"Superb, well-maintained, site but
poss unkempt & boggy LS; ltd area for tourers; friendly,
helpful staff & owner; facs clean but update req; owner
sites vans; conv base for touring Danube & Romantic
Rd; nr Danube cycle way."* **€25.00** 2019

DORTMUND *1B4* (10km SE Rural) *51.42078, 7.49514*
Camping Hohensyburg, Syburger Dorfstrasse 69,
44265 Dortmund-Hohensyburg **(0231) 774374;
info@camping-hohensyburg.de; www.camping-
hohensyburg.de**

🔢 🏕 €3 👫 ⬛ ⛺ 🅿 🚿 ⋈ 🍴 ⛲ ⌂ ⚓ ⌂

**Exit Dortmund a'bahn ring at Dortmund Sud onto
B54 sp Hohensyburg. Foll dual c'way S & strt at next
traff lts. Turn L twd Hohensyburg, up hill to Y junc.
Turn L (camping sp) & cont over hill to Gasthof.
Turn R immed bef Gasthof down narr, steep rd
(sharp bends) to site in 100m.** Lge, pt shd, pt sl, EHU
(16A) €2.50 or metered; bbq; twin axles; 80% statics;
Eng spkn; adv bkg acc; golf 3km; boat launch. *"Lovely,
friendly site; narr lane at ent not suitable lge o'fits;
excel, clean san facs; gd; lge site; immac san facs."*
€26.50 2016

DORUM *1C2* (6km NE Coastal) *53.73938, 8.51680*
Knaus Campingpark Dorum, Am Kuterhafen,
27632 Dorum/Neufeld **0049 4741 5020; dorum@
knauscamp.de; www.knauscamp.de**

🏕 👫 ⬛ ⛺ 🅿 🚿 ⋈ 🍴 ⌂ ⚓ ⌂ adj

**Fr A27 Bremerhaven-Cuxhaven, take exit 4 to
Dorum. Then foll signs to Dorum-Neufeld. Cont
over dyke to harbour, campsite on R.** Lge, unshd,
EHU (6A); twin axles; 40% statics; bus 0.5km; Eng
spkn; adv bkg acc; bike hire; CCI. *"Vg; temporary ssnal
site; scenic fishing port."* **€41.00, 1 Apr-30 Sep.**
2019

DRANSFELD *1D4* (1km S Rural) *51.49177, 9.76180*
Camping am Hohen Hagen, Hoher-Hagenstrasse 12,
37127 Dransfeld **(05502) 2147; mail@campingplatz-
dransfeld.de; www.campingplatz-dransfeld.de**

🔢 🏕 €1.50 👫 (htd) ⬛ ⛺ ♿ 🅿 🚿 ⋈ 🍴 ⋈ ⌂ ⚓ ⌂ ⌂
⚓ (htd) ⌂

**Exit A7 junc 73 onto B3 to Dransfeld; foll sp to S of
town & site.** 5*, Lge, mkd, pt shd, terr, EHU (16A) inc;
gas; bbq; cooking facs; 95% statics; Eng spkn; ccard
acc; waterslide; sauna; games area; tennis 100m.
*"Beautiful area; gd san facs; o'night m'vans area; diff
after heavy rain; helpful staff."* **€38.00** 2016

DRESDEN *2G4* (7km N Rural) *51.13833, 13.71861*
Camping Dresden Nord, Sandweg, 01471 Volkersdorf
**(035207) 81469; kontakt@dresden-camping.com;
www.cbm-camping.de/dd-nord**

🏕 €1 🚻 [wc] ♨ 🛒 🚿 ⋌ 🌊 🍴 ⅃ 🛝 /瓜\

Exit A4/E40 junc 81A (Dresden-Flughafen) onto
S81 W - Wilschdorfer Landstrasse. In approx 600m
turn R at x-rds dir Volkersdorf, then L to site on
lakeside, sp. 3*, Med, hdg, shd, pt sl, EHU (16A) €2.70
or mtrd (poss rev pol); bbq; sw; 60% statics; adv bkg
acc; CKE. *"Gd; touring pitch at lake v attractive; san
facs v clean but poss a bit distant; little Eng spkn."*
€18.00, 1 Apr-31 Oct.   **2019**

DRESDEN *2G4* (17km NE Rural) *51.12027, 13.98000*
Camping- und Freizeitpark Lux Oase,
Arnsdorferstrasse 1, 01900 Kleinröhrsdorf **(035952)
56666; info@luxoase.de; www.luxoase.de**

🏕 €3.50 🚻 ♨ 🛒 ♿ 🚿 ⋌ [MSP] 🌊 🍴 🛝 ⅃ ⅋ ⓦ ⅍ 🛒 /瓜\ ⅋

🏖 (covrd) ⅂adj

Leave A4/E40 at junc 85 dir Radeberg. S to
Leppersdorf, Kleinröhrsdorf. Sp on L end vill, well sp
fr a'bahn. 5*, Lge, mkd, pt shd, serviced pitches; EHU
(10A) inc; gas; bbq; sw nr; red long stay; twin axles; TV;
30% statics; bus to city; Eng spkn; ccard acc; fishing;
games area; horseriding; bike hire; sauna; games rm;
CKE. *"Excel site by lake; vg san facs; new luxury san
facs 2011; v helpful staff; gd rest; site bus to Dresden
Tues - 15 mins walk to reg bus; fitness cent; weekly bus
to Prague fr site & other attractions in easy reach; new
spa 2013."* **€33.60, 1 Jan-31Dec, G14.**   **2019**

DRESDEN *2G4* (7km S Urban) *51.01416, 13.7500*
Campingplatz Mockritz, Boderitzerstrasse 30,
01217 Dresden-Mockritz **(0351) 4715250; camping-
dresden@t-online.de; www.camping-dresden.de**

🏕 €1 🚻(htd) [wc] ♨ 🛒 ♿ 🚿 ⋌ [MSP] 🌊 ⅍ ⅂ ⓦ 🛒 🏖

Exit E65/A17 junc 3 onto B170 N sp Dresden. In
approx 1.5km turn E at traff lts sp Zschernitz, site sp.
2*, Med, mkd, pt shd, pt sl, EHU (10A) €2.70;
5% statics; bus; Eng spkn; adv bkg rec; site clsd
Christmas to end Jan; CKE. *"V conv city cent & buses;
poss muddy after rain; helpful staff; excel; office clsd
1300-1600 find a pitch and inform recep; highly rec."*
€21.00, 1 Jan-31 Jan, 16 Feb-31 Dec.   **2016**

DUSSELDORF *1B4* (19.5km NNW Urban) *51.30180,
6.72560* **Rheincamping Meerbusch,** Zur Rheinfähre
21, 40668 Meerbusch **(02150) 911817; info@
rheincamping.com; www.rheincamping.com**

🏕 €2.80 🚻(htd) [wc] ♨ 🛒 🚿 ⋌ [MSP] ⅍ ⅂ ⓦnr 🛒 /瓜\

Exit A44 junc 28, turn R twd Strümp. Thro vill, turn
L at sp for Kaiserswerth ferry, site on rv. Lge, pt shd,
EHU (10A) €3.50; gas; bbq; 40% statics; Eng spkn;
adv bkg acc; boat launch; CKE. *"Pleasant, busy, well-
organised, open site with gd views of Rv Rhine; all facs
up steps; ferry x-ring rv, then tram/train to Dusseldorf;
ferry/tram; site may flood when rv at v high level; long
lead req'd; gd NH."* **€28.00, 4 Apr-12 Oct.**   **2019**

ECHTERNACHERBRUCK *3A2* (1km SW Rural) *49.81240,
6.43160* **Camping Freibad Echternacherbrück,**
Mindenerstrasse 18, 54668 Echternacherbrück
**(06525) 340; info@echternacherbrueck.de;
www.echternacherbrueck.de**

🏕 €3.30-€4.70 🚻(htd) [wc] ♨ 🛒 ♿ 🚿 🌊 ⋌ 🍴 🌊 ⅍ ⅂ ⓦnr ⅍

🛒nr /瓜\ ⅋ 🏖 (covrd, htd) 🚣

Fr Bitburg on B257/E29 site is at Lux'burg border, sp.
Fr Trier take A64 dir Luxembourg; exit junc 15
onto N10 to Echternacherbrück; cross bdg dir Bitburg,
then 1st L sp camping & foll sp. 4*, Lge, pt shd, EHU
(10A) €2.70 + conn fee; sw nr; TV; 30% statics; Eng
spkn; games area; boat hire; tennis 400m; horseriding
4km; bike hire; waterslide; CKE. *"Poss flooding in v
wet weather; private bthrms avail; excel facs; o'night
m'van area; gd, well-organised site; gd bus service to
Luxembourg and Trier; ACSI card acc; rvside pitches
lger."* **€29.00, 18 Mar-15 Oct.**   **2016**

"There aren't many sites open at this time of year"

If you're travelling outside peak season
remember to call ahead to check site opening
dates – even if the entry says 'open all year'.

ECKERNFORDE *1D1* (12km NE Coastal) *54.50280,
9.95802* **Ostsee-Camping Gut Ludwigsburg,**
Ludwigsburg 4, 24369 Waabs **(49043) 58370; info@
ostseecamping-ludwigsburg.de; www.ostsee
camping-ludwigsburg.de**

🏕 €2-6 🚻 [wc] ♨ 🛒 ♿ 🚿 ⋌ [MSP] ⅍ ⅂ ⓦ 🛒 /瓜\ ⅋ ⅂adj

Fr Eckernforde take coastal rd NE, sp Ludwigsburg
& Waabs. Site sp in approx 12km on R; turn R down
single track rd. Site in 2km. Lge, mkd, hdstg, pt
shd, EHU (16A) €3; bbq; twin axles; TV; 60% statics;
Eng spkn; games area; games rm; CKE. *"Fishing in
lake adj; excel san facs; horseriding & watersports
adj; gd walking and cycling rtes nrby; gd site."*
€26.00, 28 Mar-1 Oct.   **2019**

EGING AM SEE *4G3* (1km NE Rural) *48.72135,
13.26540* **Bavaria Kur-Sport-Campingpark,**
Grafenauerstrasse 31, 94535 Eging **(08544) 8089;
info@bavaria-camping.de; www.bavaria-camping.de**

12 🏕 €2.60 🚻(htd) [wc] ♨ 🛒 🚿 ⋌ [MSP] 🌊 ⅍ ⅂ ⓦ 🛒

Exit A3 junc 113 at Garham dir Eging, site sp in
4.5km twd Thurmansbang. 4*, Med, hdg, hdg,
hdstg, pt shd, pt sl, terr, EHU (16A) €2.50; sw nr; TV;
20% statics; Eng spkn; ccard acc; games area; golf
10km; fishing; bike hire; tennis; CKE. *"Lovely site nr
Bavarian National Park; gd walking/cycling fr site; htd
pool 700m; Wild West theme town, Pullman City,
2.5km; vg NH & longer; adj to Danube llz cycleway and
other cycleways."* **€29.00**   **2015**

EISENACH *1D4* (10km S Rural) *50.90888, 10.29916*
Campingplatz Eisenach am Altenberger See, Am Altenberger See, 99819 Wilhelmsthal **(03691) 215637; campingpark-eisenach@t-online.de; www.camping park-eisenach.de**

🐕 €2 ♀♀ WD ♨ 🖲 ⊿ ⧫ 🦋 ⵙ Ⓓ ⧫ 🛒 ⚠

Leave E40/A4 at junc 39 Eisenach Ost onto B19 sp Meiningen; site 2km S of Wilhelmsthal, sp.
Med, hdstg, pt shd, pt sl, serviced pitches; EHU (16A) inc; 80% statics; bus to Eisenach nr; ccard acc; sauna; boating; site clsd Nov; CKE. *"Helpful staff; clsd 1300-1500; conv Wartburg & Thuringer Wald, Bach & Luther houses in Eisenach; lake adj; lge carpk in town suitable for MH's."* **€25.50, 1 Jan-31 Oct & 1 Dec-31 Dec.**
2017

ERFURT *4E1* (10km NW Urban) *51.03895, 10.97870*
Campingplatz "Erfurt am See", Steinfeld 4, 99189 Erfurt-Kühnhausen **(0176) 517 52386; mail@erfurt amsee.de; www.erfurtamsee.de**

12 ♀♀(htd) WD ♨ 🖲 ⊿ 🦋 ⵙ ⵙ Ⓓ 🛒adj

Fr A71 take exit 9 twds Kühnhausen. Turn L onto August-Röbling-Straße. Turn L onto Kühnhäuser Str, turn R onto Steinfeld, site on L. Med, unshd, pt sl, EHU; train 1km; CKE. *"Basic clean site bet angling & sw lakes; conv for visiting Erfurt; no laundry rm; gd site."* **€19.50**
2018

ERLANGEN *4E2* (7km NW Rural) *49.63194, 10.9425*
Camping Rangau, Campingstrasse 44, 91056 Erlangen-Dechsendorf **(09135) 8866; infos@ camping-rangau.de; www.camping-rangau.de**

🐕 €2.50 ♀♀(htd) WD ♨ 🖲 ⊿ 🦋 Ⓓ ⧫ ⵙnr ⚠ ⚓

Fr A3/E45 exit junc 81 & foll camp sp. At 1st traff lts turn L, strt on at next traff lts, then L at next traff lts, site sp. 4*, Med, pt shd, EHU (6A) €3 (long lead poss req); sw; red long stay; Eng spkn; adv bkg acc; ccard acc; boat hire; CKE. *"Gd site, espec for families; clean facs; welcoming & well-run; some sm pitches; popular NH - overflow onto adj sports field; vg, busy NH; arrive early; gates clsd 1300-1500 & 2200 hrs; dog wash facs."* **€28.50, 1 Apr-15 Oct.**
2019

ESSEN *1B4* (8km S Urban) *51.38444, 6.99388* **DCC**
Campingpark Stadtcamping, Im Löwental 67, 45239 Essen-Werden **(0201) 492978; essen@knauscamp.de; www.dcc-stadtcamping-essen-werden.de**

12 ♀♀ WD ♨ 🖲 ⊿ ⧫ 🦋 ⵙ Ⓓ 🛒 ⚠

Exit A52 junc 28 onto B224 S dir Solingen. Turn R bef bdge over Rv Ruhr at traff lts & immed sharp R into Löwental, site sp. 3*, Med, hdstg, mkd, pt shd, EHU (16A) metered; gas; 95% statics; phone; Eng spkn; adv bkg acc; games area; games rm. *"Rv trips; poss ssn workers; site clsd 1300-1500 & 2130-0700; car park adj; gd."* **€27.30**
2016

EXTERTAL *1C3* (3km SW Rural) *52.05118, 9.10223*
Camping Extertal, Eimke 4, 32699 Extertal-Eimke **(05262) 3307; info@campingpark-extertal.de; www.campingpark-extertal.de**

12 🐕 €1.50 ♀♀(htd) WD ♨ ♨ 🖲 ⊿ ⧫ 🦋 ⵙ ⵙ ⵙ Ⓓnr ⧫ 🛒
⚠ ⚓ ⚓

Fr Rinteln on B238 S twd Barntrup; about 1.5km S Bösingfeld turn L at sp to site over level x-ing.
4*, Med, mkd, hdg, pt shd, pt sl, serviced pitches; EHU (16A) €1.50 or metered; gas; cooking facs; sw; red long stay; 90% statics; bus adj; Eng spkn; games rm; CKE. *"Gd site; dry & well-drained in v wet weather; all facs clean; forest walks & cycle paths fr site; 80 touring pitches; gd facs; some rd noise in day; clsd 1300-1500."* **€15.50**
2015

FASSBERG *1D2* (6km E Rural) *52.87593, 10.22718*
Ferienpark Heidesee (Part Naturist), Lüneburger-Heidesee, 29328 Fassberg-Oberohe **(05827) 970546; heidesee@ferienpark.de; www.campingheidesee.com**

12 🐕 €2 ♀♀(htd) WD ♨ 🖲 ⊿ ⧫ 🦋 Ⓓ ⧫ ⚠ ⚓

Leave A7/E45 at exit 44 onto B71. Turn S to Müden, then dir Unterlüss. Foll site sp. V lge, pt shd, terr, EHU (10A) €3; gas; sw; 65% statics; Eng spkn; ccard acc; sauna; bike hire; fishing; horseriding; tennis; games rm; CKE. *"Naturist camping in sep area; long leads maybe req; pool 250m; friendly helpful staff; places of interest nrby; private bthrms avail; gd mkd cycling and walking rtes fr site."* **€21.00**
2019

FELDBERG *2G2* (2km NE Rural) *53.34548, 13.45626*
Camping am Bauernhof, Hof Eichholz 1-8, 17258 Feldberg **(039831) 21084; info@campingplatz-feldberg.de; www.campingplatz-am-bauernhof.de**

12 🐕 €3 ♀♀ WD ♨ 🖲 ⊿ ⧫ 🦋 Ⓓnr ⧫ ⚠

Fr B198 at Möllenbeck turn dir Feldburg, thro Feldburg dir Prenzlau, site sp. 4*, Med, mkd, unshd, pt sl, EHU (16A) metered + conn fee; sw; 30% statics; fishing; CKE. *"Well-situated, vg site among lakes; many cycle paths in area."* **€18.00**
2016

FICHTELBERG *4F2* (2.5km N Rural) *50.01673, 11.85525* **Kur-Camping Fichtelsee,** Fichtelseestrasse 30, 95686 Fichtelberg **(09272) 801; info@camping-fichtelsee.de; www.camping-fichtelsee.de**

🐕 €2.50 ♀♀ WD ♨ 🖲 ⊿ ⧫ 🦋 ⵙ Ⓓnr 🛒nr ⚠ ⚓

Exit junc 39 fr A9/E51. Foll B303 twd Marktredwitz. After Bischofsgrün take R turn sp Fichtelberg, site on L in 1km. 4*, Lge, mkd, hdstg, pt shd, pt sl, terr, EHU (16A) metered + conn fee (poss rev pol); TV; 20% statics; phone; Eng spkn; ccard acc; site clsd 7 Nov-15 Dec; dog wash; CKE. *"Gd cent for walking in pine forests round lake & winter sports; peaceful site; pool 800m; barrier clsd 1230-1430; excel san facs."* **€25.00, 1 Jan-31 Oct, 6 Dec-31 Dec.**
2018

FINSTERAU *4G3* (1km N Rural) *48.94091, 13.57180*
Camping Nationalpark-Ost, Buchwaldstrasse 52,
94151 Finsterau **(08557) 768; berghof-frank@berghof-frank.de; www.camping-nationalpark-ost.de**

12 🐾 🇪2 ♦♦ WD ♨ ♿ 🖫 ⁄ ☗ 🦋 ♈ 🖳 nr

**Fr B12 turn N dir Mauth. Cont to Finsterau & site
1km adj parking for National Park.** Sm, pt shd, EHU
(6-16A) metered + conn fee or €2.50; gas; TV; CKE.
*"Gd walking & mountain biking; site in beautiful
Bavarian forest."* **€17.60** **2016**

FREIBURG IM BREISGAU *3B4* (21km NE Rural)
48.02318, 8.03253 **Camping Steingrubenhof,**
Haldenweg 3, 79271 St Peter **(07660) 210; info@
camping-steingrubenhof.de; www.camping-
steingrubenhof.de**

🐾 🇪2.50 ♦♦ WD ♨ ♿ 🖫 ⁄ MSP 🦋 ♈ Ⴎ nr ⅁ nr 🖳 /⛰

**Exit A5 junc 61 onto B294. Turn R sp St Peter.
Steep hill to site on L at top of hill. Or fr B31 dir
Donaueschingen, after 4km outside Freiburg turn
N sp St Peter; by-pass vill on main rd, turn L under
bdge 1st R. Fr other dir by-pass St Peter heading for
Glottertal; site on R 200m after rd bdge on by-pass.**
Med, hdg, mkd, hdstg, unshd, terr, serviced pitches;
EHU (16A) €2.50; bbq; red long stay; 70% statics;
phone; Eng spkn; adv bkg acc; ccard acc; CKE. *"Peaceful
site in heart of Black Forest; wonderful location;
pleasant staff; immac facs; gate clsd 1200-1400 & 2200-
0800; v diff to manoeuvre twin axle vans onto pitches as
narr access paths; pitches are sm & few for tourers; great
site."* **€25.00, 1 Jan-10 Nov & 15 Dec-31 Dec.** **2019**

**"That's changed – Should I let
the Club know?"**

If you find something on site that's different
from the site entry, fill in a report and let us
know. See camc.com/europereport.

FREIBURG IM BREISGAU *3B4* (4km E Rural) *47.99250,
7.87330* **Camping Hirzberg,** Kartäuserstrasse 99,
79104 Freiburg-im-Breisgau **(0761) 35054; hirzburg@
freiburg-camping.de; www.freiburg-camping.de**

12 🐾 🇪1 ♦♦ (htd) WD ♨ ⁄ MSP 🦋 ♈ ♈ ⅁ 🖳 /⛰

**Exit A5 at Freiburg-Mitte & foll B31 past town cent
sp Freiburg, Titisee. Foll camping sp twd Freiburg-
Ebnet, nr rocky slopes on R. Then approx 2.5km on
narr, winding rd. Site on R just after start of blocks
of flats on L.** Med, pt shd, pt sl, terr, EHU (10A) €2.50;
gas; bbq; 40% statics; bus 300m; Eng spkn; adv bkg
acc; bike hire; CKE. *"Pleasant, v helpful owner; site
clsd 2000 - ltd outside parking; gd cycle path & easy
walk to town; busy in high ssn; clsd 1300-1500; pool
500m; excel, v clean & modern san facs; gd value rest."*
€31.00 **2018**

FREIBURG IM BREISGAU *3B4* (11km SE Rural)
47.96015, 7.95001 **Camping Kirchzarten,** Dietenbacher
strasse 17, 79199 Kirchzarten **(07661) 9040910;
info@camping-kirchzarten.de; www.camping-
kirchzarten.de**

12 🐾 🇪2.50 ♦♦ (htd) WD ♨ ♿ 🖫 ⁄ MSP 🦋 ♈ Ⴎ ⅁ nr ⅁ 🖳 nr
/⛰ 🏊

**Sp fr Freiburg-Titisee rd 31; into Kirchzarten; site sp
fr town cent.** 5*, Lge, mkd, pt shd, serviced pitches;
EHU (16A) €2.50 or metered; bbq; red long stay;
20% statics; train 500m; Eng spkn; adv bkg rec; ccard
acc; tennis adj; CKE. *"Gd size pitches; choose pitch
then register at office (clse fr 1200-1400); spacious,
well-kept site; office clsd 1300-1430; Quickstop o'night
area; excel san facs; gd rest; 3 htd pools adj; winter
sports area; site fees inc free bus & train travel in Black
Forest region; helpful staff; dogs not acc Jul/Aug."*
€35.00 **2016**

FREUDENSTADT *3C3* (8km ENE Rural) *48.48011,
8.5005* **Höhencamping Königskanzel,** Freizeitweg 1,
72280 Dornstetten-Hallwangen **(07443) 6730;
info@camping-koenigskanzel.de; www.camping-
koenigskanzel.de**

12 🐾 🇪2.50 ♦♦ WD ♨ ♿ 🖫 ⁄ MSP 🦋 ♈ Ⴎ ⅁ ⅁ /⛰ 🖳 🏊 (htd)

**Fr Freudenstadt head E on rte 28 foll sp Stuttgart
for 7km. Camping sp on R, sharp R turn foll sp,
sharp L on narr, winding track to site in 200m.
Fr Nagold on R28, 7km fr Freudenstadt fork L; sp as
bef. NB: 1st sharp R turn is v sharp - take care.**
Med, hdg, pt shd, pt sl, terr, serviced pitches; EHU
(10A) metered; gas; bbq; red long stay; 60% statics;
phone; Eng spkn; adv bkg req; site clsd 3 Nov-15 Dec;
golf 7km; sauna; bike hire; CKE. *"Pleasant owners;
friendly welcome; excel shwr facs, inc for dogs; well
run family site; hill top location with gd views of Black
Forest; bkg fee; ski lift 7km; recep clsd 1300-1400;
excel value rest."* **€30.40** **2019**

FREUDENSTADT *3C3* (5km W Rural) *48.45840,
8.37255* **Camping Langenwald,** Strassburgerstrasse
167, 72250 Freudenstadt-Langenwald **(07441) 2862;
info@camping-langenwald.de; www.camping-
langenwald.de**

🐾 🇪2 ♦♦ (htd) WD ♨ ♿ 🖫 ⁄ MSP ⅁ ⅁ 🖳 /⛰ 🏊 (htd)

Foll sp fr town on B28 dir Strassburg.
5*, Med, pt shd, terr, serviced pitches; EHU (16A)
metered; gas; red long stay; 10% statics; Eng spkn;
ccard acc; bike hire; golf 4km; CKE. *"Gd, clean san facs
& site; woodland walks fr site; gd rest; friendly owners."*
€30.00, 26 Mar-1 Nov. **2016**

FRICKENHAUSEN AM MAIN *3D2* (1km W Rural)
49.66916, 10.07444 **Knaus Campingpark Frickenhausen,** Ochsenfurterstrasse 49, 97252 Frickenhausen/Ochsenfurt **(09331) 3171; info@ knauscamp.de; www.knauscamp.de**

🔟 🐕 €3 🛉🛉 �🆆🅾 ♨ ♿ ⬛ ∅ ⬛ 🦋 ⑪ 🍴 ⬛ ⅄ ⚠ 🛥(htd)

Turn off B13 at N end of bdge over Rv Main in Ochsenfurt & foll camping sp. 4*, Lge, hdg, mkd, pt shd, serviced pitches; EHU (16A) €2.40 or metered; gas; red long stay; TV; 40% statics; Eng spkn; adv bkg acc; bike hire. *"Vg, well-managed site on rv island; excel, clean facs; located on Romantischestrasse with many medieval vills; site clsd 1300-1500; v clean, cared for site; gd rest; friendly staff; gd sized pitches; site clsd bet 1-3pm."* **€32.60**   **2018**

FRIEDRICHSHAFEN *3D4* (10km W Coastal) *47.66583, 9.37694* **Campingplatz Schloss Helmsdorf,** Friedrichshafenerstrasse, 88090 Immenstaad-am-Bodensee **(07545) 6252; info@schloss-helmsdorf.org; www.schloss-helmsdorf.org**

🐕 🛉🛉(htd) � 🆆🅾 ⬛ ♿ ⬛ ∅ ⬛ 🦋 ⑪ ⬛ 🛥

Site sp fr B31 bet Meersburg & Friedrichshafen at Immenstaad. Lge, pt shd, pt sl, EHU (6A) €2.50; sw; 80% statics; windsurfing; boating. *"Vg, well-run site; gd position on lakeside; gd, clean san facs; helpful owners; sh walk to lake ferry; no dogs high ssn; Zeppelin & Dornier museums 8km level bike rte."* **€32.00, 25 Mar-9 Oct.**   **2016**

FRIEDRICHSHAFEN *3D4* (8km W Rural) *47.66896, 9.40253* **Camping Fischbach,** Grenzösch 3, 88048 Friedrichschafen-Fischbach **(07541) 42059; info@ camping-fischbach.de; www.camping-fischbach.de**

🛉🛉 �🆆🅾 ⬛ ♿ ⬛ ∅ ⬛ 🍴 ⑪ ⬛ 🛥 sand adj

Take B31 fr Friedrichshafen to Meersburg. Site sp on L at end of vill. Turning lane avail for easy access off busy rd. 3*, Med, hdstg, mkd, pt shd, EHU (10-16A) €2 (poss rev pol); sw nr; 40% statics; phone; Eng spkn; CKE. *"Tranquil, relaxing site; some lake view pitches, worth the extra; excel, clean, modern san facs; ferries to Konstanz nrby; Zeppelin/Dornier museums nrby; cr; on Lake Constance cycle rte."* **€27.00, 14 Apr-8 Oct.**   **2017**

FRIESOYTHE *1C2* (13km SE Rural) *52.93703, 7.92923* **Campingplatz Wilken,** Thülsfelder Str. 3, 26169 Friesoythe **04 49 52 61; info@camping-wilken.de; www.camping-wilken.de**

🔟 🐕 🛉🛉(htd) �🆆🅾 ⬛ ∅ ⬛ 🦋 ⬛ ⚠

Fr B72 Cloppenburg-Friesoythe. After 13km turn L onto Thülsfelder Straße. Site next to Thülsfeld Reservoir on L. Lge, mkd, hdstg, unshd, EHU (16A) metered. *"Excel site for long stay; spacious pitches; v clean san facs; would rec."* **€13.50**   **2019**

FUSSEN *4E4* (6km N Rural) *47.61553, 10.7230* **Camping Magdalena am Forggensee,** Bachtalstrasse 10, 87669 Osterreinen **(08362) 4931; camping platz.magdalena@t-online.de; www.sonnenhof-am-forggensee.de**

🐕 €3 🛉🛉 �🆆🅾 ⬛ ∅ 🦋 🍴 ⑪ ⬛ ⚠

Fr Füssen take rd 16 sp Kaufbeuren & Forggensee for 5km; R sp Osterreinen for 500m; L at T-junc foll site sp; site on R in 50m; app rd steep with sharp bends. Site well sp. 3*, Med, hdg, mkd, pt shd, terr, EHU (10A) metered + conn fee; gas; 40% statics; Eng spkn; adv bkg rec; sailing; watersports; CKE. *"Ltd touring pitches; superb views over lake; peaceful; gd site; sm pitches; conv for Zugspitze, Royal Castles, Oberammergau; lakeside cycle track to Füssen & to Neuschwanstein Castle."* **€23.90, 1 Apr-31 Oct.**
                      2019

FUSSEN *4E4* (6km NE Rural) *47.59638, 10.73861* **Camping Brunnen,** Seestrasse 81, 87645 Brunnen **(08362) 8273; info@camping-brunnen.de; www.camping-brunnen.de**

🔟 🐕 €4.50 🛉🛉 �🆆🅾 ⬛ ♿ ⬛ ∅ ⬛ 🍴 nr ⑪ nr ⬛ ⚠ 🛥 adj

S on rte 17 twd Füssen turn R in vill of Schwangau N to Brunnen; turn R at ent to vill at Spar shop, site clearly sp. Fr Füssen N on B17; turn L in Schwangau; well sp on lakeside. 5*, Lge, mkd, hdstg, pt shd, pt sl, serviced pitches; EHU (10-16A) metered + conn fee; gas; sw nr; bus; Eng spkn; adv bkg acc; ccard acc; bike hire; golf 3km; site clsd 5 Nov-20 Dec; CKE. *"Lovely location, next to lake; o'fits poss tightly packed; steel pegs ess; excel san facs; some pitches cramped; gd for Royal castles; gd cycle rtes; 10% red visits to Neuschwanstein Castle nrby; gates clsd 2200-0700; excel, busy, vg site; yachting in Lake Forggensee adj; handy rest, supmkt & g'ge."* **€38.00**   **2019**

FUSSEN *4E4* (5km NW Rural) *47.60198, 10.68333* **Camping Hopfensee,** Fischerbichl 17/Uferstrasse, 87629 Hopfen-am-See **(08362) 917710; info@ camping-hopfensee.de; www.camping-hopfensee.com**

🐕 €4.15 🛉🛉 �🆆🅾 ⬛ ♨ ♿ ⬛ ∅ ⬛ 🦋 ⑪ ⬛ 🍴 ⬛ ⬛ ⚠ 🛥 ∅ 🛥(covrd, htd)

Fr Füssen N on B16 twd Kaufbeuren in 2km L on rd sp Hopfen-am-See, site at ent to vill on L thro c'van car park. Lge, hdstg, mkd, pt shd, serviced pitches; EHU (16A) metered; gas; sw nr; free bus to Fussen; Eng spkn; adv bkg rec; sauna; boating; fishing; CKE. *"Gd location; excel facs; helpful staff; gd rest on site; no tents allowed except for awnings; tight squeeze in high ssn; vans need manhandling; fitness cent; solarium; winter sports area; gd walking & cycling; lakeside pitches rec; excel; highly rec; 5 star facs; WiFi €2 per day; recep clsd 12-2pm."* **€43.00, 1 Jan-4 Nov & 15 Dec-31 Dec.**   **2018**

GANDERKESEE *1C2* (7km W Rural) *53.04666, 8.46388* **Ferienpark Falkensteinsee,** Am Falkensteinsee 1, 27777 Ganderkesee-Steinkimmen **(04222) 9470077; camping@falkensteinsee.de; www.falkensteinsee.de**

12 ♈ €1.50 ♏ ♨ ♿ 🗑 ⋇ ❦ ⓦ nr 🛒 ⚱

Exit A28/E22 junc 18 dir Habbrügge. Site on R in 2km. 4*, Lge, pt shd, EHU (16A) €3.50 or metered; sw nr; 70% statics; Eng spkn; golf 8km; sauna; CKE. *"Conv Oldenburg & Bremen; new owners; completely refurb (2015); lake sw with 2 sandy beaches; pleasant holiday park; well organised; o'night m'van area; friendly staff; sep naturist beach; new facs & v high quality; excel; sep sw area for dogs."* **€21.50** **2016**

GARTOW *2E2* (4km NW Rural) *53.03972, 11.41583* **Camping Laascher See,** Ortsteil Laasche 13, 29471 Gartow (05846) 342; pewsdorf@campingplatz-laascher-see.de; www.elbtalaue-camping.de

♈ €1.50 ♏ ⓦ ♨ ♿ 🗑 ⋇ ❦ Ⓨ 🛒 nr ⚱ ⚰

Fr S on B493 to Gartow, turn N on L256 (Rondelerstrasse) dir Gartower See & Laasche See, site sp on R. Or E fr Dennenberg on L256 dir Gorleben & Gartow, site sp approx 5km after Gorleben. Med, hdg, pt shd, pt sl, EHU (6A) inc; sw nr; 60% statics; adv bkg acc; CKE. *"Pleasant owners; clean, modern san facs; vg."* **€19.50, 1 Apr-31 Oct.** **2016**

GEMUNDEN AM MAIN *3D2* (5km W Rural) *50.05260, 9.65656* **Spessart-Camping Schönrain,** Schönrainstrasse 4-18, 97737 Gemünden-Hofstetten **(09351) 8645; info@spessart-camping.de; www. spessart-camping.de**

♈ €2.80 ♏ (htd) ⓦ ♨ ♿ 🗑 ⋇ ❦ Ⓨ 🛒 ⚱ ⚰ ⛴

Rd B26 to Gemünden, cross Rv Main & turn R dir Hofstetten, site sp. 5*, Lge, hdg, mkd, hdstg, pt shd, terr, EHU (10A) metered + conn fee €2.15; TV; 50% statics; phone; Eng spkn; bike hire; sauna; fitness rm; solarium; games area; CKE. *"Clean, well-kept, wooded site; interesting towns nrby; variable pitch sizes/ prices; excel; v well kept new facs block; welcoming."* **€25.00, 1 Apr-30 Sep.** **2019**

GLUCKSBURG (OSTSEE) *1D1* (6km NE Coastal) *54.85901, 9.59109* **Ostseecamp,** An der Promenade 1, 24960 Glücksburg-Holnis **(04631) 622071; info@ ostseecamp-holnis.de; www.ostseecamp-holnis.de**

♈ €2.50 ♏ (htd) ⓦ ♨ ♿ 🗑 ⋇ ⓜ ❦ Ⓨ Ⓦ nr ⚱ ⚰ ♒ ⚓ sand adj

Fr Flensburg on rd 199 turn off thro Glücksburg & further 6km to Holnis. 4*, Med, hdstg, mkd, pt shd, EHU (16A) €3; bbq; cooking facs; 30% statics; adv bkg acc; windsurfing 1km; fishing; bike hire; CKE. *"Lovely coastal loc; v friendly staff; clean facs."* **€29.00, 28 Mar-16 Oct.** **2016**

GOPPINGEN *3D3* (13.5km SW Rural) *48.63946, 9.55508* **Campingplatz Aichelberg,** Bunzenberg 1, 73101 Aichelberg **(07164) 2700**

♈ €2 ♏ ⓦ ♨ ⋇ ❦ Ⓨ Ⓦ nr ⚱

Exit E52/A8 junc 58 sp Aichelberg-Goppingen & foll sp to camp site in 1km. 3*, Med, pt shd, EHU (10A) €2; 80% statics; adv bkg acc. *"Fills up after 1600 hrs but gd overflow field with EHU for NH; family-run site; new excel facs; owner helpful; nr A8; gd conv NH."* **€20.00, 7 Apr-8 Oct.** **2017**

GOSLAR *1D3* (4km SW Rural) *51.88958, 10.39889* **Campingplatz Sennhütte,** Clausthalerstrasse 28, 38644 Goslar (05321) 22498; sennhuette@camping platz-goslar.de; www.campingplatz-goslar.de

12 ♈ ♏ ⓦ ♨ ♿ ⋇ Ⓦ ⚱

Fr Goslar on B241 twd Clausthal, Zellerfeld site on R in 2km. Ent thro car pk of Hotel Sennhütte. 2*, Med, pt shd, EHU (16A) metered + €2 conn fee (poss long lead req); 30% statics; bus at ent to town; ccard acc. *"Gd NH/sh stay nr beautiful town."* **€21.00** **2018**

GREIFSWALD *2G1* (16km NE Coastal) *54.12666, 13.52196* **Campingplatz Loissin (Part Naturist),** 17509 Loissin (038352) 243; info@campingplatz-loissin.de; www.campingplatz-loissin.de

♈ €2 ♏ ♨ ♿ 🗑 ⋇ ⓜ ❦ Ⓨ Ⓦ ⚱ ⚰ ♒ ⚓ sand adj

Fr Greifswald E to Kemnitz, then head N twds Loissin; site on coast N, well sp fr the vill. 3*, Lge, mkd, pt shd, EHU (16A) inc; 40% statics; adv bkg acc; games area; windsurfing; clsd 1300-1430 & 2200-0800; bike hire; CKE. *"Vg site; approx 40km to foot x-ing fr car park to Poland for shopping; excel san facs; sep naturist beach; main attraction is immed proximity to sea."* **€22.00, 1 Apr-31 Oct.** **2018**

GREVEN *1B3* (6km SW Rural) *52.08328, 7.55806* **Campingplatz Westheide,** Altenbergerstrasse 23, 48268 Greven **(02571) 560701; kontakt@ campingplatz-westheide.de; www.campingplatz-westheide.de**

12 ♈ €1 ♏ (htd) ⓦ ♨ ♿ 🗑 ⋇ ❦ Ⓨ ⚱ ⚰ ♒ sand adj

Exit A1 junc 76 onto B481 around E side of Greven, then turn L onto B219 for 2km. Turn R onto L555 Nordwalderstrasse & in 2km at Westerode turn L into Altenbergerstrasse, site on L in 1km. Med, hdg, pt shd, EHU (16A) metered; 80% statics; ccard acc; games rm; fishing; CKE. *"Gd for sh stay; lake adj; walks around lake."* **€18.00** **2016**

GYHUM *1D2* (4km SE Rural) *53.19308, 9.33638* **Waldcamping Hesedorf,** Zum Waldbad 3, 27404 Gyhum-Hesedorf (04286) 2252; info@waldcamping-hesedorf.de; www.waldcamping-hesedorf.de

12 ♈ €0.50 ♏ (htd) ⓦ ♨ ⋇ ⓜ ❦ Ⓨ Ⓦ ⚱ nr ⚰

Exit A1/E22 junc 49 in dir Zeven. In 1km turn R sp Gyhum & foll site sp to Hesedorf. Med, unshd, EHU (16A) inc; 70% statics; Eng spkn; CKE. *"Clean, well-kept site; attractive area; htd pool 150m inc; gd rest; lge sep area for tourers; barrier clsd 1300-1500; dated san facs but clean; gd NH."* **€20.00** **2019**

HAMBURG *1D2* (7km NW Urban) *53.5900, 9.93083*
Campingplatz Buchholz, Keilerstrasse 374, 22525
Hamburg-Stellingen **(040) 5404532; info@camping-buchholz.de; www.camping-buchholz.de**

12 🐕 €4 ♦♦ ♨ ♿ ☐ ⚡ ⊻ nr ☂ nr

**Exit A7/E45 junc 26 & foll dir 'Innenstadt' - city cent.
Site sp in 600m on L.** Sm, hdg, mkd, hdstg, pt shd,
EHU (16A) €4; 10% statics; bus, train nr; adv bkg acc.
*"Fair NH nr a'bahn & Hamburg cent; conv transport to
city - tickets fr recep; friendly management; sm pitches;
busy site, rec arr early; diff access for lge o'fits."*
€35.00   **2019**

HAMBURG *1D2* (9km NW Urban) *53.64916, 9.92970*
Knaus Campingpark Hamburg, Wunderbrunnen 2,
22457 Hamburg **(040) 5594225; service@camping
platz-hamburg.de; www.campingplatz-hamburg.de**

12 🐕 €3.50 ♦♦ ⬚ ♨ ♿ ☐ ⚡ ⊻ nr ♨ ☂ ⋔

**Heading N on A7 exit junc 23 to Schnelsen Nord; L
at traff lts, foll sp Ikea & site behind Ikea.** 4*, Med,
mkd, pt shd, EHU (6A) inc; TV; phone; bus to city; Eng
spkn; ccard acc; CKE. *"Useful NH; helpful staff; stn
adj; gates clsd 2200 hrs & 1300-1600 LS; elec pylons
& cables cross site; deposit for key to san facs & el box;
3-day Hamburg card excel value."* **€43.50**   **2019**

HAMELN *1D3* (2km W Urban) *52.10916, 9.3475*
Campingplatz zum Fährhaus, Uferstrasse 80, 31785
Hameln **(05151) 67489; info@campingplatz-hameln.
de; www.campingplatz-hameln.de**

12 🐕 €1 ♦♦ (htd) ⬚ ♨ ♿ ☐ ⚡ 🦋 ☂ Y ⊕ ☂ nr

**Fr A2/E30 at Bad Eilsen junc 35 onto B83 to Hameln
on NE side of Rv Weser; in town foll sp Detmold/
Paderborn; cross bdge to SW side (use Thiewall
Brücke); turn R on minor rd twd Rinteln; foll site sp.**
3*, Med, unshd, EHU (10-16A); 20% statics; phone;
clsd 1300-1430; CKE. *"Picturesque & historic district;
open-air performance of Pied Piper in town on Sun
to mid-Sep; sm pitches & poss uneven; helpful, lovely
owner; san facs refurb, best in Europe!(2017); gd cycle
paths by rv to town; site beautifully kept."* **€18.50**
                                                             2017

HAMELN *1D3* (8km W Rural) *52.10725, 9.29588*
Camping am Waldbad, Pferdeweg 2, 31787
Halvestorf **(05158) 2774; info@campingamwaldbad.
de; www.campingamwaldbad.de**

🐕 ♦♦ ⬚ ♨ ♿ ☐ ⚡ 🦋 ☂ Y ⋔ ☂ (htd) ⬚

**Fr Hameln on B83 dir Rinteln. In approx 10km
turn L, cross rv & foll sp Halvestorf & site.** 4*, Med,
unshd, pt sl, EHU (16A) €2; 80% statics; adv bkg acc.
"Pleasant site - better than site in Hameln; gd facs."
€19.00, 1 Apr-31 Oct.   **2018**

HAMM *1B3* (13km E Rural) *51.6939, 7.9710* **Camping
Uentrop,** Dolbergerstrasse 80, 59510 Lippetal-
Lippborg **(02388) 437 or (0172) 2300747; info@
camping-helbach.de; www.camping-helbach.de**

12 🐕 €2 ♦♦ (htd) ⬚ ♨ ♿ ☐ ⚡ ⊻ ☂ nr ☂ nr ⋔

**Exit A2/E34 junc 19, site sp; behind Hotel Helbach
1km fr a'bahn.** 3*, Lge, pt shd, pt sl, EHU (16A) €2;
gas; 90% statics; Eng spkn; ccard acc. *"Friendly; gd
security; barrier clsd 1300-1500 & 2200-0500; fair NH."*
€18.00   **2016**

> # "I like to fill in the reports as I travel from site to site"
>
> You'll find report forms at the back of this
> guide, or you can fill them in online at
> camc.com/europereport.

HAMMELBACH *3C2* (0.6km S Rural) *49.63277,
8.83000* **Camping Park Hammelbach,** Gasse 17,
64689 Grasellenbach/Hammelbach **(06253) 3831;
info@camping-hammelbach.de; www.camping-
hammelbach.de**

🐕 €2.50 ♦♦ (htd) ⬚ ♨ ♿ ☐ ⚡ 🦋 ☂ Y nr ⊕ nr ☂ nr

**Exit A5/E35 exit junc 31 onto B460 E. Turn S in
Weschnitz to Hammelbach & foll site sp.**
5*, Med, hdg, pt shd, EHU (16A) metered; gas; bbq;
70% statics; bus 300m; Eng spkn; adv bkg acc; ccard
acc; CKE. *"Excel family run site with views; sauna adj;
v pleasant, helpful staff; red for snrs; conv Heidelberg;
immac hotel like san facs; htd pool 300m; well up to CC
standards."* **€24.50, 1 Apr-31 Oct.**   **2019**

HANNOVER *1D3* (14km NE Urban) *52.45383,
9.85611* **Campingplatz Parksee Lohne,** Alter Postweg
12, 30916 Isernhagen 05139 88260; **parksee-lohne@
t-online.de; www.parksee-lohne.de**

🐕 ♦♦ (htd) ⬚ ♨ ♿ ☐ ⚡ 🦋 ☂ Y ⊕ ⬚

**Fr A2 take exit 46 to Altwarmbüchen. Cont onto
K114, turn R onto Alter Postweg & foll sp to
campsite.** V lge, pt shd, cooking facs; 95% statics; Eng
spkn. *"Vg site; next to golf course; excel san facs; narr
cobbled rd 1/2 m; under flight path, but quiet at night."*
€29.60, 1 Apr-15 Oct.   **2019**

HANNOVER *1D3* (16km SE Rural) *52.30447, 9.86216*
Camping Birkensee, 30880 Laatzen **(0511) 529962;
birkensee@camping-laatzen.de; www.camping-
laatzen.de**

12 🐕 €2.50 ♦♦ ⬚ ♨ ♿ ☐ ⚡ Y ⬚ ⋔ ☂ (covrd)

**Fr N leave A7 junc 59 dir Laatzen, turn R, then turn
L & site well sp on L after traff lts. Fr S exit junc 60
twd Laatzen, site sp on L on lakeside.** 3*, Lge, pt
shd, EHU (10A) €2.50 (poss rev pol); sw; 60% statics;
Eng spkn; fishing; games area; sauna; CKE. *"Gd, clean
facs; sm touring area; site needs TLC; v helpful staff."*
€27.00   **2019**

HANNOVER *1D3* (10km S Rural) *52.30133, 9.74716*
Campingplatz Arnumer See, Osterbruchweg 5,
30966 Hemmingen-Arnum (05101) 3534; info@
camping-hannover.de; www.camping-hannover.de

12 🐾 €1.50 ♦♦(htd) WD 🏕 ♨ 🖫 🖉 MSP 🦋 ♈ 🍽 ⓘ🍴 🎿nr 🅰

Leave A7 junc 59 onto B443 dir Pattensen, then B3
dir Hannover. Site sp in Hemmingen dir Wilkenburg.
4*, Lge, hdg, mkd, pt shd, EHU (16A) €3; gas; cooking
facs; sw; 95% statics; bus to Hannover 1.5km; tennis;
fishing; bike hire; CKE. *"Friendly staff; excel, modern,
clean san facs; sm area for tourers - gd size open
pitches; gd lake sw & boating; insect repellent ess!"*
€31.00   **2019**

HANNOVER *1D3* (16km NW Rural) *52.42083,
9.54638* **Camping Blauer See,** Am Blauen See 119,
30823 Garbsen (05137) 89960; info@camping-
blauer-see.de; www.camping-blauer-see.de

12 🐾 €2.50 ♦♦(htd) WD 🏕 ♨ 🖫 🖉 🍽 ⓘ🍴 🅰

Fr W exit A2 at junc 41 onto Garbsen rest area. Thro
service area, at exit turn R, at T-junc turn R (Alt
Garbson). All sp with int'l camp sp. Fr E exit junc 40,
cross a'bahn & go back to junc 41, then as above.
Lge, hdstg, pt shd, serviced pitches; EHU (16A) €2.70;
gas; bbq; sw nr; 90% statics; phone; bus to Hannover
1.5km; Eng spkn; ccard acc; watersports adj; CKE.
*"Excel san facs; well-organised site; helpful staff; conv
bus/train to Hannover; barrier clsd 2300-0500 & 1300-
1500; rec pitch by lake."* **€29.00**   **2019**

HANNOVERSCH MUNDEN *1D4* (0.9km W Rural)
51.41666, 9.64750 **Campingplatz Grüne Insel
Tanzwerder,** Tanzwerder 1, 34346 Hannoversch-
Münden (05541) 12257; info@busch-freizeit.de;
www.busch-freizeit.de

🐾 €2 ♦♦ WD 🏕 🖫 🖉 MSP ♈ 🍽 🎿nr ⓘ 🎿nr 🅰

A7/E45 exit junc 76 onto B496 to Hann-Münden.
Cross bdge & site sp on an island on Rv Fulda next
to town cent. App over narr swing bdge. Fr junc 75
foll sp to Hann-Münden. At Aral g'ge in town take
next L & foll sp to site (sp Weserstein). 3*, Med, mkd,
pt shd, EHU (16A) metered + conn fee; red long stay;
Eng spkn; adv bkg acc; CKE. *"Pleasant, well looked
after site on island bordered by rv both sides; noisy
bdge traff; easy stroll to historic old town."*
€21.00, 1 Apr-16 Oct.   **2016**

HARZGERODE *2E4* (8km SW Rural) *51.60833,
11.08444* **Ferienpark Birnbaumteich,** Birnbaumteich 1,
06493 Neudorf Harzgerode (03948) 46243; info@
ferienpark-birnbaumteich.de; www.ferienpark-
birnbaumteich.de

12 🐾 €4 ♦♦ WD 🏕 ♨ 🖫 🖉 MSP ♈ 🍽 ⓘ🍴 🎿nr 🅰 🖉

Fr Harzgerode on B242 dir Halle, after 1km turn R,
dir Stolberg. In 4.3km after Neudorf turn R at
camping sp. Site 1km on R. 3*, Med, pt shd, pt sl, EHU
(16A) €3; bbq; sw; twin axles; 50% statics; phone; bus
1km; Eng spkn; adv bkg acc; games rm; sauna; games
area; CKE. *"Forest walk & bike trails; steam rlwy 3km;
interesting towns nrby; vg."* **€24.00**   **2015**

HATTINGEN *1B4* (3km NW Urban) *51.40611, 7.17027*
Camping Ruhrbrücke, Ruhrstrasse 6, 45529 Hattingen
(02324) 80038; info@camping-hattingen.de;
www.camping-hattingen.de

🐾 €2 ♦♦(htd) WD 🏕 ♨ 🖉 🍽 🍽 nr ⓘ nr 🎿nr

Fr A40 bet Essen & Bochum exit junc 29 dir Höntrop
& Hattingen. Foll sp Hattingen on L651 & B1, site sp
bef rv bdge. 3*, Med, unshd, pt sl, EHU (16A) €3; bbq;
sw nr; phone; bus, train adj; Eng spkn; adv bkg acc;
windsurfing adj; canoeing adj; CKE. *"Beautiful rvside
setting; plentiful, clean facs; friendly owner; excel cycle
tracks."* **€18.00, 1 Apr-20 Oct.**   **2016**

HECHTHAUSEN *1D2* (4km SW Rural) *53.62525,
9.20298* **Ferienpark & Campingpark Geesthof,** Am
Ferienpark 1, 21755 Hechthausen-Klint (04774) 512;
info@geesthof.de; www.geesthof.de

12 🐾 €2 ♦♦ WD 🏕 ♨ 🖫 🖉 MSP 🦋 ♈ ⓘ🍴 🎿 🅰 🖉
🎣 (covrd, htd) 🚣

Site sp on B73 rd to Lamstedt. 3*, Med, hdg, mkd,
pt shd, EHU (10A) €2; 60% statics; Eng spkn; boat
hire; waterslide; watersports; fishing; bike hire; sauna.
*"Superb site with mature trees around pitches; peaceful
surroundings adj to rv, lake & woods; friendly staff."*
€22.50   **2015**

HEIDELBERG *3C2* (10km E Rural) *49.40175, 8.77916*
Campingplatz Haide, Ziegelhäuser Landstrasse 91,
69151 Neckargemünd (06223) 2111; info@camping-
haide.de; www.camping-haide.de

🐾 €2 ♦♦ WD 🏕 ♨ 🖫 🖉 MSP ♈ ⓘ🍴 🎿nr 🅰

Take B37 fr Heidelberg, cross Rv Neckar by
Ziegelhausen bdge by slip rd on R (avoid vill narr
rd); foll site sp. Site on R bet rv & rd 1km W of
Neckergemünd on rvside. Lge, hdstg, unshd, EHU
(6A) €2.50 (long lead req); bbq; 5% statics; Eng spkn;
bike hire; CKE. *"Conv Neckar Valley & Heidelberg; some
rd, rlwy (daytime) & rv noise; NH/sh stay only; long
attractive site along rv."* **€20.30, 1 Apr-31 Oct.**   **2016**

HEIDELBERG *3C2* (12km E Urban) *49.39638, 8.79472*
Campingplatz an der Friedensbrücke, Falltorstrasse 4,
69151 Neckargemünd (06223) 2178; nfo@camping
platz-am-neckar.de; www.campingplatz-am-neckar.de

🐾 €1.50 ♦♦(htd) WD 🏕 ♨ 🖫 🖉 MSP ♈ 🍽 ⓘ nr 🅰

Exit Heidelberg on S side of rv on B37; on ent
Neckargemünd site sp to L (grey sp) mkd
Poststrasse; site adj rv bdge. Fr S on B45 turn L sp
Heidelberg, then R at camping sp. Fr A6 exit junc 33
onto B45 sp Neckargemünd, then as above. Foll sp
- do not foll sat nav. 4*, Lge, unshd, EHU (6-16A) €5
or metered (poss rev pol); gas; TV; phone; Eng spkn;
adv bkg acc; tennis. *"Gd location by busy rv, poss liable
to flood; immac, well-run, relaxing site; ask for rvside
pitch (sm) - extra charge; transport to Heidelberg by
boat, bus & train 10 mins walk fr site; owner will site
o'fits; warm welcome; helpful staff; kayaking 500m;
no plastic grndsheets; 26 steps up to main san facs;
pool adj; gd rvside walks & cycling; TO 500m; gd
NH facs, nr ent; recep clsd 1-3pm; Wifi €2 per day."*
€27.00, 1 Apr-21 Oct.   **2018**

HEIDENAU *1D2* (2.6km W Rural) *53.30851, 9.62038*
Ferienzentrum Heidenau, Minkens Fuhren, 21258
Heidenau **(04182) 4272 or 4861; info@ferien
zentrum-heidenau.de; www.ferienzentrum-
heidenau.de**

12 ♥♥ (htd) wo ▲ ☐ ✗ MP ➤ ⑪ Ⴑ ⊕ ⅃ ⅄ ▲ ⅃ (htd)

**Exit A1 Hamburg-Bremen m'way junc 46 to
Heidenau; foll sp.** 4*, Lge, pt shd, EHU (16A) €2.50
(poss long lead req); bbq (sep area); 75% statics;
phone; Eng spkn; sauna; cycling; games area; tennis;
lake fishing; CKE. *"Pleasant, wooded site; tourers on
grass areas by lakes; clean, modern facs; ltd shop; gd;
visa ccards not acc; pitches maybe unusable in v wet
weather."* **€26.00** **2016**

HERSBRUCK *4E2* (6km E Rural) *49.51884, 11.49200*
Pegnitz Camping, Eschenbacherweg 4, 91224
Hohenstadt **(09154) 1500; camping.mueller@t-
online.de; urlaub.nuernberger-land.de**

♥♥ wo ▲ ☐ ✗ MP ➤ ⑪ nr Ⴑ nr

**Exit A9 junc 49 onto B14 dir Hersbruck & Sulzbach-
Rosenberg. By-pass Hersbruck & after 8km turn
L sp Hohenstadt. Bef vill, cross rv bdge & immed
turn R at site sp.** 3*, Med, pt shd, EHU (10A) inc;
gas; 10% statics; train nr; Eng spkn; adv bkg acc; bike
hire; CKE. *"Lovely, peaceful, friendly site; gd walking
& cycling area; helpful owner; vg san facs; train to
Nuremberg; gd; stn 200m; recep clsd 1230-1330,
waiting area outside."* **€19.50, 1 Mar-31 Oct.** **2019**

HOCHDONN *1D1* (1.5km E Rural) *54.02395, 9.29381*
Campingplatz Klein Westerland, Zur Holstenau 1,
25712 Hochdonn **04948 252345; info@campingplatz-
klein-westerland.de; www.campingplatz-klein-
westerland.de**

⑪ €1.50 ♥♥ ▲ ☐ ✗ ⏀ ⅄ ⑪ ⅃

**Fr A23, take exit 5 to Süderhastedt. Turn L on 431 to
Hochdonn. Site sp. Canal ferry maybe diff for trailer
c'vans, steep ramps.** Med, pt shd, EHU; 70% statics;
gd. *"Interesting canal traff & lge locks at Brunsbüttel,
20km S; noisy, passing ships; only site on the Northsea-
Baltic sea canal."* **€18.00, 1 Apr-31 Oct.** **2016**

HOF *4F2* (10km NW Rural) *50.37494, 11.83804*
Camping Auensee, 95189 Joditz-Köditz **(09295) 381;
rathaus@gemeinde-koeditz.de; www.gemeinde-
koeditz.de**

12 ⑪ €1.50 ♥♥ ▲ ☐ ✗ MP ➤ ⑪ Ⴑ nr ⅄

**Exit A9 at junc 31 Berg/Bad Steben. Turn R fr m'way
& in 200m L to Joditz, foll site sp in vill (1-way ent/
exit to site).** 3*, Med, unshd, terr, EHU (16A) €1.80 or
metered; sw; 75% statics; tennis; fishing; clsd 1230-
1500; CKE. **€16.00** **2016**

HOLZMINDEN *1D3* (10km N Rural) *51.88618,
9.44335* **Weserbergland Camping,** Weserstrasse 66,
37649 Heinsen **(05535) 8733; info@weserbergland-
camping.de; www.weserbergland-camping.de**

⑪ €3 ♥♥ (htd) wo ▲ ☆ ☐ ✗ MP ➤ ⑪ Ⴑ ⊕ ☆ Ⴑ nr ⅄ ✗
⅃ (htd)

**Fr Holzminden on B83 twd Hameln, site sp in
Heinsen cent twd rv bank.** 3*, Med, pt shd, EHU
(10A) €1.90; gas; twin axles; red long stay; 50% statics;
Eng spkn; adv bkg acc; ccard acc; bike hire; sauna;
games area; CKE. *"Beautiful site on rv bank; gd
modern san facs (2015); gd area for walking/cycling;
gd local bus service; accomodating owner; excel."*
€23.00, 1 Apr-31 Oct. **2015**

HOOKSIEL *1C2* (2km N Coastal) *53.64100, 8.03400*
Nordsee Camping Hooksiel (Part Naturist),
Bäderstrasse, 26434 Wangerland **(04425) 958080;
info@wangerland.de; www.wangerland.de**

⑪ €3.10 ♥♥ wo ▲ ☆ ☆ ☐ ✗ MP ➤ ⑪ ☆ Ⴑ ⅄ ✗ ⅃

**Exit A29 at junc 4 sp Fedderwarden to N. Thro
Hooksiel, site sp 1.5km.** 4*, V lge, hdstg, unshd, EHU
(6-10A) inc; gas; 50% statics; bike hire; fishing; games
area; watersports; sailing. *"Main san facs excel but up 2
flights steps - otherwise facs in Portakabin; naturist site
adj with same facs."* **€24.00, 25 Mar-17 Oct.** **2016**

HORB AM NECKAR *3C3* (4km W Rural) *48.44513,
8.67300* **Camping Schüttehof,** Schütteberg 7-9,
72160 Horb-am-Neckar **(07451) 3951; camping-
schuettehof@t-online.de; www.camping-
schuettehof.de**

12 ⑪ €2 ♥♥ wo ▲ ☐ ✗ ➤ ⑪ Ⴑ ⅄ ✗ ⅃ (htd) ⅃

**Fr A81/E41 exit junc 30; take Freudenstadt rd out
of Horb site sp.** Med, mkd, pt shd, pt sl, EHU (16A)
metered + conn fee; gas; 75% statics; adv bkg acc.
*"Horb delightful Black Forest town; site close to saw
mill & could be noisy; steep path to town; site clsd
1230-1430; superb, new, state of the art facs; peaceful;
v pleasant helpful staff."* **€18.50** **2017**

HOXTER *1D3* (2km S Rural) *51.76658, 9.38308*
Wesercamping Höxter, Sportzentrum 4, 37671
Höxter **(05271) 2589; info@campingplatz-hoexter.de;
www.campingplatz-hoexter.de**

⑪ €1.50 ♥♥ wo ▲ ☐ ✗ ➤ ⑪ Ⴑ ⅄ ✗

**Fr B83/64 turn E over rv sp Boffzen, turn R & site
sp almost on rv bank. Turn R in 300m at green sp,
turn L in car park.** Med, pt shd, EHU (10-16A) €2;
60% statics; CKE. *"Lge open area for tourers; clsd
1300-1500; spaces beside rv; easy walk along rv to
town."* **€19.50, 15 Mar-15 Oct.** **2019**

HUNFELD *1D4* (5km SW Rural) *50.65333, 9.72388*
Knaus Campingpark Praforst, Dr Detlev-Rudelsdorff Allee 6, 36088 Hünfeld **(06652) 749090; huenfeld@ knauscamp.de; www.knauscamp.de/huenfeld-praforst**

12 🛖 €2 ⅋⅋ WD ♨ ⅋ 🗑 ∥ MP 🦋 ⅋ 🏊 ⅍

Exit A7 junc 90 dir Hünfeld, foll sp thro golf complex. 5*, Med, mkd, pt shd, pt sl, EHU (16A) metered or €3.50; 40% statics; fishing; golf adj; games area; games rm. *"Excel san facs; gd walking/cycling."* **€33.00** **2018**

IDAR OBERSTEIN *3B2* (15km N Rural) *49.80455, 7.26986* **Camping Harfenmühle,** 55758 Asbacherhütte **(06786) 7076; mail@harfenmuehle.de; www.camping-harfenmuehle.de**

12 🛖 €3 ⅋⅋ WD ♨ ⅋ 🗑 ∥ MP ⅋ 🍷 ⅋ ⅋ 🗑 ⅍

Fr rte 41 fr Idar twd Kirn, turn L at traff lts at Fischbach by-pass sp Herrstein/Morbach, site 3km past Herrstein vill. Sharp turn to site. 4*, Med, pt shd, EHU (16A) metered; gas; sw nr; TV; 50% statics; phone; Eng spkn; adv bkg acc; tennis; games rm; sauna; fishing; games area; golf 10km; CKE. *"Vg rest; o'night m'vans area; gd san facs but poss inadequate in high ssn; sep area late arr; barrier clsd 2200; gd site."* **€31.00** **2019**

ILLERTISSEN *3D4* (11km S Rural) *48.14138, 10.10665* **Camping Christophorus Illertal,** Werte 6, 88486 Kirchberg-Sinningen **(07354) 663; info@camping-christophorus.de; www.camping-christophorus.de**

12 🛖 €3.50 ⅋⅋ (htd) WD ♨ ⅋ ∥ ⅋ 🗑 ⅍ 🏊 (covrd)

Exit A7/E43 junc 125 at Altenstadt. In cent of town turn L, then R immed after level x-ing. Foll site sp. 4*, Lge, pt shd, EHU (16A) €2.50 or metered; sw nr; 80% statics; Eng spkn; adv bkg acc; bike hire; fishing; sauna; CKE. *"Gd site; sm sep area for tourers; excel san facs."* **€26.00** **2017**

ILLERTISSEN *3D4* (2km SW Rural) *48.21221, 10.08773* **Camping Illertissen,** Dietenheimerstrasse 91, 89257 Illertissen **(07303) 7888; campingplatz-illertissen@t-online.de; www.camping-illertissen.de**

🛖 €2 ⅋⅋ WD ♨ ⅋ 🗑 ∥ MP 🦋 ⅋ 🗑 ⅍ 🏊

Leave A7 at junc 124, twd Illertissen/Dietenheim; after rlwy x-ing turn R then L foll site sp. Off main rd B19 fr Neu Ulm-Memmingen fr N, turn R in Illertissen, foll sp. 3*, Sm, mkd, pt shd, terr, EHU (16A) €2 or metered; gas; 65% statics; ccard acc; CKE. *"Trains to Ulm & Kempten; 20 mins walk to town or cycle track; some pitches poss unrel in wet; site clsd bet 1300-1500 & 2200-0700; obliging owner; conv a'bahn; vg."* **€24.50, 1 Apr-31 Oct.** **2018**

IMMENSTADT IM ALLGAU *3D4* (3km NW Rural) *47.57255, 10.19358* **Buchers Alpsee Camping,** Seestrasse 25, 87509 Bühl-am-Alpsee **(08323) 7726; mail@alpsee-camping.de; www.alpsee-camping.de**

12 🛖 €3 ⅋⅋ ♨ ⅋ ∥ 🦋 ⅋ 🗑 ⅍

Fr Immenstadt, W on B308; turn R dir Isny & Missen. In 1.3km turn L sp Bühl & site sp. 2*, Lge, unshd, EHU (16A) €2.50 (poss rev pol); gas; sw nr; Eng spkn; adv bkg acc. *"Lake sm but pleasant; gd mountain walks; friendly welcome; ski lift 3km; excel site, first class facs."* **€45.00** **2019**

INGOLSTADT *4E3* (4.5km E Rural) *48.75416, 11.46277* **Campingpark Am Auwaldsee,** 85053 Ingolstadt **(0841) 9611616; ingolstadt@azur-camping.de; www.azur-camping.de**

12 🛖 €3.50 ⅋⅋ WD ♨ ⅋ ∥ MP ⅋ 🍷 ⅋ ⅋ 🗑 nr ⅍

Exit A9/E45 junc 62 Ingolstadt Süd, foll sp for camp site & Auwaldsee. Lge, pt shd, EHU (10A) inc; gas; sw; 50% statics; bus; adv bkg rec; fishing; boating. *"Wooded site by lake; useful NH nr m'way; modern & clean san facs; gd location; excel facs; gd rest; excel."* **€27.00, G07.** **2018**

INZELL *4F4* (0.8km SW Rural) *47.76722, 12.75341* **Camping Lindlbauer,** Kreuzfeldstraße 44, 83334 Inzell **08665 928 99 88; info@camping-inzell.de; www.camping-inzell.de**

12 🛖 €4 ⅋⅋ (htd) ♨ ⅋ ♨ 🗑 ∥ MP 🦋 ⅋ 🍷 ⅋ ⅋ 🗑 ⅍ 🏊 (covrd, htd)

Fr A8 exit 112 Traunstein-Siegsdorf. Take B306 twds Inzell. Foll sp in vill to campsite. Med, hdstg, mkd, unshd, terr, EHU (16A); twin axles; bus adj; Eng spkn; adv bkg acc; games area; CCI. *"Excel site; beautiful views; friendly, family run site; excel location for walking & cycling."* **€44.70** **2019**

JENA *2E4* (2km NE Rural) *50.93583, 11.60833* **Campingplatz Unter dem Jenzig,** Am Erlkönig 3, 07749 Jena **(03641) 666688; post@camping-jena.com; www.camping-jena.com**

12 🛖 €1 ⅋⅋ ♨ ⅋ 🗑 ∥ MP 🦋 🍷 ⅋ 🗑 nr ⅋ 🗑 nr ⅍

Exit A4/E40 junc 54 to Jena, then B88 for 4m N dir Naumberg. Turn R just outside Jena at campsite sp, R over blue bdge; site nr sports stadium/sw pool on L, sp. Med, unshd, EHU (10A) €2.50; phone; bus 1km; Eng spkn; adv bkg acc. *"Gd san facs in Portakabin; pool adj; sh walk to interesting town; gd cycle paths."* **€17.00** **2019**

JESTETTEN *3C4* (0.8km SW Urban) *47.64802, 8.56648* **Campingplatz & Schwimmbad,** Waldshuterstrasse 13, 79798 Jestetten **(07745) 1220; info@jestetten.de; www.jestetten.de**

⅋⅋ (htd) WD ♨ ⅋ 🗑 ∥ 🦋 ⅋ ⅋ 🗑 nr ⅋ 🗑 nr ⅍ 🏊 (htd)

Site in town on B27 main rd, sp. Sm, pt shd, pt sl, EHU (10A) metered; bus at gate, train 500m; Eng spkn; adv bkg acc. *"Gd for walk or train Rhine Falls & Switzerland; shwr token inc; friendly; site in Schwimmbad grnds."* **€22.00, Mid May-Mid Sep.** **2015**

For a guide to symbols see the fold out on the rear cover

KALKAR *1A3* (5km N Rural) *51.76100, 6.28483*
Freitzeitpark Wisseler See, Zum Wisseler-See 15,
47546 Kalkar-Wissel **(02824) 96310; info@wisseler-see.de; www.wisseler-see.de**

🕁 🛉 €3 🛉🛉 (htd) 🆚 ♨ ⚿ 🖭 🥾 🛝 🛶 🏊

Fr A3 take junc 4 onto B67 dir Kalkar & Wissel.
Fr Kleve take B57 SE for 8km twd Kalkar, E to Wissel
& foll camp sp. V lge, mkd, hdg, pt shd, serviced
pitches; EHU (16A) inc; 75% statics; Eng spkn; adv bkg
rec; bike hire; games area; watersports; tennis.
*"Commercialised & regimented but conv NH Rotterdam
ferry; gd facs; gd for children & teenagers."*
€25.00 **2016**

KAMENZ *2G4* (7km NE Rural) *51.30465, 14.15272*
Campingplatz Deutschbaselitz, Grossteichstrasse 30,
01917 Kamenz **(03578) 301489; info@campingplatz-deutschbaselitz.com; www.campingplatz-deutsch-baselitz.com**

🛉 🛉🛉 (htd) 🆚 ♨ ⚿ 🖭 🥾 🦋 🛝 🏊

Fr Kamenz N on rd S95 dir Wittichenau; at Schiedel
turn R twd lake, site sp. 3*, Med, pt shd, EHU (16A)
€3; bbq; cooking facs; sw; 10% statics; adv bkg acc;
bike hire; games area; watersports; games rm; CKE.
€23.00, 1 Mar-31 Oct. **2016**

> ## "We must tell the Club about that great site we found"
>
> Get your site reports in by mid-August and we'll
> do our best to get your updates into the next
> edition.

KARLSHAGEN *2G1* (2km E Coastal) *54.11769,
13.84477* **Dünencamp,** Zeltplatzstraße; 17449
Ostseebad; Karlshagen 038371 20291; **camping@
karlshagen.de; www.duenencamp.de**

🕁 🛉 €4 🛉🛉 (htd) 🆚 ♨ ⚿ 🖭 🦋 🛝 🏊 adj

Site sp fr Karlshagen along Zeltplatzstrasse.
Lge, mkd, shd, pt sl, EHU (16A) €2 (or metered);
phone; Eng spkn. *"Site has direct access to long clean
sandy beach; long mains lead may be needed for
some pitches; conv for visiting Peenemünde; gd site."*
€26.00 **2016**

KARLSRUHE *3C3* (7km E Rural) *49.00788, 8.48303*
Azur Campingpark Turmbergblick, Tiengenerstrasse
40, 76227 Karlsruhe-Durlach **(0721) 497236;
karlsruhe@azur-camping.de; www.azur-camping.de**

🛉 €3.50 🛉🛉 (htd) 🆚 ♨ ⚿ 🖭 🥾 🖭 ⚓ 🛝 🏊

Exit A5/E35 junc 44 dir Durlach/Grötzingen onto
B10 & foll sp to site 3km. Lge, mkd, pt shd, EHU (10A)
€3 (long lead poss req); gas; 20% statics; Eng spkn; adv
bkg acc; ccard acc; tennis; CKE. *"NH conv to a'bahn;
adequate, clean san facs; clsd 1230-1400; expensive
for average site; Karlsruhe worth a visit."*
€32.00, 1 Apr-31 Oct. **2016**

KASSEL *1D4* (22km S Rural) *51.17757, 9.47781*
Camping Fuldaschleife, zum Bruch 6, 34302
Guxhagen-Büchenwerra **(0566) 5961044; info@
fuldaschleife.de; www.fuldaschleife.de**

🛉 €1.50 🛉🛉 (htd) 🆚 ♨ ⚿ 🖭 🥾 🖭 ⚓ 🛝 nr 🛶 🏊

Exit A7 at J81 twrds Guxhagen. Foll sp. Site in 4km.
4*, Sm, mkd, pt shd, bbq; twin axles; 60% statics;
bus adj; Eng spkn; adv bkg acc; ccard acc; games
area; CKE. *"Pleasant site adj rv; helpful staff; boating,
canoeing & cycling rtes fr site; Hann Munden &
Gottingen worth visiting; conv for N, S, E & W Germany;
excel."* **€22.00, 1 Mar-31 Oct.** **2016**

KASTELLAUN *3B2* (0.8km SE Rural) *50.06846,
7.45382* **Burgstadt Camping Park,** Südstrasse 34,
56288 Kastellaun **(06762) 40800; info@burgstadt.de;
www.burgstadt.de**

🕁 🛉 €2 🛉🛉 (htd) 🆚 ♨ ⚿ 🖭 🥾 🦋 🛝 🏊 ⚓ 🛝

Exit A61 junc 42 dir Emmelshausen onto L206/L213
for 1.2km; turn L onto B327; cont for 13.5km to
Kastellaun. Site adj hotel on B237. Med, mkd, hdstg,
unshd, terr, EHU (16A) metered; bbq; Eng spkn; adv
bkg acc; ccard acc; tennis nr; sauna; solarium; CKE.
*"Lge pitches; clean site; excel, clean san facs; o'night
m'van area; helpful staff; conv touring base; htd covrd
pool 300m; riding & kayaking nrby; fitness & beauty
cent in hotel adj; excel; v peaceful."* **€24.00** **2015**

KEHL *3B3* (3km S Urban) *48.5615, 7.80861* **DCC**
Campingpark Kehl-Strassburg, Rheindammstrasse 1,
77694 Kehl-Kronenhof **(07851) 2603; Campingpark
Kehl@aol.com; www.campingplatz-kehl.de**

🛉 €2 🛉🛉 (htd) 🆚 ♨ ⚿ 🖭 🥾 🖭 ⚓ 🛝 🏊

Fr A5/E35, take exit 54 onto B28 at Appenweier
twd Kehl & foll site sp. 4*, Lge, pt shd, EHU (16A)
metered + conn fee (long lead poss req); gas;
15% statics; bus 1km; Eng spkn; adv bkg acc; ccard
acc; CKE. *"Peaceful site adj Rv Rhine; excel rest &
modern san facs; sm pitches; pleasant rv walk & cycle
paths to town; sw pool adj; barrier clsd 1300-1500."*
€25.00, 15 Mar-31 Oct. **2019**

KELBRA *2E4* (2km W Rural) *51.42551, 11.00307*
Seecamping Kelbra, Langestrasse 150, 06537 Kelbra
(034651) 45290; info@seecampingkelbra.de

🕁 🛉 €2 🛉🛉 (htd) 🆚 ♨ ⚿ 🖭 🦋 🛝 🏊 ⚓ 🛝

🏊 sand 1km

Exit A38 at Berga (bet junc 12 & 14); on app to town
turn L at traff lts onto B85 to Kelbra; go thro
chicane in vill, then R onto L234/L1040 dir
Sonderhausen; site sp. L234 is Langestrasse.
Lge, unshd, pt sl, EHU (16A) €2; bbq (elec, gas); sw nr;
TV; phone; bus adj; Eng spkn; adv bkg acc; games area;
CKE. *"Gd touring base & walking area; boat hire on site;
vg; 2 toilet blocks now (2015); NH outside main gates."*
€18.50 **2015**

GERMANY

KEMPTEN (ALLGAU) *3D4* (25km E Rural) *47.80283, 10.55377* **Camping Platz Elbsee,** Am Elbsee 3, 87648 Aitrang 08 34 32 48; info@elbsee.de; www.elbsee.de

[12] 🕿 €4.50 ♦♦♦(htd) �🅆 🏊 ♨ ♿ 🖳 ∥ ᴹᴾ 🦋 📶 ⑭ 🛒 🛒 ⚠ ✎

S on A7. Take J134 dir Marktobedorf on B12. Take exit twd Unterthingau on OAL10. Turn L on OAL3, cont onto OAL 5. Turn R on Am Elbsee. Foll sp. 5*, Lge, hdg, mkd, hdstg, pt shd, EHU (16A); bbq; cooking facs; twin axles; bus 0.75km; Eng spkn; adv bkg acc; ccard acc; games rm; CCI. *"Excel site; gd base; lake adj; many local historical places & amazing architecture; camp has much to offer - peace & quiet, spa art, yoga."* **€29.70**   2019

KINDING *4E3* (5km E Rural) *49.00328, 11.45200* **Camping Kratzmühle,** Mühlweg 2, 85125 Kinding-Pfraundorf (08461) 64170; info@kratzmuehle.de; www.kratzmuehle.de

[12] 🕿 €2 ♦♦♦ ⅏ 🏊 ♨ ♿ 🖳 ∥ ᴹᴾ 🦋 📶 ⑭ 🛒 ⚠

Exit A9/E45 junc 58, dir Beilngries. Site sp. 4*, Lge, pt shd, serviced pitches; EHU (16A) €2.50; gas; cooking facs; sw nr; red long stay; 40% statics; adv bkg acc; ccard acc; games area; sauna; CKE. *"Beautiful situation; conv NH for a'bahn; ideal boating & bathing, public access to lake; clsd 1300-1500; poss mosquito prob; helpful staff."* **€26.00**   2018

KIRCHHEIM *1D4* (5km SW Rural) *50.81435, 9.51805* **Camping Seepark,** Reimboldshäuserstraße, 36275 Kirchheim (06628) 1525; info@campseepark.de; www.campseepark.de

[12] 🕿 €2 ♦♦♦(htd) ⅏ 🏊 ♨ ♿ 🖳 ∥ ᴹᴾ 🦋 🍴 ⑭ 🛒 ⚠ ✎
🛟 (covrd)

Exit A7 at Kirchheim junc 87, site clearly sp. 5*, Lge, mkd, pt shd, pt sl, terr, EHU (16A) €3 metered; gas; sw; red long stay; 50% statics; phone; bus 500m; adv bkg acc; ccard acc; sauna; golf 3km; games area; tennis; CKE. *"Gd walking; helpful owner; o'night m'vans area; excel site - leisure facs pt of lge hotel complex; NH only."* **€26.00**   2017

KIRKEL *3B3* (1km S Urban) *49.28175, 7.22860* **Caravanplatz Mühlenweiher,** Unnerweg 5c, 66459 Kirkel-Neuhäusel (06849) 1810555; info@camping-kirkel.de; www.caravanplatz-kirkel.de

[12] 🕿 €1.15 ♦♦♦(htd) ⅏ 🏊 ♨ ♿ 🖳 ∥ 📶 🍴 ⑭ 🛒nr

Fr A6 junc 7 & fr A8 junc 28, take dir into town & foll sp for 'schwimmbad'. Site on L past pool, well sp. 3*, Med, hdstg, mkd, pt shd, EHU (10A) €3 or metered + conn fee (poss rev pol); gas; TV (pitch); 60% statics; phone; CKE. *"Gd welcome; excel area for cycling; noise fr pool & church bells all night; pool adj; site/office clsd 1230-1500."* **€15.00**   2016

KOBLENZ *3B2* (4km NE Urban) *50.36611, 7.60361* **Camping Rhein-Mosel,** Schartwiesenweg 6, 56070 Koblenz-Lützel (0261) 82719; info@camping-rhein-mosel.de; www.camping-rhein-mosel.de

🕿 ♦♦♦ ⅏ ♿ 🖳 ∥ ᴹᴾ 🍴 ⑭ 🛒 🛒

Fr Koblenz heading N on B9 turn off dual c'way at sp for Neuendorf just bef Mosel rv bdge; foll sp to Neuendorf vill. Or heading S on B9 exit dual c'way at camping sp (2nd sp) bef Koblenz; fr Koblenz cent foll sp for 'Altstadt' until Baldwinbrücke (bdge); N over bdge instead of foll sp along S bank of Rv Mosel; R after bdge, then foll sp; site on N side of junc Rhine/Mosel rvs. 2*, Lge, hdstg, pt shd, pt sl, EHU (6-16A) €2.05 or metered (long lead poss req); cooking facs; Eng spkn; adv bkg rec; CKE. *"Pleasant, informal site in beautiful location; muddy in wet; staff helpful; no veh acc after 2200; adj ferry to city & easy cycle rte; mkt Sat; sep dog shwrs; flea mkt Sun; 'Rhine in Flames' fireworks 2nd Sat in Aug - watch fr site; MH stopover called Knaus Campingpark just outside main gates, basic price €12.50, both sites under same owner."* **€33.00, 1 May-20 Oct.**   2016

KOBLENZ *3B2* (12km SW Urban) *50.30972, 7.50166* **Campinginsel Winningen (previously Campingplatz Ziehfurt),** Inselweg 10, 56333 Winningen (02606) 357 or 1800; ferieninsel-winningen@t-online.de; www.mosel-camping.com

🕿 €3 ♦♦♦ ⅏ 🏊 🖳 ∥ ᴹᴾ ⑭ 🛒 ⚠

Exit A61/E31 junc 38 to Winningen. In Winningen turn R twds Cochem B416, then L at sw pool. In approx 100m turn R and then in 700m turn L over bdge to site recep. Lge, pt shd, EHU (16A) €2.50; 50% statics; Eng spkn. *"Cent of wine-growing country; boat trips avail fr Koblenz; cycle rtes; scenic area; poss flooding if v high water; pool 300m; lively site when busy; gd, modern san facs up steep steps but poss stretched when busy; excel rest; excel site."* **€25.00, 1 May-1 Oct.**   2017

KOBLENZ *3B2* (8km SW Rural) *50.33194, 7.55277* **Camping Gülser Moselbogen,** Am Gülser Moselbogen 20, 56072 Koblenz-Güls (0261) 44474; info@mosel bogen.de; www.moselbogen.de

[12] 🕿 €4 ♦♦♦(htd) ⅏ 🏊 ♨ ♿ 🖳 ∥ ᴹᴾ ⑭nr 🛒nr ⚠

Fr A61/E31 exit 38 dir Koblenz/Metternich. After 400m turn R at rndabt dir Winningen. Stay on this rd to T-junc in Winningen, turn L dir Koblenz-Güls, site sp on R in 3km. 4*, Med, hdg, mkd, pt shd, EHU (16A) €1.50 + conn fee; gas; TV (pitch); 50% statics; phone; Eng spkn; adv bkg acc; ccard acc; bike hire; CKE. *"High quality, high-tech san facs; no vehicles 1200-1400; poss subject to flooding; excel."* **€28.00**   2019

KOLN *1B4* (4km NE Urban) *50.96305, 6.98361*
Reisemobilhafen Köln, An der Schanz, 50735 Köln
017 84674591 (mob); info@reisemobilhafen-koeln.de
🔢 🐕 ✏ MP Ⓣ nr Ⓦ nr ⛟ nr

Fr A1 Köln ring rd exit junc 100 dir Köln 'Zentrum'
until reach rv. Turn L & foll sp to site. M'vans only.
Sm, mkd, hdstg, EHU (10A) €1 for 12 hrs; own san req;
bus, train nr. *"Adj Rv Rhine; must have change for elec*
& water (metered) - €0.50, parking (€10 note) etc; easy
access to city cent; site is unmanned; cycle rte to city,
zoo & botanic gdns." **€10.00**   **2017**

KOLN *1B4* (8km SE Rural) *50.8909, 7.02306*
Campingplatz Berger, Uferstrasse 71, 50996 Köln-
Rodenkirchen (0221) 9355240; camping.berger@t-
online.de; www.camping-berger-koeln.de
🔢 🐕 €1 ♨(htd) Ⓦ ⛺ 🚿 ♿ ✏ MP 🐩 Ⓣ Ⓦ ⛟ ⟋

Fr A4 turn S onto A555 at Köln-Sud exit 12. Leave
A555 at Rodenkirchen exit 3. At 1st junc foll site
sp to R. Fr A3 Frankfurt/Köln a'bahn, take A4 twd
Aachen (Köln ring rd); exit at Köln Sud; foll sp
Bayenthal; at lge rndabt turn R sp Rheinufer & R
again at camp sp, under a'bahn. App rd narr & lined
with parked cars. Lge, pt shd, EHU (4-10A) €1.50; gas;
cooking facs; red long stay; 80% statics; phone; bus
500m; Eng spkn; ccard acc; bike hire; CKE. *"Pleasant,*
popular, wooded site on banks of Rhine; rvside pitches
best; excel rest; helpful staff; gd dog walking; cycle
path to city cent; conv cathedral, zoo & museums;
some noise fr Rhine barges; don't arr early eve at w/end
as narr app rd v busy; pitches poss muddy after rain;
san facs up steps - poss clsd 2300-0600; gd site; vg
facs; need car/bike to get around." **€28.00**   **2018**

KOLN *1B4* (6km S Urban) *50.90263, 6.99070*
Campingplatz der Stadt Köln, Weidenweg 35, 51105
Köln-Poll (0221) 831966; info@camping-koeln.de;
www.camping-koeln.de
🐕 €2.50 ♨ ⛺ 🚿 ♿ ✏ MP Ⓦ nr ⛟

Exit fr A4 (E40) at junc 13 for Köln-Poll-Porz at E
end of bdge over Rv Rhine, 3km S of city. At end of
slip rd, turn L twd Poll & Köln. Cont about 1000m
turn L at sp just bef level x-ing, then foll site sp.
Narr lane to ent. Lge, pt shd, EHU (10A) €3.50 (some
rev pol & long lead poss req); gas; cooking facs; phone;
Eng spkn; CKE. *"Tram to city over rv bdge; rural site in*
urban setting on bank of Rv Rhine & subject to flooding;
clsd 1230-1430; gd undercover cooking facs; gd
refurbished san facs on 1st floor; friendly site; v busy at
w/end; rvside cycle track to city; cycle theft a problem
(store in caged kitchen o'night); friendly owner; site in
green zone." **€29.40, 1 Apr-15 Oct.**   **2016**

KONIGSSEE *4G4* (1km N Rural) *47.5992, 12.98933*
Camping Mühlleiten, Königsseerstrasse 70, 83471
Königssee (08652) 4584; info@muehlleiten.eu;
www.camping-muehlleiten.de
🔢 🐕 €2.50 ♟♟ Ⓦ ⛺ 🚿 ✏ MP 🐩 Ⓣ Ⓦ nr ⛟ ⛟ ✂ 🌲 1km

On on R of B20 Berchtesgaden-Königssee. 3*, Med,
unshd, EHU (16A) €3 or metered; gas; golf 6km; CKE.
"Beautiful area; friendly staff; excel san facs; excel site
with mixed MH's, c'van and camping; walking trails;
free/red bus fares with visitor card; ski lift 500m; off
clsd 1200-1500 daily." **€30.00**   **2016**

KONIGSSEE *4G4* (2km N Rural) *47.59445, 12.98583*
Camping Grafenlehen, Königsseer Fussweg 71, 83471
Königssee (08652) 6554488; camping-grafenlehen@
t-online.de; www.camping-grafenlehen.de
🐕 €2 ♟♟(htd) Ⓦ ⛺ 🚿 ♿ ✏ 🐩 ✂ ⟋

On B20 fr Berchtesgaden 5km to Königssee.
Where car park with traff lts is ahead, turn R sp
Schönau, site on R. Lge, pt shd, terr, EHU (16A)
metered; 10% statics; site clsd Nov to mid-Dec;
CKE. *"Pleasant site; spectacular views; gd san facs;*
superb walking; cycle path by rv; gd value rest; 30
mins drive Salzburg Park & Ride; conv Berchtesgaden."
€31.00, 1 Jan-1 Nov & 15 Dec-31 Dec.   **2015**

KONIGSTEIN *2G4* (1km E Rural) *50.92222, 14.08833*
Camping Königstein, Schandauerstrasse 25e,
01824 Königstein (035021) 68224; info@camping-
koenigstein.de; www.camping-koenigstein.de
🐕 €3 ♟♟ ⛺ 🚿 ♿ ✏ MP Ⓦ ⛟ nr ⟋

Foll B172 SE fr Dresden/Pirna. Site 500m past
Königstein rlwy stn. Turn L over rlwy x-ing & R
into site ent on Rv Elbe. 3*, Med, unshd, pt sl, EHU
(10-16A) €2.60; gas; red long stay; 15% statics; adv
bkg acc; sep car park. *"Gd san facs; lovely location*
nr national parks & Czech border; on Elbe cycle path;
frequent trains to Dresden; boat trips; gates clsd 1300-
1500; dogs not acc Jul/Aug; site updated to hg std
(2018)." **€24.00, 25 Mar-31 Oct.**   **2018**

KONSTANZ *3D4* (13km N Rural) *47.74596, 9.14701*
Camping Klausenhorn, Hornwiesenstrasse, 78465
Dingelsdorf (07533) 6372; info@camping-
klausenhorn.de; www.camping-klausenhorn.de
♟♟(htd) Ⓦ ⛺ 🚿 ♿ ✏ 🐩 Ⓣ Ⓦ nr ⛟ ⟋ ✂

Site sp N of Dingelsdorf on lakeside. 4*, Lge, hdstg,
mkd, pt shd, EHU (10A) inc; bbq; 50% statics; bus
500m; Eng spkn; adv bkg acc; ccard acc; boating;
games area; sep car park; CKE. *"Excel site; lake adj;*
1st class san facs; v helpful recep; free bus svrs fr site."
€30.00, 27 Mar-5 Oct.   **2016**

KONSTANZ *3D4* (12km W Rural) *47.69871, 9.04603*
Camping Sandseele, Bradlengasse 24, 78479
Niederzell **(07534) 7384; info@sandseele.de;**
www.sandseele.de

🛉🛉 ⓦⓓ ♨ ⚫ 🖥 ∥ 🅟 Ⓗ 🗑 🅩 /ⱉ\

**Clearly sp off B33 Konstanz-Radolfzell rd. Foll sp
on island & sm multiple sp.** Lge, pt shd, EHU (16A)
€3.50; gas; sw; 30% statics; watersports. *"Insect
repellent rec, excel san facs; sep car park high ssn;
excel walking & cycling all over island; poor layout."*
€33.00, 18 Mar-9 Oct. **2016**

KRANICHFELD *2E4* (4km NW Rural) *50.87216,
11.17843* **Campingplatz Stausee Hohenfelden,**
99448 Hohenfelden **(036450) 42081; info@stausse-
hohenfelden.de; www.stausee-hohenfelden.de**

12 🛉 €2.50 🛉🛉 ⓦⓓ ♨ ⚫ 🖥 ∥ 🅟 Ⓨ 🅩 /ⱉ\

**Fr A4/E40 take exit 47a S twd Kranichfeld. Site
clearly sp by lake along rough rd.** 4*, V lge, mkd, pt
shd, pt sl, terr, EHU (10A) €4.50; bbq; cooking facs; sw;
red long stay; 50% statics; adv bkg acc; ccard acc; bike
hire; boating; lake adj; CKE. *"Woodland, lakeside walks;
gd."* **€24.00** **2019**

KRESSBRONN AM BODENSEE *3D4* (9km NE Rural)
47.63395, 9.6477 **Gutshof-Camping,** Badhütten 1,
88069 Laimnau **(07543) 96330; gutshof.camping@
t-online.de; www.gutshof-camping.de**

🛉 €2 🛉🛉 ⓦⓓ ♨ ⚫ ♨ 🖥 ∥ 🅟 🦋 Ⓨ Ⓗ 🗑 🅩 /ⱉ\ ⌨ 🏊

**Fr Kressbronn take B467 to Tettnang & Ravensburg.
In 3km immed after x-ing Rv Argen turn R & site
sp for approx 3km. Take care on final app rd. Dark,
steep and twisty, great care needed.** 4*, V lge, mkd,
hdg, pt shd, serviced pitches; EHU (16A) metered;
gas; red long stay; 40% statics; adv bkg acc; CKE. *"Sep
area for naturists; gd facs; v rural site; clean, quiet &
pleasant; excel."* **€29.00, 7 Apr-3 Oct, G15.** **2016**

KRESSBRONN AM BODENSEE *3D4* (2km SW Rural)
47.58718, 9.58281 **Campingplatz Irisweise,** Tunau 16,
88079 Kressbronn **(07543) 8010; info@campingplatz-
irisweise.de; www.campingplatz-irisweise.de**

🛉 €2.50 🛉🛉 (htd) ⓦⓓ ♨ ⚫ ♨ 🖥 ∥ 🅟 🦋 ⓨ Ⓨ Ⓗ 🅩 /ⱉ\

**Fr E or W take exit off B31 bypass for Kressbronn,
site well sp.** 4*, Lge, hdg, mkd, pt shd, EHU (10A)
metered + conn fee; gas; bbq; sw nr; 10% statics;
phone; Eng spkn; watersports; sailing; CKE. *"Steamer
trips on lake; no car access 2100-0700, park outside
site; sep naturist beach; excel san facs but some dist fr
touring pitches; gd."* **€28.00, 22 Mar-21 Oct.** **2019**

KRUMBACH *4E4* (7km SW Rural) *48.22720, 10.29280*
See Camping Günztal, Oberrieder Weiherstrasse 5,
86488 Breitenthal **(08282) 881870; info@see-
camping-guenztal.de; www.see-camping-guenztal.de**

🛉 €2 🛉🛉 (htd) ⓦⓓ ♨ ⚫ ♨ 🖥 ∥ 🅟 🦋 ⓨ Ⓨ Ⓗnr 🗑 🅩nr /ⱉ\

**W fr Krumbach on rd 2018, in Breitenthal turn S twd
Oberried & Oberrieder Weiher, site sp on lakeside.**
Med, hdstg, mkd, pt shd, EHU (10A) inc; bbq; sw; TV;
30% statics; adv bkg acc; games area; watersports;
fishing. **€21.00, 15 Apr-30 Oct.** **2016**

KULMBACH *4E2* (11km NE Rural) *50.16050,
11.51605* **Campingplatz Stadtsteinach,** Badstrasse 5,
95346 Stadtsteinach **(09225) 800394; info@camping
platz-stadtsteinach.de; www.campingplatz-stadt
steinach.de**

🛉 €2 🛉🛉 (htd) ⓦⓓ ♨ ⚫ ♨ 🖥 ∥ 🅟 🦋 ⓨ Ⓨ Ⓗ 🗑 🅩nr /ⱉ\
🏊 (htd) 🛁

**Fr Kulmbach take B289 to Untersteinach (8km);
turn L to Stadtsteinach; turn R at camping sp &
foll rd for 1km. Site also sp fr N side of town on
B303. Or fr A9/E51 exit junc 39 onto B303 NW
to Stadtsteinach.** 4*, Med, mkd, pt shd, pt sl, EHU
(6-16A) €2.50; bbq (charcoal, gas); sw; 60% statics;
Eng spkn; adv bkg acc; ccard acc; rv fishing; bike
hire; tennis; CKE. *"Excel site in beautiful countryside;
htd pool adj; excel, modern facs; highly rec."*
€24.00, 1 Mar-1 Nov. **2019**

LAHNSTEIN *3B2* (6km SE Urban) *50.27393, 7.64098*
Campingplatz Uferwiese, Am Campingplatz 1,
56338 Braubach **(02627) 8762; uferwiese@web.de;
www.campingplatz-braubach.de**

🛉 €1 🛉🛉 ⓦⓓ ♨ ⚫ 🖥 ∥ 🅟 ⓨ Ⓨ Ⓗnr 🗑 🅩nr

**Take B42 S twd Rüdesheim. Site behind hotel opp
church.** Med, shd, EHU (16A) €2 (poss rev pol);
50% statics; bus; CKE. *"Scenic on Rv Rhine; poss
flooding after heavy rain; gd san facs; no shd on rvside
pitches."* **€21.50, 15 Apr-25 Oct.** **2015**

"I need an on-site restaurant"

We do our best to make sure site information
is correct, but it is always best to check any
must-have facilities are still available or will
be open during your visit.

LAHR (SCHWARZWALD) *3B3* (9km SE Rural)
48.29999, 7.94395 **Ferienparadies Schwarzwälder
Hof,** Tretenhofstrasse 76, 77960 Seelbach **(07823)
960950; info@spacamping.de; www.campingplatz-
schwarzwaelder-hof.de**

12 🛉 €3.50 🛉🛉 ⓦⓓ ♨ ⚫ ♨ 🖥 ∥ 🅟 🦋 Ⓨ Ⓗ 🅩 /ⱉ\

**Fr A5 take exit 56 to Lahr. In 5km turn R twd
Seelbach & Schuttertal. Thro town & site on S o'skts
of Seelbach just after town boundary.** 5*, Med, mkd,
hdstg, pt shd, pt sl, terr, serviced pitches; EHU (10A)
metered + conn fee; gas; 10% statics; Eng spkn; adv
bkg req; ccard acc; CKE. *"Vg touring base; o'night
m'vans area; well-laid out pitches & excel facs; many
gd mkd walks; lake adj; htd pool adj; gd programme of
events in Seelbach; within easy reach of Strasbourg."*
€37.00 **2015**

LAICHINGEN *3D3* (6km SE Rural) *48.47560, 9.7458*
Camping & Freizeitzentrum Heidehof, Heidehof
strasse 50, 89150 Laichingen-Machtolsheim **(07333)**
6408; info@heidenhof.info; www.camping-
heidehof.de

12 ♂♥ ⊞ ▲ ♿ ☐ ✗ ⌦ ⑪ 🎮 ⚠ 🦽(htd)

**Exit A8 junc 61 dir Merklingen. At T-junc turn R sp
Laichingen. In 3km site sp to L.** 4*, V lge, hdg, mkd,
hdstg, pt shd, pt sl, EHU (10-16A) €2 or metered;
gas; red long stay; 95% statics; adv bkg acc; bike hire;
sauna; CKE. *"Blaubeuren Abbey & Blautopf (blue pool
of glacial origin) worth visit; sep area for o'nighters
immed bef main camp ent - poss unrel when wet; hdstg
pitches sm & sl; vg rest; gd NH; clean modern facs; lack
of elec boxes; no water taps excep at facs; whole site
on uneven sl; arr early to get nr elec."* **€27.50**   **2019**

"Satellite navigation makes touring much easier"

Remember most sat navs don't know if you're
towing or in a larger vehicle – always use yours
alongside maps and site directions.

LANDSBERG AM LECH *4E4* (4km SE Rural) *48.03195,
10.88526* **DCC Campingpark Romantik am Lech,**
Pössinger Au 1, 86899 Landsberg-am-Lech **(08191)**
47505; campingparkgmbh@aol.com; www.camping
platz-landsberg.de

12 ♂♥ €1 ♂♥ ⊞ ▲ ♿ ☐ ✗ ⌦ 🦋 Ⴥ ⑪nr ⫯ 🎮 ⚠

**Not rec to tow thro Landsberg. If app fr S, get onto
rd fr Weilheim & foll sp on app to Landsberg.
Fr other dir, exit junc 26 fr a'bahn A96 Landsberg
Ost, then app town via Muchenstrasse. Foll sp dir
Weilheim, after 400m turn R & foll site sp.** 4*, Lge,
mkd, hdg, pt shd, pt sl, EHU (16A) metered (some
rev pol); gas; 50% statics; Eng spkn; adv bkg acc;
tennis; bike hire; CKE. *"V pleasant site; excel, clean
facs; nature reserve on 2 sides; gd walking & cycling;
attractive old town; pool 3km; site clsd 1300-1500 &
2200-0700."* **€19.00**   **2015**

LANDSHUT *4F3* (3km NE Urban) *48.55455, 12.1795*
Camping Landshut, Breslauerstrasse 122, 84028
Landshut **(0871)** 53366; www.landshut.de

♂♥ €1.50 ♂♥ ⊞ ▲ ♿ ☐ ✗ ⌦ 🦋 Ⴥ ⑪nr ⫯ 🎮

**Fr A92/E53 exit junc 14 onto B299 dir Landshut
N. After approx 5km turn L at int'l camping sp &
foll site sp.** 2*, Med, pt shd, EHU (16A) €2.50; bbq;
10% statics; CKE. *"Well-run, friendly site; gd san facs;
htd pool 3km; beautiful medieval town & castle - easy
cycle rte."* **€17.00, 1 Apr-30 Sep.**   **2016**

LECHBRUCK *4E4* (3km NE Rural) *47.71169, 10.81872*
Via Claudia Camping, Via Claudia 6, 86983 Lechbruck
(08862) 8426; info@camping-lechbruck.de;
www.via-claudia-camping.de

12 ♂♥ €3.50 ♂♥ ⊞ ▲ ♿ ☐ ✗ ⌦ 🦋 ⑪ Ⴤ ☂ ⑪ 🎮 ⚠ ✎

**A7 exit 138 Nesselwang. Sp Seeg, foll Oa1 round
Seeg to Roßhaupten. Then B16 sp Markt-Oberdorf.
1st exit to Lechbruck. Thro Lechbruch to site on R
by lake.** 4*, Lge, hdstg, mkd, pt shd, terr, EHU (10-
16A) €2.65; gas; bbq; sw; twin axles; red long stay;
TV; 50% statics; Eng spkn; adv bkg acc; ccard acc;
watersports; games rm; CKE. *"Pleasant, peaceful,
lakeside site; o'night m'van area; fac to a high standard;
pool 500m; mini golf; gd welcome; v helpful; volleyball;
archery; cont investment in site fr new owners; bus
1.5km; watersports; mountain tours; hiking; cycle trails;
model aircraft; spa; rafting; traditional craft demos;
skiing; local historic buildings; excel."* **€34.00**   **2018**

LEER (OSTFRIESLAND) *1B2* (7km W Rural) *53.22416,
7.41891* **Camping Ems-Marina Bingum,** Marinastrasse
14-16, 26789 Leer-Bingum **(0491)** 64447; into-
camping-bingum@t-online.de; www.ems-marina-
bingum.de

12 ♂♥ €3.50 ♂♥ ⊞ ▲ ♿ ☐ ✗ ⌦ 🦋 ⑪ ⫯ 🎮nr ⚠

**Leave A32/E12 junc 12; site 500m S of Bingum; well
sp.** Lge, pt shd, EHU (16A) €2.50 or metered; gas; red
long stay; 65% statics; adv bkg acc; bike hire; CKE.
"Gate clsd 1230-1500." **€23.00**   **2016**

LEIPHEIM *3D3* (3.5km NNW Rural) *48.46566, 10.2035*
Camping Schwarzfelder Hof, Schwarzfelderweg 3,
Riedheim, 89340 Leipheim **(08221)** 72628; info@
schwarzfelder-hof.de; www.schwarzfelder-hof.de

12 ♂♥ €3.90 ♂♥(htd) ⊞ ▲ ☐ ✗ ⌦ 🦋 ⑪ ⑪nr ⫯ 🎮nr ⚠

**Fr A8 exit junc 66 Leipheim onto B10. In Leipheim
foll sp Langenau & Riedheim, site sp. Do not confuse
with Laupheim 25km S of Ulm on B30.** Sm, hdstg,
pt shd, serviced pitches; EHU (16A) €2.50; bbq;
50% statics; train 1km; Eng spkn. *"Peaceful, delightful,
farm-based site on site of old quarry; ideal for children
& adults; welcoming, helpful owner; lge pitches; vg san
facs but ltd; farm animals & riding for children; conv
Ulm; recep open 0800-1000 & 1730-2000; poss noisy
youth groups; conv NH for m'way."* **€25.50**   **2019**

LEIPZIG *2F4* (7km NW Urban) *51.37030, 12.31375*
Campingplatz Auensee, Gustav-Esche Strasse 5,
04159 Leipzig **(0341)** 4651600; leipzig@knauscamp.
de; www.camping-auensee.de

12 ♂♥ €2 ♂♥(htd) ⊞ ▲ ♿ ☐ ✗ ⌦ 🎮 ⫯ 🎮nr ⚠

**Fr A9/E51 exit junc 16 onto B6 two Leipzig. In
Leipzig-Wahren turn R at 'Rathaus' sp Leutzsch
(camping symbol), site on R in 1.5km, sp.** 4*, Lge,
hdstg, mkd, pt shd, EHU (16A) €3; bbq; cooking facs;
TV; phone; bus; Eng spkn; adv bkg acc; ccard acc; CKE.
*"Roomy, well-run, clean site; plentiful, excel, modern
san facs; gd size pitches; friendly, helpful staff; Lake
Auensee 500m; tram 1.5km; 10 mins walk to tram for
city cent or bus stop at site ent; excel."* **€29.00**   **2018**

LEMGO *1C3* (0.6km E Urban) *52.02503, 8.90874*
Campingpark Lemgo, Regenstorstrasse 10, 32657
Lemgo (05261) 14858; info@camping-lemgo.de;
www.camping-lemgo.de

12 ♻ €2 �100 ♨ 🏊 🚿 🍴 ⏰ nr 🛒 nr ⚏

**Exit A2 junc 28 onto L712N to Lemgo; at traff lts
turn L following L712; at rndbt take Bismarckstrasse
exit; at traff lts turn R into Regenstorstrasse. Site sp.**
3*, Med, pt shd, EHU (6A) metered + conn fee;
25% statics; adv bkg rec. *"Pleasant site in cent of
lovely medieval town; o'night m'vans area; pool 200m;
sm, modern, clean san facs."* **€26.60**   2019

LIETZOW *2G1* (0.2km N Coastal) *54.48358, 13.50846*
Störtebecker Camp, Gästehaus Lietzow, Waldstraße
59a, 18528 Lietzow 038302 2166; info@lietzow.net;
www.lietzow.net

♻ €2.50 �100 ♨ 🏊 🚿 🍴 ▽ ⏰ 🛒 ⚏ 🏊250m

**On rd 96, E22 fr Stralsund to ferry harbour at
Sassnitz; when you arr at Lietzow site sp 'Gästehaus
Lietzow' on RH side of rd; sh, steep incline fr main rd.**
Med, hdg, pt shd, EHU inc; gas; adv bkg rec; CKE.
*"Pleasant, beautifully kept sm site in woodland; cent
for the island, sightseeing & useful stopover nr ferry
point; MV waste; many mkd cycle rtes around island;
charming owners; excel san facs; sh walk to delightful
coast."* **€33.50, 29 Mar-15 Oct.**   2015

LIMBURG AN DER LAHN *3C2* (2km SSW Urban)
50.38916, 8.07333 **Lahn Camping,** Schleusenweg 16,
65549 Limburg-an-der-Lahn (06431) 22610; info@
lahncamping.de; www.lahncamping.de

♻ €1.50 �100 ♨ 🏊 🚿 🍴 ▽ ⏰ 🛒 ⚏

**Exit A3/E35 junc 42 Limburg Nord, site sp. By Rv
Lahn in town, easy access.** 3*, Lge, pt shd, EHU (6A)
€2.60 (long lead poss req); gas; sw; 20% statics; bus;
Eng spkn; fishing; CKE. *"Busy, well-organised site;
delightful location by rv; sm pitches - some poss diff to
manoeuvre; gd views; friendly staff; poss flooding in
wet weather; htd pool 100m; sh walk to interesting
town; gates clsd 1300-1500; useful NH."*
€19.90, 28 Mar-27 Oct.   2019

LIMBURG AN DER LAHN *3C2* (9km SW Rural)
50.38151, 8.00046 **Camping Oranienstein,**
Strandbadweg, 65582 Diez (06432) 2122; info@
camping-diez.de; www.camping-diez.de

♻ ♨ ♻ ⏰ 🏊 🚿 🍴 ▽ ⏰ 🛒 ⚏ ⛵

**In Diez on L bank of Lahn. Exit A3 junc 41 Diez
or junc 43 Limburg-Süd. Site sp 1km bef Diez,
8km fr a'bahn.** 3*, Lge, pt shd, EHU (6A) inc; gas;
60% statics; adv bkg acc; ccard acc; bike hire;
watersports; CKE. *"Pleasant vill; gd rests; hot water
metered; gd NH."* **€20.00, 1 Apr-31 Oct.**   2015

LINDAU (BODENSEE) *3D4* (5km NE Rural) *47.58509,
9.70667* **Campingpark Gitzenweiler Hof,** Gitzenweiler
88, 88131 Lindau-Gitzenweiler (08382) 94940; info@
gitzenweiler-hof.de; www.gitzenweiler-hof.de

12 ♻ €3.50 �100 ♨ 🏊 🚿 🚿 🍴 ▽ ⏰ 🏊 🛒 ⚏ 🌿 🏊

**Exit A96/E43/E54 junc 4 onto B12 sp Lindau. Turn
off immed after vill of Oberreitnau twd Rehlings.
Site well sp fr all dirs.** Lge, mkd, pt shd, pt sl, serviced
pitches; EHU (6-16A) inc; gas; red long stay; TV;
50% statics; bus 1km; Eng spkn; adv bkg acc; boating;
fishing; CKE. *"Well-run, busy site in scenic area; gd
facs; friendly staff; excel site for children; max 2 dogs;
o'night facs for m'vans; gd cycling; poss prone to
flooding after v heavy rain; pitches poorly maintained;
poss cr."* **€36.00, G18.**   2019

LINDAU (BODENSEE) *3D4* (9km SE Coastal)
47.53758, 9.73143 **Park-Camping Lindau am See,**
Fraunhoferstrasse 20, 88131 Lindau-Zech (08382)
72236; info@park-camping.de; www.park-
camping.de

♻ €3 �100 ♨ 🏊 🚿 🚿 🍴 ▽ ⏰ 🏊 🛒 ⚏ 🌿 🏊shgl

**On B31 fr Bregenz to Lindau, 200m after customs
turn L to site in 150m; ent could be missed; mini-
mkt on corner; ent rd crosses main rlwy line with
auto barriers. B31 fr Friedrichshafen, site well sp
fr o'skts of Lindau.** 4*, Lge, hdstg, mkd, pt shd, EHU
(10A) €1 (long lead poss req); sw; 20% statics; Eng
spkn; bike hire; golf 3km. *"Busy site; immac san facs;
sh stay pitches poss diff to manoeuvre as v cramped;
office/gate clsd 1300-1400; helpful staff; m'van o'night
area €10; shwr rm for dogs; excel walking in Pfänder
area; excel; Korridor scheme round Bregenz abolished;
Pfander tunnels complete; Austria m'way vignette req;
cyc rtes fr site."* **€33.50, 25 Mar-10 Nov.**   2018

LINDAUNIS *1D1* (1km SSW Rural) *54.58626, 9.8173*
Camping Lindaunis, Schleistrasse 1, 24392 Lindaunis
(04641) 7317; info@camping-lindaunis.de;
www.camping-lindaunis.de

♻ €2 �100 (htd) ♨ 🏊 🚿 🚿 🍴 ▽ 🦋 🍴 ▽ 🛒 ⚏ 🌿

**Exit A7/E45 junc 5 onto B201 sp Brebel &
Süderbrarup. At Brebel turn R & foll dir Lindaunis,
site approx 12km on R beside Schlei Fjord.** 3*, Lge,
hdg, mkd, pt shd, terr, EHU (16A); bbq; twin axles; TV;
80% statics; Eng spkn; adv bkg rec; games area; boat
hire; games rm; boating; fishing; bike hire; canoeing;
CKE. *"Vg, family-run site ideally placed for exploring
Schlei fjord & conv Danish border; lakeside setting; boat
& canoe rentals; gd walks & cycle rtes; attractive area;
vg."* **€23.00, 28 Mar-15 Oct.**   2016

LINGERHAHN *3B2* (1km NE Rural) *50.09980, 7.57330* **Campingpark am Mühlenteich,** Am Mühlenteich 1, 56291 Lingerhahn **(06746) 533; info@muehlenteich.de; www.muehlenteich.de**

🔟 🐕 €3.50 � 🚰 WD 🚿 ▨ ⊘ 🥾 MSP ⊕ 🎣 🗲 ⚠ 🗲

Exit A61/E31 exit junc 44 to Laudert & Lingerhahn. In Lingerhahn foll sp Pfalzfeld, site sp. 4*, Lge, unshd, serviced pitches; EHU (6A) €2; 75% statics; adv bkg acc; golf 12km; tennis; CKE. *"Delightful rest & beer garden; ent clsd 1300-1500 & 2200; excel site."* **€22.50** 2019

LIPPSTADT *1C4* (8km NE Rural) *51.70095, 8.40808* **Campingparadies Lippstadter Seenplatte,** Seeufer Straße 16, 59558 Lippstadt **02 948 22 53; info@ camping-lippstadt.de; www.camping-lippstadt.de**

🐕 €2.50 ♨ WD 🚰 ♨ ⅙ ▨ ⊘ MSP 🦋 ⚠

Turn R off B55 to Lipperode. In town turn R onto Niederdedinghauser. After 2.5km turn L onto Seeuferstraße. Site 200m on R. Sm, mkd, pt shd, EHU (16A); twin axles; 25% statics; bus 200m; adv bkg acc; bike hire; CCI. *" Vg site; fishing in adj lake; excel modern facs; lge pitches; friendly owners; Paderborn lovely city; off clsd 1230-1430."* **€23.00, 1 Mar-31 Oct.** 2018

LORCH *3C2* (6km SE Rural) *50.01820, 7.85493* **Naturpark Camping Suleika,** Im Bodenthal 2, 65391 Lorch-bei-Rüdesheim **(06726) 839402; info@suleika-camping.de; www.suleika-camping.de**

🐕 €2 ♨ ▨ ⊘ WD 🦋 ⊕ 🎣 ⚠

Site off B42 on E bank of Rv Rhine, 3km NW of Assmannshausen. 3km SE of Lorch foll sp over rlwy x-ing on narr winding, steep rd thro vineyards to site. App poss diff & dangerous for lge o'fits. Sm, pt shd, pt sl, terr, serviced pitches; EHU (16A) metered + conn fee; bike hire; sep car park; CKE. *"Vg site in magnificent setting; excursions by Rhine steamer, local places of interest, wine district; access & exit 1-way system; helpful staff; excel rest; environmentally friendly."* **€23.00, 15 Mar-1 Nov.** 2015

LOWENSTEIN *3D3* (4km N Rural) *49.11697, 9.38321* **Camping Heilbronn Breitenauer See,** 74245 Löwenstein **(07130) 8558; info@breitenauer-see.de; www.breitenauer-see.de**

🔟 🐕 €5 ♨(htd) WD 🚰 ♨ ⅙ ▨ ⊘ MSP 🦋 ☂ ⊕ 🎣 ⚠ 🗲

Exit m'way A81 (E41) at J10, Weinsberg/Ellhofen & on B39 twd Löwenstein/Schwäbisch Hall; site in approx 8km. 5*, V lge, mkd, pt shd, EHU (16A) €2 or metered + conn fee; gas; sw nr; red long stay; 50% statics; Eng spkn; adv bkg acc; ccard acc; golf 15km; boating; watersports; dog wash; CKE. *"Lake walks; beautiful location; pleasant site close to A6 & A81; all facs highest quality & superb; some fully serviced pitches; excel."* **€25.00** 2015

LUBBEN *2G3* (1km S Urban) *51.93641, 13.89490* **Spreewald Camping,** Am Burglehn 218, 15907 Lübben **(03546) 7053 or 3335 or 8874; info@ spreewald-camping-luebben.de; www.spreewald-camping-luebben.de**

🐕 ♨ WD 🚰 ⅙ ▨ ⊘ MSP 🦋 ⊕ 🥾 nr ⚠

Fr N on A13 exit junc 7 at Freiwalde onto B115 twd Lübben. In town cent turn R to stay on B115 sp Lübbenau. Site on L - well sp. Or fr S exit junc 8 onto B87 to Lübben. Cross rlwy, cont along Luckauerstrasse. Turn R at traff lts into Puschkinstrasse, sp Cottbus. Site on L, well sp. Lge, pt shd, EHU (10A) metered; gas; 20% statics; adv bkg acc; CKE. *"Excel location; modern, clean facs; dogs free; excel cycle rtes; adj rv for boating; conv for Berlin."* **€27.00, 15 Mar-31 Oct.** 2015

LUBECK *2E2* (6km W Rural) *53.86943, 10.63086* **Campingplatz Lübeck-Schönböcken,** Steinrader Damm 12, 23556 Lübeck-Schönböcken **(0451) 893090; info@camping-luebeck.de; www.camping-luebeck.de**

🔟 🐕 €1 ♨ WD 🚰 ▨ ⊘ 🦋 ☂ 🥾 ⚠

Fr A1 exit junc 23 on sh slip rd, stay in L lane, foll sp to Schönböcken & then camp sp (not v obvious); turn R at traff lts bef Dornbreite, site in 1km on L. 3*, Med, unshd, pt sl, EHU (6A) inc; gas; bbq; bus to town; Eng spkn; ccard acc; games rm; CKE. *"Helpful owners; busy site; gd san facs but poss stretched if site full; conv Travemünde ferries; Lübeck interesting town; cycle path to town; vg; nice place; gd hypmkt nr; gd site; gd bus service to fascinating town."* **€24.00** 2019

LUNEBURG *1D2* (6km S Rural) *53.20925, 10.41000* **Camping Rote Schleuse,** Rote Schleuse 4, 21335 Lüneburg **(04131) 791500; kontakt@camp-rote-schleuse.de; www.camproteschleuse.de**

🔟 🐕 €1 ♨ WD 🚰 ♨ ⅙ ▨ ⊘ 🦋 ☂ ☕ ⊕ nr 🎣 🥾 ⚠ 🗲

Exit A250 junc 4 onto Neu Häcklingen twd Lüneburg. Site sp to R in 300m. 3*, Med, pt shd, EHU (16A) €2.50 or metered; bbq; 60% statics; bus fr site ent; Eng spkn; adv bkg acc; ccard acc; games rm; bike hire. *"Pleasant, friendly owners; clsd 1300-1500; interesting town; gd rest."* **€25.80** 2018

LUTHERSTADT WITTENBERG *2F3* (5km S Rural) *51.85465, 12.64563* **Marina-Camp Elbe,** Brückenkopf 1, 06888 Lutherstadt-Wittenberg **(03491) 4540; info@marina-camp-elbe.de; www.marina-camp-elbe.de**

🔟 🐕 €1.50 ♨ WD 🚰 ♨ ⅙ ▨ ⊘ MSP 🦋 ☂ 🥾 nr

Site on S side of Elbe bdge on B2 dir Leipzig; well sp. 5*, Med, pt shd, serviced pitches; EHU (16A)€2.50; gas; bbq; cooking facs; TV; bus at gate; ccard acc; bike hire; sauna; CKE. *"Delightful rvside site; marina adj; excel, modern san facs."* **€27.00** 2017

GERMANY

MAGDEBURG *2E3* (15km N Rural) *52.21888, 11.65944* **Campingplatz Barleber See,** Wiedersdorfer strasse, 39126 Magdeburg **(0391) 503244; camping platz@cvbs.de; www.cvbs.de**

🏕 €2 ♦♦ 🆆 ♨ & 🛒 ⚏ 🅿 🐾 🍴 ① 🅳 🛒 /Ⓜ 🛶 ⛱ sand adj

Exit A2/E30 junc 71 sp Rothensee-Barleber See; site 1km N of a'bahn. 4*, Lge, mkd, pt shd, EHU (10A) €2; gas; sw; red long stay; 80% statics; Eng spkn; bike hire; CKE. *"Gd beach & watersports; pleasant site; gd sports facs; gd touring base; v noisy due to adj gravel quarry; unhelpful staff; v busy at w/end; crowded beach."* **€22.00, 15 Apr-1 Oct.**   **2018**

MALSCH *3C3* (4km S Rural) *48.86165, 8.33789* **Campingpark Bergwiesen,** Waldenfelsstrasse 1, 76316 Malsch **(07246) 1467; email@campingpark-bergwiesen.eu; www.campingpark-bergwiesen.eu**

🕧 🏕 €2 ♦♦ 🆆 ♨ & 🛒 ⚏ 🅿 🍴 ① 🛒 nr /Ⓜ

Fr Karlsruhe on B3 thro Malsch vill over level x-ing to Waldprechtsweier. Foll site sp, take care tight L turn & steep app thro residential area. 4*, Lge, mkd, hdg, hdstg, pt shd, terr, serviced pitches; EHU (16A); gas; sw nr; 80% statics; Eng spkn; adv bkg req; CKE. *"1st class facs; well-run site in beautiful forest setting; v friendly site & owner; not rec for long o'fits or lge m'vans; gd walks fr site; no wifi."* **€19.00**   **2016**

MANNHEIM *3C2* (8km S Urban) *49.44841, 8.44806* **Camping am Strandbad,** Strandbadweg 1, 68199 Mannheim-Neckarau **(0176) 55422268; cfsm. mannheim@googlemail.com; www.campingplatz-mannheim-strandbad.de**

🏕 €1.50 ♦♦ ♨ 🛒 ⚏ 🅿 🐾 ① 🛒 nr 🛒 nr

Exit A6 Karlsruhe-Frankfurt at AB Kreuz Mannheim (junc 27) L onto A656 Mannheim-Neckarau. Exit junc 2 onto B36 dir Neckarau, site sp. 2*, Med, pt shd, EHU (16A) metered; gas; sw; 60% statics; CKE. *"Some noise fr barges on Rhine & factories opp; poss flooding at high water; interesting area; barrier down & recep clsd 1200-1500."* **€20.00, 1 Apr-15 Oct.**   **2019**

MARKTHEIDENFELD *3D2* (5km S Rural) *49.81885, 9.58851* **Camping Main-Spessart-Park,** Spessartstrasse 30, 97855 Triefenstein-Lengfurt **(09395) 1079; info@ camping-main-spessart.de; www.camping-main-spessart.de**

🕧 🏕 €2.50 ♦♦ 🆆 ♨ & 🛒 ⚏ 🅿 ① 🛒 /Ⓜ

Exit A3/E41 junc 65 or 66 sp Lengfurt. In Lengfurt foll sp Marktheidenfeld; site in 1km. 5*, Lge, pt shd, pt sl, terr, serviced pitches; EHU (6-10A) €3; 50% statics; Eng spkn; adv bkg acc; ccard acc; watersports; CKE. *"Excel, high quality site; vg rest; vg san facs; easy access A4; sep NH area; helpful owners; access diff parts of site due steep terrs; busy site; pool adj; gd facs."* **€24.00**   **2016**

MEDELBY *1D1* (0.7km W Rural) *54.81490, 9.16361* **Camping Kawan Mitte,** Sonnenhügel 1, 24994 Medelby **(04605) 189391; info@camping-mitte.de; www.camping-mitte.de**

🕧 🏕 ♦♦ (htd) 🆆 ♨ ♨ & 🛒 ⚏ 🅿 🍴 ① nr 🛒 /Ⓜ 🛶 (htd)

Exit A7 junc 2 onto B199 dir Niebüll to Wallsbüll, turn N dir Medelby, site sp. 5*, Lge, mkd, pt shd, EHU (16A) metered; bbq; cooking facs; TV; 20% statics; adv bkg acc; fitness rm; horseriding 600m; sauna; games area; bike hire; golf 12km; CKE. *"Conv m'way & Danish border; vg."* **€29.00**   **2017**

MELLE *1C3* (8km NW Rural) *52.22428, 8.2661* **Campingplatz Grönegau-Park Ludwigsee,** Nemdenerstrasse 12, 49326 Melle **(05402) 2132; info@ludwigsee.de; www.ludwigsee.de**

🕧 🏕 €3 ♦♦ 🆆 ♨ 🛒 ⚏ 🅿 🐾 🍴 ① 🅳 🛒 nr /Ⓜ ⚏

Exit A30/E30 junc 22 twd Bad Essen, site sp on lakeside. 4*, Lge, hdg, mkd, pt shd, EHU (10A) inc; sw; 80% statics; adv bkg acc; ccard acc; games area; bike hire; CKE. *"Beautiful & pleasant site; sep car park; barrier clsd 1300-1500; helpful owners; sep area for tourers."* **€30.00**   **2019**

MENDIG *3B2* (7km N Rural) *50.42151, 7.26448* **Camping Laacher See,** Am Laacher See, 56653 Wassenach **(02636) 2485; info@camping-laacher-see.de; www.camping-laacher-see.de**

🏕 €4 ♦♦ (htd) 🆆 ♨ ♨ & 🛒 ⚏ 🅿 🐾 🍴 ① 🅳 🛒 /Ⓜ

Fr A61, exit junc 34 Mendig. Foll tents sp to Maria Laach. Site on Laacher See. 4*, Lge, mkd, hdg, hdstg, pt shd, pt sl, terr, EHU (16A) metered + conn fee; gas; sw; 50% statics; bus 500m; Eng spkn; adv bkg acc; ccard acc; fishing; sailing; CKE. *"Beautiful, neat, clean, relaxing site; all pitches lake views; busy at w/end; modern, outstanding san facs; gd woodland walks, cycling & sw; excel sailing facs & sw; excel site & rest; close to m'way; rec; helpful staff; avoid arr bet 11am-2pm when recep clsd."* **€29.00, 29 Mar-25 Sep.**   **2018**

MENDIG *3B2* (2km NNW Rural) *50.38646, 7.27237* **Camping Siesta,** Laacherseestrasse 6, 56743 Mendig **(02652) 1432; service@campingsiesta.de; www.campingsiesta.de**

🕧 🏕 €2 ♦♦ ♨ 🛒 ⚏ 🍴 ① /Ⓜ ⚏

Fr A61 exit junc 34 for Mendig dir Maria Laach; foll camp sps; site on R in 300m by ent to car park. 3*, Med, hdg, sl, EHU (16A) €2.5; gas; 60% statics; Eng spkn; CKE. *"Useful NH; easy access fr A61; owner helpful in siting NH o'fits; longest waterslide in Europe; gd base for region's castles & wines; friendly owners; spotless site; gd rest; site has so much more to offer than only a NH; v welcoming; vg refurbished; new san facs (2014)."* **€24.00**   **2019**

METTINGEN *1B3* (2km SW Rural) *52.31251, 7.76202*
Camping Zur Schönen Aussicht, Schwarzestrasse 73,
49497 Mettingen **(05452) 606;** info@camping-
schoene-aussicht.de; www.camping-schoene-
aussicht.de

🄵🏕🛉🗄⬛♿🅟/🔤 🦋♈🍴⊕🛒🚿⁄🔥 (covrd, htd)

**Exit A30 junc 12 dir Mettingen. Go thro town cent,
uphill turn L at traff lts, site sp.** 3*, Med, mkd, hdg, pt
shd, pt sl, EHU (10A) €3 or metered; 50% statics; Eng
spkn; adv bkg acc; CKE. *"Nice, friendly site; gd walking,
cycling; easy walk to town; gd facs."* **€27.50**   **2015**

MITTENWALD *4E4* (4km N Rural) *47.47290, 11.27729*
Naturcamping Isarhorn, Am Horn 4, 82481 Mittenwald
(08823) 5216; camping@mittenwald.de; www.camping-
isarhorn.de

🄵🏕€2.90🛉🗄⬛♿/🔤🦋♈⊕🛒🚿

**E fr Garmisch-Partenkirchen on rd 2; at Krün turn S
on D2/E533 dir Mittenwald. Site on R in approx 2km
at int'l camping sp. Ent on R fr main rd. NB: Rd thro
to Innsbruck via Zirlerberg improved & no longer
clsd to c'vans descending S; long & steep; low gear;
not to be attempted N.** 4*, Lge, hdstg, pt shd, EHU
(16A) €2.80 or metered; bbq; bus adj; Eng spkn; ccard
acc; tennis; site clsd 1 Nov-mid Dec; site clsd 1300-
1500 & 2200-0700; canoeing. *"Relaxed, secluded site
in pines; mountain views; excel base for walking; htd
covrd pool 4km; cycle track to attractive town; poss
some noise fr nrby military base; ski lift; owner v keen
on recycling waste; facs gd but insufficient for size of
site; highly rec."* **€27.50**   **2015**

MITTENWALD *4E4* (8km N Rural) *47.49040, 11.25438*
Alpen-Caravanpark Tennsee, Am Tennsee 1, 82493
Klais-Krün **(08825) 170;** info@camping-tennsee.de;
www.camping-tennsee.de

🏕€3.30🛉(htd)⬛♿/🔤♈⊕🛒🚿🔥✏

**N fr Mittenwald on main Innsbruck-Garmisch rd
turn off for Krun, foll Tennsee & site sp. 2km SE of
Klais, not well sp.** 5*, Lge, mkd, hdstg, pt shd, terr,
serviced pitches; EHU (16A) metered; gas; phone; Eng
spkn; adv bkg acc; ccard acc; bike hire; CKE. *"Excel
area for Bavarian Alps, Tirol; barrier clsd 1200-1500;
gd size pitches; ski lift 2.5km; red snr citizens; vg, clean,
friendly, family-run site; price inc use of tourist buses."*
€35.00, 1 Jan-2 Nov, 18 Dec-31 Dec.   **2016**

MITTERTEICH *4F2* (3km NW Rural) *49.97311,
12.22497* **Campingplatz Großbüchlberg,**
Großbüchlberg 32, 95666 Mitterteich **09633 40 06
73;** camping@freizeithugl.de; www.freizeithugl.de

🄵🏕€1.50🛉(htd)⬛♿/🔤🦋♈🍴⊕🛒🚿🔥

**Fr A93 Marktredwitz-Mitterteich take exit 16
Mitterteich. At xrds in town cent foll Freizeithugl
signs. Turn L after 200m twds Grossbuchberg. Foll
sp.** 5*, Med, hdg, mkd, hdg, pt shd, pt sl, terr, EHU
(16A); twin axles; TV; bus adj; Eng spkn; adv bkg acc;
ccard acc; CCI. *"Excel site; superb htd san facs; close
to mini golf, toboggan run, etc; extensive views; v
friendly."* **€25.00**   **2019**

MONTABAUR *3C2* (8km E Rural) *50.43761, 7.90498*
Camping Eisenbachtal, 56412 Girod **(06485) 766**

🄵🏕€2🛉(htd)⬛♿🗄🛒/🔤🦋⊕nr🔥

**S on A3/E35 exit junc 41 dir Montabaur; at Girod
turn L to site, well sp.** Med, hdg, mkd, hdstg, pt
shd, pt sl, serviced pitches; EHU (10A) inc (poss rev
pol); gas; sw nr; red long stay; 75% statics; Eng spkn;
adv bkg acc; CKE. *"Beautiful, well-equipped site in
Naturpark Nassau; conv NH fr a'bahn & worth longer
stay; friendly, welcoming staff; gd for nature lovers
& children; gd walking & cycling; adj rest excel; site
clsd 1300-1500 but car park opp; conv Rhine & Mosel
valleys."* **€18.00**   **2019**

MORFELDEN *3C2* (3km E Rural) *49.97986, 8.59461*
Campingplatz Mörfelden, Am Zeltzplatz 5-15, 64546
Mörfelden-Walldorf **(06105) 22289;** info@camping
platz-moerfelden.de; www.campingplatz-
moerfelden.de

🄵🏕€1.50🛉🗄⬛♿/🔤🦋♈⊕🔥

**Fr A5 exit 24, turn W on 486 twds Morfelden. In
200m turn L, opp Holiday Inn. Site on R in 100m.**
3*, Med, pt shd, EHU (16A) metered or €2.50; gas;
phone; Eng spkn. *"Conv NH/sh stay for Frankfurt;
excel, modern san facs; helpful owner; vg."*
€26.50   **2016**

MORFELDEN *3C2* (9km S Rural) *49.94461, 8.60544*
Campingplatz Am Steinrodsee, Triftweg 33, 64331
Weiterstadt **06150 53593;** rezeption.koehres@t-
online.de; www.camping-steinrodsee.de

🏕🛉(htd)⬛♿🛒🗄/🔤🦋♈🍴⊕🔥

**Leave A5 twds Darmstadt at exit 25. L at 2nd traff
lts onto L3113. Turn R in 5km & foll signs.**
4*, Lge, mkd, hdg, pt shd, EHU (16A); bbq; twin axles;
60% statics; CCI. *"Vg site; quiet with some aircraft &
m'way noise; clean, tidy, well regulated site; immac san
facs; conv for Darmstadt."* **€23.00, 1 Jan-31 Oct.**
                                                        2015

MORITZBURG *4G1* (3km S Rural) *51.1450, 13.67444*
Campingplatz Bad Sonnenland, Dresdnerstrasse
115, 01468 Moritzburg **(0351) 8305495;** bad-
sonnenland@t-online.de; www.bad-sonnenland.de

🏕€3🛉🗄⬛/🔤🦋♈🍴⊕🛒🚿🔥

**Leave A4/E40 exit 80. Turn R sp Moritzburg, foll site
sp thro Reichenberg. Site on L 3km bef Moritzburg.**
Lge, pt shd, EHU (16A) €2.50; gas; sw nr; bus to
Dresden; Eng spkn; ccard acc; games area; games rm;
CKE. *"Scenic area; friendly staff; excel, immac facs;
site clsd 1300-1500 & 2200-0700; also holiday vill with
many huts; conv Dresden, Meissen; narr gauge steam
train Dresden-Moritzburg; day trip to Prague; statics
(sep area); many mkd walking & cycling rtes in area;
Schloss Moritzburg in vill; vg site; poss cr high ssn."*
€22.00, 1 Apr-31 Oct.   **2015**

MUHLBERG *2E4* (1.6km NW Rural) *50.87516, 10.80843* **Campingplatz Drei Gleichen,** Am Gut Ringhofen, 99869 Mühlberg **(036256) 22715; service@ campingplatz-muehlberg.de; www.campingplatz-muehlberg.de**

12 🛈 €2.20 ♦♦ wc ㅗ 🚿 🖪 / MP 🕯 Ⴧ 🛈 nr 🖳 nr 🏛

Leave A4/E40 at junc 43 (Wandersleben) S twds Mühlberg; site well sp in 2km on rd to Wechmar. Med, hdg, mkd, unshd, pt sl, EHU (16A) €1.80 + conn fee; sw nr; 50% statics; adv bkg acc; CKE. *"Gd facs; helpful staff; site clsd 1300-1500; conv a'bahn."* **€16.00**   2015

MUNCHEN *4E4* (12km NW Urban) *48.19888, 11.49694* **Campingplatz Nord-West,** Auf den Schrederwiesen 3, 80995 München-Moosach **(089) 1506936; info@campingplatz-nord-west.de; www.campingplatz-nord-west.de**

12 🛈 €2 ♦♦ (htd) wc ㅗ 🚿 🖪 / MP 🕯 Ⴧ 🛈 nr 🖳 🖋

Fr N exit A99 junc 10 Lugwigsfeld onto B304 S - Dachauerstrasse, sp München. Turn L in approx 800m at traff lts. Turn R at T-junc to site on R. Med, hdstg, shd, EHU (10-16A) €5 or metered; 50% statics; phone; bus to city; Eng spkn; adv bkg acc; ccard acc; CKE. *"Friendly, helpful welcome; enquire about public transport tickets; ltd facs LS; Dachau - pretty town 10km; gd; Dachau Concentration Camp Memorial worth a visit."* **€23.20**   2017

"That's changed – Should I let the Club know?"

If you find something on site that's different from the site entry, fill in a report and let us know. See camc.com/europereport.

MUNCHEN *4E4* (17km NW Rural) *48.19821, 11.41161* **Campingplatz am Langwieder See,** Eschenriederstrasse 119, 81249 München-Langwied **(089) 8641566; info@camping-langwieder-see.de; www.camping-langwieder-see.de**

12 🛈 €1.70 ♦♦ (htd) wc 🖪 / 🕯 🛈 🖳

Exit A8 junc 80 at Langwieder See & foll sp Dachau; site within 200m. Fr ring rd A99 junc 8 join A8 to N, then as above. Med, hdstg, pt shd, EHU (10A) metered + conn fee €1; gas; sw nr; 95% statics; Eng spkn; CKE. *"Pleasant owners; tourers in a row outside recep area parked v close together; v sm pitches, mostly on gravel; gd san facs; site used by workers; easy access to Munich by train fr Dachau; lge free car park at stn; NH/sh stay only."* **€21.50**   2016

MUNSTER *1B3* (9km SE Rural) *51.94638, 7.69027* **Camping Münster,** Laerer Wersuefer 7, 48157 Münster **(0251) 311982; mail@campingplatz-muenster.de; www.campingplatz-muenster.de**

12 🛈 €3 ♦♦ (htd) wc ㅗ 🚿 🖪 / MP 🕯 🕯 🛈 🖳 🏛

Fr A43 exit junc 2 or A1/E37 exit junc 78 onto B51 dir Münster then Bielefeld. On leaving built-up area, turn R after TV mast on R. Cross Rv Werse & turn L at 1st traff lts, site sp. (Site is also sp fr Münster S by-pass). 5*, Lge, mkd, hdstg, pt shd, serviced pitches; EHU (16A) inc; bbq; twin axles; 50% statics; bus 50m; Eng spkn; adv bkg acc; ccard acc; tennis; bike hire; fishing; CKE. *"Excel; quiet mid wk; Münster very interesting; radio/TV mast useful landmark fr S; gd cycle rtes; o'night m'van area; barrier clsd 1300-1500; htd pool adj; vg site, tokens for shwrs; sep motor parking outside camp; excel for bus to Munster; helpful staff; clean facs & plentiful; well organised; pitches cramped; gd rest."* **€24.00**   2016

MUNSTERTAL *3B4* (2km WNW Rural) *47.85995, 7.76370* **Feriencamping Münstertal,** Dietzelbach-strasse 6, 79244 Münstertal **(07636) 7080; info@ camping-muenstertal.de; www.camping-muen-stertal.de**

12 🛈 €3.50 ♦♦ wc ㅗ 🚿 🖪 / MP 🕯 🕯 🛈 🖳 🏛 🖋
🏊 (covrd, htd)

Exit A5 junc 64a at Bad Krozingen-Staufen-Münstertal. By-pass Stauffen & foll Münstertal sps. Site on L 1.5km past Camping Belchenblick off rd L123. 5*, Lge, mkd, shd, serviced pitches; EHU (16A) metered; gas; red long stay; TV (pitch); 10% statics; phone; adv bkg rec; fishing; tennis; horseriding; games area; games rm; CKE. *"Superb, well-managed site; luxurious, clean facs; beauty treatments avail; winter sports nrby; ski lift 10km; sauna; steam rm; solarium; private bthrms avail; many organised activities for all family; gd walking; vg rest; conv Freiburg & Black Forest; new premium pitches (2016); rlwy stn 200m; gates clsd 1300-1430 & 2200-0730; m'van o'night area; friendly staff."* **€36.50**   2017

See advertisement opposite

MURNAU AM STAFFELSEE *4E4* (3.5km NW Rural) *47.68493, 11.17918* **Camping Halbinsel Burg,** Burgweg 41, 82418 Murnau-Seehausen **(08841) 9870; info@camping-staffelsee.de; www.camping-staffelsee.de**

♦♦ wc ㅗ 🚿 🖪 / MP 🛈 🖳 🏛 🖋

Exit A95 junc 9 Sindelsdorf/Peissenberg to Murnau. Site sp at traff lts in cent of Murnau, dir Seehausen. 3*, Med, pt shd, EHU (16A) €2.50; sw; 20% statics; watersports; CKE. *"Wonderful sw & boating; pleasant, lovely, well-equipped site in superb location for alps, lakes & local amenities."* **€26.00, 6 Jan-25 Oct.**   2019

NAUMBURG (HESSEN) *1C4* (0.8km NW Rural)
51.25070, 9.16060 **Camping in Naumburg (formerly Kneipp Kur Camping),** Am Schwimmbad 12, 34311 Naumburg (05625) 9239670 or 0170 4418621 (mob); info@camping-naumburg.de; www.camping-naumburg.de

12 🐕 €2.50 ♦♦(htd) WD ♨ ♨ ♿ 🛒 ⊘ MSP 🦋 ♉ ⚠

Exit A44 junc 67 onto B251 thro Istha. At Bründersen foll sp Altenstadt & Naumburg. Foll int'l camping sp, well sp. 4*, Med, mkd, unshd, terr, EHU (16A) €2 or metered (poss rev pol); bbq; cooking facs; twin axles; 30% statics; bus 500m; Eng spkn; adv bkg acc; games area; golf 15km; tennis; horseriding 5km; CKE. *"Charming site; excel, modern san facs; spacious pitches; friendly, helpful staff; interesting town; clsd 1300-1500; gd walks fr site; spa treatments; rec; nr pool, smkt, Dambusters Dam; pool adj; new management."* **€22.00** 2015

NENNIG *3A2* (1.6km N Rural) *49.54195, 6.37126* Mosel-Camping Dreiländereck, Am Moselufer, 66706 Perl-Nennig (06866) 322; info@mosel-camping.de; www.mosel-camping.de

🐕 €1 ♦♦(htd) WD ♨ 🛒 ⊘ MSP 🦋 ♉ ⊕ ♨ ♨ nr ⚠

Site on bank of Mosel opp Remich (Luxembourg), access on R just bef bdge (fr German side). Fr Luxembourg cross rv bdge, turn L after former border post cont to rv & turn L under bldg; site is ahead. Med, unshd, EHU (16A) inc; bbq; red long stay; 65% statics; phone; Eng spkn; adv bkg acc; golf 15km; cycling; fishing; CKE. *"Nice, lovely site; dishwashing & chem disp adj; ltd, tired facs; conv vineyards, Roman mosaic floor in Nennig; cycle track along rv; sh walk to Remich; friendly welcome."* **€19.40, 1 Apr-15 Oct.** 2018

NENNIG *3A2* (1.8km N Rural) *49.54331, 6.37207*
Camping Mosella am Rothaus (formerly Moselplatz),
Zur Moselbrücke 15, 66706 Perl-Nennig **(06866) 510
or 26660222 (Lux'bourg); info@mosel-camping.de**
🏕 ♟(htd) 🚾 ⚠ ♿ ⚊ ✉ 🐕 ☂ ⓘ ♨ 📷 nr

Site on bank of Mosel opp Remich (Luxembourg),
access on R just bef bdge. Fr Luxembourg cross rv
bdge, turn L after former border post, site is ahead,
opp Mosel-Camping Dreiländereck. Med, hdg, pt shd,
EHU (10A) inc; bbq; 50% statics; bus 100m; Eng spkn;
CKE. *"Lovely, well placed site by rv for sh or long stay;
helpful, friendly owner; ltd facs, a bit tired; rest nr;
rvside pitch sm extra charge; gd touring base; frequent
bus to Luxembourg City."* **€22.60, 1 Apr-15 Oct.**
2017

"We must tell the Club about that great site we found"

Get your site reports in by mid-August and we'll
do our best to get your updates into the next
edition.

NEUMARKT IN DER OBERPFALZ *4E3* (10km N Rural)
49.32944, 11.42876 **Campingplatz Berg,** Hausheimer
strasse 31, 92348 Berg **(09189) 1581; campingplatz-
herteis@t-online.de; www.camping-in-berg.de**
12 🏕 €2 ♟ 🚾 ⚊ ♿ ⚊ ✉ 📷 ⓘ nr ☂ nr

Exit A3 junc 91 & foll sp Berg bei Neumarkt. In cent
of Berg, turn R, site on R in 800m, sp. On ent turn
R to tourers area & walk to recep. 3*, Med, unshd,
pt sl, EHU (20A) €2.50; 60% statics; Eng spkn; golf
8km. *"Well-run, friendly, family-owned site; excel san
facs; sh walk to Berg cent; excel touring base; gd NH
fr m'way; pleasant views of countryside; canal walk."*
€20.00 **2016**

NEUMUNSTER *1D1* (6km SW Rural) *54.04636,
9.92306* **Familien-Camping Forellensee,**
Humboldredder 5, 24634 Padenstedt **(04321) 82697;
info@familien-campingplatz.de; www.familien-
campingplatz.de**
12 🏕 €1.50 ♟ 🚾 ⚊ ♿ ⚊ ✉ 📷 ☂ ⓘ nr ♨ ☂

Exit A7 junc 14 for Padenstedt, join dual c'way for
1km & turn L sp Centrum. In 1km turn L at traff lts
sp Padenstedt for 3km, under m'way. Site on L in
vill. 4*, Lge, mkd, pt shd, EHU (16A) €3.50 or metered;
sw; 75% statics; phone; Eng spkn; tennis; trout fishing;
games area; CKE. *"Gd NH; conv for trains to Hamburg/
Lübeck; swimming lake with section for dogs."*
€26.00 **2019**

NEUREICHENAU *4G3* (8km E Urban) *48.74861,
13.81694* **Knaus Campingpark Lackenhäuser,**
Lackenhäuser 127, 94089 Neureichenau **(08583) 311;
lackenhaeuser@knauscamp.de; www.knauscamp.de**
12 🐕 €2.50 ♟ 🚾 ⚊ ♿ ⚊ ✉ 📷 ☂ ♟
☂ ⓘ ♨ 📷 ⚠ ✎ ⚊(htd) 🏊

Leave A3/E56 at junc 14 (Aicha-vorm Wald) & go E
for 50km via Waldkirchen, Jandelsbrunn, Gsenget
& Klafferstrasse to Lackenhäuser. 4*, Lge, hdg, mkd,
pt shd, pt sl, terr, serviced pitches; EHU (16A) €2.60
or metered; gas; bbq; red long stay; TV; 40% statics;
adv bkg acc; ccard acc; horseriding adj; fishing; tennis
500m; games rm; sauna; bike hire. *"Lge site with little
waterfalls & walkways; ski lift on site - equipment for
hire; mv service pnt diff to access; excel shop; 2km to 3
point border with Austria & Czech Republic; excursions
booked; solarium; hairdresser; recep clsd 1200-1500 &
after 1800."* **€34.00** **2016**

NEUSTADT *3C2* (10km SW Rural) *49.30083, 8.09027*
Campingplatz Wappenschmiede, Talstrasse 60,
67487 St Martin **(06323) 6435; cpwappenschmiede@
hotmail.de; www.campingplatz-wappenschmiede.
beep.de**
🏕 ♟ 🚾 ⚊ ✉ 📷 ☂ ⓘ ☂ nr ⚠

Exit A65 at junc 13 or 14 to Maikammer, then foll
sp St Martin & site (blue/white or yellow/brown
sp). At end houses take 1st L into touring area (do
not go up hill to statics area). 2*, Sm, shd, EHU €2;
red long stay; 50% statics; Eng spkn; adv bkg acc;
CKE. *"Poss long walk to facs; friendly site; St Martin
very picturesque; gd rests; gd walking area; gd site."*
€20.00, 1 Apr-1 Nov. **2015**

NEUSTADT AN DER AISCH *4E2* (9km N Rural)
49.64058, 10.59975 **Campingplatz Münchsteinach,**
Badstrasse 10, 91481 Münchsteinach **(09166) 750;
gemeinde@muenchsteinach.de;
www.muenchsteinach.de**
12 🐕 €2 ♟ 🚾 ⚊ ♿ ⚊ ✉ 📷 ☂ nr

Turn NW fr rd 470 Neustadt-Höchstadt at camp sp
8km fr Neustadt & thro Gutenstetten. Int'l camping
sp in 5km turn R, foll camp sp. Lge, unshd, EHU (16A)
metered; red long stay; 60% statics; CKE. *"Sm touring
area; clean facs; pool adj; site muddy when wet."*
€11.00 **2016**

NEUSTADT/HARZ *2E4* (2km NW Rural) *51.56897,
10.82836* **Campingplatz am Waldbad,** An der Burg 3,
99762 Neustadt/Harz 036331 479891; info@
neustadt-harz-camping.de; www.neustadt-harz-
camping.de
12 🏕 €2 ♟(htd) 🚾 ⚊ ♿ ⚊ ✉ 📷 ☂ ♨ ⚠

Fr A38, exit J10 for B243 to Nordhausen. Turn L
onto B4 dir Niedersachswerfen. Turn R onto L1037,
L onto Osteroder Straße and R onto Klostergasse.
Foll sp to campsite. 4*, Med, hdg, pt shd, pt sl, EHU
(10A) metered + con fee; twin axles; 50% statics;
adv bkg acc; games area; CCI. *"Gd site; conv for Harz;
helpful owners; vg san facs."* **€18.90** **2019**

NEUSTRELITZ *2F2* (10km SW Rural) *53.30895, 13.00305* **Camping- und Ferienpark Havelberge,** An der Havelbergen 1, 17237 Gross Quassow **(03981)** 24790; info@haveltourist.de; www.haveltourist.de

🐕 👫 wo ♨ ⅄ ♿ ▯ ⚟ 🐾 ❤ ♈ 🍴 ⑭ ⟟ ▤nr ⚠ ✂

Fr Neustrelitz foll sp to Userin on L25 & bef Userin turn L sp Gross Quassow. Turn S in vill at camping sp, cross rlwy line & rv, sm ent in 1.5km. Site 1.7km S of Gross Quassow twd lake, sp. 5*, Lge, pt shd, pt sl, EHU (16A) €2.90; sw; 30% statics; watersports; sauna; bike hire. *"Lovely wooded area; poss diff lge o'fits; not rec as NH."* **€33.40, 01 Apr-03 Nov, G11.**   **2016**

NIESKY *2H4* (3km W Rural) *51.30156, 14.80302* **Campingplatz Tonschächte (Part Naturist),** Raschkestrasse, 02906 Niesky **(03588)** 205771; info@campingplatz-tonschacht.de; campingplatz-tonschacht.de

🐕 👫 ♨ ⅄ ♿ ▯ ⚟ ⑭nr ⟟ ▤ ⚠

Leave A4/E40 at junc 93 onto B115 sp Niesky; cont on B115 site sp on L; do not go into Niesky but stay on B115. 2*, Lge, shd, EHU (10A); 50% statics; games area. *"Conv Polish border x-ing & a'bahn; sep naturist area."* **€12.50, 15 Apr-15 Oct.**   **2016**

NORDEN *1B2* (5km W Coastal) *53.60471, 7.13863* **Nordsee-Camp Norddeich,** Deichstrasse 21, 26506 Norden-Norddeich **(04931)** 8073; info@nordsee-camp.de; www.Nordsee-Camp.de

🐕 €3.80 👫 wo ♨ ⅄ ♿ ▯ ⚟ ❤ ♈ ⑭ ⟟ ▤ ⚠ ✂ ⚓200m

Off B70 N of Norden. Well sp. V lge, mkd, pt shd, EHU (6A) €2.20; 25% statics; ccard acc; fishing; bike hire; CKE. *"Immac san facs; friendly atmosphere; day trips to Frisian Islands; excel rest; vg site."* **€20.80, 8 Mar-25 Oct.**   **2016**

NURNBERG *4E2* (12km W Rural) *49.43174, 10.92541* **Camping Zur Mühle,** Seewaldstraße 75, 90513 Zirndorf/Leichendorf **(0911)** 693801; camping.walther@t-online.de; www.camping-zur-muehle.de

🐕 €2 👫(htd) wo ♨ ⅄ ▯ ⚟ ❤ ♈ 🍴 ⑭ ⟟ ⚠

Head W on Adlerstraße twd Stangengäßchen, cont onto Josephspl, then Vordere Lederg. Cont onto Schlotfegerg then onto Fürther Tor; Cont onto Dennerstraße then slight R onto Am Plärrer. Cont onto Rothenburger Str, turn L to stay on Rothenburger. Turn R twd Seewaldstraße, keep R. Site on L. Med, mkd, pt shd, EHU metered; bbq; ccard acc; CKE. *"Mastercard acc not Visa; local style rest in traditional building on site; conv for visiting Nurnberg; vg site."* **€24.00, 1 Apr-31 Dec.**   **2019**

OBERAMMERGAU *4E4* (1km S Rural) *47.58988, 11.0696* **Campingpark Oberammergau,** Ettalerstrasse 56B, 82487 Oberammergau **(08822)** 94105; info@camping-oberammergau.de; www.campingpark-oberammergau.de

12 🐕 €2 👫 wo ♨ ⅄ ♿ ▯ ⚟ ♈ ⑭nr ▤nr ⚠ ✂

Fr S turn R off B23, site on L in 1km. Fr N turn L at 2nd Oberammergau sp. Do not ent vill fr N - keep to bypass. 4*, Med, hdstg, hdg, mkd, pt shd, EHU (16A) metered + conn fee; gas; red long stay; 25% statics; bus; Eng spkn; adv bkg rec; sep car park; bike hire; CKE. *"Plenty of space; helpful recep; excel san facs; excel rest adj; easy walk to vill; well run site, visitor tax does not apply to one night stays."* **€29.00**   **2017**

OBERSTDORF *3D4* (2km N Rural) *47.42370, 10.27843* **Rubi-Camp,** Rubingerstrasse 34, 87561 Oberstdorf **(08322)** 959202; info@rubi-camp.de; www.rubi-camp.de

12 🐕 €4 👫(htd) wo ♨ ⅄ ♿ ▯ ⚟ ❤ 🍴 ⑭ ⟟ ▤nr ⚠

Fr Sonthofen on B19, just bef Oberstdorf at rndabt take exit sp Reichenbach, Rubi. Site in 1km over level x-ing, 2nd site on R. 5*, Med, hdstg, unshd, serviced pitches; EHU (8A) metered; bbq; TV; 10% statics; phone; bus; Eng spkn; adv bkg acc; site clsd Nov; CKE. *"Well-run, well-maintained site; immac facs; block paved paths to pitches; block hdstg with grass growing thro; ski lift 1km; excel scenery; excel facs; easy 20 min level walk to town."* **€38.80**   **2019**

OBERSTDORF *3D4* (3km N Rural) *47.42300, 10.27720* **Campingplatz Oberstdorf,** Rubingerstrasse 16, 87561 Oberstdorf **(08322)** 6525; camping-oberstdorf@t-online.de; www.camping-oberstdorf.de

🐕 €0.50 👫 wo ♨ ⅄ ▯ ⚟ ❤ 🍴 ⑭ ⟟ ▤nr

Fr B19 dir Oberstdorf, foll site sp. 3*, Med, hdstg, serviced pitches; EHU (10A) metered; 45% statics; golf 5km. *"Cable cars to Nebelhorn & Fellhorn in town; ski lift 3km; ski bus; Oberstdorf pedestrianised with elec buses fr o'skirts; vg."* **€32.00, 1 Jan-31 Oct, 15 Dec-31 Dec.**   **2017**

OBERWESEL *3B2* (7.6km SE Rural) *50.05111, 7.7750* **Camping Sonnenstrand,** Strandbadweg 9, 55422 Bacharach **(06743)** 1752; info@camping-sonnenstrand.de; www.camping-rhein.de

🐕 €1 👫 wo ♨ ⅄ ♿ ▯ ⚟ ❤ ♈ ⑭ ▤ ⚠ ⚓adj

S on A61. Exit 44 Laudert via Oberwesel to Bacharach (B9). Turn Sat Nav off after Laudert. Foll sp to Oberwesel-Bacharach. Med, mkd, hdstg, pt shd, EHU (6A); bbq; red long stay; twin axles; 25% statics; Eng spkn; boating; golf 6km; games area; bike hire; games rm; CKE. *"Helpful, knowledgeable owner; poss lge groups m'cyclists; scenic area; busy, noisy rvside site; sm pitches; wine cellar visits; shwrs/san facs ltd & poss stretched high ssn; plenty of rv activities; excel rest; sh walk to sm medieval town; sh stay/NH; gd."* **€19.50, 25 Mar-31 Oct.**   **2016**

OBERWESEL *3B2* (0.9km S Urban) *50.10251, 7.73664*
Camping Schönburgblick, Am Hafendamm 1, 55430
Oberwesel (06744) 714501; camping-oberwesel@t-
online.de; www.camping-oberwesel.de

🛉🛉 ᵂᴰ ♨ ⚊ ∅ ᴹˢᴾ ⵙ ⏦ ⓘ nr ♨ 🏊 nr

**Fr A61/E31 exit sp Oberwesel, site sp on L at ent
to sports stadium, on rvside.** Sm, pt shd, EHU (6A)
€4.20; red long stay; adv bkg acc; tennis adj; CKE.
*"Clean, modern san facs in Portacabins - stretched
when site full; o'night m'vans area; rv trips, cycling,
walking."* **€23.40, 17 Mar-1 Nov.** **2017**

OBERWESEL *3B2* (9km NW Rural) *50.14976, 7.69478*
Camping Friedenau, Gründelbach 103, 56329
St Goar-am-Rhein (06741) 368; info@camping-
friedenau.de; www.camping-friedenau.de

12 🛖 €2 🛉🛉 ᵂᴰ ♨ ⚊ 🖾 ∅ ᴹˢᴾ 🐕 🎪 ⏦ ⓘ 🏊 nr ⚠

**App on B9 fr Boppard or Bingen; turn under rlwy
bdge 1km N of St Goar; keep L; site on L in 1km.
NB - do not app fr J43 off m'way.** 3*, Sm, shd, pt sl,
EHU (16A) €2.50; gas; bus; Eng spkn; CKE. *"Quieter
than other sites in area - uphill fr busy Rhine & resorts;
some pitches uneven & poss diff after heavy rain; vg
welcome; easy walk or cycle to rv town; country walks
fr site; relaxed atmosphere; pool 1.5km; friendly staff;
gd bar/rest; san fac gd; great views fr Rheinfels Castle;
in very pleasant valley; washing up and lndry facs in
female toilet block."* **€21.50** **2016**

OLPE *1B4* (8km N Rural) *51.0736, 7.8564* **Feriencamp
Biggesee - Vier Jahreszeiten,** Am Sonderner Kopf 3,
57462 Olpe-Sondern (02761) 944111; info@
camping-sondern.de; www.camping-biggesee.de

12 🛖 €4.50 🛉🛉 ᵂᴰ ♨ ⚊ 🖾 ∅ ᴹˢᴾ 🐕 🎪 ⏦ ⓘ ♨ 🏊 ⚠ ⚓

**Exit A45/E41 junc 18 & foll sp to Biggesee. Pass
both turnings to Sondern. Take next R in 200m.
Ent on R in 100m. NB: Other sites on lake.** 4*, Lge,
mkd, pt shd, terr, EHU (16A) inc; gas; cooking facs;
sw nr; 20% statics; Eng spkn; adv bkg acc; sauna;
tennis; watersports inc diving; solarium; bike hire;
CKE. *"Gd facs; well-organised site; barrier clsd 1300-
1500 & 2200-0700; rollerskating rink; conv Panorama
Theme Park & Cologne; vg cycling area; footpaths."*
€31.50 **2019**

ORTRAND *2G4* (2km E Rural) *51.37265, 13.77956*
Ferienpark Dresden, Am Bad 1, 01990 Ortrand
35 75 56 20 00; ferienpark-dresden@themen
camping.de; www.themencamping.de

12 🛖 €2 🛉🛉 ᵂᴰ ♨ ⚊ 🖾 ∅ ᴹˢᴾ 🐕 🎪 ⏦ ⓘ ♨ 🏊 ⚠ ⚓
🏊 (htd) 🖾

**A13 Berlin-Dresden. Take exit 18 - Ortrand. At
rndabt take 2nd exit (L55) & foll signs to camp site
2km. Note tight turn L after passing thro indus
units.** Med, mkd, unshd, EHU (16A) €1.50; bbq;
cooking facs; twin axles; TV; 30% statics; phone; Eng
spkn; adv bkg acc; bike hire; games area; waterslide;
games rm; CCI. *"Vg site; volleyball; fishing adj; cls to
mkd cycle rtes; sep car park with hook-ups for late
arrs."* **€33.70** **2019**

OSNABRUCK *1C3* (14km SW Rural) *52.22944, 7.89027*
Regenbogen-Camp Tecklenburg, Grafenstrasse 31,
49545 Leeden (05405) 1007; www.regenbogen.ag

12 🛖 €4 🛉🛉 ᵂᴰ ♨ ⚊ ⚓ 🖾 ∅ ᴹˢᴾ 🐕 ⓘ ♨ 🏊 nr ⚠ ⚓
🏊 (covrd, htd) 🖾

**Exit A1/E37 junc 73 or fr A30/E30 junc 13; foll sp to
Tecklenburg, then Leeden & foll site sp.** V lge, pt shd,
pt sl, serviced pitches; EHU (16A) €2.90; 45% statics;
adv bkg acc; ccard acc; bike hire; games area; CKE. *"Gd
views; o'night area for m'vans open all yr; site clsd 1
Nov-15 Dec; clsd 1300-1500; excel san facs; gd rest."*
€36.50 **2018**

OSTERODE AM HARZ *1D4* (2km E Rural) *51.72779,
10.28281* **Camping Eulenburg,** Scheerenbergstrasse
100, 37520 Osterode-am-Harz (05522) 6611; ferien@
eulenburg-camping.de; www.eulenburg-camping.de

12 🛖 €2 🛉🛉 (htd) ᵂᴰ ♨ ⚊ ⚓ 🖾 ∅ ᴹˢᴾ 🐕 🎪 ⏦ ⓘ ♨ 🏊 nr ⚠
🏊 🖾

**Take B498 fr Osterode cent, cross by-pass at traff
lts. Site on R in 1.5km.** Med, hdstg, mkd, hdg, pt
shd, serviced pitches; EHU (6-16A) metered + conn
fee; gas; bbq (charcoal, sep area); red long stay;
50% statics; Eng spkn; CKE. *"Beautiful old town;
gd cent for Harz mountains; walks to lake fr site;
motorhome stellplatze adj."* **€21.00** **2015**

"I need an on-site restaurant"

We do our best to make sure site information
is correct, but it is always best to check any
must-have facilities are still available or will
be open during your visit.

PAPENBURG *1B2* (1km S Rural) *53.06481, 7.42691*
Camping Poggenpoel, Am Poggenpoel, 26871
Papenburg (04961) 974026; campingpcp@aol.com;
www.papenburg-camping.de

12 🛖 €2.50 🛉🛉 (htd) ᵂᴰ ♨ ⚊ ⚓ 🖾 ∅ ᴹˢᴾ 🐕 ⏦ ⓘ 🏊 ⚠ ⚓

Fr B70, site sp fr town. 4*, Med, pt shd, EHU (10A)
inc; sw nr; red long stay; TV (pitch); 40% statics;
phone; games area; golf 1km; CKE. *"O'night facs for
m'vans."* **€27.50** **2016**

PAPPENHEIM *4E3* (1.8km N Rural) *48.93471,
10.96993* **Camping Pappenheim,** Badweg 1, 91788
Pappenheim (09143) 1275; info@camping-
pappenheim.de; www.camping-pappenheim.de

🛖 €1 🛉🛉 ᵂᴰ ♨ 🖾 ∅ ᴹˢᴾ 🐕 ⓘ nr ♨ 🏊

**B2 heading S, site sp after passing thro Weissenburg,
on edge of Pappenheim.** Med, pt shd, EHU (16A) €2;
sw; 25% statics; Eng spkn. *"Mountain views; excel site
in historical town; castle worth visiting; grass pitches;
san facs dated."* **€20.00, 1 Apr-25 Oct.** **2017**

PASSAU *4G3* (10km NW Rural) *48.60605, 13.34583*
Drei-Flüsse Campingplatz, Am Sonnenhang 8, 94113
Irring **(08546) 633; dreifluessecamping@t-online.de;
www.dreifluessecamping.privat.t-online.de**

🐕 €1.50 🛉🛉 ⬚ 🛁 ⚙ ☕ ⚙ / MP ⓘ 🔌 ⚓ (covrd)

On A3/E56, junc 115 (Passau Nord); foll sps to site.
3*, Med, pt shd, pt sl, terr, serviced pitches; EHU (16A)
€4; gas; bbq; red long stay; phone; bus 200m; adv bkg
acc; ccard acc; CKE. *"Interesting grotto on site; gd rest;
rec arr early; facs need updating; poor surface drainage
after heavy rain; interesting town at confluence of
3 rvs; on Danube cycle way; conv NH fr A3/E56."*
€28.00, 1 Apr-31 Oct.   **2019**

"Satellite navigation makes touring much easier"

Remember most sat navs don't know if you're
towing or in a larger vehicle – always use yours
alongside maps and site directions.

PFALZFELD *3B2* (1km SW Rural) *50.10612, 7.56804*
Country-Camping Schinderhannes,
Hausbayerstrasse, 56291 Hausbay **(06746) 8005440;
info@countrycamping.de; www.countrycamping.de**

12 🐕 €2 🛉🛉 (htd) ⬚ 🛁 ⚙ / MP 🦊 🥢 ☕ ⓘ 🔌 nr /⚓

**Fr A61/E31 exit J43, foll sps for 3km to Pfalzfeld &
onto Hausbay, site sp.** 4*, Med, mkd, hdstg, pt shd,
terr, EHU (6-16A) inc; sw; twin axles; 10% statics; adv
bkg acc; ccard acc; fishing; games rm; tennis; CKE.
*"Pleasant, peaceful, clean site; spacious pitches, some
far fr san facs; helpful, friendly staff; sep NH area;
excel, immac san facs; htd pool 8km; scenic area close
Rv Rhine; vg cycle track; nice area for walking; conv
m'way; excel NH with sep area to stay hitched-on;
wonderful touring area; excel."* **€26.00**   **2019**

PFORZHEIM *3C3* (13km S Rural) *48.81800, 8.73400*
International Camping Schwarzwald, Freibadweg 4,
75242 Neuhausen-Schellbronn **(07234) 6517; fam.
frech@t-online.de; www.camping-schwarzwald.de**

12 🛉🛉 ⬚ 🛁 ⚙ / MP 🦊 🥢 ☕ ⓘ 🔌 /⚓ ✂

**Fr W on A8 exit junc 43 for Pforzheim; fr E exit
junc 45. In town cent take rd 463 sp Calw, but
immed after end of town sp take minor rd L thro
Huchenfeld up hill to Schellbronn; go R in vill.
Site in vill of Schellbronn on N side of rd to Bad
Liebenzell - sp at church on R.** 4*, Lge, pt shd, pt
sl, EHU (17A) €2 or metered; gas; red long stay;
80% statics; bus; adv bkg acc; bike hire; CKE. *"Scenic
area; dance & fitness cent; no vehicle access after
2200; htd pool adj; v clean, well-maintained site; vg san
facs; excel rest/takeaway; v rural."* **€22.00**   **2016**

PIELENHOFEN *4F3* (2km S Rural) *49.05896, 11.95820*
Campingplatz Naabtal, Distelhausen 2, 93188
Pielenhofen **(09409) 373; camping-pielenhofen@t-
online.de; www.camping-pielenhofen.de**

12 🐕 €2.20 🛉🛉 (htd) ⬚ 🛁 ⚙ / MP 🍽 ⓘ 🔌 /⚓

**Exit A3/E56 junc 97 onto B8 dir Etterzhausen. Thro
Etterzhausen turn L to Pielenhofen/Amberg. In
Pielenhofen turn R over bdge.** Lge, mkd, pt shd, EHU
(10A) metered + conn fee €0.60; gas; 65% statics; Eng
spkn; sauna; solarium; bike hire; games area; tennis;
CKE. *"In beautiful valley; helpful warden; v nice site in
gd location; liable to flooding; gd rv access for boating;
family-run site; lots of facs; skittle alley; summer
curling rink; spacious pitches; gd rest; conv Regensburg;
busy site."* **€17.60**   **2015**

PIRMASENS *3B3* (20km NE Rural) *49.27546, 7.72121*
Camping Clausensee, 67714 Waldfischbach-Burgalben
**(06333) 5744; info@campingclausensee.de;
www.campingclausensee.de**

12 🐕 €4.20 🛉🛉 (htd) ⬚ 🛁 ⚙ / MP 🦋 🥢 ☕ ⓘ 🔌 /⚓

**Leave a'bahn A6 at junc 15 Kaiserslautern West;
S onto B270 for 22km. E 9km on minor rd sp Leimen,
site sp.** 4*, Lge, mkd, pt shd, serviced pitches;
EHU (6-16A) inc; gas; bbq; sw nr; red long stay;
TV; 50% statics; Eng spkn; adv bkg acc; ccard acc;
fishing; games rm; boating; CKE. *"Peaceful situation
in Pfalzerwald Park; helpful staff; clean san facs; busy
at w/ends; gd walking & cycling; gd; lovely setting
on shore of Lake Clausensee; noisy at wkends when
permanent o'fits inhabited."* **€31.50**   **2016**

"There aren't many sites open at this time of year"

If you're travelling outside peak season
remember to call ahead to check site opening
dates – even if the entry says 'open all year'.

PORTA WESTFALICA *1C3* (8km SW Rural) *52.22146,
8.83995* **Camping Grosser Weserbogen,** Zum
Südlichen See 1, 32457 Porta Westfalica **(05731)
6188 or 6189; info@grosserweserbogen.de;
www.grosserweserbogen.de**

12 🐕 €1.50 🛉🛉 ⬚ 🛁 ⚙ / MP 🦋 🥢 ☕ ⓘ 🔌 /⚓

**Fr E30/A2 exit junc 33, foll sp to Vennebeck &
Costedt. Site 12km by rd fr Bad Oeynhausen. Site
sp fr m'way.** 4*, Lge, mkd, hdstg, pt shd, EHU (16A)
€2.90; bbq; sw nr; twin axles; Eng spkn; adv bkg acc;
ccard acc; fishing; watersports; games rm; CKE. *"Site
in cent of wildlife reserve; v tranquil, lovely lakeside
location; gd base Teutoburger Wald & Weser valley;
barrier clsd 1300-1500 & o'night; 80% statics; lge area
for tourers; gd for families; excel san facs & rest; shwrs
charged to electronic card; level access; highly rec."*
€27.00   **2016**

GERMANY

POTSDAM *2F3* (10km SW Rural) *52.36088, 12.94663*
Camping Riegelspitze, Fercherstrasse, 14542
Werder-Petzow **(03327) 42397; info@campingplatz-riegelspitze.de; www.campingplatz-riegelspitze.de**

🏕️ ⛺₃ 👫 wo ♨ ᕫ 🍴 ♿ ⅃ ᵐˢᵖ 🦋 ⵟ ℗ 🖫 ⛽ ⟋⟍

Fr A10/E55 Berlin ring a'bahn take exit 22 dir Glindow or Werder exits & foll sp to Werder; then foll B1 for 1.5km twd Potsdam, R after Strengbrücke bdge twd Petzow. 4*, Lge, pt shd, terr, EHU (16A) €0.50 (poss rev pol & long lead req); sw; 50% statics; bus; Eng spkn; adv bkg acc; watersports; bike hire; CKE. *"Friendly recep; haphazard pitching; no dogs high ssn; transport tickets fr recep; recep clsd 1300-1500 and 2200-0700; bus outside site; Sanssouci visit a must; train to Berlin £6; vg."*
€26.50, 1 Apr-25 Oct.   **2016**

POTSDAM *2F3* (10km SW Rural) *52.35278, 12.98981*
Naturcampingplatz Himmelreich, Wentorfinsel, 14548 Caputh **(033209) 70475; info@berlin-potsdam-camping.de; www.berlin-potsdam-camping.de**

🏕️ ⛺₂ 👫 (htd) wo ♨ ᕫ ♿ 🍴 ♿ ⵟ ℗ 🖫 🏊

Exit A10 junc 20 or 23 to Glindow. Take B1 to Geltow, turn L immed after rlwy x-ring & foll sp Caputh. 3*, Lge, shd, EHU (10A) €1.50 (poss rev-pol); 65% statics; phone; adv bkg acc; boat hire; CKE. *"Lovely position on waterfront, ferry 750m; modern san facs; poss haphazard pitching; cycle rtes & walks; lake adj; 2 pin adaptor needed for some pitches."* **€30.00, 1 Apr-31 Oct.**   **2015**

POTSDAM *2F3* (7km SW Rural) *52.36055, 13.00722*
Camping Sanssouci, An der Pirschheide 41, 14471 Potsdam **(0331) 9510988; info@camping-potsdam.de; www.camping-potsdam.de**

🏕️ ⛺₄.₉₀ 👫 wo ♨ ᕫ ♿ 🍴 ♿ ᵐˢᵖ 🦋 ⵟ ⵟ ℗ 🖫 ⟋⟍

Fr A10 Berlin ring rd take exit 22 at Gross Kreutz onto B1 twd Potsdam cent for approx 17km, past Werder (Havel) & Geltow. Site sp approx 2km after Geltow immed bef rlwy bdge. 5*, Lge, shd, serviced pitches; EHU (6A) inc (poss rev pol); gas; bbq; sw nr; 25% statics; Eng spkn; adv bkg acc; horseriding 8km; games rm; bike hire; watersports; fishing; CKE. *"V helpful, friendly owners; lovely area; sandy pitches; poss diff lge o'fits manoeuvring round trees; excel clean facs inc music & underfloor heating; camp bus to/fr stn; gate clsd 1300-1500; fitness cent; gd security; covrd pool 200m; conv Schlosses & Berlin by rail - minibus to stn; excel site and rest; 5 star facs; sm pitches; site & rest cash only; gate opens 7.30am; new kitchen, washup and dog shwr (2016); rec."*
€36.00, 18 Mar-2 Jan, G16.   **2016**

POTTENSTEIN *4E2* (3km NW Rural) *49.77942, 11.38411* **Feriencampingplatz Bärenschlucht,** 12 Weidmannsgesees, 91278 Pottenstein **(09243) 206; info@baerenschlucht-camping.de; www.baerenschlucht-camping.de**

12 🏕️ ⛺₁.₉₀ 👫 (htd) wo ♨ ᕫ ♿ 🍴 ♿ ᵐˢᵖ 🦋 ⵟ ℗ 🖫 nr

Exit A9 junc 44 onto B470 dir Forchheim; cont past Pottenstein; site in 2km on R. Med, pt shd, pt sl, EHU (8-16A) €1.90; gas; cooking facs; 40% statics. *"A naturalized quarry surrounded by trees & rocky cliffs; vg; scenic area; local caves & climbing; excel local rest and san facs; adv bkg via email."* **€20.00**   **2016**

PREETZ *1D1* (6km SE Rural) *54.21073, 10.31720* **Camp Lanker See,** Gläserkoppel 3, 24211 Preetz-Gläserkoppel **(04342) 81513; camp@lankersee.de; www.camp-lankersee.de**

🏕️ ⛺₁ 👫 wo ♨ ᕫ ♿ 🦋 ⵟ ℗ 🖫 ⛽

Sp off B76 bet Preetz & Plön. 4*, Lge, mkd, pt shd, terr, EHU (6A) metered; sw; 10% statics; phone; adv bkg acc; ccard acc; horseriding; boating; CKE. *"Barrier clsd 1300-1500 & o'night; gd."*
€19.00, 1 Apr-31 Oct.   **2016**

PRUM *3A2* (2km NE Rural) *50.21906, 6.43811* **Waldcamping Prüm,** 54591 Prüm **(06551) 2481; info@waldcamping-pruem.de; www.waldcamping-pruem.de**

12 🏕️ ⛺₂.₅₀ 👫 wo ♨ ᕫ ♿ 🍴 ♿ ᵐˢᵖ 🦋 ⵟ ℗ nr 🖫 ⛽ ⟋⟍ 🏊

Site sp fr town cent dir Dausfeld. 4*, Med, pt shd, EHU (10-16A) inc; gas; 60% statics; Eng spkn; adv bkg acc; ccard acc; tennis adj; bike hire; CKE. *"Pleasant site in lovely surroundings; pool complex adj; friendly staff; clean facs; m'van o'night facs; ski lift 2km; o'night facs for m'vans; do not arr bef 1900 on Sundays due local rd closures for family cycling event."* **€28.20**   **2019**

QUEDLINBURG *2E3* (10km SW Urban) *51.75614, 11.04956* **Kloster Camping Thale,** Burghardt Wilsdorf, Wendhusenstraße 3, 06502 Thale **(03947) 63185; info@klostercamping-thale.de; www.klostercamping-thale.de**

12 👫 (htd) wo ♨ ᕫ ♿ 🍴 ♿ ᵐˢᵖ 🦋 ⵟ ℗ nr 🖫 ⛽ nr ⟋⟍

Head S twds Steinholzstraße. 1st R onto Steinholzstraße. Bear L onto Stauffenberg-Platz. Turn L onto Weststraße cont onto Wipertistraße for 1.4km then onto Unter der Altenburg. Cont onto K2356, turn L onto Thalenser Str. Cont onto L240 then turn L onto L92. After 1.4km turn L onto Schmiedestraße. Then R onto Breiteweg & bear R onto Wendhusenstraße. Site on LH side. Med, mkd, hdstg, pt shd, EHU (10A) €2.50; 10% statics; bus 0.3km; CKE. *"San facs excel; lovely site with gdn & lake."*
€27.00   **2018**

For a guide to symbols see the fold out on the rear cover

RADEVORMWALD *1B4* (5km SW Rural) *51.18498, 7.31362* **Camping-Ferienpark Kräwinkel,** Kräwinkel 1, 42477 Radevormwald **(02195) 6887899; info@ ferienpark.de**

12 ♿ €2 ♦♦(htd) 🅦 ⚓ ♨ ⚥ 🦋 ☂ ⊕ 🏛

Exit A1 at junc 95B, take B229 sp Radevormwald, foll B229 for 6km over lake bdge to 1st rndabt, R sp Heide & Krawinkel, site on L in 3km. Sm, hdg, pt shd, terr, EHU (20A) inc; sw nr; 80% statics; Eng spkn; adv bkg acc; CKE. *"Lge pitches; pleasant area; key needed for all facs €10 deposit; friendly owner; call nbr on noticeboard for access."* **€16.00**   **2017**

RADOLFZELL AM BODENSEE *3C4* (16km S Rural) *47.65972, 8.93388* **Campingplatz Wangen,** Seeweg 32, 78337 Öhningen-Wangen **(07735) 919675; info@ camping-wangen.de www.camping-wangen.de**

♦♦ €2 ♦♦ 🅦 ⚓ ♿ ⚥ 🦋 ♊ ☂ ⊕♿ ♨nr 🏛

Site in Wangen vill, 5km E of Stein am Rhien. 4*, Med, hdstg, pt shd, EHU (10A) metered + conn fee; bbq; sw nr; twin axles; 40% statics; phone; Eng spkn; adv bkg acc; games area; fishing; CKE. *"Lovely scenery; site in vill but quiet; dogs by prior arrangement only; helpful recep; gd cycling & sw; lake steamer trips; Stein-am-Rhein 5km; watersports in adj lake."* **€22.00, 3 Apr-3 Oct.**   **2019**

RADOLFZELL AM BODENSEE *3C4* (6km SW Urban) *47.72942, 9.02432* **Campingplatz Willam,** 78315 Markelfingen **(049) 7533 6211; info@campingplatz-willam.de; www.campingplatz-willam.de**

♦♦ 🅦 ⚓ ♨ ⚥ ☂ ⊕♿ 🏛 ♊adj

Fr S on A81 at junc 40 take A98 for 9m, at end of m'way turn L, site ent on L in 0.75m. Lge, mkd, pt shd, EHU (€0.7/kWh); gas; bbq; Eng spkn; boat hire; CKE. *"Gd site; cycle track; modern san facs; some noise fr rlwy; 2.6m low bdge nr site ent (can be avoided)."* **€20.50, 23 Mar-3 Oct.**   **2016**

RAVENSBURG *3D4* (13km SW Rural) *47.73935, 9.47187* **Camping am Bauernhof,** St Georg Strasse 8, 88094 Oberteuringen-Neuhaus **(07546) 2446; kramer@camping-am-bauernhof.de; www.camping-am-bauernhof.de**

♦♦ €2 ♦♦ 🅦 ⚓ ♿ ⚥ 🦋 ♨nr 🏛

Fr Ravensburg twd Meersburg on B33. In Neuhaus foll sp on R; site bef chapel. Sm, pt shd, EHU (10A) €2.50; bbq; sw; 20% statics; Eng spkn; games rm; CKE. *"CL-type but with full facs inc shwrs for wheelchair users; vg, clean, modern san facs; volleyball; relaxed atmosphere; gd cycling area; farm with animals, fruit, distillery, herb garden, barn; sm lake on site; pre order fresh rolls/bread daily; excel site; lots of interest for kids; sep park for m'van on hdstg; friendly, helpful owners."* **€22.50, 28 Mar-15 Sep.**   **2015**

REGENSBURG *4F3* (5km NW Urban) *49.02779, 12.05899* **Azur Campingpark Regensburg,** Weinweg 40, 93049 Regensburg **(0941) 270025; regensburg@ azur-camping.de; www.azur-camping.de**

12 ♿ €3.50 ♦♦(htd) 🅦 ⚓ ♿ 🍴 ⚥ 🦋 ☂ ⊕ 🐾 🏛

Fr A93/E50 exit junc 40 Regensburg W, dir Weiden; turn W away fr town onto dual c'way; R at traff lts, site sp fr next T-junc. Lge, hdstg, pt shd, EHU (10A) €3 (poss long lead req); 40% statics; phone; bus at site ent; bike hire; CKE. *"Helpful owner; vg facs; gd, clean san facs, lge block unisex; covrd pool 300m; sm pitches poss diff lge o'fits; dist bet units minimal; o'night m'vans area; cycle path into town along Rv Danube; gates clsd 1300-1500 & 2200-0800; gd."* **€31.00**   **2015**

REINSBERG *2G4* (1km W Rural) *51.00381, 13.36012* **Campingplatz Reinsberg,** Badstrasse 17, 19629 Reinsberg **(037324) 82268; campingplatz-reinsberg@web.de; www.campingplatz-reinsberg.de**

♦♦ €2 ♦♦(htd) 🅦 ⚓ ♿ ⚥ 🦋 ♊ ♨nr ⊕nr♿ 🐾 🏛

Exit A4/E40 junc 75 Nossen. Take 1st R to Siebenlehn & foll sp Reinsberg. In Reinsberg take 1st R sp camping & 'freibad' to site. 3*, Med, pt shd, EHU (16A) €2; 40% statics; phone; Eng spkn; adv bkg acc. *"Friendly, helpful owner; sports facs adj; excel san facs; gd walking; conv Meissen, Dresden & Freiberg; v clean; peaceful; pool adj; gd for dogs, walks and cycling."* **€16.00, 25 Mar-31 Oct.**   **2016**

REMAGEN *3B1* (1km ENE Urban) *50.57666, 7.25083* **Campingplatz Goldene Meile,** Simrockweg 9-13, 53424 Remagen **(02642) 22222; info@camping-goldene-meile.de; www.camping-goldene-meile.de**

12 ♦♦ €1.70 ♦♦ 🅦 ⚓ ♿ ⚥ 🦋 ♊ ☂ ⊕♿ 🐾 🏛 ♬

Fr A61 exit dir Remagen onto B266; foll sp 'Rheinfähre Linz'; in Kripp turn L, site sp. Or fr B266 1km beyond Bad Bodendorf at rndabt take B9 (dir Bonn & Remagen); in 1km take exit Remagen Süd; foll sp to sports cent/camping. Site adj Luddendorf Bdge. Fr S on A48 exit junc 10 onto B9 twd Bonn. Site sp in 22km after junc with B266. 4*, Lge, hdstg, hdg, mkd, pt shd, serviced pitches; EHU (16A) €2.60 (50m cable rec some pitches); gas; 50% statics; train into Bonn; Eng spkn; adv bkg acc; bike hire; CKE. *"Tourers on flat field away fr rvbank; sm pitches tightly packed in high ssn; gd rest; helpful staff; EHU up ladder; access to facs not gd; cycle path along Rhine; m'van o'night area adj; site clsd 1300-1500; vg, well-organised site; pool adj; interesting old town."* **€27.50**   **2018**

RERIK *2E1* (1km NE Urban) *54.11133, 11.63234* **Campingpark Ostseebad Rerik,** Straße am Zeltplatz 18230 Ostseebad Rerik **038296 75720; info@ campingpark-rerik.de; www.campingpark-rerik.de**

12 ♦♦ €3 ♦♦(htd) 🅦 ⚓ ♿ ⚥ 🦋 ♊ ☂ ⊕♿ 🏛 ♊

Fr A20 junc 12 to Kröpelin on L12 thro Kröelin twrds Rerik then foll sp to site. 5*, Med, hdg, mkd, pt shd, EHU (16A); Eng spkn; ccard acc. *"Gd site; new modern facs."* **€27.00**   **2016**

GERMANY

RETGENDORF *2E2* (4.6km N Rural) *53.75194, 11.49638* **Seecamping Flessenow,** Am Schweriner See 1A, 19067 Flessenow **(03866) 81491; info@ seecamping.de; www.seecamping.de**

🏕 👭(htd) ⬜ 🏊 ♨ ⬇ ☐ ⚊ ⚽ 🦋 🛈 ⛱ 🛒 ⚓

Exit A14 at junc 4 Schwerin-Nord onto B104 dir Schwerin. In 2km turn R along lakeside sp Retgendorf & Flessenow, site in approx 10km. 4*, Med, mkd, pt shd, EHU (10A) €2.50; gas; bbq (charcoal); sw nr; twin axles; TV; 50% statics; phone; bus adj; adv bkg acc; ccard acc; watersports; games area; CKE. *"Fair site in gd location; gd long stay for touring."* **€30.00, 30 Mar-14 Oct.** **2018**

RHEINMUNSTER *3C3* (1km NW Rural) *48.77330, 8.04041* **Freizeitcenter Oberrhein,** Am Campingpark 1, 77836 Rheinmünster-Stollhofen **(07227) 2500; info@freizeitcenter-oberrhein.de; www.freizeit center-oberrhein.de**

12 🏕 €4.50 👭 ⬜ 🏊 ♨ ⬇ ☐ ⚊ ⚽ 🦋 🛈 🛒 ⚓ ✎

Exit A5 junc 51 at Baden Baden/Iffezheim sp to join B500. At traff lts turn L onto B36 dir Hügelsheim & Kehl. In 8km turn R at rndabt immed on ent Stollhofen & cont to end of lane. 5*, V lge, mkd, hdg, pt shd, serviced pitches; EHU (16A) €2.50 + conn fee; gas; sw; 70% statics; phone; Eng spkn; adv bkg acc; ccard acc; watersports; windsurfing; golf 6km; tennis; fishing; bike hire. *"Conv touring base Baden-Baden, Strasbourg; Black Forest; helpful, nice staff; clsd 1300-1500; m'van o'night area outside site; excel san facs; highly rec; some lovely lakeside pitches; gd cycling by Rhine."* **€32.00** **2015**

RIBNITZ DAMGARTEN *2F1* (13km NE Coastal) *5 4.28194, 12.31250* **Camping in Neuhaus,** Birkenallee 10, 18347 Dierhagen-Neuhaus **(038226) 539930; ostsee@camping-neuhaus.de; www.camping-neuhaus.de**

12 🏕 €3 👭(htd) ⬜ 🏊 ♨ ⬇ ☐ ⚊ 🦋 🛈 nr ⚓ ⚓ 🏖100m

Exit E55/A19 junc 6 onto B105 N. At Altheide turn N thro Klockenhagen dir Dierhagen, then turn L at camping sp & foll site sp to sea. Med, hdg, pt shd, EHU (16A); 40% statics; adv bkg acc. *"Friendly site; vg."* **€28.00** **2016**

RIBNITZ DAMGARTEN *2F1* (13km NW Coastal) *54.29188, 12.34375* **Ostseecamp Dierhagen,** Ernst Moritz Arndt Strasse, 18347 Dierhagen-Strand **(038226) 80778; info@ostseecamp-dierhagen.de; www.ostseecamp-dierhagen.de**

🏕 €2.80 👭 ⬜ 🏊 ⬇ ☐ ⚊ 🦋 🛈 ⚓ ⚓ 🏖sand 800m

Take B105 fr Rostock dir Stralsund. Bef Ribnitz, turn L sp Dierhagen & Wustrow & cont for 5km to traff lts & camp sp. Turn L to site on R in 300m. Lge, pt shd, EHU (6A) €3; gas; 20% statics; phone; adv bkg req; bike hire. *"Site low-lying, poss v wet after heavy rain; bkg fee; charge for chem disp."* **€34.00, 15 Mar-31 Oct.** **2016**

RIEGEL AM KAISERSTUHL *3B4* (1.5km N Rural) *48.16463, 7.74008* **Camping Müller-See,** Zum Müller-See 1, 79359 Riegel-am-Kaiserstuhl **(07642) 3694; info@muellersee.de; www.muellersee.de**

👭(htd) ⬜ 🏊 ♨ ⬇ ☐ ⚊ ⚽ 🦋 🛈 🍽 🛈 nr 🛒 ⚓

Exit A5/E35 at junc 59 dir Riegel, foll site sp. 4*, Med, pt shd, EHU (16A) €2; sw nr; phone; CKE. *"Excel cycle paths in area; excel san facs; gd NH; train to Freiburg; sep excel MH area (unshd, €10 inc acc to all facs); elec fr pay boxes."* **€25.00, 1 Apr-31 Oct.** **2019**

RIESTE *1C3* (0.2km W Rural) *52.48555, 7.99003* **Alfsee Ferien- und Erholungspark,** Am Campingpark 10, 49597 Rieste **(05464) 92120; info@alfsee.de; www.alfsee.de**

12 🏕 €3 👭(htd) ⬜ 🏊 ♨ ⬇ ☐ ⚊ ⚽ 🛒 🍽 🛈 ⚓ ⚓ ⚓

Exit A1/E37 junc 67; site in 10km, sp. 5*, V lge, mkd, pt shd, EHU (16A) metered; sw nr; 50% statics; phone; Eng spkn; ccard acc; tennis; watersports; bike hire; CKE. *"Site pt of lge watersports complex; modern san facs; gd for famiies, conv for Osnotbruk old town."* **€37.30** **2019**

"That's changed – Should I let the Club know?"

If you find something on site that's different from the site entry, fill in a report and let us know. See camc.com/europereport.

ROSENHEIM *4F4* (9km N Rural) *47.92518, 12.13571* **Camping Erlensee,** Rosenheimerstrasse 63, 83135 Schechen **(08039) 1695; campingplatz-erlensee@t-online.de; www.camping-erlensee.de**

12 🐕 €2 👭 ⬜ 🏊 ☐ ⚊ 🛈 ⚓ nr

Exit A8 junc 102, avoid Rosenheim town cent by foll B15 sp Landshut. Site on E side of B15 at S end Schechen. 3*, Med, pt shd, serviced pitches; EHU (16A) €2; sw; 60% statics; Eng spkn; adv bkg acc; CKE. *"Pleasant, gd & simple site; helpful owners; excel facs; mosquito prob."* **€25.00** **2019**

ROSENHEIM *4F4* (14km SW Rural) *47.78978, 12.00575* **Kaiser Camping (formerly known as Tenda-Park),** Reithof 2, 83075 Bad Feilnbach **(08066) 884400; info@kaiser-camping.com; www.kaiser-camping.com**

12 🏕 €3 👭 🏊 ♨ ⬇ ☐ ⚊ 🦋 🛈 ⚓ ⚓ ⚓ ✎ (htd) 🛁

Take exit 100 fr A8/E45/E52 & foll sp to Brannenburg. Site in 5km on R, 1km N of Bad Feilnbach. 4*, V lge, pt shd, EHU (16A) €2 or metered + conn fee (poss rev pol); gas; 80% statics; Eng spkn; adv bkg acc; bike hire. *"V busy, clean, well-run site; pleasant, wooded pitches; useful NH; pleasant helpful staff; some of the best san facs; ski lift 12km; discount vouchers for local shops/ rest."* **€32.00** **2017**

GERMANY

ROSTOCK *2F1* (23.5km NNE Rural/Coastal) *54.194259, 12.155333* **Camp & Ferienpark Markgrafenheide,** Budentannenweg 2, 18146 Markgrafenheide **(938166)** 11510 or (45448) 00313; info@baltic-freizeit.de; www.baltic-freizeit.de

🚲 🐕 ♦️ WD ⚐ 🚿 ♨️ ⚙️ ᴹᴾ ☂ Ⓣ Ⓗ 🍴 ᴢᴢ 🅿️ 🏊 (covrd, htd) ⬆️100m

Take B105/E22 fr Rostock twrds Stralsund. Aft 9km exit twrds Markgrafenheide & Niederhagen. Aft 3.5km turn L. Aft approx 4km sharp R, site immed on L. Lge, mkd, shd, EHU (16A); bbq; TV; Eng spkn; adv bkg acc; sauna; games area; bike hire; CKE. *"Vg site; 20mins fr ferry terminal; max 2 dog; wellness ctr."* **€36.50** 2018

ROTHENBURG OB DER TAUBER *3D2* (3km NW Rural) *49.38805, 10.16638* **Camping Tauber-Idyll,** Detwang 28, 91541 Rothenburg-ob-der-Tauber **(09861) 3177 or 6463; camping-tauber-idyll@t-online.de; www.rothenburg.de/tauberidyll**

🐕 €1 ♦️(htd) WD ⚐ 🚿 ♨️ 🍴 ᴹᴾ Ⓗ 🅿️

NW on Rothenburg-Bad Mergentheim rd in vill of Detwang. Sp. Site behind inn nr church. Care on tight R turn into ent. Sm, pt shd, EHU (6-16A) €2 or metered + conn fee; gas; bus; Eng spkn; adv bkg rec; bike hire. *"Church clock chimes each hr; clsd to vehicles 2200-0800; old walled town, gd cent for Romantische Strasse & Hohenlohe Plain; owners helpful, friendly; pleasant, peaceful, excel site; gd, clean san facs; sm c'van pitches at busy times; gd walking & cycle rte along valley; playgrnd at church; rec."* **€20.00, 23 Mar-31 Oct.** 2018

ROTHENBURG OB DER TAUBER *3D2* (3km NW Rural) *49.38888, 10.16722* **Campingplatz Tauber-Romantik,** Detwang 39, 91541 Rothenburg-ob-der-Tauber **(09861) 6191; info@camping-tauber-romantik.de; www.camping-tauberromantik.de**

🐕 €2 ♦️(htd) WD ⚐ 🚿 ♨️ 🍴 ᴹᴾ ☂ Ⓗ 🍴 ᴢᴢ 🅿️

NW on Rothenburg-Bad Mergentheim rd in vill of Detwang; turn L at camp sp & immed R; site sp fr Rothenburg. Sharp turn into site ent. Med, mkd, hdstg, pt shd, pt sl, terr, EHU (16A) €2.40; gas; 10% statics; phone; bus adj; Eng spkn; adv bkg acc; ccard acc; CKE. *"Pleasant, gd value site; excel, clean, vg facs; gd sized pitches; picturesque town; gd cycle rte; pleasant atmosphere; gd facs for children; conv NH for Rothenburg, Austria, Italy; busy over festival w/ends; vg; well managed."* **€24.00, 15 Mar-4 Nov & 30 Nov-7 Jan.** 2017

RUDESHEIM *3C2* (3km E Urban) *49.97944, 7.95777* **Camping Geisenheim Rheingau,** Am Campingplatz 1, 65366 Geisenheim **(06722) 75600; campingplatz geisenheim@t-online.de; www.rheingau-camping.de**

🐕 €1.50 ♦️(htd) WD ⚐ 🚿 ♨️ 🍴 ☂ Ⓣ Ⓗ ᴢᴢ 🅿️

Well sp fr B42, on rvside. 3*, Lge, mkd, pt shd, EHU (16A) metered €1 + 0.76 per kWh; bbq; 50% statics; bus adj; Eng spkn; adv bkg acc; games area; CKE. *"Vg site bet Rv Rhine & vineyards; walks and cycling by rv; lots to do."* **€25.00, 15 Mar-31 Oct.** 2017

RUDESHEIM *3C2* (2km SE Urban) *49.97777, 7.94083* **Camping am Rhein,** Auf der Lach, 65385 Rüdesheim-am-Rhein **(06722) 2528 or 49299 (LS); info@camping platz-ruedesheim.de; www.campingplatz-ruedes heim.de**

🐕 €3 ♦️(htd) WD ⚐ 🚿 ♨️ 🍴 ᴹᴾ ☂ Ⓗ ᴢᴢ 🅿️

Fr Koblenz (N) on B42 pass car ferry to Bingen on app to Rüdesheim; turn L & over rlwy x-ing, foll Rheinstrasse & rlwy E for 1km; cont under rlwy bdge, turn R sp to Car Park 6; turn R at T-junc, pass coach park; turn L at x-rds & foll rd to site on R. When arr via Bingen ferry turn R onto B42 & foll above dir fr level x-ing. Fr S on B42 ent Rüdesheim, turn L immed after o'head rlwy bdge (2.8m); foll camping sp. Lge, pt shd, EHU (10A) inc (poss rev pol & poss long lead req); gas; bbq (charcoal, gas); bus 500m; Eng spkn; adv bkg acc; horseriding 4km; tennis adj; bike hire; CKE. *"Pleasant, busy, family-run, well-kept site; gd, clean modern facs; poss long walk to water supply; pleasant 1km walk/cycleway by rv to town; warden sites you & connects elec - no mkd pitches; perforated grnd sheets only allowed; recep 0800-2200; rallies welcome; htd pool, paddling pool adj; Harley Davidson w/end bike festival in June; no o'fits over 11m; pool adj; shwrs far; pleasant loc by rv; shops conv."* **€31.00, 1 May-3 Oct, G08.** 2016

SAARBURG *3B2* (5km S Urban) *49.59937, 6.54143* **Camping Leukbachtal,** 54439 Saarburg **(06581) 2228; service@campingleukbachtal.de; www.camping leukbachtal.de**

🐕 €2 ♦️ WD ⚐ 🚿 🍴 ☂ Ⓗ ᴢᴢ 🅿️

Fr B51 Trier-Sarbrucken rd on S end Saarburg ring rd, take exit sp Nennig, Wincheringen, site sp. Site on o'skirts of Saarburg on L of B407. 3*, Med, hdg, pt shd, EHU (6A); bbq; sw nr; Eng spkn; adv bkg acc; CKE. *"Gd walking area; m'van o'night rate; interesting scenic town; vg."* **€19.70, 19 Mar-15 Oct.** 2016

SAARBURG *3B2* (3km W Rural) *49.60083, 6.52833* **Campingplatz Waldfrieden,** Im Fichtenhain 4, 54439 Saarburg **(06581) 2255; info@campingwaldfrieden.de; www.campingwaldfrieden.de**

🚲 🐕 €2 ♦️ WD ⚐ 🚿 🍴 ☂ ☂ Ⓗ 🍴 ᴢᴢ 🅿️

Fr B51/B407 bypass foll sp 'krankenhaus' (hospital). Site sp off L132. 4*, Med, hdg, hdstg, pt shd, pt sl, serviced pitches; EHU (16A) metered; gas; bbq; cooking facs; red long stay; TV; 60% statics; Eng spkn; adv bkg acc; bike hire; CKE. *"Highly rec; helpful owners; warm welcome; clean facs; pitches poss tight lge o'fits; Aldi & Rewe supmkt 1km."* **€24.00** 2016

SAARLOUIS *3B2* (11km NW Rural) *49.36732, 6.66043* **Camping Siersburg,** Zum Niedwehr 1, 66780 Siersburg **(06835) 2100; info@campingplatz-siersburg.de; www.campingplatz-siersburg.de**

🛏 €2 ♦♦ ⓌⒸ ♨ ♿ ⅃ ⊘ ❦ ⁂ ① ♨ ⚠

Fr Saarlouis, leave A8 at junc 7, foll Rehlingen, turn off to Siersburg. Foll sp in Siersburg for site thro town to o'skirts. Lge, mkd, pt shd, EHU (16A); bbq; twin axles; Eng spkn; games area. *"Spacious site in rv Nied; walking & cycling rtes nrby; ruined castle in town; vg."* **€19.00, 1 Apr-31 Oct.** **2015**

SAARLOUIS *3B2* (2km NW Urban) *49.31833, 6.73972* **Campingpark Saarlouis Dr Ernst Dadder,** Marschall-Ney-Weg 2, 66740 Saarlouis **(06831) 3691; info@campingplatz-saarlouis.de; www.campingplatz-saarlouis.de**

🛏 €0.60 ♦♦ ♨ ⊟ ⊘ ⁂ ❦ ⁂ ♨ ⚑ nr

Exit A620/E29 junc 2. Foll sp to city cent. At 500m approx turn L at traff lts sp 'Schiffanlegestelle'. At 500m approx site on R. 3*, Med, pt shd, EHU (16A) €2.30 or metered; gas; red long stay; 50% statics; Eng spkn; adv bkg acc; ccard acc; CKE. *"Castles, Roman remains, ruins & forest rds at Saarland & Saarbrücken; htd pool 150m; beautifully situated & clean; conv for A8; 15min walk to town; friendly, helpful owner; gd rest; cycle rte along R Saar; recep clsd 1200-1400."* **€21.00, 15 Mar-31 Oct.** **2018**

SALEM *3D4* (2.6km NE Rural) *47.76926, 9.30693* **Gern-Campinghof Salem,** Weildorferstrasse 46, 88682 Salem-Neufrach **(07553) 829695; info@campinghof-salem.de; www.campinghof-salem.de**

🛏 €2 ♦♦ (htd) ⓌⒸ ♨ ♨ ⊟ ⊘ ❦ ♨ ⁔ ① nr ⚠

Site well sp on all app to Neufrach on rvside. 4*, Med, mkd, unshd, pt sl, EHU (16A) €2; gas; bbq; cooking facs; sw nr; TV (pitch); 5% statics; phone; bus; Eng spkn; adv bkg acc; ccard acc; tennis; games rm; CKE. *"Excel touring base for Lake Constance away fr busy lakeside sites; htd covrd pool 4km; barrier clsd 1230-1500 & 2200-0700; avoid pitches by recep - noise & dust; gd, clean san facs; friendly, helpful owners; no dogs Jul/Aug; gd for families; vg."* **€25.50, 1 Apr-31 Oct.** **2018**

SCHILLINGSFURST *3D3* (2km S Rural) *49.27353, 10.26587* **Campingplatz Frankenhöhe,** Fischhaus 2, 91583 Schillingsfürst **(09868) 5111; info@campingplatz-frankenhoehe.de; www.campingplatz-frankenhoehe.de**

⑫ 🛏 €1.50 ♦♦ (htd) ⓌⒸ ♨ ♨ ♿ ⊟ ⊘ ⁂ ♨ ⚑ ⚠

Fr A7/E43 exit junc 109; fr A6/E50 exit junc 49. Site situated bet Dombühl & Schillingsfürst. 3*, Med, pt shd, pt sl, EHU (16A) €2.50 or metered + conn fee; gas; sw nr; red long stay; 40% statics; phone; adv bkg acc; CKE. *"Very clean facs; barrier clsd 1300-1500 & 2100-0700; poss unkempt early ssn (2009); gd cycle paths; ACSI prices; gd NH."* **€21.00** **2017**

SCHILTACH *3C3* (0.8km W Urban) *48.29061, 8.33746* **Camping Schiltach,** Bahnhofstrasse 6, 77761 Schiltach **(07836) 7289; campingplatz-schiltach@t-online.de**

♦♦ (htd) ⓌⒸ ♨ ♿ ⊟ ⊘ ⁂ ❦ ⁂ ♨ ① nr ⚑ ⚠ nr ⚠

Site on B294 sp on ent to vill; short, steep ent & sharp turns. 3*, Sm, mkd, pt shd, EHU (16A) metered + conn fee; bbq; 2% statics; phone; train 200m; Eng spkn; adv bkg acc; CKE. *"Vg, clean, tidy site on rv bank adj indus est; covrd pool 2km; recep clsd 1230-1430; picturesque vill; disused rlwy bdge over pt of site, 2.6m headrm; friendly staff."* **€21.70, 1 Apr-10 Oct.** **2016**

SCHLEIDEN *3B1* (6km NW Rural) *50.52752, 6.41195* **Camping Schafbachmühle,** 53937 Schleiden-Harperscheid **(02485) 268; info@schafbachmuehle.de; www.schafbachmuehle.de**

⑫ 🛏 €2.20 ♦♦ (htd) ⓌⒸ ♨ ♨ ♿ ⊟ ⊘ ⁂ ❦ ⁂ ♨ ① ⚑ ⚑ nr ⚠

Fr Schleiden take B258 twd Monschau. In 3.5km turn R sp Schafbachmühle. Site in 2.5km on L. Med, hdstg, mkd, pt shd, terr, EHU (10A) metered + conn fee; bbq; 60% statics; phone; Eng spkn; adv bkg acc; games area. *"Tranquil site; gd for touring Eifel, Mosel Valley, Rhine Valley."* **€20.50** **2016**

SCHLESWIG *1D1* (6km S Rural) *54.50111, 9.57027* **Wikinger Camping Haithabu,** 24866 Haddeby **(04621) 32450; info@campingplatz-haithabu.de; www.campingplatz-haithabu.de**

🛏 €2 ♦♦ ⓌⒸ ♨ ♨ ♿ ⊟ ⊘ ⁂ ♨ ⚑ ⚑ nr ⚠

Leave A7/45 N & S junc 6. Travel E two Schleswig & turn R onto B76 sp Kiel & Eckernförde. Site on L in 2km sp. Med, pt shd, EHU (16A) €2; bbq; sw nr; 10% statics; bus; Eng spkn; adv bkg acc; fishing; bike hire; CKE. *"Lovely site on rv with lovely views; foot & cycle paths to Schleswig (4.5km) & ferry; gd area for children; Schloss Gottorf worth visit; boating facs; vg Viking museum adj; shwrs newly refurb (2015); boating; gd."* **€23.00, 1 Mar-31 Oct.** **2017**

SCHOMBERG *3C3* (2km N Rural) *48.79820, 8.63623* **Höhen-Camping,** Schömbergstrasse 32, 75328 Langenbrand **(07084) 6131; info@hoehencamping.de; www.hoehencamping.de**

⑫ 🛏 €2 ♦♦ (htd) ⓌⒸ ♨ ♨ ⊟ ⊘ ❦ ⚑ nr ⚠

Fr N exit A8 junc 43 Pforzheim, take B463 dir Calw. Turn R sp Schömberg & foll sp Langenbrand. 5*, Med, hdg, mkd, pt shd, pt sl, EHU (10-16A) €3; TV; 70% statics; phone; adv bkg acc; CKE. *"Clean, well-maintained site in N of Black Forest; no recep, ring bell on house adj site ent; blocks req for sl pitches; vg site with excel san facs."* **€20.00** **2018**

For a guide to symbols see the fold out on the rear cover

SCHONAU IM SCHWARZWALD *3B4* (1km N Rural) *47.79127, 7.90076* **Camping Schönenbuchen,** Friedrichstrasse 58, 79677 Schönau **(07673) 7610; info@camping-schoenau.de; www.camping-schoenau.de**

🅲🅱 ⛺ ∈1 ♨ [wc] ♨ ⚓ ♿ ⊟ ⚙ [MsP] 🛒 🍸 ⊕ ♨ ⚡ nr 🏔 ⚓ (htd)

Fr Lörrach on B317 dir Todtnau for approx 23km. Site thro Schönau main rd on R on rvside, ent thro car park. Narr access diff for l'ge o'fits. 3*, Med, hdg, pt shd, EHU inc (16A) (poss rev pol); sw nr; red long stay; 70% statics; adv bkg acc; watersports adj; bike hire; horseriding; sauna; tennis; CKE. *"Friendly staff; site poss not well-kept; gd walking & cycling; lovely old town."* **€25.00** **2019**

SCHUTTORF *1B3* (2km N Rural) *52.33960, 7.22617* **Camping Quendorfer See,** Weiße Riete 3, 48465 Schüttorf **05923 90 29 39; info@camping-schuettorf.de; www.camping-schuettorf.de**

⛺ ∈2 ♨ (htd) [wc] ♨ ⚓ ♿ ⊟ ⚙ [MsP] 🛒 🍸 ♨ ⚡ nr 🏔

A1/A30, exit J4 Schüttorf-Nord. Or A31 exit J28 Schüttorf-Ost twds town cent. Foll sp to site. Sm, hdg, mkd, unshd, EHU (16A); sw nr; twin axles; adv bkg acc; ccard acc; games area; CCI. *"Excel site; immac san facs; mostly fully serviced pitches; conv NH for ferries fr Holland; flat cycling & walking."* **€26.50, 1 Apr-31 Oct.** **2019**

SCHWAAN *2F2* (3.6km S Rural) *53.92346, 12.10688* **Camping Schwaan,** Güstrowerstrasse 54/Sandgarten 17, 18258 Schwaan **(03844) 813716; info@camping platz-schwaan.de; www.campingplatz-schwaan.de**

⛺ ∈2 ♨ (htd) ♨ ⚓ ♿ ⊟ ⚙ [MsP] 🛒 ♟ 🍸 ⊕ ♨ ⚡ 🏔 ♫

Fr A20 exit junc 13 to Schwaan, site sp. Fr A19 exit junc 11 dir Bad Doberan & Schwaan. Site adj Rv Warnow. 4*, Lge, mkd, pt shd, EHU (16A) €2.20 or metered; cooking facs; TV; 30% statics; adv bkg acc; sauna; site clsd 21 Dec-4 Jan; canoeing; games area; bike hire; tennis 700m; boat hire. *"Pleasant rvside site; gd touring base; tight app thro Schwaan town (esp fr N)."* **€21.00, 1 Mar-31 Oct.** **2019**

SCHWABISCH HALL *3D3* (2km S Urban) *49.09868, 9.74288* **Camping am Steinbacher See,** Mühlsteige 26, 74523 Schwäbisch Hall-Steinbach **(0791) 2984; thomas.seitel@t-online.de; www.camping-schwaebisch-hall.de**

⛺ ∈2 ♨ (htd) [wc] ♨ ♿ ⊟ ⚙ 🍸 ⊕ nr ♨ ⚡ nr 🏔

Fr A6/E50 exit junc 43 fr W or junc 42 fr E & foll permanent diversion via new B19 rd. At x-rds at lge Lidl store, turn L twds town and foll sp S to Comburg & site. 4*, Med, mkd, pt shd, EHU (10A) metered + conn fee; bbq; 50% statics; Eng spkn; adv bkg acc; bike hire; CKE. *"Lovely well kept idiosyncratic site; friendly; clsd 1300-1500; walking dist to interesting medieval town; cycle track to town."* **€22.00, 15 Mar-15 Oct.** **2015**

SCHWEICH *3B2* (1.6km S Urban) *49.81459, 6.75019* **Campingplatz zum Fährturm,** Am Yachthafen, 54338 Schweich **(06502) 91300; camping@kreusch.de; www.kreusch.de**

⛺ ♨ [wc] ♨ ⚓ ♿ ⊟ ⚙ [MsP] 🛒 🍸 ⊕ ♨ ⚡ nr 🏔

Fr exit 129 or 130 fr A1/E44. Site by rv bank by bdge into town, sp. 4*, Lge, mkd, pt shd, EHU (16A) €1.60; gas; bbq; twin axles; bus to Trier nr; Eng spkn; adv bkg acc; bike hire; watersports; CKE. *"Poss long wait for conn to EHU; poss long walk to san facs - dated; m'van o'night area outside site - no EHU; sports cent adj; on banks of Mosel with cycle rte; yacht/boating harbour adj; gd rest/bar; pool adj; vg."* **€20.00, 8 Apr-21 Oct.** **2017**

SCHWEPPENHAUSEN *3B2* (1km N Rural) *49.93392, 7.79194* **Campingplatz Aumühle,** Naheweinstraße 65, 55444 Schweppenhausen **06724 602392; info@ camping-aumuehle.de**

⛺ ♨ (htd) [wc] ♨ ⚓ ⊟ ⚙ 🛒 🍸 ♨ 🏔

Fr A61 take exit 47 - Waldlaubersheim. Foll signs to Schweppenhausen. Sp to camp site. Med, mkd, pt shd, EHU (10A); twin axles; 50% statics; Eng spkn; adv bkg acc; CKE. *"V gd site; cycle rtes fr site; v helpful Dutch owners; gd san facs; touring vans in sep area nr m'way; excel NH; gd base for Rhine."* **€21.50, 1 Apr-31 Oct.** **2018**

SCHWERIN *2E2* (10km N Rural) *53.69725, 11.43715* **Ferienpark Seehof,** Am Zeltzplatz 1, 19069 Seehof **(0385) 512540; info@ferienparkseehof.de; www.ferienparkseehof.de**

🅲🅱 ⛺ ∈1 ♨ [wc] ♨ ⊟ ⚙ [MsP] 🛒 🍸 ⊕ ♨ ⚡ 🏔 ♫ ⚓ sand

Take B106 N fr Schwerin for approx 5km: turn R at city boundary & site within 5km at end of vill, sp. 4*, Lge, pt shd, pt sl, serviced pitches; EHU (4A) inc (poss rev pol); gas; sw; 30% statics; adv bkg acc; ccard acc; sailing school; bike hire; windsurfing. *"Lge pitches; vg."* **€33.00** **2015**

SEEBURG *2E4* (1km NW Rural) *51.49400, 11.69400* **Camping Seeburg am Süsser See,** Nordstrand 1, 06317 Seeburg **(034774) 28281; info@campingplatz-seeburg.de; www.campingplatz-seeburg.de**

🅲🅱 ⛺ ∈1.20 ♨ [wc] ♨ ♿ ⚡ ⊕ nr 🏔

W fr Halle on B80 twd Eisleben, sp fr Seeburg. Site on N shore of Lake Süsser See. 2*, Lge, pt shd, EHU (16A) €1.10; sw; 95% statics; fishing. *"Attractive, busy site by lake; excel base for medieval towns nr & 'Martin Luther country'; gd; nice site by lake; not many pitches; new immac facs (2015)."* **€19.60** **2015**

SEEFELD *4E4* (1.3km W Rural) *48.030463, 11.199018*
Camping Am Pilsensee, Am Pilseesee 2, 82229
Seefeld am Pilsensee **(08152) 7232;** info@camping-
pilsensee.de; www.camping-pilsensee.de

12 🏕 ♦♦ [wc] ♨ ♣ ♿ 🖃 ⋰ [msp] ⋔ Ⅹ ⑨ ♨ ℤ /ⱱ\

W on 96 fr Munchi, exit 31, turn R onto 2349. Aft abt
6km turn R onto 2068. Cont for 4.5km, site 500m S
of junc with 2070 to Seefeld to the R. V lge, mkd,
hdg, pt shd, EHU (10A); bbq; sw; twin axles; TV;
80% statics; phone; Eng spkn; adv bkg acc; games
area; CKE. *"Gd site; boat hire on lake; Andechs
monastery nrby."* **€26.00**   **2018**

SEESHAUPT *4E4* (4km E Rural) *47.82651, 11.33906*
Camping beim Fischer, Buchscharnstrasse 10,
82541 St Heinrich **(08801) 802;** info@camping-
beim-fischer.de; www.camping-beim-fischer.de

12 🏕 ♦♦(htd) [wc] ♨ ♣ ♿ 🖃 ⋰ 🦋 Ⅹ nr ⑨ nr /ⱱ\

Exit A95 junc 7 & foll sp Seeshaupt for 1.6km to
T-junc. Turn R, site in 200m on R. 4*, Med, mkd, unshd,
EHU (16A) metered; gas; sw nr; TV; 45% statics; bus
adj; Eng spkn; adv bkg acc; games area; CKE. *"Well-
maintained, friendly, lovely, honest family-run site;
immac facs; conv Munich & Bavarian castles."*
€26.40   **2019**

> ## "I like to fill in the reports as I travel from site to site"
>
> You'll find report forms at the back of this
> guide, or you can fill them in online at
> camc.com/europereport.

SIGMARINGEN *3D4* (2km SW Urban) *48.08366,
9.20794* **Erlebnis-Camp Sigmaringen,** Georg-
Zimmererstrasse 6, 72488 Sigmaringen **(07571)**
50411; info@outandback.de; www.erlebnis-camp.de

12 🏕 €1 ♦♦ [wc] ♨ ♣ ♿ 🖃 ⋰ [msp] ⋔ ⑨ ℤ nr /ⱱ\

App town fr N or SW, ent town over Danube bdge,
turn R into car pk (camp sp). To far end of car park,
turn R in front of supmkt. Ent camp fr far end. Site
adj to stadium by rv, sp fr town. 4*, Med, pt shd, EHU
(6-16A) €3; 10% statics; bike hire; CKE. *"On Danube
cycle way; gd outdoor activities; lovely site; htd pool
300m; clsd 12-1400; new facs; new ent."* **€26.50**
                                                     2015

SIMMERATH *1A4* (8km E Rural) *50.61777,
6.37690* **Camping Rursee,** Seerandweg 26, D
52152 Simmerath/Rurberg **(02473) 2365;** info@
camping-rursee.de; http://camping-rursee.de

♦♦ [wc] ♨ 🖃 ⋰ Ⅹ ♨ ℤ

Fr Simmerath L166 to Kesternich; R on 266 for 1
km; then L on L166 twds Rurberg. L on L128 twds
Woffelsbach then sp R to site. Sm, mkd, unshd, EHU
€3; games area. **€18.50, 1 Apr-Nov.**   **2019**

SOEST *1C4* (12km S Rural) *51.47722, 8.10055*
Camping Delecke-Südufer, Arnsbergerstrasse 8,
59519 Möhnesee-Delecke **(02924) 8784210;**
info@campingplatz-moehnesee.de; www.camping
platz-moehnesee.de

12 ♦♦ [wc] ♨ ♣ ♿ 🖃 ⋰ [msp] 🦋 Ⅹ ⑨ nr ♨ ℤ /ⱱ\

Exit A44/E331 at junc 56 onto B229 sp Arnsberg/
Mohnesee. Cont to lake, cross bdge. At next junc
turn L & site immed on L, sp. 4*, Med, hdg, unshd, pt
sl, EHU (16A); sw nr; 50% statics; phone; Eng spkn;
adv bkg acc; clsd 1300-1500 & 2000-0800; boating;
CKE. *"Excel site on boating lake; san facs locked
o'night; gd walking & sailing; v busy at w/ends; gd
disable facs."* **€25.00**   **2016**

SOTTRUM *1D2* (5km SW Rural) *53.08335,
9.17697* **Camping-Paradies Grüner Jäger,**
Everinghauser Dorfstrsse 17, 27367 Sottrum/
Everinghausen **(04205) 319113;** info@camping-
paradies.de; www.camping-paradies.de

12 🏕 ♦♦(htd) [wc] ♨ ♣ ♿ 🖃 ⋰ [msp] Ⅹ ⑨ /ⱱ\ ⚓ ⛱

Exit A1 junc 50 at Stuckenborstel onto B75 dir
Rotenburg. In approx 500m turn R & foll sp
Everinghausen. Site in 4km. Med, mkd, unshd, EHU
(16A) inc; 30% statics; Eng spkn; CKE. *"Excel NH; dogs
free; new superb facs block (2016)."* **€22.50**   **2017**

SPEYER *3C3* (3km N Rural) *49.33600, 8.44300*
Camping Speyer, Am Rübsamenwühl 31,
67346 Speyer **(06232) 42228;** info@camping-
speyer.de; www.camping-speyer.de

🏕 €2 ♣ ⋰ 🦋 Ⅹ ⑨ ♨ ℤ nr /ⱱ\

Fr Mannheim or Karlsruhe take rd 9 to exit
Speyer Nord dir Speyer. At 3rd traff lts turn L
into Auestrasse, then at 2nd rndabt L into Am
Rübsamenwühl. Site in 500m. Sm, mkd, EHU €3;
sw; red long stay; 90% statics. *"Speyer pleasant
town, cathedral & Technik Museum worth visit; v
basic site; scruffy & not well-kept; fair NH/sh stay."*
€29.00, 15 Mar-25 Sep.   **2019**

SPEYER *3C3* (1km SE Urban) *49.31250, 8.44916*
Camping Technik Museum, Am Technik Museum 1,
Geibstrasse, 67346 Speyer **(06232) 67100;** info@
hotel-speyer.de; www.hotel-speyer.de

12 🏕 ♦♦(htd) [wc] ♨ ♣ ♿ 🖃 ⋰ [msp] Ⅹ nr ⑨ nr ℤ nr

Exit A61/E34 at junc 64, foll sp to museum.
Med, unshd, EHU inc (10A); bus; Eng spkn; adv bkg
acc; ccard acc. *"Book in at hotel adj; 3 nights max stay;
excel museum & IMAX cinema on site; conv Speyer cent
and cathedral; dogs free; site unkept; excel san facs;
24hr CCTV controlled ent gate."* **€22.00**   **2016**

STAUFEN IM BREISGAU *3B4* (1.4km SE Rural)
47.87194, 7.73583 **Ferien-Campingplatz Belchenblick**, Münstertälerstrasse 43, 79219 Staufen-im-Breisgau **(07633) 7045; info@camping-belchenblick.de; www.camping-belchenblick.de**

12 ⛺ €2.50 ♦♦ (htd) ⊞ ♨ ♿ ⊠ ✉ MP ♙ ▼ ⓘ nr ♨ ♨ nr ✈
⚓ (htd, indoor)

Exit A5/E35 junc 64a dir Bad Krozingen-Staufen-Münstertal. Avoid Staufen cent, foll Münstertal sp. Camp on L 500m past Staufen. Visibility restricted fr Münstertal dir. 4*, Lge, pt shd, EHU (16A) metered; gas; bbq; TV; 60% statics; phone; Eng spkn; adv bkg rec; horseriding 500m; games rm; bike hire; sauna; tennis nr; CKE. "Well-run, family-owned site; some pitches sm; no o'fits over 8m high ssn; no veh access 1230-1500 & night time - parking area avail; strict pitching rules; beautiful area & Staufen pleasant town; beware train app round blind corner at x-ing; gd walking, cycling, horseriding; san facs tired, need refurbishing (2013); better cheaper sites close by." **€30.00, G02.** 2015

STOCKACH *3C4* (7.5km SSW Rural) *47.80860, 8.97000* **Campinggarten Wahlwies**, Stahringerstrasse 50, 78333 Stockach-Wahlwies **(07771) 3511; info@camping-wahlwies.de; www.camping-wahlwies.de**

⛺ ♦♦ (wo) ♨ ⊠ ✉ MP ❦ ▼ ⓘ nr ♨ ♨ nr

Exit A98 junc 12 Stockach West onto B313 to Wahlwies. In vill turn L immed after level x-ing, site on R bef next level x-ing, sp. 3*, Med, pt shd, EHU (16A) €2; sw nr; 50% statics; phone; Eng spkn; adv bkg rec; CKE. "Pleasantly situated, orchard site 6km fr Bodensee; friendly, helpful staff; female san facs inadequate; gd touring cent; gd local train service; excel cycle tracks." **€23.00, 1 Jan-15 Nov & 15 Dec-31 Dec.** 2016

STOCKACH *3C4* (2.5km SW Urban) *47.84194, 8.99500* **Camping Papiermühle**, Johann Glatt Strasse 3, 78333 Stockach **(07771) 9190490; campingpark-stockach@web.de; www.campingpark-stockach-de.webnode.com**

⛺ €2.20 ♦♦ (htd) (wo) ♨ ♿ ⊠ ✉ MP ❦ ▼ ⓘ nr ♨ ♨ nr ✈

Fr Stockach at junc rndabt of B31 & B313, turn L (E) to Caramobil C'van Sales Depot. Site adj under same management. Med, mkd, hdstg, pt shd, pt sl, terr, EHU (6A) €2; bbq; 50% statics; phone; bus 200m; Eng spkn; adv bkg acc; ccard acc; CKE. "Sep m'van area adj; v clean facs; helpful staff; conv location for town; gd walking & cycling; vg site." **€21.50, 1 Mar-30 Nov.** 2016

STRAUBING *4F3* (1km N Urban) *48.89346, 12.5766* **Camping Straubing**, Wundermühlweg 9, 94315 Straubing **(09421) 89794; info@campingplatz straubing.de; www.campingplatzstraubing.de**

⛺ ♦♦ (htd) (wo) ♨ ♨ ♿ ⊠ ✉ MP ♙ ▼ ⓘ ♨ nr ✈

Fr A3/E56 exit junc 105 or 106 to Straubing. Foll sp over Danube bdge, site sp on R in approx 1km. Also foll sp to stadium. 4*, Med, shd, EHU (16A) inc; bbq; cooking facs; sw nr; twin axles; phone; bus; adv bkg acc; golf 2km; CKE. "Gd, clean, well-kept site In grnds of sports stadium; quaint town with attractive shops; gd san facs; pool 5km; conv Danube cycle way; easy walk to town; dogs not acc Aug; excel stop over fr A3, gd for longer breaks; excel." **€23.50, 1 May-15 Oct.** 2018

STUTTGART *3D3* (5km E Urban) *48.79395, 9.21911* **Campingplatz Cannstatter Wasen**, Mercedesstrasse 40, 70372 Stuttgart **(0711) 556696; info@camping platz-stuttgart.de; www.campingplatz-stuttgart.de**

12 ⛺ €3 ♦♦ (htd) (wo) ♨ ♿ ⊠ ✉ MP ⓘ ♨ nr ✈

Fr B10 foll sp for stadium & Mercedes museum & then foll camping sp. Access poss diff when major events in park adj. Lge, hdstg, pt shd, serviced pitches; EHU (16A) metered + conn fee; bbq; bus nr; Eng spkn; adv bkg acc; ccard acc; CKE. "Helpful staff; clean san facs (2015); town cent best by train, tickets fr recep; cycle ride to town thro park; Mercedes museum 15 mins walk; fr Sep site/office open 0800-1000 & 1700-1900 only; site within low emission zone; camping field for tents." **€22.00** 2016

SULZBURG *3B4* (1.5km SE Rural) *47.83583, 7.72333* **Terrassen-Camping Alte Sägemühle**, Badstrasse 57, 79295 Sulzburg **(07634) 551181; info@camping-alte-saegemuehle.de; www.camping-alte-saegemuehle.de**

12 ⛺ €2 ♦♦ (htd) (wo) ♨ ✉ MP ▼ nr ⓘ nr ♨

Exit A5 junc 64a to Heitersheim & Sulzburg. Fr cent of Sulzburg, foll camp sps SE past timber yard on rd to Bad Sulzburg hotel. 3*, Sm, mkd, pt shd, terr, EHU (16A) metered + conn fee; bbq; sw nr; 10% statics; Eng spkn; CKE. "Excel san facs, poss long walk; v friendly, helpful owners site van with tractor; restful site in beautiful hilly countryside; gd walks, cycling." **€26.00** 2016

GERMANY

SULZBURG *3B4* (1km NW Rural) *47.84778, 7.69848*
Camping Sulzbachtal, Sonnmatt 4, 79295 Sulzburg
(07634) 592568; a-z@camping-sulzbachtal.de;
www.camping-sulzbachtal.de

12 🏕 €2.60 (htd) [wc] ♨ ♿ ▣ ∥ [MsP] 🦋 ♈ ⊕ nr ◧ 🔌nr ⚠ ♨

Fr A5/E35 exit junc 64a Bad Krozingen onto L120/
L123 dir Staufen-in-Breisgau. Cont on L125, site
sp on L. 5*, Med, mkd, hdstg, pt shd, terr, serviced
pitches; EHU (16A) metered; red long stay;
10% statics; phone; Eng spkn; adv bkg acc; ccard acc;
tennis; CKE. *"Gd base for S Black Forest & Vosges; well
laid-out site; clean facs; conv m'way; 45 mins to Basel;
helpful, pleasant owners; ask about bus/train pass;
m'van o'night facs; high standards; well maintained;
excel san facs; lge pitches; in wine growing area; excel
walks."* **€35.40** **2019**

TENGEN *3C4* (1km NW Rural) *47.82365, 8.65296*
Hegau Familien-Camping, An der Sonnenhalde 1,
78250 Tengen **(07736) 92470; info@hegau-camping.**
de; www.hegau-camping.de

12 🏕 €4 (htd) [wc] ♨ ♿ ▣ ∥ [MsP] 🦋 ♈ 🍽 ⊕ ◧ 🔌 ⚠ ✂ ⚓ (covrd, htd) 🛗

Exit A81 junc 39 thro Engen dir Tengen, site sp.
5*, Lge, hdstg, mkd, pt shd, pt sl, serviced pitches;
EHU (16A) metered or €2; gas; sw; red long stay;
40% statics; bus 500m; Eng spkn; adv bkg acc; ccard
acc; tennis adj; sauna; games area; horseriding 2km;
bike hire; games rm; canoeing; dog shwr; CKE. *"Site of
high standard; fairly isolated; gd family facs; clsd 1230-
1430; o'night m'vans area; excel; same price in high ssn;
beautifully maintained; well run; 1st rate pool complex;
wonderful children's play facs; rec."* **€42.00** **2016**

TITISEE NEUSTADT *3C4* (7km SW Rural) *47.88693,
8.13776* **Terrassencamping Sandbank,** Seerundweg 9,
79822 Titisee-Neustadt **(07651) 8243 or 8166; info@
camping-sandbank.de; www.camping-sandbank.de**

🏕 €1.50 (htd) [wc] ♨ ♿ ▣ ∥ [MsP] 🍽 ⊕ ◧ 🔌 ⚠

**Fr rte 31 Freiberg-Donauschingen turn S into
Titisee. Fork R after car park on R, foll sp for
Bruderhalde thro town. After youth hostel fork
L & foll sp at T junc.** 4*, Lge, mkd, hdstg, terr, EHU
(16A) €1.40; sw; red long stay; 50% statics; Eng
spkn; ccard acc; boating; bike hire; CKE. *"Ltd touring
pitches; steel pegs ess; clean, well-run, well laid-out
site in gd position; terr gives gd lake views; helpful
owner; gd welcome; larger pitches avail at extra cost;
gd touring base for Black Forest; gd walks round
lake; lakeside walk into town thru woods (approx
30 mins); ask for Konus card for free travel on local
buses; clsd 1200-1400; excel; rd to site tarmaced."*
€25.50, 1 Apr-18 Oct. **2016**

TITISEE NEUSTADT *3C4* (7.6km SW Rural) *47.89516,
8.13789* **Camping Bühlhof,** Bühlhofweg 13, 79822
Titisee-Neustadt **(07652) 1606 or (01713) 634160
(mob); info@camping-buehlhof.de; www.camping-
buehlhof.de**

12 🏕 €2.30 ♨ [wc] ♨ ♿ ▣ ∥ [MsP] 🦋 ♈ ⊕ nr ⚠

**Take rd 31 out of Freiburg to Titisee; R fork on ent
Titisee; bear R to side of lake, site on R after end
of Titisee, up steep but surfaced hill, sharp bends.**
2*, Lge, mkd, pt shd, pt sl, terr, serviced pitches;
EHU (16A) €1.80; gas; bbq; 30% statics; Eng spkn;
horseriding; boat hire; site clsd Nov to mid-Dec; tennis;
watersports; CKE. *"Beautiful situation on hillside above
Lake Titisee; 300m fr Lake Titisee (but no access; recep
0700-2200; lower terr gravel & 50% statics; top terr
for tents & vans without elec; winter sports area, ski
lift 6km; pitches sm; woodland walks; pleasant walk to
town; gd san facs."* **€25.50** **2017**

TITISEE NEUSTADT *3C4* (8.6km SW Rural) *47.88633,
8.13055* **Camping Bankenhof,** Bruderhalde 31a,
79822 Titisee-Neustadt **(07652) 1351; info@camping-
bankenhof.de; www.camping-bankenhof.de**

12 🏕 €2.80 ♨ [wc] ♨ ♿ ▣ ∥ [MsP] 🦋 ♈ 🍽 ⊕ 🔌 ⚠ ✂

**Fr B31 Frieberg-Donaueschingen, turn S into
Tittisee & fork R after car park on R, foll sp
Bruderhalde thro town. In 2.5km fork L after
youth hostel; foll sp to site in 200m. If app Titisee
fr Donausechingen (B31) do not take Titisee P
sp exit but exit with int'l camping sp only, then
as above.** 4*, Lge, mkd, hdstg, pt shd, EHU (10A)
metered (poss rev pol); gas; sw nr; 20% statics; Eng
spkn; adv bkg acc; ccard acc; bike hire; CKE. *"Gd walk
to town & in forest; o'night area for m'vans €12 - dogs
free in this area; lovely scenery; helpful staff; vg san
facs; excel rest; most pitches gravel; boat launch 200m;
ask at recep for red/free tickets on public transport;
excel, well-run, clean site, some pitches narr."*
€28.00 **2015**

TRAUNSTEIN *4F4* (8km SW Rural) *47.81116, 12.5890*
Camping Wagnerhof, Campingstrasse 11, 83346
Bergen **(08662) 8557; info@camping-bergen.de;
www.camping-bergen.de**

12 🏕 €2 ♨ [wc] ♨ ∥ 🦋 ⊕ nr 🔌 ⚠ 🎿 shgl 10km

**Exit A8/E52/E60 junc 110. On ent Bergen take 2nd
R turn (sp).** 4*, Med, mkd, pt shd, EHU (16A) metered;
red long stay; 30% statics; Eng spkn; adv bkg acc;
tennis; site clsd 1230-1500; CKE. *"Excel, v clean,
pleasant site in beautiful location; htd pool adj; debit
& euro card acc; helpful owner; when not full owner
tries to offer pitches with empty pitches adjoining; conv
a'bahn; cable car to Hockfelln."* **€23.50** **2019**

TRAVEMUNDE *2E2* (4km SW Rural) *53.94196, 10.84417* **Camping Ivendorf,** Frankenkrogweg 2, 23570 Ivendorf **(04502) 4865; mail@camping-travemuende.de; www.camping-travemuende.de**

12 🛏 €2 ♦♦ wo ⚓ ♨ ♿ 🖃 🖉 ⓌⓃnr 🛆

Fr A1 exit junc 19 take B226 to Ivendorf, then B75 dir Travemünde, site well sp. 3*, Med, mkd, pt shd, EHU €3.50 or metered; 10% statics; CKE. *"Sep disabled pitches; conv ferries to/fr Sweden; pool 4km; easy access to Lübeck, a beautiful city."* **€23.00** **2016**

TRIER *3B2* (2km SW Urban) *49.74385, 6.62523* **Camping Treviris,** Luxemburgerstrasse 81, 54290 Trier **(0651) 8200911; info@camping-treviris.de; www.camping-treviris.de**

🛏 🐕 €1.70 ♦♦ wo ⚓ ♨ ♿ 🖃 🖉 MsP ♈♈ ❞ Ⓨ Ⓦ 🛒 🐾nr 🛆

On E side of Rv Mosel on A1/A603/B49/B51 cross to W side of rv on Konrad Adenauerbrücke. Cont in R lane & foll sp Koln/Aachen - Luxemburgerstrasse. In 500m turn R to site, site on R. Well sp fr W bank of rv. Med, mkd, pt shd, EHU (10A) metered; bbq; bus 200m; ccard acc; site clsd 1-10 Jan; CKE. *"Cycle/walk to town cent; m'van park adj open all yr - ltd facs; clean, modern, clean san facs; swipe card for all facs; elec pylon in cent of site; gd touring base; gd sh stay/NH; well placed; sm pitches; 20min walk to city."* **€24.00, 18 Mar-30 Oct.** **2018**

TRIER *3B2* (9km SW Rural) *49.70555, 6.55333* **Campingplatz Igel,** Moselstrasse, 54298 Igel **(06501) 12944; info@camping-igel.de; www.camping-igel.de**

🛏 €2 ♦♦ (htd) wo ⚓ 🖉 MsP Ⓨ Ⓦ 🐾nr 🛆

SW on A49 Luxembourg rd fr Trier; in cent of Ige vill, turn L by Sparkasse Bank, thro narr tunnel (3.6m max height); in 200m turn L along rv bank; site 300m on L; café serves as recep. Med, pt shd, EHU (6A) €2 (poss rev pol); 90% statics; lake fishing adj; CKE. *"Excel, friendly, well-run site; immac san facs; gd rest; ltd touring pitches; rv bank foot & cycle path to Trier; conv Roman amphitheatre in Trier (bus/train); close to Luxembourg border for cheap petrol; conv for bus into Trier."* **€19.00, 1 Apr-31 Oct.** **2019**

TRIER *3B2* (15km W Rural) *49.75416, 6.50333* **Campingplatz Alter Bahnhof-Metzdorf,** Uferstrasse 42, 54308 Langsur-Metzdorf **(06501) 12626; info@camping-metzdorf.de; www.camping-metzdorf.de**

12 🛏 €1 ♦♦ (htd) wo ⚓ ♿ 🖃 🖉 ♈♈ ❞ Ⓨ Ⓦ 🛆

Fr W leave A64/E44 junc 15 & foll sp Wasserbillig; at T-junc in Wasserbillig turn L onto B49 sp Trier. Ignore campsite in 500m. On ent Germany at end of bdge turn sharp L onto B418 sp Ralingen/ Metternich. In 3km turn L sp Metzdorf; in 750m turn L, site in 750m. Fr N (Bitburg) join A64 at junc 3 sp Luxembourg, then as above. Fr SE on A1/E422 join A602 (Trier) & approx 1km past end of a'bahn turn R over Kaiser Wilhelm Bdge sp A64 Lux'bourg) & immed L at end of bdge. In 9km in Wasserbillig turn R under rlwy bdge & keep R on B418 sp Ralingen/ Mesenich. In 3km turn L sp Melzdorf, in 750m turn L, site in 750m. Do not use sat nav if app fr the E. 3*, Med, pt shd, pt sl, EHU (6-16A) €2 or metered (10A); red long stay; 75% statics; phone; bus 500m; Eng spkn; adv bkg acc; CKE. *"Rvside location; gd san facs but poss long walk & steep climb; m'van o'night €9; cycle rte to Trier; vg NH."* **€17.50** **2015**

TRITTENHEIM *3B2* (4km N Urban) *49.84933, 6.89283* **Camping Neumagen-Dhron,** Moselstrasse 100, 54347 Neumagen-Dhron **(06507) 5249; camping-neumagen@ t-online.de; www.campingneumagen.de**

🛏 🐕 wo ⚓ ♨ ♿ 🖃 🖉 ♈♈ ❞ Ⓨ Ⓦ 🛒 🛆

On B53 fr Trittenheim twd Piesport. Immed after x-ing rv turn R, then R again sp Neumagen. Site sp in vill on rvside. 3*, Med, mkd, pt shd, EHU (6A) metered + conn fee; bbq; 40% statics; adv bkg acc; boating; fishing; CKE. *"Gd; site clsd if rv in flood; marina adj; rvside park; excel site; interesting Roman town; poss noise fr adj rest; main san facs up 25 steps; Hot water 7am-9pm."* **€22.00, 1 Apr-31 Oct.** **2017**

TRITTENHEIM *3B2* (8km S Rural) *49.79956, 6.92715* **Campingplatz Moselhöhe,** Bucherweg 1, 54426 Heidenburg **(06509) 99016; vandijk1968@hotmail. com; www.moselhohe.de**

12 🛏 €1.70 ♦♦ (htd) wo ⚓ ♿ 🖃 🖉 MsP ♈♈ Ⓨ Ⓦ nr 🛒 nr 🛆 ⌂

Leave A1/E422 at junc 131, foll sp twd Thalfang. After 4km take 2nd L over bdge sp Heidenburg (2 hairpin bends). Thro Büdlich to Heidenbrug, foll sp in vill. 4*, Med, mkd, unshd, terr, serviced pitches; EHU (16A) metered; red long stay; 25% statics; Eng spkn; adv bkg acc; ccard acc; site clsd mid-Nov to mid-Dec; games rm; CKE. *"Excel, clean, hilltop site surrounded by meadows; well-maintained; generous terraces; excel san facs; water & waste disposal points nr every pitch; wonderful views; v friendly owner; conv Rv Mosel attractions 4km."* **€19.00** **2015**

TUBINGEN *3C3* (5km SW Rural) *48.51008, 9.03525*
Neckarcamping Tübingen, Rappenberghalde 61,
72070 Tübingen **(07071) 43145; mail@neckar
camping.de; www.neckarcamping.de**

🐕 €1.50 👫 wc ♨ & 🖳 ⊘ ⮢ 🕭 🏊 🅿 ⛟

B28 to Tübingen, site well sp fr main rds. Site on
N bank of Rv Neckar. 3*, Med, pt shd, EHU (6A)
metered + conn fee (rev pol); 70% statics; bike hire;
clsd 1230-1430 & 2200-0800; CKE. *"Easy walk to
attractive old town & lge pool complex; Neckar cycle
path rn; cramped pitches; NH only; bus stop nr camp
ent."* **€27.00, 1 Apr-30 Oct.**   **2017**

UBERLINGEN *3D4* (3km SE Coastal) *47.75186,
9.19315* **Campingplatz Nell,** Zur Barbe 7, 88662
Überlingen-Nussdorf **(07551) 4254; info@camping
platz-nell.de; www.campingplatz-nell.de**

👫 wc ♨ & ⊘ 🦋 Y nr ⊕ nr 🅿 🕭 nr

Exit B31 to Nussdorf. In vill cent turn L under rlwy
bdge at 2nd campsite sp, site on R on lakeside.
Sm, pt shd, EHU (10A) metered; bbq; sw nr; adv bkg
acc. *"Beautifully-kept site; friendly owner; all amenities
nr; gd cycling; excel; lge plots; cash only; ltd places for
tourers so arrive early."* **€21.00, 21 Mar-20 Oct.**
                                                       2016

UBERLINGEN *3D4* (13km NW Rural) *47.81720,
9.03802* **Campingplatz Schachenhorn,** Radolfzeller
Str. 23, 78351 Bodman-Ludwigshafen **07773
9376851; info@camping-schachenhorn.de;
www.camping-schachenhorn.de**

🐕 👫 wc ♨ ⚓ & ⊘ ⛵ ⊕ 🏊

Exit A98/E54 junc 12 onto B34. Site sp 1.5km on
Bodensee fr Ludwigshafen. Med, pt shd, EHU (16A);
bbq; sw nr; twin axles; TV; 20% statics; Eng spkn;
games rm. *"Taken over in 2013, formerly Camping
See-Ende; lovely location at W end of Bodensee;
excel san facs; many cycle paths; bit disorganised;
poss muddy after rain; rec visit Mainau Gdns."*
€30.00, 15 Mar-15 Oct.   **2016**

UBERLINGEN *3D4* (3km NW Rural) *47.77081,
9.13813* **Campingplatz Überlingen,** Bahnhofstrasse
57, 88662 Überlingen **(07551) 64583; info@camping
park-ueberlingen.de; www.campingpark-
ueberlingen.de**

🐕 €2.50 👫 (htd) wc ♨ ⊘ 🖳 Y ⊕ 🕭 🏊

Heading SE on B31, bef Überlingen turn R at sp
Campingplatz Goldbach down slip rd; after 1.75km
turn R; foll rd parallel with rlwy; after level x-ing
site immed on R by lakeside. 1*, Lge, pt shd, pt sl,
EHU (16A) metered; gas; bbq; sw nr; red long stay;
30% statics; bus; Eng spkn; boating adj; CKE. *"Extra
for lake pitches; high ssn poss diff for lge c'vans to
manoeuvre; gd rest; strict rule no vehicles in after
2230; rec arr early to secure pitch; boat to Insel Mainau
fr site."* **€23.50, 1 Apr-9 Oct.**   **2018**

UBERSEE *4F4* (4km N Rural) *47.8412, 12.47166*
Chiemsee-Campingplatz Rödlgries, Rödlgries
1, 83236 Übersee-Feldwies **(08642) 470; info@
chiemsee-camping.de; www.chiemsee-camping.de**

🐕 €2.50 👫 (htd) wc ♨ & 🖳 ⊘ 🖳 MP Y ⊕ 🕭 🏊 🅿 🐾 🌳 shgl

Exit A8/E52 junc 108 Übersee, foll sp
Chiemseestrand, veer L at wooden sp of sites.
4*, V lge, mkd, hdstg, pt shd, serviced pitches; EHU
(16A) metered + conn fee; gas; sw; phone; adv bkg
acc; boating. *"Superb facs; vg for children; highly
rec; extra for lakeside/serviced pitches; dogs by prior
agreement in Jul/Aug; vg touring base; v conv nr
A8; cycle track around lake; excel; lge level pitches."*
€32.50, 1 Apr-31 Oct.   **2015**

ÜBERSEE *4F4* (16km W Rural) *47.816891, 12.363742*
Camping Mariengrund, Prienerstr. 42, D-83233
Bernau am Chiemsee **(08051) 7894; mariengrund@
aol.com; campingplatz-mariengrund.de**

12 🐕 👫 wc ♨ ⊘ MP Y 🕭 🏊 nr

Exit m'waysp Bernau. Turn twrds Prien. Ent to site
v sharp R immed after Munich slip rd. Lge o'fits can
cont twrds Prien and u turn at next rndabt. Hdstg,
pt shd, EHU (16A) inc; bbq (charcoal, elec, gas); sw
nr; Eng spkn; adv bkg acc; ccard acc. *"Hdstng area
sometimes crowded with NH'ers; facs basic but ok;
vast numbers of flies & mosquitoes in summer; fair."*
€31.00   **2019**

VLOTHO *1C3* (5km NE Rural) *52.17388, 8.90666*
Camping Sonnenwiese, Borlefzen 1, 32602 Vlotho
**(05733) 8217; info@sonnenwiese.com; www.sonnen
wiese.com**

12 🐕 €2.20 👫 (htd) wc ♨ ⚓ & 🖳 ⊘ MP 🦋 ⛵ Y ⊕ 🕭 🏊 🅿
🐾 ⛴

Fr S exit A2 junc 31 to Vlotho; cross rv bdge
(Mindenerstrasse) & in 500m turn R into
Rintelnerstrasse to site - 2 sites share same access.
Fr N exit A2 junc 32 to Vlotho; turn L bef bdge into
Rintelner Strasse. 4*, Lge, hdstg, unshd, serviced
pitches; EHU (10A) inc; bbq; sw; TV (pitch);
75% statics; phone; Eng spkn; adv bkg acc; games
rm; CKE. *"Excel site; v helpful staff, abundant wildlife;
rv adj for boats/canoes; recep clsd 1300-1500."*
€25.50   **2016**

VOLKACH *3D2* (2km NW Rural) *49.869215, 10.214989*
Campingplatz Ankergrund, Fahrerstraße 7, 97332
Volkach am Main **(09381) 6713 or (09381) 4114;
info@campingplatz-ankergrund.de; www.camping
platz-ankergrund.de**

🐕 €3.50 👫 ⚓ & 🖳 ⊘ 🖳 ⛵ Y 🕭 🏊

Exit A3 J74 sp Kitzingen/Schwarzach/Volkach.
Site sp in town approx 10km fr A3. Med, mkd, hdg,
pt shd, EHU (10A) €0.60kwh; bbq; sw nr; red long
stay; twin axles; 25% statics; 800m; adv bkg acc;
games area; CKE. *"Excel; super pitches avail with
rv view; adj to Rv Main; sports ctr nrby with pool;
san facs raised with disabled access via lift; in wine
area; excel cycling & walking; gd rests; gd supmkt."*
€24.00, 1 Apr-21 Oct.   **2018**

WALDBREITBACH *3B1* (1.5km NE Rural) *50.55389, 7.42518* **Campingplatz Wiedhof,** Wiedhof 1, 56588 Waldbreitbach **(02638) 4258; camping@wiedhof.de; www.wiedhof.de**

ᛐ ᛰᚱ ᵂᴰ ♨ ♿ ⚊ ⫽ ❦ ♣ ⌂

Exit A3 junc 36 onto B256 W to Bonefeld, then take L257 Kurtscheiderstrasse to Niederbreitbach, then L255 to Waldbreitbach, site sp on rvside. This rte avoids steep hills. Sm, unshd, EHU (10A) inc; bbq; TV; 80% statics; adv bkg acc; fishing; CKE. *"Conv A3 m'way; vg, peaceful site; gd walks, quiet site next to local town."* **€13.00, 1 Apr-31 Oct.**   **2015**

WALDMUNCHEN *4F2* (3km N Rural) *49.39598, 12.69913* **Campsite Ferienpark Perlsee (formerly Camping am Perlsee),** Alte Ziegelhütte 6, 93449 Waldmünchen **(09972) 1469; info@ferienpark-perlsee.de; www.ferienpark-perlsee.de**

12 ᛐ €2 ᛰᚱ (htd) ᵂᴰ ♨ ♿ ⚊ ⫽ ᴹˢᴾ ❦ ♣ ① ♨ ♣ ⌂

N fr Cham on B22 to Schontal, NE to Waldmünchen for 10km. Foll site sp 2km. 4*, Med, hdg, mkd, pt shd, terr, EHU (16A) metered; bbq; sw nr; 50% statics; games area; watersports; CKE. *"Vg san facs; superb site; long leads poss req."* **€25.30**   **2019**

WALKENRIED *2E4* (1km NE Rural) *51.58944, 10.62472* **Knaus Campingpark Walkenried,** Ellricherstrasse 7, 37445 Walkenried **(05525) 778; walkenried@knauscamp.de; www.knauscamp.de**

12 ᛐ €2.80 ᛰᚱ ᵂᴰ ♨ ♿ ⚊ ⫽ ᴹˢᴾ ❦ ♣ ① ♨ ♣ ⌂ ♣ ⚊ (covrd, htd)

A7, exit Seesen, then B243 to Herzberg-Bad Sachsa-Walkenried, sp. 4*, Lge, mkd, pt shd, pt sl, terr, EHU (6-10A) €2.40; gas; red long stay; TV; 20% statics; Eng spkn; adv bkg acc; games area; solarium; site clsd Nov; sauna. *"Vg rest; winter sports; lovely old vill; excel site."* **€32.50**   **2018**

WARNITZ *2G2* (0.7km S Rural) *53.17754, 13.87400* **Camping Oberuckersee,** Lindenallee 2, 17291 Warnitz **(039863) 459; info@camping-oberuckersee.de; www.camping-oberuckersee.de**

ᛐ €2 ᛰᚱ ᵂᴰ ♨ ♿ ⚊ ⫽ ❦ ♣ ① nr ♣ ⌂

Fr A11/E28 exit 7. Site sp fr Warnitz on lakeside. 3*, Lge, shd, pt sl, EHU (10A) €2; sw; TV; 50% statics; fishing; bike hire; boating. *"Lovely site in pine trees on edge lge lake; conv NH en rte to Poland; deposit for san facs key; clsd 1300-1500; gd cycle rte nrby."* **€16.00, 1 Apr-5 Oct.**   **2016**

WEIKERSHEIM *3D2* (4km S Rural) *49.45640, 9.92565* **Camping Schwabenmühle,** Weikersheimer Straße 21, 97990 Weikersheim **07934 99 22 23; info@camping-schwaben-muehle.de; www.camping-schwaben muehle.de**

ᛐ €1 ᛰᚱ ᵂᴰ ♨ ♿ ⚊ ⫽ ❦ ♣ ⌂

Fr Weikersheim twd Laudenbach, site on R in 3km. 4*, Med, hdg, mkd, hdstg, pt shd, EHU (16A); twin axles; Eng spkn; bike hire; CCI. *"Excel; bread can be ordered."* **€26.00, 17 Apr-12 Oct.**   **2019**

WEILBURG *3C1* (4km SW Rural) *50.4757, 8.23966* **Campingplatz Odersbach,** Runkelerstrasse 5A, 35781 Weilburg-Odersbach **(06471) 7620; info@camping-odersbach.de; www.camping-odersbach.de**

ᛐ €1 ᛰᚱ ♨ ♿ ⚊ ⫽ ❦ ♣ ♈ ① nr ♨ ♣ ⌂ ♣ ♨

Fr Limburg exit B49 sp Weilburg & Bad Homburg, turn S (R) opp Shell stn at top of hill at Weilburg o'skts. Site on L at foot of hill in Odersbach. 4*, Lge, unshd, EHU (16A) metered + conn fee; 75% statics; ccard acc; boating; bike hire; golf 8km; CKE. **€25.00, 1 Apr-31 Oct.**   **2019**

WEIMAR *2E4* (12km S Rural) *50.92456, 11.34785* **Camping Mittleres Ilmtal,** Auf den Butterberge 1, 99438 Oettern **(036453) 80264; weil-camping@freenet.de; www.camping-oettern.de**

ᛐ €2 ᛰᚱ ᵂᴰ ♨ ⚊ ⫽ ❦ ♣ ♈ ① ♨

Exit A4/E40 junc 50 & foll B87 to SW to Oettern, take 1st L after narr bdge, site on L in 600m along narr rd, sp 'Camperbaude'. 2*, Med, hdstg, pt shd, pt sl, terr, EHU (16A) €2; 50% statics; phone. *"Conv Weimar & Buchenwald; recep open 0800-1000 & 1700-2000; welcoming; gd NH/sh stay; v pleasant rural site; gd walking & cycling fr site; statics (sep area); helpful manager; no public transport."* **€20.50, 15 Apr-31 Oct.**   **2016**

WEINHEIM *3C2* (9km N Rural) *49.59776, 8.64013* **Camping Wiesensee,** Ulmenweg 7, 69502 Hemsbach **(06201) 72619; familie.herwig@camping-wiesensee.de; www.camping-wiesensee.de**

12 ᛐ €2 ᛰᚱ ᵂᴰ ♨ ♿ ⚊ ⫽ ᴹˢᴾ ① ♨ ♣ ⌂

Exit A5/E35 junc 32; foll sp Hemsbach. On ent vill strt at 1st rndbt & traff lts, at 2nd rndabt turn L & foll camping sp about 1km. 4*, Lge, mkd, pt shd, serviced pitches; EHU (16A) €1.90 or metered + conn fee; gas; sw; 75% statics; Eng spkn; adv bkg rec; boating; tennis 100m; golf 12km; bike hire. *"Superb facs to CC standard; htd pool 100m; friendly welcome; helpful staff; supmkt in walking dist; gd NH for A5."* **€21.50**   **2019**

WERNIGERODE *2E3* (5km SE Rural) *51.81530, 10.81359* **Campingplatz Alte Waldmuhle,** Mühlental 78, 38855 Wernigerode **(03943) 266399; info@altewaldmuehle.de; www.altewaldmuehle.de**

ᛐ €1.50 ᛰᚱ ᵂᴰ ♿ ⚊ ⫽ ❦ ♣ ♈ ① ♨ ⌂

Fr Wernigerode foll B244 SE to Elbingerode. Site on R on edge of Wernigerode. Med, hdstg, pt shd, EHU (10A) inc; bbq; twin axles; TV; bus 200m; Eng spkn; adv bkg acc; games rm; CKE. *"Basic san facs; gd rest; bus free into town; beautiful town, castle & Harz rlwy stns."* **€23.00, 1 May-31 Oct.**   **2016**

WERTACH *4E4* (1km NE Rural) *47.60861, 10.41750*
Camping Waldesruh, Bahnhofstrasse 19, 87497
Wertach (08365) 1004; info@camping-wertach.de;
www.camping-wertach.de

12 🏕 €2.50 (htd) 👫 ⬛ 🚿 🛁 ♿ 🖪 ⚊ ♨ 🦋 🐕 ¶ ⓣ nr Ⓗ 🛒 nr /⧄

Fr A7 exit junc 137 at Oy & take B310 dir Wertach;
2km bef Wertach turn R into Bahnhofstrasse & foll
site sp. 4*, Med, mkd, pt shd, pt sl, EHU (16A) metered;
gas; bbq; sw nr; red long stay; TV; 50% statics; phone;
bus; Eng spkn; adv bkg acc; games area; games rm;
CKE. *"V picturesque area; friendly site; gd walks; winter
sports site & conv NH in rte Austria/Italy."* **€22.50**
2015

WERTHEIM *3D2* (11km NE Rural) *49.78097, 9.56553*
Campingpark Wertheim-Bettingen, Geiselbrunnweg
31, 97877 Wertheim-Bettingen (09342) 7077;
info@campingpark-wertheim-bettingen.de;
www.campingpark-wertheim-bettingen.de

🏕 €1 👫 🖪 ⬛ 🚿 ♿ 🖪 ⚊ ♨ 🦋 🐕 📶 🛒 /⧄

Fr A3/E41 exit junc 66 - 2nd Wertheim exit; then
turn off to vill of Bettingen; site sp. 4*, Med, pt shd,
pt sl, EHU (6A) €3.50 (long lead req for rvside pitches);
gas; red long stay; 80% statics; Eng spkn; adv bkg acc;
ccard acc; bike hire; boating; fishing; CKE. *"On bank of
Rv Main; conv, popular NH for A3 - rec arr early; NH
tourers on sep, lge, level meadow outside main site
(but within barrier); gd rest; htd pool, paddling pool
adj; waterslide adj; san facs tired, req upgrade (2014)."*
€20.50, 1 Apr-31 Nov. 2019

WESEL *1B3* (3km W Rural) *51.66795, 6.55620*
Erholungszentrum Grav-Insel, 46487 Wesel-Flüren
(0281) 972830; grav-insel@t-online.de; www.grav-
insel.com

12 🏕 €1 👫 🖪 ⬛ 🚿 ♿ 🖪 ⚊ ♨ 🦋 🐕 ¶ ⓣ Ⓗ 🛒 /⧄ 🖊

Exit A3/E35 junc 6 dir Wesel. Then foll sp Rees &
Flüren, site sp. 4*, V lge, unshd, EHU (10) €3;
65% statics; Eng spkn; tennis 3km; boat hire; fishing;
games area; bike hire; watersports; golf 7km. *"Rv
Rhine adj; many activities; gd touring base; htd pool
3km; modern san facs but pss far fr pitches; v lge site
with comprehensive facs & v well kept."* **€15.50** 2016

WESTERSTEDE *1C2* (1km S Rural) *53.2508, 7.93506*
Camping Westerstede, Süderstrasse 2, 26655
Westerstede (04488) 78234; camping@
westerstede.de; www.westerstede.de/camping

12 👫 (htd) 🖪 ⬛ 🚿 ♿ 🖪 ⚊ ♨ 🦋 🐕 Ⓗ 🛒 nr /⧄

Exit E35/A28 junc 6 to Westerstede; cont thro town
dir Bad Zwischenahn on L815 for 1km; then foll
L815 to L onto Oldenburgerstrasse (rd conts strt
on as L821); in 200m turn L to site. 3*, Med, hdstg,
mkd, pt shd, EHU (9A) inc; bus; train 400m; Eng spkn;
CKE. *"Pleasant, friendly, relaxing, well-managed site;
clsd 1300-1500; sm pitches; outer field (nr mv svc pnt
and rest) cheaper but rd noise and abt 100mtrs fr facs;
o'night m'van facs; gd touring base; many cycle paths;
gd town for shopping; gd midway stop to/fr Denmark."*
€15.50 2016

WETTRINGEN *1B3* (10km N Rural) *52.27408, 7.3204*
Campingplatz Haddorfer Seen, Haddorf 59, 48493
Wettringen (05973) 2742; info@campingplatz-
haddorf.de; www.campingplatz-haddorf.de

12 🏕 €3 👫 (htd) 🖪 ⬛ 🚿 ♿ 🖪 ⚊ ♨ 🦋 🐕 ¶ Ⓗ 🛒 /⧄

Exit A30 junc 7 at Rheine Nord dir Neuenkirchen. At
end city limits turn R dir Salzbergen then L in 4km &
foll site sp. 4*, V lge, mkd, pt shd, EHU (16A) metered
+ conn fee; sw; 90% statics; adv bkg acc; fishing; boat
hire; games area; watersports; CKE. *"Family-friendly
site; modern san facs; gd bistro; gd walking, cycling."*
€24.00 2016

WETZLAR *3C1* (13km SW Rural) *50.51155, 8.38293*
Campingpark Braunfels, Am Weiherstieg 2, 35619
Braunfels (06442) 4366; www.braunfels.de

12 🏕 €1 👫 🖪 ⬛ 🚿 ♿ 🖪 ⚊ ♨ 🦋 🐕 Ⓗ 🛒 nr

Take B49 fr Wetzlar to Braunfels. Site on R at S end
of town. 2*, Med, hdg, mkd, pt shd, pt sl, EHU (16A)
metered + conn fee; 60% statics; adv bkg acc; tennis
300m; horseriding 1km. *"Braunfels beautiful health
resort in easy reach Taunus mountains; htd pool 200m;
fair NH."* **€20.00** 2015

WIESLOCH *3C3* (8km NW Urban) *49.31643, 8.63481*
Campingplatz Walldorf-Astoria, Schwetzingerstrasse
98, 69190 Walldorf (06227) 9195

👫 🖪 ⬛ 🚿 ♿ 🖪 ♨ 🦋 🐕 🛒

Fr A5, exit junc 39 for Walldorf & Wiesloch; take
B291/L598 N sp Walldorf Nord; in 2km turn R onto
Schwetzingerstrasse; site sp in 250m. 3*, Med, pt
shd, EHU (16A) €2.50; 50% statics; Eng spkn; CKE.
*"Vg rest on site; sm zoo & sports complex adj; bus to
Heidelberg at gate; gates clsd 1200-1500; indoor pool
200m; excel NH/sh stay, busy; rec arr bef 1700 high
ssn; conv for Hockenheim Circuit; gd rest; hard working
fam run site; Heidelberg & Speyer worth visiting."*
€18.00, 15 Apr-15 Oct. 2015

WILDESHAUSEN *1C2* (6km W Rural) *52.89916,
8.35444* **Camping Auetal,** Aumühlerstrasse 75, 27793
Aumühle (04431) 1851

12 👫 🖪 ⬛ 🚿 ♿ 🖪 ⚊ ♨ Y Ⓗ /⧄

Exit a'bahn A1/E37 junc 61. Take rd B213 E; site on L
in 1.5km. 2*, Sm, pt shd, EHU (16A) €1.50; bbq; sw nr;
CKE. *"Statics site but sm field for tourers; vg rest; NH
only."* **€16.00** 2015

WINTRICH *3B2* (30km NE Rural) *49.96541, 7.10537*
Mosel Stellplatz Wintrich, Rissbacherstraße 155,
56841 Traben-Trarbach 06542 9691728; info@alf.
moselcampingplatz.de; www.mosel-camping-
platz.de

12 🏕 👫 🖪 ⬛ 🚿 ♿ 🖪 ⚊ ♨ 🦋 🐕 ¶

Fr S of A1 take exit 125 Wittlich-Mitte for B50 twds
Wittlich. Merge onto B49, cont onto L55 to Urzig,
then turn R onto B53 & foll sp to camp. 4*, Med, shd,
EHU (6A). *"Vg site."* **€8.00** 2019

WISMAR *2E2* (0.4km S Urban) *53.89388, 11.45166*
Wohnmobilpark Westhafen, Schiffbauerdamm 12,
23966 Wismar **(01723) 905368 or 884003; info@
wohnmobilpark-wismar.de; www.wohnmobilpark-
wismar.de**

🔢 ♦♦ 🏕 ⅄ ⓘ nr 🏬 nr

Exit A20/E22 junc 8 to cent of Wismar; foll sp to
'hafen', site sp. 4*, Sm, hdstg, unshd, EHU (10A) €1
for 8 hrs; adv bkg acc. *"Superb NH in stunning town;
quayside noise; m'vans only - no c'vans allowed."*
€9.00   **2016**

> ## "There aren't many sites open at this time of year"
>
> If you're travelling outside peak season
> remember to call ahead to check site opening
> dates – even if the entry says 'open all year'.

WISMAR *2E2* (9km NW Coastal) *53.93441, 11.37160*
Ostsee Camping, Sandstrasse 19c, 23968 Zierow
(038428) 36280; info@ostsee-camping.de; www.
ostsee-camping.de

🔢 🐕 €2.70 ♦♦(htd) 🆆🅳 🏕 ♨ 🚿 ⅄ 🍽 ⓘ 🥤 🏬 🛢 🐾 adj

Fr Wismar-Lübeck rd B105/22 to Gägelow, turn
N to Zierow; thro vill to site at end of rd. 4*, V lge,
unshd, EHU (16A) €2.80; TV; 75% statics; games
area; sauna; horseriding adj; bike hire; CKE. *"Busy site
in superb location; gd san facs; a first class campsite."*
€32.00   **2016**

WISSEN *1B4* (3km SW Rural) *50.76108, 7.72086* **Zum
Hahnhof,** Paffrather Str. 192, 57537 Wissen **49 27 42
56 10; info@zumhahnhof.de; www.zum-hahnhof.de**

🔢 🐕 ♦♦ 🆆🅳 🏕 ♨ 🚿 ⅄ 🍽 🦋 🍽 ⓘ 🛢 🏬

Take B62 twds Roth. After 1km turn R onto
Koblenzer Str (rd doubles back onto overpass) then
1st R onto Nistertals Str. Site approx 3km on R. Sm,
hdstg, pt shd, terr, EHU (6A) €1.50; bbq; sw nr; twin
axles; TV; 25% statics; Eng spkn; adv bkg acc; CKE.
*"Modern san facs, very clean; some hdstg pitches, rest
in meadow - long elec leads req; app rd (K133) fairly
narr in places; gd site."* **€10.00**   **2016**

WITZENHAUSEN *1D4* (2km N Rural) *51.3499,
9.86916* **Camping Werratal,** Am Sande 11, 37213
Witzenhausen (05542) 1465; info@campingplatz-
werratal.de; www.campingplatz-werratal.de

🔢 🐕 €2.30 ♦♦ 🆆🅳 🏕 ⅄ 🍽 🍽 ⓘ nr 🏬 🛢

Exit A7/E45 junc 75 to Witzenhausen. Cross rv &
immed R foll sp rte around town cent. Site nr rv,
sp. 3*, Med, unshd, EHU (16A) €2.30; red long stay;
50% statics; bike hire. *"Clean, pleasant, family-run site;
htd covrd pool 200m; poss flooding at high water; easy
walk to town; some rd & rlwy noise."* **€20.00**   **2015**

WOLFSBURG *2E3* (3km NE Urban) *52.4316, 10.8158*
Camping am Allersee, In den Allerwiesen 5, 38446
Wolfsburg (05361) 63395; allerseecamping@gmx.de;
www.camping-allersee.de

🔢 🐕 €1 ♦♦(htd) 🆆🅳 🏕 ♨ 🚿 ⅄ 🍽 🍽 nr 🏬 🐾 🛢 adj

Exit A39 junc 5 twd Zentrum, foll sp VW Autostadt
until start of flyover, keep R and foll sp. 3*, Med,
mkd, hdstg, pt shd, EHU (10A) €2.50 or metered;
cooking facs; sw nr; 80% statics; Eng spkn; adv bkg
acc; sailing; clsd 1300-1500 & 2200-0700; canoeing.
*"Vg, clean site beside lake; conv VW factory visits (not
w/end or bank hols) - check time of tour in Eng; o'night
m'vans area; gd lake perimeter path adj; friendly,
helpful owners; ice rink & indoor water cent other side
of lake."* **€19.00**   **2016**

WURZBURG *3D2* (6km NE Urban) *49.83286, 9.99783*
Camping Estenfeld, Maidbronnerstrasse 38, 97230
Estenfeld (09305) 228; cplestenfeld@freenet.de;
www.camping-estenfeld.de

🐕 €1.50 ♦♦ 🆆🅳 🏕 ⅄ 🦋 🍽 ⓘ nr 🛢 🏬 🛢

Exit A7/E45 junc 101. Foll sp to Estenfeld & site sp.
Sm, hdstg, pt shd, EHU (16A) €2.50 or metered & conn
fee; red long stay; 10% statics; Eng spkn; CKE. *"Helpful
owner; clsd 1300-1500; clean, tidy site; rec NH."*
€21.50, 29 May-14 Oct.   **2019**

WUSTENWELSBERG *4E2* (0.5km SE Rural) *50.13750,
10.82777* **Camping Rückert-Klause,** Haus Nr 16,
96190 Wüstenwelsberg (09533) 288

🐕 ♦♦ 🆆🅳 🏕 🛢 ⅄ 🦋 🍽 🛢 🏬 nr 🛢

Fr Coburg on B4, turn W at Kaltenbrunn; site sp
thro Untermerzbach & Obermerzbach. Or fr B279
fr Bamberg to Bad Königshofen, turn R just S of
Pfarrweisch, sp. Sm, pt shd, pt sl, EHU (16A) metered
+ conn fee; 50% statics; Eng spkn; adv bkg acc; games
rm; CKE. *"Many castles nrby; beautiful countryside;
super situation."* **€18.00, 1 Apr-31 Oct.**   **2016**

ZELL *3B2* (9km W Rural) *50.03305, 7.11527*
Camping Moselland, Im Planters, 56862 Pünderich
(06542) 2618; www.campingplatz-moselland.de

🐕 €2 ♦♦ 🆆🅳 🏕 🛢 ⅄ 🦋 🍽 ⓘ 🛢 🏬

Foll Rv Mosel S fr Zell on B53. In 6km turn R sp
Pünderich & site. Turn immed L, then immed R &
foll narr rd to site in 1km. Med, mkd, pt shd, EHU
(16A) metered + conn fee; 30% statics; phone; Eng
spkn; adv bkg acc; boat launch. *"Pleasant rvside
site in vineyards & orchards; vg; various odd rules."*
€18.00, 1 Apr-1 Nov.   **2015**

ZELL *3B2* (6km NW Rural) *50.05391, 7.13041*
Bären Camp, Am Moselufer 1-3, 56859 Bullay
**(06542) 900097; info@baeren-camp.de;
www.baeren-camp.de**

🏠 €2 👫 ⅏ 🛁 ♿ 🅿 ⁄ 🅼🅿 ⛅ 🐛 🏊 ⚓

Exit A1 junc 125 at Wittlich onto B49 to Alf. At Alf cross rv to Bullay & foll sp to site. 4*, Med, pt shd, EHU (16A) metered; bbq; Eng spkn. *"Conv Cochem, Bernkastel-Kues; gd cycling along tow-path; extra for rvside pitch; recep clsd 1230-1400; narr rd to recep; friendly staff; gd location on the Mosel."*
€28.50, 18 Apr-10 Nov. **2019**

ZEVEN *1D2* (2km NE Urban) *53.30401, 9.29793*
Campingplatz Sonnenkamp Zeven, Sonnenkamp 10, 27404 Zeven **(04281) 951345; info@campingplatz-sonnenkamp.de; www.campingplatz-zeven.de**

12 🏠 €0.50 👫(htd) ⅏ 🛁 ♿ 🅿 ⁄ 🅼🅿 🐛
⛅ ⛅ 🍴 Ⓙ 🏊 ⚓ 🚲 🎣

Fr A1 exit 47 or 49 to Zeven. Fr Zeven dir Heeslingen/Buxtehude rd, site sp fr all dir twd stadium. 5*, Lge, hdstg, mkd, unshd, EHU (16A) metered; gas; 75% statics; phone; Eng spkn; adv bkg acc; ccard acc; bike hire; games area; tennis; games rm; sauna; CKE. *"Sports facs adj."* **€22.60** **2016**

FEHMARN ISLAND

WULFEN *2E1* (0.6km E Coastal) *54.40611, 11.1772*
Camping-und Ferienpark Wulfener Hals (Part Naturist), Wulfener Hals Weg, 23769 Wulfen **(04371) 86280; camping@wulfenerhals.de; www.wulfener hals.de**

🏠 €10 👫(htd) ⅏ 🛁 ♿ 🅿 ⁄ 🅼🅿 ⛅ 🍴
Ⓙ 🏊 ⚓ 🚲 🎣 ⚓ 🏖sand adj

Turn off B207/E47 to Avendorf, site sp.
5*, V lge, mkd, shd, serviced pitches; EHU (160A) inc; gas; 20% statics; phone; adv bkg acc; ccard acc; golf adj; sauna; watersports; sailing; CKE. *"Excel."*
€56.00, 24 Mar-5 Nov, G10. **2017**

ZIERENBERG *1D4* (1km E Rural) *51.36809, 9.31494*
Campingplatz Zur Warme, Im Nordbruch 2, 34289 Zierenberg **(05606) 3966; campingplatz-zierenberg@t-online.de; www.campingplatz-zierenberg.de**

12 🏠 €1.50 👫(htd) ⅏ 🛁 ♿ 🅿 ⁄ 🐛
🍴 Ⓙ 🏊 ⚓ nr ⚓ 🎣(covrd)

Exit A44 at junc 67 to Zierenberg. In vill cent foll sp for Freizeit Centrum. Site on R on leaving vill, well sp. 4*, Med, mkd, hdstg, unshd, EHU (16A) €1.70 or metered; TV; 75% statics; Eng spkn; adv bkg acc; fishing. *"Scenic, well-kept site with stream & sm lake adj; clean, modern facs but poss stretched if site full."*
€16.50 **2016**

ZINGST AM DARSS *2F1* (3km W Coastal) *54.44055, 12.66031* **Camping am Freesenbruch,** Am Bahndamm 1, 18374 Zingst-am-Darss **(038232) 15786; info@ camping-zingst.de; www.camping-zingst.de**

12 🏠 €2 👫 ⅏ 🛁 ♿ 🅿 ⁄ 🅼🅿 ⛅ 🍴 Ⓙ 🏊 ⚓ 🎣 🏖adj

On rd 105/E22 at Löbnitz take rd thro Barth to Zingst; site on coast rd. 4*, Lge, mkd, pt shd, EHU (16A) metered + conn fee; 20% statics; adv bkg acc; ccard acc; games area; bike hire; CKE. *"Well-maintained site in National Park; sep car park; o'night facs for m'vans; sep fr beach by sea wall & rd; well-maintained; card operated barrier."* **€36.00** **2016**

ZISLOW *2F2* (2km N Rural) *53.44555, 12.31083*
Naturcamping Zwei Seen, Waldchaussee 2, 17209 Zislow **(039924) 2550; info@zwei-seen-naturcamping.de; www.zwei-seen-naturcamping.de**

12 🏠 €2.50 👫 ⅏ 🛁 ♿ 🅿 ⁄ 🅼🅿 ⛅ 🍴 Ⓙ 🏊 ⚓ 🎣

A19/E55 exit 17 dir Adamshoffnung. Turn R at x-rds in 4km. Site sp. Also sp fr W of Stuer on B198. 3*, Lge, pt shd, EHU (6A) €2; sw; 40% statics; phone; Eng spkn; adv bkg acc; ccard acc; games area; bike hire; watersports; CKE. *"Ideal for country lovers; remote spot; vg lakeside pitches."* **€22.70** **2016**

ZITTAU *2H4* (3km W Rural) *50.8943, 14.77005*
See-Camping Zittauer Gebirge, Zur Landesgartenschau 2, 02785 Olbersdorf **(03583) 69629-2; info@see camping-zittau.com; www.seecamping-zittau.com**

12 🏠 €2 👫 ⅏ 🛁 ♿ 🅿 ⁄ 🐛 ⛅ 🍴 nr Ⓙ 🏊 🎣

Fr Zittau foll Olbersdorfer See sp, site on lakeside. 3*, Lge, unshd, sl, EHU (10A) €2; sw; 10% statics; Eng spkn; ccard acc; CKE. *"Excel san facs; excel base for hill walking; close Polish & Czech borders."*
€23.00 **2016**

RUGEN ISLAND

ALTEFAHR *2F1* (1km NW Coastal) *54.33200, 13.12206* **Sund Camp,** Am Kurpark 1, 18573 Altefähr **(038306) 75483; info@sund-camp.de; www.sund-camp.de**

12 🏠 €2 👫 ⅏ 🛁 ♿ 🅿 ⁄ 🅼🅿 🐛 ⛅ nr 🏊 nr 🏖shgl 500m

Fr Stralsund, cross bdge on B96 to Rügen Island. Foll sp to Altefähr. Site well sp fr vill. Med, mkd, pt shd, EHU (16A) inc (poss rev pol); red long stay; TV; 15% statics; phone; sep car park; bike hire. *"Conv Rugen Is (walks, cycle tracks, beaches, steam rlwy); easy walk to vill & harbour; splendid, but busy island; well worth visit; ferry to Stralsund Altstadt nrby; excel, friendly site; muddy when wet; excel, clean san facs; ltd nbr of touring pitches."* **€24.00** **2015**

BINZ *2G1* (3km NW Coastal) *54.42315, 13.57808*
Camping Meier, Proraer Chaussee 30, 18609 Prora
**(038393) 2085; info@camping-meier-ruegen.de;
www.camping-meier-ruegen.de**

🐕 €3.50 ⵏ⟊ ⬛ ᵂᴰ ⛲ ♿ 🚻 ⟊ 🦋 💦 ⵏ 🍴 ⓘ ⛱ nr ⚠ ⛱ sand 500m

**On B96 Stralsund to Bergen cont on 196 to Karow.
Turn L on 196a to Prora, at traff lts turn R onto L29
to Binz. After 1.5km at camp sp turn R thro wood to
site.** Med, mkd, pt shd, EHU (6A) €2.50; red long stay;
phone; adv bkg req; ccard acc; bike hire; tennis. *"Gd
location for touring Rügen area; gd sandy beach 5-10
min walk thro woods; bkg fee; vg rest; vg san facs."*
€30.00, 13 Mar-1 Nov. 2016

"That's changed – Should I let the Club know?"

If you find something on site that's different
from the site entry, fill in a report and let us
know. See camc.com/europereport.

WESTERLAND *1C1* (5km N Coastal) *54.94251,
8.32685* **Camping Wenningstedt,** Am Dorfteich,
25996 Wenningstedt **(04651) 944004; camp@
wenningstedt.de; www.campingplatz.wenningstedt.
de**

🐕 €3.50 ⵏ⟊ ⬛ ᵂᴰ ⛲ ♿ 🚻 💦 ⵏ 🦋 💦 ⓘ ⛱ 🚿 ⚠ 🏊 (covrd, htd)

**Fr Westerland foll sp to Wenningstedt or List. Site
app rd on sharp bend bef Wenningstedt.** 4*, Lge,
unshd, pt sl, EHU (16A) metered; adv bkg acc; fishing
300m. **€27.00, Easter-31 Oct.** 2016

ZWEIBRUCKEN *3B3* (17km SW Rural) *49.15888,
7.24388* **Camping Walsheim(formerly Camping
am Schwimmbad),** Am Campingplatz 1, 66453
Gersheim-Walsheim **(06843) 800180; info@
campingwalsheim.de; www.campingwalsheim.de**

🐕 €0.50 ⵏ⟊ ⬛ ᵂᴰ ⛲ ♿ 🚻 ⵏ 🦋 💦 🍴 nr ⓘ nr ⛱ nr

**Fr A8/E50 exit junc 9 onto B423 dor Blieskastel. In
Webenheim turn L twd Gersheim, after 11km turn L
for Walsheim. Site on L beyond vill.** 3*, Med, pt shd,
pt sl, EHU €2 or metered (10A); bbq; 85% statics;
phone; adv bkg acc; CKE. *"Helpful warden; htd pool
adj; sep area for tourers; pleasant countryside; walking
& cycle paths nr; site barrier clsd 1300-1500 & 2200."*
€19.00, 15 Mar-31 Oct. 2019

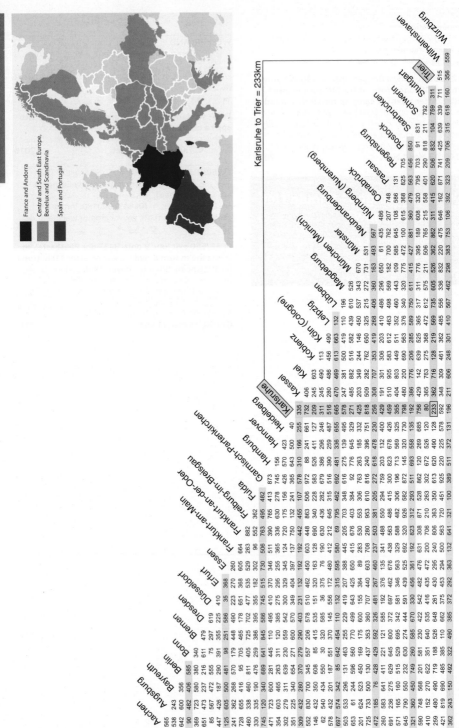

Federal States of Germany

Map 1

Map 2

Map 3

Map 4

Greece

📍 The Acropolis, Athens

Highlights

Whether you want to marvel at ancient ruins, lay on an idyllic sandy beach or sample local dishes, Greece is undoubtedly the place to be.

From rugged hillsides to the sparkling blue waters of the Mediterranean, this is a country steeped in myths of gods and heroes. The country is also famed for the friendly and hospitable nature of its people, so you're sure to receive a warm welcome.

Music is an integral part of Greek society and laïkó is a modern folk music genre that boomed in the 1960s and 70s. There are now many different forms of this music, but it still retains a sense of being a song of the people.

Greece can be considered the birthplace of wine, and the origins of wine-making in Greece go back well over 6000 years. Although not as well-known as other European nations for its wine, Greece has a thriving industry and the local varieties pair up well with food dishes from the same area.

Major towns and cities

- Athens – the cradle of Western civilization and one of the world's oldest cities.
- Thessalonika – a charming city filled with museums to explore.
- Patras – this amazing city is home to fascinating sites from ancient times.
- Larissa – surrounded by mountains and home to several ancient sites.

Attractions

- The Acropolis, Athens – an ancient citadel containing the Parthenon and other ruins.
- Meteora – stunning monasteries built on natural sandstone pillars.
- Delphi – this site boasts some of Greece's most important ancient ruins.
- Cape Sounion – fantastic views over the Aegean and the ruins of an ancient temple.

Find out more

www.visitgreece.gr
E: info@gnto.gr T: 0030 (0) 21 03 31 05 29

Country Information

Population (approx): 10.8 million

Capital: Athens

Area: 131,957 sq km

Bordered by: Albania, Bulgaria, Macedonia, Turkey

Coastline: 13,676km

Terrain: Mainly mountain ranges extending into the sea as peninsulas and chains of islands

Climate: Warm Mediterranean climate; hot, dry summers; mild, wet winters in the south, colder in the north; rainy season November to March; winter temperatures can be severe in the mountains

Highest Point: Mount Olympus 2,919m

Language: Greek

Local Time: GMT or BST + 2, i.e. 2 hours ahead of the UK all year

Currency: Euros divided into 100 cents; £1 = €1.16, €1 = £0.87 (October 2019)

Emergency numbers: Police 100; Fire brigade 199; Ambulance 166. Operators speak English. Dial 171 for emergency tourist police.

Public Holidays 2020: Jan 1, 6; Mar 2, 25; Apr 17, 20; May 1; Jun 8; Aug 15; Oct 28; Dec 25, 26.

School summer holidays run from the beginning of July to the first week in September.

Border Posts

Borders may be crossed only on official routes with a Customs office. These are usually open day and night. Customs offices at ports are open from 7.30am to 3pm Monday to Friday.

Entry Formalities

Visas are not required by British or Irish passport holders for a stay of up to three months. Visitors planning to stay longer should contact the Greek Embassy in London before they travel www.greekembassy.org.uk.

Medical Services

For minor complaints seek help at a pharmacy (farmakio). Staff are generally well trained and in major cities there is usually one member of staff in a pharmacy who speaks English. You should have no difficulty finding an English speaking doctor in large towns and resorts.

Medications containing codeine are restricted. If you are taking any medication containing it, you should carry a letter from your doctor and take no more than one month's supply into the country.

There are numerous public and private hospitals and medical centres of varying standards. Wards may be crowded and the standards of nursing and after care, particularly in the public health sector, are generally below what is normally acceptable in Britain. Doctors and facilities are generally good on the mainland, but may be limited on the islands. The public ambulance service will normally respond to any accident but there are severe shortages of ambulances on some islands.

Emergency treatment at public medical clinics (yiatria) and in state hospitals registered by the Greek Social Security Institute, IKA-ETAM, is free on presentation of a European Health Insurance Card (EHIC) but you may face a long wait. You will be charged for prescriptions so keep the adhesive labels from the medicines packages in order to claim a refund at an IKA-ETAM office. See www.ika.gr for a list of local offices.

You may consult a doctor or dentist privately but you will have to present your EHIC and pay all charges up front. You can then claim back the charges later from the IKA-ETAM.

If staying near a beach, ensure that you have plenty of insect repellent as sand flies are prevalent. Do not be tempted to befriend stray dogs as they often harbour diseases which may be passed to humans.

Opening Hours

Banks: Mon-Fri 8am-2pm (1.30pm on Friday); 8am-6pm in tourist areas.

Museums: Check locally for opening hours. Normally closed on Mon or Tues and some bank holidays.

Post Offices: Mon-Fri 8am-2pm; 8am-7pm in tourist areas; many in Athens open Sat mornings in summer.

Shops: Mon-Fri 8am/8.30am/9am-2pm/4.30pm & on some days 5pm-8.30pm; Sat 8.30am-3pm; check as hours vary according to season.

Safety and Security

Normally visits to Greece are trouble-free, but the tourist season results in an increase in incidents of theft of passports, wallets, handbags, etc, particularly in areas or at events where crowds gather.

Take care when visiting well-known historical sites; they are the favoured haunts of pickpockets, bag-snatchers and muggers. Women should not walk alone at night and lone visitors are strongly advised never to accept lifts from strangers or passing acquaintances at any time.

Since banking services were restricted in 2015, the FCO has recommended that you take enough cash to cover your needs while you are in Greece. If you are carrying large amounts of cash, make sure you take safety precautions. Be aware that tourists are expected to be carrying larger amounts of money, making them potential targets for thieves.

Multi-lingual tourist police are available in most resorts offering information and help; they can be recognised by a 'Tourist Police' badge, together with a white cap band. There is also a 24-hour emergency helpline for tourists; dial 171 from anywhere in Greece.

Certain areas near the Greek borders are militarily sensitive and you should not take photographs or take notes near military or official installations. Seek permission before photographing individuals.

There is a general threat from domestic terrorism. Attacks could be indiscriminate and against civilian targets in public places. Public protests are a standard feature of Greek politics and it is wise to avoid public gatherings and demonstrations. Domestic anarchist groups remain active but their actions are primarily directed against the Greek state.

During especially hot and dry periods there is a danger of forest fires. Take care when visiting or driving through woodland areas. Ensure that cigarette ends are properly extinguished, do not light barbecues and do not leave rubbish or empty bottles behind.

Some motorists have encountered stowaway attempts while waiting to board ferries to Italy from Patras. Keep a watch on your vehicle(s).

In order to comply with the law, always ensure that you obtain a receipt for goods purchased.

British Embassy

1 PLOUTARCHOU STREET
106 75 ATHENS
Tel: (210) 7272600
www.ukingreece.fco.gov.uk

There are also British Consulates/Vice-Consulates/Honorary Consulates in Corfu, Heraklion (Crete), Rhodes and Zakynthos.

Irish Embassy

7 LEOF.VAS
KONSTANTINOU, 106 74 ATHENA
Tel: (210) 7232771
www.embassyofireland.gr

There are also Honorary Consulates in Corfu, Crete, Rhodes and Thessaloniki.

Documents

Money

Major credit cards are accepted in hotels, restaurants and shops and at some petrol stations. They may not be accepted at shops in small towns or villages. There is an extensive network of cash machines in major cities.

Carry your credit card issuers'/banks' 24-hour UK contact numbers in case of loss or theft.

Passport

Carry your passport at all times as a means of identification.

Vehicle(s)

Carry your vehicle registration certificate (V5C), insurance certificate and MOT certificate (if applicable) at all times.

Driving

Accidents

It is not essential to call the police in the case of an accident causing material damage only, however motorists are advised to call at the nearest police station to give a description of the incident to the authorities.

Whenever an accident causes physical injury, drivers are required to stop immediately to give assistance to the injured and call the police. Drivers who fail to do this are liable to imprisonment for up to three years.

If a visiting motorist has an accident, especially one causing injuries, they should inform the motoring organisation, ELPA, preferably at its head office in Athens, on (210) 6068800, email: info@elpa.gr, as they should be able to offer you assistance.

Alcohol

The maximum permitted level of alcohol is 50 milligrams in 100 millilitres of blood, i.e. lower than that permitted in the UK (80 milligrams). A level of 20 milligrams in 100 millilitres of blood applies to drivers who have held a driving licence for less than two years and to motorcyclists. Police carry out random breath tests and refusal to take a test when asked by the police, and/or driving while over the legal limit, can incur high fines, withdrawal of your driving licence and even imprisonment.

Breakdown Service

The Automobile & Touring Club of Greece (ELPA) operates a roadside assistance service (OVELPA) 24 hours a day on all mainland Greek roads as well as on most islands. The number to dial from most towns in Greece is 10400.

Members of AIT/FIA affiliated clubs, such as The Caravan and Motorhome Club, should present their valid membership card in order to qualify for reduced charges for on-the-spot assistance and towing. Payment by credit card is accepted.

Child Restraint System

Children under three years of age must be seated in a suitable and approved child restraint. Children between the ages of 3 and 11 years old that are less than 1.35 metres in height must be seated in an appropriate child restraint for their size. From 12 years old children that are over 1.35 metres in height can wear an adult seat belt.

A rear facing child restraint can be placed in the front seat but only if the airbag is deactivated.

Fuel

Petrol stations are usually open from 7am to 7pm; a few are open 24 hours. Some will accept credit cards but those offering cut-price fuel are unlikely to do so. In rural areas petrol stations may close in the evening and at weekends, so keep your tank topped up. There are no automatic petrol pumps operated with either credit cards or bank notes.

LPG (autogas) is available from a limited number of outlets.

Motorways

There are over 2,000 km of motorways in Greece. Service areas provide petrol, a cafeteria and shops. The main motorways are A1 Agean, A2 Egnatia, A6 Attiki, A7 Peloponissos, A8 Pathe, A29 Kastorias. For further information visit www.greek-motorway.net.

Motorway Tolls

Tolls are charged according to vehicle classification and distance travelled. By European standards the tolls are generally quite low. Cash is the preferred means of payment.

The Egnatia Highway

The 804 km Egnatia Highway (the A2), part of European route E90 linking the port of Igoumenitsa with the Turkish border at Kipoi, has undergone extensive upgrade and improvement in recent years. The route includes many bridges and tunnels with frequent emergency telephones for which the number to call from a landline or mobile phone is 1077. The road provides a continuous high speed link from west to east and will eventually connect with Istanbul. An electronic toll collection system is planned for the future.

Patras – Antirrio Bridge

A 2.8 km long toll suspension bridge between Rio (near Patras) and Antirrio links the Peloponnese with western central Greece and is part of the A8/E55 motorway. It has cut the journey time across the Gulf of Corinth – formerly only possible by ferry – to just five minutes. Tolls are charged.

Preveza – Aktio Tunnel

This undersea toll tunnel links Preveza with Aktio near Agios Nikolaoș on the E55 along the west coast of mainland Greece and is part of a relatively fast, scenic route south from Igoumenitsa to central and southern regions.

Parking

Parking is only permitted in the Athens 'Green Zone' where there are parking meters. Special parking sites in other areas are reserved for short-term parking for tourists.

There may be signs on the side of the road indicating where vehicles should be parked. Parking restrictions are indicated by yellow lines at the side of the road. The police are entitled to remove vehicles. They can also confiscate the number plates of vehicles parked illegally and, while this usually applies only to Greek-registered vehicles, drivers of foreign registered vehicles should nevertheless avoid illegal parking.

Parking is not permitted within three metres of a fire hydrant, five metres of an intersection, stop sign or traffic light, and fifteen metres of a bus stop, tram stop and level crossings.

Roads

The surfaces of all major roads and of the majority of other roads are in good condition. Some mountain roads, however, may be in poor condition and drivers must beware of unexpected potholes (especially on corners), precipitous, unguarded drops and single-carriageway bridges. Even on narrow mountain roads you may well encounter buses and coaches.

British motorists visiting Greece should be extra vigilant in view of the high incidence of road accidents. Driving standards are generally poorer than in the UK and you may well have to contend with dangerous overtaking, tailgating, weaving motorcycles and scooters, constant use of the horn, roaming pedestrians and generally erratic driving. Greece has one of the highest rate of road fatalities in Europe and overtaking and speeding are common causes of accidents, particularly on single lane carriageways. Drive carefully and be aware of other drivers at all times.

August is the busiest month of the year for traffic and the A1/E75 between Athens and Thessalonika is recognised as one of the most dangerous routes, together with the road running through the Erimanthos mountains south of Kalavrita. Mountain roads in general can be dangerous owing to narrow carriageways, blind bends and unprotected embankments, so keep your speed down.

You are strongly advised against hiring motorcycles, scooters and mopeds, as drivers of these modes of transport are particularly at risk. The wearing of crash helmets is a legal requirement. Never hand over your passport when hiring a vehicle.

Greece has a high level of pedestrian fatalities. Where there is a shortage of parking spaces drivers park on pavements so pedestrians are forced to walk in the road. Collisions between pedestrians and motorcycles are common.

Road Signs and Markings

Road signs conform to international conventions. Motorway signs have white lettering on a green background, signs on other roads are on a blue background. All motorways, major and secondary roads are signposted in Greek and English.

Some open roads have a white line on the nearside, and slower-moving vehicles are expected to pull across it to allow vehicles to overtake.

Speed Limits

	Open Road (km/h)	Motorway (km/h)
Car Solo	90-110	130
Car towing caravan/trailer	80	80
Motorhome under 3500kg	80	90
Motorhome 3500-7500kg	80	80

Traffic Jams

There is heavy rush hour traffic in and around the major cities and traffic jams are the norm in central Athens any time of day. During the summer months traffic to the coast may be heavy, particularly at weekends. Traffic jams may be encountered on the A1/E75 Athens to Thessalonika road and on the A8/E65 Athens to Patras road. Traffic may also be heavy near the ferry terminals to Italy and you should allow plenty of time when travelling to catch a ferry. Delays can be expected at border crossings to Turkey and Bulgaria.

Violation of Traffic Regulations

The Greek police are authorised to impose fines in cases of violation of traffic regulations, but they are not allowed to collect fines on the spot. Motorists must pay fines within ten days, otherwise legal proceedings will be started.

Essential Equipment

First Aid Kit

All vehicles must carry a first aid kit.

Fire Extinguisher

All vehicles must carry a fire extinguisher.

Warning Triangles

The placing of a warning triangle is compulsory in the event of an accident or a breakdown. It must be placed 100 metres behind the vehicle.

Touring

Mainland Greece and most of the Greek islands that are popular with British tourists are in seismically active zones, and small earth tremors are common. Serious earthquakes are less frequent but can, and do, occur.

Smoking is prohibited in bars and restaurants. In restaurants, if the bill does not include a service charge, it is usual to leave a 10 to 20% tip. Taxi drivers do not normally expect a tip but it is customary to round up the fare.

The best known local wine is retsina but there is also a wide range of non-resinated wines. Beer is brewed under licence from German and Danish breweries; Ouzo is a popular and strong aniseed-flavoured aperitif.

The major Greek ports are Corfu, Igoumenitsa, Patras, Piraeus and Rhodes. Ferry services link these ports with Cyprus, Israel, Italy and Turkey. The routes from Ancona and Venice in Italy to Patras and Igoumenitsa are very popular and advance booking is recommended.

For further information contact:

VIAMARE LTD
SUITE 108
582 Honeypot Lane
STANMORE
MIDDX
HA7 1JY
Tel: 020 8206 3420,
www.viamare.com
Email: ferries@viamare.com

Some ferries on routes from Italy to Greece have 'camping on board' facilities whereby passengers can sleep in their outfits. Mains hook-ups, t showers and toilets are available.

There are several World Heritage Sites in Greece (with more under consideration), including such famous sites as the Acropolis in Athens, the archaeological sites at Olympia and Mistras, and the old towns of Corfu and Rhodes. See www.worldheritagesite.org for more information. When visiting churches and monasteries dress conservatively, i.e. long trousers for men and no shorts, sleeveless T-shirts or short skirts for women.

Camping and Caravanning

There are over 300 campsites licensed by the Greek National Tourist Office. These can be recognised by a sign displaying the organisation's blue emblem. Most are open from April until the end of October, but those near popular tourist areas stay open all year. There are other unlicensed sites but visitors to them cannot be assured of safe water treatment, fire prevention measures or swimming pool inspection.

Casual/wild camping is not allowed outside official sites in Greece.

Electricity and Gas

Usually current on campsites varies between 4 and 16 amps. Plugs have two round pins. There are few CEE connections.

The full range of Campingaz cylinders are available from hypermarkets and other shops, but when purchasing a cylinder you may not be given a refundable deposit receipt.

Public Transport

Greece has a modern, integrated public transport system, including an extensive metro, bus, tram and suburban railway network in and around Athens – see www.ametro.gr for a metro map.

Buy bus/tram tickets from special booths at bus stops, newspaper kiosks or from metro stations. A ticket is valid for a travel time of 90 minutes.

Taxis are relatively cheap. All licensed taxis are yellow and are equipped with meters (the fare is charged per kilometre) and display a card detailing tariffs and surcharges. In certain tourist areas, you may be asked to pay a predetermined (standard) amount for a ride to a specific destination. Taxis run on a share basis, so they often pick up other passengers on the journey.

There are many ferry and hydrofoil services from Piraeus to the Greek islands and between islands.

Meteora Monasteries

ALEXANDROUPOLI *C1* (2km W Coastal) *40.84679, 25.85614* **Camping Alexandroupolis Beach,** Makris Ave, 68100 Alexandroupoli **(25510) 28735; camping@ditea.gr; www.ditea.gr**

12 ♦†♦ wo ♨ ♪ ☂ ♈ ☂ ♨ ♨ /Λ ☂ sand adj

Site on coast - after drainage channel, at 2nd set traff lts close together. Lge, hdg, mkd, hdstg, shd, EHU (8A) €3.60; gas; 20% statics; phone; Eng spkn; watersports; games area; tennis; CKE. *"Spacious, secure, well-run site; clean, hot shwrs; easy walk to pleasant town cent."* **€18.50**   2016

ATHINA *B3* (17km NE Urban) *38.09944, 23.79166* **Camping Nea Kifissia,** Potamou 60, Adames, 14564 Athina **(210) 8075579 or 6205646; camping@hol.gr; www.camping-neakifissia.gr**

12 ☂ ♦†♦ wo ♨ ☂ ♪ ☂ nr ♨

Sp both dirs on E75 Athens-Lamia rd. Heading twd Athens exit at sp, to U-turn onto service rd then take 1st L & foll sp. Sm, hdg, hdstg, shd, terr, EHU (10A) €4; TV; 50% statics; phone; bus to metro stn 200m; Eng spkn; CCI. *"Conv base for Athens - metro at Kifissia; pleasant, quiet, well-run site; excel pool; clean san facs but tired; helpful recep staff; san facs down 30+ steps."* **€33.00**   2015

DELFI *B2* (2km.W Rural) *38.4836, 22.4755* **Camping Apollon,** 33054 Delfi **(22650) 82762 or 82750; apollon4@otenet.gr; www.apolloncamping.gr**

12 ☂ ♦†♦ wo ♨ ♨ ☂ ♪ msp ☂ ⊕ ♨ /Λ ♨

Site on N48 fr Delfi twd Itea & 1st of number of campsites on this rd. Site 25km fr Parnassus ski cent. 3*, Med, mkd, pt shd, pt sl, terr, EHU (16A) €3; gas; TV; 30% statics; phone; adv bkg acc; ccard acc; bike hire; CKE. *"Magnificent views over mountains & Gulf of Corinth; Harmonie Group site; site cooler than some other sites due to its elevation; vg site; popular with groups of students; vg campsite."* **€30.00**   2015

DELFI *B2* (5km W Rural) *38.47868, 22.47461* **Camping Delphi,** Itea Road, 33054 Delfi **(22650) 82745; info@delphicamping.com; www.delphicamping.com**

☂ ♦†♦ wo ♨ ☂ ♪ msp ☂ ♈ ⊕ ♨ ♨

App fr Itea-Amfissa rd or Levadia; well sp. Med, shd, terr, EHU (16A) €3.90; gas; TV; phone; bus to Delfi; adv bkg acc; ccard acc; tennis; CKE. *"Visit grotto, refuge of Parnassus; Delfi archaeological sites 3km; friendly, helpful staff; Sunshine Group site; magnificent views; gd pool; dogs free; tired facs; 20% discount for Minoan Line ticketholders; delightful site; san facs bit tired but clean & tidy; excel site."* **€29.00, 1 Apr-31 Oct.**   2019

DELFI *B2* (8.5km W Rural) *38.47305, 22.45926* **Chrissa Camping,** 33055 Chrissa **(22650) 82050; info@chrissacamping.gr; www.chrissacamping.gr**

12 ♦†♦ wo ♨ ♨ ♪ ☂ ♈ ☂ ⊕ ♨ ♨ /Λ ♨ ♨ ☂ shgl 10km

1st site on Itea to Delfi rd, sp. 4*, Med, shd, pt sl, terr, EHU (10A) €4 first 4KWh/day then metered; gas; TV; adv bkg acc; ccard acc; games area; tennis 300m; CKE. *"Excel, scenic site."* **€21.50**   2017

DREPANO *B3* (12km E Coastal) *37.49710, 22.99028* **Iria Beach Camping,** Iria Beach 21060, Nafplio **02 75 20 94 253; iriabeach@naf.forthnet.gr; www.iriabeach.com**

12 ☂ ♦†♦ wo ♨ ♨ ♿ ☂ ♪ msp ♈ ☂ ♨ ☂ adj

Fr Drepano head E on Epar. Od. Drepanou-Kantias. Cont onto Kantias-Irion. 800m after Iria Beach Hotel turn R. Site on L after 1.5km. Med, hdstg, shd, EHU (16A); bbq; cooking facs; twin axles; TV; 5% statics; Eng spkn; adv bkg acc; CCI. *"Opp beach; gd sw; site quiet & relaxing; helpful staff; vg site."* **€25.00**   2019

"There aren't many sites open at this time of year"

If you're travelling outside peak season remember to call ahead to check site opening dates – even if the entry says 'open all year'.

EGIO *B2* (13km NW Coastal) *38.32078, 21.97195* **Tsoli's Camping,** Lambíri Egion, 25100 Lambiri **(26910) 31469 or 31621**

12 ☂ ♦†♦ wo ♨ ☂ ♪ ☂ ⊕ ♨ ♨ /Λ ♂ ☂ shgl adj

Fr Athens: A8/E65 exit Kamaras, site clearly sp 1km W of Lambiri. Fr Patras: Leave A8/E65 at exit Longos, take the Old Nat. On L in 1.5km after Lampiri. Med, hdstg, shd, EHU (16A) inc; gas; bbq; TV; 10% statics; phone; bus; Eng spkn; adv bkg acc; ccard acc; sep car park; boat launch; fishing; watersports; CKE. *"Bus & train service to Athens & Patras; gd site with gd facs in delightful position; few shd pitches for tourers & poss diff for high o'fits."* **€24.00**   2015

FINIKOUNDAS *A3* (1km W Coastal) *36.80555, 21.79583* **Camping Thines,** 24006 Finikoundas **(27230) 71200; thines@otenet.gr; www.finikounda.com**

12 ☂ ♦†♦ wo ♨ ♨ ☂ ♪ ☂ ♈ ☂ ♨ ☂ sand adj

Fr Methoni dir Finikoundas, turn R 1km bef vill, site on L. Sm, hdg, mkd, hdstg, pt shd, EHU (6-10A); gas; bbq; cooking facs; TV; Eng spkn; ccard acc; boat launch; CKE. *"Excel facs; helpful, friendly management; wonderful scenery & beach; red winter long stay; lovely vill in walking dist; beautiful site."* **€26.50**   2015

GREECE

GERAKINI *B2* (3km SE Coastal) *40.26464, 23.46338*
Camping Kouyoni, 63100 Gerakini **(23710) 52226;**
info@kouyoni.gr; www.kouyoni.gr

🛖 👬 wc 🚿 🔁 🖉 🦋 ♈ 🍽 ⓓ ♿ 🛒 🏍 🚣 🛶 🌳 sand adj

Take main rd S fr Thessaloniki to Nea Moudania,
then turn E twd Sithonia. Site is 18km on that rd
past Gerakini on R, past filling stn. Well sp.
Med, hdg, mkd, shd, pt sl, EHU (16A) €3.30; bbq; red
long stay; TV; 30% statics; phone; adv bkg acc; games
area; boat launch; CKE. *"Gd touring base set in olive
grove; friendly owner; gd facs; gd beach; influx of w/
enders high ssn."* **€29.00, 1 May-30 Sep.** **2016**

GITHIO *B3* (5km SSW Coastal) *36.73055, 22.55305*
Camping Meltemi, Mavrovouni Gytheio Lakonias
23200 **(02733) 023260;** info@campingmeltemi.gr;
www.campingmeltemi.gr

🛖 👬 wc 🚿 🔁 🖉 🅼 ♈ ⓓ 🛒 🏍 🚣 🌳20m

Site is approx 3km S of Githio on the L of the rd to
Areopoli. Lge, mkd, shd, EHU (16A); bbq; cooking facs;
twin axles; TV; phone; Eng spkn; adv bkg acc;
waterslide; games area; CKE. *"Beach volleyball, tennis,
table tennis & basketball court; vg."*
€26.00, 1 Apr-31 Oct. **2015**

IGOUMENITSA *A2* (10km S Coastal) *39.46346,
20.26037* **Camping Elena's Beach,** 46100 Platariá
(26650) 71414; bteo@altecnet.gr or info@
campingelena.gr; www.epirus.com/campingelena

🛖 👬 wc 🚿 🔁 ♿ 🖉 🦋 ♈ ⓓ 🛒 🏍 🌳shgl adj

Sp on Igoumenitsa-Preveza rd, 2km NW of Platariá.
Med, hdstg, pt shd, terr, EHU (5A) inc; gas; bbq; red
long stay; 10% statics; phone; bus; adv bkg acc; CKE.
*"Well-maintained, family-run, friendly site; clean,
modern san facs; beautiful location with pitches next
to sea; excel rest; conv ferries Corfu, Paxos."*
€26.50, 1 Apr-31 Oct. **2019**

**"That's changed – Should I let
the Club know?"**

If you find something on site that's different
from the site entry, fill in a report and let us
know. See camc.com/europereport.

IGOUMENITSA *A2* (5km W Coastal) *39.51014,
20.22133* **Camping Drepanos,** Beach Drepanos,
46100 Igoumenitsa **(26650) 26980;** camping@
drepano.gr; www.drepano.gr

12 🛖 👬 wc 🚿 🔁 🅼 ♈ 🍽 ⓓ 🛒nr 🏍 🌳sand

Fr Igoumenitsa take coast rd N. Foll sp for Drepanos
Beach. Fr either port turn L and head N up coast.
Med, hdstg, pt shd, sl, bbq; twin axles; 10% statics;
bus adj; Eng spkn; adv bkg acc; CKE. *"Beside nature
reserve; amazing sunsets; friendly; dated san facs;
attractive walks/cycle; vg."* **€26.50** **2016**

IOANINA *A2* (2km NW Urban) *39.67799, 20.84279*
Camping Limnopoula, Kanari 10, 45000 Ioanina
(26510) 25265

🛖 👬 wc 🚿 🔁 🖉 🦋 ♈ 🍽 ☖nr ⓓnr 🛒 🏍

At Ioanina Nautical Club on Igoumenitsa rd at W
o'skts of town on rd that runs along lake fr citadel;
site well sp fr all dirs. Med, pt shd, EHU (10A) inc; gas;
bbq; phone; Eng spkn; watersports. *"Beautiful situation
on lake, mountain views; excel touring base; helpful
staff; gd facs; clean; may close earlier; adv bkg acc 1-2
days ahead only LS; popular with groups LS; dogs free;
vg."* **€27.00, 1 Apr-15 Oct.** **2015**

**"I like to fill in the reports as I
travel from site to site"**

You'll find report forms at the back of this
guide, or you can fill them in online at
camc.com/europereport.

KALAMBAKA *A2* (4km SE Rural) *39.68250, 21.65510*
Camping Philoxenia, 42200 Kalambaka **(24320)**
24466; philoxeniacamp@ath.forthnet.gr

🛖 👬(htd) 🚿 🔁 ♿ 🖉 🅼 ♈ 🍽 ☖nr 🛒 🏍 🚣

Site on N side of E92 Trikala rd, behind barrier.
3*, Med, hdstg, shd, EHU (6A) inc; gas; bbq; cooking
facs; TV; 30% statics; Eng spkn; adv bkg acc; ccard acc;
waterslide; bike hire; CKE. *"Interesting area esp during
Easter religious festivals; Still open 2016 but call bef
travelling."* **€20.00, 1 Mar-30 Nov.** **2017**

KALAMBAKA *A2* (2km NW Rural) *39.71315, 21.61588*
Camping Vrachos, Meteoron Street, 42200 Kastraki
(24320) 22293; tsourvaka@yahoo.gr;
www.campingkastraki.com

12 🛖 👬 wc 🚿 🔁 ♿ 🖉 🅼 🦋 ♈ 🍽 ⓓ 🛒 🏍 🚣(htd)

Fr cent of Kalambaka take rd at app to vill of
Kastraki. Site is 2km N of E92. Med, hdstg, mkd, hdg,
pt shd, pt sl, terr, EHU (16A) inc; gas; bbq; cooking
facs; twin axles; TV; phone; bus adj, train 1km; Eng
spkn; adv bkg acc; CKE. *"V friendly management;
clean san facs; vg views fr some pitches; ltd facs open
in winter; dogs free; Harmonie Group site; conv for
monasteries, tour bus fr camp."* **€19.00** **2017**

KAVALA *C1* (4km SW Urban/Coastal) *40.91573,
24.37851* **Camping Multiplex Batis,** 65000 Kavala
(2510) 245918; nfo@batis-sa.gr; www.batis-sa.gr

12 👬(htd) wc 🚿 🔁 ♿ 🖉 🦋 ♈ ⓓ 🛒 🏍 🚣 🌳sand adj

On W app to town on old coast rd, ent on a curving
hill. Med, hdg, mkd, shd, pt sl, EHU (6A) €4; phone;
bus; Eng spkn; adv bkg acc; ccard acc; CKE. *"Beautiful
location but v developed; conv ferry to Thassos &
archaeological sites; clean facs but site poss unkempt
LS; vg."* **€26.00** **2016**

KORINTHOS *B3* (7km W Urban/Coastal) *37.93470, 22.86543* **Blue Dolphin Camping,** 20011 Lecheon Korinth **(27410)** 25766 or 25767; info@camping-blue-dolphin.gr; www.camping-blue-dolphin.gr
🛏 ♦♦ ⓌⒹ ⚓ & ▤ ∥ ✖ ♆ Ⓣ ⑭ ▣ ▥ 🅐 🛖 shgl

Best app fr E to avoid town; Fr A8 exit sp Ancient Corinth, then N (R) to T-junc end of rd, W (R) past pipe factory, sp 400m N (R) at bottom of bdge sl. Fr W take exit sp Ancient Corinth after toll point. Fr Old National rd turn N (L) immed over rlwy bdge bef pipe factory. Fr Corinth foll old National rd twd Patras, past pipe factory. Med, mkd, hdstg, pt shd, EHU (6A) €3.50; gas; bbq; TV; Eng spkn; ccard acc; games area; CKE. *"V obliging, friendly owners; Sunshine Group site; pleasant site; sm pitches; lovely site by sea."* **€23.00, 1 Apr-31 Oct.** **2015**

KYLLINI *A3* (10km S Coastal) *37.88539, 21.11175* **Campsite Melissa,** 27050 Kastro Kyllinis Ilia **02 62 30 95 213**; camping_melissa@yahoo.gr
🛏 ♦♦ ⓌⒹ ⚓ & ▤ ∥ Ⓜ ✖ ♆ Ⓣ ⑭ ▥ 🅐 🛖

S fr Patras twd Pygros on E55. Turn R twds Lehena after 58km marker. Foll signs to Kastro Kyllinis. Med, hdg, shd, EHU (10A); bbq; cooking facs; twin axles; TV; 2% statics; Eng spkn; adv bkg acc; CCI. *"Great campsite to chill; excel rest, bar & shop; lovely sandy beach; excel sw; fabulous views across the bay."* **€25.00, 1 Apr-31 Oct.** **2019**

KYLLINI *A3* (17km S Coastal) *37.83828, 21.12972* **Camping Aginara Beach,** Lygia, 27050 Loutra Kyllinis **(26230)** 96211; info@camping-aginara.gr; www.camping-aginara.gr
⑫ 🛏 ♦♦ ⓌⒹ ⚓ & ▤ ∥ Ⓜ ✖ ♆ Ⓣ ⑭ ▣ ▥ 🅐 🛖 shgl adj

S fr Patras on E55 twds Pyrgos; exit Gastouni & turn W thro Vartholomio twd Loutra Kyllinis; turn L about 3km bef Kyllinis then foll sps. 3*, Lge, hdg, hdstg, shd, pt sl, EHU (10A); gas; bbq; TV; 25% statics; phone; Eng spkn; adv bkg acc; ccard acc; watersports; CKE. *"Friendly proprietor; excel, modern facs; site on lovely beach; beautiful views."* **€28.00** **2019**

METHONI *A3* (1km ESE Coastal) *36.81736, 21.71515* **Camp Methoni,** 24006 Methoni **(27230)** 31188
🛏 ♦♦ ⚓ ▤ ∥ Ⓣ ⑭ ▣ 🅐 🛖 sand

Fr Pylos on rd 9, strt thro Methoni to beach, turn E along beach, site sp. 2*, Med, hdstg, pt shd, EHU (10A) inc; bbq; phone; Eng spkn; adv bkg acc; CKE. *"Superb Venetian castle; close to pleasant vill; park away fr taverna & rd to avoid noise; excel sw; v dusty site; clean san facs; new owner & undergoing renovations (2013); quiet & gd site."* **€21.40, 1 May-31 Oct.** **2019**

MIKINES *B3* (0.1km E Urban) *37.71922, 22.74676* **Camping Mikines/Mykenae,** 21200 Mikines **(27510)** 76247; dars@arg.forthnet.gr; www.ecogriek.nl
⑫ 🛏 ♦♦ ⓌⒹ ⚓ & ▤ ∥ ✖ ▥ nr

In town of Mikines (Mycenae) nr bus stop. On R as heading to archeological site, sp. 2*, Sm, hdstg, mkd, pt shd, EHU (10A) €4.50; Eng spkn; CKE. *"Quaint family-run site; v warm welcome; conv ancient Mycenae; meals served; friendly staff; vg."* **€21.00** **2019**

PARGA *A2* (2km W Coastal) *39.28550, 20.38997* **Camping Valtos,** Valtos Beach, 48060 Parga **(26840)** 31287; info@campingvaltos.gr; www.campingvaltos.gr
🛏 ♦♦ ⓌⒹ ⚓ ▤ ∥ ♆ Ⓣ ⑭ ▣ ▥ 🛖 sand adj

Foll sp fr Parga twd Valtos Beach, site sp. Site at far end of beach behind bar/club. Med, mkd, shd, pt sl, EHU (10A); Eng spkn; CKE. *"Helpful owners; gd walking area; steep walk to town; poor san facs."* **€28.50, 1 May-30 Sep.** **2016**

PLAKA LITOHOROU *B2* (10km N Coastal) *40.18230, 22.55885* **Camping Stani,** 60200 Kalivia Varikou **(23520)** 61277
⑫ 🛏 ♦♦ ⓌⒹ ⚓ ▤ ∥ ♆ ⑭ ▣ ▥

Leave E75 (Athens-Thessaloniki) at N Efesos/Variko, foll sp Varikou & site. Lge, mkd, shd, EHU; TV; phone; CKE. *"Ltd facs LS; conv Dion; fair site."* **€22.00** **2019**

PYLOS *A3* (7km N Coastal) *36.94784, 21.70635* **Camping Navarino Beach,** 24001 Gialova **(27230)** 22973; info@navarino-beach.gr; www.navarino-beach.gr
⑫ 🛏 ♦♦ ⓌⒹ ⚓ ▤ ∥ Ⓜ ✖ ♆ ⑭ ▣ ▥ nr 🅐 🛖

Fr Pylos N twds Kiparissia for 5km around Navarino Bay, site at S end of Gialova vill; sp. Med, hdstg, pt shd, EHU (16A) €4; gas; bbq; cooking facs; red long stay; bus; Eng spkn; adv bkg acc; ccard acc; windsurfing; boat launch; CKE. *"Management v helpful; gd, clean, modern facs; several rest & shops in easy walking dist; some pitches on beach; vg."* **€32.50** **2019**

SPARTI *B3* (5km W Rural) *37.06941, 22.38163* **Camping Castle View,** 23100 Mistras **(27310)** 83303; info@castleview.gr; www.castleview.gr
🛏 ♦♦ ⚓ ▤ ∥ ✖ ♆ Ⓣ ⑭ ▣ ▥ 🅐 🛲

Fr Kalamata take 1st turning to Mistras, past castle then thro vill dir Sparti. Site in approx 1km on L, well sp. 3*, Med, pt shd, EHU (16A) inc; gas; TV; 10% statics; phone; Eng spkn; CKE. *"Gd clean facs; gd rest; close to archaeological remains; helpful owner."* **€26.00, 1 Apr-20 Oct.** **2016**

GREECE

STYLIDA *B2* (4km SE Coastal) *38.89638, 22.65555*
Camping Interstation, Rd Athens-Thessalonika, Km 230, 35300 Stylida **(22380) 23828; www.camping interstation.com**

12 ⛺ ♙♙ wc ♨ & ⛟ ∥ 👜 ⊕ ⛴ ⚕ ☂ adj

Fr Lamia take rd E to Stylis; cont for further 3km & site situated to side of dual-c'way opp petrol stn. Med, shd, EHU (16A); gas; TV; 10% statics; Eng spkn; adv bkg acc; tennis; watersports; CKE. *"Day visitors have access to beach via site; do not confuse with Cmp Paras adj - not rec; Sunshine Camping Group site; poss poor san facs LS; NH only."* **€27.40**   **2017**

VARTHOLOMIO *A3* (10km SW Coastal) *37.83555, 21.13333* **Camping Ionion Beach,** 27050 Glifa **(26230) 96828; iniongr@otenet.gr; www.ionion-beach.gr**

12 ⛺ ♙♙ (htd) wc ♨ & ⛟ ∥ MSP 👜 🍴 ⊕ 🛒 ⛴ nr ⛰ ⚓ 🏊 ☂ adj

Fr E55 Patras-Pirgos rd turn W to Gastouni, Ligia & Glifa, then Glifa Beach. Site is 1km SW of Glifa. Med, hdg, hdstg, pt shd, serviced pitches; EHU (16A); gas; bbq; TV; Eng spkn; adv bkg acc; ccard acc; watersports; games area; CKE. *"Excel, well-run site; superb facs."* **€30.60**   **2016**

VIVARI *B3* (1km E Coastal) *37.53421, 22.93179* **Camping Lefka Beach,** 21100 Drepanon Vivari **(27520) 92334; info@camping-lefka.gr; www.camping-lefka.gr**

⛺ ♙♙ wc ♨ & ⛟ ∥ 🍴 ⊕ 🛒 ☂ 20m

On the Nafplio-Drepanon-Iria rd. About 1km on the R after vill of Vivari. Foll sp. Med, mkd, hdstg, shd, terr, EHU (16A); bbq; twin axles; TV; Eng spkn; adv bkg acc; CKE. *"Beautiful views of bay fr site; close to antiquities; vg."* **€28.00,** 1 Apr-10 Nov.   **2015**

VOLOS *B2* (18km SE Coastal) *39.31027, 23.10972* **Camping Sikia,** 37300 Kato Gatzea **(24230) 22279 or 22081; info@camping-sikia.gr; www.camping-sikia.gr**

12 ⛺ ♙♙ wc ♨ & ⛟ ∥ 👜 ⊕ 🍴 ⚕ ☂ shgl

Fr Volos take coast rd S to Kato Gatzea site on R, sp immed next to Camping Hellas. Med, shd, terr, EHU (16A) €3; gas; red long stay; 20% statics; phone; Eng spkn; adv bkg acc; ccard acc; CKE. *"Highly rec; some beautiful, but sm, pitches with sea views; Sunshine Group site; excel, friendly family-run site; v clean; v helpful staff; take care o'hanging trees."* **€24.00** 2016

ZACHARO *A3* (8km S Coastal) *37.41068, 21.66850* **Camping Tholo Beach,** Tholo, 27054 Zacharo **(26250) 61345 or 33454 (winter); campingtholo@hotmail.com**

⛺ ♙♙ wc ♨ & ⛟ ∥ MSP 👜 🍴 ⊕ 🛒 ⛰ ☂ sand adj

S fr Pyrgos on E55 dir Kyparissia, 8km S of Zacharo turn R to Tholo. Site sp in 500m on L. Med, shd, EHU €4; bbq; TV; Eng spkn; adv bkg acc; CKE. *"Excel, quiet, clean site; gd, clean san facs; friendly staff; excel sandy beach where loggerhead turtles lay eggs; dolphins off shore; san facs need updating; great location; excel mkt on Tuesdays; Ancient Olympia about an hr's drive."* **€24.50,** 1 May-30 Oct.   **2015**

GREEK ISLANDS

AGIA GALINI (CRETE) *C4* (2km E Rural/Coastal) *35.10004, 24.69514* **Camping No Problem!,** 74056 Agia Galini **(28320) 91386; www.agia-galini.com**

12 ⛺ ♙♙ wc ♨ & ⛟ ∥ 👜 🍴 ⊕ 🛒 🏊 ⛴ ☂ shgl 500m

Site sp on Tympaki rd. Sm, mkd, pt shd, EHU (6A) €4; bbq; 10% statics; bus 500m; Eng spkn; adv bkg acc. *"Vg, family-run site; dogs free; gd walks."* **€22.00**   **2016**

ERETRIA (EVIA) *B2* (11km NE Coastal) *38.39148, 23.77562* **Milos Camping,** 34008 Eretria **(22290) 60420; info@camping-in-evia.gr; www.camping-in-evia.gr**

⛺ ♙♙ wc ♨ & ⛟ ∥ MSP 👜 🍴 ⊕ 🛒 ⛴ ☂ shgl adj

Fr Chalkida for 20km; ignore any previous sp for Milos Camping. Med, mkd, pt shd, terr, EHU (16A) inc; gas; bbq; TV; 70% statics; phone; Eng spkn; CKE. *"Friendly site; excel rest; rather scruffy (5/09) but gd san facs."* **€25.00,** 15 Apr-30 Sep.   **2015**

LEFKADA (LEFKAS) *A2* (26km SE Coastal) *38.67511, 20.71475* **Camping Santa Maura,** Dessimi, 31100 Vlycho **(26450) 95007, (00306) 976085621, (00306) 932902309; campingsantamavra@yahoo.gr; www.campingsantamaura.com**

⛺ ♙♙ wc ♨ & ⛟ ∥ MSP 👜 🍴 ⊕ 🛒 ☂ shgl adj

Take coast rd S fr Lefkada to Vlycho, turn L for Dessimi, site in 2.5km (after Camping Dessimi). Access via v steep hill - severe gradients both sides. 3*, Med, mkd, pt shd, terr, EHU (6A) inc; gas; bbq; TV; phone; CKE. *"Excel site & beach; gd, clean san facs; friendly owners; pls call for prices."* 1 Apr-31 Oct.   **2016**

PEFKARI (THASSOS) *C2* (0.3km W Coastal) *40.61630, 24.60021* **Camping Pefkari Beach,** 64002 Pefkari **(25930) 51190; info@camping-pefkari.gr; www.camping-pefkari.gr**

wc ♨ ⛟ ∥ 👜 🍴 ⊕ 🛒 ☂ sand adj

SW fr Thassos port approx 43km to Limenaria, Pefkari is next sm vill. Site well sp in vill. Med, hdstg, pt shd, EHU (6A) €2.90; own san req; bbq; 5% statics; bus 1km; Eng spkn; CKE. *"Lovely spot; worth putting up with poor, dated san facs; gd local rest; vg; improving site; beautiful; easy walk to Pefkari and Potos; excel on site rest; lovely spot."* **€31.00,** 1 May-30 Sep.   **2019**

For a guide to symbols see the fold out on the rear cover

RETHYMNO (CRETE) *C4* (3km E Coastal) *35.36795, 24.51487* **Camping Elizabeth,** Ionias 84 Terma, 74100 Missiria **(28310) 28694; wallydewever@yahoo.gr; www.camping-elizabeth.com**

🔢 🛖 👥 wc ⛺ ♿ 🚿 ♨ MP 🛒 ☂ 🍴 ⑭ 🏊 🏖 ⚓adj

W fr Iraklio/Heraklion exit Platanes/Arkadi. Site 1km bef Platanes, on R on sh unsurfaced rd. Lge, hdg, shd, EHU (12A) inc; bbq; cooking facs; 3% statics; phone; bus 500m; Eng spkn; adv bkg acc; CKE. *"Gd walking on mkd rtes; gd cycling; excursion programme; vg."* **€29.50** 2016

TINOS (TINOS) *C3* (0.5km E Coastal) *37.53994, 25.16377* **Tinos Camping Bungalows,** Louizas Sohou 5, 84200 Tinos **(22830) 22344 or 23548; tinos camping@thn.forthnet.gr; tinoscamping.gr**

🛖 👥 wc ⛺ ♿ 🚿 ♨ ⑭ 🏊 🏖 ⚓shgl 500m

Clearly sp fr port. Sm, hdg, mkd, hdstg, shd, EHU €4.50; bbq; cooking facs; red long stay; phone; Eng spkn; adv bkg acc; ccard acc; CKE. *"1,600 Venetian dovecots & 600 churches on island; monastery with healing icon."* **€21.50, 1 May-31 Oct.** 2016

"I need an on-site restaurant"

We do our best to make sure site information is correct, but it is always best to check any must-have facilities are still available or will be open during your visit.

MONTENEGRO

SERBIA

KOSOVO

SOFIYA

BULGARIA

Burgas

SKOPJE

Blagoevgrad

Plovdiv

NORTH
MACEDONIA

TIRANË

Edirne

ALBANIA

Bitola

14

Gjirokastër

FLORINA

12

KAVALA

51

A25

A1

THESSALONIKI

ALEXANDROUPOLI

KASTORIA

A29

Pefkári

THASSOS

Plaka Litohoro

A2

16

Gerakini

NEOS
MARMARAS

LEMNOS

IOANINA

Kalambaka

20

A2

LARISA

IGOUMENITSA

6

TRIKALA

A1

Parga

VOLOS

CORFU/
KERKIRA

TRIKALA

A3

LESBOS

AEGEAN
SEA

38

LAMIA

Stylida

EUBOEA
EVIA

Lefkada

LEVKAS

CHIOS

İzmir

48

Delfi

Eretria

CEPHALONIA

PATRA

Egio

TURKEY

Kyllini

A8

KORINTHOS

ATHINA

Vartholomio

Olimbia

Mikines

ZANTE

PYRGOS

A7

7

NAFPLIO

TINOS

Zacharo

TRIPOLI

Drepano

Vivari

Tinos

KALAMATA

A71

CYCLADES

Pylos

SPARTI

Bodrum

Methoni

Finikoundas

Githio

KOS

RHODES

MEDITERRANEAN SEA

N

Rethymno

90

Sisi

Agia Galini

CRETE

W   E

S

● All year site(s)

○ Seasonal site(s)

○ No sites listed

200m +

0–200m

| 0 | 50 | 100 | 150 | 200 | 250 kms |

| 0 | 50 | 100 | 150 mls |

Motorways

Major roads

Main roads

© Collins Bartholomew Ltd 2020

267

Budapest

Highlights

Hungary is home to some of the most dramatic and exotic architecture found in Europe, with buildings spanning from the Art Nouveau era to Ancient Rome. Turkish, Slavic, Magyar and Roman influences entwine with its own unique culture to make Hungary a fascinating place.

There are more medicinal spas in Hungary than anywhere else in Europe and spa culture is an important part both of tourism and everyday life. You can enjoy spas that range from traditional bathhouses to modern wellness centres that cater for the whole family.

Many folk festivals are celebrated in Hungary throughout the year, the biggest of which is the Festival of Folk Arts/Crafts held every August in Buda Castle. Thousands of visitors attend to view the fantastic traditional crafts on offer.

One of the most renowned crafts is pottery making, with Hungary having a long tradition of creating both fine porcelain, such as Herend, and tiling and stoneware, such as Zsolnay produces.

Major towns and cities

- Budapest – an enchanting city full of galleries, theatres and museums.
- Debrecen – this former capital is one of Hungary's most important cultural centres.
- Pécs – an ancient city with countless things to see and do.
- Eger – a city famous for its fine red wines.

Attractions

- Fisherman's Bastion, Budapest – enjoy unmatched views over the city.
- Hungarian Parliament Building, Budapest – a magnificent building on the banks of the Danube.
- Lake Hévíz – one of the largest thermal lakes in the world with its own unique ecosystem.
- Esztergom Basilica – a spectacularly enormous cathedral with Renaissance art.

Find out more

www.gotohungary.com
E: info@mtu.gov.hu T: 0036 (0) 14 88 87 00

Country Information

Population (approx): 9.9 million

Capital: Budapest

Area: 93,000 sq km

Bordered by: Austria, Croatia, Romania, Serbia, Slovakia, Slovenia, Ukraine

Terrain: Mostly flat and rolling plains; hills and low mountains to the north

Climate: Temperate, continental climate; cold, cloudy winters; warm, sunny summers; changeable in spring and early summer with heavy rain and storms. The best times to visit are spring and autumn

Highest Point: Kekes 1,014m

Language: Hungarian

Local Time: GMT or BST + 1, i.e. 1 hour ahead of the UK all year

Currency: Forint (HUF); £1 = HUF 383, HUF 1000 = £2.61 (October 2019)

Emergency numbers: Police 107; Fire brigade 105; Ambulance 104. Operators speak English.

Public Holidays 2020: Jan 1; Mar 15; Apr 10, 13; May 1; Jun 1; Aug 20; Oct 23; Nov 1; Dec 24, 25, 26, 27.

School summer holidays are from mid-June to the end of August

Entry Formalities

Due to the current migrant crisis in Europe some countries have temporarily restored their borders. A current list of countries affected is available on the EU website: **ec.europa. eu/home-affairs/what-we-do/policies/ borders-and-visas/schengen/reintroduction-border-control_en**. At the time of going to print Austria has restored their borders with Hungary.

British and Irish passport holders may stay for a period of three months without a visa. Your passport needs to be valid for the duration of your stay and it is always recommended when visiting a foreign country to have an additional period of validity on your passport in case of any unforeseen delays. Anyone planning to stay longer than three months should contact the Hungarian Embassy for further information

There are no immigration or Customs checks at borders with other EU countries, i.e. Slovakia, Slovenia and Austria. Border crossings with other countries are generally open 24 hours.

Medical Services

British nationals may obtain emergency medical and dental treatment from practitioners contracted to the national health insurance scheme, Országos Egészségbiztosítási (OEP), together with emergency hospital treatment, on presentation of a European Health Insurance Card (EHIC) and a British passport.

Fees are payable for treatment and prescribed medicines, and are not refundable in Hungary. You may be able to apply for reimbursement when back in the UK.

Pharmacies (gyógyszertár) are well stocked. The location of the nearest all-night pharmacy is displayed on the door of every pharmacy.

Opening Hours

Banks: Mon-Thurs 8am-3pm. Fri 8am - 1pm. Hours may vary slightly.

Museums: Tue-Sun 10am-6pm; closed Mon.

Post Offices: Mon-Fri 8am-6pm; post office at Budapest open Mon-Sat 7am-9pm.

Shops: Mon-Fri 10am-6pm (supermarkets from 7am-7pm with some grocery stores open 24 hours); open half day Saturdays.

Safety and Security

Petty theft in Budapest is common in areas frequented by tourists, particularly on busy public transport, at markets and at popular tourist sites. Beware of pickpockets and bag snatchers.

Do not carry large amounts of cash. Take care when receiving bank notes and change as some that are no longer valid are still in circulation, e.g. HUF 200 notes were withdrawn in 2009. There has been a small number of instances of taxi drivers deliberately passing these notes to tourists. Be aware especially when paying with a HUF 10,000 or 20,000 bank note.

Theft of and from vehicles is common. Do not leave your belongings, car registration documents or mobile phones in your car and ensure that it is properly locked with the alarm on, even if leaving it for just a moment. Beware of contrived 'incidents', particularly on the Vienna-Budapest motorway, designed to stop motorists and expose them to robbery.

Visitors have reported in the past that motorists may be pestered at service areas on the Vienna to Budapest motorway by people insisting on washing windscreens and demanding money.

During the summer season in Budapest, uniformed tourist police patrol the most frequently visited areas of the city. Criminals sometimes pose as tourist police and ask for visitors' money, credit cards or travel documents in order to check them. Always ensure that a uniformed police officer is wearing a badge displaying the word 'Rendörség' and a five-digit identification number, together with a name badge. Plain clothes police carry a badge and an ID card with picture, hologram and rank. If in doubt, insist on going to the nearest police station.

There are still occasional incidents of exorbitant overcharging in certain restaurants, bars and clubs in Budapest, accompanied by threats of violence. Individuals who have been unable to settle their bill have frequently been accompanied by the establishment's security guards to a cash machine and made to withdraw funds. Visitors are advised to ask for a menu and only order items which are priced realistically. A five digit price for one dish is too high. Never accept menus which do not display prices and check your bill carefully.

Taxi drivers are sometimes accomplices to these frauds, receiving 'commission' for recommending restaurants and bars which charge extortionate prices to visitors. Never ask a taxi driver to recommend a bar, club or restaurant. If a driver takes you to one or you are approached on the street with an invitation to an unfamiliar bar or restaurant, you should treat such advice with extreme caution.

Do not change money or get involved in gambling in the street; which are both illegal.

If you need help, go to the nearest police station or the Tourist Information Point open 8am - 8pm, Deák Ferenc Square, 1052 Budapest, Sütő Street 2 (1) 438 8080

There is a low threat from terrorism.

British Embassy
FUGE UTCA 5-7 BUDAPEST 1022
Tel: (1) 2662888
www.ukinhungary.fco.gov.uk

Irish Embassy
SZABADSÁG TÉR 7, BANK CENTRE, GRANIT TOWER, V. FLOOR
1054 BUDAPEST
Tel: (1) 3014960
www.embassyofireland.hu

Documents

Money

Hungarian currency is available from banks in Austria before crossing the border. For emergency cash reserves, it is advisable to have euros, rather than sterling. Foreign currency is best exchanged at banks as they are not allowed to charge commission. Private bureaux de change do charge commission, but the rate of exchange may be better.

Credit cards are accepted at many outlets in large towns and cities and cash dispensers, 'bankomats', are widespread even in small towns. There is a high incidence of credit card fraud and payment in cash wherever possible is advisable. Carry your credit card issuers'/banks' 24 hour UK contact numbers separately in case of loss or theft of your cards.

Recent visitors report that some newer types of debit and credit cards issued in the UK do not work in certain cash machines in Hungary. The banks are working on a solution but, in the meantime, if you encounter this problem you should try a cash machine at a different bank. It is possible to obtain cash from post offices with a debit or credit card.

Euros are widely accepted in shops and restaurants frequented by tourists, but check the exchange rate.

When leaving Hungary on the MI motorway (Budapest-Vienna), it is important to change back your forints on the Hungarian side of the border by crossing the carriageway to the left at the designated crossing-point, as visitors report that there are no facilities on the right hand side and none on the other side in Austria.

Passport

Carry your passport at all times. A photocopy is not acceptable.

Vehicle(s)

Carry your vehicle registration certificate (V5C), vehicle insurance certificate and MOT certificate (if applicable) with you when driving.

Driving

Accidents

Accidents causing damage to vehicles or injury to persons must be reported to the nearest police station and to the Hungarian State Insurance Company (Hungária Biztositó) within 24 hours. The police will issue a statement which you may be asked to show when leaving the country.

If entering Hungary with a conspicuously damaged vehicle, it is recommended that you obtain a report confirming the damage from the police in the country where the damage occurred, otherwise difficulties may arise when leaving Hungary.

Alcohol

It is illegal to drive after consuming any alcohol whatsoever.

Breakdown Service

The motoring organisation, Magyar Autóklub (MAK), operates a breakdown service 24 hours a day on all roads. Drivers in need of assistance should telephone 188 or (1) 3451680. The number (1) is the area code for Budapest. On motorways emergency phones are placed at 2km intervals.

MAK road patrol cars are yellow and marked 'Segélyszolgálat'. Their registration numbers begin with the letters MAK.

The roadside breakdown service is chargeable, higher charges applying at night. There is a scale of charges by vehicle weight and distance for towing vehicles to a garage. Payment is required in cash.

Child Restraint System

Children under the height of 1.5m must be seated in a suitable child restraint system appropriate for their size in the rear of the vehicle.

If no child restraint is available a child over 3 who is over 1.35m in height may travel in the rear seat with a seatbelt. Children younger or shorter than this may not ever travel without a suitable restraint system in the vehicle.

Fuel

Leaded petrol is no longer available. The sign 'Ólommentes üzemanyag' or 'Bleifrei 95' indicates unleaded petrol. LPG is widely available.

Most petrol stations are open from 6am to 8pm. Along motorways and in large towns they are often open 24 hours. Some petrol stations accept credit and debit cards but cash is the most usual means of payment.

Lights

Outside built-up areas dipped headlights are compulsory at all times, regardless of weather conditions. Bulbs are more likely to fail with constant use and you are recommended to carry spares. At night in built-up areas dipped headlights must be used as full beam is prohibited.

Headlight flashing often means that a driver is giving way, but do not carry out a manoeuvre unless you are sure that this is the case.

Motorways

All motorways (autópálya) and main connecting roads run to or from Budapest. In recent years the road network has been extended and improved and there are now approximately 1500 kilometres of motorway and dual carriageways or semi-motorways. However, most roads are still single carriageway, single lane and care is recommended. The M0 motorway is a 75km ringroad around Budapest which links the M1, M7, M6, M5 and Highway 11. The recently built Megyeri Bridge on the Danube is part of the M0 and its opening has considerably reduced traffic congestion to the north of Budapest.

Emergency corridors are compulsory on motorways and dual carriageways. Drivers are required to create a precautionary emergency corridor to provide access for emergency vehicles whenever congestion occurs. Drivers in the left-hand lane must move as far over to the left as possible, and drivers in the central and right-hand lanes must move as far over to the right as possible.

Motorway Vignettes

Approximately 30% of motorways are toll-free; otherwise you must purchase an electronic vignette (matrica) or e-vignette (sticker) before entering the motorway.

They are available online, from motorway customer service offices and at large petrol stations near the motorways.
You can pay in forints or by credit card.

Leaflets are distributed to motorists at the border and a telephone information centre is available in Hungary – tel 36 58 75 00. Vignettes should only be purchased from outlets where the prices are clearly displayed at the set rates. For full details (in English), including how to buy online and toll-free sections, see www.motorway.hu

When purchasing an e-vignette a confirmation message will be sent or a coupon issued and this must be kept for a year after its expiry date. There is no need to display the vignette in your windscreen as the motorway authorities check all vehicles electronically (without the need for you to stop your vehicle) and verify registration number, category of toll paid and validity of an e-vignette. Charges in forints (2015 charges, subject to change) are shown below:

Category of Vehicle	Period of Validity	
	10 Days	1 month
Vehicle up to 3,500kg with or without caravan or trailer	2,975	4,780
Motorhome	5,950	9,560

Since the beginning of 2013 Hungary's State Motorway Management company (AAK) have been imposing on-the-spot fines for motorists who do not have a vignette. Fines amount to HUF 14,875 (around £40) for vehicles under 3,500kg or HUF 66,925 (around £178) for vehicles between 3,500kg and 7,500kg if paid within 30 days. 78% of the motorists fined so far have been foreign nationals, so ensure you have a vignette before travelling on motorways.

Parking

Zigzag lines on the carriageway and road signs indicate a stopping/parking prohibition. Illegally-parked vehicles will be towed away or clamped. On two-way roads, vehicles must park in the direction of traffic; they may park on either side in one-way streets. In certain circumstances, parking on the pavement is allowed.

Budapest is divided into various time restricted parking zones (maximum three hours) where tickets must be purchased from Monday to Friday from a machine. For longer periods you are advised to use 'Park and Ride' car parks located near major metro stations and bus terminals.

Priority

Pedestrians have priority over traffic at pedestrian crossings and at intersections. They do not have priority on the roadway between central tram loading islands and pavements, and drivers must exercise care on these sections. Major roads are indicated by a priority road ahead sign. At the intersection of two roads of equal importance, where there is no sign, vehicles coming from the right have priority. Trams and buses have priority at any intersection on any road and buses have right of way when leaving bus stops after the driver has signalled his intention to pull out.

Roads

Hungary has a good system of well surfaced main roads and driving standards are higher than in many other parts of Europe. There are few dual carriageways and care is required, therefore, when overtaking with a right-hand drive vehicle. Extra care is required on provincial roads which may be badly lit, poorly maintained and narrow. In the countryside at night be on the alert for unlit cycles and horse drawn vehicles

Road Signs and Markings

Road signs and markings conform to international conventions. Square green road signs indicate the number of km to the next town. At traffic lights a flashing amber light indicates a dangerous intersection. Destination signs feature road numbers rather than the names of towns, so it is essential to equip yourself with an up-to-date road map or atlas. Signs for motorways have white lettering on a blue background; on other roads signs are white and green.

Speed Limits

	Open Road (km/h)	Motorway (km/h)
Car Solo	90-110	130
Car towing caravan/trailer	70	80
Motorhome under 3500kg	90-110	130
Motorhome 3500-7500kg	70	80

A speed limit of 30 km/h (18 mph) is in force in many residential, city centre and tourist resort areas.

Traffic Jams

Roads around Budapest are busy on Friday and Sunday afternoons. In the holiday season roads to Lake Balaton (M7) and around the lake (N7 and N71) may be congested. There are regular traffic hold ups at weekends at the border crossings to Austria, the Czech Republic and Serbia. Motorway traffic information (in English) is available on www.motorway.hu

Violation of Traffic Regulations

The police make spot vehicle document checks and are keen to enforce speed limits. They are permitted to impose on-the-spot fines of up to HUF300,000. Credit cards are accepted for the payment of fines in some circumstances.

Winter Driving

The use of snow chains can be made compulsory on some roads when there is severe winter weather.

Essential Equipment

First Aid Kit

It is a legal requirement that all vehicles should carry a first aid kit.

Reflective Jackets/ Waistcoats

If your vehicle is immobilised on the carriageway outside a built-up area, or if visibility is poor, you must wear a reflective jacket or waistcoat when getting out of your vehicle. Passengers who leave the vehicle, for example, to assist with a repair, should also wear one. Keep the jackets inside your vehicle, not in the boot.

In addition, pedestrians and cyclists walking or cycling at night or in poor visibility along unlit roads outside a built-up area must also wear a reflective jacket.

Warning Triangles

In the event of accident, it is compulsory to place a warning triangle 100 metres behind the vehicle on motorways and 50 metres on other roads.

Touring

Hungary boasts eight World Heritage sites including the national park at Aggtelek which contains Europe's largest cave network, the Christian cemetery at Pécs and the monastery at Pannonhalma. Lake Balaton, the largest lake in Central Europe, offers swimming, sailing, fishing and windsurfing. With 200km of sandy shoreline and shallow warm waters, it is very popular with families.

A Budapest Card is available, allowing unlimited travel on public transport for two or three consecutive days, free city walking tours, discounted entry to museums and other attractions, plus discounts on many guided tours, events, shops and restaurants. Cards are available from metro stations, tourist information offices, many travel agencies, hotels, museums and main Budapest transport ticket offices, as well as from the Hungarian National Tourist Office in London. You can also order online from www.budapest-card.com.

A tip of 10-15% of the bill is expected in restaurants. Check your bill first to ensure that a service charge has not already been added.

Hungarian is a notoriously difficult language for native English speakers to decipher and pronounce. English is not widely spoken in rural areas, but it is becoming increasingly widespread elsewhere as it is now taught in schools. German is widely spoken and a dictionary may be helpful.

Camping and Caravanning

There are approximately 100 organised campsites in Hungary rated from 1 to 4 stars. These are generally well signposted off main routes, with the site name shown below a blue camping sign. Most campsites open from May to September and the most popular sites are situated by Lake Balaton and the Danube. A Camping Key Europe (CKE) or Camping Card International (CCI) is essential.

Facilities vary from site to site, but visitors will find it useful to carry their own flat universal sink plug. There has been much improvement in recent years in the general standard of campsites, but communal changing areas for showers are not uncommon. Many sites have communal kitchen facilities which enable visitors to make great savings on their own gas supply.

Many campsites require payment in cash. Prices have risen sharply in recent years. Therefore, prices in this guide for sites not reported on for some time might not reflect the current prices. Casual/wild camping is prohibited.

Cycling

There are approximately 2,000km of cycle tracks, 100km of which are in Budapest and 200km around Lake Balaton. Tourinform offices in Hungary provide maps of cycling routes.

Children under 14 years are not allowed to ride on the road and all cyclists must wear a reflective jacket at night and in poor daytime visibility.

Electricity and Gas

Current on campsites varies between 6 and 16 amps. Plugs have two round pins. There are some sites that do not have CEE connections.

Only non-returnable and/or non-exchangeable Campingaz cylinders are available.

Public Transport & Local Travel

Cars are not permitted within the Castle District and on Margaret Island in Budapest. It is advisable to use public transport when travelling into the city and there is an excellent network of bus, tram and metro routes (BKV). All public transport in Hungary is free for over 65s, and this also applies to foreign visitors with proof of age (passport).

There are a number of ticket options, including family tickets, 1, 3 and 7 day tickets, and they can be bought at metro stations, ticket machines, tobacconists and newsagents. Validate your bus and metro tickets before use at each stage of your journey and every time you change metro lines at the red machines provided. Tickets are often checked on vehicles or at metro station exits by controllers wearing arm bands and carrying photo ID. For further information on public transport in Budapest see www.bkv.hu

As a general rule, it is better to phone for taxis operated by reputable local companies, rather than flag them down in the street, and always ensure that fares are metered. A tip of approximately 10% of the fare is customary.

Mahart, the Hungarian Shipping Company, operates a regular hydrofoil service from April to October along the Danube between Budapest and Vienna. The journey lasts six hours and covers 288km.

Local companies Legenda (www.legenda.hu) and Mahart also offer city cruises between May and October, as well as regular trips to tourist attractions outside Budapest, such as Szentendre, Visegrád and Esztergom.

A ferry service takes cars across Lake Balaton from Szántód to Tihany. There are crossings every 10 minutes from June to September and every hour during the low season. Regular bus and train services link the towns and villages along the lakeside.

AGGTELEK *A3* (1km NW Rural) *48.47094, 20.49446*
Baradla Camping, Baradla Oldal 1, 3759 Aggtelek
(06) 308619427; szallas@anp.hu
♦↟↟ ♨ ⩕ ☂ ⊤ nr ⓦ nr ⚏

**Fr Slovakia turn off E571/A50 at Plesivec onto rd
587 S via Dlha Ves to border x-ing. Cont S for approx
800m & hotel/campsite complex is on L. Fr Miskolc
45km N on rte 26, turn onto rte 27 sp Perkupa then
foll sp Nemzeti National Park & Aggtelek. Site sp in
vill.** 1*, Med, pt shd, pt sl, EHU (16A) inc; bbq; cooking
facs; 10% statics. *"Gd NH to/fr Slovakia; ent to lge
Barlang Caves system adj; facs poss stretched high
ssn."* **HUF 4366, 15 Apr-15 Oct.** 2016

BALATONAKALI *C1* (1km SW Rural) *46.87939,
17.74190* **Balatontourist Camping Levendula
(Naturist),** Hókuli u 25, 8243 Balatonakali **36 30 309
7797; info@levendulacamp.com; levendulacamp.com**
↟ HUF950 ♦↟↟ ⬚ ♨ ⩕ ⌖ ⚏ ⊤ ⓦ ♟ ⚏ ⚏

**NE on rte 71 on N shore of Lake Balaton twds
Tihany. Site sp on W app to Balatonakali. Turn R
twds lake; go over level x-ing, site ent on R.**
3*, Med, mkd, pt shd, EHU (4A) inc; gas; sw; TV; Eng
spkn; adv bkg acc; ccard acc; fishing; games area; bike
hire; windsurfing school; sauna; CKE. *"Superb site."*
HUF 7500, 7 May-12 Sep. 2016

BALATONFURED *C2* (9km NE Rural) *46.99184,
17.98698* **Présház Camping,** Présház út 1, 8226 Alsóörs
(87) 447736
12 ↟ ♦↟↟ ⬚ ♨ ⩕ ⚏

**Rd 71 fr Balatonfüred, site just past vill of Alsóörs
on L.** Sm, pt shd, pt sl, EHU (10A) inc; sw nr; games
area. *"Vg, lovely, CL-type site in orchard of wine shop;
friendly owner; wine-tasting; paid in Euros but Forint
preferred; sighting of wild boar nrby!"* **HUF 4360**
2015

BUDAPEST *B2* (14km N Rural) *47.6013, 19.0191*
Jumbo Camping, Budakalászi út 23, 2096 Üröm
(26) 351251; jumbo@campingbudapest.com;
www.jumbocamping.hu
↟ ♦↟↟ ⬚ ♨ ⩕ ⚏ ⚏ ⊤ ⓦ nr ♟ ⚏ nr ⚏ ⚏ (htd)

**Best app fr N on rd 10 or 11. Fr M1 take Zsámbék
exit thro Perbál to join rd 10 & turn W twd Budapest.
After Pilisvörösvar turn L in 8km sp Üröm Site
well sp.** 3*, Med, hdg, hdstg, pt shd, pt sl, terr,
EHU (6-10A) inc; TV; 10% statics; bus to Budapest
fr vill; Eng spkn; adv bkg acc. *"Highly rec; clean,
modern facs; immac, family-run site, v helpful."*
HUF 6495, 1 Apr-31 Oct. 2017

BUDAPEST *B2* (10km E Urban) *47.50421, 19.15834*
Camping Arena, Pilisi Str 7, 1106 Budapest **06 30 29
691 29; info@budapestcamping.hu; www.budapest
camping.hu**
12 ↟ ♦↟↟ ⬚ ♨ ⩕ ⚏ ⚏ (yp)

**Do not use Sat Nav. Leave M0 at exit 60 Kistarcsa
& foll Rd 3 twd city cent for 7.5km. Turn L just bef
rlwy bdge. Site 200m on R.** Sm, hdg, pt shd, EHU
(16A) inc; cooking facs; 10% statics; bus 400m; Eng
spkn; adv bkg acc; CCI. *"Some rlwy & aircraft noise;
supmkt 400m; shopping arcade 1km; metro 1km; rec
all day travel card for metro, trams & busses; vg; v
helpful staff."* **HUF 7650** 2019

BUDAPEST *B2* (7km WNW Rural) *47.514437,
18.972951* **Ave Natura Camping,** Csermely u. 3, 1121
Budapest (36) 12003470 or (36) 705507069;
campingavenatura@gmail.com; www.camping
avenatura.hu
↟ ♦↟↟ ⬚ ♨ ⩕ ⚏ ⚏ ⚏ (yp)

**Fr Austria via M1/M7 fr Balaton exit 14 Budakeszi.
Fr M0, foll rd to end then Route 1 direction
Budakeszi. Fr Budakeszi foll camping sp. Fr city
to Moskva Ter then foll sp.** Sm, hdstg, hdg, pt shd,
terr, EHU (16A) HUF1200; bbq; cooking facs; phone;
bus 300m; Eng spkn; adv bkg acc; CKE. *"Guaranteed
warm and informative welcome by family run peaceful,
wooded site; 10min downhill walk to bus into Budapest;
vg."* **HUF 5800, 1 Apr-31 Oct.** 2018

BUK *B1* (4km E Rural) *47.38433, 16.79051* **Romantik
Camping,** Thermál Krt 12, 9740 Bükfürdő (94) 558050;
info@romantikcamping.com; www.romantik
camping.com
12 ↟ €2 ♦↟↟ (htd) ⬚ ♨ ⩕ ⚏ ⚏ ⊤ nr ⓦ ⚏ ⚏ ⚏ ⚏

**Fr Sopron on rte 84 twd Lake Balaton for approx
45km, foll sp & exit Bükfürdő. After service stn turn
R then cont for 5km sp Thermalbad & site.**
3*, Lge, pt shd, EHU (10-16A) metered; red long stay;
10% statics; adv bkg acc; ccard acc; bike hire; tennis
500m; CKE. *"Quiet and peaceful an ideal place to
unwind; thermal cent 500m."* **HUF 5604** 2015

CSERKESZOLO *C3* (0.8km S Urban) *46.86386,
20.2019* **Thermal Camping Cserkeszölö,** Beton út 5,
5465 Cserkeszölö (6) 56568450; hotelcamping@
cserkeszolo.hu; www.touring-hotel.hu/en
12 ↟ ♦↟↟ (htd) ⬚ ♨ ⩕ ⚏ ⚏ ⚏ ⓦ ⚏ ♟ nr ⚏ (covrd, htd) ⚏

**On rte 44 bet Kecksemet & Kunszentmárton. Site
sp in Cserkeszölö.** 4*, Lge, pt shd, EHU (10A) inc;
bbq; cooking facs; 10% statics; phone; bus 200m;
waterslide; sauna; tennis; games area; CKE. *"Use of sw
pools & thermal pools inc in site fee; gd."*
HUF 6226 2016

DOMOS *B2* (0.5km E Rural) *47.7661, 18.91495*
Dömös Camping, Dömös Dunapart, 2027 Dömös
**(33) 482319; info@domoscamping.hu; www.domos
camping.hu**

🐾 HUF500 ♚♛♟ ⚏ ♨ Ⅎ 💧 ⚒ ⊙♨ ⚏ ⚒ ⚑

**On rd 11 fr Budapest, site on R on ent Dömös, adj
Rv Danube.** 3*, Med, hdg, pt shd, EHU (10A) HUF950;
cooking facs; red long stay; TV; phone; bus to
Budapest; Eng spkn; adv bkg acc; CKE. *"Delightful site
with views Danube bend; spacious pitches - lower ones
poss subject to flooding; excel, clean facs & rest."*
HUF 6150, 1 May-30 Sep. **2017**

DUNAFOLDVAR *C2* (2km NE Rural) *46.81227,
18.92664* **Kék-Duna Camping,** Hösök Tere 23, 7020
Dunafoldvár **(75) 541107; ddifzrt@freemail.hu**

12 ♚♟ ♨ ⚏ ⚑ 💧 ⚑ ⊙ ⚒ ⚒ (covrd) ⚑

**Fr rndabt S of Dunafoldvár turn twd town cent. At
traff lts turn R down to rv, then turn L, under green
bdge & foll towpath 300m to site.** 2*, Sm, shd, EHU
(16A) inc; bbq; adv bkg acc; fishing; bike hire; tennis;
watersports; CKE. *"Pleasant position o'looking Danube;
adequate, clean san facs but dated; gd touring base
Transdanubia."* **HUF 4100** **2016**

GYOR *B1* (7km NE Rural) *47.72547, 17.71446* **Piheno
Camping,** Weg 10, 9011 Gyor **(96) 523008; piheno@
piheno.hu; www.piheno.hu**

🐾 HUF1000 ♚♟ (htd) ⚏ ♨ ⚏ 💧 ⚒ Ⅎ ⊙ ⚑ ⚒ ⚑

**E fr Gyor on rte 1 twds Budapest, stay on rte 1 for
Komarom. Site on L 3km past m'way (M1) junc.**
Sm, hdg, mkd, pt shd, pt sl, EHU (16A); gas; bbq;
cooking facs; TV; 10% statics; phone; bus; Eng spkn;
adv bkg acc; ccard acc; CKE. *"Gd facs; fair."*
HUF 4593, 1 May-30 Sep. **2017**

HAJDUSZOBOSZLO *B4* (2km N Urban) *47.45756,
21.39396* **Thermál Camping,** Böszörményi út 35A,
4200 Hajdúszoboszló **(52) 558552; thermalcamping@
hungarospa.hu; www.hungarospa.hu**

12 🐾 HUF440 ♚♟ ⚏ ♨ ⚏ 💧 ⚑ ⚒ ⊙ ⚒ ⚑ ⚑

**Fr W on rte 4/E573 thro town, site sp on L. Fr
Debrecen, turn R 500m past Camping Hadjdútourist
on lakeside.** 3*, Lge, hdg, pt shd, EHU (12A) inc; bbq;
cooking facs; TV; phone; Eng spkn; ccard acc;
waterslide; CKE. *"Pleasant site; htd covrd pool adj;
sm naturist island in lake; thermal baths adj."*
HUF 9136 **2016**

JASZAPATI *B3* (1.5km S Urban) *47.50537, 20.14012*
Tölgyes Strand Camping, Gyöngyvirág u 11, 5130
Jászapáti **(57) 441187; info@tolgyesstrand.hu;
www.tolgyesstrand.hu**

🐾 ♚♟ ⚏ ♨ ⚏ 💧 ⚒ Ⅎ ⊙ ⚑ ⚒ (covrd, htd)

**Fr Budapest E on M3, exit at Hatvan & take rd 32
to Jászberény then foll rd 31 to Jászapáti. Site sp
fr town cent.** 3*, Med, mkd, pt shd, EHU (10A); TV;
10% statics; adv bkg acc; games area; site clsd 1
Nov to mid-Dec; bike hire; tennis 200m. *"Gd, modern
facs."* **1 Apr-30 Nov.** **2016**

KESZTHELY *C1* (8.5km N Rural) *46.80803, 17.21248*
Camping Panoráma, Köz 1, 8372 Cserszegtomaj
**(83) 314412; matuska78@freemail.hu;
www.panoramacamping.com**

🐾 €1 ♚♟ (htd) ⚏ ♨ ⚏ 💧 ⚒ ⊙ ⚒ nr

**Exit Keszthely by direct rd to Sümeg. After turn
to Hévíz (Thermal Spa). Clearly sp on R of side rd.**
3*, Med, pt shd, terr, EHU (16A) €2.50; sw nr; TV;
30% statics; phone; CKE. *"Conv Lake Balaton area; v
friendly & clean; remedial massage avail; gd views."*
HUF 4000, 1 Apr-31 Oct. **2015**

MANFA *D2* (18km NE Rural) *46.23372, 18.30844*
Campsite Mare Vara, Varvolgyi utca 2, 7332
Magyaregregy **(72) 420126; info@camping-
marevara.com; www.camping-marevara.com**

🐾 ♚♟ (htd) ⚏ ♨ ⚏ ⚏ 💧 ⚑ ⚒ Ⅎ ⚏ ⚒

**Fr Pecs head N on 6. Turn L onto Cseresznyes ut,
which then becomes Komlo-Zobakpuszta. In 6.8km
turn R onto Varvolgyi u. Site in 120m.** Sm, pt shd, pt
sl, EHU (10A) inc; bbq; 1% statics; Eng spkn; adv bkg
acc; games area; CKE. *"Dutch owners, warm welcome;
ample space to pitch; almost an orchard setting; vg."*
HUF 5499, 15 Apr-30 Sep. **2015**

MATRAFURED *B3* (4km N Rural) *47.84416, 19.95725*
Mátra Camping Sástó, Farkas út 4, 3232 Mátrafüred
(37) 374025; www.matrakemping.hu

🐾 ♚♟ ♨ ⚑ Ⅎ ⊙ ⚒ nr ⊙ nr ⚒ nr

**Take rte 24 N fr Gyöngyös. Site on L 2km after
Mátrafüred.** 4*, Med, hdstg, pt shd, pt sl, EHU (10A)
inc; cooking facs; TV; 10% statics; ccard acc. *"Site
pt of controlled sports complex; vg secure site."*
HUF 5543, 1 Apr-31 Oct. **2016**

MOSONMAGYAROVAR *B1* (1km E Urban) *47.87718,
17.27874* **Termál Aqua Camping,** Kigyó út 1, 9200
Mosonmagyaróvár **(96) 579168; aquahotel@t-
online.hu; www.tha.hu**

🐾 €2 ♚♟ (htd) ⚏ ♨ ⚏ 💧 ⚑ ⚒ Ⅎ ⊙ ⚏ ⚒ nr

**Foll sp fr town cent to Termál Hotel Aqua; site
in grnds, just behind lge thermal baths.** Sm, hdg,
mkd, shd, EHU €3; bbq; cooking facs; phone; bus;
train 1km; Eng spkn. *"Vg site; htd covrd thermal
adj; pool adj; price inc ent to thermals & sauna."*
HUF 9028, 1 Apr-30 Oct. **2016**

MOSONMAGYAROVAR *B1* (3km SE Urban) *47.84224,
17.28591* **Camping Kis-Duna,** Gabonarakpart 6,
9200 Mosonmagyaróvár **(96) 216433**

12 🐾 HUF500 ♚♟ ⚏ ♨ ⚏ 💧 ⚑ ⚒ nr

**Site on L of M1 Mosonmagyaróvár-Györ in grnds of
motel & rest, 15km fr border.** 2*, Sm, hdstg, unshd,
EHU (16A) HUF500; TV. *"Gd, clean, facs; thermal
pool 2.5km; rest gd but busy; gd alt to Bratislava site
(Slovakia); ideal NH."* **HUF 6113** **2018**

PAPA *B1* (2km N Urban) *47.33797, 17.47367* **Termál Camping Pápa,** Várkert út 7, 8500 Pápa **36 89 320 735; info@thermalkemping.hu; www.thermalkemping.hu**

🔢 🐕 €2 👭 (htd) 🆆 ⬆ ♨ ⚡ 🐟 ⚜ 〰 ♛ 🍽 ⊕ 🚲 ⛟nr ⟁ 🖌 🗑

Fr 83 exit at Gyori Way. Foll sp. Lge, hdstg, mkd, hdg, pt shd, EHU (16A); gas; bbq; cooking facs; sw nr; twin axles; 20% statics; phone; bus 500m; Eng spkn; adv bkg acc; games rm; games area; CCI. *"Onsite kids club; boccia; basketball; archery; disco adj; thermal baths with indoor & outdoor pools, slides; excel; htd pool adj; well managed site; gd area for long stay & touring; very helpful staff."* **HUF 11570**   **2019**

SAROSPATAK *A4* (2km NE Rural) *48.33274, 21.58245* **Tengerszem Camping,** Herceg Ferenc ut 2, 3950 Sárospatak **(47) 312744; info@tengerszem-camping. hu; www.tengerszem-camping.hu**

👭 ⬆ ⚜ 〰 ⊕ 🚲 🎾 ⟁ 🛶

NW fr Tokaj on R38; then NE on R37 to Sárospatak; foll camp sp. 3*, Med, hdg, pt shd, EHU (10A) inc; TV; games area; tennis; CKE. *"Refurbished thermal sw baths next door; gd site for mountains."* **HUF 6441, 30 Apr-15 Oct.**   **2016**

> ## "There aren't many sites open at this time of year"
>
> If you're travelling outside peak season remember to call ahead to check site opening dates – even if the entry says 'open all year'.

SARVAR *B1* (2km SE Urban) *47.24671, 16.9473* **Sárvár Thermal Camping,** Vadkert út 1, 9600 Sárvár **(95) 523610; info@thermalcamping.com; www.thermalcamping.com**

🔢 🐕 €2 👭 (htd) 🆆 ⬆ ♨ ⚡ 🐟 ⚜ 〰 ♛ ⊕nr 🚲 ⟁ 🗑

E fr Szombathely via rtes 86 & 88. Site on Sopron-Lake Balaton rte 84. 4*, Med, hdstg, pt shd, EHU 16A) €3; bbq; cooking facs; red long stay; 10% statics; ccard acc; waterslide; lake fishing; tennis 500m; sauna; CKE. *"Barrier clsd 1330-1500; htd thermal pools adj; private san facs avail; free ent to spa & fitness cent adj."* **HUF 13007   2016**

SOPRON *B1* (8km SE Rural) *47.6525, 16.6575* **Kurcamping Castrum Balf-Sopron,** Fürdö Sor 59-61, 9494 Balf **(99) 339124; balfcamping@gmail.com; sopron-balf-camping.hu**

🐕 €2.50 👭 (htd) 🆆 ⬆ ⚜ ♛ ⊕nr 🚲nr 🛶

On rte 84 S of Sopron turn E sp Balf. In 2km turn N sp Sopron & foll sps. Site at W end Balf vill. 3*, Med, hdg, mkd, pt shd, EHU (6A) HUF800; TV; phone; Eng spkn; ccard acc; bike hire; sauna; CKE. *"Thermal baths avail; Tesco hypmkt on app to Sopron 6km, with ATM; pitches uneven; ltd facs LS & poss unkempt; poss cold shwrs; site in need of maintenance; overpriced NH."* **HUF 4770, 1 Apr-31 Oct.**   **2016**

SZIGETVAR *D1* (14km E Rural) *46.059598, 17.933796* **Camping Idyll,** Petofi S.u.28, 7912 Nagyvaty **(73) 546612; info@campingidyll.hu; www.camping idyll.hu**

🐕 👭 🆆 ⬆ 🐟 〰 ♛ 🍽

Rte 6 Szigetvar to Pecs. Turn L to Nagyvaty after km marker 222. Foll sp fr vill. Sm, hdstg, hdg, pt shd, EHU (6-10A); bbq; red long stay; twin axles; TV; 10% statics; bus 500m; Eng spkn; adv bkg acc; Spa 12km; CCI. *"Local walks, cycle rides fr site; clse to Rv Drava nature & forest area; excel."* **HUF 6302, 1 May-1 Oct.**   **2018**

TATABANYA *B2* (14km N Rural) *47.6679, 18.3090* **Fényes Camping,** Környei út 24, 2890 Tata **(34) 481208; fenyesfurdo@tata.hu; www.fenyesfurdo.hu**

🐕 HUF500 👭 ⬆ ⚜ ⊕ 🚲 ⟁ 🛶

Exit junc 67 fr M1 to Tata town cent; foll sp for 3km E to site. Lge, shd, EHU; own san rec; Eng spkn; games area; CKE. *"Tata interesting town; fair site set in lge park."* **HUF 1800, 1 May-15 Sep.**   **2016**

TOKAJ *A4* (1km NE Rural) *48.12306, 21.41806* **Tiszavirág Camping,** Horgász út 11a, 3910 Tokaj **(06) 709344175; tiszavir@axelero.hu; www.tokaj.hu**

🐕 HUF400 👭 🆆 ⬆ ⚜ 〰 🍽 🚲nr

Fr town cent turn E over rv on rte 38 sp Nyiregyháza. Camp ent 100m over bdge on L. Med, shd, EHU (10A) HUF450; fishing. *"On rv bank; wine cellars in walking dist; ltd facs on Sun."* **HUF 4200, 1 Apr-30 Oct.**   **2015**

TURISTVANDI *A4* (1km SW Rural) *48.04710, 22.64300* **Vizimalom Camping,** Malom út 3, 4944 Túrístvándi **(30) 289 9808; turvizimalom@freemail.hu; www.turvizimalom.hu**

🐕 👭 ⬆ 〰 ♛ 🍽 ⊕ 🚲nr ⟁

Fr Fehérgyarmat foll rd 491 NE for 4km to Penyige, turn L to Túristvándi. After approx 12km site on R adj 18thC water mill on Rv Túr. Sm, hdstg, pt shd, EHU (10A); bbq; TV; games rm; canoeing; games area. *"Excel location; no hdstg."* **HUF 5853, 1 Mar-1 Nov.**   **2016**

ZALAKAROS *C1* (3km S Rural) *46.53165, 17.12443* **Kurcamping Castrum,** Ady Endre út, 8754 Galambok **(93) 358610; zalakaros@castrum.eu; www.castrum-group.hu**

🐕 👭 (htd) 🆆 ⬆ ♨ 🐟 ⚜ 〰 ♛ 🍽 ⊕nr 🚲 ⛟nr 🛶 (covrd, htd)

Fr rte 7 N dir Zalakaros, site sp. 4*, Med, mkd, hdg, pt shd, EHU (6A) inc; bbq; 10% statics; bus; ccard acc; sauna; CKE. *"Thermal complex 2km."* **HUF 8000, 1 Mar-31 Oct.**   **2016**

UKRAINE

Berehove

Turistvándi

SatuMare

ROMANIA

N
W E
S

Oradea

© Collins Bartholomew Ltd 2020

| 0 | 10 | 20 | 30 | 40 | 50 kms |

| 10 | 20 | 30 mls |

Motorways
Major roads
Main roads

Košice

Sárospatak

Tokaj

M3

M35

DEBRECEN

Hajdúszoboszló

42

Arad

Timișoara

MISKOLC

M30

Aggtelek

28

Lučenec

SALGÓTARJÁN

M3

32

Jászapáti

SZOLNOK

Békéscsaba

BÉKÉSCSABA

Cserkeszőlő

M43

SLOVAKIA

Mátrafüred

21

4

M5

SERBIA

M0

Nové Zámky

2

BUDAPEST

M5

Subotica

Dömös

M7

M6

Dunaföldvár

9

SZEKSZÁRD

M6

55

Osijek

10

M1

TATABÁNYA

Pannonhalma

M7

M0

SZÉKESFEHÉRVÁR

Balatonalmádi
Balatonkenese
Balatonfüred

VESZPRÉM

Tamási

M60

PÉCS

Manfa

MOSONMAGYARÓVÁR

GYŐR

14

M2

Papa

8

Balatonakali

Balatonberény

Balatonszárszó

Szigetvár

Vinovitica

BRATISLAVA

M15

Eisenstadt

SOPRON

Bük

84

86

Sárvár

ZALAEGERSZEG

KESZTHELY

Zalakaros

M7

Varaždin

AUSTRIA

WIEN

CROATIA

●	All year site(s)
●	Seasonal site(s)
○	No sites listed

| | 200m + |
| | 0–200m |

Italy

Clinque Terre

Highlights

One of the greatest cultural jewels in Europe's crown has to be Italy. It is a country alive with art and fashion that is envied across the world, and boasts some of the most extraordinary architectural masterpieces in existence.

Alongside the grandeur is a country with great natural diversity, from the snow-capped Alps in the north to the stunning Mediterranean coastline. The variety of local customs and traditions encountered through the different regions are always captivating.

Italy is often considered the fashion capital of the world, and leather working has often been at the forefront of its fashion industry. The Italian tanning industry is considered a world leader and there are many products available from bags to belts which showcase this skill.

Italy is also a country of celebration, with hundreds of festivals and carnivals taking place. One of the most famous is the Carnival of Venice, where traditional masks and costumes are worn by attendees.

Major towns and cities

- Rome – this remarkable city is known as the "Capital of the World".
- Milan – a global centre of fashion and known for its exquisite galleries.
- Turin – famous for its baroque architecture and monuments.
- Naples – boasting a wealth of historical buildings from a variety of periods.

Attractions

- Venice – one of the world's most beautiful cities and boasting a wealth of historic sites.
- Santa Maria del Fiore, Florence – one of the most recognisable cathedrals that houses several important works of art.
- Pompeii – the remains of an ancient Roman town in the shadow of Mount Vesuvius.
- Cinque Terre – five beautiful and traditional villages that lie on the Italian Riviera.

Find out more

www.enit.it
E: sedecentrale@enit.it   T: 0039 (0) 06 49 711

Country Information

Population (approx): 61.8 million

Capital: Rome

Area: 301,318 sq km (inc Sardinia & Sicily)

Bordered by: France, Switzerland, Austria, Slovenia

Terrain: Mountainous in the north descending to rolling hills in the centre; some plains and coastal lowlands

Climate: Predominantly Mediterranean climate, alpine in the far north, hot and dry in the south

Coastline: 7,600km

Highest Point: Monte Bianco (Mont Blanc) 4,810m

Language: Italian, German (in the northern Alps)

Local Time: GMT or BST + 1, i.e. 1 hour ahead of the UK all year

Currency: Euros divided into 100 cents; £1 = €1.16, €1 = £0.87 (October 2019)

Emergency numbers: Police 113; Fire brigade 115; Ambulance 118

Public Holidays 2020: Jan 1, 6; Apr 12, 13, 25; May 1; Jun 2; Aug 15; Nov 1; Dec 8, 25, 26.

Each locality also celebrates its patron saint's day. School summer holidays run from mid June to mid September.

Entry Formalities

Due to the current migrant crisis in Europe some countries have temporarily restored their borders. A current list of countries affected is available on the EU website: **ec.europa. eu/home-affairs/what-we-do/policies/ borders-and-visas/schengen/reintroduction- border-control_en**. At the time of going to print Italy hasn't reinstated their borders, but neighbouring Austria has so check before you travel.

British and Irish passport holders may stay in Italy for up to three months without a visa.

Medical Services

Ask at a pharmacy (farmacia) for the nearest doctor registered with the state health care scheme (SSN) or look in the telephone directory under 'Unita Sanitaria Locale'. The services of a national health service doctor are normally free of charge.

A European Health Insurance Card (EHIC) entitles you to emergency treatment and medication at local rates and to hospital treatment under the state healthcare scheme. Any charges you do incur are non-refundable in Italy but you may be able to make a claim on your return to the UK. Dental treatment is expensive and you will be charged the full fee.

Emergency services (Guardia Medica) are available at weekends and at night and there are first aid posts at major train stations and airports. Staff at pharmacies can advise on minor ailments and at least one pharmacy remains open 24 hours in major towns.

Opening Hours

Banks: Mon-Fri 8.30am-1.30pm & 3pm-4pm.

Museums: Check locally as may vary. The Vatican museums and Sistine Chapel are not open to visitors Sun. Visitors under 18 or over 60 are admitted free to State museums on production of a passport.

Post Offices: Mon-Fri 8.30am-2pm/5.30pm, Sat 8.30am-12 noon.

Shops: Mon-Sat 8.30am/9am-1pm & 3.30pm/ 4pm-7.30pm/8pm. In southern Italy and tourist areas shops may stay open later. There is no lunch time closing in large cities. Shops are closed half a day each week (variable by region).

Regulations for Pets

All dogs, including those temporarily imported, must be on a leash at all times. It is advisable to carry a muzzle as the police/authorities can insist on your dog wearing one if they consider your dog to be dangerous. Some sites and some public transport operators insist that all dogs are muzzled at all times - check local requirements on arrival.

A domestic animal may be transported in a car provided it does not distract the driver. More than one animal may be transported provided they are kept in the rear of the car, separated from the driver by bars, or kept in special cages.

Safety and Security

Most visits to Italy are trouble free and, in general, levels of crime are low, but visitors should take care on public transport and in crowded areas where pickpockets and bag snatchers may operate. In Rome take particular care around the main railway station, Roma Termini, and on the bus to and from St Peter's Square. Also take care in and around railway stations in large cities. Be particularly wary of groups of children who may try to distract your attention while attempting to steal from you. Do not carry your passport, credit cards and cash all together in one bag or pocket and only carry what you need for the day. Do not wear expensive jewellery, particularly in the south of Italy.

Take care in bars and don't leave drinks unattended. Recently there have been cases of drinks being spiked. Check prices before ordering food and insist on seeing a priced menu. Be particularly careful when ordering items, such as lobster, which are charged by weight.

When driving in towns keep your car windows shut and doors locked and never leave valuables on display. Around Rome and Naples moped riders may attempt to snatch bags from stationary cars at traffic lights. Always lock your vehicle and never leave valuables in it, even if you will only be away for a short time or are nearby. Avoid leaving luggage in cars for any length of time or overnight.

Increasingly robberies are taking place from cars at rest stops and service stations on motorways. Treat offers of help with caution, for example with a flat tyre, particularly on the motorway, as sometimes the tyre will have been punctured deliberately.

Do not be tempted to enter or bathe in Italy's many fountains – there are heavy fines if you do. Dress conservatively when visiting places of worship, i.e. cover shoulders and upper arms and do not wear shorts. Avoid queues in the peak season by visiting early in the morning.

The authorities are making strenuous efforts to stamp out the illegal production and sale of counterfeit goods. Illegal traders operate on the streets of all major cities, particularly tourist cities such as Florence and Rome. You are advised not to buy from them at the risk of incurring a fine.

Italy shares with the rest of Europe a general threat from terrorism. Attacks could be indiscriminate and against civilian targets in public places, including tourist sites. There continue to be isolated cases of domestic terrorism by extreme left wing and secessionist groups, aimed primarily at official Italian targets.

British Embassy

VIA XX SETTEMBRE 80A, I-00187 ROMA RM
Tel: 06 4220 0001 (24 hour emergency number)
www.ukinitaly.fco.gov.uk/en

British Consulate-General

VIA SAN PAOLO 7, I-20121 MILANO MI
Tel: 02 7230 01
There is also a British Consulates in Naples.

Irish Embassy

VILLA SPADA, VIA GIACOMO MEDICI
1 - 00153 ROMA
Tel: 06 5852 381
www.embassyofireland.it
There is also an Irish Honorary Consulate in Milan.

Documents

Driving Licence

The standard pink UK paper driving licence is recognised in Italy but holders of the old-style green UK licence are recommended to change it for a photocard licence. Alternatively an International Driving Permit may be purchased from the AA, the RAC or selected Post Offices.

Money

There are few bureaux de change, so change cash at a bank.

Major credit cards are widely accepted including at petrol stations, but not as widely as in some other European countries. Automatic cash machines (Bancomat) are widespread. Carry your credit card issuers'/banks' 24-hour UK contact numbers in case of loss or theft of your cards.

Vehicle(s)

You must be able to present to the police on demand your vehicle and insurance documents, i.e. vehicle registration certificate (V5C), insurance certificate and MOT certificate (if applicable) and, if you are not the owner of your vehicle(s), authorisation for its use from the owner.

Driving

Alcohol

The maximum permitted level of alcohol is 50 milligrams in 100 millilitres of blood, i.e. less than in the UK (80 milligrams). For drivers with less than three years' driving experience, the limit is zero. It is advisable to adopt the 'no drink and drive' rule at all times as penalties are severe.

Breakdown Service

The motoring organisation, Automobile Club d'Italia (ACI) operates a breakdown service 24 hours a day throughout Italy, including San Marino and Vatican City. Telephone 803116 from a landline or mobile phone. ACI staff speak English. This number also gives access to the ACI emergency information service, operated by multi-lingual staff, for urgent medical or legal advice. There are emergency phones placed every 2km on motorways.

On all roads, including motorways, standard charges are made for assistance and/or recovering a vehicle weighing up to 2,500kg to the nearest ACI garage. Higher charges apply for vehicles over 2,500kg, at night, over weekends and public holidays and for towing to anywhere other than the nearest ACI garage. Payment is required in cash.

Road police, 'Polizia Stradale', constantly patrol all roads and motorways and can assist when vehicles break down.

Congestion Charge

To access the historical centre of Milan (Area C) from 7.30am – 7.30pm on Monday, Tuesday, Wednesday and Friday and from 7.30am- 6pm on Thursday you must pay a fee of €5 a day.

You can buy a ticket for entrance from parking meters, newsagents and some ATM points or online at www.areac.it – tickets must then be activated on the day before you plan to drive into the area. You can activate the ticket via text message or telephone. Visit the above website address to find out more. Petrol vehicles classed as Euro 0 and diesel vehicles in classes Euro 0 - 3 are not allowed to enter Area C at all during the above times.

Child Restraint System

Children travelling in UK registered vehicles must be secured according to UK legislation.

Fuel

Unleaded petrol is sold from pumps marked 'Super Unleaded' or 'Super Sensa Piombo'. Diesel is called 'gasolio' and LPG is known as 'gas auto' or 'GPL'.

Fuel is sold 24 hours a day on motorways but elsewhere petrol stations may close for an extended lunch break and overnight from approximately 7pm. Opening hours are clearly displayed, as are the addresses of the nearest garages which are open.

Major credit cards are accepted, but possibly not in rural areas, so always carry some cash. Look for the 'Carta Si' sign. Recent visitors report that many petrol stations in rural areas and on major routes between towns are now unmanned and automated. Payment may be made with bank notes but the machines will usually only accept credit cards issued by Italian banks.

Lights

It is compulsory for all vehicles to have dipped headlights at all times when driving outside built-up areas, on motorways and major roads, when driving in tunnels and when visibility is poor, e.g. in rain or snow. Bulbs are more likely to fail with constant use so you are advised to carry spares.

Low Emission Zones

Many Italian cities and towns operate low emission zones. They often affect all vehicles, but rules vary from city to city. For more information visit www.lowemissionzones.eu.

Motorways

There are approximately 6,700km of motorway (autostrade) in Italy. Tolls (pedaggio) are levied on most of them.

On some motorways, tolls are payable at intermediate toll booths for each section of the motorway used. On a few others the toll must be paid on entering the motorway.

Motorway Tolls

Category A Cars with height from front axle less than 1.30m.

Category B Motor vehicles with 2 axles with height from front axle over 1.30m including motorhomes.

Category C Motor vehicles with 3 axles, e.g. car plus caravan.

Category D Motor vehicles with 4 axles, e.g. car plus twin-axle caravan.

To calculate the tolls payable and find traffic and motorway services information see www.autostrade.it which allows you to enter your route and class of vehicle.

Tolls can prove to be expensive especially over long distances.

Cash (euro only), debit and credit cards are accepted. Credit cards are also accepted for payment in the Fréjus, Mont-Blanc and Grand St Bernard tunnels. However, visitors advise that on some stretches of motorway automated pay desks which accept credit cards will only do so for solo vehicles. If you are towing a caravan it is advisable to have cash available as you may need to pass through the manned white channel for cash payments.

The prepaid Viacard, available in values of €25, €50 and €75, is also accepted on the majority of motorways and is obtainable from motorway toll booths, service areas and PuntoBlu points of sale along the motorways. The card may be used for any vehicle. When leaving a motorway on which the Viacard is accepted (use the blue or white lanes – do not use the yellow 'Telepass' lanes), insert your entry ticket and card into the machine or give them to the attendant who will deduct the amount due. A Viacard is valid until the credit expires and may be used on a subsequent visit to Italy but cannot be refunded. Viacards are not accepted on Sicilian motorways.

Overtaking

On roads with three traffic lanes, the middle lane is reserved for overtaking, but overtaking is only allowed if a vehicle travelling in the opposite direction is not already overtaking.

When pulling out to overtake on motorways check for cars travelling at well over the maximum speed limit of 130km/h (81 mph).

Parking

In major towns there are parking zones where payment is required and these are indicated by blue road signs. Pay either at a machine with coins or buy a card from local tobacconists or newspaper shops and display it inside your vehicle. Some cities also have green zones where parking is prohibited on working days during the morning and afternoon rush hours.

Parking against the traffic flow and parking on the pavement are not allowed. Illegally parked vehicles may be clamped or towed away.

Priority

In general, priority must be given to traffic coming from the right except if indicated by road signs. At traffic lights a flashing amber light indicates that traffic must slow down and proceed with caution, respecting the priority rules.

Roads

The road network is of a high standard and main and secondary roads are generally good. Many main roads are winding and hilly but provide a more interesting route than the motorways. Stopping places for refreshments may be few and far between in some areas.

Standards of driving may be erratic, especially overtaking, and lane discipline poor; some roads have a particularly bad reputation for accidents. Those where special vigilance is called for include the Via Aurelia between Rome and Pisa, which is mostly two lane and is extremely busy at weekends, the A12 to the north with its series of tunnels and curves, the A1 between Florence and Bologna, the Rome ring road, roads around Naples and Palermo, and mountain roads in the south and in Sicily.

Road Signs and Markings

Road signs conform to international standards. White lettering on a green background indicates motorways (autostrada), whereas state and provincial roads outside built-up areas have white lettering on a blue background.

Snow chains required

Horizontal traffic light

Carabinieri (police)

Ecopass zone (Milan)

Other frequently encountered signs include the following:

Italian	English Translation
Attenzione	Caution
Autocarro	Lorries
Coda	Traffic jam
Curva pericolosa	Dangerous bend
Destra	Right
Deviazione	Diversion
Divieto di accesso	No entry
Divieto di sorpasso	No overtaking
Divieto di sosta	No parking
Ghiaia	Gravel
Incidente	Accident
Incrocio	Crossroads
Lavori in corso	Roadworks ahead
Pericoloso	Danger
Rallentare	Slow down
Restringimento	Narrow lane
Senso unico	One-way street
Senso vietato	No entry
Sinistra	Left
Sosta autorizzata	Parking permitted (times shown)

Italian	English Translation
Sosta aietata	No parking
Svolta	Bend
Uscita	Exit
Vietato ingresso veicili	No entry for vehicles

A single or double unbroken line in the centre of the carriageway must not be crossed.

Speed Limits

	Open Road (km/h)	Motorway (km/h)
Car Solo	90-110	130
Car towing caravan/trailer	70	80
Motorhome under 3500kg	90-110	130
Motorhome 3500-7500kg	80	100

Motorhomes over 3,500kg are restricted to 80 km/h (50 mph) outside built-up areas and 100 km/h (62 mph) on motorways.

Speed on some sections of Italian motorways is electronically controlled. When you leave a motorway the toll booth calculates the distance a vehicle has travelled and the journey time. The police are automatically informed if speeding has taken place, and fines are imposed.

In bad weather the maximum speed is 90 km/h (56 mph) on roads outside built-up areas and 110 km/h (68 mph) on motorways.

The transportation or use of radar detectors is prohibited.

Traffic Jams

During the summer months, particularly at weekends, the roads to the Ligurian and Adriatic coasts and to the Italian lakes are particularly busy, as are the narrow roads around the lakes. Travelling mid week may help a little. Bottlenecks are likely to occur on the A1 north-south motorway at stretches between Milan and Bologna, Rioveggio and Incisa and on the ring road around Rome. Other traffic jams occur on the A14 to the Adriatic coast; on the A4 between Milan and Brescia caused by heavy traffic to Lakes Iseo and Garda; the A11 Florence to Pisa (before the A12 junction); the A12 Rome to Civitavecchia; the A23 Udine to Tarvisio and before the tunnels on the A26 between Alessandria and Voltri.

Italians traditionally go on holiday during the first weekend of August when traffic density is at its worst. Rush hour traffic jams regularly occur on the ring roads for Milan, Rome and Naples.

Violation of Traffic Regulations

The police may impose on the spot fines, which are particularly heavy for speeding and drink and/or drug related driving offences. Payment is required in cash and a receipt must be given. It can take up to a year for notice of a traffic violation and resulting fine to reach the owner of a foreign registered vehicle.

Winter Driving

In the area of Val d'Aosta vehicles must be equipped with winter tyres or snow chains must be carried between 15 October and 15 April. This rule may apply in other areas and over other periods as conditions dictate.

Essential Equipment

Reflective Jackets/ Waistcoats

If your vehicle is immobilised on the carriageway outside a built-up area at night, or in poor visibility, you must wear a reflective jacket or waistcoat when getting out of your vehicle. This rule also applies to passengers who may leave the vehicle, for example, to assist with a repair. Keep the jackets to hand inside your vehicle, not in the boot.

Warning Triangle

At night a warning triangle must be used to give advance warning of any vehicle parked outside a built-up area near a bend, or on a hill if rear side lights have failed, or in fog. Place the triangle at least 50 metres behind the vehicle (100 metres on motorways). Failure to use a triangle may result in a fine.

Touring

Italy's great cities, with their religious, artistic and historic treasures, are high on the short break list and are worthy destinations in their own right. Visitors over 65 often qualify for reduced or free entrance to museums and other attractions, so carry your passport as proof of age.

In Rome an Archaeological Card is available, valid for up to seven days, offering entry (ahead of any queues) to many of the most famous sites, together with discounts on guided tours. The cards are available from participating sites and museums.

Smoking is not permitted in public places including restaurants and bars.

In bars prices shown are for drinks taken standing at the bar. Prices are higher if you are seated at a table. In restaurants a service or cover charge is usually added to the bill but it is customary to add 50 cents or €1 per person if you are happy with the service provided. Not all restaurants accept credit cards; check before ordering.

The east coast of Italy has many holiday resorts with fine, sandy beaches, from Ravenna, to Pescara and beyond. However, most beaches in Italy are commercially managed and unless a campsite or hotel has its own private beach, be prepared to pay to enjoy a day by the sea. By law a part of every beach must have free access, but usually it is the least attractive part.

Many parts of Italy lie on a major seismic fault line and tremors and minor earthquakes are common. Visitors climbing Mount Etna should follow the marked routes and heed the advice of guides. There is also ongoing low-intensity volcanic activity on the island of Stromboli.

Visitors to Venice should note that parts of the city are liable to flood in late autumn and early spring.

There are more than 40 World Heritage Sites in Italy (more than any other country) including the historic centres of Florence, Siena, Naples, Pienza, Urbino and the Vatican City.

The Vatican museums and Sistine Chapel are closed on Sundays, except on the last Sunday of the month. When visiting art galleries in Florence, in particular the Uffizi and Accademia, you are advised to buy timed tickets in advance, either online or in person. Otherwise you will encounter long queues.

There are numerous ferry services transporting passengers and vehicles between Italy and neighbouring countries. Major ports of departure for Croatia, Greece and Turkey are Ancona, Bari, Brindisi, Trieste and Venice. Services also operate to Corsica from Citavecchia, Genoa, Livorno, Porto Torres (Sardinia), Santa Teresa di Gallura (Sardinia) and Savona.

For further information contact:

VIAMARE LTD
SUITE 108, 582 HONEYPOT LANE
STANMORE
MIDDX HA7 1JS
Tel: 020 8206 3420, Fax: 020 8206 1332
www.viamare.com
Email: ferries@viamare.com

If you are planning a skiing holiday contact the Italian State Tourist Board for advice on safety and weather conditions before travelling.

Italy has introduced a law requiring skiers and snowboarders to carry tracking equipment if going off-piste. The law also obliges children up to 14 years of age to wear a helmet. There are plans for snowboarders to be banned from certain slopes, check local news for updates.

Camping and Caravanning

There are approximately 2,000 organised and supervised campsites in Italy. They are usually well signposted and are open from April to September. Advance booking is recommended in high season, especially by the lakes and along the Adriatic coast. About 20% of campsites are open all year including some in the mountains and around large towns. Campsites organised by the Touring Club Italiano (TCI) and the Federcampeggio are particularly well equipped.

In general pitch sizes are small at about 80 square metres and it may be difficult to fit a large outfit plus an awning onto a pitch. You will frequently find that hot water is supplied to showers only, for which you will be charged. Published opening and closing dates may be unreliable - phone ahead if travelling during the low season.

It is not compulsory to have a Camping Key Europe (CKE) or Camping Card International (CCI), but it is recommended as a means of identification. If for any reason details are missing from the CKE or CCI a site will insist on holding a visitor's passport instead.

Casual camping is not recommended and is not permitted in national parks or in state forests.

Motorhomes

Many local authorities permit motorhomes to park overnight in specially designated places known as 'Camper Stops' or 'Aree di Sosta' and a list of their locations and the services provided are contained in a number of publications and on a number of websites including the French 'Guide Officiel Aires de Service Camping-Car' published by the Fédération Française de Camping et de Caravaning, www.ffcc.fr. You will also find a list of 'Camper Stops' on www.turismoitinerante.com.

Transportation of bicycles

An overhanging load must be indicated by an aluminium square panel (panello) measuring 50cm x 50cm with reflective red and white diagonal stripes. The load must not exceed 30% of the length of the vehicle, may only overhang at the rear and the regulation applies to a car or caravan carrying bicycles at the rear or windsurf boards on the roof. A fine may be imposed for failure to display the approved sign which is made by Fiamma and in the UK may be purchased from or ordered through motorhome or caravan dealers/accessory shops. For a list of Fiamma stockists please see www.fiamma.com.

At night, outside built up areas, cyclists must wear a reflective jacket and must ride in single file.

Electricity and Gas

Current at campsites varies between 2 and 16 amps and often it is very low, offering a maximum of only 4 amps across the whole site. Many sites have CEE connections. Plugs have three round pins in line.

Campingaz cylinders are generally available, except in the south of Italy, Sardinia and Sicily where exchange may be difficult outside of marinas and holiday resorts.

Public Transport & Local Travel

Traffic is restricted in the historical centre of most Italian cities in order to reduce congestion and pollution levels, and you are advised to use out of centre car parks and public transport. The boundaries of historic centres are usually marked with signs displaying the letters ZTL (zona traffico limitato). A crossed hammer on the sign means the restriction does not apply on Sundays and public holidays. Do not pass the ZTL sign as your registration number is likely to be caught on camera and fined. Fines are around €100 each time you enter a ZTL.

In addition many northern Italian regions have banned traffic, except buses and taxis, in town and city centres on Sundays.

Public transport is usually cheap and efficient. All the major cities have extensive bus networks and Messina, Milan, Padova, Rome and Turin also have trams. At present only Rome and Milan have an underground network and Perugia has a 'minimetro'. Bus and metro tickets cannot be purchased on board and must be obtained prior to boarding from newsagents, tobacconists, ticket kiosks or bars. Books of tickets and daily, weekly and monthly passes are also available. Validate your ticket at the yellow machines positioned at the entrance to platforms in railway stations, in the entrance hall of metro stations and on board buses and trams. Officials patrol all means of public transport and will issue an on the spot fine if you do not hold a validated ticket. Tickets for buses and the metro tend to be time limited (75 minutes) and it is therefore necessary to complete your journey within the allotted time and purchase a new ticket for any additional travel.

Only use taxis which are officially licensed. They will have a neon taxi sign on the roof and are generally white or yellow. Also ensure that the meter in the taxi has been reset before starting your journey. Fares are quite high and there are additional charges for luggage and pets, at night and on public holidays. A tip is expected (up to 10%) and this is sometimes already added to the fares for foreigners.

Car ferry services operate between Venice and the Lido, the Italian mainland and the Aeolian Islands, Sardinia, Sicily, Elba and Capri, Corsica (France) and on Lakes Maggiore, Como and Garda. Parking in Venice is very difficult; instead park at a mainland car park and use a bus or ferry to the city. However, be aware that thieves may operate in car parks in Mestre. Driving and parking in Naples are not recommended in any circumstances.

Cars towing caravans are prohibited from using the S163 south of Naples because it is narrow and has many bends. Motorhomes are prohibited in summer between Positano and Vietri-a-Mare.

Venice

AGEROLA 3A3 (3.5km SE Urban) 40.62537, 14.56761
Camping Beata Solitudo, Piazza Generale Avitabile 4, San Lazzaro, 80051 Agerola (NA) **081 8025048; beatasol@gmail.com; www.beatasolitudo.it**

12 ⚰ ♦♦(cont) ⬚ ♨ ⬚ ∥ ⬚ ✖ ⟟ ♈ nr ⓌŊ nr ♨nr ⚟

Exit A3/S145 at Castellammare-di-Stabia & foll dirs S on S366 to Agerola. Turn L sp San Lazzaro, site in vill sq - narr access rds. Do not app via Amalfi coast rd. Sm, shd, terr, EHU (3A) inc; 70% statics; bus adj; Eng spkn; adv bkg acc; CKE. *"Vg access to Amalfi coast via bus; site at 650m - sea views; v helpful owner; bungalows & hostel accomm avail in restored castle building on site; vg but suitable m'vans only; facs tired."* **€20.00** **2016**

ALBA 1B2 (1km SW Urban) 44.68507, 8.01019
Camping Village Alba, Corso Piave 219, San Cassiano, 12051 Alba (CN) **0173 280972; info@albavillage hotel.it; www.albavillagehotel.it**

12 ⚰ ♦♦(htd) ⬚ ♨ ♿ ⬚ ∥ ✖ ♈ ⟟ Ⓦ ♨nr ▨

Fr A21 exit Asti Est onto S231 to Alba ring rd. Take Corso Piave dir Roddi & Castiglione Falletto, site sp (Campo Sportivo) on L - red block. Or fr A6 exit at SP662 & foll sp Cherasco & Marene, then at rndabt foll sp Pollenza, then Roddi. Fr Roddi site sp dir Alba. 3*, Med, mkd, hdg, pt shd, EHU (16A) €2.50; bbq; red long stay; bus; Eng spkn; adv bkg acc; ccard acc; games area; bike hire; CKE. *"Excel, friendly, clean site; mv service pnt adj; open country to rear; htd pool adj; vg facs; some statics or apartmnts; sports cent adj; conv Barolo vineyards; attractive town & area; camper van stop adj €5."* **€30.00** **2017**

ALBEROBELLO 3A4 (1.5km N Rural) 40.80194, 17.25055 **Camping Dei Trulli,** Via Castellana Grotte, Km 1.5, 70011 Alberobello (BA) **0804 323699; info@ campingdeitrulli.it; www.campingdeitrulli.com**

♦♦ ♨ ∥ ♈ ⟟ Ⓦ♨ Ⓓ♨ ▨ nr ▨ ♨

Fr Alberobello, site sp on R. Lift barrier to ent if clsd. 3*, Med, mkd, hdstg, pt shd, EHU (6A) €2.50; red long stay; phone; Eng spkn; ccard acc; bike hire; CKE. *"Gd touring base; some pitches sm due to trees; mv service pnt nr; ltd, basic facs LS; hot water to shwrs only; site run-down."* **€29.50, 1 Apr-30 Oct.** **2019**

ALBEROBELLO 3A4 (1km S Rural) 40.77507, 17.24040 **Camping Bosco Selva,** 27 Via Bosco Selva, 70011 Alberobello (BA) **080 4323726; info@camping boscoselva.it; www.campingboscoselva.it**

12 ♦♦ Ⓦ ♨ ⬚ ∥ ⬚ ✖ ♈ ⟟ Ⓦ♨ nr

Sp fr S172/S239 Alberobello ring rd. 3*, Med, hdstg, shd, pt sl, EHU (2A) inc; Eng spkn; CKE. *"In heart of 'Trulli' region of sm beehive-shaped houses; wooded site; friendly owner; vg facs; v nice site; tennis courts; walks in forest adj."* **€23.00** **2019**

AOSTA 1B1 (5km SW Rural) 45.71706, 7.26161
Camping Monte Bianco, St Maurice 15, 11010 Sarre (AO) **0165 258514; info@campingmontebianco.it; www.campingmontebianco.it**

♦♦ Ⓦ ♨ ⬚ ∥ ⬚ ✖ ⟟ ♈ nr Ⓦ♨ nr ♨nr ⚟

Fr A5/E25 exit Aosta W twd Aosta, site on R, well sp. Fr Mont Blanc tunnel on S26 site on R at Sarre 500m past St Maurice sp. W fr Aosta, site on L 100m past boundary sp St Maurice/Sarre, yellow sp. Turn into site poss tight for lge o'fits. 2*, Sm, pt shd, terr, EHU (6-10A) €2.80; gas; red long stay; phone; bus fr site to Aosta; Eng spkn; adv bkg acc; CKE. *"Sm, gd, family-run site set in orchard on rv; friendly, helpful; excel tourist info; beautiful alpine scenery & walks; last tunnel is close to exit when coming fr Mont Blanc do not rely on sat nav to restart in time; bar 100m; pool 4km; pleasant site; supmkt 2km; fascinating walled Roman town; many archaeological sites to visit."* **€25.00, 15 May-30 Sep.** **2018**

ARCO 2D1 (6km SSW Coastal) 45.87614, 10.86779
Camping Bellavista, Via Gardesana, 31 - Arco 0464 505644; www.camping-bellavista.it

🏇 €3.50 ♦♦ Ⓦ ♨ ♨ ♿ ⬚ ∥ ⬚ ♈ ⟟ Ⓦ Ⓓ♨ ▨ ♨

Fr A22 take exit for Roveretto Sud-Lago di Garda; at rndabt take 4th exit twrds Riva Del Garda; in 3km turn L onto SS240. After town cent in 8km take L into site bef lakeside tunnel, just after Lidl supmkt on L. Med, mkd, shd, EHU (3A) inc; bbq; twin axles; phone; bus 100m; Eng spkn; bike hire. *"Lakeside; v busy but v pleasant site; direct access to beach; takeaway; excel, immac san facs; vg & reasonable rest; next to supmkt; town cent 5 min walk along lakeside path; vg touring area for northern towns of lake Garda; excel site."* **€38.00, 1 Apr-30 Oct.** **2019**

AREZZO 1D3 (10km SW Rural) 43.44982, 11.78990
Camping Villaggio Le Ginestre, Loc Ruscello 100, 52100 Arezzo 0575 363566; info@campingle ginestre.it; www.campingleginestre.it

🏇 ♦♦(htd) Ⓦ ♨ ♿ ⬚ ∥ ⬚ ♈ ⟟ Ⓓ♨ ▨ nr ⚟ ♨

Onto A1 sp Arezzo. Foll sp to Battifolle & Ruscello, proceed for 2km to rndabt, turn L to Ruscello and foll sp to site which is on the L. 3*, Med, hdstg, pt shd, pt sl, terr, EHU (5-10A) inc; 5% statics; bus; adv bkg acc; ccard acc; tennis; site clsd Jan; games area; games rm; CKE. *"Pleasant tiered grassy site with views; friendly owner; gd rest (clsd Mon); trains fr Arezzo to Florence, Rome etc; gd touring base/NH."* **€29.00, 1 Mar-5 Nov.** **2018**

ITALY

ARONA *1B1* (8km N Rural) *45.81583, 8.54992*
Camping Solcio, Via al Campeggio, 28040 Solcio-de-Lesa (NO) **0322 7497; info@campingsolcio.com; www.campingsolcio.com**

🐕 €3.80 � (htd) 🆆 ♨ 🚿 🖂 ∥ 🅼🅿 ⛲ 🍴 Ⓗ 🛒 ⏚ ♒

Foll S33 N fr Arona, thro Meina campsite on R of rd app Solcio; well sp, adj boatyard. 2*, Med, mkd, pt shd, EHU (6A) inc; gas; bbq; sw nr; red long stay; 40% statics; phone; Eng spkn; adv bkg acc; fishing; boat hire; watersports; CKE. *"Gd site adj lake; some sm pitches; premium for lakeside pitches; gd rest; gd cent for area; conv Stresa and Borromeo Islands; friendly; highly rec; beach has permanent wooden parasols; immac san facs; lovely site."*
€39.40, 8 Mar-22 Oct. 2018

ARSIE *1D1* (3km S Rural) *45.96333, 11.76027*
Camping Al Lago, Via Campagna 14, 32030 Rocca di Arsie (BL) **0439 58540; info@campingallago.bl.it; www.campingallago.bl.it**

🐕 ♟👪 🆆 ♨ ∥ 🐕 🍴 Ⓗ 🛒 nr ⏚

Fr Trento on S47, turn E dir Feltre/Belluno rd SS50B, take 1st exit after long tunnel. Fr Belluno on S50 & S50B take Arsié exit & foll site sp. 2*, Med, pt shd, EHU (4A) inc; gas; sw nr; 15% statics; phone; adv bkg acc; ccard acc; CKE. *"Excel, well-run, clean, tidy site in unspoilt area of historical & cultural interest; simple facs, basic but clean; boat hire locally; ent clsd 1400-1530 & 0000-0800; passport req to register."*
€26.00, 20 Apr-18 Sep. 2016

"There aren't many sites open at this time of year"

If you're travelling outside peak season remember to call ahead to check site opening dates – even if the entry says 'open all year'.

ASSISI *2E3* (1km SE Rural) *43.06605, 12.63056*
Camping Fontemaggio, Via Eremo delle Carceri, 24 Assisi 06081 (PG) **075 813636 or 812317; info@fontemaggio.it; www.fontemaggio.it**

12 🐕 ♟👪 (htd) 🆆 ♨ 🚿 🖂 ∥ 🐕 🍴 Ⓗ 🛒

Fr Perugia on S75, turn L onto rd SS147 twd Assisi; keeping Assisi walls on L past coach car park & foll sp to Porta Nuova. In sq at front of gate turn R & foll sp to Eremo delle Carceri, Foligno & Cmp Fontemaggio. Foll sp 1km to sq in front of next gate, turn R (sharp hairpin), site sp 800m on R at gate with narr arch, site 800m on R. Diff long, winding uphill app; recep in hotel. Pls do not use sat nav. 2*, Lge, hdstg, pt shd, terr, serviced pitches; EHU (6A) inc (long lead req); gas; TV (pitch); 10% statics; phone; Eng spkn; adv bkg acc; ccard acc; CKE. *"Lovely, spacious site in olive grove; views; footpath to attractive town; steep site rds diff when wet; order bread at hotel recep; htd pool 3km; firefly displays on site; facs tired; great rest."* **€25.50** 2015

ASTI *1B2* (15km S Rural) *44.79688, 8.24183*
International Camping Le Fonti, Via Alle Fontane 54, 14041 Agliano Terme **0141 954820; info@campinglefonti.eu; www.campinglefonti.eu**

🐕 ♟👪 🆆 ♨ 🚿 ♿ 🖂 ∥ 🅼🅿 ⛲ 🍴 Ⓗ 🛒 ⏚ ♒ (htd) 🛁

Fr A21 Torino to Alessandria exit Asti Est, dir Alba. Then Isola d'Asti exit, rd 456. Camp sp at the end of Montegrosso d'Asti vill, R twds Agliano Terme. 3*, Med, mkd, shd, terr, EHU (6A) inc; bbq; twin axles; TV; 10% statics; Eng spkn; games area. *"Beautiful (if challenging) area for cycling; v friendly & helpful staff; some pitches small & diff to access; v gd."*
€28.50, 25 Mar-30 Oct. 2016

BARDOLINO *1D2* (2km S Rural) *45.52525, 10.72977*
Camping Cisano/San Vito, Via Peschiera 48, 37011 Cisano (VR) **045 6229098; cisano@camping-cisano.it; www.camping-cisano.it**

♟👪 🆆 ♨ ♿ 🖂 ∥ 🅼🅿 🐕 🍴 Ⓗ 🛒 ♒ 🛁 ⏚

Sites on S boundary of Cisano, on SE shore of Lake Garda. 5*, V lge, mkd, shd, sl, terr, EHU (16A) inc; gas; sw nr; TV; Eng spkn; windsurfing; canoeing; waterskiing; waterslide; bike hire; games area; tennis. *"Two lovely, clean, lakeside sites run as one - San Vito smaller/quieter; helpful staff; san facs in need of refurb; some pitches diff access & chocks req; passport req at site check-in; Verona Opera excursions arranged high ssn; gd; v popular; helpful staff; gd walking/cycling; gd rest."* **€50.00, 17 Mar-8 Oct.** 2018

BARDONECCHIA *1A2* (5km SW Rural) *45.04954, 6.66510* **Camping Bokki**, Loc Pian del Colle, 10052 Bardonecchia (TO) **0122 99893; info@bokki.it; www.bokki.it**

12 🐕 €1 ♟👪 (htd) 🆆 ♨ 🚿 🖂 ∥ 🅼🅿 🐕 🍴 Ⓗ 🛒 nr ⏚

Fr A32 ent Bardonecchia & foll sp Melezet. After Melezet foll rd uphill for 1.5km. Bokki is 2nd site on R. 2*, Med, mkd, pt shd, pt sl, EHU (2A) inc; sw nr; TV; 95% statics; phone; Eng spkn; adv bkg acc; CKE. *"Helpful owners; beautiful location; conv Fréjus tunnel; diff ent to v sm sl, uneven pitch; no red in LS."*
€31.00 2019

BAROLO *1B2* (1km W Rural) *44.61246, 7.92106*
Camping Sole Langhe, Piazza della Vite e Del Vino, Frazione Vergne, 12060 Barolo (CN) **0173 560510; info@solelanghe.com; www.campingsolelanghe.it**

🐕 ♟👪 🆆 ♨ 🖂 ∥ 🅼🅿 🐕 🍴 nr Ⓗ 🛒 ⏚

Fr S exit A6 E sp Carru. At Carru turn N onto SP12 & foll sp Barolo. Site sp on ent Barolo. Sm, hdg, pt shd, EHU (6A) inc; bbq; Eng spkn; games area. *"Lovely orchard site in cent Barolo wine region; v helpful owner; highly rec."* **€26.00, 1 Mar-30 Nov.** 2017

BARREA *2F4* (2km S Rural) *41.74978, 13.99128*
Camping La Genziana, Loc Tre Croci 1, 67030 Barrea
(AQ) **0864 88101; pasettanet@tiscalinet.it;**
www.campinglagenzianapasetta.it

🐕 ℇ3 ♦♦ wd ▲ 🗐 ✗ MSP 🦋 Ⴤ Ⴢ nr 🐂 /M

**Fr S83 to S end Lago di Barrea, thro Barrea S, site
immed on L on uphill L-hand bend.** 2*, Med, mkd, pt
shd, terr, EHU (3A) €2.60; bbq; sw nr; bus; Eng spkn;
adv bkg acc. *"Knowledgeable owner; delightful site;
excel area cycling; trekking, skiing; ltd shops Barrea 10
mins walk; conv Abruzzi National Park; updated facs
(2015)."* **€33.50, 5 Apr-20 Oct.** 2016

BASCHI *2E3* (13km NE Rural) *42.70722, 12.2920*
Camping Il Falcone, Loc Vallonganino 2A, Loc
Civitella-del-Lago, 05023 Baschi (TR) **0744 950249;
info@campingilfalcone.com; www.campingil
falcone.com**

🐕 ♦♦ wd ▲ 🗐 ✗ MSP Ⴤ Ⴢ ✄

**Fr Orvieto take SS205 dir Baschi then S448 alongside
Lago di Corbaro. Turn R sp Civitella. Uphill for 4km
to site.** 2*, Sm, hdstg, mkd, pt shd, terr, EHU (3A) inc;
gas; bbq; red long stay; TV; Eng spkn; adv bkg acc;
ccard acc; games rm; sep car park; CKE. *"Lovely site in
olive grove & woods; quiet; excel clean san facs; some
pitches poss diff lge o'fits."* **€32.00, 1 Apr-30 Sep.**
2018

BELLAGIO *1C1* (1.8km S Rural) *45.97093, 9.25381*
Clarke Camping, Via Valassina 170/C, 22021 Bellagio,
Como **031 951325; elizabethclarke54@icloud.com;
www.bellagio-camping.com**

♦♦ wd ▲ ✗ MSP 🦋 Ⴘ Ⴤ nr ⒣nr 🐂 nr

**Fr Como, on arr in Bellagio foll sp Lecco to R, foll
site sps uphill. Narr rds & site ent.** Med, pt shd, terr,
EHU (16A) €2; sw nr. *"Friendly British owner; views
over lake; uphill walk fr town to campsite; town is
on lakeside; site & ent not suitable for o'fits over 7m;
ferries, water taxis 1.5km; no twin axles; beautiful,
peaceful site; basic san facs but clean; use vehicle ferry
fr Cadenabbis or Varenne €20 for m'van & 2 people,
then foll dirs."* **€34.00, 1 May-20 Sep.** 2016

BERGAMO *2C1* (25km N Rural) *45.78866, 9.94705*
Camping La Tartufaia, Via Nazionale 2519, 24060
Ranzanico al Lago di Endine **39 035 819 259; info@
latartufaia.com; www.latartufaia.com**

🐕 ♦♦ wd ▲ ♿ 🗐 ✗ MSP Ⴘ Ⴤ ⒣ 🐂 nr ✄ Ⴇadj

**Fr A4 Milan-Venice, exit at Seriate. Take SS42 dir
Lovere. Campsite on L past Ranzanico exit.** 3*, Med,
mkd, hdstg, pt shd, terr, EHU (6A) inc; gas; bbq; sw
nr; twin axles; bus adj; Eng spkn; ccard acc; games rm;
CCI. *"Excel site; beautiful views over lake & mountains;
gd bus conns; footpath around lake; v friendly &
helpful owners."* **€41.50, 1 May-22 Sep.** 2019

BEVAGNA *2E3* (4.5km SW Rural) *42.91236, 12.58622*
Camping Pian di Boccio, Via Pian de Boccio 10, 06031
Bevagna **0742 360 164; info@piandiboccio.com;
www.piandiboccio.com**

🐕 ♦♦ wd ▲ ♿ 🗐 ✗ MSP 🦋 Ⴘ Ⴤ ⒣ Ⴢ /M ✄ (htd) 📶

**Fr Foligno to Bevagna in c'van strt on S316 & turn R
after 3km, foll signs. In car - just past Bevagna 1st
rd on the R past the bdge.** 3*, Med, hdg, hdstg, shd,
pt sl, terr, EHU (6A); phone; Eng spkn; adv bkg acc;
games rm; games area. *"Excel site; beautiful location;
conv for Assis and historic hill towns; dated san facs."*
€26.50, 1 Apr-30 Sep. 2015

BIBIONE *2E1* (6km W Coastal) *45.63055, 12.99444*
Camping Village Capalonga, Viale della Laguna 16,
30020 Bibione-Pineda (VE) **0431 438351 or 0431
447190 LS; capalonga@bibionemare.com;
www.capalonga.com**

♦♦ wd ▲ ♿ 🗐 ✗ MSP 🦋 Ⴘ Ⴤ ⒣ Ⴢ 🐂 /M ✎ ✄ Ⴇsand adj

Well sp approx 6km fr Bibione dir Bibione Pineda.
4*, V lge, shd, EHU (10A) inc; gas; bbq; TV; 25%
statics; phone; adv bkg acc; ccard acc; excursions;
watersports; games rm; archery; horseriding 6km;
fishing; golf 10km; tennis. *"Well-organised site; gd for
families; various activities; extra for pitches on beach;
spacious, clean san facs; no o'fits over 10m high ssn;
rest o'looking lagoon; blue flag sand beach; voracious
mosquitoes!"* **€52.00, 24 Apr-21 Sep, Y15.** 2016

BIELLA *1B1* (88km NNW Rural) *45.84781, 7.93980*
Campeggio Alagna, Localita Miniere, 3, 13020 Riva
Valdobbia VC **0163 922947; info@campeggio
alagna.it; www.campeggioalagna.it**

12 🐕 wd ▲ 🗐 ✗ 🦋 Ⴤ ⒣ 🐂 /M

**Site on R hand side up valley on the S299 at Riva
Valdobbia, just bef Alagna Valsesia.** 2*, Sm, shd,
EHU; twin axles; phone; bus adj; Eng spkn; adv bkg
acc; ccard acc; games area. *"Excel site."* **€20.00**
2016

BOLOGNA *1D2* (2km NE Rural) *44.52333, 11.37388*
Centro Turistico Campeggio Città di Bologna,
Via Romita 12/4a, 40127 Bologna **051 325016; info@
hotelcamping.com; www.hotelcamping.com**

🐕 ℇ2 ♦♦ (htd) wd ▲ ♿ 🗐 ✗ MSP Ⴘ Ⴤ ⒣ 🐂 /M ✄

**Access is fr A14 Bologna to Ancona. Leave at junc
7 sp Fiera & Via Stalingrado. Can be accessed fr the
parallel 'Tangenziale' at same junc. Sp at 1st junc
after toll.** 3*, Med, mkd, pt shd, EHU (6A) inc; bbq
(charcoal, gas); red long stay; TV; bus to city; Eng spkn;
adv bkg acc; ccard acc; site clsd 20 Dec-9 Jan; games
rm; CKE. *"Conv Bologna Trade Fair & Exhibition cent;
friendly, helpful staff; excel, clean san facs; fitness cent;
excel pool; tourist pitches at rear nr san facs block; no
o'fits over 15m on hdstg & over 9m on grass; gd bus
service fr ent into city; access to pitches poss diff lge
o'fits; sat nav dir may take you down narr rds; poss
lots mosquitoes; excel site."* **€36.00, 20 Jan-18 Dec,
Y14.** 2019

ITALY

BOLSENA *1D3* (2km S Rural) *42.62722, 11.99444*
Camping Village Lido di Bolsena, Via Cassia, Km 111,
01023 Bolsena (VT) **0761 799258; info@bolsena
camping.it; www.bolsenacamping.it**

🏕🚿 ⚿ 🅆🄳 📶 🖥 ⚿ 🄼🄿 🦋 🍴 Ⓗ🍴🅿 🛁 🚤 ⚓ sand adj

Fr S on a'strada A1 foll sp Viterbo & Lago di Bolsena,
then take SR2 N to site; sp. Fr N exit A1 at Orvieto
onto SS71 to Bolsena. At traff lts in cent of town
turn L, site on R in approx 2km. 4*, V lge, pt shd,
EHU (3A) inc (poss rev pol); gas; sw; 10% statics;
phone; Eng spkn; adv bkg acc; tennis; games area; sep
car park; bike hire; watersports. *"Beautiful lakeside
location; gd size pitches; all facs excel; cycle path
around lake to town; private bthrms avail; sm dogs acc;
charge for pool."* **€34.50, 18 Apr-30 Sep.** **2019**

BOLSENA *1D3* (1.8km SW Rural) *42.63039, 11.99802*
Camping Le Calle, Via Cassia, Km 111.2, 01023 Bolsena
(VT) **0761 797041**

🐕€2 🏕🚿 🅆🄳 📶 ♿ ⚿ 🄼🄿 🦋 Ⓗnr

On S2 bet Lido Camping Vill & Camping Blu, ent by
Fornacella rest. Sm, mkd, pt shd, EHU (6A) inc; sw nr;
adv bkg acc; CKE. *"Family-run CL-type 'Agrituristico'
site; friendly, helpful owners offer own produce inc
wine & olive oil; vg san facs; foot/cycle path to Bolsena;
excel sm site."* **€17.00, 1 Mar-31 Oct.** **2015**

BOLZANO/BOZEN *1D1* (10km S Rural) *46.42982,
11.34357* **Camping-Park Steiner,** Kennedystrasse 32,
39055 Laives/Leifers (BZ) **0471 950105; info@
campingsteiner.com; www.campingsteiner.com**

🐕€5 🏕🚿(htd) 🅆🄳 📶 ♿ 🖥 ⚿ 🄼🄿 ♟ 🍴 Ⓗ🍴🅿 🄼 🚤 (covrd)

Fr N take Bolzano/Bozen-Sud exit fr A22/E45 & pick
up rd S12 twd Trento to site; site on R on ent Laives
at N edge of vill. Fr S leave A22 at junc for Egna
onto rd S12 dir Bolzano. Poorly sp. 3*, Lge, hdg, mkd,
shd, pt sl, EHU (6A) inc; gas; TV; 10% statics; phone;
Eng spkn; adv bkg rec; bike hire; CKE. *"Pleasant, well-
run, excel site on edge of Dolomites; attractive pitches;
helpful staff; gd, clean, modern san facs; gates clsd
1300-1500 & 2200-0700; no dogs high ssn; beautiful
area; vg walking; well stocked shop; highly rec; easy
5 min walk into town; excel rest; busy in high ssn;
excel value transport passes fr TO."*
€40.00, 12 Mar-31 Oct. **2016**

BORGO SAN LORENZO *1D3* (7km SE Rural) *43.93087,
11.46426* **Camping Vicchio Ponte,** Via Costoli 16,
50039 Vicchio **055 8448306; info@campingvecchio
ponte.it; www.campingvecchioponte.it**

🐕 🏕🚿(cont) 🅆🄳 📶 ⚿ 🄼🄿 🦋 🍴nr Ⓗnr 🛁nr

On SP551 adj to sw pool in Vicchio. 3*, Med, pt shd,
EHU (4A) inc; train to Florence 1km; Eng spkn; CKE.
*"Simple, municipal site; htd pool adj inc in price; v clean
san facs; v helpful staff."* **€24.00, 1 Jun-15 Sep.** **2016**

BORGO SAN LORENZO *1D3* (5km W Rural) *43.96144,
11.30918* **Camping Mugello Verde,** Via Massorondinaio
39, 50038 San Piero-a-Sieve (FI) **055 848511;
mugelloverde@florencecamping.com;
www.florencecamping.com**

🏕🚿(htd) 🅆🄳 📶 ♿ 🖥 ⚿ 🄼🄿 🦋 🍴 Ⓗ🍴🅿 🄼 🚤

Exit A1 at Barberino exit & foll Barberino sp twd
San Piero-a-Sieve & Borgo San Lorenzo. Turn S on
S65 twd Florence. Site sp immed after Cafaggiolo.
3*, Lge, pt shd, sl, terr, EHU (6A) inc; gas; 50% statics;
bus/train; ccard acc; tennis; bike hire; CKE. *"Hillside
site; bus to Florence high ssn (fr vill LS) or 20 mins
drive; hard grnd diff for awnings; poss long walk to
recep & shop; helpful, friendly staff; refurbed, gd,
clean san facs; avoid early Jun - Italian Grand Prix!."*
€34.00, 16 Mar-3 Nov. **2019**

BORGO SAN LORENZO *1D3* (28km NW Rural)
44.09810, 011.26836 **Camping La Futa,** Via Bruscoli
Futa, 889/h, Firenzuola **3289248746; info@camping
lafuta.it; www.campinglafuta.it**

🐕€2 🏕🚿 🅆🄳 📶 ♿ ⚿ 🍴 Ⓗ🍴 🄼 🚤(htd)

A1 Bologna to Firenze - exit Roncobiaccio SS65 to
Passo Della Futa. Site close to pass. 2*, Med, mkd, pt
shd, terr, EHU (10A); bbq; twin axles; TV; 25% statics;
phone; Eng spkn; adv bkg acc; games rm; games area;
CKE. *"Excel site."* **€28.00, 15 Apr-30 Sep.** **2016**

CANAZEI *1D1* (2km W Rural) *46.47479, 11.74067*
Camping Miravalle, Strèda de Greva 39, 38031
Campitello-di-Fassa (TN) **0462 750502; info@
campingmiravalle.it; www.campingmiravalle.it**

🐕€4 🏕🚿 📶 ♿ 🖥 ⚿ 🄼🄿 🦋 🍴 Ⓗnr 🛁nr

In vill cent on rte 48 site sp down side rd.
3*, Lge, unshd, sl, EHU (6A) inc (poss rev pol),
extra €2 for 6A; Eng spkn; adv bkg acc; ccard acc;
CKE. *"Excel new san facs 2015; conv cable car."*
€37.00, 1 Jan-30 Mar, 1 Jun-30 Sep & 1 Dec-31 Dec.
2015

CANNOBIO *1C1* (0.5km N Urban) *46.06678, 8.69507*
Camping Del Sole, Via Sotto i Chiosi 81/A, 28822
Cannobio (VB) **0323 70732; info@campingsole.it;
www.campingsole.it**

🐕€3 🏕🚿 📶 ⚿ 🄼🄿 ♟ 🍴 Ⓗ🍴🅿 🛁nr 🄼 🚤

Fr S fr A26 foll Verbania sp then sp Cannobio or
Locarno. Ent vill, over cobbles, 2nd R in 750m. Bef
rv bdge immed sharp R under main rd, site on L
after quick R turn. Fr N ent Cannobio, 1st L after
x-ing rv, then as above. 2*, Lge, hdg, mkd, hdstg,
pt shd, EHU (4A) €3; gas; sw nr; red long stay;
60% statics; Eng spkn; CKE. *"Attractive vill & lake
frontage; friendly, family-run site; poss tight access
some pitches; lovely pool area; cramped pitches; diff to
park m'van; dated clean san facs; close to town; fair."*
€34.00, 1 Mar-3 Nov. **2019**

CANNOBIO 1C1 (1km N Rural) 46.07791, 8.69345
Villaggio Camping Bosco, Punta Bragone, 28822
Cannobio (VB) **0323 71597; bosco@boschetto
holiday.it; www.boschettoholiday.it/bosco**

🐕₄ ♂♀ ⓌⒸ ♨ ⏚ ⎕ ∅ 👜 ☂ 🦐 ⚠ ⚓shgl

On W side of lakeshore rd bet Cannobio & Swiss
frontier. Sh steep app to site & hairpin bend fr narr
rd, unsuitable for car/c'van o'fits & diff for m'vans.
2*, Med, pt shd, terr, EHU (3A) €3.90; gas; bbq; sw;
Eng spkn; adv bkg rec; CKE. *"All pitches with
magnificent lake view; beautiful town; hot water to
shwrs only."* **€32.30, 1 Apr-22 Oct.** **2017**

CANNOBIO 1C1 (1.5km SW Rural) 46.05756, 8.67831
Camping Valle Romantica, Via Valle Cannobina,
28822 Cannobio (VB) **0323 71249; valleromantica@
riviera-valleromantica.com; www.riviera-valle
romantica.com**

🐕₄ ♂♀ ⓌⒸ ♨ ⏚ ⎕ ∅ 👜 ☂ 🦐 ⚠ ⚓

Turn W on S o'skirts of Cannobio, sp Valle
Cannobina. In 1.5km at fork keep L. Site immed
on R. On ent site cont to bottom of hill to park &
walk back to recep. 2*, Lge, hdg, mkd, pt shd, pt sl,
terr, EHU (4-6A) €4.50; 25% statics; adv bkg acc; golf
12km. *"Vg; some sm pitches; particularly helpful&
friendly staff; narr site rds poss diff m'vans; masses
of flowers; beautiful situation; footpath to town,
poss cr high ssn; v well kept; req to show passport."*
€41.50, 1 Apr-11 Sep. **2017**

CAORLE 2E2 (5km SW Coastal) 45.56694, 12.79416
Camping Villaggio San Francesco, Via Selva Rosata 1,
Duna Verde, 30020 Porto-Santa-Margherita (VE)
**0421 299333; info@villaggiosfrancesco.com;
www.villaggiosfrancesco.com**

🐕₃ ♂♀ ⓌⒸ ♨ ⏚ ⎕ ∅ 👜 ☂ ♈ 🦐 ⚠ 🏊 ⚓adj

Fr A4/E70 exit Santo Stino di Livenza, then dir
Caorle. By-pass town & cont on coast rd, site sp on
L. 4*, V lge, shd, EHU (6A) inc; gas; TV; 60% statics;
phone; waterslide; windsurfing; games area; solarium;
bike hire; games rm; tennis; boat hire; waterskiing;
CKE. *"Excel family facs; min 2 nights' stay."*
€44.60, 24 Apr-25 Sep. **2016**

CASALBORDINO 2F4 (7km NE Coastal) 42.20018,
14.60897 **Camping Village Santo Stefano,** S16, Km 498,
66020 Marina-di-Casalbordino (CH) **0873 918118;
info@campingsantostefano.com; www.camping
santostefano.com**

♂♀ ⓌⒸ ♨ ∅ ☂ ⚠ 🦐 🏊 ⚓adj

Exit A14 Vasto N onto S16 dir Pescara, site at
km 498 on R. 3*, Med, mkd, shd, EHU (6A) inc;
10% statics; Eng spkn; adv bkg acc; CKE. *"Pleasant,
well-maintained, family-run site; sm pitches; beautiful
private beach & pool area; gd rest."*
€48.00, 21 Apr-23 Sep. **2019**

CASTELSANTANGELO SUL NERA 2E3 (4km S Rural)
42.88223, 13.18181 **Camping Monte Prata,** Loc.
Schianceto, 62030 Castel S Angelo Sul Nera **33 86 54
49 24 or 33 32 95 18 60 (mob); sostare@camping
monteprata.it; www.campingmonteprata.it**

🐕 ♂♀(htd) ⓌⒸ ♨ ⏚ ⎕ ∅ 👜 ☂ ⚠

Fr SP209 Muccia-Visso. Thro Visso on the Strada
Provinciale 134 twds Castelsangangelo Sur
Nera. Aft vill slight R onto SP 136. Campsite
on L after vill of Gualdo. 3*, Med, mkd, hdstg, pt
shd, terr, EHU; bbq; Eng spkn; ccard acc; games
area. *"Gd site; excel position nr top of Monte Prata;
guided walks & other excursions fr site in Nat Park."*
€33.00, 15 Jun-15 Sep. **2019**

CASTIGLIONE DEL LAGO 2E3 (1km N Rural) 43.13460,
12.04383 **Camping Listro,** Via Lungolago, Lido Arezzo,
06061 Castiglione-del-Lago (PG) **075 951193;
listro@listro.it; www.listro.it**

♂♀ ⓌⒸ ♨ ⏚ ⎕ ∅ ☂ ⚠nr 🦐 ⚠

Fr N A1 Val di Chiana exit 75 bis Perugia, site clearly
sp on N edge of town on lakeside. 2*, Med, mkd, pt
shd, EHU (3A) inc (poss rev pol); gas; sw nr; red long
stay; Eng spkn; adv bkg acc; ccard acc; tennis nr; bike
hire; CKE. *"On W shore of Lake Trasimeno; facs
stretched when site full; v helpful staff; sand beach &
lake sw adj; bus to Perugia; rlwy stn 1km for train to
Rome; 'tree fluff' a problem in spring; new san facs
(2016); poor elecs."* **€22.30, 1 Apr-30 Sep.** **2016**

**"That's changed – Should I let
the Club know?"**

If you find something on site that's different
from the site entry, fill in a report and let us
know. See camc.com/europereport.

CAVALLINO 2E2 (2.5km S Coastal) 45.46726,
12.53006 **Union Lido Park & Resort,** Via Fausta
258, 30013 Cavallino (VE) **041 968080 or 2575111;
info@unionlido.com; www.unionlido.com**

♂♀(htd) ⓌⒸ ♨ ⏚ ⎕ ∅ 👜 ♈ ☂ ⚠ 🦐 ♿ 🏊 ⚓

Exit a'strada A4 (Mestre-Trieste) at exit for airport
or Quarto d'Altino & foll sp for Jesolo & then Punta
Sabbioni; site on L 2.5km after Cavallino.
V lge, mkd, shd, serviced pitches; EHU (6A) inc; gas;
50% statics; Eng spkn; adv bkg acc; ccard acc; gym;
bike hire; watersports; horseriding; tennis; boating;
golf; sauna; fishing. *"Variable pitch size; sat TV; late arr
(after 2100) area with EHU; min stay 7 days high ssn;
children's lagoon with slides; some pitches soft sand
(a spade useful!); church; banking facs; Italian lessons;
wellness cent; many long-stay campers; skating rink;
hairdresser; babysitting; no admissions 1230-1500
(poss busy w/end); excursions; varied entmnt
programme high ssn; well-organised, well-run; clean
facs; worth every penny! excel."*
€66.00, 21 Apr-10 Oct. **2017**

ITALY

CAVALLINO *2E2* (5km SW Coastal) *45.45638, 12.4960* **Camping Enzo Stella Maris,** Via delle Batterie 100, 30013 Cavallino-Treporti (VE) **041 966030; info@enzostellamaris.com; www.enzostellamaris.com**

🏕 WD ⚊ ♨ ⚹ ⚽ / MSP 🐕 ⛱ Y ⓗ ♨ 🛒 ⋔ 🚿 ✎ ⚓ (htd) ⚓ sand adj

Exit A4 at sp for airport. Foll sp Jesolo, Cavallino, Punta Sabbioni rd SW. Site sp after Ca'Ballarin. 5*, Lge, mkd, pt shd, serviced pitches; EHU (10A) inc; gas; red long stay; TV; 25% statics; phone; Eng spkn; ccard acc; fitness rm; clsd 1230-1600 & 2300-0700; games area; CKE. *"Well-run, friendly, family-owned site; excel facs; beware mosquitoes; indoor htd pool; wellness cent; €30 in LS."* **€60.00, 29 Apr-22 Oct.**
2017

CAVALLINO *2E2* (6km SW Coastal) *45.44872, 12.47116* **Camping Dei Fiori,** Via Vettor Pisani 52, 30010 Cavallino-Treporti (VE) **041 966448; fiori@vacanze-natura.it; www.deifiori.it**

🏕 WD ⚊ ♨ ⚹ ⚽ / MSP 🦋 🐕 Y ⓗ ♨ 🛒 ⋔ ✎ ⚓ 🚿 ⚓ sand adj

Fr Lido di Jesolo foll sp to Cavallino; site on L approx 6km past Cavallino & bef Ca'Vio. 4*, Lge, mkd, shd, serviced pitches; EHU (5A) inc (poss rev pol); gas; red long stay; Eng spkn; adv bkg req; ccard acc; games area. *"V clean & quiet even in Aug; excel facs & amenities; conv water bus stop at Port Sabbioni; hydro massage therapy; 3/5 day min stay med/high ssn; highly rec; excel."* **€22.50, 19 Apr-30 Sep.**
2016

CECINA *1D3* (3km NW Coastal) *43.31850, 10.47440* **Camping Mareblu,** Via dei Campilunghi, Mazzanta, 57023 Cecina Mare (Li) **0586 629191; info@campingmareblu.com; www.campingmareblu.com**

🐕 🏕 WD ⚊ ♨ ⚹ ⚽ / MSP 🐕 Y ⓗ ♨ 🛒 ⋔ 🚿 ⛱ 🏊 ⚓ sand adj

Fr S on SS1 exit sp Cecina Nord & foll dir Mazzanta, site sp. Fr N exit sp Vada then Mazzanta. 3*, Lge, hdg, mkd, pt shd, EHU (3A) inc; gas; bbq (gas); 10% statics; phone; Eng spkn; adv bkg acc; ccard acc; CKE. *"Lge pitches; gd facs & pool area; car must be parked in sep car park; no dogs Jul/Aug; ATM; well-organised, friendly site."* **€42.50, 1 Apr-21 Oct.** **2017**

CERVIA *2E2* (3.6km S Coastal) *44.24760, 12.35901* **Camping Adriatico,** Via Pinarella 90, 48015 Cervia (RA) **0544 71537; info@campingadriatico.net; www.campingadriatico.net**

🐕 €6 🏕 WD ⚊ ♨ ⚹ ⚽ / MSP Y ⓗ ♨ 🛒 ⋔ ✎ 🏊 (htd) 🏖 ⚓ sand 600m

On SS16 S fr Cervia twd Pinarella, turn L at km post 175, over rlwy line & take 1st R, site sp. 3*, Lge, shd, EHU (6A) inc; TV; 40% statics; Eng spkn; adv bkg acc; ccard acc; fishing; tennis 900m; golf 5km; CKE. *"V pleasant site; friendly staff; gd san facs; excel pizza at rest; ACSI acc."* **€33.70, 14 Apr-19 Sep.** **2016**

CESENATICO *2E2* (2km N Coastal) *44.21584, 12.37798* **Camping Zadina,** Via Mazzini 184, 47042 Cesenatico (FC) **0547 82310; info@campingzadina.it; www.campingzadina.it**

🐕 €7 🏕 WD ⚊ ♨ ⚹ ⚽ / MSP 🐕 Y ⓗ ♨ 🛒 ⋔ ✎ ⚓ sand

Leave A14 at Cesena Sud; foll sp Cesenático; after 10.5km turn R at T-junc onto SS16; after 2km fork L over level x-ing; site on L. Lge, mkd, pt shd, terr, EHU (6A) inc; gas; bbq; 80% statics; Eng spkn; adv bkg acc; sep car park; fishing. *"Sea water canal runs thro site; pitches poss tight lge o'fits; gd."* **€43.00, 18 Apr-22 Sep.** **2019**

CHIOGGIA *2E2* (2km E Urban/Coastal) *45.19027, 12.30361* **Camping Miramare,** Via A. Barbarigo 103, 30015 Sottomarina (VE) **041 490610; campmir@tin.it; www.miramarecamping.com**

🐕 €3.50 🏕 WD ⚊ ♨ ⚹ ⚽ / MSP 🐕 Y ⓗ ♨ 🛒 ⋔ ✎ 🏖 ⚓ sand

Fr SS309 foll sp Sottomarina. In town foll brown sp to site. 3*, Lge, mkd, pt shd, EHU (6A) inc; gas; 75% statics; adv bkg acc; ccard acc; games area; CKE. *"Busy site; friendly staff; gd entmnt facs for children; cycle tracks to picturesque Chioggia; site 10 min walk fr ferry point and beach or free shuttle bus service until mid Sept; free sun umbrella for the beach front; rec; visit Venice by bus/ferry; pitches generous; private beach beautifully kept; site rest vg."* **€38.00, 19 Apr-24 Sep.** **2018**

CHIUSA/KLAUSEN *1D1* (0.7km E Rural) *46.64119, 11.57332* **Camping Gamp,** Via Griesbruck 10, 39043 Chiusa/Klausen (BZ) **0472 847425; info@camping-gamp.com; www.camping-gamp.com**

12 🐕 €3.50 🏕 (htd) WD ⚊ ♨ ⚹ ⚽ / MSP 🐕 Y ⓗ ♨ 🛒 ⋔ 🏊

Exit A22 Chiusa/Klausen & bear L at end of slip rd (sp Val Gardena). Site on L at rd fork 800m, sp. 3*, Sm, mkd, pt shd, EHU (6A) €2.60; TV (pitch); phone; Eng spkn; CKE. *"Excel cent for mountain walks; Chiusa attractive town; immac facs, sep m'van o'night area; busy site; table tennis; htd ski & boot rm; some pitches sm for lge o'fits; sep m'van o'night facs; discount with Camping Euro card."* **€34.00** **2019**

COMO *1C1* (5km S Urban) *45.78385, 9.06034* **Camping No Stress (formerly International Camp-Sud),** Breccia, Via Cecilio, 22100 Como **031 521435; campingint@hotmail.com; camping-internazionale.business.site**

🐕 €2 🏕 ⚊ ♨ ⚽ / Y ⓗ ♨ 🛒 ⋔ 🏊

Fr E to Como, on SS35 Milano rd foll sp a'strada Milano; site on Como side of rndabt at junc S35 & S432; ent/exit diff unless turn R. Or take 2nd exit off m'way after border (Como S), site sp. 2*, Med, pt shd, pt sl, EHU (4-6A) €2.50 (rev pol); gas; ccard acc; golf 5km; bike hire. *"Conv NH for m'way."* **€24.00, 1 Apr-31 Oct.** **2019**

ITALY

CORIGLIANO CALABRO *3A4* (10km N Coastal) *39.69130, 16.52233* **Camping Thurium,** Contrada Ricota Grande, 87060 Ricota Grande (CS) **0983 851101; info@campingthurium.com; www.camping thurium.com**

12 ⚡ €4.80 ♛♛ wo ⚓ ⚒ ⚑ ✉ msp ♔ ☂ ⑪ ♨ ⚓ ⚟ ⚓ ✕ ☕ ☂ sand adj

Exit SS106 at km stone 21. Site sp on gd app rd for 2km. Rd narr and bumpy in places. Do not foll sat nav. 4*, Lge, mkd, pt shd, EHU inc (3-6A); gas; twin axles; 20% statics; Eng spkn; games area; tennis; bike hire; CKE. *"Vg well-run site; windsurfing lessons; site rdways narr on corner, tight for lge o'fits; fair."* **€49.00**　　**2019**

> ## "I like to fill in the reports as I travel from site to site"
>
> You'll find report forms at the back of this guide, or you can fill them in online at camc.com/europereport.

CORIGLIANO CALABRO *3A4* (7km N Coastal) *39.70333, 16.52583* **Camping Onda Azzurra,** Contrada Foggia, 87064 Corigliano-Calabro (CS) **0983 851157; info@onda-azzurra.it; www.onda-azzurra.it**

12 ⚡ €3 ♛♛ (htd) wo ⚓ ⚒ ⚑ ✉ ☂ ⑪ ♨ ⚓ ⚟ ☂ sand adj

On SS106-bis Taranto to Crotone rd, after turn off for Sibari, cont S for 6km. Turn L at 4 lge sp on 1 notice board by lge sep building, 2km to site on beach. 3*, Lge, mkd, shd, EHU (6-10A) €3-4; red long stay; 10% statics; adv bkg acc; ccard acc; tennis; bike hire; CKE. *"Excel, well-run site all ssns - facs open all yr; popular long stay; clean facs; lge pitches; water not drinkable; v friendly helpful owner; popular in winter; special meals Xmas/New Year; site conv Sybaris & Rossano; high standard site; excel friendly welcome; free acitivities LS."* **€31.00**　　**2019**

CORTINA D'AMPEZZO *2E1* (3.5km S Rural) *46.51858, 12.1370* **Camping Dolomiti,** Via Campo di Sotto, 32043 Cortina-d'Ampezzo (BL) **0436 2485; campeggio dolomiti@tin.it; www.campeggiodolomiti.it**

⚡ ♛♛ (htd) ⚓ ⚒ ⚑ ✉ ♔ ☂ ⑪ ♨ ☂ ⚟ ✕ (htd)

2km S of Cortina turn R off S51. Site beyond Camping Cortina & Rocchetta. 4*, Lge, mkd, pt shd, EHU (4A) inc (check earth); gas; 10% statics; phone; bus; Eng spkn; ccard acc; games area; games rm. *"Superb scenery in mountains, gd walks; cycle rte into Cortina; helpful owner; beautiful setting; choice of open meadow or shd woodland pitches; gd facs; excel shwrs."* **€24.00, 1 Jun-20 Sep.**　　**2019**

CORVARA IN BADIA *1D1* (2km W Rural) *46.55111, 11.8575* **Camping Colfosco,** Via Sorega 15, 39030 Corvara-in-Badìa (BZ) **0471 836515; info@camping colfosco.org; www.campingcolfosco.org**

⚡ €4 ♛♛ wo ⚓ ⚒ ⚑ ✉ msp ⚟ ♔ ☂ ⑪ nr ☂ ⚟

Leave A22 (m'way fr Brenner) at Bressanone exit foll E66/S49 E. At San Lorenzo turn S on S244 for 28km to Corvara. In town turn R dir Colfosco, foll sp. 1*, Lge, hdstg, unshd, pt sl, EHU (16A) €0.70 per kWh; bbq; twin axles; Eng spkn; adv bkg acc; ccard acc; sep car park; golf 4km; site clsd 1200-1500; games rm. *"Fine scenery & walks; well-managed site; sh walk to vill; gd base for skiing (ski in & out of site) & mountain biking; ski lift 300m; ski bus; lift/bus passes avail; vg san facs; somewhat bleak hdstg area; site lies at 5000ft - cool nights; cycle track, walking routes nr; gd base for Passo Pordoi; vg."* **€35.50, 5 Jan-6 Apr & 7 Jun-20 Dec.**　　**2018**

COURMAYEUR *1A1* (6.2km NE Rural) *45.83293, 6.99095* **Campsite Grandes Jorasses,** Via per la Val Ferret 53, 11013 Courmayeur (Valle d'Aosta) **0165 869708; info@grandesjorasses.com; www.grandes jorasses.com**

♛♛ wo ⚓ ⚒ ⚑ ✉ msp ♔ ☂ ⑪ ♨ ☂

Foll the brown 'Val Ferret' signs bet Courmayeur and the Mont Blanc tunnel, and the campsite is located a few km on the L of the rd. Med, hdstg, pt shd,; games rm; CKE. *"Beautiful site at the foot of Mt Blanc; nature trails thro forest; trekking expeditions arranged; gd rest."* **€26.00, 20 Jun-15 Sep.**　　**2019**

COURMAYEUR *1A1* (6km SE Rural) *45.76333, 7.01055* **Camping Arc en Ciel,** Loc Feysoulles, 11017 Morgex (AO) **0165 809257; info@campingarcenciel.it; www.campingarcenciel.it**

12 ⚡ €1 ♛♛ (htd) wo ⚓ ⚒ ♨ ⚑ ✉ msp ♔ ☂ ⑪ ♨ nr

Fr A5/E25 take Morgex exit, turn L to vill & foll sp dir Dailley. Site in 1km on L, sp. Fr tunnel take SS25 to Morgex, then as above. 1*, Med, pt shd, terr, EHU (3-6A) €1-€2; bbq; 30% statics; adv bkg acc; ccard acc; sep car park; site clsd 6 Nov-8 Dec; rafting; CKE. *"Gd, clean san facs; views Mont Blanc fr some pitches; vg; ski lift 8km; mountain climbing; ski bus; views of the mountains marvellous; helpful manager."* **€27.00**
　　2019

DEIVA MARINA *1C2* (3km E Coastal) *44.22476, 9.55146* **Villaggio Camping Valdeiva,** Loc Ronco, 19013 Deiva-Marina (SP) **0187 824174; camping@ valdeiva.it; www.valdeiva.it**

⚡ ♛♛ wo ⚓ ⚒ ⚑ ♔ ☂ ⑪ ♨ ☂ ⚟ ⚓ ✕ ☂ shgl 3km

Fr A12 exit Deiva Marina, site sp on L in approx 4km by town sp. 2*, Med, hdstg, mkd, pt shd, pt sl, EHU (3-6A) inc; bbq; TV (pitch); 90% statics; phone; bus to stn; Eng spkn; adv bkg rec; ccard acc; CKE. *"Free minibus to stn - conv Cinque Terre or Portofino; helpful, friendly staff; gd rest; sep car park high ssn; excel walking; v quiet LS & shwrs ltd; gd facs."* **€36.00, 1 Jan-8 Jan, 5 Feb-15 Nov & 3 Dec-31 Dec.**
　　2018

ITALY

DESENZANO DEL GARDA *1D2* (5km SE Rural) *45.46565, 10.59443* **Camping San Francesco,** Strada V San Francesco, 25015 Desenzano-del-Garda (BS) **030 9110245; booking@campingsanfrancesco.com; www.campingsanfrancesco.com**

🏠 👬 wo ♨ ⛱ ♿ 🖥 🛝 ⚑ 🍽 Ⓣ ⑨ 🐕 ♨ ⚠ ♫ 🏊 ⛵

E fr Milan on A4 a'strada take exit Sirmione & foll sp twd Sirmione town; join S11 twd Desenzano & after Garden Center Flowers site 1st campsite on R after rndabt; site sp twd lake bet Sirmione & Desanzano. Or fr Desenzano, site just after Rivoltella.
5*, Lge, mkd, shd, pt sl, EHU (6A) inc; gas; bbq (charcoal, gas); sw; TV; 50% statics; phone; Eng spkn; adv bkg acc; ccard acc; games area; sailing; boat hire; windsurfing; canoe hire; golf 10km; fishing; bike hire; tennis; CKE. *"Lovely lakeside pitches for tourers (extra); no o'fits over 6m high ssn; muddy if wet; poss diff lge o'fits due trees; helpful staff; well managed site; gd position on edge of lake; recep clsd 1300-1500 & no vehicle movement; handy for local bus; excel site; v clean facs; gd rest."* **€53.70, 1 Apr-30 Sep.** **2019**

> ## "We must tell the Club about that great site we found"
>
> Get your site reports in by mid-August and we'll do our best to get your updates into the next edition.

DIANO MARINA *1B3* (4km NE Coastal) *43.92177, 8.10831* **Camping del Mare,** Via alla Foce 29, 18010 Cervo (IM) **0183 400130 or 0183 405556; info@campingdelmare-cervo.com; www.campingdelmare-cervo.com**

🏠 👬 wo ♨ ⛱ ♿ 🖥 🛝 ⚑ 🍽 Ⓣ ♨ 🛒 ᴛ shgl adj

Exit A10/E80 at San Bartolomeo/Cervo onto Via Aurelia. Turn L at traff lts twd Cervo. Sp adj rv bdge. R turn acute - long o'fits app fr NE. 2*, Med, hdstg, hdg, mkd, shd, EHU (6A) €2; gas; TV; 40% statics; phone; Eng spkn; adv bkg rec; ccard acc. *"Immac site; spacious pitches; friendly, helpful staff; picturesque beach & perched vill (Cervo); easy walk San Bartolomeo; gd mkts; highly rec site; pitches close together; office closes 1200-1500."* **€45.00, 1 Apr-15 Oct.** **2019**

EDOLO *1D1* (1.5km W Rural) *46.17648, 10.31333* **Camping Adamello,** Via Campeggio 10, Loc Nembra, 25048 Edolo (BS) **0364 71694 or 0333 8275354; info@campingadamello.it; www.campingadamello.it**

12 🐕 €3 👬 wo ♨ ⛱ ♿ 🖥 🛝 🍽 Ⓣ ⑨nr 🛒

On rd 39 fr Edolo to Aprica; after 1.5km turn sharp L down narr lane by rest; camping sp on rd; diff app.
3*, Med, pt shd, pt sl, terr, EHU (6A) €1.50; 50% statics. *"Useful NH; beautiful mountain site; steep rds all round; v diff app fr W; quiet for couples; nothing for children."* **€27.00** **2016**

FALZE DI PIAVE *2E1* (0.7km S Rural) *45.85674, 12.16565* **Parking Le Grave,** Via Passo Barca, 31020 Falze-di-Piave (TV) **0390 43886896; belleluigi@libero.it; www.legrave.it**

12 wo ♫ 🍽 🦋 ⚠

Fr A27 exit Conegliano & turn R onto SP15 then SS13 to Susegana. At Ponte-della-Priula turn onto SP34 to Falze-di-Piave. Fr town cent turn L just past war memorial into Via Passo Barca, site on R.
Sm, unshd, EHU (4A) inc; bbq. *"CL-type site in delightful area; no wc or shwrs; friendly, helpful owner; gd walking/cycling; wine tasting last w/end May."* **€10.00** **2016**

FERRARA *1D2* (3km NE Rural) *44.85303, 11.63328* **Campeggio Comunale Estense,** Via Gramicia 76, 44100 Ferrara **0532 752396; campeggio.estense@freeinternet.it or idem@libero.it**

12 🐕 €1.50 👬 (htd) wo ♨ ⛱ ♿ 🖥 🛝 🍽 Ⓣ ⑨nr 🛒nr

Exit A13 Ferrara N. After Motel Nord Ovest on L turn L at next traff lts into Via Porta Catena. Rd is 500m fr city wall around town; foll brown/yellow sps - well sp fr all dirs. 3*, Med, pt shd, EHU (6A) €3.50; Eng spkn; ccard acc; golf adj; site clsd early-Jan to end-Feb; bike hire; CKE. *"Peaceful, well-kept, clean site; helpful staff; lge pitches; ltd privacy in shwrs; pool in park nrby; interesting, beautiful town; gd cycle tracks round town; some stored c'vans; rlwy stn in town for trains to Venice; gd NH; watch out for low branches when driving thro site."* **€24.50, 1 Jan-11 Jan & 1 Mar-31 Dec.** **2016**

FIANO ROMANO *2E4* (2km W Rural) *42.15167, 12.57670* **Camping I Pini,** Via delle Sassete 1/A, 00065 Fiano-Romano **0765 453349; ipini@camping.it; www.camping.it/roma/ipini**

🐕 €2 👬 (htd) wo ♨ ⛱ ♿ 🖥 🛝 🍽 🦋 Ⓣ ⑨ 🐕 ♨ ⚠ ♫ 🏊 🛝

Fr A1/E35 exit sp Roma Nord/Fiano Romano (use R-hand lane for cash toll), foll sp Fiano at rndabt. Take 1st exit at next rndabt sp I Pini & stay on this rd for approx 2km. Take 2nd exit at next rndabt, L at T-junc under bdge, site sp on R. 4*, Med, mkd, hdg, pt shd, pt sl, terr, EHU (6A) inc (poss rev pol); bbq; TV; 60% statics; phone; bus; Eng spkn; adv bkg rec; ccard acc; fishing; games rm; tennis; horseriding nr; bike hire; CKE. *"Well-run, clean, excel san facs; helpful, friendly staff; excel rest; access poss diff lge o'fits; kerbs to all pitches; most pitches slope badly side to side req double height ramps; no o'fits over 10m high ssn; excursions by coach inc daily to Rome or gd train service; super site."* **€37.50, 18 Apr-30 Sep, Y13.** **2019**

FIE/VOLS *1D1* (3km N Rural) *46.53334, 11.53335* **Camping Alpe di Siusi/Seiser Alm,** Loc San Constantino 16, 39050 Fiè-allo-Sciliar/Völs-am-Schlern (BZ) 0471 706459; info@camping-seiseralm.com; www.camping-seiseralm.com

🏠 €4.50 ♦♦(htd) [wc] 🏕 ♨ 🚻 🖪 🗐 ✏ [MSF] 🦋 ♈ ⓣ ⑭ ♨ 🗲 ⚠

Leave Bolzano on SS12 (not A22) sp Brixen & Brenner. After approx 7km take L fork in tunnel mouth sp Tiers, Fiè. Foll rd thro Fiè, site in 3km dir Castelrotto, sp on L. 4*, Lge, mkd, hdstg, unshd, terr, EHU (16A) metered; TV (pitch); 20% statics; phone; bus; Eng spkn; adv bkg acc; golf 1km; sauna; site clsd 5 Nov to 20 Dec; CKE. *"Well-organised site with gd views; impressive, luxury undergrnd san facs block; private san facs avail; vg walking/skiing; an amazing experience; v popular site; efficiently run!"* **€47.00, 1 Jan-2 Nov & 20 Dec-31 Dec.** **2019**

FIGLINE VALDARNO *1D3* (20km SW Rural) *43.53847, 11.41380* **Camping Orlando in Chianti,** Localita Caffggiolo, 52022 Cavriglia 055 967 422; info@ campingorlandoinchianti.it; www.campingorlandoin chianti.it

♦♦ [wc] 🏕 ♨ 🚻 🖪 ✏ [MSF] 🦋 ⓣ ⑭ ♨ 🗲

Fr A1 Firenze-Roma, exit Incisa. Foll Figline Val d'Arno. Dir Greve in Chianti, exit at Lucolena, then foll signs to 'Piano Orlando Parco Cavriglia'. Med, hdstg, mkd, shd, pt sl, EHU (16A); bbq; 10% statics; Eng spkn; adv bkg acc; CCI. *"Vg site; excel priced rest; rural; v friendly staff."* **€40.00, 25 May-13 Oct.** **2019**

FIGLINE VALDARNO *1D3* (2.5km W Rural) *43.61111, 11.44940* **Camping Norcenni Girasole Club,** Via Norcenni 7, 50063 Figline-Valdarno (FI) 055 915141; girasole@ecvacanze.it; www.ecvacanze.it

🏠 ♦♦ [wc] 🏕 ♨ 🚻 🖪 ✏ 🦋 ♈ ⓣ ⑭ ♨ 🗲 ⚠ ⚡ 🗲(covrd) 🛶

Fr a'strada A1, dir Rome, take exit 24 (sp Incisa SS69) to Figline-Valdarno; turn R in vill & foll sp to Greve; site sp Girasole; steep app rd to site with some twists for 3km. 4*, V lge, hdg, pt shd, terr, EHU (6A) inc; gas; bbq; twin axles; TV; bus to Florence; Eng spkn; adv bkg acc; ccard acc; sauna; horseriding; games area; tennis; excursions; jacuzzi; games rm; bike hire. *"Excel, well-run site; some pitches sm; fitness cent; steep site rds poss diff lge o'fits; private bthrm extra; steel pegs rec; upper level pool area excel for children; site clsd 1330-1530; site hilly; gd touring base."* **€50.00, 19 Apr-13 Oct, Y07.** **2017**

FINALE LIGURE *1B2* (1.5km N Rural) *44.18395, 8.35349* **Eurocamping Calvisio,** Via Calvisio 37, 17024 Finale-Ligure (SV) 019 601240; info@eurocamping calvisio.it; www.eurocampingcalvisio.it

🏠 ♦♦ [wc] 🏕 ♨ 🚻 🖪 ✏ 🦋 ♈ ⓣ ⑭ ♨ 🗲 ⚠ ⚡ 🗲 🛶 🏖 1 sand 2km

On SS1 Savona-Imperia, turn R at ent to Finale-Ligure; sp to site in Calvisio vill. 3*, Med, mkd, hdg, shd, EHU (6A) inc; 80% statics; adv bkg acc; ccard acc; solarium. *"Security guard at night; sep car park high ssn; clean, well-maintained san facs."* **€54.50, Easter-5 Nov.** **2016**

FIRENZE *1D3* (24km SE Rural) *43.70138, 11.40527* **Camping Village Il Poggetto,** Strada Provinciale Nr1 Aretina Km14, 50067 Troghi 055 8307323; info@campingilpoggetto.com; www.campingil poggetto.com

🏠 €2.20 ♦♦ [wc] 🏕 ♨ 🚻 🖪 ✏ [MSF] 🦋 ♈ ⓣ ⑭ ♨ 🗲 ⚠ 🛶

Fr S on E35/A1 a'strada take Incisa exit & turn L dir Incisa. After 400m turn R dir Firenze, site in 5km on L. Fr N on A1 exit Firenze-Sud dir Bagno a Ripoli/S. Donato; go thro S. Donato to Troghi, site on R, well sp. Narr, hilly app rd & sharp turn - app fr S easier. Lge, mkd, hdg, pt shd, pt sl, terr, EHU (7A) inc (poss rev pol); gas; red long stay; 5% statics; phone; bus adj; Eng spkn; adv bkg req; ccard acc; table tennis; bike hire; CKE. *"Superb, picturesque, family-run site in attractive location inc vineyard; clean, modern facs; lovely pool; bus to Florence 45mins - tickets fr recep; trains fr Incisa Valdarno (free parking at stn); excursions; gd rest; LS offers for long stay (7+ days); money exchange; vg site; helpful staff; private san facs avail; lge o'fits come fr S; highly rec."* **€37.00, 1 Apr-15 Oct.** **2017**

FORNI DI SOPRA *2E1* (2km E Rural) *46.42564, 12.56928* **Camping Tornerai,** Stinsans. Via Nazionale, 33024 Forni-di-Sopra (UD) 0433 88035; www.camping tornerai.it

12 🏠 €2 ♦♦(cont) [wc] ✏ 🦋

Site sp on SS52 Tolmezzo-Pieve di Cadore rd, 2km E of Forni-di-Sopra (approx 35km by rd fr Pieve-di-Cadore). Sm, pt shd, pt sl, EHU (2A) €1 (extra for 6A) (long lead poss req); 50% statics; Eng spkn; ccard acc. *"Conv CL-type site for Forni-di-Sopra chairlift & Passo-della-Mauria; gd san facs."* **€20.00** **2016**

GALLIPOLI *3A4* (4km SE Coastal) *39.99870, 18.02590* **Camping Baia di Gallipoli,** Litoranea per Santa Maria di Leuca, 73014 Gallipoli (LE) 0833 273210 or 338 8322910 LS; info@baiadigallipoli.com; www.baiadi gallipoli.com

🏠 €3 ♦♦(htd) [wc] 🏕 ♨ 🚻 🖪 ✏ [MSF] 🦋 ♈ ⓣ ⑭ ♨ 🗲 ⚠ ⚡ 🗲 🏖 1 sand 800m

Fr Brindisi/Lecce take S101 to Gallipoli. Exit at sp Matino-Lido Pizzo & foll sp to site, on coast rd bet Gallipoli & Sta Maria di Leuca. 4*, V lge, pt shd, EHU (6A) inc; bbq; TV; ccard acc; tennis; excursions; games area; sep car park. *"Gd site; small dogs only."* **€32.00, 1 Apr-31 Oct.** **2019**

GENOVA *1C2* (15km W Coastal) *44.41437, 8.70475* **Caravan Park La Vesima,** Via Aurelia, Km 547, 16100 Arenzano (GE) 010 6199672; info@caravanpark lavesima.it; www.caravanparklavesima.it

12 ♦♦(htd) [wc] 🏕 ♨ ✏ 🏖 ⓣ ⑭ ♨ 🗲 🏖 1 shgl adj

E of Arenzano on coast rd, clearly sp. Or leave A10 at Arenzano & go E on coast rd. 2*, Med, mkd, hdstg, unshd, EHU (3A) inc (poss rev pol); gas; 90% statics; Eng spkn; adv bkg acc; CKE. *"Useful LS NH/sh stay; gd security; gd, clean san facs; v cr, noisy high ssn; some pitches sm; vg site."* **€35.00** **2018**

GOLDRAIN 1D1 (1km SW Urban) 46.61762, 10.81859
Camping Cevedale, Via Val Venosta 59, 39021
Goldrain 0473 742132; info@camping-cevedale.com;
www.camping-cevedale.com
€4 (covrd, htd)

**SS38 Merano-Silandro, pass Latsch/Laces to rndabt
sp Goldrain/Martelltal, sp on R (do not confuse
vill of Lasa/Laas).** Med, hdg, pt shd, EHU (6A); bbq;
phone; bus/train 50m; Eng spkn; adv bkg acc. *"Excel
site."* €35.50, 15 Mar-7 Nov. 2015

GOREGLIA ANTELMINELLI 1D2 (0.8km N Rural)
44.06642, 10.52879 **Camping Pian d'Amora,** Via
Crocifisso, Loc. Pian d'Amora, 55025 Coreglia
Antelminelli 0583 78334; info@campingpiandamora.
nl; www.campingpiandamora.nl
(covrd, htd)

**Fr A11 at Lucca foll sp Val Gaifagnama SS12. After
30km at Piano di Coreglia turn N on minor rd 7km to
Coreglia Antelminelli. Site top of town.** Sm, shd, terr,
EHU (10A); Eng spkn; adv bkg acc. *"Beautiful historic
hill top town, 5 min walk; gd walking area; conv Lucca;
sm c'vans rec; excel."* €35.50, 15 Apr-1 Oct. 2015

GRAVEDONA 1C1 (3km SW Rural) 46.13268, 9.28954
Camping Magic Lake, Via Vigna del Lago 60, 22014
Dongo (CO) 034 480282; camping@magiclake.it;
www.magiclake.it
€3 (htd)

Site sp on S340d adj Lake Como. 2*, Sm, pt shd, pt sl,
EHU (6A) inc; bbq; sw nr; red long stay; TV; 40%
statics; bus 100m; Eng spkn; adv bkg acc; CKE. *"Excel,
friendly, family-run site; walk, cycle to adj vills along
lake; excel facs; v clean mod facs; bike/kayak hire on
site; bike repairs on site; helpful staff."*
€30.00, 1 Apr-10 Oct. 2016

GUBBIO 2E3 (1.2km W Urban) 43.35213, 12.56704
Camping Parking Gubbio, Via Bottagnone 06024
Area Communale P4 07 59 27 20 37
12

**Head NW on SR298 twd Via Bruno Buozzi, at rndbt
take 2nd exit onto Viale Parruccini cont for 500m,
take 1st exit at rndbt onto Viale Leonardo da Vinci,
after 250m turn L onto Via Botagore.** Sm, pt shd,.
*"Only campervan parking allowed; no san facs; gd NH;
historical town worth a visit."* €5.00 2019

IDRO 1D1 (2km NE Rural) 45.7540, 10.4981 **Rio
Vantone,** Via Vantone 45, 25074 Idro (BS) 0365 83125;
idro@azur-camping.de; www.idrosee.eu
€5

**Fr Brescia, take S237 N. At S tip of Lago d'Idro, turn
E to Idro. thro Crone, on E shore of lake, thro sh
tunnel, site 1km on L, last of 3 sites.** 4*, Lge, shd,
serviced pitches; EHU (6A) inc; gas; TV; phone; adv
bkg acc; ccard acc; games area; boat hire; windsurfing;
bike hire; tennis; CKE. *"Idyllic on lakeside with
beautiful scenery; lake adj; superb san facs; excel."*
€45.00, 20 Apr-30 Sept, Y08. 2017

IMPERIA 1B3 (1km SW Coastal) 43.86952, 7.99810
Camping de Wijnstok, Via Poggi 2, 18100 Porto-
Maurizio (IM) 0183 64986; info@campingdewijnstok.
com; www.campingdewijnstok.com
12 shgl 500m

**Exit A10/E80 Imperia W twds sea, take coast rd
SS1 Via Aurelia dir San Remo. At km 651/1 turn
dir Poggi, site sp.** Med, shd, EHU (3A) €2; gas; TV;
80% statics; phone; ccard acc; sep car park; site clsd
mid-Dec to mid-Jan. *"Shabby facs ltd LS; sm pitches
diff for lge o'fits; sh walk to town; NH only."*
€31.00 2016

ISEO 1C1 (0.5km NE Rural) 45.66416, 10.05722
Camping Iseo, Via Antonioli 57, 25049 Iseo (BS)
030 980213; info@campingiseo.it; www.camping
iseo.com
€3.50 adj

**Fr A4 exit sp Rovato & immed foll brown sp Lago
d'Iseo. Site well sp in vill.** 3*, Med, hdg, pt shd,
serviced pitches; EHU (6-10A) €2; gas; 10% statics;
phone; Eng spkn; adv bkg acc; windsurfing; golf 3km
(red for campers); games area; bike hire; CKE. *"V
scenic; friendly, welcoming owner; well-organised,
smart site; sm pitches; extra for lakeside pitches; well-
maintained, clean facs but ltd; cruises on lake; many
rests nr; excel; site next to a rlwy line, poss sm noise;
sm pitches."* €37.00, 1 Apr-1 Nov. 2017

ISEO 1C1 (0.5km NE Rural) 45.66388, 10.05638
Camping Punta d'Oro, Via Antonioli 51-53, 25049
Iseo (BS) 030 980084; info@camping-puntadoro.com;
www.puntadoro.com
€5 shgl

**Fr Brescia-Boario Terme into Iseo, look for `Camping
d'Iseo' sp on corner; after 200m cross rlwy, 1st R to
site in 400m on lakeside.** Med, pt shd, pt sl, EHU (4A)
inc; sw; Eng spkn; boating; golf 6km; CKE. *"Gd security;
beautiful area; friendly family run site, eager to help."*
€35.50, 1 Apr-15 Oct. 2017

ISEO 1C1 (1km NE Rural) 45.66527, 10.06277
Camping Quai, Via Antonioli 73, 25049 Iseo (BS) 030
9821610; info@campingquai.it; www.campingquai.it

**Fr Brescia-Boario Terme rd by-passing Iseo, take NE
exit; look for 'Camping d'Iseo' sp on corner. After
200m cross rlwy, site sp (sps obscured - go slow).
Site adj Punta d'Oro on lakeside.** 3*, Med, mkd, shd,
EHU (4A) inc (poss rev pol); bbq; sw nr; red long stay;
25% statics; phone; bus, train 1km; Eng spkn; adv bkg
acc; ccard acc; watersports; boat launch; sep car park;
games area. *"Well-kept; lake views fr some pitches;
helpful manager; some noise fr nrby rlwy."*
€35.00, 20 Apr-20 Sep. 2019

ISEO *2F2* (1km E Urban) *45.66700, 10.06766*
Camping Covelo, Via Covelo 18, 25049 Iseo **030 982
13 05**; info@campingcovelo.it; www.camping
covelo.it

♈ ⌾€3.50 ⵌ ⬛ ▲ ⬛ ⟋ ♈ ⵌ ⓗ ⬛ ⬛ ⛰

Fr A4 Bergamo-Brescia, take exit Palazzolo/SP469.
Cont Onto SP12. At rndabt take 2nd exit SPxi. Take
3rd exit at next rndabt and foll sp to camp.
Med, pt shd, EHU (6A); sw nr; Eng spkn; adv bkg acc;
ccard acc; games area. *"Excel site; v well run; adj to
lake; beautiful views; range of watersports; v helpful
staff."* **€36.00, 18 Apr-3 Nov.**   **2019**

ISEO *1C1* (1.5km W Rural) *45.65689, 10.03739*
Camping Del Sole, Via per Rovato 26, 25049 Iseo (BS)
030 980288; info@campingdelsole.it; www.camping
delsole.it

♈ ⌾€3.50 ⵌ ⬛ ▲ ⬛ ⟋ ⬛ ✦ ♈ ⓗ ⬛ ⬛ ⛰ ⌾(htd) ⬛

Exit Brescia-Milan a'strada at Rivato-Lago d'Iseo exit
& foll sp to Iseo. At complex rd junc with rndabts on
Iseo o'skirts, site ent on L (lge sp). Site bet lakeside
& rd, bef API petrol stn on R. 4*, Lge, mkd, shd, EHU
(6A) inc; sw; TV; 75% statics; Eng spkn; adv bkg acc;
ccard acc; sep car park; bike hire; waterskiing; tennis;
games area. *"Glorious views; excel facs; htd private
bthrms avail; well-run, pleasant, popular lakeside site;
pitches poss closely packed; ltd waste/water disposal;
no dogs high ssn; narr site rds."*
€46.00, 15 Apr-25 Sep.   **2017**

ISEO *1C1* (1.5km W Rural) *45.65690, 10.03429*
Camping Sassabanek, Via Colombera 2, 25049 Iseo (BS)
030 980300; sassabanek@sassabanek.it; www.sassa
banek.it

ⵌ ⬛ ▲ ⬛ ⟋ ⬛ ✦ ♈ ⓗ ⬛ ⛰ ⬛ ⬛

On periphery of Iseo by lakeside. 4*, Lge, pt shd, EHU
(6A) inc; gas; bbq; TV; 50% statics; phone; adv bkg acc;
ccard acc; boating; sep car park; bike hire; tennis;
windsurfing; sauna. *"Clean facs; sh walk to pretty
lakeside & vill; helpful staff; gd NH/sh stay; nice
location; cramped pitches; vg."*
€39.00, 1 Apr-30 Sep.   **2017**

LAZISE *1D2* (1.5km N Urban) *45.50807, 10.73166*
**Camping Lazise Campeggio Comunale (former
Municipale),** Via Roma 1, 37017 Lazise (VR) **045
7580020**; camping.municipale@comune.lazise.vr.it;
www.comune.lazise.vr.it

♈ ⌾€3 ⵌ ⬛ ▲ ⬛ ⟋ ⬛ ✦ ♈ nr ⓗ nr ⬛ nr

N on S249 fr Peschiera, thro Pacengo & Lazise, at
rndabt cont on S249 then turn L into Via Roma.
Site sp at end of rd. Care req in 100m, sharp R turn;
site ent pt hidden. 2*, Med, hdg, mkd, pt shd, EHU
(10A) inc; sw nr; 5% statics; Eng spkn; ccard acc. *"Gd
touring cent; some pitches v muddy; gd, clean facs;
friendly staff; avoid arr bef 1500 Wed (mkt on app
rd); easy walk along lake to interesting sm town."*
€33.00, 22 Mar-2 Nov.   **2018**

LAZISE *1D2* (0.9km S Rural) *45.49861, 10.7375*
Camping Du Parc, Via Gardesana, 110 I, 37017 Lazise
(VR) **045 7580127**; duparc@campingduparc.com;
www.campingduparc.com

♈ ⌾€5.70 ⵌ ⬛ ▲ ⬛ ⟋ ⬛ ♈ ♈ ⓗ ⬛ ⬛ ⛰ ⬛ ⬛

Site on W side of lakeside rd SR249. 3*, Lge, hdg, pt
shd, pt sl, EHU (5A) inc (rev pol); sw; 15% statics; Eng
spkn; adv bkg acc; ccard acc; boat hire; waterslide;
gym; bike hire; watersports. *"Sh walk to old town &
ferry terminal; lovely lakeside position; excel, well-
maintained site; vg san facs; gd size pitches, some
on lake - long walk to water point; vg pizzeria & pool;
quiet; ideal for families; gd security; Magic of Europe
discount; vg; site improved every year; most pitches
have water & drain."* **€50.00, 15 Mar-4 Nov.**   **2017**

LAZISE *1D2* (3.5km S Urban) *45.47912, 10.72635*
Camping Amici di Lazise, Loc Fossalta Nuova, Strada
del Roccolo 8, 37017 Lazise (VR) **045 6490146**; info@
campingamicidilazise.it; www.campingamicidi
lazise.it

⬛12 ♈ ⌾€4.50 ⵌ ⬛ ▲ ⬛ ⟋ ⬛ ✦ ♈ ⓗ ⬛ ⛰ ⬛ ⬛ ⬛
⬛ shgl 300m

S fr Lazise, immed bef high rest with Greek columns
(bef Gardaland) take side rd on R, site on R. 3*, Med,
pt shd, serviced pitches; EHU (6A) inc; 40% statics;
Eng spkn; adv bkg acc. *"Gd; nice friendly site; gd pool;
noise fr theme pk next door."* **€34.00**   **2016**

LECCE *3A4* (10km W Rural) *40.36417, 18.09889*
Camping Lecce Namaste, 73100 Lecce **0832 329647**;
info@camping-lecce.it; www.camping-lecce.it

⬛12 ⵌ ▲ ⟋ ✦ ⬛ nr

Fr Lecce ring rd exit junc 15 W dir Novoli, in 5km
immed after (abandoned) sm petrol stn turn R at
sp Namaste. App rd to site potholed/gravelled. Site
may appear clsd - sound horn for attention.
Sm, hdstg, pt shd, EHU (10A) inc; bus to Lecce. *"Gd,
clean site but dated facs; conv for Baroque city of
Lecce & coast around heel of Italy."* **€21.00**   **2015**

LECCO *1C1* (6km S Coastal) *45.81555, 9.39969*
Camping Village Riviera, Via Foppaola 113, 23852,
Garlate **0341 680346**; info@campingvillageriviera.
com; www.campingvillageriviera.com

♈ ⵌ (htd) ⬛ ▲ ⬛ ⟋ ♈ ⬛ nr ⬛

Head S on SS36, take exit Pescate/Lecco, cont strt,
at rndabt take 3rd exit onto Via Roma, over rndbt,
cont onto Via Statale, turn L onto Via Foppaola, site
on L. Sm, hdg, pt shd, pt sl, EHU (10A); bbq (sep area);
sw; bus; adv bkg acc; CKE. *"Lake location with free
kayak, pedalo, gym, site poor; facs dirty and unkept
(2019); very noisy day and night."* **€25.00**   **2019**

LECCO *1C1* (4km W Rural) *45.81730, 9.34307*
Camping Due Laghi, Via Isella 34, 23862 Civate (LC)
0341 550101; erealin@tin.it; www.duelaghi
camping.com

🐕 €3 ♦♦ (cont) ♨ 🖫 ∦ ⩊ 🍴 Ⓣ Ⓓ å 🛒 🚣 ⛱

S side of Lecco-Como rd on lake. Use slip rd mkd
Isella/Civate. Turn L at T-junc, then L over bdge; foll
v narr app rd to site, sp. 2*, Med, shd, pt sl, EHU (10A)
inc; gas; 80% statics; Eng spkn; games area. *"Lovely
lakeside pitches; gd facs; quiet except weekends; app to
site is v narr."* **€29.00, 28 Mar-15 Sep.** **2019**

LEVANTO *1C2* (0.4km SE Urban/Coastal) *44.16656,
9.61366* **Camping Acqua Dolce,** Via Guido Semenza 5,
19015 Levanto (SP) 0187 808465; mail@camping
acquadolce.com; www.campingacquadolce.com

12 🐕 ♦♦ 🐾 ᵬ å 🖫 ∦ 🍴 Ⓓ å 🛒 nr 🏔 🌲 sand 300m

Site sp fr town cent, app rd to Levanto steep &
winding. Site ent steep. Pls do not use sat nav fr
town. 1*, Med, hdstg, mkd, shd, terr, serviced pitches;
EHU (6A) €2.50 (rev pol); phone; Eng spkn; adv bkg
acc; ccard acc; site clsd mid-Jan to end Feb; sep car
park. *"Site ent poss diff; sm pitches; vg, modern san
facs but unisex; o'fits parked v close high ssn; pool
250m; not rec c'vans over 6m; gd touring base Cinque
Terre vills; gd walks fr site; lovely, clean beach; easy
walk to boat terminal & rlwy stn."* **€38.50** **2015**

LEVICO TERME *1D1* (1km S Rural) *46.00638, 11.28944*
Camping Lago Levico, Via Pleina 5, 38056 Levico-
Terme (TN) 0461 706934; info@campinglevico.com;
www.campinglevico.com

🐕 €2-6 ♦♦ 🐾 ♨ ᵬ å 🖫 ∦ ⩊ 🦋 ⅌ 🍴 Ⓓ å 🛒 🏔 ∥ 🚣
⛱ 🌲 shgl 200m

Foll sp to Levico fr A22 or SS12 onto SS27; site sp.
Lge, mkd, shd, serviced pitches; EHU (6A) inc; gas; bbq;
30% statics; adv bkg acc; golf 7km. *"Health spa nr;
vg; supp for lakeside pitch (no dogs on these pitches)."*
€38.00, 1 Apr-10 Oct. **2017**

LEVICO TERME *1D1* (5km SW Rural) *46.00392,
11.25838* **Camping Spiaggia,** Viale Venezia 12,
38050 Calceranica al Lago (TN) 0461 723037; info@
campingspiaggia.net; www.campingspiaggia.net

🐕 €3 ♦♦ 🐾 ♨ ∦ 🍴 🦋 🏔

Foll sp to Levico fr Trento; after exit rd turn L &
in 400m turn L foll sp to site. Site after Camping
Jolly on S side of lake. Med, mkd, hdg, pt shd, EHU
inc; sw nr; 10% statics; Eng spkn. *"Gd site; private
san facs avail; new san facs (2015) & private bthrms."*
€22.50, 10 Apr-27 Sep. **2015**

LEVICO TERME *1D1* (6km SW Urban) *46.00574,
11.24698* **Camping Penisola Verde,** Via Penisola
Verde, 5 38050 Galceranica Al Lago 0461 723272;
info@penisolaverde.it; www.penisolaverde.it

🐕 €3 ♦♦ 🐾 ♨ å ∦ 🍴 🦋 ⅌ 🍴 Ⓓ å 🏔

Exit Trento-Padova SS47 either end of lake for
Calceranica. Turn W in vill at camping sp, over rlwy
x-ing and immed L to lakeside site. 2*, Med, mkd,
hdstg, pt shd, EHU (6A); bbq; sw; twin axles;
10% statics; train 200m, bus 100m; Eng spkn; adv bkg
acc; games area. *"Mountain views across lake; beach
has sep area for sw, fishing & boating; excel."*
€36.00, 9 May-13 Sep. **2015**

LIDO DI JESOLO *2E2* (5.8km NE Coastal) *45.52862,
12.69693* **Campsite Parco Capraro,** Via Corer 2 ramo,
4 30016 Lido di Jesolo 0421 961073; info@parco
capraro.it; www.parcocapraro.it

🐕 ♦♦ 🐾 ♨ ᵬ å ∦ 🍴 🦋 ⅌ 🍴 Ⓓ å 🏔 ∥ 🚣 (htd)

Fr Jesolo head NE on Via Roma Destra twrds Via
Giotto da Bondone. Cont onto Via Loghetto, then
onto Via Cà Gamba, L onto Via Corer. Site on L.
3*, Lge, pt shd, EHU (16A); bbq; twin axles; TV; Eng
spkn; games rm; bike hire. *"Vg; v well kept family site;
public transport 1km; takeaway; path thro sm pine
forest leads to beach & bus stop to cent of town; vg
rest/bar; superb sw pool."* **€41.00, 5 Apr-15 Sep.**
2019

LIMONE SUL GARDA *1D1* (0.7km S Rural) *45.80555,
10.7875* **Camping Garda,** Via 4 Novembre, 25010
Limone-sul-Garda (TN) 0365 954550; horstmann.
hotel@tin.it

🐕 €4 ♦♦ (cont) 🐾 ♨ ᵬ å 🖫 ∦ 🦋 Ⓓ å 🛒 nr 🚣 ⛱

Site sp fr SS45b. 3*, Sm, hdstg, mkd, pt shd, pt sl, terr,
EHU (3A) €1; sw; 10% statics; Eng spkn; adv bkg acc;
bike hire; CKE. *"Splendid views; v friendly owner; clean,
well-kept site adj to lake; excel pool; tired facs but OK
(2014)."* **€38.00, 1 Apr-31 Oct.** **2015**

LUINO *1C1* (6km N Rural) *46.04189, 8.73279*
Camping Lido Boschetto Holiday, Via Pietraperzia
13, 21010 Maccagno (VA) 0332 560250; lido@
boschettoholiday.it; www.boschettoholiday.it/lido

🐕 €3 ♦♦ 🐾 ♨ ∦ 🦋 🛒 🏔

On E shore of Lake Maggiore on SS394 bet
Bellinzona & Laveno. Fr Luino pass under 2 rlwy
bdges & foll sp L twd lake, site clearly sp. Med, pt
shd, EHU (3-4A) €3.50 (poss rev pol); sw nr; 4% statics;
adv bkg acc; ccard acc; watersports; CKE. *"Hydrofoil/
ferries fr vill to all parts of lake; trains to Locarno;
barrier clsd 1300-1500, no place to pk outside; well
kept."* **€31.00, 31 Mar-22 Oct.** **2017**

MALCESINE *1D1* (0km N Urban) *45.76583, 10.81096*
Camping Villaggio Turistico Priori, Via Navene 31,
37018 Malcesine (VR) **045 7400503; info@
appartement-prioriantonio.it; www.appartement-
prioriantonio.it**

⚌⚌ [wc] ⚌ ⚌ ⚋ T nr ⊕ nr ⚌ nr

Well sp in town cent. Take care if app fr N.
1*, Sm, mkd, hdstg, pt shd, pt sl, terr, EHU (3A) inc;
sw nr; phone; Eng spkn; adv bkg acc; CKE. *"Vg; conv all
amenities & Monte Baldo funicular."*
€24.00, 15 Apr-16 Oct. 2016

"I need an on-site restaurant"

We do our best to make sure site information
is correct, but it is always best to check any
must-have facilities are still available or will
be open during your visit.

MALCESINE *1D1* (3km N Rural) *45.78971, 10.82609*
Camping Martora, Campagnola, Martora 2, 37018
Malcesine (VR) **045 4856733 or 338 1453795;
martora@martora.it; www.martora.it**

⚌⚌ [wc] ⚌ ⚋ T ⚌ ⊕ nr

**On E side of lake on rd SS249 at km 86/11. Ent up
concrete rd bet iron gates at 'Prinz Blau' sp.**
2*, Med, mkd, pt shd, pt sl, EHU (4A) inc; sw nr;
10% statics; adv bkg acc; windsurfing adj. *"Lakeside
cycle path to town."* **€27.00, 1 Apr-3 Oct.** 2016

MALS/MALLES VENOSTA *1D1* (3km S Rural)
46.67305, 10.5700 **Campingpark Gloria Vallis,**
Wiesenweg 5, 39020 Glurns/Glorenza (BZ) **0473
835160; info@gloriavallis.it; www.gloriavallis.it**

⚌ €4 ⚌⚌(htd) [wc] ⚌ ⚌ ⚋ ⚌ [MSP] ⚌ T ⚌ ⚌ /⚌ ⚋

Sp on rd S41 E of Glorenza. 4*, Med, mkd, unshd, terr,
EHU (10A) inc; gas; 5% statics; phone; Eng spkn; adv
bkg acc; ccard acc; tennis; games area; CKE. *"Excel
mountain views; dog shwr rm; higher prices in winter;
excel well run site; serviced pitches; 7 day travel pass in
'all inc' package."* **€37.00, 23 Mar-31 Oct.** 2016

MANERBA DEL GARDA *1D2* (2.5km N Rural)
45.56333, 10.56611 **Camping San Biagio,** Via Cavalle
19, 25080 Manerba-del-Garda (BS) **0365 551549;
info@campingsanbiagio.net; www.campingsan
biagio.net**

⚌ €5 ⚌⚌(htd) ⚌ ⚌ ⚋ ⚌ ⚌ /⚌ ⚌ ⚌ T ⊕ ⚌ ⚌ /⚌

**Fr S572 rd turn E at sp Manerba, site sp 1.5km N
fr Manerba.** 3*, Lge, hdstg, mkd, shd, terr, EHU (16A)
metered; bbq; sw; Eng spkn; adv bkg acc; ccard acc.
*"Terr pitches with views over Lake Garda; v clean,
modern san facs; easily got twin axle into lge pitch
(reserved); beautiful site; extra for lakeside pitches; gd
cent for touring area - Verona, Mantua, Sigurta, Torri."*
€31.00, 23 Mar-30 Sep. 2016

MANERBA DEL GARDA *1D2* (3km S Rural) *45.52555,
10.54333* **Camping Fontanelle,** Via del Magone 13,
25080 Moniga-del-Garda (BS) **0365 502079; info@
campingfontanelle.it; www.campingfontanelle.it**

⚌ €7 ⚌⚌ [wc] ⚌ ⚌ ⚋ ⚌ /⚌ [MSP] ⚌ T ⊕ ⚌ ⚌ /⚌ ⚌ ⚌

**Exit A4 m'way dir Desenzano del Garda & foll sp
Salo. In 10km arr at Moniga del Garda take 2nd exit
off 1st rndabt twd Salo, then 1st R into Via Roma sp
Moniga Centro. Immed after 'Api' g'ge on L turn R
into into Via Caccinelli; at end of this narr rd turn R
into Via del Magone; site on L by lake. Access poss
diff lge o'fits due narr vill rds.** 4*, Lge, mkd, pt shd, sl,
terr, EHU (6A) inc; gas; bbq (charcoal, gas); sw; TV;
20% statics; phone; Eng spkn; adv bkg acc; ccard acc;
tennis; fishing; golf 5km; games rm; horseriding 8km;
watersports; boat trips; CKE. *"Vg site; excursions to
Venice, Florence, Verona; bike hire 2km; friendly,
helpful staff; excel san facs; no o'fits over 6.5m high
ssn; levellers needed all pitches; extra for lakeside
pitches; pitches poss tight lge o'fits due trees; mkt Mon;
lovely site."* **€45.00, 18 Apr-26 Sep, Y01.** 2017

MANFREDONIA *2G4* (10.5km SSW Coastal)
41.55477, 15.88794 **Camping Lido Salpi,** SS159 delle
Saline Km 6,200, 71043 Manfredonia **0884 571160;
lidosalpi@alice.it; www.lidosalpi.it**

[12] ⚌ ⚌⚌ [wc] ⚌ ⚋ ⚌ /⚌ [MSP] ⚌ T ⚌ ⚌ ⚌ ⚋

**Head S on A14, exit at Foggia dir Manfredonia/
SS89. Take ramp to Manfredonia Sud and cont strt.
Turn R onto SS159, site on the R.** Sm, mkd, pt shd,
EHU (6A) €2; bbq; twin axles; 10% statics; bus 0.5km;
Eng spkn. *"V well located for San Giovanni Rotondo &
Gargano; gd o'night stop fr A14; some pitches awkward
for lge o'fits due to trees & site furniture; gd site."*
€24.00 2019

"Satellite navigation makes touring much easier"

Remember most sat navs don't know if you're
towing or in a larger vehicle – always use yours
alongside maps and site directions.

MARINA DI MINTURNO *2F4* (6km SE Coastal)
41.20731, 13.79138 **Camping Villlagio Baia Domizia,**
Via Pietre Bianche, 81030 Baia-Domizia (CE) **0823
930164; info@baiadomizia.it; www.baiadomizia.it**

⚌⚌ [wc] ⚌ ⚌ ⚋ ⚌ /⚌ [MSP] ⚌ T ⊕ ⚌ ⚌ /⚌ ⚌ ⚌ ⚌ sand adj

**Exit A1 at Cassino onto S630, twd Minturno on S7
& S7quater, turn off at km 2, then foll sp Baia
Domizia, site in 1.5km N of Baia-Domizia.** 4*, V lge,
hdg, shd, EHU (10A) inc (poss rev pol); gas; TV; ccard
acc; boat hire; windsurfing; games area; tennis; bike
hire. *"Excel facs; 30/7-16/8 min 7 night stay; site clsd
1400-1600 but adequate parking area; top class site
with all facs; gd security."* **€56.00, 19 Apr-23 Sep,
Y10.** 2017

ITALY

MARINA DI MONTENERO *2F4* (1km NW Coastal) *42.06500, 14.77700* **Centro Vacanze Molise,** SS Adriatica, Km 525, 86036 Montenero di Bisaccia **0873 803570 or 3385 408323 (mob); info@camping molise.it; www.campingmolise.it**

🏕 €1 🏃 wo 🟰 🛒 🚻 ✉ MsP ✉ 🟰 🟰 🟰 🏕 sand adj

Exit A14 at Vasto Sud to SS16 dir S. On R Centro Commerciale Costa Verde, site opp on L.
4*, Med, mkd, pt shd, EHU (3A) inc; gas; phone; bus; Eng spkn; adv bkg acc; games area; tennis; CKE. *"Excel site; helpful staff; vg beach; Aqualand Water Park nr; Tremiti Isands rec; gd touring base; conv for m'way A14."* **€33.00, 1 Jun-8 Sep.** 2015

MARTINSICURO *2F3* (1km S Urban/Coastal) *42.88027, 13.92055* **Camping Riva Nuova,** Via dei Pioppi 6, 64014 Martinsicuro (TE) **0861 797515; info@riva nuova.it; www.rivanuova.it**

🚻 wo 🟰 🛒 🚻 ✉ MsP ✉ 🟰 🟰 🟰 🟰 🟰 🟰 🟰 🏕 sand adj

Fr N exit A14/E55 sp San Benedetto-del-Tronto onto S16 dir Pescara to Martinsicuro, site sp.
3*, Lge, shd, EHU inc; TV; adv bkg acc; ccard acc; games area; excursions; gym; watersports; bike hire. *"San facs were exceptionally gd & spotless; quiet."* **€43.00, 14 May-18 Sep.** 2016

MENAGGIO *1C1* (0.5km N Rural) *46.02516, 9.23996* **Camping Europa,** Loc Leray, Via dei Cipressi 12, 22017 Menaggio (CO) **344 31187; europamenaggio@ hotmail.it**

🏕 🚻 🚻 🟰 ✉ ✉ 🟰 🟰 🟰

On ent Menaggio fr S (Como) on S240 turn R & foll 'Campeggio' sp along lakeside prom. On ent fr N turn L at 'Campeggio' sp, pass site ent & turn in boatyard. 1*, Sm, mkd, pt shd, terr, EHU; sw; 80% statics; Eng spkn; adv bkg acc; bike hire; boat hire; CKE. *"V sm pitches cramped high ssn; narr site rds diff for lge o'fits; old-fashioned facs but clean; poor security; helpful owner; m'vans rec to arr full of water & empty of waste; hardly any rd noise, Menaggio delightful place; v friendly."* **€26.50, 25 Mar-30 Sep.** 2016

MERANO/MERAN *1D1* (5km E Rural) *46.67144, 11.20091* **Camping Hermitage,** Via Val di Nova 29, 39012 Meran **0473 232191; info@einsiedler.com; www.einsiedler.com**

🏕 €3 🚻 wo 🟰 🟰 🟰 ✉ MsP 🟰 ✉ ✉ 🟰 🟰

Exit SS38 at Meran Süd & foll sp twds Merano to Meran 2000 past Trautmannsdorf. Site sp.
4*, Med, mkd, hdstg, pt shd, terr, EHU (10-16A); bbq; twin axles; phone; bus 100m; adv bkg acc; bike hire; sauna. *"Tennis; serviced pitches; mountain views; hotel facs avail to campers; forest walk; ACSI site; excel."* **€40.00, 8 Apr-5 Nov.** 2018

MERANO/MERAN *1D1* (1km S Urban) *46.66361, 11.15638* **Camping Merano,** Via Piave/Piavestrasse 44, 39012 Merano/Meran (BZ) **0473 231249; info@meran.eu; www.merano-suedtirol.it**

12 🐕 €3.30 🚻 wo 🟰 ✉ ✉ ✉ nr ✉ nr 🟰 🟰 (htd)

Exit S38 at Merano Sud & foll rd into town. Brown site sps to Camping & Tennis (no name at main juncs in town cent). Site ent mkd 'Camping Tennis'. Site also sp fr N. 3*, Med, hdstg, pt shd, EHU (6A) €3; red long stay; phone; tennis adj; CKE. *"Sh walk to town cent; fine site surrounded by spectacular mountain scenery; helpful staff; pitches soft after rain; gd clean san facs; helpful staff; 10% surcharge for 1 night; excel thermal baths; take car pk ticket to acc site recep at barrier, ticket to exit car park provided free at recep."* **€29.00** 2015

MERANO/MERAN *1D1* (15km S Rural) *46.59861, 11.14527* **Camping Völlan,** Zehentweg 6, 39011 Völlan/Foiana **0473 568056; info@camping-voellan.com; www.camping-voellan.com**

🏕 €3 🚻 wo 🟰 🟰 ✉ MsP 🦋 ✉ nr ✉ 🟰 🟰

Leave S38 dual c'way (Merano-Bolzano) S of Merano sp Lana. Drive thro Lana, turn uphill sp Gampenpass. Turn R sp Foliana/Völlan & foll sp to site. 3*, Sm, mkd, pt shd, terr, serviced pitches; EHU (4A) €2.50; 10% statics; phone; Eng spkn; golf 6km; CKE. *"Long drag up to site fr Lana, but worth it; beautiful situation o'looking Adige Valley; excel facs & pool; barriers clsd 1300-1500 & 2200-0700; v helpful owners; some pitches with steep acc & tight for lge units."* **€42.80, 23 Mar-4 Nov.** 2019

MESTRE *2E2* (4km E Urban) *45.48425, 12.28227* **Camping Rialto,** 16 Via Orlanda, Loc Campalto, 30175 Mestre (VE) **041 5420295; rialto@camping.it; www.campingrialto.com**

🏕 €3 🚻 wo 🟰 🟰 ✉ MsP 🟰 🟰

Fr A4 take Marco Polo Airport exit, then fork R onto SS14 dir Venice. Site on L 1km past Campalto opp lge car sales area, well sp. Do not enter Mestre. Med, pt shd, EHU (15A) €1.50; phone; bus to Venice; Eng spkn; adv bkg acc; CKE. *"Site in need of refurb but v conv Venice; bus tickets fr recep; friendly, helpful staff; vg san facs, vg rest; rec."* **€33.00, 7 Apr-31 Oct.** 2019

MESTRE *2E2* (5.5km SW Urban) *45.47138, 12.21166* **Camping Jolly delle Querce,** Via G De Marchi 7, 30175 Marghera (VE) **041 920312; campingjolly@ ecvacanze.it; www.ecvacanze.it**

12 🐕 🚻 wo 🟰 🟰 ✉ ✉ MsP 🟰 ✉ ✉ 🟰 🟰 🟰 🟰

App fr Milan, exit A4/E70 immed after toll, sp Mestre/Ferrovia/Marghera, then onto SS309 at rndabt sp Chioggia, then 1st R, site sp on R. 2*, Med, hdg, hdstg, mkd, unshd, EHU (4-16A) inc (rev pol); gas; bbq; twin axles; 50% statics; Eng spkn; adv bkg acc. *"Bus to Venice 15 min walk; excel modern facs block; v noisy fr adj airport & m'way; beach volleyball court; hydromassage tub; gd."* **€38.00** 2016

MILANO *1C2* (8km W Urban) *45.47390, 9.08233*
Camping Citta di Milano, Via Gaetano Airaghi 61,
20153 Milano **0248 207017; info@campingmilano.it;**
www.campingmilano.it

12 ⛺ 🚐 €3.50 ♦♦♦ [wc] 🚿 ♨ 🛒 ⊘ / [MP] 🍴 ⓘ 🐾 nr

Fr E35/E62/A50 Tangentiale Ovest ring rd take
Settimo-Milanese exit & foll sp San Siro along Via
Novara (SS11). Turn R in 2km at Shell petrol stn,
then R at traff lts in 500m & L to site in 600m. Site
ent at Gardaland Waterpark, poorly sp. 4*, Lge, mkd,
hdstg, pt shd, EHU (6A) inc; phone; bus 500m; Eng
spkn; ccard acc; CKE. *"Gd san facs; noise fr adj concerts*
high ssn; conv bus/metro Milan; penned animals for kid
to enjoy; rd, aircraft noise, disco at w/end & waterpark
adj; gd security; peacocks roaming site; excel well
organised site; gd for NH." **€33.00** **2018**

MONTEFORTINO *2E3* (0.8km W Rural) *42.94495,*
13.34017 **Camping Sibilla,** Via Tenna, 63858
Montefortino FM **3387695040; info@camping**
sibilla.it; www.campingsibilla.it

⛺ ♦♦♦ [wc] 🚿 ♨ 🛒 ⊘ / [MP] 🍴

A14 exit Civitanova Marche. M'way Macerata take
Sarnano exit and on to Amondola. Foll sp for
Montefortino. In about 5km, fork R after IP g'ge.
Site 200m on L. Med, mkd, hdstg, pt shd, terr, EHU
(6A) inc; bbq; twin axles; TV; bus 0.8km; Eng spkn; adv
bkg acc; CKE. *"New site opened June 2016; great*
mountain views; family owned; excel site."
€25.00, 1 May-10 Nov. **2016**

NATURNO/NATURNS *1D1* (0.5km S Rural) *46.6475,*
11.00722 **Camping Adler,** Via Lido 14, 39025
Naturno (BZ) **0473 667242; info@campingadler.com;**
www.campingadler.com

⛺ 🚐 €2.50 ♦♦♦ (htd) [wc] 🚿 ♨ 🛒 ⊘ / [MP] 🦋 🍴 ⓘ nr 🐾 nr

Fr E on SS38 turn L at rndabt into Naturno, L at traff
lts & foll sp to site. Fr W after passing thro tunnel
bypass, turn R at rndabt then as above.
4*, Med, mkd, pt shd, EHU (4-6A) €3.90; twin axles;
TV; 10% statics; bus/train 500m; Eng spkn; adv bkg
acc; ccard acc; CKE. *"Well-kept site; conv town cent;*
gd hill walks; htd pool 300m; friendly staff; off clsd
1230-1500; cable car nrby; excel."
€33.00, 15 Mar-15 Nov. **2015**

NICOTERA *3B4* (3km S Coastal) *38.50755, 15.92666*
Camping Villaggio Mimosa, Mortelletto, 89844
Nicotera Marina (VV) **0963 81397; info@villaggio**
mimosa.com

12 🐕 ⛺ ♦♦♦ [wc] 🚿 ♨ 🛒 ⊘ / [MP] 🍴 🍴 ⓘ 🐾 /□ 🏊 🚣 🛶

🏖 sand adj

Exit A3/E45 at Rosarno exit. Cross S18 & site sp dir
San Ferdinando Porto. Foll sp on SP50 for approx
7km. 3*, Sm, mkd, pt shd, EHU (12A); gas; bbq; twin
axles; 40% statics; Eng spkn; games area; tennis; bike
hire; boat hire; windsurfing; CKE. *"Some pitches have*
tight corners for lge o'fits; gd site." **€42.00** **2019**

ORBETELLO *1D4* (5.5km N Coastal) *42.46341,*
11.18597 **Camping Village Obertello,** Strada Gianella
166, 58015 Orbetello **0564 820 201; orbetello**
campingvillage@clubdelsole.com; www.orbetello
campingvillage.it

♦♦♦ [wc] 🚿 ♨ 🛒 🛒 ⊘ / [MP] 🦋 🍴 ⓘ 🐾 /□ 🛶 (htd)

📷 🐾 adj

Fr SS1 Aurelia take exit Albinia. Cont twds Porto
Santo Stefano. Campsite on L after 5km.
V lge, hdstg, mkd, pt shd, EHU (6A); bbq; cooking facs;
TV; Eng spkn; adv bkg acc; games area; bike hire; CCI.
€62.00, 19 Apr-27 Sep. **2019**

ORTA SAN GIULIO *1B1* (0.5km N Rural) *45.80125,*
8.42093 **Camping Orta,** Via Domodossola 28, Loc
Bagnera, 28016 Orta San Giulio (NO) **0322 90267;**
info@campingorta.it; www.campingorta.it

⛺ 🚐 €4 ♦♦♦ (htd) [wc] 🚿 ♨ 🛒 ⊘ / 🍴 ⓘ nr 🐾 /□

Fr Omegna take rd on SS229 for 10km to km 44.5 sp
Novara. Site both sides of rd 500m bef rndabt at
Orta x-rds. Recep on L if heading S; poor access
immed off rd. Med, pt shd, pt sl, terr, EHU (3-6A)
€2.50; gas; sw nr; Eng spkn; adv bkg acc. *"Popular site*
in beautiful location; sm pitches; narr site rds & tight
corners; arr early for lakeside pitch (extra charge);
slipway to lake; friendly, helpful owner; Orta a gem;
waterskiing; noise fr Beach Club at night; €4.50 for
lakeside pitches; lakeside walk round peninsular;
rec Sacre Monte for St Francis."
€38.00, 8 Mar-31 Dec. **2019**

ORTA SAN GIULIO *1B1* (2km N Rural) *45.81212,*
8.41076 **Camping Verde Lago,** Corso Roma 76, 28028
Pettenasco (NO) **0323 89257; campingverdelago@**
campingverdelago.it; www.campingverdelago.it

♦♦♦ [wc] 🚿 ♨ 🛒 ⊘ / 🍴 ⓘ 🐾 /□

Site bet SS229 & lake at km 46, 500m S of
Pettenasco on Orta Lake. Gd access. Sm, pt shd, pt
sl, EHU (6A) €2.50; bbq; sw nr; TV; 60% statics; Eng
spkn; ccard acc; games rm. *"Vg family-run site; friendly,*
helpful; clean facs but dated; beach; boat mooring;
recep 0930-1200 & 1630-1900; excel rest; beautiful
setting by lake; if visiting Orta by car take lots of €1
coins for parking; excel." **€38.00, 25 Mar-16 Oct.**
2016

OSTRA *2E3* (0.2km SW Rural) *43.61032, 13.15351*
Camping 'L Prè, Viale Matteotti 45, 60010 Ostra
(AN) **071 68045; info@lpre.it; www.lpre.it**

⛺ ♦♦♦ [wc] 🚿 ⊘ / ⓘ nr 🐾 nr

Exit A14 at Senigallia onto S360. After approx 10km
turn R to Ostra. Sp in vill. 2*, Sm, pt shd, terr, EHU
(3A) €2.50; red long stay; games rm. *"Gd san facs;*
very friendly owners; lovely, quiet, simple site with
easy access Ancona, Esini Valley; beautiful views over
valley; gd for cyclists; gd place to relax after Venice."
€24.00, 1 Apr-30 Sep. **2019**

ITALY

PAESTUM *3A3* (4km N Coastal) *40.42780, 14.98244*
Camping Villaggio Ulisse, Via Ponte di Ferro, 84063 Paestum (SA) **0828 851095; info@campingulisse.com; www.campingulisse.com**

🛖 🏕 ⬥ 🆑 🚿 ⚕ 📶 🐕 ⟟ ⓗ 🗑 🕱 🅿 🛒 sand adj

Foll site sp in cent Paestum, well sp. 3*, Lge, shd, EHU (3A) inc; 80% statics; games area; CKE. *"Direct access to beautiful beach; gd, clean, lovely, friendly site; cash only; gd rest."* **€36.00, 1 Apr-30 Sep.** **2018**

PAESTUM *3A3* (5km WNW Coastal) *40.42896, 14.98214*
Campsite Athena, Via Ponte di Ferro, 84063 Paestum **0828 851105; vathena@tiscali.it; www.camping athena.com**

🛖 🏕 wc ⬥ 🆑 🚿 ⚕ 📶 ⟟ 🕱 ⓗ 🗑 🛒

Site 50km S of Salerno. Foll a'strada to Battipaglia onto main rd to Paestum. Head S on SS18. At rndabt take 1st exit onto SP276, then at next rndabt take 1st exit onto Via della Repubblica. Go thro 1 rndabt, turn L onto SP175, at rndabt take 1st exit onto Via Marittima, L onto Via Poseidonia and 1st L onto Via Ponte di Ferro. Site on R. 3*, Med, pt shd, EHU (5A); twin axles; Eng spkn; CKE. *"Gd site, direct access to beach; takeaway."* **€36.00, 1 Apr-31 Oct.** **2019**

PAESTUM *3A3* (5km NW Coastal) *40.41330, 14.99140*
Camping Villaggio Dei Pini, Via Torre, 84063 Paestum (SA) **0828 811030; info@campingvillaggiodeipini. com; www.campingvillaggiodeipini.com**

12 🛖 🏕 wc ⬥ 🆑 🚿 ⚕ 📶 🐕 ⟟ ⓗ 🗑 🕱 🅿 🛒 🚣 🅿 sand adj

Site 50km S of Salerno in vill of Torre-de-Paestum. Foll a'strada to Battipaglia onto main rd to Paestum, site sp bef Paestum on rd S18, foll to beach. 3*, Med, hdg, mkd, shd, EHU (6A) inc; bbq; 30% statics; phone; adv bkg acc; ccard acc; games area; CKE. *"Historical ruins nr; narr access rd fr vill due parked cars; lge o'fits may grnd at ent; some sm pitches - c'vans manhandled onto pitches; no dogs Jul/Aug; pleasant site by beach; gd rest; helpful owner; rec."* **€45.00** **2019**

PALMI *3B4* (7km N Coastal) *38.39317, 15.86280*
Sosta Camper Prajola, Lungomare Costa Viola, 4, 89015 Palmi RC **03662 529692; sostacamper.praiola@ gmail.com**

12 🐕 🏕 wc ⬥ 🚿 📶 ⟟ 🅿 opp

Sp fr camp site San Fantino (Palmi), on beach front, down the hill in 2km. Sm, hdstg, pt shd, EHU (6A); bbq; twin axles. *"Gd basic NH to & fr Sicily; fair."* **2016**

PALMI *3B4* (9.5km N Coastal) *38.40676, 15.86912*
Villaggio Camping La Quiete, Contrada Scinà, 89015 Palmi (RC) **0966 479400; info@villaggio laquiete.it; www.villaggiolaquiete.it**

🛖 🏕 wc ⬥ 🆑 🚿 ⚕ ⟟ 🕱 ⓗ 🗑 🅿 sand 200m

N fr Lido-di-Palmi on Contrada Pietrenere coast rd dir Gioia Tauro, site sp. 3*, Lge, hdstg, pt shd, EHU (10A) €3; gas; red long stay; 5% statics; phone; Eng spkn; adv bkg acc; ccard acc; CKE. *"Sm pitches; fair sh stay/NH; friendly owner; pitches in ctr of little cottages."* **€30.00, 1 May-31 Oct.** **2018**

PASSIGNANO SUL TRASIMENO *2E3* (1km E Rural) *43.18338, 12.15085* **Camping Kursaal,** Viale Europa 24, 06065 Passignano-sul-Trasimeno (PG) **075 828085; info@campingkursaal.it; www.camping kursaal.it**

🛖 €1.50 🏕 wc ⬥ 🆑 🚿 ⚕ 📶 ⟟ 🕱 ⓗ 🗑 🕱 🅿 🚣

Fr Perugia on S75 to Lake Trasimeno. Exit at Passignano-Est twd lake; site on L past level x-ing adj hotel, well sp. 3*, Med, mkd, hdg, pt shd, pt sl, EHU (6A) €2 (poss rev pol); TV; phone; Eng spkn; adv bkg req; ccard acc; bike hire; CKE. *"Pleasant, lovely site in gd position; vg rest; some pitches have lake view; ltd space & pitches tight; gd clean site; vg san facs; great pool."* **€36.00, 24 Mar-04 Nov.** **2018**

PERTICARA *2E3* (2km N Rural) *43.89608, 12.24302*
Camping Perticara, Via Serra Masini 10/d, 47863 Perticara (PS) **0335 7062260; info@camping perticara.com; www.campingperticara.com**

🛖 🏕 (htd) wc ⬥ 🚿 🆑 📶 🐕 ⟟ 🕱 🗑 🕱 🅿 🚣 🅿 ⛴

Fr A14 at Rimini take S258 to Novafeltria. Foll sp Perticara & site. Steep, hairpins on pt of rte. 3*, Med, hdstg, hdg, mkd, unshd, terr, serviced pitches; EHU (10A) inc; gas; TV; 5% statics; phone; bus; Eng spkn; adv bkg acc; ccard acc; CKE. *"Clean, well-maintained, scenic site; hospitable Dutch owners; many activities arranged; immac san facs; poss diff egress to SW (hairpins with passing places) - staff help with 4x4 if necessary; rough terrain; excl; well run."* **€38.00, 13 May-20 Sep.** **2016**

PESCHIERA DEL GARDA *1D2* (1km N Urban) *45.44780, 10.70195* **Camping del Garda,** Via Marzan 6, 37019 Castelnuovo-del-Garda (VR) **045 7551682; info@camping-delgarda.com; www.camping delgarda.it**

🏕 wc ⬥ 🆑 🚿 ⚕ 📶 🐕 🕱 ⓗ 🗑 🕱 🅿 🅿 🚣 shgl

Exit A4/E70 dir Peschiera onto SR249 dir Lazise. Turn L in 500m dir Lido Campanello, site in 1km on L on lakeside. 4*, V lge, shd, EHU (4A) inc; gas; sw; 60% statics; phone; adv bkg acc; games area; tennis. *"Busy, well-organised site; helpful staff, discount snr citizens; gd rest; walking & cycling rtes adj; conv Verona."* **€60.00, 1 Apr-5 Nov.** **2017**

PESCHIERA DEL GARDA *1D2* (1km N Rural) *45.46722, 10.71638* **Eurocamping Pacengo,** Via del Porto 13, 37010 Pacengo (VR) **045 7590012; info@ eurocampingpacengo.it; www.eurocamping pacengo.it**

🛖 €2.40 🏕 wc ⬥ 🆑 🚿 ⚕ 📶 🐕 🕱 ⓗ 🗑 🕱 🅿 🅿

On SS249 fr Peschiera foll sp to Gardaland, Pacengo in 1km. Turn L at traff lts in cent of vill, site on L. 3*, Lge, mkd, pt shd, sl, EHU (4A) inc; sw nr; 25% statics; phone; Eng spkn; adv bkg acc; boat launch; CKE. *"Well-equipped site on shore Lake Garda; helpful staff; some sm pitches; pool adj; espec gd end of ssn; excel rest; conv Verona."* **€36.50, 11 Apr-30 Sep.** **2019**

For a guide to symbols see the fold out on the rear cover

PESCHIERA DEL GARDA *1D2* (6km NE Rural) *45.46472, 10.71416* **Camping Le Palme,** Via del Tronchetto 2, 37017 Pacengo (VR) **045 7590019; info@lepalmecamping.it; www.lepalmecamping.it**

🏕 €4.60 ‖‖ ⅏ ♨ ♿ ⊟ ⩕ ⌘ ⵏ ⊕nr ⫯ ⵤ ⚠ ⵘ(htd) ⌂

A4/E70 exit at Peschiera onto SS249, sp Lazise. Site sp bef Pacengo in approx 5km. 3*, Lge, mkd, pt shd, terr, serviced pitches; EHU (6A) inc; sw nr; 40% statics; Eng spkn; adv bkg acc; ccard acc; waterslide. *"Well-maintained site; excel, clean facs; extra for lakeside pitches; helpful staff; sh walk to vill; 4 theme parks nr; excel."* **€37.00, 27 Mar-26 Oct.** **2015**

PESCHIERA DEL GARDA *1D2* (6km W Coastal) *45.45120, 10.66557* **Camping Wien,** Loc. Fornaci, 37019 Peschiera (VR) **045 7550379; info@camping wien.it**

🏕 ‖‖ ⅏ ♿ ⩕ ⌘ 🦋 ♔ ⵏ ⊕ ⫯ ⵤ ⚠ ⵙ ⵘ ⵏshgl adj

On Verona-Brescia rd (not a'strada) W of Peschiera, turn R at San Benedetto, turn R 400m after traff lts, site has 2 ents 100m apart. Med, mkd, hdstg, shd, pt sl, EHU inc (3A); gas; red long stay; 50% statics; phone; bus adj; Eng spkn; adv bkg acc; boating; games area; fishing; ice; CKE. *"Wonderful pool o'looking Lake Garda; walking/cycle path into town; vg site; busy high ssn."* **€40.00, 9 Apr-30 Sep.** **2017**

PESCHIERA DEL GARDA *1D2* (2km NW Urban) *45.44825, 10.66978* **Camping San Benedetto,** Strada Bergamini 14, 37019 San Benedetto (VR) **045 7550544; info@campingsanbenedetto.it; www.campingsanbenedetto.it**

🏕 €1.50-2 ‖‖ ⅏ ⩕ ⌘ 🦋 ♔ ⵏ ⊕ ⫯ ⵤ ⚠ ⵙ ⵘ

Exit A4/E70 dir Peschiera-del-Garda, turn N at traff lts in cent of vill, site on lake at km 274/V111 on rd S11. 3*, Lge, shd, pt sl, EHU (3A) inc; 30% statics; adv bkg acc; games area; bike hire; boat hire; canoeing; windsurfing. *"Pleasant, well-run; sm harbour; site clsd 1300-1500; excel modern rest beside lake; excel new san facs (2017)."* **€44.60, 1 Apr-8 Oct.** **2017**

PIEVE TESINO *1D1* (6km N Rural) *46.11361, 11.61944* **Villaggio Camping Valmalene,** Loc Valmalene, 38050 Pieve-Tesino (TN) **0461 594214; info@valmalene.com; www.valmalene.com**

12 🏕 €5 ‖‖(htd) ⅏ ♨ ♿ ⩕ ⌘ 🦋 ♔ ⵏ ⊕ ⫯ ⵤ ⚠ ⵙ(htd) ⌂

Fr Trento E for 50km on S47. Turn N at Strigno to Pieve-Tesino, site sp. 3*, Med, mkd, pt shd, EHU inc; 10% statics; adv bkg rec; ccard acc; site clsd Nov; sauna; fitness rm; bike hire; games area; tennis. *"Gd base for summer & winter hols; private bthrms avail."* **€32.00** **2016**

PISA *1C3* (1km N Urban) *43.72416, 10.3830* **Camp Torre Pendente,** Viale delle Cascine 86, 56122 Pisa **050 561704; info@campingtorrependente.com; www.campingtorrependente.com**

🏕 €1.60 ‖‖ ⅏ ♨ ♿ ⊟ ⩕ ⌘ ♔ ⵏ ⊕ ⫯ ⵤ ⚠ ⵙ

Exit A12/E80 Pisa Nord onto Via Aurelia (SS1). After 8km & after x-ing rlwy bdge, turn L after passing Pisa sp at traff lts. Site on L, sp. 1*, Lge, mkd, pt shd, EHU (5A) inc (poss rev pol); gas; bbq; red long stay; TV; phone; Eng spkn; ccard acc; bike hire; CKE. *"Gd base Pisa; leaning tower 15 mins walk; immac, modern, well-maintained san facs; private san facs avail; pitches typically 50sqm; poss tight lge o'fits due narr site rds & corners; many pitches shd by netting; site rds muddy after rain; friendly staff; excel, well-run site; 300m fr Pisa San Rossore rlwy stn, trains to Lucca etc."* **€39.00, 1 Apr-4 Nov.** **2019**

PISTOIA *1D3* (10km S Rural) *43.84174, 10.91049* **Camping Barco Reale,** Via Nardini 11, 51030 San Baronto-Lamporecchio (PT) **0573 88332; info@ barcoreale.com; www.barcoreale.com**

🏕 ‖‖ ⅏ ♨ ♿ ⊟ ⩕ ⌘ 🦋 ♔ ⵏ ⊕ ⫯ ⵤ ⚠ ⵙ

Leave A11 at Pistoia junc onto P9 & foll sp to Vinci, Empoli & Lamporecchio to San Baronto. In vill turn into rd by Monti Hotel & Rest, site sp. Last 3km steep climb. 4*, Lge, mkd, shd, pt sl, terr, serviced pitches; EHU (3-6A) inc (poss rev pol); gas; red long stay; phone; Eng spkn; adv bkg req; ccard acc; bike hire; games area; CKE. *"Excel site in Tuscan hills; helpful staff; gd touring base; excel mother & fam bthrm; vg rest; poss diff access some pitches but towing help provided on request; unsuitable lge o'fits; well-organised walking & bus trips; excel pool."* **€45.50, 1 Apr-30 Sep.** **2019**

POGGIBONSI *1D3* (12km N Rural) *43.58198, 11.13801* **Camping Panorama Del Chianti,** Via Marcialla 349, 50020 Marcialla-Certaldo (FI) **0571 669334; info@ campingchianti.it; www.campingchianti.it**

🏕 €2 ‖‖ ⅏ ⩕ ⌘ 🦋 ♔ ⵏ ⊕nr ⵤ ⵙ

Fr Florence-Siena a'strada exit sp Tavarnelle. On reaching Tavernelle turn R sp Tutti Direzione/ Certaldo & foll by-pass to far end of town. Turn R sp to Marcialla, in Marcialla turn R to Fiano, site in 1km. NB Some steep hairpins app site fr E. 2*, Med, mkd, hdstg, pt shd, terr, EHU (3A) inc; red long stay; phone; Eng spkn; adv bkg acc; bike hire; CKE. *"Gd tourist info (in Eng); sports facs in area; cultural sites; helpful staff; friendly owner; san facs clean - hot water to shwrs only; 4 excel rests nr; panaromic views; midway bet Siena & Florence; popular site - arr early to get pitch; facs need updating."* **€36.00, 1 Apr-1 Nov.** **2019**

ITALY

ITALY

POMPEI *3A3* (1km S Urban) *40.74638, 14.48388*
Camping Spartacus, Loc Pompei Scavi, Via Plinio 127,
80045 Pompei (NA) **081 8624078; staff@camping
spartacus.it; www.campingspartacus.it**

12 ♦♦ ⌷ wo ♨ ♿ ◨ ⊘ ∥ MSP ♈ 🐾 nr

Fr N on A3 exit Pompei Ovest. At T-junc turn L & site
on R just after passing under rlwy bdge. Fr S exit
Pompei Est & foll sp Pompei Scavi (ruins). Sat nav
may lead to low bdge. 3*, Sm, mkd, shd, EHU (5A)
€2.3.(poss rev pol); gas; TV; Eng spkn; adv bkg acc;
ccard acc; CKE. *"Nice, family-run, welcoming site, 50m
fr historical ruins; conv train to Naples, boats to Capri;
stray dogs poss roam site & ruins; v popular with
students high ssn; rest, snacks, bar in high ssn; best of
3 town sites; gd site for exploring area; friendly owners;
clean san facs; steep access rd."* **€34.00** 2015

PORLEZZA *1C1* (4km E Rural) *46.04074, 9.16827*
Camping Ranocchio, Via Al Lago 7,22010 Loc Piano
di Porlezza, Carlazzo (CO) **0344 70385 or 62611;
campeggioranocchio@gmail.com; www.camping
ranocchio.com**

🐕 €2 ♦♦ ⌷ (htd) wo ♨ ♨ ♿ ◨ ⊘ ∥ 🦋 ♈ 🍴 ⵉ ⊕ ♨ 🐾 ⛰ 🚣 ⛵

On main rd bet Menaggio & Porlezza. Ent in vill of
Piano on S side. Sp. Steep app in Lugano with
hairpin bends; 15% gradient. V narr rd fr Lugano
- clsd to c'vans at peak times. 2*, Lge, mkd, unshd,
pt sl, terr, EHU inc (6A); gas; sw; TV; Eng spkn;
horseriding 2km; fishing; CKE. *"Friendly recep; gd for
exploring Como & Lugano; steamer trips on both lakes;
lovely, v attractive site; helpful recep; excel corner shop
& rest; vg."* **€29.50, 1 Apr-30 Sep.** 2019

PORTO RECANATI *2F3* (4km N Coastal) *43.47123,
13.64150* **Camping Bellamare,** Lungomare Scarfiotti
13, 62017 Porto-Recanati (MC) **071 976628; info@
bellamare.it; www.bellamare.it**

♦♦ ⌷ wo ♨ ♿ ◨ ∥ ♈ ⵉ ⊕ ♨ 🐾 ⛰ 🚣 ⛵ ♈ shgl

Exit A14/E55 Loreto/Porto-Recanati; foll sp
Numana & Sirolo; camp on R in 4km on coast rd.
3*, Lge, unshd, EHU (6A) €3; gas; 10% statics; phone;
Eng spkn; ccard acc; games area; games rm; bike
hire; CKE. *"V well-run & laid out site on beach; NH
tariff of €17-28 (inc elec) for a pitch at the edge of
the site but OK; beach access; gd facs & security."*
€39.00, 29 Mar-7 Oct. 2018

PORTOFERRAIO *1C3* (9km E Rural) *42.80072,
10.36452* **Rosselba Le Palme,** Loc. Ottone 3, 57037
Elba Portoferraio **0565 933 101; info@rosselbale
palme.it; www.rosselbalepalme.it**

♦♦ ⌷ wo ♨ ◨ ∥ MSP 🦋 ♈ ⵉ ⊕ ♨ 🐾 ⛰ ♈ ⛵ ♈ sand 0.5km

Fr ferry terminal foll signs 'tutti direzioni'. At 3rd
rndabt head twds Porto Azzurro. Take L fork to
Bagnaia. Site sp. 3*, Sm, hdg, pt shd, terr, EHU (6A);
twin axles; 80% statics; bus adj; Eng spkn; adv bkg acc;
CCI. *"Ferry service fr Piombino every 1/2 hr; statics
enhance site facs."* **€55.00, 20 Apr-30 Sep.** 2019

POZZA DI FASSA *1D1* (0.5km SW Rural) *46.42638,
11.68527* **Camping Catinaccio Rosengarten,** Via
Avisio 15, 38036 Pozza-di-Fassa (TN) **0462 763305;
info@catinacciorosengarten.com; www.catinaccio
rosengarten.com**

🐕 €4 ♦♦ ⌷ ♨ ◨ ⊘ ∥ MSP 🦋 ♈ ⵉ ⊕ nr 🐾 nr

Fr S SS48 site sp just after San Giovanni.
1*, Lge, hdstg, pt shd, EHU (2A) inc (extra for higher
amperage); red long stay; 30% statics; Eng spkn; adv
bkg req; ccard acc; site clsd Oct; CKE. *"Superb scenery;
helpful staff; luxury san facs; free taxi (2018) to Vigo
di Fassa cable car; ski lift 1km; pool 300m; excel site; v
convly sited for access to vill & public transport; 20 min
walk to Buffaure cable car; ski bus; off clsd 1230-1500."*
€35.50, 1 Jan-30 Apr, 1 Jun-15 Oct, 1 Dec-31 Dec.
2018

PRATO ALLO STELVIO *1D1* (0.5km NW Rural)
46.62472, 10.59388 **Camping Kiefernhain,** Via Pineta
37, 39026 Prato-allo-Stélvio (BZ) **0473 616422;
reception@camping-kiefernhain.it; www.camping-
kiefernhain.it**

🐕 €4 ♦♦ ⌷ ♨ ♨ ♿ ◨ ∥ MSP 🦋 ♈ ⵉ ⊕ nr ♨ 🐾 ⛰ 🚣 (htd)

Fr rd S40 turn SW at Spondigna onto rd S38 dir
Stélvio, site sp in vill. Lge, mkd, pt shd, EHU (6A)
€2.50; bbq; red long stay; phone; Eng spkn; adv bkg
rec; waterslide; dog shwrs. *"V modern, clean san facs;
superb views; sports cent adj; private bthrms avail;
facs stretched high ssn; vg value."*
€52.50, 1 May-4 Oct. 2019

PRECI *2E3* (3km NW Rural) *42.88808, 13.01483*
Camping Il Collaccio, 06047 Castelvecchio-di-Preci
(PG) **0743 665108; info@ilcollaccio.com;
www.ilcollaccio.com**

🐕 ♦♦ ⌷ (htd) wo ♨ ♨ ♿ ◨ ∥ MSP 🦋 ⵉ ⊕ ♨ 🐾 ⛰ 🚣

S fr Assisi on S75 & S3, turn off E sp Norcia, Cascia.
Then foll sp for Visso on S209. In approx 30km turn
R for Preci, then L, site sp. Rte is hilly.
4*, Med, mkd, pt shd, terr, EHU (6A) inc (long lead
poss req); TV; 20% statics; phone; Eng spkn; adv bkg
acc; ccard acc; bike hire; horseriding; tennis; games
area; CKE. *"Beautiful views; well-maintained, clean
site; pleasant rest; maganificent pool area; sm pitches;
gd walking in Monti Sibillini National Park; paragliding;
conv Assisi & historic hill towns; excel; well run."*
€35.00, 1 Apr-30 Sep. 2015

PREDAZZO *1D1* (2.5km E Rural) *46.31027, 11.63138*
Camping Valle Verde, Loc Ischia 2, Sotto Sassa, 38037
Predazzo (TN) **0462 502394; info@campingvalle
verde.it; www.campingvalleverde.it**

🐕 €3.50 ♦♦ ⌷ (htd) wo ♨ ♿ ◨ ∥ MSP 🦋 ♈ ⵉ ⊕ ♨ ⛰

Exit A22 dir Ora onto rd S48 dir Cavalese/Predazzo.
Fr Predazzo take SS50 E, turn R in 1.5km, site on L
in 500m. 2*, Med, mkd, pt sl, EHU (6A) €2; bbq;
sw nr; twin axles; 5% statics; bus 0.5km; Eng spkn; adv
bkg acc; ccard acc; games area. *"Excel; bus & cable car
rides; walks, cycle tracks & mountain climbs nrby; mini
train adj; beautiful site."* **€32.00, 28 Apr-30 Sep.**
2018

Make sure you check any essential information with the site before you travel

PUNTA SABBIONI *2E2* (1.6km SSW Coastal) *45.44035, 12.4211* **Camping Miramare,** Lungomare Dante Alighieri 29, 30013 Punta-Sabbioni (VE) **041 966150; info@camping-miramare.it; www.miramare venezia.it**

🐕 €4 ♦♦♦(htd) 🗚 ♨ ⅃ 📖 ⁄ 🔉 🐾 ♀♀ ⑪nr 🏖 ⚠ 🏊

Take rd Jesolo to Punta-Sabbioni, pass all camps & go to end of peninsula. Turn L at boat piers & foll rd alongside beach; site 500m on L. 3*, Med, hdg, mkd, pt shd, EHU (6A) inc (rev pol); gas; phone; Eng spkn; adv bkg acc; ccard acc. *"Excel, well-organised, helpful, caring, friendly family-owned site - 10 mins walk for Venice (tickets fr recep) - can leave bikes at terminal; gd security; new pt of site v pleasant wooded area; clean facs; poss mosquito problem; min 3 nights stay high ssn; superior to other sites in area; min stay 2 nights Jul/Aug; sm dogs only; don't miss camping supmkt on way in - an Aladdin's cave; bus to beach; avoid dep on Sat due traff; ferry; Magic of Italy site; highly rec, reasonable mob home rentals; excel staff; close to beach and ferries."* **€41.40, 1 Apr-3 Nov.**
2019

PUNTA SABBIONI *2E2* (1km SW Rural) *45.44236, 12.42251* **Al Batèo,** via Lungomare Dante Alighieri 19/A, 30013 Cavallino Treporti Venice **040 5301 455 or 041 5301 564; info@albateo.it; www.albateo.it**

12 ♦♦♦(htd) 📖 ♨ ⅃ 🔉 🐾 🐾

Take rd Jesolo to Punta Sabbioni and go to end of the peninsula. Turn L at boat piers and foll rd along side beach. Site 300 on L. Sm, hdg, shd, bus; Eng spkn; adv bkg acc. *"M'vans only; gd value; Vapporetti to Venice 300m."* **€25.00**
2019

"There aren't many sites open at this time of year"

If you're travelling outside peak season remember to call ahead to check site opening dates – even if the entry says 'open all year'.

RAPALLO *1C2* (2km N Urban) *44.35805, 9.2100* **Camping Miraflores,** Via Savagna 10, 16035 Rapallo (GE) **0185 263000; info@campingmiraflores.it; www.campingmiraflores.it**

🐕 ♦♦♦ 📖 ♨ ⅃ 🔉 ⁄ 🔉 ⅄ ⑪ 🐾 🐾 nr ⚠ 🏊

Exit A12/E80 at Rapallo. In 100m fr toll gate sharp L across main rd, sharp L again, site sp 200m on R. Site almost immed beside toll gate but not easily seen. Sp fr town. 1*, Med, hdg, mkd, hdstg, pt shd, terr, EHU (3A) €1.80; gas; red long stay; 10% statics; bus 200m to stn & town cent; ccard acc; sep car park; CKE. *"Excel htd pool adj; gd, modern san facs; refurb (2018); grass pitches for tents, earth only for m'vans & c'vans; v noisy & dusty as under m'way; v friendly staff; ferries to Portofino fr town; conv NH; rec phone ahead if lge o'fit."* **€32.00, 1 Mar-31 Dec.**
2018

RAPALLO *1C2* (2.5km W Urban) *44.35691, 9.1992* **Camping Rapallo,** Via San Lazzaro 4, 16035 Rapallo (GE) **0185 262018; campingrapallo@libero.it; www.campingrapallo.it**

🐕 ♦♦♦ 📖 ♨ ⅃ ⁄ 🔉 ⅄ ⑪nr 🐾 nr 🏖(htd) ⌖shgl 2.5km

Exit A12/E80 dir Rapallo, turn immed R on leaving tolls. Site sp in 500m on L at bend (care), over bdge then R. Narr app rd. Site sp. 2*, Med, hdg, mkd, pt shd, EHU (3A) €2.20; gas; 10% statics; bus (tickets fr recep); Eng spkn; adv bkg acc; ccard acc; bike hire; CKE. *"Clean, family-run site; conv Portofino (boat trip) & train to Cinque Terre; beautiful coastlline; shwrs clsd during day but hot shwrs at pool; v busy public hols - adv bkg rec; awkward exit, not suitable for lge o'fits; NH only."* **€28.50, 15 Mar-15 Nov.**
2019

RAVENNA *2E2* (10.6km E Coastal) *44.43335, 12.29680* **Camping Park Adriano,** Via dei Campeggi 7, 48122 Punta-Marina-Terme (RN) **0544 437230; info@ adrianocampingvillage.com; www.camping adriano.com**

🐕 €3 ♦♦♦ 📖 ♨ ⅃ 🔉 ⁄ 🔉 ♀♀ ⅄ ⑪ 🐾 🐾 ⚠ ⁄ 🏊 🎣 ⌖300m

Fr S309 Ravenna-Venezia rd foll sp to Lido Adriano. Site at N end of Lido. 4*, Lge, shd, EHU (5A) inc (poss rev pol/no earth); bbq; TV; 70% statics; bus to Ravenna; Eng spkn; adv bkg acc; ccard acc; bike hire; golf 10km; CKE. *"Site in pine forest; excel san facs; ATM; sh walk to beach."* **€43.00, 20 Apr-18 Sep.** **2015**

RHEMES ST GEORGE *1B1* (3km N Rural) *45.64966, 7.15150* **Camping Val di Rhemes,** Loc Voix 1, 11010 Rhêmes-St George (AO) **0165 907648; info@camping valdirhemes.com; www.campingvaldirhemes.com**

🐕 €2.50 ♦♦♦(htd) 📖 ♨ ⅃ 🔉 ⁄ 🔉 🐾 ♀♀ ⅄ 🐾 ⚠

Fr S26 or A54/E25 turn S at Introd dir Rhêmes-St George & Rhêmes-Notre-Dame; site on R in 10km past PO; app is diff climb with hairpins. 2*, Med, pt shd, pt sl, EHU (2-6A) €2; 10% statics; Eng spkn; adv bkg acc; ccard acc; CCI. *"Peaceful, family-run site; nr Gran Paradiso National Park; gd walking; excel."* **€26.40, 20 May-10 Sep.**
2019

RIVA DEL GARDA *1D1* (2.5km E Rural) *45.88111, 10.86194* **Camping Monte Brione,** Via Brione 32, 38066 Riva-del-Garda (TN) **0464 520885; info@ campingbrione.com; www.campingbrione.com**

🐕 €4 ♦♦♦ 📖 ♨ ⅃ 🔉 ⁄ 🔉 🐾 ♀♀ ⅄ ⑪nr 🐾 🐾 ⚠ 🏊(htd)

Exit A22 Garda Nord onto SS240 to Torbole & Riva; on app to Riva thro open-sided tunnel; immed R after enclosed tunnel opp Marina; site ent 700m on R. 4*, Med, mkd, pt shd, terr, EHU (6A) inc; gas; bbq; sw nr; Eng spkn; adv bkg acc; ccard acc; watersports; bike hire; solarium; CKE. *"Olive groves adj; barriers clsd 1300-1500 & 2300-0700; pleasant site with lge pitches; gd, modern san facs."* **€31.50, 15 Apr-16 Oct.** **2016**

ITALY

ROMA *2E4* (9km N Rural) *42.00353, 12.45283* **Happy Village & Camping,** Via Prato della Corte 1915, 00123 Roma **06 33626401 or 06 33614596; info@happy camping.net; www.happycamping.net**

🚶 ♦♦ ��🅦🅓 🏊 ♿ 🖃 ✓ 🅜🅟 🍽 🛉 ⓘ ♨ 🦌 ⚟ 🏖

Take exit 5 fr Rome ring rd sp Viterbo. Site sp on ring rd, fr N & S on dual c'way Rome/Viterbo at 1st exit N of ring rd. 3*, Lge, pt shd, terr, EHU (6A) inc; gas; bbq; 10% statics; train into Rome; adv bkg acc; ccard acc; CKE. *"Friendly, busy site in hills; sm pitches; vg rest; mini bus shuttle to train stn; gd site; v nice well kept site; steep access rd."* **€25.00, 1 Mar-6 Jan.**
2015

ROMA *2E4* (10km SW Rural) *41.77730, 12.39605* **Camping Fabulous,** Via Cristoforo Colombo, Km 18, 00125 Acilia (RM) **06 5259354; fabulous@ecvacanze. it; www.ecvacanze.it**

🚶 €1.50 ♦♦ (htd) 🏊 ♿ 🖃 ✓ 🛉 ⓘ ♨ 🦌 ⚟ 🏖 🏖

Exit junc 27 fr Rome ring rd into Via C Colombo. At 18km marker turn R at traff lts, site 200m on R. V lge, mkd, shd, pt sl, EHU (6-10A) inc; bbq; 80% statics; phone; bus on main rd; Eng spkn; adv bkg acc; ccard acc; tennis; games area; waterslide; CKE. *"Set in pinewoods; gd sh stay; ltd facs in LS; helpful staff."* **€40.00, 14 Apr-31 Oct.**
2017

ROSETO DEGLI ABRUZZI *2F3* (3km S Coastal) *42.65748, 14.03568* **Eurcamping Roseto,** Lungomare Trieste Sud 90, 64026 Roseto-degli-Abruzzi (TE) **085 8993179; info@eurcamping.it; www.eurcamping.it**

🚶 €5 ♦♦ 🅦🅓 🏊 🖃 ✓ 🛉 ⓘ ♨ 🦌 ⚟ 🏖 🏖 ⛵ shgl adj

Fr A14 exit dir Roseto-degli-Abruzzi to SS16. At rndabt turn R, next L & under rlwy bdge to promenade. Turn R at sea front, site at end of promenade. 3*, Med, hdg, mkd, shd, EHU (3A) inc; 20% statics; Eng spkn; adv bkg acc; bike hire; tennis; games area; CKE. *"Phone to check if open LS; gates close 2300; pitches poss flood after heavy rainfall; Roseto excel resort."* **€43.50, 1 May-24 Oct.**
2015

SALBERTRAND *1A2* (1km SW Rural) *45.06200, 6.86821* **Camping Gran Bosco,** SS24, Km 75, Monginevro, 10050 Salbertrand (TO) **0122 854653; info@camping granbosco.it; www.campinggranbosco.it**

12 ♦♦ (htd) 🅦🅓 🏊 🖃 ✓ 🅜🅟 🍽 ⓘ nr 🦌 ⚟ 🏖

Leave A32/E70 (Torino-Fréjus Tunnel) at Oulx Ouest junc & foll SS24/SS335 sp Salbertrand. Site sp 1.5km twd Salbertrand at km 75. Fr S (Briançon in France) on N94/SS24 to Oulx cent, foll SS24 thro town & foll sp Salbertrand, then as above. 3*, Lge, pt shd, EHU (3-6A) inc; gas; 80% statics; ccard acc; tennis; games area. *"Beautiful setting; excel NH bef/after Fréjus Tunnel or pass to/fr Briançon; gates open 0830-2300; excel, modern, clean san facs; sm pitches; grnd soft in wet - no hdstg; conv for m'way; popular with m'cyclists but quiet at night."* **€29.00**
2016

SALSOMAGGIORE TERME *1C2* (3km E Rural) *44.80635, 10.00931* **Camping Arizona,** Via Tabiano 42, 43039 Tabiano-Salsomaggiore Terme (PR) **0524 565648; info@camping-arizona.it; www.camping-arizona.it**

🚶 €3 ♦♦ 🏊 ♿ 🖃 ✓ 🅜🅟 🦋 🛉 🍽 ⓘ ♨ 🦌 ⚟ 🏖 🏖

Fr fidenza foll sp Salsomaggiore and then at rndabt to Tabiano. Go thro Tabiano and site 500m on L. 4*, Lge, shd, pt sl, EHU (3A) inc (rev pol); 30% statics; phone; bus to Salsomaggiore; waterslide; games area; jacuzzi; sep car park; games rm; tennis; bike hire; golf 7km; fishing. *"Vg site; friendly, helpful staff; interesting, smart spa town; excel touring base; gd for families; san facs vg; best campsite shop; vg rest."* **€37.00, 1 Apr-6 Oct.**
2019

SAN FELICE DEL BENACO *1D2* (1km E Rural) *45.58500, 10.56583* **Camping Fornella,** Via Fornella 1, 25010 San Felice-del-Benaco (BS) **0365 62294; fornella@fornella.it; www.fornella.it**

🚶 €7 ♦♦ (htd) 🅦🅓 🏊 ♿ 🖃 ✓ 🅜🅟 🦋 🛉 🍽 ⓘ ♨ 🦌 ⚟ 🏖 🏖 🏖

N fr Desenzano on S572 twd Salo. Turn R to San Felice-del-Benaco, over x-rds & take 2nd R turn at sp to site. R into app rd, L into site. Rd narr but accessible. Avoid vill cent, site sp (with several others) fr vill by-pass just bef g'ge. 5*, Lge, pt shd, pt sl, terr, EHU (6A) inc; gas; bbq (charcoal); sw; TV; 20% statics; Eng spkn; adv bkg acc; ccard acc; games area; bike hire; games rm; boat hire; windsurfing; tennis; fishing; CKE. *"Family-run site in vg location by Lake Garda; park outside until checked in; recep 0800-1200 & 1400-2000; no o'fits over 7m high ssn; sep car park; excel pool; extra for lge pitches & lakeside pitches; excursions to Venice, Florence & Verona opera; excel rest; gd san facs."* **€54.40, 13 Apr-13 Oct, Y11.**
2019

SAN MARINO *2E3* (7km N Rural) *43.95990, 12.46090* **Centro Vacanze San Marino,** Strada San Michele 50, 47893 Cailungo, Repubblica di San Marino **0549 903964; info@centrovacanzesanmarino.com; www.centrovacanzesanmarino.com**

12 🚶 €5 ♦♦ (htd) 🅦🅓 🏊 ♿ 🖃 ✓ 🦋 🛉 🍽 🛉 ⓘ ♨ 🦌 ⚟ 🏖 (htd) 🏖

Exit A14 at Rimini Sud, foll rd S72 to San Marino. Pass under 2 curved footbdges, then 800m after 2nd & 13km after leaving a'strada, fork R. Cont uphill for 1.5km then turn R at Brico building, site sp. Steep long-haul climb. 4*, Lge, hdstg, hdg, pt shd, terr, serviced pitches; EHU (6A) inc (poss rev pol); bbq; cooking facs; red long stay; TV (pitch); 10% statics; bus; Eng spkn; adv bkg acc; ccard acc; bike hire; games area; tennis; CKE. *"V busy at w/end - rec arr early; superb hill fort town; excel rest & pool; sm pitches; conv Rimini 24km; solarium; mini zoo; excel, clean site; bus calls at site ent for San Marino."* **€37.00, Y04.**
2016

For a guide to symbols see the fold out on the rear cover

SAN MICHELE ALL'ADIGE *1D1* (3km SW Rural) *46.16789, 11.11452* **Camping Moser,** Via Nazionale 64, 38015 Nave San Felice (TN) **0461 870248**

🛉 ⁕ ᵂᴰ ♨ ♂ 𝖸 ⊕ 🐚 nr

12km N of Trento on SS12. Sm, mkd, shd, EHU inc; bus 500m; Eng spkn; adv bkg acc; ccard acc. *"Gd, friendly NH; site run by Hotel Moser (well sp on S12); scruffy & run down but busy; new san facs block almost completed (2014)."* **€18.00, 1 May-31 Oct.** **2015**

SAN VALENTINO ALLA MUTA *1D1* (0.7km N Rural) *46.7700, 10.5325* **Camping Thöni,** Landstrasse 83, 39020 St Valentin-an-der-Haide, Graun **0473 634020; thoeni.h@rolmail.net; www.camping-thoeni.it**

12 🛉 ⁕ (htd) ᵂᴰ ♨ ♂ 𝖸 nr ⊕ nr 🐚 nr

N twd Austrian border site on L on edge of vill on S edge of Lago di Resia. 2*, Sm, unshd, pt sl, EHU 6-16A; site clsd Nov. *"Conv sh stay/NH en rte Austria; cycle rte around lake; scenic area; off open 0900-1000 & 1700-1800; numbered pitches; views; walking rte rnd Haidensee below vill; cable car opens late June."* **€26.00** **2018**

SARNANO *2E3* (3km SSW Rural) *43.01743, 13.28358* **Quattro Stagioni,** Contrada Brilli, 62028 Sarnano **0733 651147; quattrostagioni@camping.it; www.camping4stagioni.it**

12 🛉 ⁕ ᵂᴰ ♨ ♿ 🖥 ♂ 🦋 𝖸 ⊕ 🐚 nr 🏔 ⛵ ⛏

A14 exit Civitanova Marche. M'way to Macerata as far as Sarnano exit. In Sarnano turn R at sq, foll main rd. Site approx 3km outside Sarnano to the W. 3*, Sm, mkd, pt shd, pt sl, EHU; bbq; twin axles; 60% statics; Eng spkn; adv bkg acc; games area; CKE. *"Fair site."* **€30.00** **2019**

SARTEANO *1D3* (0km W Rural) *42.9875, 11.86444* **Camping Parco Delle Piscine,** Via del Bagno Santo, 53047 Sarteano (SI) **0578 26971; info@parcodelle piscine.it; www.parcodellepiscine.it**

⁕ ᵂᴰ ♨ ♿ 🖥 ♂ 🦋 𝖸 ⊕ 🐚 nr 🏔 ⛏

Exit A1/E35 onto S478 at Chiusi & foll sp to Sarteano. Site at W end of vill, sp. 4*, Lge, pt shd, serviced pitches; EHU (6A) inc; 50% statics; Eng spkn; ccard acc; solarium; tennis. *"Clean, well-run; security guard 24 hrs; no vehicles during quiet periods 1400-1600 & 2300-0700; poss long walk to wc/shwrs; Florence 90 mins on m'way, Siena 1 hr; site at 600m, so cool at night; excel."* **€70.00, 14 Apr-30 Sep, Y17.** **2017**

SARZANA *1C2* (4km SE Coastal) *44.076651, 9.981182* **Camping Iron Gate Marina 3B,** Viale XXV Aprile 54 19038, Sarzana **0187 676370; info@marina3b.it; www.marina3b.com**

🛉 ⁕ (htd) ᵂᴰ ♨ ♿ 🦋 𝖸 ⊕ 🐚 ⛵ 🏖 1km

Fr A12 exit Sarzana dir S. TR at 4th rndabt (2nd after dble rndabt). 3.1 km or R. Lge, mkd, shd, 65% statics; Eng spkn; ccard acc. *"VG, nice site; gd facs; conv for Cinque Terre towns."* **€20.00, 15 Mar-30 Sep.** **2019**

SARZANA *1C2* (8km S Rural/Coastal) *44.07638, 9.97027* **Camping River,** Loc Armezzone, 19031 Ameglia (SP) **0187 65920; info@campingriver.com; www.campingriver.com**

🛉 €3 ⁕ ᵂᴰ ♨ ♿ 🖥 ♂ ᴹˢᴾ 𝖸 ⊕ 🐚 nr 🏔 ♂ ⛏ 🏖 2km

Exit A12 at Sarzana & foll sp Ameglia & Bocca di Magra on SP432. In 7km turn L into Via Crociata to site (blue sp). Narr app rd with few passing places. 3*, Lge, mkd, pt shd, EHU (3-6A) inc; TV; 50% statics; adv bkg acc; bike hire; games area; tennis 200m; boat hire; golf driving range; rv fishing; horseriding 200m; sauna. *"Gd touring base Cinque Terre; pleasant, helpful staff; vg, well-situated site; gd shop & rest; bus to beach; nice location by rv; dated facs; gd pools."* **€44.00, 12 Apr-30 Sep.** **2019**

SAVONA *1B2* (13km SW Coastal) *44.224200, 8.41032* **Camping Leo,** Via Siaggia 4, 17028 Spotorno **019 745184; info@campingleo.it; www.campingleo.it**

🛉 ⁕ ᵂᴰ ♨ ♿ 🖥 ♂ ᴹˢᴾ 🦋 𝖸 🐚 nr 🏔

Leave A10 sp S8 Spotorno. Immed after rlwy bdge turn R at rndabt into site. Med, hdstg, pt shd, serviced pitches; EHU (3A); bbq (gas, sep area); sw nr; 500m; Eng spkn; adv bkg rec; games area; bike hire. *"Excel."* **€25.00, 1 Feb-4 Nov.** **2019**

SAVONA *1B2* (13km SW Coastal) *44.22731, 8.40795* **Camping Rustia,** Via La Torre 4, 17028 Spotorno (SV) **019 745042 or 019 741446; info@campingrustia.it; www.campingrustia.it**

🛉 ⁕ ♨ ♿ ♂ 𝖸 ⊕ nr 🐚 ♂ sand 600m

Exit A10/E80 for Spotorno, site sp on app rd to m'way. V steep app rd. C'vans returning to m'way use ent at Albissola Marina. 1*, Lge, shd, EHU (3A) €3; 30% statics; Eng spkn; ccard acc. *"Site diff for lge o'fits due narr paths & many trees - manhandling necessary onto pitches; gd san facs; gates locked at night; busy, well laid out site; helpful staff."* **€32.00, 1 Mar-30 Sep.** **2015**

SESTO CALENDE *1B1* (4km N Rural) *45.74892, 8.59698* **Camping Okay Lido,** Via per Angera 115, Loc Lisanza, 21018 Sesto Calende (VA) **0331 974235; campingokay@camping-okay.com; www.camping-okay.com**

🛉 €5 ⁕ ᵂᴰ ♨ ♿ 🖥 ♂ ᴹˢᴾ 🦋 𝖸 ⊕ 🐚 nr 🏔 ♂ ⛏ (htd) ⛏

Exit A8 at Sesto Calende onto SP69 N dir Angera, site sp. 4*, Med, mkd, pt shd, terr, EHU (6A) €3; sw; TV; 10% statics; Eng spkn; adv bkg acc; watersports; games rm; games area. *"Friendly, welcoming site; private san facs avail; NH pitches by lakeside; gd NH for Amsterdam ferry."* **€42.00, 30 Mar-13 Oct.** **2019**

SESTO CALENDE *1B1* (7.5km N Rural) *45.82712, 8.62722* **International Camping Ispra,** Via Carducci, 21027 Ispra (VA) **0332 780458; info@international campingispra.it; www.internationalcampingispra.it**

🐕 €6 ♛♛(cont) ▲ ⊡ ∅ ✖ ⊺ ⊕ ♨ ⚍ ⚟ ⚓

Site 1km NE of Ispra on E side of lake. 4*, Med, shd, terr, EHU (6A) €3; own san req; bbq; sw; TV; 90% statics; Eng spkn; adv bkg acc; fishing; boating; games area; CKE. *"Gd views of lake; muddy beach; vg rest; nice, peaceful site; friendly, helpful staff; lovely situation on banks of Lake Maggiore; well run; loud music fr bar till midnight."* **€32.00, 18 Mar-2 Nov.**
2016

SESTO/SEXTEN *2E1* (3km SE Rural) *46.66806, 12.39935* **Caravan Park Sexten,** St. Josefstr. 54, 39030 Sexten / Moos **0474 710444; info@caravan parksexten.it; www.caravanparksexten.it**

🔢12 🐕 €6 ♛♛ ⊡ ▲ ♿ ⊡ ∅ ⌨ ✖ ⊺ ⊕ ⚍ ♣ ⚓ ⛖

Fr S49 take S52 SE fr San Candido thro Sexten & Moos. After sh, steep climb site on W of S52 midway bet Moos & Kreuzberg pass. 4*, Lge, mkd, pt shd, pt sl, serviced pitches; EHU (16A) metered; gas; TV; Eng spkn; adv bkg req; tennis; sauna; solarium; CKE. *"Excel, clean facs; Waldbad worth visit; rock climbing wall; lovely scenery; mountain walks; beauty & wellness treatments; v popular & busy site; private bthrms avail; winter sports; v well managed & equipped; rest worth a visit."* **€54.70, Y03.**
2019

SETTIMO VITTONE *1B1* (2.5km N Rural) *45.56474, 7.81668* **Camping Mombarone,** Torre Daniele, 10010 Settimo-Vittone (TO) **0125 757907; info@camping mombarone.it; www.campingmombarone.it**

🔢12 ♛♛ ⊡ ▲ ♿ ⊡ ∅ ⌨ ⊺ ⊕ nr ♨ ⚍ nr ⚓

On E side of Ivrea-Aosta rd (SS26), 100m S of Pont-St Martin. Exit A5 at Quincinetto, turn R onto SP69 across bdge, R at end onto SP26 & site on L in 150m. (App fr S, sp at ent but if overshoot go on 100m to rndabt to turn). Tight ent off busy rd. 2*, Med, pt shd, pt sl, EHU (6A) €2.50; 80% statics; games area; CKE. *"Gd base Aosta valley; superb views; Quincinetto medieval vill walking dist; lovely, grassy, well-kept site; ltd space for tourers; v pleasant, helpful owner who speaks gd Eng, friendly welcome; san facs immac; gd NH; rlwy stn nrby."* **€22.50**
2019

SIBARI *3A4* (4km E Coastal) *39.77944, 16.47889* **Camping Villaggio Pineta di Sibari,** 87070 Sibari (CS) **0981 74135; info@pinetadisibari.it; www.pinetadi sibari.it**

🐕 €5 ♛♛ ▲ ♿ ⊡ ∅ ⌨ ⊺ ⊕ ♨ ⚍ ⚟ ♣ 🌴 sand adj

Exit A3 at Frascineto onto SS106, then exit at Villapiana-Scalo. Site sp on beach. 3*, Lge, pt shd, EHU (4A) inc; TV; 20% statics; ccard acc; tennis; bike hire. *"Vg beach; site in pine forest; noisy bar/music; gd touring base; watch out for low bdge on app."* **€44.00, 19 Apr-29 Sep.**
2019

SIENA *1D3* (7.4km N Urban) *43.33750, 11.33055* **Camping Siena Colleverde,** Via Scacciapensieri 47, 53100 Siena **0577 334080; info@sienacamping.com; www.sienacamping.com**

🐕 ♛♛(htd) ⊡ ▲ ♿ ⊡ ∅ ⌨ ⊺ ⊺ ⊕ ♨ ⚍ ⚟ ⚓

Site sp ('Camping' or symbol) on all app to Siena, foll sp for 'Ospedale' (hospital). Use exit Siena Nord & foll site sp, but take care as some sp misleadingly positioned. 3*, Lge, hdg, mkd, hdstg, pt shd, pt sl, terr, EHU (10A) inc; gas; TV; phone; bus; Eng spkn; adv bkg acc; CKE. *"Attractive location; gd views old town wall fr upper pitches (no shd); excel touring base; upgraded, well-run site - gd, well kept; modern san facs; easy access by bus to town fr site ent; excel; pt of 'We Love Camping' group; some lge unmkd pitches."* **€37.00, 1 Mar-31 Dec.**
2015

SIENA *1D3* (21km W Rural) *43.2815, 11.21905* **Camping La Montagnola,** Strada della Montagnola 139, 53100 Sovicille (SI) **0577 314473; info@camping lamontagnola.it; www.campinglamontagnola.it**

🐕 ♛♛ ⊡ ▲ ⊡ ∅ ⌨ ✖ ⊺ ⊺ ⊕ nr ♨ ⚍ ⊡

Fr N on S2 or S on S223 site well sp fr junc with S73. Avoid Siena town cent. 2*, Med, hdstg, mkd, pt shd, terr, EHU (6A) inc; gas; 7% statics; phone; bus to Siena; Eng spkn; adv bkg rec; ccard acc; games area; sep car park; CKE. *"Super site; sm pitches; sharp stone chippings on hdstg pitches; v clean facs; vg refuge fr summer heat in wooded hills; facs poss stretched high ssn & rubbish bins o'flowing; gd walks fr site (booklet fr recep); Magic of Italy disc, conv bus service to Siena fr site."* **€29.00, 1 Apr-30 Sep.**
2015

SIRMIONE *2G2* (3km E Coastal) *45.45738, 10.64025* **Tiglio,** Loc. Punta Grò, 25019 Sirmione **030 990 4009; info@campingtiglio.it; www.campingtiglio.it**

♛♛ ⊡ ∅ ⌨ ⊺ ⊕ ♨ ⚟

A4 Milan-Verona, exit Sirmione. 1st exit at rndabt onto SP13. 1st exit at next rndabt. Turn L twds Via San Martino. 1st exit at rndabt onto Via Verona. Foll sp to camp. Lge, mkd, shd, EHU inc (4A); bbq; twin axles; 50% statics; bus adj; Eng spkn; adv bkg acc; ccard acc; CKE. *"Gd site; noisy & busy but friendly; on bus rte to Verona."* **€36.00, 18 Apr-30 Sep.**
2019

SIRMIONE *1D2* (3km S Rural) *45.46845, 10.61028* **Camping Sirmione,** Via Sirmioncino 9, 25010 Colombare-di-Sirmione (BS) **030 99 04 665; info@ camping-sirmione.it; www.camping-sirmione.it**

🐕 ♛♛(cont) ▲ ♿ ⊡ ∅ ⌨ ✖ ⊺ ⊕ ♨ ⚍ ⚟ ⛖

Exit S11 at traff lts sp Sirmione, in 500m R at site sp. 3*, Lge, mkd, hdstg, pt shd, pt sl, EHU (6A) inc; sw; 30% statics; adv bkg acc; ccard acc; games area; watersports. *"Excel lakeside site; facs poss stretched when site busy; excel rest, bar, pool & san facs; lovely walk to Sirmione; highly rec."* **€43.60, 17 Apr-5 Oct.**
2019

SORRENTO *3A3* (3km N Coastal) *40.63541, 14.41758*
Camping I Pini, Corso Italia 242, 80063 Piano-di-Sorrento (NA) **081 8786891; info@campingipini.com; www.campingipini.com**

🏕12 🏪 👭 wc ▲ ᷂ 🗑 ⁄ MSP 🦋 ▼ ⓘ ♨ 🛒 nr 🚣 🌳 1km

S fr Naples on A3; Exit A3 sp Castellammare di Stabia & take SS145 sp to Sorrento; pass thro vill of Meta; site on R immed over bdge; lge sp on main **rd.** 1*, Med, hdg, mkd, pt shd, pt sl, EHU (4A) inc; red long stay; 50% statics; bus 50m; Eng spkn; adv bkg acc; ccard acc; CKE. *"Spacious site in mountains bet 2 vills; pool restricted to campers; sh walk to public transport to sites of interest; best site in Sorrento to avoid narr gridlocked rds; old, tired facs (2013); tight narr pitches."* **€47.50**   **2019**

"That's changed – Should I let the Club know?"

If you find something on site that's different from the site entry, fill in a report and let us know. See camc.com/europereport.

SORRENTO *3A3* (2km W Coastal) *40.62818, 14.35816*
Camping Villaggio Santa Fortunata, Via Capo 39, 80067 Capo-de-Sorrento (NA) **081 8073579 or 081 8073574; info@santafortunata.com; www.santa fortunata.com**

🏕 👭 wc ▲ ᷂ 🗑 ⁄ MSP ♨ ▼ ⓘ 🛒 🏔 🦋 🚣 🌳 shgl

Only app fr a'strada, exit Castellamare. Foll sp into Sorrento then sp Massa-Lubrense. Site poorly sp fr Sorrento on R, gd wide ent. 4*, V lge, mkd, hdg, shd, pt sl, terr, EHU (6A) inc; gas; red long stay; TV; 50% statics; phone; bus adj; Eng spkn; sep car park; CKE. *"Gd, clean facs; pitches sm for lge o'fits (7m+) & poss dusty; bus fr gate, ticket fr recep; boat trips to Capri fr site beach; noisy nr gd rest, disco & 18-30 tours; many scruffy statics; facs dated; steep access & tight hairpins to some pitches; friendly, vg site."*
€46.00, 30 Mar-3 Nov.   **2019**

SPERLONGA *2E4* (1km SE Coastal) *41.25514, 13.44625*
Camping Villaggio Nord-Sud, Via Flacca, Km 15.5, 04029 Sperlonga (LT) **0771 548255; info@camping nordsud.it; www.campingnordsud.it**

👭 wc ▲ ᷂ 🗑 ⁄ MSP ▼ ⓘ ♨ 🛒 🌳 sand

Site on seaward side of S213 at km post 15.9. Lge sp visible fr both dirs. Lge, mkd, hdstg, shd, EHU (4A) inc; 10% statics; adv bkg acc; tennis; games area; windsurfing; fitness rm. *"Mostly statics but great location; pleasant site; picturesque beach."*
€48.00, 1 Apr-31 Oct.   **2016**

STRESA *1B1* (3.4km NW Urban) *45.91246, 8.50410*
Camping Parisi, Via Piave 50, 28831 Baveno (VB) **0323 924160; campingparisi@tiscalinet.it; www.campingparisi.it**

🏕 €4 👭 wc ▲ ᷂ 🗑 ⁄ MSP ♈ ▼ nr ⓘ nr 🛒 nr 🏔

Exit A26 at Baveno, after x-ing bdge on o'skirts Baveno, turn L off main rd bet Hotel Simplon & Agip g'ge & foll sp. Fr Stresa drive thro Baveno. At end of prom, take R fork at Dino Hotel up a minor 1-way rd (poss congested by parked cars); foll Parisi sp.
2*, Med, pt shd, pt sl, EHU (6A) €3.50; sw; 10% statics; phone; bus; Eng spkn; adv bkg acc; boat launch; fishing; CKE. *"Well-managed site on Lake Maggiore; fine views; extra for lakeside pitches; frequent lake steamers nr site; gd rests adj; long hose rec for m'van fill up; sm pitches; busy at w/end; sw in lake - supervise children; many repeat visitors; bar adj; clean facs; welcoming recep; conv base for visiting Borromeo Islands."* **€34.00, 25 Mar-30 Sep.**   **2015**

STRESA *1B1* (4km NW Rural) *45.91185, 8.48913*
Camping Tranquilla, Via Cave 2, Oltrefuime, 28831 Baveno (VB) **0323 923452; info@tranquilla.com; www.tranquilla.com**

🏕 €2.50 👭 wc ▲ 🗑 ⁄ MSP 🦋 ▼ 🛒 nr 🚣

Fr N go into Baveno & turn R 200m past Hotel Splendide; fr S turn L immed after x-ing bdge. Foll brown sp to site up steep hill 1km. 2*, Med, hdg, mkd, hdstg, pt shd, pt sl, terr, serviced pitches; EHU (6A) €2.60; red long stay; 25% statics; train to Milan 2km; Eng spkn; adv bkg acc; watersports; bike hire; car wash; CKE. *"Clean, comfortable, well-managed, pleasant, family-owned site; entmnt (w/end); v helpful staff; sm pitches; conv Lake Maggiore; day trip by train to Milan."* **€33.50, 19 Mar-16 Oct.**   **2016**

TORBOLE *1D1* (0.4km N Urban) *45.8725, 10.87361*
Camping Al Porto, Via Al Cor, 38069 Tórbole (TN) **0464 505891; info@campingalporto.it; www.campingalporto.it**

🏕 €2.50 👭 wc ▲ ᷂ 🗑 ⁄ MSP 🦋 ▼ ⓘ nr ♨ 🛒 nr 🏔

On ent Tórbole fr S take rd twd Riva-del-Garda for approx 600m. Petrol stn & car park on R, turn L into narr lane after shops; site sp. 3*, Med, mkd, pt shd, EHU (5A) inc; bbq; sw nr; red long stay; watersports; CKE. *"Excel san facs; excel site; secure; helpful staff; vill has many rest & sportling locations."*
€39.00, 10 Apr-3 Nov.   **2019**

TRAFOI *1D1* (0.9km S Rural) *46.54332, 10.50750*
Camping Trafoi, Drei Brunnen Weg 1, 39020 Trafoi **0473 611533; info@camping-trafoi.com; www.camping-trafoi.com**

🏕 €3 👭 wc ▲ ᷂ 🗑 ⁄ MSP 🦋 🛒

Fr SS40 turn SW at Spondigna onto SS38 dir Stelvio to Trafoi. Site thro vill sp on L. Sm, pt shd, pt sl, EHU (4A); bbq; bus 500m; Eng spkn. *"Excel cycle rtes, mountaineering; chair lift for skiing; excel."*
€30.00, 15 Jun-15 Sep.   **2015**

TRENTO *1D1* (12km NW Rural) *46.11111, 11.04805*
Camping Laghi di Lamar, Via alla Selva Faeda 15,
38070 Terlago (TN) **0461 860423; campeggio@
laghidilamar.com; www.laghidilamar.com**

🐕 €2.50 ⚌ wo ♨ & ◻ ⧄ MSP 🌁 ⛱ 🍽 ⑨ å 🛒 ⚗ ⚓

Head W fr Trento for 10km on SS45b dir Riva-del-
Garda/Brescia. Turn R twd Monte-Terlago; site sp on
R. Last section via SS45 v steep. 3*, Med, pt shd, terr,
EHU (10A) inc; gas; bbq; sw nr; TV; 30% statics; phone;
Eng spkn; ccard acc; games rm; bike hire; games area;
CKE. *"Excel site; excel new san facs."*
€35.00, 1 Apr-30 Oct. **2017**

TRIESTE *2F1* (5.5km N Rural) *45.67974, 13.78387*
Camping Obelisco, Strada Nuova Opicina 37, 34016
Opicina (TS) **040 212744; campeggioobelisco@
gmail.com; www.campeggiobelisco.it**

12 🐕 €2.50 ⚌(cont) ♨ ⧄ 🌁 ⛱ Ⴒ nr ⑨ å ⚗

Sp fr S58. 2*, Med, hdstg, shd, pt sl, terr, EHU €2.50;
own san req; 95% statics; Eng spkn; CKE. *"V steep,
narr, twisting ent/exit to site - suitable sm c'vans only
& diff in wet; excel views Trieste harbour; interesting
tram ride into city fr obelisk; demanding up hill walk to
top of site, both Turkish & European wcs."* **€18.00**
2016

VENEZIA *2E2* (18km SW Coastal) *45.41916, 12.25666*
Camping Fusina, Via Moranzani 79, 30030 Fusina (VE)
041 5470055; info@campingfusina.com;
www.campingfusina.com**

12 🐕 ⚌(htd) wo ♨ ⧄ 🌁 ⑨ å 🛒 ⚗ ⚓

Exit A4 at sp Ravenna/Chiogga onto SS309 S, & foll
sp to site. Take care when turning into rd leading
to Fusina as L-hand turning lane used by locals for
o'taking. 3*, Lge, pt shd, EHU (6A) inc (poss rev pol);
gas; TV; 50% statics; ccard acc; games area; boat
hire; CKE. *"Pleasant, busy site; some pitches o'looking
lagoon; many backpackers, educational groups & 18-
30s; gd san facs; gd public transport/boat dir to Venice;
ferry to Greece adj; helpful staff; poss mosquitoes;
some ship & aircraft noise + noise fr bar & adj indus
complex; some pitches diff due trees & soft when wet;
ltd facs LS & poss travellers; refurb in progress (2017)."*
€35.00 **2017**

VENEZIA *2E2* (16km W Rural) *45.45222, 12.18305*
Camping Serenissima, Via Padana 334/A, 30176
Malcontenta **041 5386498 or 041 921850; info@
campingserenissima.it; www.campingserenissima.com**

🐕 ⚌(htd) wo ♨ ⧄ 🌁 MSP 🍽 ⑨ å 🛒 ⚗ ⚓

Exit A4 at Oriago/Mira exit. At 1st rndabt foll sp
Ravenna/Venezia; at next rndabt take 1st exit sp
Padova/Riviera del Brenta (SR11) twd Oriago. Rv
on L, site on R in approx 2km. 3*, Med, mkd, pt shd,
EHU (10-16A) inc; gas; 25% statics; phone; Eng spkn;
adv bkg acc; ccard acc; boat hire; bike hire; CKE. *"Bus
to Venice/Padua - buy tickets on site; friendly, helpful
owners; efficient recep; some sm pitches; excel, v clean
san facs; poss mosquitoes; conv Padova; highly rec for
Venice; supmkt 3km; vg."* **€34.00, 26 Mar-5 Nov.**
2018

VERBANIA *1B1* (6km W Rural) *45.93731, 8.48615*
Camping Conca d'Oro, Via 42 Martiri 26, 28835
Feriolo di Baveno (VB) **0323 28116; info@conca
doro.it; www.concadoro.it**

🐕 €5 ⚌ ♨ ⧄ & ◻ ⧄ MSP 🌁 ⛱ 🍽 ⑨ å 🛒 ⚗ 🔥 ⚓ sand adj

Foll S33 NW fr Stresa, thro Bavena to Feriolo. At
traff lts in Feriolo fork R, sp Verbania & in 800m
immed over rv bdge, turn R into site. Clearly sp.
3*, Lge, mkd, shd, pt sl, EHU (6A) inc; 10% statics;
Eng spkn; adv bkg acc; ccard acc; games area;
windsurfing; bike hire; CKE. *"Helpful staff; excel,
clean, modern san facs; discount for local services;
dogs not acc Jul/Aug; extra for lakeside pitches;
excel, v well run site; beautiful location; busy site."*
€48.00, 1 Apr-10 Sep. **2019**

VERBANIA *1B1* (9km NW Urban) *45.96111, 8.45694*
Camping Lago delle Fate, La Quartina, Via Pallanza
22, 28802 Mergozzo (VB) **0323 80326; info@lago
dellefate.com; www.lagodellefate.com**

⚌(cont) wo ♨ ⧄ & ◻ ⧄ 🌁 ⛱ Ⴒ ⑨ nr å 🛒 nr 🔥 shgl

1km E of vill of Mergozzo which is 2nd L after exit
Gravellona on S34 to Verbania. 2*, Med, hdstg, pt
shd, EHU (6A); gas; bbq; sw; twin axles; 10% statics;
Eng spkn; adv bkg acc; boat hire; CKE. *"Extra charge
for lakeside pitches, slightly bigger with superb views;
gd sh stay; town, 5 min walk; gd walking & cycling."*
€43.00, 2 Apr-4 Oct. **2015**

VERONA *1D2* (1.5km N Rural) *45.44985, 11.00415*
Camping San Pietro, Via Castel San Pietro 2, 37129
Verona **045 592037; info@campingcastelsanpietro.
com; www.campingcastelsanpietro.com**

🐕 ⚌(cont) wo ♨ ⧄ & ◻ ⧄ 🌁 ⑨ nr å 🛒

Exit A4/E70 to San Martino-Buon-Albergo & foll S11
dir Verona cent, site sp adj Castel San Pietro.
1*, Sm, mkd, hdstg, shd, EHU; bbq; 10% statics; bus
1km; adv bkg req. *"Basic site in park, more suited to
tents or sm m'vans only; no vehicles/o'fits over 7m;
beautiful views over city; easy walk to town cent, but
many steps or use funicular 300mtrs; poor & ltd san
facs."* **€41.00, 2 May-30 Sep.** **2018**

VERONA *1D2* (15km W Rural) *45.44557, 10.83447*
Camping El Bacàn, Via Verona 11, 37010 Palazzolo
di Sona (VR) **348 9317204; info@el-bacan.it;
www.el-bacan.it**

12 🐕 ⚌(cont) wo ♨ ⧄ & ◻ ⧄ 🌁 Ⴒ nr ⑨ nr 🛒 ⚗

Exit A4 onto A22 N & foll sp for Brescia (W) on SR11.
Site in 7km on R, sp 150m bef site ent. Sm, hdg, mkd,
pt shd, EHU (16A) inc; bbq; TV; bus 1km; Eng spkn;
adv bkg acc; ccard acc; CKE. *"Charming, pleasant site
on wkg farm; conv Verona, Lake Garda; friendly owner
& staff; excel farm shop; highly rec; easy access; vg; gd
san facs."* **€23.00** **2017**

VERONA *1D2* (7km W Rural) *45.446075, 10.918951*
Agricamping Corte Finiletto, Strada Bresciana 41,
37139 Verona **340 6075017; info@cortefiniletto.it;**
www.cortefiniletto.it

🔢 ⛺ 🅦 ♨ ⊘ 🄼 ♈ ⛰

Exit A4 onto A22 N & foll sp for Brescia (W) on SR11.
Site approx 3km on R. Lge sp with flags flying.
Sm, mkd, pt shd, EHU (6A) inc; bbq; bus; Eng spkn; adv
bkg acc; ccard acc. *"Kiwi fruit fm; site OAY except for*
1st 2 weeks in Nov (harvest time); gd." **€25.50** **2018**

VIAREGGIO *1C3* (2km S Coastal) *43.85133, 10.25963*
Camping Viareggio, Via Comparini 1, 55049 Viareggio
(LU) **0584 391012; info@campingviareggio.it;**
www.campingviareggio.it

🐕€4 ⛺ 🅦 ♨ ♿ ⊘ ⊘ 🄼 🦋 ♈ 🍴 ⓘ 🄿 ⋔ ⚓ ⛱800m

Fr sea front at Viareggio, take rd on canal sp
Livorno; after x-ing canal bdge turn L (but not
immed on canal) & 2nd R to site in 2km. 1*, Lge, shd,
EHU (4A) (poss rev pol); gas; TV; phone; adv bkg acc;
games area; CKE. *"Gd site & facs; no dogs Aug; hot*
water to shwrs only; cycle rte/footpath to town."
€32.00, 19 Apr-30 Sep. **2019**

VIAREGGIO *1C3* (5km S Coastal) *43.82920, 10.2727*
Camping Italia, Viale dei Tigli 52, 55048 Torre-del-
Lago Puccini (LU) **0584 359828; info@camping**
italia.net; www.campingitalia.net

🐕 ⛺ 🅦 ♨ ♿ ⊘ ⊘ ♈ 🍴 ⓘ 🄿 🄼 ♂ ⚓ ⛱sand 1.5km

Fr A12 N exit sp Viareggio, fr S exit Pisa N onto SS1
& turn twd Torre del Lago at S junc, site well sp thro
vill. Do not turn L at vill cent but cont for 2km N,
then L at rlwy bdge. At rndabt turn L, site on R in
250m. Avoid Viareggio town cent.
Med, shd, EHU (6A) €1.30; gas; TV; 10% statics; Eng
spkn; adv bkg acc; ccard acc; sep car park; bike hire;
tennis. *"Vg for Lucca - Puccini's birthplace; bus tickets*
fr site for Pisa & Lucca; dogs not acc Jun-Aug; some
pitches diff for lge o'fits due trees & low branches; gd
clean facs; poss problem with mosquitoes."
€32.50, 17 Apr-27 Sep. **2019**

VICENZA *1D2* (9km SE Urban) *45.5175, 11.60222*
Camping Vicenza, Strada Pelosa 239, 36100 Vicenza
0444 582311; info@campingvicenza.it; www.camping
vicenza.it

⛺ 🅦 ♨ ♿ ⊘ ⊘ ♈ 🍴 ⓘnr 🄿nr 🄼 ♂

Exit A4 Vicenza Est dir Torri di Quartesole; turn R
immed after toll; site on L 300m fr Vicenza exit,
hidden behind Viest Quality Inn. Fr city foll sp Padua
& a'strada; sp. 4*, Med, pt shd, pt sl, EHU (3A) inc
(rev pol); bbq; red long stay; TV; bus; Eng spkn; adv bkg
acc; ccard acc; bike hire; tennis; CKE. *"Cycle path to*
interesting town; functional site; clean san facs; friendly,
helpful staff; pleasant site." **€38.00, 1 Apr-18 Oct.**
2016

VIESTE *2G4* (2km N Coastal) *41.89901, 16.14964*
Camping Punta Lunga, Loc Defensola, 71019 Vieste
(FG) **0884 706031 or 03466 403894; info@punta**
lung.it; www.puntalunga.it

⛺ (htd) 🅦 ♨ ♿ ⊘ ⊘ 🄼 🦋 ♈ ⓘ 🄿 🄼 ⋔ ♂ ⛱adj

N fr Vieste 1.5km fr end of long beach, turn R at
traff lts down narr lane. Site sp. 3*, Lge, mkd, pt shd,
terr, EHU (3-5A) inc; gas; TV; 15% statics; phone; bus;
Eng spkn; adv bkg acc; ccard acc; canoeing;
windsurfing; sep car park; bike hire; CKE. *"Friendly,*
helpful staff; well-run site on lovely cove; tight pitches -
beware pitch marker posts; v clean facs; rec use bottled
water; beautiful coastal area; statics sep area; gd rest;
lovely cove; excel beaches."
€49.00, 30 May-15 Sep. **2019**

> ## "I like to fill in the reports as I travel from site to site"
>
> You'll find report forms at the back of this
> guide, or you can fill them in online at
> camc.com/europereport.

VIPITENO/STERZING *1D1* (1km S Urban) *46.88737,*
11.43098 **Autoporto,** 00098 Vipiteno **0472 760620;**
info@hotel-brenner.com

🔢 ⛺ ♨ ♂ 🄼 ⓘnr 🄿nr

S fr Brenner Pass approx 17km, take exit immed
bef toll booths Vipiteno & foll sp 'Autoporto'. Site
well sp fr toll booth - 500m. Can also be accessed
fr SS12. Push button on site barrier if office clsd.
Med, hdstg, pt shd, EHU inc. *"Excel NH for c'vans*
or m'vans; conv Austrian border; all facs in services."
€15.00 **2015**

VOLTERRA *1D3* (1km NW Rural) *43.41271, 10.8509*
Camping Le Balze, Via di Mandringa 15, 56048
Volterra (PI) **0588 87880; campinglebalze@**
hotmail.it; www.campinglebalze.com

🐕 ⛺ 🅦 ♨ ♿ ⊘ 🦋 ♈ ⓘnr 🄿 ⚓ 🏊

Take Pisa rd (S68) fr town; site clearly sp ('Camping'
or symbol) after 1km. Watch out for R turn at sharp
L corner. 2*, Med, pt shd, pt sl, terr, EHU (6A) inc; gas;
bus adj; Eng spkn; ccard acc; CKE. *"Beautifully situated*
with views of Volterra & hills; gd, adequate san facs;
select own pitch; Etruscan walls just outside site; excel
site; helpful staff." **€33.00, 1 Apr-15 Oct.** **2018**

ITALY

SARDINIA

ALGHERO *3A1* (1.5km N Coastal) *40.57916, 8.31222*
Camping La Mariposa, Via Lido 22, 07041 Alghero (SS)
079 9950480; info@lamariposa.it; www.lamariposa.it
🐕 👫 wc 🏊 🖪 ⚡ MP ⛺ 🍴 ⑭ 🍴 🍽 🐾 🌲 sand adj

N fr Alghero on coast rd dir Fertilia. Site on L just
beyond pool. 3*, Lge, hdstg, pt shd, pt sl, terr, EHU
(6-10A) €3; gas; bbq; TV; 20% statics; bus nr; Eng spkn;
ccard acc; bike hire; watersports; games rm; sep car
park; CKE. *"Lovely wooded site; gd clean facs; gd
security; friendly staff; boat fr Alghero to caves at Cape
Caccia or by rd + 625 steps."*
€41.00, 1 Apr-15 Oct. 2016

CAGLIARI *3B1* (1km SE Urban) *39.21129, 9.12883*
Camper Cagliari Park, 13 Via Stanislao Caboni, 09125
Cagliari 329 6713141 or 070 303147 or 0328 3348847
(mob); info@campercagliaripark.it; www.camper
cagliaripark.it
12 👫 wc 🚐 MP

Well sp on main rds into Cagliari. Sm, unshd, EHU
(10A) €4; bus 200m; Eng spkn; CKE. *"Gd secure site;
v helpful owner; walking dist historical cent, rests etc;
c'vans enquire 1st."* **€21.00** 2019

DORGALI *3A2* (7km W Coastal) *40.28486, 9.63370*
Camping Villaggio Calagonone, Via Collodi 1, 08022
Cala-Gonone (NU) 0784 93476; info@calagonone
camping.com; www.calagononecamping.com
🐕 €5 👫 wc ♿ ⚡ MP 🍴 ⑭ 🍴 🍽 Ⓜ 🌲 🌲 shgl 400m

Fr S125 turn E twd Cala Gonone, thro tunnel. Site sp
on L of main rd. 4*, Med, shd, terr, EHU (6A) €5; bbq;
30% statics; phone; adv bkg acc; ccard acc; games
area; tennis. *"Beautiful situation in pine forest on edge
of pretty town; nrby coves & grottoes accessible by
boat or on foot."* **€44.00, 1 Apr-3 Nov.** 2019

NARBOLIA *3A1* (6km W Coastal) *40.06956, 8.48375*
Camping Nurapolis, Loc Is Arenas, 09070 Narbolia (OR)
0783 52283 or 348 8080839(mob); info@nurapolis.it;
www.nurapolis.it
12 🐕 👫 ♿ ⚡ 🍴 ⑭ 🍴 🍽 🐾 🌲 sand adj

Fr Oristano take sp to Cuglier on rd SS292i. Site sp
fr rd approx 5km fr S. Caterina-di-Pittinura. 3*, Lge,
pt shd, EHU (3A) €3; gas; adv bkg acc; ccard acc;
tennis; watersports; CKE. *"Site in pine forest; many
sports, guided walks Easter to Oct; very pleasant
owners."* **€36.50** 2019

PORTO SAN PAOLO *3A2* (2km S Coastal) *40.85870,
9.64296* **Camping Tavolara,** Loc Porto Taverna,
07020 Loiri-Porta San Paolo (SS) 0789 40166; info@
camping-tavolara.it; www.camping-tavolara.it
🐕 €3 👫 wc 🏊 ♿ 🖪 ⚡ MP 🍴 🍴 ⑭ 🍽 Ⓜ 🐾 🌲 sand 500m

On SS125, sp. 3*, Lge, hdg, unshd, EHU (3-6A) €3.50;
25% statics; Eng spkn; adv bkg acc; ccard acc; tennis;
bike hire; site clsd Dec & early Jan; CKE. *"Friendly
staff; conv ferries & boat trips; pleasant, well managed
site; 16km fr Olbia ferries; lovely beach; siesta 1@30-
3:30pm; vg."* **€50.00, 19 Apr-13 Oct.** 2019

PORTO TORRES *3A1* (7km E Coastal) *40.81607,
8.48541* **Camping Golfo dell'Asinara-Cristina,**
Loc Platamona, 07037 Sorso (SS) 079 310230;
info@campingasinara.it; www.campingasinara.it
👫 🏊 🖪 ⚡ MP 🍴 🍴 ⑭ 🍴 🍽 🐾 🌲 sand adj

Foll coast rd SP81 E fr Porto-Torres to site. Sp.
4*, Lge, pt shd, EHU (4A) €4; gas; red long stay;
40% statics; ccard acc; bike hire; tennis; games area;
sep car park; CKE. *"Gd position."*
€35.00, 15 May-30 Sep. 2016

PULA *3B1* (4km S Coastal) *38.96779, 8.97799*
Camping Flumendosa, Santa Margherita, Km 33.800,
09010 Pula (CA) 070 4615332 or 392 9623094;
info@campingflumendosa.com; www.camping
flumendosa.com
🐕 €2.50 👫 (htd) wc 🏊 ♿ 🖪 ⚡ MP 🍴 🍴 🍴 ⑭ 🍽 🐾 🌲
🌲 sand

Fr Cagliari take SS195 past Pula, sp. Turn L, foll
track for 500m to site ent. Lge, hdstg, mkd, pt shd,
EHU (8A); gas; bbq; cooking facs; TV; 30% statics;
Eng spkn; adv bkg acc; ccard acc; fishing; guided
walks; jeu de boules alley; beach volleyball. *"Beautiful
coastline; excel for children; sand flies abound;
good, pleasant, friendly site; gd bar/rest; rec Nora
for Roman city & beach; conv fr lovely coast to W."*
€43.00, 1 Apr-13 Nov. 2019

> ## "We must tell the Club about that great site we found"
>
> Get your site reports in by mid-August and we'll
> do our best to get your updates into the next
> edition.

TONARA *3A1* (0.9km NE Rural) *40.02812,
9.17647* **Camping Sa Colonia,** Via
Muggianeddu 4, 08039 Tonara (NU) 03921
282340; info@campingsacolonia.it
12 👫 wc 🏊 ⚡ 🍴 🍴 🍴 ⑭ 🍴 🐾 nr Ⓜ

Fr S fr Cagliari on SS128/SS295, site sp. Sp rte
unsuitable lge car + c'van o'fits or v lge m'vans.
Avoid town cent rds - v narr & steep. Med, mkd, shd,
terr, EHU (5A) inc; Eng spkn; CKE. *"Mountain scenery;
rds gd but steep, twisty & slow; welcoming owners."*
€20.00 2016

SICILY

ACIREALE *3C4* (1.5km NE Coastal) *37.62015, 15.17320* **La Timpa International Camping,** Via Santa Maria La Scala 25, 95024 Acireale **095 7648155; info @campinglatimpa.com; www.campinglatimpa.com**

⊞ 🛏 €4 ♦♦♦ 🚿 🕭 🗐 ⁄ 🍴 ⊕ 🏊 🚉 ⁄ 🅿 adj

Exit A18/E45 onto rd S114 dir Acireale. Foll sp for Santa Maria La Scala; site on L after 1.5km; steep & diff access rds. 3*, Med, pt shd, EHU (6A) €3.50; 60% statics; ccard acc; sep car park; CKE. *"Lovely site in orchard, o'looking sea, surfaced in black volcanic ash; hot & cold shwrs; no dogs Jul/Aug; chem displ; trips to Etna; lift down to rocky beach; sh, steep walk to vill & harbour; v quiet; gd rest."* **€30.50**   **2018**

AGRIGENTO *3C3* (8km S Urban/Coastal) *37.26936, 13.58299* **Camping Valle dei Templi,** Viale Emporium 95, 92100 San Leone **0922 411115; info@camping velledeitempli.com; www.campingvalledeitempli.com**

⊞ 🐕 ♦♦♦ 🚿 🕭 🕭 🗐 ⁄ 🅼🆂🅿 🍴 ⊕ 🏊 🚉 nr 🅿 800m

Sp S of Agrigento, foll sp San Leone, site on L bef beach. Lge, hdstg, pt shd, pt sl, terr, EHU (6A) €3; red long stay; 20% statics; bus; Eng spkn; adv bkg acc; ccard acc; tennis; bike hire; site clsd 8 Dec-15 Jan; CKE. *"Gd modern facs; friendly staff; bus to temples fr site ent."* **€40.50**   **2018**

AVOLA *3C4* (4km N Coastal) *36.93631, 15.17462* **Camping Sabbiadoro,** Via Chiusa di Carlo 45, 96012 Avola (SR) **0931 822415; info@campeggio sabbiadoro.com; www.campeggiosabbiadoro.com**

⊞ 🛏 ♦♦♦ 🚿 🕭 ⁄ 🅼🆂🅿 🍴 🏊 🚉 🅿 sand

Fr N exit A18/E45 at Cassibile onto S115 dir Avola, site sp in 4km. Last 500m on narr, winding rd. 3*, Med, mkd, shd, pt sl, terr, EHU (2A) €4; 20% statics; phone; adv bkg acc; ccard acc; horseriding. *"V attractive site with clean, ltd facs; rec visit Noto; well run; dir access to beach; sep car park Jul-Aug; poss muddy pitches after heavy rain."* **€41.00**   **2019**

AVOLA *3C4* (5km NE Coastal) *36.93853, 15.17756* **Camping Paradiso del Mare,** Contrada Gallinara Fondolupo, 96012 Avola (SR) **0931 561147; info@ paradisodelmare.com; www.paradisodelmare.com**

🛏 ♦♦♦ 🚿 🕭 🕭 🗐 ⁄ 🍴 ⊕ nr 🚉 🅿 adj

Best app fr N on S115 fr Siracusa, site on L, well sp. Tight turn if app fr Avola. 2*, Sm, mkd, pt shd, EHU (5A) €3; bus 200m; Eng spkn; CKE. *"Pleasant lovely site by beautiful beach; friendly helpful owners."* **€27.50, 14 Apr-31 Oct.**   **2018**

CASTELLAMMARE DEL GOLFO *3C3* (1km E Coastal) *38.02393, 12.89348* **Nausicaa Camping,** C/da Spiaggia-Plaia, Loc Forgia, 91014 Castellammare-del-Golfo (TP) **0924 33030; info@nausicaa-camping.it; www.nausicaa-camping.it**

♦♦♦ 🚿 🕭 🕭 ⁄ 🐕 ⊕ nr 🚉 🅿 sand adj

Site 1km E fr Castellammare on R of rte 187. Well sp. Awkward ent for lge o'fits as steep ramp. 3*, Sm, hdstg, mkd, pt shd, EHU €3; gas; 10% statics; ccard acc; tennis; CKE. *"Nr Roman temple at Segesta; gd 1st stop fr Palermo if touring historical sites; lovely site on cliff; easy walk to town & access to beach."* **€41.00, 1 Apr-15 Oct.**   **2018**

CATANIA *3C4* (6km NE Coastal) *37.53279, 15.12012* **Camping Jonio,** Loc Ognina, Via Villini a Mare 2, 95126 Catania **095 491139; info@campingjonio.com; www.campingjonio.com**

⊞ 🛏 ♦♦♦ 🚿 🕭 🕭 🗐 ⁄ 🅼🆂🅿 🍴 ⊕ 🏊 🚉 nr 🅿 shgl

SS114 N of Catania, exit Ognina. Fr the Catania ring rd, take exit Catania Centro (San Gregorio) and then Catania E. Foll sp to site. 3*, Med, hdstg, pt shd, terr, EHU (6A) €4; gas; bbq; twin axles; 20% statics; bus to Catania; Eng spkn; adv bkg acc; ccard acc; waterskiing; games area; sep car park; CKE. *"Mt Etna 45 mins drive N; owner v helpful; some pitches sm; subways, scubadiving; gd."* **€39.00**   **2016**

CEFALU *3B3* (5km W Rural) *38.02700, 13.98247* **Camping Sanfilippo,** Ogliastrillo SS113, 90015 Cefalù **0921 420 184; info@campingsanfilippo.com; www.campingsanfilippo.com**

🛏 €3.50 ♦♦♦ 🚿 🕭 🕭 🗐 ⁄ 🅼🆂🅿 🐕 🏊 🚉 🛆 🅿 150m

Fr Palermo E twds Cafalu on rd SS113. 2*, Med, hdstg, mkd, shd, terr, EHU (4A) inc; bbq; twin axles; 50% statics; bus 300m; Eng spkn; adv bkg acc; games area; games rm; CCI. *"Vg, beautiful site; sea views fr pitches; newly renovated (2016)."* **€28.50, 1 Apr-31 Oct.**   **2018**

MARINA DI RAGUSA *3C3* (2km E Coastal) *36.78116, 14.56697* **Camping Baia del Sole,** Lungomare Andrea Doria, 97010 Marina-di-Ragusa (RG) **03495 116018 or 03393 471986; info@campingbaiadelsole.it; www.campingbaiadelsole.it**

⊞ ♦♦♦ 🕭 🕭 ⁄ 🍴 ⊕ 🏊 🚉 🛆 🐕 🅿 adj

Foll sp in Marina di Ragusa for Hotel Baia del Sole. Site in hotel grnds on dual c'way on seafront. 3*, Med, shd, EHU (4A) inc; adv bkg acc; ccard acc; bike hire; tennis. *"Go to recep 1st; no height barrier; sep car park; v quiet."* **€19.00**   **2018**

MENFI *3C3* (6km S Coastal) *37.56500, 12.96416*
Camping La Palma, Contrada Fiore, Via delle Palme
29, 92013 Menfi (AG) **0925 78392; campinglapalma@
libero.it; www.campinglapalma.com**

🏕12 🐕 👫 ⬦ ♨ ⛄ 🍴 ⚥ 🦋 ⛲ 🍽 🍹 ① ♨ 🛒 ⛁ 🚿 sand adj

Foll sp fr SS115 past Menfi to coast. In abt 3-4km
look for campsite sp. 1*, Med, hdstg, shd, EHU 16A;
gas; bbq; twin axles; TV; 5% statics; Eng spkn; adv bkg
acc; games area; CKE. *"Lovely, unspoilt quiet beach
(blue flag) with dunes; v helpful owner & staff; family
run site; excel."* **€30.00** **2018**

MILAZZO *3B4* (2km N Coastal) *38.26090, 15.24335*
Camping Villaggio Riva Smeralda, Strada
Panoramica 64, 98057 Milazzo (ME) **090 9282980;
info@rivasmeralda.it; www.rivasmeralda.it**

🏕12 👫 ⬦ ♨ ⛄ 🍴 ⚥ 🍽 🍹 ① ♨ 🛒 ⛁ 🚿 ⛵ shgl adj

Clearly sp in Milazzo; foll sp Capo-di-Milazzo. Diff
app. 1*, Med, hdstg, shd, pt sl, terr, EHU (6A) €3; bbq;
twin axles; 5% statics; Eng spkn; adv bkg acc; CKE. *"Gd
base for trips to adj isles; site a bit run down; 1 in 5 sl
access to pitches, ltd turning space; best for sm m'vans;
diving cent on site; excel; v nice site with beautiful
views of sea; pitches tight; extremely helpful owners;
€3 a night to leave camper to go to Aeolian Islands;
vg."* **€33.50** **2017**

"I need an on-site restaurant"

We do our best to make sure site information
is correct, but it is always best to check any
must-have facilities are still available or will
be open during your visit.

PALERMO *3B3* (16km NW Urban/Coastal) *38.19805,
13.28083* **Camping Degli Ulivi,** Via Pegaso 25, 90148
Sferracavallo (PA) **091 533021 or 091 530247;
mporion@libero.it; www.campingdegliulivi.com**

🏕12 🐕 👫 ⬦ ♨ ⛄ 🍴 ⚥ 🍽 🍹 ① ♨ 🛒 ⛁ shgl 300m

Fr W on A29 exit sp Tommaso & foll dual c'way twd
Mondello. Do U-turn at 1st opportunity to
Sferracavallo. Downhill thro vill, site sp, R turn off
hg street. 1*, Sm, hdg, pt shd, pt sl, EHU (6-10A) €3;
bbq; twin axles; 10% statics; bus to Palermo; Eng spkn;
sep car park; CKE. *"Helpful staff; pleasant ambience;
beach sand 700m; well-maintained site nr nature park -
excel views, popular site."* **€20.50** **2016**

PATTI *B4* (4.8km NNW Coastal) *38.169266, 14.948943*
Camping IL Cicero, Via Pola 98, 98063 San Giorgio
**094 139551 or 347 9989530; info@ilcicero.it;
www.ilcicero.it**

🐕 👫(htd) ⬦ ♨ ⛄ 🍴 ⚥ 🦋 🍹 🍴 ① nr 🛒 ⛁ nr ⛲ 🚿

🏖 sand; adj

Fr E90 take SS113 to San Giorgio. Site on seafront
Med, mkd, shd, EHU (6A) inc; twin axles; 20% statics;
0.5km; games area; games rm. *"V friendly, helpful
staff; gd for kids; vg site."* **€36.00, 1 May-30 Sep.**
2018

PIAZZA ARMERINA *3C3* (4km SE Rural) *37.20239,
14.23155* **Camping Agriturismo Agricasale,** C da
Ciavarini, 94015 Piazza-Armerina (EN) **0935 686034;
www.agricasale.it**

🏕12 🐕 👫 ⬦ ♨ ⛄ 🍴 ⚥ 🍽 🦋 🍹 🍴 ① 🛒 nr ⛲ 🚿

In Piazza-Armerina town foll sp twd Mirabella but at
rndabt with stone cross bear R (red fox sign) & foll
red fox down nar rd to wooded site. Park with care.
Sm, pt shd, pt sl, EHU (4A) inc; bbq; TV; Eng spkn;
adv bkg acc; CKE. *"Excel site close Palazzo Romana
mosaics; pony-trekking, archery & other activities high
ssn; all inc rate of €50 avail per day inc excel banquet;
site run down."* **€15.00** **2019**

PUNTA BRACCETTO *3C3* (0km E Urban/Coastal)
36.81713, 14.46736 **Camping Scarabeo,** Via dei
Canaletti 120, Punta-Braccetto, 97017 Santa Croce
Camerina (RG) **0932 918096; info@scarabeo
camping.it; www.scarabeocamping.it**

🏕12 🐕 €2.50 👫 ⬦ ♨ ⛄ 🍴 ⚥ 🍽 🦋 🍹 🍴 nr ① nr ⛁ ⚥

🏖 sand adj

W fr Marina di Ragusa on SP80/SC25 coast rd. Site sp.
2*, Sm, hdstg, hdg, pt shd, pt sl, EHU (3-6A); bbq; red
long stay; twin axles; 5% statics; phone; Eng spkn; adv
bkg acc; ccard acc; CKE. *"Beautiful situation; private
bthrm €4; well-maintained, friendly, family-run site; gd,
clean, modern facs; vg security; friendly, helpful staff;
cars parked sep across rd; excel."* **€41.50** **2017**

PUNTA BRACCETTO *3C3* (0km S Urban/Coastal)
36.81722, 14.46583 **Camping Luminoso,** Viale dei
Canalotti, 97017 Punta Braccetto - Santa Croce
Camerina (RG) **0932 918401; info@camping
luminoso.com; www.campingluminoso.com**

🏕12 🐕 👫 ⬦ ♨ ⛄ 🍴 ⚥ 🍽 🍹 🍴 ① ♨ 🛒 ⛲ ⚥ 🏖 sand adj

W fr Marina di Ragusa on SP80/SC25 coast rd.
Site sp. 3*, Med, mkd, hdstg, shd, EHU (6A) €5; TV;
adv bkg rec; ccard acc; bike hire; CKE. *"Well-run site
in gd location; easy access to pitches - suitable lge
o'fits/m'vans; excel; modern, immac facs; spacious level
hdstg pitches; reliable wifi; helpful English manager;
private bthrms avail; direct access to sandy beach; mob
shops call daily; ideal long stay in winter."* **€46.00**
2019

PUNTA BRACCETTO *3C3* (4km SW Coastal) *36.81661, 14.46895* **Camping Baia Dei Coralli,** Punta Braccetto, 97017 Santa Croce Camerina **0932 91 81 92; info@baiadeicoralli.it; www.baiadeicoralli.it**
12 🐕 ♦♦♦ wd ♨ ♿ ⬛ ✉ MP 🦋 ♈ ⍟ ⊕ ♨ ᾼ ♪ ⚓ 🖈 sand

Fr Agrigento take SS115 twds Sircusa to Gela. Turn L onto SP14, cont onto SP13. At rndabt take 3rd exit onto SP20, R onto SP85, L twd Strada Regionale 25. R onto Strada Regionale 24. Campsite on L. 3*, Lge, hdg, hdstg, unshd, EHU (6A); bbq; twin axles; TV; bus; Eng spkn; adv bkg acc; ccard acc; CCI. *"Excel site; v busy in summer."* **€35.00**   2019

> ## "Satellite navigation makes touring much easier"
>
> Remember most sat navs don't know if you're towing or in a larger vehicle – always use yours alongside maps and site directions.

SAN VITO LO CAPO *3B3* (3km S Coastal) *38.15067, 12.73184* **El Bahira Camping Village,** Contrada Salinella, 91010 San Vito-lo-Capo (TP) **0923 972577; info@elbahira.it; www.elbahira.it**
12 ♦♦♦ wd ♿ ⬛ ✉ 🦋 ⍟ ⊕ ♨ ᾼ ♪ ⚓ 🖈 🏠 shgl adj

W fr Palermo on A29 dir Trapani. Exit at Castellammare del Golfo onto SS187, then turn N onto SP16 sp San Vito-lo-Capo. At Isolidda foll site sp. 4*, Lge, mkd, shd, EHU (6A) inc; bbq; TV; 10% statics; phone; bus nr; Eng spkn; ccard acc; watersports; games rm; sep car park; tennis; excursions; games area; CKE. *"Excel, secure site in vg location; gd facs for families; san facs tired need updating (2014)."* **€26.00**   2019

SECCAGRANDE *3C3* (2km SE Coastal) *37.43833, 13.2450* **Kamemi Camping Village,** Contrada Camemi Superiore, 92016 Seccagrande-di-Ribera (AG) **0925 69212; info@kamemicamping.it; www.kamemi camping.it**
12 🐕 ♦♦♦ ♿ ⬛ ✉ ⍟ Y ⊕ ♨ ᾼ ♪ ⚓ 🖈 sand 1km

Foll sp fr S115 to Seccagrande & site. 2*, Med, hdstg, pt shd, EHU (6A) €5; 40% statics; Eng spkn; adv bkg rec; tennis; games area. **€37.00**   2019

SIRACUSA *3C4* (4km SW Rural) *37.03841, 15.25063* **Camping Agritourist Rinaura,** Strada Laganelli, Loc Rinaura, SS115, 96100 Siracusa **0931 721224; sindona.marina@virgilio.it; www.campingrinaura.it**
12 🐕 ♦♦♦ wd ♨ ♿ ⬛ ✉ 🦋 ⍟ ⊕ nr ♨ ᾼ 🖈 sand 2km

S fr Siracusa on S115 twd Avola. Turn R 300m past Hotel Albatros then immed R after rlwy x-ing. Narr lane to site in 300m. 2*, Lge, pt shd, EHU (16A) €3; red long stay; phone; bus 1km; Eng spkn; adv bkg acc; bike hire; CKE. *"CL-type site in lge orchard; basic but adequate san facs; rather neglected LS; helpful owners."* **€27.00**   2019

TAORMINA *3C4* (10km NE Coastal) *37.93159, 15.35560* **Camping La Focetta Sicula,** Via Torrente Agro, 98030 Sant' Alessio Siculo (ME) **0942 751657; info@lafocetta.it; www.lafocetta.it**
12 🐕 ♦♦♦ wd ♨ ♿ ⬛ ✉ MP 🦋 ♈ Y ⊕ ♨ ᾼ ♪ 🖈 sand

A'strada fr Messina to Catania, exit Roccalumera. SS114 thro Sta Teresa-di-Riva to vill of Sant' Alessio-Siculo. Sp at beg of vill. NB Many towns poorly sp. 2*, Med, mkd, pt shd, EHU (6A) €3 gas; red long stay; sep car park; bike hire; games area; CKE. *"Popular winter site; v helpful owner."* **€26.00**   2018

TAORMINA *3C4* (12km S Coastal) *37.74928, 15.20616* **Camping Mokambo,** Via Spiaggia 211, Fondachello, 95016 Máscali (CT) **095 938731; info@ campingmokambo.it; www.campingmokambo.it**
🐕 ♦♦♦ wd ♨ ♿ ✉ ⍟ ⊕ nr ♨ nr ᾼ 🖈 adj

Exit A18/E45 at Fiumefreddo & take S114 sp Catania. In Máscali turn L twd Fondachello. At Fondachello turn R & foll site sp, site 1km on R. 2*, Med, hdstg, pt shd, EHU (3A) €4; bbq; 10% statics; Eng spkn; adv bkg acc; ccard acc; games area; CKE. *"Gd views Etna; conv beach & Taormina; wifi unreliable; no dogs Jul/Aug; poor."* **€43.20, 1 Apr-30 Sep.**   2017

Map I

Map 2

Map 3

A

TARANTO

Alberobello
Matera
Corigliano Calabro
Sibari

901
407
107
280
18
106
E45

Marina di Caulonia

Nicotera
Palmi
MESSINA
REGGIO DI CALABRIA

Milazzo
Oliveri
Patti
Finale
Taormina
Acireale
A18

SIRACUSA
Avola
Donnalucata

Piazza Armerina

Agrigento
A19
189

Punta Braccetto

Menfi
Seccagrande

Castellammare del Golfo
Cefalù
PALERMO

San Vito lo Capo

SICILY

IONIAN SEA

TYRRHENIAN SEA

NAPOLI
Pompei
Sorrento
Agerola
SALERNO
Paestum

SARDINIA

Porto San Paolo
Dorgali
Tonara

Porto Torres
199
129
131
130
Cagliari
Pula

Alghero
Narbolia

TUNISIA

ALGERIA

MALTA

N
W E
S

200m +
0–200m

Motorways
Major roads
Main roads

All year site(s)
Seasonal site(s)
No sites listed

© Collins Bartholomew Ltd 2020

0   50   100   150 kms
0   50   100 mls

ABRUZZO
Chieti
L'Aquila
Pescara
Teramo

BASILICATA
Matera
Potenza

CALABRIA
Catanzaro
Cosenza
Crotone
Reggio di Calabria
Vibo Valentia

CAMPANIA
Avellino
Benevento
Caserta
Napoli
Salerno

EMILIA-ROMAGNA
Bologna
Ferrara
Forli
Modena
Parma
Piacenza
Ravenna
Reggio Emilia
Rimini

FRIULI-VENEZIA GIULIA
Gorizia
Pordenone
Trieste
Udine

LAZIO
Frosinone
Latina
Rieti
Roma
Viterbo

LIGURIA
Genova
Imperia
La Spezia
Savona

LOMBARDIA
Bergamo
Brescia
Como
Cremona
Lecco
Lodi
Mantova
Milano
Pavia
Sondrio
Varese

MARCHE
Ancona
Ascoli Piceno
Macerata
Pesaro e Urbino

MOLISE
Campobasso
Isernia

PIEMONTE
Alessandria
Asti
Biella
Cuneo
Novara
Torino
Verbano-Cusio-Ossola
Vercelli

PUGLIA
Bari
Brindisi
Foggia
Lecce
Taranto

SARDEGNA
Cagliari
Nuoro
Oristano
Sassari

SICILIA
Agrigento
Caltanissetta
Catania
Enna
Messina
Palermo
Ragusa
Siracusa
Trapani

TOSCANA
Arezzo
Firenze
Grosseto
Livorno
Lucca
Massa Carrara
Pisa
Pistoia
Prato
Siena

TRENTINO-ALTO ADIGE
Bolzano
Trento

UMBRIA
Perugia
Terni

VALLE D'AOSTA
Aosta/Aoste

VENETO
Belluno
Padova
Rovigo
Treviso
Venezia
Verona
Vicenza

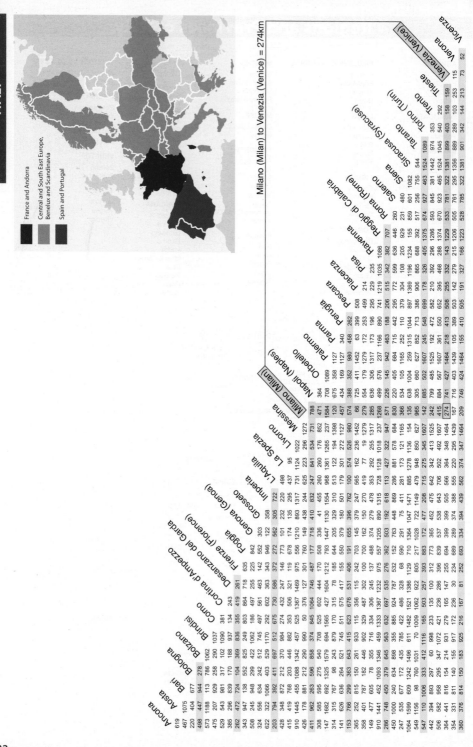

France and Andorra

Central and South East Europe, Benelux and Scandinavia

Spain and Portugal

Milano (Milan) to Venezia (Venice) = 274km

Luxembourg

Luxembourg City

Highlights

Although a tiny country just over 50 miles long, Luxembourg is an economic powerhouse. Luxembourg City is famous for its stunning, medieval old town and for the number of notable museums and galleries that it boasts.

Most of the country is rural, and the beautiful landscapes vary from the micro-gorges of Müllerthal to the vineyards of the Moselle wine region.

Luxembourg cuisine is heavily influenced by its neighbours and in particular has many Germanic influences. Judd mat Gaardebounen, a smoked collar of pork with broad beans, is a particularly popular meal and is widely recognised as one of the country's national dishes.

The Festival of Wiltz is an annual affair that celebrates some of the most talented international musicians. With its open air setting and castle backdrop, it attracts large audiences each year and is considered to be a cultural highlight.

Major towns and cities

- Luxembourg City – this fascinating capital offers UNESCo sites and gastronomy.
- Esch-sur-Alzette – this city has the longest shopping street in the country.
- Diekirck – a city with charming old streets.
- Dudelange – a cultural centre with lots to see including Mount St. Jean.

Attractions

- Mullerthal Trail – explore 112km of varied landscape, from forests to rock formations.
- Vianden Castle, Vianden – a grand building that originates from the 10th century.
- National Museum of Art and History, Luxembourg City – enjoy a fascinating range of exhibitions from archaeology to fine arts.
- Holy Ghost Citadel, Luxembourg City – a majestic fortress with stunning views.

Find out more

www.visitluxembourg.lu
E: info@visitluxembourg.lu
T: +352 (0) 42 82 82 10

323

Country Information

Population (approx): 570,000

Capital: Luxembourg City

Area: 2,586 sq km

Bordered by: Belgium, France, Germany

Terrain: Rolling hills to north with broad, shallow valleys; steep slope to Moselle valley in south-east

Climate: Temperate climate without extremes of heat or cold; mild winters; warm, wet summers; July and August are the hottest months; May and June have the most hours of sunshine.

Highest Point: Kneiff 560m

Languages: French, German, Lëtzebuergesch (Luxembourgish)

Local Time: GMT or BST + 1, i.e. 1 hour ahead of the UK all year

Currency: Euros divided into 100 cents; £1 = €1.16, €1 = £0.87 (October 2019)

Emergency numbers: Police 113; Fire brigade 112; Ambulance 112. Operators speak English

Public Holidays 2020: Jan 1; Apr 13; May 1, 21; Jun 1, 23; Aug 15; Nov 1; Dec 25, 26.

There are other dates such as Luxembourg City Fete and 2 Nov which are not official holidays but many businesses, banks and shops may close. School summer holidays run from mid-July to mid-September.

Entry Formalities

British and Irish passport holders may stay for up to three months without a visa.

Medical Services

Emergency medical treatment is available on presentation of a European Health Insurance Card (EHIC) but you will be charged both for treatment and prescriptions. Refunds can be obtained from a local sickness insurance fund office, Caisse de Maladie des Ouvriers (CMO). Emergency hospital treatment is normally free apart from a non-refundable standard daily fee.

Opening Hours

Banks: Mon-Fri 8.30am-12 noon & 1.30pm-4.30pm.Some stay open to 6pm and open Sat 9am-12 noon.

Museums: Tue-Sun 10am-6pm, Thurs late opening 5pm-8pm (check locally); most close Mon.

Post Offices: Mon-Fri 8am-12 noon & 1.30pm-4.30pm/5pm; the central post office in Luxembourg City is open 7am-7pm Mon to Fri & 7am-5pm Sat.

Shops: Mon-Sat 9am/10am-6pm/6.30pm. Some close for lunch and Mon mornings. Large malls may be open to 8pm or 9pm.

Safety and Security

There are few reports of crime but visitors should take the usual commonsense precautions against pickpockets. Do not leave valuables in your car.

Luxembourg shares with the rest of Europe an underlying threat from terrorism. Attacks could be indiscriminate and against civilian targets in public places, including tourist sites.

British Embassy

BOULEVARD JOSEPH II, L-1840 LUXEMBOURG
Tel: 22 98 64
www.ukinluxembourg.fco.gov.uk

Irish Embassy

Résidence Christina (2nd floor)

28 ROUTE D'ARLON, L-1140 LUXEMBOURG
Tel: 450 6101
www.embassyofireland.lu

Documents

Money

Major credit cards are widely accepted although there are often minimum amount requirements. Cash machines are widespread. Carry your credit card issuers'/banks' 24-hour UK contact numbers in case of loss or theft of your cards.

Passport

When driving it is easy to cross into neighbouring countries without realising it. Although you are unlikely to be asked for it, you must have your valid passport with you.

Vehicle(s)

Drivers of foreign-registered vehicles must be able to produce on demand a current driving licence, vehicle registration document (V5C) insurance certificate, insurance certificate and MOT certificate (if applicable).

Driving

Alcohol

The maximum permitted level of alcohol is 50 milligrams in 100 millilitres of blood, i.e. lower than that permitted in the UK (80 milligrams). For drivers who have held a driving licence for less than two years the permitted level is 20 milligrams i.e. virtually nil. Breath tests are compulsory following serious road accidents and road offences.

Breakdown Service

A 24-hour breakdown service 'Service Routier' is operated by the Automobile Club De Grand-Duche de Luxembourg (ACL) on all roads, telephone 26000. Operators speak English. Payment by credit card is accepted.

Child Restraint System

Children under the age of 3 years old must be seated in an approved child restraint system.

Children from the ages of 3 to 17 and/or under the height of 1.5m must be seated in an appropriate restraint system. If they are over 36kg in weight they can use a seat belt but only if they are in the rear of the vehicle.

Rear-facing child restraint systems are not allowed on seats with front airbags unless the airbag has been deactivated.

Fuel

Petrol stations are generally open from 8am to 8pm with 24 hour service on motorways. Most accept credit cards and many have automatic pumps operated with a credit card.

It is illegal to carry petrol in a can.

LPG is available at a handful of petrol stations – see www.mylpg.eu and use the drop down menu listed under LPG stations.

Motorways

There are approximately 152km of motorways, all of which are toll-free for private vehicles. Motorway service areas are situated at Capellen on the A6 near Mamer, at Pontpierre on the A4, and at Berchem near Bettenbourg on the A3.

Emergency telephones are situated every 1.5km along main roads and motorways and link motorists to the 'Protection Civile'.

Overtaking

When overtaking at night outside built-up areas it is compulsory to flash headlights.

Parking

Parking is prohibited where there are yellow lines or zigzag white lines. Blue zone parking areas exist in Luxembourg City, Esch-sur-Elzette, Dudelange and Wiltz. Parking discs are available from the ACL, police stations, tourist offices and shops. Parking meters operate in Luxembourg City. Police will clamp or remove illegally parked vehicles.

There are free car parks two to three kilometres outside Luxembourg City and Esch-sur-Elzette from which regular buses leave for the city.

If there is no public lighting when parking on a public road sidelights must be switched on.

Priority

Where two roads of the same category intersect, traffic from the right has priority. In towns give priority to traffic coming from the right, unless there is a 'priority road' sign (yellow diamond with white border) indicating that the driver using that road has right of way.

Road Signs and Markings

Road signs and markings conform to international standards and are shown in French and German. Traffic lights pass from red immediately to green (no red and amber phase). A flashing amber light allows traffic to turn in the direction indicated, traffic permitting. In Luxembourg City some bus lanes and cycle lanes are marked in red.

Speed Limits

	Open Road (km/h)	Motorway (km/h)
Car Solo	90	130
Car towing caravan/trailer	75	90
Motorhome under 3500kg	90	130
Motorhome 3500-7500kg	90	130

The solo car top speed of 130 km/h (80 mph) is reduced to 110 km/h (68 mph) in wet weather. The speed limit for drivers who have held a licence for less than a year is 90 km/h (56 mph) on motorways and 75 km/h (47 mph) outside built-up areas. In some residential areas called 'Zones de Rencontre' the maximum permitted speed is 20 km/h (13 mph).

Traffic Jams

Many people travel through Luxembourg in order to take advantage of cheaper fuel and queues at petrol stations often cause jams, in particular along the 'petrol route' past Martelange (N4 in Belgium), at Dudelange on the A3/E25 at the Belgium-Luxembourg border, and near Steinfort on the A6.

Other bottlenecks occur, particularly during weekends in July and August, at the junctions on the A1/E44 near Gasperich to the south of Luxembourg City, and the exit from the A3/E25 at Dudelange. To avoid traffic jams between Luxembourg City and Thionville (France), leave the western ring road around Luxembourg and take the A4 to Esch-sur-Alzette and then the D16. When past Aumetz join the N52 which then connects to the A30 to Metz.

The website www.cita.lu provides webcam views of all motorways and traffic information.

Violation of Traffic Regulations

Police officers may impose on the spot fines for infringement of regulations. These must be settled in cash and a receipt given. Non-residents of Luxembourg are liable to receive penalty points for serious infringements of traffic law.

Winter Driving

Vehicles are required to have M&S (Mud and Snow) marked tyres fitted when driving in wintery conditions (frost, snow, ice etc.). This regulation applies to all drivers, regardless of where the vehicle is registered.

Essential Equipment

Lights

The use of dipped headlights in the daytime is recommended for all vehicles.

Reflective Jacket/ Waistcoat

It is compulsory to wear a reflective jacket when getting out of your vehicle on a motorway or main road. Pedestrians walking at night or in bad visibility outside built-up areas must also wear one.

Warning Triangle

A warning triangle must be used if the vehicle is immobilised on the roadway.

Touring

Luxembourg is the only Grand Duchy in the world and measures a maximum of 81km (51 miles) from north to south and 51km (32 miles) from east to west. The fortifications and old town of Luxembourg City have been designated as a UNESCO World Heritage site.

Smoking is not allowed in bars and restaurants. A service charge is usually added to restaurant bills and it is normal practice to leave a little extra if the service is good.

The Luxembourg Card is valid for one, two or three days, and entitles the holder to free public transport, admission to numerous museums and tourist attractions, and discounts on sightseeing trips. It is available from tourist offices, campsites, hotels, information and public transport offices as well as from participating attractions. You can also buy it online at www.ont.lu.

There are many marked walking trails throughout the country – see www.hiking-in-luxembourg.co.uk for full details. A Christmas market is held in the pedestrianised Place d'Armes in Luxembourg City. Others are held in towns and villages throughout the country.

French is the official language, but Luxembourgish is the language most commonly used. English is widely spoken in Luxembourg City, but less so elsewhere.

Camping and Caravanning

There are approximately 120 campsites in Luxembourg; most are open from April to October. Apart from in the industrial south, campsites are found all over the country. The Ardennes, the river banks along the Moselle and the Sûre and the immediate surroundings of Luxembourg City are particularly popular.

Casual/wild camping is only permitted with a tent, not a caravan, but permission must first be sought from the landowner.

Motorhomes

Many campsites have motorhome amenities and some offer Quick Stop overnight facilities at reduced rates.

Electricity and Gas

Most campsites have a supply of between 6 and 16 amps and many have CEE connections. Plugs have two round pins. The full range of Campingaz cylinders is widely available.

Public Transport & Local Travel

A transport network ticket (billet réseau) is available at railway stations throughout the country and at the airport. It allows unlimited travel on city buses, trains and country coaches for one day (until 8am the next morning) throughout Luxembourg. Public transport maps can be downloaded from the Luxembourg Tourist Office website, www.luxembourg.co.uk.

Luxembourg is a compact city and walking around it is easy and pleasant. It is served by an efficient network of buses. You can buy bus tickets valid either for two hours (billet de courte durée) or one day (billet de longue durée). A discount is offered on a block of 10 tickets. Tickets must be validated at the machines on buses and train platforms. Dogs are allowed free of charge on city buses. People over 65 years of age may qualify for travel concessions; show your passport as proof of age.

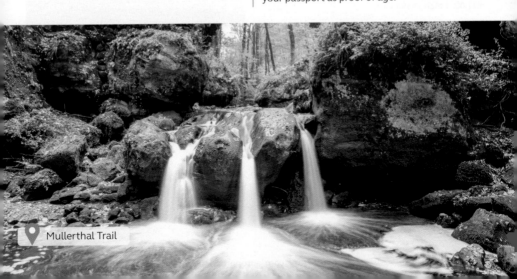

Mullerthal Trail

BORN SUR SURE *C3* (0.5km NE Rural) *49.76081,
6.51672* **Camping Officiel Born-Sûre,** 9 Rue du
Camping, 6660 Born-sur-Sûre **tel** 730144; syndicat@
gmx.lu; www.camping-born.lu

🐕 €2.50 ♦♦ (wo) ⛲ ⚒ 🗐 ⁄ 🍴 ⛽ ⓘ ⚓

E along E44 sp Trier; leave immed bef ent Germany.
On N10 go N sp Echternach; ignore sat nav & drive
to end of vill, site sp. Med, mkd, pt shd, EHU (6A);
bbq; 70% statics; phone; Eng spkn; adv bkg acc; ccard
acc; boating; fishing; CKE. *"Gd, clean site; all tourers on
rvside; htd pool 8km; if barrier clsd find contact in bar;
excel."* **€23.00, 1 Apr-1 Oct.** **2019**

CLERVAUX *B2* (16km SW Rural) *49.97045, 5.93450*
Camping Kaul, Rue Joseph Simon, 9554 Wiltz
tel 9503591; info@kaul.lu; www.kaul.lu

🐕 €1.50 ♦♦ (htd) (wo) ⛲ ♨ ⚒ 🗐 ⁄ 🦋 ⚓ 🌊 /Ɫ

Turn N off rd 15 (Bastogne-Ettelbruck) to Wiltz,
foll sp N to Ville Basse & Camping. Lge, mkd, unshd,
EHU (6-10A) €2.50-2.75; gas; adv bkg rec; tennis;
waterslide. *"Gd site; pitches tight for awnings if site
full; excel san facs & takeaway; pool adj; local children
use playgrnd."* **€30.00, 15 Feb-31 Dec.** **2019**

DIEKIRCH *C2* (0.9km S Rural) *49.86768, 6.16984*
Camping op der Sauer, Route de Gilsdorf, L 9234
Diekirch **tel** 808590; info@campsauer.lu;
www.campsauer.lu

🐕 €2.50 ♦♦ (htd) (wo) ⛲ 🗐 ⁄ 🍴 ⓘ ⚓ 🌊 /Ɫ

On rd 14 to Larochette, on S o'skts of Diekirch. 1st L
after x-ing rv bdge, site well sp on L past Camping
de la Sûre and behind sports facs. Lge, mkd, pt shd,
EHU (6A) €3; gas; bus 800m; Eng spkn; adv bkg acc;
CKE. *"On banks Rv Sûre; sh walk/cycle to town;
spacious site; friendly owners; ltd facs LS; gd, basic site;
helpful recep; pool 400m; clean san facs with plenty of
hot water; vet is 20 mins walk."*
€21.00, 1 Mar-31 Oct. **2015**

ECHTERNACH *C3* (2km SE Rural) *49.79681, 6.43122*
Camping Alferweiher, Alferweiher 1, 6412 Echternach
tel 720271; info@camping-alferweiher.lu;
www.camping-alferweiher.lu

🐕 €2 ♦♦ (htd) (wo) ⛲ ♨ ⚒ 🗐 ⁄ 🌊 🦋 🍴 ⚓ /Ɫ ✎

Fr S on N10 turn R at traff lts & pictogram fishing/
camping. Then L at sp to Alferweiher. 3*, Lge, mkd,
pt shd, EHU (10A) €2.75; gas; TV; Eng spkn; adv bkg
acc; bike hire; CKE. *"Gd walking; office open 0900-1300
& 1400-1800; if shut site yourself - elec boxes not
locked; hot water in individ cubicles in san facs block
only, other basins cold water; popular site but in need
of some tlc (2017)."* **€24.00, 21 Apr-17 Sep.** **2017**

ECHTERNACH *C3* (6km NW Rural) *49.81958, 6.34737*
Camping Belle-Vue 2000, 29 Rue de Consdorf, 6551
Berdorf **tel** 790635 or 808149; campbv2000@
gmail.com

(12) 🐕 ♦♦ (htd) (wo) ⛲ ♨ 🗐 ⁄ 🌊 🦋 ⚓ 🌊 /Ɫ

Nr cent of vill on rd to Consdorf. 2nd of 3 adj sites
with facs on L on way out of vill. Lge, hdg, pt shd,
terr, EHU (6A) €2.5; gas; bbq; 50% statics; phone; adv
bkg acc; games rm; CKE. *"Gd walking; attractive vill
with gd rests; open in Jan only if no snow; pitches poss
soft after rain; pool 500m; owner's son now running &
improving site (2017)."* **€19.00** **2017**

ECHTERNACH *C3* (6km NW Rural) *49.81904, 6.34694*
Camping Bon Repos, 39 Rue de Consdorf, 6551
Berdorf **tel** 790631; irma@bonrepos.lu;
www.bonrepos.lu

♦♦ (htd) (wo) ⛲ ♨ 🗐 ⁄ 🦋 🍴 ⓘ nr ⚓ nr /Ɫ

In cent Echternach at x-rds take Vianden rd, then
in 2km turn L to Berdorf thro vill twds Consdorf.
Site nr cent vill on L adj Camping Belle-Vue.
Fr Luxembourg thro Consdorf to Berdorf, site on
R on ent to vill, clearly sp. Med, hdg, mkd, pt shd, pt
sl, terr, EHU (16A) €2.80 (poss rev pol); gas; red long
stay; TV; bus 100m; Eng spkn; adv bkg acc; games rm;
CKE. *"Clean, tidy site - best in area; clean facs; helpful,
friendly owners; some pitches sm; forest walks fr site;
conv for trips to Germany; pool 5km; pleasant site but v
small pitches."* **€18.00, 1 Apr-4 Nov.** **2017**

"There aren't many sites open at this time of year"

If you're travelling outside peak season
remember to call ahead to check site opening
dates – even if the entry says 'open all year'.

ESCH SUR SURE *B2* (1km SE Rural) *49.90693,
5.94220* **Camping Im Aal,** 7 Rue du Moulin, 9650
Esch-sur-Sûre **tel** 839514; info@camping-im-aal.lu;
www.campingaal.lu

🐕 €2 ♦♦ (htd) (wo) ⛲ ♨ ⚒ 🗐 ⁄ 🦋 🍴 ⚓ /Ɫ

Fr N turn R off N15 onto N27 sp Esch-sur-Sûre. Pass
thro sh tunnel, site on L in 500m on banks of Rv
Sûre. 3*, Lge, hdg, mkd, pt shd, pt sl, EHU (6A) €2;
50% statics; Eng spkn; site clsd 1 Jan-14 Feb; fishing;
CKE. *"Well-kept, clean site; gd welcome; gd, modern
facs; some rvside pitches; walks along towpath & in
woods; cash only; gd for wheelchair users; gd fishing,
walking; gd NH & longer."* **€24.00, 12 Feb-11 Dec.**
2016

ETTELBRUCK *B2* (4km E Rural) *49.85043, 6.13461*
Camping Gritt, 2 Rue Gritt, 9161 Ingeldorf
tel 802018; info@camping-gritt.lu; www.camping-gritt.lu

符 €2 ♦♦(htd) ⓌⒹ ▲ ♨ ♿ ▣ ✉ ⓂⓅ ₩ ♈ ▾ ♨ ⚏nr ⚠ ✎

**On N15 fr Bastogne turn R at rndabt in Ettelbrück
sp Diekirch, go under A7 sp Diekirch. In 3km at end
of elevated section foll slip rd sp Diekirch,
Ettelbrück, Ingeldorf. At rndabt take 2nd exit sp
Ingledorf, site on R over narr rv bdge. Fr Diekirch on
N7 fork L twd Ingeldorf. Site on L over rv bdge.**
Lge, mkd, pt shd, EHU (6A) €2.80; gas; bbq; sw nr; twin
axles; TV; 30% statics; bus/train to Luxembourg City;
Eng spkn; adv bkg acc; games rm; tennis nr; fishing nr;
CKE. *"Peaceful site; helpful, welcoming Dutch owners;
lge pitches with open aspect; gd, modern san facs;
recep 0900-1800 high ssn; canoe hire nr; red for
groups; pitching still OK after heavy rain; on banks
of Rv Sûre (swift-flowing & unfenced); gd walking &
sightseeing; rest vg; vg site."*
€28.00, 17 Apr-27 Oct. 2019

ETTELBRUCK *B2* (1.5km W Rural) *49.84600, 6.08193*
Camping Ettelbruck (formerly Kalkesdelt),
88 Chemin du Camping, 9022 Ettelbrück **tel 00 352 81
21 85;** ellen.ringelberg@gmx.de; www.campingettel
bruck.com

符 €2.50 ♦♦(htd) ⓌⒹ ▲ ♨ ♿ ▣ ✉ ⓂⓅ ₩ ▾ ♨ ▣ ⚠

**Exit Ettelbrück on Bastogne rd N15. Site visible as
app town; approx 200m fr town cent fork L into
lane, turn R at sp at foot of hill, steep & narr rd.
Site sp fr town.** 4*, Lge, mkd, pt shd, terr, EHU (16A)
€2.90; TV; 15% statics; phone; Eng spkn; adv bkg
acc; CKE. *"Gd, well-maintained, friendly, family-run
site in woods; excel san facs; lge pitches; gd walks;
train to Luxembourg city fr town; pool 3km; vg rest."*
€30.00, 1 Apr-1 Oct. 2016

GREVENMACHER *C3* (0.8km N Urban) *49.68302,
6.44891* **Camping La Route du Vin,** 10 route du Vin, L
6794 Grevenmacher **tel 750234 or 758275;** campvin@
pt.lu; grevenmacher-tourist.lu/unterkuenfte/camping

符 €1 ♦♦ ⓌⒹ ▲ ♿ ▣ ✉ ♨ ▾ ♨nr ⚏nr ✎

**Fr E44/A1 exit junc 14 onto N1 to Grevenmacher.
After 1km turn R at T-junc opp Esso g'ge. Site sp in
town, ent off rndabt.** Med, mkd, pt shd, pt sl, EHU
(16A) €2.50; 60% statics; Eng spkn; adv bkg acc;
games area; games rm; tennis; CKE. *"Easy walk to
town cent; wine festival in Sep; pleasant, well kept site;
excel new san facs (2015); boat trips; rvside walks;
excel base for touring Moselle & Luxembourg; pool adj;
views; helpful staff; excel."* **€19.40, 1 Apr-30 Sep.**
2017

KAUTENBACH *B2* (1km E Rural) *49.95387, 6.02730*
Camping Kautenbach, An der Weierbaach, 9663
Kautenbach **tel 950303;** campkaut@pt.lu;
www.campingkautenbach.lu

12 符 ♦♦(htd) ⓌⒹ ▲ ♨ ♿ ▣ ✉ ⓂⓅ ♨ Ⓗ ♨ ▣ ⚠ ✎

**Travelling E fr Bastogne on N84, approx 5km after
Luxembourg border take N26 to Wiltz & foll sp to
Kautenbach/Kiischpelt. In 10km turn L over bdge
into vill, site sp 800m.** 3*, Lge, mkd, pt shd, EHU (6A)
inc; gas; bbq; TV; 20% statics; phone; Eng spkn; adv
bkg acc; pool clsd 21 Dec-14 Jan; bike hire.
*"Gd for walking & mountain biking; long site along
beautiful, secluded rv valley."* **€26.00** 2016

LAROCHETTE *C3* (2km W Rural) *49.78525, 6.21010*
Iris Parc Camping Birkelt, 1 Um Birkelt, 7633
Larochette **tel 879040;** info@camping-birkelt.lu;
www.camping-birkelt.lu

符 €2.50 ♦♦(htd) ⓌⒹ ▲ ♨ ♿ ▣ ✉ ⓂⓅ ♨ ▾ Ⓗ ♨ ▣ ⚠ ✎
♨(covrd, htd) ⛱

**Fr Diekirch take N14 to Larochette; turn R in town
on CR118 (N8), foll sp for Mersch. At top of hill foll
site sp. Fr Luxembourg take N7 foll sp for Mersch &
Ettelbruck (ignore Larochette sp bef Mersch). Turn
R bef rv bdge at Mersch onto CR118 & foll rd to
o'skts of town. Site on R beyond municipal sports
cent - fairly steep, winding app rd.** 5*, Lge, mkd,
hdg, pt shd, pt sl, serviced pitches; EHU (16A) inc;
gas; bbq (charcoal, gas); TV; 50% statics; Eng spkn;
ccard acc; golf 5km; tennis; games rm; horseriding;
bike hire; sauna; fishing; games area; CKE. *"Excel,
well-kept, busy site in pleasant wooded hilltop location;
friendly, helpful staff; ideal for families; fitness rm;
no o'fits over 9m; canoeing 5km; gd san facs, poss
stretched high ssn; access poss diff lge o'fits, care req;
late arr report to rest/bar; gd bar & rest, open in LS."*
€39.00, 12 Apr-29 Sep, H08. 2019

LAROCHETTE *C3* (7km W Rural) *49.78521, 6.16596*
Camping Nommerlayen, Rue Nommerlayen, 7465
Nommern **tel 878078;** info@nommerlayen-ec.lu;
www.nommerlayen-ec.lu

符 €3 ♦♦(htd) ⓌⒹ ▲ ♨ ♿ ▣ ✉ ⓂⓅ ♨ ▾ Ⓗ ♨ ▣ ⚠ ✎
♨(htd) ⛱

**N7 Luxembourg to Diekirch. At Mersch N8 E dir
Larochette & Nommern. Site is 1km S of Nommern.**
5*, Lge, hdg, mkd, pt shd, terr, EHU (10A) inc; gas; TV;
40% statics; Eng spkn; adv bkg acc; sauna; games rm;
tennis; bike hire; games area. *"Superb site & facs;
private bthrms avail; ideal for families; acc to some
pitches diff, site staff will help."* **€40.00, 1 Mar-5 Nov,
H20.** 2018

LUXEMBOURG

LAROCHETTE *C3 (3km NW Rural) 49.79991, 6.19816*
Camping auf Kengert, Kengert, 7633 Larochette
tel 837186; info@kengert.lu; www.kengert.lu
🐕 €2 ♦♦(htd) ⓌⒹ ▲ ♨ & ▣ ◢ ◪ 🦋 ♈ ♈ 🍽 ♈ ⑪ ♨ 🎆 🛶 (htd)

N8 dir Mersch, CR19 dir Schrondweiler. Site sp fr
cent Larochette. 5*, Lge, mkd, shd, sl, EHU (4-16A)
€2; gas; 10% statics; Eng spkn; adv bkg acc; solarium;
sauna; CKE. *"Vg facs; Luxembourg Card (red on
attractions & public transport) avail at recep; peaceful,
friendly site; indoor playgrnd; excel rest; gd local
walks/cycle rtes; ltd hdstg for MH's."*
€34.50, 1 Mar-8 Nov.   **2017**

"That's changed – Should I let the Club know?"

If you find something on site that's different
from the site entry, fill in a report and let us
know. See camc.com/europereport.

LIELER *B2 (0.5km SW Rural) 50.12365, 6.10509*
Camping Trois Frontières, Hauptstroos 12, 9972
Lieler **tel** 998608; info@troisfrontieres.lu; www.trois
frontieres.lu
12 🐕 €2.20 ♦♦(htd) ⓌⒹ ▲ ♨ ▣ ◢ ◪ 🦋 ♈ 🍽 ♈ ⑪ ♨ 🎆 ✎
🎆 🛶

Fr N7/E421 turn E sp Lieler, site sp. 4*, Med, mkd,
pt shd, EHU (6A) €2.75; TV; 10% statics; adv bkg acc;
bike hire; games area; games rm. *"V pleasant site; gd
touring base; site under new ownership (2014); ACSI
registered; discount in LS."* **€32.80**   **2019**

LUXEMBOURG CITY *C3 (7km S Rural) 49.57220,
6.10857* **Camping Kockelscheuer,** 22 Route de
Bettembourg, 1899 Kockelscheuer **tel** 471815;
caravani@pt.lu; www.ccclv.lu/site/index.php/en
🐕 ♦♦(htd) ▲ ♨ & ▣ ◢ ◪ ♈ ♈ ⑪ nr ♨ 🎆

Fr N on A6 then A4 exit junc 1 sp Leudelange/
Kockelscheuer, at top of slip rd turn L N4. After
about 1.5km turn R N186 sp Bettembourg/
Kockelscheuer & foll camp sp. Foll sp 'Park & Ride',
site is 1st R. Fr S exit A3 junc 2 sp Bettembourg &
Kockelscheuer. In 700m turn R dir Kockelscheuer &
in 3km turn L & foll site sp, rd numberd CR196.
4*, Lge, hdg, mkd, pt shd, terr, EHU (10-16A) metered
(check pol); gas; TV (pitch); bus to city 400m (tickets
fr site recep); Eng spkn; adv bkg acc; CKE. *"Rec arr
early afternoon as popular; well-run, clean, pretty site;
helpful, pleasant staff; office & gates clsd 1200-1400
& 2230-0700; gd san facs; pitch access on lower level
needs care; gd size pitches on terr; poss boggy after
rain; sports complex adj; gd dog walks nrby; useful NH
for Zeebrugge; pool 4km; excel site; poss to cycle into
Luxembourg city."* **€18.50, 24 Mar-31 Oct.**   **2018**

LUXEMBOURG CITY *C3 (9km S Rural) 49.56907,
6.16010* **Camping Bon Accueil,** 2 Rue du Camping,
5815 Alzingen **tel** 367069; www.camping-alzingen.lu
🐕 €3 ♦♦(htd) ⓌⒹ ▲ ♨ & ▣ ◢ ◪ 🦋 ♈ 🍽 ♈ 🎆 ♨

Fr Luxembourg city take A3/E25 S, exit junc 1 sp
Hespérange. Cont thro town to Alzingen, site sp
on R after Mairie, well sp. Med, hdg, mkd, hdstg,
pt shd, EHU (16A) inc (poss rev pol); gas; bbq; twin
axles; phone; bus to city adj; Eng spkn; adv bkg acc;
ccard acc; games area; CCI. *"Pleasant, open, clean, tidy
site; gd size pitches; friendly staff; vg, clean, modern
san facs; hot water metered; lovely gardens adj; clsd
1200-1400 - ltd waiting space; excel base for city;
spotlessly clean; vg site; pool 3km; rec arrive early."*
€16.00, 1 Apr-15 Oct.   **2015**

MERSCH *B3 (2km SW Urban) 49.74339, 6.08963*
Camping Um Krounebierg, Rue du Camping, 7572
Mersch **tel** 352329756; contact@camping
krounebierg.lu; www.campingkrounebierg.lu
🐕 €2.50 ♦♦(htd) ⓌⒹ ▲ ♨ & ▣ ◢ ◪ 🦋 ♈ 🍽 ♈ ⑪ ♨ 🎆 🎆

In Mersch town cent fr main N7 foll site ss. Fr A7,
exit Kopstal dir Mersch, then foll site sps. 5*, Lge,
mkd, hdstg, hdg, pt shd, pt sl, terr, EHU (10A) inc; gas;
bbq; twin axles; TV; 20% statics; phone; Eng spkn; adv
bkg acc; tennis. *"Gd touring & walking cent; conv for
trains to Luxembourg City; htd covrd pool adj; warden v
helpful - only on site 2 hrs morning & 2 hrs evening LS;
site guarded; excel clean facs; skate park; nice site close
to a pleasant town; well laid out; beautiful location; san
facs clean."* **€35.00, 25 Mar-31 Oct.**   **2017**

REISDORF *C2 (0.1km W Urban) 49.86958, 6.26746*
Camping De La Sure, 23 Route de la Sure, L-9390
Reisdorf **tel** 661-151358; reisdorfcamp@gmail.com;
www.campingdelasure.lu
🐕 ♦♦♦ ⓌⒹ ▲ ♨ & ▣ ◢ ◪ 🦋 ♈ 🍽 ♈ ⑪ ♨ nr 🎆

Reisdorf is bet Diekirch & Echternach. Site sp off
the N10 in Reisdorf. NB-2nd site on L after the bdge
driving fr Diekirch. Med, pt shd, EHU (10A); bbq
(charcoal, gas); TV; 10% statics; bus adj; Eng spkn;
adv bkg acc; games area; games rm; CKE. *"V friendly
& helpful; gd cycle paths along rv; ACSI; site being
upgraded to a hg standard (2015); vg; lovely site by rv;
easy walk to town."* **€27.00, 30 Mar-16 Oct.**   **2018**

REMICH *C3 (4km S Rural) 49.5106, 6.36302* **Camping
Le Port,** 5447 Schwebsange **tel** 23664460;
commune@wellenstein.lu or info@camping-port.lu
🐕 ♦♦♦ ⓌⒹ ▲ & ▣ ◢ ◪ ♈ 🍽 ♈ nr 🎆

Fr Remich take N10 S on W bank of Moselle. Site
1km E of Schwebsange. Or fr S leave A13 at junc 13
onto N10. Site sp. Lge, mkd, pt shd, serviced pitches;
EHU (10A) inc; gas; 80% statics; Eng spkn; adv bkg
rec; CKE. *"Busy transit site for Austria/Italy; clean facs;
helpful staff; office open 0800-1200, 1350-1800; rd,
rv & port noise; sep area for m'vans on far side of port;
marina & rv activities; red facs LS; pool 4km; gd cycle
rtes fr site."* **€20.50, 1 Apr-31 Oct.**   **2018**

SEPTFONTAINES *B3* (2.5km NE Rural) *49.69274, 5.98514* **Camping Simmerschmelz,** Rue de Simmerschmelz 1, 8363 Septfontaines **tel 307072; info@simmerschmelz.com; simmerschmelz.com**

[12] 🐕 €3 �04(htd) [WD] ♨ ▦ ∥ 🦋 ♍ ₫ 🎿 ⛱

Head NE fr Arlon sp Mersch. In 4km at Gaichel (Bel/ Lux frontier) foll valley of Rv Eisch thro Hobscheid, Septfontaines & in 2km at rd junc turn R. Site on L in 100m. Or fr E25 m'way exit at Windhof. Head N to Koerich & onto Septfontaines, as above. Med, pt shd, pt sl, EHU (6A) €2.50; gas; TV; 40% statics; phone; Eng spkn; adv bkg acc. *"Pleasant site in valley, wet in winter; 1 hdstg pitch; helpful owner."* **€25.80   2017**

TROISVIERGES *B2* (0.4km S Urban) *50.11908, 6.00251* **Camping Troisvierges (formerly Walensbongert),** Rue de Binsfeld, 9912 Troisvierges tel 997141; info@camping-troisvierges.lu; www.camping-troisvierges.lu

🐕 €2 �04(htd) [WD] ♨ ▦ ♿ 🖫 ∥ [MSP] 🦋 ♍ ⑪nr ₫ 🎿nr ⛵

Fr Belgium on E42/A27 exit at junc 15 St Vith on N62 sp Troisvierges. Site sp. 1*, Med, hdg, mkd, pt shd, EHU (16A) €2.50; 10% statics; phone; train 1km; Eng spkn; adv bkg acc; ccard acc; games rm; tennis; CKE. *"Pretty town; pools adj; gd hiking; charming, helpful owners."* **€23.50, 1 Apr-30 Sep.   2019**

> ## "I like to fill in the reports as I travel from site to site"
>
> You'll find report forms at the back of this guide, or you can fill them in online at camc.com/europereport.

VIANDEN *C2* (1km E Rural) *49.93213, 6.21554* **Camping op dem Deich,** Rue Neugarten, 9420 Vianden

[12] 🐕 [WD] ♨ ∥ [MSP] 🦋 ♍ ♈nr ⑪nr 🎿nr

Fr Diekirch take N19 E for 3km. Turn L on N17 to Vianden. Site sp 500m fr town cent twd Bitburg. 1*, Sm, hdstg, unshd, EHU (16A) inc. *"Site no longer camp site but an Aire de Service for MH's; 16 hdstdg pitches with ehu; water, waste and cassette services avail at ent; payment by machine; €15 per 24hrs; all pitches line the rv bank; easy walk to sm town with cafes, rest & shops as well as castles; excel scenery."* **€15.00   2018**

VIANDEN *C2* (2km SE Rural) *49.92673, 6.21990* **Camping du Moulin,** Rue de Bettel, 9415 Vianden tel 834501; campingdumoulin@vianden-info.lu; www.campingdumoulin-vianden.lu

🐕 €1.50 �04(htd) [WD] ♨ ♿ 🖫 ∥ [MSP] 🦋 ♍ ♈ ₮ ⑪ 🎿 ⛰

Fr Diekirch take N17 dir Vianden. In 8km at Fouhren take rd N17B sp Bettel then sp Vianden. Site on R behind yellow Vianden sp. Lge, mkd, pt shd, EHU (10-16A) €2.20; TV (pitch); phone; Eng spkn; CKE. *"Lovely location; spacious pitches, some on rv bank; gd, modern san facs; superb children's san facs; rv adj; interesting area; rec."* **€24.00, 14 Apr-3 Apr.   2017**

WASSERBILLIG *C3* (2km SW Rural) *49.70241, 6.47717* **Camping Mertert,** Rue du Parc, 6684 Mertert **tel 748174**

�04(htd) [WD] ♨ ♿ 🖫 ∥ 🦋 🎿nr ⛰

On E of rte 1 (Wasserbillig-Luxembourg), clearly sp in both dir. Immed R after rlwy x-ing. Site on rv. 3*, Med, mkd, shd, EHU (10A) inc; 70% statics; buses & trains nr; adv bkg acc. *"Grassed tourer area open fr Apr, but owner allows pitching on tarmac rd adj office; excel, clean facs; scruffy statics area; sm boating pond; pool 4km; recep clsd 1300-1500; vg."* **€12.50, 15 Apr-15 Oct.   2019**

Motorways
Major roads
Main roads

All year site(s)
Seasonal site(s)
No sites listed

200m +
0–200m

BELGIUM

GERMANY

FRANCE

Liège
Malmedy
Troisvierges
Lieler
CLERVAUX
Bastogne
Kautenbach
Bitburg
Esch-sur-Sûre
Vianden
Bettendorf
Diekirch
Reisdorf
Ettelbruck
Echternach
Larochette
Born-sur-Sûre
MERSCH
Wasserbillig
Septfontaines
Gravenmacher
Trier
Arlon
LUXEMBOURG CITY
Saarburg
Longwy
Remich
Esch-sur-Alzette
Thionville
Metz

N7
N15
N7
N11
N1
N6
A6
N5
N4
A1
A3
N2
N10
A13
A4
A13

0   10   20   30   40   50 kms

0   10   20   30 mls

© Collins Bartholomew Ltd 2020

N
W   E
S

Netherlands

📍 Tulip fields near Zaanse Schans

Highlights

With a flat landscape that's covered in tulips and windmills, the Netherlands is an enchanting country to explore and is ideal for cyclists. Amsterdam is often the main draw for tourists, and is the home of several museums, including one dedicated to Van Gogh.

The Netherlands is also well known for its beaches, and the coast is a great place to visit for nature lover and sports enthusiasts alike.

The Netherlands has produced some of the greatest painters in the world, from Rembrandt to Vermeer and Van Gogh to Escher. The Mauritschuis in The Hague houses many famous works of art from the Dutch golden age and is well worth a visit.

Christmas is a time of great celebration for the Dutch, with Sinterklaas a traditional holiday figure based on Saint Nicholas. The giving of gifts on December 5th is a long-held tradition, as is the Sinterklaas parade in mid-November, which is broadcast live on national TV.

Major towns and cities

- Amsterdam – this beautiful capital is filled with canals, galleries and pretty buildings.
- Rotterdam – a city famous for its museums and landmark architecture.
- The Hague – a historic city of political and cultural significance.
- Leiden – home of the oldest university in the Netherlands the birthplace of Rembrandt.

Attractions

- Keukenhof, Lisse – one of the world's largest flower gardens and a must-see in the spring.
- Hoge Veluwe, Gelderland – this National Park is a great place for walking or cycling.
- Rijksmuseum, Amsterdam – a national museum dedicated to arts and history.
- Kinderdijk – a beautiful village with the largest collection of old windmills in the Netherlands.

Find out more

www.holland.com
E: info@holland.com T: 0031 (0) 70 37 05 705

Country Information

Population (approx): 16.9million

Capital: Amsterdam

Area: 33,939 sqkm

Bordered by: Belgium, Germany

Terrain: Mostly coastal lowland and reclaimed land (polders) dissected by rivers and canals; hills in the south-east

Climate: Temperate maritime climate; warm, changeable summers; cold/mild winters; spring is the driest season

Coastline: 451km

Highest Point: Vaalserberg 322m

Language: Dutch

Local Time: GMT or BST + 1, i.e. 1 hour ahead of the UK all year

Currency: Euros divided into 100 cents; £1 = €1.16, €1 = £0.87 (October 2019)

Emergency numbers: Police 112; Fire brigade 112; Ambulance 112. Operators speak English

Public Holidays 2020: Jan 1; Apr 10, 12, 13, 27; May 5, 21, 31; Jun 1; Dec 25, 26

School summer holidays vary by region, but are roughly early/mid July to end August/early September

Entry Formalities

British and Irish passport holders may stay in the Netherlands for up to three months without a visa.

Medical Services

Pharmacies (apotheek) dispense prescriptions whereas drugstores (drogisterij) sell only over-the-counter remedies. Pharmacies may require a photocopy of the details on your European Health Insurance Card (EHIC). You will need to show your EHIC to obtain treatment by a doctor contracted to the state health care system (AGIS Zorgverzekeringen) and you will probably have to pay a fee. You will be charged for emergency dental treatment. Charges for prescriptions vary. Treatment refunds are obtained from AGIS.

Inpatient hospital treatment is free provided it is authorised by AGIS. Local state health insurance fund offices can give advice on obtaining emergency medical services and provide names and addresses of doctors, health centres and hospitals. Tourist Information offices also keep lists of local doctors.

Opening Hours

Banks: Mon-Fri 9am-4pm/5pm (some open Sat).

Museums: Tue-Fri 10am-5pm; Sat & Sun 11am/1pm-5pm.

Post Offices: Mon-Fri 9am-5pm; some Sat 9am-12 noon/1.30pm.

Shops: Mon-Fri 8am/8.30am-6pm/8pm; Sat 8am/8.30am-4pm/5pm; late night shopping in many towns on Thursday or Friday to 9pm. Shops close one day or half day in the week in addition to Sunday.

Safety and Security

In relative terms there is little crime but visitors should take the usual precautions in central Amsterdam (particularly in and around Central Station), in Rotterdam and The Hague. As in many large cities, pickpocketing and bag snatching are more common. Pickpockets operate on trams, especially on numbers 2 and 5 in Amsterdam.

Ensure you keep your valuables safely with you at all times and do not leave them unattended or hanging on the back of a chair. Bicycle theft is a common occurrence in the major cities.

Fake, plain clothes policemen carrying badges are in action pretending to be investigating counterfeit money and false credit cards. Dutch police do not have badges and plain clothes police will rarely carry out this kind of inspection. Always ask for identity, check it thoroughly and do not allow yourself to be intimidated. Call 0900 8844 to contact the nearest police station if you are concerned or suspicious.

Several deaths occur each year due to drowning in canals. Take particular care when driving, cycling or walking alongside canals.

Avoid confrontation with anyone offering to sell you drugs and stay away from quiet or dark alleys, particularly late at night.

There have been incidences of drinks being spiked in city centre locations. Always be aware of your drink and do not leave it unattended. Young women and lone travellers need to be especially vigilant in these situations.

The Netherlands shares with the rest of Europe a general threat from terrorism. Attacks could be indiscriminate and against civilian targets in public places, including tourist sites.

British Embassy

LANGE VOORHOUT 10, 2514 ED THE HAAG
Tel: (070) 4270427
www.ukinnl.fco.gov.uk

British Consulate-General

KONINGSLAAN 44,1075 AE AMSTERDAM
Tel: (020) 6764343

Irish Embassy

SCHEVENINGSEWEG 112, 2584 AE THE HAGUE
Tel: (070) 3630993
www.embassyofireland.nl

Documents

Passport

Everyone from the age of 14 is required to show a valid identity document to police officers on request and you should, therefore, carry your passport at all times.

Vehicle(s)

When driving carry your driving licence, vehicle registration certificate (V5C), insurance certificate and MOT certificate, if applicable. If driving a vehicle that does not belong to you, carry a letter of authority from the owner.

Money

Money may be exchanged at main border crossing posts, major post offices, banks, VVV tourist information offices and some ANWB offices. Other bureaux de change may not give such favourable rates.

The major credit and debit cards are widely accepted but supermarkets will not generally accept credit cards. As a precaution carry enough cash to cover your purchases as you may find that debit cards issued by banks outside the Netherlands are not accepted. Cash machines are widespread.

Driving

The Dutch drive assertively and are not renowned for their road courtesy. Pedestrians should be very careful when crossing roads, including on zebra crossings.

Accidents

All accidents which cause injuries or major damage must be reported to the police. Drivers involved in an accident must exchange their identity details and their insurance company contact information.

Alcohol

The maximum permitted level of alcohol is 50 milligrams in 100 millilitres of blood, i.e. lower than that permitted in the UK (80 milligrams). Penalties for driving under the influence of alcohol can be severe. A lower level of 20 milligrams applies to drivers who have held a driving licence for less than five years. It is wisest to adopt a 'no drinking and driving' rule.

Breakdown Service

There are emergency telephones every 2km on all motorways and they are directly linked to the nearest breakdown centre.

ANWB, the motoring and leisure organisation, has a road patrol service which operates 24 hours a day on all roads. Drivers requiring assistance may call the 'Wegenwacht' road patrol centre by telephoning 088 2692888. Alternatively call the ANWB Emergency Centre on (070) 3141414. Operators speak English.

Charges apply for breakdown assistance and towing is charged according to distance and time of day. Members of clubs affiliated to the AIT/FIA, such as The Caravan and Motorhome Club, incur lower charges. Payment by credit card is accepted. In some areas the ANWB Wegenwacht has contracts with local garages to provide assistance to its members and affiliates.

Child Restraint System

Children under the age of 18 years, measuring less than 1.35m, must be seated in an approved child restraint adapted to their size (ECE 44/03 or 44/04 safety approved). Children under 3 years old are able to travel in the front if they are seated in a rear facing child seat with the airbag deactivated, and under no circumstances are they allowed to travel in a car with no child restraint system fitted.

Fuel

Unleaded petrol is available from green pumps marked 'Loodvrije Benzine'. LPG (autogas) is widely available along main roads and motorways.

Petrol stations along motorways and main roads and in main towns are open 24 hours, except in parts of the north of the country where they close at 11pm. Credit cards are accepted but some all night petrol stations only have automatic pumps which may operate with bank notes only.

Lights

The use of dipped headlights during the day is recommended.

Low Emission Zones

Low Emission Zones are in operation in 16 cities in the Netherlands. Restrictions only apply to freight vehicles over 3500kg, however currently all foreign vehicles are able to enter the Low Emission Zone without any restrictions. Check www.urbanaccessregulations.eu before you travel.

Motorways

There are over 2,750 kilometres of toll-free motorway. There are rest areas along the motorways, most of which have a petrol station and a small shop. Tolls are charged on some bridges and tunnels, notably the Westerschelde Toll Tunnel. This road tunnel links Terneuzen (north of Gent) and Ellewoutsdijk (south of Goes) across the Westerschelde. It provides a short, fast route between Channel ports and the road network in the west of the country. The tunnel is 6.6km long (just over 4 miles) and the toll for a car + caravan (maximum height 3m measured from front axle) is €7.45 and for a motorhome €7.45

height under 2.5m) or €18.20 (height over 3m) (all prices for 2015). Credit cards are accepted. For more information go to www.westerscheldetunnel.nl.

Parking

Parking meters or discs are in use in many towns allowing parking for between 30 minutes and two or three hours; discs can be obtained from local shops. A sign 'parkeerschijf' indicates times when a disc is compulsory. Paid parking is expensive and there are insufficient parking spaces to meet demand. Clamping and towing away of vehicles are commonplace and fines are high. Check signs for the precise times you are allowed to park, particularly on main roads in Amsterdam.

Priority

Yellow diamond shaped signs with a white border indicate priority roads. In the absence of such signs drivers must give way to all traffic approaching from the right. At the intersection of two roads of the same class where there are no signs, traffic from the right has priority.

At junctions marked with a 'priority road ahead' sign, a stop sign or a line of white painted triangles ('shark's teeth') across the road, drivers must give way to all vehicles on the priority road, including bicycles and mopeds.

Be particularly careful when using roundabouts as on some you have the right of way when on them, but on others you must give way to vehicles entering the roundabout, i.e. on your right.

Trams have priority at the intersection of roads of equal importance, but they must give way to traffic on priority roads. If a tram or bus stops in the middle of the road to allow passengers on and off, you must stop. Buses have right of way over all other vehicles when leaving bus stops in built-up areas.

Roads

Roads are generally good and well maintained, but are overcrowded and are frequently subject to strong winds. Most cities have a policy of reducing the amount of nonessential traffic within their boundaries. Narrowing roads, obstacles, traffic lights and speed cameras are often in place to achieve this.

Road Signs and Markings

National motorways are distinguished by red signs, and prefixed with the letter A, whereas European motorways have green signs and are prefixed E. Dual carriageways and other main roads have yellow signs with the letter N and secondary roads are prefixed B.

In general road signs and markings conform to international standards. The following are some road signs which may also be seen:

Cycle path

Cycle route

District Numbers

Hard shoulder open as rush-hour lane

Dutch	English Translation
Afrit	Exit
Doorgaand verkeer gestremd	No throughway
Drempels	Humps
Langzaam rijden	Slow down
Omleiding	Detour
Oprit	Entrance
Ousteek u lichten	Switch on lights
Parkeerplaats	Parking
Pas op!	Attention
Stop-verbod	No parking
Wegomlegging	Detour
Werk in uitvoering	Road works
Woonerven	Slow down (in built-up area)

A continuous central white line should not be crossed even to make a left turn.

Speed Limits

	Open Road (km/h)	Motorway (km/h)
Car Solo	80-100	130*
Car towing caravan/trailer	80-90	90
Motorhome under 3500kg	80-100	130*
Motorhome 3500-7500kg	80	80

*Unless otherwise indicated.

Be vigilant and observe the overhead illuminated lane indicators when they are in use, as speed limits on motorways are variable. Speed cameras, speed traps and unmarked police vehicles are widely used. Radar detectors are illegal, with use resulting in a heavy fine.

Motorhomes over 3,500kg are restricted to 50 km/h (31 mph) in built-up areas and to 80 km/h (50 mph) on all other roads. The beginning of a built up area is indicated by a rectangular blue sign with the name of the locality in white. The end of a built up area is indicated by the same sign with a white diagonal lines across it.

Traffic Jams

The greatest traffic congestion occurs on weekdays at rush hours around the major cities of Amsterdam, Den Bosch, Eindhoven, Rotterdam, Utrecht, The Hague and Eindhoven.

Summer holidays in the Netherlands are staggered and, as a result, traffic congestion is not too severe. However during the Christmas, Easter and Whitsun holiday periods, traffic jams are common and bottlenecks regularly occur on the A2 (Maastricht to Amsterdam), the A12 (Utrecht to the German border) and on the A50 (Arnhem to Apeldoorn). Roads to the Zeeland coast, e.g. the A58, N57 and N59, may become congested during periods of fine weather.

Many Germans head for the Netherlands on their own public holidays and the roads are particularly busy during these periods.

Violation of Traffic Regulations

Police are empowered to impose on-the-spot fines (or confiscate vehicles) for violation of traffic regulations and fines for speeding can be severe. If you are fined always ask for a receipt.

Touring

The southern Netherlands is the most densely populated part of the country but, despite the modern sprawl, ancient towns such as Dordrecht, Gouda, Delft and Leiden have retained their individuality and charm. Rotterdam is a modern, commercial centre and a tour of its harbour – the busiest in Europe – makes a fascinating excursion. The scenery in the north of the country is the most typically Dutch – vast, flat landscapes, largely reclaimed from the sea, dotted with windmills.

Some of the most charming towns and villages are Marken, Volendam and Alkmaar (famous for its cheese market). Aalsmeer, situated south of Amsterdam, stages the world's largest daily flower auction.

It is worth spending time to visit the hilly provinces in the east such as Gelderland, known for its castles, country houses and its major city, Arnhem, which has many links with the Second World War. Overijssel is a region of great variety and the old Hanseatic towns of Zwolle and Kampen have splendid quays and historic buildings. Friesland is the Netherland's lake district.

An Amsterdam Card entitles you to free admission to many of the city's famous museums, including the Rijksmuseum and Van Gogh Museum, and to discounts in many restaurants, shops, attractions and at Park & Ride car parks. It also entitles you to discounts on tours as well as free travel on public transport and a free canal cruise. The Card is valid for one, two or three days and is available from tourist information offices, some Shell petrol stations, Canal Bus kiosks, Park & Ride car parks and some hotels. Alternatively purchase online from www.iamsterdamcard.com.

Service charges are included in restaurant bills and tips are not necessary. Smoking is not permitted in bars or restaurants.

Spring is one of the most popular times to visit the Netherlands, in particular the famous Keukenhof Gardens near Lisse, open from 24 March to 16 May in 2016, see www.keukenhof. nl. Visitors enjoy a display of over seven million flowering bulbs, trees and shrubs. Special events take place here at other times of the year, including a National Bulb Market in October.

Camping and Caravanning

There are approximately 2,500 officially classified campsites which offer a wide variety of facilities. Most are well equipped with modern sanitary facilities and they generally have a bar, shop and leisure facilities.

A number of sites require cars to be parked on a separate area away from pitches and this can present a problem for motorhomes. Some sites allow motorhomes to park on pitches without restrictions, but others will only accept them on pitches if they are not moved during the duration of your stay. Check before booking in.

A tourist tax is levied at campsites of approximately €1.00 per person per night. It is not generally included in the prices quoted in the Site Entry listings which follow this chapter.

The periods over, and immediately after, the Ascension Day holiday and the Whitsun weekend are very busy for Dutch sites and you can expect to find many of them full. Advance booking is highly recommended.

Casual/wild camping is prohibited as is overnight camping by the roadside or in car parks. There are overnight parking places specifically for motorhomes all over the country – see the website of the Camper Club Nederland, www.campervriendelijk. nl and look under 'camperplaatsen NL' or write to CCN at Postbus 115, 7480 AC Haaksbergen, tel:(0)634 492 913. Alternatively see www.campercontact.nl or email cnn@ camperclubnetherland.nl

Many campsites also have motorhome amenities and some offer Quick Stop overnight facilities at reduced rates.

Cycling

There are twice as many bicycles as cars in the Netherlands and as a result cyclists are catered for better than in any other country. There are 15,000 km of well-maintained cycle tracks in both town and country, all marked with red and white road signs and mushroom-shaped posts indicating the quickest and/or most scenic routes. Local tourist information centres (VVV) sell maps of a wide range of cycling tours and cycling fact sheets and maps are available from the Netherlands Board of Tourism in London. Motorists should expect to encounter heavy cycle traffic, particularly during rush hours.

Obligatory separate bicycle lanes for cyclists are indicated by circular blue signs displaying a white bicycle. Small oblong signs with the word 'fietspad' or 'rijwielpad' indicate optional bicycle lanes. White bicycles and dotted white lines painted on the road surface indicate cycle lanes which may be used by motor vehicles providing they do not obstruct cyclists. Cycle lanes marked by continuous white lines are prohibited for use by motor vehicles.

Cyclists must obey traffic light signals at crossroads and junctions; elsewhere, where no traffic lights are in operation, they must give way to traffic from the right.

Cycle tracks are also used by mobility scooters and mopeds. Pedestrians should be especially cautious when crossing roads, especially on zebra crossings. Look out for both cyclists and riders of mopeds, who often ignore traffic rules as well as red lights. In Amsterdam in particular, many cyclists do not use lights at night.

Bicycles may be carried on the roof of a car providing the total height does not exceed 4 metres. They may also be carried at the rear providing the width does not extend more than 20cm beyond the width of the vehicle.

Electricity and Gas

Most campsites have a supply ranging from 4 to 10 amps and almost all have CEE connections. Plugs have two round pins.

The full range of Campingaz cylinders is available.

Public Transport

There is an excellent network of buses and trams, together with metro systems in Amsterdam (called the GVB), Rotterdam and The Hague. An electronic card 'OV Chipkaart' is gradually replacing the previous system of 'Strippenkaart' which were strips of 15 or 45 tickets valid throughout the country.

OV-Chip cards can be bought at vending machines at stations or ticket offices and on board buses and trams and are available for periods from one hour to seven days allowing unlimited travel on trams, buses and the metro. Children under 12 and people over the age of 65 qualify for reduced fares (show your passport as proof of age). See www.gvb.nl for more information.

Tickets must be validated before travel either at the yellow machines on trams and at metro stations or by your bus driver or conductor.

In Amsterdam canal transport includes a regular canal shuttle between Centraal Station and the Rijksmuseum. A 'circle tram' travels from Centraal Station through the centre of Amsterdam past a number of local visitor attractions, such as Anne Frank's house, the Rijksmuseum, Van Gogh museum and Rembrandthuis.

There are Park & Ride facilities at most railway stations. Secure parking is also offered at 'transferiums', a scheme offering reasonably priced guarded parking in secure areas on the outskirts of major towns with easy access by road and close to public transport hubs. Transferiums have heated waiting rooms and rest rooms as well as information for travellers, and some even have a shop.

Frequent car ferry services operate on routes to the Frisian (or Wadden) Islands off the north west coast, for example, from Den Helder to Texel Island, Harlingen to Terschelling Island and Holwerd to Ameland Island. Other islands in the group do not allow cars but there are passenger ferry services. In the summer island-hopping round tickets are available to foot passengers and cyclists and are popular for exploring the country.

ALKMAAR *B2* (7.7km W Rural/Coastal) *52.634290, 4.660384* **De Markiess,** Driehuizerweg 1A, 1934 PR Egmond aan den Hoef **(072) 5062274; info@ demarkiess.nl; www.demarkiess.nl**

🐕 ♦♦(htd) 🅦 ♨ ♻ ♿ 🗐 ∥ 🅼🅿 ☀ ♈ ⵏ nr ⊕ nr ⵏ nr ⚲

↑ 2km; sand

N9 W of Alkmaar. Take Egmond sp. Turn R aft petrol stn. Foll sp to site. Med, unshd, EHU (6A) inc; bbq; TV; bus 2km; Eng spkn; games rm. *"One of best maintained sites; grass like bowling green; no grass cuttings left; spotless facs; recycling; excel."* **€24.00, 30 Mar-30 Sep.** **2018**

ALKMAAR *B2* (2.6km NW Urban) *52.64205, 4.72407* **Camping Alkmaar,** Bergerweg 201, 1817 ML Alkmaar **(072) 5116924; info@campingalkmaar.nl; www.campingalkmaar.nl**

🐕 €3 ♦♦(htd) 🅦 ♨ ♻ ♿ 🗐 ∥ 🅼🅿 ☀ ⵏ nr ⚲

Fr W ring rd (Martin Luther Kingweg) foll Bergen sp, bear R at T-junc & site 150m on L. Site well sp. Med, hdstg, mkd, pt shd, EHU (4-10A) inc; bbq; TV (pitch); 10% statics; bus at gate; Eng spkn; adv bkg acc; ccard acc; golf 2km; CKE. *"Clean, friendly site; decent sized pitches; buses to town; 20 min walk to town cent; cheese mkt on Friday in ssn; pool adj; vg cycling rte into centre; cash/mastercard; gd san facs."* **€29.00, 1 Mar-1 Oct.** **2019**

ALMERE *C3* (7km W Rural) *52.35688, 5.22505* **Camping Waterhout,** Archerpad 6, 1324 ZZ Almere **(036) 5470632; info@waterhout.nl; www.waterhout.nl**

🐕 €2.50 ♦♦ 🅦 ♨ ♻ 🗐 ∥ ☀ ♈ ⊕ ♨ ⵏ ⚲ ✎

Exit A6 junc 4, site sp fr slip rd on S edge Weerwater. Med, mkd, shd, EHU (10A) inc; sw nr; TV; 30% statics; phone; bus 200m; Eng spkn; adv bkg acc; CKE. *"Well laid-out site; conv Amsterdam by bus or train - 30 mins; Almere ultra-modern city."* **€27.00, 19 Apr-27 Oct.** **2019**

AMSTERDAM *B3* (12km N Rural) *52.43649, 4.91445* **Camping Het Rietveen,** Noordeinde 130, 1121 AL Landsmeer **(020) 4821468; info@campinghet rietveen.nl; www.campinghetrietveen.nl**

12 🐕 ♦♦ 🅦 ♨ ∥ 🗐 ☀ ♈ ⵏ nr ⊕ nr ⵏ nr

Fr A10 ring rd exit junc 117. At junc off slip rd turn L dir Landsmeer, site sp. Sm, mkd, EHU (10A) inc; sw; bus to Amsterdam 200m; Eng spkn; tennis; adv bkg adv; fishing; bike hire; CKE. *"Vg, pretty lakeside site, like lge CL, in well-kept vill; no recep - site yourself & owner will call; sep field avail for rallies; excel touring base; city 30 mins by bus; san facs inadequate; no wifi; dogs free."* **€27.00** **2018**

AMSTERDAM *B3* (5km NE Urban) *52.38907, 4.92532* **Camping Vliegenbos,** Meeuwenlaan 138, 1022 AM Amsterdam **(020) 6368855; vliegenbos@ noord.amsterdam.nl; www.vliegenbos.com**

♦♦(htd) 🅦 ♨ ♻ ♿ 🗐 ∥ 🅼🅿 ☀ ⊕ nr ⵏ ⵏ

Fr A10 Amsterdam ring rd, take exit S116 Amsterdam Noord, at 2nd slip rd turn R sp Noord over rndabt, turn L at next rndabt, then immed sharp R, L onto service rd, site sp. 2*, Lge, hdstg, pt shd, pt sl, EHU (6A) inc; gas; phone; bus to city nr; Eng spkn; ccard acc. *"Sm pitches mainly for tents; ltd EHU; m'vans & c'vans park outside barrier; friendly staff; pool 1.5km; bus tickets to city cent fr recep; cycle path to city cent via free ferry; clean, modern san facs; v well set up."* **€30.00, 1 Apr-1 Oct.** **2016**

AMSTERDAM *B3* (6km E Urban) *52.36555, 4.95829* **Camping Zeeburg,** Zuider IJdijk 20, 1095 KN Amsterdam **(020) 6944430; info@camping zeeburg.nl; www.campingzeeburg.nl**

12 🐕 €3 ♦♦ 🅦 ♨ 🗐 ∥ 🅼🅿 ♨ ⵏ

Fr A10 ring rd exit at S114 & foll site sps. Lge, unshd, EHU (6-16A) inc; gas; 10% statics; bus/tram to city nr; adv bkg rec; bike hire. *"Used mainly by tents in summer, but rest of year suitable for c'vans; conv city cent."* **€29.00** **2016**

AMSTERDAM *B3* (12km SE Urban) *52.31258, 4.99035* **Gaasper Camping,** Loosdrechtdreef 7, 1108 AZ Amsterdam-Zuidoost **(020) 6967326; info@ gaaspercamping.nl; www.gaaspercamping.nl**

🐕 €2.50 ♦♦(htd) 🅦 ♨ 🗐 ∥ 🅼🅿 ☀ ♈ ⊕ ♨ ⵏ ⚲

Fr A2 take A9 E sp Amersfoort. After about 5km take 3rd exit sp Gaasperplas/Weesp S113. Cross S113 into site, sp. 2*, Lge, hdg, mkd, hdstg, pt shd, serviced pitches; EHU (10A) €3.50 (care needed); gas; 20% statics; Eng spkn; CKE. *"Immac site set in beautiful parkland; well-run with strict rules; night guard at barrier (high ssn); vans must be manhandled onto pitch (help avail); high ssn arr early to ensure pitch - no adv bkg for fewer than 7 nights; metro 5 mins walk (tickets fr site recep); poss cold shwrs & ltd shop LS; gd security; well run site; conv for metro; adv bkg rec high ssn."* **€30.00, 1 Jan-4 Jan, 15 Mar-1 Nov, 28 Dec-31 Dec.** **2017**

AMSTERDAM *B3* (15km SW Rural) *52.29366, 4.82316*
Camping Het Amsterdamse Bos, Kleine Noorddijk 1,
1187 NZ Amstelveen **(020) 6416868; info@camping
amsterdam.com; www.campingamsterdamsebos.com**

🏕 €3 ♟(htd) ⬜ 🚿 ♨ 🗑 ⚫ MSP ♟ ⛳ Ⓓ 🍴

Foll A10 & A4 twd Schiphol Airport. Fr junc on A4 &
A9 m'way, take A9 E twd Amstelveen; at next exit
(junc 6) exit sp Aalsmeer. Foll Aalsmeer sp for 1km
bearing R at traff lts then at next traff lts turn L
over canal bdge onto N231. In 1.5km turn L at 2nd
traff lts into site. Fr S exit A4 junc 3 onto N201 dir
Hilversum (ignore other camp sps). Turn L onto
N231 dir Amstelveen, at rd junc Bovenkirk take
N231 dir Schiphol, site on R in 200m, sp. 1*, V lge,
pt shd, EHU (10A) €4.50; gas; 20% statics; bus to
city; Eng spkn; adv bkg acc; ccard acc; CKE. *"Conv
Amsterdam by bus - tickets sold on site; poss migrant
workers resident on site; san facs stretched high ssn;
gd walking & cycling paths; spectacular daily flower
auctions at Aalsmeer; waterpark nr; conv bulbfields."*
€25.50, 18 Mar-3 Nov. **2019**

"That's changed – Should I let the Club know?"

If you find something on site that's different
from the site entry, fill in a report and let us
know. See camc.com/europereport.

ANNEN *D2* (3.7km S Rural) *53.03017, 6.73912*
De Baldwin Hoeve, Annerweg 9, 9463 TB Eext
**05 92 27 16 29; baldwinhoeve@hetnet.nl;
www.baldwinhoeve.nl**

🔢 🐕 ♟ ⬜ 🚿 ⚫ 🦋

Fr N34 take Annen exit. Turn R onto Anlooerweg.
At rndabt take R dir Eext. Bef underpass take sm
service rd on L to campsite. Sm, mkd, unshd, EHU
(10A); bbq; twin axles; bus adj; Eng spkn; adv bkg acc;
CCI. *"CL type farm site with excel san facs; friendly
owners; horses & other livestock; lg group
accomodation avail; vg."* **€16.50** **2019**

APELDOORN *C3* (10km N Rural) *52.29066, 5.94520*
Camping De Helfterkamp, Gortelseweg 24, 8171 RA
Vaassen **(0578) 571839; info@helfterkamp.nl;
www.helfterkamp.nl**

🏕 €1.75 ♟(htd) ⬜ 🚿 ♨ ♿ 🗑 ⚫ 🦋 ♟ 🛁 /A

Leave A50 junc 26; foll sp to Vaassen; site sp on ent
to town - 2.5km W of Vaassen. Med, mkd, pt shd,
EHU (16A) metered (poss rev pol); gas; sw nr; red long
stay; 40% statics; phone; Eng spkn; adv bkg req; ccard
acc; bike hire; CKE. *"Excel, immac, well-maintained,
busy site in beautiful woodland area; key for shwrs
& hot water; v friendly owners; conv for Apeldoorn/
Arnhem areas & De Hooge Veluwe National Park; gd
walking/cycling."* **€25.00, 1 Mar-31 Oct.** **2017**

APELDOORN *C3* (10km S Rural) *52.11771, 5.90641*
Camping De Pampel, Woeste Hoefweg 35, 7351 TN
Hoenderloo **(055) 3781760; info@pampel.nl;
www.pampel.nl**

🔢 🏕 €3 ♟(htd) ⬜ 🚿 ♨ 🗑 ⚫ MSP 🦋 ⛳ Ⓓ 🛁 /A 🚣

Exit A1 Amersfoort-Apeldoorn m'way at junc 19
Hoenderloo. Fr Hoenderloo dir Loenen, site sp.
Lge, mkd, hdg, pt shd, serviced pitches; EHU (6-16A);
adv bkg req; bike hire. *"V pleasant setting 2km fr
National Park; go-kart hire; excel facs; free 1-day bus
ticket; private bthrms avail; same site rds diff for lge
o'fits; vg for children; no dogs high ssn; many mkd
walks/cycle paths; friendly staff."* **€32.30** **2018**

APPELSCHA *D2* (4.5km S Rural) *52.92134, 6.34447*
Boscamping Appelscha, Oude Willem 3, 8426 SM
Appelscha **(0516) 431391; info@boscamping
appelscha.nl; www.campingalkenhaer.nl**

♟ ⬜ 🚿 ♨ 🗑 ⚫ 🦋 ♟ 🛁 /A 🚣

A28 junc 31 sp Drachten. Turn L onto N381. About
13km turn L onto Oude Willem then take 3rd R,
site on L. Lge, mkd, pt shd, EHU (16A); 60% statics;
Eng spkn; CKE. *"Neat, friendly, well run site; takeaway;
many walking, cycling & riding trails in nrby national
park; vg site."* **€24.50, 1 Apr-1 Oct.** **2019**

ARNHEM *C3* (6km W Rural) *51.99365, 5.82203*
Camping Aan Veluwe, Sportlaan 1, 6861 AG
Oosterbeek **(0224) 563109; info@aannoordzee.nl;
www.aanveluwe.nl**

🏕 €1.80 ♟(htd) ⬜ 🗑 ⚫ 🦋 ⛳ 🛁 /A

Fr S fr Nijmegen, cross new bdge at Arnhem. Foll
Oosterbeek sp for 5km, cont past memorial in
Oosterbeek, in 1km turn R at rndabt, 500m L to site.
Or fr A50 exit junc 19 onto N225 twd Osterbeek/
Arnhem. In 3km at rndabt turn L, site on L in 500m.
Med, pt shd, pt sl, EHU (16A) inc; gas; red long stay;
10% statics; adv bkg acc; sep car park. *"Conv Airborne
Museum & Cemetery & Dutch Open Air Museum; sports
club bar open to site guests; shwr facs for each pitch;
pool 3km; lovely walks."* **€21.00, 29 Mar-28 Oct.**
2019

ARNHEM *C3* (5km NW Rural) *52.0072, 5.8714*
Camping Warnsborn, Bakenbergseweg 257, 6816
PB Arnhem **(026) 4423469; info@camping
warnsborn.nl; www.campingwarnsborn.nl**

🏕 €3 ♟(htd) ⬜ 🚿 ♨ ♿ 🗑 ⚫ MSP 🦋 ♟ Ⓓ nr 🛁 /A

Fr Utrecht on E35/A12, exit junc 25 Ede (if coming
fr opp dir, beware unnumbered m'way junc 200m
prior to junc 25). Take N224 dual c'way twd Arnhem
& foll sp Burgers Zoo, site sp. Beware oncoming
traff & sleeping policeman nr site ent. Med, pt shd,
EHU (6A) inc; gas; bbq; red long stay; 5% statics;
phone; bus 100m; Eng spkn; adv bkg acc; ccard acc;
CKE. *"Excel, spacious, clean, well-maintained, wooded
site; san facs clean; friendly, helpful family owners &
staff; airborne museum & cemetery; cycle rtes direct fr
site; conv Hooge Veluwe National Park & Kröller-Müller
museum (Van Gogh paintings); super site but busy; bus
into Arnhem."* **€19.50, 24 Mar-30 Oct.** **2016**

ASSEN *D2* (16km NW Rural) *53.07783, 6.44870*
Camping de Norgerberg, Langeloërweg 63. 9331 VA
Norg **(0592)** 612281; info@norgerberg.nl;
www.norgerberg.nl

🐕 €2.30 ♦♦(htd) ⍵ᴅ ≛ ♨ ᴔ ⎕ ⁄ ⍟ 🦋 ⍦ 𝖸 ⑪ ⍛ ⍿ ⚲

**Fr Leeuwarden, N31 S to junc 30(20km). Then N381
sp Emmen for 10km, L twrds Waskemeer/Norg on
N917. Turn L at Norg onto N373. Site on L in 1km.**
Med, hdg, mkd, pt shd, EHU (10A); gas; bbq; TV; bus
adj; Eng spkn; adv bkg acc; games area; games rm;
CCI. *"Vg cycling trails including forest; easy access to
town, rest & shops; excel."* **€28.00, 27 Mar-1 Nov.**
2015

BERGEN OP ZOOM *B4* (5km SE Rural) *51.46913,
4.32236* **Camping Uit en Thuis,** Heimolen 56, 4625 DD
Bergen op Zoom **(0164)** 233391; info@
campinguitenthuis.nl; www.campinguitenthuis.nl

🐕 €2.80 ♦♦(htd) ⍵ᴅ ≛ ♨ ᴔ ⎕ ⁄ ⍟ 🦋 𝖸 ⑪ ⍛ ⍿

Exit A4/E312 at junc 29 sp Huijbergen & foll site sp.
Lge, hdg, pt shd, EHU (4-6A) €2; red long stay; TV;
75% statics; Eng spkn; adv bkg acc; tennis; games
area; CKE. *"Spacious site in woodland; gd cycle paths to
pleasant town; sep mv places; excel site, v pretty; lge
pitches."* **€22.00, 1 Apr-1 Oct.** **2017**

BLADEL *C4* (1.6km S Rural) *51.35388, 5.22254* **Mini-
Camping De Hooiberg,** Bredasebaan 20, 5531 NB
Bladel **(0497)** 369619 or 06 54341822 (mob); info@
minicampingdehooiberg.nl; www.minicampingde
hooiberg.nl

🐕 ♦♦(htd) ⍵ᴅ ≛ ᴔ ⎕ ⁄ 🦋

**Exit A67 junc 32 onto N284 to Bladel, turn L at traff
lts to Bladel-Zuid, site on L in 2km.** Sm, pt shd, EHU
(6A) inc; bus adj; Eng spkn; adv bkg acc; sep car park.
*"Gd, quiet site; clean san fac; v friendly owner; dogs
free; farm shop selling local produce adj; 10 mins fr
A67; conv NH & for Eindhoven & Efteling theme park."*
€18.00, 15 Mar-31 Oct. **2019**

BLADEL *C4* (3km S Rural) *51.34325, 5.22740*
Camping De Achterste Hoef, Troprijt 10, 5531 NA
Bladel **(0497)** 381579; info@achterstehoef.nl;
www.achterstehoef.nl

🐕 ♦♦(htd) ⍵ᴅ ≛ ♨ ᴔ ⎕ ⁄ ⍟ ⍦ 𝖸 ⑪ ⍛ ⍿ ⚲
🏊(covrd, htd) 🎿

**Fr A67 exit junc 32 onto N284 to Bladel, then
Bladel-Zuid, site sp.** 5*, V lge, pt shd, EHU (6A) inc;
70% statics; adv bkg acc; ccard acc; waterslide; games
area; tennis; games rm; bike hire. *"Private san facs
avail."* **€41.70, 5 Apr-29 Sep.** **2019**

BRIELLE *B3* (1km E Urban) *51.90666, 4.17527*
Camping de Meeuw, Batterijweg 1, 3231 AA Brielle
(0181) 412777; info@demeeuw.nl; www.demeeuw.nl

🐕 €3.75 ♦♦♦ ⍵ᴅ ≛ ᴔ ⎕ ⁄ ⍟ 𝖸 ⑪ ⍛ ⍿ ⚲ 𝟐sand

**On A15/N57 foll sp to Brielle. Turn R after passing
thro town gates & foll sp to site.** Lge, pt shd, EHU
(10A) €2 (poss rev pol); gas; 70% statics; phone; Eng
spkn; bike hire; CKE. *"Historic fortified town; attractive
area for tourers; conv Europoort ferry terminal; gd NH/
sh stay; phone warden fr recep when arr after 5pm."*
€28.00, 31 Mar-30 Oct. **2017**

CADZAND *A4* (2km SE Rural) *51.36099, 3.42503*
Camping De Wielewaal, Zuidzandseweg 20, 4506 HC
Cadzand **(0117)** 391216; info@campingwielewaal.nl;
www.campingwielewaal.nl

🐕 €2 ♦♦♦ ⍵ᴅ ≛ ♨ ᴔ ⎕ ⁄ ⍟ ⍦ 𝖸nr ⑪nr ⍛nr ⍿ ⚲ 𝟐3km

**Head to Cadzand. Travel 1km SE, site ent on L,
3km NW of Zuidzande.** Med, hdg, mkd, pt shd,
EHU; bbq; Eng spkn; adv bkg acc; ccard acc; games
rm. *"Many cycle tracks; walks fr site; friendly,
helpful owners; windmill 1km; highly rec; excel."*
€18.70, 19 Mar-31 Oct. **2016**

CADZAND *A4* (5km S Rural/Coastal) *51.344562,
3.429860* **Minicamping de Hullu,** Kokersweg 1,
4505 PK Zuidzande **(3111)** 7452842; www.camping
dehullu.nl

🐕 ♦♦(htd) ⍵ᴅ ≛ ᴔ ⎕ ⁄ ⍟ 🦋 ⍦ 𝟐4km

**Do not use SatNav. Fr Bruge A11 (new) N253 to
Oostburg. N674 thro Zuidzande. Site on L.** Sm, shd,
EHU (6A) inc; bbq; Eng spkn; adv bkg acc; games
area. *"Excel; feels like camping in gdn of stately home;
16 vans when full; views; lawned; no passing traff;
spacious."* **NP 20, 20 Apr-15 Sep.** **2018**

> ## "I like to fill in the reports as I travel from site to site"
>
> You'll find report forms at the back of this guide, or you can fill them in online at camc.com/europereport.

CALLANTSOOG *B2* (2.5km NE Coastal) *52.84627,
4.71549* **Camping Tempelhof,** Westerweg 2, 1759 JD
Callantsoog **(0224)** 581522; info@tempelhof.nl;
www.tempelhof.nl

12 🐕 €3.50 ♦♦(htd) ⍵ᴅ ≛ ♨ ᴔ ⎕ ⁄ ⍟ ⍦ 𝖸 ⑪ ⍛ ⍿ ⚲
🏊(covrd, htd) 🎿 𝟐sand 1km

**Fr A9 Alkmaar-Den Helder exit Callantsoog, site sp
to NE of vill.** 5*, Lge, mkd, pt shd, serviced pitches;
EHU (10A) inc; gas; TV (pitch); 50% statics; phone;
adv bkg rec; sauna; gym; bike hire; games area; tennis.
*"Superb, well-run site & facs; private bthrms avail; ACSI
acc."* **€43.00** **2017**

For a guide to symbols see the fold out on the rear cover

CALLANTSOOG *B2* (3km NE Coastal) *52.84143, 4.71909* **NCC Camping De Ooster Nollen,** Westerweg 8, 1759 JD Callantsoog **(0224) 581281 or 561351; info@denollen.nl; www.denollen.nl**

🐕 €3 ♙♙ (htd) ⬜ ♨ 🔥 🚿 🛁 / MSP 🦋 ⓦ 🍴 🛒 🎣 🛱 /Ⅲ 🚲

🏖 sand 1.5km

N fr Alkmaar on A9; turn L sp Callantsoog. Site sp 1km E of Callantsoog. Lge, mkd, pt shd, EHU (10A) inc; gas; red long stay; TV; 40% statics; phone; Eng spkn; adv bkg acc; ccard acc; bike hire; games area; CKE. *"Nature area nr; cheese mkt; clean & superb san facs; pool 400m; supmkt 3km."* **€34.00, 1 Apr-29 Oct.** **2017**

"We must tell the Club about that great site we found"

Get your site reports in by mid-August and we'll do our best to get your updates into the next edition.

DELFT *B3* (4km NE Urban) *52.01769, 4.37945* **Camping Delftse Hout,** Korftlaan 5, 2616 LJ Delft **(015) 2130040; info@delftsehout.nl; www.delftse hout.co.uk**

🐕 €3.25 ♙♙ (htd) ⬜ ♨ 🔥 🚿 🛁 / MSP 🍴 ⓦ 🎣 🛱 /Ⅲ 🚲

🏖 (htd) 🏊

Fr Hook of Holland take N220 twd Rotterdam; after Maasdijk turn R onto A20 m'way. Take A13 twd Den Haag at v lge Kleinpolderplein interchange. Take exit 9 sp Delft (Ikea on R). Turn R twrds Ikea then L at rndabt. Foll sp. Do not use Sat Nav. 4*, Lge, hdstg, mkd, hdg, pt shd, EHU (10A) inc; gas; bbq; red long stay; TV; 50% statics; phone; bus to Delft; Eng spkn; adv bkg rec; ccard acc; bike hire; fishing nr; golf 5km; watersports nr; games rm; CKE. *"Located by pleasant park; gd quality, secure, busy site with excel facs; Holland Tulip Parcs site; helpful, friendly staff; little shd; no o'fits over 7.5m; excursions by bike & on foot; easy access Delft cent; sm m'van o'night area outside site; mkt Thur; excel; site clean & well maintained; gd rest; vg play areas for kids; flea mkt on Sat; gd tram and train svcs to the Hague, Leiden and Gouda fr Delft stn; gd sized pitches; vg MH svr pnt; well stocked shop."* **€37.60, 22 Mar-3 Nov, H06.** **2019**

DELFT *B3* (9.4km SW Rural) *51.95450, 4.28833* **Hoeve Bouwlust,** Oostgaag 31, 3155 CE Maasland **(0105) 912775; info@hoevebouwlust.nl; www.hoeve bouwlust.nl**

♙♙ ⬜ ♨ 🔥 🛱 / MSP 🍴 ⓦ 🎣 /Ⅲ

Fr Hofh on A20 turn N at junc 7. Go thro Maasland on N468. Site on L in 3km. Sm, hdg, pt shd, EHU; bbq; twin axles; 10% statics; bus adj; Eng spkn; adv bkg acc; CKE. *"Lots of outdoor activities inc tandem, boating & scooters; v friendly & helpful owners; vg site."* **€19.00, 1 Apr-31 Oct.** **2018**

DEN HELDER *B2* (3.5km SW Coastal) *52.93672, 4.73377* **Camping de Donkere Duinen,** Jan Verfailleweg 616, 1783 BW Den Helder **(0223) 614731; info@donkereduinen.nl; www.donkereduinen.nl**

🐕 €2.75 ♙♙ ⬜ ♨ 🔥 🚿 🛁 / MSP 🦋 ⓦ 🍴 🛒 nr /Ⅲ 🌳 sand 800m

Fr S turn L off N9 sp Julianadorp (Schoolweg), strt over at x-rds in Julianadorp (Van Foreestweg). Turn R at t-junc onto N502, site on L in approx 4km. 2*, Lge, pt shd, EHU (4-16A) inc; gas; 10% statics; Eng spkn; adv bkg req; ccard acc; tennis; bike hire; CKE. *"V helpful owner; excel walking/cycling; ferry to Texel Is; bkg fee; lge naval museum & submarine; opp Heldersee Valley Adventure (treetop) Pk."* **€25.50, 13 Apr-12 Sep.** **2017**

DENEKAMP *D3* (4km NE Rural) *52.39190, 7.04890* **Camping De Papillon,** Kanaalweg 30, 7591 NH Denekamp **(0541) 351670; info@depapillon.nl; www.depapillon.nl**

🐕 €4.50 ♙♙ (htd) ⬜ ♨ 🔥 🚿 🛁 / MSP 🦋 🍴 ⓦ 🎣 /Ⅲ

🏖 (covrd, htd)

Fr A1 take exit 32 onto N342 Oldenzaal-Denekamp, dir Nordhorn, site sp on left just bef German border. 4*, Lge, mkd, hdg, pt shd, EHU (6-10A) inc; gas; bbq; sw; red long stay; TV; 5% statics; phone; Eng spkn; tennis; pool paddling; bike hire. *"Super, clean site; friendly site; helpful owners; man-made lake; vg."* **€35.00, 29 Mar-30 Sep, H18.** **2018**

DEVENTER *C3* (11km E Rural) *52.25591, 6.29205* **Camping De Flierweide,** Traasterdijk 16, 7437 Bathmen **31 570 541478; info@flierweide.nl; www.flierweide.nl**

🐕 ♙♙♙ ⬜ ♨ 🔥 🚿 🛁 / 🦋 ⓦ 🍴 /Ⅲ

Fr A1 junc 25 dir Bathmen. After 1km turn R sp De Flierweide, 800m L onto Laurensweg, thro vill. Cross rlwy, 1st R ontp Traasterdijk. Site on R after 500m at fm buildings. Med, hdg, mkd, hdstg, pt shd, EHU (4-16A) €2.50; bbq; red long stay; 1% statics; Eng spkn; adv bkg acc; bike hire; games area; CKE. *"Walking & cycle rtes; golf nr; boules onsite; excel."* **€23.00, 15 Mar-1 Nov.** **2016**

DIEREN *C3* (2.5km NW Rural) *52.06908, 6.07705* **De Jutberg Vakantiedorp,** Jutberg 78, 6957 DP Laag-Soeren **03 13 61 92 20; jutberg@ardoer.com; www.ardoer.com/jutberg**

12 🐕 ♙♙ (htd) ⬜ ♨ 🔥 🛱 / 🦋 🍴 ⓦ 🎣 🛒 /Ⅲ 🚲

🏖 (covrd, htd)

Fr A12 take exit 27 onto the A348. Turn L on the N348 into Dieren. Turn L at petrol stn, cont for 2.7km. Foll sp to site. V lge, mkd, shd, pt sl, EHU (6A); bbq; Eng spkn; adv bkg acc; games rm; games area; CCI. *"Hugh pitches, fully serviced; v lively but noisy; excursions for adults & kids in summer; wet weather diversions; excel san facs; extensive cycle paths thro countryside & forest; excel site."* **€35.20** **2019**

DOKKUM *C2* (0.4km E Urban) *53.32611, 6.00468*
Camping Harddraverspark, Harddraversdijk 1a,
9101 XA Dokkum **(0519)** 294445; info@camping
dokkum.nl; www.campingdokkum.nl

🐕 ε2 👫 wo ⛱ 🛢 ∥ MSP 🐾 ♀ Ⴑ nr ⊕ nr 🛢 nr ⏞

Best app fr E fr ring rd N361 onto Harddraversdijk
alongside rv, site sp. Do not app thro town - narr
rds. Med, hdg, mkd, hdstg, pt shd, EHU (6A) €2.50;
gas; Eng spkn; tennis. *"Excel location in cent of
pleasant town; conv for ferry to Ameland Island
(12km)."* **€19.00, 1 Apr-31 Oct.** **2015**

DORDRECHT *B3* (13km N Rural) *51.89530, 4.72209*
Camping en Feestzall Landhoeve, Lekdijk 15,
2957 CA Nieuw-Lekkerland **(3184)** 684137 or **(316)**
40487201; info@landhoeve.info; www.landhoeve.com

🐕 👫 (htd) wo ⛱ க் ∥ 🐾 ♀

Fr A15 take exit 23. Take 2nd exit at rndabt and
then 3rd exit at next rndabt twrds New Lekkerland.
Turn R onto the N480 twrds Streefkerk. Then L
onto Zijdeweg & L again at the end of rd. Site in
400mtrs. Sm, unshd, EHU; bbq; Eng spkn; adv bkg
acc. *"New htd toilet facilities (2017); views; 19 windmills
at Kinderdijk nrby, Unesco site; like lge CL; vg."*
€22.00, 1 Apr-1 Oct. **2017**

DORDRECHT *B3* (3km SE Rural) *51.80738, 4.71862*
Camping Het Loze Vissertje, Loswalweg 3, 3315 LB
Dordrecht **(078)** 6162751; info@campinghet
vissertje.nl; www.campinghetvissertje.nl

🐕 ε1 👫 wo ⛱ ∥ 🐾 ♀

Fr Rotterdam across Brienenoord Bdge foll sp
Gorinchem & Nijmegen A15. Exit junc 23
Papendrecht & turn R onto N3 until exit
Werkendam. Turn R & foll sp 'Het Vissertje'. Sm,
pt shd, EHU (6A) inc; red long stay; 20% statics; Eng
spkn. *"Lovely, delightful site; friendly, helpful manager;
modern, clean san facs; gd cycle rtes nr; vg; easy acc to
town on local train."* **€21.00, 15 Apr-15 Sep.** **2019**

DRACHTEN *C2* (10km W Rural) *53.09696, 5.94695*
Camping De Veenhoop Watersport & Recreatie,
Eijzengapaed 5, 9215 VV De Veenhoop **(0512)**
462289; info@de-veenhoop.nl; www.de-veenhoop.nl

🐕 👫 (htd) wo ⛱ 🛢 ∥ 🐾 ♀ ⊕ nr Ⴑ nr ⏞

Exit A7 junc 28 dir Nij Beets, foll De Veenhoop sp
to site. Or exit A32 junc 13 & turn W for approx
6km via Aldeboarn. Turn L at Pieter's Rest to De
Veenhoop, site on L bef sm bdge. Med, pt shd, EHU
(6-10A) €4; bbq; sw; 50% statics; bus adj; Eng spkn;
adv bkg acc; boat hire. *"Excel, peaceful, friendly site;
helpful owners; clean & well-maintained; excel sailing,
cycling, walking; well situated for lakes & N N'lands; gd
NH & longer stays; MH beware some soft (peat) grnd."*
€24.00, 1 Apr-1 Oct. **2018**

DROONENBURGH *C3* (3km NNW Rural) *51.90416,
5.98529* **Camping de Waay,** Rijndijk 67A, 6686 MC
Doornenburg **(048)** 1421256; info@de-waay.nl;
www.de-waay.nl

🐕 👫 wo ⛱ க் ⚥ 🛢 ∥ ♀ ♀ ⊕ க் Ⴑ ⏞ ⚓ (htd) ⛴

A325 S fr Arnhem for 12km turn R onto A15 twrds
Tiel, take exit N839 Bemmel. At t-junc foll sp to
Gendt. In Gendt take N838. Foll ANWB de Waay sp
twrds Angeren. Turn R onto the dyke and site on R.
Sm, pt shd, EHU 6A; bbq; TV; 60% statics; Eng spkn;
adv bkg acc; waterslide; games rm; bike hire; games
area; CKE. *"V helpful staff; takeaway; gd for Arnhem &
Nijmegen; ACSI acc; vg."* **€33.50, 25 Mar-1 Oct.**
2016

DWINGELOO *D2* (2km SE Rural) *52.82216, 6.39258*
Camping De Olde Bârgen, Oude Hoogeveensedijk
1, 7991 PD Dwingeloo **(0521)** 597261; info@
oldebargen.nl; www.oldebargen.nl

12 🐕 ε2 👫 wo ⛱ க் ⚥ 🛢 ∥ 🐾 ♀ Ⴑ nr ⏞

Exit A28 Zwolle/Assen rd at Spier, turn W sp
Dwingeloo, site clearly sp, in wooded area. Sm, mkd,
pt shd, EHU (4-6A) inc; 10% statics; Eng spkn; adv
bkg acc; CKE. *"Excel, v clean, well-run site on N side
Dwingelderveld National Park; gd for walkers & cyclists;
v friendly, helpful owners; pool 1.5km; delightful, quiet
sitewarden avail 1 hr each morning LS, pitch & pay next
day."* **€21.00** **2017**

EDAM *B2* (2km NE Coastal) *52.51853, 5.07286*
Camping Strandbad Edam, Zeevangszeedijk 7A,
1135 PZ Edam **(0299)** 371994; info@
campingstrandbad.nl; www.campingstrandbad.nl

👫 (htd) wo ⛱ க் ⚥ 🛢 ∥ MSP 🐾 ♀ ♀ ⊕ க் Ⴑ ⏞ 🖭 ⚓ sand adj

Foll N247 Amsterdam-Hoorn; after sp for Edam foll
site sp. At traff lts in Edam keep on N247 past bus
stn on R, then R at next rndabt. Last 100m to site is
single track opp marina. Access thro public car park.
2*, Lge, pt shd, EHU (10A) €2.90; gas; red long stay;
TV; 40% statics; phone; Eng spkn; adv bkg acc; ccard
acc; watersports; bike hire. *"Walking dist Edam; landing
stage for boats; excel san facs; pool 3km; sm, poss
cramped pitches high ssn."* **€20.00, 1 Apr-30 Sep.**
2018

EDAM *B2* (2.5km NE Coastal) *52.52472, 5.06472*
Camping Zeevangshoeve, Zeevangszeedijk 5-C,
1135 PZ Edam **(061)** 7864374; info@
zeevangshoeve.nl; www.zeevangshoeve.nl

🐕 ε1.50 👫 wo ⛱ க் ⚥ ∥ MSP ♀ ⏞ ⚓ opp

Foll coast rd out of Nof old part of Edam past
marina along edge of the Markermeer dyke. Site is
on L opp the Zeedijk. Sm, pt shd, EHU 6A; bbq; Eng
spkn; adv bkg acc. *"Easy walk/cycle to historic cent of
Edam; vg."* **€20.00, 30 Mar-31 Oct.** **2018**

EERSEL *C4* (4km SE Rural) *51.33635, 5.35552*
Camping De Paal, De Paaldreef 14, 5571 TN Bergeijk
(0497) 571977; info@depaal.nl; www.depaal.nl
🐕 €5 👪(htd) 🆆 ▲ ♨ ⚴ 🗑 ⁄ 🅼🆂🅿 ⁈ 🍽 ⑪ 🍴 🇿 ⚠ ✿
🏊(covrd, htd) 🛶

Fr A67/E34 Antwerp/Eindoven exit junc 32 sp Eersel
& bear R onto N284 & stay in R-hand lane. At rndabt
take 1st exit onto Eijkereind. In 500m after rndbt
turn L at traff lts & foll rd around R & L bend. Take R
turn sp Bergeijk after lge church (sm sp on sharp L
bend). After approx 5km turn L into site rd.
5*, V lge, pt shd, EHU (6A) inc; gas; bbq (charcoal,
gas); TV; 10% statics; phone; games rm; sep car
park; bike hire; tennis; watersports 10km; fishing;
horseriding 500m; sauna. *"Excel, family-run site set in
woodland; espec gd for young children; lge pitches in
groups with sep sm play areas; excursions; recep 0900-
1800; sm children's zoo; fitness cent; no o'fits over 8m
high ssn; conv Efteling theme park, Hilvarenbeek safari
park, Oisterwijk bird park; mkt Mon & Tue pm; 1st class
facs."* **€25.00, 25 Mar-30 Oct, H04.** **2016**

EINDHOVEN *C4* (16km S Rural) *51.32887, 5.46160*
Recreatiepark Brugse Heide, Maastrichterweg 183,
5556 VB Valkenswaard **(040) 2018304; info@
vakantieparkbrugseheide.nl; www.vakantiepark
brugseheide.nl**
🐕 👪(htd) 🆆 ▲ ♨ ⚴ 🗑 ⁄ 🅼🆂🅿 ⁈ 🍽 🍴 🇿nr ⚠ ✿ 🏊(htd) 🛶

S fr Eindhoven, exit Waalre; take N69
Valkenswaard; drive thro to rndabt, turn L. At next
rndabt strt ahead, at next rndabt turn R, foll sp
Achel. Site on L in 1km. 3*, Lge, mkd, shd, serviced
pitches; EHU (6A) inc (rev pol); gas; bbq; TV;
40% statics; phone; Eng spkn; adv bkg req; ccard acc;
bike hire. *"Excel, friendly site; gd NH en rte Germany;
excel san facs."* **€34.00, 18 Mar-31 Oct.** **2016**

EMMEN *D2* (6km N Rural) *52.82861, 6.85714*
Vakantiecentrum De Fruithof, Melkweg 2, 7871 PE
Klijndijk **(0591) 512427; info@fruithof.nl;
www.fruithof.nl**
🐕 👪(htd) 🆆 ▲ ♨ ⚴ 🗑 ⁄ 🅼🆂🅿 ⁈ 🍽 ⑪ 🍴 🇿 ⚠ ✿ 🏊(htd) 🛶

On N34 N fr Emmen dir Borger, turn R sp Klijndijk,
foll site sp. 5*, Lge, mkd, hdg, pt shd, serviced
pitches; EHU (6A) inc; gas; bbq; sw nr; red long stay; TV;
50% statics; Eng spkn; adv bkg acc; tennis; games
area; bike hire; CKE. *"Excel; v lge busy site; gd san
facs."* **€38.80, 5 Apr-23 Sep.** **2019**

ENKHUIZEN *C2* (1km N Coastal) *52.70888, 5.28830*
Camping De Vest, Noorderweg 31, 1601 PC Enkhuizen
**(0228) 321221; info@campingdevest.nl; www.camping
devest.nl**
🐕 👪 🆆 ▲ ⁄ 🏖 sand 800m

When N302 turns R at traff lts, keep strt on to
T-junc. Foll site sp to R, site on R in 50m.
Sm, pt shd, EHU (4A) inc; 25% statics; Eng spkn; adv
bkg acc. *"Gates clsd 2300-0800; easy walk to town
cent; lively jazz festival last w/end in May; facs old but
clean, well-kept - poss stretched when site full; site
inside town walls."* **€21.00, 30 Mar-30 Sep.** **2018**

ENSCHEDE *D3* (6km E Urban) *52.21034, 6.95127*
Euregio Camping de Twentse Es, Keppelerdijk 200,
7534 PA Enschede **(053) 4611372; info@twentse-es.nl;
www.twentse-es.nl**
⓬ 🐕 👪(htd) 🆆 ▲ ♨ ⚴ 🗑 ⁄ 🦋 ⁈ 🍽 ⑪ 🍴 🇿 ⚠ ✿ 🏊 🛶

Fr Germany, cross border at Gronau on B54/N35;
twd Enschede. In 2.5km turn R into Oostweg, then
in 2km turn R into Gronausestraat, then in 800m
turn R into Esmarkelaan. Foll rd thro residential
area, turn L at end, site on R. Not rec to foll sat nav
due rd building, rec foll rd signs. 3*, Lge, pt shd, EHU
(10A) inc; gas; TV; 70% statics; adv bkg acc; ccard acc;
bike hire; games area; CKE. *"Excel site; modern facs;
15% discount with CCI card; local tourist tax of €0.76
pppn."* **€24.00** **2018**

EXLOO *D2* (2km SE Rural) *52.86841, 6.88496*
Camping Exloo, Valtherweg 37, 7875 TA Exloo
**05 91 54 91 47 or 05 91 56 40 14; info@camping
exloo.nl; www.campingexloo.nl**
⓬ 🐕 €1 👪 🆆 ▲ ♨ 🗑 ⁄ 🅼🆂🅿 🦋 ⁈

N34 fr Groningen, exit Exloo. Turn R after vill twd
Valthe. Site 2km on L. Sm, pt shd, EHU (6A); bbq;
twin axles; TV; Eng spkn; adv bkg acc; CCI. *"Friendly
recreation rm; vg site."* **€20.20** **2019**

GENDT *C3* (1km E Rural) *51.87599, 5.98900*
Waalstrand Camping, Waaldijk 23, 6691 MB Gendt
**(0481) 421604; info@waalstrand.nl;
www.waalstrand.nl**
🐕 €3 👪 🆆 ♨ 🗑 ⁄ ⁈ 🍽 🇿nr ⚠ 🛶

Exit A15 to Bemmel, then Gendt. In Gendt foll sp to
site on Rv Waal. Med, mkd, unshd, terr, EHU (6A) inc;
gas; TV (pitch); 50% statics; Eng spkn; adv bkg acc;
bike hire; tennis. *"Excel, well-kept site; clean, modern
san facs; interesting rv traff; v friendly owners; lovely
position; gd walks; 6 fully serviced camper van pitches;
good views; excel site."* **€29.50, 1 Apr-30 Sep.** **2018**

GOUDA *B3* (10km E Rural) *52.01719, 4.82943*
Camping De Mulderije, Hekendorpsebuurt 33, 3467
PA Hekendorp **(0348) 563233 or 06 20680521
(mob); info@demulderije.nl; demulderije.nl**
⓬ 🐕 👪 🆆 ▲ ⚴ ⁄ 🦋 🍴nr ⑪nr 🇿nr

Exit A12 junc 14 Woerden onto N204 S. In 5km turn
R to Oudewater N228. Cont dir Hekendorp & in
approx 2km site sp on R. Narr rd to site.
1*, Sm, hdstg, pt shd, EHU (6A) inc; Eng spkn. *"Vg,
clean, friendly site in nature reserve; cycle or boat to
Gouda; facs clean attractive position; gd base; narr rd
to site not suitable for lge o'fits; no passing places; do
not use sat nav."* **€17.00** **2017**

GOUDA *B3* (2km E Urban) *52.01226, 4.71544*
Klein Amerika Parking, 2806 Gouda
⓬ 👪 🆆 ⁄

500m fr Gouda town cent, sp off Blekerssingel/
Fluwelensingel. EHU (16A). *"30 spaces in car pk at
Klein Amerika supervised by Gouda City Council; 12
EHU sockets; max stay 3 days; normal car parking fees
applicable; poorly maintained."* **€8.00** **2016**

GRONINGEN *D2* (6km SW Urban) *53.20128, 6.53577*
Camping Stadspark, Campinglaan 6, 9727 KH
Groningen (050) 5251624; info@campingstadspark.nl;
www.campingstadspark.nl

🛉 €2 ⬜ WD ♨ ⚲ ∥ MSP ✿ ⓣ Ⅰ â 🏊 ⚠

Take exit 36-A (dir Drachten) and foll 'Stadspark'.
In the park go to the L and foll the sp. Fr Drachten/
Winsum, take exit 36. 2*, Med, shd, EHU (6A) €2.50
(poss rev pol); gas; TV; 20% statics; phone; Eng spkn;
adv bkg acc; bike hire; sep car park. *"Municipal site adj
parkland with gd sports facs; park & ride into town;
plenty of space, tents & vans mixed; extensive cycle
paths; car park adj to each set of pitches; gd san facs;
well run site; interesting town; pool 3km; friendly
helpful staff."* **€24.00, 15 Mar-15 Oct.** **2017**

GULPEN *C4* (1.5km S Rural) *50.80720, 5.89430*
Panorama Camping Gulperberg, Berghem 1, 6271
NP Gulpen (043) 4502330; info@gulperberg.nl;
www.gulperberg.nl

🛉 €4.50 🛉🛉 (htd) WD ♨ ⚲ 🗎 ∥ ✿ ⓣ Ⅰ ⓗ â 🏊 ⚠ 🏊 🛶

Fr Maastricht on N278 twd Aachen. At 1st traff lts
in Gulpen turn sharp R & foll site sp for 2km (past
sports complex). Narr final app. 4*, Lge, hdstg,
mkd, pt shd, terr, EHU (10A) inc; gas; bbq; TV (pitch);
10% statics; phone; Eng spkn; adv bkg acc; games
area; bike hire; CKE. *"Nr Maastricht with gd walking/
views; mkd cycle rtes & footpaths; modern, clean facs
- poss long walk; beautiful views; v popular site; busy
even in LS; excel."* **€37.00, 17 Mar-3 Nov, H12.** **2017**

HARDERWIJK *C3* (13.6km W Rural) *52.340102,
5.505166* **Camping Het Groene Bos,** Green
Woudseweg 98, 3896 LS Zeewolde (036) 5236366;
info@hetgroenebos.nl; www.hetgroenebos.nl

🛉🛉 (htd) WD ♨ ⚲ ∥ MSP ✿ ⓣ ⚠

Off A305 on minor rd between Kampen & A27. Exit
A27 J26 onto 305. Med, mkd, hdg, pt shd, EHU inc;
Eng spkn; CKE. *"Vg site; surrounded by woodland."*
€21.60, 1 Apr-11 Oct. **2018**

HARLINGEN *C2* (2km SW Coastal) *53.16253, 5.41653*
Camping De Zeehoeve, Westerzeedijk 45, 8862 PK
Harlingen (0517) 413465; info@zeehoeve.nl;
www.zeehoeve.nl

🛉 €3.50 🛉🛉 (htd) WD ♨ ⚲ ⚲ ∥ ∥ MSP ⓣ Ⅰ ⓗ â 🏊 nr ⚠ ✐
🏊 adj

Leave N31 N'bound at sp Kimswerd. At rndabt turn
L under N31 & foll site sp. Site on R in 1.6km. 3*,
Lge, pt shd, EHU (6A) inc; gas; TV; 30% statics;
phone; Eng spkn; ccard acc; fishing; bike hire; games
area; watersports. *"Roomy, well-maintained, well run,
open site; clean modern facs; easy walk to historic
town & harbour; interesting area; vg; ACSI acc."*
€26.00, 1 Apr-31 Oct. **2018**

HAVELTE *D2* (1km SE Rural) *52.76820, 6.24987*
Campsite Jelly's Hoeve, Raadhuislaan 2, 7971 CT
Havelte (052) 1342808; info@jellyshoeve.nl;
www.jellyshoeve.nl

🛉 €2 ⬜ WD ♨ ⚲ ∥ ✿ ⓤ

Take exit 4 on A32. Then N371 twrds Havelte/
Diever. After 4km cross the bdge and take immed
R, foll rd for 1km. Turn L at canal bdge, bear R &
after 75m turn R. Site on R after 100m. Sm, mkd,
hdg, pt shd, EHU (10A) €2; bbq; twin axles; Eng spkn;
games area. *"Plenty of walks & cycle tracks; excel."*
€21.00, 1 Apr-30 Sep. **2015**

HELDEN *C4* (2km E Rural) *51.31813, 6.0235* **Camping
De Heldense Bossen,** De Heldense Bossen 6, 5988
NH Helden 07 73 07 24 76; heldensebossen@
ardoer.com; www.ardoer.com/heldensebossen

🛉 🛉🛉 WD ♨ ⚲ ⚲ ∥ MSP ⓣ Ⅰ ⓗ â 🏊 ⚠ 🏊 (covrd, htd) 🛏

Fr A67 Eindhoven-Venlo, take exit 38 (Helden). Turn
R onto N277 twds Maasbreeseweg. Cont onto N562.
Fr Helden dir Kessel. Turn L after 1km. Campsite
1km further on. 5*, V lge, mkd, pt shd, EHU (10A);
bbq; twin axles; 65% statics; Eng spkn; adv bkg acc;
games area; waterslide; bike hire; CCI. *"Excel site."*
€34.50, 29 Mar-27 Oct. **2019**

HENGELO *D3* (7km W Rural) *52.25451, 6.72704*
Park Camping Mooi Delden, De Mors 6, 7491 DZ
Delden (074) 3761922; info@parkcamping.nl;
www.parkcamping.nl

🛉 €3.15 🛉🛉 (htd) WD ♨ ⚲ ⚲ 🗎 ∥ ✿ ⓣ Ⅰ â 🏊 ⚠ 🏊

Exit A35 junc 28 onto N346 dir Delden. Fr Delden-
Oost, site sp. Site ent is R-hand of 2 via barrier
(use intercom on arr.) If you have a high vehicle
take the turning after Delden-Oost to avoid low
rail bdge (3.2m); turn L immed aft lge rv bdge &
foll site sp. 3*, Med, mkd, pt shd, EHU (6-10A) €3.40
(poss rev pol); 50% statics; Eng spkn; adv bkg acc;
tennis. *"Ideal for touring beautiful pt of Holland; sports
complex adj; pleasant, well-kept site; clean facs."*
€28.00, 25 Mar-1 Oct. **2016**

HEUMEN *C3* (2km NW Rural) *51.76890, 5.82140*
Camping Heumens Bos, Vosseneindseweg 46, 6582
BR Heumen (024) 3581481; info@heumensbos.nl;
www.heumensbos.nl

12 🛉 €4 🛉🛉 (htd) WD ♨ ⚲ ⚲ 🗎 ∥ MSP ✿ ⓣ Ⅰ ⓗ â 🏊 ⚠
✐ 🏊 (covrd, htd) 🛏

Take A73/E31 Nijmegen-Venlo m'way, leave at exit
3 sp Heumen/Overasselt. Do not re-cross m'way.
After 500m turn R at camp sp. Site on R in approx
1.5km, 1km S of Heumen. 5*, V lge, mkd, hdg,
shd, EHU (6A) inc; gas; bbq; sw nr; TV; 60% statics;
phone; Eng spkn; adv bkg acc; ccard acc; games area;
horseriding 100m; games rm; bike hire; tennis; fishing
2km; watersports 6km; jacuzzi; sep car park; CCI.
*"Excel, busy, family-run site; modern san facs; lots to
do on site & in area - info fr recep; no o'fits over 14m;
ideal for Arnhem; WW2 museums nr; activities in ssn;
extra €3 for m'vans; noise fr bar high ssn; mkt Sat &
Mon in Nijmegen."* **€31.50, H01.** **2019**

HOEK *A4* (7km W Rural) *51.31464, 3.72618*
Oostappen Vakantiepark Marina Beach (formerly Braakman), Middenweg 1, 4542 PN Hoek **(0115) 481730; info@vakantieparkmarinabeach.nl; www.vakantieparkmarinabeach.nl**

🚶€5 👪(htd) ⬜ ♨☀⌂⚟/☂ ▼ ⑨▯🎿⛰♿🏊

Sp fr N61. V lge, mkd, pt shd, serviced pitches; EHU (4A) inc; gas; TV (pitch); 50% statics; phone; Eng spkn; adv bkg acc; ccard acc; squash; sailing; tennis. *"Excel for families; lake beach; extensive recreation facs; conv Bruges/Antwerp; extra for lake view pitches."* **€46.00, 18 Mar-31 Oct.**   **2016**

HOEK VAN HOLLAND *B3* (1.5km N Urban) *51.98953, 4.12767* **Camping Hoek van Holland,** Wierstraat 100, 3151 VP Hoek van Holland **(0174) 382550; info@campinghoekvanholland.nl; www.campinghoekvanholland.nl**

👪(htd) ⬜ ♨☀⌂♿⚟/ ▼ ▼ ⑨▯🎿⛰♿🏊 ⏟sand nrby

Fr ferry foll N211/220 Rotterdam. After 2.4km turn L, 50m bef petrol stn on R, sp 'Camping Strand', site 400m on R. 3*, Lge, mkd, hdstg, pt shd, EHU (6A) inc; gas; TV; 60% statics; phone; bus; Eng spkn; sep car park; bike hire; tennis; CKE. *"Open 0800-2300; modern san facs but poss inadequate when site full & long walk fr m'van area; conv ferry."* **€34.00, 19 Mar-16 Oct.**   **2016**

HOEK VAN HOLLAND *B3* (3km N Coastal) *51.99685, 4.13347* **Camping Jagtveld,** Nieuwlandsedijk 41, KV 2691 'S-Gravenzande **(0174) 413479; info@jagtveld.nl; www.jagtveld.nl**

👪⬜ ♨☀/ ▼ ▯🎿⛰♿🏊 ⏟sand 400m

Fr ferry foll N211/220 sp Rotterdam. After 3.2km, turn L at junc with traff lts gantry into cul-de-sac. Site 200m on L. 2*, Med, unshd, EHU (16A) poss rev pol €2; gas; 80% statics; phone; Eng spkn; sep car park. *"Ideal for ferry port; conv Den Haag & Delft; gd, clean, level, family-run site; diff when wet; helpful owners; excel 8km long beach."* **€33.30,** 1 Apr-1 Oct.   2019

HOEK VAN HOLLAND *B3* (3.4km N Rural/Coastal) *52.002950, 4.138390* **Strandpark Vlugtenburg,** 't Louwtje 10, 2691 KR/'s-Gravenzande **(017) 4412420**

12 🚶 👪⬜ ♨☀⌂⚟/☂ ▼ ⑨▯ ▼ ⏟sand; adj

Fr ferry take N211. After passing N220 junc. After tight R-hand bend immed take L between petrol stn & bus shelter. Lge, mkd, unshd, EHU (16A) inc; bbq; 70% statics (sep area); bus adj; Eng spkn; adv bkg acc; ccard acc. *"Vg site; excel for kite & wind surfing; restrictions on dog breeds - check bef travel; conv fr ferry; easy for Delft, The Hague."* **€36.20**   **2018**

HOORN *B2* (5km SW Rural) *52.63085, 5.00920*
Camping 't Venhop, De Hulk 6a, 1622GJ, Berkhout **(0229) 551371; info@venhop.nl; www.venhop.nl**

12 🚶€1.50 👪(htd) ⬜ ♨☀⌂/☂ ▼ ⑨▯ nr ⑨nr 🎿⛰

Fr A7, exit junc 7 dir Avenhorn. Turn L under A7, site sp on R. Med, mkd, hdg, pt shd, serviced pitches; EHU (10A) inc; 60% statics; Eng spkn; ccard acc; sep car park; boat, electric bike & scooter hire; CKE. *"Friendly owner; pleasant, well-run site nr canal; full facs LS; vg, delightful waterside camp; fishing in canal fr some pitches."* **€27.00**   **2019**

KATWIJK AAN ZEE *B3* (6km E Rural) *52.19990, 4.45625* **Camping Koningshof,** Elsgeesterweg 8, 2331 NW Rijnsburg **(071) 4026051; info@koningshofholland.nl; www.koningshofholland.nl**

🚶€3.25 👪(htd) ⬜ ♨☀⌂♿⚟/☂ ▼ ▼ ▼ ⑨
▯🎿⛰♿🏊(covrd, htd) 🛶⏟sand 5km

Fr A44 (Den Haag/Wassenaar-Amsterdam) exit junc 7 (Rijnsburg-Oegstgeest). In Rijnsburg cont twd Noordwijk. Foll blue & white sps thro Rijnsburg, across a bdge & then R twd Voorhout. Site in 2km. 4*, Lge, hdstg, mkd, hdg, pt shd, EHU (16A) inc; gas; bbq; red long stay; TV (pitch); 35% statics; phone; Eng spkn; adv bkg acc; games rm; bike hire; fishing; tennis; CKE. *"Vg, well-run, busy, friendly site; o'fits over 8m by request; gd for families; excel rest; Holland Tulip Parcs site; excel facs & pool; recep 0900-1230 & 1330-2000 high ssn; sep car park for some pitches; useful tour base for bulb fields; mkt Tues; well maintained; close to beaches and town; rec cash as few cards acc."* **€35.00, 17 Apr-3 Nov, H03.**   **2019**

KORTGENE *A3* (0.5km S Rural) *51.55446, 3.80483*
Camping Villa Park de Pardakreek, Havenweg 1, NL 4484, N Beevland **0113-302051; paardekreek@ardoer.com; www.ardoer.com/nl/camping/paardekreek**

🚶👪⬜ ♨☀⌂⚟/ ▼ ▼ ⑨▯🎿⛰♿🏊

Take the N256 to Zierikzee, exit Kortgene foll sps to camp. Med, hdg, mkd, pt shd, EHU (16A); bbq; 40% statics; bus 0.5km; Eng spkn; sauna; games rm; CKE. *"Excel site; boat slipway & storage; adj Lake Veerse Meer; lake adj; water playgrnd; many places to visit."* **€43.00, 27 Mar-1 Nov.**   **2015**

KOUDUM *C2* (2km S Rural) *52.90290, 5.46625* **Kawan Village De Kuilart,** De Kuilart 1, 8723 CG Koudum **(0514) 522221; info@kuilart.nl; www.kuilart.nl**

12 🚶€3.35 👪(htd) ♨☀⌂♿⚟/☂ ⑨
⑨▯🎿⛰♿🏊(covrd, htd)

Fr A50 exit sp Lemmer/Balk. Foll N359 over Galamadammen bdge, site sp. 5*, Lge, mkd, pt shd, serviced pitches; EHU (6-16A) €1.50-3.60; gas; TV; 50% statics; phone; Eng spkn; adv bkg acc; sailing; watersports; sauna; games area; sep car park; waterslide; CKE. *"Holland Tulip Parcs site; dogs by prior agreement only; private bthrms some pitches; marina."* **€26.00**   **2016**

NETHERLANDS

LAUWERSOOG *D1* (0.5km SE Coastal) *53.40250,
6.21740* **Camping Beleef Lauwersoog,** Strandweg 5,
9976 VS Lauwersoog **(0519)** 349133; info@
lauwersoog.nl; www.lauwersoog.nl

[icons] €4.75 (htd)

Fr N355 Leeuwarden-Groningen rd, take N361
Dokkum exit. Foll rd to Lauwersoog, site sp.
4*, V lge, unshd, serviced pitches; EHU (10A) inc; gas;
TV; 50% statics; phone; Eng spkn; adv bkg acc; ccard
acc; bike hire; tennis; sep car park; CKE. *"Excel, well-
maintained site; Holland Tulip Parcs site; vg rest; gd
facs; next to historic boat harbour."* **€28.50**   **2017**

LEEK *D2* (1.6km N Rural) *53.171114, 6.382174*
Landgoedcamping Nienoord, Midwolderweg 19,
9351 PG Leek **(0159)** 4580898; info@camping
nienoord.nl; www.campingnienoord.nl

[icons] nr

A7 exit 34 Leek. Foll sp immed; Ent to site along
slip rd. Med, hdstg, mkd, pt shd, EHU (10A); Eng spkn;
ccard acc. *"Site on edge of Nienoord pk; gd fr cycling or
walks; vg."* **€22.00, 30 Mar-31 Oct.**   **2019**

LEIDEN *B3* (8km N Rural) *52.20984, 4.51370*
Camping De Wasbeek, Wasbeeklaan 5b, 2361 HG
Warmond **(071)** 3011380; dewasbeek@hetnet.nl

[icons] nr nr

Exit A44 junc 4 dir Warmond; in 200m turn L into
Wasbeeklaan, then R in 50m. Site sp. Sm, pt shd,
bbq; 40% statics; bus 500m; Eng spkn; adv bkg acc;
sep car park. *"Attractive, lawned site close to bulb
fields; m'vans by arrangement; friendly, helpful staff;
some aircraft noise; gd cycling (track to Leiden); dogs
free; fishing; boating; birdwatching; lovely sm tidy site;
nice area."* **€26.00, 1 Apr-1 Oct.**   **2019**

LISSE *B3* (6km S Rural) *52.22175, 4.55418* **Camping
De Hof van Eeden,** Hellegatspolder 2, 2160 AZ
Lisse **(0252)** 212573; info@dehofvaneeden.nl;
www.dehofvaneeden.nl

[icons]

Exit A44 junc 3 & turn N onto N208 dir Lisse. Turn R
at rest on R bef 1st set traff lts into narr rd, foll rd
to end (under A44) to site. 3*, Sm, unshd, EHU (16A)
inc; 90% statics; Eng spkn. *"Gd CL-type site, space for
10 tourers (sep area) - rec phone or email bef arr;
interesting location by waterway & lifting rlwy bdge;
conv Keukenhof; helpful owners; cycling ctr among
bulb fields & around lake; excel site; lots of room for
MH."* **€17.50, 15 Apr-15 Oct.**   **2018**

MAASTRICHT *C4* (10km E Rural) *50.84468, 5.77994*
Boerderijcamping Gasthoes, Gasthuis 1, 6268 NN
Bemelen **(043)** 4071346 or **(06)** 54717951; info@
boerderijcamping-gasthoes.nl; www.boerderij
camping-gasthoes.nl

[icons]

Head for Bemelen, site is sp. Sm, pt shd, EHU (10A);
bbq; twin axles; bus; Eng spkn; adv bkg acc; CKE.
"Excel." **€18.00**   **2017**

MAURIK *C3* (2km NE Rural) *51.97605, 5.43020*
Recreatiepark Eiland van Maurik, Rijnbandijk 20,
4021 GH Maurik **(0344)** 691502; receptie@eiland
vanmaurik.nl; www.eilandvanmaurik.nl

[icons] €4 (htd)

Exit A15 junc 33 at Tiel onto B835 N & foll sp
to Maurik & site on rvside. Or exit A2 junc 13 at
Culembourg onto N320 to Maurik. 4*, Lge, pt shd,
EHU (10A) inc; gas; TV; 50% statics; Eng spkn; adv
bkg acc; tennis; fishing; horseriding; games area;
watersports. *"Covrd play area; Holland Tulip Parcs
site."* **€42.00, 29 Mar-1 Nov.**   **2019**

MEERSSEN *C4* (1.6km ESE Rural) *50.87851, 5.77112*
Camping Meerssen, Houthemerweg 95, 6231 KT
Meerssen **(0433)** 654743 or **(0651)** 970389; info@
campingmeerssen.nl; www.campingmeerssen.nl

[icons] nr nr nr

Fr Eindhoven A2, take exit 51, foll Valkenburg sp.
Take A79 to Hellen exit 2 Meerssen. L at junc after
400m, site on R. Sm, mkd, pt shd, EHU (6A); gas; bbq;
twin axles; 2% statics; Eng spkn. *"Nice, peaceful &
relaxing site; v popular with Dutch people; cent for
touring the area; excel site."*
€35.00, 1 Apr-30 Sep.   **2019**

"I need an on-site restaurant"

We do our best to make sure site information
is correct, but it is always best to check any
must-have facilities are still available or will
be open during your visit.

MEPPEL *C2* (15km W Rural) *52.72164, 6.07484*
Passantenhaven Zuiderkluft, Jonenweg, 8355 LG
Giethoorn **(0521)** 362312

[icons]

Turn off N334 sp Dwarsgracht, over lifting bdge, 1st
L over bdge, 1st L again, site on R. Sm, unshd, EHU
(10A) metered; Eng spkn. *"M'vans only; site run by
VVV (tourist board) for m'vans only; ltd EHU; walking
dist fr delightful vill on water; all svrs accessed by
smartcard purchased from machine on site; CC only."*
€11.00, 1 Apr-1 Nov.   **2018**

MIDDELBURG *A4* (8km N Rural) *51.55005, 3.64022*
Mini Camping Hoekvliet, Meiwerfweg 3, 4352 SC
Gapinge **(0118)** 501615 or **(0621)** 957185;
copgapinge@zeelandnet.nl; www.hoekvliet.nl

[icons] €1 nr nr sand 5km

Fr Middleburg turn R off N57 at traff lts sp Veere &
Gapinge, site sp after Gapinge vill. Sm, mkd, hdstg,
pt shd, EHU (10A) inc; bbq; TV (pitch); 20% statics;
Eng spkn; bike hire; CKE. *"Superb little (25 o'fits) farm
site; excel, modern san facs; sep car park; helpful
owner; immac san facs; fully serviced pitches; great
value."* **€23.00, 1 Apr-31 Oct.**   **2017**

NETHERLANDS

MIDDELBURG *A4* (7km NE Rural) *51.53863, 3.65394*
Minicamping Trouw Vóór Goud, Veerseweg 66,
4351 SJ Veere **(0118) 501373; info@trouwvoor
goud.nl; www.trouwvoorgoud.nl**

🐕 €0.80 ♦♦ wo ♨ ⬛ 🗑 /🏠

Take Veere rd N out of Middleburg. Site on L in 4km,
bef lge g'ge, sp 'Minicamping'. 1.5km SW of Veere.
Sm, pt shd, EHU (6A) €4.95; 10% statics; Eng spkn.
*"Excel facs; friendly, tidy, spacious, CL-type site;
walking dist Veere; no wifi."*
€16.00, 15 Mar-31 Oct. **2018**

MIDWOLDA *D2* (2km W Urban) *53.18900, 6.99053*
Camping de Bouwte, Hoofdweg 20A, 9681 AH
Midwolda 05 97 59 17 06; info@campingdebouwte.nl;
www.campingdebouwte.nl

🐕 €1.75 ♦♦ wo ♨ ♁ ♂ 🗑 /🏠 ! 🛒 Y ⓘ 🛒 /🏠 🖊

Via A7 dir Groningen-Winschoten or via N33 Assen-
Delfzil, then onto A7. Exit 45 Scheemda-Midwolda.
Foll camping signs. Turn R at traff lts, site on R in
500m. Med, pt shd, EHU (10A); bbq; sw; twin axles;
TV; 50% statics; phone; bus adj; Eng spkn; adv bkg acc;
bike hire; games area; games rm; CCI. *"Vg walking/
cycling area with mkd rtes; horseriding 1km; WWll
Museum in vill; watersports on Oldambtmeer 2km; vg
site."* **€25.00, 29 Mar-21 Oct.** **2019**

MIERLO *C4* (1.5km S Rural) *51.43250, 5.61694*
Camping De Sprink, Kasteelweg 21, 5731 PK Mierlo
**(0492) 661503; info@campingdesprink.nl;
www.campingdesprink.nl**

🐕 €0.75 ♦♦ wo ♨ ♁ ♂ 🗑 /🏠 ! 🛒 Y ⓘ 🛒 🛒nr /🏠

Take A67 and exit at Geldrop/Mierlo. Foll sp for
Mierlo. Turn R at rndabt onto Santheuvel West
fr Geldropseweg. R onto Heer de Heuschweg,
R onto Kasteelweg. Site on the L. Med, mkd,
hdstg, unshd, EHU (6A); bbq; Eng spkn; adv bkg
acc. *"Friendly, helpful staff; all facs immac; excel."*
€20.00, 31 Mar-30 Oct. **2017**

NOORDWIJK AAN ZEE *B3* (5km NE Urban) *52.26580,
4.47376* **De Wijde Blick,** Schulpweg 60, 2211 XM
Noordwijkerhout **(0252) 372246; info@bungalowpark
dewijdeblick.nl; www.bungalowparkdewijdeblick.nl**

12 ♦♦ wo ♨ ⬛ 🗑 / MSP 🛒 /🏠 🏕2km

Fr Hague exit L fr N206 at Noordwijkerhout Zuid.
Shortly turn R at rndabt 1.3km, turn L at rndabt.
Site on Rin 1km (1st bldg after felds).
Med, mkd, unshd, EHU; 90% statics; train 10km; Eng
spkn; CKE. *"Site with bungalows + statics; very clean
facs; friendly, helpful staff; excel wifi; conv for
Keukenhof; Flora Holland at Aalsmeer nrby; train to
Amsterdam; excel."* **€25.00** **2017**

OIRSCHOT *C3* (1km N Rural) *51.51684, 5.30854*
Camping De Bocht, Oude Grintweg 69, 5688 MB
Oirschot **(0499) 550855; info@campingdebocht.nl;
www.campingdebocht.nl**

12 🐕 €2.50 ♦♦(htd) wo ♨ ♁ ♂ 🗑 /🏠 ! 🛒 Y ⓘ 🛒 🛒 /🏠 🖊 🛶 🛒

Fr A58/E312 take exit 8 to Oirschot. Site in 4km on
Boxtel rd. Site sp. 3*, Med, hdg, shd, EHU (10A) €3;
gas; TV; 60% statics; phone; Eng spkn; adv bkg acc;
bike hire. *"Gd touring base; gd for families; pleasant
town; helpful family run site."* **€30.50** **2019**

OMMEN *D2* (6km W Rural) *52.51911, 6.36461*
Resort de Arendshorst, Arendshorsterweg 3A,
7731 RC Ommen **(0529) 453248; info@resort-de-
arendshorst.nl; www.resort-de-arendshorst.nl**

12 🐕 €4 ♦♦(htd) wo ♨ ♁ ♂ 🗑 /🏠 ! 🛒 Y ⓘ 🛒 🛒 /🏠 🖊

W fr Ommen on N34/N340 turn L at site sp, then
500m along lane past farm, site on rvside.
5*, Lge, mkd, pt shd, serviced pitches; EHU (10A)
inc; gas; sw; red long stay; TV; 50% statics; phone;
Eng spkn; adv bkg req; bike hire; games area; CKE.
*"Beautiful area; bkg fee; many cycle rtes; pool 3km; gd
children's facs."* **€39.00, H02.** **2017**

OMMEN *D2* (4km WNW Rural) *52.532519, 6.385082*
Boerderijcamping Het Varsenerveld, Emslandweg 14,
7731 RP Ommen **(0529) 453300; boerderijcamping@
varsenerveld.nl; www.varsenerveld.nl**

12 🐕 ♦♦(htd) wo ♨ 🗑 / MSP 🛒 🛒 /🏠

W fr Ommen on N340 turn R after 2km at 1st minor
x-rds. Take 2nd L and site on L at flagpole.
Sm, pt shd, EHU (10A); bbq (charcoal, gas); twin axles;
bus 2km; Eng spkn; adv bkg acc; ccard acc. *"Wkg fm;
goats and chickens contained within child petting area;
excel."* **€21.00** **2019**

OOSTERHOUT *B3* (6km W Rural) *51.64658, 4.80818*
Koeckers Camping 't Kopske, Ruiterspoor 75, 4911
BA Den Hout **(0613) 142151; info@camping
tkopske.nl; www.campingtkopske.nl**

♦♦ wo ♨ 🛒 Y ⓘ

Leave A59 at junc 32 to Oosterhout W. At rndabt
take R for Den Hout. In Den Hout R opp Church.
1st site on L after 1km. Sm, mkd, unshd, Eng
spkn. *"Gd cycling area; activity ctr; rest nr; gd."*
€19.00, 26 Mar-2 Oct. **2016**

OOTMARSUM *D3* (2.5km S Rural) *52.38959, 6.90016*
Camping De Haer, Rossummerstraat 22, 7636 PL
Agelo 0541 291847; info@dehaer.nl; www.dehaer.nl

🐕 €1.50 ♦♦ wo ♨ ♁ ♂ 🗑 /🏠 ! Y ⓘ 🛒 /🏠 🖊 🛶

Site sp 3km S of Ootmarsum. Lge, hdg, mkd, pt shd,
EHU (6-10A); bbq; twin axles; TV; 30% statics; bus adj;
Eng spkn; adv bkg acc; games rm; bike hire; games
area; CKE. *"Many cycle paths fr site; vg."*
€21.00, 1 Apr-1 Nov. **2016**

OPENDE *D2* (3km SE Rural) *53.16465, 6.22275*
NCC Camping de Watermolen, Openderweg 26,
9865 XE Opende **(0594) 659144; info@camping
dewatermolen.nl; www.campingdewatermolen.nl**

🐕€2.50 ♂♀(htd) 🅆🄳 ⚐ ♨ 🖀 ☏ ∥ 🅼🅿 📶 ⍾ ￦ Ⓗⓓ⚡nr ⛽ ⍾

**Exit A7 junc 32 dir Kornhorn. In Noordwijk turn L at
church & in 2 km turn R into Openderweg. Site in
700m on L.** Med, hdstg, mkd, pt shd, EHU (16A); bbq;
sw; twin axles; TV; 10% statics; phone; Eng spkn; adv
bkg acc; ccard acc; CKE. *"Friendly owners; pt of site
for NCC members - CMC members welcome but must
book ahead; brilliant site with lakes to walk around &
woods; hide for bird watching; dogs not acc high ssn;
excel; fishing on site; bike hire; €10 dep for key; car free
pitches."* **€25.30, 1 Apr-1 Oct.** **2017**

OTTERLO *C3* (2km S Rural) *52.08657, 5.76934*
Europarcs Resort De Wije Werelt, Arnhemseweg
100-102, 6731 BV Otterlo **(0880) 708090; kcc@euro
parcs.nl; www.europarcs.nl/vakantiepark/resort-de-
wije-werelt**

🗓12 🐕€4 ♂♀(htd) 🅆🄳 ⚐ ♨ 🖀 ∥ 🅼🅿 ￦ ☏ Ⓗⓓ⚡ 📶 ⛄ ⍾

**Exit A50 junc 22 dir Hoenderlo & N304 to Otterlo.
Site on R after Camping de Zanding.** 4*, Lge, mkd,
unshd, EHU (6-10A) inc; 40% statics; phone; Eng spkn;
adv bkg acc; ccard acc; games area. *"Excel, well-run
site; immac; gd san facs; vg for families; conv Arnhem;
gd access to Kroller-Muller Museum; helpful staff."*
€35.00 **2019**

OTTERLO *C3* (2km NW Rural) *52.10878, 5.76040*
Camping 't Kikkergat, Lange Heideweg 7, 6731 EG
Otterlo **(0318) 591794; contact@kikkergat.nl;
www.kikkergat.nl**

🗓12 🐕 ♂♀⛑ ⚐ ♨ ♿ ∥ 🅼🅿 📶 ⍾

**Exit A1/E30 at J17 dir Harskamp. Site on R in 12km,
unmade rd.** Sm, pt shd, EHU (10A); twin axles; Eng
spkn; adv bkg acc; CKE. *"Excel site."* **€18.00** **2017**

PANNINGEN *C4* (4km NW Rural) *51.34894, 5.96111*
Beringerzand Camping, Heide 5, 5981 NX Panningen
**07 73 07 20 95; info@beringerzand.nl;
www.beringerzand.nl**

🗓12 🐕€4.85 ♂♀⛑ 🅆🄳 ⚐ ♿ 🖀 ∥ 🅼🅿 📶 ☏
⍾ ⛽ 🅰 ⛄(covrd, htd) 📶

**Fr A67 exit at junc 38 twd S, dir Koningslust/
Panningen. Site is 3km NW Panningen, down narr
lane thro asparagus fields.** Med, mkd, pt shd, EHU
(10A); bbq; twin axles; Eng spkn; adv bkg rec; games
rm; games area; bike hire; waterslide. *"Max 2 dogs per
pitch."* **€36.80** **2019**

RENSWOUDE *C3* (2km NE Rural) *52.08435, 5.55069*
Camping de Grebbelinie, Ubbeschoterweg 12, 3927
CJ Renswoude **(0318) 591073; info@campingde
grebbelinie.nl; www.campingdegrebbelinie.nl**

🐕€1.75 ♂♀⛑ 🅆🄳 ⚐ ♨ 🖀 ∥ ￦ ☏ 📶 nr Ⓗⓓnr ⛽nr 🅰

**Head NW on Dorpsstraat/N224, at rndabt take 1st
exit onto Barneveldsestraat, turn R onto Bekerweg,
R onto Ubbeschoterweg then turn L. Site on the R.**
Med, unshd, EHU; Eng spkn; adv bkg acc; games area;
CKE. *"Friendly owners; excel cycling with cycle rte adj;
conv for Arnhem & Utrecht; peaceful site on former
farm; in open countryside; excel value for money."*
€22.60, 19 Mar-15 Oct. **2016**

RIJSSEN *D3* (7km S Rural) *52.265473, 6.520075*
Camping De Bovenberg, Bovenbergweg 14, 7475
ST/Markelo **(0547) 361781; info@debovenberg.nl;
www.debovenberg.nl**

♂♀⛑(htd) 🅆🄳 ⚐ ♨ ∥ 🖀 ￦ ☏ 🅰 ⍾ ⛄ sand; adj

**Fr A1 J26, foll sp for Markelo. Site name on brown
sp.** Med, hdstg, mkd, hdg, pt shd, EHU (10A) inc;
5% statics; Eng spkn; CKE. *"Vg; ideal for restful stay;
gd NH; away fr rd noise; ideal cycling area; Markelo
nrby."* **NP 24.4, 30 Mar-16 Oct.** **2018**

> ## "Satellite navigation makes touring much easier"
>
> Remember most sat navs don't know if you're
> towing or in a larger vehicle – always use yours
> alongside maps and site directions.

ROCKANJE *A3* (2km NW Coastal) *51.88000, 4.05422*
Molecaten Park Waterbos, Duinrand 11, 3235 CC
Rockanje **(0181) 401900; info@waterboscamping.nl;
www.waterboscamping.nl**

♂♀⛑(htd) 🅆🄳 ⚐ ♨ ♿ 🖀 ∥ 🅼🅿 ￦ ☏ Ⓗⓓ⚡ 🅰 ⍾
⛄ sand 1km

Site clearly sp fr Rockanje vill. 4*, Lge, hdg, pt shd,
EHU (6A) inc; TV (pitch); 80% statics; phone; adv bkg
acc; CKE. *"Lovely base for Voorne area; private san facs
avail."* **€33.00, 25 Mar-31 Oct.** **2016**

ROERMOND *C4* (15km W Rural) *51.20947, 5.83008*
Camping Geelenhoof, Grathemerweg 16, 6037 NR
Kelpen-Oler (Limburg) **(0495) 651858; info@
geelenhoof.nl; www.geelenhoof.nl**

🐕€2.50 ♂♀⛑(htd) 🅆🄳 ⚐ ∥ 🖀 🅼🅿 ￦ ☏ Ⓗⓓ⚡ 🅰

**1km S of Kelpen-Oler; bet Roermond & Weert; exit
N280 foll sp; well mkd.** Med, mkd, hdg, pt shd, EHU
(6A) inc; Eng spkn; adv bkg acc; games area; games rm;
CKE. *"Cars not to be parked with c'van; dogs on req;
vg site; semi serviced pitches; sep NH; keycard barrier;
no twin axles; lake fishing; warm welcome; excel site."*
€25.00, 1 Mar-31 Oct. **2017**

ROTTERDAM *B3* (17km SE Rural) 51.83454, 4.54673
Camping De Oude Maas, Achterzeedijk 1A, 2991 SB Barendrecht **(078) 6772445; www.campingdeoude maas.nl**

Leave A29 (Rotterdam-Bergen op Zoom) junc 20 Barendrecht, foll sp for Heerjansdam, site sp. Fr A16 (Breda-Dordrecht) foll Europort sp, then Zierikzee, Barendrecht, site sp. 3*, Lge, pt shd, EHU (10A) inc; TV; 80% statics; phone; ccard acc. *"Excel site on Rv Maas inc sm marina & joins rec park; excel facs; some pitches rough & long way fr facs; ferry fr site in ssn; check recep opening time if planning dep bef midday (espec Sun) for return of deposit & barrier key (€35); entry via new ent past old."* **€22.00**　2016

ROTTERDAM *B3* (3km W Urban) 51.93100, 4.44200
Stadscamping Rotterdam, Kanaalweg 84, 3041 JE Rotterdam **(010) 4153440; info@stadscamping-rotterdam.nl; www.stadscamping-rotterdam.nl**

Adj to junc of A13 & A20, take slip rd sp Rotterdam Centrum & Camping Kanaalweg sp to site. Dist fr m'way 2.5km with 3 L turns. 2*, Lge, pt shd, EHU (6A) €3.75; gas; bus; adv bkg acc; ccard acc. *"Gd bus service to city cent; few water taps; pool 500m; friendly staff."* **€25.00**　2016

SCHIMMERT *C4* (0.6km E Rural) 50.90746, 5.83122
Camping Mareveld, Mareweg 23, 6333 BR Schimmert South Limburg **(045) 4041269; info@mareveld.nl; www.campingmareveld.nl**

A76 exit Spaubeek, turn R twd Schimmert. 2nd on the L in Schimmert. Campsite sp. Sm, pt shd, EHU (6A) €2.10; TV; 80% statics; Eng spkn; adv bkg acc; games area. *"Gd cycling/walking fr site; gd site; popular with families; open plan, grassy site."* **€24.00**　2019

SEVENUM *C4* (5km SW Rural) 51.38310, 5.97590
Camping De Schatberg, Midden Peelweg 1, 5975 MZ Sevenum **(077) 4677777; receptie@schatberg.nl; www.schatberg.nl**

Fr A2/A67 exit junc 38 for Helden; foll sp Sevenum & site by sm lake. 5*, V lge, shd, EHU (6-10A) inc; gas; sw; TV; 60% statics; phone; Eng spkn; adv bkg acc; fishing; bike hire; waterslide; games area; tennis; jacuzzi; sauna; watersports; CKE. *"Excel leisure facs, espec for children; sep pitches for dogs; private san facs some pitches; vg site but impersonal; Holland Tulip Parcs site; tourers pitched amongst statics; Venlo Sat mkt worth visit."* **€41.00**　2019

See advertisement

'S-HERTOGENBOSCH *C3* (10km E Rural) 51.6938, 5.4148 **Camping de Hooghe Heide,** Werstkant 17, 5258 TC Berlicum **(073) 5031522; info@hooghe heide.nl; www.hoogheheide.nl**

Fr A59/A2 circular rd around 's-Hertogenbosch exit junc 21 dir Berlicum. Foll sp Berlicum & site. Site is NE of Berlicum. 4*, Med, mkd, pt shd, EHU (10A) €3; TV; 70% statics; phone; Eng spkn; adv bkg req; games area; CKE. *"Nice, peaceful wooded site; narr site rds for lge o'fits; tourers on open field; excel."* **€32.40, 26 Mar-1 Nov.**　2016

'S-HERTOGENBOSCH *C3* (10km SW Rural) 51.65507, 5.23520 **Topparken Résidence de Leuvert,** Loverensestraat 11, 5266 Cromvoirt **088 5002473; info@deleuvert.nl; www.deleuvert.nl**

Exit for Cromvoirt fr A59 or A65. Med, mkd, pt shd, EHU (10A) inc; bbq; twin axles; TV; 75% statics; bus 0.5km; Eng spkn; adv bkg acc; games area; games rm; CKE. *"Gd bus access to 's-Hertogenbosch; vg site."* **€28.40, 1 Jan-31 Oct.**　2016

SINT OEDENRODE *C3* (3km N Rural) *51.57800, 5.4400* **NCC Camping 't Roois Klumpke,** Vliegden 1, 5491 VS Sint Oedenrode **(0413) 474702; www.ncc.nl**

12 ♦♦♦(htd) WD ♨ ⚲ & ▭ ∥ ❦

Exit A2 junc 26 to Sint Oedenrode; site sp on Schijndel rd - 100m bef Camping Kienehoef turn R onto Vliegden, site 400m on L. Med, mkd, pt shd, EHU (10A); bbq; Eng spkn; adv bkg acc; CKE. *"Members only - CC members welcome but must pre-book; shop, rest, snacks avail at Camping de Kienehoef; run by volunteers; spacious; woodland."* **€11.00 2017**

SINT OEDENRODE *C3* (3.7km SE Urban) *51.54780, 5.48703* **Camping De Graspol,** Bakkerpad 17, 5492 TL Sint Oedenrode **(0413) 474133 or (0653) 224220; info@campingdegraspol.nl; www.campingde graspol.nl**

♈ ♦♦♦(htd) WD ♨ ⚲ ▭ ∥ MSP ❦ ♔

Fr A50 take exit St Oedenrode, dir Nijnsel. Foll sp to site. Med, mkd, pt shd, EHU (16A); gas; bbq; red long stay; TV; Eng spkn; adv bkg rec; bike hire; fishing; games rm. *"Well kept; gd for NH or longer; ACSI; warm welcome; wild flower nature walk."* **€35.50, 1 Mar-1 Oct.**   **2019**

"There aren't many sites open at this time of year"

If you're travelling outside peak season remember to call ahead to check site opening dates – even if the entry says 'open all year'.

SNEEK *C2* (2km E Urban) *53.03557, 5.67630* **Jachthaven Camping De Domp,** De Domp 4, 8605 CP Sneek **(0515) 412559; www.dedomp.nl**

♈ ♦♦♦(htd) WD ♨ ⚲ & ▭ ∥ MSP ♔ ♀ ⊕ ⛴ ▤nr ⚴

Fr cent of Sneek on Leeuwarden rd, turn R sp De Domp. 3*, Med, pt shd, serviced pitches; EHU (16A) inc; gas; Eng spkn; adv bkg acc; boating; sep car park. *"Many canals in Sneek; marina on site; easy walk to pleasant town; gd cycling cent; v helpful staff."* **€24.50, 25 Mar-1 Nov.**   **2018**

STEENBERGEN *B3* (5km NW Rural) *51.60887, 4.27303* **Camping De Uitwijk,** Dorpsweg 136, 4655 AH De Heen **(0167) 560000; info@de-uitwijk.nl; www.camping deuitwijk.nl**

♈ €3.20 ♦♦♦(htd) WD ♨ ⚲ ▭ ∥ MSP ♀ ♔ ♀ ⊕ ⛴ ▤nr ⚴ ✎

Fr N259 at Steenbergen turn W onto N257 dir Zierikzee. In 2km turn N thro De Heen & turn R at T-junc. Site recep on R, site on L. Do not take c'van to recep, but ent site, park on R & walk back. Med, mkd, pt shd, EHU (4-10A) inc; TV (pitch); 60% statics; bus 750m; Eng spkn; adv bkg acc; games rm; CKE. *"Pleasant, well run, quiet site adj marina; friendly staff; excel; excel cycle rtes; conv for ferry."* **€24.00, 23 Mar-29 Sep.**   **2019**

TUITJENHORN *B2* (4km SE Rural) *52.73495, 4.77612* **Campingpark de Bongerd,** Bongerdlaan 3, 1747 CA Tuitjenhorn **(0226) 391481; info@bongerd.nl; www.bongerd.nl**

♈ €1.90 ♦♦♦(htd) WD ♨ ⚲ & ▭ ∥ ❦ ♔ ♀ ⊕ ⛴ ▤ ⚴ ✎ ⚲ (covrd, htd) ⛵

N fr Alkmaar on N245, exit at Dirkshorn & foll sp to site. 5*, V lge, mkd, pt shd, EHU (10A) inc; gas; bbq; 60% statics; Eng spkn; adv bkg acc; ccard acc; games area; lake fishing; bike hire; waterslide; tennis. *"Excel, attractive family site; vg facs."* **€56.50, 5 Apr-1 Oct.**   **2019**

UDEN *C3* (14km E Rural) *51.66309, 5.77641* **Mini Camping Boszicht,** Tipweg 10, 5455 RC Wilbertoord **(0485) 451565 or (06) 12957217; boszicht-wilbertoord@planet.nl; www.boszichtcamping.nl**

♈ €2 ♦♦♦ ♨ ▭ ∥ ❦ ♔ ⊕nr ⚴ ⚴

Fr 's-Hertogenbosch on N279 dir Helmond. At Veghel turn L onto N265. Bef Uden turn R onto N264 to Wilbertoord in 11km. Sm, hdg, mkd, unshd, EHU (6A) metered; Eng spkn; games area. *"Family-run farm site in woodland; conv Arnhem, Nijmegen; delightful site."* **€17.00, 20 Mar-19 Oct.**   **2016**

UTRECHT *B3* (10km NE Rural) *52.13123, 5.22024* **Camping Bospark Bilthoven,** Burg van der Borchlaan 7, 3722 GZ Bilthoven **(030) 2286777; info@bosparkbilthoven.nl; www.bosparkbilthoven.nl**

♈ €3.50 ♦♦♦(htd) WD ♨ ⚲ & ▭ ∥ MSP ♀ ▤ ⊕nr ⚴ ⛵(htd)

Exit A28/E30 Utrecht-Amersfoort at exit sp De Bilt & strt to Bilthoven. Approx 3km after leaving m'way (400m S of level x-ing) turn R sp De Bospark Bilthoven. At edge of town foll sps twd lge brown tower & golf course. Site on L. 2*, V lge, pt shd, serviced pitches; EHU (4-6A) inc (poss rev pol); gas; TV; 60% statics; phone; Eng spkn; adv bkg acc. *"Helpful management; quiet but some noise fr air base; 20 mins walk to stn for trains to Utrecht cent; few facs for size of site."* **€29.40, 29 Mar-20 Oct.**   **2018**

VAALS *C4* (1.5km N Rural) *50.78159, 6.00694* **Camping Hoeve de Gastmolen,** Lemierserberg 23, 6291 NM Vaals **(043) 3065755; info@gastmolen.nl; www.gastmolen.nl**

♈ €2.70 ♦♦♦ WD ♨ ▭ ∥ ❦ ⊕nr ⚴ ▤nr ⚴

Fr A76 exit at Knooppunt Bocholtz onto N281 SW to join N278, turn L twd Aachen. Site on L just bef 1st rndabt as ent Vaals. 2*, Med, mkd, hdg, pt shd, pt sl, EHU (6A) €2.70; 10% statics; bus 500m; Eng spkn; adv bkg rec; sep car park; CKE. *"Sm rural site; conv Aachen; vg san facs; diff in wet - tractor avail; mosquitoes; Drielandenpunt 4km, in walking dist (where Netherlands, Germany & Belgium meet); excel."* **€20.50, 25 Mar-31 Oct.**   **2016**

VALKENBURG AAN DE GEUL *C4* (13km N Rural)
50.94973, 5.87883 **De Botkoel,** Kerkpad 2, 6155 KJ
Puth **(0464)** 432374; camping@botkoel.nl;
www.botkoel.nl

🐕 ⛺(htd) ⓌⒹ 🏕 ⚖ 🛁 🍽 ⁄ ⒨ 🍴 🛒 nr ⑪ nr 🛒 nr ⛰ 🏊

Fr W on A2 exit at J4 sp Schinnen. At end of rd turn
L, cross x-rds and turn R again on the R until you
cross rlwy x-ing, then R on the R. Cont on Stn Street
until T-junc, turn L twrds Puth. Uphill to Puth then
turn R. At S-turn, turn R into narr rd. Site 200m on L.
Sm, unshd, pt sl, terr, EHU; bbq; twin axles; train
1km; Eng spkn; adv bkg acc; games area; CKE. *"Site
on fruit fm; views; bike hire; clean facs, rebuilt 2017;
excel; conv for Sittard, Maastricht & Aachen; vg; Zoover
award site."* **€22.50, 15 Mar-31 Oct.** **2018**

"That's changed – Should I let the Club know?"

If you find something on site that's different
from the site entry, fill in a report and let us
know. See camc.com/europereport.

VALKENBURG AAN DE GEUL *C4* (2km N Rural)
50.88013, 5.83466 **Familie Camping De Bron,**
Stoepertweg 5, 6301 WP Valkenburg **(045)** 4059292;
info@camping-debron.nl; www.camping-debron.nl

🐕 €3.50 ⛺(htd) ⓌⒹ 🏕 ⚖ 🛁 🍽 ⁄ ⒨ 🍴 ⑪ 🛒 🛒 ⛰ 🎣 🏊

Fr A79 exit junc 4 dir Hulsberg. Take 3rd exit
fr rndabt onto N298, across next rndabt, then L
onto N584, site sp. Fr A76 exit junc 3 dir Schimmert,
foll sp Valkenburg & site. 4*, Lge, mkd, pt shd, EHU
(4-6A) €3-4.50; TV; 30% statics; phone; adv bkg acc;
bike hire; games area; CKE. *"Vg, well laid-out site;
gd facs; muddy in wet weather; 2 pools with lots of
equipment for kids; statics hidden away in the greenery;
helpful staff."* **€30.00, 1 Apr-20 Dec.** **2019**

VALKENBURG AAN DE GEUL *C4* (3km S Urban)
50.85972, 5.83138 **Stadscamping Den Driesch,**
Heunsbergerweg 1, 6301 BN Valkenburg **(043)**
6012025; info@campingdendriesch.nl;
www.campingdendriesch.nl

🐕 €3 ⛺(htd) ⓌⒹ 🏕 🍽 ⁄ ⒨ 🦋 ⑪ nr 🛒

Fr A2 dir Maastricht exit sp Valkenburg-Cauberg.
Foll sp Valkenburg N590 & take turning sp Sibbe-
Margraten. At rndabt foll sp Valkenburg, pass coal
mine & turn R in 250m into sm, sl, unmkd ent. Steep
turn off main rd into ent. NB L turn into site diff -
proceed to rndabt at top of hill & return downhill
to site. 2*, Med, hdstg, mkd, pt shd, pt sl, terr, EHU
(10A) inc; 10% statics; phone; Eng spkn; adv bkg acc;
ccard acc; bike hire; CKE. *"Castle & caves adj; other
attractions nr; gd Xmas mkts in caves; easy access
Maastricht by bus/train; vg."* **€42.00, 23 Mar-31 Dec,
H10.** **2017**

VALKENBURG AAN DE GEUL *C4* (1km SW Rural)
50.85672, 5.81891 **Camping De Cauberg,** Rijksweg
171, 6325 AD Valkenburg **(043)** 6012344; info@
campingdecauberg.nl; www.campingdecauberg.nl

🐕 €3.10 ⛺(htd) ⓌⒹ 🏕 ⚖ 🛁 🍽 ⁄ 🦋 ⑪ 🛒 🛒 ⛰

Exit A79 sp Valkenburg, foll Sibbe & Margraten sp
to town cent. Take R fork in town sp De Cauberg,
site on R at top of hill just past end Valkenburg sp.
Med, mkd, shd, pt sl, EHU (10A) inc; red long stay;
10% statics; phone; bus; Eng spkn; adv bkg acc; site
clsd 1-15 Nov; CKE. *"Excel pool 1km; excel, modern,
clean san facs; htd pool 1km; friendly, helpful owner;
conv Maastricht; many rests, cafes in Valkenburg."*
€33.00, 22 Mar-27 Oct & 16 Nov-23 Dec. **2019**

VENLO *D4* (10km NW Rural) *51.42029, 6.10675*
Camping Californië, Horsterweg 23, 5971 ND
Grubbenvorst **(077)** 3662049; info@limburgse
camping.nl; www.limburgsecamping.nl

⛺(htd) ⓌⒹ 🏕 🍽 ⁄ 🦋 ⛰

Exit A73 at Grubbenvorst junc 12 dir Sevenum, site
sp. Med, pt shd, EHU (4-10A); Eng spkn. *"Pleasant,
peaceful, warm welcome; unisex shwrs; CL style site
with grass cut reg."* **€18.00, 15 Mar-15 Oct.** **2019**

VIERHUIZEN *D1* (0.3km E Rural) *53.36011, 6.29505*
Camping Lauwerszee, Hoofdstraat 49, 9975 VR
Vierhuizen 05 95 40 16 57; info@camping-
lauwerszee.nl; www.camping-lauwerszee.nl

🐕 ⛺(htd) ⓌⒹ 🏕 ⚖ 🛁 🍽 ⁄ ⒨ 🦋 🍴 ⑪ ⛰

Fr A7/E22 Amsterdam-Groningen take exit 33
Oude Riet onto N388 Grijpskerk. Turn L on N355
then R onto N388. 2.5km after Zoutcamp turn L
to Vierhuizen. Site on R in 1km. Med, mkd, hdg, pt
shd, EHU (6A); bbq; twin axles; bus 0.5km; Eng spkn;
adv bkg acc; bike hire; CCI. *"Sep field with lge pitches
avail for CC memb at red price; helpful owner; vg."*
€21.00, 1 Apr-1 Nov. **2019**

"I like to fill in the reports as I travel from site to site"

You'll find report forms at the back of this
guide, or you can fill them in online at
camc.com/europereport.

VORDEN *D3* (5km SE Rural) *52.08379, 6.35510* **'t
Lebbink,** Lindense Enkweg 1, 7251 NH Vorden **(0575)**
556680; harmsen@tlebbink.nl; www.tlebbink.nl

🐕 ⛺(htd) ⓌⒹ 🏕 ⚖ 🛁 ⁄ 🦋 ⑪

Fr Vordon N316 S for 1.6km. L onto Lindeseweg
for 3km to Linde. L just bef windmill along access
rd to campsite on R. Med, hdg, mkd, pt shd, EHU
(6-16A); bbq; twin axles; adv bkg acc; bike hire;
CKE. *"On numbered cycle rte & walking rte; vg."*
€16.00, 15 Mar-1 Nov. **2015**

NETHERLANDS

WASSENAAR *B3* (1km NW Rural) *52.14638, 4.38750*
Camping Duinrell, Duinrell 1, 2242 JP Wassenaar
**(070) 5155147 or (070) 5155255; touroperator@
duinrell.nl; www.duinrell.nl**

12 🐕 €6 ♻️(htd) 🅆 ⛲ ♨ ♿ 🍳 ✉ 🅼 🦋 ⛲ 🍸 🕮 🍴 🧺 ⛏ 🖊
🏊(covrd) 🎣 🏖 sand 3km

Fr Rotterdam in dir Den Haag on A13/E19, then on
A4/E19 foll sp for Amsterdam. On A4 keep R onto
A12 in dir Voorburg/Den Haag. At end m'way turn
R onto N44 sp Wassenaar. In 8km turn L at traff
lts immed bef Mercedes g'ge, foll site sp. On arr at
site foll sp to campsite not coach park. Not rec to
arrive mid-afternoon/early evening due to heavy
traff leaving amusement park. 4*, V lge, mkd, hdg,
pt shd, serviced pitches; EHU (6A) inc; gas; bbq; TV;
30% statics; phone; Eng spkn; adv bkg acc; ccard acc;
waterslide; tennis; sauna; golf 1km; fishing nr; bike
hire; games rm; horseriding nr. *"Popular, busy site;
no o'fits over 7.75m high ssn; some pitches poss diff
access, check bef siting; superb, modern facs; tropical
indoor pool; free ent adj amusement park; private san
facs avail; sep car park for some pitches; vg security;
excel."* **€33.50, H13.** **2016**

**"We must tell the Club about
that great site we found"**

Get your site reports in by mid-August and we'll
do our best to get your updates into the next
edition.

WEZUPERBRUG *D2* (9km SW Rural) *52.77911,
6.68607* **Camping De Bronzen Emmer,** Mepperstraat
41, 7855 TA Meppen **(0591) 371543; info@de-
bronzen-emmer.nl; www.bronzenemmer.nl**

🐕 ♻️(htd) 🅆 ⛲ ♨ ♿ 🍳 ✉ 🦋 ⛲ 🍸 🕮 🍴 🧺 nr 🛝

🏊(covrd, htd)

Exit the A37 at Oosterhesselen (N854) twrds
Meppen. Foll sp to site. Lge, mkd, pt shd, EHU (10A)
€0.40/Kwh; gas; TV; 10% statics; Eng spkn; adv bkg
acc; tennis; games area; games rm. *"Cycling off-rd to
supmkt; friendly, family site; excel facs; sauna; excel."*
€34.00, 1 Apr-28 Oct. **2017**

WINTERSWIJK *D3* (5km N Rural) *52.00878, 6.73850*
Poelhuis Boerderijcamping, Poolserweg 3, 7104 DC
Winterswijk **(0543) 569246; info@poelhuis.nl;
www.poelhuis.nl**

♻️(htd) 🅆 ⛲ ♨ 🍳 ✉ 🦋 🍸

N on Meddosweg to Meddo, R on Wandersweg to
x-rds, Poolseweg, L and site on R in 500m. Sm, mkd,
hdstg, pt shd, EHU (6A); bbq; TV; Eng spkn; adv bkg
acc; bike hire; games rm; CKE. *"Numbered cycle rte;
close to German border; flamingo nature park with
walking rtes; vg."* **€18.00, 15 Mar-31 Oct.** **2015**

WOERDEN *B3* (4km NE Rural) *52.09280, 4.88530*
Camping Batenstein, Van Helvoortlaan 37, 3443 AP
Woerden **(0348) 421320; campingbatenstein@
planet.nl; www.camping-batenstein.nl**

🐕 €1.50 ♻️ 🅆 ⛲ ♨ 🍳 ✉ 🅼 🦋 ⛲ 🧺 nr 🛝 🏊(covrd, htd)
🎣

Fr A12 exit junc 14 sp Woerden. Twd cent of town,
L at rndabt, R at next rndabt, thro rlwy tunnel. L
at traff lts, L again at next traff lts, R at camping
sp. Ent narr & sm sp. 1*, Med, pt shd, EHU (6-10A)
inc; gas; red long stay; 75% statics; phone; bus
750m; Eng spkn; adv bkg acc; ccard acc; sep car park;
waterslide; sauna; games area; CKE. *"Gd touring
base; el conn by site staff only (locked boxes); san
facs cramped but gd quality & clean; conv for ferries."*
€20.80, 29 Mar-27 Oct. **2019**

AMELAND ISLAND

BUREN *C1* (1km N Coastal) *53.45355, 5.80460*
Camping Klein Vaarwater, Klein Vaarwaterweg
114, 9164 ME Buren **(0519) 542156; info@
kleinvaarwater.nl; www.kleinvaarwater.nl**

12 ♻️(htd) 🅆 ⛲ ♨ ♿ 🍳 ✉ 🅼 🍸 🕮 🍴 🧺 🛝 🖊
🏊(covrd, htd) 🎣 🏖 sand 800m

Take ferry fr Holwerd to Nes on Ameland Island.
Turn R at rndabt twd Buren & strt on to supmkt.
At 3-lane intersection turn L twd beach rd & site.
4*, Med, mkd, pt shd, EHU (16A); gas; bbq; TV;
75% statics; adv bkg acc; tennis; fitness rm; games
area; waterslide. *"Nature park adj; site in dunes &
forest; ATM; Holland Tulip Parcs site; 10-pin bowling."*
€20.00 **2016**

ZANDVOORT *B3* (5km N Coastal) *52.40415, 4.55180*
Kennemer Duincamping De Lakens, Zeeweg 60, 2051
EC Bloemendaal aan Zee **(023) 5411570; delakens@
kennemerduincampings.nl; www.kennemerduin
campings.nl**

♻️(htd) 🅆 ⛲ ♨ ♿ 🍳 ✉ 🅼 🦋 ⛲ 🕮 🍴 🧺 🛝 🏖 sand 200m

Site sp N of Zaandvoort on coast rd, site in sand
dunes. 4*, V lge, unshd, EHU (4-10A) inc; gas; TV;
50% statics; Eng spkn; adv bkg rec; ccard acc;
horseriding 300m; games area; windsurfing 2km. *"V
busy May/June public holidays; gd facs; excel walking,
cycling fr site; welcoming helpful staff; excel spar
shop; gd position in National Park; pool 4km; gd for
sightseeing in Amsterdam, Haarlem, Aalsmeer flower
mkt as well as outdoor pursuits."*
€54.00, 29 Mar-28 Oct. **2019**

ZEVENAAR C3 (8km S Rural) 51.89666, 6.07041
Camping De Rijnstrangen, Beuningsestraat 4, 6913
KH Aerdt **(0316) 371941 or (0612) 559464; info@
derijnstrangen.nl; www.derijnstrangen.nl**

🔢 �11(htd) ⭐ ♿ 🚿 ⛽ ✉ ☕ 🦋 ⛳ 🎣nr

Exit A12 junc 29 onto N 336 Elten & Lobith. At sp
Aerdt turn R onto dyke (narr) & cont approx 1.5km
to church. Turn L in 100m, site on R (500m W of
Aerdt). Sm, hdg, mkd, hdstg, pt shd, EHU (6A); bbq;
cooking facs; twin axles; Eng spkn; adv bkg acc; games
rm; bike hire; CKE. "Friendly, welcoming, helpful
owners; gd cycling area with numbered rte; excel htd
facs; excel; sep carpark." **€20.50** 2018

ZIERIKZEE A3 (5km N Rural) 51.68048, 3.89847
Mini-Camping Appelgaerd, Zandweg 6, 4321 TA
Kerkwerve **(0614) 449924; info@appelgaerd.nl;
www.appelgaerd.nl**

🔢 ♦11 🦋 ⛳ 🏔 🎣4km

Fr Zierikzee take N59 dir Serooskerke. Immed
turn R onto Zandwek. Cont for 3km, site on L bef
vill of Kerkwerve. Sm, hdg, pt shd, EHU (6A) inc;
bbq; twin axles; bus 250m; Eng spkn; adv bkg acc.
"Gd cycling, walking & bird watching area; excel site."
€20.50, 1 Apr-30 Oct. 2019

"I need an on-site restaurant"

We do our best to make sure site information
is correct, but it is always best to check any
must-have facilities are still available or will
be open during your visit.

TERSCHELLING ISLAND

OOSTEREND C1 (0.2km N Rural) 53.40562, 5.37947
Camping 't Wantij, Oosterend 41, 8897 HX Oosterend
**(0562) 448522 or (06) 20396345 (mob); info@
wantij-terschelling.nl; www.wantij-terschelling.nl**

🔢 🐕€1.75 ♦11(htd) ⭐ ♿ ✉ 🦋 ⛳ 🎣nr 🏔

🌴sand 2km

Fr Harlingen to Terschelling by ferry. Take rd to
Oosterend, site ent on L 250m after vill sp, past bus
stop & phone box. Sm, mkd, pt shd, EHU (6A) €3
(poss rev pol); cooking facs; TV; bus adj; Eng spkn; adv
bkg acc; CKE. "Gd area for birdwatching; many cycle/
foot paths across dunes; horsedrawn vehicles for
conducted tours; Elvis memorabilia 2km at Heartbreak
Hotel - rest on stilts; excel site." **€18.00** 2016

TEXEL ISLAND

DE KOOG B2 (0.5km E Rural) 53.09610, 4.76500
**Camping Coogherveld Texel (formerly De Luwe
Boshoek),** Kamperfoelieweg 3, 1796 MT De Koog
02 22 31 77 28; www.coogherveld-texel.nl

🐕 ♦11(htd) ⭐ ♿ ✉ 🦋 ⛳ 🎣nr 🌴sandy 1km

Fr ferry take 501 to De Koog. Sp after ref point 17. R
at De Zwaluw Hotel. Site on L after 100m. Med, mkd,
unshd, EHU (16A); bbq; 10% statics. "Excel; gd base to
stay; bike hire 0.5 km." **€32.50, 12 Apr-25 Oct.** 2019

DEN BURG B2 (16km N Rural) 53.16987, 4.86072
Camping de Hoek, Vuurtorenweg 83, 1795 LK De
Cocksdorp **(0222) 316236; saaldehoek@tele2.nl;
www.campingdehoek.nl**

🐕 ♦11(htd) ⭐ ✉ 🦋 ⛳ 🎣nr 🌴sandy 1km

Take the main rd fr ferry to top of island, past exit
35, site on L nr end of rd. Sm, pt shd, EHU (16A); bbq;
Eng spkn; adv bkg acc. "Farm site; beatifully kept;
lovely fam; by rd but v quiet; cycle path; excel."
€25.00, 1 Apr-1 Oct. 2017

ZUIDWOLDE D2 (2km S Rural) 52.65822, 6.42726
NCC Camping De Krententerp, Ekelenbergweg 2,
7921 RH Zuidwolde DR **(0528) 372847; zuidwolde@
ncc.nl; www.ncc.nl**

🐕 ♦11(htd) ⭐ ✉ 🦋 🏔nr 🎣nr

Fr S fr Zwolle exit A28 junc 22 dir Dedemsvaart.
Turn L at Balkbrug onto N48, then L at junc
Alteveer-Linde to site. Sm, mkd, shd, EHU (4A) €2.75
(long lead poss req); bus 200m; adv bkg acc. "Peaceful
site; friendly, helpful staff; CC members welcome;
phone ahead bet 1700 & 1800; htd covrd pool 2km;
excel cycling, walking; Zuidwolde beautiful town."
€12.50, 1 Apr-31 Oct. 2016

ZWOLLE C2 (5km NE Urban) 52.53690, 6.12954
Camping De Agnietenberg, Haerstveerweg 27,
8034 PJ Zwolle **(038) 4531530; info@camping
agnietenberg.nl; www.campingagnietenberg.nl**

🐕€3.50 ♦11(htd) ⭐ ✉ 🦋 ⛳ 🏔 🎣 📶

N fr Zwolle on A28 exit junc 20 Zwolle Oost & turn
R at end of slip rd then immed L. In 400m turn L at
traff lts into Haerstveerweg & foll site sp.
Lge, mkd, pt shd, EHU (10A); bbq; sw nr; TV;
60% statics; Eng spkn; ccard acc; fishing; tennis.
"Excel, family site in pleasant area; gd walking, cycling,
water recreation; cars parked in sep areas; single track
rd to site." **€30.00, 29 Mar-31 Oct.** 2019

ZWOLLE C2 (6.5km E Urban) 52.524253, 6.167658
Vecht & Zo, Hessenweg 14, 8028 PA Zwolle **(06)
24332462; info@vechtenzo.nl; www.vechtenzo.nl**

🐕 ♦11(htd) ⭐ ✉ 🦋 ⛳ 🏔

Fr J21 on A28 N of Zwolle take N340 in 2km R at
sp onto cycleway (row of shops). Sm, mkd, pt shd,
EHU (6A) inc (rev pol); bbq; sw; Eng spkn; adv bkg acc;
games area; canoes. "Gd for Gelderland, Kampen,
Zwolle; traff noise in day; spotless facs; vg."
€20.00, 1 Apr-31 Oct. 2018

France and Andorra

Central and South East Europe, Benelux and Scandinavia

Spain and Portugal

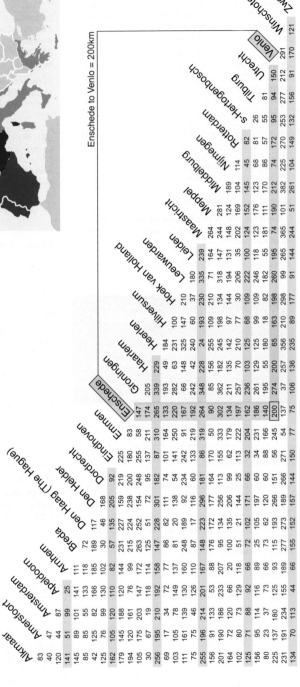

Enschede to Venlo = 200km

Legend

- All year site(s)
- Seasonal site(s)
- No sites listed

200m +
0–200m

0   50   100 kms

0   25   50 mls

N
W   E
S

© Collins Bartholomew Ltd 2020

Motorways
Major roads
Main roads

NORTH SEA

Newcastle upon Tyne

Hull

Harwich

Hull

AMELAND
TERSCHELLING
Buren
Oosterend
Lauwersoog
Vierhuizen
VLIELAND
Dokkum
LEEUWARDEN
GRONINGEN
Midwolda
Emden
N46
Harlingen
N31
WINSCHOTEN
TEXEL
De Koog
Sneek
Drachten
A7
A28
Annen
DEN BURG
A7
N371
Assen
Exloo
DEN HELDER
Koudum
A32
Appelscha
N34
Wezuperbrug
Callantsoog
Dwingeloo
EMMEN
Tuitjenhorn
Enkhuizen
MEPPEL
Havelte
ALKMAAR
A37
Zuidwolde
A9
Edam
N50
ZWOLLE
A28
Ootmarsum
Nordhorn
A7
Denekamp
Zandvoort
AMSTERDAM
Harderwijk
Rijssen
Weerselo
Noordwijk aan Zee
Almere
A50
Hengelo
Lisse
HILVERSUM
APELDOORN
Katwijk aan Zee
A30
A1
ENSCHEDE
Wassenaar
LEIDEN
Otterlo
DEN HAAG
UTRECHT
Renswoude
Dieren
Zoetermeer
Woerden
ARNHEM
Winterswijk
Delft
Gouda
Maurik
Zevenaar
HOEK VAN HOLLAND
A2
Gendt
A18
Rockanje
NIJMEGEN
Droonenburgh
A15
ROTTERDAM
Heumen
Hellevoetsluis
Wesel
Burgh-Hammstede
A29
DORDRECHT
'S-HERTOGENBOSCH
N59
A16
A27
Zierikzee
Oosterhout
Uden
Steenbergen
BREDA
Kortgene
TILBURG
Sint
GERMANY
Goes
A58
Oedenrode
MIDDELBURG
Bergen
EINDHOVEN
op Zoom
A73
Cadzand
Bladel
MIERLO
Sluis
Eersel
Panningen
A67
Hoek
A2
Weert
Helden
VENLO
Antwerpen
Düsseldorf
Roermond
Gent
Echt
A2
GERMANY
BELGIUM
Schimmert
Köln
Meerssen
HEERLEN
BRUSSEL/
MAASTRICHT
Valkenburg aan de Geul
BRUXELLES
Vaals
Aachen
Liège

Norway

Geirangerfjord

Highlights

Home to soaring fjords, glaciers and polar bears juxtaposed with cosmopolitan cities and vibrant festivals, Norway truly is a remarkable country. The natural landscape must rank as one of the most beautiful in the world, it is easy to see why people become entranced.

With a rich culture spanning centuries from the ancient Vikings to the present day, and plenty of legends, folklore and fairytales in between, Norway is a magical place that invariably delights and inspires its visitors.

The Nobel Peace Prize has, since its inception, been awarded in Oslo by the Norwegian Nobel Committee. Oslo City Hall, where the ceremony is held, is now one of Norway's most famous buildings.

As a country steeped in myths and legends, Norway has a vibrant heritage of story-telling. Trolls are some of the most talked about fairytale creatures, and statues, books and pictures of them can be found all over the country.

Major towns and cities

- Oslo – Norway's capital city hosts numerous festivals throughout the year.
- Bergen – a colourful and peaceful city surrounded by mountains.
- Trondheim – home to the world's most northerly medieval cathedral.
- Drammen – a city with plenty of attractions such as the oldest brewery in Norway.

Attractions

- Heddal Stave Church, Notodden – Norway's largest medieval wooden church.
- Geirangerfjord, Sunnmøre – one of Norway's most breathtaking fjords and a UNESCO site.
- Jostedal Glacier – Europe's largest glacier and an outstanding natural environment.
- The Royal Palace, Oslo - take a tour through some of the most beautiful state rooms.

Find out more

www.visitnorway.com
E: info@visitoslo.com T: 0047 (0) 22 00 25 00

Country Information

Population (approx): 5.3 million

Capital: Oslo

Area: 328,878 sqkm

Bordered by: Finland, Russia, Sweden

Terrain: Mostly high plateaux and mountain ranges broken by fertile valleys; deeply indented coastline; arctic tundra in the north

Climate: Moderate climate along coastal areas; more extreme inland with snowy/rainy winters; arctic conditions in the north; summers can be unpredictable and May and June can be cool

Coastline: 25,148km (including islands/fjords)

Highest Point: Galdhøpiggen 2,469m

Language: Norwegian; Sami in some areas

Local Time: GMT or BST + 1, i.e. 1 hour ahead of the UK all year

Currency: Krone (NOK) divided into 100 øre; £1 = NOK 11.82, NOK 10 = £0.85 (October 2019)

Emergency numbers: Police 112, with mobile phone 911; Fire brigade 110; Ambulance 113. From a mobile phone dial 112 for any service.

Public Holidays 2020: Jan 1; Apr 9,10, 12, 13; May 1, 17, 21, 31; Jun 1; Dec 25, 26.

School summer holidays run from mid-June to mid-August.

Border Posts

Borders with Sweden and Finland may be crossed on all main roads. Storskog on the E105, east of Kirkenes, is the only border crossing for tourist traffic from Norway into Russia (visa required).

Duty-Free Allowances

Norway isn't a member of the EU and therefore it is possible to import goods duty-free into the country from the EU. Duty-free allowances, which are strictly enforced, are as follows:

200 cigarettes or 250gm tobacco

1 litre spirits and 1½ litres wine

or 1 litre spirits and 3.5 litres beer

or 3 litres wine and 2 litres beer

or 5 litres beer

Goods to the value of NOK 6,000 (including alcohol and tobacco products)

Visitors must be aged 20 years and over to import spirits and 18 years and over for wine, beer and cigarettes.

Entry Formalities

Holders of British and Irish passports may visit Norway for up to three months without a visa.

Food and Medicines

Up to 10kg (combined weight) of meat, meat products and cheese can be imported into Norway from EU countries for personal consumption. The import of potatoes is not permitted but you can take in up to 10kg of fruit, berries and other vegetables. Visitors may only take in medicines for their own personal use with a covering letter from a doctor stating their requirements.

Medical Services

British visitors are entitled to the same basic emergency medical and dental treatment as Norwegian citizens, on production of a UK passport or European Health Insurance Card (EHIC), but you will have to pay the standard fees. Ensure you consult a doctor who has a reimbursement arrangement with the NAV (Norwegian Employment and Welfare Organisation). Hotels and tourist offices have lists of local doctors and dentists.

You will have to pay in full for most prescribed medicines which are available from pharmacies (apotek). Emergency in-patient hospital treatment at public hospitals, including necessary medication, is free of charge but you will have to pay for out-patient treatment. NAV Health Service Agencies will reimburse any payments that are refundable.

Mosquitos and midges may be a nuisance at certain times of the year, especially near lakes.

Money

Travellers may import or export currency up to the equivalent of NOK 25,000 in Norwegian and/or foreign notes and coins. Any amount above this must be declared to Customs.

Opening Hours

Banks: Mon-Fri 8am-3.30pm and some open until 5pm on Thurs.

Museums: 9am/10am-4pm/5pm; no regular closing day.

Post Offices: Mon-Fri 8am/8.30am-4pm/5pm; Sat 8am-1pm.

Shops: Mon-Fri 9am-4pm/5pm (Thurs until 6pm/8pm); Sat 9am/10am-1pm/3pm. Some supermarkets and shopping centres are open longer and some open Sun.

Refund of VAT on Export

Some shops have a blue and red sign in their window indicating that visitors may purchase goods free of VAT. For visitors from the UK the purchase price of individual items (exclusive of VAT) must be at least NOK 250. Shop assistants will issue a voucher and on departure from Norway visitors must present goods and vouchers at a tax-free counter situated on ferries, at airports and at main border crossings where a refund of 11-18% will be made.

Regulations for Pets

For details of the regulations regarding the import of pets into Norway, see website www. mattilsynet.no (English option) or contact the Norwegian Embassy in London.

Safety and Security

Norway is considered to have lower crime rates than some other European countries, even in the large cities, however you should always take the usual precautions against pickpockets and petty theft, especially in crowded areas. Do not leave valuables in your car.

Following some recent incidents of robbery, the police are warning motorists not to stop in lay-bys overnight. The Norwegian Automobile Association, Norges Automobilforbund (NAF), has also sent out warnings to campsites urging campers to be careful.

If you plan to go off the beaten track or out to sea you should take local advice about weather conditions, have suitable specialist equipment and respect warning signs. Because of Norway's northerly latitude the weather can change rapidly, producing sudden arctic conditions on exposed mountains – even in summer. The winter is long (it can last well into April) and temperatures can drop to minus 25º celcius and below, plus any wind chill factor.

Norway shares with the rest of Europe an underlying threat from terrorism. Attacks could be indiscriminate and against civilian targets in public places, including tourist sites.

British Embassy

THOMAS HEFTYES GATE 8, OSLO
Tel: 23 13 27 00
www.ukinnorway.fco.gov.uk/en/

Irish Embassy

HAAKON VIIS GATE 1, N-0244 OSLO
Tel: 22 01 72 00
www.embassyofireland.no

Documents

Money

Norway is expensive; bring or have electronic access to plenty of money, especially if you are intending to eat and drink in restaurants and bars.

Bank opening hours are shorter than in the UK, especially in summer, but cash machines are widespread. Bureaux de change are found in banks, post offices, airports, stations, hotels and some tourist offices.

The major credit cards are widely accepted (although some supermarkets and petrol stations do not accept credit cards) and may be used at cash machines (minibanks) throughout the country. In remote areas banks and cash machines may be few and far between.

It is advisable to carry your passport or photocard driving licence if paying with a credit card as you may well be asked for photographic proof of your identity. Carry your credit card issuers'/banks' 24-hour UK contact numbers in case of loss or theft of your cards.

Vehicle(s)

Carry your vehicle registration document (V5C), insurance certificate and MOT certificate (if applicable). If driving a borrowed vehicle carry a letter of authority from the owner.

Driving

Alcohol

Norwegian law is very strict: do not drink and drive. Fines and imprisonment await those who exceed the legal limit of 20 milligrams of alcohol in 100 millilitres of blood, which is considerably lower than that permitted in the UK (80 milligrams), and equates to virtually zero for at least 12 hours before driving. Random roadside breath tests are frequent.

If you are involved in a road accident which causes damage to property or vehicles or injuries you should not drink any alcohol for six hours following the accident as the police may wish to carry out blood alcohol tests.

If purchasing medicines in Norway you should be aware that some containing alcohol should be avoided if you intend to drive. These are marked with a red triangle.

Breakdown Service

Norges Automobilforbund (NAF) operates a 24-hour breakdown service nationwide. Call 08505 from a landline or 0926 08505 from a mobile phone. Emergency yellow telephones have been installed on difficult stretches of road.

NAF Veipatrulje (road patrols) operates from mid-June to mid-August on mountain passes and in remote areas but in Oslo, Stavanger and Bergen, they operate all year round.

If you're a member of The Caravan and Motorhome Club show your membership card in order to benefit from special NAF rates for breakdown assistance. Some breakdown vehicles have credit card payment terminals; otherwise payment is required in cash.

Child Restraint System

Children of four years and under 135cm must be seated in a special child restraint system. If in a rear facing system on the front seat, the airbag must be deactivated. A child between 135-150cm should use a booster seat with an adult seatbelt.

All child restraints must conform to ECE R44-03 or 04 regulations.

Fuel

Prices vary according to region - they are slightly higher in the north and in mountainous areas. Prices can also vary on different days and fuel tends to be cheaper on Sunday and Monday. There are automatic petrol pumps where payment is made by credit card or cash.

Petrol stations are generally open from 7am to 10pm on weekdays, but in cities you might find some open 24 hours. Petrol stations maybe scarce, particularly in the north.

Unleaded petrol is dispensed from pumps marked 'Blyfri'. Not all petrol stations stock diesel. If you fill up with it, ensure that you use the correct pump and do not inadvertently fill with 'Afgift Diesel' (red diesel for agricultural vehicles). LPG is available at a limited number of outlets – see www.visitnorway.com for a list.

Lights

The use of dipped headlights is compulsory at all times, regardless of weather conditions. Bulbs are more likely to fail with constant use and it is recommended that you carry spares.

Mountain Passes

Always check that any mountain passes you intend to use are open. Some high mountain roads close during the winter, the duration of the closure depending on weather conditions, but many others remain open all year. Other passes may close at short notice, at night or during periods of bad weather. Yellow emergency telephones are installed on mountain passes.

The Norwegian Tourist Board can provide a list of roads which normally close in winter, or contact the Road User Information Centre (Vegtrafikksentralen) for information about roads, road conditions, mountain passes, tunnels, border crossings, etc. The Centre is open round the clock all year, telephone 02030 within Norway or (0047) 91 50 20 30 from abroad. Alternatively a list of roads that are closed in winter or which have limited accessibility can be found at www.vegvesen.no/en/traffic and click on Truckers' Guide, or email firmapost@vegvesen.no.

Motorways

There are 300km of 4 lane motorways signposted by the prefix A, which are situated around the towns of Bergen and Oslo. In addition there are category B motorways with 2 lanes. There are normally no emergency telephones on motorways.

There are many toll roads throughout the country and most have an electronic toll system. Vehicles are categorised as follows:

Class 1 – Motorcycles

Class 2 – Car, with or without trailer, with a total weight less than 3,500kg and maximum length of 6m.

Class 3 – Vehicle with or without trailer and a total weight of more than 3,500kg or between 6m and 12.4m in length.

Motorway tolls

If you have not registered your credit card under the Visitors' Payment scheme (see below) you would normally pass through tolls in the lanes marked 'Mynt/Coin' or 'Manuell'. You either pay manually or at a coin machine – keep a supply of small change handy as it is understood that the machines do not issue change. Most toll roads have a facility for credit card payment. Drivers of vehicles over 3,500kg must drive through the 'Manuell' lane.

Don't be tempted to pass through unmanned tolls without paying, as checks are made. However, many toll road operators have installed fully automatic toll stations – AutoPASS – where a sign indicates that you should not stop. Drivers without an AutoPASS can stop and pay at Esso stations (following the 'KR-Service' signs) within three days of being eligible to pay a toll, or they will receive an invoice at their home address. This also applies to drivers of foreign-registered vehicles.

Alternatively, and more conveniently, there is now a 'Visitors' Payment' system for which you register and pay NOK 300 (vehicles below 3,500kg) or NOK 1,000 (over 3,500kg) by credit card. You specify how long your account is to be operative (maximum three months) and it is then automatically debited when you pass a pay point. Three months after your 'Visitors' Payment' has expired your account will be credited with any balance remaining. See www.autopass.no (English option) for more information and to open an account.

This system means you can drive through all toll roads in the AutoPASS lane and pay automatically at toll stations and pay points

Parking

A white line on the edge of the carriageway indicates a parking restriction. Do not park on main roads if visibility is restricted or where there is a sign 'All Stans Førbudt' (no stopping allowed). If you do so you may have your vehicle towed away. Parking regulations in towns are very strict and offences are invariably subject to fines. Pay and display car parks are in use in the main towns.

Priority

Priority roads (main roads) are indicated by a road sign bearing a yellow diamond on a white background. A black diagonal bar through the sign indicates the end of the priority rule. If you are not travelling on a priority road then vehicles coming from the right have priority. Traffic already on a roundabout has priority and trams always have priority.

Narrow roads have passing places (møteplass) to allow vehicles to pass. The driver on the side of the road where there is a passing place must stop for an oncoming vehicle. However heavy goods vehicles tend to take right of way on narrow roads, especially if travelling uphill, and it may be necessary to reverse to a passing place to allow one to pass.

Roads

The standard of roads is generally good but stretches of major roads may be bumpy and rutted as a result of use by heavy freight traffic. Caravanners in particular should take care to avoid wheels being caught in ruts.

Some roads are narrow, especially in the mountains, and may not have a central yellow line. State roads are shown in red on maps and are asphalted but may not have kerbs and may, therefore, easily become cracked and rutted. Many roads have barriers mounted close to the side of the road.

Secondary roads have a gravel surface that can be tricky when wet and may be in poor condition for some weeks during and after the spring thaw.

Don't assume that roads with an E prefix are major roads - sections of the E39, for example, are single-track with passing places. The E6 road is asphalted all the way to the Swedish border in the south and to Kirkenes in the north.

Some roads in the fjord region have many hairpin bends and can be challenging. Roads may narrow to a single carriageway and single-track bridges often have no advance warning.

Gradients on main highways are generally moderate, not over 10%, but the inside of hairpin bends may be much steeper. There is a gradient of 20% on the E68 from Gudvangen (on the southern tip of the Sognefjord) to Stalheim, but a tunnel under the steepest section of the Stalheim road eliminates this difficult section.

Maps showing roads closed to caravans and those only recommended for use by experienced caravanners, together with rest stops, may be obtained from the Norwegian Tourist Board, Norwegian local road authority offices and from the NAF.

Because of the nature of the country's roads – and the beauty of the scenery – average daily mileage may be less than anticipated. Major repairs to roads and tunnels take place during the summer months and traffic controls may cause delays. Ferries make up an integral part of a number of routes, particularly when travelling north along the coast.

Care should be taken to avoid collisions with elk, deer and reindeer, particularly at dawn and dusk. Accidents involving any kind of animal must be reported to the police.

A number of roads are closed in winter, including the E69 to the North Cape, due to snow conditions; some do not open until late May or early June.

Road Signs and Markings

European highways are prefixed with the letter E and are indicated by signs bearing white letters and figures on a green background, national highways (Riksvei or Stamvei) are indicated by black figures prefixed Rv on a yellow background and local, county roads (Fylkesvei) by black figures on a white background. County road numbers do not generally appear on maps.

Lines in the middle of the carriageway are yellow. Bus, cycle and taxi lanes are marked in white.

Some signs have been introduced, for example a square blue sign showing a car and '2+' in white means that cars carrying more than two people can use bus lanes. Square signs indicate the presence of speed cameras, small rectangular signs indicate the exit numbers on highways and main roads, and a number of triangular signs with a yellow background indicate a temporary danger. Signs advising maximum speeds on bends, obstructions, etc, should be respected.

In addition to international road signs, the following signs may also be seen:

Passing place

Place of intrest

Norwegian	English Translation
All stans førbudt	No stopping allowed
Arbeide pa vegen	Roadworks ahead
Enveiskjøring	One-way traffic
Ikke møte	No passing, single line traffic
Kjør sakte	Drive slowly
Løs grus	Loose chippings
Møteplass	Passing place
Omkjøring	Diversion
Rasteplass	Lay-by

Speed Limits

	Open Road (km/h)	Motorway (km/h)
Car Solo	80	90-100
Car towing caravan/ trailer	80	80
Motorhome under 3500kg	80	90-100
Motorhome 3500-7500kg	80	80

Drivers should pay close attention to speed limits, which are in general significantly lower than in the UK. Fines for exceeding speed limits are high and often have to be paid on the spot. Radar detectors are illegal.

In residential areas the speed limit may be as low as 30 km/h (18 mph). Frequent speed controls are in operation. Ramps and speed control bumps are not always signposted.

Vehicles over 3,500kg are restricted to 80 km/h (50 mph) on motorways and highways, regardless of signs showing higher general limits.

Tolls

Toll ring roads are in place around major cities charging drivers to take their vehicles into city centres. There are 3 zones (rings) of toll points in Oslo. In the outer zone you are only charged on entry. In the two inner zones you are charged every time you pass a toll point. Surcharges apply from 6.30-9am and 3-5pm, and for diesel vehicles - see www.fjellinjen.no/private/prices for full details.

Because of the mountainous terrain and the numerous fjords and streams, there are many bridges and tunnels where tolls are normally payable. Tunnels may be narrow and unlit and care is needed when suddenly entering an unlit tunnel from bright daylight. Alternative routes to avoid tolls can be full of obstacles which are not marked on a map, e.g. narrow stretches with sharp turns and/or poor road surface, and are best avoided.

Svinesund Bridge

There is a 700 metre long bridge linking Norway and Sweden on the E6 at Svinesund (Sweden) – the busiest border crossing between the two countries. Tolls are NOK20 for vehicles up to 3,500kg and NOK100 for vehicles over 3,500kgs (2019 prices).

Towing

Drivers of cars and caravans with a combined length of more than 12.4 metres must check from the list of national highways and/or municipal roads may not be allowed on some routes.

You can check this information with the Road User Information Centre (Vegtrafikksentralen),

tel: 02030 within Norway or (0047) 91 50 20 30 from abroad, www.vegvesen.no/en/Traffic and click on Truckers' Guide, or from the Norwegian Tourist Board or NAF. For a motorhome the maximum length is 12 metres (12.4 metres for those registered before September 1997).

Any vehicle towing must have extended towing mirrors fitted.

Some secondary roads have a maximum width of less than 2.55 metres. If your caravan is wider than 2.3 metres and more than 50cm wider than your car, white reflectors must be mounted on the front of your car mirrors. More information is available from the Road User Information Centre.

It is understood that the Rv55 from Sogndal to Lom and the Rv63 north from Geiranger are not suitable for caravans exceeding 5 metres in length, or those without an adequate power/weight ratio.

Traffic Jams

Roads in general are rarely busy but the roads in and around the cities of Oslo, Bergen, Kristiansand and Trondheim suffer traffic jams during rush hours and at the beginning and end of the holiday season. The E6 Oslo-Svinesund road at the border with Sweden and the E18 Oslo-Kristiansand road are generally busy during the June to August holiday period. During the summer you should also expect delays at ferry terminals.

Tunnels

The road network includes approximately 950 tunnels, most of which can be found in the counties of Hordaland and Sogn og Fjordane in western Norway. Most tunnels are illuminated and about half are ventilated. There are emergency telephones at the entrance to tunnels and inside them. Tunnels also have refuges which can be used by motorists in the event of an emergency.

Laersdal Tunnel

The Lærsdal road tunnel links the Rv50 from just east of Aurlandsvangen to the E16 east of Lærdalsoyri, by-passing the ferry link from Gudvangen to Lærsdal. The toll-free 24.5km long tunnel is illuminated and ventilated throughout and has a number of caverns at regular intervals which act as turning points and, it is reported, help dispel any feelings of claustrophobia. An alternative route is to take the Rødnes tunnel and then the Rv53, but this involves a steep climb beyond Øvre Ardal.

Lofoten and Vesterålen Islands

The Lofoten Islands can be reached by ferries from Bodø & Skutvik and the Vesteralen Islands can be reached by road (E10) west of Narvik. The individual islands of the Lofoten and Vesterålen groups are connected to each other by bridge or tunnel and the two groups of islands are linked by the E10 Lofast route from Gullesfjordbotn in Vesterålen to Fiskebøl in Lofoten. This route was formerly only possible by ferry.

Oslo Tunnel

A 3km long toll-free tunnel runs from east to west Oslo.

Violation of Traffic Regulations

The police are empowered to impose and collect on-the-spot fines for infringement of traffic regulations.

where there is no option for manual payment. You do not need an AutoPASS tag which is designed for residents and long-stay visitors and for which you have to enter into a contract.

Winter Driving

Vehicles with a total weight of 3,500kg or more must carry chains during the winter season, regardless of road conditions. Checks are often carried out.

Generally spiked tyres can be used from 1st November to the first Sunday after Easter. In an effort to discourage the use of spiked tyres in Bergen, Oslo and Trondheim a tax is levied on vehicles equipped with them. For vehicles up to 3,500kg the tax is NOK 30 for one day and NOK 400 for a month. For vehicles over 3,500kg the fee is doubled. Daily permits are available from vending machines along major roads into the city marked 'Frisk luft i byen'. Vehicles over 3,500 kg must be equipped with winter tyres on all axles between 15th November and 31st March.

Essential Equipment

Reflective Jacket/Waistcoat

Owners of vehicles registered in Norway are required to carry a reflective jacket to be worn if their vehicle is immobilised on the carriageway following a breakdown or accident. This legislation does not yet apply to foreign registered vehicles but you are strongly advised to carry at least one such jacket. Passengers who leave the vehicle, for example to assist with a repair, should also wear one.

Warning Triangle

An warning triangle must be used if the vehicle has broken down, punctures or is involved in an accident, and could cause danger to other road users.

Touring

International ferry services operate between Norway and Denmark, Germany, Iceland and Sweden. Routes from Harwich to Denmark and Newcastle to the Netherlands are in operation as gateways to Europe and, in addition, a daily overnight ferry service connects Copenhagen and Oslo.

A green 'i' sign indicates a tourist information office which is open all year with extended opening hours in summer, whereas a red sign means that the office is only open during the summer season.

Norwegians take their school and industrial holidays from mid-June to mid-August; travelling outside this season will ensure that facilities are less crowded and more economically priced. Winter brings the inevitable snowfall with some of the most reliable snow conditions in Europe. The winter sports season is from November to April.

Alta, on the coast north of the Arctic Circle, boasts the most extensive prehistoric rock carvings in Europe and has been declared a UNESCO World Heritage Site. Other World Heritage Sites include Geirangerfjord, Nærøyfjord, Bryggen in Bergen and the wooden buildings in Røros.

City cards are available for Oslo and Bergen, giving unlimited free travel on public transport, free public parking and free or discounted admission to museums and tourist attractions. They can be bought from tourist information centres, hotels and campsites in or near the city, from some kiosks or online at www.visitoslo.com or www.visitbergen.com.

Wine and spirits are only available from special, state-owned shops (vinmonopolet) usually found in larger towns, and are expensive, as are cigarettes. Beer is available from supermarkets. Smoking in bars, restaurants and public places is prohibited. Tipping is not expected in restaurants.

English is widely spoken, often fluently, by virtually everyone under the age of 60.

Camping and Caravanning

There are more than 1,000 campsites in Norway which are classified 1 to 5 stars and which are generally open between June and mid August. A camping guide listing 300 sites is available from the Norwegian Automobile Association, Norges Automobilforbund (NAF), see www.nafcamp.no. The Norwegian Tourist Board also distributes a camping guide free of charge – see www.camping.no. Most 3 star sites and all 4 and 5 star sites have sanitary facilities for the disabled and all classified sites have cooking facilities.

Many sites do not open until mid-June and do not fully function until the beginning of July, particularly if the winter has been prolonged. Sites with published opening dates earlier than June may not open on time if the weather has been particularly bad and if, for example, there has been heavy rain and flooding near rivers or lakes where campsites are situated. Campsites which are open all year will usually have very limited facilities for most of the year outside the short holiday season.

Facilities vary; in main tourist centres there are large, well-equipped sites with good sanitary facilities, grocery shops, leisure facilities and attendants permanently on duty. Sites are generally maintained to a high standard of cleanliness. In more remote areas, sites are small and facilities can be very simple.

Many small campsites have no chemical disposal point. Roadside notice boards at the entrance to each local area (kommune) indicate campsites,

chemical disposal points (normally sited at petrol stations) and other local amenities. These disposal facilities are usually coin-operated and have instructions in English. In some areas in the north, there may be no adequate arrangements for the disposal of waste water, either on site or in the immediate area, and you are advised enquire when arriving at a campsite.

The Camping Key Europe, which replaced the Camping Card Scandinavia (CCS) in 2012, may be required at some sites. You can buy the Camping Key Europe on arrival at your first site and will be issued with a temporary card. Alternatively, you can order the card before you travel from www.camping.no/en/cke and click on 'Bestillig av Kort' where you can then select to view the order form in English. If ordering in advance allow at least three weeks for the card to arrive.

There are many sites on the E6 to the North Cape, seldom more than 30km apart. These sites may be subject to road noise. Caravans are allowed to stay at the North Cape but no facilities are available – see Nordkapp later in this chapter and in the Site Entry listing.

In the short summer season campsites can be crowded and facilities stretched and you are recommended to arrive before 3pm (many sites have a latest arrival time of 4pm) in order to have a better choice of pitches and have the opportunity to erect an awning.

Casual/wild camping is not actively encouraged but the Norwegian 'Right of Access' allows visitors to explore the countryside freely, except for cultivated land, farmland, gardens, nurseries, etc. Off-road driving is not allowed. Visitors must respect nature and take their rubbish away with them when they leave. Open fires (which include Primus stoves) are prohibited in forests or on open land between 15 April and 15 September.

Cycling

Cyclists are fairly well catered for and some areas, such as Vestfold, Rogaland and the Lillehammer area, have a well-developed network of cycle paths. Some old roads have been converted into cycle paths in the mountains and along western fjords. Paths run through magnificent scenery in the Lofoten and Vesterålen Islands in particular, and from Haugastøl in the Hardangervidda National Park to Flåm. A number of tunnels are prohibited to cyclists, but local detours are generally signposted. Information is available at www.cyclingnorway.no

Electricity and Gas

Campsites usually have a minimum 10 amp supply. Plugs are the continental type and have two round pins plus two earth strips. Some sites do not yet have CEE connections. It is recommended that you take an extension cable of at least 50 metres.

There are often problems with both polarity and the earthing of the electrical supply on some sites. Due to its geology and mountainous nature, Norway's electricity supply network is quite different from that found elsewhere in Europe. There is no national grid and electricity systems vary from place to place throughout the country. Any polarity testing system is likely to give false readings. It is understood that progress is being made to improve and standardise the electrical supply throughout the country but you should exercise caution and, if in any doubt, ask site staff to demonstrate the integrity of the earthing system before connecting.

Propane gas cylinders are generally widely available from Esso and Statoil petrol stations. You will need to buy an appropriate adaptor, available from camping shops or Statoil garages. AGA AS dealers will allow you to sell back propane cylinders within six months of purchase prior to leaving Norway at approximately 80% of the purchase price. It is understood that Statoil garages no longer buy them back. Some Statoil garages and AGA AS dealers will exchange Swedish Primus propane cylinders for their Norwegian version but will not accept other foreign propane cylinders. There is no refund for the adaptor.

Gas supplies can be conserved by taking advantage of the kitchens and/or cooking facilities available at classified campsites, and using electrical hook-ups at every opportunity.

Motorhomes

Many towns provide parking places for motorhomes close to city centres, known as Bobil Parks, which are open in June, July and August. In general these parking areas provide limited facilities and car and caravan outfits are not permitted. Details, where known, are listed in the Site Entry pages.

Apart from at campsites, motorhome service points are reported to be few and far between and are generally to be found at petrol stations, where water refill may also be available.

The Midnight Sun and Northern Lights

The best time to experience the midnight sun is early or high summer. The sun does not sink below the horizon at the North Cape (Nordkapp) from the second week in May to the last week in July.

Midsummer Night's Eve is celebrated all over the country with thousands of bonfires along the fjords.

You can hope to see the Northern Lights (Aurora Borealis) between November and February depending on weather conditions. You need to go north of the Arctic Circle, which crosses Norway, just south of Bodø on the Nordland coast. Occasionally the Northern Lights may be seen in southern Norway, again depending on weather conditions.

North Cape (Nordkapp)

A tunnel links the island of Magerøya, on which the North Cape is situated, to the mainland.

North Cape is open from the beginning of May until the end of September. It is possible to visit in winter; contact the Nordkapp Tourist Office, www.nordkapp.no or tel: (0047) 78 47 70 30. This is a tourist centre where there are exhibitions, displays, restaurants, shops and a post office, as well as an area of hardstanding for parking. This charge covers a stay of up to 48 hours. More information is given in the campsite entry for Nordkapp or on the website www.nordnorge.com. There are no cash machines at North Cape but credit cards are accepted in shops and restaurants, as are euros and sterling.

The true northernmost point of Norway is in fact at Knivskjellodden on a peninsular to the west of North Cape which is marked by a modest monument and a wooden box where you can record your name in a log book. It is possible to walk the 18km round trip from a car park on the E69 to Knivskjellodden but the walk should not be undertaken lightly. Later you can claim a certificate to mark your achievement from the tourist office in

Honningsvåg by quoting the reference number of your signed entry in the log book.

The Order of Bluenosed Caravanners

Visitors to the Arctic Circle from anywhere in the world may apply for membership of the Order of Bluenosed Caravanners which will be recognised by the issue of a certificate by the International Caravanning Association (ICA).

For more information contact bluenosed@icacaravanning.org and attach a photograph of yourselves and your outfit under any Arctic Circle signpost, together with the date and country of crossing and the names of those who made the crossing.

This service is free to members of the ICA (annual membership £20); the fee for non-members is £5. Coloured plastic decals for your outfit, indicating membership of the Order, are also available at a cost of £4. Cheques should be payable to the ICA. For more information visit www.icacaravanning.org.

Public Transport

The public transport network is excellent and efficient with bus routes extending to remote villages. For economical travel buy a 24 hour bus pass (campsites often sell them), valid when stamped for the first time. Many train routes run through very scenic countryside and special offers and discounts mean that train travel is reasonably priced. Only Oslo has a metro system. Trams operate in Bergen and Trondheim.

Using domestic public ferry services is often the quickest way of travelling around Norway and from place to place along the coast and within fjords. Most operate from very early in the morning until late at night. Booking is not normally necessary except in the height of the holiday season when there may be long queues to the more popular destinations. However, internal ferries can be expensive in high season and you may wish to plan your route carefully in order to avoid them.

The ultimate ferry journey is the Norwegian steamer trip (hurtigrute) up the coast from Bergen to Kirkenes. A daily service operates in both directions and the steamer stops at about 30 ports on the way. The round trip lasts eleven days.

The scenic round trip from Bergen or Oslo, 'Norway in a Nutshell', takes you through some of the most beautiful scenery in the country. It combines rail, boat and coach travel on the scenic Bergen railway, the breathtaking Flåm Railway, and takes in the Aurlandsfjord, the narrow Naerøyfjord and the steep Stalheimskleiva. Further details are available from the Norwegian Tourist Board.

You can safely hail a taxi off the street or take one from a taxi stand. Most drivers speak English and all taxis are equipped for taking payment by credit card.

Bergen

ALESUND *1B1* (1km N Coastal) *62.47571, 6.15688*
Ålesund Bobilsenter, Storgata 39, 6015 Ålesund
(Møre og Romsdal)
♦♦♦ ♨ ♿ ⚑

Foll coast to N of town cent & m'van sps; well sp.
Sm, hdstg, unshd, EHU; ccard acc. *"No on-site warden; motor c'vans only; site on water's edge adj sea wall; conv town cent; v nice facs in wonderful location."*
NOK 200, May-Sep. 2019

ALESUND *1B1* (3km E Urban/Coastal) *62.46986, 6.19839* **Volsdalen Camping,** Sjømannsveien, 6008
Ålesund (Møre og Romsdal) **tel 70 12 58 90; post@
volsdalencamping.no; www.volsdalencamping.no**
🐕 ♦♦♦(htd) ⬚ ♨ ⚭ ⚑ ♿ ⚑ ⚑ 🏍

**Foll Rv136 two Centrum, ignore 1st camping sp
(Prinsen), take 2nd site sp Volsdalsberga to exit
R, up slip rd. At top turn L over E136 then immed
R, site on L.** 3*, Sm, mkd, hdstg, unshd, terr, EHU
(10A) NOK30 (no earth); gas; cooking facs; red long
stay; TV; 40% statics; bus 600m; Eng spkn; adv bkg
acc; ccard acc. *"Stunning location; some pitches
o'looking fjord; sm pitches not suitable lge o'fits high
ssn; 75% travellers; site unkempt; new san facs being
built (2013); rec NH; only site for c'van nr Alesund,
so adv bkg strongly advised; town 30 min walk."*
NOK 350, 1 May-1 Sep. 2019

ALTA *2G1* (6km S Rural) *69.92904, 23.26136* **Alta
River Camping,** Steinfossveien 5, 9518 Øvre Alta
(Finnmark) **tel 07 94 03 27 99; post@alta-river-
camping.no; www.alta-river-camping.no**
[12] ♦♦♦(htd) ⬚ ♨ ⚭ ⚑ ⚑ 🐕 ♈ ⚑ 🏍

**Fr E6 (by-passing Alta), take E93 S sp Kautokeino.
Site clearly sp on L (opp information board).**
Med, pt shd, EHU (10-16A) NOK30; cooking facs; TV;
Eng spkn; adv bkg acc; ccard acc; sauna; CKE. *"Excel
facs; o'looks salmon rv; pitches not mkd and close
together, some hdstg; elec point poss no earth; facs
dated but clean; elec poss no earth."* **NOK 279** 2019

ALTA *2G1* (7km S Rural) *69.92735, 23.27075* **Alta
Strand Camping & Apartments,** Stenfossveien 29,
9518 Øvre Alta (Finnmark) **tel 78 43 40 22; mail@
altacamping.no; www.altacamping.no**
[12] 🐕 ♦♦♦(htd) ⬚ ♨ ⚭ ⚑ ⚑ ♈ ⟐ ⚑ nr 🏍

**Fr E6 (W of Alta) take Rv93 S sp Kautokeino. Three
sites adj in 3km on L, clearly sp, Strand is last one.**
3*, Sm, hdstg, unshd, EHU (16A) NOK50 (poss no
earth); bbq; cooking facs; twin axles; 20% statics;
phone; Eng spkn; adv bkg acc; ccard acc; sauna; car
wash; CKE. *"Gd for visiting rock carvings; midnight sun
visible fr nrby Alta museum; excel."* **NOK 272** 2017

ALVDAL *1C2* (5km NE Rural) *62.13115, 10.56896*
Gjelten Bru Camping, 2560 Alvdal (Hedmark) **tel
62 48 74 44; www.nafcamp.com/gjelten-camping**
[12] 🐕 ♦♦♦ ⬚ ♨ ⚭ ⚑ ⚑ ⚑ 🏍

**Fr Rv3 join rd 29 at Alvdal. Cross rv opp general
store to site on rv bank.** 3*, Sm, mkd, pt shd, EHU
(10A) NOK40; Eng spkn; fishing; games area. *"V
pleasant site; friendly owner."* **NOK 237** 2016

ANDALSNES *1B1* (11km S Rural) *62.4940, 7.75846*
Trollveggen Camping, Horgheimseidet, 6300
Åndalsnes (Møre og Romsdal) **tel 07 40 09 20 02;
post@trollveggen.com; www.trollveggen.com**
🐕 ♦♦♦(htd) ⬚ ♨ ⚭ ⚑ ⚑ ⚑ ♈ ⊕ nr 🏍

Sp on W side of E136, dir Dombås. 3*, Sm, mkd, pt
shd, terr, EHU (16A) NOK40; bbq; cooking facs; Eng
spkn; adv bkg acc; ccard acc; fishing; bike hire; golf
10km. *"Friendly, family-run site; excel touring base;
outstanding scenery; at foot of Trollveggen wall - shd
fr late afternoon; ideal site for walking in Romsal; on
Trollsteig classic rte."* **NOK 294, 10 May-20 Sep.**
2019

"There aren't many sites open at this time of year"

If you're travelling outside peak season
remember to call ahead to check site opening
dates – even if the entry says 'open all year'.

ANDALSNES *1B1* (3km S Rural) *62.55223, 7.70394*
Åndalsnes Camping & Motell, 6300 Åndalsnes (Møre
og Romsdal) **tel 71 22 16 29; epost@andalsnes-
camping.no; www.andalsnes-camping.com**
♦♦♦ ⬚ ♨ ⚭ ⚑ ⚑ ♈ ⊕ ⚑ 🏍

**Foll E136 to o'skirts of Åndalsnes. Foll sp Ålesund
x-ing rv bdge twd W & L immed.** Lge, pt shd, EHU
(10-16A) NOK40 (check earth); TV; ccard acc; fishing;
boating; CKE. *"Excel facs; rvside, excel mountain
scenery; nr Troll Rd & Wall; nice site; grnd can be
soft; poss long lead req (poss no earth); gd cent site."*
NOK 284, 1 May-30 Sep. 2019

ANDALSNES *1B1* (23km NW Rural/Coastal) *62.58720,
7.53004* **Saltkjelsnes Camping,** N-6350 Eidsbygda
**tel 71 22 39 00; camping@saltkjelsnes.no;
www.saltkjelsnes.no**
🐕 ♦♦♦(htd) ⬚ ♨ ⚑ ⚑ 🐕 ♈

FV64 twds Molde, site on L sp Eidsbyga. 3*, Sm,
pt shd, pt sl, terr, EHU (10A) 40 NOK; bbq; cooking
facs; twin axles; 60% statics; Eng spkn; boat hire;
fishing. *"Lovely location; site small & space ltd,
but 1st class facs; Rodven Stavkirke 10km; vg."*
NOK 287, 1 Apr-1 Oct. 2015

BERGEN *1A3* (21km E Rural) *60.37381, 5.45768* **Lone Camping,** Hardangerveien 697, 5268 Haukeland (Horda-Rogaland) **tel 55 39 29 60; booking@lone camping.no; www.lonecamping.no**

🏕️ WC 🗑️ ⌂ ∥ MSP 🦋 ⚲ ♿ 🏰

Fr N on E39 until junc with E16. foll sp Voss to rndabt junc with Rv580 sp Nesttun. Foll Rv580 S for approx 5km, site sp on L. Fr S on E39 until Nesttun, foll Rv580 N sp Indre Arna for approx 6km, site sp on R. Recep is sm bureau adj g'ge or, if unmanned, in g'ge. Do NOT go into Bergen city cent. Site is 20km by rd fr Bergen. 3*, Lge, hdstg, pt shd, pt sl, EHU (16A) NOK40; gas; sw; red long stay; TV; 10% statics; phone; bus to Bergen; Eng spkn; ccard acc; site clsd 5 Nov-19 Dec & New Year; fishing; boating; CKE. *"Well-organised; helpful staff; peaceful lakeside setting; superb views; lakeside pitches diff when wet; bus at camp ent for Bergen (35 mins)."* **NOK 326, 5 Jan-19 Apr & 29 Apr-20 Dec.**   **2019**

BERGEN *1A3* (17km SE Rural) *60.35220, 5.43520* **Bratland Camping,** Bratlandsveien 6, 5268 Haukeland (Hordaland) **tel 55 10 13 38 & 92 61 52 00 (mob); post@bratlandcamping.no; www.bratlandcamping.no**

🏕️ WC ⌂ ♿ ⌂ ∥ MSP ⚲ 🚆

Fr N on E39 until junc with E16, foll sp Voss to rndabt junc with Rv580 sp Nesttun. Foll Rv580 S for approx 4km; site sp on L. Fr Voss on E16, emerge fr tunnel to rndabt, turn L onto Rv580. Then as above. Site 16km by rd fr Bergen. 3*, Sm, hdstg, unshd, EHU (10A) NOK40; cooking facs; TV; 10% statics; bus to Bergen at site ent; Eng spkn; ccard acc; CKE. *"Clean, family-run site; gd, modern san facs; v helpful, friendly owners; conv Bergen, nrby stave church & Grieg's home; great loc."* **NOK 267, 1 May-15 Sep.**   **2016**

BERLEVAG *2H1* (0.6km E Coastal) *70.85716, 29.09933* **Berlevåg Pensjonat Camping,** Havnagata 8, 9980 Berlevåg (Finnmark) **tel 41 54 42 55; post@berlevag-pensjonat.no; www.berlevag-pensjonat.no**

🏕️ (htd) WC ⌂ ♿ ⌂ ∥ MSP ⚲ 🚆 nr 🏰 ⛺

Leave E6 at Tanabru, foll Rv890 to Berlevåg. Site sp at beg of vill. 3*, Sm, unshd, EHU (16A) NOK40; bbq; cooking facs; TV; phone; Eng spkn; adv bkg acc; ccard acc; CKE. *"Busy fishing port on edge of Barents Sea; museum, glassworks, WW2 resistance history; v helpful staff as site is also TO; site will open outside Jun-Sep on request if contacted ahead; library & lounge; rec arr early; excel site."* **NOK 237, 1 Jun-30 Sep.   2016**

BIRTAVARRE *2G1* (0.7km S Rural) *69.49051, 20.82976* **Camping Birtavarre (TR34),** 9147 Birtavarre (Troms) **tel 47 40 00 34 34; https://eng.high-north.com/camp-birtavarre/**

🏕️ WC ⌂ ♿ ⌂ ∥ MSP ⚲ 🚆 nr

On E6 Olderdalen to Nordkjsobotn, sp. Or foll sp fr vill. 3*, Med, unshd, EHU NOK45; cooking facs; sw; Eng spkn; ccard acc; CKE. *"Basic site; OK for NH."* **NOK 195, 1 May-15 Oct.**   **2019**

BO *1C3* (9km SE Rural) *59.38478, 9.18171* **Teksten Camping AS,** Strannavegen 140, 3810 Gvary **tel 35 95 55 96; teksten@barnascamping.no; www.barnas camping.no**

🏕️ (htd) WC ⌂ ♿ ⌂ MSP 🦋 🏰

On 36 dir Skien. Go thro Gvarv. Site sp on L. 700m fr main rd by rv. Med, mkd, pt shd, terr, cooking facs; sw nr; twin axles; 30% statics; Eng spkn; adv bkg acc; ccard acc; games area; games rm; CKE. *"Vg site for children."* **NOK 258, 1 May-9 Sep.**   **2015**

BODO *2F2* (28km SE Coastal) *67.23545, 14.62125* **Saltstraumen Camping,** Knapplund, 8056 Saltstraumen (Nordland) **tel 75 58 75 60; saltstraumen@pluscamp.no; www.saltstraumen-camping.no**

12 🎣 🏕️ (htd) WC ⌂ ♿ ⌂ ∥ MSP ⚲ ⑪ nr 🚆 nr 🏰

Fr Bodø take Rv80 for 19km; turn S onto rte 17 at Løding; site sp in Saltstraumen. 3*, Med, hdstg, unshd, EHU (16A) NOK30; gas; bbq; cooking facs; twin axles; TV; 50% statics; phone; bus 300m; Eng spkn; adv bkg acc; ccard acc; fishing; bike hire; boating; CKE. *"5 min walk to Mælstrom, the 'angler's paradise'; v busy high ssn - rec arr early; site a bit tired."* **NOK 330**   **2019**

BREMSNES *1B1* (6km W Coastal) *63.08043, 7.59535* **Skjerneset Brygge Camping,** Ekkilsøy, 6530 Averøy (Møre og Romsdal) **tel 71 51 18 94; info@skjerneset.com; www.skjerneset.com**

12 🏕️ (htd) WC ⌂ ⌂ ∥ MSP 🦋 🚆

Foll sp to Ekkilsøya Island on Rv64 (off Averøy Island). Site on R over bdge. Sm, hdstg, pt shd, EHU (10-16A) NOK30; cooking facs; TV (pitch); boat hire; fishing. *"Charming, clean, peaceful site adj working harbour; beautiful outlook; apartments to rent; basic san facs; waterside pitches - unfenced deep water in places; museum adj."* **NOK 200**   **2015**

BRONNOYSUND *2E3* (14km SW Coastal) *65.39340, 12.09920* **Torghatten Camping,** 8900 Torghatten (Nordland) **tel 75 02 54 95; post@torghatten.net; www.rv17.no/torghatten-camping/**

12 🏕️ WC ⌂ ♿ ⌂ ∥ MSP 🦋 🍴 ⌂ 🚆 🏰 ⛺ adj

Fr Rv17 onto Rv76 to Brønnøysund, foll sp Torghatten. Site at base of Torghatten mountain. Sm, unshd, pt sl, EHU (16A) NOK30; phone; bus; Eng spkn. *"Take care speed humps in/out Brønnøysund; sea water pool adj; vg."* **NOK 280**   **2019**

BRUFLAT *1C2* (10km SE Rural) *60.82932, 9.75050* **Etna Familiecamping,** Maslangrudvegen 50, 2890 Etnedal **tel 61 12 17 55 or 94 81 90 56 (mob); info@etnacamping.no; www.etnacamping.no**

12 🏕️ (htd) WC ⌂ ♿ ⌂ MSP 🦋 ⌂ ⛷️

Fr Gjovik, W on 33 past Dokka. Site on R approx 2 km past 251. Downhill to ent. Lge, pt shd, pt sl, terr, twin axles; TV; 20% statics; Eng spkn; adv bkg acc; ccard acc; games rm; CKE. *"Relaxing site; sep area for touring; may need long lead, some still 2 pin; vg."* **NOK 276**   **2015**

BUD *1B1* (1km SE Coastal) *62.9040, 6.92866*
PlusCamp Bud (MR11), 6430 Bud (Møre og Romsdal)
tel 71 26 10 23 or 97 70 05 44 (mob); bud@pluscamp.
no; www.budcamping.no

🐾 ♨️(htd) [wo] 🛁 ♨️ ♿ ℹ️ 🚿 [MSP] 🏕️ ♈ 🖥️ 🍴 ⚠️ 🏖️sand adj

Site on Rv664, sp fr Bud. 4*, Med, unshd, pt sl, EHU
(16A) NOK40; cooking facs; TV; 50% statics; Eng spkn;
ccard acc; fishing; boat hire; CKE. *"Waterfront site with
beautiful views; 20 min walk to vill shops/rest; gd facs;
gd location for start of Atlantic Highway, National
Tourist Rte & for cycling; vg site."*
NOK 270, 20 Apr-1 Oct. **2015**

BYGLANDSFJORD *1B4* (3km N Rural) *58.68895,
7.80322* **Neset Camping,** 4741 Byglandsfjord (Aust-
Agder) tel 37 93 40 50; post@neset.no; www.neset.no

[12] 🐾 ♨️(htd) [wo] 🛁 ♨️ ♿ ℹ️ 🚿 [MSP] 🏕️ 🍴 ⓘ 🍴 🖥️ ⚠️

N on Rv9 fr Evje, thro Byglandsfjord, site on L.
4*, Lge, unshd, pt sl, EHU (10A) NOK30; gas; bbq;
cooking facs; sw nr; TV; 40% statics; Eng spkn; adv bkg
acc; ccard acc; windsurfing; bike hire; fishing; sauna;
boat hire. *"Wonderful location on lakeside; elk safaris;
walks; rafting nr; check elec earth."* **NOK 352** **2019**

BYRKJELO *1B2* (0.3km S Rural) *61.73026, 6.50843*
Byrkjelo Camping & Hytter, 6826 Byrkjelo (Sogn og
Fjordane) tel 91 73 65 97; mail@byrkjelo-camping.no;
www.byrkjelo-camping.tefre.com

♨️ [wo] 🛁 ♨️ ♿ ℹ️ 🚿 [MSP] 🏕️ ♈ ⓘ nr 🖥️ nr ⚠️ 🚣(htd) 🛶

Fr S site ent on L as ent town, clearly sp.
3*, Sm, hdstg, pt shd, EHU (10A) NOK30; cooking facs;
25% statics; phone; Eng spkn; adv bkg acc; ccard acc;
solarium; fishing; cycling; CKE. *"Horseriding, mountain
& glacier walking; excel, well kept site; great facs."*
NOK 278, 1 May-24 Sep. **2019**

"That's changed – Should I let the Club know?"

If you find something on site that's different
from the site entry, fill in a report and let us
know. See camc.com/europereport.

DRAMMEN *1C3* (25km SE Coastal) *59.60003, 10.40383*
Homannsberget Camping, Strømmveien 55, 3060
Svelvik (Vestfold) tel 33 77 25 63 or 91 30 98 52 (mob);
post@homannsberget.no; www.homannsberget.no

🛁 🍴 🚿 [MSP] 🏕️ ♈ 🍴 🖥️ ⚠️ 🏖️adj

Head SW on E18, take exit 25 twr Svelvik/RV319, at
rndabt take 3rd exit onto E134. At next rndabt take
1st exit onto Bjørnsons gate/Rv282. Turn L onto
Havnegata/Rv319. Cont on Rv319, go thro 1 rndabt.
Site on the L. Med, mkd, unshd, EHU; twin axles; adv
bkg acc; ccard acc; games area; CKE. *"Vg site; train
stn within 20 mins; site is also a strawberry farm &
orchard."* **NOK 245, 1 May-1 Sep.** **2019**

EDLAND *1B3* (6km E Rural) *59.72378, 7.69712*
Velemoen Camping, 3895 Edland Vinje i Telemark
tel 35 07 01 09 or 90 89 40 49 (mob); velemoen@
frisurf.no; www.velemoen.no

🐾 ♨️ 🛁 ♨️ ♿ ℹ️ 🚿 [MSP] 🏕️ 🖥️nr ⚠️

Fr E site on L off E134 bef Edland; Fr W site is on R,
8km after Haukeligrend on Lake Tveitevatnet.
2*, Sm, hdstg, unshd, pt sl, EHU (16A, no earth); bbq;
cooking facs; sw nr; red long stay; twin axles; TV;
10% statics; phone; Eng spkn; adv bkg acc. *"V helpful
owner; immac san facs; beautiful lakeside/mountain
location; on S side of Hardangervidda National Park;
on main E-W rte Oslo-Bergen; excel."*
NOK 250, 15 May-1 Oct. **2017**

"I like to fill in the reports as I travel from site to site"

You'll find report forms at the back of this
guide, or you can fill them in online at
camc.com/europereport.

EIDFJORD *1B3* (7km SE Rural) *60.42563, 7.12318*
Sæbø Camping (HO11), 5784 Øvre-Eidfjord
(Hordaland) tel 53 66 59 27 or 55 10 20 48;
scampi@online.no; www.saebocamping.com

♨️(htd) [wo] 🛁 ♨️ ♿ ℹ️ 🚿 [MSP] 🏕️ ⓘnr 🖥️ ⚠️

Site N of Rv7 bet Eidfjord & Geilo, 2nd on L after
tunnel & bdge; clearly sp. 3*, Med, pt shd, EHU (10A)
NOK40 (earth fault); cooking facs; boating; CKE. *"Vg;
beautiful lakeside setting; adj to excel nature cent with
museum/shop/theatre; clean san facs; helpful staff; gd
location for walking & cycling."*
NOK 240, 1 May-30 Sep. **2019**

ELVERUM *1D2* (2km S Rural) *60.86701, 11.55623*
Elverum Camping, Halvdan Gransvei 6, 2407 Elverum
(Hedmark) tel 62 41 67 16; booking@elverum
camping.no; www.elverumcamping.no

[12] 🐾 ♨️(htd) [wo] 🛁 🍴 🚿 [MSP] 🏕️ ♈ 🍴nr ⓘnr 🖥️nr ⚠️

Site sp fr Rv20 dir Kongsvinger. Lge, pt shd, EHU
(10A); bbq; 20% statics; phone; Eng spkn; adv bkg acc.
*"Vg; museum of forestry adj; rlwy museum at Hamar
(30km)."* **NOK 300** **2019**

FAGERNES *1C2* (0.6km S Rural) *60.98189, 9.23125*
Camping Fagernes, Tyinvegen 23, 2900 Fagernes
(Oppland) tel 61 36 05 10; post@fagernes-camping.no;
www.fagernes-camping.no

[12] 🐾 ♨️(htd) [wo] 🛁 ♨️ ♿ ℹ️ 🚿 [MSP] 🏕️ 🍴 ⓘ 🍴 🖥️ ⚠️

Site on N side of Fagernes on E16. 4*, Lge, hdg, pt
shd, pt sl, EHU (10-16A) NOK30; cooking facs; sw;
TV; 90% statics; phone; Eng spkn; ccard acc; cycling;
fishing; CKE. *"Helpful owner; car wash; activity cent;
ltd water pnts; Valdres folk museum park adj highly rec;
fjord views; skiing; excel new san facs & site refurbished
(2015); vg."* **NOK 275** **2015**

NORWAY

FARSUND *1A4* (6km S Coastal) *58.0663, 6.7957*
Lomsesanden Familiecamping, Loshavneveien 228,
4550 Farsund (Vest-Agder) **tel 38 39 09 13;**
e-vetlan@online.no; www.lomsesanden.no

🐕 ⚎ ⓦ ♨ ♿ 🍴 ⅃ ✉ 🦋 ♨ 🏛 ⚓ sand adj

Exit E39 at Lyngdal onto Rv43 to Farsund & foll
camp sps. (NB Rv465 fr Kvinesdal not suitable for
c'vans.) 2*, Med, pt shd, EHU (10A) NOK45; TV; 95%
statics; Eng spkn; adv bkg rec; ccard acc; fishing. *"Gd
site in beautiful location."*
NOK 200, 1 May-15 Sep.   **2016**

FAUSKE *2F2* (5km S Urban) *67.23988, 15.41961*
Fauske Camping & Motel, Leivset, 8201 Fauske
(Nordland) **tel 75 64 84 01;** fausm@online.no

12 🐕 ⚎ ♨ ♿ 🍴 ⅃ ✉ 🦋 ♨ nr 🏛

Fr S site on R of E6, approx 6km fr exit of Kvenflåg
rd tunnel, & 2km bef Finneid town board. Fr N site
on L approx 1km after rv bdge. 3*, Sm, pt shd, sl,
EHU (10A) NOK40; cooking facs; sw nr; Eng spkn; adv
bkg acc; ccard acc; fishing; cycling. *"Vg; phone ahead
LS to check open; v close to E6 rd."* **NOK 267**   **2016**

FJAERLAND *1B2* (4km N Rural) *61.42758, 6.76211*
Bøyum Camping, 5855 Fjærland (Sogn og Fjordane)
tel 57 69 32 52; post@boyumcamping.no; www.boyum
camping.no

12 ⚎ (htd) ⓦ ♨ ♿ 🍴 ⅃ ✉ 🦋 ♨ 🏛

On Rv5 Sogndal to Skei. Shortly after end of toll
tunnel on L, well sp. 4*, Sm, hdstg, unshd, EHU;
cooking facs; TV; 30% statics; phone; Eng spkn; adv
bkg acc; ccard acc; bike hire; CKE. *"Adj glacier museum,
conv for glacier & fjord trips; beautiful location nr fjord
(no views); visit Mundal for 2nd hand books; helpful
owner; superb, clean site; vg."* **NOK 270**   **2017**

FLAM *1B2* (1km WNW Urban) *60.86296, 7.10985*
Flåm Camping, Nedre Brekkevegen 12, 5743 Flåm
(Sogn og Fjordane) **tel 57 63 21 21;** camping@flaam-
camping.no; www.flaam-camping.no

🐕 ⚎ (htd) ⓦ ♨ ♿ 🍴 ⅃ ✉ ⅃ nr ✉ nr ✉ 🏛

Fr Lærdal Tunnel cont on E16 thro 2 more tunnels.
At end of 2nd tunnel (Fretheim Tunnel) turn L
immed to Sentrum. Turn L at x-rds, site on L.
4*, Med, hdstg, pt shd, pt sl, terr, serviced pitches; EHU
(10A) inc; bbq; cooking facs; red long stay; phone;
Eng spkn; ccard acc; bike hire; boating; fishing;
watersports; CKE. *"Well-kept, friendly, busy, family-run
site; no o'fits over 8.5m; excel san facs; conv mountain
walks, excel location for Flambana rlwy,
Aurlandsvangen 7km - gd shops; gd cycling base;
excel."* **NOK 300, 1 Mar-31 Oct.**   **2015**

FLEKKEFJORD *1A4* (6km ESE Rural) *58.28868,
6.7173* **Egenes Camping (VA7),** 4400 Flekkefjord
(Vest-Agder) **tel 38 32 01 48;** post@egenescamping.
no; http://2017.egenescamping.no/

12 ⚎ (htd) ⓦ ♨ ♿ 🍴 ⅃ ✉ 🦋 ♨ 🏛

Located N of E39 dir Seland. 4*, Med, mkd, pt shd,
EHU (5A) NOK40; TV; 75% statics; phone; ccard acc;
CKE. *"Ltd facs LS; overflow car park area with facs for
tourers 0.5km; lovely situation."* **NOK 250**   **2019**

FLORO *1A2* (2km E Coastal) *61.59420, 5.07244*
Pluscamp Krokane (SF15), Strandgt 30, 6900 Florø
(Sogn og Fjordane) **tel 57 75 22 50;** post@krocamp.no;
www.krocamp.no

12 ⚎ (htd) ⓦ ♨ ♿ 🍴 ⅃ ✉ 🦋 ♈

⅃ nr ⓗ nr ✉ nr 🏛 ⚓ sand adj

On Rv5 Forde to Florø, on ent town turn L at rndabt
sp Krokane, then immed R & foll rd to coast. Turn
L, pass marina to site, sp. Steep ent/exit. Sm, hdstg,
pt shd, pt sl, EHU (10A) NOK30; 80% statics; phone;
bus; Eng spkn; boat hire; fishing; CKE. *"V sm area for
tourers; Florø interesting fishing town with boat trips
etc."* **NOK 130**   **2016**

FREDRIKSTAD *1C4* (16km SE Coastal) *59.13942,
11.03855* **Bevo Camping,** Bevoveien 31, 1634 Gamle
Fredrikstad **tel 69 34 92 15;** info@bevo.no;
www.bevo.no

⚎ ⓦ ♨ ♿ 🍴 ✉ 🦋 ♨ ⚓ sand adj

Avoid app fr Fredrikstad. Fr E6 junc 4, take RV110
(Fredrikstad) then L on RV111 & L on RV107
(Torsnesveien). Foll signs to campsite.
3*, Sm, mkd, pt shd, EHU; CCI. *"Isolated site on Oslo
Fjord; 15 mins to Gamle Frederikstad by car."*
NOK 280, 28 Apr-8 Sep.   **2019**

GEILO *1B3* (2km NE Rural) *60.54422, 8.23637* **Øen
Turistsenter & Geilo Vandrerhjem,** Lienvegen 139,
3580 Geilo **tel 32 08 70 60;** post@oenturist.no;
www.oenturist.no

12 🐕 ⚎ ♨ ✉ 🦋 ♈ ⓗ

Fr Geilo on Rv.7 twds Gol. Turn L onto Lienvegen &
site. Med, hdg, pt shd, pt sl, EHU (10A) 30 NOK; bbq;
cooking facs; 30% statics; Eng spkn; sauna; CKE. *"Vg
site."* **NOK 230**   **2015**

GEIRANGER *1B1* (0.4km S Rural) *62.09998, 7.20421*
Camping Geiranger, 6216 Geiranger (Møre og
Romsdal) **tel 70 26 31 20;** post@geirangercamping.
no; www.geirangercamping.no

🐕 ⚎ ⓦ ♨ ♿ 🍴 ✉ 🦋 ♈ 🏛

Site on fjord edge in vill. On Rv63 Eidsdal-Geiranger
take lower rd thro vill to site on R & on both sides
of rv. Rv63 not suitable for c'vans - steep hill &
hairpins, use ferry fr Hellesylt. 2*, Lge, unshd, pt sl,
EHU ltd (16A) NOK35; bbq; cooking facs; Eng spkn;
ccard acc; CKE. *"Busy site in superb location, gd touring
base, gd boat trips on fjord, facs (inc EHU) ltd if site
full; gd facs."* **NOK 270, 10 May-20 Sep.**   **2015**

GEIRANGER *1B1* (2km NNW Rural) *62.11548, 7.18437* **Grande Hytteutleige og Camping,** 6216 Geiranger (Møre og Romsdal) **tel 70 26 30 68; office@grande-hytteutleige.no; www.grande-hytteutleige.no**

♦♦♦(htd) 🏕 ⊟ ∥ ⊌ ⍢

Head N on Rv63, in 2.3km turn L at the foot of zigzags, then 1st R. Site on the L. Sm, pt sl, EHU (16A); cooking facs; Eng spkn; ccard acc. *"Friendly staff; conv for Fjord cruise, vg site."* **NOK 310, 15 May-15 Sep.   2019**

GOL *1C2* (3km S Rural) *60.70023, 9.00416* **Gol Campingsenter (BU17),** Heradveien 7, 3550 Gol (Buskerud) **tel 32 07 41 44; gol@pluscamp.no; www.golcamp.no**

12 ♦♦♦(htd) 🆆 🏕 ♨ ⅏ ⊟ ∥ ⍢ ⍢ 🍽 ⊕ 🐕 ⊒ ⍂ 🌊(htd) 🛝

Ent on R of Rv7 fr Gol twd Nesbyen. 4*, Lge, unshd, pt sl, EHU (16A) inc; gas; cooking facs; sw nr; TV; ccard acc; sauna; games area; CKE. *"Excel; lge extn with full facs across main rd - modern & clean."* **NOK 245   2016**

GOL *1C2* (2km SW Rural) *60.69161, 8.91909* **Personbråten Camping,** 3550 Gol (Buskerud) **tel 90 78 32 73; leif.personbraten@c2i.net**

12 ♦♦♦ 🆆 🏕 ⊟ ∥ ⍢ ⍂

Fr Gol to Geilo on Rv7, on L on rvside. 2*, Med, pt shd, EHU (10A); bbq; cooking facs; sw nr; Eng spkn; adv bkg acc; fishing; cycling; CKE. *"On rvside; v pleasant; poss noise fr rd & rv; honesty box if office unmanned; excel NH."* **NOK 217**   **2016**

"We must tell the Club about that great site we found"

Get your site reports in by mid-August and we'll do our best to get your updates into the next edition.

GRIMSBU *1C2* (0km N Rural) *62.15546, 10.17198* **Grimsbu Turistsenter,** 2582 Grimsbu (Oppland) **tel 62 49 35 29; mail@grimsbu.no; www.grimsbu.no**

12 ♦♦♦(htd) 🆆 🏕 ♨ ⅏ ⊟ ∥ 🅼 ⍢ ⍢ ⊕ 🐕 ⊒ ⍂

On Rv29 11km E of Folldal, well sp. 4*, Med, pt shd, pt sl, EHU (16A) NOK30; bbq; cooking facs; sw nr; TV; Eng spkn; adv bkg acc; ccard acc; sauna; boat hire; bike hire; rv fishing. *"Family-run site; fitness rm; private san facs avail; beautiful situation."* **NOK 310   2019**

GRIMSTAD *1B4* (5km NE Coastal) *58.36888, 8.63722* **Moysand Familiecamping,** Moy, 4885 Grimstad (Aust-Agder) **tel 90 53 55 93; mail@moysand-familie camping.no; www.moysand-familiecamping.no**

12 🐕 ♦♦♦(htd) 🏕 ♨ ⅏ ⊟ ∥ ⍢ ⊕ ⊒ ⍂

Exit A18 junc 78 onto Rv420 E twd Fevik. Foll site sp on rd to Riksveien, site 2km after Riksveien. Lge, mkd, pt shd, EHU metered; bbq; cooking facs; TV; 10% statics; adv bkg acc; fishing; boat hire. *"Private san facs avail."* **NOK 190**   **2016**

GRONG *2E3* (2km S Rural) *64.4604, 12.3137* **Langnes Camping,** 7870 Grong (Nord-Trøndelag) **tel 47 68 83 33; post@langnescamping.no; langnescamping.no**

♦♦♦(htd) 🆆 🏕 ♨ ⅏ ⊟ ∥ 🅼 ⍢ ⍢ ⊕ nr ⍂ ⍂

N on E6 turn off S of bdge over rv on by-pass, site sp. 4*, Med, mkd, hdstg, unshd, EHU (10A) NOK50; bbq; cooking facs; sw nr; TV; 10% statics; Eng spkn; adv bkg acc; games area; rv fishing; games rm. *"Helpful staff; drying rm for skiers; pleasant, family-run site; Quick Stop pitches; free phone to owner if site clsd; gd facs; access via gravel track."* **NOK 296, 1 Jun-31 Aug.**

2018

GUDVANGEN *1B2* (1km SW Rural) *60.87206, 6.82873* **Vang Camping,** 5747 Gudvangen (Sogn og Fjordane) **tel 57 63 39 26; post@vang-camping.no; www.vang-camping.no**

♦♦♦ 🏕 ⊟ ∥ ⍢ ⊕ nr ⊒ nr

At S end of of Nærøy Fjord on E16 at edge of vill. 3*, Sm, hdstg, unshd, EHU (16A) NOK30 (poss no earth); Eng spkn; CKE. *"Immac site in beautiful valley with waterfalls; spectacular scenery; cruises on adj fjord; bus to Flam; poor san facs (2015)."*

NOK 225, 1 May-15 Sep.   **2015**

HELLESYLT *1B1* (0.4km S Coastal) *62.08329, 6.87224* **Hellesylt Camping,** 6218 Hellesylt (Møre og Romsdal) **tel 90 20 68 85; postmottak@hellesyltturistsenter. no; www.hellesyltturistsenter.no**

🐕 ♦♦♦(htd) 🆆 🏕 ♨ ⅏ ⊟ ∥ 🅼 ⍢ ⍢ ⊕ nr ⊒ nr ⍂ shgl

Site on edge of fjord, sp fr cent of vill dir Geiranger. 2*, Sm, unshd, EHU (10A) NOK30; 40% statics; Eng spkn; adv bkg acc; CKE. *"Conv ferry to Geiranger; adj fjord surrounded by mountains - great views; gd rest in local hotel; beautiful church nr."* **NOK 140, 15 Apr-30 Sep.**   **2019**

HONNINGSVAG *2H1* (8km NW Coastal) *71.02625, 25.89091* **Nordkapp Camping,** 9751 Honningsvåg (Finnmark) **tel 78 47 33 77; post@nordkappcamping. no; www.nordkappcamping.no**

🐕 NOK10 ♦♦♦(htd) 🆆 🏕 ♨ ⅏ ⊟ ∥ 🅼 ⍢ ⍢ ⊕ ⍢

En rte Nordkapp on E69, site clearly sp. 3*, Sm, unshd, EHU (16A) NOK40; bbq; cooking facs; twin axles; 10% statics; bus 100m; Eng spkn; ccard acc; CKE. *"Vg; reindeer on site."* **NOK 319, 1 May-30 Sep.**   **2017**

HORTEN *1C3* (3km S Rural/Coastal) *59.39776, 10.47582* **Rørestrand Camping,** Parkveien 34, 3186 Horten (Vestfold) **tel 33 07 33 40; booking@ rorestrandcamping.no; rorestrandcamping.no**

🐕 ♦♦♦(htd) 🆆 🏕 ♨ ⅏ ⊟ ∥ ⍢ ⍂ ⍂

Fr Horten foll Rv19 for 500m S to rndabt, then foll sp. 3*, Sm, unshd, sl, EHU (10A) NOK40; 90% statics; phone; Eng spkn; ccard acc; games area; CKE. *"Conv NH en rte Oslo; facs stretched high ssn."* **NOK 250, 1 May-15 Sep.**   **2016**

NORWAY

JORPELAND 1A3 (5km SE Rural) 58.99925, 6.0922
Preikestolen Camping (RO17), Preikestolvegan 97,
4100 Jørpeland (Horda-Rogaland) **tel 47 48 19 39 50;**
info@preikestolencamping.com; www.preikestolen
camping.com

[icons]

**Fr S exit Rv13 to Preikestolen to R, site sp. Rd narr
in places, care needed.** Med, hdstg, unshd, EHU (16A)
NOK40; sw nr; red long stay; phone; bus to Preikestolen
parking; Eng spkn; adv bkg acc; ccard acc; games area;
CKE. *"Marvellous views; poss walk to Pulpit Rock but
not easy; conv Stavanger by ferry; excel facs, esp shwrs;
midge repellent ess; long lead poss needed; poss no
earth."* **NOK 322**   **2016**

KARASJOK 2H1 (1km SW Rural) 69.46888, 25.48908
Camping Karasjok, Kautokeinoveien, 9730 Karasjok
(Finnmark) **tel 97 07 22 25; karasjokcamping@**
runbox.no or booking@karacamp.no

[icons]

**Sp in town; fr x-rds in town & N of rv bdge take Rv92
W dir Kautokeino, site 900m on L.** 3*, Sm, pt shd,
EHU (10A) NOK40; Eng spkn; adv bkg acc; ccard acc;
CKE. *"Youth hostel & cabins on site; gd, clean site &
facs; lge pitches suitable RVs & lge o'fits; sh walk to
Sami park & museum."* **NOK 241**   **2018**

KAUTOKEINO 2G1 (2.5km S Rural) 68.99760, 23.03662
Arctic Motell & Kautokeino Camping, Suomaluodda
16, 9520 Kautokeino (Finnmark) **tel 78 48 54 00;**
samicamp@me.com; www.kautokeinocamping.no

[icons]

Well sp fr Rv93. Sm, unshd, pt sl, EHU (10A);
20% statics; Eng spkn. *"No chem disp; Juhls silver
gallery worth visit; gd, friendly site."* **NOK 325**   **2019**

KILBOGHAMN 2E2 (3km S Coastal) 66.50667,
13.21608 **Hilstad Camping,** 8752 Kilboghamn
(Nordland) **tel 75 09 71 86; post@polarcamp.com** or
booking@polarcamp.com; www.polarcamp.com

[icons] shgl adj

N on Rv17 sp to L just bef Kilboghamn ferry.
Sm, hdstg, unshd, terr, EHU (16A); 40% statics; phone;
Eng spkn; fishing. *"Superb location on Arctic Circle; ltd
san facs in high ssn; fishing/boat trips arranged; helpful
owner."* **NOK 300**   **2019**

KIRKENES 2H1 (92km SSW Rural) 69.21283, 29.15560
Ovre Pasvik Camping, Vaggetem, 9925 Svanvik
tel 95 91 13 05; atle.randa@pasvikcamping.no;
www.pasvikcamping.no

[icons]

On the R of Rte 885. Sp fr rd. Sm, hdstg, pt shd, pt sl,
EHU; bbq; cooking facs; 50% statics; Eng spkn; sauna;
CKE. *"Clean facs, dated & basic; gd for birdwatching;
fishing; canoeing; gd."*
NOK 250, Mid Apr-Mid Oct.   **2016**

KONGSBERG 1C3 (7km N Rural) 59.71683, 9.61133
Pikerfoss Camping, Svendsplassveien 2, 3614
Kongsberg (Buskerud) **tel 32 72 49 78 or 91 19 07 41;**
mail@pikerfoss.no or erikfred@online.no;
www.pikerfoss.no

[icons]

**Fr E134 in Kongsberg turn N bef x-ring rv & go N bet
rv (on L) & rlwy line (on R) on Bærvergrendveien.
Site on R just after x-ing rlwy line.** Sm, mkd, pt shd,
EHU (10A) NOK30; 75% statics; Eng spkn; ccard acc.
*"Modern, clean facs; lge pitches; facs stretched high
ssn; excel."* **NOK 160**   **2019**

KONGSVINGER 1D3 (10km S Rural) 60.11786,
12.05208 **Sigernessjøen Familiecamping,** Strenelsrud
Gård, Arko-Vegen, 2210 Granli (Hedmark) **tel 40 60 11
22; post@sigernescamp.no; www.sigernescamp.no**

[icons]

**On N side of Rv2 Kongsvinger to Swedish border,
well sp.** 3*, Med, pt shd, pt sl, EHU (10A) NOK40;
sw nr; 30% statics; Eng spkn; golf adj. *"Gd."*
NOK 250, 1 May-30 Sep.   **2018**

KOPPANG 1D2 (3km W Rural) 61.57163, 11.01745
Camping Koppang, 2480 Koppang (Hedmark) **tel 62
46 02 34; info@koppangcamping.no;**
www.koppangcamping.no

[icons]

**Fr Rv3, 25km S of Atna, turn onto Rv30; site on L
immed bef rv bdge.** 4*, Med, pt shd, pt sl, EHU (16A)
NOK30; gas; cooking facs; TV; 10% statics; Eng spkn;
adv bkg acc; ccard acc; fishing.
NOK 256, 1 May-30 Sep.   **2018**

KRISTIANSAND 1B4 (12km E Rural) 58.12187,
8.06568 **Kristiansand Feriesenter,** Dvergsnesveien
571, 4639 Kristiansand (Vest-Agder) **tel 38 04 19 80;**
post@kristiansandferiesenter.no;
www.dvergsnestangen.no

[icons]

**Turn S off E18 jnc 91, 6km E of Kristiansand after
Varoddbrua onto Rv401, cont for 5.5km foll sps
to site. Rd narr last 3km.** 5*, Lge, mkd, shd, sl, EHU
(16A) inc; cooking facs; sw; TV; phone; ccard acc;
boat hire; fishing; CKE. *"Gd NH; conv for ferry (20
mins); beautiful location; helpful, friendly staff."*
NOK 506, 16 Apr-16 Sep.   **2019**

KROKSTRANDA 2F2 (0.3km SE Rural) 66.46233,
15.09344 **Krokstrand Camping,** Saltfjellveien 1573,
8630 Krokstranda (Nordland) **tel 75 16 60 02;**
toverakvaag@msn.com

[icons]

**Nr Krokstrand bdge on E6, 18km S of Artic Circle
& approx 50km N of Mo i Rana.** 2*, Med, pt shd, pt
sl, EHU (10A) NOK40; cooking facs; 20% statics;
phone; train; Eng spkn; adv bkg acc; ccard acc; fishing;
CKE. *"Conv Polar Circle Cent; gd; recep in café opp."*
NOK 256, 1 Jun-20 Sep.   **2018**

KVISVIKA *1B1* (8km NE Coastal) *63.10910, 8.07875*
Magnillen Camping, 6674 Kvisvika (Møre og Romsdal)
tel 71 53 25 59; jarl-mo@online.no; www.magnillen.no

Fr W turn L off E39 approx 5km after Vettafjellet (N); thro Kvisvika & after another 9km turn L into site; sp. Sm, unshd, serviced pitches; EHU (10A) NOK30; gas; bbq; sw nr; red long stay; 50% statics; Eng spkn; adv bkg acc; ccard acc; boat hire; CKE. *"Site adj sm harbour; gd views."* **NOK 170**   **2016**

LAERDALSOYRI *1B2* (26km E Rural) *61.06725, 7.82170* **Borgund Hyttesenter and Camping,** 6888 Borgund in Laerdal **tel** 57 66 81 71 or 90 62 08 59 (mob); ovoldum@alb.no; hyttesenter.com

Site on L of E16 just aft Borgunds Tunnel. Well sp in adv aft rd to Borgund Stave Church. Sm, hdstg, unshd, EHU (16A) no earth; bbq; cooking facs; red long stay; TV; 10% statics; phone; bus 500m; Eng spkn; adv bkg acc; bike hire. *"Gd for Borgund Stave Church, Laerdal tunnel, Glacier ctr & historic rtes; gd."* **NOK 220**   **2017**

LAERDALSOYRI *1B2* (0.8km NW Rural/Coastal) *61.10056, 7.47031* **Lærdal Ferie & Fritidspark,** Grandavegen 5, 6886 Lærdal (Sogn og Fjordane) **tel** 57 66 66 95; info@laerdalferiepark.com; www.laerdalferiepark.com

Site on N side of Lærdal off Rv5/E16 adj Sognefjord. 4*, Med, unshd, EHU NOK40 (poss no earth); bbq; cooking facs; red long stay; TV; phone; Eng spkn; ccard acc; games rm; bike hire; golf 12km; boat hire; games area; tennis; CKE. *"Modern, clean, gd value site; excel san & cooking facs; lovely location adj fjord ferry terminal & nr attractive vill; gd touring base; friendly, helpful owners - will open on request outside dates shown; nice site next to Fjord; 10% discount for CAMC members; nr worlds longest tunnel."* **NOK 270, 27 Mar-25 Oct.**   **2019**

LANGFJORDBOTN *2G1* (1km S Rural) *70.02781, 22.2817* **Altafjord Camping,** 9545 Langfjordbotn (Finnmark) **tel** 78 43 80 00; booking@altafjord-camping.no; www.altafjord-camping.no

On E6, 600m S of exit to Bognelv, site adj to fjord across E6. Dist by rd fr Alta 80km. 3*, Med, hdstg, unshd, terr, serviced pitches; EHU (16A); gas; cooking facs; sw; TV; 50% statics; phone; Eng spkn; ccard acc; fishing; sauna; bike hire. *"Friendly owner; excel views; boat hire; mountaineering."*
NOK 271, 1 Jun-1 Sep.   **2016**

LARVIK *1C4* (1km S Urban) *59.04902, 10.03330* **Larvic Bobilparkering,** Tollerudden, Larvik (Vestfold) www.bobilplassen.no

Fr E18 exit at Rv303 twd Larvik. At rndabt take 1st exit onto Strandpromenaden. Sm, hdstg, unshd, EHU (3A); bbq. *"Gd; parking lot for m'vans; NH only; 8 mkd pitches, honesty box for payment."* **NOK 137**   **2016**

LILLEHAMMER *1C2* (10km S Urban) *61.10275, 10.46278* **Camping Lillehammer,** Dampsagveien 47, 2609 Lillehammer (Oppland) **tel** 61 25 33 33; resepsjon@lillehammer-camping.no; www.lillehammer-camping.no

Exit E6 at Lillehammer Sentrum. Turn 1st R at 1st rndabt, foll rd around Strandtorget shopping cent, cont approx 1.5km along lakeside rd. 4*, Med, hdstg, mkd, unshd, EHU (10A) inc (check earth); gas; TV; phone; Eng spkn; adv bkg acc; ccard acc; CKE. *"Excel san facs, site adj Lake Mjøsa; gd views, conv town & skiing areas; site adj to c'van cent, spare parts etc; facs need updating."* **NOK 300**   **2016**

LOM *1C2* (0.1km E Rural) *61.83812, 8.56969* **Camping Nordal Turistsenter,** 2686 Lom (Oppland) **tel** 61 21 93 00; booking@nordalturistsenter.no; www.nordalturistsenter.no

In cent Lom at x-rds R of Rv15. Ent by rndabt bet Esso stn & recep. Site at foot of Sognefjell Pass. 4*, Med, pt shd, EHU (10A) (no earth); cooking facs; TV; 10% statics; Eng spkn; adv bkg acc; ccard acc; sauna; CKE. *"Split level site; bottom level quiet; top level adj to recep - often noisy due to rd noise & w/ end coach parties; gd, modern san facs; mosquitoes troublesome in hot weather; busy tourist area; pleasant site; nice vill."* **NOK 356, 15 May-30 Sep.**   **2015**

LUNDE *1C3* (0.8km W Rural) *59.29844, 9.09041* **Telemark Kanalcamping,** Slusevegen 21, 3825 Lunde **tel** 91 57 54 21; post@kanalcamping.no; www.kanalcamping.no

Fr Rv 359 foll sp to Lunde slues. Site on L 1km fr cent of Lunde. Med, hdstg, unshd, sl, EHU (16A); bbq; twin axles; bus/train 1km; Eng spkn; adv bkg acc; boat hire; CKE. *"Site on Telemark canal; lovely position; gd cycling/walking; lake adj; site & san facs being developed, current san facs adequate (2015); vg."*
NOK 210, Mar-Sep.   **2015**

NORWAY

MALVIK *1D1* (2km E Rural) *63.43243, 10.70778*
Storsand Gård Camping (ST68), 7563 Malvik
(Sør-Trøndelag) **tel 73 97 63 60; post@storsand
camping.no; www.storsandcamping.no**
🚻 ⓦ 🏕 ♿ 🍴 🔌 🅿️ ⛰ 🅃 shgl

On N side of E6 N, site sp. Rec use E6 toll rd fr S, 2nd
exit after tunnel. Many lge speed humps on local
rd Rv950, care needed. 4*, Lge, unshd, EHU (16A);
cooking facs; TV; 10% statics; phone; games area;
fishing. **NOK 364, 15 May-1 Sep.**   **2015**

MALVIK *1D1* (2km W Coastal) *63.44064, 10.63978*
Vikhammer Camping, Vikhammerløkka 4, 7560
Vikhammer **tel 73 97 61 64; vikcampi@online.no;
www.vikhammer.no**
🗓12 🚻 ♿ 🍴(htd) ⓦ 🏕 ♿ 🅿️ ⒨ᵖ ⛲ 🍴 🅿️nr

E fr Trondheim on E6. Immed bef toll plaza take
ramp sp Vikhammer/Ransheim & turn R, then foll
sp Vikhammer. After 6km at traff lts cont strt on
Rv950 to rndabt & take 3rd exit sp motel & site.
Fr N exit E6 after airport sp Hell, then Malvik/
Hommelvik. Then take Rv950 to site. NB Many lge
speed humps on Rv950, care req. RV950 appears as
24 on Sat Nav. 3*, Sm, unshd, terr, EHU (16A) NOK30,
no earth; bbq; 75% statics; phone; bus adj; Eng spkn;
adv bkg acc; ccard acc; CKE. *"Insufficient san facs;
site muddy after rain; migrant workers in statics."*
NOK 240   **2015**

MANDAL *1B4* (3.5km N Rural) *58.04213, 7.49436*
Sandnes Camping, Holumsveien 133, 4516 Mandal
(Vest-Agder) **tel 98 88 73 66; sandnescamping@
online.no; www.sandnescamping.com**
🐕 🚻(htd) ⓦ 🏕 ♿ 🍴 🔌 🦋 ⛲ 🅿️nr 🅿️nr 🅃 sand 2.5km

On E39 Kristiansand to Stavanger. Turn N onto
Rv455, site on R 1.4km. 3*, Med, hdstg, pt shd, EHU
(16A) NOK40 (poss rev pol); bbq; cooking facs; sw
nr; 5% statics; phone; Eng spkn; adv bkg acc;
boating; CKE. *"Excel, well-kept site; friendly, helpful
owners; superb scenery; nature trails thro adj pine
forest; Mandal pretty town with longest sandy beach in
Norway, conv Kristiansand ferry & Lindesnes, Norway's
most S point."* **NOK 284, 1 May-1 Sep.**   **2019**

MAURVANGEN *1C2* (0.1km SW Rural) *61.48838,
8.84176* **Maurvangen Hyttegrend Camping,** Besseggen
Fjellpark, 2680 Maurvangen VÅGÅ (Oppland) **tel 61 23
89 22; post@maurvangen.no; www.maurvangen.no**
🗓12 🚻 ⓦ 🏕 ♿ 🍴 🔌 ⒨ᵖ 🦋 ⛲ 🅿️ 🅿️ ⛰

At rv bdge turn off Rv51. Foll sp. Med, hdstg, pt shd,
pt sl, EHU (10A) inc; bbq; cooking facs; sw nr; TV;
phone; Eng spkn; adv bkg acc; cycling; fishing; CKE.
*"White water rafting; gd views; rd 51 poss clsd Nov to
mid-May; gd hill walking cent; lovely site."*
NOK 300   **2016**

MELHUS *1C1* (8km NW Coastal) *63.32635, 10.21564*
Øysand Camping (ST38), Øysandan, 7224 Melhus
(Sør-Trøndelag) **tel 72 87 24 15 or 92 08 71 74 (mob);
post@oysandcamping.no; www.oysandcamping.no**
🐕 🚻 ⓦ 🏕 ♿ 🍴 🔌 ⛲ 🍴 Ⓘ 🅿️ ⛰ 🅃 adj

Fr Melhus, N on E6; then L (W) onto E39; site sp.
2*, Med, mkd, unshd, EHU (10A) NOK50; bbq; cooking
facs; sw nr; red long stay; phone; Eng spkn; ccard
acc; games area; fishing adj; boating adj; CKE. *"Fair
site with gd views; facs stretched if full; next to Fjord;
beach open to day trippers; barrier clsd at night."*
NOK 240, 1 May-1 Sep.   **2019**

MO I RANA *2F2* (17km SW Rural) *66.23307,
13.89178* **Yttervik Camping,** Sørlandsveien 874, 8617
Dalsgrenda (Nordland) **tel 75 16 45 65 or 90 98 73 55
(mob); ranjas@online.no; www.yttervikcamping.no**
🐕 🚻(htd) ⓦ 🏕 🔌 🦋 Ⓘ 🅿️ ⛰

Sp S of Mo i Rana, on W side of E6, cross sm bdge
over rlwy, diff for long o'fits. Sm, mkd, hdstg, unshd,
EHU (16A) NOK40 (no earth); 50% statics; Eng spkn;
adv bkg acc; ccard acc; fishing; CKE. *"Pleasant location
on edge fjord; friendly owners; clean, well-run site; gd
new facs (2015); rd works on E6, easier access to site in
2017."* **NOK 248, 1 Jun-15 Sep.**   **2016**

MOLDE *1B1* (4km E Rural) *62.74258, 7.2333* **Camping
Kviltorp,** Fannestrandveien 140, 6400 Molde (Møre og
Romsdal) **tel 71 21 17 42 or 47 90 14 83 05 (mob);
kviltorp.camping@online.no; www.kviltorpcamping.no**
🗓12 🚻(htd) 🏕 ♿ 🍴 🔌 Ⓘ 🅿️ 🅿️

On app fr S, Rv64 (toll) turn L onto E39/Rv62, site
on L, sp. Nr airport. 3*, Med, pt shd, pt sl, EHU (16A)
NOK35; gas; sw nr; TV; phone; Eng spkn; ccard acc;
solarium; boating; fishing; CKE. *"Conv Molde; adj
Romsdal Fjord (some pitches avail on fjord-side);
wonderful mountain views; excel, clean facs; poor
security - site open to rd on 1 side; helpful owners;
aircraft & rd noise; gd site; pool 3km; cycle track into
Molde."* **NOK 370**   **2019**

MOSJOEN *2E3* (2km E Rural) *65.83453, 13.21971*
Mosjøen Camping & Hotel, Kippermoen, 8657
Mosjøen (Nordland) **tel 75 17 79 00; mosjoen-
camping@hotmail.com; www.mosjoencamping.no**
🗓12 🐕 🚻(htd) ⓦ 🏕 ♿ 🍴 🔌 ⒨ᵖ ⛲ 🍴 Ⓘ 🅿️ 🅿️nr ⛰ 🚣

E6 by-passes town, well sp on W side of E6 by
rndabt. Fr S only mkd by flag 500m bef rndabt at
start Mosjøen bypass. 4*, Med, hdstg, unshd, terr,
EHU (16A) NOK40; twin axles; TV; 40% statics; phone;
Eng spkn; adv bkg acc; ccard acc; games rm; CKE.
*"Clean, v basic san facs; gd site; gd kitchen facs and san
facs, friendly staff; lge spmkt nrby; pizza rest; bowling
alley; lively local ctr; gd."* **NOK 298**   **2017**

NORDKAPP *2H1* (0.1km S Rural/Coastal) *71.16795, 25.78174* **Nordkapphallen Carpark,** 9764 Nordkapp (Finnmark) **tel** 78 47 68 60; nordkapphallen@rica.no; www.rica.no

🏕 ♦♦♦ ⵟ ⓦ ⵛ

N on E69. Hdstg, unshd, pt sl, own san req. *"NOK 285 per person for 24hrs (max stay); no other o'night or site charges; 1 Nov-1 Apr private vehicles not permitted - buses in convoy (daily) only; price inc visit to Nordkapp Cent; no facs; very exposed gravel surface; excel for viewing midnight sun."* **NOK 285**　　　　**2019**

NOTODDEN *1C3* (1km W Rural) *59.55850, 9.24878* **Notodden Bobilcamp,** Nesøya 11, 3674 Notodden **tel** 47 35 01 33 10; notcamp@notoddencamping.com; www.notoddencamping.com

♦♦♦ ⵏⴅ ⵛ ⵉ

1km W of Notodden on the E134. Sm, hdstg, pt shd, bus/tram 1km. *"City run stop over; low charge for all facs except electric; no one on site, owner calls in evening."* **NOK 130**　　　　**2019**

ODDA *1A3* (2km S Rural) *60.0533, 6.5426* **Odda Camping,** Jordalsveien 29, 5750 Odda (Hordaland) **tel** 94 14 12 79; post@oddacamping.no; www.odda camping.no

🏕 ⵟ ♦♦♦(htd) ⵏ ⵙ ⵛ ⵉ ⵉ ⵿ ⓦ ⵕ ⵛⵕ

Sp on Rv13; adj sports complex, nr lakeside. 3*, Med, pt shd, EHU (16A) NOK40; bbq; Eng spkn; games area; bike hire; watersports; lake fishing. *"Beautiful area; nr Hardanger Fjord; watersports with canoes for hire; private san facs avail; owner owns a guesthouse where you can use wifi & organise trips."* **NOK 150**　**2016**

OPPDAL *1C1* (13km SW Rural) *62.49886, 9.58853* **Magalaupe Camping,** 7340 Oppdal (Sør-Trøndelag) **tel** 72 42 46 84 or 99 25 99 93 (mob); anja.moene@ gmail.com; www.magalaupe.no

🏕 ⵟ ♦♦♦(htd) ⵏ ⵙ ⵛ ⵉ ⵉ ⵕ ⵟ ⵙ ⵛ ⵿

On W side of E6 Dombås to Trondheim rd, sp on side of Rv Driva. 2*, Med, unshd, pt sl, EHU (10-16A) NOK20; cooking facs; TV; 10% statics; Eng spkn; sauna; bike hire; fishing. *"Sh walk to waterfalls; musk oxen safaries run by owner; excel; facs satisfactory; quiet site."* **NOK 158**　　　　**2015**

OPPDAL *1C1* (12km W Rural) *62.61640, 9.47845* **Trollheimsporten Turistsenter Bobil Plass,** Festa, 7340 Oppdal **tel** 47 48464241 or 41339130; turist@ oppdal.com; campingoppdal.no

🏕 ♦♦♦ ⵏ ⵙ ⵛ ⵉ ⵟ ⵙ

In Oppal on E6 take turning onto Rte 70. Site on R of Rte 70 in about 15km. Sm, hdstg, pt sl, EHU; TV; 50% statics; Eng spkn. *"This site is only for MH; vg."* **NOK 150**　　　　**2016**

ORNES *2E2* (7km NW Rural) *66.91327, 13.62995* **Reipa Camping,** N 8146 Reipa **tel** 75 75 57 74 or 90 95 60 47; post@reipacamping.com; www.reipa camping.com

🏕 ⵟ ♦♦♦(htd) ⵏ ⵙ ⵛ ⵛ ⵉ ⵟ ⵿

Head NE on Havneveien twd Chr. Tidemanns vei/ Rv17, then turn R onto Havneveien/Fv456. Sm, EHU inc (16A); Eng spkn; adv bkg acc; ccard acc; CKE. *"Gd NH on classic Rv17."* **NOK 230**　　　　**2019**

OS I OSTERDALEN *1D1* (2km NE Rural) *62.50430, 11.25938* **Røste Hyttetun & Camping,** 2550 Os I Østerdalen (Sør-Trøndelag) **tel** 62 49 70 55; post@ rostecamping.no; www.rostecamping.no

🏕 ♦♦♦ ⵏ ⵙ ⵛ ⵉ ⵿ ⵕ ⵟ ⵿

Sp on Rv30. 3*, Sm, EHU NOK40; cooking facs; TV; 10% statics; fishing 150m. **NOK 207**　　　　**2016**

"I need an on-site restaurant"

We do our best to make sure site information is correct, but it is always best to check any must-have facilities are still available or will be open during your visit.

OSLO *1C3* (5km W Urban) *59.91802, 10.67554* **Sjølyst Marina Campervan Parking,** Drammensveien 160, Sjølyst Båtopplag, 0273 Oslo **tel** 22 50 91 93; post@bobilparkering.no; www.bobilparkering.no

ⵟ ⓦ ⵏ ⵙ ⵛ ⵉ ⵿ ⵕ ⵛ

Fr E exit E18 at junc after Bygdøy (museums) junc. At rndabt take last exit, go under E18 & into site. Fr W leave E18 at Sjølyst junc, at bottom of slip rd turn R into site. Sm, hdstg, unshd, EHU inc; own san rec; bbq; bus adj; Eng spkn; clsd 2300-0700. *"Gd, basic site, pt of marina; m'vans only - pay at machine; san facs clsd o'night; 30 min walk city cent."* **NOK 300, 1 Jun-15 Sep.**　　　　**2016**

OSLO *1C3* (9km NW Urban) *59.9623, 10.6429* **NAF Camping Bogstad,** Ankerveien 117, Røa, 0766 Oslo **tel** 22 51 08 00; bogstad@naf.no; www.bogstad camping.no

🏕 ⵟ ♦♦♦(htd) ⵏ ⵙ ⵛ ⵉ ⵉ ⵿ ⵕ ⵛⵕ

Fr N on E16 cont to E18 & turn E twd Oslo. After approx 7km exit & proceed N twds Røa and Bogstad. Site sp adj Oslo golf club. 4*, V lge, mkd, pt shd, pt sl, EHU (10A) NOK50 (long lead poss req); 25% statics; bus to Oslo 100m; Eng spkn; adv bkg acc; ccard acc; CKE. *"Beautiful area with walking trails; avoid area of site with statics & many ssn workers (behind recep), far end OK with lake views; modern, clean san facs; helpful staff; recep open 24 hrs; conv Oslo cent; bus stop nrby, bus every 10 mins; lake nrby; 30 mins to cent; gd."* **NOK 434**　　　　**2019**

OYSTESE *1A3* (2.4km SSW Coastal) *60.36828, 6.18969* **Hardanger Feriesenter,** Hardangerfjordvegen 341, 5600 Norheimsund **tel 92 05 09 55; booking@ hardangerferiesenter.no; www.hardanger-resort. com**

12 🎪 ♍️ 🛁 🔲 ∥ MP 🦋 ⊕ ♒︎

Directly at Rv7 in Kvam, app 2.5km E of Norheimsund on the shores of Hardangerfjord. Sm, unshd, pt sl, EHU (10A); bbq; cooking facs; 50% statics; Eng spkn; CKE. *"Boat hire & pier on site; vg."* **NOK 250** **2015**

PORSGRUNN *1C4* (5km SE Rural) *59.11183, 9.71208* **Camping Olavsberget,** Nystrandveien 64, 3944 Porsgrunn (Vestfold) **tel 35 51 12 05; irene@ olavsbergetcamping.no**

12 ♯♯ ♍️ 🛁 ♿ 🔲 ∥ ∥ ♒︎ ♒︎ sand adj

Leave E18 at Eidanger onto Rv354 N; foll camp sp for 1km; site on L. Fr Porsgrunn foll Rv36 S; just bef E18 junc turn L; foll sp as above. Med, unshd, pt sl, EHU (16A) NOK30 (no earth); 60% statics; Eng spkn; clsd 2300-0700; CKE. *"Well-run site; public access to beach thro site; gd walks in wood; visits to Maritime Brevik & mineral mine, Porsgrunn porcelain factory & shop, Telemark Canal inc boat tour."* **NOK 200** **2019**

RANDSVERK *1C2* (0.8km NE Rural) *61.73016, 9.08155* **Randsverk Camping,** Fjellvegen 1972 Randsverk (Oppland) **tel 61 23 87 45; randsverk. kiosk@c2i.net; www.randsverk-camping.no**

12 ♯♯ (htd) wc 🛁 🔲 ∥ MP 🦋 ♈︎ ⊕ 🔥 ⚠️

Heading S on Rv51, 20km fr junc with Rv15, site on L on ent vill of Randsverk. Med, hdstg, unshd, sl, terr, EHU (10A) inc (long lead poss req); bbq; cooking facs; twin axles; Eng spkn. *"V scenic rds; excel area for walking or driving excursions; excel san facs; vg site in area."* **NOK 270** **2015**

RISOR *1C4* (18km SW Coastal) *58.69083, 9.16333* **Sørlandet Feriecenter,** Sandnes, 4950 Risør **tel 37 15 40 80; sorferie@online.no; www.sorlandet-feriesenter.no**

12 🎪 ♯♯ (htd) wc 🛁 ♒︎ ♿ 🔲 ∥ 🦋 ♈︎ 🍽️ ⊕ 🔥 ⚠️ ♒︎ sand

Fr N take E18 to Sørlandsporten then Rv416 to Risør, then Rv411 to Laget. Foll sp Sørlandet. Fr S exit E18 at Tvedestrand & cont to Laget, then foll site sp. Site is 20km by rd fr Risør. 4*, Med, mkd, pt shd, EHU inc; cooking facs; TV (pitch); 10% statics; Eng spkn; adv bkg acc; bike hire; games rm; boat hire; tennis 1km; watersports. *"Fitness rm; private san facs avail."* **NOK 392** **2019**

RODBERG *1C3* (6.5km SE Rural) *60.23533, 9.0040* **Fjordgløtt Camping,** Vrenne, 3630 Rødberg (Buskerud) **tel 32 74 13 35 or 97 15 96 53 (mob); info@fjordglott. net; www.fjordglott.net**

12 ♯♯ (htd) wc 🛁 ♒︎ ♿ 🔲 ∥ 🦋 ♈︎ 🔥 ⚠️

Fr Rødberg on Rv40 dir Kongsberg, take R turn sp Vrenne, cross bdge & foll sp past power stn. 4*, Med, mkd, pt shd, terr, serviced pitches; EHU (16A) NOK30; sw; 40% statics; phone; Eng spkn; ccard acc; fishing; sauna; CKE. *"Lovely views of fjord; excel facs; well kept."* **NOK 268** **2019**

ROLDAL *1B3* (0.5km E Rural) *59.83103, 6.82888* **Røldal Hyttegrend & Camping,** Kyrkjevegen 49, 5760 Røldal (Hordaland) **tel 07 90 05 44 64; adm@ roldal-camping.no; www.roldal-camping.no**

12 🎪 ♯♯ (htd) wc 🛁 ♒︎ ♿ 🔲 ∥ 🦋 ♈︎ 🔥 ⚠️

Fr E on E134 turn L on ent vill, site sp. 4*, Sm, pt shd, EHU (10A) NOK30; gas; cooking facs; sw nr; TV; 20% statics; phone; Eng spkn; adv bkg acc; ccard acc; CKE. *"Gd walking, angling."* **NOK 206** **2019**

ROLDAL *1B3* (1km SW Rural) *59.83012, 6.81061* **Seim Camping,** 5760 Røldal (Horda-Rogaland) **tel 53 64 73 71 or 97 53 35 17 (mob) or 90 91 90 63 (mob); seim@seimcamp.no; www.seimcamp.no**

12 🎪 ♯♯ (htd) wc 🛁 ♒︎ ♿ 🔲 ∥ ♈︎ nr ⊕ nr 🔥 nr ⚠️

App fr SW on E134, site sp at ent town. Turn R off main rd & R again. 3*, Med, pt shd, pt sl, EHU (20A) NOK40; Eng spkn; boating; fishing; CKE. *"Gd walks; beautiful views; prehistoric burial mounds & museum on site; poss rd noise."* **NOK 258** **2019**

ROROS *1D1* (0.6km S Urban) *62.57078, 11.38295* **Idrettsparken Hotel & Camping,** Øra 25, 7374 Røros (Sør-Trøndelag) **tel 72 41 10 89; ihotell@online.no; www.idrettsparken.no**

♯♯ (htd) 🛁 ♒︎ ∥ 🦋 🔥 nr

Heading twd Trondheim on Rv30 to Røros cent, turn L at rndabt into Peter Møllersvei, over rlwy line, L again & foll sp to site. Sm, unshd, EHU (16A) NOK35. *"Tours of museums & mines; nature reserve & nature park nr; no chem disp - use dump point at fire stn on Rv30; fair NH."* **NOK 300, 1 May-30 Sep.** **2019**

RORVIK *2E3* (2km NE Coastal) *64.8729, 11.2609* **Nesset Camping,** Engan, 7900 Rørvik (Nord-Trøndelag) **tel 74 39 06 60**

♯♯ (htd) wc 🛁 ∥ 🦋

Fr cent of Rørvik on Rv770, foll sp to site. Med, hdstg, hdg, pt shd, pt sl, terr, EHU (10A); sw nr; 10% statics; Eng spkn. *"Many pitches with fjord view; facs stretched high ssn; beware of speed bumps on app rd."* **NOK 250, May-Sep.** **2019**

NORWAY

SARPSBORG *1C3* (10km NW Rural) *59.31800, 10.98049* **Utne Camping,** Desideriasvei 43, 1719 Greaker **tel** 47 69 14 71 26; post@utnecamping.no; www.utnecamping.no

12 🐩 ♦♦(htd) ᵂᴰ ⚐ 🖵 🗑 ✓ 🦋 ⦿ 🏧

Leave E6 at junc 9 sp Sollikrysset. Take 118 S (Desiderias vei), 2km to site on R. 3*, Sm, unshd, pt sl, EHU (10A) NOK60; bbq; twin axles; TV; bus adj; Eng spkn; adv bkg acc; ccard acc; games area; CKE. *"Conv acc fr E6; pleasant open site; excel."* **NOK 294   2017**

"Satellite navigation makes touring much easier"

Remember most sat navs don't know if you're towing or in a larger vehicle – always use yours alongside maps and site directions.

SKARNES *1D3* (10km SW Rural) *60.19910, 11.58054* **Sanngrund Camping,** Oslovegen 910, 2100 Skarnes (Hedmark) **tel** 62 96 46 60; booking@sanngrund.no; www.sanngrund.no

12 ♦♦(htd) ᵂᴰ ⚐ 🖵 🗑 ✓ ᴹˢᴾ ⦿ 🏧

Fr Skarnes foll Rv2 S; site sp on L. Sm, mkd, pt shd, EHU inc; bbq; cooking facs; sw nr; TV; 50% statics; Eng spkn; fishing adj; CKE. *"Conv NH to/fr Oslo (approx 70km); pleasant rest; fair site."* **NOK 235   2016**

SKARSVAG *2G1* (1km SW Coastal) *71.1073, 25.81238* **Kirkeporten Camping,** 9763 Skarsvåg (Finnmark) **tel** 90 96 06 48; kipo@kirkeporten.no; www.kirkeporten.no

♦♦(htd) ᵂᴰ ⚐ 🖵 🗑 ✓ ᴹˢᴾ 🦋 ⦿ 🏧

Foll E69 fr Honningsvåg for 20km to Skarsvåg junc; site sp at junc & on L after 2km immed bef vill. 3*, Sm, hdstg, unshd, pt sl, EHU (16A) NOK35; TV; Eng spkn; adv bkg acc; ccard acc; sauna; CKE. *"Site on edge sm fishing vill 10km fr N Cape, ringed by mountains; exposed location; claims to be world's most N site; helpful, knowledgeable owner; vg rest; clean facs but stretched if site full; poss reindeer on site; highly rec; arr early; camping area extended & modernised (2016)."* **NOK 247, 15 May-15 Sep.   2016**

SKIBOTN *2G1* (1km SE Rural) *69.38166, 20.29528* **Olderelv Camping (TR30),** 9048 Skibotn (Troms) **tel** 77 71 54 44 or 91 13 17 00 (mob); firmapost@olderelv.no; www.olderelv.no

♦♦(htd) ᵂᴰ ⚐ 🖵 🗑 ✓ ᴹˢᴾ 🦋 ⦿ 🏧

W of E6 1km N of junc at E8. 4*, Lge, mkd, hdstg, unshd, pt sl, EHU (16A) NOK40; bbq; cooking facs; twin axles; 80% statics; phone; Eng spkn; adv bkg acc; ccard acc; solarium; sauna. *"Well-maintained & clean; dryest area of Troms; vg walking; v busy; vg; car wash."* **NOK 290, 15 May-1 Sep.   2019**

SOGNDALSFJORA *1B2* (4.5km SE Coastal) *61.2118, 7.12106* **Camping Kjørnes,** 6856 Sogndal (Sogn og Fjordane) **tel** 57 67 45 80 or 975 44 156 (mob); camping@kjornes.no; www.kjornes.no

12 🐩 ♦♦(htd) ᵂᴰ ⚐ 🖵 🗑 ✓ ᴹˢᴾ ⦿ 🏧

Fr W foll sp in Sogndal for Kaupanger/Lærdal (Rv5) over bdge. Fr E (Rv55) turn L at T-junc with rd 5 over bdge. Site on R; sharp R turn into narr lane (passing places); site ent on R in approx 500m. 4*, Med, hdstg, unshd, pt sl, terr, EHU (10-16A) NOK40 (no earth); cooking facs; twin axles; red long stay; 20% statics; phone; bus 500m; Eng spkn; adv bkg acc; ccard acc; boat launch; fishing; CKE. *"Useful for ferries; stunning location on edge of fjord; superb san facs, the best!; excel site; v highly rec."* **NOK 290   2019**

STAVANGER *1A3* (3.5km SW Rural) *58.9525, 5.71388* **Mosvangen Camping,** Henrik Ibsens Gate, 4021 Stavanger (Rogaland) **tel** 51 53 29 71; info@mosvangencamping.no; www.mosvangencamping.no

🐩 ♦♦ ᵂᴰ ⚐ 🖵 🗑 ✓ 🦋 ⦿ 🏧

Fr Stavanger foll sp E39/Rv510; site well sp. Fr Sandnes on E39 exit Ullandhaug; foll camp sp. Med, hdstg, pt shd, sl, EHU (10A) NOK40 (no earth & poss intermittent supply); cooking facs; sw nr; phone; bus; Eng spkn; ccard acc; CKE. *"Excel for wooden city of Stavanger; easy, pleasant walk to town cent; soft grnd in wet weather; facs well used but clean but stretched when site full; helpful manager; excel rustic type of site; bus to cent nr ent."* **NOK 250, 1 Apr-1 Oct.   2016**

STEINKJER *2E3* (14km N Rural) *64.10977, 11.57816* **Follingstua Camping,** Haugåshalla 6, 7732 Steinkjer (Nord-Trøndelag) **tel** 74 14 71 90; post@follingstua.no; www.follingstua.com

12 🐩 ♦♦(htd) ᵂᴰ ⚐ 🖵 🗑 ✓ 🦋 ⦿ 🏧

N on E6, site on R, well sp. 3*, Sm, mkd, hdstg, unshd, terr, EHU (16A) NOK40; bbq; twin axles; TV; 60% statics; phone; bus 200m; Eng spkn; adv bkg acc; bike hire; boating; fishing. *"Excel san facs down 10 steps; lake adj; some lakeside pitches; nr Gold Rd tour of local craft & food producers; excel."* **NOK 292   2017**

STORJORD *2F2* (1km SSE Rural) *66.81317, 15.40055* **Saltdal Turistsenter,** 8255 Storjord (Nordland) **tel** 75 68 24 50; firmapost@saltdal-turistsenter.no; www.saltdal-turistsenter.no

12 ♦♦(htd) ᵂᴰ ⚐ 🖵 🗑 ✓ ᴹˢᴾ 🦋 ⦿ 🏧

Site is 35km S of Rognan by-pass on E6, 700m N of junc of Rv77, adj filling stn. Med, mkd, hdstg, pt shd, terr, EHU (10A) NOK25; bbq; cooking facs; 99% statics; phone; Eng spkn; adv bkg acc; CKE. *"M'way-style service stn & lorry park; tightly packed cabins & statics; 10 pitches only for tourers; excel rv walks fr site; beautiful area; NH only; secure barrier; clean facs, could be stretched if full."* **NOK 305   2019**

STRYN *1B2* (10km E Rural) *61.93347, 6.88640*
Mindresunde Camping (SF43), 6783 Stryn (Sogn og Fjordane) **tel 57 87 75 32 or 41 56 63 16 (mob); post@mindresunde.no; www.mindresunde.no**

👫♿(htd) 🅆 ⛺ ♨ ♿ 🗑 ∥ 🌳 ⏏shgl

2nd site on Rv15 on N side of rd. 3*, Sm, mkd, unshd, pt sl, EHU inc (earth prob); TV; Eng spkn; adv bkg acc; car wash; CKE. *"Well-kept, pleasant site; many pitches on lake; friendly staff; site yourself; vg views; excel facs; conv Geiranger, Briksdal glacier & Strynefjellet summer ski cent; gd walking."* **NOK 289, 1 May-31 Oct.**

2019

STRYN *1B2* (12km E Rural) *61.9314, 6.92121*
Strynsvatn Camping, Meland, 6783 Stryn (Sogn og Fjordane) **tel 57 87 75 43; camping@strynsvatn.no; www.strynsvatn.no**

👫♿(htd) 🅆 ⛺ ♿ 🗑 ∥ 🅼🅿 🦋 ⛽ 🏊 🌳

On Rv15 Lom to Stryn, on L. 4*, Sm, unshd, terr, EHU (10A) inc (poss earth fault); TV; 20% statics; Eng spkn; adv bkg acc; ccard acc; sauna; CKE. *"Superb site; lake adj; excel facs & v clean, gd views/walking; v friendly owners."* **NOK 247, 1 May-30 Sep.** **2016**

TANA *2H1* (5km SE Rural) *70.1663, 28.2279* **Tana Familiecamping,** Skiippagurra, 9845 Tana (Finnmark) **tel 78 92 86 30; tana@famcamp.net**

👫♿(htd) 🅆 ⛺ 🗑 ∥ 🅼🅿 🦋 ⓗ 🌳

On ent Tana fr W, cross bdge on E6, heading E sp Kirkenes; site on L in approx 4km. 3*, Sm, unshd, pt sl, EHU (16A); bbq; Eng spkn; ccard acc; sauna. **NOK 217, 20 May-1 Oct.** **2016**

TENNEVOLL *2F2* (5km SW Rural) *68.67881, 17.91421*
Lapphaugen Turiststasjon, General Fleischers Vei 365, 9357 Tennevoll **tel 77 17 71 27; postmaster@ lapphaugen.no; www.lapphaugen.no**

🐕 👫♿ 🅆 ⛺ ♨ ♿ 🗑 ∥ 🅼🅿 ⓗ 🌳

On the L of E6 approx 60km N of Narvik. Sm, hdstg, unshd, pt sl, terr, EHU (16A) NOK40; bbq; cooking facs; twin axles; red long stay; 50% statics; Eng spkn; adv bkg acc. *"Gd."* **NOK 200, 12 Feb-16 Dec.** **2017**

TINN AUSTBYGD *1B3* (8km S Rural) *59.98903, 8.81665* **Sandviken Camping (TE13),** 3650 Tinn Austbygd (Telemark) **tel 35 09 81 73; post@ sandviken-camping.no; www.sandviken-camping.no**

12 🐕 👫♿(htd) 🅆 ⛺ ♨ ♿ 🗑 ∥ 🅼🅿 🏊 🌳

Site is off Rv364 on L after passing thro Tinn Austbygd. 4*, Med, pt shd, EHU (10A) NOK35 (check earth); gas; bbq; cooking facs; sw; TV; 10% statics; phone; Eng spkn; games area; boat hire; sauna; games rm; CKE. *"Superb, peaceful location at head of Lake Tinnsjø; sh walk thro woods to shops & bank; conv for museum at Rjukan heavy water plant."* **NOK 245**

2016

TJOTTA *2E3* (26km N Rural) *65.94692, 12.46255*
Sandnessjøen Camping, Steiro, 8800 Sandnessjøen, Norge **tel 97 56 20 50 or 75 04 54 40; post@ssj.no; www.ssj.no**

🐕 👫♿(htd) 🅆 ⛺ ♿ 🗑 ∥

Head NW on Rv17 twrds Parkveien. Site is on R. Sm, unshd, pt sl, EHU; bbq; cooking facs; Eng spkn; ccard acc. *"Excel san facs; fjord views; gd hiking & fishing; excel site."* **NOK 250, 1 May-31 Aug.** **2019**

TREUNGEN *1B4* (18km N Rural) *59.15560, 8.50611*
Søftestad Camping, Nissedal, 3855 Treungen (Aust-Agder) **tel 41 92 76 20; www.facebook.com/Softestad**

👫♿ 🅆 ⛺ ♨ ♿ 🗑 ∥ 🦋 🌳

N fr Kristiansand on Rv41 to Treungen, then alongside E edge of Nisser Water to Nissedal, site sp. Sm, shd, EHU (10A) inc; bbq; red long stay; phone; bus adj; Eng spkn; adv bkg acc; CKE. *"Close to Telemarken heavy water plant; beautiful alt rte N fr Kristiansand - rd suitable for towed c'vans; gorgeous views over lake."* **NOK 162, 1 May-1 Sep.** **2019**

TROGSTAD *1D3* (6km N Rural) *59.68888, 11.29275*
Olberg Camping, Olberg, 1860 Trøgstad (Østfold) **tel 07 41 76 56 72**

👫♿(htd) 🅆 ⛺ ♨ ♿ 🗑 ∥ 🦋 ⓗ 🌳 ⛽ ⏏3km

Fr Mysen on E18 go N on Rv22 for approx 20km dir Lillestrøm. Site is 2km 2 of Båstad. 3*, Sm, hdg, pt shd, EHU (10-16A) NOK35; bbq; red long stay; TV; phone; Eng spkn; adv bkg acc; ccard acc; tennis 200m; fishing; CKE. *"Site on lge, working farm with elk safaris; local bread & crafts; farm museum; conv Oslo (40km); v helpful staff; ice-skating; gd for NH or longer."* **NOK 274, 1 May-1 Oct.** **2019**

TROMSO *2F1* (27km NE Coastal) *69.77765, 19.38273*
Skittenelv Camping, Ullstindveien 736, 9022 Krokelvdalen (Troms) **tel 46 85 80 00; post@ skittenelvcamping.no; www.skittenelvcamping.no**

🐕 👫♿(htd) 🅆 ⛺ ♿ 🗑 ∥ 🦋 ⓗ 🌳 ⛽ (htd) 🈴

Fr S end of Tromsø Bdge on E8, foll sps to Kroken & Oldervik. Site on N side of rd Fv53. 4*, Med, hdstg, unshd, EHU (10A) NOK50; bbq; TV; 10% statics; ccard acc; waterslide; fishing; sauna; games rm; CKE. *"Beautiful situation on edge of fjord; arctic sea birds; some facs dated but nice; location o'looking Fjord."* **NOK 320, 15 May-30 Sep.** **2019**

TROMSO *2F1* (5km E Rural) *69.64735, 19.01505*
Tromsø Camping, 9020 Tromsdalen (Troms) **tel 77 63 80 37; post@tromsocamping.no; www.tromso camping.no**

12 🐕 👫♿(htd) 🅆 ⛺ 🗑 ∥ 🅼🅿 ⓗ 🌳nr 🌳

At rndabt on edge of Tromsø take 2nd exit under E8 bdge. Shortly turn R & foll sp. Do not cross narr bdge but turn R then fork L to site. 3*, Sm, unshd, EHU (10-16A) NOK50; Eng spkn; CKE. *"V busy site; surrounded by fast rv after rain; poss mkt traders on site; rec visit to Arctic church at midnight; many improvements; excel san facs (2016)."* **NOK 356**

2016

For a guide to symbols see the fold out on the rear cover

TRONDHEIM *1C1* (14km W Rural) *63.45004, 10.20230*
Flakk Camping (ST19), 7070 Flakk (Sør-Trøndelag)
tel 07 94 05 46 85; contact@flakk-camping.no;
www.flakk-camping.no

🐕 ♦♦ WD ⚍ 🛇 🖮 ⬚ ∥ ☀ 🏊nr

**Fr N on E6 to Trondheim cent, then foll sp Fosen
onto Rv715 W; site sp & adj Flakk ferry terminal; fr S
to Trondheim take Rv707 to site & ferry.** 3*, Med,
unshd, pt sl, EHU (10A) NOK40 (check earth); bus to
city; Eng spkn; adv bkg acc; ccard acc; CKE. *"V well-
kept site; clean facs; pleasant view over fjord; parts
poss muddy after rain; site by ferry terminal (Need to
be on R), some ferry noise at night; helpful owner; no
earth on elec."* **NOK 361, 1 May-1 Sep.** **2019**

ULSVAG *2F2* (3km NE Coastal) *68.13273, 15.89699*
Sorkil Fjordcamping, Sorkil 8276 **tel 75 77 16 60 or
41 66 08 42 (mob);** kontakt@sorkil.no; www.sorkil.no

♦♦(htd) WD ⚍ ⬚ ∥ ☀ 🏊 🐕adj

**Head NE fr Ulsvag on E6, turn R in abt 2.7km onto
site.** Sm, mkd, unshd, pt sl, EHU (16A) NOK40; bbq;
Eng spkn. *"Lovely site S of ferry; adj Fjord excel for
midnight sun and fishing."* **1 May-30 Sep.** **2019**

UTVIKA *1C3* (0.5km N Rural) *60.02972, 10.26316*
Utvika Camping (BU14), Utstranda 263, 3531 Utvika
(Buskerud) **tel 32 16 06 70;** post@utvika.no;
www.utvika.no

♦♦ WD ⚍ 🛇 🖮 ⬚ ∥ ☀ ☀ 🏊 ⚏

**Site on loop rd fr E16 N of Nes twd Hønefoss. Site
sp but sp opp site ent v sm.** Med, mkd, hdstg, unshd,
pt sl, EHU (10A) NOK40; sw nr; twin axles; TV (pitch);
80% statics; Eng spkn; adv bkg acc; CKE. *"Conv Oslo
(40km) & better than Oslo city sites; busy, friendly site;
san facs inadequate when busy."*
NOK 289, 1 May-1 Oct. **2017**

VADSO *2H1* (18km W Coastal) *70.11935, 29.33155*
Vestre Jakobselv Camping, Lilledalsveien 6, 9801
Vestre Jakobselv (Finnmark) **tel 78 95 60 64;** post@
vj-camping.no; www.vj-camping.no

🔢 🐕 ♦♦ WD ⚍ ⬚ ∥ ☀ ☀ 🏊nr

**E fr Tana for approx 50km on E6/E75 dir Vadsø, site
sp, 1km N of Vestre Jakobselv.** Sm, hdstg, pt shd,
EHU (10A) NOK40; cooking facs; 10% statics; bus
1km; Eng spkn; ccard acc; CKE. *"Conv Vadsø & Vardø -
interesting towns."* **NOK 150** **2016**

VAGAMO *1C2* (1km S Rural) *61.86950, 9.10291*
Smedsmo Camping, Vågåvegen 80, 2680 Vågåmo
(Oppland) **tel 61 23 74 50;** smedsmo@online.no

🐕 ♦♦ WD ⚍ 🛇 🖮 ⬚ ∥ ☀ ⚏

Behind petrol stn on Rv15 twd Lom. 3*, Med, hdstg,
unshd, EHU (16A) NOK40; bbq; cooking facs; twin
axles; TV; 50% statics; Eng spkn; ccard acc; CKE.
"Gd touring base; site now sep fr g'ge; fair."
NOK 290, 1 May-30 Sep. **2017**

VALLE *1B3* (12km N Rural) *59.2441, 7.4753* **Flateland
Camping & Hyttesenter,** 4747 Valle (Aust-Agder)
tel 95 00 55 00; flateland.camping@broadpark.no;
www.flatelandcamping.no

🐕 ♦♦(htd) WD ⚍ ⬚ ∥ ☀ ☀ 🐾 🏊nr ⚏

**On W side of Rv9 to Bykle, 1km N of junc with Rv45
Dalen.** 2*, Med, pt shd, pt sl, EHU (10A) NOK30; bbq;
cooking facs; 20% statics; Eng spkn; ccard acc; boat
hire; CKE. *"Pleasant; site yourself; fee collected pm;
water trampolin; rvside walks; climbing; excel site."*
NOK 160, 1 Jun-1 Sep. **2019**

VANG *1B2* (1.7km NW Rural) *61.13032, 8.54352*
Bøflaten Camping, 2975 Vang I Valdres (Sogn og
Fjordane) **tel 61 36 74 20;** info@boflaten.com;
www.boflaten.com

🔢 🐕 ♦♦ WD ⚍ 🛇 🖮 ⬚ ∥ ☀ ☀ 🏊nr ⚏

Sp on E16 55km NW of Fagernes. 4*, Sm, pt shd,
EHU (10A) NOK40; bbq (charcoal, gas); cooking facs;
sw nr; twin axles; 10% statics; phone; Eng spkn;
ccard acc; games area; CKE. *"Beautiful area; lakeside;
useful NH & gd winter sports site; walks nrby; guided
excursions; boat, canoe, bike & TV hire; excel."*
NOK 237 **2016**

VANGSNES *1B2* (0km N Rural/Coastal) *61.17483,
6.63729* **Solvang Camping & Motel,** 6894 Vangsnes
(Sogn og Fjordane) **tel 57 69 66 20;** post@solvang
camping.com; www.solvangcamping.com

🔢 ♦♦ ⚍ 🛇 🖮 ∥ 🍽 ⬚ 🏊nr ⚏ ⚒

**Site at end of peninsula, on S side of Sognefjord on
Rv13, immed overlkg ferry terminal.** 4*, Sm, pt shd,
sl, EHU NOK30; sw; TV; boating; fishing. *"Wonderful
views; useful sh stay/NH for x-ing Sognefjord; some
noise fr ferries; delightful."* **NOK 185** **2016**

VANGSNES *1B2* (3km S Rural) *61.14515, 6.62330*
Tveit Camping (SF32), 6894 Vangsnes (Sogn og
Fjordane) **tel 57 69 66 00;** tveitca@online.no;
www.tveitcamping.no

🐕 ♦♦(htd) WD ⚍ 🛇 🖮 ⬚ ∥ ☀ ☀ ⏰nr 🏊nr ⚏

On Rv13; sp. 3*, Sm, pt shd, terr, EHU (10A) NOK25;
red long stay; TV; 30% statics; phone; boating; bike
hire; boat hire; CKE. *"Sw poss off rocky shore; views of
Sognefjord."* **NOK 192, 1 May-1 Oct.** **2016**

VASSENDEN *1A2* (2km SW Rural) *61.48785, 6.08366*
PlusCamp Jølstraholmen, 6847 Vassenden (Sogn og
Fjordane) **tel 57 72 88 79;** post@jolstraholmen.no;
www.jolstraholmen.no

🔢 🐕 ♦♦(htd) WD ⚍ 🛇 🖮 ⬚ ∥ ☀ ☀ ⏰ 🏊 ⚏ ⚒

**On R of E39, site is 2km SW of Vassenden at Statoil
petrol stn.** 4*, Med, hdg, pt shd, pt sl, terr, EHU (10-
16A) NOK40; bbq; sw; TV (pitch); 70% statics; Eng
spkn; ccard acc; fishing; CKE. *"Rv flows thro site; gd
facs; ski lift 500m; friendly site; ltd facs for tourers;
NH."* **NOK 286** **2016**

VEGA *2E3* (6km S Rural) *65.64353, 11.95110* **Vega Camping,** 8980 Vega **tel 47 94 35 00 80; post@ vegacamping.no; www.vegacamping.no**

12 🐎 ♥♥(htd) ᵂᴰ ♨ ℐ 🦋

Fr Fv90 head NW, take 1st L onto Fv90, turn L twd Fv84, turn R onto Fv84. After 1.6km turn L, then take 2nd L. Site in 450m. Sm, unshd, EHU (16A) inc; cooking facs; sw; Eng spkn. *"Island ideal for cycling/ walking; Elder Duck cent; beautiful location; cash only; excel site."* **NOK 250**   **2019**

VESTBY *1C3* (3km N Rural) *59.62620, 10.73126* **Vestby Gjestegard & Hyttepark,** Hytteveien 11, 1540 Vestby **tel 47 64 95 98 00; info@vestbyhytte park.co; www.vestbyhyttepark.no**

12 ♥♥♨ 🖵 ♨ ⚠

Junc 17 on E6. Foll sp. Site behind Esso stn on W of E6. Sm, hdstg, unshd, pt sl, 90% statics; Eng spkn; ccard acc; CKE. *"Limited touring space, mainly chalets; NH only."* **NOK 210**   **2016**

VIKØYRI *1B2* (0.2km N Rural) *61.08884, 6.57721* **Vik Camping,** 6891 Vikøyri (Sogn og Fjordane) **tel 57 69 51 25; grolilje@hotmail.com**

🐎 ♥♥(htd) ᵂᴰ ♨ ♿ 🖵 ℐ 🦋 ♈ 🗝nr

Sp in cent of Vikøyri dir Ligtvor; 67km N of Voss on Rv13. 2*, Sm, unshd, EHU (10A) (no earth); Eng spkn; CKE. *"Conv for ferry fr Vangsnes, easier access than other sites; gd NH."* **NOK 178, 1 May-30 Sep.**   **2016**

VOSS *1A2* (0.3km S Rural) *60.62476, 6.42235* **Voss Camping,** Prestegardsmoen 40, 5700 Voss (Hordaland) **tel 56 51 15 97; post@vosscamping.no; www.voss camping.no**

♥♥(htd) ᵂᴰ ♨ 🖵 ℐ 🗝nr ⚠ 🛷(htd)

Exit town on E16 & camping sp; by lake nr cent of Voss; app fr W on E16, site visible by lake on R; 2nd turn on R in town to site in 300m. Sm, mkd, hdstg, pt shd, terr, EHU (10A) NOK45; 10% statics; phone; Eng spkn; ccard acc; watersports; bike hire; boat hire; CKE. *"Excel cent for fjords; cable car stn in walking dist; tourist bureau; lake adj; most pitches hdstg gravel but narr/sm."* **NOK 408, 1 May-1 Oct.**   **2019**

LOFOTEN ISLANDS

RAMBERG *2E2* (7km W Rural) *68.0975, 13.1619* **Strand & Skærgårdscamping,** 8387 Fredvang **tel 76 09 42 33 or 76 09 46 46; mail@fredvang camping.no; www.fredvangcamp.no**

♥♥(htd) ♨ 🖵 ℐ ᴹˢᴾ 🦋 ♨ ♈ sand adj

Foll Fredvang sp fr E10; site sp in vill cent. Sm, unshd, EHU (16A) NOK25; cooking facs; TV (pitch); Eng spkn; boat launch; boat hire; washing machine NOK20; dryer NOK20; CKE. *"View of midnight sun; surrounded by sand beach, sea & mountains; peaceful; gd san facs, tired (unisex), stretched when busy; friendly."* **NOK 300, 20 May-31 Aug.**   **2019**

SORVAGEN *2E2* (3km N Coastal) *67.90017, 13.04656* **Moskenes Camping,** 8392 Sørvågen **tel 99 48 94 05; info@moskenescamping.no; www.moskenes camping.no**

♥♥(htd) ᵂᴰ 🖵 ℐ ᴹˢᴾ 🦋 ♈ ♈ 🍸 🗝nr

Fr ferry turn L, then immed R opp terminal exit, site up sh unmade rd, sp. Med, hdstg, unshd, terr, EHU (16A) NOK20 (no earth); Eng spkn. *"Excel NH; gd san facs."* **NOK 283, 1 May-15 Sep.**   **2018**

STAMSUND *2F2* (15km N Rural/Coastal) *68.20429, 13.88580* **Brustranda Sjøcamping,** Rolfsfjord, 8356 Leknes **tel 76 08 71 00; post@brustranda.no; www.brustranda.no**

🐎 ♥♥ ᵂᴰ 🖵 ℐ 🦋 ♨ ♈ shgl adj

Take E10 W fr Svolvaer ferry for approx 19km. After 3rd bdge turn L onto Rv815. Site on L in 22km. 4*, Sm, pt shd, EHU (10A) NOK50 (poss rev pol); 30% statics; Eng spkn; boat hire; fishing. *"Idyllic setting; mountain views; beach sand 2km; v helpful staff; san facs stretched when site full; highly rec."* **NOK 200, 1 Jun-31 Aug.**   **2018**

> ## "There aren't many sites open at this time of year"
>
> If you're travelling outside peak season remember to call ahead to check site opening dates – even if the entry says 'open all year'.

SVOLVAER *2F2* (15km W Coastal) *68.20573, 14.42576* **Sandvika Fjord & Sjøhuscamping (N09),** Ørsvågveien 45, 8310 Kabelvåg **tel 76 07 81 45; post@sandvika-camping.no; www.sandvika-camping.no**

♥♥ ᵂᴰ ♨ ♨ ♿ 🖵 ℐ ᴹˢᴾ 🦋 ♈ ⊕ ♨ 🗝 ⚠ 🛷

Sp on S of E10; app lane thro 1 other site. 4*, Lge, mkd, unshd, terr, EHU (16A) NOK35 (poss rev pol); TV; phone; bus nr; Eng spkn; ccard acc; fishing; sauna; bike hire; boating. *"Ideal for trip thro Lofoten Islands; conv Svolvær main fishing port; vg; beautiful views; helpful staff; currency exchange; san facs stretched in high ssn."* **NOK 330, 15 Apr-30 Sep.**   **2019**

SVOLVAER *2F2* (26km NW Coastal) *68.27619, 14.30207* **Rystad Lofoten Camping,** Brennaveien 235, 8313 Kleppstad **tel 47 91658954; kwes_8@ hotmail.com; www.rystadcamping.com**

♥♥ ᵂᴰ ♨ 🖵 ℐ ᴹˢᴾ 🦋 ♈

Foll E10 W out of Svolvaer. Just bef bdge to Grimsoya Island turn R, sp to Rystad. Site sp fr this junc, about 2km on L. Sm, pt sl, EHU; bbq; sw nr; Eng spkn; CKE. *"Gd for birdwatching; lovely sea views; gd for photographing midnight sun; vg site."* **NOK 220, 1 May-30 Sep.**   **2016**

RUNDE ISLAND

RUNDE *1A1* (4km NW Rural/Coastal) *62.40416,
5.62525* **Camping Goksøyr,** 6096 Runde (Møre og
Romsdal) **tel 70 08 59 05 or 924 12 298 (mob);**
camping@goksoyr.no; www.goksoeyr-camping.com
12 ⚭ ⬚ ♨ ⬚ ⬚ ✦ ⬚ ✖ ⬚ ⬚

Take causeway/bdge to Runde Island. Turn R off
bdge & foll rd round island, thro tunnel. Rd ends
1km after site. 3*, Sm, hdstg, unshd, EHU (16A)
NOK30; phone; Eng spkn; adv bkg acc; fishing; bike
hire; CKE. *"Excel birdwatching (inc puffins); site
on water's edge; boat trips avail; basic facs poss
inadequate when site full; owner helps with pitching;
vg."* **NOK 222** 2019

VESTERALEN ISLANDS

ANDENES *2F1* (21km SW Coastal) *69.20410,
15.84674* **Stave Camping & Hot Pools,** Stave 8489
Nordmela **tel 92 60 12 57; info@stavecamping.no;**
www.stavecamping.no
⚭ (htd) ⬚ ♨ ✦ ⬚ ⬚ adj

Head S on Storgata/Rv82 twds Stadionveien, cont
to foll Rv82, turn R onto Fv976, bear L onto
Laksebakkveien, cont onto Fv976; site on L.
Sm, unshd, EHU (16A) 40NOK; cooking facs; Eng spkn;
ccard acc. *"Excel for midnight sun, hot tubs 250NOK
pn."* **NOK 268, 17 May-1 Sep.** 2019

ANDENES *2F1* (9.6km SW Coastal) *69.27552,
15.96372* **Midnattsol Camping,** Gardsveien 8, 8481
Bleik **tel 47 47 84 32 19; midnattsol.camping@
gmail.com; www.midnattsolcamping.com**
12 ♘ ⚭ ⬚ ♨ ⬚ ⬚ ✦ ⬚ ✖ ⬚ ⬚ ⬚ sand

Take Rte 82 S. Then turn R onto Rte 976 sp Bleik.
Site at side of Rte 976 just bef Bleik. Med, mkd,
unshd, terr, EHU 16A (NOK50); bbq; cooking facs;
TV; Eng spkn; adv bkg acc; recep open 0930-1200;
CKE. *"Sea adj; walks; birdwatching; conv for puffin &
whale safaris & fishing boat trips; golf & sports grnd
adj; lovely site; sea views; friendly owner; lovely setting
bet mountain & sea; easy walk to vill shop; excel."*
NOK 235 2019

GULLESFJORDBOTN *2F2* (1km NW Coastal) *68.53213,
15.72611* **Gullesfjordbotn Camping,** Våtvoll, 8409
Gullesfjordbotn **tel 47 91 59 75 50; post@
gullesfjordcamping.no; www.gullesfjordcamping.no**
⚭ (htd) ⬚ ♨ ⬚ ✦ ⬚ ⬚ ⬚ shgl adj

Fr S on E10 then rd 85. At rndabt just bef
Gullesfjordbotn take 2nd exit sp Sortland rd 85.
Site on R 1km, well sp. 3*, Sm, hdstg, unshd, EHU
(16A, poss rev pol) NOK50; cooking facs; phone; Eng
spkn; ccard acc; fishing; boat hire; sauna; CKE. *"On
edge of fjord; liable to flood after heavy rain; mountain
views; gd san facs; friendly owners."*
NOK 256, 15 May-15 Sep. 2018

HARSTAD *2F2* (5km S Coastal) *68.77231, 16.57878*
Harstad Camping, Nessevegen 55, 9411 Harstad
tel 77 07 36 62; postmaster@harstad-camping.no;
www.harstad-camping.no
12 ⚭ ⬚ ♨ ⬚ ⬚ ✦ ⬚ ⬚ nr ✖ ⬚

Sp fr E10/Rv83. 3*, Med, unshd, pt sl, EHU (16A)
NOK50; ccard acc; fishing; boating; CKE. *"San facs
poss stretched high ssn; lovely situation."*
NOK 315 2019

RISØYHAMN *2F1* (13km S Coastal) *68.88408, 15.60304*
Andøy Friluftssenter & Camping, Buksnesfjord, 8484
Risøyhamn **tel 76 14 88 04; firmapost@andoy-
friluftssenter.no; www.andoy-friluftssenter.no**
12 ⚭ (htd) ⬚ ♨ ⬚ ⬚ ✦ ⬚ ⬚ ⬚ ⬚

Exit E10 onto Rv82 sp Sortland; in 31km at bdge
to Sortland do not cross bdge but cont N on Rv82
sp Andenes. Site on R in 38km at Buknesfjord.
Sm, hdstg, unshd, pt sl, EHU (10A) NOK50; sw;
50% statics; Eng spkn; adv bkg acc; ccard acc; fishing;
CKE. *"Lake fishing; guided mountain walks; easy access
for whale-watching; v clean facs; gourmet meals."*
NOK 250 2016

SORTLAND *2F2* (2km NW Rural) *68.70286, 15.3919*
Camping Sortland & Motel, Vesterveien 51, 8400
Sortland **tel 76 11 03 00; hj.bergseng@sortland-
camping.no; www.sortland-camping.no**
12 ⚭ ⬚ ♨ ⬚ ⬚ ✦ ⬚ ✖ ⬚ ⬚ ⬚

Exit E10 onto Rv82/85 sp Sortland; in 31km turn L
over bdge to Sortland, L again at end bdge. Site sp
in approx 1km immed past church. Foll rd uphill for
1km, site on R. 4*, Med, hdstg, pt shd, EHU (16A) (no
earth) NOK30; gas; cooking facs; TV; phone; Eng spkn;
ccard acc; fishing; cycling; gym; solarium; boating;
CKE. *"Basic, clean site; v helpful staff; gd base to tour
islands; walking; skiing; facs stretched when full; red
facs LS."* **NOK 250** 2019

STO *2F1* (0.7km W Coastal) *69.01922, 15.10894*
Stø Bobilcamp, 8438 Stø **tel 97 63 36 48;**
stobobilcamp@gmail.com; www.stobobilcamp.no
⚭ (htd) ⬚ ♨ ⬚ ✦ ⬚ ⬚ ✖ ⬚

Site sp fr cent of Stø. Sm, hdstg, unshd, EHU (16A)
NOK30; cooking facs; 10% statics; Eng spkn; fishing;
bike hire. *"View of midnight sun; 10min walk to whale
boat safari; coastal walks, Queen Sonja's walk fr site,
v scenic but poss strenuous; facs stretched high ssn;
site open to public for parking."*
NOK 130, 1 May-10 Sep. 2016

NORWAY

Map 1

Map 2

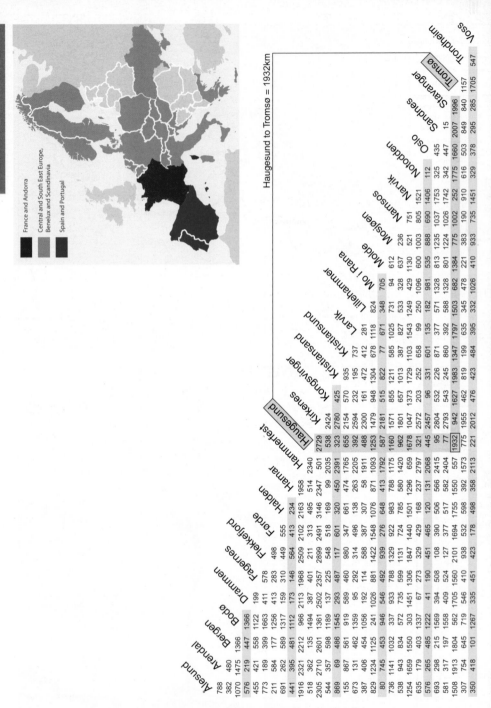

France and Andorra

Central and South East Europe,
Benelux and Scandinavia

Spain and Portugal

Haugesund to Tromsø = 1932km

Voss
Trondheim
Tromsø
Stavanger
Sandnes
Oslo
Notodden
Narvik
Namsos
Mosjøen
Molde
Mo i Rana
Lillehammer
Larvik
Kristiansund
Kristiansand
Kongsvinger
Kirkenes
Haugesund
Hammerfest
Hamar
Halden
Førde
Flekkefjord
Fagernes
Drammen
Bodø
Bergen
Arendal
Ålesund

Poland

Market Square, Wroclaw

Highlights

Poland is a country with a deep sense of history, cultural identity and resilience that has been built over thousands of years. The historic and beautiful centre of Kraków is a must see, while the engaging and fascinating museums of Warsaw are also a fantastic experience.

For those looking for relaxation, the Polish countryside is peaceful and unspoilt. There are many hiking trails scattered around the country taking you alongside rivers, through thick forests and around mountains.

Amber, sometimes called the gold of the Baltic, has been crafted in Poland for centuries. Amber products are still produced and sold with the best place to shop being Cloth Hall in the heart of Kraków.

Poland has been producing vodka since the early Middle Ages, and is the birthplace of this spirit. The vodka distilled in Poland is considered some of the finest in the world and vodka tasting events are held around the country.

Major towns and cities

- Warsaw – Poland's capital and the largest city in the country.
- Kraków – a charming and beautiful place that has retained its historic feel.
- Łódź – the high street is one of the longest in the world.
- Wrocław – a city with plenty of landmarks and wonderful buildings.

Attractions

- Main Square, Kraków – a bustling, medieval market square filled with historic buildings and monuments.
- Białowiⱬea Forest – the remains of a primeval forest, home to European bison, ancient oaks and a magical beauty.
- Wieliczka Salt Mine – discover a fascinating mix of history, art and industry in one of Poland's oldest salt mines.

Find out more

www.poland.travel
E: pot@pot.gov.pl T: 0048 (0) 22 53 67 070

Country Information

Population (approx): 38.3 million

Capital: Warsaw

Area: 312,685 sq km

Bordered by: Belarus, Czech Republic, Germany, Lithuania, Russia, Slovakia, Ukraine

Terrain: Mostly flat plain with many lakes; mountains along southern border

Climate: Changeable continental climate with cold, often severe winters and hot summers; rainfall spread throughout the year; late spring and early autumn are the best times to visit

Coastline: 440km

Highest Point: Rysy 2,499m

Language: Polish

Local Time: GMT or BST + 1, i.e. 1 hour ahead of the UK all year

Currency: Zloty (PLN) divided into 100 groszy; £1 = PLN 4.97; PLN10 = £2.01 (October 2018)

Emergency numbers: Police 997; Fire brigade 998; Ambulance 999. Call 112 for any service.

Public Holidays 2020: Jan 1, 6; Apr 12, 13; May 1, 3 (Constitution Day); Jun 11; Aug 15; Nov 1, 11 (Independence Day); Dec 25, 26.

School summer holidays run from the last week of June to the end of August.

Border Posts

Customs posts are open 24 hours a day throughout the year. Cars crossing the eastern borders, especially to Lithuania and Belarus, are usually intensively scrutinised by the Polish authorities in an effort to combat widespread smuggling of stolen cars. Travellers should ensure all documents are in order.

Borders may be busy at weekends with cross border shoppers, and in particular the crossing from Germany via Frankfurt-on-Oder can be heavily congested on Saturday mornings.

Entry Formalities

British and Irish passport holders may visit Poland for up to three months without a visa. At campsites reception staff should look after any required registration with local authorities.

Medical Services

For simple complaints and basic advice visit a pharmacy (apteka). In general, medical facilities are comparatively inexpensive and of a good standard. Medical staff are well qualified. English is not always widely spoken so you may face language difficulties.

You will need a European Health Insurance Card (EHIC) to obtain emergency treatment from doctors, dentists and hospitals contracted to the state health care system, the NFZ. Reimbursements for any charges that you incur can be claimed from the NFZ office in Warsaw. You will have to pay a proportion of the cost of prescriptions, which is not refundable in Poland.

Private health clinics, found in large cities, offer a good standard of medical care.

Opening Hours

Banks: Mon-Fri 9am-4pm; Sat 9am-1pm.

Museums:Tue-Sun 10am-5pm; closed Mon.

Post Offices: Mon-Fri 8am-6pm; Sat 8am-2pm (on rota basis).

Shops: Mon-Fri 11am-8pm; Sat 9am-2pm/4pm; food shops open and close earlier; supermarkets open until 9pm/10pm.

Safety and Security

Most visits to Poland are trouble free and violent crime is rare, but there is a risk of robbery in tourist areas, particularly near hotels, at main railway stations and on public transport. Passengers are most at risk when boarding and leaving trains or trams. Avoid walking alone at night, particularly in dark or poorly-lit streets or in public parks.

Some tourists have been the target of a scam in which men claiming to be plain clothes police officers ask visitors to show their identity documents and bank cards, and then ask for their PIN(s).

Theft of and from vehicles is common so do not leave vehicle documentation or valuables in your car. Foreign registered cars may be targeted, especially in large, busy supermarket car parks.

Cases have been reported of vehicles with foreign number plates being stopped by gangs posing as police officers, either claiming a routine traffic control or at the scene of fake accidents, particularly in rural and tourist areas. If in doubt, when flagged down keep all doors and windows locked, remain in your vehicle and ask to see identification. The motoring organisation, PZM, advises that any car or document inspection performed outside built-up areas can only be carried out by uniformed police officers and at night these officials must use a police patrol car. Although police officers do not have to be in uniform within built-up areas, they must always present their police identity card. More details are available to motorists at Polish road borders.

An emergency helpline has been set up to assist visitors who have been victims of crime or who require assistance tel: 0800 200300 (freephone) or +48 608 599999 (mobile number). The helpline operates from 1 June to 30 September between 10am and 10pm.

Do not leave drinks or food unattended or accept drinks from strangers. There has been a small number of reports of drinks being spiked and of visitors having their valuables stolen whilst drugged.

British Embassy

UL KAWALERII 12
00-468 WARSZAWA
Tel: (022) 3110000
www.ukinpoland.fco.gov.uk

Irish Embassy

UL MYSIA 5, 00-496 WARSZAWA
Tel: (022) 5642200
www.embassyofireland.pl.

Documents

Driving Licence

The standard pink UK paper driving licence is recognised, but if you hold the old style green UK licence or a Northern Irish licence you are advised to update it to a photocard licence in order to avoid any local difficulties.

Passport

You should carry your passport with you at all times.

Vehicle(s)

You must carry your original vehicle registration certificate (V5C), insurance documentation and MOT certificate (if applicable) at all times. You may be asked for these if you are stopped by the police and, in particular, when crossing borders. If you do not own the vehicle(s) you will need a letter of authority from the owner, together with the vehicle's original documentation.

Money

Cash can easily be obtained from ATMs in banks and shopping centres. ATMs offer an English option.

Major credit cards are widely accepted in hotels, restaurants and shops but you may find that supermarkets do not accept them. Take particular care with credit/debit cards and don't lose sight of them during transactions.

Sterling and euros are readily accepted at exchange bureaux but Scottish and Northern Irish bank notes are not generally recognised and you may have difficulties trying to exchange them.

Carry your credit card issuers'/banks' 24-hour UK contact numbers in case of loss or theft of your cards.

Driving

Poland is a major route for heavy vehicles travelling between eastern and western Europe and driving can be hazardous. There are few dual carriageways and even main roads between large towns can be narrow and poorly surfaced. Slow moving agricultural and horse-drawn vehicles are common in rural areas. Street lighting is weak even in major cities.

Local driving standards are poor and speed limits, traffic lights and road signs are often ignored. Drivers rarely indicate before manoeuvring and you may encounter aggressive tailgating, overtaking on blind bends and overtaking on the inside. Take particular care on national holiday weekends when there is a surge in road accidents.

It isn't advisable to drive a right hand drive vehicle alone for long distances or to drive long distances at night.

At dusk watch out for cyclists riding without lights along the edge of the road or on its shoulder.

Hitchhikers use an up and down motion of the hand to ask for a lift. This may be confused with flagging down.

Accidents

Drivers involved in accidents must call the police, obtain an official record of damages and forward it to the insurance company of the Polish driver involved (if applicable). Members of AIT/FIA affiliated clubs, such as The Caravan and Motorhome Club, can obtain help from the touring office ('Autotour') of the Polish motoring organisation, Polski Zwiazek Motorowy (PZM), tel: (022) 8496904 or (022) 8499361.

If people are injured, you must call an ambulance or doctor. By law, it is an offence for a driver not to obtain first aid for accident victims or to leave the scene of an accident. In such circumstances the authorities may withdraw a tourist's passport and driving licence, vehicle registration certificate or even the vehicle itself and the penalties can be a prison sentence and a fine.

Alcohol

The permitted level of alcohol is 20 milligrams in 100 millilitres of blood, which in practice equates to zero. At the request of the police or if an accident has occurred a driver must undergo a blood test which, if positive, may lead to a prison sentence, withdrawal of driving licence and a fine. Penalty points will be notified to the authorities in the motorist's home country.

Breakdown Service

The toll free telephone number for breakdown assistance throughout the country is 981.

The PZM runs a breakdown service covering the entire country 24 hours a day. Members of AIT and FIA affiliated clubs, such as The Caravan and Motorhome Club, should call the PZM Emergency Centre on (022) 5328433. Staff speak English. Roadside assistance must be paid for in cash.

Child Restraint System

Children under the age of 12 years old and under the height of 1.5m must use a suitable restraint system that has been adapted to their size. It is prohibited to place a child in a rear facing seat in the front of the vehicle if the car is equipped with airbags.

Fuel

The usual opening hours for petrol stations are from 8am to 7pm; many on main roads and international routes and in large towns are open 24 hours. Credit cards are widely accepted. LPG (Autogas) is widely available from service stations.

Motorways and Tolls

There are approximately 3000km of motorways in Poland. Tolls are levied on sections and vary in price, for example, the A1 Rusocin to Nowe Marzy is PLN 41.80 (2015 prices) for a car towing a caravan weighing under 3500kg.

An electronic toll system is in place for vehicles which weigh over 3,500kg, including motorhomes and car and caravan combinations if the total weight is over 3,500kg. These vehicles will need to be equipped with an electronic device called a viaBOX. Visit www.viatoll.pl/en and select the 'Trucks' option for details of toll costs for motorhomes and car/caravan combinations weighing over 3500kg.

An electronic option is also available for vehicles and car/caravan combinations which weigh under 3500kg - go to the above website and choose the 'Cars' options for details.

There are emergency telephones every 2km along motorways. Recent visitors report that newer stretches of motorway have rest areas with chemical disposal and waste water disposal facilities.

Parking

There are parking meters in many towns and signs display parking restrictions or prohibitions. There are many supervised car parks charging an hourly rate. Illegally parked cars causing an obstruction may be towed away and impounded, in which case the driver will be fined. Wheel clamps are in use.

Sidelights must be used when parking in unlit streets during the hours of darkness.

Priority

Priority should be given to traffic coming from the right at intersections of roads of equal importance, however vehicles on rails always have priority. At roundabouts traffic already on a roundabout has priority.

Give way to buses pulling out from bus stops. Trams have priority over other vehicles at all times. Where there is no central reservation or island you should stop to allow passengers alighting from trams to cross to the pavement.

Roads

All roads are hard surfaced and the majority of them are asphalted. However, actual road surfaces may be poor; even some major roads are constructed of cement or cobbles and heavily rutted. Average journey speed is about 50 km/h (31 mph).

Some roads, notably those running into Warsaw, have a two metre wide strip on the nearside to pull onto in order to allow other vehicles to overtake. Oncoming lorries expect other motorists to pull over when they are overtaking.

Overtake trams on the right unless in a one-way street.

Road Signs and Markings

Road signs and markings conform to international standards. Motorway and national road numbers are indicated in red and white, and local roads by yellow signs with black numbering. Signs on motorways are blue with white lettering and on main roads they are green and white.

The following road signs may be seen:

Polish	English Translation
Rondzie	Roundabout
Wstep szbroniony	No Entry
Wyjscie	Exit

You may also encounter the following:

Paid parking between 7am and 6pm

Residential area-predestrians have priority

Toll road

Rutted road

Winding road

Emergency vehicles

Crossroads and road junctions may not be marked with white 'stop' lines, and other road markings in general may be well worn and all but invisible, so always take extra care.

Speed Limits

	Open Road (km/h)	Motorway (km/h)
Car Solo	90	140
Car towing caravan/trailer	70	80
Motorhome under 3500kg	90	140
Motorhome 3500-7500kg	70	80

In built up areas the speed limit is 50 km/h (31 mph) between 5am and 11pm, and 60 km/h (37 mph) between 11pm and 5am.

For vehicles over 3,500kg all speed limits are the same as for a car and caravan outfit. In residential zones indicated by entry/exit signs, the maximum speed is 20 km/h (13 mph). The use of radar detectors is illegal.

Traffic Lights

Look out for a small, non-illuminated green arrow under traffic lights, which permits a right turn against a red traffic light if the junction is clear.

Violation of Traffic Regulations

Motorists must not cross a road's solid central white line or even allow wheels to run on it. Radar speed traps are frequently in place on blind corners where speed restrictions apply. Police are very keen to enforce traffic regulations with verbal warnings and/or on the spot fines. Fines are heavy and drivers of foreign registered vehicles will be required to pay in cash. Always obtain an official receipt.

Touring

The national drinks of Poland include varieties of vodka and plum brandy. When dining and drinking in restaurants it is usual to leave a tip of between 10 to 15%.

There are over 9,000 lakes in Poland, mostly in the north. The regions of Western Pomerania, Kaszubia and Mazuria are a paradise for sailing enthusiasts, anglers and nature lovers. In order to protect areas of natural beauty, national parks and nature reserves have been created, two of the most interesting of which are the Tatra National Park covering the whole of the Polish Tatra mountains, and the Slowinksi National Park with its 'shifting' sand dunes.

There are 14 UNESCO World Heritage sites including the restored historic centres of Warsaw and Kraków, the medieval, walled town of Toruń and Auschwitz Concentration Camp. Other towns worth a visit are Chopin's birthplace at Zelazowa Wola, Wieliczka with its salt mines where statues and a chapel are carved out of salt, and Wrocław.

White and brown signs in cities and near sites of interest indicate architectural and natural landmarks, places of religious worship, etc. Each sign includes not only information on the name of and distance to a particular attraction, but also a pictogram of the attraction, e.g. Jasna Góra monastery. Themed routes, such as the trail of the wooden churches in the Małopolska Region (south of Kraków), are marked in a similar way.

A Warsaw Tourist Card and a Kraków Tourist Card are available, both valid for up to three days and offering free travel on public transport and free entry to many museums, together with discounts at selected restaurants and shops and on sightseeing and local excursions. Buy the cards from tourist information centres, travel agents or hotels.

The Polish people are generally friendly, helpful and polite. English is becoming increasingly widely spoken in major cities.

Camping and Caravanning

There are around 250 organised campsites throughout Poland, with the most attractive areas being the Mazurian lake district and along the coast. Campsites are usually open from the beginning of May or June to the middle or end of September, but the season only really starts towards the end of June. Until then facilities may be very limited and grass may not be cut, etc.

You can download details of approximately 160 sites (including GPS co-ordinates) from the website of the Polish Federation of Camping & Caravanning, www.pfcc.eu.

Campsites are classified from one to four stars. Category one sites provide larger pitches and better amenities, but it may still be advisable to use your own facilities. There are also some basic sites which are not supervised and are equipped only with drinking water, toilets and washing facilities. Sites may be in need of modernisation but, on the whole, sanitary facilities are clean although they may provide little privacy. Some new sites are being built to higher standards. A site may close earlier than its published date if the weather is bad.

Many sites are not signposted from main roads and may be difficult to find. It is advisable to obtain a large scale atlas or good maps of the areas to be visited and not rely on one map covering the whole of Poland.

Casual/wild camping is not recommended and is prohibited in national parks (except on organised sites) and in sand dunes along the coast.

Cycling

There are several long-distance cycle routes using a combination of roads with light motor traffic, forest trails or tracks along waterways. There are some cycle lanes on main roads where cyclists must ride in single file.

Electricity and Gas

The current on most campsites is 10 amps. Plugs have two round pins. There are some CEE connections.

It is understood that both propane and butane supplies are widely available, but cylinders are not exchangeable and it may be necessary to refill. The Caravan and Motorhome Club does not recommend this practice and you should aim to take enough gas to last during your stay. Some campsites have kitchens which you may use to conserve your gas supplies.

Public Transport & Local Travel

For security reasons recent visitors recommend using guarded car parks such as those in Warsaw on the embankment below the Old Town, in the Palace of Culture and near the Tomb of the Unknown Soldier.

Use only taxis from official ranks whose vehicles have the name and telephone number of the taxi company on the door and on the roof (beside the occupied/unoccupied light). They also display a rate card in the window of the vehicle. Taxis with a crest but no company name are not officially registered.

There are frequent ferries from Gydnia, Swinoujscie and Gdansk to Denmark, Germany and Sweden. Passenger services operate along the Baltic Coast, on the Mazurian lakes and on some rivers, for example, between Warsaw and Gdansk.

There is a metro system in Warsaw. It is possible to buy a daily or weekly tourist pass which is valid for all means of public transport – bus, tram and metro. Buy tickets at newspaper stands and kiosks displaying a sign 'bilety'. Tickets must be punched before travelling at the yellow machines at the entrance to metro stations or on board buses and trams. You will incur an on the spot fine if you are caught travelling without a valid ticket.

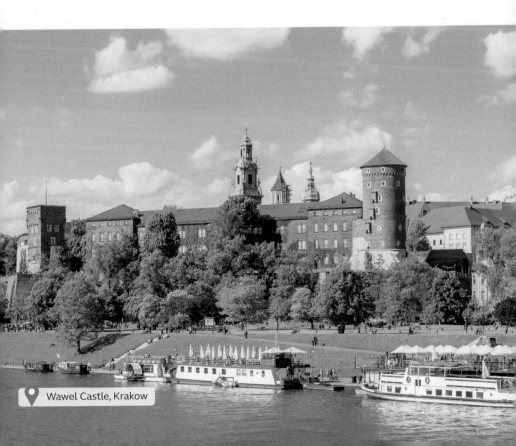

Wawel Castle, Krakow

BIALOWIEZA *B4* (3km W Rural) *52.69395, 23.83088*
Camping U Michała (No. 124), ul Krzyże 11, 17-230
Białowieża **(085) 6812703; info@bialowieza-forest.
com; http://bialowieza-forest.com/miejsce/camping-
u-michala-bialowieza**

🏕 ⌷ᵂᴰ 🏛 ☖ 🖵 ⫽ 🦋 ⚘

Exit Bielsk Podlaski onto rd 689; cont past Hajnówka
for 17m; site on R at end of vill. Sm, mkd, pt shd, EHU
(16A); bike hire. *"Gd san facs."*
PLN 50, 15 Apr-30 Sep. 2016

CZESTOCHOWA *C3* (4km W Urban) *50.81122,
19.09131* **Camping Oleńka (No. 76),** ul Oleńki 10,
42-200 Częstochowa **(034) 3606066; camping@
mosir.pl; www.mosir.pl**

🐕 🏕 ⌷ᵂᴰ 🏛 ☖ 🖵 ⫽ 🦋 ♈ 🍴 Ⓖ 🏧ⁿʳ ⚘

Fr A1/E75 foll sp Jasna Góra monastery, pick up sm
white camping sp to site. Lge, pt shd, EHU (20A);
TV; 20% statics; phone; Eng spkn; ccard acc; CKE.
*"Guided tours; monastery worth visit; gd NH/sh stay
nr Jasna Góra & Black Madonna painting; poor security;
san facs unclean & poorly maintained."*
PLN 58, 1 May-15 Oct. 2016

ELK *A3* (3km SW Urban) *53.81545, 22.35215*
Camping Plaża Miejska (No. 62), ul Parkowa 2,
19-300 Ełk **(087) 6109700; mosir@elk.com.pl;
http://mosir.elk.pl/plaza-miejska/camping/**

🏕 (htd) 🏛 ☖ ⫽ 🦋 ♈ 🏧 🏧ⁿʳ

Fr town cent on rd 16 take rd 65/669 dir Białystok.
After 200m cross rv & immed turn R, site 100m on L.
3*, Sm, mkd, hdstg, pt shd, EHU (10A) inc; cooking
facs; sw nr; CKE. *"Gd security; well-maintained, clean
site adj town cent & attractive lake; gd touring base
lake district."* **PLN 65, 1 Jun-1 Sep.** 2016

JELENIA GORA *C2* (2km SE Urban) *50.89638,
15.74266* **Auto-Camping Park (No. 130),** ul Sudecka
42, 58-500 Jelenia Góra **(075) 7524525; camping
park@interia.pl; www.camping.karkonosz.pl**

⑫ 🐕 PLN5 🏕 🏛 ☖ ⫽ 🦋 ♈ Ⓖ 🏧ⁿʳ

In town foll sp to Karpacz on rd 367. Site 100m fr
hotel. Well sp. Med, hdstg, pt shd, terr, EHU (6-10A)
PLN10 (poss rev pol); TV; 20% statics; adv bkg acc;
ccard acc; tennis 500m; CKE. *"Conv Karkanosze
mountains & Czech border; well-run, clean, neat site
nr hotel with gd, modern facs; 20 min walk to pleasant
town; pool 500m; sports facs 500m; staff friendly,
helpful & obliging; conv NH; gd facs."* **PLN 53** 2015

KATOWICE *D3* (4km SE Rural) *50.24355, 19.04795*
Camping Dolina Trzech Statow (No. 215), ul Trzech
Stawow 23, 40-291 Katowice **(032) 2565939 or (032)
2555388; camping@mosir.katowice.pl; camping.
mosir.katowice.pl**

🐕 PLN5 🏕 (htd) 🏛 ☖ ⫽ 🦋 ♈ Ⓖ 🏧 🏧ⁿʳ ⚘

Exit A4 at junc Murckowska & foll sp on rd 86
Sosnowiec. In 500m turn R & foll site sp. Med, shd, pt
sl, EHU (16A) PLN2.50/kwh; cooking facs; Eng spkn;
adv bkg acc; ccard acc; tennis; CKE. *"V clean facs but
basic & little privacy; vg."* **PLN 45, 1 May-30 Sep.** 2016

KAZIMIERZ DOLNY *C3* (2km N Rural) *51.33106,
21.95879* **Campsite Pielak,** Pulawska 82, 24-120
Kazimierz Dolny (Lubelskie) **(069) 1047409**

🐕 🏕 ⌷ᵂᴰ 🏛 ☖ 🖵 ⫽ 🦋 ♈ 🌲 50m

Site sp on the S824 300m N of the town. Sm, pt shd,
pt sl, EHU (16A); bbq; cooking facs; twin axles; bus adj;
Eng spkn; kayaking; CCI. *"V friendly owners, warm
welcome; pool 50m; walking dist to town; close to rv;
open grassy site; historic town; excel."*
PLN 72, 1 May-30 Oct. 2016

"There aren't many sites open at this time of year"

If you're travelling outside peak season
remember to call ahead to check site opening
dates – even if the entry says 'open all year'.

KLODZKO *D2* (13km W Urban) *50.41502, 16.51335*
Camping Polanica-Zdroj (No. 169), ul Sportowa 7,
57-320 Polanica-Zdrój **(074) 8681210; osir.polanica@
neostrada.pl; www.osir.polanica.net/pl**

⑫ 🐕 PLN5 🏕 (htd) 🏛 ⫽ 🦋 Ⓖ 🏧

Foll sp fr rd 8/E67. Site is 1km N of Polanica-Zdrój.
Med, pt shd, EHU (6A) PLN9.50; Eng spkn; ccard acc;
tennis; CKE. *"Well-run site; clean san facs; helpful
warden; many statics adj; easy walk to pleasant spa
town - many rests/cafés; wifi free in recep."*
PLN 69.3 2019

KRAKOW *D3* (5km N Urban) *50.09454, 19.94127*
Camping Clepardia (No. 103), ul Pachońskiego 28A,
31-223 Kraków **(012) 4159672; clepardia@gmail.
com; www.clepardia.com.pl**

🐕 ♟ [wo] ♨ 🖥 ⁄ 🍴 ⑪ nr 🔦 nr

Fr Kraków cent take rd 7/E77 N twds Warsaw for
3km. Turn L onto rd 79 'Opolska' & foll sp 'Domki
Kempingowe - Bungalows'. Fr A4/E40 exit onto
E462 then S on rd 79 'Pasternik' thro to 'J Conrada
& foll sp. Site is nr lge Elea supmkt & Clepardia
Basen (sw pools).** Med, mkd, pt shd, EHU (6A) PLN12;
phone; bus 250m; Eng spkn; CKE. *"Busy site with
tightly packed pitches - rec arr bef 1700 high ssn to
secure pitch; excel, clean, modern san facs; ltd EHU
if site full; muddy in wet weather; dogs free; pool adj;
friendly, helpful staff; gd security; well maintained."*
PLN 94, 15 Apr-15 Oct.   **2017**

KRAKOW *D3* (7km SW Rural) *50.04638, 19.88111*
Camping Smok (No. 46), ul Kamedulska 18, 30-252
Kraków **48 12 429 88 00; info@smok.krakow.pl;
www.smok.krakow.pl**

[12] 🐕 PLN5 ♟ [wo] ♨ 🖥 ⁄ [MSP] 🦋 ⑪ nr 🔦 /🏔

Fr Kraków W ring rd site sp as No 46. Fr S 1st exit
immed after x-ing rv onto rd 780 twd Kraków.
3*, Med, shd, pt sl, EHU (5-10A) PLN12; red long stay;
Eng spkn; adv bkg rec; windsurfing 6km; CKE. *"On rd
to Auschwitz; salt mine at Wieliczka; friendly, well-kept
site; spotless san facs; lower field (m'vans) poss muddy
after rain - tractor tow avail; poss rallies on site; gd tour
base; frequent bus to Krakow connects with trams to
cent; cycle rte to cent; gd security; tours with pick-up fr
site; excel; v helpful and friendly."* **PLN 111**   **2018**

"That's changed – Should I let the Club know?"

If you find something on site that's different
from the site entry, fill in a report and let us
know. See camc.com/europereport.

LANCUT *D3* (2km E Urban) *50.070940, 22.254689*
Camping Lancut, ul. Kazimierza Wielkiego 20, 37-
100 Łańcut **(604) 915112 or (602) 252909; biuro@
campinglancut.pl; www.campinglancut.pl**

🐕 PLN 5 ♟ [wo] ♨ 🔥 ⁄ [MSP] 🍴 🍽 ⑪ nr 🔦 nr

On 94 between Rzeszow and Przeworks. Sm, mkd,
hdg, pt shd, serviced pitches; EHU; bbq (charcoal,
elec, gas, sep area); cooking facs; twin axles; red long
stay; phone; bus; Eng spkn; adv bkg acc. *"Excel; lots
to see locally; bike ride off rd; lovely site, 2 years old
(2019); modern; helpful American owner; v well kept."*
PLN 51, 1 Apr-30 Oct.   **2019**

LEBA *A2* (2km NE Urban) *54.76580, 17.57145*
Camping Przymorze Nr. 48, ul. Nadmorska 9, 84-360
Leba **059 866 1304; biuro@camping.leba.pl; http://
camping-leba.pl/kamery.asp**

🐕 ♟ (htd) [wo] ♨ 🔥 ⑇ 🍴 🦋 🍽 ⑪ 🔦 /🏔 🌲 sand 0.5km

Take DW214 dir Leba, at rndabt take 1st exit onto
aleja swietego Jakuba. Turn R onto Nadmorska
& foll sp to camp.** Lge, mkd, pt shd, EHU; bbq; TV;
10% statics; phone; bus adj; Eng spkn; ccard acc; CCI.
*"Excel site; shops & rest in walking dist; interesting
harbour with fresh fish for sale; windsurfing; lovely
sandy beach."* **PLN 110, 1 May-30 Sep.**   **2019**

LEGNICA *C2* (13km SE Rural) *51.14216, 16.24006*
Camping Legnickie Pole (No. 234), Ul Henryka
Brodatego 7, 59-241 Legnickie Pole **(076) 8582397;
osir.legnica@wp.pl; www.osir.legnica.pl**

🐕 PLN8 ♟ 🔥 ⁄ 🍴 🍽 🔦 nr /🏔

Fr A4/E40 fr Görlitz take exit dir Legnickie Pole/
Jawor, foll sp to vill & site. Sharp L turn after leaving
main rd. Site sp on S o'skirts of Legnica on E65 &
fr m'way.** Sm, pt shd, EHU (10A) inc; CKE. *"Helpful,
friendly welcome; clean, basic facs (hot water to shwrs
only); poss diff after heavy rain; gd NH on way S;
pleasant vill."* **PLN 44, 1 May-30 Sep.**   **2017**

LEZAJSK *C4* (12km ENE Rural) *50.280257, 22.514233*
Pole Biwakowe Laguna, 37-303 Kuryłówka **(602)
717262; marianszktanny.wp.pl**

🐕 ♟ (htd) ♨ ⚲ 🖥 ⁄ 🍴 ⑪ nr 🔦 nr /🏔 🌲 sand adj

Thro Kurylowka town. At edge of town foll sp left
to Ozanna-Stron. Site on L.** 5*, Sm, pt shd, EHU
(16A); bbq (charcoal, elec, gas); cooking facs; sw; twin
axles; bus; Eng spkn; adv bkg acc; games area. *"Site on
lakeside; fishing; grass mowed short; peaceful; Lezajsk
monastery 20 mins; cycle path around lake; v friendly;
sailing ok; vg."* **PLN 30, 1 May-30 Sep.**   **2019**

LUBLIN *C4* (8km S Rural) *51.19186, 22.52725*
Camping Graf Marina (No. 65), ul Krężnicka 6, 20-518
Lublin **(081) 7441070 or (0607) 455320; info@graf-
marina.pl; grafmarina.obitur.pl**

♟ 🔥 ⁄ ⑪ 🔦 nr

Take rd 19 S & cross rlwy line; lge parking area after
1.8km then L after 300m (no sp but leads to
Zemborzyce); in 5km cross rlwy then L at T-junc; site
on R in 5km on lakeside.** Med, mkd, hdg, unshd, EHU
(10A); own san req; sw nr; Eng spkn; CKE. *"Marina adj;
sailing; fishing; site run down (early ssn 2011); sodden
after rain."* **PLN 71, 1 May-30 Sep.**   **2016**

POLAND

NIEDZICA *D3* (3.5km SE Urban) *49.40477, 20.33411*
Camping Polana Sosny (No. 38), Osiedle Na Polanie
Sosny, 34-441 Niedzica **(018) 2629403; polana.sosny@
niedzica.pl; www.niedzica.pl**

12 ♦♦♦(htd) WD ▲ ♣ ♿ ▣ ∥ ▼ Ⴤ ⊕ nr ॐ ᴣ nr

**Rte 969 fr Nowy Targ. At Dębno turn R & foll sp to
border (lake on L). At 11km pass castle & 1st dam
on L twds 2nd Dunajec dam. Site sp.** 2*, Sm, mkd,
unshd, EHU inc; cooking facs; red long stay; phone;
adv bkg acc; watersports; games area; CKE. *"Beautiful,
well-maintained site in superb location; friendly, helpful
staff; clean, modern san facs; excel walks in mountains;
2km to Slovakian border; quiet but noise fr dam; vg
touring base."* **PLN 50**   2016

OSWIECIM *D3* (4km S Rural) *50.02262, 19.19891*
Centre for Dialogue & Prayer in Auschwitz,
ul Maksymiliana Kolbego 1, 32-600 Oświęcim **(033)
8431000; biuro@centrum-dialogu.oswiecim.pl;
www.centrum-dialogu.oswiecim.pl**

12 ♦♦♦ ▲ ♿ ∥ ⊕ ᴣ nr

**700m fr Auschwitz 1 museum car park on parallel rd
to S, on forecourt of hotel-like building.** Sm, hdstg,
unshd, EHU inc; bbq; phone; Eng spkn; CKE. *"Conv
Auschwitz museum & Auschwitz-Birkenau (3km); clean,
modern, lovely site on lawn & among trees; all site
powered; gd, clean san facs, similar quality to UK CC
sites; friendly, helpful staff; very nice site; excel facs; a
gem of a site; highly rec."* **PLN 84**   2018

POZNAN *B2* (5km E Urban) *52.40343, 16.98399*
Camping Malta (No. 155), ul Krańcowa 98, 61-036
Poznań-Malta **(061) 8766203; camping@malta.
poznan.pl; www.poznan.pl**

12 ♦♦♦(htd) WD ▲ ♿ ▣ ∥ ▼ Ⴤ ॐ ᴣ

**Fr A2/E30 Poznań bypass leave at rte 2/11 dir
Poznań. Turn R at traff lts onto rte 5/E261 sp Malta,
Zoo & camping, site sp.** 4*, Sm, hdg, pt shd, EHU
(16A) inc; 80% statics; tram to city; Eng spkn; ccard
acc; CKE. *"Clean tidy site on lake with sports but poss
unkempt pitches LS; 6 tram stops to Poznań Sq; vg 24-
hr security; lake adj; helpful staff; site amongst sports
facs by lake."* **PLN 102**   2019

SANDOMIERZ *C3* (1km E Urban) *50.68010, 21.75502*
Camping Browarny (No. 201), ul Żwirki I Wigury 1,
27-600 Sandomierz **(015) 8332703; wmajsak@
poczta.fm; www.majsak.pl**

♔ ♦♦♦ WD ▲ ♿ ▣ ∥ MSP Ⴤ ⊕ nr ᴣ nr ⌂

**Diff app to site off dual c'way. App on rd 77 fr N only.
Avoid town ctr, 2.5 tonne weight limit.** 3*, Sm, pt shd,
EHU (16A) PLN10; bbq; cooking facs; phone; bus adj;
Eng spkn; adv bkg acc; games rm; CKE. *"Attractive sm
town in walking dist; vg site; helpful staff; red for 'vans
under 5mtrs."* **PLN 57, 1 May-30 Sep.**   2017

SUWALKI *A3* (11km SE Rural) *54.0767, 23.0742*
Kajaki Camping Pokoje, 16-412 Stary Folwark 44, Wigry
(087) 5637789; wigry@wigry.info; www.wigry.info

♦♦♦ WD ▲ ▣ ∥ ▼ ♔

**Fr Suwalki take 653 dir Sejny. In about 11km turn
R in Stary Folwark at PTTK sp. Site on R in approx
100m.** Sm, unshd, EHU (10A) inc; bbq; sw nr; Eng
spkn. *"Nr lake in National Park; kayaking fr site; vg site."*
PLN 40, 1 May-30 Sep.   2016

SZCZECIN/STETTIN *B1* (8km SE Rural) *53.39505,
14.63640* **Marina Camping (No. 25),** ul Przestrzenna
23, 70-800 Szczecin-Dabie **(091) 4601165; camping.
marina@pro.onet.pl; www.campingmarina.pl**

12 ♔ ♦♦♦(htd) ▲ ♣ ▣ ∥ MSP ♔ Ⴤ ⊕ ॐ ᴣ nr

**Fr E28/A6 take A10 sp Szczecin. Immed after rlwy
bdge turn R sp Dąbie. At traff lts in cent Dąbie turn
L, site on R in approx 2km on lake.** 3*, Med, pt shd,
EHU (6A) inc; sw; bus to Stettin; tennis; boat hire;
games area; CKE. *"Pleasant, lakeside site; clean,
modern san facs but inadequate if site full; bus tickets
fr recep; helpful staff; vg site on lake side."*
PLN 85   2018

TORUN *B2* (2km S Urban) *53.00062, 18.60847*
Camping Tramp (No. 33), ul Kujawska 14, 87-100
Toruń **(056) 6547187; tramp@mosir.torun.pl;
www.mosir.torun.pl**

12 ♔ PLN4.50 ♦♦♦ WD ▲ ♿ ▣ ∥ ♔ Ⴤ ⊕ nr ᴣ ᴣ nr

**Cross bdge S of town & take 1st L at traff lts, site
sp in 500m on rvside.** 3*, Med, shd, EHU (10A) inc;
10% statics; games area; CKE. *"Noisy, busy site but
reasonable; walking dist fr interesting old town across
bdge; gd security; NH/sh stay only."* **PLN 76**   2018

WARSZAWA *B3* (13km SE Urban) *52.17798, 21.14727*
Camping Wok (No. 90), ul Odrębna 16, 04-867
Warszawa **(022) 6127951; wok@campingwok.
warszawa.pl; www.campingwok.warszawa.pl**

♦♦♦(htd) WD ▲ ♣ ▣ ∥ MSP ▼ ♔ Ⴤ ⊕ nr ᴣ nr ⌂

**Fr city cent or fr W on E30, take bdge on E30 over
Rv Wisła to E side of rv. Then take rte 801 for
approx 8km (dual c'way). At rndabt double back
for 600m & take 3rd R into Odrębna. Site 200m
on R.** 4*, Sm, shd, EHU (10-16A) PLN15; gas; bbq;
cooking facs; TV; bus/tram adj; Eng spkn; adv bkg
acc; ccard acc; games area; CKE. *"Lovely little site;
v secure; spotless, modern san facs; helpful staff."*
PLN 125, 1 Apr-31 Oct.   2018

WARSZAWA *B3* (17km W Rural) *52.23066, 20.79196*
Campsite Kaputy 222, Sochaczewska 222, 05-850
Kreczki, (Mazowieckie) **(860) 1088112; biuro@camping
222.pl; www.camping222.pl**

PLN5 ⋔⋔(htd) ⓌⒹ ♨ ᵭ ⬛ ⫻ ₩ ⧉

Head S on SS36, take exit Pescate twd Pescate/
Lecco/Malgrate/SS583/Bellagio/Calco, cont strt;
at rndabt take 3rd exit via Roma, go thro 1 rndabt;
cont onto Via Statale, turn L onto Via Foppaola, site
on L. Med, mkd, EHU 15PLN; bus adj; Eng spkn; CCI.
*"Fishing lake on site; NH or visit to Warsaw; excel san
facs; bread on site; clean, spacious site & easy to find."*
PLN 138, 15 Apr-30 Sep. **2019**

WARSZAWA *B3* (4km W Urban) *52.2144, 20.96575*
Majawa Camping (No. 123), ul Bitwy Warszawskiej
19/20, 02-366 Warszawa-Szczęśliwice **(022)
8229121; biuro@majawa.pl; www.majawa.pl**

⋔⋔ ⓌⒹ ♨ ⬛ ⫻ ₩ ⓊLnr ⧉nr

Fr W on E30/rd 2 at junc with E67/rd 8 rd goes S
thro tunnel under rlwy then strt on under new overpass. Site on R in 100m. On E67/rd 8 fr Wrocław app
concrete monument 3m high in middle of tramway;
turn L at traff lts. Hotel Vera on R, site on L. Fr cent
of Warsaw, take rd no. 7/8 700m twds Katowice.
Not v well sp fr cent of town. Ent & exit diff due
v busy rd. 1*, Sm, pt shd, EHU (6A) PLN15; bbq;
10% statics; phone; bus 500m; Eng spkn; ccard acc;
tennis; CKE. *"Easy access to Warsaw & Royal Castle; gd
meals at adj bowling alley or Vera hotel; poss lge rallies
on site; friendly; poor condition but well positioned to
get into city."* **PLN 138, 1 May-30 Sep.** **2019**

WIELICZKA *D3* (1.5km SE Urban) *49.98273, 20.07611*
Motel Camping Wierzynka, ul Wierzynka 9, 32-020
Wieliczka **(012) 2783614; motel@nawierzynka.pl;
www.nawierzynka.pl**

⋔⋔ ♨ ⫻ ₩ ⧉ ▽ Ⓤ🛒Lnr

Site sp fr E40/rte 4 about 2km fr salt mine.
Sm, hdstg, pt shd, pt sl, EHU (10A) PLN10 (rev pol);
bus to Krakow, train 1km; Eng spkn; ccard acc; bike
hire; CKE. *"10 pitches in pleasant setting; helpful staff;
facs basic but clean; shwrs erratic; 2km fr salt mines;
vg site, local to salt mines; shwr portacabin, but clean."*
PLN 80, 1 May-30 Sep. **2019**

WROCLAW *C2* (4km NE Urban) *51.11722, 17.09138*
Stadion Olimpijski Camp (No. 117), ul Padarewskiego
35, 51-620 Wrocław **(071) 3484651**

⧉ ⋔⋔ ♨ ⬛ ⫻ ▽ Ⓤnr 🛒 Lnr ⧉

Fr A4 into Wrocław foll N8 sp Warszawa thro city.
On N8 dir Warszawa, pass McDonalds, at fork in
rd take Sienkiewicza to end, then Rozyckiego to
stadium, site on R. If poss foll sp 'stadion' to camp;
head for lighting towers of sports stadium if seen
thro trees. 2*, Lge, pt shd, EHU (16A) PLN7.50; bbq;
10% statics; phone; tram nr; CKE. *"San facs basic but
clean; site run down (2017); gd security; poss noise fr
stadium; v conv for city; stop for tram v handy; pool
700m; carpk outside site."* **PLN 77, 1 May-15 Oct.**
2018

ZAKOPANE *D3* (4km NE Rural) *49.32415, 19.98506*
Camping Harenda (No. 160), Oś Harenda 51B,
34-500 Zakopane **(018) 2014700; harenda51b@
gmail.com; www.harenda.tatrynet.pl**

12 ⧉ ⋔⋔(htd) ⓌⒹ ♨ ⬛ ⫻ ₩ ⧉ Ⓤ 🛒nr ⧉

On main rd to Zakopane fr N, after town sp turn
R into petrol stn with McDonalds. Cont to R, pass
Cmp Ustep on L then turn L over rv bdge to site in
200m on R. 2*, Med, pt shd, pt sl, EHU (10A) PLN10
(long lead req); bbq; Eng spkn; CKE. *"Gd views Tatra
mountains fr site; superb walking; poss rallies on site;
poss unkempt LS; laundry done at modest cost; vg
rest; rafting (not white water) on Dunajec Rv; Nowy
Targ rec; lower site poss muddy in wet weather."*
PLN 52 **2019**

ZAKOPANE *D3* (4km NE Rural) *49.32229, 19.98550*
Camping Ustup (No. 207), ul Ustup K/5, 34-500
Zakopane-Ustup **(08667) 477791; camping.ustup@
gmail.com**

⋔⋔ ⓌⒹ ♨ ᵭ ⫻ ₩ Ⓤnr 🛒nr ⧉

Turn R off Kraków-Zakopane rd 47 at petrol stn/
McDonalds just after 1st town sp. Turn R again
immed (also sp Cmg Harenda), site on L in 200m.
Sm, unshd, pt sl, EHU (10A) inc; bus to town cent; adv
bkg acc; CKE. *"Ideal cent for Tatra region; mountain
views; excel, family-run site; v welcoming, friendly
& helpful owner (ltd Eng); vg, clean san facs; grassy
pitches; coach tours arranged fr adj g'ge info desk."*
PLN 81, 1 May-30 Sep. **2019**

ZAMOSC *C4* (1km SW Rural) *50.71919, 23.23908*
Camping Duet (No. 253), ul Królowej Jadwigi 14,
22-400 Zamość **(084) 6392499; duet@virgo.com.pl**

12 ⧉ ⋔⋔ ⓌⒹ ♨ ⫻ ₩ ▽ Ⓤᵭ 🛒

Fr Zamość cent W on rd 74, site on R bef Castorama.
1*, Sm, pt shd, EHU PLN12; 10% statics; CKE. *"Walk
to attractive town; pool 150m; fair sh stay/NH."*
PLN 59 **2016**

France and Andorra
Central and South East Europe, Benelux and Scandinavia
Spain and Portugal

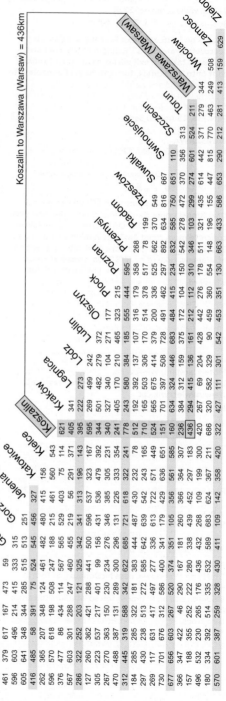

Koszalin to Warszawa (Warsaw) = 436km

Biala Podlaska
Bialystok
Bielsko-Biala
Bydgoszcz
Czestochowa
Elblag
Gdansk
Gorzów Wielkopolski
Jelenia Gora
Katowice
Kielce
Koszalin
Kraków
Legnica
Lódz
Lublin
Olsztyn
Plock
Poznan
Przemysl
Radom
Rzeszów
Suwalki
Swinoujscie
Szczecin
Torun
Wroclaw
Zamosc
Zielona Gora
Warszawa (Warsaw)

POLAND

© Collins Bartholomew Ltd 2020

Motorways
Major roads
Main roads

50 kms
30 mls
0

BALTIC SEA

BORNHOLM
(Denmark)

LITHUANIA
VILNIUS
Marijampole

BELARUS
Slonim
Hrodna

RUSSIA
Kaliningrad

LITHUANIA

SUWAŁKI
Ełk
Mikołajki
Ruciane-Nida

BIAŁYSTOK

Białowieża
Brest

BIAŁA
PODLASKA

LUBLIN

ZAMOSĆ

Kovel'

UKRAINE

Przeworsk

RZESZÓW

Tarnów

KRAKÓW
Wieliczka

BIELSKO-BIAŁA

Oświęcim

Zakopane

Niedzica

SLOVAKIA

Žilina

Ostrava

CZECHIA
(CZECH REPUBLIC)

Hradec
Králové

PRAHA

Liberec
Karpacz
Kłodzko

Görlitz

Cottbus

Frankfurt
an der Oder

BERLIN

Dresden

GERMANY

N
W   E
S

Frombork
Morąg
OLSZTYN
PLOCK
WARSZAWA
RADOM
Kazimierz
Dolny
Sandomierz
KIELCE
CZĘSTOCHOWA
KATOWICE

ŁÓDŹ
Uciechów
WROCŁAW
LEGNICA
JELENIA
GÓRA

POZNAŃ
BYDGOSZCZ
TORUŃ
GDAŃSK
Łeba
Ustka
Mielno
Kołobrzeg
KOSZALIN
ŚWINOUJŚCIE
Paslewalk
SZCZECIN
GORZÓW
WIELKOPOLSKI
Sulęcin
ZIELONA GÓRA

Sassnitz
Rostock
Greifswald

Rostock

No sites listed
All year site(s)
Seasonal site(s)
200m +
0–200m

Slovakia

📍 Bojnice Castle

Highlights

Well known for the sheer volume of castles to be found, Slovakia is a country rich in culture. It retains much of its sense of tradition, both in its beautiful medieval towns such as Levoča or Bardejov and in the small villages dotted around the countryside.

A relatively small country with an untamed and diverse wilderness, Slovakia is a great place for those wanting to experience new and different landscapes on a daily basis.

Slovakia has a rich tradition of folklore, and festivals celebrating local folk customs are found throughout the country. The oldest of these is held in Východná, and showcases parades, music, costumes and local crafts.

There are several speciality foods found in Slovakia, one of which is bryndza, a creamy sheep's cheese known for its strong smell. It is the main ingredient of Bryndzové Halušky, a dish made of potato dumplings, bryndza and bacon and considered the national speciality.

Major towns and cities

- Bratislava – a unique capital with a hill-top castle overlooking the city.
- Košice – the well-preserved historical centre is full of heritage sites.
- Prešov – a tourist favourite with many attractions.
- Žilina – packed with museums and historic buildings.

Attractions

- Tatras National Park – with a rich variety of flora and fauna there is plenty to discover in this gorgeous landscape.
- Spiš Castle – the sprawling remains of a 12th century castle that now houses a fascinating museum.
- Nedbalka Gallery, Bratislava – admire the works of major modern artists from Slovakia from the 19th century to the present day.

Find out more

www.slovakia.travel
E: touristinfo@visitbratislavia.com
T: 0042 (0) 14 84 13 61 46

Country Information

Population (approx): 5.4 million

Capital: Bratislava

Area: 49,036 sq km

Bordered by: Austria, Czech Republic, Hungary, Poland, Ukraine

Terrain: Rugged mountains in the centre and north; lowlands in the south

Climate: Continental climate; warm, showery summers; cold, cloudy, snowy winters; best months to visit are May, June and September

Highest Point: Gerlachovský štít 2,655m

Languages: Slovak, Hungarian, German

Local Time: GMT or BST + 1, i.e. 1 hour ahead of the UK all year

Currency: Euros divided into 100 cents; £1 = €1.16, €1 = £0.87 (October 2019)

Emergency numbers: Police 112; Fire brigade 112; Ambulance 112

Public Holidays 2020: Jan 1, 6; Apr 10, 13; May 1, 8; Jul 5; Aug 29; Sep 1, 15; Nov 1, 17; Dec 24,25,26

School summer holidays are from the beginning of July to the end of August

Entry Formalities

Holders of valid British and Irish passports may visit Slovakia for up to three months without a visa. There are no registration formalities for short stay visitors.

All foreign visitors are required to show proof of medical insurance cover on entry.

Medical Services

Medical facilities are variable. Whereas the standard of care from doctors is good, many hospitals suffer from a lack of maintenance. The biggest problem you will probably encounter is language, as nurses and ancillary workers may not speak English.

There is a reciprocal health care agreement with the UK for urgent medical treatment and you should present a European Health Insurance Card (EHIC). Emergency treatment is from doctors and dentists contracted to the Slovak health insurance system, but you will be asked for payment and follow on costs could be considerable. Hospital patients are required to make a financial contribution towards costs. Charges incurred are not refundable in Slovakia.

A 24 hour first aid service exists in all provincial and district towns, as well as in some small communities. For minor ailments, the first call should be to a pharmacy (lekáren) where staff are qualified to give advice and may be able to prescribe drugs normally available only on prescription in the UK.

Hepatitis A immunisation is advised for long stay travellers to rural areas, and those who plan to travel outside tourist areas.

Opening Hours

Banks: Mon-Fri 8am-3pm/5pm.

Museums: Tue-Sun 10am-5pm; closed Mon.

Post Offices: Mon-Fri 8am-6pm; Sat 8am-1pm.

Shops: Mon-Fri 7am-6pm; Sat 7am-12 noon. Hypermarkets usually open Sun.

Food Shops: Mon-Fri 7am-6pm; Sat 7am-12pm. Department Stores - Mon-Sat 9am-9pm

Safety and Security

Most visits to Slovakia are trouble free. However, there is a risk of being a victim of petty theft, particularly in Bratislava, and pickpocketing is common at tourist attractions and in some bars. When placing your jacket on the back of a chair in a restaurant make sure you don't leave valuables in the pockets. Don't put handbags on the floor or under chairs, where they may be vulnerable to theft. There have been occurrences in Bratislava of visitors being offered 'spiked' drinks and subsequently being robbed.

Visitors entering Slovakia via the border crossings on the D2 and D4 motorways should be extremely vigilant. While you leave your vehicle to buy petrol or a motorway vignette, a tyre may be deliberately damaged. Once you are back on the road and have driven a few kilometres other motorists will flag you down under the pretext of offering assistance. In these circumstances you should stay in your vehicle with the doors locked and call the police (dial 112) or the emergency service of the Slovensky Autoturist Klub (SATC) on 18124 or (02) 68249211.

Robberies from parked cars are on the increase. Cameras, mobile phones and tablets are as attractive as cash and credit cards; don't leave them or other valuables unattended.

If you intend to ski or hike in the Slovak mountains you are recommended to have sufficient insurance to cover rescue costs should the Slovak Mountain Rescue (HZS) be called out. Take heed of any instructions issued by HZS; if you ignore their advice you may be liable to a heavy fine.

Taking photos of anything that could be perceived as a military establishment or of security interest may result in problems with the authorities.

Slovakia shares with the rest of Europe an underlying threat from terrorism. Attacks, although unlikely, could be indiscriminate and against civilian targets, including places frequented by tourists.

British Embassy

PANSKA 16, 81101 BRATISLAVA
Tel: (02) 59982000
www.ukinslovakia.fco.gov.uk/en/

Irish Embassy

MOSTOVA 2, 81102 BRATISLAVA
Tel: (02) 32338700
www.embassyofireland.sk

Documents

Passport

Carry your passport at all times as it is an offence to be without it and you may be fined and held in custody for up to 24 hours. Keep a photocopy of the details page separately. Ensure your passport is in a presentable state as the authorities can refuse you entry if it is worn or damaged or looks as if it may have been tampered with.

Vehicle(s)

You should carry your vehicle registration certificate (V5C), at all times together with your driving licence, insurance certificate and your vehicle's MOT certificate (if applicable). Fines may be imposed by police patrols if you cannot produce these documents on request.

Money

Exchange kiosks often offer poor exchange rates and there is a risk of being robbed by thieves nearby. Scottish and Northern Irish bank notes will not be exchanged.

Cash machines which accept UK debit or credit cards are common but do not rely on finding one in remote areas. Shops, particularly in the main tourist areas, increasingly accept credit cards but are sometimes reluctant to accept cards issued by foreign banks. If you intend to pay for something by card do check first that the shop will accept it and that it can be read. You should also check your statements carefully for transactions you did not make.

Driving

The standard of driving is not high and sometimes aggressive with drivers going too fast, especially in bad weather, tailgating and overtaking dangerously. Drive defensively and allow yourself more 'thinking time'. Beware of oncoming cars overtaking on your side of the road, especially on bends and hills.

Accidents

If your vehicle is damaged when you enter Slovakia the border authorities must issue a certificate confirming the visible damage. While in the country if an accident causes bodily injury or material damage exceeding a value of approximately €4,000 it must be reported to the police immediately. If a vehicle is only slightly damaged both drivers should complete a European Accident Report. In the case of foreign motorists driving vehicles registered abroad, it is advisable to report the accident to the police who will issue a certificate which will facilitate the exportation of the vehicle.

Alcohol

Slovakia has a policy of zero tolerance for drinking or consuming drugs before driving. There is no permitted level of alcohol in the bloodstream. Police carry out random breath tests and you will be heavily penalised if there is any trace of alcohol in your system.

Breakdown Service

The motoring organisation, Slovensky Autoturist Klub (SATC), operates an emergency centre which can be contacted 24 hours a day by dialling (0)18124 or (02) 68249211. Operators speak English.

Child Restraint System

Children under the age of 12 years and anyone under 1.5m in height must not travel in the front seat of a vehicle. Child restraint seats must be used for any children weighing less than 36kg.

Fuel

Diesel is sold in service stations with the sign 'TT Diesel' or 'Nafta'. LPG is widely available and is sold under the name ECO Auto-gas or ECO Car-Gas – see www.lpg.szm.sk/slovensko_5.pdf for a list of outlets. If driving a vehicle converted to use LPG you must be in possession of a safety certificate covering the combustion equipment in your vehicle.

Some service stations on international roads and in main towns are open 24 hours but in other areas they may close by 6pm. Credit cards are generally accepted. Service stations may be hard to find in rural areas.

Lights

All vehicles must use dipped headlights at all times.

Motorways

There are 432km of motorways. Bratislava has direct motorway connections with Prague and Vienna and a new motorway is planned to connect it with Budapest.

Emergency phones are placed along motorways and callers are connected directly to the police.

Vehicles using motorways and selected highways must display a vignette (windscreen sticker), which may be purchased at border crossings, petrol stations and post offices. Charges for vehicles up to 3,500kg with or without a caravan or trailer are as follows (2015 prices): €10 for a period of 10 days and €14 for one month. Fines are payable for non-display and old stickers must be removed. The road from the Austrian border crossing at Berg to Bratislava is free of charge.

Motorhomes over 3,500kg are considered private vehicles and can buy the above vignettes as long as you are able to show the Vehicle Registration Certificate (V5) and it shows that the vehicle has fewer than 9 seats. Without the V5, drivers of vehicles over 3,500kg must pay motorway tolls by means of an electronic toll collection unit fitted to their vehicle. Tolls vary according to distance driven, vehicle weight and emissions classification. For information see www.emyto.sk or telephone 00421 235 111111.

Parking

Visitors are warned to park only in officially controlled parking areas since cars belonging to tourists may be targeted for robbery. There are many restrictions on parking in Bratislava and fines are imposed. Wheel clamps are used in main towns and vehicles may be towed away.

Continuous white/yellow lines indicate that parking is prohibited and broken white/yellow lines indicate parking restrictions.

Priority

At uncontrolled crossroads or intersections not marked by a priority sign, priority must be given to vehicles coming from the right. Drivers must not enter an intersection unless the exit beyond the crossing is clear.

Drivers must slow down and, if necessary, stop to allow buses and trams to move off from stops and to allow buses to merge with general traffic at the end of a bus lane. A tram turning right and crossing the line of travel of a vehicle moving on its right has priority once the driver has signalled his intention to turn. Trams must be overtaken on the right but do not overtake near a tram refuge.

Roads

Roads are relatively quiet and are generally well maintained. They often follow routes through towns and villages, resulting in sharp bends and reduced speed limits.

Many main roads, although reasonably good, have only a single carriageway in each direction making overtaking difficult.

In winter, north-south routes through Slovakia can be challenging as they pass through mountain ranges. The passes of Donovaly (Ružomberok to Banská Bystrica), Veľký Šturec (Martin to Banská Bystrica), and Čertovica (Liptovský Mikuláš to Brezno) are the most frequented. Slow moving vehicles travelling uphill should pull over at suitable stopping places to allow vehicles behind to pass.

Road Signs and Markings

Road signs and markings conform to international standards. The following signs may also be seen:

Slovak	English Translation
Dialkova premavka	By-pass
Hnemocnica	Hospital
Jednosmerny premavka	One-way traffic
Obchadzka	Diversion
Průjezd zakázaný	Closed to all vehicles
Zákaz parkovania	No parking
Zákaz vjazdu	No entry

Signs indicating motorways are red and white and signs on motorways or semi-motorways have a green or blue background; on other roads signs have a blue background.

Sat Nav/GPS Device

A GPS device must not be placed in the middle of the windscreen. The driver's view must not be impeded.

Speed Limits

	Open Road (km/h)	Motorway (km/h)
Car Solo	90	130
Car towing caravan/trailer	90	90
Motorhome under 3500kg	90	130
Motorhome 3500-7500kg	80	90

Motorhomes over 3,500kg are restricted to 80/90 km/h (56 mph) on motorways and to 80 km/h (50 mph) on other main roads and dual carriageways. Do not exceed 30 km/h (18 mph) when approaching and going over level crossings.

Speed limits are strictly enforced. Carrying and/or use of radar detectors is prohibited.

Traffic Lights

A green arrow together with a red or amber light indicates that drivers may turn in the direction indicated by the arrow provided they give way to other traffic and to pedestrians. A green arrow accompanied by an amber light in the form of a walking figure means that pedestrians have right of way.

Violation of Traffic Regulations

Police are empowered to collect on the spot fines for contravention of driving regulations. An official receipt should be obtained.

Winter Driving

In winter equip your vehicle(s) for severe driving conditions and fit winter tyres, which are compulsory when roads are covered in snow or ice. Carry snow chains and use them when there is enough snow to protect the road surface.

Essential Equipment

First aid kit

A first aid kit is compulsory in all vehicles.

Reflective Jacket/ Waistcoat

If your vehicle is immobilised on the carriageway outside a built up area, or if visibility is poor, you must wear a reflective jacket or waistcoat when getting out of your vehicle. Passengers who leave the vehicle, for example, to assist with a repair, should also wear one.

Warning Triangles

Carry a warning triangle which, in an emergency or in case of breakdown, must be placed at least 100 metres behind your vehicle on motorways and highways, and 50 metres behind on other roads.

The triangle may be placed closer to the vehicle in built-up areas. Drivers may use hazard-warning lights until the triangle is in position.

In case of breakdown, vehicles left on the edge of the carriageway will be towed away after three hours by the organisation in charge of the motorway or road at the owner's expense.

Touring

Smoking is not allowed on the premises where food is served and a partial smoking ban is in force in some bars and cafés which have a dedicated area for smokers. A tip of between 5 to 10% is usual in restaurants. It is normal to give taxi drivers a small tip by rounding up fares to the nearest 50 cents.

Mains water is heavily chlorinated and may cause stomach upsets. Bottled water is available.

The highest peaks of the Tatras mountains are covered with snow for approximately four months of the year and offer ample scope for winter sports. There are plenty of cableways and ski-lifts.

There are a number of UNESCO World Heritage sites in Slovakia including the town of Bardejov, the mining centre of Banská Štiavnica, the 'gingerbread houses' of Vlkolínec village, Spiš Castle, wooden churches in the Carpathian mountains and the caves of Aggtelek Karst and Slovak Karst.

Slovakia has over a thousand curative mineral and thermal springs, together with extensive deposits of high quality healing peat and mud reputed to cure a variety of diseases and ailments. Visitors from all over the world attend these spas every year.

The Bratislava City Card valid for one, two or three days, offers discounts and benefits at approximately 60 attractions and at restaurants and cafés. In addition, it offers free access to public transport and a free one hour walking tour of the Old Town. The card can be obtained at tourist information centres, at the central railway station and at hotels.

In general Slovakia does not cater for the physically handicapped. For example, it is normal for cars to park on the pavement and dropped kerbs are perceived as helping drivers to achieve this without damaging tyres or suspension! Public transport invariably requires large steps to be climbed and bus and tram drivers tend to accelerate from stops at great speed, catching passengers by surprise. Access to most buildings is by steps, rather than ramps. However effort is now being taken to make buildings more accessible.

German is the most common second language, English is not widely understood or spoken.

Camping and Caravanning

There are approximately 175 campsites (Kemping or Autocamp) which are classified into four categories. Sites generally open from mid-June until mid-September, although some are open all year. The season is slow to get going and sites which claim to open in May may not do so or offer only minimal facilities.

Campsites' standards vary and facilities may be basic. Many consist mainly of cabins and chalets in various states of repair, while others form part of the facilities offered by hotels, guest houses or leisure/thermal spa complexes. Casual/wild camping is not permitted; it is prohibited to sleep in a caravan or motorhome outside a campsite.

Campsite prices and the cost of living are still relatively low. Some of the prices shown in the campsite entries have been directly converted from prices previously shown in koruna (crowns) and rounded up. You may find actual prices somewhat higher now that the official currency is the euro. Prices charged include a tourist tax.

Cycling

There are a number of long distance cycle tracks throughout the country (visit the website www.slovakia.travel for more information) including alongside the River Danube between Bratislava and the Gabčikovo Dam.

Cyclists must ride in single file on the right hand side of the road or may use the verge outside built up areas. Children under 10 years of age may not ride on the road unless accompanied by a person over 15 years of age.

Electricity and Gas

Usually the current on campsites varies between 10 and 16 amps. Plugs have two round pins. Some campsites, but not all, have CEE connections.

It is not possible to purchase Campingaz International or any other of the gas cylinders normally available in the UK. Sufficient supplies for your stay should be taken with you. Many sites have communal kitchen facilities which enable visitors to make great savings on their own gas supply.

Public Transport

From April to September hydrofoil services operate from Bratislava to Vienna and Budapest.

In Bratislava bus, trolley bus and tram tickets are valid for periods of up to 60 minutes, extending to up to 90 minutes at night and weekends. Buy them from kiosks and yellow ticket machines. Alternatively you can buy tickets valid for one or several city zones for a fixed period, e.g. 24, 48 or 72 hours or for seven days. Ensure that you validate your ticket on boarding the bus or tram.

Passengers aged 70 and over travel free; carry your passport as proof of age. You must buy a ticket for dogs travelling on public transport and they must be muzzled. You must also purchase a ticket for large items of luggage. For more information see www.imhd.zoznam.sk/ba.

Bratislava

BANSKA BYSTRICA *B2* (11km W Rural) *48.7540, 19.0552* **Autocamping Tajov,** 97634 Tajov **(048) 4197320; ks.rovdyklev@rovdyklev; www.velkydvor. sk/en**

12 �11(htd) wo ♨ ∥ 🐾 ♈ 〒 ① nr ♨ 🗲 🕭

Fr Tajov dir Kordíky. Site well sp 2km NW of Tajov. Sm, unshd, pt sl, EHU (6-10A) inc; TV; bus; CKE. *"Lovely setting in wooded valley; friendly welcome."*
€16.00 2016

BANSKÁ ŠTIAVNICA *C2* (6.7km E Rural) *48.447462, 18.983303* **Camping Studenec,** 969 01 Banský Studenec **907 418 033 or 907 746 303; info@ campingstudenec.eu; www.campingstudenec.eu**

🐾 �11 wo ∥ 🐾 ♈ 🕭

Fr Banska Stiavnica take 2536 (sp Bansky Studenec) for 5km. At end of vill turn L sp Studenec. At next junc go strt on gravel track for 50m. Sm, unshd, pt sl, EHU (16A); bbq; cooking facs; sw nr; bus 500m; Eng spkn. *"Well run new (2018) site; excel facs; extensive views; rural walks & biking; conv Bansky Stiavnica; poss open off ssn esp w/ends; excel."*
€21.00, 1 Jul-31 Aug. 2018

"I need an on-site restaurant"

We do our best to make sure site information is correct, but it is always best to check any must-have facilities are still available or will be open during your visit.

BRATISLAVA *C1* (9km NE Urban) *48.18801, 17.18488* **Autocamping Zlaté Piesky,** Senecká Cesta 12, 82104 Bratislava **(02) 44257373 or 44450592; kempi@ netax.sk; www.intercamp.sk**

🐾 €2 �11 ♨ ∥ 〒 ① ♨ 🗲 🕭 ✎

Exit D1/E75 junc sp Zlaté Piesky. Site on S side of rd 61 (E75) at NE edge of Bratislava. Look for pedestrian bdge over rd to tram terminus, ent thro adj traff lts. If x-ing Bratislava foll sp for Žilina. In summer a 2nd, quieter, drier site is opened. For 1st site turn L when ent leisure complex; for 2nd site carry strt on then turn R. Med, shd, EHU (10A) €3 (long lead poss req); sw; phone; tram to city; Eng spkn; golf 10km; tennis; fishing; CKE. *"Basic site on lge leisure complex; no privacy in shwrs; ltd hot water; muddy in wet; security guard at night & secure rm for bikes etc but reg, major security problems as site grnds open to public; pedalos on lake; helpful, friendly staff; interesting city."* **€13.00, 1 May-15 Oct.** 2016

LEVOCA *B3* (5km N Rural) *49.04982, 20.58727* **Autocamping Levočská Dolina,** 05401 Levoča **(053) 4512705 or 4512701; rzlevoca@pobox.sk**

12 🐾 €1.50 �11 ♨ ♨ 🖃 ∥ 🐾 ♈ 〒 ① ♨ 🗲 nr 🕭

Site on E side of minor rd 533 running N fr E50 at Dolina to Levočská Dolina. Steep ent; ltd access lge o'fits. Med, pt shd, sl, EHU (16A) €3; TV; Eng spkn; CKE. *"Diff in wet weather due v sl grnd; friendly staff; interesting old town; ski lift 2.5km; Spišský Hrad castle worth visit; walks in forests around site."* **€18.00**
2016

LIPTOVSKY MIKULAS *B3* (11km NW Rural) *49.13608, 19.5125* **Resort Villa Betula (formerly Penzión),** 03223 Liptovský Sielnica **(907) 812327; villabetula@villabetula.sk; www.villabetula.sk**

12 🐾 €7 �11 wo ♨ ♨ ∥ 🐾 ♈ 〒 ① 🗲 🕭

Fr rd 18/E50 exit onto R584 to Liptovský Mikuláš, site on N of lake 6km past Autocamp. 3*, Med, unshd, EHU (10A) inc; sw nr; phone; Eng spkn; ccard acc; bike hire; jacuzzi; sauna; CKE. *"Family-friendly, gem of a site in wonderful area of lakes, mountains & forest; welcoming, helpful owners; v clean & well-kept; vg rest; site at rear of hotel; excel for long or sh stay."*
€26.00 2015

MARTIN *B2* (5km NW Rural) *49.1082, 18.89888* **Autocamping Turiec,** Kolónia Hviezda 92, 03608 Martin **(421) 907 539178; recepcia@autocamping turiec.sk; www.autocampingturiec.sk**

🐾 €0.70 �11 wo ♨ 🖃 ∥ msf ♈ ① 🗲 nr

Site in town of Vrútky 3km NW of Martin. Foll Autocamping Turiec sps fr rd 18/E50 Žilina-Poprad. Site approx 1km S of this rd on o'skts Vrútky. 3*, Med, pt shd, sl, EHU (10A); 50% statics; Eng spkn; adv bkg acc; CKE. *"Warm welcome; excel security; pleasant wooded setting; excel art galleries/museums in Martin; vg."* **€17.00, 1 May-31 Oct.** 2018

NITRIANSKE RUDNO *B2* (1km N Rural) *48.80457, 18.47601* **Autocamping Nitrianske Rudno,** 97226 Nitrianske Rudno **(090) 5204739; info@camping-nrudno.sk; www.camping-nrudno.sk**

🐾 €1 �11 ♨ ♨ ∥ 🐾 ♈ 〒 ♨ 🕭 ✎

E fr Bánovce & Dolné Vestenice on rd 50, turn N onto rd 574. Site on shore of Lake Nitrianske Rudno, sp in vill. 2*, Med, pt shd, EHU €2.50; cooking facs; sw; 10% statics; adv bkg acc; watersports; games area; CKE. *"Welcoming, helpful owner; pleasant location."*
€13.00, 1 Jun-30 Sep. 2016

SLOVAKIA

PIESTANY *B1* (2.6km S Urban) *48.576469, 17.833889*
Camping Pullman, Cesta Janka Alexyho 2, 92101
Piešťany **(033) 7623563; info@campingpiestany.sk;
www.campingpiestany.sk**

🛐 ♗ 👪 ⱳ 🌡 ⱳ 🍽 ⯒ 🏊 ⯒ ⯒ ⯒

On rd 507 500m Sof junc with 499 (immed E of rv
bdge). Sm, unshd, EHU (6A); bbq; cooking facs; TV;
20% statics; train 2km; Eng spkn; adv bkg acc; games
rm; bike hire; CCI. *"Canoing on rv adj; rvside walk to
town; reg trains to Bratislava 50mins (taxi to stn €8 or
free parking nr stn); pleasant parks in town ctr; bar/rest
in town; vg."* **€15.00, 15 Apr-15 Oct.** **2018**

"Satellite navigation makes touring much easier"

Remember most sat navs don't know if you're
towing or in a larger vehicle – always use yours
alongside maps and site directions.

PREŠOV *B4* (13km W Rural) *49.00386, 21.08145*
Autokemping A Motorest Kemp, Chminianske Nová
Ves, District Prešov 082 33 **0517 795190 or 0905
191056 (mob); kemppo@kemppo.sk; www.kemppo.sk**

🛐 ♗ 👪 ♗ 🌡 ⱳ 🍽 ⯒ 🏊 ⯒ ⯒

Fr W on Rte 18/D1/E50, take exit twd Vit'az/
Hrabkov, site on R. Sm, pt shd, EHU €4; gas; bbq;
cooking facs; twin axles; Eng spkn; ccard acc; games
area; CKE. *"Site behind motorest Kemp on Rte 18;
campers kitchen; recep in rest; 5 chalets for rent on
site; fair site."* **€15.00, Feb-Dec.** **2019**

TATRANSKA LOMNICA *B3* (2.5km ESE Rural)
49.15830, 20.30979 **Intercamp Tatranec,** 05960
Tatranská Lomnica **(052) 4467092; hoteltatranec@
hoteltatranec.com**

🔢 ♗ 👪 ♗ 🌡 ⱳ 🍽 ⯒ 🍽 ⯒ ⯒ 🏊 ⯒ ⯒

NE fr Poprad on rd 67, after 8km turn L over level
x-ing, thro Vel'ká Lomnica twds Tatranská Lomnica
on rd 540. Site on L. 3*, Lge, unshd, pt sl, EHU (6A)
inc; Eng spkn; adv bkg acc; CKE. *"Superb views of High
Tatras; conv cable car, train etc; excel base for walking
& holiday resort; hotel adj; poor, dated facs & ltd
privacy."* **€18.50** **2015**

TERCHOVA *B2* (3km SW Rural) *49.24779, 18.98866*
Autocamp Belá, Nižné Kamence, 01305 Belá **(041)
5695135 or (905) 742514; camp@bela.sk;
www.campingbela.eu**

🛐 ♗ 👪 ⱳ 🌡 ⱳ 🍽 ⯒ 🏊 ⯒

Fr Zilina foll rd 583 twd Terchová. Site on L 3km
after vill of Belá. 2*, Med, pt shd, EHU (10A) €3; bbq;
cooking facs; 10% statics; tennis. *"Delightful rvside
site; gd welcome; clean, modern san facs; conv walking
in Malá Fatra mountains."* **€11.50, 1 May-15 Oct.**
2016

"There aren't many sites open at this time of year"

If you're travelling outside peak season
remember to call ahead to check site opening
dates – even if the entry says 'open all year'.

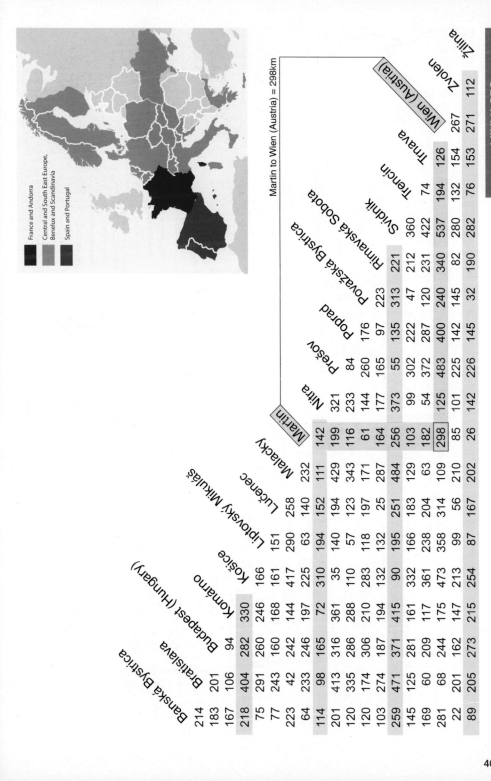

Map legend:
- France and Andorra
- Central and South East Europe, Benelux and Scandinavia
- Spain and Portugal

Martin to Wien (Austria) = 298km

Distance chart (km). Each origin city is followed by the road distances to the cities listed after it.

Origin	Bratislava	Budapest (Hungary)	Komárno	Košice	Liptovský Mikuláš	Lučenec	Malacky	Martin	Nitra	Prešov	Poprad	Považská Bystrica	Rimavská Sobota	Svidník	Trenčín	Trnava	Wien (Austria)	Zvolen	Žilina
Banská Bystrica	214	183	167	218	75	77	223	64	114	201	120	120	103	259	145	169	281	22	89
Bratislava		201	106	282	260	243	42	233	98	316	335	174	274	471	125	60	68	201	205
Budapest (Hungary)			94	330	168	160	144	246	165	361	288	210	187	415	161	209	244	162	273
Komárno				246	161	417	242	197	72	35	286	306	194	371	281	117	175	147	215
Košice					166	290	63	140	152	194	57	118	132	195	166	238	358	99	254
Liptovský Mikuláš						151	258	140	197	123	57	118	132	195	166	238	314	56	87
Lučenec							258	140	152	194	57	118	25	197	287	132	132	56	167
Malacky								232	111	429	343	171	287	484	129	63	109	210	202
Martin									142	199	116	61	164	256	103	182	298	85	26
Nitra										321	233	144	177	373	99	54	125	101	142
Prešov											84	260	165	55	302	372	483	225	226
Poprad												176	97	135	222	287	400	142	145
Považská Bystrica													223	313	47	120	240	145	32
Rimavská Sobota														221	212	231	340	82	190
Svidník															360	422	537	280	282
Trenčín																74	194	132	76
Trnava																	126	154	153
Wien (Austria)																		267	271
Zvolen																			112

Slovenia

Lake Bled

Highlights

Equipped with an extraordinarily pretty landscape, Slovenia is deeply in tune with its natural surroundings and is one of the greenest countries in Europe. Outdoor pursuits are wholeheartedly embraced here and are top of the list when it comes to attractions.

There is also plenty to see and do for history fans to see and do - this small country boasts around 500 castles and manor houses. Not to be missed are the hilltop castles of Bled, Ljubljana and Predjama.

Slovenia is one of the world's most biologically diverse countries, and despite its small size is home to an estimated total of 45,000 – 120,000 species.

Slovenia is also a key centre for winter sports, with major competitions and events held in the country on a regular basis. Kanin, the highest ski centre in Slovenia, offers the opportunity to ski to neighbouring Italy.

Major towns and cities

- Ljubljana – a charming capital with an old-world feel.
- Maribor – this vibrant city holds many events throughout the year.
- Celje – an ancient settlement with Celtic and Roman origins.
- Kranj – a lively city with a castle and 14th century church.

Attractions

- Bled Castle – a medieval castle overlooking the popular Lake Bled, and one of the most visited attractions in the country.
- Tivoli Park, Ljubljana - home to botanical gardens and a museum.
- Škocjan Caves – an extraordinary series of caves renowned as a natural treasure.
- Predjama Castle, Postojna – a gothic castle built 700 years ago into the mouth of a cave.

Find out more

www.slovenia.info
E: info@slovenia.info T: 0038 (0) 61 58 98 550

Country Information

Population (approx): 2 million

Capital: Ljubljana

Area: 20,273 sqkm

Bordered by: Austria, Croatia, Hungary, Italy

Coastline: 46.6km

Terrain: Coastal strip on the Adriatic; alpine mountains in west and north; many rivers and forests

Climate: Mediterranean climate on the coast; hot summers and cold winters in the plateaux and valleys in the east; spring and early autumn are the best times to visit

Highest Point: Triglav 2,864m

Languages: Slovenian; Serbo-Croat

Local Time: GMT or BST + 1, i.e. 1 hour ahead of the UK all year

Currency: Euros divided into 100 cents; £1 = €1.16, €1 = £0.87 (October 2019)

Emergency numbers: Police 113; Fire brigade 112; Ambulance 112. Operators speak English

Public Holidays 2020: Jan 1, 2; Feb 8; Apr 13, 27; May 1, 2; Jun 25; Aug 15; Oct 31; Nov 1; Dec 25, 26.

School summer holidays are from the last week in June to the end of August

Entry Formalities

All foreign nationals must register with the police within three days of arrival in Slovenia. Campsites carry out registration formalities, but if you are staying with friends or family you or your host will need to visit the nearest police station to register your presence in the country.

British and Irish passport holders may stay in Slovenia for up to three months without a visa. For longer stays contact the Slovenian Embassy for further information.

Medical Services

British visitors may obtain emergency medical, hospital and dental treatment from practitioners registered with the public health service, Health Institute of Slovenia (HIIS) on presentation of a European Health Insurance Card (EHIC). You will have to make a contribution towards costs which will not be refunded in Slovenia. Full fees are payable for private medical and dental treatment.

Health resorts and spas are popular and the medical profession uses them extensively for treatment of a wide variety of complaints.

Opening Hours

Banks: Mon-Fri 9am-12 noon & 2pm-5pm; closed Sat/Sun

Museums: Tues-Sun 9/10am-5/6pm. Most closed Mon.

Post Offices: Mon-Fri 8am-6pm; Sat 8am-12noon.

Shops: Mon-Fri 8am-7pm/9pm; Sat 8am-1pm.

Safety and Security

Slovenia is relatively safe for visitors but the usual sensible precautions should be taken against pickpockets in large towns and cities. Do not leave valuables in your car.

Western Slovenia is on an earthquake fault line and is subject to occasional tremors.

If you are planning a skiing or mountaineering holiday, contact the Slovenian Tourist Board for advice on weather and safety conditions before travelling. You should follow all safety instructions meticulously, given the danger of avalanches in some areas. Off-piste skiing is highly dangerous.

There is a low threat from terrorism but attacks could be indiscriminate and against civilian targets, including places frequented by tourists.

British Embassy

4TH FLOOR, TRG REPUBLIKE 3, 1000 LJUBLJANA
Tel: (01) 2003910
www.ukinslovenia.fco.gov.uk/en

Irish Embassy

Palaca Kapitelj, 1st floor
POLJANSKI NASIP 6
1000 Ljubljana
Tel: (01) 3008970
www.embassyofireland.si

Documents

Driving Licence

All European countries recognise the EU format paper UK driving licence introduced in 1990. However, it is a legal requirement to show your driving license with a form of photographic identification, such as your passport, if your driving licence does not include a photograph.

Passport

Carry a copy of your passport at all times as a form of identification.

Vehicle(s)

You should carry your vehicle documentation, i.e. vehicle registration certificate (V5C), insurance certificate, MOT certificate (if applicable) and driver's licence.

If you are driving a hired or borrowed vehicle, you must be in possession of a letter of authorisation from the owner or a hire agreement.

Money

Cash machines are widespread and the major credit cards are widely accepted. Carry your credit card issuers'/banks' 24-hour UK contact numbers in case of loss or theft of your cards.

Driving

Accidents

Any visible damage to a vehicle entering Slovenia must be certified by authorities at the border. All drivers involved in an accident while in the country should inform the police and obtain a written report (Potrdilo). Drivers of vehicles which have been damaged will need to present this police report to Customs on departure.

Alcohol

The maximum permitted level of alcohol is 50 milligrams in 100 millilitres of blood, i.e. lower than the limit in the UK (80 milligrams).

If a driver is under the age of 21 or has held a driving licence for less than three years the permitted level of alcohol is zero. The police carry out tests at random.

Breakdown Service

The motoring organisation, Avto-Moto Zveza Slovenije (AMZS), operates a 24 hour breakdown service which can be contacted by telephoning 1987. On motorways, using a mobile phone, call the AMZS Alarm Centre in Ljubljana on (01) 5305353 or use the emergency telephones and ask for AMZS assistance.

Charges apply for repairs or towing, plus supplements at night, weekends and on public holidays. Credit cards are accepted.

Child Restraint System

Children under 12 years of age and under the height of 1.5 metres must use a suitable child restraint system for their size and age.

Fuel

Petrol stations are generally open from 7am to 8pm Monday to Saturday. Many near border crossings, on motorways and near large towns are open 24 hours. Credit cards are accepted. It is understood that few petrol stations sell LPG.

Lights

Dipped headlights are compulsory at all times, regardless of weather conditions. Bulbs are more likely to fail with constant use and you are required to carry spares. Hazard warning lights must be used when reversing.

Motorways

There are about 620km of motorways (autoceste) and expressways (hitre ceste) with more under construction. For more information about motorways see the website www.dars.si.

There are service areas and petrol stations along the motorways and emergency telephones are situated every 2km.

Emergency corridors are compulsory on motorways and dual carriageways. Drivers are required to create a precautionary emergency corridor to provide access for emergency vehicles whenever congestion occurs. Drivers in the left-hand lane must move as far over to the left as possible, and drivers in the central and right-hand lanes must move as far over to the right as possible.

Motorway Tolls

Drivers of vehicles weighing up to 3,500kg must purchase a vignette (windscreen sticker) for use on motorways and expressways. Caravans/trailers don't need an additional vignette and the weight of the caravan/trailer isn't taken into account. The vignette is available from petrol stations in Slovenia, neighbouring countries and at border posts. The cost of a 7 day vignette is €15, 1 month is €30 and an annual is €110 (2015 charges). For vehicles over 3,500kg tolls are payable with cash or credit card.

Karawanken Tunnel

The 8km Karawanken Tunnel links the E61/A11 in Austria and E61/A2 in Slovenia. The toll is €7.20 for car and caravan or motorhome up to 3,500kg and €9.38 for a motorhome over 3,500kg (2018 charges).

Parking

Parking meters are used in towns. In city centres white lines indicate that parking is permitted for a maximum of two hours between 7am and 7pm, a parking ticket must be purchased from a machine. Blue lines indicate places where parking is allowed free of charge for up to 30 minutes. Vehicles parked illegally may be towed away or clamped.

Priority

At intersections drivers must give way to traffic from the right, unless a priority road is indicated. The same rule applies to roundabouts, i.e. traffic entering a roundabout has priority.

Roads

Slovenia has a well-developed road system, and international and main roads are in good condition. Secondary roads may still be poorly maintained and generally unlit. Minor roads are often gravelled and are known locally as 'white

roads'. Road numbers are rarely mentioned on road signs and it is advisable to navigate using place names in the direction you are travelling.

Roadside verges are uncommon, or may be lined with bollards which make pulling over difficult. Where there is a hard shoulder it is usual for slow vehicles to pull over to allow faster traffic to overtake.

The capital, Ljubljana, can be reached from Munich, Milan, Vienna and Budapest in less than five hours. There are numerous border crossings for entry into Slovenia.

Care should be taken, especially on narrow secondary roads, where tailgating and overtaking on blind bends are not unknown. Drive defensively and take extra care when driving at night. Be prepared for severe weather in winter.

Information on roads may be obtained by telephoning the AMZS Information Centre on (01) 5305300.

Road Signs and Markings

Road signs conform to international standards. Motorway signs have a green background and national road signs a blue background. On your travels you may see the following signs:

Mountain pass

School area

Toll: Vignette/card or cash

Speed Limits

	Open Road (km/h)	Motorway (km/h)
Car Solo	90-110	130
Car towing caravan/trailer	90	100
Motorhome under 3500kg	90-110	130
Vehicle over 3500-7500kg	80	80

Motorhomes over 3,500kg are restricted to 80 km/h (50 mph) on open roads, including motorways. Other speed limits are the same as for solo cars.

Areas where speed is restricted to 30 km/h (18 mph) are indicated by the sign 'Zone 30'. In bad weather when visibility is reduced to 50 metres the maximum speed limit is 50 km/h (31 mph).

Traffic Jams

Slovenia is a major international through-route and bottlenecks do occur on the roads to and from Ljubljana, such as the E61/A2 from Jesinice and the E57 from Maribor. Traffic queues can be expected from May to August on the roads around Lake Bled and to the Adriatic and on the E70/A1 motorway near the Razdrto toll station and near Kozina and Koper. Tailbacks also occur at border posts near the Karawanken Tunnel, Ljubelj and Šentilj/Spielfeld particularly at weekends. The motoring organisation, AMZS, provides traffic information in English – telephone (01) 5305300 or see their website www.amzs.si.

Violation of Traffic Regulations

The police have powers to stop drivers and levy heavy on-the-spot fines, including penalties for speeding, driving under the influence of alcohol and for using mobile phones without properly installed wireless headsets (bluetooth). Jaywalking is an offence and you could be fined if caught. Fines must be paid in local currency and you should obtain an official receipt.

Winter Driving

From 15 November to 15 March, and beyond those dates during winter weather conditions (snowfalls, black ice, etc), private cars and vehicles up to 3,500kg must have winter tyres on all four wheels or, alternatively, carry snow chains. Minimum tread depth of tyres is 3mm.

Essential Equipment

First aid kit

Although a first aid kit is not compulsory in all vehicles, it is recommended.

Reflective Jacket/ Waistcoat

In the event of vehicle breakdown on a motorway, anyone who leaves the vehicle must wear a reflective jacket.

Warning Triangles

Vehicles towing a trailer must carry two warning triangles (single vehicles require only one). In the event of a breakdown to vehicle and trailer combinations, one triangle must be placed at the rear of the towed vehicle and another at the front of the towing vehicle at a distance which ensures maximum safety and visibility. At night, drivers must use hazard warning lights or a torch in addition to the warning triangles.

Touring

A 10% tip is usual in restaurants and for taxi drivers.

The capital, Ljubljana, is a gem of a city with many Baroque and Art Nouveau influences. The works of the world renowned architect Jože Plecnik are among the finest urban monuments in the city. A Ljubljana Card is available for one, two or three days and offers free travel on city buses, tourist boat trips, the funicular, guided tours and the tourist train to Ljubljana Castle, plus free admission to museums and discounts at a wide range of shops, restaurants and bars. You can buy the card at the main bus and railway stations, hotels and tourist information centres or from www.visitljubljana.si.

Visit the largest cave in Europe is situated at Postojna, south west of Ljubljana. Also worth visiting are the mountains, rivers and woods of Triglav National Park, which covers the major part of the Julian Alps, together with the oldest town in Slovenia, Ptuj, and the city of Maribor. In Lipica take a guided tour around the stud, home to the world famous Lipizzaner horses.

There is a hydrofoil service between Portorož and Venice from April to November.

Slovenian is the official language although most Slovenians speak at least one other major European language and many, especially the young, speak English.

Camping and Caravanning

There are over 60 organised campsites in Slovenia rated one to five stars. They are usually open from May to October but a few are open all year. Standards of sites and their sanitary facilities are generally good. Campsites on the coast consist mostly of statics and can be overcrowded during the peak summer season. Casual/wild camping is not permitted.

Cycling

There are some cycle lanes which are also used by mopeds. Cyclists under the age of 15 must wear a safety helmet.

If using a vehicle bike carrier which overhangs by over one metre at the rear of a vehicle, you need to affix a 30cm square red flag or panel. At night the overhanging load must be indicated by a red light and a reflector. Loads may only project rearwards; they must not overhang the sides of vehicles.

Electricity and Gas

Usually the current on campsites varies between 6 and 16 amps. Plugs have two round pins. Hook-up points on most campsites conform to CEE standards.

Campingaz cylinders cannot be purchased or exchanged. Recent visitors report that it is possible to have gas cylinders refilled at premises on Verovškova Ulica 70, Ljubljana. The company's name is Butan-Plin. However, The Caravan and Motorhome Club does not recommend this practice and you should aim to take enough gas to last during your stay.

Public Transport

There is an extensive bus network in Ljubljana. Buy a yellow 'top-up' Urbana card for a one-off payment of €2 from news-stands, tobacconists, tourist information offices or the central bus station and add credit (between €1 and €50) at the same locations or at the green Urbanomati machines around the city. When boarding a bus simply touch the card to one of the card readers at the front of the bus and €1.20 will be deducted allowing 90 minutes of unlimited travel regardless of how many changes you make. Taxis are generally safe, clean and reliable. Fares are metered. For longer distances ordering a taxi by phone will attract lower rates.

Ljubljana

Bled

BLED *B2* (12.5km SE Rural) *46.326170, 14.234771*
Turistična kmetija Hribar, Brezje 14, 4243 Brezje
(04) 0260414; breda.policar@gmail.com;
www.turisticna-kmetija-hribar.si

🄁 🕅 ⬜ 🚻 🛒 ∥ 🗺 🦋 ⵌ ℔ nr ⓝ nr ℞ nr

**Exit m'way sp Brezje and turn L to Brezje. Turn R
at rndabt sp Brezje. On reaching Brezje bear R and
cont past firestn. At T-junc turn R. Cont for 300m
(ignoring Sat Nav) until you see sm residential
carpk on R. Now turn sharp L and go straight thro
metal gates to site.** Sm, pt shd, EHU (16A) €3.50;
bbq (charcoal, elec, gas); cooking facs; red long stay;
5% statics; bus 1km; Eng spkn; adv bkg acc; ccard acc.
€24.40 2019

"That's changed – Should I let the Club know?"

If you find something on site that's different
from the site entry, fill in a report and let us
know. See camc.com/europereport.

BLED *B2* (4km SE Rural) *46.35527, 14.14833*
Camping Šobec, Šobčeva Cesta 25, 4248 Lesce
(04) 5353700; sobec@siol.net; www.sobec.si

🐕 €3.50 🕅 ⬜ 🚻 ⬝ ⅋ 🗺 ⵌ ℔ ⓝ ⟟ ℞ /ⵥ

Exit rte 1 at Lesce, site sp. 5*, Lge, pt shd, pt sl, EHU
(16A) €3.70 (poss long lead req); red long stay; TV;
Eng spkn; ccard acc; bike hire; CKE. *"Excel, tranquil
rvside site in wooded area surrounded by rv; friendly,
helpful staff; lge pitches; clean san facs; gd rest; gd
walking/cycling; many sports & activities; real camping
atmosphere, plenty of space; def rec; rv pool; beautiful
area; conv NH en-rte to Croatia."*
€35.00, 15 Apr-1 Oct. 2017

BLED *B2* (4km SW Rural) *46.36155, 14.08066*
Camping Bled, Kidričeva 10c, SI 4260 Bled
04 5752000; info@camping-bled.com;
www.camping-bled.com

🐕 €3 🕅 ⬜ 🚻 ⬝ ♿ 🛒 ∥ 🗺 ⵌ ℔ nr ⟟ ℞ nr /ⵥ ⵌ 🌳 shgl

**Fr Ljubljana take E16/A2 & exit dir Bled/Lesce. At
rndabt take 2nd exit for Bled & cont along rd 209.
In Bled take rd around lake on L (lake on R), site sp
- winding rd.** 5*, Lge, mkd, pt shd, pt sl, EHU (16A)
inc (long lead req some pitches - fr recep); gas; bbq;
sw nr; twin axles; red long stay; TV; bus to Ljubljana
adj; Eng spkn; ccard acc; games rm; fishing; white
water rafting; games area; horseriding; bike hire;
dog shwrs; CKE. *"Beautifully situated nr lake; m'van
& car wash; busy, popular, well-run site; well-drained
in bad weather altho lower pitches poss muddy; v
gd, modern, clean san facs, stretched in ssn; helpful,
efficient, friendly staff; spa cent nrby; paragliding;
conv Vintgar Gorge, Bled Castle, Lake Bohinj, Dragna
Valley; excel walking/cycling around lake; excel
rest; arr acc anytime; free WiFi throughout site."*
€34.00, 1 Apr-15 Oct, X03. 2018

See advertisement

BOHINJSKA BISTRICA *B1* (0.8km NW Rural)
46.27438, 13.94798 **Camping Danica Bohinj,**
Triglavska 60, 4264 Bohinjska Bistrica (04) 5721702;
info@camp-danica.si; www.camp-danica.si

🄁 🐕 €2 🕅 ⬜ 🚻 ⬝ ∥ 🗺 🦋 ⵌ ℔ ⟟ ℞ nr /ⵥ

Site on o'skts of vill clearly sp. 3*, Med, pt shd,
EHU (6A) inc (long lead poss req); gas; red long stay;
10% statics; Eng spkn; ccard acc; tennis; canoe hire;
kayak hire; fishing; CCI. *"Excel site, spacious, open,
attractive site in beautiful valley; fly-fishing; gd walking
& climbing; gd, clean san facs but poss stretched high
ssn; conv bus to Ljubljana & Lake Bohinji."* **€33.00**
2018

SLOVENIA

KAMNIK *B2* (1km NE Urban) *46.22724, 14.61902*
Kamp Resnik, Nevlje 1a, 1240 Kamnik **(01) 8317314;**
info@kampresnik.com; www.kampresnik.com

🐾 ♦♦ ⱳ ⚲ 🛒 ⊿ ᴹˢᴾ ⴹ ⓗ nr 🐕 nr 🏛

Fr Ljubljana foll rd sp Celje then turn N for Kamnik.
Fr Kemnik by-pass (E side of rv) bear R thro 2 sets
traff lts, site 200m on L just after sports cent - site
ent not obvious, turn bef zebra x-ing opp pub. Fr E
on rd 414, site sp. 2*, Med, pt shd, EHU (10A) €3;
gas; 5% statics; bus; Eng spkn; adv bkg acc; ccard
acc; golf nr; CKE. "*Conv Ljubljana & Kamnik Alps;
friendly staff; pleasant, well-kept; thermal spa nrby;
pool adj; new excel extra shwrs (2018); views of
Kamniska Alps; short stroll into town; rly stn 1km.*"
€17.00, 1 May-30 Sep. **2019**

KOBARID *B1* (1km NE Rural) *46.25070, 13.58664*
Kamp Koren, Drežniške Ravne 33, 5222 Kobarid (05)
3891311; info@kamp-koren.si; www.kamp-koren.si

12 🐾 €2 ♦♦(htd) ⱳ ⚲ 🛒 ⊿ ᴹˢᴾ 🦋 ⴹ ⓗ nr 🐕 🏛

Turn E fr main rd in town, site well sp dir Drežnica.
4*, Med, pt shd, EHU (16A) €4; red long stay; TV; Eng
spkn; ccard acc; bike hire; canoeing; CKE. "*Vg, clean
facs but stretched; friendly, helpful staff; pitches
cramped; pleasant location in beautiful rv valley; excel
walk to waterfall (3hrs); WW1 museum in town; lge
elec lead poss req.*" **€30.00** **2017**

KOPER *D1* (7km N Coastal) *45.57818, 13.73573*
Camping Adria, Jadranska Zesta 25, 6280 Ankaran
(05) 6637350; camp@adria-ankaran.si; www.adria-
ankaran.si

🐾 €4 ♦♦ ⱳ ⚲ 🛒 ⊿ ᴹˢᴾ ⴹ ⓗ ⊿ 🐕 🏛 ⊿ 🏊 ⊤ adj

Fr A1/E70/E61 onto rd 10 then rd 406 to Ankaran.
Or cross Italian border at Lazzaretto & foll sp to site
in 3km. Site sp in vill. 4*, Lge, mkd, shd, EHU (10A)
€3; bbq; 60% statics; bus 500m; ccard acc; tennis;
bike hire; waterslide; sauna. "*Old town of Koper worth
a visit;1 Olympic-size pool; Vinakoper winery rec N of
site on dual c'way; poss noisy groups high ssn; insect
repellent req; private san facs avail; clean san facs but
red LS; gd rest; has beach but not picturesque; vg.*"
€35.00, 8 Apr-15 Oct. **2018**

KRANJSKA GORA *B1* (14km E Rural) *46.46446,
13.95773* **Camping Kamne,** Dovje 9, 4281 Mojstrana
(04) 5891105; info@campingkamne.com;
www.campingkamne.com

12 🐾 €2 ♦♦(htd) ⱳ ⚲ 🛒 ⊿ ᴹˢᴾ 🦋 ⴹ ⓗ nr 🐕 nr 🏛 ⊿

Sp fr rd 201 bet Jesenice & Kranjska Gora, 2km E
of Mojstrana. Do not go thro vill of Dovje. 3*, Sm,
hdstg, pt shd, terr, EHU (6A) €2.50-3.50; red long stay;
TV; 10% statics; bus to Kranjska Gora fr site; Eng spkn;
bike hire; tennis; fishing; CKE. "*Conv Triglav National
Park & border; views Mount Triglav; warm welcome;
ltd san facs stretched high ssn; hiking; friendly helpful
staff; gd cycling along old rlwy track; steep site; some
pitches sm, some with good views; tap for filling
aquarolls at bottom of site.*" **€31.00** **2019**

KRANJSKA GORA *B1* (4km E Rural) *46.484438,
13.837885* **Camping Spik,** Jezerci 21, 4282 Godz
Martuljek **(51) 634466; info@camp-spik.si;**
www.camp-spik.com

12 🐾 ♦♦(htd) ⱳ ⚲ 🛒 ⊿ 🛒 ⊿ ᴹˢᴾ ⴹ ⴹ ⓗ 🐕 🏛 ⊿(htd) 🛏

Fr Ratece foll rd past Kranjska Gora to Gozd. Thro
vill, bear L over rv bdge, site ent immed on L adj
hotel. 3*, Lge, mkd, shd, EHU (10A); bbq (charcoal,
elec, gas); red long stay; twin axles; 40% statics;
phone; adv bkg acc; ccard acc; bike hire; fitness rm;
tennis adj; sauna; climbing wall. "*Conv Kranska Gora
National Park; max 2 dogs; vg rests in KG; gd walking
& cycling; LS check in at hotel; gd facs; next to Spa
Hotel.*" **€33.70** **2019**

LJUBLJANA *C2* (5km N Urban) *46.09752, 14.51870*
Ljubljana Resort, Dunajska Cesta 270, 1000 Ljubljana
(01) 5890130; ljubljana.resort@gpl.si; www.ljubljana
resort.si

12 🐾 €3 ♦♦(htd) ⱳ ⚲ 🛒 ⊿ ᴹˢᴾ ⴹ ⴹ ⓗ 🐕 🏛 ⊿ 🛏

Fr Maribor take A1 twd Ljubljana, at junc Zadobrova
take Ljubljana ring rd twd Kranj & exit junc 3 sp Lj -
Ježica, Bežigrad. At x-rds turn R twd Črnuče along
Dunajska Cesta, turn R 100m bef rlwy x-ing. Fr N
(Jesenica/Karawanken tunnel) exit A2/E66 at junc
13 sp Ljubljana Črnuče & foll rd for 3.5km; at rndabt
junc with Dunajska Cesta rd turn R (1st exit); site on
L in 200m. 4*, Lge, mkd, hdg, pt shd, EHU (10A) €4.50;
bbq (elec, gas, sep area); 10% statics; phone; bus to
city at site ent (tickets at recep); Eng spkn; ccard acc;
horseriding 500m; rv fishing; tennis; bike hire; games
rm; CKE. "*Busy site by rv; gd rest; naturist sunbathing
adj pool; dishwash area; red facs LS; archery; fitness
club; pitches nr hotel poss noisy due late-night
functions; whirlpools; htd pool complex adj; some
pitches muddy when wet; conv for city; cycle & walking
path along Rv Sava; friendly, helpful staff.*" **€33.00,
X04.** **2018**

MARIBOR *B3* (5km SW Urban) *46.5355, 15.60508*
Camping Centre Kekec, Pohorska ulica 35c, 2000
Maribor **040 665 732; info@cck.si or bernard@cck.si;**
www.cck.si

12 🐾 €1.50 ♦♦(htd) ⱳ ⊿ ᴹˢᴾ ⴹ ⴹ nr ⓗ nr

Fr S on A1 exit Maribor Jug; foll rd until you see
Bauhaus shopping cent on the R, turn L at this x-rd;
turn R after approx 400m; turn L after approx 100m;
site on L after approx 3km opp the Terano Hotel.
Sm, mkd, hdstg, unshd, pt sl, terr, EHU (25A) €3; bbq;
Eng spkn; adv bkg acc; ccard acc; CKE. "*Rec for larger
o'fits as lge pitches avail but care with narr ent rd; v
nice site.*" **€23.00** **2017**

NAZARJE *B2* (7km W Rural) *46.31166, 14.90916*
Camping Menina, Varpolje 105, 3332 Rečica ob
Savinji **(0)** 40525266; info@campingmenina.com

🈯 🐕 €3 ⛺ ⚌ ♨ 🍽 ⚡ 🔵 🦋 ⛲ 🍴 ⊕ 🍴 ⛰

Fr rte E57 bet Ljubljana & Celje, turn N twd Nazarje,
then dir Ljubno for 3km. Site sp. 4*, Med, hdstg, mkd,
shd, EHU (6-16A) €3; sw nr; 10% statics; Eng spkn; adv
bkg acc; bike hire; CKE. *"Helpful owners; delightful site
in woodland; very ltd facs in winter."* **€26.00**   2016

> ## "I like to fill in the reports as I travel from site to site"
>
> You'll find report forms at the back of this guide, or you can fill them in online at camc.com/europereport.

NOVO MESTO *C3* (11km SW Rural) *45.76735,
15.05150* **Campsite Polje,** Meniška vas 47, 8350
Dolenjske Toplice **(0)** 40466589; info@kamp-polje.si;
kamp-polje.si

🐕 ⛺ (htd) ♨ ⚌ ♨ 🦋 ⚡ 🔵nr

W fr Novo Mesto on 419 to Dolenjske Toplice. Foll
sp. Hdstg, mkd, pt shd, EHU (16A); bbq (charcoal, elec,
gas); sw nr; twin axles; Eng spkn; adv bkg rec; ccard
acc; bike, canoe and scooter hire; fishing. *"Ideal NH or
longer; forest on one side, fields other; ACSI discount."*
€18.00, 1 Apr-5 Nov.   2019

PIVKA *D2* (3km S Rural) *45.708997, 14.192552*
Camp Plana, Selce 66, 6257 Pivka **(07)** 0668668;
camp.plana@gmail.com; camping-plana.com

🐕 ⛺ ♨ ⚌ ♨ 🔵 🍽 ⚡ 🔵 ⛰

Fr the border with Croatia at the end of E61/A7
foll rte 6 to Pivka. Site sp on R off rte 6. Sm, hdstg,
pt shd, EHU (10A); cooking facs; sw nr; twin axles;
TV; Eng spkn; adv bkg acc; games area. *"Excel."*
€25.00, 1 Apr-31 Oct.   2018

PORTOROZ *D1* (3km S Coastal) *45.50138, 13.59388*
Camping Lucija, Obala 77, 6320 Portorož
(05) 6906000; camp.lucija@bernardingroup.si;
www.camp-lucija.si

🐕 €5 ⛺ ♨ ⚌ ♨ 🍽 🍽 🍽 ⚡ 🔵 🚣 🏊adj

Fr Koper (N) on rd 111, turn R at traff lts in Lucija.
Take next L, then 2nd L into site. Nr Metropol Hotel,
site sp. 3*, Lge, pt shd, serviced pitches; EHU (6-10A)
€4.50; 60% statics; Eng spkn; ccard acc; bike hire; CKE.
*"Conv Piran old town by bike or bus; sea views; sep area
for tourers, extra for beach pitch; sm pitches; vg facs;
busy site; gd public beach; noise fr disco opp till 4am."*
€37.00, 11 Mar-2 Nov.   2016

POSTOJNA *C2* (5km NW Rural) *45.80551, 14.20470*
Camping Pivka Jama, Veliki Otok 50, 6230 Postojna
(05) 7203993; avtokamp.pivka.jama@siol.net;
www.camping-postojna.com

🐕 ⛺ (htd) ♨ ⚌ ♨ 🦋 🍽 ⚡ 🔵 🍴 ⊕ ⛰ 🏊 🍴

Fr N or S Exit A1/E61 strt over traff lts, R at
rdbt then bear L at next, foll sp to caves grotto
(Postojnska Jama). Pass caves on R & then foll signs
for Predjama Castle. 3km after caves site sp. Narr,
winding app rd. 3*, Lge, hdstg, shd, pt sl, terr, EHU
(6A) €3.70 (rev pol); cooking facs; 50% statics; Eng
spkn; adv bkg acc; ccard acc; tennis; CKE. *"Gd forest
site; gd rest with live Tirolean music; gd san facs, needs
updating (2017); used as transit to Croatia, open 24
hrs; caves 4km a must visit (take warm clothing!)."*
€29.00, 1 Apr-31 Oct, X09.   2018

PREBOLD *B3* (0.2km N Rural) *46.24027, 15.08790*
Camping Dolina, Dolenja Vas 147, 3312 Prebold
(03) 5724378; camp@dolina.si; www.dolina.si

🈯 🐕 €2 ⛺ ⚌ ♨ 🦋 🍽 ⚡ 🔵nr 🔵nr 🍴(htd)

On A1/E57 turn R 16km fr Celje sp Prebold & foll
sp, site on N edge of vill. 3*, Sm, unshd, EHU (6-10A)
€3.30; gas; red long stay; bike hire; CKE. *"Gd clean facs
but no changing area in shwrs; helpful, friendly owner;
conv Savinja valley; gd walking."* **€20.00**   2016

> ## "We must tell the Club about that great site we found"
>
> Get your site reports in by mid-August and we'll do our best to get your updates into the next edition.

PREBOLD *B3* (15km W Rural) *46.24458, 14.943502*
Camping Podgrad Vransko, Praprece 30, 3305
Vransko **(386)** 51229155; www.camp-vransko.com

🈯 🐕 ⛺ (htd) ♨ ♨ ⚌ 🦋 ⚡ ⛰

Foll sp off A1 at Vransko. Site 0.5km NW of town.
Well sp. Sm, hdstg, mkd, pt shd, EHU (16A); bbq
(charcoal, elec, gas); Eng spkn; ccard acc; games rm;
games rm. *" New site (2018); v friendly, helpful owners;
MH disposal; panaramic views."* **€23.00**   2019

ROGASKA SLATINA *B3* (12km S Rural) *46.16499,
15.60495* **Camping Natura Terme Olimia,** Zdraviliška
Cesta 24, 3254 Podčetrtek **(03)** 8297000; info@
terme-olimia.com; www.terme-olimia.com

⛺ (htd) ♨ ♨ ⚌ ♨ 🍽 ⚡ 🔵 🍽 🔵nr 🍴 🍴 ⛰ 🏊 (covrd, htd) 🍴

Fr Celje take rte E dir Rogaška Slatina. Turn S sp
Podčetrtek just bef Rogaška. Site on L (waterchutes)
alongside Rv Solta on Croatian border in approx
10km. 5*, Sm, unshd, EHU (10-16A) €3.20; TV; phone;
adv bkg acc; ccard acc; bike hire; waterslide; golf
4km; tennis; horseriding 2km; sauna; fitness rm; CKE.
*"Aqualuna Thermal Pk adj; vg walking country with
wooded hillsides."* **€32.00, 15 Apr-15 Oct.**   2016

SLOVENIA

VELENJE *B3* (2km NW Rural) *46.36832, 15.08864*
Autocamp Jezero, Cesta Simona Blatnika 26, 3320
Velenje **(03) 5866466; mastodontbar@gmail.com**
🐾 €1.50 👫 📶 🏕 ♿ 🖻 ✦ 🅿 🦋 ⁇ ⑪ nr ⛟ 💺 nr ⛺

**Exit A1/E57 at Velenje & cont to 2nd traff lts,
then turn R. Turn L at 3rd traff lts & foll site sp.
Site on lakeside.** Med, mkd, pt shd, EHU (10A) inc;
sw; 10% statics; fitness rm; tennis; games area;
watersports. *"Lovely location but nr coal-powered
power stn; poss unkempt LS; Velenje coal mining
museum worth visit 1km; san facs need refurb (2015);
poor."* **€22.00, 1 May-30 Sep.** **2015**

VIPAVA *C1* (2km S Rural) *45.832168, 13.971053*
Kamp Tura, Gradišče pri Vipavi 14a, 5271 Vipava
**(08563) 96320; info@kamp-tura.si; www.kamp-
tura.si**
12 🐾 👫 📶 🏕 ♿ 🖻 ⁇ ⑪ 💺 ⛺

**Foll sp fr Vipava. Steep, narr approach, not suitable
for units over 5m.** TV; Eng spkn; Ccard acc. *"Gd facs;
helpful owner; gd walks/climbing."* **€32.00** **2019**

"I need an on-site restaurant"

We do our best to make sure site information
is correct, but it is always best to check any
must-have facilities are still available or will
be open during your visit.

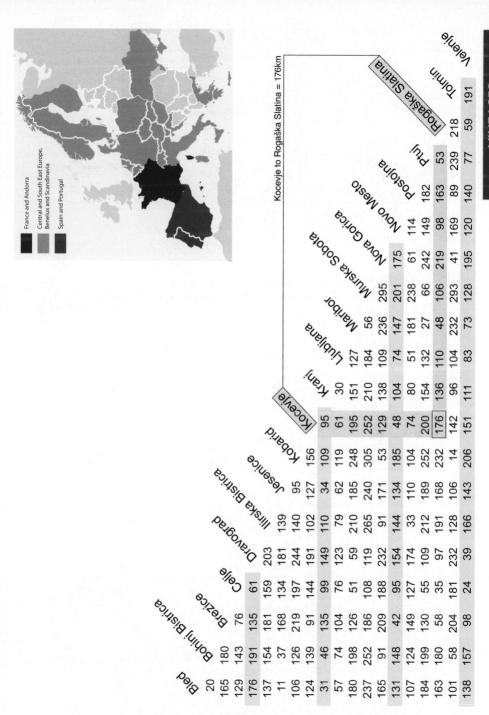

Kocevje to Rogaška Slatina = 176km

Sweden

Stockholm

Highlights

Renowned for combining simple beauty with functionality, Sweden is one of the design capitals of the world. This is shown in everything from gothic cathedrals and baroque palaces to its more modern creations.

As one of Europe's largest, least populated countries Sweden has a lot of green space to enjoy. An extensive network of national parks and trails mean even the most remote parts of the country are easily accessible.

Due to its shorter summers, Sweden makes the most of the long days by packing as many events into them as possible. One of these is a crayfish party, which is a traditional summertime eating and drinking celebration.

Sweden is also celebrated for its rich variety of children's literature, with Astrid Lindgren's Pippi Longstocking, or Pippi Långstrump, one of the most well-known creations.

Major towns and cities

- Stockholm – a dynamic capital city which is the home of the Nobel Prize.
- Gothenburg – this port city has plenty of history on show.
- Malmö – a green city with plenty of beautiful parks.
- Uppsala – this city has ancient roots and boast a dominating cathedral and castle.

Attractions

- Vasa Museum, Stockholm – This fascinating museum features a fantastically preserved shipwreck from the 17th century
- Sigtuna – the oldest town in Sweden, boasting a picturesque medieval centre filled with restaurants, shops and cafés.
- Drottningholm Palace – A residence of the Swedish royal family, this stunning palace has beautiful gardens.

Find out more

www.visitsweden.com
E: info@visitsweden.com T: 0046 (0) 87 89 10 00

Country Information

Population (approx): 9.9 million

Capital: Stockholm

Area: 450,000 sqkm

Bordered by: Finland, Norway

Terrain: Mostly flat or gently rolling lowlands; mountains in the west

Climate: Cold, cloudy winters, sub-arctic in the north; cool/warm summers. The best time to visit is between May and September; August can be hot and wet. Be prepared for occasional sub-zero temperatures and snowfalls, even in summer months

Coastline: 3,218km

Highest Point: Kebnekaise 2,104m

Language: Swedish

Local Time: GMT or BST + 1, i.e. 1 hour ahead of the UK all year

Currency: Krona (SEK) divided into 100 öre; £1 = SEK 12.47, SEK 100 = £8.02 (October 2019)

Emergency Numbers: Police 112 (or 11414 for non-emergency calls); Fire Brigade 112; Ambulance 112. Operators speak English

Public Holidays 2020: Jan 1, 6; Apr 10, 12, 13; May 1, 21; Jun 6, 19, 20; Nov 1; Dec 24, 25, 26.

School summer holidays are from early June to the second or third week of August

Border Posts

There are approximately 40 Customs posts along the Swedish/Norwegian border. They are situated on all main roads and are normally open Mon to Fri from 8.30am - 4pm/5pm.

Travellers with dutiable goods must cross the land borders during hours when the Customs posts are open. However, travellers without dutiable goods may cross the border outside Customs post opening hours.

The main border posts with Finland are at Haparanda, Övertornea, Pajala and Karesuando.

Customs Regulations

Visitors arriving from an EU country via a non-EU country (e.g. Norway) may bring quantities of tobacco and alcohol obtained in EU countries, plus the amounts allowed duty-free from non-EU countries. However, you must be able to produce proof of purchase for goods from EU countries and goods must be for your personal use.

Entry Formalities

Holders of valid British and Irish passports may visit for up to three months without a visa.

Medical Services

Health care facilities are generally very good and most medical staff speak English. Thre is no GP system; instead visit the nearest hospital clinic (Akutmottagning or Värdcentral) and present your passport and European Health Insurance Card (EHIC). You will be charged a fee for the clinic visit (free for anyone under 20) plus a daily standard charge if it is necessary to stay in hospital.

Prescriptions are dispensed at pharmacies (apotek) which are open during normal shopping hours. Emergency prescriptions can be obtained at hospitals. Dentists (tandläkare or folktandvård) offer emergency out-of-hours services in major cities but you may have to pay the full cost of treatment.

The use of mosquito repellent is recommended, particularly from mid June to September when mosquitos are most common. Mosquitos are generally more often encountered in the north of Sweden rather than the south.

Visitors to remote areas should consider the relative inaccessibility of the emergency services. In northern Sweden mobile phone coverage does not generally extend beyond main roads and the coast.

Opening Hours

Banks: Mon-Fri 9.30am-3pm or 5pm and until 5.30pm one day a week in larger towns. Many banks do not handle cash after 3pm and some banks will not handle cash at all.

Museums: Check locally, opening hours can vary.

Post Offices: Post offices no longer exist. Mail is dealt with at local shops, kiosks and petrol stations; opening hours vary.

Shops: 8am-8pm every day. Shops generally close early the day before a public holiday.

Regulations for Pets

In order to protect the countryside and wildlife, dogs are not allowed to run off the lead from 1 March to 20 August and at other times in certain areas.

Dogs travelling directly from the UK and Ireland must be microchipped and have an EU pet passport. For more information please visit www.jordbruksverket.se (english option) and go to the 'Animals' section.

Safety and Security

Petty crime levels are much lower than in most other European countries but you should take the usual commonsense precautions. Pickpocketing is common in the summer months in major cities where tourists may be targeted for their passports and cash.

In recent years there have been incidents of 'highway robbery' from motorhomes parked on the roadside, especially on the west coast between Malmö and Gothenburg.

Sweden shares with the rest of Europe an underlying threat from terrorism. Attacks could be indiscriminate and against civilian targets in public places, including tourist sites.

British Embassy

SKARPÖGATAN 6-8,115 93 STOCKHOLM
Tel: (08) 6713000
www.ukinsweden.fco.gov.uk/en/

Irish Embassy

Hovslagargatan 5, 111 48 STOCKHOLM
Tel: (08) 54504040
www.dfa.ie/sweden

Documents

Driving Licence

A UK driving licence is only valid when it bears a photograph of the holder, i.e. a photocard licence, or when it is carried together with photographic proof of identity, such as a passport.

Money

Foreign currency may be exchanged in banks and bureaux de change.

Major credit cards are widely used both for major and minor transactions and cash machines (Bankomat or Minuten) are widespread. It is advisable to carry your passport or photocard driving licence if paying with a credit card as you may be asked for photographic proof of identity.

Driving

Accidents

In the case of an accident it is not necessary to call the police unless there are injuries to drivers or passengers and/or vehicles are badly damaged, but drivers are required to give their details to the other persons involved before leaving the accident scene. A driver leaving the scene of an accident without following this procedure may be fined.

If you are involved in an accident with a possible third party claim, you are strongly recommended to report the accident to the national Swedish insurance bureau which will act as claims agent. Contact Trafikförsäkringsforeningen in Stockholm, tel: 08 522 78100, info@ tff.se, www.tff.se.

Accidents involving wild animals (e.g. elk, reindeer, bear, wolf, etc) must be reported to the police immediately by calling 112 or 11414 and the spot where the accident took place must be marked by putting up reflective tape or anything clearly noticeable so that the police can find it easily. Collisions must be reported even if the animal involved is not injured. After reporting the accident and marking out the place, a driver may leave. Accidents involving smaller animals (badgers, foxes, etc) need not be reported.

Alcohol

Penalties for driving a motor vehicle under the influence of alcohol are extremely severe. The police carry out random breath tests. If the level of alcohol exceeds 20 milligrams in 100 millilitres of blood a fine will be imposed and driving licence withdrawn. This level is considerably lower than that permitted in the UK (80 milligrams) and equates to virtually zero. A level exceeding 100 milligrams is considered to be severe drink driving for which a jail sentence of up to two years may be imposed and licence withdrawn.

Breakdown Service

The motoring organisation, Motormännens Riksförbund (known as the 'M'), does not operate a breakdown service. It does, however, have an agreement with 'AssistanceKåren' (a nationwide road service company) which operates a 24-hour, all-year service and can be contacted free on (020) 912912 or 08 6275757 from a foreign-registered mobile phone. Phone boxes are becoming quite scarce and it is advisable to carry a mobile phone. There are normally no emergency telephones along motorways or dual carriageways. Charges for assistance and towing vary according to day and time and payment by credit card is accepted.

Child Restraint System

Children under the height of 135cm must be seated in a child restraint or child seat. A child aged 15 or over, or 135cm in height or taller, can use normal seat belts in the car.

Children under the height of 140cm are only allowed in the front seat if the passenger seat airbag has been deactivated.

Fuel

Petrol stations are usually open from 7am to 9pm. Near motorways and main roads and in most cities they may remain open until 10pm or even for 24 hours. Outside large towns garages seldom stay open all night but

most have self-service pumps (possibly not for diesel) which accept credit cards. In the far north filling stations may be few and far between so keep your tank topped up. Credit cards are accepted.

LPG (known as gasol) is sold at a very limited number of petrol stations mainly located in central and southern Sweden.

Lights

Dipped headlights are compulsory at all times, regardless of weather conditions. Bulbs are more likely to fail with constant use and you are recommended to carry spares. Fog lights may be used when visibility is poor but they must not be used together with dipped headlights.

Vehicles parked or stopped on a poorly lit road at night, including dawn, dusk and bad weather, must have their parking lights switched on.

Low Emission Zones

There are Low Emission Zones (Miljözen) in Sweden. Please see www.lowemissionzones.eu for the most up-to-date information.

Motorways

There are approximately 1,900 kms of motorway and 560 kms of semi-motorway or dual carriageway, all confined to the south of the country and relatively free of heavy traffic by UK standards. There are no service areas or petrol stations on motorways; these are situated near the exits and are indicated on motorway exit signs. Please note that there are no petrol stations close to the 110km long Uppsala to Gälve motorway.

Overtaking

Take care when overtaking long vehicles. A typical long-distance Swedish truck is a six-wheeled unit towing a huge articulated trailer, i.e. a very long load.

Many roads in Sweden have wide shoulders or a climbing lane to the right of the regular lane and these permit drivers of slow moving vehicles or wide vehicles to pull over to allow other traffic to pass. These climbing lanes and shoulders should not be used as another traffic lane.

Parking

Parking meters and other parking restrictions are in use in several large towns. Vehicles must be parked facing the direction of the flow of traffic. Wheel clamps are not in use but illegally parked vehicles may be towed away and, in addition to a parking fine, a release fee will be charged.

In an area signposted 'P' parking is permitted for a maximum of 24 hours, unless otherwise stated.

Priority

Vehicles driving on roads designated and signposted (with a yellow diamond on a black background) as primary roads always have priority. On all other roads, as a general rule, vehicles coming from the right have priority, unless signs indicate otherwise. This rule is sometimes ignored however, especially by vehicles on roads regarded as major roads but not signposted as such.

At most roundabouts signs indicate that traffic already on the roundabout has priority, i.e. from the left.

Give trams priority at all times. Where there is no refuge at a tram stop, you must stop to allow passengers to board and alight from the tram.

Roads

The condition of national and country roads is good although some minor roads may be covered with oil-gravel only. Road surfaces may be damaged following the spring thaw, and some may be closed or have weight restrictions imposed during that period. Gradients are generally slight and there are no roads that need to be avoided for vehicles towing a caravan.

Road repairs tend to be intensive during the short summer season. Information on major roadworks and road conditions on E roads and major national roads can be obtained from www.trafikverket.se.

There is a good road link with Norway in the far north of Sweden. The Kiruna-Narvik road is open all year from Kiruna to the border. It is a wide road with no steep gradients.

There is generally little or no heavy goods traffic on roads during the Christmas, Easter and midsummer holidays or on the days preceding these holidays so good progress can be made.

Road Signs and Markings

Road signs and markings conform to international standards. Warning lines (usually on narrow roads) are broken lines with short intervals which indicate that visibility is limited in one or both directions; they may be crossed when overtaking. Unbroken lines should not be crossed at any time.

National roads (riksvägar) have two-digit numbers and country roads (länsvägar) have three-digit numbers. Roads which have been incorporated into the European road network – E roads – generally have no other national number.

Direction and information signs for motorways and roads which form part of the European road network are green. Signs for national roads and the more important country roads are blue. Signs for local roads are white with black numerals.

The following are some other signs that you may see:

Passing place

Additional stop sign

Accident

Swedish	English Tanslation
Enkelriktat	One way
Farlig kurva	Dangerous bend
Grusad väg	Loose chippings
Höger	Right
Ingen infart	No entrance
Parkering förbjuden	No parking
Vänster	Left

Speed Limits

	Open Road (km/h)	Motorway (km/h)
Car Solo	60-100	90-120
Car towing caravan/trailer	70-80	80
Motorhome under 3500kg	60-100	90-120
Motorhome 3500-7500kg	70-100	90-120

Speed limits are no longer based on the category of road but on the quality and safety level of the roads themselves. As a result limits may vary from one town to another and along stretches of the same road. It is advisable, therefore, to pay close attention to road signs as speed limits are strictly enforced. If in doubt, or if no speed limit is indicated, you are advised to keep to 70 km/h (44 mph) until you see a speed limit sign.

Outside built-up areas, including expressways, speeds up to 100 km/h (62 mph) may be permitted according to road signs, providing a lower maximum speed is not applicable for certain vehicle categories. Vehicles with trailers must never exceed 80 km/h (49mph). On motorways the maximum permitted speed is 110 or 120 km/h (68 or 74 mph). During the winter a speed limit of 90 km/h (56 mph) is in force on some motorways and dual carriageways. This limit is signposted.

In most residential areas and during certain periods in areas near schools, speed is limited to 30 km/h (18 mph) according to road signs. Periods indicated in black mean Monday to Friday, those in black in brackets mean Saturday and the eves of public holidays, and those indicated in red mean Sunday and public holidays.

Speed limits for motorhomes under 3,500kg and privately registered motorhomes over 3,500kg are the same as for solo cars. Speed cameras are in use on many roads. The use of radar detectors is not permitted.

Tolls

Tolls for private vehicles have now been introduced. The Motala by-pass (on road 50m in central Sweden) the toll will be 5 SEK and for the Sundsvall by-pass (on E4 in northern Sweden) the toll will be 9 SEK. Göteborg(E6) 9-22 SEK.

Toll Bridges

The Øresund Bridge links Malmö in Sweden with Copenhagen in Denmark and means that it is possible to drive all the way from mainland Europe by motorway. The crossing is via a 7.8 km bridge to the artificial island of Peberholm and a 4 km tunnel. Tolls (payable in cash, including EUR, SEK or DKK or by credit card) are levied on the Swedish side and are as follows for single journeys (2018 prices subject to change)

Vehicle(s)	Price
Solo car or motorhome up to 6 metres	€55 online €59 at toll
Car + caravan/trailer or motorhome over 6 metres	€110 online €118 at toll

Vehicle length is measured electronically and even a slight overhang over six metres will result in payment of the higher tariff.

Speed limits apply in the tunnel and on the bridge, and during periods of high wind the bridge is closed to caravans. Bicycles are not allowed. Information on the Øresund Bridge can be found on www.oeresundsbron.com.

Svinesund Bridge

There is a 700 metre long bridge linking Sweden and Norway on the E6, at Svinesund. Tolls are SEK24 (NOK20) for light vehicles and SEK120 (NOK100) for vehicles over 3,500kgs (2018).

Traffic Lights

A green arrow indicates that traffic may proceed with caution in the direction of the arrow but pedestrians must be given priority. A flashing amber light indicates that a crossing/turning must be made with caution.

Violation of Traffic Regulations

Police are authorised to impose and collect fines for violation of minor traffic offences which must be paid at a bank, normally within two to three weeks. Offences, which may qualify for a fine include driving without lights in daylight, speeding, lack of a warning triangle or nationality plate (GB or IRL) or a dirty or missing number plate.

If a fine is not paid and the driver is a resident of another EU country, notice of the fine will be forwarded to the authorities in the driver's country of residence. Jaywalking is not permitted; pedestrians must use official crossings.

Winter Driving

The winter months are periods of severe cold and you should be prepared for harsh conditions. The fitting of winter tyres is compulsory for vehicles from 1st December to 31st March in the event of severe winter road conditions, i.e. the road is covered with ice or snow, or if the road is wet and the temperature is around freezing point. Trailers towed by these vehicles must also be equipped with winter tyres. These regulations apply to foreign registered vehicles.

Essential Equipment

Warning Triangle

It is compulsory for foreign registered vehicles to carry a warning triangle. They should be placed as a distance of 50 meters behind the vehicle on ordinary roads and 100 meters on motorways.

Touring

Ferry services connect Sweden with Denmark, Estonia, Finland, Germany, Latvia, Lithuania, Norway and Poland; some services only operate in the summer. Full details are available from Visit Sweden, www.visitsweden.com. Scheduled car ferry services also operate between the mainland and the island of Gotland during the summer season.

In the south and centre the touring season lasts from May to September. In the north it is a little shorter, the countryside being particularly beautiful at each end of the season. Campsites are most crowded over the midsummer holiday period and during the Swedish industrial holidays in the last two weeks of July and first week of August. Tourist attractions may close before the end of August or operate on reduced opening hours.

Sweden has 15 UNESCO World Heritage sites and 29 national parks which, together with nature reserves, cover eight percent of the country. Information on national parks and nature reserves is available on www.naturvardsverket.se.

Inland, particularly near lakes, visitors should be armed with spray-on, rub-on and electric plug-in insect repellent devices as mosquitoes and midges are a problem.

Discount cards are available in Stockholm and Gothenburg offering free public transport and free admission to many museums and other attractions, plus free boat and canal sightseeing trips. Buy the cards at tourist information offices, hotels, kiosks, some campsites and online – see www.stockholmtown.com or www.goteborg.com.

Local tourist offices are excellent sources of information and advice; look for the blue and yellow 'i' signs. Information points at lay-bys at the entrance to many towns are good sources of street maps.

A good-value 'dagens rätt' (dish of the day) is available in most restaurants at lunchtime. A service charge is usually included in restaurant bills but an additional small tip is normal if you have received good service.

The most popular alcoholic drink is lager, available in five strengths. Wines, spirits and strong beer are sold only through the state-owned 'Systembolaget' shops, open from Monday to Friday and on Saturday morning, with branches all over the country. Light beer can be bought from grocery shops and supermarkets. The minimum age for buying alcoholic drinks is 20 years at Systembolaget and 18 years in pubs, bars and licensed restaurants.

It is not permitted to smoke in restaurants, pubs or bars or in any place where food and drinks are served.

Camping and Caravanning

Camping and caravanning are very popular, but because summer is short the season is brief - from May to early September, although winter caravanning is increasing in popularity. High season on most sites ends around the middle of August when prices and site office opening hours are reduced or sites close altogether. There are more than 1,000 campsites, about 350 of which remain open during the winter particularly in mountainous regions near to ski resorts. Those that are open all year may offer fewer or no facilities from mid-September to April and advance booking may be required.

In late June and July advance booking is recommended, especially at campsites along the west coast (north and south of Göteborg), on the islands of Öland and Gotland and near other popular tourist areas.

Approximately 500 campsites are members of the SCR (Svenska Campingvärdars Riksfärbund – Swedish Campsite Owners' Association), which are classified from 1 to 5 stars. Visitors wishing to use these sites must have a Camping Key Europe card. You can buy the Camping Key Europe at campsites and you will be given a temporary card, or you can order it in advance from www.camping.se/en for 150 SEK (2018 prices). If ordering in advance you should allow at least 3 weeks for delivery.

Also aim to arrive by mid afternoon to get a better pitch, since many Swedes arrive late. It is reported that hand basins on sites often do not have plugs so it is advisable to carry a flat universal plug when touring.

Many sites have a 'Quick Stop' amenity which provides safe, secure overnight facilities on, or adjacent to, a site. This normally includes the use of sanitary facilities. 'Quick Stop' rates are about two thirds of the regular camping rate if you arrive after 9pm and leave before 9am.

Casual/wild camping is normally permitted (except in National Parks and recreational areas), however for security reasons it is not recommended to spend the night in a vehicle on the roadside or in a public car park. Instead use the 'Quick Stop' amenity at campsites. In any event local parking rules and signposting should always be observed.

Alternatively there are around 150 organised 'ställplatser' mainly intended for motorhomes but generally car and caravan outfits may also use them for an overnight stay at the discretion of the site's manager. For a list of 'ställplatser' see www.campinggladje.se/resa.

Most designated rest areas along highways are owned and managed by the Vågverket (Swedish Roads Administration) which, although not officially ranked as 'ställplatser', offer adequate parking space and various facilities for motorhomes staying overnight. A map showing these rest areas is available at local tourist offices.

Cycling

The network of cycle lanes in Sweden is growing rapidly and many cycle routes are named and signposted. In some cases cycle lanes are combined with foot paths. See www.svenska-cykelsallskapet.se.

The 'Sverigeleden' cycle trail covers the whole country and connects all major ports and cities. The 190km cycle route along the Göta Canal from Sjötorp on Lake Vänern to Mem on the Baltic coast is relatively flat and hence a very popular route.

The wearing of a safety helmet is compulsory for children up to the age of 15 and is recommended for everyone.

Electricity and Gas

On campsites the current is usually 10 amps or more and round two-pin plugs are used. CEE connections are becoming standard.

Propane (gasol) is the gas most widely obtainable at more than 2,000 Primus dealers; you will need to buy an appropriate adaptor. It is understood that it is possible to sell back your propane cylinder at the end of your holiday and outlets will also exchange the corresponding Norwegian Progas cylinders. Recent visitors report that major distributors will refill cylinders but they must be of a recognised make/type and in perfect condition.

Butane gas is available from a number of outlets including some petrol stations. It is understood that Campingaz 904 and 907 cylinders are available but recent visitors report that they may be difficult to find, and virtually impossible in the north of the country.

For more information on butane suppliers contact the Swedish Campsite Owners' Association (SCR) by email: info@scr.se

Ensure that you are well-equipped with gas if venturing north of central Sweden as it may be difficult to find an exchange point. Many sites have communal kitchen facilities which enable visitors to make great savings on their own gas supply.

The Midnight Sun and Northern Lights

The Midnight Sun is visible north of the Arctic Circle from about the end of May until the middle of July.

The Northern Lights (Aurora Borealis) are often visible during the winter from early evening until midnight. They are seen more frequently the further north you travel. The best viewing areas in Sweden are north of the Arctic Circle between September and March.

The Order of Bluenosed Caravanners

Visitors to the Arctic Circle from anywhere in the world may apply for membership of the Order of Bluenosed Caravanners which will be recognised by the issue of a certificate by the International Caravanning Association (ICA).

For more information contact bluenosed@ icacaravanning.org and attach a photograph of yourselves and your outfit under any Arctic Circle signpost, together with the date and country of crossing and the names of those who made the crossing.

This service is free to members of the ICA (annual membership £20); the fee for non-members is £5. Coloured plastic decals for your outfit, indicating membership of the Order, are also available at a cost of £4. Cheques should be payable to the ICA. For more information visit www.icacaravanning.org.

Public Transport & Local Travel

Stockholm has an extensive network of underground trains (T-bana), commuter trains, buses and trams. Underground station entrances are marked with a blue 'T' on a white background. You can buy single tickets for one of three zones at the time of your journey, or save money by buying tickets in advance. A discount applies if you are aged 65 or over. Single tickets and prepaid tickets are valid for one hour after beginning your journey. Travel cards offer reduced price public transport in Stockholm for periods of 1, 3, 7 or 30 days – see www.sl.se (click on 'Visitor') for details of routes, fares and tickets.

For information on public transport systems in Göteborg and Malmö, see www.vasttrafik.se and www.skanetrafiken.se.

Stockholm is built on an archipelago of islands and island hopping ferries operate all year. You can buy single tickets or an island hopping pass for use on the Waxholmsbolaget and Cinderella fleet of ferries.

Confirm your taxi fare before setting off in the vehicle. Some companies have fixed fares which vary according to the day of the week and time of day. A full price list must be on display. Payment by credit card is generally accepted. It is usual to round up the fare shown on the meter by way of a tip.

Sweden is a country of lakes, rivers and archipelagos and, as a result, there are over 12,000 bridges. Road ferries, which form part of the national road network, make up the majority of other crossings. Most ferries are free of charge and services are frequent and crossings very short.

A congestion charge was introduced in Stockholm in 2007. Drivers of foreign-registered vehicles are exempt from the charge. For more information go to www. visitstockholm.com. In some other towns traffic restrictions may apply during certain periods and these are signposted.

When giving directions Swedes will often refer to distances in 'miles'. A Swedish 'mile' is, in fact, approximately ten kilometres. All road signs are in kilometres so if a Swede tells you it is 3 miles to a town, expect the journey to be around 30km.

Sites in Sweden

AHUS *2F4* (1km NE Urban/Coastal) *55.94118, 14.31286* **First Camp Ahus (formerly Regenbogen),** Kolonivägen 59, 29633 Åhus **(044) 248969; ahus@ firstcamp.se; firstcamp.se**

🔢 🐕 👫(htd) 🅆 ♨ ♿ 🚽 ⚊ 🅼 🐾 ⛴ Tnr ⊕nr 🛒 ⚗

🏖️sand 150m

Take rd 118 fr Kristianstad SE twd Åhus. Site well sp fr ent to town. 3*, Lge, mkd, hdstg, pt shd, EHU (10A) SEK29; bbq; 10% statics; Eng spkn; ccard acc; sauna; site clsd 3 Nov-16 Dec; CKE. *"Gd base for walking, cycling, watersports; htd pool 300m; excel fishing; famous area for artists."* **SEK 260**   **2016**

ALMHULT *2F3* (2km N Rural) *56.56818, 14.13217* **Sjöstugans Camping (G5),** Campingvägen, Bökhult, 34394 Älmhult **(0476) 71600; info@sjostugan.com; www.sjostugan.com**

🐕 👫(htd) 🅆 ♨ ♿ 🚽 ⚊ 🅼 🐾 ℗ T ⊕ à 🛒nr ⚗ 🏖️sand adj

Fr Växjö SW on rd 23, at rndabt turn W to Älmhult. Fr town cent turn N on Ljungbyvägen, site in 1.5km on lakeside, well sp. 3*, Med, pt shd, pt sl, EHU (16A) SEK45; bbq; cooking facs; twin axles; 25% statics; bus 500m; Eng spkn; adv bkg acc; ccard acc; canoe hire; sauna; games area; CKE. *"Some lakeside pitches; well-kept site; lake adj; 1st Ikea store opened here in 1958; v helpful staff; excel."* **SEK 283, 1 May-30 Sep.**   **2017**

AMAL *2E2* (1km SE Urban) *59.0465, 12.7236* **Örnäs Camping (P2),** Gamla Örnäsgatan, 66222 Åmål **(0532) 17097; ornascamping@amal.se; www.amal.se**

🔢 🐕 👫(htd) 🅆 ♨ ♿ ⚊ 🅼 🐾 T ⊕nr à 🛒nr ⚗

Leave rd 45 to Åmål, site sp. 4*, Med, mkd, hdstg, pt shd, pt sl, terr, EHU (10A) inc; red long stay; 10% statics; Eng spkn; ccard acc; boat hire; fishing; bike hire; tennis; CCS; sauna. *"Gd views Lake Vänern; lake adj."* **SEK 275**   **2017**

ARBOGA *2G1* (13km S Rural) *59.28134, 15.90509* **Herrfallets Camping (U14),** 73293 Arboga **(0589) 40110; reception@herrfallet.se; www.herrfallet.se**

🔢 🐕 👫(htd) 🅆 ♨ ♿ 🚽 ⚊ 🅼 🐾 ℗ T ⊕ ⚗ 🎣

Foll sp fr E20/E18, turn off at Sätra junc twd Arboga, cross rv. Foll sp to Herrfallet/Västermo. 4*, Med, mkd, pt shd, serviced pitches; EHU (10A) SEK40; bbq; sw; phone; ccard acc; boating; bike hire; sauna; CKE. *"Lovely spot on edge Lake Hjälmaren."* **SEK 270**   **2016**

ARJANG *2E1* (26km SE Rural) *59.30399, 12.44662* **Camping Grinsby,** Grindsbyn 100, Sillerud, 67295 Årjäng **(0573) 42022; campgrinsby@telia.com; www.campgrinsby.se**

🐕 👫(htd) 🅆 ♨ ♿ 🚽 ⚊ 🅼 🐾 🛒 ⚗

On E18 SE fr Årjäng & Sillerud, turn L at site sp. Site in 2km on Stora Bör lake. Med, hdstg, pt shd, terr, EHU (10A) SEK40; bbq; cooking facs; sw nr; 10% statics; phone; Eng spkn; adv bkg acc; ccard acc; games rm; bike hire; boat hire; CKE. *"A 'wilderness' site in beautiful setting; many walking paths; friendly, helpful staff; vg san facs."* **SEK 231, 1 May-3 Sep.**   **2017**

ARJEPLOG *1C2* (1.5km W Rural) *66.05007, 17.86298* **Kraja Camping (BD1),** Krajaudden, 93090 Arjeplog **(0961) 31500; kraja@silverresort.se; www.kraja.se**

🔢 🐕 👫(htd) 🅆 ♨ ♿ 🚽 ⚊ 🅼 🐾 ℗ T ⊕ 🛒nr ⚗ 🎿(htd) ⛷ 🏖️sand

NW fr Arvidsjaur thro Arjeplog vill to site on R. 3*, Lge, unshd, EHU (16A) SEK40; bbq; cooking facs; sw nr; twin axles; TV; 90% statics; phone; bus 500m; Eng spkn; adv bkg acc; sauna; boating; fishing; CKE. *"Gd cent for local Lapp area; hotel on site with full facs; 20 touring pitches; v pleasant & helpful staff; keypad security at night; excel Sami silver museum in town."* **SEK 235**   **2017**

ASARNA *1B3* (9km S Rural) *62.56340, 14.38786* **Kvarnsjö Camp,** Kvarnsjö 696, 84031 Åsarna **(0682) 22016; info@kvarnsjocamp.com; www.kvarnsjo camp.com**

🔢 🐕 👫(htd) 🅆 ♨ ⚊ 🅼 🐾

Fr N on E45 3km after Åsarna turn R onto rd 316 dir Klövsjo. In 8km turn L sp Cmp Kvarnsjö. In 8km cross rlwy, thro vill, site on L in 1km. Fr S 9km after Rätan turn L dir Klövsjo. In 1.5km bear R at Y-junc site in 4km. 3*, Sm, hdstg, unshd, terr, EHU (10A) SEK40; Eng spkn; adv bkg acc; sauna; CKE. *"CL-type family-run site o'looking woods & mountains; excel walking, fishing; boating, fresh bread/breakfast in high ssn."* **SEK 200**   **2017**

BOCKSJO *2F2* (5km NW Rural) *58.68058, 14.59911* **Stenkällegårdens Camping i Tiveden,** 54695 Stenkällegården **(0505) 60015; stenkallegarden@ swipnet.se; www.stenkallegarden.se**

🔢 🐕 👫(htd) 🅆 ♨ ♿ 🚽 ⚊ 🅼 🐾 ℗ ⊕ 🛒 ⚗

N on rd 49 fr Karlsborg, turn L at Bocksjö, site sp on L in 2km. Pt of rte single track with passing places. 4*, Med, mkd, pt shd, pt sl, terr, EHU (10A) SEK40; bbq; cooking facs; sw; TV; 30% statics; Eng spkn; ccard acc; fishing; boat hire; sauna; site clsd last 2 weeks Apr & 1st 2 weeks Oct; CKE. *"Gd cycling; mkd walking trails; spacious, sheltered site; clean san facs; skiing on site in winter; Tiveden National Park 5km."* **SEK 250**   **2016**

BORAS *2E3* (2.5km N Urban) *57.73885, 12.93608*
Caming Borås Salteman (P11), Campinggatan 25,
50602 Borås **(033) 353280; info@borascamping.com;
www.borascamping.com**

12 🛉 🛉🛉 WD 🛁 🛆 🖫 / MP 💗 ⊕ 🐕 🏂nr /🏔

**Exit N40 fr Göteborg for Borås Centrum; foll sps to
Djur Park R42 to Trollhätten thro town; well sp.**
4*, Med, mkd, pt shd, pt sl, EHU (10A) SEK30; cooking
facs; twin axles; TV; 10% statics; bus 350m; Eng
spkn; adv bkg acc; boating; CKE. *"Gd pitches adj rv
with paths; quickstop o'night facs; gd zoo 500m; pool
500m; gd, clean facs; nr sports stadium/tennis courts."*
SEK 270 **2017**

BORENSBERG *2G2* (1.5km S Rural) *58.55663,
15.27911* **Strandbadets Camping,** 59030 Borensberg
**(0141) 40385; info@strandbadetscamping.se;
www.strandbadetscamping.se**

🛉🛉 WD 🛁 🛆 🖫 / MP 💗 ⊕ 🐕 🏂nr /🏔

**Foll sp for Camping Gota Canal fr Rd 34 thro town &
across canal. Site 2nd site on R.** 3*, Med, pt shd, EHU
(10A) SEK50; cooking facs; sw; 10% statics; fishing.
*"Gd base for Östergötland & Lake Vättern area; cycle
rte along Göta Canal."* **SEK 190, 22 Apr-11 Sep.** **2018**

DOROTEA *1C3* (0.5km SW Rural) *64.25850, 16.38833*
Doro Camping, Storgatan 1A, 91731 Dorotea **(0942)
10238; reception@dorocamp.com; www.doro
camping.com**

12 🛉🛉 WD 🛁 🛆 🖫 / 💗 💗 ⊕ 🐕 🏂 /🏔

Site on E side of E45. 3*, Med, pt shd, pt sl, EHU (10A)
SEK50; cooking facs; sw; 10% statics; Eng spkn;
sauna; site clsd Nov; golf; fishing. *"Site being
extensively redeveloped (2019); most impressive rest."*
SEK 218 **2019**

ED *2E2* (2km E Rural) *58.89931, 11.93486* **Gröne
Backe Camping (P8),** Södra Moränvägen 64, 66832
Ed **(0534) 10144; gronebackecamping@telia.com**

12 🛉🛉 WD 🛁 🛆 / 💗 💗 ⊕ nr 🏂nr /🏔

App Ed on rd 164/166, site sp on Lake Lilla Le.
3*, Med, shd, pt sl, EHU (10A) SEK40; sw; ccard acc;
sauna; bike hire; CKE. *"Excel for boating."*
SEK 291 **2016**

EKSJO *2F3* (1km E Rural) *57.66766, 14.98923* **Eksjö
Camping (F13),** Prästängsvägen 5, 57536 Eksjö **(0381)
39500; info@eksjocamping.se; www.eksjocamping.se**

12 🐕 🛉🛉 WD 🛁 🛆 🖫 / MP 💗 💗 ⏳ ⊕ 🐕 🏂 /🏔

**Site sp fr town cent on rd 33 twd Västervik, on
lakeside.** 3*, Med, shd, EHU (10A) SEK45; sw nr;
10% statics; phone; ccard acc; boating; fishing; bike
hire; CKE. *"Gd cent glass region; attractive countryside
& old town."* **SEK 250** **2016**

ENKOPING *2H1* (6km S Rural) *59.59334, 17.07146*
Bredsand Camping & Stugby, Bredsandsvägen 22,
74948 Enköping **(0171) 80011; bredsand@nordic
camping.se; www.nordiccamping.se**

12 🐕 🛉🛉(htd) WD 🛁 🛆 🖫 / 💗 💗 ⊕ 🐕 🏂nr

**Fr E18 or rd 55 foll sp to site, well sp on Lake
Mälaren.** 3*, Med, mkd, pt shd, pt sl, EHU (10A)
SEK50; sw nr; 50% statics; CKE. *"Vg site."*
SEK 287 **2015**

FALKOPING *2F2* (2km W Rural) *58.17595, 13.52726*
Mössebergs Camping & Stugby (R7), Scheelegatan,
52130 Falkoping **(0515) 17349 or 07072 56493;
mossebergscamping@telia.com; www.mossebergs
camping.se**

12 🐕 🛉🛉 🛁 🛆 🖫 / MP 💗 💗 🏂nr /🏔

**Exit rd 184 at Falköping; foll Int'l Camping sps or
sps to Mösseberg; site also sp fr rds 46 & 47 & in
town. Site on plateau overlkg town.** 3*, Med, mkd,
pt shd, EHU SEK40; cooking facs; sw nr; 10% statics;
phone; ccard acc; sauna; CKE. *"Pool 400m; site has
barrier."* **SEK 230** **2018**

FILIPSTAD *2F1* (1km N Rural) *59.72035, 14.15899*
Munkeberg Camping (S5), Skillervägen, 68233
Filipstad **(0590) 50100; alterschwede@telia.com;
www.munkeberg.com**

12 🐕 🛉🛉(htd) WD 🛁 🛆 🖫 / 💗 💗 💗 🐕 🏂nr /🏔

**Fr Karlstad take rd 63 to Filipstad. In town foll sp
for rd 246 twd Hagfors, site sp in town.** 3*, Med, pt
shd, pt sl, EHU (10A) SEK30; sw; 10% statics; adv bkg
acc; fishing; boating; CKE. *"Beautiful lakeside site; gd
for touring old mining district."* **SEK 208** **2016**

GADDEDE *1B2* (0.4km NE Rural) *64.50400, 14.14900*
Gäddede Camping & Stugby, Sagavägen 9, 83090
Gäddede **(0672) 10035; info@gaddedecamping.se;
www.gaddedecamping.se**

12 🐕 🛉🛉(htd) 🛁 🛆 🖫 / 💗 💗 ⊕ nr 🏂nr /🏔 🎣(htd) 🚣

**On ent Gäddede cent on rd 342, turn R & site in
500m on R, sp.** 3*, Med, mkd, pt shd, EHU (10A)
SEK50; TV; 40% statics; Eng spkn; adv bkg acc; ccard
acc; games area; canoe hire; games rm; sauna; fishing;
CKE. *"Gd touring base 'Wilderness Way'."*
SEK 198 **2016**

GALLIVARE *1C2* (1km S Urban) *67.1290, 20.6776*
Gällivare Campingplats (BD5), Kvarnbacksvägen 2,
98231 Gällivare **(0970) 10010; info@gellivare
camping.com; www.gellivarecamping.com**

🐕 🛉🛉(htd) WD 🛁 🛆 🖫 / MP 💗 💗 ⊕ nr 🏂 /🏔

On E45 app fr SW on R immed after bdge. 3*, Sm,
hdstg, mkd, unshd, EHU (10A) SEK30; bbq; cooking
facs; sw nr; twin axles; TV; 50% statics; phone; Eng
spkn; ccard acc; bike hire; sauna; games area; CKE.
*"Helpful, friendly owners; pleasant pitches on rvside; gd
facs; daytime cafe opp; rest & shops 1km; sep car pk."*
SEK 160, 13 May-27 Sep. **2018**

SWEDEN

GAMLEBY *2G2* (1km SE Coastal) *57.88475, 16.41373*
KustCamp Gamleby (formerly Hammarsbadets),
Hammarsvägen 10, 59432 Gamleby **(0493) 10221;**
info@campa.se; www.campa.se

🏕 👬 ⓦ 🛉 ♿ ⌷ ∥ 🅼🅿 🦋 ♒ 🍽 ⓐ 🅓 🏔 🛥 ⅋ sand adj

On E22 Kalmar-Norrköping, foll sp to site 2km off
main rd. 4*, Med, mkd, pt shd, terr, EHU (10A) SEK45;
sw; 10% statics; phone; ccard acc; boat hire; tennis;
Quickstop o'night facs; sauna; bike hire; CKE. *"Clean,
well-kept, relaxing site."* **SEK 312, 1 May-15 Sep.**
2016

GESUNDA *1B4* (2km N Rural) *60.90100, 14.58500*
Sollerö Camping (W60), Levsnäs, 79290 Sollerön
(0250) 22230; info@sollerocamping.se; www.sollero
camping.se

🄬 👬 ⓦ 🍴 🛉 ♿ ∥ 🅼🅿 🦋 ♒ 🍽 ⓐ 🅓 🏔

Fr Gesunda take bdge to Sollerön Island in Lake
Siljan. Site immed on R on reaching island; clearly
visible fr bdge. 3*, Lge, pt shd, pt sl, EHU (16A); sw nr;
adv bkg acc; ccard acc; tennis; boat hire; sauna; canoe
hire; CKE. *"Beautiful outlook to S across lake; gd base
for Dalarna folklore area; gd site & facs; every 7th day
is free."* **SEK 260**   **2019**

GOTEBORG *2E3* (22km ENE Rural) *57.758329,
12.252601* **Aspen Camping,** Seglarvagen 25, 443 30
Lerum **(0302) 71166;** info@aspencamping.se;
www.aspencamping.se

🏕 ⓦ 🍴 🛉 ♿ ∥ 🅼🅿 ♒ 🅓 🏔

E20 exit 84. Foll sp to Lerum Centrum. At next
rndabt turn L under rly, then L at next rndabt. Site
on R after 600m. Med, hdstg, mkd, pt shd, pt sl, EHU
(10-16A) inc; bbq; cooking facs; sw nr; twin axles;
50% statics; train 600m; Eng spkn; games area; CCI.
*"Vg site; fishing & boat hire; mini golf on site; some
pitches clse to rlwy."* **SEK 230, 1 May-30 Sep.**   **2018**

GOTEBORG *2E3* (4km E Rural) *57.7053, 12.0286*
Lisebergsbyn Camping Kärralund (O39),
Olbersgatan 1, 41655 Göteborg **(031) 840200;**
lisebergsbyn@liseberg.se; www.liseberg.se

🄬 🐕 👬 ⓦ 🍴 🛉 ♿ ∥ 🅼🅿 ♒ 🍽 ⓐ 🅓 🏔

Exit E6/E20 junc 71 onto rd 40 E & foll sp
Lisebergsbyn, site well sp. Lge, unshd, pt sl, terr,
EHU (16A) inc; gas; bbq; cooking facs; twin axles;
TV; 25% statics; phone; tram 400m; Eng spkn; adv
bkg rec; ccard acc; games area; CKE. *"Boat trips
arranged; vg, well-run site; LS arr early to obtain barrier
key; poss travellers on site; cycle path to Liseberg
amusement park & town cent; impressive, organised &
professional staff; red LS & Sun-Fri; lovely site; san facs
outstanding."* **SEK 450**   **2017**

GOTEBORG *2E3* (7km W Urban) *57.70413, 12.02989*
Lisebergs Ställplats, Olbersgatan 9, 416 55 Göteborg
031 840 200; lisebergsbyn@liseberg.se; www.liseberg.se

🄬 🏕 ⓦ ∥ 🅼🅿 ♒ 🏔

Take Backebogatan to Litteraturgatan. Then E6
and Delsjövägen to Olbersgatan. At rndabt take 1st
exit to Olbersgatan, Turn R & R again, site on L. Sm,
mkd, hdstg, pt shd, EHU (10A) inc; own san rec; bbq;
Eng spkn; adv bkg acc; ccard acc. *"Tram at bottom of
hill past main site ent, main site off will help with travel
info etc; excel."* **SEK 240**   **2016**

GRANNA *2F2* (0.5km NW Rural) *58.02783, 14.45821*
Grännastrandens Familjecamping (F3), Hamnen,
56300 Gränna **(0390) 10706;** info@grannacamping.se;
www.grannacamping.se

🏕 👬 ⓦ 🍴 🛉 ♿ ∥ 🅼🅿 🦋 ♒ ⓐnr 🅓 🏔

In cent of Gränna down rd twd Lake Vättern, sp
Visingsö Island. 3*, Lge, unshd, EHU (10A) metered
+ conn fee; sw; TV (pitch); CKE. *"Ballooning cent
of Sweden; Visingsö Island, Brahehus ruined castle,
glass-blowing 3km; vg site; gd location; some
cottages; excel, clean san facs, excel camp kitchen."*
SEK 300, 30 Apr-3 Oct.   **2016**

HALMSTAD *2E3* (10km S Coastal) *56.59033,
12.94430* **Gullbrannagården Camping (N27),** 31031
Eldsbërga **(035) 42180;** mail@gullbrannagarden.se;
www.gullbrannagarden.se

🄬 🏕 👬 ⓦ 🍴 🛉 ♿ ∥ 🅼🅿 🦋 ♒ 🅓 🏔 ⅋ 🛥 sand 500m

Fr S site sp on E6. Lge, pt shd, pt sl, EHU SEK45;
cooking facs; 60% statics; Eng spkn; adv bkg acc;
games rm. *"Christian-run site; church & bible classes;
alcohol discouraged; OK for those of like mind."*
SEK 290   **2016**

HAMBURGSUND *2E2* (1km S Coastal) *58.54075,
11.28240* **Rorviks Camping,** Rorviksangen 15 45747
Hamburgsund **05 25 33 573;** info@rorrvikscamping.se;
www.rorvikscamping.se

🏕 🐕 👬 ⓦ 🍴 🛉 ∥ 🅼🅿 🅓 ⅋

Take exit 103 on the E6 (bet Tatum V-Munkedal).
Foll 163 W to Kville. Turn L to Hamburgsund,
cont S 1km. Campsite on R. Lge, hdstg, mkd, pt
shd, EHU (10A) inc; bbq; cooking facs; twin axles;
10% statics; bus 1km; Eng spkn; adv bkg acc; games
area; CCI. *"Quiet, low key site in a great area; vg."*
SEK 350, 1 May-31 Aug.   **2019**

HAPARANDA *1D2* (15km N Rural) *65.9620, 24.0378*
Kukkolaforsen Camping (BD27), Kukkolaforsen
184, 95391 Haparanda **(0922) 31000;** info@
kukkolaforsen.se; www.kukkolaforsen.se

🄬 👬 (htd) ⓦ 🛉 ♿ ∥ ♒ 🍽 ⓐ 🅓 🏔

On rd 99 on banks of Rv Tornionjoki. 3*, Med, pt shd,
EHU (10A) SEK40; TV; phone; adv bkg acc; ccard acc;
sauna; bike hire; fishing; CKE. *"Friendly staff; rv rapids."*
SEK 280   **2016**

SWEDEN

HARNOSAND *1C3* (2.5km NE Coastal) *62.64451, 17.97123* **Sälstens Camping (Y21),** Sälsten 22, 87133 Härnösand **(0611) 18150; salsten.camping@telia.com**

👫(htd) ⚓ ♿ 🅿 ⚙ 🐾 ♟ ♨ 🎿 ⛺

On Gulf of Bothnia, E of town & on S side of inlet; exit off E4; foll sp for Härnösand town cent, then intn'l camping sp; then site. 3*, Sm, mkd, pt shd, terr, EHU (10A); TV; Eng spkn; CKE. *"Folk museum in town; excel site."* **SEK 250, 15 May-31 Aug.** 2016

HEDESUNDA *2G1* (5km SE Rural) *60.35000, 17.02100* **Hedesunda Camping (formerly Sandsnäs),** Övägen 68, 81040 Hedesunda **(0291) 44123; info@hedesunda camping.se; www.hedesundacamping.se**

👫(htd) ⚓ ♿ 🅿 ⚙ 🐾 ♟ ⊕ ♨ ⛽nr ⛺

Exit rd 67 L at sp Hedesunda. Foll camp sp thro Hedesunda; past church, cont about 4km to Hedesunda Island. 3*, Sm, pt shd, EHU (6A) SEK30; gas; cooking facs; sw nr; red long stay; TV; Eng spkn; fishing; boat hire; CKE. *"Peaceful, lakeside site; organised activities in ssn; helpful staff."* **SEK 260, 1 May-31 Oct.** 2016

"There aren't many sites open at this time of year"

If you're travelling outside peak season remember to call ahead to check site opening dates – even if the entry says 'open all year'.

HELSINGBORG *2E4* (5km S Coastal) *56.0034, 12.7300* **Campingplatsen Råå Vallar (M3),** Kustgatan, 25270 Råå **(042) 182600; raavallar@nordiccamping.se; www.nordiccamping.se**

12 👫(htd) ⚓ ♿ 🅿 ⚙ 🐾 ♟ ♨ ⊕ ♨ ⛺ 🎿 ⛱ ⛺sand

Exit E6 into Helsingborg onto rd 111 to Råå, foll sp to camp. 3*, Lge, pt shd, EHU (10A) SEK50; gas; 10% statics; phone; ccard acc; Quickstop o'night facs; golf 5km; fishing; sauna; CKE. *"Excel, secure site with gd facs; sports cent 2km; friendly, helpful staff; excursions to Copenhagen via Helsingør or Landskrona; town bus excursions to King's Summer Palace daily; boat trips to glass works at Hyllinge."* **SEK 410** 2016

HOGANAS *2E4* (8km N Rural) *56.27061, 12.52981* **FirstCamp Mölle (M1),** Kullabergsvägen, 26042 Mölle **(042) 347384; molle@firstcamp.se; www.firstcamp.se**

🐾 👫(htd) ⚓ ♿ 🅿 ⚙ 🐾 ♟ ♨ ⊕ ♨ ⛺ 🐾 ⛺1.5km

Site is S of Mölle at junc of rds 11 & 111, at foot of Kullaberg. 5*, Lge, unshd, pt sl, EHU (10A) inc; cooking facs; 10% statics; Eng spkn; ccard acc; games area; golf; Quickstop o'night facs; sauna; fishing. *"Steep slope to san facs; walking; Krapperups Castle & park sh walk fr site; excel outdoor activities."* **SEK 417, 1 Apr-30 Sep.** 2016

HOVA *2F2* (8.7km NE Coastal) *58.90998, 14.28995* **Otterbergets Bad & Camping,** 54891 Hova **050633 127 or 0738064 935; info@otterbergetscamping. com; www.otterbergetscamping.com**

🐾 👫 WD ⚓ ♟ ♿ 🅿 ⚙ MSP 🐾 ♟ ⊕ ♨ ⛺adj

Fr Laxa take E20 rd; site sp approx 4km fr Hova; drive 2 km thro woods to site. Med, mkd, pt shd, EHU (16A) SEK 40; bbq; cooking facs; 10% statics; Eng spkn; adv bkg rec; sauna; CCI. *"Attractive site with private access to lake; events held such as fishing competition & trade fairs (when site may be busy); v helpful Dutch owners; recep 0800-2200; san facs vg; excel."* **SEK 253, 15 Apr-1 Nov.** 2017

JOKKMOKK *1C2* (3km SE Rural) *66.59453, 19.89145* **Arctic Camp Jokkmokk,** Notudden, 96222 Jokkmokk **(0971) 12370; arcticcamp@jokkmokk.com; arctic campjokkmokk.se/en/**

12 🐾 👫(htd) WD ⚓ ♿ 🅿 ⚙ MSP 🐾 ♟ ♨ ⊕ ♨ ⛺ 🎿(htd)

Sp fr rd 45. In Jokkmokk take rd 97 E, site in 3km on N side of rd situated bet rv & rd. 4*, Lge, mkd, pt shd, EHU (10A) SEK40 (poss rev pol); sw nr; 10% statics; Eng spkn; adv bkg acc; ccard acc; bike hire; waterslide; fishing; sauna; CKE. *"Friendly, clean, well-maintained site 5km inside Arctic Circle; gd area for Sami culture; excel playgrnd; lakeside setting, gd pool; late arrival area."* **SEK 290** 2018

JOKKMOKK *1C2* (3km W Rural) *66.60500, 19.76200* **Skabram Stugby & Camping,** Skabram 206, 96299 Jokkmokk **(0971) 10752; info@skabram.se; www.skabram.se**

12 🐾 👫(htd) WD ⚓ ♿ 🅿 ⚙ 🐾 ♟

Site sp fr E45 along rd 97, Storgatan. Sm, hdstg, pt shd, EHU (16A) SEK25; bbq; cooking facs; sw nr; twin axles; 10% statics; Eng spkn; adv bkg acc; sauna; fishing; boating. *"Vg; canoe & dog sleigh trips; relaxing site; lovely sm fm type site; v quiet location; gd san facs."* **SEK 185** 2017

JONKOPING *2F3* (15km S Rural) *57.66245, 14.18407* **Lovsjöbadens Camping (F7),** Hyltena, 55592 Jönköping **(036) 182010; info@lovsjocamping.se; www.lovsjocamping.se**

🐾 👫 WD ⚓ ♟ ♿ 🅿 ⚙ 🐾 ♟ ♨

Exit E4 at Hyltena, site sp on lakeside. 3*, Sm, mkd, pt sl, terr, EHU (10-16A) SEK30; bbq; cooking facs; sw; TV; 10% statics; Eng spkn; adv bkg acc; ccard acc; bike hire; boat hire; games rm; CKE. *"V friendly owners; vg site by sm lake; busy in high ssn; sm sw beach; rowing boats for hire."* **SEK 260, 15 May-15 Sep.** 2015

SWEDEN

KALMAR *2G3* (2km S Coastal) *56.64975, 16.32705*
Stensö Camping (H12), Stensövägen, 39247 Kalmar
(0480) 88803; info@stensocamping.se; www.stenso
camping.se

🏕🚻 wc ⚓ ♨ 🚿 🔥 🍴 MSP 🏋 Ỵ ⊕ 🛒 ⚫ /ⁿ 🌲 sand adj

Fr E22 foll sp Sjukhus (hosp) then camping sp - this
avoids town cent. Fr town cent, site sp. 4*, Lge, mkd,
shd, pt sl, EHU (10A) SEK40 (check pol); cooking facs;
10% statics; phone; Eng spkn; ccard acc; boating;
fishing; Quickstop o'night facs; cycling; CKE. *"Conv
Öland Island (over bdge); glass factories in vicinity;
walking dist to town; helpful, friendly staff; new clean
san facs (2014); excel."* **SEK 276, 27 Mar-30 Sep.**
2016

KAPPELLSKAR *2H1* (0.5km W Rural) *59.72046,
19.05045* **Camping Kapellskär (B9)**, Riddersholm 985,
76015 Gräddö (0176) 44233

🏕🚻(htd) wc ⚓ ♨ 🚿 🔥 MSP 🏋 Ỵ ⊕ nr 🛒 ⚫ /ⁿ

Fr Norrtälje take E18 E sp Kapellskär. At ferry sp
turn R, site in 1km, sp. Last 700m on unmade rd.
3*, Med, mkd, hdstg, pt shd, terr, EHU (10A) SEK40;
60% statics; Eng spkn; adv bkg acc; ccard acc; games
area; bike hire; CKE. *"Conv for ferry terminal; fair site."*
SEK 272, 1 May-29 Sep. **2015**

KARESUANDO *1D1* (2km SE Rural) *68.43396,
22.51577* **Karesuando Camping**, Laestadiusvagen
185, 98016 Karesuando (0981) 20139; karesuando.
camping@hotmail.com; www.karesuando.se/
foretag/camping/camping.htm

🏕🚻 wc ⚓ 🚿 🔥 MSP 🏋 🛒 /ⁿ

Travelling N on E45, in town cont past bdge to
Finland onto rd 99 for approx 2km; site on L. App
fr Finland, turn L after x-ing bdge; cont on 99 for
2km. Sm, unshd, EHU (10A) inc; bbq; twin axles;
50% statics; Eng spkn; adv bkg acc; sauna; games
area; CKE. *"Model Sami vill on site; cash point in PO;
poss mosquito prob; canoe hire avail; gd view of
midnight sun on rv; unmkd pitches, fills up quickly."*
SEK 230, 18 May-18 Sep. **2018**

KATRINEHOLM *2G2* (2km S Rural) *58.9696, 16.21035*
Djulö Camping (D6), Djulögatan 51, 64192 Katrineholm
(0150) 57242; info@djulocamping.se; www.djulo
camping.se

12 🏕🚻 ⚓ ♨ 🚿 🔥 MSP 🏋 ⊕ nr 🛒 nr /ⁿ

At Norrköping on E4 cont twd Stockholm for about
3km, turn L onto rd 55 N twd Katrineholm. Camping
site sp in 2km. 3*, Lge, hdstg, pt sl, EHU (10A) SEK35;
gas; sw; adv bkg acc; ccard acc; games area; bike hire;
fishing; boating; CKE. *"On lakeside in lge park; well-run,
friendly site."* **SEK 291** **2016**

KIL *2F1* (7km N Rural) *59.54603, 13.34145*
Frykenbadens Camping (S17), Stubberud, 66591 Kil
(0554) 40940; info@frykenbaden.se; www.fryken
baden.se

12 🏕🚻 ⚓ ♨ 🚿 🔥 MSP 🏋 Ỵ 🛒 /ⁿ

Fr Karlstad take rd 61 to Kil, site clearly sp on
lakeside. 4*, Lge, pt shd, pt sl, EHU (10A) SEK40;
sw; TV; phone; adv bkg acc; fishing; Quickstop
o'night facs; boat launch; bike hire; CKE. *"Very clean,
spacious waterfront site; sauna SEK5; barrier key."*
SEK 376 **2018**

KIRUNA *1C1* (1.6km NE Urban) *67.8604, 20.2405*
Ripan Hotel & Camping, Campingvägen 5, 98135
Kiruna (0980) 63000; info@ripan.se; www.ripan.se

12 🏕🚻(htd) wc ⚓ 🚿 🔥 MSP 🏋 Ỵ 🛒 nr /ⁿ 🎿(htd)

Site sp fr town cent. 3*, Med, hdstg, mkd, unshd, EHU
(10A) inc; TV (pitch); Eng spkn; ccard acc; sauna. *"No
privacy in shwrs; easy walk to town; public footpath
thro site (top end) - poss v noisy & disruptive; trips to
Kirunavaara Deep Mine fr tourist info office; no security
fence."* **SEK 323** **2016**

KIVIK *2F4* (1.6km N Rural/Coastal) *55.69135,
14.21373* **Kiviks Familjecamping (L35)**, Väg 9, 27732
Kivik (0414) 70930; info@kivikscamping.se;
www.kivikscamping.se

🏕🚻 wc ⚓ ♨ 🚿 🔥 MSP 🏋 ⊕ 🛒 /ⁿ 🌲 shgl 1km

On rd 9 o'looking sea, sp. 3*, Med, mkd, unshd, EHU
SEK35; bbq; cooking facs; TV; 20% statics; phone; Eng
spkn; ccard acc; CKE. *"Steam rlwy w/end in summer at
Brösarp; cider/apple area; easy walk to town; rev pol
certain pitches."* **SEK 230, 16 Apr-9 Oct.** **2016**

KOLMARDEN *2G2* (2km SE Coastal) *58.6597, 16.4006*
First Camp Kolmården (E3), 61834 Kolmården
(011) 398250; kolmarden@firstcamp.se; www.first
camp.se

🏕🚻(htd) wc ⚓ ♨ 🚿 🔥 MSP 🏋 Ỵ ⊕ 🛒 ⚫ /ⁿ 🌲 adj

Fr E4 NE fr Norrköping take 1st Kolmården exit
sp Kolmården Djur & Naturpark. Site on sea 2km
bef Naturpark. 4*, Lge, pt shd, terr, EHU (10A);
cooking facs; TV; 10% statics; phone; ccard acc;
waterslide; sauna; bike hire; boat hire; CKE. *"Gd site;
nr to Kilmarden zoo & aquarium; well mkd pitches."*
SEK 457, 1 Apr-30 Sep. **2019**

KUNGALV *2E2* (1km SE Rural) *57.86211, 11.99613*
Kungälvs Vandrarhem & Camping (O37), Färjevägen
2, 44231 Kungälv (0303) 18900; info@kungalvs
vandrarhem.se; www.kungalvsvandrarhem.se

🏕🚻(htd) wc ⚓ ♨ 🚿 🔥 MSP 🏋 Ỵ ⊕ 🛒 /ⁿ

Exit E6 junc 85 or 86 & foll sp Kungälv cent, then sp
'Bohus Fästning'. Site sp. 3*, Sm, mkd, hdstg, shd,
EHU (12A) SEK40; bbq (gas); red long stay;
10% statics; bus adj; Eng spkn; ccard acc; CCI. *"Site
adj Bonus Fästning (fort) & Kungälv Church (17th C)
on rv bank; find pitch & check in at recep 0800-1000
& 1700-1900; door code fr recep for san facs; gd NH."*
SEK 250, 15 Apr-30 Sep. **2019**

KUNGSBACKA *2E3* (5km SE Rural) *57.42492, 12.15860* **Silverlyckans Camping,** Varbergsvägen 875, 43433 Fjärås **(0300) 541349; www.silverlyckan.eu**

🐕 � (htd) 🅦 ⚏ ♨ ✓ 🦋 ⓦ nr ⚏ nr 🏔 ⟋ sand 4km

Exit E6/E20 junc 58 dir Åsa. Site in 400m on L.
Med, unshd, pt sl, EHU (10A) SEK30; cooking facs; 10% statics; bus adj; Eng spkn; adv bkg acc. *"Vg site; htd pool 3km; mv service pnt (refill only); rec visit Tjölöholms Slott (castle)."*
SEK 180, 1 May-15 Sep. 2019

KUNGSHAMN *2E2* (2km NE Coastal) *58.36569, 11.28077* **Swecamp Johannesvik,** Wagga Nordgard 1, 45634 Kungshamn **(0523) 32387; info@johannesvik. nu; www.johannesvik.nu**

12 🐕 ♻ (htd) 🅦 ⚏ ♨ ⚏ ✓ 🄼 🦋 ⟋ ⓦ ♨ ⚏ 🏔 ⟋ shgl adj

Fr E6 rte 171 to Askum, dir Kungshamn, thro Hovenaset, over bdge. Ent to site on R (sp). 4*, Lge, mkd, unshd, terr, EHU inc; gas; bbq; cooking facs; red long stay; TV; Eng spkn; adv bkg acc; CKE. *"Barrier card SEK150 dep; dep req; shwr card SEK6 (3mins); gd."* **SEK 381** 2017

LANDSKRONA *2E4* (4km N Rural) *55.90098, 12.8042* **Borstahusens Camping (M5),** Campingvägen, 26161 Landskrona **(0418) 10837; bokning@motesplats borstahusen.se; www.motesplatsborstahusen.se**

♻ (htd) 🅦 ⚏ ♨ ⚏ ✓ 🄼 🦋 ♨ ⓦ ♨ ⚏ 🏔 ⟋ adj

Exit E6/E20 at 'Landskrona N' & foll sp for Borstahusen 4.5km fr E6/D20. 3*, Lge, unshd, EHU (10A) SEK40; TV; 50% statics; phone; Eng spkn; ccard acc; tennis; golf; bike hire; CKE. *"Gd, pleasant, well run site on edge of Kattegat; htd pool 2km; sm pitches; game reserve; boat to Ven Island fr town; adj sea but no views; chalets & holiday packages."*
SEK 320, 21 Apr-11 Sep. 2019

LIDKOPING *2F2* (3km N Rural) *58.51375, 13.14008* **Krono Camping (R3),** Läckögaten, 53154 Lidköping **(0510) 26804; info@kronocamping.com; www.krono camping.com**

12 ♻ 🅦 ⚏ ♨ ⚏ ✓ 🄼 🦋 ♨ ⓦ nr ⚏ 🏔

On Lake Vänern nr Folkparken, on rd to Läckö; at Lidköping ring rd foll int'l camping sp. 5*, Lge, pt shd, serviced pitches; EHU (10A) inc; gas; sw nr; TV (pitch); ccard acc; watersports; CKE. *"V clean, friendly, well-run site; open pinewoods on lakeside; htd pool 300m; interesting area."* **SEK 412** 2015

LIDKOPING *2F2* (32km NE Rural) *58.624003, 13.383631* **Kinnekulle Camping & Stugby,** Strandvägen, 53394 Hällekis **(0510) 544102; info@ kinnekullecamping.se; www.kinnekullecamping.se**

♻ (htd) 🅦 ⚏ ✓ 🄼 🦋 ⟋ adj, sand

Turn off E20 at Gotene for Hallekis. Outskirts of Hallekis foll sp (ignore MH NH sp) rd passes factory & heads into woods. Site in 3km. 4*, Lge, mkd, pt shd, pt sl, terr, EHU (10A) inc; 30% statics; Eng spkn; ccard acc; CKE. *"Vg; local walks in woods & hillside; barrier key card."* **SEK 298, 13 Apr-9 Sep.** 2018

LJUNGBY *2F3* (1km N Urban) *56.84228, 13.95251* **Ljungby Camping Park,** Campingvägen 1, 34122 Ljungby **(0372) 10350; reservation@ljungby-semesterby.se; www.ljungby-semesterby.se**

♻ (htd) 🅦 ⚏ ♨ ✓ ⓦ ⚏ 🏔 ⟋

Exit E4 at Ljungby N, site sp. 3*, Med, shd, EHU (10A) SEK35; ccard acc; cycling; CKE. *"Adv bkg ess high ssn; htd pool adj."* **SEK 256, 1 May-31 Aug.** 2016

LJUSDAL *1B3* (3km W Rural) *61.83894, 16.04059* **Ljusdals Camping (X21),** Ramsjövägen 56, 82730 Ljusdal **(0651) 12958; info@ljusdalscamping.se; www.ljusdalscamping.se**

12 🐕 ♻ (htd) 🅦 ⚏ ♨ ⚏ ✓ 🄼 ♨ 🍽 ⓦ ♨ 🏔 ⟋

Leave Ljusdal on Rv83 dir Ånge, site on R in 3km. 3*, Med, pt shd, EHU (10A) SEK40; cooking facs; sw nr; 10% statics; Eng spkn; adv bkg acc; ccard acc; bike hire; games area; sauna; CKE. **SEK 295** 2019

"That's changed – Should I let the Club know?"

If you find something on site that's different from the site entry, fill in a report and let us know. See camc.com/europereport.

LULEA *1D2* (8km W Coastal) *65.59565, 22.07221* **First Camp Luleå (BD18),** Arcusvägen 110, 97594 Luleå **(0920) 60300; lulea@firstcamp.se; www.first camp.se/lulea**

12 🐕 ♻ (htd) 🅦 ⚏ ♨ ⚏ ✓ 🄼 🦋 ♨ 🍽 ⓦ ♨ ⚏ 🏔
⟋ sand adj

Exit E4 on R 500m N of Luleälv Rv bdge. Foll sp 'Arcus' (recreation complex). 3*, V lge, mkd, pt shd, EHU (10A) inc; cooking facs; TV; phone; Eng spkn; adv bkg acc; ccard acc; tennis 300m; car wash; sauna; bike hire; CKE. *"Excel family site; many sports facs; san facs poss stretched high ssn; htd pool complex 700m; suitable RVs & twin axles; adj rlwy museum."*
SEK 365 2019

MALMO *2E4* (11km N Coastal) *55.68873, 13.05756* **Habo-Ljung Camping (M23),** Södra Västkustvägen 12, 23434 Lomma **(040) 411210; info@haboljung camping.se; www.haboljungcamping.se**

♻ (htd) 🅦 ⚏ ♨ ⚏ ✓ 🄼 ♨ ⚏ 🏔 ⟋ ⟋ sand adj

Turn off E6 dir Lomma, head N for Bjärred, site on L. 3*, Lge, pt shd, EHU (10A) SEK40; bbq; cooking facs; 5% statics; phone; Eng spkn; ccard acc; CKE. *"Conv NH; vg; location for wind & kite surfing; 20 min walk along beach to town."* **SEK 396, 15 Apr-15 Sep.**
2019

MALMO *2E4* (7km SW Urban) *55.5722, 12.90686*
Malmö Camping & Feriesenter (M8), Strandgatan
101, Sibbarp, 21611 Limhamn **(040) 155165;**
malmocamping@malmo.se; www.firstcamp.se

🏕 12 ♿ 👭(htd) 🆆 ♨ 🚿 ♿ 🚮 🍽 🦋 📶 🛗🅟🛒 ⚓ 🛝 🏊

⛱ sand 250m

Fr Öresund Bdge take 1st exit & foll sp Limhamn &
Sibbarp, then int'l campsite sp. Fr N on E6 round
Malmö until last exit bef bdge (sp), then as above.
Fr Dragør-Limnhamn ferry turn R on exit dock. Site
in 1km on R, nr sea, in park-like setting. 4*, V lge,
hdg, mkd, pt shd, pt sl, EHU (16A) inc (poss rev pol);
gas; bbq; cooking facs; twin axles; TV; 20% statics;
phone; bus to Malmo; Eng spkn; ccard acc; games rm;
windsurfing; games area; bike hire; CKE. *"Easy cycle to
town cent; facs poss stretched high ssn; v busy city site;
well-laid out; pool 400m; conv Öresund Bdge; lovely
site; v friendly, helpful staff; gd clean new (2016) san
facs blocks."* **SEK 395** **2017**

MALUNG *2F1* (1km W Rural) *60.68296, 13.70243*
Malungs Camping (W22), Bullsjövägen, 78235
Malung **(0280) 18650;** info@malungscamping.se;
www.malungscamping.se

🏕 12 👭(htd) 🆆 ♨ 🚿 ♿ 🚮 🍽 🦋 📶 🛗🛒 🚣

Fr Stöllet take rd 45 to Malung, site sp.
3*, Lge, pt shd, EHU (10A) SEK40; TV; ccard acc; car
wash; fishing; Quickstop o'night facs; bike hire;
boating; CKE. **SEK 260** **2016**

MARIESTAD *2F2* (2km NW Rural) *58.7154, 13.79516*
Ekuddens Camping (R2), 54245 Mariestad **(0771)
101200;** www.ekuddenscamping.se

🏕 12 🐕 👭 ♨ 🚿 ♿ 🚮 🍽 Y 🛗🅟🛒 🛗 🛝(htd) 🎿

Fr E20 take turn off twd Mariestad. At 1st rndabt
foll ring rd clockwise until site sp on Lake Vänern.
4*, Lge, shd, EHU (10A) SEK40; gas; phone; ccard acc;
bike hire; golf 2km; sauna; Quickstop o'night facs; CKE.
*"Gd views fr lakeside pitches; friendly, helpful staff; gd
san facs."* **SEK 294** **2019**

MARKARYD *2F3* (0.5km N Urban) *56.46475,
13.60066* **Camping Park Sjötorpet (G4)**, Strandvägen
4, 28531 Markaryd **(0433) 10316;** reservation@
sjotorpet-roc.se; www.sjotorpet-roc.se

🐕 👭(htd) 🆆 ♨ 🚿 ♿ 🚮 🍽 🦋 📶 Y 🛗🅟🛒 🛗

E4 fr Helsingborg (ferry) site is bet E4 N turn to
Markaryd & rd 117, sp. Narr app. 3*, Sm, pt shd, pt
sl, EHU (10A) SEK40; cooking facs; sw; 10% statics;
phone; Eng spkn; ccard acc; boating; fishing; bike
hire; CKE. *"Excel san & cooking facs; well-run site; new
owners (2017), helpful."* **SEK 270, 1 Apr-31 Oct.**
2017

MARSTRAND *2E2* (1.4km NE Coastal) *57.89380,
11.60510* **Marstrands Camping (036)**, Långedalsvägen
16, 44030 Marstrand **(0303) 60584; info@marstrand
camping.se; www.marstrandscamping.se**

🐕 👭(htd) 🆆 ♨ 🚿 ♿ 🚮 🍽 🦋 📶 🅟 🛗 🛝 shgl

Exit A6 dir Kungsälv/Marstrand & foll rd 168 to
Marstrand. Site sp on Koön Island. App rd to site v
narr. 4*, Med, pt shd, pt sl, EHU (10A) SEK45; cooking
facs; TV; 50% statics; adv bkg acc; ccard acc; CKE.
"Ferry to Marstrand Island; recep not staffed in LS."
SEK 350, 12 Apr-2 Oct. **2017**

MELLERUD *2E2* (15km N Rural) *58.81968, 12.41519*
Haverud Camping, Kanalvagen 4, 464 72 Haverud
(0530) 30770; hafrestromsif@telia.com;
www.hafrestromsif.se

👭 ♨ 🚿 ♿ 🚮 🦋 🛗 nr 🛗

Signposted in Haverund. Sm, mkd, hdstg, unshd,
terr, EHU; sw nr; Eng spkn; CKE. *"Self pitch on arr,
fees collected am or pay at visitors ctr at canal; gd."*
SEK 220, 25 Apr-14 Sep. **2017**

MELLERUD *2E2* (2km W Rural) *58.71288, 12.43231*
Kerstins Camping (P21), Hålsungebyn 1, 46494
Mellerud **(0530) 12715; epost@kerstinscamping.se;**
www.kerstinscamping.se

🐕 👭(htd) 🆆 ♨ 🚿 ♿ 🚮 🍽 🦋 🛗 🛝

Fr Mellerud on rd 166 dir Bäckefors & Ed, site sp.
3*, Sm, hdg, mkd, pt shd, EHU (10A) SEK45; bbq (sep
area); cooking facs; TV; 15% statics; phone; Eng spkn;
adv bkg acc; games rm; CKE. *"Pleasant area; excel;
sm site with open outlook to fmland on 1 side; vg site."*
SEK 282, 14 May-9 Sep. **2018**

MORA *1B4* (0.5km N Urban) *61.00853, 14.53178*
Mora Parkens Camping, Parkvägen 1, 79237 Mora
**(0250) 27600; info@moraparken.se; www.mora
parken.se**

🏕 12 👭(htd) 🆆 ♨ 🚿 ♿ 🚮 🍽 🦋 📶 🛗 nr 🛗 nr 🛝(covrd, htd)
⛸

Fr SW site sp on rd 45. Or foll sp in town cent; site in
400m. Recep in adj hotel. 4*, Lge, mkd, pt shd, pt sl,
EHU (10A) inc; TV; 10% statics; Eng spkn; ccard acc;
sports facs; Quickstop o'night facs; fishing; waterslide;
games rm; CKE. *"Excel site; ltd facs LS & poss unclean;
suitable RVs & twin axles; conv for bear sanctuary at
Orsa."* **SEK 433** **2018**

NYNASHAMN *2H2* (1km NW Coastal) *58.90717,
17.93805* **Nicksta Camping (B8)**, Nickstabadsvägen
17, 14943 Nynäshamn **(08) 52012780; info@nicksta
camping.se; www.nickstacamping.se**

🏕 12 🐕 👭(htd) 🆆 ♨ 🚿 ♿ 🚮 🍽 🦋 🛗 nr 🛗 🛝 adj

Fr Stockholm on Rv 73 to Nynäshamn. Foll site
sp, turning R at ICA supmkt, then immed L (sp
poss cov'rd by hedge.) 4*, Med, pt shd, pt sl, EHU
(10A) SEK50; cooking facs; 10% statics; train 600m;
Eng spkn; games area; site clsd mid-Dec to mid-Jan;
Quickstop o'night facs; waterslide; bike hire; CKE. *"Gd
site; ferries to Gotland & Poland."* **SEK 343** **2016**

OREBRO *2G2* (3km S Rural) *59.2554, 15.18955*
Gustavsviks Camping (T2), Sommarrovägen, 70229
Örebro **(019) 196950; camping@gustavsvik.com;**
www.gustavsvik.com

🐕 ⁇(htd) ⓦ ♨ 🚿 🛁 🖨 ⌁ ⁇ ⁇ ⁇ 🍽 ⓗ 🛒 🏚 ⁇
🏊(covrd, htd) 🛗

Foll sp fr E18/E20 & rd 51 to site. 5*, V lge, mkd, pt
shd, pt sl, serviced pitches; EHU (10A) SEK80 (poss rev
pol); gas; bbq; cooking facs; sw nr; TV (pitch);
10% statics; phone; bus; Eng spkn; ccard acc;
waterslide; solarium; gym; golf nr; CKE. *"Excel family
site; excel facs; gentle stroll to town; very highly rec;
beautiful site."* SEK 240, 15 Apr-6 Nov. **2016**

ORSA *1B4* (1km W Rural) *61.12090, 14.59890* **Orsa
Camping (W3),** Timmervägen 1, 79421 Orsa **(0250)**
46200; info@orsacamping.se; www.orsacamping.se

⁇ ⁇(htd) ♨ 🚿 🛁 🖨 ⌁ ⁇ ⁇ ⁇ 🍽 ⓗ 🛒 nr 🏚 ⁇ 🏊(htd)

Sp fr town cent & fr rd 45. 4*, V lge, pt shd, EHU
(10A) SEK50; cooking facs; sw; TV (pitch); 5% statics;
phone; tennis; canoe hire; fishing; waterslide; bike hire;
sauna; CKE. *"Excel countryside; bear reserve 15km; gd
general facs but ltd LS."* SEK 375 **2016**

OSKARSHAMN *2G3* (3km SE Coastal) *57.2517,
16.49206* **Gunnarsö Camping (H7),** Östersjövägen
103, 57263 Oskarshamn **(0491) 77220; gunnarso@
oskarshamn.se; www.oskarshamn.se**

🐕 ⁇(htd) ⓦ ♨ 🚿 🛁 🖨 ⌁ ⁇ ⁇ ⁇ 🛒 🏚 🏊

Fr E22 dir Oskarshamn, site sp on Kalmar Sound.
4*, Med, pt shd, EHU (10A) SEK35; TV; 40% statics;
phone; adv bkg acc; ccard acc; watersports; sauna;
CKE. *"Beautiful location; many pitches with gd views;
gd walking/cycling."* SEK 332, 1 May-15 Sep. **2016**

OSTERSUND *1B3* (3km SE Rural) *63.15955, 14.6731*
Östersunds Camping (Z11), Krondikesvägen 95, 83146
Östersund **(063) 144615; ostersundscamping@
ostersund.se; www.ostersundscamping.se**

⁇ 🐕 ⁇(htd) ⓦ ♨ 🚿 🛁 🖨 ⌁ ⁇ ⁇ ⁇ 🍽 🛒 nr 🏚 🏊 🛗

At Odensala on lakeside, well sp fr E14. 4*, Lge, mkd,
hdstg, pt shd, pt sl, EHU (10A) SEK60 (poss rev pol);
cooking facs; TV (pitch); 80% statics; phone; bus; ccard
acc; sauna; tennis; CKE. *"Gd NH; very helpful staff."*
SEK 200 **2019**

PAJALA *1D1* (1.5km SE Rural) *67.20381, 23.4084*
Pajala Camping (BD8), Tannavägen 65, 98431 Pajala
**(0978) 74180 or (0702) 107448; pajalacamping@
gmail.com; www.pajalacamping.se**

⁇ 🐕 ⁇(htd) ⓦ ♨ 🚿 🛁 🖨 ⌁ ⁇ ⁇ 🛒 🏚

Site sp fr rd 99. 2*, Med, mkd, hdstg, pt shd, EHU
(10A) SEK30; cooking facs; red long stay; TV; Eng
spkn; adv bkg acc; ccard acc; sauna; tennis; bike
hire; CKE. *"Clean, well-presented site; delightful
owner; salmon-fishing in rv in ssn (mid-Jun approx)."*
SEK 190 **2016**

RATTVIK *1B4* (1km W Rural) *60.88891, 15.10881*
Siljansbadets Camping (W8), Långbryggevägen 4,
79532 Rättvik **(0248) 56118; camp@siljansbadet.com;**
www.siljansbadet.com

🐕 ⁇(htd) ⓦ ♨ 🚿 🛁 🖨 ⌁ ⁇ ⁇ ⁇ 🍽 ⓗ 🛒 nr 🏚

**Fr S on rd 70 thro Rättvik. Immed outside town turn
L at rndabt, site sp on Lake Siljan. Height restriction
3.5m.** 4*, V lge, mkd, pt shd, EHU (16A) SEK50; bbq;
cooking facs; sw; twin axles; TV; 15% statics; bus/train;
Eng spkn; ccard acc; games area; boat hire. *"Lovely
scenic lakeside location; conv town cent; excel san facs;
excel site."* SEK 355, 26 Apr-6 Oct. **2017**

SAFFLE *2F2* (6km S Rural) *59.08326, 12.88616* **Duse
Udde Camping (S11),** 66180 Säffle **(0533) 42000;
duseudde@krokstad.se; www.duseudde.se**

⁇ 🐕 ⁇ ♨ 🚿 🛁 🖨 ⌁ ⁇ ⁇ ⁇ 🍽 ⓗ 🛒 🏚 ⁇ ⁇

Site sp fr rd 45. 4*, Med, shd, pt sl, EHU (10A) SEK50;
sw; red long stay; 20% statics; phone; bus; ccard
acc; watersports; sauna; bike hire; Quickstop o'night
facs; CKE. *"Place to relax; pool 6km; useful base for
Värmland area with nature walks."* SEK 180 **2016**

SARNA *1B3* (1km S Rural) *61.69281, 13.14696*
Särna Camping (W32), Särnavägen 6, 79090 Särna
**(0253) 10851; camping@sarnacamping.se;
www.sarnacamping.se**

⁇ ⓦ ♨ 🚿 🛁 ⌁ ⁇ ⁇ ⁇ ⓗ nr 🛒 nr 🏚 ⁇ shgl

Turn R off rd 70 opp fire stn. 3*, Med, pt shd, terr,
EHU (10A) SEK35; adv bkg acc; sauna; bike hire.
"Beautiful setting o'looking lake; pleasant town."
SEK 245, 19 May-30 Sep. **2016**

SIMRISHAMN *2F4* (2km N Coastal) *55.57021,
14.33611* **Tobisviks Camping (L14),** Tobisvägen,
27294 Simrishamn **(0414) 412778; info@tobisviks
camping.se; http://tobisviks camping.se**

⁇ ⁇ ♨ 🛁 ⌁ ⁇ ⓗ nr 🛒 nr 🏊(htd)

By sea at N app to town. 4*, Lge, pt shd, EHU (10A)
SEK50; TV; phone; ccard acc; watersports; CKE.
SEK 210 **2016**

SKANOR *2E4* (2km SE Coastal) *55.39750, 12.86555*
**Calsterbo Camping & Resort (formerly Ljungens
Camping),** Strandbadsvägen, 23942 Falsterbo **(040)
6024020 or (414) 401180; info@falsterboresort.se;
falsterboresort.se**

🐕 ⁇(htd) ⓦ ♨ 🚿 🛁 ⌁ ⁇ 🛒 🏚 ⁇ sand 200m

**Fr E6/E22 exit to W sp Höllviken onto rd 100. Foll
sp Skanör/Falsterbo. Site sp on L at rndabt at ent to
town, dir Falsterbo.** 4*, Lge, mkd, hdstg, pt shd, EHU
(10A) SEK40; bbq; cooking facs; TV; 50% statics; bus;
Eng spkn; ccard acc; CKE. *"Conv Viking Vill museum;
nature reserve adj; gd birdwatching, cycling; vg;
aircraft noise (under flight path Copenhagen airport);
new management, new recep & ongoing work on facs
(2017)."* SEK 290, 29 Apr-28 Sep. **2017**

SWEDEN

SKELLEFTEA *1C2* (1.5km N Rural) *64.76156, 20.97513* **Skellefteå Camping (AC18),** Mossgaten, 93170 Skellefteå **(0910) 735500; skellefteacamping@ skelleftea.se; www.skelleftea.se/skellefteacamping**

12 🏕 ⚏(htd) wc ⚏ ⚏ ⚏ ✓ MSP 🐕 ⚏ 🏊 nr

⚏nr 🏊 ⚏ ⚏(htd) 🏖 sand 5km

Turn W off E4; well sp behind g'ge. Also sp as Camping Stugby. 4*, Lge, mkd, unshd, pt sl, EHU (10A) SEK60; bbq; cooking facs; TV; 10% statics; phone; Eng spkn; ccard acc; waterslide; tennis 150m; sauna; fishing; bike hire; games area; CKE. *"Friendly, clean site in pine trees on sheltered inlet; lge pitches suitable RVs & twin axles; Nordanå Cultural Cent & Bonnstan Church Vill in walking dist; if site clsd book in at Statoil stn 500m S on E4 at rndabt; excel san facs, lgr camp kitchen, helpful staff, lge supmkt nrby."* **SEK 330** **2017**

SODERHAMN *1C4* (10km SE Coastal) *61.24843, 17.19506* **Stenö Havsbad Camping (X9),** Stenövägen, 82022 Sandarne **(0270) 60000; steno@nordic camping.se; www.nordiccamping.se**

12 ⚏ wc ⚏ ⚏ ⚏ ✓ MSP 🐕 ⚏ ⚏ ⚏ 🏊 ⚏ 🏖 sand

Exit E4 at sp Bollnäs-Sandarne (S of Söderhamn turn), foll sp Sandarne at Östansjö, turn L at camping sp. 4*, Lge, shd, EHU (10A) SEK50; cooking facs; TV; 10% statics; phone; bus; adv bkg acc; ccard acc; games area; CKE. *"Adj nature reserve."* **SEK 307** **2016**

SODERKOPING *2G2* (1km N Rural) *58.49163, 16.30618* **Skeppsdockans Camping (E34),** Dockan 1, 61421 Söderköping **(0121) 21630; korskullenscamp@ hotmail.com; www.soderkopingscamping.se**

⚏(htd) wc ⚏ ⚏ ⚏ ✓ 🐕 ⚏nr 🏊nr

On E22 immed N of canal bdge. 2*, Sm, mkd, unshd, EHU SEK40; cooking facs; sw; TV; Eng spkn; ccard acc; bike hire; CKE. *"On side of Gota Canal; peaceful."* **SEK 220, 30 Apr-2 Oct.** **2016**

SORSELE *1C2* (0.4km W Rural) *65.53428, 17.52663* **Sorsele Camping (AC21),** Fritidsvägen, Näset, 92070 Sorsele **(0952) 10124; info@lapplandskatan.nu; www.lapplandskatan.nu**

12 🏕 ⚏(htd) wc ⚏ ⚏ ⚏ ✓ 🐕 ⚏ ⚏nr ⚏ 🏖 🏊

N on rd 45/363 fr Storuman to Arvidsjaur. In Sorsele vill turn W for 500m; site sp. 2*, Med, unshd, EHU (16A) SEK35; TV; 10% statics; phone; ccard acc; bike hire; canoeing; fishing; CKE. *"Nature reserve; hiking; interesting ancient Lapp vill; friendly, welcoming; attractive site."* **SEK 249** **2019**

STOCKHOLM *2H2* (15km N Rural) *59.43821, 17.99223* **Rösjöbadens Camping (B1),** Lomvägen100, 19256 Sollentuna **(08) 962184; info@rosjobaden.se; www.rosjobaden.se**

12 🏕 ⚏ wc ⚏ ⚏ ⚏ ✓ MSP 🐕 ⚏ 🏊 ⚏

Take E18 m'way N fr Stockholm, sp Norrtälje. Pass Morby Centrum on L after 7km. Take Sollentuna exit, turn L & foll Sollentuna rd 265/262 for approx 5km. At 2nd set of traff lts with pylons adj, turn R on sm rd, clear sp to site. 3*, Lge, pt shd, pt sl, EHU (16A); bbq; cooking facs; twin axles; TV (pitch); 90% statics; bus 150m; Eng spkn; adv bkg acc; Quickstop o'night facs; boating; fishing; CKE. *"Conv Morby Centrum, lge shopping cent, petrol, metro to city; pleasant walks in woods & lakeside; lake sw fr pontoons; san facs adequate; staff uninterested; site run as a residential site; fair."* **SEK 330** **2017**

STOCKHOLM *2H2* (12km SW Urban) *59.29558, 17.92300* **Bredäng Camping (A4),** Stora Sällskapetväg, 12731 Skärholmen **(08) 977071; bredangcamping@telia.com; www.bredangcamping.se**

🐕 ⚏(htd) wc ⚏ ⚏ ⚏ ✓ MSP 🐕 ⚏ ⚏ ⚏ ⚏ ⚏

🏖 ⚏(htd) ⚏ adj

Exit E4/E20 to Bredäng junc 152 & foll sp to site. 3*, Lge, hdstg, mkd, pt shd, serviced pitches; EHU (16A) SEK40; cooking facs; TV; 30% statics; Eng spkn; adv bkg acc; ccard acc; Quickstop o'night facs; bike hire; sauna. *"Facs ltd LS & poss stretched in ssn; v helpful staff; overspill 3km at Sätra Camping; battery-charging; conv for Stockholm; shopping cent & metro with free car park about 700m; lake adj; access to Stockholm also poss by lake steamer fr pier (high ssn) - 10 min walk; well-run site; metro 700m; vg forest walks."* **SEK 358, 18 Apr-9 Oct.** **2016**

STOCKHOLM *2H2* (10km W Rural) *59.33731, 17.90105* **Ängby Campingplats (A3),** Blackebergsvägen 25, 16850 Bromma **(08) 370420; reservation@angbycamping.se; www.angby camping.se**

12 🐕 ⚏ wc ⚏ ⚏ ⚏ ✓ MSP ⚏ ⚏ ⚏ ⚏

On E4 fr Stockholm take rd 275 W twd Vällingby. At rndabt turn L for rd 261 dir Ekerö, then R sp Sodra Ängby, site sp. 3*, Med, mkd, pt shd, pt sl, EHU SEK35; sw nr; TV (pitch); 10% statics; phone; train; Eng spkn; ccard acc; waterslide; tennis; sauna; CKE. *"Sh walk to metro stn, 20 mins to city; gd situation; walk/cycle to Drottningsholm Palace; some sm pitches; poss diff pitching for lge o'fits; lack of privacy in shwrs; san facs stretched high ssn & need update; ltd facs LS; workers living on site; site poss muddy after rain; helpful staff."* **SEK 333** **2016**

STROMSTAD 2E2 (3km S Coastal) 58.91350, 11.20531 **Lagunen Camping & Stugor,** Skärsbygdsvägen 40, 45297 Strömstad **(0526) 755000; info@lagunen.se; www.lagunen.se**

🏕 🐕 ♿ 🅿 ⛽ 🛒 🦋 ⛺ 🍴 ⓘ 🛒 ⚓ 🏔 ⚓ adj

On Uddevalla rd 176 out of Strömstad. Site on L. 4*, Lge, pt shd, pt sl, EHU inc; cooking facs; TV; 10% statics; adv bkg acc; ccard acc; bike hire; boat hire. *"By lakeside (long stay); barrier card preloaded with shwr money."* **SEK 490** **2017**

STROMSUND 1B3 (1km SW Rural) 63.84651, 15.53378 **Strömsunds Camping (Z3),** Näsviken, 83324 Strömsund **(0670) 16410; turism@stromsund. se or stromsunds.turistbyra@stromsund.se; www.stromsund.se/stromsundscamping**

🏕 🐕 🍴(htd) 🔲 ♿ 🛒 🅿 ⛽ 🛒 ⛺ ⓘ 🛒 ⚓nr 🏔 ⚓ ⚓

W of rd 45, over bdge S of main town on lakeside. 4*, Lge, pt shd, pt sl, EHU (10A) SEK30; cooking facs; 10% statics; phone; ccard acc; bike hire; fishing; boat hire; CKE. *"In 2 parts: W side has main facs but E quieter; go to g'ge adj when site office clsd."* **SEK 274** **2018**

SUNDSVALL 1C3 (4km SE Urban/Coastal) 62.3585, 17.37016 **Fläsians Camping & Stugor (Y26),** Norrstigen 15, 85468 Sundsvall **(060) 554475; bernt.ostling@ gmail.com**

🏕 ♿(htd) 🔲 ♿ 🛒 ♿ 🅿 ⛽ 🦋 ⓘ ⚓ 🏔 ⚓ sand adj

Clear sps on E4 in both dirs; site on E coast side of rd. 3*, Med, mkd, pt shd, terr, EHU (10A) SEK35; cooking facs; Eng spkn; adv bkg acc; ccard acc; fishing; CKE. *"Sea view all pitches; gd access even in wet; suitable RVs & twin axles; if recep clsd, site yourself & pay later; helpful staff; some traff noise; sw pools in Sundsvall; clean san facs."* **SEK 300** **2017**

SVEG 1B3 (0.6km S Rural) 62.03241, 14.36496 **Svegs Camping (Z32),** Kyrkogränd 1, 84232 Sveg **(0680) 13025; info@svegscamping.se; www.svegscamping. se**

🏕 🐕 ♿(htd) 🔲 ♿ 🛒 ♿ 🅿 ⛽ 🛒 ⛺ 🍴nr ⓘnr ♿ 🏔

Just S of traff lts at junc rds 45 & 84. Opp Statoil at rear of rest, well sp. 2*, Med, mkd, pt shd, EHU (16A) SEK50; bbq; cooking facs; twin axles; TV; 15% statics; phone; bus 300m; Eng spkn; adv bkg acc; ccard acc; games area; bike hire; CKE. *"Gd for sh stay/NH; htd pool 500m; many cabins used as long stay family units; san facs excel; well organised & run."* **SEK 285** **2017**

TIMMERNABBEN 2G3 (1.5km S Rural/Coastal) 56.94405, 16.46708 **Camping Timmernabben,** Varvsvägen 29, 38052 Timmernabben **(0499) 23861; timmernabben-camp@telia.com**

🏕 ♿(htd) 🔲 ♿ 🛒 🅿 ⛽ 🦋 ⛺ 🏔 ⚓ shgl adj

Turn off E22, site sp. Med, mkd, shd, pt sl, EHU (10A) inc; bbq; Eng spkn; games area; tennis; CKE. *"Tranquil site; delightful views; gd walking & windsurfing; paths on site not wheelchair-friendly."* **SEK 271** **2016**

TORSBY 2F1 (16km N Rural) 60.275763, 13.029961 **Camping 45,** Overbyn 53, 68594 Torsby **(560) 31169; kontakt01@camping45.com; www.camping45.com**

🏕 🐕 ♿ 🔲 🅿 ⛽ ⛺ (htd)

18km N fr Torsby on L of E45 immed after g'ge. Sm, pt shd, EHU (10A) inc; bbq; cooking facs; sw nr; twin axles; TV; 30% statics; bus 100m; Eng spkn; adv bkg acc; sauna; games rm; bike hire. *"Vg site; green key eco award site; guided walks; canoe hire; friendly, helpful staff."* **SEK 240** **2018**

TRANAS 2F2 (3km E Rural) 58.03548, 15.0309 **Hättebadens Camping (F1),** Hätte, 57393 Tranås **(0140) 17482; info@hattecamping.se; www.hatte camping.se**

🏕 🐕 ♿ 🛒 ♿ 🛒 🅿 ⛽ 🛒 ⛺ 🍴 ⓘnr ♿nr 🏔

On W edge Lake Sommen on rd 131, sp. 4*, Med, mkd, pt shd, EHU (10A) SEK40; sw; 20% statics; phone; Eng spkn; ccard acc; boating; fishing; Quickstop o'night facs; bike hire; CKE. *"Generous pitches; spacious site; gd, clean facs."* **SEK 220** **2016**

TRELLEBORG 2E4 (4km E Coastal) 55.3638, 13.20933 **Camping Dalabadet,** Dalköpingestrandväg 2, 23132 Trelleborg **(0410) 14905; www.dalabadets camping.se**

🐕 ♿(htd) 🔲 ♿ 🛒 ♿ 🅿 ⛽ 🛒 ⓘnr ♿nr 🏔 ⚓

Bet sea shore & rd 9 (Trelleborg-Ystad), E of town. Foll sp fr town. 4*, Med, pt shd, EHU (10A) SEK30; cooking facs; TV (pitch); 20% statics; phone; ccard acc; tennis; sauna. *"Conv for ferries; gd; helpful recep; ltd fac LS."* **SEK 290, 27 Apr-30 Sep.** **2017**

TROLLHATTAN 2E2 (1km N Urban) 58.29206, 12.29848 **Trollhättans Camping Hjulkvarnelund (P7),** Kungsportsvägen 7, 46139 Trollhättan **(0520) 30613**

🐕 ♿(htd) 🔲 ♿ 🛒 ♿ 🅿 ⛽ 🛒 ⓘ ♿nr 🏔

Foll rd 45, site sp adj rv/canal. 3*, Med, pt shd, pt sl, EHU (10A) SEK40; Eng spkn; tennis; CKE. *"Access to Trollhätte Canal; beautiful, spacious wooded site; cycles; easy walk to town & impressive gorge/waterfall; htd pool 300m; modern, clean san facs poss stretched high ssn."* **SEK 246, 1 May-6 Sep.** **2017**

UDDEVALLA 2E2 (9.5km W Rural) 58.3306, 11.8222 **Unda Camping (O30),** Unda 149, 45194 Uddevalla **(0522) 86347; info@undacamping.se; www.unda camping.se**

🏕 ♿(htd) 🔲 ♿ 🛒 ♿ 🅿 ⛽ 🛒 ⛺ 🍴 ⓘ ♿ 🏔 ⚓ ⚓

Exit E6 junc 96 Uddevalla N onto rte 44 twd Uddevalla Centrum. Site sp in 1km on R. 4*, Lge, pt shd, pt sl, EHU (10A) SEK50; cooking facs; TV; 80% statics; phone; adv bkg acc; ccard acc; boat hire; fishing; sauna; bike hire; CKE. *"Lovely situation in nature reserve; o'flow area when full; Quickstop o'night facs; recep hrs erratic LS; cr in high ssn."* **SEK 310** **2015**

SWEDEN

SWEDEN

ULRICEHAMN *2F3* (3km S Rural) *57.77055, 13.40173*
Camping Skotteksgården (P34), Gamla Marbäcksvägen, 52390 Ulricehamn **(0321) 13184 or (0705) 613184;** skotteksgarden@telia.com; www.skottek.cc

🛏 ♨(htd) 🏊 ♿ 🗲 ⊟ ✉ 🦋 ⊕ ♨ 🐾 ⚠

On rd 40 take dir Centrum. Foll sp Skotteksgården to Tranemo. 4*, Sm, mkd, hdstg, unshd, serviced pitches; EHU SEK70; cooking facs; sw nr; 10% statics; phone; ccard acc; boat hire; sauna; fishing; bike hire; CKE. *"Friendly, helpful owner; cycle path adj; OAY, winter on req."* **SEK 302, 1 May-30 Sep.**   2018

UMEA *1C3* (6km NE Coastal) *63.84210, 20.33815*
FirstCamp Umeå (AC12), Nydalasjön 2, 90654 Umeå **(090) 702600; umea@firstcamp.se; www.firstcamp.se**

12 🛏 ♨(wc) 🏊 ♿ ⊟ ✓ (MSP) 🍴 🐾 ⚠ 🏊(htd)

Sp fr E4 to N of town on lakeside. 5*, Lge, mkd, pt shd, serviced pitches; EHU (10A) inc; sw nr; 10% statics; bus; ccard acc; tennis; games rm; waterslide; games area; CKE. *"Attractive site; lge pitches suitable RVs & twin axles; excel service block; conv E4; pitches muddy in wet weather; shop, rest & pool clsd in LS."*
SEK 299   2016

UNDERSAKER *1B3* (22km SW Rural) *63.1660, 13.0590* **Camping Vålågården,** Östra Vålådalen 120, 83012 Vålådalen **(0647) 35173; marie@valagarden.se;** www.valagarden.se

12 🛏 ♨(htd) 🏊 ♿ ⊟ ✓ 🦋 ♨ 🐾 ⚠

E14 to Undersåker, turn S at hotel sp Vålådalen. Site on L. Sm, pt shd, EHU (10A); cooking facs; TV; 20% statics; Eng spkn; ccard acc; sauna; CKE. *"Hiking in surrounding nature reserve; magnificent mountain scenery; friendly owners."* **SEK 210**   2016

UPPSALA *2H1* (2km N Urban) *59.87133, 17.61923*
Fyrishov Camping (C12), Idrottsgatan 2, 75333 Uppsala **(018) 7274950; info@fyrishov.se;** www.fyrishov.se

12 ♨ (wc) 🏊 ♿ ⊟ ✓ (MSP) ⊕ nr ♨ 🐾 nr ⚠

Exit E4 Uppsala N; in 300m at rndabt foll sp Strangnas, Sala. In 2.25km exit via slip rd sp Bjorklinge, Fyrishov. At rndabt foll sp Fyrishov, in 1.6km to traff lts turn R & immed R. Site in Fyrishov Park adj sw & sports complex. 3*, Med, unshd, EHU (10A) SEK45; bus; ccard acc; CKE. *"Within easy access of city cent; pool adj (sports complex behind pool); fair NH."* **SEK 225**   2016

URSHULT *2F3* (1km N Rural) *56.54476, 14.80703*
Urshults Camping (G7), Sirkövägen 19, 36013 Urshult **(0477) 20243; info@urshult-camping.com;** www.urshult-camping.com

🛏 ♨(htd) (wc) 🏊 ♨ ♿ ⊟ ✓ (MSP) 🦋 ♨ 🐾 ⚠

Rd 30 S fr Växjö, turn W onto rd 120 at Tingsryd. In 10km at Urshult turn R, site sp on lakeside. 3*, Med, pt shd, EHU (10A) SEK45; cooking facs; sw nr; 10% statics; Eng spkn; CKE. *"Well-run site; nr Kurrebo gardens & museum; vg."* **SEK 245, 27 Apr-15 Oct.**
          2018

URSHULT *2F3* (10km NW Rural) *56.58466, 14.69491*
Getnö Gård Naturcamping (G24), Lake Åsnen Resort, 36010 Ryd **(0477) 24011; info@getnogard.se;** www.getnogard.se

🛏 ♨(htd) (wc) 🏊 ♨ ♿ ⊟ ✓ (MSP) 🦋 🍴 ⊕ ♨ 🐾 ⚠

W fr Urshult on rte 120 to junc with rte 126; turn NW onto rte 126, site in 7km via Ålshult to Getnö Gård. Site on shore Lake Åsnen. 4*, Med, mkd, pt shd, pt sl, EHU (10A) SEK45; cooking facs; red long stay; 10% statics; phone; Eng spkn; adv bkg acc; fishing; canoe hire; CKE. *"Beautiful location in private nature reserve; lake adj; needs care & attention; facs dated."* **SEK 245, 1 May-10 Oct.**   2017

VADSTENA *2F2* (4km NE Rural) *58.46448, 14.9334*
Vadstena Camping (E9), Vätterviksbadets, 59230 Vadstena **(0143) 12730; info@vadstenacamping.se;** www.vadstenacamping.se

🛏 ♨(wc) 🏊 ♿ ⊟ ✓ (MSP) 🍴 ♨ 🐾 ⚠

On rd 50, 3km N of Vadstena by Lake Vattern. 4*, Lge, mkd, pt shd, EHU (10A) SEK50; cooking facs; 20% statics; Eng spkn; adv bkg acc; ccard acc; sauna; fishing; tennis; waterslide; CKE. *"Many local attractions; lake adj; vg family site; htd pool 3km; cycle path to town; gd birdwatching nrby; lakeside site with beach."* **SEK 346, 1 May-12 Sep.**   2015

VARBERG *2E3* (5km NW Coastal) *57.1165, 12.21426*
Getteröns Camping (N6), Valvikavägen 1-3, 43293 Varberg **(0340) 16885; info@getteronscamping.se;** www.getteronscamping.se

🛏 ♨(htd) 🏊 ♨ ♿ ⊟ ✓ (MSP) 🍴 ♨ 🐾 nr ⚠ ♨ 🏊 sand 200m

Exit E6/E20 junc 54 Varberg Centrum, then W dir Getterön, site sp. 3*, V lge, mkd, unshd, EHU (6A) SEK45; 50% statics; phone; ccard acc; sauna; bike hire; fishing; CKE. *"Conv ferry to Denmark; Varberg pleasant town; lge nature reserve nr; gd beach walk; clean san facs; well laid-out site."* **SEK 290, 25 Apr-14 Sep.**   2015

VASTERVIK *2G3* (3km SE Coastal) *57.73823, 16.66846*
Camping Lysingsbadets (H3), Lysingsvägen, 593 53 Västervik **(0490) 258000; lysingsbadet@vastervik.se;** www.lysingsbadet.se

12 🛏 ♨(htd) (wc) 🏊 ♿ ⊟ ✓ (MSP) 🍴 🍴 ⊕ ♨ 🐾 ⚠ ♨ 🏊(htd) 🏊 sand adj

On coast 3km SE of town. Fr E22 foll sp around S ring rd; on app to Västervik. Site well sp fr E22. 5*, V lge, pt shd, serviced pitches; EHU (10A) inc; cooking facs; 10% statics; ccard acc; tennis; bike hire; sauna; boat hire; waterslide; golf. *"Lovely, family site in landscaped, coastal woodland; easy access to islands by wooden footbdge fr site; o'night m'vans area; adj to bay; in HS EHU's taken by late afternoon."* **SEK 450**   2016

VAXHOLM *2H1* (2km W Coastal) *59.40508, 18.3047*
Waxholm Strand & Camping (B6), Eriksövägen, 18521
Vaxholm **(08) 54130101; info@waxholmstrand.com;**
www.waxholmstrand.com

🐕 👫👫 wo ♨ ⚒ ♿ 🛒 ✉ MP 🛜 ♦ 🍴 🔋 nr ⚟ 🌲 sand adj

**On rd 274 turn R immed after x-ing bdge to
Vaxholm Island, foll sp 'Eriksö Camping'.** 3*, Med,
mkd, unshd, pt sl, EHU SEK40; 10% statics; phone; adv
bkg acc; ccard acc; CKE. *"35 mins drive fr Stockholm;
boat trips, bike hire, ferry terminal Vaxholm-Stockholm
3.3km."* **SEK 210, 30 Apr-25 Sep.**   **2015**

VILHELMINA *1C2* (1.5km SE Rural) *64.62131,
16.67846* **Saiva Camping (AC4),** Baksjön 1, 91231
Vilhelmina **(0940) 10760; info@saiva.se; www.saiva.se**

🐕 👫👫 (htd) wo ♨ ⚒ ♿ 🛒 ✉ 🦋 🛜 🍴 🔋 ⚟

Sp on E site of rd 45. 3*, Med, pt shd, EHU (10A)
SEK30; TV; 10% statics; phone; ccard acc; tennis;
bike hire; CKE. *"Gd; excel san facs in log style cabins,
v helpful staff, lovely lakeside setting; lake beach."*
SEK 180, 20 May-1 Oct.   **2016**

VILHELMINA *1C2* (5km NW Rural) *64.64998,
16.59240* **Kolgärdens Camping,** Lövliden 16, 91292
Vilhelmina **(0940) 10304; kolgarden@vilhelmina.ac;
www.kolgarden.se**

12 🐕 👫👫 (htd) wo ♨ ⚒ ♿ 🛒 ✉ MP 🦋 🔋 nr

Site sp fr E45 N of Vilhelmina. Sm, pt shd, EHU (10A)
SEK35; cooking facs; TV; 50% statics; Eng spkn; sauna;
fishing. *"Wonderful lakeside location; clean san facs;
helpful, pleasant owner; highly rec."* **SEK 240   2017**

VINSLOV *2F4* (0.5km N Rural) *56.10988, 13.91245*
Vinslövs Camping (L2), Troed Nelsongatan 18, 28834
Vinslöv **(070) 2077679; info@vinslovscamping.se;
vinslovscamping.se**

12 🐕 👫👫 wo ♨ ⚒ ♿ 🛒 ✉ 🦋 🍴 nr ⊕ nr 🔋 nr ⚟

Site sp of rte 21. 2*, Sm, mkd, pt shd, EHU (6A)
SEK40; cooking facs; 20% statics; bus 500m; CKE.
"Htd pool adj." **SEK 120**   **2016**

YSTAD *2F4* (3km E Coastal) *55.43286, 13.8650*
Camping Sandskogens (M15), Österleden, 27160
Ystad **(0411) 19270; info@sandskogenscamping.se;
www.sandskogenscamping.se**

🐕 👫👫 wo ♨ ⚒ ♿ 🛒 ✉ MP 🛜 ⊕ nr 🔋 ⚟ 🌲 sand 100m

On N side of rd 9. 4*, Lge, mkd, shd, EHU (10A)
SEK40; TV; 10% statics; phone; ccard acc; CKE. *"On
Baltic coast; cycle path to beautiful town; mkd walks
nrby; gd site, well-managed site; extremely helpful Eng
spkn staff; high ssn expect queues checking in; CKE
card req; metered shwrs; Wallander TV series studios
site nr site, tours avail; cramped pithces; san facs
stretched when busy."* **SEK 350, 17 Apr-21 Sep.**
                                                                 2017

OLAND ISLAND

BYXELKROK *2G3* (1km N Coastal) *57.33013,
17.01211* **Neptuni Camping (H41),** Småskogsvägen
2, 38075 Byxelkrok **(0485) 28495 or 070 5428495
(mob); info@neptunicamping.se; www.neptuni
camping.se**

🐕 👫👫 wo ♨ ⚒ ♿ 🛒 ✉ MP 🦋 🔋 ⚟ 🌲 adj

**Fr S on rd 136 thro Böda, at Byxelkrok turn R past
harbour for 200m. Site on R.** 4*, Med, pt shd, EHU
(16A) SEK40; phone; Eng spkn; ccard acc; games area;
CKE. *"Conv touring base N Öland, sh walk to harbour,
rest & supmkt."* **SEK 230, 29 Apr-2 Oct.**   **2017**

DEGERHAMN *2G4* (12km S Rural) *56.23778, 16.4530*
Ottenby Vandrarhem & Camping (H57), Ottenby
106, 38065 Degerhamn **(0485) 662062; info@
ottenbyvandrarhem.se; www.ottenbyvandrarhem.se**

12 🐕 👫👫 (htd) wo ♨ ⚒ ♿ 🛒 ✉ MP 🛜 🔋 nr ♨ (htd) 🚿

**Rd 36 S to Ottenby, bear R for 4km, site on R at
youth hostel.** Sm, unshd, EHU (10A) SEK40; cooking
facs; 10% statics; phone; ccard acc; bike hire. *"On edge
Ottenby nature reserve; excel walks & birdwatching
- ssn geared to bird migration; poss noise fr late arr &
early risers as no barrier; dogs free; World Heritage Site
on S pt of island."* **SEK 220**   **2017**

LOTTORP *2G3* (3km N Coastal) *57.17876, 17.03746*
Sonjas Camping (H39), John Emils Gata 43, 38074
Löttorp **(0485) 23212; info@sonjascamping.se;
www.sonjascamping.oland.com**

👫👫 (htd) wo ♨ ⚒ ♿ 🛒 ✉ MP 🦋 🛜 🍴 ⊕ 🍴 🔋 ⚟ 🚴 🏊 (htd)
🚿 🌲 sand adj

**Fr Kalmar over bdge to Öland Island, take rd 136
N thro Borgholm. Cont to Löttorp, site sp.** 5*,
Lge, mkd, pt shd, EHU (10A) SEK45; cooking facs;
10% statics; adv bkg acc; bike hire; sauna; tennis;
fishing; CKE. *"Vg beach; excel family site; vg touring
base."* **SEK 364, 1 May-4 Oct.**   **2016**

Map 1

Map 2

445

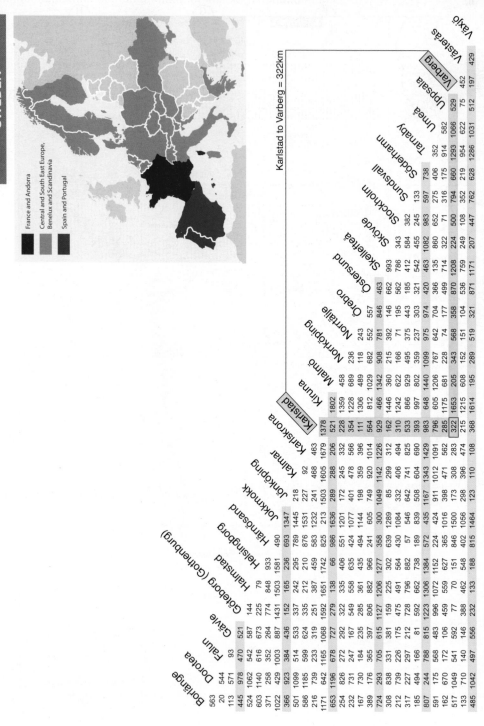

France and Andorra
Central and South East Europe, Benelux and Scandinavia
Spain and Portugal

Karlstad to Varberg = 322km

Basel

Highlights

A country of mountains, lakes and natural beauty, Switzerland's high alpine peaks make it one of the world's top destinations for winter sports.

Inside the cities, you will find a world that compliments the outstanding landscape while providing a modern and vibrant outlook on life.

There is an endless supply of places to visit and experience, with mouth-watering chocolates and cuckoo clocks just the tip of the cultural iceberg.

Switzerland is renowned for being a hub for winter sports enthusiasts, but there are also a variety of traditional competitions such as Schwingen, a type of Swiss wrestling and Hornussen, a strange mixture of golf and baseball, which are still practiced today.

Switzerland also produces a delicious variety of food, with cheese being one of its specialities. Types such as Emmental and Gruyère are used to make fondue, which is often associated with the skiing culture of the Alps.

Major towns and cities

- Zürich – there are tons of museums and cultural sites in this metropolitan capital.

- Geneva – this breathtaking city is one of the world's most diverse.

- Basel – a world-leading city of culture and arts.

- Lausanne – this city has a stunning view of Lake Geneva and the Alps.

Attractions

- Jungfraujoch – admire unrivalled views from the highest railway station in Europe.

- Château de Chillon, Veytaux – an island castle on Lake Geneva.

- Kapellbrücke, Lucerne – Europe's oldest wooden covered bridge.

- Rhine Falls, Shaffhausen – discover Europe's largest waterfall.

Find out more

www.myswitzerland.com
E: info@myswitzerland.com
T: 0041 (0) 80 01 00 20 029

Country Information

Population: 8.2 million

Capital: Bern

Area: 41,285 sq km

Bordered by: Austria, France, Germany, Italy, Liechtenstein

Terrain: Mostly mountainous; Alps in the south, Jura in the north-west; central plateau of rolling hills, plains and large lakes

Climate: Temperate climate varying with altitude; cold, cloudy, rainy or snowy winters; cool to warm summers with occasional showers

Highest Point: Dufourspitze 4,634m

Languages: French, German, Italian, Romansch

Local Time: GMT or BST + 1, i.e. 1 hour ahead of the UK all year

Currency: Swiss Franc (CHF) divided into 100 centimes; £1 = CHF 1.27, CHF 10 = £7.86 (October 2019)

Emergency numbers: Police 117; Fire brigade 118; Ambulance 144 or 112 for any service

Public Holidays 2020: Jan 1, 2; Apr 10, 13; May 1, 21; June1, 11; Aug 1 (National Day), 15; Nov 1; Dec 25, 26.

School summer holidays vary by canton but are approximately from early July to mid/end August.

Entry Formalities

Holders of valid British or Irish passports may enter without a visa for up to 3 months.

Medical Services

There are reciprocal emergency health care arrangements with Switzerland for EU citizens. A European Health Insurance Card (EHIC) will enable you to get reduced cost for emergency treatment in a public hospital but you will be required to pay the full cost of treatment and apply afterwards for a refund from the Department for Work & Pensions on your return to the UK. Ensure that any doctor you visit is registered with the national Swiss Health Insurance Scheme. Dental treatment is not covered.

You will have to pay 50% of the costs of any medically-required ambulance transport within Switzerland and/or Liechtenstein, including air ambulance.

If you are planning sports activities, such as skiing and mountaineering, your holiday insurance should be extended to cover these activities and should also include cover for mountain rescue and helicopter rescue costs.

Opening Hours

Banks: Mon-Fri 8.30am-4.30pm (some close for lunch; late opening once a week to 5.30pm/6pm in some towns).

Museums: Check locally as times vary.

Post Offices: Mon-Fri 7.30am-6pm (smaller branches may close for lunch); Sat 7.30am-11am.

Shops: Mon-Fri 8am/8.30am-6.30pm/7pm (closed lunch time) & Sat 8am-4pm/7pm; shops close early on the eve of a public holiday.

Safety and Security

Most visits to Switzerland and Liechtenstein are trouble-free and the crime rate is low. However, petty theft is on the increase and you should be alert to pickpockets and thieves in city centres, railway stations and public places.

You should be aware of the risks involved in the more hazardous sports activities and take note of weather forecasts and conditions, which can change rapidly in the mountains. You should be well-equipped; do not undertake the activity alone, study the itinerary and inform someone of your plans. Off-piste skiers should follow the advice given by local authorities and guides; to ignore such advice could put yourselves and other mountain users in danger.

Switzerland and Liechtenstein share with the rest of Europe an underlying threat from terrorism. Attacks could be indiscriminate and against civilian targets in public places.

British Embassy
THUNSTRASSE 50, CH-3005 BERN
Tel: 031 3597700
www.ukinswitzerland.fco.gov.uk/en

Irish Embassy
KIRCHENFELDSTRASSE 68, CH-3000 BERN 6
Tel: 031 3521442
www.embassyofireland.ch

Customs

Alcohol and Tobacco

Switzerland is not a member of the EU and visitors aged 17 years and over may import the following items duty-free:

200 cigarettes or 50 cigars or
250 g tobacco

2 litres of alcoholic drink up to 15% proof
1 litre of alcoholic drink over 15% proof

All goods are duty free up to a total combined value of CHF300, including alcohol and tobacco products.

Caravans and Motorhomes

Caravans registered outside Switzerland may be imported without formality up to a height of 4 metres, width of 2.55 metres and length of 12 metres (including towbar). The total length of car + caravan/trailer must not exceed 18.75 metres.

Food

From EU countries you may import per person 1 kg of meat and/or meat products (excluding game).

Refund of VAT on Export

A foreign visitor who buys goods in Switzerland in a 'Tax-Back SA' or 'Global Refund Schweiz AG' shop may obtain a VAT refund (7.6%) on condition that the value of the goods is at least CHF 300 including VAT. Visitors should complete a form in the shop and produce it, together with the goods purchased, at Customs on leaving Switzerland. See www.globalrefund.com for more information.

Documents

Vehicle(s)

Carry your original vehicle registration certificate (V5C), MOT certificate (if applicable) and insurance documentation at all times. Recent visitors report that drivers may be asked to produce proof of vehicle ownership at the border and failure to do so may mean that entry into Switzerland is refused. If you are driving a vehicle which does not belong to you, you should be in possession of a letter of authorisation from the owner.

Money

Prices in shops are often displayed in both Swiss francs and euros. Major credit cards are widely accepted, although you may find small supermarkets and restaurants do not accept them. Recent visitors report that some retail outlets may accept only one kind of credit card (MasterCard or VISA), not both, and it may be advisable to carry one of each. You may occasionally find that a surcharge is imposed for the use of credit cards.

Carry your credit card issuers'/banks' 24-hour UK contact numbers in case of loss or theft of your cards.

Driving

Accidents

In the case of accidents involving property damage only, when drivers decide not to call the police, a European Accident Statement must be completed.

In the case of injury or of damage to the road, road signs, lights etc, the police must be called.

Alcohol

The maximum permitted level of alcohol is 50 milligrams in 100 millilitres of blood, i.e. lower than that permitted in the UK (80 milligrams). A lower limit of 10 milligrams in 100 millilitres applies for new drivers of up to three years. A blood test may be required after an accident, and if found positive, the penalty is either a fine or a prison sentence, plus withdrawal of permission to drive in Switzerland for at least two months. Police carry out random breath tests.

Breakdown Service

The motoring and leisure organisation Touring Club Suisse (TCS) operates a 24-hour breakdown service, 'Patrouille TCS'. To call for help throughout Switzerland and

Liechtenstein, dial 140. On motorways use emergency phones and ask for TCS.

Members of clubs affiliated to the AIT, such as Tthe Caravan and Motorhome Club, who can show a current membership card will be charged reduced rates for breakdown assistance and towing, according to the time of day and/or the distance towed. Payment by credit card is accepted.

Child Restraint System

Vehicles registered outside of Switzerland that are temporarily imported into the country, have to comply with the country of registration with regards to safety belt equipment and child restraint regulations. All children up to 12 years of age must be placed in an approved UN ECE 44.03 regulation child restraint, unless they measure more than 150cm and are over seven years old.

Fuel

Prices of petrol vary according to the brand and region, being slightly cheaper in self-service stations. Credit cards are generally accepted.

On motorways, where prices are slightly higher, some service stations are open 24 hours and others are open from 6am to 10pm or 11pm only, but petrol is available outside these hours from automatic pumps where payment can be made by means of bank notes or credit cards.

There are 44 outlets (August 2015) selling LPG (GPL) – see www.jaquet-ge.ch for a list of outlets and a map showing their location.

Lights

Dipped headlights are compulsory at all times, even during the day. Bulbs are more likely to fail with constant use and you are recommended to carry spares.

Motorways

There are 1,700 km of motorways and dual carriageways. To use these roads motor vehicles and trailers up to a total weight of 3,500kg must display a vignette. Motorists using roads to avoid motorways and dual carriageways may find it necessary to detour through small villages, often with poor signposting. In addition, due to a diversion, you may be re-routed onto roads where the motorway vignette is required.

If you have visited Switzerland before, make sure you remove your old sticker from your windscreen.

There are emergency telephones along the motorways.

Mountain Roads and Tunnels

One of the most attractive features of Switzerland for motorists is the network of finely engineered mountain passes, ranging from easy main road routes to high passes that may be open only from June to October. In the Alps most roads over passes have been modernised; only the Umbrail Pass, which is not recommended for caravans, is not completely tarred. Passes have a good roadside telephone service for calling aid quickly in the event of trouble.

A blue rectangular sign depicting a yellow horn indicates a mountain postal road and the same sign with a red diagonal stripe indicates the end of the postal road. On such roads, vehicles belonging to the postal services have priority.

During certain hours, one-way traffic only is permitted on certain mountain roads. The hours during which traffic may proceed in either or both directions are posted at each end of the road. The TCS road map of Switzerland, scale 1:300,000, indicates this type of road.

Speed must always be moderate on mountain passes, very steep roads and roads with numerous bends. Drivers must not travel at a speed which would prevent them from stopping within the distance they can see ahead.

When it is difficult to pass oncoming vehicles, the heavier vehicle has priority.

Slow-moving vehicles are required by law to use the lay-bys provided on alpine roads to allow the free flow of faster traffic. This is the case where a car towing a caravan causes a queue of vehicles capable of a higher speed.

Parking

Parking in cities is difficult and it is worth using the numerous Park & Ride schemes which operate around major towns and cities. Illegal parking of any kind is much less tolerated in Switzerland than in any of its neighbours and fines are common for even minor violations.

Pay and display car parks and parking meters are used throughout the country and permitted parking time varies from 15 minutes to 2 hours. Feeding meters is not allowed. Wheel clamps are not used, but vehicles causing an obstruction may be removed to a car pound.

You may park in a 'blue zone' for limited periods free of charge providing you display a parking disc in your vehicle. These are available from petrol stations, kiosks, restaurants and police stations. Parking in a red zone is free for up to 15 hours with a red parking disc available from police stations, tourist offices, etc.

Parking on pavements is not allowed. Do not park where there is a sign 'Stationierungsverbot' or 'Interdiction de Stationner'. Continuous or broken yellow lines and crosses at the side of the road and any other yellow markings also indicate that parking is prohibited.

Priority

In general, traffic (including bicycles) coming from the right has priority at intersections but drivers approaching a roundabout must give way to all traffic already on the roundabout, i.e. from the left, unless otherwise indicated by signs. However, vehicles on main roads – indicated by a yellow diamond with a white border or a white triangle with a red border and an arrow pointing upwards – have priority over traffic entering from secondary roads.

Please be aware sometimes pedestrians have right of way and will expect vehicles to stop for them.

Roads

Switzerland has some 72,000 kilometres of well-surfaced roads, from motorways to local municipal roads, all well-signposted. Four-wheel drive vehicles must not be driven off road local authority permission.

During daylight hours outside built-up areas you must sound your horn before sharp bends where visibility is limited. After dark

this warning must be given by flashing your headlights.

Dial the following numbers for information:

162: Weather information

163: Road conditions, mountain passes, access to tunnels and traffic news

187: In winter, avalanche bulletins; in summer, wind forecasts for Swiss lakes

It is also possible to obtain updated information on road conditions via teletext in larger motorway service areas.

Motorway Tax

To be able to use national roads (motorways and semi-motorways) in Switzerland, motor vehicles and trailers up to a total weight of 3,500kg must have a vehicle sticker (vignette). The ticket is valid for 14 months from 1st December every year and costs CHF40 (2015). An additional fee is charged for caravans and trailers. The sticker allows multiple re-entry into Switzerland during the period of validity.

If you enter a motorway or semi-motorway without a sticker you will be fined CHF200 and also the cost of the sticker. The stickers can be bought from custom offices, petrol stations or TCS offices in Switzerland or alternatively they can be purchased from the UK before travelling by calling the Swiss Travel Centre on 0207 420 4934.

Heavy Vehicle Tax

Vehicles (including motorhomes) over 3,500kg must pay a heavy vehicle tax on entry into Switzerland which is applicable for all roads. This charge applies for every day you are in Switzerland and your vehicle is on the road. For a 10-day pass (valid for a year) you self-select the days that your vehicle is on the road and, therefore, you are not penalised if your motorhome is parked at a campsite and not driven on a public road. This heavy vehicle tax applies to any Swiss road and replaces the need for a motorway vignette.

This particular tax is only payable at the border on entry into Switzerland and if there is any doubt about the exact weight of your vehicle it will be weighed. An inspection may be carried out at any time and is likely at the exit border. Failure to pay the tax can result in an immediate fine.

Road Signs and Markings

Road signs and markings conform to international standards.

White lettering on a green background indicates motorways, whereas state and provincial main roads outside built-up areas have white lettering on a blue background. This is the reverse of the colouring used in France and Germany and may initially cause confusion when driving from one country to the other. Road signs on secondary roads are white with black lettering.

The following are some road signs which you may encounter:

Postal vehicles have priority

Parking disc compulsory

Slow lane

One-way street with a two-way cycle lane

Speed Limits

	Open Road (km/h)	Motorway (km/h)
Car Solo	80-100	120
Car towing caravan/trailer	80	80
Motorhome under 3500kg	80-100	120
Motorhome 3500-7500kg	80	80

The fundamental rule, which applies to all motor vehicles and bicycles, is that you must always have the speed of your vehicle under control and must adapt your speed to the conditions of the road, traffic and visibility. On minor secondary roads without speed limit signs speed should be reduced to 50 km/h (31 mph) where the road enters a built-up area. The speed limit in residential areas is 30 km/h (18 mph). Speeding fines are severe.

When travelling solo the speed limit on dual carriageways is 100 km/h (62 mph) and on motorways, 120 km/h (74 mph) unless otherwise indicated by signs. On motorways with at least three lanes in the same direction, the left outside lane may only be used by vehicles which can exceed 80 km/h (50 mph).

Motorhomes with a laden weight of under 3,500 kg are not subject to any special regulations. Those over 3,500 kg may not exceed 80 km/h (50 mph) on motorways.

In road tunnels with two lanes in each direction, speed is limited to 100 km/h (62 mph); in the St Gotthard tunnel and San Bernardino tunnels the limit is 80 km/h (50 mph).

It is illegal to transport or use radar detection devices. If your GPS navigation system has a function to identify the location of fixed speed cameras, this must be deactivated.

Traffic Jams

Traffic congestion occurs near tunnels in particular, during the busy summer months, at the St Gotthard tunnel on Friday afternoons and Saturday mornings. When congestion is severe and in order to prevent motorists coming to a standstill in the tunnel, traffic police stop vehicles before the tunnel entrance and direct them through in groups.

Other bottlenecks occur on the roads around Luzern (A2) and Bern (A1, A6 and A12), the border crossing at Chiasso (A2), the A9 around Lausanne and between Vevey and Chexbres, and the A13 BellinzonaSargans, mainly before the San Bernardino tunnel.

Traffic Lights

Outside peak rush hours traffic lights flashing amber mean proceed with caution.

Violation of Traffic Regulations

The police may impose and collect on-the-spot fines for minor infringements. In the case of more serious violations, they may require a deposit equal to the estimated amount of the fine. Fines for serious offences are set according to the income of the offender. Drivers of foreign-registered vehicles may be asked for a cash deposit against the value of the fine.

Winter Driving

Alpine winters often make driving more difficult. You should equip your vehicle(s) with winter tyres and snow chains and check road conditions prior to departure.

A sign depicting a wheel and chains indicates where snow chains are required for the mountain road ahead.

Snow chains are compulsory in areas where indicated by the appropriate road sign. They must be fitted on at least two drive wheels.

Essential Equipment

Nationality Plate (GB or IRL Stickers)

Strictly-speaking, it is necessary to display a conventional nationality plate or sticker when driving outside EU member states, even when vehicle number plates incorporate the GB or IRL Euro-symbol. However, the Swiss authorities have adopted a commonsense approach and confirm that it is not necessary to display a separate GB or IRL sticker if your number plates display the GB or IRL Euro-symbol. If your number plates do not incorporate this symbol then you will need a separate sticker.

Warning Triangles

All vehicles must be equipped with a warning triangle which has to be within easy reach and not in the boot.

Touring

The peak season for winter sports is from December to the end of April in all major resorts. February and March are the months with the most hours of winter sunshine and good snow for skiing. Summer skiing is also possible in a few resorts. Information on snow conditions, including avalanche bulletins, is available in English from www.slf.ch.

Besides being famous for watches, chocolate and cheese, the Swiss have a fine reputation as restaurateurs, but eating out can be expensive. Local beers are light but pleasant and some very drinkable wines are produced.

There are a number of UNESCO World Heritage Sites in Switzerland including the three castles of Bellinzona, Bern Old Town, the Monastery of St John at Müstair, the Jungfrau, the Aletsch Glacier and the Bietschhoorn region.

Liechtenstein is a principality of 160 sq km sharing borders with Switzerland and Austria. The capital, Vaduz, has a population of approximately 5,500 and German is the official language. The official currency is the Swiss franc. There are no passport or Customs controls on the border between Switzerland and Liechtenstein.

Camping and Caravanning

There are approximately 340 campsites available to touring caravanners, with around 100 sites remaining open in winter. Some sites may be nearly full with statics, with only a small area for tourers.

There are 27 Touring Club Suisse (TCS) sites and affiliated sites classified into five categories according to amenities available. All TCS campsites have a service station with facilities for emptying sanitary tanks. For further information and current rates see www.reise-tcs ch. The Swiss Camp Sites Association (VSC/ACS) produces a camping and road map covering approximately 180 sites, including charges and classification. See www.swisscamps.ch.

To download a guide to more than 40 campsites, including those open in winter, in the Bernese Oberland region of Switzerland see www.camping-bo.ch.

The Swiss are environmentally conscious with only limited scope for removing waste. Recycling is vigorously promoted and it is normal to have to put rubbish in special plastic bags obtainable from campsites. A 'rubbish charge' or 'entsorgungstaxe' of approximately CHF 3 per person per day is commonly charged.

A visitors' tax, varying according to the area, is levied in addition to the site charges.

The rules on casual/wild camping differ from canton to canton. It may be tolerated in some areas with the permission of the landowner or local police, or in motorway service areas, but local laws – particularly on hygiene – must not be contravened. For reasons of security the Caravan and Motorhome Club recommends that overnight stops should always be at recognised campsites.

Cycling

Switzerland has 9,000 km of cycle trails, including nine national cycle routes, which have been planned to suit all categories of cyclist from families to sports cyclists. Maps of cycle routes are available from www.schweizmobil.ch. Routes are marked by red and white signs. The problem of strenuous uphill gradients can be overcome by using trails routed near railway lines. Most trains will transport bicycles and often bicycles are available for hire at stations. Switzerland Tourism can provide more information.

Children under the age of 6 may only cycle on the road if accompanied by a person over 16 years of age.

Bikes may be carried on the roof of a car providing they are attached to an adequate roof rack and providing the total height does not exceed 4 metres. Bicycles carried on special carriers at the rear of a vehicle can exceed the width of the vehicle by 20 cm on each side, but the total width must not exceed 2 metres. The rear lights and number plate must remain visible and the driver's view must not be obstructed.

Electricity and Gas

Usually current on campsites varies between 4 and 16 amps. Plugs have two or, more usually, three round pins. Some campsites have CEE connections. Some may lend or hire out adaptors – but do not rely on it – and it may be advisable to purchase an appropriate adaptor cable with a Swiss 3-pin plug. Adaptors are readily available in local supermarkets.

The full range of Campingaz cylinders is available from large supermarkets.

Public Transport & Local Travel

Some towns are inaccessible by road, e.g. Zermatt and Wengen, and can only be reached by train or tram.

The Swiss integrated transport system is well known for its efficiency, convenience and punctuality. Co-ordinated timetables ensure fast, trouble-free interchange from one means of transport to another. Yellow post buses take travellers off the beaten track to the remotest regions. As far as railways are concerned, in addition to efficient inter-city travel, there is an extensive network of mountain railways, including aerial cableways, funiculars and ski-lifts.

Half-fare tickets are available for attractions such as cable cars, railways and lake steamers. In addition, Switzerland Tourism offers a public transport map and a number of other useful publications. See www.swisstravelsystem.com.

All visitors to campsites and hotels in Interlaken are issued with a pass allowing free bus and train travel in the area.

A ferry operates on Lake Constance (Bodensee) between Romanshorn and Friedrichshafen (Germany) saving a 70km drive. The crossing takes 40 minutes. Telephone 071 4667888 for more information; www.bodensee-schiffe.ch. A frequent ferry service also operates between Konstanz and Meersburg on the main route between Zürich, Ulm, Augsburg and Munich (Germany); information is available on a German telephone number, 0049 7531 8030; www.stadtwerke.konstanz.de. The crossing takes 20 minutes. Principal internal ferry services are on Lake Lucerne between Beckenried and Gersau, www.autofaehre.ch, and on Lake Zürich between Horgen and Meilen, www.faehre.ch. All these services transport cars and caravans.

AARBURG A2 (1km SW Rural) 47.31601, 7.89488
Camping Wiggerspitz, Hofmattstrasse 40, 4663
Aarburg 062 7915810; info@camping-aarburg.ch;
www.camping-aarburg.ch

🎪 CHF1 ♦♦ (htd) 🆆🅳 🔺 🖃 ⁄ MsP ⊤ ⊕ nr ♨ 🝭

Exit A1/A2/E35 junc 46 sp Rothrist/Olten, foll sp to site. 3*, Med, mkd, pt shd, EHU (6A) CHF3 (rev pol); long lead req; gas; bbq; 25% statics; phone; CKE. *"Conv Luzern, Zürich, Bern; picturesque, walled town; excel, clean site; htd pool adj; friendly warden; excel san facs; site is popular so rec adv bkg."*
CHF 29, 1 May-15 Sep. 2015

ALTDORF B3 (2km N Rural) 46.89256, 8.62800
Remo-Camp Moosbad, Flüelerstrsse 122, 6460 Altdorf
041 8708541

12 🎪 ♦♦ 🆆🅳 🔺 🖃 ⁄ MsP ⊤ ⊕ 🝭

Exit A2 at Altdorf junc 36. Foll sp Altdorf to rndabt & turn R. Site 200m on L adj cable car & sports cent. 2*, Sm, pt shd, EHU (10A) CHF3 (adaptor loan); bbq; 80% statics; phone; Eng spkn; CKE. *"Ideal windsurfing; useful NH en rte Italy; friendly welcome; excel san facs; excel rest; superb views; gd base for train trip over St Gotthard pass; plenty to see & do in Altdorf; public pool & waterslide adj; bus & cable car combos avail."*
CHF 35 2016

BASEL A2 (18km S Rural) 47.45806, 7.63545 **TCS**
Camping Uf der Hollen, Auf der Hollen, 4146
Hochwald 061 7120240; buero@tcscampingbasel.ch;
www.tcscampingbasel.ch

12 ♦♦ (htd) 🆆🅳 🔺 🕭 ⁄ 🦋 ⚁

Exit A18 at Reinach-Sud dir Dornach, S thro Dornach dir Hochwald, uphill thro forest to site. 2*, Med, mkd, pt shd, EHU CHF3; 90% statics; adv bkg acc; games area; CKE. *"Gd views; peaceful, pleasant site; buy day pass on bus."* **CHF 35** 2016

BERN B2 (8km NW Rural) 46.96375, 7.38420 **TCS**
Camping Bern-Eymatt, Wohlenstrasse 62C, 3032
Hinterkappelen 031 9011007; camping.bern@tcs.ch;
www.campingtcs.ch/bern

🎪 CHF5 ♦♦ (htd) 🆆🅳 🔺 ♨ 🕭 ⁄ MsP ⁇ ⊤ ⊕ ♨ 🝭 ⚁ ✎
♨ (htd) 🕭

Fr E on A1 exit junc 33 sp Bern-Bethlehem; foll sp for Wohlen & site. In 200m turn R at bottom of hill into site on shores Wohlensee. Fr W take Brunnen-Bern exit, then sp to Wohlen. Access for lge o'fits poss diff. 4*, Lge, hdstg, pt shd, EHU (6A) inc; gas; bbq (charcoal, gas); TV; 80% statics; bus to Bern nrby; ccard acc; sep car park; games area; games rm; bike hire; fishing; CKE. *"Recep 0830-1100 & 1700-2000 high ssn, but site yourself; various pitch sizes; clean facs; no o'fits over 8m high ssn; helpful staff; daily mkt in Bern; 2 supmkt nrby; excel."* **CHF 56, 1 Mar-10 Nov.**
2018

BOURG ST PIERRE D2 (0.5km N Rural) 45.95265, 7.20740 **Camping du Grand St Bernard,** 1946 Bourg-St Pierre 0 79 370 98 22; reservation@camping grand-st-bernard.ch; www.campinggrand-st-bernard.ch

🎪 ♦♦ 🆆🅳 🔺 🖃 ⁄ ⁇ ⊤ nr ⊕ nr 🝭 nr

Fr Martigny S to Grand St Bernard Tunnel. Site well sp in cent of vill. 1*, Med, unshd, EHU (4A) CHF3.50; gas; Eng spkn; ccard acc; CKE. *"Conv St Bernard Tunnel; htd pool adj; gd views."*
CHF 32, 1 Jun-30 Sep. 2016

BRIENZ B2 (2km SE Rural) 46.75069, 8.04838
Camping Seegartli, 3855 Brienz 033 9511351;
www.camping-seegaertli.ch

♦♦ 🆆🅳 🔺 🖃 ⁄ MsP 🦋 ⚁ 🝭

Fr Interlaken take N8 sp Luzern/Brienz. Take Brienz exit, ignore sp to site to R & take L in 1km bef Esso stn, sp Axalp. Site in 500m on R immed after passing under rlwy. Site on E shore of lake, next to sawmill. 2*, Sm, pt shd, pt sl, EHU (10A) CHF3; sw; Eng spkn; fishing; watersports; tennis; CKE. *"Beautiful lakeside situation; well-kept site; friendly owner; lakeside pitches boggy in wet weather; long hose req for m'van fill-up; arr bef noon in ssn; no dogs."*
CHF 33, 1 Apr-31 Oct. 2016

BRIENZ B2 (3km SE Urban) 46.74811, 8.04769
Camping Aaregg, Seestrasse 22, 3855 Brienz
033 9511843; mail@aaregg.ch; www.aaregg.ch

🎪 CHF5 ♦♦ (htd) 🆆🅳 🔺 🖃 ⁄ MsP ⁇ 🦋 ⊤ ⊕ ♨ 🝭

Fr Interlaken take N8 sp Luzern/Brienz. Take Brienz exit, ignore sp to site to R & take L in 1km bef Esso stn, sp Axalp. Site in 500m on R after passing under rlwy. Site on E shore of lake, next to sawmill. 5*, Med, mkd, hdstg, pt shd, serviced pitches; EHU (10A) CHF5; sw nr; red long stay; train nr; Eng spkn; adv bkg rec; ccard acc; CKE. *"Excel, busy site on lakeside; lakeside pitches sm; pool 500m; ideal touring base; excel, modern san facs; many attractions nrby."*
CHF 55, 1 Apr-31 Oct, S02. 2017

BRIG C2 (1km S Rural) 46.30838, 7.99338 **Camping Geschina,** Geschinastrasse 41, 3900 Brig 027 9230688; www.geschina.ch

🎪 CHF2 ♦♦ 🆆🅳 🖃 ⁄ 🦋 ⊤ 🝭 ⚁ /🅰

Foll sps twd Simplon Pass, site on R at 700m, behind pool at rv bdge. Best app fr Glis. 4*, Med, pt shd, pt sl, EHU (10A) CHF2.50; gas; red long stay; Eng spkn; adv bkg acc; fishing; CKE. *"Friendly, well-kept, family-run site; vg san facs; superb mountain & glacier views; ideal for Rhône Valley & Simplon Pass; pool adj; sh walk to town."* **CHF 29, 1 Apr-15 Oct.** 2016

BRIG *C2* (6km SW Rural) *46.30177, 7.93010* **Camping Thermal Brigerbad,** Thermalbad 1, 3900 Brigerbad 027 9484837; camping@brigerbad.ch; www.thermal bad-wallis.ch

🏕 ⓌⒹ 🏊 🔲 ⚊ 🍴 ⓗⓐ 🔄 🅼 🖊 ⚓ (covrd, htd) 🛝

To ent Brigerbad, access the "Kantonsstrasse", which is the main rd bet Visp and Brig. Once on this rd look out for blue bdge which leads directly to the Brigerbad. Lge, pt shd, EHU €3.60; bbq; twin axles; Eng spkn; adv bkg rec; waterslide; games area; bike hire. *"Sauna landscape; fitness rm; vg."*
CHF 40, 1 May-31 Oct. 2017

BUOCHS *B3* (1km N Rural) *46.97950, 8.41860* **TCS Camping Buochs Vierwaldstattersee (formerly Sportzentrum),** Seefeldstrasse, 6374 Buochs-Ennetbürgen 041 6203474; camping.buochs@tcs.ch; www.campingtcs.ch

🐕 CHF4 🏕 ⓌⒹ 🏊 🔲 🖊 🅼 🦋 🍴 ⓣ 🔲 ⚊ nr 🅼

Fr W on N2 m'way, exit junc 33 Stans-Süd & bear L. Foll sp Buochs. At 1st x-rds in Buochs, turn L to Ennetbürgen, in approx 1km R twd lake, sp. Fr E exit junc 34 for Buochs, turn L onto Beckenriederstrasse; at x-rds in cent of town turn R dir Ennetbürgen & foll sp as above. 3*, Med, mkd, pt shd, EHU (10A) CHF3.50 (adaptor avail); gas; sw nr; TV; 50% statics; Eng spkn; ccard acc; tennis; games rm; bike hire; fishing; CKE. *"Gd NH twd Italy; helpful staff; well-maintained facs; fine views; boat trip tickets sold on site; ferry close by; if recep clsd find own pitch & sign in later; pitches not draining well after heavy rains; v friendly staff; picturesque site; pool adj; site being redeveloped winter 2016-17."*
CHF 50, 4 Apr-4 Oct. 2016

BURGDORF *B2* (1.4km SE Rural) *47.05241, 7.63350* **TCS Camping Waldegg,** Waldeggweg, 3400 Burgdorf 344 222460; www.campingtcs.ch

🐕 🏕 ⓌⒹ 🏊 🔲 🖊 🅼 🦋 🍴 ⓗ nr ⚊ nr 🅼

Exit Bern-Basel N1 m'way at sp Kirchberg. Site in Burgdorf clearly sp. App over narr (2.7m) humpback bdge. 3*, Med, pt shd, EHU (10A) CHF4; adv bkg acc; golf; tennis; fishing. *"Conv Bern; old town of Burgdorf v interesting; pool 200m; friendly staff; clean san facs; gd NH."* **CHF 35, 1 Apr-30 Oct.** 2016

CHAUX DE FONDS, LA *B1* (15km SW Rural) *47.06568, 6.69856* **Camping Lac des Brenets,** 2416 Les Brenets 032 9321618; campinglesbrenets@kfnmail.ch; www.camping-brenets.ch

12 🐕 CHF3 🏕 (htd) ⓌⒹ 🏊 ⚊ 🔲 🖊 🅼 🦋 🍴 ⓗ ⚊ ⚓

Take rd 20 fr La Chaux-de-Fonds to Le Locle, foll sp Les Brenets. Foll twisting rd downhill to lake, turn & ascend to ent site on R. NB Diff L turn on descent. 5*, Med, hdstg, unshd, terr, EHU (12A) CHF4; gas; sw nr; red long stay; 80% statics; Eng spkn; adv bkg acc; ccard acc; tennis; CKE. *"Gd site o'looking Lac des Brenets & Rv Doubs; beautiful views; watch/clock museum 3km; friendly owner; ltd recep hrs, site yourself; sm pitches; excel rest; scenic touring & walking area."* **CHF 34** 2015

CHUR *B4* (2.6km W Rural) *46.85605, 9.50435* **Camping Au Chur,** Felsenaustrasse 61, Obere Au, 7000 Chur 081 2842283; info@camping-chur.ch; www.camping-chur.ch

12 🐕 CHF3 🏕 (htd) ⓌⒹ 🏊 ⚊ 🔲 🖊 🅼 🍴 🍴 ⓗ nr ⚊ 🅼

Site sp fr Chur Süd a'bahn exit, foll sp with tent pictogram (easily missed). 3*, Lge, pt shd, EHU (10A) CHF3.50; gas; TV; 65% statics; bus nr; Eng spkn; ccard acc; tennis; games area; CKE. *"Well-ordered, clean site; sm area for tourers; htd pool 200m; sm pitches; gd, modern facs; v soft when wet; helpful, friendly owners; interesting, old town."* **CHF 16** 2016

DISENTIS MUSTER *C3* (1.6km S Rural) *46.69620, 8.85270* **TCS Camping Fontanivas,** Via Fontanivas 9, 7180 Disentis-Mustèr 081 9474422; camping. disentis@tcs.ch; www.campingtcs.ch

🐕 CHF6 🏕 (htd) ⓌⒹ 🏊 ⚊ 🔲 🖊 🅼 🦋 🍴 ⓗ ⚊ 🅼

Fr Disentis S twd Lukmanier Pass for 2.5km. Site on L. 3*, Lge, pt shd, EHU (6-10A) CHF4; gas; bbq; cooking facs; sw; TV; 25% statics; Eng spkn; adv bkg acc; ccard acc; tennis; bike hire; CKE. *"Excel san facs; pool 2.5km; historic old town; gd walks."*
CHF 56, 26 Apr-29 Sep. 2016

ERLACH *B2* (0.5km N Rural) *47.04649, 7.09812* **Camping Erlach,** Stadtgraben 23, 3235 Erlach 032 3381646; camping@erlach.ch; www.erlach.ch

🐕 CHF3 🏕 ⓌⒹ 🏊 ⚊ 🔲 🖊 🅼 🦋 🍴 ⓗ ⚊ 🅼 🖊

Fr any dir foll sp for sm town of Ins; fr there foll sp Erlach. In Erlach turn L dir Le Landeron, then R twd Hotel du Port; turn L at hotel, site 200m on L by pier. 4*, Med, mkd, shd, EHU inc; gas; sw; TV; 60% statics; Eng spkn; adv bkg rec; ccard acc; games area; tennis; bike hire; CKE. *"Scenic area; gd for walking & sightseeing; pleasure steamers on lake; gd, superb modern san facs; charming site; sep car park - no cars on pitch; busy, friendly; pool 3km; rec."*
CHF 55, 31 Mar-15 Oct. 2015

FAIDO *C3* (2.4km SE Rural) *46.47134, 8.81771* **Camping Gottardo,** 6764 Chiggiogna 091 8661562; schroeder.camp@vtxmail.ch; www.camping ottardo.ch

🐕 CHF2 🏕 (htd) ⓌⒹ 🏊 🔲 🖊 🍴 ⓗ ⚊ 🅼 ⚓

Exit A2/E35 at Faido, site on R in 500m, sp immed bef Faido. 3*, Med, pt shd, terr, EHU (6A) CHF4; gas; red long stay; 10% statics; phone; bus 400m; Eng spkn. *"On main rd fr Italian lakes to St Gotthard Pass; interesting vill; poss diff for lge o'fits, espec upper terrs (rec pitch bef white building); excel facs; gd bar & rest - home cooking inc bread, pastries; friendly, helpful staff; access to pitches v ltd in snowy conditions; excel NH."*
CHF 33.7, 1 Mar-1 Nov. 2019

FLEURIER *B1* (1.4km NW Rural) *46.90643, 6.57508*
Camping Val de Travers, Belle Roche 15, 2114
Fleurier **032 8614262; camping.fleurier@tcs.ch;**
www.camping-val-de-travers.ch

🛖 CHF3 ♗ wd ♨ ⊟ ⁄ ✕ ☂ ⊕ ♨ ⚘

**On Pontarlier (France) to Neuchâtel rd, site sp in
Fleurier to L at start of vill.** 2*, Med, pt shd, EHU (4A)
CHF3; gas; 15% statics; Eng spkn; adv bkg acc; ccard
acc; rv fishing; tennis; games area; bike hire. *"Helpful
owners; htd pool 2km; wild chamois on rocks behind
site visible early morning; vg."*
CHF 22, 17 Apr-26 Sep.   **2016**

FRIBOURG *B2* (13km N Rural) *46.87827, 7.19121*
Camping Schiffenensee, Schiffenen 15, 3186
Düdingen **026 4933486; info@camping-schiffenen.ch;**
www.camping-schiffenen.ch

🛖 CHF3 ♗ wd ♨ ⊟ ⁄ ✕ ☂ ⊕ ♨ ⚘ ⛵

**Exit A12 Bern-Fribourg at Düdingen & foll rd for
Murten (sp). Ent poss tight lge o'fits.** 4*, Lge, mkd, pt
shd, EHU (10A) CHF3; 80% statics; bus; Eng spkn; adv
bkg acc; tennis; CKE. **CHF 27, 1 Apr-31 Oct.**   **2016**

"We must tell the Club about that great site we found"

Get your site reports in by mid-August and we'll do our best to get your updates into the next edition.

GENEVE *C1* (8km NE Urban) *46.24465, 6.19433*
TCS Camping Pointe à la Bise, Chemin de la Bise, 1222
Vésenaz **022 7521296; camping.geneve@tcs.ch;**
www.campingtcs.ch

🛖 CHF5 ♗ wd ♨ ⊞ ⊟ ⁄ ✕ ☂ ⊕ ♨ ⚘ ⛵

**Fr Geneva take S lakeside rd N5 sp Evian to Vésanez
4km. Turn L on Rte d'Hermance (D25) at traff lts &
foll sp to site in 1km.** 4*, Med, pt shd, EHU (4-10A)
CHF4.50 (adaptor on loan, rev pol); gas; sw; TV;
60% statics; bus to Geneva; Eng spkn; ccard acc; bike
hire; fishing; CKE. *"Pleasant, lovely site; excel lake &
mountain excursions; helpful staff; muddy when wet;
bus & boat pass fr recep; some early morning aircraft
noise."* **CHF 80, 28 Mar-6 Oct.**   **2018**

GRUYERES *C2* (2km N Rural) *46.59515, 7.08069*
Camping Les Sapins, 1664 Epagny-Gruyères **026
9129575; info@gruyeres-camping.ch; www.gruyeres-
camping.ch**

♗ (htd) wd ♨ ⊞ ⊟ ⁄ ✕ ☂ ⊕ ♨ ⚘

**Foll rd S fr Bulle sp Châteaux d'Oex. Site on L
of rd sp Gruyères-Moléson.** 3*, Med, pt shd, EHU
(10A) CHF3; 60% statics; phone; adv bkg acc;
tennis. *"Neat, tidy site; Gruyères lovely medieval
town; visits to cheese factory; lovely countryside;
easy reach E end Lake Geneva; supmkt & fuel 2km."*
CHF 38, 1 Apr-30 Sep.   **2017**

GRUYERES *C2* (6km S Rural) *46.56080, 7.08740*
Camping Haute Gruyère, Chemin du Camping 18,
1667 Enney **026 9212260; camping.enney@
bluewin.ch; www.camping-gruyere.ch**

12 🛖 CHF4 ♗ (htd) wd ♨ ⊞ ⊟ ⁄ ✕ ☂ ⊕ ♨ nr ⚘ ✂

**Well sp fr N (Gruyères) but not by name - foll TCS
sp, not well sp fr S. Site E of rd fr Bulle to Château
d'Oex, 1km S of Enney vill. Beware trains on x-ing
at turn in. Diff final app, single track around blind
bend.** 3*, Med, hdstg, unshd, EHU (6-10A) CHF4.50
(adaptor on loan); gas; red long stay; fishing; bike hire. *"Vg, modern
san facs; minimal area for tourers; bread to order;
mainly level cycle rte to Gruyeres; new management
(2016); not rec, NH only."* **CHF 45**   **2017**

GSTAAD *C2* (2km NW Rural) *46.48119, 7.27269*
Camping Bellerive, Bellerivestrasse 38, 3780 Gstaad
**033 7446330; bellerive.camping@bluewin.ch;
www.bellerivecamping.ch**

12 🛖 CHF2.70 ♗ (htd) wd ♨ ⊟ ⁄ ✕ ☂ ⚘

App fr Saanen turn R bef Gstaad, sp. 3*, Sm, hdstg,
mkd, pt shd, EHU (12A) CHF2.70; gas; TV; 60% statics;
Eng spkn; adv bkg acc; tennis; fishing. *"Gd touring,
walking, winter sports; rvside site; sm pitches; pool
700m; skiing; buy Gstaad Card for rd, rail & mountain
transport."* **CHF 29**   **2016**

HAUDERES, LES *D2* (2km N Rural) *46.09303,
7.50560* **Camping Molignon,** Route de Molignon
183, 1984 Les Haudères **027 2831240; info@
molignon.ch; www.molignon.ch**

12 🛖 CHF3.20 ♗ wd ♨ ⊞ ⊟ ⁄ ✕ ☂ ⊕ ♨ ⚘ ✂ (htd)

**Fr Sion take rd to Val d'Hérens, turn R 2.5km after
Evolène. Site sp. Rd fr Sion steep, twisting & narr
in places.** 4*, Med, mkd, pt shd, terr, EHU (10A)
CHF3.80; gas; TV; 15% statics; phone; Eng spkn; adv
bkg acc; ccard acc; CKE. *"V friendly owner; ski lift
3km; ideal for mountain climbing & walking; beautiful
location."* **CHF 35**   **2019**

INNERTKIRCHEN *C3* (1.5km NW Rural) *46.70938,
8.21519* **Camping Aareschlucht,** Hauptstrasse 34,
3862 Innertkirchen **033 9712714;
campaareschlucht@bluewin.ch; www.camping-
aareschlucht.ch**

🛖 CHF2 ♗ (htd) wd ♨ ⊟ ⁄ ✕ ⊕ nr ♨ nr ⚘

On Meiringen rd out of town on R. 3*, Sm, pt shd,
EHU (6-10A) CHF3; gas; bbq; 30% statics; Eng
spkn; adv bkg acc; ccard acc; games rm; sep car
park; CKE. *"Excel site; clean facs; gd walking; gd
touring base Interlaken, Jungfrau region; pool 5km;
conv Grimsel & Susten passes; rv walk to town."*
CHF 24, 1 May-31 Oct.   **2016**

INTERLAKEN C2 (5km NE Rural) 46.70761, 7.91330
Camp au Lac, 3852 Ringgenberg **033 8222616;**
camping@au-lac.ch

12 🐕 CHF2 🛉🛉 WD ♨ ⚲ & ☕ ⚡ MSP 🦋 ▼ ⊕ 🏊

**Fr Ringgenberg to Brienz, site sp on R when exit
Ringgenberg. Cont under rlwy viaduct to site.**
3*, Med, pt shd, pt sl, EHU (6A) CHF3 (long cable
poss req); 25% statics; bus; Eng spkn; adv bkg acc;
ccard acc; CKE. "Excel site; private access to lake;
magnificent setting." **CHF 36**   2016

INTERLAKEN (NO. 01) C2 (8km W Rural) 46.68004,
7.81669 **Camping Manor Farm**, Seestrasse 201,
3800 Interlaken-Thunersee **033 8222264; info@**
manorfarm.ch; www.manorfarm.ch

12 🐕 CHF5 🛉🛉 WD ♨ ⚲ & ☕ ⚡ 🌱 ♥ ▼ ⊕ nr 🌳 🏊 ⚓ 🚲 ⛵

**Fr W on A8 exit junc 24 Interlaken West & foll sp
Thun & Gunten. At rndabt take 2nd exit twd Thun,
sp Gunten; pass Camping Alpenblick on R, then
site on L after bdge.** 5*, V lge, mkd, pt shd, serviced
pitches; EHU (6A) inc (adaptor avail); gas; bbq
(charcoal, gas); sw nr; TV; 25% statics; Eng spkn;
adv bkg req; ccard acc; watersports; boat hire; golf
300m; fishing; games rm; horseriding 3km; bike hire;
CKE. "Site on banks of Lake Thun; excel views; gd
sized pitches; helpful staff; immac san facs; o'fits over
8m by request; money exchange; variable pitch price;
excel facs for children; steamer boat trips; excursions;
bkg fee; cable car & chairlift nrby; local bus pass
provided free; gd walking; if staying on Super pitch,
water hose with pressurised valve fitting req; site
v easy to find; v pleasant and well looked after; if
taking an awning a storm strap req." **CHF 66**   2019

See advertisement

INTERLAKEN (NO. 02) C2 (5km W Rural) 46.67969,
7.81764 **Camping Alpenblick**, Seestrasse 130, 3800
Unterseen-Interlaken **033 8227757 or 8231470; info@**
camping-alpenblick.ch; www.camping-alpenblick.ch

12 🐕 CHF3 🛉🛉 (htd) WD ♨ ⚲ & ☕ ⚡ MSP 🛜 🌳 🏊 🏔

**Fr W on A8 exit junc 24 Interlaken West & foll sp
Thun & Gunten. At rndabt take 2nd exit twd Thun,
sp Gunten. Site adj Motel Neuhaus & Rest Strandbad
on Gunten-Thun rd.** 4*, Lge, mkd, pt shd, EHU (10A)
CHF4.50 (rev pol); gas; bbq; sw nr; 30% statics; phone;
bus fr site ent; Eng spkn; ccard acc; watersports;
fishing; golf adj; CKE. "In beautiful situation; mountain
views; excel, modern facs; bread baked on site; lake
steamers fr hotel opp; gd walks nr; free bus pass to
town; cycle rte to Interlaken; CHF1 to fill m'van water
tank; adv bkg attracts surchage; pool 3km; site next to
shooting club, poss noisy." **CHF 55**   2018

INTERLAKEN (NO. 04) C2 (4.2km W Rural) 46.68555,
7.83083 **Camping Lazy Rancho**, Lehnweg 6, 3800
Unterseen-Interlaken **033 8228716; info@lazy**
rancho.ch; www.lazyrancho.ch

🐕 CHF3 🛉🛉 (htd) WD ♨ ⚲ & ☕ ⚡ MSP 🛜 ▼ 🌳 🏔 ⛷

**Fr W on app to Interlaken, exit A8/A6 junc 24 sp
Interlaken West. Turn L at slip rd rndabt then at
rndabt take a sharp R turn (foll camping sp Nos.
3-5); at Migrol petrol stn foll sp for Lazy Rancho
4 (narr rd on L just bef Landhotel Golf); it is 2nd
site. Cent of Interlaken best avoided with c'vans
or lge m'vans. Rec arr bef 1900 hrs.** 4*, Med, hdg,
mkd, hdstg, pt shd, serviced pitches; EHU (10A) inc
(adaptors provided); gas; bbq; cooking facs; TV (pitch);
30% statics; phone; Eng spkn; ccard acc; bike hire;
horseriding 500m; fishing nr; tennis 2.5km; games rm;
watersports nr; CKE. "Superb views Eiger, Monch &
Jungfrau; no o'fits over 7.5m high ssn; ideal for touring
Interlaken, Bernese Oberland; fitness cent/spa; friendly,
caring, helpful owners; sm pitches; recep 0900-1200
& 1330-2100 high ssn; 5 mins to bus stop nr Cmp
Jungfrau; ask about Swiss red fare rlwy services - excel
value; immac, outstanding, well-maintained site & facs;
brilliant site." **CHF 54, 18 Apr-15 Oct, S01.**   2019

INTERLAKEN (NO. 05) *C2* (2km W Rural) *46.68688, 7.83411* **Jungfrau Camp,** Steindlerstrasse 60, 3800 Unterseen-Interlaken **033 8225730; info@jungfrau camp.ch; www.campinginterlaken.ch or www.jungfraucamp.ch**

CHF4 (htd)

Leave N8 at exit Unterseen. In approx 600m turn R at rndabt & foll sp to site. 4*, Med, pt shd, EHU (10A) CHF4; gas; sw nr; 40% statics; bus adj; Eng spkn; adv bkg acc; tennis. *"Visits to all Bernese Oberland vills; views of Jungfrau, Mönch & Eiger; some noise fr shooting range at w/end; town in walking dist; excel, relaxing, well-run site; high standard san facs; poss ssn workers in summer."* **CHF 50, 15 Jun-20 Sep. 2016**

INTERLAKEN (NO. 08) *C2* (3km S Rural) *46.66111, 7.86453* **Camping Oberei,** Obereigasse 9, 3812 Wilderswil-Interlaken **033 8221335; info@camping wilderswil.ch; www.campinginterlaken.ch or www.campingwilderswil.ch**

CHF2 (htd) nr

Fr Interlaken by-pass take rd sp Grindelwald & Lauterbrunnen. Site sp 800m past stn on R in vill. Narr ent. 3*, Med, mkd, pt shd, pt sl, EHU (6A) CHF3; gas; TV; bus adj, bus/train nr; Eng spkn; adv bkg acc; CKE. *"Well-managed, relaxing, family-run site in superb scenic location; helpful owners; grnd sheets supplied if wet/muddy; blocks provided; gd, clean facs; gd touring cent; easy walk to rlwy stn; guest card gives free local train & bus travel; pool 3km; excel rec high ssn."* **CHF 41.6, 1 May-15 Oct. 2016**

KANDERSTEG *C2* (15km N Rural) *46.58188, 7.64150* **Camping Grassi,** 3714 Frutigen **033 6711149; campinggrassi@bluewin.ch; www.camping-grassi.ch**

CHF1.50 (htd) nr

Exit rd to Kandersteg at Frutigen-Dorf & in 400m L to site in 500m. 4*, Med, pt shd, EHU (10A) CHF3; gas; red long stay; TV; 50% statics; phone; Eng spkn; adv bkg acc; tennis; bike hire; fishing. *"Walking rte dir fr site to spectacular pedestrian suspension bdge; htd covrd pool 1km; 10 min walk to town."* **CHF 34 2019**

KANDERSTEG *C2* (1.3km NE Rural) *46.49800, 7.68519* **Camping Rendez-Vous,** 3718 Kandersteg **033 6751534; rendez-vous.camping@bluewin.ch; www.camping-kandersteg.ch**

12 CHF3 (htd)

In middle of Kandersteg turn E dir Sesselbahn Öschinensee; site sp. 3*, Med, hdstg, pt shd, pt sl, terr, EHU (10A) (adaptors avail); gas; bbq; Eng spkn; adv bkg acc; ccard acc; games rm; bike hire; CKE. *"Excel, well-supervised site; htd pool 800m; chair-lift adj; excel walking."* **CHF 41 2019**

KREUZLINGEN *A3* (0km E Rural) *47.64676, 9.19810* **Camping Fischerhaus,** Promenadenstrasse 52, 8280 Kreuzlingen **071 6884903; info@camping-fischer haus.ch; www.camping-fischerhaus.ch**

(htd)

Fr Konstanz take rd 13 dir Romanshorn. Turn L at sp 'Hafen/Indus Est' off main lakeside rd, Kreuzlingen-Arbon. Camping sps fr 5km SE at Customs in Konstanz. 4*, Med, unshd, EHU (10A) inc; gas; bbq; twin axles; 60% statics; phone; bus 100m; train 1km; Eng spkn; adv bkg acc; fishing; tennis; games area. *"Facs for statics excel, but for tourers v basic; gates clsd 1200-1400 & 2200-0700; gd cycle paths."* **CHF 44, 28 Mar-21 Oct. 2018**

LANDERON, LE *B2* (0.3km S Rural) *47.05216, 7.06975* **Camping des Pêches,** Route du Port, 2525 Le Landeron **032 7512900; info@camping-leland eron.ch; www.camping-lelanderon.ch**

A5 fr Neuchâtel, exit Le Landeron or La Neuveville; foll site sp. 4*, Med, mkd, pt shd, serviced pitches; EHU (15A) CHF3.50; gas; TV; 60% statics; Eng spkn; adv bkg acc; ccard acc; sep car park; bike hire; tennis; fishing; CKE. *"Sep touring section on busy site; htd pool 100m; walks by lake & rv; interesting old town."* **CHF 32, 1 Apr-15 Oct. 2016**

See advertisement

LANDQUART *B4* (3km E Rural) *46.97040, 9.59620*
TCS Camping Neue Ganda, Ganda 21, 7302
Landquart **081 3223955; camping.landquart@tcs.ch;**
www.campingtcs.ch

🏠 CHF4 ♦♦(htd) ⬛ ♨ ♿ ⬛ ∥ ᴹᴾ ☂ ⅄ ⌂ 🗲 ⚠ ♪

Exit A13/E43 dir Landquart, site sp on rd to Davos.
3*, Lge, pt shd, pt sl, EHU (6-10A) CHF4; gas; bbq;
cooking facs; 60% statics; ccard acc; rv fishing; bike
hire; canoeing; tennis 300m; games rm; CKE. *"Immac
san facs; excel site; v helpful owner & staff; poss
uneven pitches, mainly grass; if recep clsd find pitch &
sign in later; many mkd walks fr site."*
CHF 46, 10 Dec-28 Feb & 19 Mar-17 Oct.   **2015**

LAUSANNE *C1* (9km E Rural) *46.48973, 6.73786*
Camping de Moratel, Route de Moratel 2, 1096
Cully **021 7991914; camping.moratel@bluewin.ch**

♦♦ ⬛ ♨ ⬛ ∥ ᴹᴾ ⅄ ⌂ ⌂

**Fr Lausanne-Vevey lakeside rd (not m/way), turn R
to Cully; sp thro town; site on R on lake shore. Ent
not sp.** 3*, Sm, mkd, hdstg, hdg, pt shd, EHU (3-5A)
metered (adaptor provided); gas; sw; 80% statics; bus,
train, ferry; adv bkg acc; boating; fishing. *"Vg value;
attractive, clean site with beautiful views; rec adv bkg
for lakeside pitch; friendly staff; siting poss diff for lge
o'fits; pool 3km; gd location for best pt Lake Geneva; vg
value."* **CHF 26, 20 Mar-20 Oct.**   **2018**

> ## "Satellite navigation makes touring much easier"
>
> Remember most sat navs don't know if you're
> towing or in a larger vehicle – always use yours
> alongside maps and site directions.

LAUSANNE *C1* (3km W Rural) *46.51769, 6.59766*
Camping de Vidy, Chemin du Camping 3, 1007
Lausanne (Genferseegebiet) **021 6225000; info@clv.ch;**
www.clv.ch

12 🏠 CHF2 ♦♦(htd) ⬛ ♨ ♿ ⬛ ∥ ᴹᴾ ☂ ⅄ ⌂ ⌂ ⚠ ⅄adj

**Leave A1 at Lausanne Süd/Ouchy exit; take 4th
exit at rndabt (Rte de Chavannes); in 100m filter L
at traff lts & foll site sp to L. Site adj to HQ of Int'l
Olympic Organisation, well sp all over Lausanne.**
4*, Lge, mkd, pt shd, EHU (10A) inc; gas; bbq; TV;
80% statics; bus to Lausanne 400m; Eng spkn; adv
bkg acc; ccard acc; watersports; bike hire; games rm;
tennis 1km; CKE. *"Excel lakeside site in attractive park;
friendly staff; sm pitches; gd train service to Geneva;
sports & recreation area adj; conv m'way; recep 0800-
2100 high ssn; no o'fits over 8m high ssn; free bus
passes for unltd bus & Metro tavel in Lausanne; gd san
facs (updated 2018); gd cycling."* **CHF 42**   **2018**

LAUTERBRUNNEN *C2* (1km S Rural) *46.58788,
7.91030* **Camping Jungfrau,** Weid 406, 3822
Lauterbrunnen **033 8562010; info@camping-
jungfrau.ch;** www.camping-jungfrau.ch

12 🏠 CHF3 ♦♦(htd) ⬛ ♨ ♿ ⬛ ∥ ᴹᴾ ⅄ ☂ ⌂ ⚠

**S o'skirts of Lauterbrunnen sp at R fork, site in
500m.** 5*, Lge, hdstg, pt shd, terr, serviced pitches;
EHU (16A) CHF2.5 (metered in winter, poss rev pol);
gas; red long stay; TV; 30% statics; phone; Eng spkn;
adv bkg rec; ccard acc; tennis; bike hire; CKE. *"Friendly,
helpful welcome; fine scenery, superb situation in
vertical walled valley; rlwy tickets sold; sep car park
when site full; ski bus; ATM; close to town & rlwy stn to
high alpine resorts; ski & boot rm; superb facs; clean;
shop gd; pool 600m; excel site."* **CHF 45.6, S15.**
    2018

> ## "There aren't many sites open at this time of year"
>
> If you're travelling outside peak season
> remember to call ahead to check site opening
> dates – even if the entry says 'open all year'.

LAUTERBRUNNEN *C2* (3.6km S Rural) *46.56838,
7.90869* **Camping Breithorn,** Sandbach, 3824
Stechelberg **033 8551225; breithorn@stechelberg.ch;**
www.campingbreithorn.ch

12 🏠 CHF1 ♦♦ ⬛ ♨ ⬛ ∥ ᴹᴾ ⅄ ⌂nr ⌂ ⚠

**Up valley thro Lauterbrunnen, 300m past
Trümmelbach Falls to ent on R.** 3*, Med, unshd, EHU
(10A); gas; bbq; 60% statics; phone; Eng spkn; adv bkg
acc; tennis; fishing; CKE. *"Quiet site in lovely area; arr
early high ssn; fine scenery & gd touring base; friendly
helpful owners; frequent trains, funiculars & cable cars
fr Lauterbrunnen stn (4km); Schilthorn cable car 1.5km;
excel cent for mountain walking & cycling; pool 3km;
excel, clean facs; cash only."* **CHF 29**   **2018**

LEUK *C2* (12km E Rural) *46.30667, 7.74117*
Camping Rhône, 3945 Gampel **027 9322041; info@
campingrhone.ch; www.campingrhone.ch**

🏠 CHF3 ♦♦ ⬛ ♨ ♿ ⬛ ∥ ᴹᴾ ⅄ ⅄ ⌂ ⚠ 🗲(htd) 🏠

**Fr rd A9/E62 exit dir Gampel, site well sp on R bank
of Rv Rhône.** 3*, Lge, pt shd, EHU CHF3.20; gas;
30% statics; adv bkg acc; tennis; golf; fishing. *"Superb
location & touring base; gd walking, cycling; driest pt of
Switzerland; modern, clean san facs; friendly owners;
well maintained; gd pool; beautiful views; supmkt 1km."*
CHF 31, 25 Mar-31 Oct.   **2016**

LEUK C2 (4km SE Rural) 46.29780, 7.65936 **Camping Gemmi,** Briannenstrasse 4, 3952 Susten **027 4731154 or 4734295; info@campgemmi.ch; www.campgemmi.ch**

CHF3 ⚡ WD ⚡ 🚻 🔄 ⚡ MP 🦋 ⚡ ⚡ ⚡ 🚲 🅿 /Λ\

Foll A9/E27 SE; then nr Martigny take A9/E62 to Sierre; then take E62 thro Susten. After 2km, by Hotel Relais Bayard, take R lane (Agarn, Feithieren), ignoring sp Camping Torrent, & foll Alte Kantonstrasse sp Agarn. **Turn R at site sp into Briannenstrasse; site in 200m.** 4*, Med, mkd, pt shd, pt sl, serviced pitches; EHU (16A) inc; gas; bbq (elec, gas); TV (pitch); 5% statics; Eng spkn; adv bkg acc; ccard acc; tennis; golf; bike hire; horseriding nr; CKE. *"Outstanding site; friendly, helpful, hardworking owners; excel facs some pitches; no o'fits over 9m high ssn; private bthrms avail; gd stop on way Simplon Pass; various pitch prices; barrier clsd 2200-0800; pool 600m; excel walking; conv A9."* **CHF 41, 30 Mar-7 Oct, S12.** 2017

LOCARNO C3 (14km E Rural) 46.16978, 8.91396 **Park-Camping Riarena,** Via Campeggio, 6516 Cugnasco **091 8591688; info@campingriarena.ch; www.campingriarena.ch**

CHF4 ⚡ WD ⚡ 🚻 🔄 ⚡ MP 🦋 ⚡ ⚡ 🚲 🅿 /Λ\ ⚡ 🏊 ⚡

Exit A2/E35 Bellinzona-Süd & foll sp dir airport. Bear R at rndabt & foll site sp to Gudo, site on R in 2km. 4*, Med, mkd, shd, EHU (10A) CHF5 (adaptor avail); gas; red long stay; twin axles; bus 0.5km; Eng spkn; adv bkg acc; ccard acc; bike hire; games area. *"Friendly, family-run site; excursions arranged; gd cycle rtes; gate shut 1300-1500; clean san facs; dusty site; beware acorn drop September; vg."* **CHF 53, 21 Mar-17 Oct.** 2019

LUGANO D3 (7km W Rural) 45.99534, 8.90845 **Lugano,** Via alla Force 14, 6933 Muzzano-Lugano **091 9947788 or 091 9858070 LS; camping.muzzano@ tcs.ch; www.campingtcs.ch/muzzano**

12 🐕 CHF5.50 ⚡ WD 🚻 🔄 ⚡ ⚡ MP ⚡ ⚡ ⚡ 🚲 🅿 /Λ\ ⚡
⚡ (htd) 🔥

Leave A2 at Lugano Nord & foll sp Ponte Tresa & airport. In Agno turn L at traff island; foll camping sp. In 800m, just after La Piodella town sp, look for sm sp at rd junc with tent symbol & TCS sticker. NB This may appear to direct you to your R but you must make a 180° turn & take slip rd along R-hand side of rd you have just come along - app rd to site. 4*, Lge, mkd, pt shd, serviced pitches; EHU (10A) inc (long lead poss req, avail fr recep); gas; bbq; TV; 10% statics; Eng spkn; adv bkg acc; ccard acc; watersports; games area; horseriding 6km; tennis; games rm; fishing; CKE. *"Idyllic location; pitches nr lake higher price; o'fits over 7.5m HS; sep car park; modern san facs; no cats; access to pitches poss diff lge o'fits; boating 6km; train to Lugano 1km, or easy drive; ideal for Ticino Lakes; day/eve aircraft noise; barrier clsd 1200-1400."* **CHF 49, S10.** 2016

LUZERN B3 (3km E Rural) 47.0500, 8.33833 **Camping International Lido,** Lidostrasse 19, 6006 Luzern **041 3702146; luzern@camping-international.ch; www.camping-international.ch**

12 ⚡ CHF4 ⚡ (htd) WD 🚻 🔄 ⚡ ⚡ MP ⚡ ⚡ ⚡ nr 🚲 🅿 /Λ\

Fr bdge on lake edge in city cent foll sp Küssnacht & Verkehrshaus. Turn R off Küssnacht rd at traff lts by transport museum (sp Lido), site 50m on L beyond lido parking. Fr A2/E35 exit Luzern Centrum. 4*, Lge, mkd, hdstg, pt shd, EHU (16A) CHF4.60; gas; bbq; sw nr; 10% statics; phone; bus, 200mtrs; Eng spkn; adv bkg rec; ccard acc; boat trips; boat launch; CKE. *"Ltd touring pitches cr in peak ssn, early arr rec; pool adj (May-Sep); recep open 0830-1200 & 1400-1800 high ssn; money exchange; recep in bar LS; clean, well-maintained facs stretched high ssn; lake ferry 200m; helpful staff; pleasant lakeside walk to Luzern; conv location; excel rest in Wurzenbach; transport museum worth a visit; well-run site; free local bus tickets avail."* **CHF 50** 2018

MADULAIN C4 (0.3km N Rural) 46.58764, 9.94004 **Camping Madulain,** Via Vallatscha, 7523 Madulain **081 8540161; mail@campingmadulain.ch; www.campingmadulain.ch**

⚡ (htd) WD 🚻 🔄 ⚡ ⚡ ⚡ Y nr ⚡ nr 🅿 nr

Sp fr N27 at foot of Albula Pass. 3*, Sm, pt shd, pt sl, terr, EHU (10A) CHF2; 70% statics; Eng spkn. *"Simple CL-type site; excel san facs; helpful owner."* **CHF 35, 19 Dec-10 Apr & 27 May-18 Oct.** 2015

MEIERSKAPPEL B3 (1km S Rural) 47.12175, 8.44670 **Campingplatz Gerbe,** Landiswilerstrasse, 6344 Meierskappel **041 7904534; info@swiss-bauernhof.ch; www.swiss-bauernhof.ch**

🐕 CHF2.50 ⚡ (htd) WD 🚻 🔄 ⚡ ⚡ MP 🦋 ⚡ ⚡ ⚡ 🚲 /Λ\
⚡ (covrd, htd)

Exit A4/E41 at Küssnacht & foll sp N to Meierskappel. Bef ent Meierskappel turn L into farm ent for site (sp.) Med, pt shd, pt sl, EHU (10A) CHF3.50 (poss rev pol); bbq; 5% statics; CKE. *"Vg, basic farm site, poor facs (unisex), in need of refurb; lge field - choose own pitch; conv Luzerne & Zurich."* **CHF 25, 1 Mar-1 Nov.** 2015

MEIRINGEN C3 (1.5km NW Rural) 46.73431, 8.17139 **Alpencamping,** Brünigstrasse 47, 3860 Meiringen **033 9713676; info@alpencamping.ch; www.alpencamping.ch**

🐕 CHF3 ⚡ (htd) WD 🚻 🔄 ⚡ ⚡ MP ⚡ ⚡ ⚡ nr 🚲 /Λ\ ⚡

Leave A8, then take rd11/6 twd Brünig Pass. On entering Meiringen, at 1st rndabt foll camp sp L to site. 4*, Med, unshd, EHU (10A) CHF5.50; gas; bbq; cooking facs; 70% statics; bus 200m, train 1.3km; Eng spkn; adv bkg acc; site clsd Nov; CKE. *"Meeting point of alpine passes; friendly, family-run site; excel, modern san facs; vg walking/cycling; beautiful site with gd views; fair."* **CHF 47, 1 Jan-31 Oct & 1 Dec-31 Dec.** 2018

MENDRISIO *D3* (8km NW Rural) *45.88921, 8.94841*
Camping TCS Meride-Mendrisio (formerly Parco al Sole), Via Ala Caraa 2, 6866 Meride **091 6464330; camping.meride@tcs.ch; www.campingtcs.ch**

🛠CHF5 ♦♦♦ 🆆🅾 ♨️ ♿ 🔄 🚿 ⧫ ᴹˢᴾ ☂️ 🍴

ⓦ 🃏 🌡️ nr /🏔 ⚓ 🛶 (htd)

Fr A2/E35 exit Mendrisio, then foll sp Rancate & Serpiano. Steep climb. Site on L to S of vill. 4*, Med, hdstg, pt shd, pt sl, EHU (4A) CHF4.50; gas; TV; 20% statics; Eng spkn; adv bkg acc; ccard acc; lake fishing; sep car park. *"Attractive, peaceful setting away fr traff; Unesco World Heritage vill; pitches uneven in parts & v sm, some surrounded by other pitches - make sure you can get off with o'fit; site clsd to arr 1100-1700; conv Milan by train."*
CHF 49, 1 May-26 Sep.   **2016**

MORGES *C1* (2km S Rural) *46.50360, 6.48760*
Morges, Promenade du Petit-Bois 15, 1110 Morges **021 8011270 or 091 9858070 LS; camping. morges@tcs.ch; www.campingtcs.ch/morges**

🛠CHF5 ♦♦♦ 🆆🅾 ♨️ ♿ 🔄 ᴹˢᴾ ☂️ 🍴 ⓦ 🃏 /🏔 ⚓

Exit A1/E25 at Morges Ouest, then foll sp to lake. Site well sp on Lake Léman N shore adj pool. 3*, Lge, hdg, mkd, pt shd, EHU (6A) inc (adaptor/long lead avail); gas; bbq; sw nr; TV; 50% statics; Eng spkn; adv bkg acc; games rm; bike hire; watersports; tennis 500m; boating. *"Pleasant site but sm pitches; htd pool in complex 200m (high ssn) inc; helpful staff; clean san facs; conv Lausanne, Geneva & some Alpine passes; o'fits over 8m on req; m'van o'night/late arr area; easy walk to town & stn; cycle path around lake; vg."*
CHF 60, 29 Mar-9 Oct, S14.   **2017**

MURG *B3* (0.5km N Rural) *47.11543, 9.21445*
Camping Murg am Walensee, 8877 Murg **081 7381530; info@camping-murg.ch; www.murg-camping.ch**

🛠CHF4.50 ♦♦♦ 🆆🅾 ♨️ /🏔 ⓦ nr 🃏

Exit A3 junc 47 dir Murg, site sp on lake. Med, pt shd, EHU (10A) CHF3.70; sw nr; 30% statics; phone; adv bkg req. *"Spectacular outlook at water's edge; sm pitches; beautiful setting; boat trips adj; cable car 4km; vg."* **CHF 49, 1 Apr-15 Oct.**   **2019**

MUSTAIR *B4* (0.5km E Rural) *46.62405, 10.44933*
Camping Muglin, Via Muglin 223, 7537 Mustair **081 8585990; info@campingmuglin.ch; www.campingmuglin.ch**

♦♦♦ 🆆🅾 ♨️ 🔄 /🏔 ᴹˢᴾ ☂️ 🍴 🃏 /🏔

On rd 28 to Mustair. Foll sp. Med, mkd, unshd, EHU (13A); bbq; TV; adv bkg acc; games rm. *"Beautiful views; serviced pithces; walking rte fr site; lge sauna."*
CHF 42, 22 Apr-29 Oct.   **2017**

NEUCHATEL *B1* (13km NE Rural) *47.00198, 7.04145*
TCS Camping Gampelen (formerly Camp Fanel), Seestrasse 50, 3236 Gampelen **032 3132333; camping.gampelen@tcs.ch; www.campingtcs.ch**

🛠CHF4 ♦♦♦ 🆆🅾 ♨️ 🔄 🚿 /🏔 ᴹˢᴾ ☂️ 🍴 ⓦ 🃏 /🏔 ⚓ 🛶 (htd)

Foll TCS camping sp fr turning off N5 in Gampelen - approx 4km fr vill, on lakeside. 3*, V lge, mkd, pt shd, serviced pitches; EHU (4-6A) CHF 3.50-4.50 (adaptor on loan, rev pol); gas; bbq; sw; red long stay; 80% statics; Eng spkn; adv bkg acc; ccard acc; tennis; archery; golf; fishing; watersports; CKE. *"In nature reserve; office/barrier clsd 1200-1400; office & shop hrs vary with ssn; gd, modern facs; helpful staff; Euros also acc; vg cycling around lakes."*
CHF 55, 10 Apr-13 Oct.   **2018**

PRESE, LE *C4* (0.5km N Rural) *46.29490, 10.08010*
Camping Cavresc, 7746 Le Prese **081 8440259; camping.cavresc@bluewin.ch; www.camping sertori.ch**

12 🛠CHF2 ♦♦♦ (htd) 🆆🅾 ♨️ ♿ 🔄 /🏔 ᴹˢᴾ ☂️ 🍴 ⓦ 🃏 nr /🏔 🛶

S fr Pontresina on N29 site sp on L 5km S of Poschiavo adj Lake Poschiavo. 4*, Med, shd, EHU (10A) CHF4; gas; bbq; red long stay; TV; bus/train adj; adv bkg acc; ccard acc; games area; CKE. *"Stunning scenery; htd covrd pool 5km; walking/cycling rtes; excel; friendly owners."* **CHF 36**   **2015**

ROMANSHORN *A4* (5km SE Rural) *47.53620, 9.39885*
Camping Seehorn (formerly Wiedehorn), Wiedehorn, 9322 Egnach **071 4771006; info@seehorn.ch; www.seehorn.ch**

🛠CHF4 ♦♦♦ 🆆🅾 ♨️ 🔄 /🏔 ☂️ 🍴 ⓦ 🃏 /🏔

Site is 2km E of Egnach, dir Arbon. 4*, Med, mkd, pt shd, pt sl, serviced pitches; EHU (16A) CHF2.50; gas; TV; 60% statics; phone; adv bkg acc; fishing. *"Direct access Lake Constance; sep car park high ssn; statics sep; excel facs; great loc; cycle paths around lake; friendly recep; ACSI acc."* **CHF 50, 1 Mar-31 Oct.**
                                                   2018

SAAS FEE *D2* (4.6km NE Rural) *46.11588, 7.93819*
Camping am Kapellenweg, 3910 Saas-Grund **027 9574997; camping@kapellenweg.ch; www.kapellenweg.ch**

🛠CHF2.50 ♦♦♦ 🆆🅾 ♨️ ♿ 🔄 /🏔 ⓦ 🃏

Fr Visp, take Saas Fee rd to Saas Grund, cont twd Saas Almagell, site on R after 1km. 3*, Sm, pt shd, pt sl, EHU CHF3; gas; Eng spkn; fishing; golf. *"Ideal for walking; family-run site; clean san facs; beautiful scenery; if recep clsd, site yourself; bus or walk (50 mins) into town; excel site."* **CHF 49, 10 May-13 Oct.**   **2019**

ST GALLEN *A4* (9km N Rural) *47.46191, 9.36371*
Camping St Gallen-Wittenbach, Leebrücke, 9304
Bernhardzell **071 2984969; campingplatz.stgallen@
ccc-stgallen.ch; www.ccc-stgallen.ch**

🐕 CHF3 👫 �wo ♨ ⚓ ⊙ ✂ 🦋 Ⴘ ♨ ⅀ ⚑

Exit A1/E60 St Fiden. L in Wittenbach cent at site sp.
Cross Rv Sitter on sharp R bend, turn sharp R at sp.
3*, Med, hdstg, pt shd, EHU (6A) CHF4 (adaptor loan);
gas; bbq; TV; 30% statics; bus; Eng spkn; adv bkg acc;
ccard acc; canoeing; golf 10km; bike hire; CKE. *"Gd
base for S shore of Bodensee; pleasant rvside setting;
friendly staff."* **CHF 32, 12 Apr-4 Oct.** 2016

ST MARGRETHEN *A4* (3km E Rural) *47.45114,
9.65650* **Strandbad Camping Bruggerhorn,** 9430 St
Margrethen **071 7442201**

👫 wo ♨ ⚓ ⊙ ✂ ⊙ nr ♨ ⅀ ⚑ ⎈

Exit N1/E60 dir St Margrethen, site well sp. 3*, Med,
pt shd, EHU (10A) CHF2.50 (adaptor avail); gas; sw;
Eng spkn; adv bkg acc; tennis; CKE. *"Picturesque,
clean site; vg shwrs; sports cent adj; helpful staff."*
CHF 36, 1 Apr-31 Oct. 2016

ST MORITZ *C4* (1km S Rural) *46.47843, 9.82511*
TCS Camping Olympiaschanze, 7500 St Moritz
**081 8334090; camping.stmoritz@tcs.ch;
www.campingtcs.ch**

🐕 CHF4 👫 (htd) ♨ ⚓ ⊙ ✂ 🦋 Ⴘ ⊙ nr ♨ ⅀ ⚑ ✎

Turn S off rd N27 immed after park & ride car park.
Site 1km fr vill of Champfer. 3*, Med, mkd, pt sl, EHU
(6A) CHF4 (adaptor on loan); gas; sw nr; Eng spkn;
ccard acc; bike hire; tennis; CKE. *"Gd walking area, nr
St Moritz & Maloja & Julier passes; site v high & cold
(poss snow in Aug); san facs stretched when site full; sh
walk town cent."* **CHF 52, 20 May-28 Sep.** 2016

SEMPACH *B3* (1.5km S Rural) *47.12447, 8.18924* **TCS
Camping Sempach,** Seelandstrasse, 6204 Sempach
Stadt **041 4601466 or 091 9858070; camping.
sempach@tcs.ch; www.campingtcs.ch/sempach**

🐕 CHF5 👫 (htd) wo ♨ ⚓ ⚒ ⊙ ✂ ⟨MSP⟩ 🦋 Ⴘ ⊙ ♨ ⅀ ⚑ ✎ ⎈

Fr Luzern on A2 take exit sp Emmen N, Basel, Bern.
Join E35 & cont on this rd to exit at Sempach sp. Site
well sp. 4*, Lge, mkd, unshd, EHU (13A) inc (adaptor
avail); gas; bbq (charcoal, gas); sw nr; TV; 60% statics;
Eng spkn; adv bkg acc; ccard acc; bike hire;
watersports; fishing; golf 5km; tennis; games rm; CKE.
*"Excel location on Sempacher See, 10 mins drive fr
m'way & attractive town; no o'fits over 9m high ssn;
sep car parks high ssn; sm pitches; helpful staff; rest &
beach open to public; water & bins far fr many pitches;
poss tight parking; ltd facs LS; private san facs avail;
lakeside walk to Sempach."* **CHF 56, 4 Apr-7 Oct,
S08.** 2016

SIERRE *C2* (3km NE Rural) *46.30215, 7.56420*
Camping Swiss Plage, Campingweg 3, 3970 Salgesch
**027 4556608; info@swissplage.ch; www.swiss
plage.ch**

🐕 CHF3.50 👫 wo ♨ ⚓ ⊙ ✂ ⟨MSP⟩ 🦋 Ⴘ ⊙ ♨ ⅀ ⚑

Fr A9/E62 exit at Sierre, turn L & go over bdge, Foll
sp Salgesch & Site. Fr town site well sp. 4*, Lge, shd,
EHU (10A) CHF3.60; gas; sw; Eng spkn; adv bkg req;
ccard acc; tennis. *"Pleasant site in lovely location."*
CHF 39, Easter-15 Oct. 2016

SION *C2* (9km SW Rural) *46.20578, 7.27855* **Camping
du Botza,** Route du Camping 1, 1963 Vétroz **027
3461940 or 079 2203575 (mob); info@botza.ch;
www.botza.ch**

⟨12⟩ 🐕 CHF3.50 👫 wo ♨ ⚓ ⚒ ⊙ ✂ ⟨MSP⟩ 🦋 Ⴘ Ⴘ ⊙ ♨ ⅀ ⚑ ✎
⎈ (htd) ⎙

Exit A9/E62 junc 25 S'wards over a'bahn. Site adj
Vétroz indus est, foll sp 'CP Nr.33'. 5*, Lge, mkd,
pt shd, serviced pitches; EHU (10A) CHF3.70; gas;
30% statics; adv bkg acc; ccard acc; fishing; squash;
tennis; golf 8km. *"Superb site conv m'way & ski resorts;
excel facs; gd security; organised excursions; vg rest;
fine mountain views; cycle track along Rhone nrby;
some noise fr nrby airport."* **CHF 34.3** 2019

SOLOTHURN *B2* (2km SW Rural) *47.19883, 7.52288*
TCS Camping Lido Solothurn, Glutzenhofstrasse 5,
4500 Solothurn **032 6218935 or 091 9858070 LS;
camping.solothurn@tcs.ch; www.campingtcs.ch/
solothurn**

🐕 CHF5 👫 (htd) wo ♨ ⚓ ⚒ ⊙ ✂ ⟨MSP⟩ 🦋 Ⴘ Ⴘ Ⴘ ⊙ ♨ ⅀ ⚑ ✎
⎙

Exit A5 dir Solothurn W, cross rv bdge. At traff lts
turn L & foll sp to site (new rd 2009). 4*, Lge, mkd, pt
shd, serviced pitches; EHU (16A) inc; gas; bbq; cooking
facs; TV; 20% statics; bus 200m; Eng spkn; adv bkg
acc; ccard acc; games rm; bike hire; tennis 200m;
fishing; boat hire; golf 100m; games area; CKE. *"Gd
touring base by Rv Aare; no o'fits over 12m high ssn;
lge pitches; htd pool adj; excel facs; helpful staff; 20
mins walk to picturesque town; excel cycling paths."*
CHF 58, 28 Feb-29 Nov, S13. 2019

campofelice.ch/tcc | Tenero · Ticino · Switzerland | +41 91 745 14 17

SPIEZ *C2* (6km SE Rural) *46.65880, 7.71688* **Camping Stuhlegg,** Stueleggstrasse 7, 3704 Krattigen **033 6542723; campstuhlegg@bluewin.ch; www.camping-stuhlegg.ch**

12 🐕 CHF3 ♗♗(htd) 🆆🅳 ♨ ⚓ 👪 ⚡ 🅼🅿 🦋 ⚟ ⑪nr 🍴 🛒 ∕⌂ ✎ 🏊(htd)

13km fr Interlaken on hillside on S side of Lake Thun. Advise app fr Spiez. Fr Spiez rlwy stn heading SE turn R over rlwy bdge; foll sp Leissigen & Krattigen for 5km. In Krattigen after modern church turn R (low gear), site 500m on R. To avoid going thro Spiez town, leave Bern-Interlaken m'way at junc 19. Foll dir to Aeschi. At rndabt in Aeschi turn L to Krattigen. Turn L after 1m opp wood yard into Stuhleggstrasse. Site in 300 yds. 4*, Lge, pt shd, pt sl, terr, EHU (10A) CHF4 (some rev pol); gas; 60% statics; phone; adv bkg acc; ccard acc; site clsd last week Oct to end Nov; CKE. *"Excel well-kept, well run site; immac facs; helpful friendly staff; recep clsd 1300-1500; mountain views; gd dog-walking in area; scenic rtes fr site; ski bus; free bus service with Guest Card; gd rest; bread can be ordered."* **CHF 40** **2019**

> ## "I like to fill in the reports as I travel from site to site"
>
> You'll find report forms at the back of this guide, or you can fill them in online at camc.com/europereport.

SUMVITG *C3* (0.9km SW Rural) *46.72439, 8.92968* **Camping Garvera,** Campadi alla Staziun, 7175 Sumvitg **081 9431922; info@garvera.ch; www.garvera.ch**

🐕 CHF4 ♗♗(htd) 🆆🅳 ♨ ⚓ 👪 ⚟ 🅘 🛒nr

Fr Chur on rd 19, site well sp in Sumvitg. 2*, Sm, pt shd, terr, EHU (10A) CHF4; bus/train adj; Eng spkn. *"Excel, clean, well cared for site; friendly, helpful owners, who run nrby rest; beautiful area; gd walking; excel facs, inc a natural spring water pond; highly rec."* **CHF 34, 1 May-1 Oct.** **2015**

SURSEE *B2* (3km W Rural) *47.17505, 8.08685* **Camping Sursee Waldheim,** Baslerstrasse, 6210 Sursee **041 9211161; info@camping-sursee.ch; www.camping-sursee.ch**

🐕 CHF1 ♗♗ 🆆🅳 ♨ ⚓ 👪 ⚟ 🅼🅿 🦋 ⚟ ⑪nr 🍴 🛒 ∕⌂

Exit A2 at junc 20 & take L lane onto rd 24 dir Basel/Luzern. Turn R at traff lts, foll rd 2 turn R at 2nd rndabt dir Basel to site. 3*, Sm, hdstg, pt shd, pt sl, EHU (10A); gas; bbq; sw nr; TV; 60% statics; Eng spkn; adv bkg acc; games rm; bike hire; CKE. *"Pretty site; excel san facs; gd train service to Luzern; sh walk to town cent; popular NH; gd touring base; v helpful owner; acc Euros."* **CHF 30, 1 Apr-29 Oct.** **2017**

TENERO *C3* (1.5km E Rural) *46.16890, 8.85561* **Camping Campofelice,** Via alle Brere, 6598 Tenero **091 7451417; camping@campofelice.ch; www.campofelice.ch**

♗♗ 🆆🅳 ♨ ⚓ 👪 ⚟ 🅼🅿 ⚟ ⑪nr 🍴 🛒 ∕⌂ ✎

Fr A2 take Bellinzona S exit & foll sp Locarno on A13. In about 12km take Tenero exit, at end slip rd foll sp to site. V lge, mkd, pt shd, serviced pitches; EHU (10A) inc; gas; red long stay; 10% statics; Eng spkn; ccard acc; tennis; CKE. *"Expensive but superb, attractive & well-equipped, v clean facs; boat moorings; pool 8km; min stay 3+ nights high ssn."* **CHF 55, 14 Mar-27 Oct.** **2017**

See advertisement

TENERO *C3* (1km SW Urban) *46.17292, 8.84808* **Camping Miralago,** Via Roncaccio 20, 6598 Tenero **091 7451255; info@camping-miralago.ch; www.camping-miralago.ch**

12 🐕 CHF3 ♗♗(htd) 🆆🅳 ♨ ⚓ 👪 ⚡ 🅼🅿 🦋 ⚟ ⚟ 🅘 🍴 🛒 ∕⌂ 🏊(htd) 🛥

Turn L off A13 Bellinzona/Locarno rd at Tenero & foll camping sps. 5*, Med, mkd, unshd, EHU (10A) inc; bbq; sw nr; bus adj; Eng spkn; adv bkg acc; ccard acc; games area; CKE. *"Beautiful area; ltd facs LS; lake steamer pier lakefront camping; sm pitches with no privacy hdgs; fairly new san facs; beautiful location, no rd noise."* **CHF 93** **2019**

ULRICHEN *C3* (1km SE Rural) *46.50369, 8.30969*
Camping Nufenen, 3988 Ulrichen **027 9731437;**
info@camping-nufenen.ch; www.camping-
nufenen.ch

🐕 CHF2 � [wc] ⚡ ⚐ ✉ 🦋 ♈ ⑨ nr 🛁

On NE end of Ulrichen turn R on Nufenen pass rd.
After rlwy & rv x-ing (1km), site on R. 3*, Med, pt shd,
EHU (8A) CHF3.50; red long stay; 50% statics; phone;
adv bkg acc; tennis 2km; CKE. *"Pleasantly situated,*
mountainous site with gd local facs; gd walking; san
facs basic but clean; pool 6km; recep open 0800-2100,
clsd 1230-1400; gd NH." **CHF 35, 1 Jun-30 Sep.**
2018

ULRICHEN *C3* (8km SW Rural) *46.46480, 8.24469*
Camping Augenstern, 3988 Reckingen **027**
9731395; info@campingaugenstern.ch;
www.campingaugenstern.ch

🐕 CHF2 ♔ [wc] ⚡ ⚐ ✉ 🦋 ♈ 🍴 ⑨ ♣ 🛁

On Brig-Gletsch rd turn R in Reckingen over rlwy
& rv, site sp. 3*, Med, unshd, EHU (10A) CHF4.50;
20% statics; golf; fishing; CKE. *"Nr Rv Rhône &*
mountains; htd pool adj." **CHF 37, 1 Jan-15 Mar,**
11 May-16 Oct & 14 Dec-31 Dec. **2016**

VADUZ (LIECHTENSTEIN) *B4* (7km S Rural)
47.0866, 9.52666 **Camping Mittagspitze,**
Saga 29, 9495 Triesen **3923677; info@**
campingtriesen.li; www.campingtriesen.li

🐕 CHF4 ♔ [wc] ⚡ ⚐ ✉ 🦋 ♈ ⑨ 🛁 ⋒

On rd 28 bet Vaduz & Balzers, sp. Poss diff for
lge o'fits. 4*, Med, hdstg, pt shd, terr, EHU (6A)
CHF5; gas; bbq; 80% statics; Eng spkn; ccard
acc; fishing. *"Pretty site in lovely location; excel*
touring base; site yourself, recep open 0800-0830
& 1900-1930 only; fitness trail; steep, diff access to
pitches & slippery when wet; beer garden; gd rest."
CHF 42, 1 Mar-31 Dec. **2016**

VALLORBE *B1* (0.7km SW Urban) *46.71055, 6.37472*
Camping Pré Sous Ville, 10 Rue des Fontaines, 1337
Vallorbe **021 8432309; yvan.favre@vallorbe.com**

🐕 ♔ [wc] ⚡ ⚐ ✉ 🦋 ♈ 🍴 ⑨ nr ⋒

Foll camping sp in town. 3*, Med, mkd, pt shd, EHU
(10A) CHF5; gas; 20% statics; Eng spkn; fishing; games
area; tennis; CKE. *"Gd, clean facs; gd size pitches; site*
yourself if warden absent; htd pool adj; conv for Vallée
de Joux, Lake Geneva & Jura; views down valley."
CHF 37, 15 Apr-15 Oct. **2016**

VILLENEUVE *C1* (12km W Rural) *46.38666,*
6.86055 **Camping Rive-Bleue,** Case postale 68,
1897 Le Bouveret **024 4812161; info@camping-**
rive-bleue.ch; www.camping-rive-bleue.ch

🐕 CHF3.20 ♔ [wc] ⚡ ⚐ ✉ 🦋 ♈ ⑨ nr 🛁 ⋒

Fr Montreux foll sp to Evian to S side of Lake
Geneva. Turn R after sp 'Bienvenue Bouveret'. Foll
camp sp to Aqua Park. Site on R approx 1km fr main
rd. 4*, Lge, mkd, pt shd, EHU (10A) CHF4.20 (adaptor
avail - check earth); gas; sw; 20% statics; Eng spkn; adv
bkg acc; watersports; tennis; waterslide; sep car park;
CKE. *"Well-maintained, well-ordered, completely flat*
site in lovely setting on lake; friendly staff; water/waste
pnts scarce; vg facs but red LS; 15 mins walk to vill with
supmkt; conv ferries around Lake Geneva; cars must
be parked in sep public car park; gd cyling area; free
bicycles for 4 hrs fr vill; pool adj; 1st class san block."
CHF 43, 1 Apr-12 Oct. **2018**

VILLENEUVE *C1* (5km W Rural) *46.39333,*
6.89527 **Camping Les Grangettes,** Rue des
Grangettes, 1845 Noville **021 9601503; noville@**
treyvaud.com; www.les-grangettes.ch

[12] 🐕 CHF3 ♔ (htd) ⚡ ⚐ ✉ 🦋 🍴 ⑨ ♣ 🛁

Fr N9 Montreux-Aigle rd, take Villeneuve exit, at
end slip rd turn N twds Villeneuve. At 1st traff
lts turn L to Noville, turn R by PO, site sp. Narr
app rd. 4*, Med, unshd, EHU (10A) CHF4; sw;
80% statics; phone; Eng spkn; sep car park; fishing;
boating. *"Beautifully situated on SE corner Lake*
Geneva o'looking Montreux; sep tourer area; pool 3km;
poss noisy in high ssn." **CHF 39** **2019**

VISP *C2* (1.6km NW Rural) *46.29730,*
7.87269 **Camping Schwimmbad Mühleye,**
3930 Visp **027 9462084; info@camping-**
visp.ch; www.camping-visp.ch

🐕 CHF2 ♔ [wc] ⚡ ⚐ ✉ 🍴 ♣ 🛁 nr ⋒

Exit main rd E2 at W end of town bet Esso petrol
stn & rv bdge at Camping sp. Site nr pool. 3*, Lge,
pt shd, EHU (13A) CHF3.50; gas; red long stay;
20% statics; Eng spkn; fishing; tennis; CKE. *"Gd*
for Zermatt & Matterhorn; lge pool adj; recep at
sw pool ent; gd value espec LS; suitable lge o'fits."
CHF 35, 10 Mar-31 Oct. **2015**

VITZNAU *B3* (0.5km SE Rural) *47.00683, 8.48621* **Camping Vitznau,** Altdorfstrasse, 6354 Vitznau **041 3971280; info@camping-vitznau.ch; www.camping-vitznau.ch**

🛖 CHF5 ♦♦ ⬜ 🛁 ♿ 🖂 ✎ MSP 🦋 Y 🛒 🏊

On E edge of Vitznau, sp. Fr Küssnacht twd Brunnen turn L at RC church with tall clock tower. 4*, Lge, hdstg, pt shd, terr, EHU (16A) CHF4 (adaptors on loan); gas; sw nr; red long stay; 40% statics; Eng spkn; adv bkg rec; ccard acc; tennis; CKE. *"Excel, v clean, family-run site; friendly owner will help with pitching; max c'van length 7m high ssn; sm pitches; some site rds tight & steep; recep closes 1830 hrs; fine views lakes & mountains; Quickstop o'night facs CHF20; many activities inc walking; gd dog-walking; conv ferry terminal, cable cars & mountain rlwy (tickets avail on site); gd saving by using 'tell-pass'; lake steamer to Luzern 500m; gd pool, sm shop."* **CHF 53, 30 Mar-7 Oct, S05.** **2018**

WINTERTHUR *A3* (3km N Rural) *47.51965, 8.71655* **Camping am Schützenweiher,** Eichliwaldstrasse 4, 8400 Winterthur **052 2125260; campingplatz@win.ch; www.camping-winterthur.info**

12 🛖 CHF4 ♦♦ (htd) ⬜ 🛁 🖂 ✎ 🕈 ⑨ 🛒 nr 🏔

Fr A1/E60 exit Winterthur-Ohringen dir Winterthur, turn R & foll site sp, site adj police stn in about 200m. 2*, Sm, shd, EHU CHF3; gas; 8% statics; phone; bus 250m, train; Eng spkn; CKE. *"Helpful owner; office open 0900-1100 & 1830-1930 to register & pay; find own pitch outside these hrs; sm pitches; pool 3km; gd NH; fairly gd site."* **CHF 39** **2018**

ZUG *B3* (2km E Rural) *47.17806, 8.49438* **TCS Camping Zug,** Chamer Fussweg 36, 6300 Zug **041 7418422; camping.zug@tcs.ch; www.campingtcs.ch**

🛖 CHF5 ♦♦ (htd) ⬜ 🛁 🖂 ✎ MSP Y ⑨ 🅰 🛒 🏔

Fr A4/E41 take A4a Zug-West, site sp on R in 3km on lakeside. Fr Zug take Luzern rd for 2km. Site on L under rlwy. 3*, Med, mkd, pt shd, EHU (6A) CHF4; gas; sw; 40% statics; phone; Eng spkn; ccard acc; tennis; fishing; games area; bike hire; CKE. *"Easy walk to town; pool 3km; new (2018) young owners; v clean & tidy; lovely location."* **CHF 36, 29 Mar-14 Oct.** **2018**

ZUG *B3* (11km SE Rural) *47.127781, 8.591945* **Campsite Unterägeri,** Wilbrunnenstraße 81, 6314 Unterägeri **041 7503928; info@campingunteraegeri.ch; www.campingunteraegeri.ch**

12 ♦♦ (htd) ⬜ 🛁 ♿ 🖂 ✎ MSP 🦋 🕈 ⑨ 🛒 🏔 🏊 pebble lake adj

Fr Zug take rd to Unterageri. Site sp fr vill. 4*, Lge, hdstg, mkd, pt shd, EHU (rev pol); gas; sw; 40% statics; Eng spkn; adv bkg acc; ccard acc. *"Excellent sw in lake; cycling/walking; recep clsd 1200-1400; vg."* **CHF 46** **2018**

ZURICH *A3* (4km S Rural) *47.33633, 8.54167* **Camping Zurich Fischers Fritz (formerly Camp Seebucht),** Seestrasse 559, 8038 Zürich-Wollishofen **044 4821612; camping@fischers-fritz.ch; www.fischers-fritz.ch**

🛖 CHF3 ♦♦ ⬜ 🛁 ♿ 🖂 ✎ Y ⑨ 🅰 🛒 🏔

Fr city foll rd 3 (twd Chur) on S side of lake; foll camping sp. 1*, Lge, hdstg, pt shd, EHU (6A) CHF5; gas; bbq; sw; 80% statics; bus; Eng spkn; ccard acc; tennis; fishing; watersports. *"Parking in Zürich v diff, use bus; sm area for tourers; pool 3km; conv NH, v sm pitches; cycling into Zurich poss; only 52 plots; tent spaces."* **CHF 39, 1 May-30 Sep.** **2018**

ZWEISIMMEN *C2* (1km N Rural) *46.56338, 7.37691* **Camping Fankhauser,** Ey Gässli 2, 3770 Zweisimmen **033 7221356; info@camping-fankhauser.ch; www.camping-fankhauser.ch**

12 🛖 (htd) ⬜ 🛁 🖂 ✎ Y nr ⑨ nr 🛒 nr 🏔

N6 exit Spiez, then foll sp Zweisimmen. On o'skts of town turn L at camping sp immed bef Agip petrol stn, site on L immed after rlwy x-ing. 4*, Med, pt sl, EHU (10A) CHF3.50 or metered; bbq; 90% statics; phone; Eng spkn; adv bkg acc; fishing; golf; CKE. *"Gd NH; pool 800m."* **CHF 28** **2016**

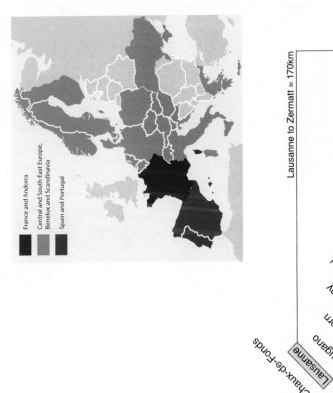

Legend
- France and Andorra
- Central and South East Europe, Benelux and Scandinavia
- Spain and Portugal

Distances (km)

Note: Lausanne to Zermatt = 170 km

Distance chart (road distances in km). Origin cities across the top, destination cities down the left; read the value at the intersection.

	Altdorf	Basel	Bellinzona	Bern	Brig	Chur	Delémont	Disentis	Fribourg	Genève (Geneva)	Gstaad	Interlaken	La Chaux-de-Fonds	Lausanne	Lugano	Luzern	Martigny	Neuchâtel	Olten	St. Gallen	St. Moritz	Schaffhausen	Scuol/Schuls	Sion	Vaduz (Liechtenstein)	Winterthur	Zermatt	Zug
Basel	144																											
Bellinzona	110	244																										
Bern	155	98	255																									
Brig	118	230	115	166																								
Chur	181	103	292	243	175																							
Delémont	151	44	80	93	182	239																						
Disentis	62	159	132	177	108	66	268																					
Fribourg	188	204	420	108	66	275	124	211																				
Genève (Geneva)	319	187	223	35	275	261	268	324	141																			
Gstaad	159	155	126	172	410	348	124	183	126	145																		
Interlaken	68	195	195	91	268	201	261	88	93	263	97																	
La Chaux-de-Fonds	99	291	291	77	211	223	201	108	230	230	63	34																
Lausanne	189	205	358	68	141	160	188	103	66	66	149	156	74															
Lugano	257	264	29	107	159	105	169	145	145	149	138	138	23	172														
Luzern	132	231	281	281	181	401	209	188	312	284	154	104	104	220	250													
Martigny	42	142	240	29	285	32	315	225	108	134	46	122	122	177	155	146												
Neuchâtel	281	102	295	142	105	158	161	98	449	74	156	103	103	275	57	139	336											
Olten	196	313	47	47	181	206	213	177	280	156	74	156	99	279	245	218	332	145										
St. Gallen	179	147	327	205	245	135	141	206	136	74	149	122	188	275	110	369	305	268	62									
St. Moritz	201	206	203	152	186	115	180	204	101	149	114	229	104	425	215	216	337	115	181	252								
Schaffhausen	147	133	232	145	262	117	136	169	188	235	138	23	23	99	273	362	166	260	326	62	317							
Scuol/Schuls	253	212	219	219	79	206	204	130	223	156	44	122	122	310	115	225	249	225	181	296	136	99						
Sion	110	253	185	185	115	135	135	127	160	284	122	104	310	249	81	262	188	160	296	58	233	72	221					
Vaduz (Liechtenstein)	119	125	215	202	181	115	122	204	129	375	215	188	279	279	81	279	89	186	278	99	313	299	82	84				
Winterthur	245	196	166	137	211	117	169	169	161	164	114	103	224	249	28	99	265	79	325	197	82	72	189	86	267			
Zermatt	67	112	196	123	211	117	130	130	305	164	75	128	188	241	59	174	182	66	197	112	293	293	293	293	51	22		
Zug	65	112	196	123	211	117	122	127	158	191	105	156	172	228	59	28	258	165	201	83	201	51	194	280	93	51	219	
Zürich	65	112	196	123	211	117	122	127	158	292	191	128	156	228	223	59	258	165	66	83	201	51	194	280	93	22	245	30

Site Report Form

If campsite is already listed, complete only those sections of the form where changes apply
or alternatively use the Abbreviated Site Report form on the following pages.

Sites not reported on for 5 years may be deleted from the guide

Year of guide used	20.........	Is site listed?	Listed on page no...........	Unlisted	Date of visit	......../......../.........

A – CAMPSITE NAME AND LOCATION

Country		Name of town/village site listed under *(see Sites Location Maps)*				

Distance & direction from centre of town site is listed under *(in a straight line)*		...................km	eg N, NE, S, SW	Urban	Rural	Coastal

Site open all year?	Y / N	Period site is open *(if not all year)*	................/................ to ..../................

Site name			Naturist site	Y / N

Site address	

Telephone		Fax	
E-mail		Website	

B – CAMPSITE CHARGES

Charge for outfit + 2 adults in local currency	PRICE	

C – DIRECTIONS

Brief, specific directions to site (in km) *To convert miles to kilometres multiply by 8 and divide by 5 or use Conversion Table in guide*	
GPS	Latitude..(eg 12.34567) Longitude...(eg 1.23456 or -1.23456)

D – SITE INFORMATION

Dogs allowed	DOGS	Y / N	Price per night .... *(if allowed)*	
Facilities for disabled				
Public Transport within 5km	BUS / TRAM / TRAIN		Adj	Nearby
Reduction long stay	RED LONG STAY	Credit Card accepted		CCARD ACC
Advance bookings accepted/recommended/required		ADV BKG ACC / REC / REQ		
Camping Key Europe or Camping Card International accepted in lieu of passport				CKE/CCI

E – SITE DESCRIPTION

SITE size ie number of pitches	Small Max 50	SM	Medium 51-150	MED	Large 151-500	LGE	Very large 500+	V LGE	Unchanged
Pitch features if **NOT** open-plan/grassy	HDG PITCH	Hedged	HDG PITCH	Marked or numbered	MKD PITCH	Hardstanding or gravel		HDSTG	Unchanged
If site is **NOT** level, is it	PT SL	Part sloping	PT SL	Sloping	SL	Terraced		TERR	Unchanged
Is site shaded?		SHD	Shaded	SHD	Part shaded	PT SHD	Unshaded	UNSHD	Unchanged
ELECTRIC HOOK UP *if not included in price above*	EL PNTS			Price...		Amps......................			
% Static caravans / mobile homes / chalets / cottages / fixed tents on site							................% STATICS		
Serviced Pitched		Y / N		Twin axles caravans allowed?		TWIN AXLES Y / N			

You can also complete forms online: camc.com/europereport

E – SITE DESCRIPTION CONTINUED...

Phone on site	PHONE		Wifi Internet	WIFI
Television	TV RM	TV CAB / SAT	Playground	PLAYGRND
Entertainment in high season	ENTMNT		English spoken	ENG SPKN
Motorhome Service Point	Y / N			

F – CATERING

Bar	BAR	On site	or		Within 2km
Restaurant	REST	On site	or		Within 2km
Shop(s)	SHOP(S)	On site	or		Within 2km
Snack bar / take-away	SNACKS	On site	Y / N		
Cooking facilities	COOKING FACS	On site	Y / N		
Supplies of bottled gas on site	GAS	Y / N			
Barbecue allowed	BBQ	Charcoal	Gas	Elec	Sep area

G – SANITARY FACILITIES

WC	Heated	HTD WC	Continental	CONT	Own San recommended	OWN SAN REC
Chemical disposal point		CHEM DISP				
Hot shower(s)	SHWR(S)	Inc in site fee?		Y / N		
Child / baby facilities *(bathroom)*		FAM BTHRM		Launderette / Washing Machine		LNDRY

H – OTHER INFORMATION

Swimming pool	POOL	HEATED	COVERED	INDOOR	PADDLING POOL	
Beach	BEACH	Adj	or ....km	Sand	Shingle	
Alternative swimming *(lake)*	SW	Adj	or ....km	Sand	Shingle	
Games /sports area / Games room	GAMES AREA		GAMES ROOM			

I – ADDITIONAL REMARKS AND/OR ITEMS OF INTEREST

Tourist attractions, unusual features or other facilities, eg waterslide, tennis, cycle hire, watersports, horseriding, separate car park, walking distance to shops etc	YOUR OPINION OF THE SITE:
	EXCEL
	VERY GOOD
	GOOD
	FAIR / POOR
	NIGHT HALT ONLY

Your comments & opinions may be used in future editions of the guide, if you do not wish them to be used please tick ....

J – MEMBER DETAILS

ARE YOU A:	Caravanner		Motorhomer		Trailer-tenter?	
NAME:			MEMBERSHIP NO:			
			POST CODE:			
DO YOU NEED MORE BLANK SITE REPORT FORMS?		YES			NO	

Please use a separate form for each campsite and do not send receipts. Owing to the large number of site reports received, it is not possible to enter into correspondence. Please return completed form to:

The Editor, Overseas Touring Guides, East Grinstead House
East Grinstead, West Sussex RH19 1UA

Please note that due to changes in the rules regarding freepost we are no longer able to provide a freepost address for the return of Site Report Forms. You can still supply your site reports free online by visiting camc.com/europereport. We apologise for any inconvenience this may cause.

Site Report Form

If campsite is already listed, complete only those sections of the form where changes apply
or alternatively use the Abbreviated Site Report form on the following pages.

Sites not reported on for 5 years may be deleted from the guide

Year of guide used	20..........	Is site listed?	Listed on page no............	Unlisted	Date of visit	........./........./.........

A – CAMPSITE NAME AND LOCATION

Country		Name of town/village site listed under *(see Sites Location Maps)*					
Distance & direction from centre of town site is listed under *(in a straight line)*		....................km	eg N, NE, S, SW		Urban	Rural	Coastal
Site open all year?	Y / N	Period site is open *(if not all year)*	.................../................. to ..../.................				
Site name						Naturist site	Y / N
Site address							
Telephone				Fax			
E-mail				Website			

B – CAMPSITE CHARGES

Charge for outfit + 2 adults in local currency	PRICE		

C – DIRECTIONS

Brief, specific directions to site (in km) *To convert miles to kilometres multiply by 8 and divide by 5 or use Conversion Table in guide*	
GPS	Latitude...(eg 12.34567) Longitude...(eg 1.23456 or -1.23456)

D – SITE INFORMATION

Dogs allowed	DOGS	Y / N	Price per night .... *(if allowed)*	
Facilities for disabled				
Public Transport within 5km	BUS / TRAM / TRAIN	Adj		Nearby
Reduction long stay	RED LONG STAY	Credit Card accepted		CCARD ACC
Advance bookings accepted/recommended/required		ADV BKG ACC / REC / REQ		
Camping Key Europe or Camping Card International accepted in lieu of passport		CKE/CCI		

E – SITE DESCRIPTION

SITE size ie number of pitches	Small Max 50	SM	Medium 51-150	MED	Large 151-500	LGE	Very large 500+	V LGE	Unchanged
Pitch features if **NOT** open-plan/grassy		HDG PITCH	Hedged	HDG PITCH	Marked or numbered	MKD PITCH	Hardstanding or gravel	HDSTG	Unchanged
If site is **NOT** level, is it		PT SL	Part sloping	PT SL	Sloping	SL	Terraced	TERR	Unchanged
Is site shaded?		SHD	Shaded	SHD	Part shaded	PT SHD	Unshaded	UNSHD	Unchanged
ELECTRIC HOOK UP *if not included in price above*		EL PNTS			Price..			Amps........................	
% Static caravans / mobile homes / chalets / cottages / fixed tents on site								.................% STATICS	
Serviced Pitched		Y / N			Twin axles caravans allowed?			TWIN AXLES Y / N	

CUT ALONG DOTTED LINE

You can also complete forms online: camc.com/europereport

E – SITE DESCRIPTION CONTINUED...

Phone on site	PHONE			Wifi Internet	WIFI
Television	TV RM		TV CAB / SAT	Playground	PLAYGRND
Entertainment in high season	ENTMNT			English spoken	ENG SPKN
Motorhome Service Point	Y / N				

F – CATERING

Bar	BAR	On site		or		Within 2km
Restaurant	REST	On site		or		Within 2km
Shop(s)	SHOP(S)	On site		or		Within 2km
Snack bar / take-away	SNACKS	On site	Y / N			
Cooking facilities	COOKING FACS	On site	Y / N			
Supplies of bottled gas on site	GAS	Y / N				
Barbecue allowed	BBQ	Charcoal	Gas	Elec	Sep area	

G – SANITARY FACILITIES

WC		Heated	HTD WC	Continental	CONT	Own San recommended	OWN SAN REC
Chemical disposal point			CHEM DISP				
Hot shower(s)		SHWR(S)	Inc in site fee?		Y / N		
Child / baby facilities *(bathroom)*			FAM BTHRM		Launderette / Washing Machine		LNDRY

H – OTHER INFORMATION

Swimming pool	POOL	HEATED	COVERED	INDOOR		PADDLING POOL
Beach	BEACH	Adj	or ....km	Sand		Shingle
Alternative swimming *(lake)*	SW	Adj	or ....km	Sand		Shingle
Games /sports area / Games room	GAMES AREA		GAMES ROOM			

I – ADDITIONAL REMARKS AND/OR ITEMS OF INTEREST

Tourist attractions, unusual features or other facilities, eg waterslide, tennis, cycle hire, watersports, horseriding, separate car park, walking distance to shops etc	YOUR OPINION OF THE SITE:	
	EXCEL	
	VERY GOOD	
	GOOD	
	FAIR	POOR
	NIGHT HALT ONLY	
Your comments & opinions may be used in future editions of the guide, if you do not wish them to be used please tick		

J – MEMBER DETAILS

ARE YOU A:	Caravanner		Motorhomer		Trailer-tenter?	
NAME:			MEMBERSHIP NO:			
			POST CODE:			
DO YOU NEED MORE BLANK SITE REPORT FORMS?		YES			NO	

Please use a separate form for each campsite and do not send receipts. Owing to the large number of site reports received, it is not possible to enter into correspondence. Please return completed form to:

**The Editor, Overseas Touring Guides, East Grinstead House
East Grinstead, West Sussex RH19 1UA**

Please note that due to changes in the rules regarding freepost we are no longer able to provide a freepost address for the return of Site Report Forms. You can still supply your site reports free online by visiting camc.com/europereport. We apologise for any inconvenience this may cause.

Site Report Form

If campsite is already listed, complete only those sections of the form where changes apply
or alternatively use the Abbreviated Site Report form on the following pages.

Sites not reported on for 5 years may be deleted from the guide

Year of guide used	20……….	Is site listed?	Listed on page no…………	Unlisted	Date of visit	………/………/………

A – CAMPSITE NAME AND LOCATION

Country		Name of town/village site listed under *(see Sites Location Maps)*					
Distance & direction from centre of town site is listed under *(in a straight line)*		…………………….km	eg N, NE, S, SW	Urban		Rural	Coastal
Site open all year?	Y / N	Period site is open *(if not all year)*	……………./……………. to ……………./…………….				
Site name					Naturist site		Y / N
Site address							
Telephone			Fax				
E-mail			Website				

B – CAMPSITE CHARGES

Charge for outfit + 2 adults in local currency	PRICE	

C – DIRECTIONS

Brief, specific directions to site (in km) *To convert miles to kilometres multiply by 8 and divide by 5 or use Conversion Table in guide*	
GPS	Latitude………………………………….(eg 12.34567) Longitude…………………………………….(eg 1.23456 or -1.23456)

D – SITE INFORMATION

Dogs allowed	DOGS	Y / N	Price per night ……………………………. *(if allowed)*	
Facilities for disabled				
Public Transport within 5km	BUS / TRAM / TRAIN	Adj		Nearby
Reduction long stay	RED LONG STAY	Credit Card accepted		CCARD ACC
Advance bookings accepted/recommended/required		ADV BKG ACC / REC / REQ		
Camping Key Europe or Camping Card International accepted in lieu of passport		CKE/CCI		

E – SITE DESCRIPTION

SITE size ie number of pitches	Small Max 50	SM	Medium 51-150	MED	Large 151-500	LGE	Very large 500+	V LGE	Unchanged
Pitch features if NOT open-plan/grassy		HDG PITCH	Hedged	HDG PITCH	Marked or numbered	MKD PITCH	Hardstanding or gravel	HDSTG	Unchanged
If site is NOT level, is it		PT SL	Part sloping	PT SL	Sloping	SL	Terraced	TERR	Unchanged
Is site shaded?		SHD	Shaded	SHD	Part shaded	PT SHD	Unshaded	UNSHD	Unchanged
ELECTRIC HOOK UP *if not included in price above*		EL PNTS			Price…………………………………			Amps……………………	
% Static caravans / mobile homes / chalets / cottages / fixed tents on site								……………….% STATICS	
Serviced Pitched		Y / N			Twin axles caravans allowed?			TWIN AXLES Y / N	

CUT ALONG DOTTED LINE

You can also complete forms online: camc.com/europereport

E – SITE DESCRIPTION CONTINUED...

Phone on site	PHONE		Wifi Internet	WIFI
Television	TV RM	TV CAB / SAT	Playground	PLAYGRND
Entertainment in high season	ENTMNT		English spoken	ENG SPKN
Motorhome Service Point	Y / N			

F – CATERING

Bar	BAR	On site	or		Within 2km
Restaurant	REST	On site	or		Within 2km
Shop(s)	SHOP(S)	On site	or		Within 2km
Snack bar / take-away	SNACKS	On site	Y / N		
Cooking facilities	COOKING FACS	On site	Y / N		
Supplies of bottled gas on site	GAS	Y / N			
Barbecue allowed	BBQ	Charcoal	Gas	Elec	Sep area

G – SANITARY FACILITIES

WC	Heated	HTD WC	Continental	CONT	Own San recommended	OWN SAN REC
Chemical disposal point		CHEM DISP				
Hot shower(s)	SHWR(S)	Inc in site fee?		Y / N		
Child / baby facilities (bathroom)		FAM BTHRM		Launderette / Washing Machine		LNDRY

H – OTHER INFORMATION

Swimming pool	POOL	HEATED	COVERED	INDOOR	PADDLING POOL	
Beach	BEACH	Adj	or ....km	Sand	Shingle	
Alternative swimming (lake)	SW	Adj	or ....km	Sand	Shingle	
Games /sports area / Games room	GAMES AREA		GAMES ROOM			

I – ADDITIONAL REMARKS AND/OR ITEMS OF INTEREST

Tourist attractions, unusual features or other facilities, eg waterslide, tennis, cycle hire, watersports, horseriding, separate car park, walking distance to shops etc	YOUR OPINION OF THE SITE:
	EXCEL
	VERY GOOD
	GOOD
	FAIR / POOR
	NIGHT HALT ONLY

Your comments & opinions may be used in future editions of the guide, if you do not wish them to be used please tick ....

J – MEMBER DETAILS

ARE YOU A:	Caravanner		Motorhomer		Trailer-tenter?
NAME:			MEMBERSHIP NO:		
			POST CODE:		
DO YOU NEED MORE BLANK SITE REPORT FORMS?		YES		NO	

Please use a separate form for each campsite and do not send receipts. Owing to the large number of site reports received, it is not possible to enter into correspondence. Please return completed form to:

The Editor, Overseas Touring Guides, East Grinstead House
East Grinstead, West Sussex RH19 1UA

Please note that due to changes in the rules regarding freepost we are no longer able to provide a freepost address for the return of Site Report Forms. You can still supply your site reports free online by visiting camc.com/europereport. We apologise for any inconvenience this may cause.

Abbreviated Site Report Form

Use this abbreviated Site Report Form if you have visited a number of sites and there are no changes (or only small changes) to their entries in the guide. If reporting on a new site, or reporting several changes, please use the full version of the report form. If advising prices, these should be for an outfit, and 2 adults for one night's stay. Please indicate high or low season prices and whether electricity is included.

Remember, if you don't tell us about sites you have visited, they may eventually be deleted from the guide.

Year of guide used	20..........	Page No.	....	Name of town/village site listed under		
Site Name					Date of visit	......./......./........
GPS	Latitude...(eg 12.34567) Longitude...(eg 1.23456 or -1.23456)					
Site is in: Andorra / Austria / Belgium / Croatia / Czech Republic / Denmark / Finland / France / Germany / Greece / Hungary / Italy / Luxembourg / Netherlands / Norway / Poland / Portugal / Slovakia / Slovenia / Spain / Sweden / Switzerland						
Comments:						

Charge for outfit + 2 adults in local currency	High Season	Low Season	Elec inc in price?	Y / N	.............amps
			Price of elec (if not inc)		.............amps

Year of guide used	20..........	Page No.	....	Name of town/village site listed under		
Site Name					Date of visit	......./......./........
GPS	Latitude...(eg 12.34567) Longitude...(eg 1.23456 or -1.23456)					
Site is in: Andorra / Austria / Belgium / Croatia / Czech Republic / Denmark / Finland / France / Germany / Greece / Hungary / Italy / Luxembourg / Netherlands / Norway / Poland / Portugal / Slovakia / Slovenia / Spain / Sweden / Switzerland						
Comments:						

Charge for outfit + 2 adults in local currency	High Season	Low Season	Elec inc in price?	Y / N	.............amps
			Price of elec (if not inc)		.............amps

Year of guide used	20..........	Page No.	....	Name of town/village site listed under		
Site Name					Date of visit	......./......./........
GPS	Latitude...(eg 12.34567) Longitude...(eg 1.23456 or -1.23456)					
Site is in: Andorra / Austria / Belgium / Croatia / Czech Republic / Denmark / Finland / France / Germany / Greece / Hungary / Italy / Luxembourg / Netherlands / Norway / Poland / Portugal / Slovakia / Slovenia / Spain / Sweden / Switzerland						
Comments:						

Charge for car, caravan & 2 adults in local currency	High Season	Low Season	Elec inc in price?	Y / N	.............amps
			Price of elec (if not inc)		.............amps

Please fill in your details and send to the address on the reverse of this form.
You can also complete forms online: camc.com/europereport

CUT ALONG DOTTED LINE

Year of guide used	20..........	Page No.	....	Name of town/village site listed under			
Site Name						Date of visit	......./......./.......
GPS	Latitude...(eg 12.34567) Longitude...(eg 1.23456 or -1.23456)						

Site is in: Andorra / Austria / Belgium / Croatia / Czech Republic / Denmark / Finland / France / Germany / Greece / Hungary / Italy / Luxembourg / Netherlands / Norway / Poland / Portugal / Slovakia / Slovenia / Spain / Sweden / Switzerland

Comments:

Charge for outfit + 2 adults in local currency	High Season	Low Season	Elec inc in price?		Y / N	............amps
			Price of elec (if not inc)			............amps

Year of guide used	20..........	Page No.	....	Name of town/village site listed under			
Site Name						Date of visit	......./......./.......
GPS	Latitude...(eg 12.34567) Longitude...(eg 1.23456 or -1.23456)						

Site is in: Andorra / Austria / Belgium / Croatia / Czech Republic / Denmark / Finland / France / Germany / Greece / Hungary / Italy / Luxembourg / Netherlands / Norway / Poland / Portugal / Slovakia / Slovenia / Spain / Sweden / Switzerland

Comments:

Charge for outfit + 2 adults in local currency	High Season	Low Season	Elec inc in price?		Y / N	............amps
			Price of elec (if not inc)			............amps

Year of guide used	20..........	Page No.	....	Name of town/village site listed under			
Site Name						Date of visit	......./......./.......
GPS	Latitude...(eg 12.34567) Longitude...(eg 1.23456 or -1.23456)						

Site is in: Andorra / Austria / Belgium / Croatia / Czech Republic / Denmark / Finland / France / Germany / Greece / Hungary / Italy / Luxembourg / Netherlands / Norway / Poland / Portugal / Slovakia / Slovenia / Spain / Sweden / Switzerland

Comments:

Charge for outfit + 2 adults in local currency	High Season	Low Season	Elec inc in price?		Y / N	............amps
			Price of elec (if not inc)			............amps

Your comments & opinions may be used in future editions of the guide, if you do not wish them to be used please tick ....

Name ....

Membership No. ....

Post Code ....

Are you a Caravanner / Motorhomer / Trailer-Tenter?

Do you need more blank Site Report forms?   YES / NO

Please return completed forms to:
The Editor – Overseas Touring Guides
East Grinstead House
East Grinstead
West Sussex
RH19 1FH
Please note that due to changes in the rules regarding freepost we are no longer able to provide a freepost address for the return of Site Report Forms. You can still supply your site reports free online by visiting camc.com/europereport. We apologise for any inconvenience this may cause.

You can also complete forms online: camc.com/europereport

Abbreviated Site Report Form

Use this abbreviated Site Report Form if you have visited a number of sites and there are no changes (or only small changes) to their entries in the guide. If reporting on a new site, or reporting several changes, please use the full version of the report form. If advising prices, these should be for an outfit, and 2 adults for one night's stay. **Please indicate high or low season prices and whether electricity is included.**

Remember, if you don't tell us about sites you have visited, they may eventually be deleted from the guide.

Year of guide used	20..........	Page No.	....	Name of town/village site listed under		
Site Name					Date of visit	......./......./........
GPS	Latitude..(eg 12.34567) Longitude..(eg 1.23456 or -1.23456)					

Site is in: Andorra / Austria / Belgium / Croatia / Czech Republic / Denmark / Finland / France / Germany / Greece / Hungary / Italy / Luxembourg / Netherlands / Norway / Poland / Portugal / Slovakia / Slovenia / Spain / Sweden / Switzerland

Comments:

Charge for outfit + 2 adults in local currency	High Season	Low Season	Elec inc in price?		Y / N	.............amps
			Price of elec (if not inc)			.............amps

Year of guide used	20..........	Page No.	....	Name of town/village site listed under		
Site Name					Date of visit	......./......./........
GPS	Latitude..(eg 12.34567) Longitude..(eg 1.23456 or -1.23456)					

Site is in: Andorra / Austria / Belgium / Croatia / Czech Republic / Denmark / Finland / France / Germany / Greece / Hungary / Italy / Luxembourg / Netherlands / Norway / Poland / Portugal / Slovakia / Slovenia / Spain / Sweden / Switzerland

Comments:

Charge for outfit + 2 adults in local currency	High Season	Low Season	Elec inc in price?		Y / N	.............amps
			Price of elec (if not inc)			.............amps

Year of guide used	20..........	Page No.	....	Name of town/village site listed under		
Site Name					Date of visit	......./......./........
GPS	Latitude..(eg 12.34567) Longitude..(eg 1.23456 or -1.23456)					

Site is in: Andorra / Austria / Belgium / Croatia / Czech Republic / Denmark / Finland / France / Germany / Greece / Hungary / Italy / Luxembourg / Netherlands / Norway / Poland / Portugal / Slovakia / Slovenia / Spain / Sweden / Switzerland

Comments:

Charge for car, caravan & 2 adults in local currency	High Season	Low Season	Elec inc in price?		Y / N	.............amps
			Price of elec (if not inc)			.............amps

Please fill in your details and send to the address on the reverse of this form.
You can also complete forms online: camc.com/europereport

CUT ALONG DOTTED LINE

Year of guide used	20..........	Page No.	....	Name of town/village site listed under	

Site Name				Date of visit	......./......./........

GPS	Latitude................................(eg 12.34567) Longitude..................................(eg 1.23456 or -1.23456)

Site is in: Andorra / Austria / Belgium / Croatia / Czech Republic / Denmark / Finland / France / Germany / Greece / Hungary / Italy / Luxembourg / Netherlands / Norway / Poland / Portugal / Slovakia / Slovenia / Spain / Sweden / Switzerland

Comments:

Charge for outfit + 2 adults in local currency	High Season	Low Season	Elec inc in price?	Y / N	.............amps
			Price of elec (if not inc)		.............amps

Year of guide used	20..........	Page No.	....	Name of town/village site listed under	

Site Name				Date of visit	......./......./........

GPS	Latitude................................(eg 12.34567) Longitude..................................(eg 1.23456 or -1.23456)

Site is in: Andorra / Austria / Belgium / Croatia / Czech Republic / Denmark / Finland / France / Germany / Greece / Hungary / Italy / Luxembourg / Netherlands / Norway / Poland / Portugal / Slovakia / Slovenia / Spain / Sweden / Switzerland

Comments:

Charge for outfit + 2 adults in local currency	High Season	Low Season	Elec inc in price?	Y / N	.............amps
			Price of elec (if not inc)		.............amps

Year of guide used	20..........	Page No.	....	Name of town/village site listed under	

Site Name				Date of visit	......./......./........

GPS	Latitude................................(eg 12.34567) Longitude..................................(eg 1.23456 or -1.23456)

Site is in: Andorra / Austria / Belgium / Croatia / Czech Republic / Denmark / Finland / France / Germany / Greece / Hungary / Italy / Luxembourg / Netherlands / Norway / Poland / Portugal / Slovakia / Slovenia / Spain / Sweden / Switzerland

Comments:

Charge for outfit + 2 adults in local currency	High Season	Low Season	Elec inc in price?	Y / N	.............amps
			Price of elec (if not inc)		.............amps

Your comments & opinions may be used in future editions of the guide, if you do not wish them to be used please tick ....

Name ....

Membership No. ....

Post Code ....

Are you a Caravanner / Motorhomer / Trailer-Tenter?

Do you need more blank Site Report forms?　　YES / NO

Please return completed forms to:
The Editor – Overseas Touring Guides
East Grinstead House
East Grinstead
West Sussex
RH19 1FH
Please note that due to changes in the rules regarding freepost we are no longer able to provide a freepost address for the return of Site Report Forms. You can still supply your site reports free online by visiting camc.com/europereport. We apologise for any inconvenience this may cause.

Index

A

Abbreviated Site Report Forms .... Back of guide
Abbreviations 11
Abbreviations (mountain passes & tunnels) 48
Accessing the Internet 65
Accidents and Emergencies .... 68 & country intros
Acknowledgements 8
Alcohol (legal limits) .... Country Intros
Alps (passes & tunnels) 48
AUSTRIA 86

B

Beaches (Safety) 74
BELGIUM 110
Breakdown Service .... Country Intros
Booking a Campsite 80
Booking your Ferry 26
British Consular Services Abroad 79
British & Irish Embassy Contacts .... Country Intros

C

Camping & Caravanning .... Country Intros
Camping Key Europe 14
Campsite Entries (explanation) 9
Campsite Fees .... 6 & 84
Campsite Groups 85
Campsite Safety 74
Caravan Spares 36
Caravan Storage Abroad 81
Car Spare Kits 36
Channel Tunnel 27
Club Sites Near Ports 28
Club Together 65
Complaints 85
Contact Details - Sites .... Individual Site Entries
Converting Gradients 47
Counrty Highlights .... Country Intros
Country Information .... Country Intros
Credit and Debit Cards 25
CRIS document 17
CROATIA 127
Currency .... Country Intros
Customs Allowances 21
Customs Regulations 21
Cycling .... COuntry Intros
CZECH REPUBLIC 142

D

DENMARK 156
Documents .... 14 & Country Intros
Driving in Europe 31
Driving Licence 14
Dynamic Currency Conversion 25

E

E10 Petrol 31
Electrical Connections 70
Electricity .... 70 & Country Intros
Emergency Cash 25

E cont...

Emergency Services .... Country Intros
Essential Equipment .... 34, 38 & Country Intros
European Accident Statement 19
European Health Insurance Card (EHIC) 67
Explanation of a Campsite Entry 9

F

Facilities and Site Description 81
Ferry routes and Operators 29
Final Checks (motoring) 30
Finding a Campsite 82
FINLAND 176
Fire Extinguisher 34
First Aid 68
Food (Customs) 23
Foreign Currency Bank Accounts 24
Fuel .... 31 & Country Intros

G

Gas .... 72 & Country Intros
Gas on Ferries and Eurotunnel 27
General Advice (campsites) 83
GERMANY 189
Global SIM Cards 64
GREECE 254

H

Hands-free 65
Hazard Warning Lights 35
Headlight flashing 35
Hired or Borrowed Vehicles 17
HMRC Advice Service 23
Hooking up to the Mains 71
HUNGARY 268

I

Insurance: 18
  – Car, Motorhome & Caravan 18
  – Holiday .... 19 & 68
  – Home 20
International direct dial calls 64
Internet access 65
ITALY 280

L

Lakes (Safety) 74
Legal Costs Abroad 19
Lights 34
Liquified Petroleum Gas (LPG) 32
Local Currency 24
Low Emission Zones .... 32 & Country Intros
LUXEMBOURG 323
Lyme disease 69

M

Major Alpine Mountain Passes 48
Major Alpine Rail Tunnels 57
Major Alpine Road Tunnels 58
Major Towns & Cities .... Country Intros

Index

M cont...

Medical Services .... 67 & Country Intros
Medicines (Customs) 22
Mobile Internet 65
Mobile Phones 64
Money .... 24 & Country Intros
Money Security 78
MOT Certificate 17
Motorhomes Towing Cars 32
Motoring .... Country Intros
Motorway Tolls .... Country Intros
Motorways .... Country Intros
Mountain Passes & Tunnels .... 50 & 58
Mountain Pass and Tunnel Maps .... 54 & 60
Mountain Pass Information 46
Municipal Campsites 82

N

Nationality Plate 35
Naturist Campsites 82
NETHERLANDS 333
NORWAY 358

O

On the Ferry 26
On the Road Safety 76
Opening Hours .... 83 & Country Intros
Overnight Stops 82
Overseas Site Night Vouchers 80
Overseas Travel Service 80
Overtaking .... Country Intros

P

Parking .... Country Intros
Passport 15
Pedestrian Crossings 33
Personal Possessions (Customs) 23
Personal Security 77
Pets on Campsites 83
Pets on Ferries and Eurotunnel 27
Pet Travel Scheme 16
Plants (Customs) 23
POLAND 387
Preparing for your Journey 30
Prices 84
Priority .... 32 & Country Intros
Public Holidays .... Country Intros
Public Transport .... 33 & Country Intros
Punctures 37

R

Radar Detectors .... Country Intros
Radio and Television 65
Reflective Jackets/Waistcoats 35
Registering on Arrival 84
Returning Home (Medical Advice) 69
Reversed Polarity 72
Rivers (Safety) 74
Roads .... Country Intros

R cont...

Road Signs and Markings .... Country Intros
Route Planning 35
Route Planning Maps 40

S

Safety and Security .... 74 & Country Intros
Sanitary Facilities 81
Satellite Navigation/GPS .... 7 & 36
Satellite Television 66
Schengen agreement 15
Seat Belts 36
Shaver Sockets 72
Site Hooking up Adaptor 72
Site Location Maps .... End of Site Entries
Site Opening Dates .... Individual Site Entries
Site Prices .... Individual Site Entries
Site Report Forms .... 7 & 469
SLOVAKIA 400
SLOVENIA 411
Spare Wheel 36
Spares 36
Speed Limits .... Country Intros
Sun Protection 69
SWEDEN 423
SWITZERLAND 447

T

Telephones and Calling 66
Television 64
Tick-Borne Encephalitis 69
Touring .... Country Intros
Tourist Information .... Country Intros
Towbar 37
Traffic Jams .... Country Intros
Traffic Lights .... 33 & Country Intros
Travelling with Children 16
Travel Money Cards 25
Tyre Pressure 37
Tyres 37

V

Vehicle Tax 17
Vehicle Registration Certificate (V5C) 17
Vehicles left behind abroad 19
Violation of Traffic Regulations .... Country Intros
Visas 17

W

Warning Triangles 38
Water 69
Weight Limits 30
Winter Driving 37
Winter Sports 79

PEFC Certified

This product is
from sustainably
managed forests and
controlled sources

PEFC

PEFC/16-33-254   www.pefc.org